Personality-Guided Therapy

THEODORE MILLON

Personality-Guided Therapy

with Contributing Associates

Seth Grossman
Sarah Meagher
Carrie Millon
George Everly

Foreword by Roger D. Davis

John Wiley & Sons, Inc.

New York • Chichester • Weinheim • Brisbane • Singapore • Toronto

Library of Congress Cataloging-in-Publication Data:

Millon, Theodore.
    Personality-guided therapy / Theodore Millon.
       p.   cm.
    Includes index.
    ISBN 0-471-52807-2 (alk. paper)
    1. Psychotherapy—Handbooks, manuals, etc.   2. Personality disorders—Treatment—Handbooks, manuals, etc.   I. Title.
    [DNLM: 1. Psychotherapy—methods.   2. Personality Disorders.   WM 420 M656p 1999]
    RC480.5.M54   1999
    616.89′14—dc21
    DNLM/DLC
    for Library of Congress   99-10439

Printed in the United States of America.

10 9 8 7 6 5 4 3 2 1

To all of my past students, supervisees,
and patients from whom I have learned
more than I can ever say or thank.

Foreword

This book fills a gaping hole in clinical practice. In an age when the forces of managed care drive clinicians more and more to treat only the most immediate and dramatic outcroppings of pathology, Millon maintains that therapists should understand the presenting problem by understanding the whole person. Personality-guided therapy not only addresses the most pressing issues, but also treats the potential for pathology, the only foundation of an ethical psychotherapy. No longer is the focus on superficial, manualized psychotherapies that "bleed" patients of symptom severity while leaving intact the underlying potential for disease—the ways of thinking, feeling, perceiving, and relating that we call personality. By seeking to understand the whole person, therapy is shifted back to the humanistic values that, throughout most of its history, have formed our discipline's core mission: a patient's return to long-term healthy functioning. No one would dare disagree with such a noble purpose, but it is strange that contemporary times are marked by such a discrepancy between practicing and preaching.

The explanation for this discrepancy can be located in the disconnectedness of the diagnostic landscape itself. Apart from the seminal contributions of Ted Millon, beginning with *Modern Psychopathology* (1969) and continuing through *Disorders of Personality* (1981, 1996) and *Toward a New Personology* (1990), the conceptual foundations of the personality disorders have remained poorly articulated. The *DSM* itself has been both a blessing and a curse. The current edition puts the personality disorders in a place of prominence on Axis II, but syndromizes them as diagnostic entities in the Neo-Kraepelinian tradition, just like Axis I. Rather than focus the clinician on how personality might contextualize and color the expression of depression or anxiety, for example, the *DSM* implies that Axis I and Axis II are largely independent (and only incidentally interacting) entities that must be defeated through independent methods. As a result, discussions of treatment have tended to remain construct-centered, focused on some singular disorder, and therapy has remained what it was and always will be: person-centered. Without a coherent logic for bridging the two, practitioners are mainly left with only the trivial contributions of the common factors movement, the atheoretical pragmatism of technical eclecticism, or the dogmatism of the pre-*DSM* school-oriented past. By knowing that folks usually like a warm therapist and that one must borrow whatever, from wherever, to get the job done, any practitioner could be considered close to state-of-the-art and would probably be just as effective as any of his or her colleagues.

But no more. With this book, the logic that connects constructs to persons has been specified in detail. The psychotherapy advocated is genuinely *integrative,* but in a sense that differs from the term as it is now casually thrown around. For Millon, integration refers to an understanding that issues from an explicit theory of personality, the Evolutionary Model (Millon, 1990). The goal is to put forward a taxonomy of personality constructs that resembles the periodic table of chemistry or the standard model of physics. The value of such a system would seem self-evident, but it has been overlooked by so-called integrationists. Yet, if it is essential to understand persons through constructs, as it always is in therapy, then we must first determine what constructs are essential to such an understanding. The theory is the Evolutionary Model; the constructs it generates are personality styles and disorders of Axis II; and the goal is understanding the patient's personality and how his or her interactions with the surrounding world create difficulties that result in anxiety, depression, and other disorders of Axis I. As Millon shows, only then can techniques be chosen scientifically—that is, logically integrated in accordance with the person's problems and needs.

Beyond specifying the logic that links constructs and persons, Millon also applies previously published concepts that remain far ahead of their time. Among these are potentiated pairings and catalytic sequences. The heart of the matter, as Millon explains, is that personality disorders are disorders of the entire matrix of the person. The various facets of personality sustain and perpetuate themselves across multiple domains of functioning—cognitive style, defense mechanisms, self-image, and interpersonal relationships, for example. Personality disorders take on an emergent tenacity that makes them more difficult to treat than depression or anxiety. The content of therapy—the specific techniques to be applied—can be chosen on the basis of a theoretical portrait of the person. The form of therapy, however, must be dictated by the nature of the problem. If personality possesses an emergent tenacity, then therapeutic techniques must be applied with an emergent efficacy. Therapy must be more than the sum of its parts because it must treat something that is more than the sum of its parts. Any eclectically minded person could argue that different techniques should be applied, but Millon frames the problem and links its resolution to the nature of personality itself. Many famous figures have noted that vicious circles and neurotic paradoxes represent a defining feature of personality pathology, but somehow they all missed the necessary analogues on the therapeutic side of the equation. Millon does not. By bringing such conceptual innovations to bear, Millon is empowered to go beyond generalities, to dive into the specifics of therapeutic integration, and to apply the insights in this latest classic to Axis I *and* Axis II, in a way that other thinkers have only begun to appreciate.

ROGER D. DAVIS

Preface

The great philosophers and clinicians of the past viewed their task as creating a rationale that took into account *all* of the complexities of human nature: the biological, the phenomenological, the developmental, and so on. Modern conceptual thinkers have actively avoided this complex and broad vision. They appear to favor one-dimensional schemata—conceptual frameworks that intentionally leave out much that may bear significantly on the reality of human life. In this book, we join with thinkers of the past and argue that no part of human nature should lie outside the scope of a clinician's regard (e.g., the family and culture, neurobiological processes, unconscious memories, and so on).

It is my hope that the book will lead us back to "reality" by exploring both the natural intricacy and the diversity of the patients we treat. Despite their frequent brilliance, most schools of therapy have become inbred; more importantly, they persist in narrowing clinicians' attention to just one or another facet of their patients' psychological makeup, thereby wandering ever farther from human reality. They cease to represent the fullness of patients' lives when they consider as significant only one of several psychic spheres—the unconscious, biochemical processes, cognitive schemata, and so on. In effect, what has been taught to most fledgling therapists is an artificial reality. It may have been formulated in its early stages as an original perspective and one insightful methodology, but, over time, it has drifted increasingly from its moorings and is no longer anchored to the clinical reality from which it was abstracted.

If my wish takes root, this book will serve as a revolutionary call for a renaissance that brings therapy back to the natural reality of patients' lives. I hold to the proposition that the diagnostic categories that comprise our nosology (e.g., *DSM-IV*) are not composed of distinct disease entities or separable statistical factors; rather, they represent splendid fictions and *arbitrary* distinctions that can often mislead young therapists into making compartmentalized or, worse yet, manualized interventions. Fledgling therapists must learn that *the symptoms and disorders we "diagnose" represent one or another segment of a complex of organically interwoven elements*. The significance of each clinical component can best be grasped by reviewing a patient's unique psychological experiences and his or her pattern of configurational dynamics, of which this component is but one part.

A patient's totality can present a bewildering if not chaotic array of possibilities. Even the most motivated young clinician may wish to back off into a more manageable and simpler worldview, be it cognitive, pharmacologic, or otherwise. But, as I will contend here, complexity need not be experienced as overwhelming or chaotic, if the treatment plan that is created has logic and order. This I have sought to do by illustrating, for example, that the systematic integration of Axis I syndromes and Axis II disorders is not only feasible, but is conducive to briefer and more effective therapy. Therapeutic concepts and methods can never achieve the precision and idealized model of the physical sciences. Instead, we must deal with subtle variations and sequences, as well as constantly changing forces that comprise the natural state of human life.

As I trust will be evident, this book, despite its primary title, does not limit its focus to the treatment of personality disorders. I will attempt to show that *all the clinical syndromes that comprise Axis I can be understood more clearly and treated more effectively when conceived as an outgrowth of a patient's overall personality style*. To say that depression is experienced and expressed differently from one patient to the next is a truism; so general a statement, however, will not suffice for a book such as this. Our task requires much more. This book provides extensive information, often with accompanying illustrations, on how patients with different personality vulnerabilities perceive and cope with life's stressors. With this body of knowledge in hand, therapists should be guided to undertake more precise and effective treatment plans. For example, a dependent person will often respond to a divorce situation with feelings of helplessness and hopelessness, whereas a narcissist, faced with similar circumstances, may respond in a disdainful and cavalier way. Even when both a dependent and a narcissist exhibit depressive symptoms in common, the precipitant of these symptoms will likely have been quite different. Treatment—its goals and methods—should likewise differ. In effect, similar symptoms do not call for the same treatment *if* the pattern of patient vulnerabilities and coping styles differs. In dependents, the emotional turmoil may arise from feelings of low self-esteem and an inability to function autonomously; in narcissists, depression may be the outcropping of failed cognitive denials, as well as a consequent collapse of habitual interpersonal arrogance.

Current debates regarding whether "technical eclecticism" or "integrative therapy" is the more suitable designation for our approach are mistaken. The discussants have things backward, so to speak; they start the task of intervention by focusing first on technique or methodology. Integration does not inhere in treatment methods or their theories—eclectic or otherwise. *Integration inheres in the person, not in our theories or the modalities we prefer.* It stems from the dynamics and interwoven character of the patient's traits and symptoms. Our task as therapists is *not* to see how we can blend intrinsically discordant models of therapeutic technique, but to match the integrated pattern of features that characterize each patient, and *then* to select treatment goals and tactics that mirror this pattern optimally. For this reason, among others, we have chosen to employ the label "personality-guided synergistic therapy" to represent our brand of integrative treatment.

Integration is an important concept not only for the psychotherapy of an individual case but also for the role of psychotherapy in the broad sphere of clinical science. For the treatment of a particular patient to be integrated, the several elements of a clinical science should be integrated as well. One of the arguments advanced against technical eclecticism is that it explicitly insulates therapy from the broad context of clinical science. In contrast to eclecticism, where techniques are justified methodologically or empirically, integrative treatment reflects the logic of a comprehensive and relevant theory of human nature. Comprehensive theories are inviting because they seek to encompass the full multidimensionality of human behavior; personality-guided therapy grows out of such a theory. Let me elaborate its rationale briefly.

Whether we work with "part functions" that focus on behaviors, cognitions, unconscious processes, or biological defects, and the like, or whether we address contextual systems that focus on the larger environment, the family, the group, or the socioeconomic and political conditions of life, the crossover point, the unit that links parts to contexts, is the person. The individual is the intersecting medium that brings them together. Persons, however, are more than just crossover mediums. As will be elaborated in this book, they are the only organically integrated system in the psychological domain. Persons are inherently created from birth as natural entities rather than experience-derived gestalts constructed through cognitive attribution. Moreover, persons are at the heart of the therapeutic experience. A person is a substantive being who gives meaning and coherence to symptoms and traits—whether they are behaviors, affects, or mechanisms—as well as a being, a singular entity, who gives life and expression to family interactions and social processes.

I contend that therapists should be cognizant of the person from the start because the parts and the contexts take on different meanings and call for different interventions in terms of the person to whom they are anchored. To focus on one social structure or one psychic form of expression, without understanding its undergirding or reference base, is to engage in potentially misguided, if not random, therapeutic techniques.

Personality-guided therapy insists on the primacy of the overarching gestalt of the whole person. The gestalt gives coherence, provides an interactive framework, and creates an organic order among otherwise discrete clinical techniques. Each personality is a synthesized and substantive system; the whole is greater than the sum of its parts. The problems that our patients bring to us form an inextricably interwoven structure of behaviors, cognitions, and intrapsychic processes, all bound together by feedback loops and serially unfolding concatenations that emerge at different times and in dynamic and changing configurations. The interpretation of one of my psychological inventories, the MCMI, for example, does not proceed through a linear sequence of its single scales. Instead, each scale contextualizes and transforms the meaning of the others in the profile. In parallel form, personality-guided therapy should be conceived as a configuration of strategies and tactics in which each intervention technique is selected not only for its efficacy in resolving singular pathological features but also for its contribution to the overall constellation of treatment procedures, of which it is but one.

All psychic pathologies represent disorders for which the logic of the integrative mindset is the optimal therapeutic choice. The cohesion (or lack thereof) of complexly interwoven psychic structures and functions is what distinguishes our model of therapy from other clinical forms of treatment; the careful orchestration of diverse, yet synthesized techniques that mirror the characteristics of each patient's psychological makeup differentiates personality-guided psychotherapy from its integrative counterparts. The interwoven nature of the components comprising personality-guided treatment makes a multifaceted and synergistic approach a necessity. Therapies that conceptualize clinical disorders from a single perspective—be it psychodynamic, cognitive, behavioral, or physiological—may be useful, and even necessary, but are not sufficient in themselves to undertake a therapy of a patient, disordered or not. The "revolution" I propose asserts that clinical disorders are not exclusively behavioral or cognitive or unconscious—that is, confined to particular expressive form. The overall pattern of a person's traits and psychic expressions is systemic and multioperational. No part of the system exists in complete isolation from the others. Every part is directly or indirectly tied to every other, so that an emergent synergism accounts for a disorder's clinical tenacity. Personality is "real"; it is a composite of intertwined elements whose totality must be reckoned with in all therapeutic enterprises. The key to treating our patients, therefore, lies in *therapy that is designed to be as organismically complex as the persons themselves.* This form of therapy should generate more than the sum of its parts. I am aware that this may sound difficult. I hope to demonstrate its ease and utility.

Personality-guided synergism employs two basic strategies. In the *first,* which I have termed "potentiated pairings," treatment methods are combined simultaneously to overcome problematic characteristics that may be refractory to each technique if administered separately. These composites pull and push for change on several fronts. Treatment is then oriented to *more than one* expressive domain of clinical dysfunction. A currently popular form of treatment pairing is found in "cognitive-behavioral" therapy. The *second* synergistic procedure, labeled "catalytic sequences," considers the order in which coordinated treatments are executed. Therapeutic combinations and progressions are designed to optimize the impact of changes in a manner that would be more effective than if the order were otherwise arranged. In a catalytic sequence, for example, one might seek first to alter a patient's stuttering by direct behavioral modification procedures. The alteration, if achieved, would facilitate the use of cognitive methods in producing self-image changes in confidence, which, in turn, would foster the utility of interpersonal techniques to effect social skill improvement. Personality-guided therapy is conceived, therefore, as a configuration of strategies and tactics in which each intervention technique is selected not only for its efficacy in resolving particular pathological difficulties, but also for its contribution to the overall constellation of treatment procedures, of which it is but one.

The logic for combining therapies has now become a central theme for a wide variety of health problems.

- A recent study of *depression* among the elderly has shown that those given both medication and psychotherapy recovered more than twice as frequently as did those who received either medication or psychotherapy alone.
- In treating *AIDS,* it has been found that a cocktail of three drugs in combination works appreciably better than any of the drugs alone; moreover, these data have held up with patients at different stages of the HIV disease.
- In difficulties such as *smoking cessation,* recent studies have shown that a combination of an antidepressant, nicotine replacement, and psychological counseling sharply increases (40–60%) success with cessation, as compared to utilizing only one of these methods (5%).
- *Diabetes* is a disease in which any of several anatomic structures and physiochemical processes can go awry. Standard practice with diabetes patients is to administer two or more medications, each of which addresses one or another of the possible inherent defects. The goal is to cover *all* potentially contributing biophysical difficulties, and the consequent drop in blood sugar levels among multitreated patients is nothing less than miraculous.

- Recent studies demonstrate that the combination of smaller-than-usual dosages of two or more drugs for *hypertension* has proven much more effective than administering just one of the antihypertensives.

The logic here, which is no less applicable to mental disorders, is that the action of certain modality combinations broadens the range of efficacy to include a variety of potential clinical dysfunctions; taken together, these combinations complement each other and, most importantly, they produce a synergistic result. The reduced dosage combination causes fewer side effects *and* achieves a greater level of efficacy than each modality could attain on its own.

Eclectic combinations of several treatment modalities, such as those proposed by Lazarus, are a good start toward the goal of synergizing therapy. Combining methods that are mutually reinforcing strengthens what each modality can achieve separately. The logic for selecting modalities, however, should not be based on "school-oriented" habits, random choice, or superficial analyses, but rather on a knowledge of the inherent traits and psychic processes that characterize different personality styles or disorders. Whether we employ a cognitive modality first, followed by a behavioral, or a family-oriented, or an intrapsychic approach, should be determined by knowing the structure and the character of the patient's personality makeup.

The combinational revolution in general health treatment has been proposed as a first-line approach to the treatment of psychological disorders as well as medical conditions. This book strongly favors this new model, proposing to guide not just any therapeutic combination, but one built on, and informed by, a thoughtful examination of all of the expressive features (domains) that characterize the person being treated—his or her cognitive distortions, interpersonal conduct, self-image, and the like. Just as medications for diabetes or hypertension are not randomly or habitually chosen, so, too, the several spheres of psychic function that characterize our patient's difficulties must be recognized. A focused assessment should enable us to identify which specific vulnerabilities and styles prove troublesome, and to understand how they synergistically relate in a pathological manner. With this knowledge as a guide, we can begin to approach our therapeutic task with a justifiably high measure of confidence. As health professionals in other fields have argued, informed combinational therapy is the "wave of the future."

Many persons have contributed to my thinking and my writing over the past several years. In the Preface to *Disorders of Personality* (1996), I recorded and thanked the majority of that valued group. I shall be briefer in my comments here. The scientific groundwork for a therapeutic approach is no less important than its guiding principles, its undergirding theory, its assessment tools, or its diagnostic classifications—the first four components of my conception of a clinical science. This Preface has offered an opportunity to outline the overall rationale of "personality-guided therapy," the final constituent of the fivefold program that I have referred to recently as *psychosynergy*.

Most relevant in this latest phase of my work are those contributors listed on the title page. Seth Grossman and Sarah Meagher, current graduate students of mine, have been of inestimable value in researching the literature and in writing partial drafts to camouflage each of the over-100 case histories that comprise the book's "illustrations." As I have noted in earlier writings, it is not merely a charitable act that prompts me to record their important contributions. George Everly, a post-doctoral colleague some two decades ago, was the first of my associates to utilize the concept of "personologic psychotherapy," an early and insightful forerunner of personality-guided therapy. My daughter, Carrie, has continued to contribute her creative endeavors to all aspects of my work, both substantive and aesthetic. She joins with my wife, Renée, in providing editorial skills that enrich and clarify my often impenetrable prose. Lastly, I repeat the tribute noted in this book's dedication: To all of my past Students, Supervisees, and Patients, from whom I have learned more than I can ever say or give thanks for.

THEODORE MILLON

Coral Gables, Florida

Contents

xvi   **Contents**

PART I

Foundations

CHAPTER ONE

A Brief Review of Modern Treatment Modalities

Current theories and known facts about human behavior are the product of a long and continuing history of curiosity and achievement. Although dependence on the past cannot be denied, progress also occurs because dissatisfaction with the "truths" of yesterday stimulates our search for better answers today. Hopefully, a perspective of historical trends will enable us to decide which achievements are worthy of acceptance and which require further investigation.

As we look back over the long course of scientific history, we see patterns of progress and regress, brilliant leaps alternating with foolish pursuits and blind stumblings. Significant discoveries often were made by capitalizing on accidental observation; at other times, progress required the clearing away of deeply entrenched but erroneous beliefs.

Despite these erratic pathways to knowledge, scientists have returned time and time again to certain central themes: What are the causes of abnormal behavior? How can we best conceptualize the structure and dynamics of psychopathology? Are there but a few basic processes underlying all behavior? What therapeutic methods are best for alleviating these disorders? As the study of the sciences of psychopathology and psychotherapy progressed, different and occasionally insular traditions and terminology evolved to answer these questions. Separate disciplines with specialized educational and training procedures developed, until today we have divergent professional groups involved in the enactment of psychotherapy, for example, the medically oriented psychiatrist with a tradition in biology and physiology; the psychodynamic psychiatrist with a concern for unconscious intrapsychic processes; the clinical-personology psychologist with an interest in cognitive functions and the measurement of personality; and the academic psychologist with experimental approaches to the basic processes and modification of behavior. Each has studied these complex questions with a different emphasis and focus. Yet, the central issues remain the same. By tracing the history of each of these diverging trends, we will clearly see how different modes of thought today have their roots in cultural ideologies and accidental discoveries, as well as in brilliant and creative innovation.

3

Until that day in the distant future when practitioners can specify exactly which "pill" will dissolve the discomforts of psychopathology, patients will continue to be treated with drugs whose mode of action is only partially understood and whose effectiveness is highly limited. Unfortunately, this state of confusion and minimal efficacy is paralleled among the equally perplexing psychosocial therapies.

Beset with troublesome "mental" difficulties, patients are given a bewildering "choice" of therapeutic alternatives that might prove emotionally upsetting in itself, even to the well-balanced individual. Thus, patients may not only be advised to purchase this tranquilizer rather than that one, or told to take vacations or leave their jobs or go to church more often, but if they explore the possibilities of formal psychological therapy, they must choose among myriad "schools" of treatment, each of which is claimed by its adherents to be the most efficacious, and by its detractors to be both unscientific and ineffective.

Should a patient or his or her family evidence a rare degree of "scientific sophistication," they will inquire into the efficacy of alternative therapeutic approaches. What they will learn, assuming they chance upon an objective informant, is that the "outcome" of different treatment approaches is strikingly similar, and that there is little data available to indicate which method is "best" for the particular difficulty they face. Moreover, they will learn the troublesome fact that many patients improve *without benefit of psychotherapy*.

This state of affairs is most discouraging. However, the science as opposed to the art of psychotherapy is relatively new, perhaps no older than three or four decades. Discontent concerning the shoddy empirical foundations of therapeutic practices was registered in the literature as early as 1910 (Patrick & Bassoe), but systematic research did not begin in earnest until the early 1950s and has become a primary interest of able investigators only in the past thirty to forty years (Frank & Frank, 1991; Garfield & Bergen, 1994; A. Goldstein & Dean, 1966; Gottschalk & Auerbach, 1966; Hoch & Zubin, 1964; Lazarus & Messer, 1991; Norcross & Goldfried, 1992; Rubinstein & Parloff, 1959; Shlien, 1968; Stollak, Guerney, & Rothberg, 1966; Strupp & Luborsky, 1962)

It may be appropriate to comment on the reader's desire to find a single, preferred "definition" of psychotherapy. It should be evident from the foregoing discussion of treatment traditions that no single description will do. Wolberg (1967), for example, listed 26 different definitions in the recent literature, and Corsini (1981) proposed over 200 others. Obviously, psychotherapy means different things to different people. Definitions of psychotherapy cannot be formulated by reference to an abstract set of principles; rather, therapy is more or less whatever data, goals, setting, and process a therapist employs in his or her practice. Thus, a behaviorally oriented therapist who adheres to an action-suppressive process will define psychotherapy differently from an intrapsychically oriented therapist who is inclined to follow an insight-expressive procedure. Definitions follow, then, rather than precede the orientation adopted by the therapist. No single definition can fully convey the variety of philosophies and techniques with which psychotherapy is executed.

Because there is no simple way to define therapeutic techniques, it may be argued that it would be best simply to catalogue the myriad approaches currently in use, leaving their classification to some later date when a clear-cut organizational logic may have evolved. However, as was noted in earlier books (Millon & Davis, 1996a) concerning the classification of pathological syndromes, no format will ever be fully satisfactory because it is impossible to encompass all of the many dimensions and features by which a complex set of phenomena can be grouped.

Despite the inevitable limitations of classification, there are certain logical relationships among therapies that enable us to coordinate techniques in a reasonably systematic fashion. Unless we employ some rational format, advances in therapeutic science will become lost in a sea of incidental and scattered observations. Some frame of reference must be employed, then, to ensure that alternative techniques will be differentiated; in this way, we may accumulate a body of evaluative data that will enable therapists to determine the methods that are "best" for different types of psychopathology.

For the remainder of this section of the chapter, we will classify psychological therapies into several categories. The first, termed environmental management, refers to procedures that are designed to change the patient indirectly by manipulating and exploiting the surrounding conditions of his or her life for therapeutic purposes. The second, labeled supportive therapy, focuses directly on the patient; however, these procedures seek only to reestablish the patient's equilibrium without altering his or her premorbid makeup. The next sections comprise techniques that are designed to promote fundamental changes in the patient. Most deal with therapies that are practiced most often in the setting of an individual patient-therapist relationship.

The varied settings, goals, processes, and orientation that differentiate psychological treatment methods may lead one to conclude that the field of psychotherapy comprises a motley assemblage of techniques. However, despite substantive differences in verbalized rationales and technical procedures, psychotherapies "sound" more dissimilar than they are in practice. Close inspection reveals that the aims of many are fundamentally alike and that their methods, although focusing on different facets or levels of psychological functioning, deal essentially with similar pathological processes.

Given the confusing picture that prevails among psychological treatment methods, it may appear that a logical ordering of techniques at this time would be both unwise and premature. Nevertheless, it is necessary that we set forth as clearly as possible the basic rationales that differentiate the alternative traditions of therapies as we practice them today. To accomplish this in a reasonably useful pedagogical fashion requires first that we review briefly the historical development of psychotherapy. With this as a foundation, we will have a perspective from which modern schools of treatment may be more completely described and evaluated.

A BRIEF HISTORICAL PRÉCIS

Psychotherapy has a long history, although the concept of treatment by psychological methods was first formally proposed in 1803 by Johannes Reil. In this section, we review some of the relevant highlights of the history of psychotherapy, arranging them into several phases or periods, some of which extend into the present. With this as a base, we then elaborate the traditions of this history in a more formal manner.

"Psychological" treatment was first recorded in the temple practices of early Greeks and Egyptians in the eighth century B.C. In Egyptian "hospices," physician-priests interpreted dreams and suggested solutions to both earthly and heavenly problems. In the Grecian Asclepiad temples, located in regions remote from sources of stress, the sick were provided with rest, given various nourishing herbs, massaged, and surrounded with soothing music. During the fifth century B.C., Hippocrates suggested that exercise and physical tranquillity should be employed to supplant the more prevalent practices of exorcism and punishment. Asclepiades, a Roman in the first century B.C., devised a variety of measures to relax patients and openly condemned harsh "therapeutic" methods such as bloodletting and mechanical restraints. The influential practitioner Soranus (A.D. 120) suggested methods to "exercise" the mind by having the patient participate in discussions with philosophers who could aid him or her in banishing fears and sorrows. Although doubting the value of "love" and "sympathy" as a therapeutic vehicle, Soranus denounced the common practices of keeping patients in fetters and darkness and depleting their strength by bleeding and fasting. The value of philosophical discussions espoused by Soranus may be viewed as a forerunner of many contemporary psychological therapies.

Humane approaches to the treatment of the mentally ill were totally abandoned during medieval times, when witchcraft and other cruel and regressive acts were employed as "therapy." In the early years of the Renaissance, medical scientists were preoccupied with the study of the body and its workings and paid little attention to matters of the mind or the care of the mentally ill. Institutions for the insane were prevalent throughout the continent, but they continued to serve as places to incarcerate and isolate the deranged rather than as settings for medical or humane care.

A second phase of psychological treatment, what may be termed the period of "hospital reformation" and "moral treatment," began with the pioneering efforts of Philippe Pinel following the French Revolution. Guided by the belief that institutionalized patients could be brought from their state of degradation and depravity by exposure to a physically attractive environment and by contact with socially kind and moralistically proper hospital personnel, Pinel initiated an approach to mental hospital care that took hold, albeit gradually and fitfully. Moral treatment as practiced by responsible and considerate hospital personnel failed to take root for many years. This occurred for several reasons: there was a decline in the nineteenth century of psychiatric "idealism"; innumerable practical difficulties prevented the staffing of institutions with adequately motivated workers; and there was a resurgence from the mid-nineteenth to the early twentieth century of the medical disease model, turning the attention of psychiatrists to methods of physical rather than psychological treatment.

The practice of office psychiatry, characterized by treatment techniques that focus on one patient at a time and attempt to uncover the unconscious basis of problems, may be said to have begun with Mesmer's eighteenth-century investigations of *animal magnetism,* that is, hypnotism. Although the concept of magnetic forces was soon dispelled, Mesmer's occult procedures set the stage for a more scientific study of unconscious processes and strengthened the view that *suggestion* can be a potent factor in influencing mental symptoms. Moreover, Mesmer's enormous success with well-to-do "neurotics" in his private salon may be viewed as a precursor of modern-day office practice.

Charcot, the great French neurologist, explored the use of hypnotism in his studies of hysteria. Exposed to the ideas of Charcot and Bernheim and to the discovery by Breuer of emotional *abreaction,* Freud elaborated an intricate theory of psychic development and a highly original system of therapeutic practice, both of which he termed *psycho-analysis.* Subjected soon thereafter to dissenting views, even among its early adherents, the practice of psychoanalysis splintered into numerous subvarieties. Despite these deviations, the focus on unconscious processes and the office practice model with individual patients remained well entrenched as a major treatment model until quite recently.

Concurrent with the development of "office psychoanalysis," laboratory scientists were gathering a body of empirical data on basic biological processes and methods of learning and behavior change. It was many years, however, before the early work of biochemical studies and the concepts of learning theory were translated into principles and procedures applicable to therapy. By the mid-1950s, a variety of pharmacologic and behavior modification techniques, employing technical procedures of neurochemistry and systematic desensitization and eschewing notions such as *unconscious forces*, were devised and promulgated by medical and learning researchers. The emergence of these biological and behavioral treatment methods, in contrast to other psychological techniques, grew not so much out of clinical need and observation as out of systematic research. Although less than four or five decades old, biomedical and behavior techniques quickly rose to the status of major alternatives of psychotherapy.

As just noted, the most recent stage in this historical progression has been not only the development of new therapeutic procedures, but the application of research methodology in the evaluation of the *efficacy* and *process* of established procedures. Until the 1970s, the efficacy of alternative therapies was, for the most part, an article of faith rather than proof. At best, the merits of these techniques were "demonstrated" in crudely designed and easily faulted clinical studies. "Success" was gauged subjectively by the therapist according to ambiguous criteria rather than through objective measures undertaken by independent judges. Rarely were controls employed, and improvement rates were presented without reference to such relevant variables as chronicity, symptomatology, and so on. In short, what little had been done was done poorly. Despite questions concerning effectiveness, proponents of each technique were not only convinced of the utility of their cherished procedures, but prospered and confidently inculcated each new generation of fledgling clinicians. Disputes among "schools" of therapy were evident, of course, but they were handled by verbal polemics rather than empirical research.

As long ago as 1910, Hoche noted that therapists were not scientists but cultists, willing promulgators of dubious measures that rested on the most unreasonable of assumptions. Despite these early warnings, it was not until the late 1940s that clinicians such as Carl Rogers and J. McV. Hunt, trained both in scientific method and therapeutic practice, pioneered the first controlled studies of psychological therapy (Hunt, 1952; Rogers & Dymond, 1954). Spurred further by the critical reviews of Eysenck (1952), Zubin (1953), and Levitt (1957), increasing numbers of investigators began to reexamine the empirical underpinnings of psychotherapy and set out to design efficacy and process studies that employed proper controls, criteria, and measurement techniques. The fruits of this newest phase in the history of psychotherapy have only recently begun to materialize, but the seeds of the "scientific" era of psychotherapy were finally well planted.

It must be noted that psychotherapy is a constantly changing science of treatment. As new research, theory, and clinical experience enlarge our range of knowledge, many of the treatment techniques described in this book may call for modification. The text is intended exclusively for graduate students and clinical professionals; moreover, the reader is not expected to utilize its suggestions without an extensive range of information about a patient to guide his or her treatment. Although every effort has been made to furnish guidelines that live up to medical and psychological standards, the author makes no warranty with regard to the effectiveness of the methods contained herein. This caveat is especially addressed to the nonprofessional who may be seeking methods for self-treatment: nonprofessionals are urged to consult their psychologist and/or physician for advice and treatment.

We now turn to a more comprehensive elaboration of the preceding, organizing them into the foundations of modern and contemporary schools of therapy.

ENVIRONMENTAL MANAGEMENT

Little progress can be expected in therapy if the patient's everyday environment provides few gratifications and is filled with tension and conflict. Like the proverbial high-priced automobile that uses up gasoline faster than it can be pumped in, an unwholesome life situation may set the patient back faster than therapy can move him or her forward. For these reasons, it may be necessary to control or modify disruptive home or work influences or perhaps remove the patient entirely from these disorganizing effects.

Beyond relief and protection, environmental manipulation may be employed to achieve positive therapeutic ends such as *releasing* potentials or developing social skills. These two elements, the alleviation of situational stress and the exploitation of situational opportunities for constructive change, constitute the chief goals of environmental management.

The profession of social work has traditionally played a central role in planning and controlling extratherapeutic elements of patient life that influence the progress of formal treatment; appropriately, social workers are viewed as integral members of the total therapeutic team. Among the numerous goals of clinical social work is to assist either the patient or the family in removing deleterious economic and interpersonal conditions. More recently, social casework is oriented to facilitate the patient to cope with significant affairs of life.

Achieving these ends may entail direct counseling on practical matters such as daily habits and routines and the budgeting of family finances. More important, mental health workers can be of considerable assistance in pointing out to relatives how they may be contributing to interpersonal tensions and resentments within the family. The one or two hours of face-to-face therapy with the patient may be completely negated by the attitudes of relatives whose verbalized good intentions are no guarantee that they will be carried out. Where necessary, then, direct intervention in the form of weekly counseling sessions may be recommended for relatives who precipitate difficulties. The efforts of a skillful mental health worker can be of inestimable value in this regard.

Where occupational or social problems exist, mental health workers may be instrumental in arranging patient participation in community agencies such as sheltered workshops and recreational centers. In sheltered occupational programs, the patient may learn to cope with tensions he or she may have experienced in relating to fellow employees and employers; the understanding and tolerant attitudes of the professional supervisory staff at these centers ensure against harsh reprimands for poor performance, which reinforce feelings of self-inadequacy. For essentially similar goals, clinicians may recommend participation in recreational clubs to remotivate social interests and develop interpersonal skills; these settings are relatively free of the personal and competitive tensions of normal group relationships.

Clinical staff can be of invaluable service in smoothing the transition of patients from hospital to home and community. Practical arrangements may be made for the patient's employment, follow-up therapy, and guidance to the family as to their expectations and ways of reacting to the patient. To ease the strain of resuming normal responsibilities that may be too taxing for the patient, arrangements may be made for halfway house or night or day hospital programs.

Except in cases of transient situational stress, environmental vexations and complications are often only precipitants, tending merely to aggravate deeply established pathological patterns. In other words, the source of the patient's difficulties either are *internal*, ingrained personal attitudes and interpersonal habits that persist and perpetuate themselves, or *relational*. Thus, clinicians often find that following the removal of one environmental irritant, the patient involves himself or herself in another relational problem that is as destructive as the first. Without modifications of the patient's pathological expectancies and behaviors, the benefits of surface "management" alone, in all likelihood, will prove short-lived.

Until the past three or four decades, institutionalized patients were provided with kind and thoughtful custodial care at best, and at worst were incarcerated in filthy wards, shackled, crammed together, and isolated from the interests and activities of the larger community. Even in the better hospitals, little effort was expended to see that the setting, routines, and personnel of the institution provided more than a comfortable asylum, a refuge from strains of everyday existence, a place where patients could withdraw quietly into themselves. Despite the pioneering efforts of Pinel in the eighteenth century and Dorothea Dix in the nineteenth, Deutsch (1948) could report in his book, *The Shame of the States,* that most hospital patients in the mid-twentieth century sat out their lives in dreary environments, abandoned by unsympathetic families and exposed to uninterested personnel.

The change from inhumane to custodial to genuine therapeutic environments came about, not through public outcries, but through the fortuitous advent of psychopharmacological treatment. These drugs "contained" difficult patients, encouraging and enabling hospital workers to turn their attention from problems of restraint to those of therapy. At the same time, state legislative bodies became convinced that a massive infusion of funds for psychopharmaceuticals might ultimately unburden the taxpayer of costly long-term patient incarceration. The increased ease of patient management, together with the influx of additional funds, combined to spur a new attitude on the part of both public and hospital personnel.

SUPPORTIVE THERAPY

Whereas the procedures of environmental management focus on the situational context of the patient, seeking to exploit the persons and activities surrounding his or her daily life for therapeutic purposes, the procedures of supportive therapy focus directly on the patient. In contrast to other individual treatment approaches, however, supportive therapy does not seek to make fundamental changes in patients' premorbid attitudes and strategies, but to strengthen these patterns so that patients can again function as they did prior to their current disorder.

Supportive procedures are employed either as the principal mode of therapy or as adjuncts to other treatment methods. Central to the varied techniques that constitute supportive therapy is the patient's acceptance of the therapist's "benevolent authority," as Wolberg (1967) put it. The therapist must maintain a sympathetic but firm attitude, exhibiting a tolerance of the patient's deviance, yet inspiring strength through the force of his or her authority and forthright honesty. As a consequence, the patient will be inclined to trust the therapist's judgments and view the therapist as an ally worthy of identification and respect. With this as a foundation, the therapist may achieve the ends sought.

Supportive therapy may be separated into three basic procedures: *ventilation, reassurance,* and *persuasion.* These may be employed separately, concurrently, or sequentially. Let us examine each.

Ventilation

People often gain a measure of emotional relief by simply unburdening their woes to a sympathetic listener; the therapeutic value of much of what a friendly physician or minister achieves is obtained by the expedient of listening without reproval as the troubled person "gets things off his chest."

Emotional ventilation comprises an important element of supportive therapy. Distressing ideas and impulses often cannot be banished from one's thoughts and keep cropping up to disrupt one's daily life. To relieve the pressure of these "bottled-up" emotions, patients are encouraged to share their thoughts with the therapist and to feel free to express the pent-up tensions these thoughts generate. Patients are assured that everyone experiences disconcerting impulses and ideas, and that they can feel confident that they will be accepted and understood by the therapist without reproach. It is hoped that exposure of these suppressed conflicts and urges will not only serve to decrease tension, but also assist the patient in learning to accept them and develop a more constructive approach to their solution.

Where therapeutic goals are limited to the restitution of equilibrium without changes in premorbid behavior and personality, the patient is *not* urged to reveal more than he or she is inclined to do. Although patients are encouraged to express whatever they desire, the therapist refrains from probing and uncovering repressed emotions and thoughts that can aggravate the very discomforts therapy is seeking to relieve.

Reassurance

The mere act of participating in therapy is a form of implicit reassurance that all is not hopeless, that there is someone knowledgeable and understanding who can be turned to for solace and strength in moments of anxiety and despondency.

Supportive therapists provide reassurance in more direct ways by pointing out how baseless are the patient's beliefs and feelings, such as unwarranted apprehensions of "going insane," and how unjust the patient has been in condemning himself or herself for minor social digressions or excesses. Therapists divert patients' preoccupations with past regrets, ask them to recall their more commendable achievements, and direct their attention to potentially constructive and self-enhancing activities in the present.

Although reassurance is part and parcel of every therapeutic encounter, its indiscriminate use can only backfire. A consistent Pollyanna-like approach to therapy will ultimately raise questions in the patient's mind as to the therapist's grasp and appreciation of his or her problems; even worse, it may lead the patient to doubt the therapist's sincerity or judgment. On the other hand, should the patient learn to accept these superficial pacifications, he or she may become unduly dependent on them and be unwilling to face reality or to examine genuine solutions to problems. Inevitably, the patient will be in for rude shocks when objective difficulties and personal inadequacies simply cannot be "reassured" away.

Persuasion

In this supportive technique, the therapist seeks to convince patients that they possess within them the will and the wherewithal to reorient their pathological attitudes and behaviors. By dint of authority and by the use of subtle ploys, the therapist enjoins patients to "get a hold of" themselves and reject the irrational assumptions and habits that consistently disrupt their life. By appealing to patients' reason and common sense, the therapist leads them to see the logic of abandoning deviant ways, developing a fresh outlook on life, and rebuilding a sense of self-esteem. Concrete suggestions are made to aid patients in redirecting goals, dissipating worrisome habits, mastering muddled thoughts, assuming responsibilities with confidence and authority, and facing adversity with an objective attitude. By the sheer force of the therapist's convictions and the picture of self-assurance and firm resolve that he or she paints, patients are inspired to see the virtues and rewards of a poised and outgoing style of life and to exhibit a high self-regard; hopefully, others will view them equally positively.

Persuasive measures often reap immediate benefits in that they strengthen the patient's self-confidence and brace weakened coping defenses. But not all patients possess the means for reorienting themselves successfully or the competence to master their distraught emotions effectively; moreover, for a variety of both conscious and unconscious reasons, many will resist the therapist's facile prescriptions. Although persuasion can serve as a fruitful if temporary expedient for well-integrated persons, the probability is small that its benefits can long be sustained even in these cases, or that mere exhortation can make any inroads with patients who suffer severe forms of pathology. As with reassurance, persuasion often backfires; thus, patients may lose their "faith" in all types of psychotherapy should the exhortations of their therapist come to naught.

BEHAVIOR MODIFICATION MODALITIES

Change behavior and you have "cured" the patient's problems.

It was the great Russian physiologist, Ivan Petrovitch Pavlov, who demonstrated experimentally that behavior is modified as a function of learning. Pavlov recognized late in his life that Thorndike had preceded him regarding the concept of reinforced learning by two or three years (1928). Pavlov was preceded also by Ivan Sechenov, the father of Russian neurology, who stated as early as 1863 that all animal and human acts were partly cerebral and partly learned or trained.

As is well-known, Pavlov's discoveries resulted from an unanticipated observation made during studies of digestive reflexes. In the year 1902, while measuring saliva secreted by dogs in response to food, he noticed that dogs salivated either at the sight of the food dish or on hearing the footsteps of the attendant who brought it in. Pavlov realized that the stimulus of the dish or the footsteps had become, through experience, a substitute or signal for the stimulus of food. He soon concluded that this signaling or learning process must play a central part in the adaptive capacity of animals. Because of his physiological orientation, however, he conceived these observations as processes of the brain. Initially, he referred to them as "psychic secretions." When he presented his findings in 1903 before the fourteenth International Congress of Medicine in Madrid, he coined the term *conditioned reflex* (cr) for the learned response and labeled the learned signal a *conditioned stimulus* (cs). As his work progressed, Pavlov noted that conditioned reflexes persisted over long periods of disuse. They could be inhibited briefly by various distractions and completely extinguished by repeated failure to follow the signal or conditioned stimulus with the usual reinforcement.

Pavlov's early experiments served to replace the focus on subjective introspection that had been favored by most psychologists at the turn of the century. In his substitution of measurable and objective reactions to stimuli, he laid the groundwork, not only for the next half century of Russian research, but for American Behaviorism and modern learning theory as well. But before we discuss the impact of Pavlov's ideas on others, we note two of his later contributions that are relevant to the history of psychotherapy.

Pavlov came to realize that words could replace physical stimuli as signals for conditioned learning. He divided human thought into two signal systems:

> Sensations, perceptions and direct impressions of the surrounding world are primary signals of reality. Words are secondary signals. They represent themselves as abstractions of reality and permit generalizations. The human brain is composed of the animal brain, the first signaling system, and the purely human part related to speech, the second signaling system. (1928, p. 88)

Pavlov noted that under emotional distress, behavior shifts from the symbols of the second signal system to the bodily expression of the first signal system. Not only did he recognize this "regression" as a part of pathology, but he also used the concept of the second signal to show how verbal therapy can influence the underlying first signal system it represents. Thus, words can alter defective or malfunctioning brain processes in the "neurotic" individual via persuasion and suggestion.

Another of Pavlov's important contributions to psychopathology, his studies of experimentally produced "neuroses" in animals, was prompted directly by his acquaintance with Freud's writings. In this work, agitation and anger are created in previously cooperative animals by presenting them with conflicting or intense stimuli. These studies generated a marked enthusiasm among a small group of American psychiatrists desirous of finding a more rigorous foundation for psychodynamic theory. The investigations undertaken by W. Horsley Gantt and Howard Liddell in the 1930s derive largely from their attempt to bridge the ideas of Pavlov and Freud.

Theories possessing a common basis in Pavlovian concepts and behavioristic objectivity provided new principles for understanding psychopathology and psychotherapy. Primary attention was given to the processes of conditioning and reinforcement because they are the mediating agents through which response habits are acquired and extinguished.

Although anticipated to some degree by William James's chapter on habits in his 1890 textbook *Principles of Psychology*, Knight Dunlap was in many regards the first systematic theorist utilizing behavioral and learning principles (Dunlap, 1932). Even John Watson in his autobiography acknowledges that Dunlap was the person who convinced him that behavior should comprise the basic data for psychology. A follower of Pavlov, Dunlap outlined a variety of processes that were significant to understanding pathological learning. Unfortunately, he restrained the impulse to report his methods until he felt they had been fully perfected; hence, his primary method, termed *negative practice,* remained largely unknown to the clinical world. Interestingly, however, Dunlap anticipated important trends in therapeutic practice (e.g., Bandura, 1969) by proposing that conditioning is invariably embedded in a cognitive context.

Another early behaviorist, preceding the work of Dollard and Miller (1950) by a year or two, was Andrew Salter (1949). A firm believer in the role of conditioning, he sought to build therapeutic methods on the scientific bedrock of Pavlov's conditioning research. Ranging across a broad variety of mental disorders, such as stuttering, shyness, anxiety, masochism, and the psychopathic personality, his well-organized techniques were firmly grounded in what he preferred to term "conditioned reflex therapy." In reading both Dunlap and Salter, one cannot help but recognize that the foundations of behavioral therapy were well set many decades earlier than we tend to think.

The small number of concepts employed in these theories to account for the diverse behaviors involved in psychopathology and psychotherapy was an achievement of considerable merit and made them especially attractive to psychologists tired of the obscure and complex explanatory concepts of the psychoanalytic schools. But of even greater importance was the hope that new insights regarding the development and modification of behavioral pathology could also be provided. For our present purposes, it will suffice to note briefly the major ideas of this approach to psychotherapy; more detailed illustrations will follow in later chapters.

Behavior therapists do not postulate the existence of underlying causes or intrapsychic conflicts to account for pathology. Rather, mental disorders are simply a composite of the person's response habits learned as a result of reinforcements experienced throughout life. Distinctions between adaptive and maladaptive behaviors reflect differences only in the reinforcing experiences to which the individual was exposed. There are no "neuroses," "repressions," or "diseases" underlying pathological symptoms, as symptoms are merely habits developed and maintained by environmental reinforcements.

The behaviorist's approach to therapy follows logically from a view of pathology; modify the behavior designated as the symptom and "pathology" is eliminated. Therapy, or behavior modification as it is called, specifies first which behaviors are maladaptive and which behaviors should be reinforced to supplant them. Psychodynamic statements such as *Strengthen the patient's ego* are translated into the question *What differences in behavior would enable the patient to function more adequately?* Once the desired changes are specified, a program of reinforcements to shape the new behavior is devised. These reinforcements are given in the form of words, images, or direct experience. By creating imaginary or real parallels to situations that previously had evoked maladaptive responses, these responses are extinguished and new, more adaptive ones learned in their stead. Through this *behavior modification,* the individual is "cured" of his or her disorder.

As we conceive the *behavioral* construct, it includes both concrete and observable actions, the prime subject for modification among *pure* behaviorists, as well as the expressive significance of these actions, and the transactive meaning of these behaviors in social interactions, the prime subject of *interpersonally oriented* therapists. In a later section, we discuss what is commonly referred to as *cognitive* therapists, those who are primarily concerned with how cognitive processes affect actions.

The feature that most clearly distinguishes pure behavior therapies from other approaches is their commitment to an action-suppressive process. Behaviorists consider emotional ventilation and insight, the bedrocks of other schools of therapy, to be of dubious value; not only are these two procedures viewed as time-consuming digressions, but they are often thought to be counterproductive, that is, to strengthen rather than weaken maladaptive behaviors (Bandura, 1969; Davison, 1968; Goldfreid & Davison, 1976; Kahn, 1960; Linehan, 1993). As behaviorists see it, the task of therapy is to achieve as directly as possible changes in real-life action, not greater self-understanding or affective expression.

During the late 1950s, stimulated largely by the provocative writings of Skinner (1953), Wolpe (1958), and Eysenck (1959), the coalescence of learning and psychotherapy took a new turn. Instead of merely restating accepted forms of treatment in the vernacular of learning concepts, as was done by Dollard and Miller (1950), investigators began to utilize principles that were derived first in behavioral learning research to create entirely new forms of therapy. It is these new approaches, based on the direct application of experimental learning principles, that constitute the treatment methods discussed in this section.

In the following sections, we follow a classificatory format that emphasizes the primary *objectives* of therapeutic intervention. The first set of approaches, termed *behavior elimination methods,* consists of procedures that are limited to but especially well-suited for the task of weakening existent pathological responses. The second group, labeled *behavior formation techniques,* includes procedures that can fulfill several goals; they can be employed not only to eliminate pathological behaviors but also to strengthen existent and acquire entirely new adaptive responses. Although this twofold division is not without overlap, it possesses the merit of stressing the utility of methods as instruments for achieving the two primary objectives of behavior modification: the elimination of maladaptive behaviors and the formation or strengthening of adaptive ones.

Methods of Behavior Elimination

The most expedient and direct procedures for eliminating or overcoming maladaptive responses have been termed *counterconditioning* and *extinction.* Let us review some of the techniques classed under these labels.

Counterconditioning methods.   The rationale of counterconditioning is based on the fact that incompatible responses cannot coexist; for example, you can walk forward or backward, but you cannot do both at the same time. Translating this into therapeutic terms, if a patient exhibits a maladaptive feeling or behavior in response to certain stimuli, that response can be neutralized or blocked by evoking responses that are antithetical to it; for example, if a particular stimulus habitually elicited an anxiety response in a patient, the therapist may train the patient to associate an incompatible response to that stimulus, such as intense pleasure or deep relaxation, in the hope of precluding or counteracting anxiety.

Counterconditioning methods have been employed to achieve two goals: eliminating feelings and thoughts, such as anxiety or fear, that inhibit desirable and adaptive behaviors; and eliminating personally objectionable or socially unacceptable behaviors, such as compulsive rituals or alcoholism. To countercondition an emotion that inhibits an adaptive response, the technique of *desensitization* may fruitfully be applied; to countercondition a maladaptive response itself, methods of *aversive learning* can be used. Let us examine both procedures.

Relaxation and desensitization.   This technique, most fully developed by Joseph Wolpe (1958), seeks to counteract the discomforting and inhibitory effects of fear-producing stimuli by interposing and associating a relaxation response to these stimuli; hopefully, by repeated counterconditioning, the fear response will be replaced by its antagonist, relaxation. Not only are the discomforts of fear eliminated thereby, but the patient may now be free to acquire adaptive responses that had previously been blocked.

As noted, relaxation is a technique that is often used as a competing response to overcome the anxious arousal that patients experience when faced with stressful situations. In early work by Jacobsen (1929) and subsequent modifications by Benson (1975), the patient learns to alternately tense and relax all major muscle groups of the body (Bernstein & Borkovec, 1973). After relaxation methods have been practiced under nonstressful conditions, the counterconditioning and systematic desensitization procedures are employed to aid the patient in reducing anxiety during threatening situations. These techniques are central elements in most stress management programs.

Wolpe's procedure follows a precise and well-planned sequence. The logic of Wolpe's counterconditioning procedure is simple and straightforward: relaxation is incompatible with fear; by arranging a properly graded sequence, the previously conditioned association between each stimulus item and the response of fear is eliminated. Wolpe claims with some justification that the relaxed attitude acquired in the consulting room generalizes to real-life situations; that is, patients are able to face the actual, previously feared environmental event without reacting as they had in the past.

Although Wolpe considers his method to be a behavioral approach, it should be noted that his desensitization technique deals essentially with cognitive processes. His procedure employs the data of symbolic imagination, not overt behavior. Perhaps it would be more correct, therefore, to classify his therapeutic technique among the cognitive procedures. The status of Wolpe's formulations as a behavioral approach may be seriously questioned also on the grounds of his partial allegiance to a neurological etiology, a view that contrasts sharply with the "pure behaviorism" of Skinner, for example. Nevertheless, tradition, brief though it has been in this field, assigns Wolpe's methods to the behavior classification.

Aversive learning.   Whereas desensitization attempts to eliminate responses (e.g., fear) that inhibit desirable behaviors (e.g., facing and solving previously feared situations), aversive learning seeks only to eliminate undesirable responses (e.g., aggressive sexual acts). This distinction may be seen more clearly by the fact that desensitization achieves its aims by counterconditioning an unpleasant response (fear) with a pleasant one (relaxation); in contrast, aversive learning counterconditions a formerly pleasant response (drinking or sexual excitement) with an unpleasant one (nausea or pain).

The classic example of aversion therapy is the use of nauseant drugs in the treatment of alcoholism. In this procedure, patients first ingest the drug. Then, moments prior to the onset of nausea, they are given a drink of liquor. Because the drink immediately precedes the sickening nausea and vomiting, patients learn over a number of such sessions to associate drinking with an unpleasant rather than a pleasant experience.

Extinction methods.   Counterconditioning procedures eliminate inhibitory emotions and maladaptive behaviors indirectly; that is, they do not attack the response itself, but interpose an incompatible response to a formerly provocative stimulus. Extinction procedures, in contrast, work directly on the disruptive behavior itself, that is, without employing an antithetical response.

There is a parallel between the two major forms of extinction and the two methods of counterconditioning. *Implosive therapy* is akin to desensitization, in that it has as its primary utility the elimination of responses that inhibit adaptive behaviors. *Reinforcement withdrawal* is similar to aversive learning, in that it is most useful in eliminating socially undesirable behaviors. A forerunner of both methods was known as *negative practice* (Dunlap, 1932), a procedure in which the patient voluntarily produced the unacceptable response, time and again, until he or she "got tired of it" or began to think it was "pretty silly" or "stupid"; negative practice was employed most frequently in extinguishing speech difficulties and other motor disturbances, such as tics.

Exposure therapy.   This technique is similar to desensitization in that it has as its goal the elimination of inhibitory responses such as fear and anxiety. The procedural steps of these two methods are quite alike also in that the patient's most disturbing thoughts and feelings are identified, and he or she is asked to imagine them during treatment sessions. In contrast to desensitization, however, Stampfl (London, 1964; Stampfl & Levis, 1967), the innovator of the *implosive* technique, the forerunner of exposure therapy, introduces the most anxiety-arousing event immediately, seeking thereby to frighten overwhelmingly rather than to calm and relax the patient. Stampfl argued that by flooding the patient's imagination with the very worst of his or her fears in a setting in which no actual harm does occur, the patient will gradually learn that those fears are unfounded (unreinforced) as nothing really detrimental happens.

A more modern variant of implosive therapy was developed by Agras, Leitenberg, and Barlow (1968) in which patients, under the supervision of clinicians, were involved in a series of situational in vivo exposure exercises (Barlow, 1988). Here, they were expected to engage in exposure practices in which they systematically ventured away from "safe places" and into situations (e.g., those presenting anxiety-arousing phobic objects) that they had been avoiding. The success rate for this procedure has been especially high with the anxiety-based phobias. The addition of certain cognitive techniques to in vivo exposure appears to add to its overall treatment efficacy.

Reinforcement withdrawal.   Rather than forcing the patient to be flooded and overwhelmed by disturbing thoughts and feelings as in implosive therapy, the reinforcement withdrawal tactic allows the undesirable behavior to dissipate naturally, simply by failing to provide the reinforcements it previously evoked. In further contrast to implosive therapy, in which the therapist seeks to overcome inhibiting responses such as fear, reinforcement withdrawal is most suitable for combating behaviors that should be inhibited, such as aggression and compulsive acts. To illustrate, Walton (1960) was able to extinguish a woman's severe habit of scratching her skin by advising her family to refrain from providing sympathy and attention in conjunction with her ailment; withdrawal of these positive reinforcements led to a rapid cessation of the habit. In another study, the control of bedtime tantrum behavior was achieved in a child by advising his parents to pay no attention to him as he cried and raged; by the eighth night, the youngster not only failed to whimper, but even smiled as he quietly went to bed.

Methods of Behavior Formation

Until recently, most types of therapy had as their principal goal the elimination of faulty attitudes, feelings, and behaviors. It was argued or assumed implicitly that when these symptoms were removed, the patient would be "free" to utilize or develop more adaptive habits. Such constructive consequences do follow for many patients, but not all. Many lack the means for acquiring new adaptive habits, for example, autistic children or other patients whose past experiences may not have supplied them with a repertoire of healthy behaviors that will flourish, so to speak, when their inhibiting fears and maladaptive responses are removed.

The notion of "forming" new constructive behaviors by direct procedures is an important departure from more traditional therapeutic methods. Although many therapies have positive growth as a desired aim, few are designed to achieve this goal explicitly and in a systematically planned fashion.

Our attention turns in this section to two behavioral methods employed to achieve the goal of response formation: *selective positive reinforcement,* including *self-assertion training* and *social skills training,* and *model imitation.* Although acquisition and strengthening of adaptive behaviors are the distinguishing objectives of these procedures, either may be used to eliminate maladaptive responses as well.

Selective positive reinforcement.   "Pure" behaviorists believe that the patient's actions are best conceived as a product *not* of intrapsychic conflicts or cognitive attitudes but of observable environmental conditions. Accordingly, changes in behavior must be achieved by manipulating external events. Central to these manipulations are reinforcements, that is, environmental rewards and punishments. By a judicious arrangement of reinforcing consequences, behaviors can be either strengthened or weakened.

The most fully developed schema based on the selective reinforcement model is operant conditioning, a technique devised by B.F. Skinner (1938) and his many associates and disciples (e.g., Ayllon & Michael, 1959; Ferster, 1958, 1964). Briefly, operant methods provide rewards when the patient exhibits the desired behavior and withholds them when undesired responses occur. Through this selective application of positive reinforcement, present adaptive behaviors are fortified, and through sequences of *successive approximation* and *shaping,* new adaptive responses are built into the patient's behavioral repertoire.

Self-assertion training.   The early and highly creative behavior therapist Andrew Salter (1949) was the first of the behavior theorists to identify personal assertiveness as an important positive goal for his patients. Although adhering rigidly to Pavlovian conceptions of cortical excitation and inhibition, he encouraged "inhibited" individuals to vent their emotions to others in a spontaneous and open manner. He suggested that his patients express their feelings verbally, that is, tell people when they felt good, bad, angry, or annoyed. For these persons, Salter recommended that they should openly disagree with others and to speak out when they felt unjustly treated or overlooked. Furthermore, they should focus on themselves and their wishes rather than the desires of others. Similarly, Salter further encouraged patients to respond with their feelings quickly, that is, at the moment their emotions surged forward and without reflection or hesitation. Although he anchored his model in Pavlovian classical conditioning, Salter believed that assertiveness would overcome the same reservations that self-actualizing therapists refer to in their treatment goals. Lazarus (1971), for example, extended Salter's ideas by developing assertion training groups. Here, the problems that unassertiveness may create for shy and inhibited persons is utilized in a setting in which assertion skills are discussed and rehearsed together.

Social skills training.   Numerous patients, for one reason or another, have failed to develop adequate social skills. For example, activities involving interpersonal behavior (e.g., job interviews, dating inquiries, general social conversation) are seriously deficient in many personality disorders (e.g., avoidant, schizoid, schizotypal). In this model, patients rehearse relevant social behaviors together with their therapist, thereby practicing specific behaviors that will overcome their prior limitations. As with assertion training programs, group social skills training has been developed (J. Kelly, 1985). These groups are composed of individuals with comparable social limitations, enabling them to provide one another with opportunities to acquire new skills that may enhance their self-esteem as well as their social adequacy.

Model imitation.   According to Bandura (1962; Bandura & Walters, 1965), the primary exponent of behavior modification through imitative modeling, selective positive reinforcement is an exceedingly inefficient method for promoting the acquisition of new adaptive learnings. Effective though operant procedures may be for strengthening and building on responses that *already exist* in the patient's behavioral repertoire, they demand extremely ingenious and time-consuming manipulations to generate new response patterns. Contributing to this difficulty is the fact that the patient must perform the desired response or some close approximation of it *before* the therapist can apply the appropriate reinforcement. Where the sought for response is highly complex (e.g., speaking meaningful sentences), the probability is likely to be zero that it will be spontaneously emitted. Approximations of complicated responses may be achieved by an intricate chain of reinforced steps, but this sequence is bound to be both laborious and prolonged. Rather than struggle through this tiresome and at best unreliable procedure, the task of forming new responses can be abbreviated and accelerated by arranging conditions in which the desired act is performed. Modeling sequences are often designed in combination with reinforcement; thus, in a typical procedure, patients obtain a reward when they imitate an act performed by a model.

Let us summarize our review of the behavior modification approach with the following observations. The techniques of behavior modification have been subjected to more systematic research, despite their brief history, than all other psychological treatment approaches combined. This reflects, in part, the strong academic-experimental orientation of those who practice behavior therapy; most behaviorists have sought to provide a firm link between the scientific discipline of psychology proper and the applied problems of clinical treatment. Because behavior therapies will continue to be rigorously examined at each stage of their development, it is likely that most of them, once established, will withstand the test of time.

Despite the fact that most published studies of behavior therapy represent reports of clinical rather than controlled experimental research, the overall picture of efficacy that emerges is extremely impressive. More specifically, the effectiveness of counterconditioning methods for eliminating simple reactions and complex syndromes is well documented (see Chapters 5 through 9). Similarly, selective reinforcement and imitative modeling techniques have proved suitable for strengthening and forming adaptive social behaviors among several patient groups (e.g., severely decompensated and antisocial syndromes) that have failed to yield to other therapeutic approaches. That these attainments have been achieved rapidly, economically, and in the hands of only moderately sophisticated agents (e.g., nurses or attendants) adds further to the value of these methods.

On the debit side of the ledger, behavioral approaches have not demonstrated efficacy with diffuse and pervasive pathological impairments such as personality patterns, maladaptive coping strategies, and "existential crises." Many of these difficult-to-pinpoint problems simply do not lend themselves to the sharply focused procedures of behavior therapy. Although advances in treatment methodology may ultimately bring these forms of disturbed functioning within the purview of behavior therapy, for the present they seem more suitably handled by cognitive and intrapsychic approaches.

INTERPERSONAL AND RELATIONAL MODALITIES

It is how we change everyday relationships that matters most in therapy.

On the basis of his clinical observations, Alfred Adler (1929) concluded that superiority and power strivings were more fundamental to pathology than was sexuality. Although many of his patients were not overtly assertive, he observed that their disorder enabled them to dominate others in devious and subtle ways. Phobias and hypochondriasis, for example, not only excused a patient from disagreeable tasks but allowed him or her to control and manipulate others. Adler hypothesized that these strivings for superiority were a consequence of the inevitable and universally experienced weakness and inferiority in early childhood. In this conception, Adler attempted to formulate a universal drive that would serve as an alternative to Freud's universal sexual strivings. According to Adler, basic feelings of inferiority led to persistent and unconscious compensatory efforts. These were manifested as pathological struggles for power and triumph if the individual experienced unusual deficiencies or weaknesses in childhood. Among healthier personalities, compensation accounted for strivings at self-improvement and interests in social change and welfare. These compensatory strivings, acquired by all individuals as a reaction to the restrictions imposed by their more powerful parents, led to a general pattern of behavior that Adler called the *style of life.*

Adler's view that the character of human development is rooted in social strivings served to guide the ideas of Karen Horney and Erich Fromm. Although both took issue with Freud's biological orientation, preferring to emphasize sociocultural factors instead, they regarded themselves as renovators of rather than deviators from his theories. Along with Harry Stack Sullivan, they have been called neo-Freudian social theorists.

Horney's main contention was that disorders reflected cultural trends learned within the family; biological determinants were minimized and interpersonal relationships stressed. Anxiety and repressed anger were generated in rejected children and led to feelings of helplessness, hostility, and isolation. As these children matured, they developed an intricate defensive pattern of either withdrawal, acquiescence, or aggression as a means of handling their basic anxiety. Although Horney felt that adult patterns resulted largely from early experience, she believed, in contrast to Freud, that therapy should focus on its adult form of expression. First, the intervening years between childhood and adulthood caused important changes in adaptive behavior. And second, present-day realities had to be accepted and the goals of therapy had to take them into account. Although many of Horney's ideas were presented in an unsystematic and unscientific fashion, the clarity of her expositions and their appropriateness to modern-day life influenced the practice and thought of psychodynamic psychiatry in many important ways.

Erich Fromm, a neo-Freudian social philosopher and psychologist, was the first of Freud's disciples to concentrate his writings on the role of society in mental disorder. He advocated the view that the impositions of social conformity force individuals to relinquish their natural spontaneity and freedom. To Fromm, neurotic behavior is a consequence of insufficient encouragement and warmth from one's parents, which could have strengthened the individual against the demands of society. Fromm perceived the goal of therapy to be a bolstering of the individual's capacities for self-responsibility, and not the facilitation of a conformist adjustment. Fromm's interest in societal influences led him to modify Freud's neurotic character types into social character types. Along with similar modifications formulated by Horney, these types depicted contemporary patterns of personality disorder with extraordinary clarity.

Dyadic Treatment Models

Broadening the therapeutic focus in significant ways are therapists who describe themselves as *interpersonally oriented*. Although they address the behavioral conduct of the patient, it is their assertion that behaviors that relate to and transact communications with others are by far the most significant. Preceded by several theorists around mid-century, there has been a marked upsurge in the use of formal interpersonal and relational therapies in recent decades (Anchin & Kiesler, 1982; L.S. Benjamin, 1993; Kaslow, 1996; Kiesler, 1997; Klerman, Weissman, Rounsaville, & Chevron, 1984).

Sullivan's interpersonal model. Foremost among the early interpersonal therapists was Harry Stack Sullivan (1953, 1954). He was influenced first by the American psychiatrists Adolf Meyer and William Alanson White, but later adopted many of Freud's concepts regarding intrapsychic processes and early childhood development. His emphasis on the interpersonal aspects of growth and his contributions to the communication process in therapy classify him properly among neo-Freudian social theorists. Because of Sullivan's exposure to the linguist Edward Sapir and the positivist philosopher Percy Bridgman, he became especially critical of the conceptually awkward and frequently obscure formulations of psychoanalysis. As a remedy, he created his own system and terminology. With few exceptions, his terminology has failed to replace that of Freud. However, his highly original studies, especially regarding early development, schizophrenia, and the process of therapy, have had a marked impact on the thinking and practice of contemporary psychodynamic psychiatry.

He directed his efforts not only to *parataxic distortion,* a process akin to the classical transference phenomenon, but to a host of other habitual maneuvers such as selective inattention, memory dissociation, and inaccurate social evaluations. The task of his therapy was to unravel this pattern of self-protective but ultimately self-defeating interpersonal measures. At times, Sullivan, a former psychoanalyst, sought to elicit child-hood memories and dream materials; however, his focus was directed primarily to current interpersonal problems. Sullivan believed that the classical passive or blank-screen attitude should be replaced by a more natural expression of the therapist's *real* feelings and thoughts. Beyond this, he proposed that certain attitudes be simulated by the therapist so as to throw the patient off guard, thereby provoking interpersonally illuminating responses. In short, Sullivan tried to participate actively in an interpersonal treatment relationship, exploiting his own reactions and feigning others, both designed to uncover the patient's distortions and unconscious styles of behavior. The primary instrument of Sullivan's therapy was skillful interviewing. The interview interaction, then, rather than the passive free association technique, was considered by Sullivan to be the most fruitful means of disentangling the web of interpersonal distortions.

Berne's transactional analysis.   A progressive shift from a biological to a socio-cultural orientation may be seen in several therapies. Employing patient-therapist communications as their data and drawing their models from either mathematical game theorists or social role theorists such as Mead (1934), a number of modern therapists have formulated an approach to treatment that is best depicted by the label *transactional analysis*. Among them are Berne (1961, 1964), and Haley (1963); the best known of these men, due largely to the witty and phrase-making character of his popular works, was Eric Berne.

According to Berne, patient-therapist interactions provide insight into the patient's characteristic interpersonal maneuvers and mirror the several varieties of his or her everyday social behaviors. These maneuvers are translated into caricature forms known as "pastimes" or "games," each of which highlights an unconscious strategy of the patient to defend against "childish" anxieties or to secure other equally immature rewards. This analytical process is akin to that contained in the analysis of transference phenomena, although Berne dramatizes these operations by tagging them with rather clever and humorous labels (e.g., "schlemiel," "ain't it wonderful," or "do me something").

Berne contended that contradictory character trends coexist within the patient; however, no single trend or "ego state," as Berne puts it, achieves dominance. Three ego states were elicited as a consequence of these reciprocal maneuvers or "transactions": archaic or infantile behaviors, known as the *child* state within the patient; attitudes reflecting either both or one's parent's orientation, termed the *parent* ego state; and mature qualities the patient has acquired throughout life, termed the *adult* state. The unconscious attitudes and strategies of these conflicting ego states are exposed and interpreted in transactional analyses. To promote insight into the patient's more immature maneuvers, therapists allow their own parent, child, and adult states to transact with those of the patient.

Benjamin's structural analysis of social behavior.   In perhaps the most detailed model of dyadic interactions, Benjamin bridges both intrapsychic and interpersonal realms of functioning. Her key medium for exploring these functions is the interview process, which Benjamin believes should contain several key features. First, a collaboration must be established in which the therapist can affirm the patient's views and responses. Second, unconscious processes should be tracked in a "free-form" flow of conversation. Third, the therapist should assume that the narrative story line that unfolds "makes sense." Fourth, Benjamin refers to gaining an awareness of patterns of interpersonal behavior as they relate to dimensions such as love-hate and enmeshment-differentiation. Fifth, the therapist should avoid reinforcing preexisting destructive patterns. Last, Benjamin enjoins the therapist to correct "errors" as quickly as possible. In Benjamin's model, the key role is that of establishing a collaboration, one in which empathic processes may or may not be appropriate. She stresses the importance of facilitating the patient's recognition of his or her interpersonal patterns of behavior. Equally significant is the task of "blocking maladaptive patterns" and the necessity of addressing the patient's underlying fears and wishes. Finally, new learning should be facilitated, that is, therapists should encourage the acquisition of interpersonal behaviors that are more adaptive and more gratifying than those previously employed.

Kiesler's interpersonal communication model.   Employing what has been termed *interpersonal communication theory,* Kiesler (1986b, 1997) has centered attention on the transactions that occur between individuals and others throughout their life experiences. As he has formulated it, people transmit an *evoking message* to others through various verbal and nonverbal channels; the message is intended to create a particular encoder-decoder relationship. Kiesler conceptualizes the emotional and personality difficulties of individuals as stemming from problematic countercommunications they unknowingly elicit from others.

The goal of Kiesler's Interpersonal Therapy is for the therapist to assist patients to identify, clarify, and establish alternatives to supplant their established, frequently rigid, and typically self-defeating evoking style. The intent is to utilize the central, recurrent, and thematic relationships that emerge between patient and therapist during their sessions. The task is to replace a patient's constricted transactional messages with communications that are more flexible and adaptive to the changing realities of life. A major priority of the therapist is to stop responding in ways akin to the way others have responded to the patient in the past. These habitual *transaction cycles* that are activated by the patient's behaviors and communications characteristically intensify and aggravate the patient's problematic relationships.

Klerman-Weissman interpersonal approach.   What sets the Klerman-Weissman (1982) approach apart from other interpersonal therapies is its emphasis on brevity and its proactive rather than reactive stance. Also distinctive is its narrow focus on resolving only interpersonal relationships and its attention to current rather than past events. Treatment sessions deal entirely with interpersonal transactions and social roles. Also notable is the avoidance of inner conflicts or the historic sources of difficulty. In addition to distancing from intrapsychic processes, little attention is given to the role of distorted thinking or cognitive schemas. Minimal note is made of the impact of non-interpersonal facets of everyday life, nor are efforts expended to appraise or modify personality traits and their disorders. Although recognition is given to the fact that interpersonal difficulties stem in part from personality characteristics, attention is not directed to their features or their contribution to interpersonal problems; rather, the focus is on the problems themselves. In short, unconscious mental processes, cognitive distortions, and personality traits are bypassed in order to effect short-term achievements. To illustrate their focus, Klerman and his associates write:

> The psychodynamic therapist is concerned with object relations while the interpersonal therapist faces interpersonal relations. The psychodynamic therapist listens for the

patent's intrapsychic wishes and conflicts; the interpersonal therapist listens for the patient's role expectations and disputes. (1984, p. 18)

Group Psychotherapy

A small band of therapists had begun to employ group procedures almost a century ago. J. H. Pratt, a Boston physician, held special classes as early as 1905 for tubercular patients, advising them not only on proper habits of physical care, but on methods to deal with the emotional complications that accompanied their illness. In 1909, L.C. Marsh, a minister, delivered inspirational lectures to groups of state hospital patients; he noted that therapeutic benefits were greatly enhanced if patients were enjoined to participate in discussions following his talks. Similar group discussion therapies were instituted by J.L. Moreno, a Viennese psychiatrist, in 1910. In the late 1920s, S.R. Slavson initiated programs of *activity group therapy* for children between 8 and 15 years of age. In the early 1930s, L. Wender and P. Schilder employed a psychoanalytically oriented approach in the treatment of hospital groups. From their earliest development in the United States, methods of group treatment were enthusiastically embraced by Alfred Adler's disciples. Viewing humans as social creatures who need support and corrective opportunities from others, noting that many disorders stem from undo self-absorption to the neglect of social interests, Adlerians regarded group processes as an effective therapeutic setting. Although psychoanalysis, in general, was loath in midcentury to focus its attentions on group processes, Foulkes and Anthony (1965), two British therapists, sought to integrate psychoanalytic theorizing with the approaches of Lewin's Group Dynamic Approach; a similar effort was made by Bach (1954) in this country.

There has been growing support for the use of trained personnel to meet an increasing number of patients who cannot afford or are not adequately covered financially by an ever-tightening managed care environment. Spurred by these practical considerations, therapists appear to be turning increasingly to more expeditious ways of treating patients for whom individual therapy is neither available nor economically feasible. The manifest need for more efficient forms of therapy may lead to a rapid growth of group treatment methods in the 1990s.

Group therapists contend that in the semirealistic group setting, patients display most clearly those attitudes and habits that intrude and complicate their real, everyday relationships with others. The interplay among group members provides numerous opportunities to observe distortions in perception and behavior that aggravate and perpetuate interpersonal difficulties. Because the atmosphere and intent of the group are characterized by mutual support, these distortions can be rectified and more socially adaptive alternatives acquired in their stead. Moreover, because each patient expresses deep feelings and attitudes with the knowledge that similar experiences are shared by fellow group members, patients gradually learn to tolerate themselves and to be sympathetic to the needs of others. As a consequence, they develop greater self-acceptance, a capacity to view things from the perspective of others, a freedom from self-defeating interpersonal strategies, and the ability to participate more effectively in social relationships.

Let us relate the advantages of group therapy. First is the fact that patients acquire new learnings in a setting that is similar to their "natural" interpersonal world; relating to peer group members is a more realistic experience than that of the authoritarian therapist-patient relationship. It is easier to "generalize" to the extratherapeutic world what one learns in a peer group setting because it is closer to "reality" than is the individual treatment setting. Second, because patients must cope with a host of different personalities in the group, they acquire a range of flexible interpersonal skills; in this way, they learn to relate not only to the neutral or uniform style of a single therapist, but to a variety of disparate personality types. Third, the semirealistic atmosphere of the group provides patients with ample opportunities to try out their new attitudes and behaviors; group therapy serves, then, as a proving ground, an experimental laboratory within which the formative stages of new learnings can be rehearsed and refined. Fourth, by observing that one's feelings are shared by others, patients are not only reassured that they are not alone in their suffering, but regain thereby some of their former self-confidence and self-respect. Fifth, no longer ashamed of their thoughts and emotions, patients can give up the barriers they have defensively placed between themselves and others, enabling them to relate to others without fear and embarrassment. Sixth, able to accept criticism and to forego their pathological interpersonal defenses, patients begin to see themselves as others do and develop a more realistic appraisal than heretofore of their social strengths and weaknesses. Seventh, concurrent with increased accuracy of self-perception, patients learn to observe others more objectively and gradually relinquish their previous tendencies to distort their interpersonal judgments. Eighth, now able to respect the feelings of others, patients can share others' perspectives and begin to assist others in resolving *their* difficulties.

An innovative way to differentiate the theories of group process was outlined by Parloff (1968). Each of the three perspectives that he outlined illustrated the unique benefits of group treatment relative to other modes of therapy. The first, termed *the intrapersonalists,* has as its primary goal the resolution of intrapsychic conflicts, given that the group is a particularly effective medium for dealing with issues of transference and resistance. In these intrapersonal settings, patients are able to recognize that they are not alone in experiencing deep unconscious problems and that they gain insight into the various ways in which people express their individual styles of relating a very concrete and efficient manner, as well as experiencing a measure of safety while they express impulses and feelings.

The second category of group theorists, according to Parloff (1968), *the transactionalists,* are characterized by their primary interest in member-to-member relationships. Here, the group is viewed as a unique setting for understanding how people relate to others. Much is gained, according to Parloff, by the opportunity to vicariously learn about their social selves by participating in this mini social setting. Similarly, each group member has the opportunity to be both a helper and a helpee, giving and receiving emotional and interpersonal feedback to other members in the group.

The third dimension in which group theorists may be differentiated according to Parloff is termed *the integralists.* Here the primary emphasis is on the group as a whole. From this vantage point, all members of the group share aspects of their unconscious world together, particularly their relationship to authority figures, including impulses related to aggression and intimacy. By interpreting these impulses to the group as a whole rather than to each individual, the impact of interventions will be broad and seen as appropriate to each patient's specific concerns. By speaking in therapeutic generalities, patients can selectively focus on those aspects of their shared experiences that are most relevant to themselves individually.

Some therapists employ group methods as adjuncts to concurrent individual treatment; others dispense entirely with individual sessions. Many recommend that group members meet in sessions without the therapist; others oppose such meetings. There are closed and open groups, the former maintaining the same group members through fixed periods of treatment, the latter continuing indefinitely with new members added as old members "graduate." Some groups are formed on the basis of a common problem such as delinquency or marital difficulties; others are planned to be as heterogeneous as possible. Obviously, no simple classification is possible (Dies, 1986; Rutan & Stone, 1984).

In contrast to analytical groups, no effort is made in open discussion therapies to uncover and trace the childhood roots of interpersonal distortions. Rather, the focus is on the here and now and, quite often, on just those events that take place in the ongoing interactions within the group itself.

Analytical groups take their inspiration from one or another of the many varieties of intrapsychic theory. In common with individual analytical approaches, the focus of group analysis is the exposure of unconscious attitudes and strategies, the discharge of repressed emotions, and the reconstruction of childhood-rooted pathological trends. This is accomplished, as in classical techniques, by the use of free association, the interpretation of dreams, and the analysis of the complex network of multiple transference relationships that emerge between patients.

Slavson, the founder of activity therapy, in both early and later writings (1943, 1964) contributed a systematic rationale for resolving the multiple transferences that arise in group settings. More recently, Wolf (1949, 1950; Wolf & Schwartz, 1962) advanced a step-by-step technique for uprooting early memories, penetrating unconscious conflicts and defenses, and working through the intricate pattern of group transference relationships. He contends that the exposure and resolution of unconscious materials and transference phenomena occur more rapidly and thoroughly in groups than is possible in individual analytical treatment.

Perhaps the original model for the analytic group approach is Moreno's technique of *psychodrama* (1934, 1946), a method designed to stimulate the open portrayal of unconscious attitudes and emotions through spontaneous playacting. In a typical procedure, several patients and therapists enact an unrehearsed series of scenes in which they assume roles simulating people who are significant in their real lives. Patients are encouraged to relive and express with dramatic intensity feelings and thoughts that ostensibly could not be tapped or vented through normal conversational methods.

The primary value of the role-playing group is that it simulates more closely than conversational expression ever can real problem situations; in other words, generalization from the therapeutic situation to the extratherapeutic world can readily be achieved. Additionally, patients can be "carried away" in their role portrayals, enabling their deepest emotions and attitudes to be brought to the surface. As a consequence, unconscious forces surge forth, come into sharp focus, and can be dealt with immediately and effectively through "on-the-spot" manipulations by therapeutic coactors. Thus, its exponents contend, psychodramatic methods are more powerful and efficient than are the "pallid" insight discussion techniques for exposing and resolving deeply repressed unconscious materials. An especially informative and eloquent portrayal of various group procedures may be found in Yalom (1986).

Family Therapies

The patient who seeks therapy is often but one member of a pathological family unit. Not uncommonly, interactions among family members form a complex of shared psychopathology, the patient being merely its most dramatic "symptom."

The *primary patient* is enmeshed in daily encounters in a system of interlocking attitudes and behaviors that not only intensify his or her illness, but sustain the pathological family unit. Each member, through reciprocal perceptual and behavioral distortions, reinforces pathogenic reactions in others, thus contributing to a vicious circle of self-perpetuating responses. It follows logically from this premise that therapy must intervene not only with the patient himself or herself, but with the total family; in short, what is needed is family therapy, not individual therapy.

Several variants in technique have been proposed to achieve the goal of disentangling these reciprocally reinforcing pathological family relations. Essentially, the therapist brings several members of the family together, explores major areas of conflict, and exposes the destructive behaviors that have perpetuated their difficulties. The therapist clarifies misunderstandings, dissolves barriers to communication, and neutralizes areas of prejudice, hostility, guilt, and fear. In this manner, the therapist gradually disengages the pathogenic machinery of the family system and enables its members to explore healthier patterns of relating. By recommending new, more wholesome attitudes and behaviors and by supporting family members as they test out these patterns, the therapist may succeed in resolving not only the difficulties of the primary patient, but pathological trends that have taken root in all members.

It may be useful to summarize some of the major thinkers who have contributed to the development of formal approaches to family therapy.

Bateson's communication model.   In the late 1950s, Gregory Bateson led a group at the Mental Research Institute in California charged with the task of studying communication among schizophrenic families. Included in this group were future contributors such as Don Jackson, John Weekland, Jay Haley, and Virginia Satir. Influenced by the General Systems Theory of von Bertalanffy (1933, 1950), Bateson stressed the importance of circular causality in communication; he noted, however, that there were no right or wrong ways in which family communications should be expressed. As he and his associates stated, all human interactions depend on the key premises and assumptions that people hold, rather than fitting some ideal model. The goal of this form of therapy is to resolve problems emanating from faulty interpersonal communication. Efforts are made to reduce the likelihood of intensifying problems owing to errors of interpretation and their potential spiraling. The task of a therapist is to clarify erroneous communications by exposing their consequences and undoing repetitive errors of miscommunication.

Ackerman's psychoanalytic approach.   Anticipating the emergence of the object-relations movement in psychodynamic theory in the mid-1950s, Nathan Ackerman (1958, 1966) instituted a nameless but formal technique that became one of the more well-received approaches to family treatment; a recent extension of his object-relations model has been formulated by D. Scharff and J.S. Scharff (1991).

Recognizing that all infants and children internalize their early perceptions and experiences with their parents, Ackerman and his associates conceived family therapy to be a replication of early gratifying and discomforting relationships between children and their parents. These internalized relationships form the basis for all subsequent intimate relationships, especially those that develop in later family life. It is the "unpacking" of these early templates that serves as the primary task of the family therapist. The disentangling of internalized experiences that have erroneously and distortingly created new family difficulties is what calls for Ackerman's approach. Following the traditional analytic model, therapists assume a neutral, blank approach so as to encourage patients to transfer their intrapsychic images; these can then be exposed and remedied within the family context.

Whitaker's modeling approach.   The emphasis for Carl Whitaker was to facilitate individual autonomy, done best by eliciting the emotional feelings that patients experience regarding their relationships. Whitaker considered conceptual understandings to be of minor if not negative utility. The central focus of his treatment approach was himself, to utilize his own creativity and spontaneity as a model for family members to emulate. Behaving in an irreverent and joyful manner in the therapeutic setting, Whitaker hoped to demonstrate through his own behavior a style for dysfunctional families to use in their interactions. The objective was to undo the rigidity of their dysfunctional ways of relating, to create a toleration for free expression, and to liberate each member to be more self-fulfilling and expressive in the family context (Whitaker & Keith, 1981; Whitaker & Malone, 1953). In his freewheeling personal style, Whitaker spontaneously expressed his own feelings, exposing the absurdity of his own impulses and thoughts, as well as confronting family members to be liberated from their "emotional deadness" and thereby promote their individual growth.

Satir's conjoint approach.   Drawing upon the Human Potential Movement, then popular in California and elsewhere in the 1960s, Satir generated a variety of innovative in-session techniques to illustrate the impact of family members on one another (Satir, 1972; Satir & Baldwin, 1983). For example, Satir utilized ropes and blindfolds to illustrate the constraints in which family members restrict and trap each other. Other methods of a more encounter and experiential nature were likewise employed, along with what she termed the *family sculpture* method; here, family members are arranged in a physical setting, using distance and body positions to illustrate the several ways in which they habitually relate to one another.

Although Satir was disinclined to utilize theory as a primary guide, she did enunciate several premises in her work. First, a strong emphasis was given to the potential of individual self-actualization, which, in turn, derived from high positive self-esteem. Next, she emphasized the clarity and character of communication patterns among members of a family. Additionally, she sought to expose the rules by which family members interacted with one another. Satir's concept of a *healthy family* is one in which individual members have positive self-esteem and intrafamily communications that are direct, honest, and clear. By contrast, Satir believes that *families in trouble* fail to encourage positive self-worth, express communications that are indirect and vague, impose rules are absolute rather than flexible, and function as a closed emotional system, highly defensive and negative in its outlook.

Minuchin's structural therapy.   Beginning in the mid-1960s, Salvador Minuchin, an analytically trained child psychiatrist, developed an approach to family treatment based on his experiences with delinquent youngsters whose difficulties appeared to stem from the dysfunctional structure of the families in which they were raised. The model that he and his associates developed soon became a general framework for family treatment. As Minuchin views it, the task of therapists is to alter the formal or structural relationships that exist within the family through a variety of in-session manipulations (Minuchin, 1974; Minuchin & Fishman, 1981).

Minuchin groups dysfunctional structures into two categories. In what he terms *enmeshed* families, the boundaries within the family are either highly permeable or absent. Conversely, Minuchin selects the term *disengaged* for families with rigid boundaries that prevent the necessary flexibility for warmth and sensitivity to develop. By modifying structural permeabilities and misalignments, Minuchin seeks to rearrange the entire pattern of communications and interactions that perpetuate the family system's difficulties. Only by modifying established boundaries and hierarchies into a more flexible schema can ultimate resolutions be achieved.

Haley's strategic therapy.   Drawing on the ideas of Bateson and his communication model, as well as the methods of Milton Erickson and Salvador Minuchin, J. Haley (1973, 1987) developed an amalgam of techniques that have become a popular approach to family treatment. Emphasizing hierarchical structures and power relationships, Haley states that families are unable to resolve their difficulties because they are locked in a deeply embedded pattern of dysfunctional relationships.

Haley emphasized the *power struggle* for control in families. He viewed psychological symptoms as a strategy for obtaining control and recognized that the power struggle is typically implicit if not covert. As such, confronting these symptoms and manipulations is likely to be unwise and fruitless. Haley was willing to undo or bypass the family organization, and also to create conditions that produce chaos and disarray. This level of disorder, Haley hoped, allows for opportunities to reorganize the system more effectively. Haley states that difficulties within an individual cannot be modified unless the entire family system is altered. Tensions between any two persons become intensified or problematically diffused when third or fourth persons are brought into play. Haley recommends that a series of provocative challenges and paradoxical directives be employed to get patients to abandon undesirable attitudes and behaviors. Ambiguous tasks are assigned and conflict-generating directives are produced to demonstrate dysfunctional family styles so that they may be understood and serve as a basis for direct resolution.

Bowen's multigenerational model.   Expanding on the object-relations notions of Ackerman, Murray Bowen (1976, 1978) traced the multigenerational transmission of family pathology as a continuing series of problematic relationships that persist through the years. Bowen's background was psychoanalytic in nature, but he developed his own comprehensive model of family systems theory, defining a number of concepts and specifying clinical approaches that are linked closely to the model. In contrast to most of his family therapy associates at the time, Bowen believed that if one person in a family could become free of the reactive processes and entrapment structures of the system, a potential chain reaction may help resolve the problematic character of the system. The central thesis of Bowen's approach relates to the "fusion" that emerges among family members, one that results in a lack of personal individuation from the family of origin, that is, an inability to differentiate self from others. This lack of differentiation, according to Bowen, leads the individual to cut all emotional bonds with parents, which, in turn, leads to an excessive degree of fusion in new family or marital arrangements. Utilizing genograms to outline multigenerational relationships, Bowen's goal is to assist members to become more self-differentiated and, hence, achieve greater personal expression. Differing from most other family therapists, Bowen prefers to work with only one family member at a time, while the others either are not present or are silently observing.

The Milan systemic approach.   Although separating this past decade into two or more separate schools of practice, the primary one led by Mara Selvini-Palazzoli and Viaro (1988), there are sufficient commonalities among the systemic models to describe them as singular in their logic and methodology. Meeting with the family but a few times in total, often four to six weeks apart, the Milan approach assumes that any individual's dysfunction plays an important role within the problematic family system; as is often seen, one member of the family is typically "sacrificed" to enable the whole family system to survive intact. Paradoxical questions and injunctions are introduced by the therapist to disrupt established interaction patterns. In many circumstances, invariant prescriptions are specifically communicated to alter the so-called myths that family members hold regarding one another. New rituals are introduced to force the family to modify its pattern of interactions and to alter those myths the family has developed to maintain its dysfunctional system. In effect, interventions are designed to undo the "primitive" myths and rules that have intensified the family's established homeostatic pattern.

DeShazer's and O'Hanlon's solution-oriented approach.   Borrowing from earlier ideas of Milton Erickson (deShazer 1982, 1988; O'Hanlon, 1987; O'Hanlon & Weiner-Davis, 1989), each family member is seen as possessing strengths that may facilitate the development of constructive attitudes and healthy styles of problem resolution. Both de-Shazer and O'Hanlon shift radically from the traditional focus of therapists on family problems and difficulties. Instead, primary attention is given to outlining examples where individuals successfully avoided or solved problems faced within the family interaction. Individual competencies and group effectiveness, not their dysfunctions, are the focus. The therapeutic task is to bring to the forefront latent capacities rather than latent conflicts and dysfunctions. Looking for "miracle" solutions to persistent difficulties serves to promote constructive outlooks and innovative changes. It is the task of the therapist to skillfully elicit from family members the positive resources necessary to achieve their mutual goals. No longer looking at their tensions and quarreling, family members can focus on what has worked previously and what can be implemented currently to create gratifying solutions.

COGNITIVE REORIENTATION MODALITIES

How we think about our lives calls for methods specifically designed to alter problematic beliefs and attitudes.

In this section, as previously in differentiating the clinical domains, we turn our attention to several spheres of pathologic structure and functioning that may be considered significant targets of therapeutic intervention, notably *cognitive modes* and, indirectly, aspects of the content areas of *self-image* and *object-representations.* Important modalities of intervention have been developed with each of the preceding in mind, albeit somewhat tangentially.

Cognitive reorientation therapies seek to address how patients perceive the events of their life, focus their attentions, process information, organize their thoughts, and communicate their reactions and ideas to others. They provide some of the most useful indices to the clinician regarding patients' distinctive way of functioning. By synthesizing these data, it may be possible to identify such general features as constricted thought, cognitive distractibility, impoverished thinking, and so on.

The philosophy underlying these procedures contrasts in emphasis with those of *self-actualizing* methods, to be discussed in the next section. They are not *primarily* concerned with nor do they limit their focus on the person's self-conception. Rather, their efforts are more general, to counteract the patient's erroneous or distorted ways of thinking, whatever realm may be involved.

Some Early Cognitivists

The first modern formulation of what may be called a direct approach to modifying a patient's cognitive assumptions was published by DuBois (1909) and Dejerine and Gawkler (1913), both of whom sought to impart *reason* to patients whose emotions had confused or distorted their capacity to think sensibly. It was their belief that mental disorders were irrational preoccupations with minor symptoms, causing these symptoms to become "mountains, instead of molehills."

In the mid-1940s, Thorne (1944, 1948), viewing the growth of what he considered to be the sentimentalistic practices of most therapists, proposed an approach that revived modern cognitive procedures. In contrast to DuBois, who sought to smooth over the strains and vexations of life, Thorne induced conflicts deliberately by confronting patients with their contradictory and self-defeating attitudes.

In the mid-1950s, George Kelly, Gardner Murphy, and Jerome Bruner revived the Functionalist idea that cognition and perception were learned and adaptive acts. To this they added the notion of unconscious motivation stressed by the psychoanalysts. Perception, as elaborated by these theorists, was an expression of the individual's cognitive schemas, which, in turn, reflected his or her unconscious drives and adaptive defenses. In attempting to maintain an equilibrium between inner strivings and objective reality, individuals develop cognitive hypotheses or expectancies that enable them to select those aspects of reality that reflect their deeper needs. In this fashion, cognition attunes needs, healthy or maladaptive, to reality, serving as a guide or template to the future. An important synthesis was achieved in these personologic theories between the schemas of the unconscious posited by psychodynamicists and the cognitive expectations stressed by clinical psychologists.

Other cognitive style approaches gained favor in the 1950s and 1960s owing to the fact that they sought to bridge the gap between well-known "principles of learning" and the primary vehicle of most therapies, that of verbal interaction. Several semiformal systems were proposed along these lines (Breger & McGaugh, 1965; Kanfer & Saslow, 1965; J. Kelly, 1955; Miller, Galanter, & Pribam, 1960; Rotter, 1954). We cannot expand on these interesting proposals, given limitations in space.

Ellis's Confrontation-Directive Procedures

A major cognitive approach, what we term *confrontation-directive,* is in many ways opposite in style to that of *cognitive reframing* procedures, where the therapist takes a more neutral stance and where treatment gives the client the basis for deciding what course to take.

In the confrontation-directive group, the therapist assumes an authoritarian role; patients are, at least implicitly, considered to be inept, irresponsible, or sick, unable or unwilling to choose for themselves what their goals should be. Not only does the therapist take an active part in deciding the objectives of treatment, but he or she employs persuasive or commanding tactics to influence the patient to adopt a system of values that is deemed more or less universally appropriate. The major theorist of this procedure has been Albert Ellis.

Ellis (1958, 1962, 1967, 1979, 1980) considers the primary objective of therapy to be countering the patient's tendency to perpetuate difficulties through illogical and negative thinking. Patients, by reiterating these unrealistic and self-defeating beliefs in a self-dialogue, constantly reaffirm their irrationality and aggravate their distress. To overcome these implicit but pervasive attitudes, the therapist confronts the patient with them and induces him or her to think about them consciously and concertedly, as well as to "attack them" forcefully and unequivocally until they no longer influence behavior. By revealing and assailing these beliefs and by "commanding" the patient to engage in activities that run counter to them, their hold on the patient's life is broken and new directions become possible.

Based on the writings of Alfred Adler, Ellis's premise in *rational-emotive therapy* is that we are too harsh with ourselves, tending to blame and judge our actions more severely than is necessary. Underlying these destructive attitudes, according to Ellis, is the tendency of patients to blame themselves for their limitations and wrongdoings, that is, to subscribe to the false and self-defeating assumption that they are "no good and therefore deserve to suffer." The principal goal of therapy is to challenge and destroy this belief, to liberate patients, to free them from such irrational notions as shame and sin, and to live life to the fullest, despite social shortcomings or the disapproval of others.

At the core of Ellis's therapeutic approach is the assertion that thoughts and emotions are invariably intertwined. Phrasing the components of his assertion as the *ABC* model, he states that most forms of psychopathology (C) are determined by a person's irrational belief systems (B), which stem from misbegotten life events or experiences (A). His goal is not only to identify the irrational beliefs that lie at the root of the patient's disturbances, but to challenge and to expunge them. To maintain psychic balance, patients must constantly monitor and challenge these difficult-to-uproot belief systems.

Ellis (1970) outlined some twelve irrational beliefs that create unrealistic standards that patients typically live by. Among the most pernicious are: (a) it is essential that a person be loved or approved by virtually everyone; (b) one must be perfectly competent, adequate, and achieving to be considered worthwhile; (c) some people are wicked or villainous and therefore should be blamed and punished; (d) unhappiness is caused by outside circumstances and a person has no control over them; (e) it is easier to avoid certain difficulties and responsibilities than to face them; (f) a person should be dependent on others and should have someone stronger on whom to rely; and (g) there is always a right or perfect solution to every problem, and it must be found or the results will be catastrophic.

Although listed in the cognitive group owing to the central role given to distorting belief systems, Ellis employs a wide range of emotive and behavioral as well as cognitive techniques as therapeutic tools. Among them, Ellis selectively employs such methods as the self-monitoring of thoughts, role playing, modeling, imagery, relaxation techniques, operant conditioning, and skill training. In contrast to other directive cognitivists, Ellis's philosophical outlook clearly espouses self-acceptance, self-interest, and self-direction. Despite this primary focus, Ellis also seeks to help patients develop a tolerance for others, to acquire a commitment to social concerns, and to learn social flexibility and accept the uncertainties of life.

Beck's Cognitive-Reframing Methods

Therapists grouped in this category are neither directive nor nondirective insofar as treatment goals or style of therapeutic interaction is concerned. Rather, therapist and patient conjointly agree that the latter possesses attitudes that promote and perpetuate his or her difficulties in life.

Cognitive-reframing therapists are more active in the treatment process than those who follow the self-actualization philosophy, to be discussed in the next section; they encourage patients to alter self-defeating perceptions and cognitions instead of allowing them to work things out for themselves. In contrast to confrontation-directive therapists, however, they do not prejudge the patient's problem in accord with a fixed philosophy such as *integrity* or *rationality;* they have no particular "axe to grind," so to speak, no set of beliefs they seek to inculcate. Rather, they plan merely to reorient the patient's misguided attitudes, whatever these may be and toward whatever direction may prove constructive, given the patient's personal life circumstances.

Although subscribing to cognitive learning principles, these therapists differ from behavior-learning therapists in that treatment is focused not on overt symptoms or behaviors, but on those internal mediating processes (perceptions and attitudes) that give rise to and perpetuate behaviors. These more neutral cognitive approaches have recently begun to gain favor among many professionals because they bridge the gap between laboratory cognitive principles and the primary vehicle of most therapies, verbal discussion. Several formal cognitive theoretical models have been proposed along these lines (Breger & McGaugh, 1965; M. Hamilton, 1980; Kanfer & Saslow, 1965; J. Kelly, 1955; Lazarus, 1965; Miller et al., 1960; Neisser, 1967; Paivio, 1971; Phillips, 1956; Rotter, 1954, 1962).

A currently highly regarded cognitive approach has been developed by Beck and his associates (Beck, 1970, 1976, 1991; Beck & Freeman, 1990b). Central to Beck's approach is the concept of *schemata,* that is, specific rules that govern information processing and behavior. The concept of schemata derives originally from the writing of Kant. More recently it has been utilized by Piagetian psychologists and other cognitive network theorists to represent tacit internal structures that reflect abstractions about the stimulus world and their relationships. These schemata are stored in memory as generalizations or prototypes of specific life experiences; they serve as a template that provides an orientation, focus, and meaning for all sources of incoming information. Despite their unconscious character, they direct attention to aspects of ongoing experiences that are important for survival and adaptation. In effect, these broad-ranging schemata orient conscious cognitive processes such as attention, encoding, retrieval, and inference. Importantly, schemata incorporate not only cognitive but emotional and affective valences as well. No less significant, schemata relate to self. These *self-schematas* serve as a gauge for appraising and valuing aspects of self.

Schemata may be classified in a variety of categories, such as personal, familial, cultural, and so on. They are inferred directly from behavior or from interviews and history taking. To Beck, the disentangling and clarification of these schemata lie at the heart of therapeutic work. They persist, despite their dysfunctional consequences, owing largely to the fact that they enable the patient to find ways to extract short-term benefits from them, thereby diverting him or her from pursuing more effective, long-term solutions. Beck recognizes that an important treatment consideration is recognizing that cognitive restructuring will inevitably evoke problematic anxieties, owing to the fact that patients are forced to reexamine or reframe their schemata.

Beck has been most fortunate in the number and quality of his disciples, many of whom have made significant contributions to the cognitive model on their own. Thus, Freeman and Reinecke (1995) provide a variety of classical distortions that patients utilize as maladaptive ways of processing information: (a) dichotomous thinking ("You are either with me or against me"); (b) emotional reasoning ("Because I feel inadequate, I am inadequate"); (c) personalization ("I know that comment was directed toward me"); (d) overgeneralization ("Everything I do turns out wrong"); and (e) catastrophizing ("I better not try because I might fail, and that would be awful").

Beck sets out a sequence of necessary steps in his cognitive therapy. Not only must one first conceptualize the core schemata that undergird the patient's pathological outlook, but the therapist must keep in mind the underlying goals for reframing them. As with other sophisticated therapists, Beck emphasizes the therapist-patient relationship as central to the therapeutic endeavor. As he notes further, considerable "artistry" is involved in unraveling the origins of the patient's beliefs and in exploring the meaning of significant past events. Toward this goal, therapists must examine "transference-like" reactions, but never be judgmental or pejorative in their responses. A list of 18 problems in establishing a good collaboration is described to illustrate issues that can undo this constructive process. Potentially problematic also are procedures for confronting schemata that repetitively distort the expectancies and assumptions of patients. A variety of *schematic restructuring* techniques are outlined to help build new schemata or to shore up defective ones. Role playing, imagery, and the reliving of childhood experiences are recommended by Beck as a means of schema modification and decision making. Important cognitive therapy developments have recently been introduced by Meichenbaum (1977), Mahoney (1974, 1977), Young (1990), and Wessler (1993), expanding the range of recommended procedures in this realm.

SELF-IMAGE MODALITIES

What is central to therapeutic success is not chemistry or unconscious resolutions, but treatment methods that foster and enhance each patient's self-esteem.

There are those who believe that personality can be understood only in terms of the intrinsic unity between biological functions and environmental stimulation. This view was fostered by the late-nineteenth-century writings of Hughlings Jackson and Theodor von Uexkuell. Its most convincing exposition in personality was made, however, in the brilliant work of Kurt Goldstein (1876–1965) and Kurt Lewin (1890–1947). Although both were influenced by the early Gestaltists, they extended the holistic idea along different lines. Goldstein, an eminent neurosurgeon, stressed the internal unity of biological functioning, whereas Lewin, a social psychologist, focused on the interdependencies of personality and environment.

To Goldstein, personality could not be understood by studying isolated behaviors or functions because the organism operated as a unit that could not be analyzed in terms of its parts. As evidence for his thesis, Goldstein illustrated numerous cases in which neurological damage to the individual led, not to a loss of the affected function, but to a reorganization of total functioning. This reorganization enabled individuals to keep their drives and goals intact, although more primitively. From this evidence, Goldstein suggested that individuals possess a sovereign motive, that of *self-actualization*. Through this concept, he proposed that our central motive is to realize our inherent potentials by whatever means and capacities available to us.

Kurt Lewin, following a similar philosophy, portrayed personality as a structure composed of interdependent and communicating regions interacting in a dynamic equilibrium with a psychological environment. Of particular note was Lewin's contention that events must be conceived in terms of how each individual consciously perceives them, rather than how they objectively exist; this phenomenological viewpoint has grown into the major cognitive orientation of contemporary psychotherapy.

Placed also among the holistic-personological theorists are other psychologists of the 1930s and 1940s, notably Henry Murray, who coined the term *personology* and whose contribution lies in the scope and depth of his writings. Drawing on a wide knowledge of neurological development, psychodynamic theory, academic psychology, and cultural anthropology, Murray formulated highly useful theories that represented the most sophisticated conceptions of personality integration of his day.

As touched on in books relating to developmental processes, the diffuse swirl of events that buffet the young child gives way over time to an increasing sense of order and continuity. The most significant configuration that imposes a measure of sameness on a previously more fluid environment is self-as-object, a distinct, ever-present, and identifiable "I" or "me." Self-identity, the image of who we are, provides a stable anchor to serve as a guidepost that creates continuity in an ever-changing world. Although few can articulate clearly the psychic elements that constitute this sense of self, it serves to color favorably or unfavorably the nature of one's continuing experiences. For some, the character and valuation of one's self image is a problematic one, an unhappy and dismaying self-reality, such as may be seen in the *avoidant's* feeling of being alienated, or the *depressive's* image of worthlessness, or the *negativist's* sense of self-discontent. On the other hand, there are those whose self-image is one of complacence, as is seen in the *schizoid*, or that of being gregarious among *histrionics*, or admirable among *narcissists*. Thus, self-image, despite the many particulars of its character, appears to be predominantly either of a positive or a negative quality. The self-actualizing techniques we describe next appear to fall into the same positive and negative division.

One group of therapists, labeled *self-actualization* types, assume that each person possesses an inherent wisdom for choosing a life course that is most suitable for him or her. Psychopathology arises because this capacity for self-fulfillment has been blocked or distorted by adverse circumstances. The task of therapy is to provide patients with a permissive and encouraging atmosphere that will facilitate the emergence of their potentials. By behaving in a nondirective and egalitarian manner, and by respecting patients' capacity to choose their own goals, the therapist encourages patients ultimately to discover ways to actualize the promise that inheres within them. We elaborate on these theorists, led by Carl Rogers.

Rogers's Client-Centered Therapy

The goal of self-actualization is most prominent in the *client-centered* therapeutic approach of Rogers's *self theory* (1942, 1959, 1961, 1967). This variant of the self-actualization therapies is based on the optimistic premise that we possess an innate drive for socially constructive behaviors; the task of therapy is to "unleash" these wholesome growth forces.

According to Rogers, patient *growth* is a product neither of special treatment procedures nor professional know-how; rather, it emerges from the quality and character of the therapeutic relationship. More specifically, it occurs as a consequence of certain attitudes of the therapist, notably *genuineness,* that is, therapists' ability to "be themselves" in therapy and to express their feelings and thoughts without pretensions or the cloak of professional authority; *unconditional positive regard,* that is, their capacity to feel respect for the patient as a worthy being, no matter how unappealing and destructive his or her behaviors may be; and *accurate empathic understanding,* that is, sensitivity to the patient's subjective world and the ability to communicate this awareness to the patient. In line with Rogers's therapeutic model, the patient assumes full responsibility for the subject and goals of therapeutic discussion; the therapist reflects rather than interprets the patient's thoughts and feelings and encourages, but does not recommend, efforts toward growth and individual expression. Experience appears to show that these techniques work best with patients who are already endowed with a positive sense of self-worth.

Kohut's Self-Analysis

It was Kohut (1971, 1977) who developed an influential variant of analytic theory; it furnished a special role for the self-construct as the major organizer of psychological development. To him, self-psychology was the proper next step following the earlier orientations of id-psychology and ego-psychology. Kohut's primary focus was on the development of self from its infantile state of fragility and fragmentation to that of a stable and cohesive adult structure. Disagreeing with classical analytic views concerning the role of conflicts as central to pathology, Kohut asserted that most disorders stemmed from deficits in the structure of the self. Owing to failures in empathic mothering, aspects of the self remain fragile and enfeebled, resulting in a variety of "narcissistically injured" personality disorders. Paying special attention to the importance of empathic responsiveness as a foundation for effective psychotherapy, Kohut added a new group of populations treatable by psychoanalytic methods. Unfortunately, Kohut was unable to continue his important contributions and, hence, may remain a less-than-significant figure in the development of psychoanalytic characterology.

Existential-Humanistic Therapy

Therapists of this persuasion are committed to the view that we must confront and accept the inevitable dilemmas of life if we are to achieve a measure of *authentic* self-realization. Themes such as these were first formulated in the philosophical writings of Kierkegaard, Nietzsche, Husserl, Heidegger, and, more recently, in those of Jaspers, Buber, Sartre, and Tillich. From these sources also may be traced the foundations of existential therapy, notably those advanced by Ludwig Binswanger (1942, 1947, 1956),

Medard Boss (1957, 1963), Viktor Frankl (1955, 1965), Rollo May (May et al., 1958, May & van Kaam, 1963), and Irvin Yalom (1980). Despite differences in terminology and philosophical emphasis, these existential variants are very similar insofar as their approach to therapy.

It may be useful, however, to illustrate differences between the European-engendered existential approach and that of the American-generated humanistic "third force" with reference to Yalom's (1980) incisive distinction:

> The existential tradition in Europe has always emphasized human limitations and the tragic dimensions of existence. Perhaps it has done so because Europeans have had a greater familiarity with geographic and ethnic confinement, with war, death and an uncertain existence. The United States (and the humanistic psychology it spawned) [is] bathed in a zeitgeist of expansiveness, optimism, limitless horizons, and pragmatism . . . the European focus is on limits, on facing and taking into one's self the anxiety of uncertainty and non-being. The Humanistic psychologists, on the other hand, speak less of limits and contingency than of developmental potential, less of acceptance than of awareness, less of anxiety than of peak experiences and oceanic oneness, less of life meaning than of self-realization. (p. 19)

Important to all existential therapists is the *being-together encounter* between patient and therapist. This encounter, characterized by mutual acceptance and self-revelation, enables patients to find an authentic meaning to their existence, despite the profound and inescapable contradictions that life presents.

Although the existential-humanistic approach consists essentially of a philosophical outlook, there are some clear-cut therapeutic goals and purposes. Most central is the desire to free individuals to relate *authentically* to others, to lead them to become more aware of their own potentials for choice and growth, and to realize that they can help redefine who they are and what their life course may be.

Glasser's Reality Therapy

The underlying assumption of client-centered, perhaps even rational-emotive therapy is that we are too harsh with ourselves, tending to blame and judge our actions more severely than is necessary. No more opposite a philosophy could be found than that espoused in Glasser's reality therapy (1961, 1965) or Mowrer's integrity therapy (1965, 1966). In effect, these men have claimed that patients are sick because they are irresponsible; they are *not* "oversocialized" victims of too rigid standards, but "undersocialized" victims of a failure to adhere to worthy social or moralistic standards. Anguish stems not from too much guilt and self-derogation but from an unwillingness to admit guilt and irresponsibility, such as may be found among *antisocials, sadists,* and *paranoids.* The task of therapy, according to this approach to altering self-image, is to confront patients with their misbehaviors and irresponsibilities and to make them "confess" their wrongdoings. The therapist does not accept patients' facile rationalizations or other efforts to find scapegoats for their misfortunes. Only by facing and admitting the "reality" of their deceit and guilt can patients regain self-integrity and learn to deal with the future truthfully and objectively. No longer needing to hide their sins, they can rectify past mistakes and find a more socially responsible style of life, without shame or the fear of being discovered. Therapists of this persuasion would not be suitable for dealing with a variety of personality disorders such as avoidants, dependents, and masochists. Moreover, where their philosophy may seem appropriate, such as noted above, there may be some difficulty in getting these patients to agree that they possess attitudes that promote and perpetuate their difficulties. Nevertheless, their methods may prove to be a useful entree into the self-image conceptions these troublesome patients possess.

Expanding on his original reality model, Glasser proposes a more general treatment framework in which one's behaviors are seen as purposeful in that their motivation stems from within the individual rather than from external forces; that is, causality is internal rather than environmentally determined. Addressing all syndromes and personality styles, Glasser states that people who wish to make the effort are able to change themselves and to live more adaptively. He speaks of patients, not as depressed, but as depressing; thus, rather than being angry, for example, they are angering themselves. Whatever form of behavior is manifest, it is a product of self-creation. People *choose* misery by developing a range of "misering" behaviors. From Glasser's point of view, depression, anxiety, and irresponsibility can be explained as an active, if unconscious, choice. The task of therapy is to help individuals become sensitive to their own inner strivings and wishes, and then to help them match their actions to these desires. However, when people take action that infringes on the freedom of others, their behavior is judged to be irresponsible.

Gestalt Therapy

What is known as Gestalt therapy may be credited to the ideas and methods of Friedrich (Fritz) Perls. Initially trained as a psychoanalyst, as well as a disciple of a number of Gestalt psychologists (Kohler, Wertheimer, Lewin), he was influenced significantly also by Wilhelm Reich and Kurt Goldstein during his early years as a psychiatric trainee in Germany. As with many innovative thinkers of his time, he left Berlin following the advent of Hitler, traveling in South Africa for several years and then on to the United States. For various reasons, Perls became anathema to his analytic colleagues, adopting as a result a number of Reich's more "radical" viewpoints. Notable at that time was his growing emphasis on affect, bodily experiences, the form rather than the content of therapeutic communication, and the use of confrontation as a treatment element.

Perls rejected the view that individuals' lives were controlled by either external or internal forces. Adopting a philosophy consistent with his own personal independence, Perls asserted that humans should be responsible for themselves and their lives. Implicit in this view was the belief that humans are free to change and to develop their own inherent potentials, a view shared by all self-actualizing theorists.

Perls contended that "neuroses" are an arrest or stagnation in growth. The goal of therapy, therefore, was to facilitate patients' control over their course of action and to actualize the "real self" rather than some fabricated "self-image." Moreover, Perls viewed psychopathology as a sign of immaturity and dependence; hence, therapy should be designed to foster maturation and independence, thereby facilitating the transition from external support to self-support.

Somewhat paradoxically, Perls and his associates did not view the therapist as a helper. In their view, "The very worst thing you can do for people is to help them." The function of the therapist is to frustrate the demands for help from patients so that they can learn that the resources for resolving problems are in themselves. In effect, patients are forced to find their own way, to discover their own potentials, and to learn that whatever they wish the therapist to do for them, they can do just as well by themselves.

Experiential Therapy

Viewing much of psychopathology to be a result of failing to experience or to dampen one's inner feelings, experiential therapists not only distrust intellectual exploration and analysis but seek to emphasize the spontaneous experience of life events. In this regard, they carry forward ideas first articulated by Aristotle in his examination of the cathartic value of drama and the powerful results that Breuer and Freud achieved in their method of abreactive treatment.

Experiential psychotherapy refers to a variety of techniques whose focus centers on the direct experience of emotions. Among current contributors to this perspective are Eugene Gendlin (1979), Alvin Mahrer (1996), and Leslie Greenberg, North, and Elliott (1993). Although their techniques differ, they seek to facilitate an inward focus on feeling experiences within the treatment context. It is their shared view that patients will not progress, much less actualize themselves, if they discuss their problems in a distanced, abstract, and intellectual way; similarly, little will be accomplished if they focus exclusively on the objective circumstances of their everyday or past lives.

Primary attention is directed to the felt or affective aspects of a patient's problematic experiences. Utilizing a technique called *focusing* (Gendlin, 1979), patients are asked to look inward and to "clear a space" so as to put aside all problems for the moment. Then, one by one, they are asked to focus on a single problem. Attention is directed to how the elements of that experience feel as a whole, to see whether certain words or themes emerge from the feeling generated by that problem. As a consequence, it is hoped that a "shift" may take place such that the character of the problem will take on a new quality by virtue of its associated feeling.

The role of the therapist is to utilize any of a variety of different methods to facilitate the task of eliciting the emotional tone of a problem situation. The therapist guides the patient through these different interventions, attempting to locate those methods that achieve the goal of enhancing a deep and sensitive exploration of feelings. As Greenberg (1993) noted, the therapist can use *evocative unfolding* to explore the emotional "edges" of a problematic experience. In this manner, patients are led to discover how they actually felt and construed a situation, and to better understand what really led to their response to that situation. No matter how dysfunctional that response may have been, it at least was "sensible" in that it reflected their real feelings about the matter. As a consequence of this discovery, new options presumably will open up for behavioral change. For experiential therapists, the process of treatment communication is one in which the topic stays in the moment, so to speak, that is, "in the flow" of what is being experienced within the session.

INTRAPSYCHIC RECONSTRUCTION MODALITIES

Behavioral expressions and conscious cognitions are but surface manifestations
of more hidden and more central forces that reside in the unconscious.

The position that mental disorders are primarily caused by internal psychological conflicts is well-established in formal studies of psychopathology and psychotherapy. The patient's chemistry and nervous system function normally, according to this view, but inner thoughts and feelings are distorted and behavior is maladaptive. The major theory espousing this position is, of course, psychoanalysis, first formulated by Sigmund Freud (1856–1939). Few other schools of medicine have had so pervasive an influence on the traditions of their society.

Intrapsychic therapy had its formal beginning in the last decade of the nineteenth century. Most readers are acquainted with the history, rationale, and variants of intrapsychic theory; more will be said concerning this model of the mind in each of the clinical chapters later in the book. However, and despite inevitable controversies and divergencies in emphasis, often appearing more divisive on first than later examination, intrapsychic therapists do share certain beliefs and goals in common that are worthy of note and distinguish them from other modality orientations.

Intrapsychic therapists focus on *internal mediating* processes and structures that ostensibly underlie and give rise to overt behavior. In contrast to cognitivists, however, their attention is directed to those mediating events that operate at the *unconscious* rather than the conscious level. To them, overt behaviors and conscious reports are merely "surface" expressions of dynamically orchestrated but deeply repressed emotions and associated defensive strategies, all framed in a distinctive structural morphology. Because these unconscious processes and structures are essentially impervious to surface maneuvers, techniques of behavior modification are seen as mere palliatives, and methods of cognitive reorientation are thought to resolve only those difficulties that are so trivial or painless as to be tolerated consciously. "True" therapy occurs only when these deeply ingrained elements of the unconscious are fully unearthed and analyzed. The task of intrapsychic therapy, then, is to circumvent or pierce resistances that shield these insidious structures and processes, bring them into consciousness, and rework them into more constructive forms.

Intrapsychic therapists also see as their goal the *reconstruction* of the patient's personality, *not* the removal of a symptom or the reframing of an attitude. Disentangling the underlying structure of personality pathology, forged of many interlocking elements that build into a network of pervasive strategies and mechanisms, is the object of their therapy. To extinguish an isolated behavior or to redirect this or that belief or assumption is too limited an aim, one that touches but a mere fraction of a formidable pathological system whose very foundations must be reworked. Wolberg (1967) illustrated this philosophy in the following analogy:

> A leaky roof can expeditiously be repaired with tar paper and asphalt shingles. This will help not only to keep the rain out, but also ultimately to dry out and to eliminate some of the water damage to the entire house. We have a different set of conditions if we undertake to tear down the structure and to rebuild the dwelling. We will not only have a water-tight roof, but we will have a better house. . . . If our object is merely to keep the rain out of the house, we will do better with the short-term repair focused on the roof, and not bother with the more hazardous, albeit ultimately more substantial reconstruction. (p. 137)

Reconstruction, then, rather than repair is the option chosen by intrapsychic therapists. They set for themselves the laborious task of rebuilding those functions (regulatory mechanisms) and structures (morphologic organization) that constitute the substance of personality, not merely its "façade."

In brief, intrapsychic therapists contend that treatment approaches designed "merely" to modify behavioral conduct and cognitive complaints or distortions fail to deal with the root source of pathology and are bound therefore to be of short-lived efficacy. As they view it, therapy must reconstruct the "inner" structures and processes that underlie overt behaviors and beliefs. It does not sacrifice the goal of personality reconstruction for short-term behavioral or cognitive relief. Reworking the source of the problem rather than controlling its effects is what distinguishes intrapsychic therapy as a treatment procedure. Once the unconscious roots of the impairment are disclosed and dislodged, patients should no longer precipitate new difficulties for themselves and will be free to develop strategies that are consonant with their healthy potentials.

Freud's views on therapy followed logically from his theories of personality and its development: replace the unconscious with the conscious, eliminate conflicts generated during the infantile stages of psychosexual development, and redress imbalances between id and superego by strengthening the resources of the ego. Maladaptive behaviors were eliminated by eliciting memories and developing insights into the past through the techniques of free association and dream analysis; the major goal was the extinction of the patient's disposition to reactivate childhood difficulties in current life experiences. This was achieved by an analysis of the *transference phenomenon*, that is, patients' tendency to act toward the therapist with the same attitudes and feelings they developed in relation to their parents. Through this procedure, patients became aware of the roots and the persistence of their maladaptive behavior; with these insights, the ego could be reorganized into a more efficient and adaptive pattern.

Freud devoted his long and fruitful life to the development and elaboration of his theories and techniques. Unlike his German contemporary Kraepelin, who sought to classify broad groups of disorders with common symptoms, Freud stressed the personal experience and uniqueness of each patient. And unlike Janet, his French contemporary, who viewed conflicts as precipitants that activate an underlying constitutional deficiency, Freud traced the psychogenic and unconscious processes he perceived as fundamental to each disorder. It was not only the specifics of his findings that proved so epochal; his individualistic philosophy and his orientation toward psychodynamic causation served as the foundation for our twentieth-century understanding of human nature.

Classical Psychoanalysis

Psychoanalytic therapy had its formal beginning in the pioneering studies of Freud during the last decade of the nineteenth century. Despite inevitable controversies and divergences in emphasis, often appearing more divisive on first than later examination, intrapsychic therapists share certain beliefs and goals in common that distinguish them from other orientations; two were discussed in prior paragraphs.

Despite commonalities in data focus and reconstructive goals, psychoanalytic therapists part company on several matters, notably the extent to which they emphasize the developmental roots of pathology and the particular techniques they employ in conducting treatment. Let us briefly examine these differences.

First, a significant number of psychoanalytic therapists believe that successful treatment is contingent on the exploration and resolution of the infantile origins of adult psychopathology. This necessitates probing and uncovering the *conflicts* of early instinctual *psychosexual* development and the myriad *neurotic* defenses that the patient has devised to keep them from consciousness.

This emphasis on uprooting the past is not shared by all who follow the psychoanalytic persuasion. Rather than attending to childhood experiences, some therapists focus on current-day events and relationships. Efforts are directed toward the end of re-fashioning the patient's unconscious style of interpersonal behavior, rather than to tracing its origins in infantile development.

Second, therapists who seek to revive the infantile roots of pathology depend exclusively on treatment techniques that are employed only occasionally by those who concentrate on contemporary events. Those who focus on infantile conflicts maintain total passivity in the treatment relationship; the therapist becomes a "blank screen" upon which patients *transfer* the feelings and attitudes they acquired toward significant persons of their childhood. To further facilitate the reliving of the past, patients recline on a couch, face away from the therapist, become immersed in their own reveries, and are allowed to wander in their thoughts, undistracted by external promptings. Significant childhood memories and emotions are revived during these *free associations,* guided only by the therapist's occasional questions and carefully phrased interpretations; these comments are employed selectively to circumvent or pierce the patient's defensive resistances to the recall of repressed material.

The last major feature of what Freud termed his therapy of psychoanalysis followed from his observation that patients often expressed totally unwarranted attitudes toward the therapist. Freud noted that these seemingly irrational emotions and thoughts reflected hidden attitudes toward significant persons of the past. This transference phenomenon, which illuminated important aspects of the repressed unconscious, could be facilitated if the therapist remained a totally neutral object; by assuming this passive role, the therapist "forced" the patient to attribute traits to him or her drawn from earlier relationships with parents or other significant childhood figures.

To classical analysts, psychopathology represents the persistence of repressed instinctual drives that had generated severe conflicts during psychosexual development. Not only did the individual expend energies to control the resurgence of these memories, but because the conflicts they engendered remained unresolved, they persisted into adulthood and caused the individual to act as if he or she were living in the past. The task of therapy was to uproot the unconscious and to free potentially constructive energies that had been tied up in the task of keeping it repressed. To do this, classical analysts employed the procedures of free association, dream interpretation, and most important, the analysis of the *transference neurosis.*

Ego Analysis

These theorists believe that infants possess innate adaptive capacities which, if properly stimulated, enable them to develop in a healthy fashion. Although ego theorists accept Freud's *id* theory, which states that the seeds of pathology are the conflicts between libidinous instincts and the demands of society, they assert that an equal if not greater cause of pathology is the failure of adaptive potentials to develop adequately. Accordingly, ego therapy focuses not only on the resolution of the infantile neurosis, but also on the reconstruction of the patient's deficient adaptive capacities.

Although ego analysts pay less attention to infantile id conflicts than to infantile ego deficiencies, they retain the classical psychoanalyst's emphasis on the revivification and resolution of the past. To elicit early memories and provide patients with insights into the roots of their difficulties, ego analysts adhere closely to the classical techniques of free association, recumbent position, dream interpretation, and transference analysis. However, in addition to these procedures, they actively promote the strengthening and expansion of the patient's repertoire of adaptive behaviors. By various interpretive suggestions, they seek not only to eliminate the destructive and energy-consuming consequences of id conflicts, but also to build up the patient's deficient ego capacities. The manner in which this is done and how these active steps intermesh with the passive procedures required to foster transference have not been spelled out fully in the writings of the ego analysts.

Object-Relations Analysis

Significant experiences from the past, especially those involving important figures of childhood, leave an inner imprint, a structural residue composed of memories, attitudes, and affects that serve as a substrate of dispositions for anticipating, perceiving, and reacting to life's ongoing events, especially those related to significant persons in one's current world. The character and specifics of these internalized representations of others from the past remain as templates for interpreting and reacting to new relationships in the present. It is this inner template that shapes our perceptions of other persons that requires identification and analysis. These *object-representations* are, along with self-image, the major components and content of the mind. They bridge the division we have made between the cognitive and intrapsychic realms in that they are essentially unconscious images, assumptions, and emotions that persistently intrude in the patient's ongoing relationships. Moreover, they can be readily reactivated into consciousness and thereby be available for phenomenologic analysis and intervention.

Object-representations follow from Freud's observation that patients often expressed totally unwarranted beliefs and attitudes toward him. He noted that these seemingly irrational thoughts and assumptions reflected deeply embedded and usually hidden anticipations and feelings toward significant persons from the patient's past. This transference phenomenon, which illuminated important aspects of the repressed unconscious, could be facilitated if the therapist remained a totally neutral object; by assuming this passive role, the therapist "forced" the patient to attribute traits to him or her drawn from earlier relationships with parents or other significant childhood figures.

All modern intrapsychic therapists (Cashdan, 1988; J. Greenberg & Mitchell, 1983; Horner, 1990) recognize that patients project onto the therapist attitudes and emotions that derive from past relationships. Object-relations therapists consider these transference phenomena to represent the nucleus of the patient's infantile conflicts and pathological defenses. More than classical analytic therapists, however, they not only seek to foster the expression of transference materials and reveal their current manifestations, but center their attentions on making them conscious and to subject them to careful reworking in present life circumstances.

Although the uncovering of unconscious materials is a necessary phase in their work, object-relations therapists pay less heed to matters of the past than they do to the resolution of present difficulties. In another deviation from classical psychoanalytic doctrines, they assert that adult pathology is not simply a repetition of "nuclear" infantile neuroses. Early experiences are recognized as the basis for later difficulties, but intervening events are thought to modify their impact; problematic learnings and anticipations acquired early in life promote new difficulties, which, in turn, provoke new maladaptive strategies. By adulthood, then, an extensive series of events have occurred, making present behaviors and cognitions far removed from their initial childhood origins. Consequently, and in contrast to classical analysts, they consider it digressive, if not wasteful, to become enmeshed in the details of the roots of infantile neuroses. Instead, efforts can more fruitfully be expended in uncovering and resolving the patient's *current cognitive* schemata and strategies.

The therapist actively interprets the patient's object-relations distortions, not only in the treatment interaction, but as they are expressed in the patient's everyday relationships with others. The focus on the current ramifications of distorted phenomenologic assumptions, and the direct mode of attack on the vicious circles they engender, further distinguish the object-relations treatment approach from both other phenomenological methods and classical analysis.

BIOLOGIC REMEDIATION MODALITIES

Many biologically oriented therapists believe that all matters of a psychological nature (depression, anxiety) are epiphenomena, that is, superficial outcroppings of problematic neurochemical deficits and dysfunctions. As stated earlier, until that day in the distant future when practitioners can specify exactly which "pill" will dissolve the discomforts of psychopathology, patients will continue to be treated with drugs whose mode of action is only partially understood and whose effectiveness is limited. Unfortunately, this state of confusion and modest efficacy is paralleled among the equally perplexing and inefficacious psychological therapies.

Early Somatotherapies

From the early successes of surgery to the more recent advent of antibiotic medicines, the conviction has grown that treatment is most effective when directed at the root of a disorder and not its surface symptomatology. An assumption made in psychiatric somatic therapy is that the overt behaviors and feelings of the patient are expressions of an underlying biological affliction best treated at its source. The fact that few if any biological causes have been identified has not deterred the search for such therapies. Somatic treatments that have proved useful have resulted from *serendipity,* the art of accidental discovery. Perhaps the most striking fact about the history of somatotherapy is its progress through error and misconception. Speculative theories regarding new therapies were often far afield, and those who discovered effective treatment agents were usually blazing trails to other diseases. By good fortune and happy accident, alert clinical observers noted unanticipated effects that proved empirically useful for mental disorders.

Fortunately, new speculations regarding biological therapy are subject to the scrutiny of a sophisticated professional and scientific public today. The early history of somatotherapy, a curious mixture of humor and horror, did not have these needed controls.

Not all of the biological techniques used in former centuries should be considered forerunners of our present-day somatotherapy. Trephining was a religious and magical punishment to allow evil spirits to escape the possessed head of the patient, not to relieve a deficit in the brain. The medications of lizard's blood, crocodile dung and fly specs, prescribed by Egyptian physicians in 1500 B.C., were not disease cures, but magic potions.

Hippocrates, despite his part in specifying the brain as the locus of mental disorder, offered no biological treatment for the disorders he observed. Although the rationale for treating the underlying disease was established in the Renaissance, medical reasoning was naïve. For example, the lungs of the fox were given to consumptives to eat because the fox was a long-winded animal, and the fat of a bear, a hairy animal, was prescribed as a cure for baldness. Paracelsus, in the sixteenth century, classified diseases according to the treatments that "cured" them, but the universal remedies of the day included powdered Egyptian mummy, unicorn's horn, bezoar stones, and theriac. Several of these contained more than 60 ingredients, all of which were worthless. As a passing note of humor, conferences were held complaining of flagrant tampering with these medications; to the physician of that early day, failures in treatment were best explained by the "pharmaceutical" adulteration of ingredients.

Not all physicians of past centuries were so naïve. Many astute observers recognized the crudeness of therapies. Maimonides, in the twelfth century, said rather facetiously, "I call him a perfect physician who judges it better to abstain from treatment rather than prescribe one which might perturb the course of the malady." And Oliver Wendell Holmes, the physician-father of the eminent judge, said as recently as 1860 that nearly all the drugs then in use "should be thrown in the sea where it would be the better for mankind, and all the worse for the fishes." Despite commentaries such as these, patients were subjected to fright, blistering, chloroform, castration, cupping, bleeding, ducking, and twirling well into the nineteenth century.

Somatic therapy for a disorder required that a disease first be identified. After syphilis had been established as the cause for general paresis, Julius Wagner-Jauregg, operating more on the basis of a hunch than scientific logic, inoculated paretic patients with malaria in 1917 and successfully cured them of their disease. His effort to extend this treatment technique to other psychotic disorders failed, and he concluded correctly that malarial action was specific to the underlying paretic infection and was not a general cure-all for mental disorders.

In 1922, Jacob Klaesi used barbiturates to produce continuous sleep treatment. Although this technique may be considered the precursor to modern "shock" therapy, it was designed to rest fatigued or irritated nerve cells. It was in the mid-1930s that the modern era of somatotherapies started with the almost simultaneous development of insulin coma therapy, convulsion treatment, and cerebral surgery.

Insulin coma therapy.   Insulin was first administered to mental patients to increase their weight and inhibit their excitement. The step from this symptom-oriented approach to one based on "curing" the disease was made in the early 1930s by Manfred Sakel (1900–1957). He observed that unintentional comas induced by excessive insulin benefited patients. From this observation Sakel was led to the rather extreme hypothesis that psychotic behavior resulted from an overproduction of adrenaline, which caused cerebral nerve cells to become hyperactive. This excessive adrenaline made the patient oversensitive to everyday stimulation; insulin was effective because it neutralized adrenaline and restored normal functioning. Sakel's hypothesis was a simple one and easy to test. In a brief time, it was established that psychotic patients do not overproduce adrenaline. Furthermore, adrenaline is increased rather than decreased during insulin coma. Sakel realized the weakness of his theory and subsequently wrote, "The mistakes in theory should not be counted against the treatment itself, which seems to be accomplishing more than the theory behind it."

The convulsion therapies.   In 1934, Laszlo Joseph von Meduna (1896–1964) reported the successful treatment of schizophrenia by inducing convulsions with a camphor mixture, known in its synthetic form as metrazol. His rationale for its presumed effectiveness was quite different from the one proposed by Sakel. Meduna's (1935) thesis was derived from two observations that had been noted frequently in psychiatric literature: that epilepsy and schizophrenia rarely coexist, and that schizophrenic symptoms often disappear following spontaneous convulsions. This same observation had led Nyiro and Jablonsky in 1929 to administer blood transfusions from epileptics to schizophrenics, without therapeutic success. Nevertheless, Meduna was convinced that the biochemistry of these two disorders was antagonistic. Subsequent research has entirely disproved Meduna's thesis. First, epilepsy and schizophrenia are neither related nor opposed. Second, clinical experience has shown convulsive treatment to be useful primarily in depressive disorders and only rarely in schizophrenia.

Prior to the advent of pharmacologic agents in the mid-1950s, *electroconvulsive therapy* was the most widely used method of biological treatment in psychiatry. The technique of electrical convulsion, developed as early as 1900 by Leduc and Robinovitch with animals, was well-known to Ugo Cerletti (1877–1963) when he first used it with psychotic subjects in 1937. After his initial success, Cerletti formulated his own theory regarding its effectiveness; it was quite different from the ones proposed by Meduna and Sakel. He speculated that the convulsion brought the patient close to a state of death. This aroused extraordinary biological defenses, which led, in turn, to therapeutic recovery. Whether Cerletti's speculation regarding biological defensive action is correct remains unclear today. Other speculations proposed to account for the beneficial results of convulsive treatment are equally unverified.

Surgical therapies.   One of the many hypotheses advanced to explain the successful effects of convulsive therapy served to spur the development of psychosurgery. This notion states that psychotic behavior derives from abnormally fixed arrangements in the organization of the brain. It was first proposed by Herman Boerhaave in the early eighteenth century when he devised a special twirling cage in which patients were spun to rearrange connections within the brain. This idea was approached surgically in 1890 when the Swiss psychiatrist G. Burkhardt removed portions of the brain cortex to rid patients of their fixed hallucinations.

Egas Moniz (1874–1955), unaware of Burkhardt's earlier work, reactivated this method of treatment in 1935 in what is known as the *prefrontal leucotomy.* This surgical separation of the frontal lobes (thought) from the thalamus (emotion) ostensibly minimized emotional preoccupations. Although the technique was used extensively in this country in the 1940s and 1950s, its effectiveness was always in doubt. Its use was sharply curtailed when pharmacologic approaches to somatotherapy emerged in the mid-1950s.

Pharmacological Therapies

The search for biological therapies was given a marked boost in 1952 when two entirely different drugs were discovered accidentally to have beneficial effects in tranquilizing anxious patients. In France, Delay and Deniker reported on the effectiveness of *chlorpromazine,* a drug originally synthesized for hypertensive and surgical patients. Almost simultaneously, another drug, *reserpine,* a product of the Rauwolfia snakeroot that had been used since the 1920s by Indian physicians, was found to calm hyperactive and assaultive patients. Interest in these drugs quickly swept the psychiatric world. Although they possessed undeniable chemical effects, much of their initial success in treating psychotic patients stemmed from *placebo* action—beneficial results arising from increased enthusiasm and high therapeutic expectations. After the early wave of excitement subsided, these agents, along with others since devised, have taken an impressive and useful place in the physician's kit.

The genuine beneficial effects of these agents encouraged a new wave of biochemical research. The action of many of the new drugs has been deciphered. More important, the search for natural biochemical dysfunctions has been intensified. The growing expectation that a scientific rationale for somatotherapy will be found accounts in large measure for the present strength of the biomedical tradition.

We need not be committed to the view that psychopathology is of biogenic origin to believe that biological therapies may be usefully employed; biological methods may prove efficacious in conditions in which the etiology is unequivocally psychogenic. For example, pharmacological anxiolytics may be fruitfully employed to ease "psychological" tension caused by the loss of a job or the death of a relative.

Biologically oriented procedures are only one of several sets of tools that make up the multitherapeutic armamentarium of an experienced and well-rounded therapist. They should not be employed to the exclusion of other therapeutic modalities and methods, as is too often the case. The practice of applying a single cherished treatment procedure, whether biological or psychological, to every form and variety of pathological condition is a sad commentary on the maturity of the profession, a sign of cognitive and behavioral rigidity most unbefitting to those who seek to aid others in achieving adaptive flexibility.

If the chief offense of psychodynamic theorists is the grandiloquence of their system and the tenuous connection between their concepts and the empirical world, the converse may be said for biologically oriented theorists. Medical scientists propose theories of limited scope and anchor their concepts closely to the observational world. Although these features are commendable, these theorists rarely propose hypotheses that go beyond established facts and thereby often fail to generate new knowledge.

At one time, biophysical treatment included only the use of electroconvulsive and psychosurgical procedures; these were never fully suitable for most syndromes and disorders and, with rare exceptions, are judged today to be technologies of the past. An early period of unjustified optimism in the 1950s and 1960s, characterized by the belief that pharmacologic "wonder drugs" would cure all mental illnesses and deplete the rolls of every state hospital, has also passed. Nevertheless, the field continues to be subjected to a flood of new products, each of which is preceded by massive and tantalizing advertisements that promise "a new life" for the mentally disordered patient. Despite this bewildering array of highly touted medications, we note that psychotherapists' offices, community clinics, and mental health hospitals are no less busy than before. Formerly agitated and assaultive patients are easier to handle, as are anxious and depressed syndromes less severe and of briefer duration, but there has been no sweeping change in the prevalence or variety of most psychopathological conditions. In short, these "wonder drugs" have assumed a solid scientific and commercially successful place as one of many tools in the broadly trained therapist's treatment kit.

The availability of efficacious medications in recent decades has signaled a major advance in the transformation of psychopharmacology from a hit-or-miss activity into one that has a scientific groundwork. Whereas there were only four or five general groups of medications available for psychotherapy a decade or two ago, each of which had many side effects and diffuse main effects, more and more of the newer drug medications have been developed with few side effects and highly specific indications. In the past, the concurrent use of more than one class of medications often led to adverse effects; today, a wise choice of several agents often may be employed for optimal efficacy. Not that there are currently available pharmacologic treatments for all aspects of pathologic emotion, thought, and behavior; for example, there are no medications for the antisocial's conscience deficits, lying and stealing, but there appear to be useful drugs that may limit parallel symptoms such as irritability and impulsivity. Owing to these or other limitations of pharmacologic management, it is usually necessary to include one or another variant of psychotherapy to achieve optimal treatment outcomes. Specific symptoms may be satisfactorily controlled with medications, but the full range of most patients' psychosocial difficulties will call for a range of psychotherapeutic interventions. The specific goal of pharmacologic therapy is to eliminate focal symptoms such as dysfunctional behaviors and attitudes by modifying neurochemical balances and processes in the brain. The most relevant task in choosing a medication is to identify the primary and focal symptoms that the patient is manifesting.

When a pharmacological agent has been shown to exert an effect on a patient, questions arise as to the precise nature of its psychological consequences: whether it influences, singly or in combination, motor behavior, sensory processes, perception, discrimination, learning, memory, conceptual thinking, and so on; the specific biophysical mechanisms altered by the drug, for example, whether it activates or inhibits certain neurohormonal transmitter substances or has different kinds of effects on cortical regions, reticular pathways, limbic divisions, and so on; and the relationship between these psychological and biophysical changes and the "final" clinical effect.

Answers to the first question are largely obtained through animal laboratory studies, although certain functions, for example, higher cognitive processes, can be appraised only in human clinical trials. Answers to the second question involve the use of exceedingly complex technical procedures that specify the anatomical site of action and trace the precise character and sequence of the induced chemical changes; the task of unraveling the neurophysiological concomitants of drugs must disentangle effects throughout the awesomely intricate histological structure of the brain and the complicated network of interactions that operates among its diverse components. Attempts to answer the third question are even more difficult because the observed "final" clinical outcome reflects not only the action of interacting chemical and neurological pathways, but the individual's learning and adaptive history and the conditions prevailing in his or her current environment.

Because of the varied questions that can be posed regarding the nature of pharmacological action, and because of the complexity of the factors involved, theorists have had a relatively open field to speculate on why and how these drugs produce their effects. These formulations fall essentially into three categories: *neurohormonal defect theories,* which hypothesize that drugs overcome endogenous chemical dysfunctions in synaptic transmission; *neurophysiological imbalance theories,* which assume that these agents reestablish equilibrium among ill-matched functional systems; and *psychological reaction theories,* which posit that these substances result in energy and temperament changes that alter the patients' coping competencies and lead them to modify their self-image.

There are several ways in which drugs have been classified. For certain purposes, they are grouped according to their chemical structure (e.g., phenothiazines, SSRIs, tricyclics); for other purposes, they may be categorized according to their neurochemical mode of action (e.g., monoamines, oxidase inhibitors, neuroleptics); and in most cases, they are best classified according to their psychological mode of action (e.g., antipsychotics, antidepressants). It is this third, the most common basis for distinguishing and grouping pharmacological agents, that we utilize in the following sections.

Efforts to classify drugs in terms of "target" symptoms or broad clinical syndromes, however, tend to be misleading. Rarely is just one target symptom affected; rather, these drugs have a pervasive impact, influencing several clinical features simultaneously. In a different way, classifying drugs in terms of which clinical syndromes they influence implies incorrectly that the drug deals with all facets of that diagnostic group. Moreover, it implies that the drug does not produce meaningful effects with patients in other diagnostic categories; for various reasons, notably the heterogeneity and unreliability of diagnostic categories, such drug classifications are bound to be partially ill-conceived and often invalid.

More in line with clinical evidence is the view that some drugs tend to decrease activity and subdue mood, whereas others appear to increase activity and brighten mood. But even this gross differentiation fails to account for individual variations in reaction that are due to personality factors such as coping styles and a host of relevant socioenvironmental conditions.

Despite difficulties in establishing uniform criteria for classification, some schema must be employed for pedagogical purposes. We therefore turn briefly to the three principal drug types, antipsychotics, anxiolytics, and antidepressants, and review their distinguishing features and clinical indications. We mention only a few examples of each for illustrative purposes.

Antipsychotics.   The discovery of the clinical utility of chlorpromazine and reserpine, reported in 1952, ushered in a new wave of optimism in psychiatric medicine. Many investigators, spurred by the impressive results of these two agents, began to manipulate their basic molecular structure in the hope of discovering variants that would be even more efficacious than the parent models. Modifications of these as well as other chemical substances have resulted in over 100 new psychopharmacological products in the past 45 years. Despite differences in structure, most of these agents affect essentially the same clinical behaviors as do chlorpromazine and reserpine, that is, they are antipsychotic *tranquilizers.*

Antipsychotics may be distinguished from a variety of compounds that have been used for over a century to moderate tension and agitation. In contrast to most of these medications, antipsychotics relieve anxiety and reduce hyperactivity without markedly dulling cognitive alertness and clarity; thus, they appear more selective in their dampening effects than sedatives, focusing on emotional and motor functions and operating modestly on cognitive functions. Let us briefly discuss the major subtypes of the tranquilizer group.

Chlorpromazine, chemically part of the dimethylamine series, was the first and is still thought to be among the most effective phenothiazines for handling markedly disturbed patients characterized by emotional tension, cognitive confusion, and motor hyperactivity. Numerous structural modifications of the basic chlorpromazine molecule have been made, producing drugs that differ from the parent model in both potency and side effects. In general, the greater the potency, the more severe and dangerous are the toxic consequences. For example, the addition of a piperazine ring to the basic molecule, as in prochlorperazine, results in a compound that is 5 to 10 times more potent than chlorpromazine, but increases the incidence of severe secondary complications. At the other end of the scale, in the piperidine series, significant alterations are made in the basic side chain and nucleus of chlorpromazine, decreasing both the potency of the compound and its associated side effects.

In the main, the various phenothiazine derivatives are alike in their clinical utility. Their primary indication is with the more severe reactions, disorders, and patterns in which a reduction in activity level and a dampening of heightened moods, such as anxiety and hostility, is desired.

Since the 1970s, a variety of new medications has been developed that parallels the effectiveness of the phenothiazines. For example, a major variant are the butyrophenones, generically known as haloperidol, or its trade name Haldol. Another relatively recent antipsychotic are the thioxanthenes; perhaps the best known variant is the piperazine group, among which is the prescriptive name Navane.

A more recent development, chemically somewhat atypical among the major antipsychotics, is the generic medication clozapine, given the trade name Clozaril. This medication appears to be especially useful if not superior to all previous antipsychotics; it has been successful especially in dealing with both positive and negative symptoms, and in the treatment of schizoaffective and complicated bipolar disorders. Particularly notable is its utility in combination with other antipsychotics and its minimal and low frequency of side effects.

Another recent antipsychotic derives from a combination of various neurohormones. It is judged a serotonin/dopamine antagonist; chemically termed risperidone, it is given the trade name Risperdal. A significant advantage appears to be its effectiveness in treating positive symptoms such as delusions and agitation; it also exhibits somewhat effective results for improving negative symptoms such as apathy and social withdrawal. There is a low incidence of extrapyramidal symptoms, as well as a low risk of inducing tardive dyskinesia. Care must be taken with both clozapine and risperidone not to abruptly terminate treatment, lest patients quickly relapse to their prior psychotic state.

A very recent chemical, termed olanzapine, possesses the prescriptive name Zyprexa, and has shown greater efficacy than certain antipsychotic forerunners (e.g., Haldol), as well as demonstrating fewer side effects. Quetiapine, another recent antipsychotic, known by the trade name Seroquel, likewise is proving useful in moderating both positive and negative symptoms of severe cognitive dysfunctions (e.g., schizophrenia). Another new agent, sertindole, labeled Serlect, is similar to olanzapine and may compare favorably to risperidone. Expected soon on the market is another antipsychotic, ziprasidone, to be prescribed as Zeldox; its efficacy is promising, but it has not been adequately evaluated as of this writing.

Each of these latter medications has proven to be useful in reducing psychotic thought and behavior. However, it should be noted that close observation is called for with several of these medications, notably their potential to produce syncope, orthostatic hypertension, and, most important, tardive dyskinesia.

Anxiolytics.   For the most part, anxiolytic agents are both less potent and produce fewer troublesome side effects than the major antipsychotic derivatives. These drugs are of lesser utility than antipsychotics in treating markedly disturbed patients, but they do fulfill a function with moderately anxious and agitated patients. They appear to influence the same spectrum of symptoms as do the antipsychotics, but to a lesser degree.

These medications, once termed minor tranquilizers, grew in use during the 1960s and 1970s, especially with the introduction of the benzodiazepines. Perhaps the best known of these medications was chlordiazepoxide, better known as Librium, its trade name. Similarly popular was diazepam, known in the trade as Valium. Although preceded by the anxiolytic medication known as meprobamate (trade name Miltown), these benzodiazapines became highly popular treatments for run-of-the-mill emotionally distressed patients. Recently developed are anxiolytic agents of the buspirone chemical group, given the trade name Buspar. Each of these pharmaceuticals has achieved considerable support in the profession by virtue of their capacity to moderate minor levels of discomfort.

Antidepressants.   An early report indicating that the antitubercular drug, isoniazid, produced a beneficial stimulant effect among psychiatric patients was lost in the vast sea of a growing medical literature on the "wonder drugs" (Flaherty, 1952). It was not until the late 1950s that the role of a similar drug, Iproniazid, was recognized as an agent that could produce "euphoric" behaviors. Evidence was gathered shortly thereafter that these drugs inhibit monoamine oxidase, an enzyme centrally involved in the metabolism of neurohormonal transmitter substances. This discovery in part gave impetus to the neurohormonal defect theories touched on previously.

Also in the late 1950s, several Swiss chemists synthesizing new variants of phenothiazine noted that one of their compounds, imipramine, produced an effect opposite to what they anticipated; it did not decrease tension or control hyperactivity, as was expected, but did appear to brighten the mood of depressed patients. New *antidepressant* compounds were quickly formulated on the basis of modifications of the iproniazid and imipramine molecular structures.

Antidepressants should be distinguished from compounds known as stimulants that have been employed for over a century to increase motor activity and mental alertness. In contrast to stimulants, the effects of antidepressants begin slowly and last appreciably beyond the termination of treatment. Also, and more important, antidepressants not only activate cognitive alertness and motor behavior, but favorably influence the mood of the patient; stimulants, in contrast, often aggravate negative moods. Let us outline the major categories of antidepressant drugs.

Iproniazid, the first widely used monoamine oxidase inhibitor (MAOI), produced dangerous side effects, notably liver toxicity; this led to its early removal from the prescription market. In the interim, several chemically similar substances were synthesized, of which several were hydrazine compounds, such as iproniazid (e.g., isocarboxazid and phenelzine) and other nonhydrazines (e.g., pargyline). The therapeutic effect of these agents on retarded depressive symptomatology appears to be well established. In general, tranylcypromine (Parnate) appears effective; its clinical efficacy, however, is somewhat dampened by discomfiting physical side effects. It should be noted also that MAO inhibitors frequently convert a retarded depression into an agitated one, and on occasion, patients may be precipitated into disorganized or hostile manic disorders.

Well established by now are the tricyclic antidepressants (TCAs). Among these apparently effective treatments are a number of tertiary amines; best known among them is amitriptyline (Elavil), imipramine (Tofranil), and doxepin (Sinequan). In a somewhat different family of chemicals is bupropion, known by the brand name Wellbutrin. This latter antidepressant appears to be effective for patients who experience apathy, anhedonia, and decreased physical energy; similarly, it may be a good choice for depressed patients who also exhibit milder bipolar disorders such as hypomania and cyclothymia.

Especially impressive in the past decade or so are the selective serotonin reuptake inhibitors (SSRIs). These have achieved impressive results and appear to have become the treatment of choice of late among the antidepressants. Used perhaps more frequently than would be appropriate, the trade names Prozac (fluoxetine), Paxil (paroxetine), Zoloft (sertraline), and Effexor (venlafaxine) are well-known among psychiatrists, family physicians, and their patients.

Other pharmaceuticals.   Brief mention should be made of a variety of sedatives that have been employed for over 70 years prior to the development of the recent anxiolytics. Among them are sodium and potassium bromides and the many barbiturates (e.g., phenobarbital).

Similarly, drugs have been introduced to control various manic states. Notable here are the lithiums (Eskalith), and the carbamazepines (Tegretol).

Not to be overlooked is the utilization of a variety of medications to counter panic states and minor phobias. Among them are the anxiolytic alprazolam (Xanax), the MAO inhibitor phenelzine (Nardil), and the tricyclic antidepressant, imipramine (Tofranil).

In Chapter 2 we turn to contemporary trends. Particularly significant are efforts to abbreviate the length of psychotherapy and movements to make treatment more relevant to the concerns of various minorities and genders, as well as to integrate in some systematic manner the many modalities discussed in this chapter.

CHAPTER TWO

A Perspective on Contemporary Trends

As outlined in Chapter 1, therapy has been dominated by what might be termed *domain* or *modality-oriented* treatment. That is, therapists identified themselves with a single-realm focus or a theoretical school (behavioral, intrapsychic) and attempted to practice within whatever prescriptions for therapy it made. Rapid changes in the therapeutic milieu, all interrelated through economic pressures, conceptual shifts, and diagnostic innovations, have taken place in the past decade or two. For better or worse, these changes show no sign of decelerating, and have become a context to which therapists, far from reversing, must now themselves adapt.

Ironically, changes wrought by the confluence of economics, the diagnostic revolution that began with the third edition of the *Diagnostic and Statistical Manual of Mental Disorders (DSM-III)*, the increasing awareness of minority- and gender-related issues, and the managed-care revolution in the 1980s perhaps represent an accidental example of the emergent synergism for which the author believes therapists should strive in their everyday work. Alone, the reinvention of the form and substance of the official nosology that occurred with the *DSM-III* in 1980 probably would not have been enough to overturn domain or school-oriented psychotherapy, though certainly the emancipation of the *DSM* from the psychodynamic paradigm and in favor of an atheoretical posture did in fact hold the philosophical seeds of the coup that followed. Nonetheless, it may be argued that the essential force that provided, and continues to provide, the latent agenda for therapeutic innovation came from without, in the form of reluctance on the part of almost all third-party payers to reimburse psychosocially grounded psychotherapy. The study of such economic influences—through which the substance of what a discipline postures as truth changes to conform with new requirements for its continued existence—is worthy of a treatise in itself. Here, however, I sketch only a few broad strokes, the ultimate goal being to deduce new forms of psychotherapy from the nature of psychopathology as a construct, an agenda motivated by the field's recent push for more effacious therapies, to be sure, but one founded on several fundamental principles that are as eternal as psychopathology itself.

Today, it is economic forces, not theoretical developments and empirical research, that increasingly drive the direction of developments in psychotherapy. Although modern times continue to see an explosion in the total number of all therapies, it is the demands of managed care that require efficacy, presumably through patient selectivity and therapeutic structure and specificity equal to or greater than the longer-term, more inclusive therapies of the past. The message to psychotherapists today is Do more with less, meaning, unfortunately, not only fewer sessions, but more patients, and therefore less time spent thinking about the dynamics of any one patient's problems. The emphasis on efficiency is today the primary impetus in the development of programmatic forms of therapy across the spectrum of disorders. Moreover, these forms have been adapted to variables at levels of analysis congruent with what is afforded by current economic constraints. So, therapy becomes more behavioral and operational and less dynamic and inferential.

TREND TOWARD BRIEFER THERAPIES

Whatever the economic constraints, psychopathology would seem to stand squarely and intrinsically in opposition, not just to managed therapies, but to most forms of brief therapy. The more concentrated Axis I disorders do admit to more focal, and therefore briefer, interventions. The disorders of Axis II, however, essentially more long-standing and pervasive disorders constituting the entire matrix of the patient, may stand like stone monoliths unmoved in the face of fiscal realities. Is it reasonable to expect 10, or even fewer, hours with a therapist to "cure" such complex disorders? These disorders are not clay to be passively resculpted. Functioning in a manner similar to the immune system, the psychic system actively resists any external influence that would disrupt its homeostasis. To uproot a complex disorder, one must wrangle with the ballast of a lifetime, a developmental pathology that has grown to become the entire structure of the person, manifested and perpetuated across a lifetime. By any reasoning, the pervasiveness and entrenched tenacity of the psychic pathology is likely to soak up therapeutic resources without end, leading inevitably to pessimism and disaffection for both therapists and payers.

Bypassing the many concerns that have been recorded concerning the effectiveness of brief therapy, it behooves us to provide the contemporary reader with a short review of the history and methods that represent this very important trend in our field. The general term *brief therapy* encompasses a wide range of approaches, techniques, and philosophical orientations, often obscuring important elements more than it may actually reveal. Similarly, despite its relative recency, segments signifying brief approaches to treatment can be traced back to the earliest of therapeutic efforts at the beginning of the twentieth century. We begin our coverage with theorists not especially thought of as brief therapists.

Early Contributors to Brief Therapy

Soon after Freud renounced the hypnotic method as a major tool of analytic treatment, he initiated a procedure of rapid diagnosis and interpretive resolution of unconscious conflicts. For example, in a series of brief treatments, he successfully resolved the symptoms of the conductor Bruno Walter in but six sessions, and those of the composer Gustav Mahler in only four.

Two disciples of Freud, Sandor Ferenczi and Otto Rank, followed his early model of brief treatment and formulated what they perceived to be short but effective therapeutic forms. Ferenczi (1921, 1926) took a vigorous stance against the passivity that had become characteristic of the analytic model by the 1920s. Anticipating later work by Sifneos in the 1960s, Ferenczi encouraged a high measure of activity on the part of the therapist. This was designed to expose the unconscious conflicts and fears that patients normally avoided in order to bring them to light for purposes of a more direct analysis. To Ferenczi, interpretation, important though it may be, was insufficient to effect a cure.

Concurrent with Ferenczi's active stance were similar ideas proposed by Otto Rank (1936); these signified his progressive dissatisfaction with the slow and tentative methodology that characterized the work of his analytic colleagues. It was his judgment that setting a time period for the end of treatment would be a key to its effectiveness. Likewise, he emphasized the importance of current life experiences rather than the pursuit of distant infantile memories. In his judgment, psychoanalysis was an excellent procedure for in-depth investigations of patients' psyches, but an ineffective tool for resolving their distress in an efficient and rapid manner. Anticipating methods adopted by others in later years, Rank stressed that patients assume responsibility for their life's resolutions. Further, he sought to guide patients into recognizing how their own attitudes and behaviors perpetuated their problems.

Franz Alexander (Alexander & French, 1944) conceived his own work on short-term analytic therapy to be a continuation of the ideas proposed by Rank and Ferenczi. Together with his Chicago colleague, Thomas French, in the late 1930s, Alexander stressed the special importance of evoking an *emotional experience* in treatment as a counterbalance to the classical analytic focus on intellectual exploration. Alexander did not abandon the importance of understanding the early development of a patient's life. Rather, he sought to revive the emotional aspects of early conflict situations. To achieve change, Alexander sought to provide new experiences and attitudes. This he considered to be the cornerstone of successful treatment, terming this process the *corrective emotional experience*. Another central theme of Alexander's was the principle of *therapeutic flexibility*. To him, psychoanalysis was too rigid in its procedure; in its stead, he proposed that therapists utilize a variety of techniques that were designed to fit the patient's psychological outlook, as contrasted with the analytic model of selecting patients who fit their preferred and singular technique.

Malan's focused approach.   David Malan picked up many of the ideas proposed by Alexander in the early 1960s, differentiating the goals and methods appropriate to time-limited psychotherapy and those more suitable to long-term treatment. In contrast to Alexander and his analytic forebears, Malan (1963) took an eloquent stance against the open-time policy and the effectiveness of analytic therapy. In 1980, he stated his position:

> It needs to be stated categorically that in the early part of this century Freud unwittingly took a wrong turning which led to disastrous consequences for the future of psychotherapy. . . . the most obvious effect has been an enormous increase in the duration of treatment—from a few weeks or months to many years. A less obvious development is that the method has become, to say the least, of doubtful therapeutic effectiveness, a matter which has received little attention or proper investigation. (p. 13)

What made Malan's approach a brief one was its limited and focused aim. In his judgment, the patient must recognize that the number of sessions were limited and that only one core conflict was to be the focus of treatment.

Wolberg's short-term orientation.   Reflecting the views of Alexander, Lewis Wolberg (1965, 1980) gave special allegiance to the importance of a high degree of therapeutic activity on the part of the clinician, and a willingness to explore a variety of therapeutic methods rather than adhering rigidly to a passive and a single therapeutic approach. Although adhering to a broad psychodynamic perspective, Wolberg asserted that clinical evidence could not support the view that discussions regarding the past are necessarily more therapeutic than discussions of the present. Further, he was not convinced that unconscious material was necessarily more significant than that within conscious awareness. Similarly, and in contrast to traditional psychoanalytic belief, he did not judge that transference interactions with the therapist were necessarily more therapeutic than those expressed toward other significant figures in the patient's life. Also, Wolberg sought to enlist the patient to become an active participant in therapy and to agree to an initial verbal contract concerning the goals of treatment and the number of sessions to be scheduled. In summary, he felt that it was necessary for therapists to overcome "the prejudice of depth."

Bellak's emergency model.   Along with his colleague Leonard Small (1978), Bellak wrote that brief therapy was especially useful in dealing with both minor and major emotional problems, especially in settings such as emergency rooms in general hospitals. Here, he sought to provide immediate, walk-in care, ranging from advice to the lovelorn to the amelioration of acute psychoses.

Writing with Siegal (1983), Bellak stated that emergency psychotherapy, with its goal defined by whatever emotional difficulty a patient presented, can achieve more than symptom removal; he believed that it provided an opportunity to assist the patient in achieving a better level of adjustment than may have been the case prior to the circumstances of emergency. Moreover, Bellak made an effort to achieve preventive goals by helping patients work through the circumstances that prompted their going to the emergency ward. Seeking to realize these gains in five or six sessions, Bellak believed that effective brief treatments were especially appropriate in cases of suicidal threat, marked depression, catastrophic life events, and acute psychotic states.

Sifneos's anxiety-provoking approach.   Following the views originally proposed by Ferenczi and Alexander, patients should experience an optimal level of anxiety for achieving the treatment aims of brief therapy, according to Peter Sifneos (1967, 1968, 1972). If anxiety is too high, it should be decreased; if it is too low, it should be increased. In cases calling for brief intervention, Sifneos attempts to provoke patient anxiety so as to intensify motivation and achieve a measure of emotional reeducation and problem-solving skill. Recommending a course of 12 to 15 sessions, Sifneos confronts patients in the service of reeducating them, especially to assist them in giving up their infantile beliefs and to stimulate more realistic thinking. In many ways, Sifneos plays the roles of both therapist and teacher, placing the patient into a parallel part-patient, part-student role. Nevertheless, Sifneos retains his analytic orientation, seeking to establish a therapeutic alliance, to explore the patient's psychodynamic difficulties through a careful developmental history, to interpret positive transference reactions, and to resolve the patient's "deeper neurotic" problem. Sifneos considers both milder and more severe disorders to be appropriate for his anxiety-provoking approach, selecting patients with relatively circumscribed complaints, a reasonable level of ego strength, and high motivation for exploring change.

Farrelly's provocative model.   Taking a different approach from Sifneos regarding the use of provocation in brief therapy, Frank Farrelly (Farrelly & Brandsma, 1974) intentionally introduces, through humor and paradoxical communications, various messages designed to upset and counteract the patient's persistent self-defeating attitudes and deviant behaviors. He recommends the use of almost any tactic—even lying and absurdity—to shame or otherwise affect patients' established characteristics. Farrelly has concluded that "softer" therapeutic tactics such as warmth and empathic understanding are often insufficient to achieve therapeutic gains. The intent of provocation is to lead patients to affirm their own self-worth, to defend themselves appropriately, and to be willing to engage in risk-taking relationships. "Attacked" in this provocative manner, patients come to assert that the therapist has distorted their thoughts and behaviors. In time, there are successive clarifications and more realistic self-appraisals. Moreover, therapists come to the belief that patients are *not* psychically fragile or incapable of functioning in a competent manner. Less uneasy about their own provocative behaviors, therapists are able to assist patients in viewing themselves as more competent and more able than heretofore.

Davanloo's confrontational approach.   Habib Davanloo (1978, 1980) has gained increasing recognition in recent years owing to the use of brief analytically oriented therapeutic techniques that are highly charged, personally challenging, and confrontational. A follower of Malan in his critique of the long-term analytic methods that have dominated the therapeutic field, Davanloo speaks of his own approach as "relentless"; others have termed it remorseless, even bullying. Unwilling to see his short-term dynamic therapy as limited in its utility, Davanloo has been convinced that brief approaches may actually be the treatment of choice for patients suffering severe neurotic disorders that may have paralyzed their lives over many years. Davanloo believes that improvement increases up to approximately 20 sessions and then fades thereafter; after the short-term period, therapists may lose their focus and thereby diffuse treatment effectiveness. Recognizing that it may be difficult for many patients to tolerate persistent confrontations and demands, Davanloo nevertheless contends that those who can meet his expectations have an unparalleled opportunity to achieve significant learnings and adaptive skills.

Budman's experiential group therapy.   As noted in Chapter 1, group psychotherapy has numerous forbearers, going back to the mid-1920s. In the past decade or two, several therapists have begun to utilize the short-term model to deal with dysfunctional groups and families. We highlight the work of Simon Budman to illustrate this useful application of brief therapy (Budman, 1981; Budman & Gurman, 1988). Working out of the Harvard Community Health Plan, Budman employs the term *experiential* to characterize his brief group treatment approach. To quote Budman and Gurman:

> It is more than simply an economical way to treat several unrelated individual patients or couples simultaneously, rather the emphasis is upon those interpersonal factors (e.g.,

cohesion, group development, feedback, self-disclosure, etc.) that are believed to be pivotal elements of any experiential group treatment. (p. 247)

Several principles guide Budman's approach. First, there must be a series of pre-group preparations to screen and orient prospective participants. Second, it is important to establish and then maintain the subject focus of the group. Third, a sense of cohesion among group members must be developed. And fourth, a clear and definite time limit must be set. As Budman conceives it, a fixed period may serve to "get members moving," especially those who may previously have been too fearful or too resistant to attempt even modest changes.

Bloom's planned single-session therapy.   Given the fact that the majority of patients fail to show up for a second therapeutic session, it appears wise to consider the possibility that single sessions may be all that therapists have available to achieve useful goals. Although popularized by Talmon (1990) this past decade, a very creative approach to single-session therapies was developed by Bernard Bloom (1981, 1992) some 20 years ago in conjunction with the emergence of the community mental health movement. Preceded in earlier years by therapists reporting on the potential impact of single sessions (e.g., E. Jacobson, D. Malan, and others), Bloom contends that therapists often overlook the fact that valuable therapeutic consequences may be associated with single sessions.

Strange as it may initially appear, Bloom's treatment model is psychodynamically informed. Hence, an effort is made to identify a central or focal problem, and then to engage in an interpretive process that seeks to bring some clarity and a measure of resolution to its essence. Although interpretations are central to Bloom's single-session task, they are presented rather tentatively. Nevertheless, therapists are advised to not underestimate patient strengths. Important to Bloom are efforts to build a follow-up plan and to mobilize social supports that may facilitate and maintain continuity of the achievements of the single session. Recognizing reality, Bloom does not seek to be overly ambitious. Similarly, he speaks of therapists as being "prudently active."

Horowitz's brief personality approach.   In previous sections, we have seen a number of innovations in brief therapy, notably as found in several group and family approaches, as well as in the dramatic developments of planned single-session therapy. Here, we briefly summarize the work of Mardi Horowitz and his associates (1984) owing to their efforts to employ short-term techniques with a variety of deeply embedded and problematic personality styles. Although the methods they have employed were developed in studies associated with a stressful catastrophic event shared by all, individual reactions and the treatment approach utilized differed substantially depending on the patient's established personality style. Horowitz elaborated a number of these differences among histrionic, compulsive, narcissistic, and borderline personality patients. He recognized that personality style differences would have significant implications for how one should conduct short-term psychotherapy.

The recognition of personality style variations and how different character types can best be treated is a theme that the present text considers extremely important. As Bloom has written (1992):

Few other time-limited psychotherapy theorists have yet given significant consideration to how their ideas about therapeutic technique should be modified by diagnostic considerations, and this work (by Horowitz) may be the harbinger of similar efforts in the future. (p. 145)

TREND TOWARD CULTURALLY SENSITIVE THERAPIES

Psychotherapists in Western societies are faced with an increasing challenge of cultural diversity and gender issues in their work. The profession has been remiss in taking cognizance of these factors in the past, displaying indifference, neglect, or inadequate preparation in our graduate training programs and in our daily practice. The part that these sociocultural issues play in our work have become more fully recognized in recent times. Numerous books and papers on socially relevant topics have been published this past decade; many compensate for the almost pernicious character of our multicultural insensitivities of the past. Fortunately, the special roles and perspectives required on the part of therapists dealing with increasingly diverse societal subgroups have become a significant trend in our professional work.

Minority Perspectives

As in the past, the United States continues to be enriched by its growing diversity of ethnic and racial minorities.

A transformation is rapidly taking place in our society. Close to 80% of those entering the United States and its labor force are composed of minorities, drawn from a vast arena of other countries and cultures. Further, owing to the fact that the fertility rate of the dominant American culture has been declining, and that the newborn population of ethnic/racial minorities continues to grow, it is clear that minority groups will become the numerical majority early this next century. This trend calls for an important reassessment of our traditional therapeutic attitudes and responsibilities. Psychotherapists are now being prepared for diverse patient populations with appreciably different cultural values and social experiences than has typified our practice in earlier years.

A few words should be recorded here concerning the several major racial/ethnic groups whose presence as patients must be given serious consideration in our plans.

Blacks or African Americans currently comprise this country's largest and relatively distinct minority group, numbering close to 30 million persons, or approximately 12% of the population of the United States. Despite significant intracultural differences among them, African Americans as a whole, owing to the superficial element of a darker skin, have been subjected to generations of social injustice, if not oppression. The effects of this historical prejudice, combined with problematic current life circumstances (lower economic and educational opportunities), dispose many to high levels of psychosocial stress.

Hispanic Americans are an unusually diverse group, comprising numerous subcultures, from Mexico, Puerto Rico, Cuba, South and Central America, and elsewhere. Hispanics are the fastest growing racial/ethnic group in the United States, with approximately 20 million residing here currently. Notable are the marked differences in cultural values and outlooks that add to the considerable heterogeneity within each Hispanic subgroup. Demographically, the Hispanic population as a whole tends to be less educated, younger, and poorer than the larger society, and more likely to live in congested inner cities. The stresses of this life setting, added to their linguistic minority status, contribute significantly to why they may be vulnerable to psychosocial problems that call for therapeutic services.

In a manner similar to Hispanics, Asian Americans comprise several major subcultures, including Japanese, Chinese, Filipino, Korean, Vietnamese, Cambodians, and Malaysians. Though heterogeneous in their country of origin, this broad-based minority group now comprises the third largest racial/ethnic population in the United States, numbering approximately 5.5 million persons and growing. Within each subgroup, there are different levels of acculturation, ranging from third-generation professionals of high status and income, to recent immigrants struggling with language difficulties and problematic employment. As with other minority groups, a large proportion of these individuals have been subjected to societal discrimination and misunderstanding.

Native Americans include American Indians, Eskimos, and Aleuts. Coming from tribes dispersed throughout the continent, Native Americans are culturally diverse as well as heterogeneous in terms of their opportunities to assimilate within the wider society. A recent census reports that their population numbers roughly 2 million, with only about 20% living on reservations. A notably young population, Native Americans fall near the low end of the educational, economic, and political power spectrum in the United States. Their poverty levels, unemployment, poor health care, shortened life expectancy, substance abuse, and suicide rate contribute significantly to the type of stresses they endure that require therapeutic assistance.

It may be useful to contrast the value system of the dominant White American male culture, and those of the minority groups to whom we have referred. For example, the dominant White culture strongly encourages the value of *individualism;* that is, that the person in treatment learn to act in an independent and autonomous fashion, that the individual carry major responsibility for the course of his or her own life, and that a primary goal of therapy should be increased self-esteem and self-actualization. By contrast, persons from several, perhaps most, minority groups in the United States regularly de-emphasize individualism. For example, American Indians value the collective group or tribe rather than each individual operating as a separate person; in other words, what is best for the group takes precedence over what is best for the individual. Similarly, many Hispanic subcultures place emphasis on the role of the family rather than the individual. Therapists would be wise, therefore, to recognize that an individualistic focus reflects the dominant White male cultural value system, but is not culturally universal.

Another value characterizing the dominant group is the role given *competition.* Primary and secondary schools in America are preoccupied with awarding grades and listing relative standings. Over time, intense competition comes into play as people seek prestigious schools of higher education and the status of a high-paying job. Our sports preoccupation, with its emphasis on winning and championships, is a central theme in the dominant culture. This competitive attitude encourages therapists to foster self-advancement and personal achievement in their therapeutic efforts. Here again, we see a sharp contrast to many racial/ethnic groups, several of whom feel quite uncomfortable with competitive activities. Many segments of both the Hispanic and Asian American cultures are oriented to joint cooperative efforts in their work habits and attitudes. Their cooperative orientation is likely to prove more motivating to them than values geared to the dominant society's focus on competitiveness.

Closely related to the preceding is the value orientation of *material achievement* that typifies the dominant culture. Wealth and status are central aspects in determining a person's worth in American society. Though these values may be experienced as comfortable to most, they are not necessarily shared by nondominant racial/ethnic groups. For example, among traditional American Indians, one's standing is measured by what one has given to others rather than by what one has gained for oneself.

The core unit in the dominant society is the nuclear family; here, parents live alone with their children, while other significant relatives (aunts, uncles, grandparents) live separately in independent family units. Many racial/ethnic subgroups, however, live in extended family systems, with diverse relatives of all ages living together or in very close proximity. Family therapy in the dominant social system tends to include only members of the nuclear family; other relatives are rarely brought into treatment. For example, the central role that grandparents have may be overlooked in treating Asian American families.

As a consequence of the diversity of racial/ethnic value systems, the primary orientation of many established therapeutic schools of thought may not prove as relevant and suitable as one might hope. We must recognize that the ancestry of many of the therapeutic theories we utilize is to be found in Europe and, hence, they reflect an English/European cultural perspective, with their implicit goals, values, and attitudes. The suitability of psychodynamic therapy, for example, is questionable owing to its focus on the key role of the individual, the desire to aid the person to "know oneself," to recognize that the problem that faces the patient is one that inheres within the self, with the consequent task of working through intrapsychic or unconscious mental distortions. This contrasts sharply with minority patient values and experiences in which primary attention may best be placed on the key role of sociocultural factors, such as racism, poverty, and social marginality. Similarly, the orientation in cognitive approaches stresses thought distortions that undermine the patient's effective functioning; in fact, the troublesome cognitions of the patient may represent the awful but actual realities experienced in everyday life. Similarly, self-actualizing modalities orient patients toward achieving psychic growth and self-esteem, but such an emphasis may cause considerable conflict or guilt for patients who come from cultural groups that are grounded in the importance of the collective, the family, or the traditional community.

Feminist Perspectives

Although the United States has benefited greatly these past three decades by the emergence of the feminist movement, especially as manifested in an increase in women's rights and opportunities, this valued progress has been a mixed blessing for some.

It wasn't until some years after the first women's rights convention at Seneca Falls in 1848 that an independent movement was established in America to set the foundation for achieving the women's right to vote in the twentieth century. Progress has been slow, but the past several decades have seen considerable movement on the part of women toward equality. Although a full measure of parity has yet to be attained, numerous intrapersonal and interpersonal complications have arisen in the course of this progression.

For both men and women, there is a deep struggle between the wish for mastery and self-determination on the one hand, and the wish for protection and security on the other. The feminist movement has sought to facilitate the development of women's autonomy, self-assertion, and psychic independence. This same ideal, however, is often experienced as a threat when it opposes the female tradition of enjoying protection from the uncertainties of a complex and competitive world. Success and achievement, therefore, can be sources of discomfort, if not anxiety, because they may threaten to disrupt the fulfillment of conflicting life-nurturing needs. Despite the worthy values of the feminist movement, many women have been socialized to develop social rather than professional and competitive skills. Behaviors that run contrary to traditional feminine roles are a special problem for women who often see their efforts at autonomy and achievement as a sign of rebelliousness, if not deviance, in contemporary society.

Therapists have observed that women, in efforts to compete with men, often anticipate troublesome social consequences. Whereas men assume that success will lead to further opportunities and cultural rewards, women are often in conflict about achievement, such as feeling guilty about surpassing their mothers, fear of losing a less adequate male partner, and consequent anxieties about aloneness in a less-than-accepting world. Historically, female identity has been shaped to be pleasing to men and to downgrade women's own abilities and confidence. It has been difficult, therefore, to integrate a sense of work achievement as a source of self-identity; in achievement, some women may be depriving themselves of a fundamental component of their self-esteem. Moreover, ambition is often complicated by the questioning attitudes of a larger society that makes aspiration a dubious motive in women; these attitudes can only create inner conflicts that may undermine the ability of women to pursue clear-cut goals.

For some, the conception of self in the liberated female appears to mirror what has historically typified males; that is, it is based on the need to separate oneself from the mother, the prime caretaker, the person of one's childhood who is tender, empathic, warm, and intimate. By jettisoning the traditional mother's role and adopting that of the father, women often develop a sense of separateness from others, a developmental trend in which they may deny their own tenderness and empathic sensitivity. No longer responsive to the needs of others, women may begin to feel alienated from themselves, isolated from what may be more congruent with their inherent maternal orientation. Male bravado and machismo may be attractive concepts, but may prove a deep source of personal alienation among those women who take them seriously.

No therapist would wish to return to the days when women were encouraged to be quiet and sedate, to be seen and not heard, to be obedient and passive. On the other hand, a good therapist must recognize that ours is a time of cultural transition when countervailing voices are to be heard, hence creating internalized conflicts for many women who will come to seek their guidance and support. There is little doubt that part of the conflict that women face stems from a social system sharply divided in its attitudes. However, in a society in which women are denied equal access to opportunities and resources, it should be a priority of therapists to help resolve the conflicts in those able women who struggle with their role-breaking efforts to find a more egalitarian life that will enable them to synthesize their deeper emotional needs with the authenticity of autonomy and independence.

Several contrasting orientations in feminist therapy have come to the foreground within the past two decades (Marececk & Hare-Mustin, 1987; Worell & Remer, 1992). One, termed *radical feminism,* attributes the struggle for women as deriving from the unequal distribution of power that exists within our society. Radical feminist therapists believe they should encourage women to assert themselves and gain increasing power in all of society's institutions. Its most significant form is seen among those who follow what has been called an *empowerment model* of therapy. A second group of feminist therapies, termed *gender-role treatment,* seeks to have patients understand that males and females have been socialized differently. The focus here is not to foster sociocultural change, but to resocialize women patients. The task is to make female clients more androgynous and thereby facilitate a broadening of their personal development and outlook. A third group, termed *women-centered therapy,* believes that differences in the psychological makeup of women and men are fundamental and not due solely to cultural socialization. Therapists of this persuasion seek to give a positive interpretation to "genuine" female traits rather than to judge them as misguided, troublesome, or signifying deficiencies. Hence, they honor as desirable such behaviors as cooperation, altruism, and empathy, and so facilitate their patients' increased valuation of their essential femaleness.

Gay/Lesbian Perspectives

There is a growing receptiveness and open-mindedness in the United States today regarding the diverse forms of gender proclivity and sexual preference. Although this trend has numerous benefits for many, problematic residuals remain for some that may call for therapeutic action.

Although gay men and lesbians constitute some 10–15% of the overall population in the United States, their status, until the past decade or so, has been that of "an invisible minority." Pervasive negative attitudes within society and insufficient professional training have prevented the delivery of thoughtful and sensitive therapeutic services to this subculture group. The trend toward greater knowledge and more egalitarian attitudes has only recently led to increased knowledge and skills necessary to work effectively with these patients.

Gay people, both male and female, experience a unique position among the socially rejected groups in that they are reared largely in nongay families, families who fail to provide adequate models of self-respect and self-esteem, and rarely provide an attitude of acceptance and affirmation for their progeny's socially problematic identity. Homophobia is commonplace and characterizes how most families and others react to gay people. Moreover, gay men and lesbians often grow up learning the same rejecting and hostile attitudes toward same-sex intimacies as do nongays. This internalization of homophobia is distressing for many gays, and further complicates their already troubled self-identity.

Historically, homoerotic attachments were viewed in a highly tolerant manner during the period of classical Greece. It was not until the sixteenth century when intense conflicts arose between Protestants and Catholics that legal action against same-sex behaviors became prominent. By the seventeenth century, same-sex relationships were viewed as a "crime against nature," and were classified with other forms of socially reprehensible behavior. The American colonies not only discouraged same-sex intimacies, but instituted legal prohibitions against such activities, often identified as a form of sodomy. Although legal punishment has abated in current times, there remains considerable social and religious discrimination in many quarters.

Promising signs have begun to emerge in the past few decades. For example, the American Psychiatric Association declassified homosexuality as a mental illness in 1973, followed in turn by a similar move on the part of the American Psychological Association in 1975. Most significantly, mental health professionals now treat the run-of-the-mill problems of gay men and lesbians, whatever their source or character, rather than concentrating their efforts on reversing their sexual orientation. These promising changes are encouraging, but they do not necessarily reflect an increased sensitivity on the part of practitioners. Research suggests that many mental health professionals carry with them rather archaic heterosexist assumptions. That is, they not only hold traditional stereotypes about gay people but are rather uninformed about gay and lesbian lifestyles, as well as harbor distorted beliefs concerning the issues that arise in the lives of these patients. Moreover, traditional homophobic assumptions invariably confound therapeutic work with complex transference and countertransference issues.

The problems presented by gay persons are not unexpected. Not untypical is a young person who might come to a therapist because he has been degraded, if not beaten, by his family, has been thrown out of his home, and is now homeless. The most frequent presenting problem among young gays is that of isolation. Youngsters report having no one to talk to and feeling alone in most social situations, especially within the family, at school, and in church or temple. Such isolation is usually associated with their fear of discovery and the constant need to hide. Even where a network of gay social companions is available, there is often a sense that others are interested only in exploiting them. Not to be overlooked is a sense of deep emotional isolation, the belief that one cannot trust bonding or attaching to others, owing to the assumption that the gay lifestyle tends to be transient and incidental rather than genuine and enduring. Lacking a consistent and appropriate role model, many young gays often demonstrate an appalling ignorance regarding what it is to be homosexual, frequently holding to the worst stereotypes about homosexuals—and therefore about themselves.

Over a third of gays and lesbians coming for therapy have suffered violence at the hands of others. There is a high percentage of suicide attempts during the teenage years as the early crisis of homosexual inclinations becomes inescapable. It is not until they move beyond the narrow confines of their early life settings, as they leave their communities or enter college or find distant jobs, that these young people begin to make contact with a more sophisticated and more homosexually oriented community. Nevertheless, many remain troubled and in conflict.

Coping with the problems of stigmatization is not an easy task in these days when the AIDS virus is so closely identified with homosexuality. Developing a close alliance with a single other person is perhaps their most important coping strategy. But the problems of being stigmatized, the remaining feelings of internal dissonance, and the need to deceive and hide one's inclination remain a serious part of the everyday life of many young gays.

There is no reason to believe that the homosexually oriented, as a group, are less well-adjusted than their heterosexual counterparts, but there are specific factors that typify the problems that gays experience when difficulties have arisen. Isolation, family rejection, abuse, and intrapsychic identity conflicts represent the problems for which they seek guidance. The task of therapists is not invariably a complex one. Many gays simply need access to accurate information; others need opportunities for socialization with a wider network of peers than achieved in same-sex settings. Of course, it is extremely difficult for gays to "actualize" themselves in a social context of public rejection. Moreover, gays and lesbians need support before they can fully express themselves and their individuality. Therapists must also learn to feel comfortable with their own sexuality and seek to rid themselves of homophobic feelings if they are to work openly and honestly with gay and lesbian patients. Most important, they must aid their patients to be free of their own homophobic stereotypes and conflicts, enabling them to develop a healthier attitude toward their own genuine feelings and authentic identities.

As with all issues discussed in this section on minority, feminist, and gay/lesbian perspectives, most of the "standard" therapeutic approaches discussed in this and the previous chapter can be carefully examined so as to reorient underlying biases and assumptions and thereby not only prove useful, but be applied with an informed sensitivity to patients' special life conditions.

TREND TOWARD INTEGRATIVE THERAPIES

The simplest way to practice psychotherapy is to approach all patients as possessing essentially the same disorder, and then utilizing one standard modality of therapy for their treatment. Many therapists still employ these simplistic models. Everything we have learned in the past two or three decades tells us that this approach is only minimally effective, an approach that deprives patients of other more sensitive and effective approaches to treatment. In the past two decades, we have come to recognize that patients differ substantially in the clinical syndromes and personality disorders they present. It is clear that not all treatment modalities are equally effective for all patients, be it pharmacologic, cognitive, intrapsychic, or other. *The task that we set before us for this chapter is to maximize our effectiveness, beginning with efforts to abbreviate treatment, to recognize significant cultural considerations, to combine treatment, and to outline a synergistic model for selective therapeutics based on each patient's personal trait configuration.*

Present knowledge about combinational and integrative therapeutics has only begun to be developed. The reader must recognize, therefore, that much of what is contained in this book is clinically and theoretically driven rather than empirically validated. It is the plan of this section to help overcome the resistance of many psychotherapists to the idea of utilizing treatment combinations comprising modalities they have not been trained to exercise. Most therapists have worked long and hard to become experts in a particular technique or two. Though they are committed to what they know and do best, they are likely to approach their patients' problems with techniques consonant with their prior training. Unfortunately, most modern therapists have become expert in only a few of the increasingly diverse approaches to treatment, much less be open to exploring interactive combinations that may be suitable for the complex configuration of symptoms that most patients bring to treatment.

In line with this theme, Frances, Clarkin, and Perry (1984) have written:

> Many of us were trained, and not so very long ago, to be quite skeptical about any use of combined therapies and to regard them as a sure sign of sloppy and inelegant practice. . . . [For example], the prescription of a combined drug regimen invited a variety of mocking nicknames like "polypharmacy," "cocktails," "shotguns," and "the kitchen sink." . . .
>
> The proponents of the various developing schools of psychotherapy tended to maintain the pristine and competitive purity of their technical innovations, rather than attempt to determine how these could best be combined with one another. There have always been a few synthesizers and bridgebuilders (often derided from all sides as "eclectic") but, for the most part, clinicians who were trained in one form of therapy tended to regard other types with disdain and suspicion. (p. 195)

The inclination of proponents of one or another modality of therapy to remain separate was only in part an expression of treatment rivalries. During the early phases of their development, innovators, quite appropriately, sought to establish a measure of effectiveness without having their investigations confounded by the intrusion of other modalities. No less important was that each treatment domain was but a single dimension in the complex of elements that patients bring to therapy. As we move away from a simple medical model to one that recognizes the psychological complexity of patients' symptoms and causes, it appears wise to *mirror* patients' complexities by developing therapies that are comparably complex. As will be noted in this chapter, the modern modalities discussed in Chapter 1 are not to be replaced but combined with one another, each addressing one or another facet of each patient's complex problems.

As will be elaborated throughout the text, certain combinational approaches have an *additive* effect; others may prove to possess a *synergistic* effect (Klerman, 1984). The term additive describes a situation in which the combined benefits of two or more treatments are at least equal to the sum of their individual benefits. The term synergistic describes a situation in which the combined benefits of several treatment modalities exceed the sum of their individual components; that is, their effects are potentiated. This entire book is intended to show that the several modalities covered in Chapter 1— pharmacotherapy, cognitive therapy, family therapy, intrapsychic therapy—may be combined and integrated to achieve additive if not synergistic effects.

There are, of course, some problems that should be noted as we reflect on integrative/combinational treatment. For example, if two different therapeutic approaches are employed, it is not possible without extensive research to know which treatment is working and how. If improvement occurs, is the primary reason the effectiveness of treatment A, treatment B, treatment C, perhaps some combination, or spontaneous remission? Part of this puzzle may be resolved by what we have termed *catalytic sequences.* Here, different modalities may be sequentially ordered so that we may determine what works and what does not.

It is our aim throughout the book to provide a deeper logic for the sequences that might be employed. For example, a self-conscious stutterer with an avoidant personality disorder might be treated first for his stuttering through behavioral techniques. Once the stuttering difficulty has been resolved effectively by a behavioral method, this patient will no longer feel especially self-conscious about his problematic stuttering and hence may be increasingly receptive to cognitive, self-actualizing, and interpersonal techniques, sequenced in that order. Cognitive reorientation may prove useful in helping undo erroneous beliefs about himself and others. Self-actualizing methods may next be employed, now that the distorting effects of his prior belief system have been worked through. And with the elimination of his stuttering behaviors, the clarification of misbegotten beliefs and assumptions, and the development of increased self-esteem, the technique of interpersonal therapy may successfully come into play for learning new social skills in relevant situations and relationships.

The *integrative* treatment trends in this section combine the various modalities described in Chapter 1. As Schacht (1984) has noted, different theorists and clinicians have referred to the integrative trend by looking at different levels or units of analysis. The most elementary of the integrative trends may be seen as *translation* of one set of concepts into the language of another; this is best illustrated by the writings of Dollard and Miller (1950). Schacht notes a second differentiation, one we see as the essence of empirical eclecticism. This he terms the *complementary integration;* here, one recognizes that different modalities may be appropriate for dealing with different problems in the same patient (e.g., a cognitive confrontation method for helping resolve excessive dependency and a psychopharmacologic treatment for underlying anxiety problems). The third of Schacht's models, which he terms *synergistic,* is an approach in which two or more therapies are applied to the same psychological problem; these are expected to interact to produce therapeutic results superior to what might be obtained by one therapy alone. (It is a variant of this model that will be elaborated shortly and that guides our approach to treatment.) Next, Schacht speaks of what he calls the *emergent* model in which different therapies blend to generate a novel hybrid of treatment features that were not seen in either therapy alone; this, too, appears to characterize what we believe occurs in what we termed the *personality-guided approach.* Last, Schacht proposes the level of *theoretical integration* in which various schools of thought are synthesized in the hope that emergent qualities will develop and treatment efficacy be enhanced; we have introduced the designation *theoretical synthesis* to reflect this orientation.

The following sections of the chapter are divided into several parts. The first is composed of several broad overviews of what have become major integrative treatment philosophies; the last outlines details concerning one of these philosophies.

In "Eclecticism," we discuss the amalgamation of different modalities to fit a case in hand; what is notable here is the decision to employ techniques that have been validated through systematic research and to leave aside those lacking in such validation. The second grouping refers to the concept of "Common Factors"; here, we include writers who are searching for underlying similarities among diverse techniques. The third category we have termed "Theoretical Syntheses"; here, an attempt is made to bring together one overarching treatment combination composed of different guiding theoretical models (e.g., psychoanalysis, cognitive reorientation, behavioral modification). It is the author's belief that none of these three integrative approaches is likely to derive an emergent form of therapy that will be both maximally useful clinically as well as theoretically consonant.

It is our view that psychopathology itself contains structural implications that legislate over the form of any therapy that would propose to remedy its constituents. Thus, the fourth philosophy we will present derives from several of these implications and proposes a new integrative model for therapeutic action; an approach that we have called "Person-Oriented Integration." This model, which is guided by the psychic makeup of a patient's personality, and not a preferred theory or modality or technique, gives promise, we believe, of a new level of efficacy and may, in fact, contribute to making therapy briefer. Far from being merely a theoretical rationale or a justification for adhering to one or another treatment modality, it should optimize psychotherapy by *tailoring* treatment interventions *to fit* the patient's specific form of pathology. It is not a ploy to be adopted or dismissed as congruent or incongruent with established therapeutic preferences or modality styles. Despite its name, we believe that what we have termed a personality-guided approach will be effective with both Axis II personality disorders and Axis I clinical syndromes.

Early Integrationists

The notion of integrating the several approaches to psychotherapy may be traced back to the 1930s. Despite its early origins, it must be clear that the modern modality focus, the first stage of analysis, will have to attain a reasonable level of achievement before the possibility of synthesizing approaches begins to emerge.

Heinz Werner (1940), the developmental theorist, held that development proceeds in three stages: (a) from the relatively global to (b) the relatively differentiated to (c) an integrated totality. Had the development of psychotherapy followed this model, integrative therapies would not only address psychological problems with unprecedented specificity and therapeutic efficacy, but they would do so from the vantage point of an overarching and unifying theoretical perspective.

Unfortunately, clinical science has not yet developed into Werner's integrative totality, for at least two reasons. First, the original clinical theory within which therapy developed, psychoanalysis, ultimately proved to be only a partial theory of human nature, and one beset with terminological ambiguities that have proven highly resistant to clarification and operationalization. In fact, the case has been made that "progress" in psychoanalysis is an evolution away from what Freud had originally conceptualized. Thus hobbled by metatheoretical obscurities, psychoanalysis did not give birth to a true taxonomy of psychopathology, one of both precision and coverage. Psychopathology and the personality disorders are multireferential constructs. Though some disorders display themselves with a greater degree of salience in some domains rather than others, a taxonomy cannot be generated that encompasses all of the disorders on the basis of a single perspective or domain alone. Consequently, psychoanalysis largely failed to profit from the synergism between theory and empirical research of the kind begun by the *DSM-III* and continues through *DSM-IV.*

Second, other modality domains, some primarily from academic psychology and others from clinical science, also gave rise to sophisticated philosophies of human nature that were just as imperious, totalistic, and exclusionary as psychoanalysis. Behaviorism emerged and dominated for a time, only to eventually give way to cognitive psychology, which today may itself be considered a subdiscipline of cognitive science. Other perspectives oriented both to harder (e.g., the neurobiologic) and softer (e.g., interpersonal) levels of organization have also emerged and flourished. Each of these spawned its own schools of intervention and theoretically derived techniques (in the neurobiologic perspectives, these techniques take the form of medications). For the most part, each also became submerged in the specificities of its own program and so developed largely in isolation, transfixed by its own internal consistency and, thus, was either not attentive to or was dismissive of the advances of alternative perspectives on the same field.

The first formal recommendation of an integrative nature was presented by Thomas French (1933), who suggested that concepts of Freudian psychoanalysis and Pavlovian conditioning, though discrepant overtly, had many fundamental similarities. Adolf Meyer suggested (see French, 1933) that the potential for convergences are worth pursuing; however, he believed that theoreticians should continue their separate lines of development and not attempt to bridge them prematurely. Adding to these early integrative proposals was Lawrence Kubie (1943), who recognized that several psychoanalytic techniques might readily be explained in terms of Pavlov's conditioned reflexology.

In 1936, Rosenzweig proposed that *common factors* were shared among most effective therapies; whereas French and Kubie attempted to bring together two separate theoretical orientations, Rosenzweig averred that treatment similarities had more to do with certain common elements of practice than with their theoretical systems. Rosenzweig suggested three common factors among effective psychotherapies: (a) it is the personality of the therapist that has most to do with treatment effectiveness, and not the preferred and habitual treatment modality; (b) interpretations provide patients with alternative modes of thought and action, as well as making their problems more understandable; and (c) different theoretical orientations focus on different domains, but all may be effective because of the synergistic effect any one area of functioning might have on the others.

Perhaps the most significant work leading to an integrative perspective was John Dollard and Neal Miller's classic *Personality and Psychotherapy* (1950). In this book, Dollard and Miller outlined in considerable detail how psychoanalytic concepts such as anxiety, displacement, regression, and repression might be more readily understood within a learning theory/behavioral model. Dollard and Miller appear to many to have merely translated one theoretical language system into another. Although this assertion is not an accurate one, most contemporary behaviorists assert that Dollard and Miller had little impact on the development of behavior therapy.

In the 1960s, Jerome Frank authored an especially insightful book, *Persuasion and Healing* (1961). Frank's primary themes related to the commonalities among diverse methods of *personal influence*. He viewed psychotherapy as but one method for persuading people to adopt certain beliefs. Personal influence with beneficial healing properties could be seen, according to Frank, in such diverse methods as brainwashing, religious conversion, primitive healing, and the placebo effects that stem from the "authority" of the medical practitioner.

The 1960s provided the groundwork for numerous papers and books seeking to synthesize several theoretical orientations, most notably the behavioral-learning and psychoanalytic. Lee Birk (1970) proposed the use of both behavior therapy and psychodynamic methods in the treatment of two complex cases. Arnold Lazarus (1971) detailed ways that behavior and cognitive techniques may be brought together; more will be said of Lazarus's ideas in the next section. Victor Raimy (1975), following Jerome Frank, Albert Ellis, and Aaron Beck, proposed that all therapies appear to be directed toward changing patients' misconceptions of themselves and others. Any differences among treatment techniques, according to Raimy, stem from the fact that different levels of functioning are addressed in different languages and are explored at different points in the therapeutic sequence.

Eclecticism

Although the goals of eclecticism in general are laudable, they are largely bound by what has been empirically established. As alluded earlier, the view of eclecticism is essentially that there exists a constellation of therapies and a separate constellation of disorders and that these should be matched empirically. In its beginning phases, however, science consists almost exclusively of descriptive terms. At its most incipient, science is mainly concerned with the questions What is there? and What is it like?, a strategy designed to inventory and specify the phenomena of a subject domain. Little more can be done at this stage, because no other terms yet exist and, moreover, the paradigms that lend scientific terms their compelling quality have not yet been formulated.

In the following sections, we briefly discuss the views of three key figures who have argued in favor of the use of modalities and techniques whose primary virtue is that they have ostensibly been empirically validated. The views of these theorists are highly similar, although we will begin with the earliest.

Thorne's clinical eclecticism.   Frederick C. Thorne was among the first of the eclectic thinkers (1950, 1961, 1967; Thorne & Pishkin, 1968). Although trained by many of the distinguished psychologists and psychiatrists of his day—Adolf Meyer, Alfred Adler, Carl Rogers—Thorne did not intend his ideas to be a compilation of all established theories about therapy, but an original synthesis of his own. As he described it, he was "determined to make a fresh start right from the beginning, accepting nothing on authority alone, and to formulate an eclectic system integrating all pertinent scientific information available at this time and place" (1968, p. v). Noting that the scientific validation of different modalities had only rarely been established, Thorne proposed:

> At this early stage in the development of clinical psychological science, the most profitable approach appears to be to attempt an eclectic collection. . . . our main objective is to simply present an eclectic collection of methods which may be applied rationally according to their indications and contraindications. To us, this is all a clinical science can ever do. How these methods are combined and used is a function of the art of clinical practice. (pp. 12–13)

Despite Thorne's seeming openness to all possible methods and observations, his eclectic view was not an unsystematic, ragtag collection that would result in a patchwork of treatment techniques. Anticipating the views of the personality-guided approach in the 1990s, Thorne asserted that personality was an integrative whole, and therefore, therapeutic efforts should likewise be integrated and systematic.

In Thorne's model, all forms of psychopathology are essentially disorders of integration. The task of the therapist is not only to strengthen and improve the reintegration of personality, but to foster increasing levels of self-actualization. In what he terms the *principle of unification,* Thorne sought to encourage the resolution of factors that disrupt the positive features of integration within each patient. This involved methods that optimize the patient's control and organization of his or her life, especially by managing the disordering effects of any affective-impulsive characteristics. No less important is that patients should first be led to experience a degree of *positive disintegration* so that they can reorganize and reintegrate their psychic state. In many ways, his thesis regarding the role of reintegration anticipated ideas that became increasingly relevant to what was subsequently called the borderline personality.

Lazarus's empirical eclecticism.   The major contributor to empirically based eclecticism is Arnold Lazarus and his *multimodal therapy* (Lazarus, 1973, 1976, 1981). Initially trained as a behavioral therapist, Lazarus came to believe that clinicians should employ modalities from different therapy systems, without necessarily accepting the theoretical orientation with which they were associated. Arguing for the importance of a full psychological assessment as a prelude to intervention, Lazarus developed a sevenfold schema for evaluating each patient's difficulties. Termed BASIC IB, this scheme included, in sequence: behavior, affect, sensation, imagery, cognition, interpersonal relationships, and biology (originally listed as drugs). As with other eclectic thinkers of his day, Lazarus emphasized the matching of treatment techniques to the patient's problems. Most important, treatments were to be selected on the basis of evidence for their effectiveness.

As noted, empirical eclecticism holds that therapeutic procedures may be divorced from their generative theories without the need for either endorsing the theory or subjecting it to validation (e.g., Beutler, Consoli, & Williams, 1994; Lazarus, 1973, 1976). Only the efficacy of specific techniques need be justified. Empirical eclecticism has struggled to move forward as a therapeutic philosophy in the face of stubborn difficulties, not the least of which is the climate of hundreds of competing approaches. However, by promising an independence of technique and theory, the problem of coordinating theories and therapies has been bypassed.

As Thorne suggested years earlier, Lazarus claimed that efforts should be made to avoid a random melange of techniques based on subjective preferences. Knowledge, they both asserted, should be based not only on experimental evidence, but also on formal measurement procedures to appraise the success of each technique. It was Lazarus's belief also that by employing terms and data that were experimentally derived, clinical science may replace "metaphysical" concepts and theories.

Although eschewing the role of theory in psychotherapy, Lazarus acknowledged that most clinicians used a rough outline of theory to orient their treatment choices and decisions. Lazarus (1986) himself recognized that his own orientation derived from a mix of social learning, communications, and general systems syntheses; his therapy was shaped by his early preference for behavioral modalities and a later expansion into the cognitive therapies. His focus on assessment through the BASIC IB model attempts to take the vague and diffuse problems of anxiety, family dysfunctions, vocational unhappiness, and so on and reduce them to specific and discrete problems.

Anticipating aspects of the person-centered integrative models of the 1990s, Lazarus recommended that the "firing order" of the different treatment modalities be given serious consideration. He referred to this sequencing model as *tracking:*

> For example, some clients tend to generate negative emotions by dwelling first on aversive images (I) (e.g., pictures of dire consequences befalling them), followed by unpleasant sensations (S) (e.g., muscle tension and heart palpitations) to which they attach negative cognitions (C) (e.g., ideas about imminent cardiac arrest), culminating in maladaptive behavior (B) (e.g., unnecessary avoidance). A person who usually adheres to such an ISCB pattern (Imagery-Sensory-Cognitive-Behavioral) tends to require a different treatment sequence then say a CISB reactor (Cognitive-Imagery-Sensory-Behavior) or someone with yet a different firing order. (1986, p. 80)

Beutler's systematic eclecticism.   Developing a model akin to those proposed by Thorne and Lazarus before him, Larry Beutler (1979, 1981, 1983, 1991) has organized an empirically oriented eclecticism that is unusually comprehensive in its scope. He emphasizes treatment specificity and the matching of techniques to the person and the problem he or she possesses. As did his forerunners, Beutler reviews empirical data to select his choice of therapy, placing only minimal emphasis on the guidance of theory. Whereas Lazarus appears to utilize behavioral and cognitive methods rather heavily, Beutler's formulations draw on a much wider range of therapeutic modalities, including the psychodynamic.

Beutler recognizes that the outcome of psychotherapy results from numerous factors other than any specific treatment technique. Beyond focusing on the match between a problematic dysfunction and a specific modality or technique, he (Beutler & Clarkin, 1990) includes such variables as the therapist's outlook (e.g., attitudes, experiences), patient personality and past history (e.g., coping style, symptom complexity, resistance), as well as other specific and interactive aspects among treatment methods.

The number and diversity of variables that could be considered in a matrix that includes patient, therapist, situation, and past history are nearly limitless. As a result of the inability to locate empirical support for many therapeutic approaches, Beutler (1986), in contrast to other empirically oriented eclecticists, willingly turns to theory to guide these choices. Here, he bases his work on social-psychological models of *persuasion*. Following the ideas of Jerome Frank (1973), Beutler has adopted a philosophy that psychotherapy is a social-influence or persuasion process. As he describes it, the therapist's guiding theory establishes the content of *what* is persuaded, and the therapist's technology serves as the *means* of influence.

Beutler's eclecticism operates from his *theory of change,* which gives substance and direction to a variety of technical procedures. He writes that eclecticism is more a collection of empirical observations than of explanatory constructs. Hence, models of social influence are not only useful for eclectic choices but sufficiently flexible to encompass a broad variety of explanatory theories (e.g., cognitive, psychodynamic, and behavioral). As such, his theory of social persuasion may be able to circumvent many of the problems of intertheory translation.

Consistent with the importance he gives to proper assessment, Beutler has tried to identify patient qualities that are conducive to positive outcomes. Somewhat to his surprise, he found that the results of his outcome research were accounted for more by such variables as problem severity, coping style, and motivating distress than by technique alone.

Comment. An independence of theory and technique entails a clinical science that is specifically unintegrated. What would clinical science look like if the two were in fact entirely disjoint, that is, if techniques were truly theory-free? Most important, there would be no scientific basis on which to choose a particular technique, only an empirical one. Deprived of the guidance of theory, clinical science would then be completely in bondage to methodology. Where empirical evidence *did not exist* to guide the therapist, there would be no reason to decide between one technique and any other, for there would be no theory, however implicit, on which to base the decision or narrow the range of options. Those patients experiencing difficulties as yet unresearched would either be assigned to the experimental or control group or simply be dismissed from the office as possessing problems outside the scope of psychology in its then current form. Psychotherapy research would consist exclusively of filling in the cells of a problems-by-techniques matrix with empirical findings (which would then be compulsively "refined" by repeated meta-analyses).

Just as philosophers of science recognize that there are no theory-neutral facts, we would argue that there are no theory- and therapy-neutral techniques, either in content or in application. Undoubtedly, those therapeutic techniques that have been derived from the propositions of a particular modality will be most efficacious for problems anchored primarily in that modality, for example, the treatment of phobias from a behavioral perspective, or the use of cognitive techniques to reframe a patient's distorted expectancies. However, the odds and ends of diverse schemata and perspectives no more form a theory than do several techniques, randomly chosen, form a therapy. Such a hodgepodge will lead only to illusory syntheses and interventions that cannot long hold together. Sechrest and Smith (1994, p. 2), for example, note that the addition of relaxation training to psychodynamic therapy "does not constitute integration unless relaxation itself has been integrated into psychodynamic theory as a construct and as an aim of therapy." Again, the problem is that different perspectives on human nature come with different sets of assumptions. By virtue of its internal consistency, each set of assumptions carves out its own universe of discourse, the terms and propositions of which are not readily translatable into those of any other. Like theoretical constructs, each technique is embedded in a particular perspective, a preformed body of nomological relationships. To lift it out of that perspective is to dissociate it from the assumptive world from whence it takes its meaning. If applied in another context, the technique must either be translated or be applied meaninglessly, without regard to the antecedent conditions that might justify its use or the consequences that might follow.

It may be useful to quote the ideas of Murray (1986) at this point:

> No one can doubt the reality of eclectic therapy used in a systematic, and apparently, effective way. But what is the system? How do you know when to use what? To many outsiders, and certainly to the beginning therapy student, it all seems chaotic and capricious. Indeed, many eclectic therapists insist on flexibility and creativity. (p. 401)

Eclecticism at least has the virtue of humility. Modality-bound eclectic therapies are a "compromise," usually intended to veil underlying self-doubt and insecurity concerning one's own deeper convictions. Alternatively, it can also derive from a fear of growth, in that growth points to the insufficiency or inadequacy of what currently exists. Epistemologically, it is found in its most obtuse form in debates concerning which treatment orientation (cognitive, behavioral, biologic, intrapsychic) is "closer to the truth," or which therapeutic method is the most intrinsically efficacious. What differentiates these orientations and treatment methods has little to do with their theoretical underpinnings *or* their empirical support. Their differences are akin to physicists, chemists, and biologists arguing over which of their fields is a more "true" representation of nature. Such schisms have been constructed less by philosophical considerations or pragmatic goals than by the accidents of history and professional rivalries.

Today, the compensating insecurity of modality-bound therapies has succumbed to an eclecticism of practical necessity; the tendency is to conceptualize cases "completely," even if internal consistency is sacrificed. No one on a treatment team waits until a common vocabulary has been evolved that bridges and unifies the perspectives of the team members in a single overarching framework. Each person simply presents his or her own opinion where his or her perspective informs the case, a practice that recognizes, if only in practice, that there is something about the totality of human nature that resists being put into a single conceptual system or taxonomy. Unlike modality-bound psychotherapies, eclecticism is viewed as being atheoretical, as encouraging research of all kinds, and as being devoted pragmatically to what actually helps people (Lambert, 1992). In contrast, modality-bound forms of psychotherapy make strong prescriptions about the perspectives from which cases are conceptualized and the techniques that may be used in psychotherapy.

What is ironic about empirically based eclecticism, however, is that it has itself become dogmatic, a virtuous kind of psychotherapeutic liberalism. The irony lies in the contrast between the intent of eclecticism and what has become of it. As we see it, there are two preconditions for intelligent eclecticism: first, practical necessity, and second, a measure of ignorance concerning the nature of the subject at hand. In the absence of a theory of human nature that is both complete and internally consistent, one that would exhaust individuality in every case, we must all remain eclectics. To this extent, eclecticism, far from being dogmatic, simply co-opts whatever present theory seems to go the farthest given the difficulties to be resolved. As a form of psychotherapeutic pragmatism, eclecticism is motivated by self-conscious ignorance; it essentially functions as a means of coping with complexity until better and more integrative schemas come along. Eclecticism, then, is a movement, not a theoretical orientation.

Like pragmatism, eclecticism prescribes whatever works, and whatever works is "the truth." In the case of psychotherapy, this means recording those techniques that have proven efficacious thus far with certain types of persons. When eclecticism begins to exist as a self-conscious movement and sets up first principles, including "Thou shall be an eclectic," it has made the transition to dogmatism, and makes no more sense than an agnostic church. Eclecticism prescribes nothing.

There are reasons for preferring an integrative approach to disorders that go beyond the sufficiencies of eclecticism. While eclecticism is motivated by the necessity of action in the face of insufficient knowledge, no such state exists with regard to theories of psychopathology; the structural properties of psychopathology are intrinsically integrative and are characteristic of the definition of the construct *person* itself. In a generic sense, these structural properties set up what we believe to be synergistic forms of therapy, which we discuss in later chapters.

Common Factors

Whereas empirical eclecticism emphasizes the coordination of *different* approaches to therapy, the movement known as common factors attempts to identify *similarities* among divergent therapies. The essential goal of the common factors approach is to discover those treatment elements that are especially associated with positive outcomes.

If development does proceed from the relatively global to the relatively differentiated, then perhaps it is possible to look for commonalities among the many differentiated schools as a means of identifying the core features that drive successful psychotherapy. This is a reasonable and honest point of beginning. Like Descartes, the common factors approach seeks to jettison the entire corpus of accumulated conceptual heterogeneities and specificities to discover a small number of fundamental truths from which to begin again with a firm foundation.

In an impressive book that outlined a common factors rationale, Jerome D. Frank (1973) proposed a series of recommendations that proved highly instructive to the profession of psychotherapy. In his search for general principles that might account for the fact that all psychotherapies appear to be equally effective, Frank (1961, 1968, 1984) suggested a variety of components that encompassed the common assertions among diverse techniques or theories:

> One way to identify some of these components would be to ask yourself what qualities you would seek in a guide if you were a tenderfoot about to embark on an exploration into unknown territory with various unknown dangers. Two qualities you would certainly want in a guide would be trustworthiness and competence. You would expect to be able to rely fully on the guide's concern about your welfare. . . . You would want the guide to be thoroughly familiar with the terrain and how to cope with the hardships and angers you might meet. (1984, p. 422)

It is Frank's belief that a therapist's trustworthiness, competence, and caring are the fundamentals for effective psychotherapy. As he viewed the psychotherapeutic problem, these fundamental common factors are extratheoretical, applying with equal force regardless of any theoretical approach. Also significant to Frank's thesis were the following elements that he believed constituted the basic ingredients of all therapies: arousing hope, encouraging changed behaviors, stimulating emotional arousal, encouraging new ways of understanding oneself, and the introduction of corrective emotional experiences. Most significantly, Frank hypothesized that there is a common problem that all therapies share: the "demoralization" of patients, owing to their loss of self-esteem and their subjective feelings of incompetence, alienation, and hopelessness. Consistent with his main theme of persuasion and healing, Frank asserted that all therapies may be equally effective in restoring a patient's morale, although they employ different ways to do so. Both before and after Frank's useful presentation of the threads of effective treatment that the various psychotherapies share, a number of other authors wrote about these common factors. We discuss three of these authors in the following sections.

Garfield's treatment commonalities. Tracing his notions to the ideas of Rosenzweig (1936) and Rosenthal and Frank (1956), Sol Garfield (1957) makes reference to several factors that the different psychotherapies share in common, that is, that are not specific to any particular form of therapy. Furthermore, it seemed plausible to Garfield that there are variables or processes common to most treatment approaches that are, in fact, the truly operative ones, instead of the many varieties advanced by theoretical separatists.

In specifying psychotherapies' common factors, Garfield notes that treatment begins when an individual experiences a degree of discomfort that finally motivates him or her to consult a therapist; thus, all forms of psychotherapy have in common a disturbed individual who seeks assistance. Further, individuals attempt to locate a therapist who is generally perceived as a socially sanctioned healer. Also in all therapies, patients are afforded the opportunity to tell the "healer" about their difficulties, to confide personal matters, and to unburden themselves of those thoughts and feelings that have been perplexing and troubling. The therapist, in return, will exhibit an attentive interest in what the patient is saying, and may ask questions or seek elaborations of what the patient has presented. No less important as a common factor is that the patient develops a relationship with the therapist; most relationships that last more than a session or two are essentially good alliances in which there is a reasonable level of mutual respect and trust. A measure of catharsis is shared in common among most verbal therapies; hence, most therapists permit the patient to achieve a degree of emotional release as therapy progresses. No less important, from the therapist's point of view, is the opportunity to directly observe and respond to characteristic behaviors of the patient. Most significant is the opportunity afforded patients to rethink their image of themselves and the world in which they live, thereby gaining a measure of reality and hope by virtue of a sense of increased competence and good fortune. Last, insofar as the therapist's sense of mission, most believe in the utility and effectiveness of their own form of therapy, a positive outlook that often is conveyed to the patient, an outlook that may strengthen the patient's conviction that *this* form of therapy will prove best for his or her search for healing.

Garfield discusses the initial sessions of therapy at considerable length, suggesting a variety of themes that are encountered during the preliminary phases of treatment. Regarding the mechanisms that Garfield suggests for evoking change, he believes that the personality and psychological health of the therapist are key components. He does recognize, however, that therapists may work successfully with some patients and not with others. Thus, it is the interaction between therapist and patient that can make this factor a crucial one. As he wrote (1992):

> The therapist, who is perceived favorably by the client, first of all provides a source of hope for the client. If a positive relationship develops, the initial hope is reinforced and increases the client's confidence in the therapist and in himself. This, in turn, helps to foster the possibility for release of a number of other potentially therapeutic variables. (p. 184)

Garfield goes on to note that the particular explanations or interpretations offered by the therapist are not of primary importance. Rather, the essential factor appears to be whether the patient finds them to be credible and acceptable. Should the explanation be unconvincing or incomprehensible, it is likely that the patient will reject it and, hence, it will have little positive effect. Among other elements significant to treatment success, according to Garfield, is the presence of positive reinforcements, the use of desensitizing techniques, the willingness to confront problems directly, and the opportunity to acquire information and skills.

Goldfried's common clinical strategies thesis.   Marvin Goldfried began his career as a behavior therapist writing about a number of useful methods in which the behavioral framework was central. By the 1970s, however, Goldfried (1971) began to challenge the adequacy of behavioral approaches to therapy and to advocate the inclusion of cognitive processes both in the conceptualization and the implementation of psychotherapy. His work during this period shifted emphasis from a focus on discrete, situation-specific behaviors to a broad-based, problem-specific model, one in which coping skills may be developed and usefully applied across a variety of situations, response modalities, and personal difficulties.

Working together with several associates, Goldfried (D'Zurilla & Goldfried, 1971) developed what he termed *social problem solving*. Patients were trained in a series of steps to acquire *not* specific responses, but problem-solving skills. They were taught first to perceive their difficulties as responses to unsolved problems; next, they were led to regard these difficulties either as challenges or as opportunities. Further, they were led to generate as many alternative solutions to the problem as possible, without judging their feasibility or potential effectiveness. Third, they were to appraise the likely consequences of each of these solutions. And fourth, they were to enact the selected solution and to evaluate its effectiveness in achieving their goals.

During the 1970s, Goldfried (1971) proposed that Wolpe's method of systematic desensitization be reconceptualized in mediational terms. He saw Wolpe's method to be a specific technique in which patients often develop a general self-relaxation skill. In a similar inventive mode, Goldfried and his associates sought to integrate Ellis's rational-emotive cognitive therapy within a social learning framework; he termed this a *systematic rational restructuring* approach (SRR). Goldfried also sought to emphasize the importance of conscious self-statements. In an earlier paper with Sobosinsky, Goldfried suggested that early learning experiences teach individuals to label situations in different ways. For him, emotional reactions may be understood best by the way individuals label situations in contrast to their behavioral response to those situations. It was

Goldfried's belief that persons can acquire more effective ways to cope by learning to modify their way of interpreting distressing events rather than automatically responding as they had in the past.

By the early 1980s, Goldfried (1980, 1991; Goldfried & Padawer, 1982) suggested that the notion of common factors be viewed at an intermediary level of abstraction, that is, between broad theories and specific techniques. He termed this intermediary level *clinical strategies* for changing patients in psychotherapy. Two strategies were proposed as central to all therapies. The first strategy is in having the patient engage in new and potentially corrective experiences. The second consists of direct feedback; here, patients are "helped to become more aware of what they are doing and not doing, thinking and not thinking, and feeling and not feeling in various situations" (1980, p. 992). Seeking to identify both common and unique elements in different therapeutic approaches, Goldfried focused his efforts increasingly on the feedback process and on coding systems by which feedback was measured.

Goldfried has suggested that the traditional way of conceptualizing common factors may be too unitary and simplistic. Moreover, he believed that it may be necessary to recognize the role of contextual factors as well. In addition to the two central strategies of engaging in new, corrective experiences and being open to feedback, Goldfried has identified a number of other similarities that characterize an intermediary level of abstraction among common factors. Reflecting the work of Frank (1961), he notes the expectation that therapy can be helpful; in line with Garfield's ideas, he judges the mere participation in a therapeutic relationship to be central. In addition, Goldfried notes the possibility of gaining an external perspective on one's self and one's world. And last, therapy provides an opportunity to test reality repeatedly.

Prochaska's transtheoretical model.   What distinguishes Prochaska's (1984, 1995) model regarding common factors is that he has specified and organized a number of basic factors in a systematic fashion, executing in a series of papers and research investigations how these elements interrelate to increase the effectiveness of treatment. With his associates (1984) he has articulated a series of commonalities that stem from what he terms the *processes of change*. Prochaska has noted several stages of change in therapy (e.g., contemplation, maintenance), a number of levels of change (e.g., symptoms, maladaptive cognitions, intrapersonal conflicts), and a set of change processes (e.g., stimulus control, self-reevaluation). Seeking to demonstrate the interplay of these elements in a systematic way, Prochaska has sought to devise ways to measure stages, levels, and processes, as well as their interactions. In describing Prochaska's approach, Arkowitz (1997) writes:

> The central idea is deceptively simple: change will be most likely to occur when there is a correspondence between stages and processes of change. Their research has revealed that certain processes of change are maximally effective only when used at certain stages of change, and that when there is a mismatch between processes and stages, change is less likely to occur. Furthermore, their stage model suggests that we need to understand the sequence of stages that people must pass through in order to accomplish enduring change. (pp. 249–250)

In discussing the stages of change, Prochaska and DiClemente (1982, 1983, 1984, 1985) have discovered that therapeutic change appears to unfold over a series of six stages: precontemplation, contemplation, preparation, action, maintenance, and termination. Among Prochaska's other inventive notions, he proposed that the frequency of sessions also depend on the patient's stage of change. For example, patients at the point of precontemplation or contemplation are expected to see the therapist weekly; for those who are in the action stage, sessions may be scheduled biweekly, and those approaching the maintenance stage may be scheduled on a monthly basis.

Although Prochaska believes that therapeutic change is sequential and predictable, he does not assert that change is linear. Rather, he notes that patients spiral in and out of these stages as life's successes and failures are encountered.

Comment.   In our judgment, and as with eclecticism, a major problem with the common factors approach is that it is insufficiently theoretical; it is a necessary, but not sufficient, basis for a comprehensive scientific psychotherapy. Even if these common factors could be concretely and consensually defined either across theories of psychotherapy or even across very good therapists, merely identifying common factors does not explicate the underlying mechanisms that mediate their efficacy. Most readers probably know therapists whose clinical intuition is so incisive that they almost instinctively know exactly what to say and do in therapy, yet cannot fully explain the rational basis on which their actions are narrowed from an almost infinite constellation of possibilities. For these individuals, attempts to link explanatory schemata directly to intervention, what we would think of as the very substance of a scientific psychotherapy, may be experienced as counterproductive, in that they disrupt a graceful automaticity that the rest of us are still struggling to achieve. Nevertheless, the fact that some psychotherapists are apparently "loaded" with common factors and are so good at what they do begs the questions How do they do it? and Why does it work?, questions that bring the insufficiency of a common factors approach to the foreground. As noted earlier, there are no theory-neutral observations; in this sense, the common factors approach suffers the problems of any inductive methodology. Once regularities or patterns have been observed again and again, their existence is clear but not why they exist, what creates them, or how they work. We might say that common factors are to psychotherapy what factor analysis is to personality.

Despite its problems, the common factors approach has generated innovative ideas about which elements cut across therapeutic schools, as well as the possibility of correlating common factors to therapy outcome. This last point has not been adequately researched, but is crucial to the assumption that the more salient of the common factors will relate directly to therapy outcome. On the other hand, a reasonably high correlation between a common factor and therapy outcome still leaves us with questions about causality. Such findings are of considerable value, but they are insufficient if one wishes to trace the *hows* and *whys* of treatment effectiveness. Arkowitz writes (1997): "What common factors shall we examine? We can search for commonalities in therapist characteristics, patient characteristics and processes, setting characteristics, change processes, relationship processes, clinical techniques, and theories of change" (p. 247).

Another issue raised by Arkowitz concerns the unidimensional and linear view of causality as conceived in most common factors proposals. Most theorists of this persuasion do not recognize that these factors not only relate to one another as well as to different forms of psychopathology, but they also interact with a variety of contextual variables over the course of therapy.

In sum, the common factors approach is useful as a gauge by which to estimate the incremental efficacy achieved by theoretically integrative efforts. Because of their distilled quality, the common factors become a kind of lowest common denominator of psychotherapies. As such, they constitute the bare minimum of what good therapy should embody, but not the maximum of what it might achieve. If a common factors therapy could be manualized, a useful point of reference would be created for outcome studies. Ideally, the waiting-list control group would show some or no improvement, the common-factors therapy group would show significant gains, and the more integrative-therapy group would show the greatest gains. Nevertheless, the fact is that technique seems to account for only a small portion of variance in outcome, about 15% of the improvement. Lambert (1992) argues that, beyond merely distilling therapy, common factors have not yet made much of a contribution to its planning or its actual conduct.

There are compelling reasons why a synthesis of technique and theory might make a contribution to the success of therapy. Most clinicians are quite capable of grasping abstract principles of the various theoretical orientations. Most clinicians are also intuitively sensitive to what their patients need at the moment. However, especially where the theory is rich, clinicians may not be good at integrating these two levels, such that their interventions are explicitly guided by and consonant with their avowed theoretical persuasion. All interpersonal interactions are highly contextualized, with communications taking place at many different levels. Psychotherapy is even more complex. Truly integrative synthesis, where the therapist has one mind on the patient's behaviors and communications, one mind on the diverse elements of theory, and one mind on how his or her own ideas are being received by the patient, may require an almost "instinctive" knowledge of human relations that the mind may not access very easily.

Theoretical Syntheses

Integration is an important concept in the psychotherapy of the individual case, but it is also important when considering the role of therapy in clinical science. For the treatment of a particular patient to be integrated, each element of a clinical science should be integrated as well. One of the arguments advanced against eclecticism is that it explicitly insulates therapy from its base in clinical science. In contrast to eclecticism, where techniques are justified empirically, integrative syntheses take place by coordinating several theories of human nature. All of these combinations, the so-called grand theories, are seductive because they attempt to explain the totality of human behavior; from this perspective, psychotherapy appears to grow naturally out of the theory. In empirical eclecticism, however, theory is actively dissociated from technique. In the common factors approach, theory is ostensibly "eliminated" by aggregating across various psychotherapies. Though we may have our doubts about whether the various grand theories in fact fulfill their promise, they nevertheless stand as an ideal, one that integrates two or more theoretical orientations.

If therapy and theory are to be part of a single integrated clinical science, then diagnoses should in fact prescribe certain forms of intervention, based on theory. In an atheoretical empirical classification, such as the *DSM-IV*, where diagnostic syndromes are inductive summaries of observations rather than validated latent taxa, the linkage between theory and therapy will probably be weak. Taxons formed on the basis of overt similarities alone, that is, by inductive methods, risk classifying together individuals who look alike but whose pathologies are actually radically different in terms of the diverse forms in which pathological processes take form. In turn, these latent heterogeneities frustrate outcome research, if only because the statistics that evaluate efficacy aggregate over individuals who do not form a homogeneous group, thus muddying up the design and affecting the magnitude of the statistical error term in unpredictable ways. It is impossible to know with certainty the extent to which the manifest taxa of *DSM-IV* in fact classify ostensibly similar but pathologically different groups of individuals together. No outcome study classifying psychotically depressed individuals and schizophrenics as a single group would be acceptable today. Exclusionary criteria are used to make a distinction that might not otherwise be made given the salience of psychotic thinking. How often we fail to make distinctions that future *DSM*s will someday observe can only be known in time. We can say, however, that manifest taxa as inductive summaries draw diagnostic boundaries with imprecision, and also lump together distinct pathological processes that should in fact be separated.

What exactly do we mean when we say that therapy must be integrated and must be grounded in a logical and coordinated theory (Arkowitz, 1992; Millon, 1988)? Unfortunately, much of what travels under the eclectic or integrative banner sounds like the talk of a "goody-goody": a desire to be nice to all sides, and to say that everybody is right. These labels have become platitudinous buzzwords, philosophies with which open-minded people certainly would wish to ally themselves. But *integrative theory and psychotherapy* must signify more than that (Beutler & Clarkin, 1990; Norcross & Goldfried, 1992; Stricker & Gold, 1993).

First, it is not eclecticism. Perhaps it might be considered posteclecticism, if we may borrow a notion used to characterize modern art just a century ago. Eclecticism is not a matter of choice. We all must be eclectics, engaging in differential (Frances et al., 1984) and multimodal (Lazarus, 1981) therapeutics, selecting the techniques that are empirically the most efficacious for the problems at hand (Beutler & Clarkin, 1990).

Integration should be more than the coexistence of two or three previously discordant orientations or techniques. We cannot simply piece together the odds and ends of several theoretical schemata, each internally consistent and oriented to different data domains. Such a hodgepodge will lead only to illusory syntheses that cannot long hold together (Messer, 1986, 1992). Efforts such as these, meritorious as they may be in some regards, represent the work of peacemakers, not innovators and not integrationists. Integration is eclectic, of course, but more.

It is our belief that integration should be a synthesized and substantive system that coordinates treatment so it will *mirror* the problematic configuration of traits (personality) and symptoms (clinical syndromes) of a *specific patient at hand.* In the next section, we discuss integration from this view. For the present, we focus on *theoretical synthesizers,* those who seek to coalesce differing theoretical orientations and treatment modalities with interconnecting bridges. By contrasting those of the *personality-guided* persuasion, to be discussed next, we bypass the *synthesis of theory;* rather, primary attention is given to the *natural synthesis or integration that inheres within the patient* himself or herself. More will be said about this most recent group of integrationists in the section that follows the three theoretical integrationists discussed in the following paragraphs.

Klerman/Beitman's pharmacology-psychotherapy synthesis.   Early ideas concerning the synthesis of pharmacotherapy and psychotherapy exhibited an intense rivalry and competition, if not hostility. Such combinations no longer appear an issue today. The antagonistic atmosphere is now largely one of historic interest only. As Gerald Klerman (1991), an innovator in the synthesis of these two modalities, has noted, many theorists believe that psychotherapy alone could provide "a true cure," whereas medication was seen as a palliative at best, or an inhibitor of treatment motivation at worst.

Psychiatrists now routinely employ treatments that are both pharmacologic and psychotherapeutic, but are still unprepared to deal with the diverse effects of both techniques, possessing no clear guideline for their combined implementation. As Beitman has written (1992):

> In part, this stems from the fact that designing research to study the relevant variables and combined regimens . . . is such a daunting task. The list of factors to be taken into account is lengthy and would include diagnosis, severity, chronicity, treatment setting, goals, stage, and type of psychotherapy. Furthermore, research would need to control such issues as the different "active ingredients" for each modality, different mechanisms of delivery, time, course of response, outcome criteria, therapist attitude, and patient expectation. (p. 535)

Since the introduction of pharmacologic agents some four decades ago, their use has increased substantially; perhaps it is too frequently prescribed in this psychological age. Despite this proliferation, medications are utilized by professionals in an increasingly sophisticated and problem-specific way. In parallel, the modalities and techniques of psychotherapy have not only broadened, but now are highly selective when applied to different syndromes and disorders. It is the additive, if not synergistic, advantages of combining these treatment modalities that will need to be developed and more finely tuned to specific diagnostic groups.

Insofar as particular disorders are concerned, there appears to be good reason to think that severely depressed persons respond better to the synthesis of pharmacology and psychotherapy than to pharmacology alone. Moreover, it has been suggested that combining these two modalities may reduce symptoms more quickly than either treatment alone. As a synthesized unit, the pharmacology-psychotherapy approach suggests that medications are especially helpful in dealing with somatic symptoms, whereas psychotherapy helps to strengthen cognitive outlook and social adjustment. Experience has shown us that medication is often a necessary element in the treatment of schizophrenia. On the other hand, such patients may acquire a variety of social skills in psychotherapy that may reduce the likelihood of repetitive relapses; this may be achieved by identifying behaviors and assumptions that perpetuate their difficulties, and by helping implement stress-control strategies to anticipate and prevent troublesome events.

Klerman (1986) has outlined a variety of factors that may result from efforts to synthesize these two broad modalities. First, he notes that there may be *no effect* of a therapy synthesis; that is, the effects of combined treatment provide no greater benefit than one or another of these treatments, both of which are themselves better than the outcome for a control group. Second, Klerman refers to the *additive effects* that may derive from modality syntheses. Here, the sum of the techniques employed is equal to its parts; that is, it produces a magnitude of effect greater than each of the two individual treatments. The third positive effect would be what Klerman and Millon have termed *synergistic*. Here, the effect of modality combinations proves to be greater than the sum of both components. As Klerman describes it: "This can also be called a cocktail or martini effect. The assumption in a cocktail is that the combination of gin plus vermouth will produce greater psychopharmacologic 'punch' than if an equal amount of gin and vermouth were taken separately" (1986, p. 795).

Another intriguing result of psychotherapeutic-pharmacologic combinations is called *facilitation* by Klerman. Here, we find that one of the treatments is effective *only* when it is combined with the other. For example, individual psychotherapy is often ineffective with hospitalized schizophrenics, but becomes a significant contributor to long-term efficacy when it is synthesized with pharmacotherapy.

Klerman notes a number of interactions between pharmacology and psychotherapy that prove useful for therapeutic efficacy. Among these is the fact that many drugs will facilitate psychotherapeutic accessibility. For example, medications may help patients uncover memories and bring into consciousness experiences against which the patient would otherwise resist acknowledging.

Turning matters around, in what ways may psychotherapy produce positive effects on pharmacologic therapy? First, such techniques as reassurance and support should enhance compliance on the part of the patient. Second, and we need not pose questions here about what is fundamental and what is secondary, psychotherapy may help resolve difficulties that transcend biological mechanisms, such as interpersonal relationships, self-esteem, and cognitive orientation.

A word or two should be offered about the potential negative effects of the synthesis of drugs and psychotherapy. First, there is the possible emergence of a degree of passivity and general compliance that may deter the development of a more proactive stance in dealing with life's difficulties. Second, as a result of pharmacologic treatment, the patient's symptoms might be reduced and hence diminish the patient's motivation for continued treatment. Some psychiatrists believe that psychotherapy may be deleterious to drug treatment, given that psychological procedures may aggravate symptoms by excessive probing and exposing of psychological defenses.

Wachtel's analytic-behavioral-family synthesis. As noted earlier, a major contribution to the history of theoretical synthesis took place in 1950 with the publication of John Dollard and Neal Miller's *Personality and Psychotherapy.* Although this book went beyond an attempt to translate psychoanalytic concepts into behavioral language, it was a truly heroic effort to synthesize notions about neurosis and psychotherapy and to provide a theory unifying both subject domains. One of Dollard and Miller's outstanding students, Paul Wachtel, carried the thinking of his mentors forward in his book *Psychoanalysis and Behavior Therapy: Toward an Integration* (1977). Hardly naïve about the difficulty of building a theoretical synthesis between the concepts of psychoanalysis and learning theory, Wachtel asserted that integrationists would need to acknowledge the diversity within each approach, as well as the need to be specific about which elements can be integrated in fact. Wachtel (1984) identified the virtues of both theoretical schools in a framework that could incorporate these elements in an internally consistent way. It was his desire to draw on the complementary strengths of both perspectives, hoping thereby to outline a new theory for understanding psychopathology and a sound clinical strategy to effect change.

The central thesis underlying all aspects of pathologic processes—behavioral, psychoanalytic, family—was termed *cyclical psychodynamics.* Wachtel sought to expand the realm of his synthesis to include family systems theories in the mid-1980s (P. Wachtel & E. Wachtel, 1986). He has stated unequivocally that cyclical psychodynamics is the theoretical basis for an integrative therapy. As he has written recently (P. Wachtel 1992):

In contrast to a technically eclectic approach, which might consist of a hodgepodge of techniques selected probabilistically because they have seemed to work with patients with similar characteristics, cyclical psychodynamics seeks to develop a coherent theoretical structure that can guide both clinical decision making and general principles. . . .

Cyclical psychodynamics attempts to forge a new, more inclusive synthesis—a synthesis that can encompass the full range of observations addressed by its contributory sources and also provide a context for as wide a range of clinical interventions as can be coherently employed. (pp. 335–336)

The inclusion of the family systems tradition has expanded the applicability of cyclical psychodynamic theory. Similarly, the inclusion of a family approach provides insights into how and when pathologic behavior is evoked, as well as furnishing a social context within which the patient functions.

As noted earlier, Wachtel does not deny that differences exist among alternative perspectives. However, he rejects the view that fundamental incompatibilities exist; theoretical differences are present, but selecting facets from among them is conceptually possible and therapeutically useful.

Cyclical psychodynamics is not a new concept, although the term is distinctively Wachtel's. Horney (1945) spoke of *the tendency to foster vicious circles,* and Millon (1969) spoke of *self-perpetuation processes* in the persistence and intensification of early learned behaviors, behaviors that set into motion negative feedback to self and from others. It is these cyclical processes, vicious circle tendencies, and self-perpetuation cognitions and behaviors that play a key role in the etiologic or causal process. More will be said about these important features of human functioning in later chapters.

It was P. Wachtel's original intent to simply *combine* methods derived from different theoretical perspectives. His cyclical model, however, has provided him with a genuine model of synthesis. He writes (1992): "In much of the work presently approached from a cyclical psychodynamic viewpoint, it is hard to say which is the psychodynamics part and which is the behavioral. The work, one might say, is becoming more seamless" (p. 347).

Safran's cognitive-interpersonal-emotional synthesis.   Drawing on Wachtel's efforts at synthesis and the ascendancy of cognitive therapies some decade or two earlier, Jeremy Safran (1984) authored a series of papers and books to show how cognition, emotion, and interpersonal behavior may be brought together into a more inclusive synthesis than heretofore. In one of his books (Safran & Segal, 1990), he sought to show how cognitive techniques could readily blend with those of an interpersonal character. Similarly, he worked together with associates (L. Greenberg & Safran, 1987) to explore the role of emotion (or affect) in psychotherapy. Illustrating his early attachment to the cognitive perspective, yet his receptivity to a broadened perspective, Safran (1984) asserted that integration can provide:

a systematic framework which will allow cognitive-behavior therapists to broaden their conceptualization of the role of emotions in psychotherapy from one which views emotions only as undesirable experiences which should be controlled to one which recognizes the adaptive role of emotions in human functioning. (p. 335)

Although Safran clearly favors psychotherapeutic synthesis, he is resistant to the creation of new treatment schools, whether integrative or not. Rather, it was his intent to initiate a process of conceptual and technical expansion in cognitive therapy that would be informed by other therapeutic perspectives. Thus, a fundamental postulate of his approach, though anchored firmly in a cognitive model, is that the individual must be understood as part of an interpersonal system. Further, and in contrast to the classical analytic model, Safran asserts that therapeutic change requires more than conceptual understandings or rational analysis. Taking a distinct phenomenological stance, Safran recognizes that people view both themselves and others through concepts, and treat these concepts as real. By reifying experience this way, however, people blind themselves to the ever-changing nature of objective reality. Patients who hold fast to their dysfunctional conceptions of reality provide us with a basis for understanding their psychological disorder.

Illustrating his integrative conception, Safran goes beyond the purely cognitive task of correcting erroneous beliefs. He takes a more "constructivist" position in which the patient is recognized as the person who should actively reconstruct reality. As Safran and Segal write (1990):

> More important than purely philosophical reasons for abandoning the perspective that therapy involves the correction of cognitive distortions are the therapeutic implications of such a position. . . . When a patient lives in a dysfunctional interpersonal situation, the assumption that depression results from cognitive distortions can have potentially pernicious effects. . . . a perspective that views psychological problems as resulting from cognitive distortions encounters the unanswerable question of who ultimately will decide what constitutes a distortion. . . . Perhaps the clearest position comes from the experiential tradition, which has always emphasized that only the patient can be the expert on his or her reality. (p. 9)

To Safran, a broadened theoretical synthesis must be able to clarify not only cognitive processes, but also the ways in which affective, cognitive, and behavioral features develop and interact in an interpersonal context. There is a clear advantage to the provision of multiple perspectives regarding the same phenomenon. As illustrated in physics, the ostensive properties of light can be perceived as either a particle or a wave. So too in psychotherapy, different lenses may enable us to see the same clinical phenomenon as a multiply structured object, sometimes seen cognitively, at other times and for other purposes as interpersonal, even from a third or fourth perspective as emotional or intrapsychic.

A major task for the therapist is to avoid perpetuating a patient's *cognitive-interpersonal-affective cycles* and to seek to *disconfirm* these interactions in the treatment setting. Among other steps taken is *unhooking,* where the therapist turns inward as a means of detecting subtle feelings and thoughts in response to the patient's attitudes and behaviors. In what he termed *decentering,* Safran encourages patients to recognize their own role in constructing their experiences. Phrased differently, therapists seek to assist patients in understanding how their expectations, tacit feelings, and interpersonal conduct create and activate their immediate experiences in the treatment setting.

Comment. As Arkowitz (1997) has noted, efforts at theoretical synthesis are not particularly integrative in that most theorists do not draw on component approaches equally. Most are oriented to one particular theory or modality, and then seek to assimilate other strategies and notions to that core approach. Moreover, assimilated theories and techniques are invariably changed by the core model into which they have been imported. In other words, the assimilated orientation or methodology is frequently transformed from its original intent. As Messer (1992) wrote: "when incorporating elements of other therapies into one's own, a procedure takes its meaning not only from its point of origin, but even more so from the structure of the therapy into which it is imported" (p. 151). The example that Messer utilizes to illustrate this point is one in which a two-chair Gestalt procedure is brought into a primary social-learning model; in this assimilation, the two-chair procedure will likely be utilized differently and achieve different goals than would occur in the hands of a Gestalt therapist using the same technique.

Furthermore, by seeking to impose an integrative synthesis, therapists may lose the context and thematic logic that each of the standard modality approaches has built up over its history. In essence, this broad context of intrinsically coherent theories and facts is disassembled by the effort to interweave their many bits and pieces. An integrative model composed of such distinct alternative models (behavioral, psychoanalytic) is pedagogically pluralistic, a collection of separate modalities with varying conceptual networks and a number of unconnected studies and findings. As such, integrative syntheses do not discover what is inherent in nature, but merely invent a schema for interweaving what is, in fact, essentially discrete.

As will be discussed in the following section, particularly in the views of Millon, it is argued that intrinsic unity cannot be invented, but can be discovered in nature by focusing on the intrinsic unity of the person, that is, the full scope of a patient's psychic being. It will be asserted that *integration based on the natural order and unity of the person* avoids the rather arbitrary efforts at synthesizing disparate and sometimes disjunctive theoretical schemata.

Efforts at synthesizing therapeutic models have been most successful in *desegregating* the field rather than truly integrating it. As phrased by Arkowitz (1997):

> Integrative perspectives have been catalytic in the search for new ways of thinking about and doing psychotherapy that go beyond the confines of single-school approaches. Practitioners and researchers are examining what other theories and therapies have to offer. . . .
>
> Several promising starts have been made in clinical proposals for integrative therapies, but it is clear that much more work needs to be done. (pp. 256–257)

As noted, it is the belief of the author that integration cannot stem from an intellectual synthesis of different theories, but from the inherent integration that is discovered in each patient's personal style of functioning, a topic to which we turn next.

Person-Oriented Integration

Unlike eclecticism, integration insists on the primacy of an overarching gestalt that gives coherence, provides an interactive framework, and creates an organic order among otherwise discrete units or elements. Whereas the theoretical syntheses previously discussed attempt to provide an intellectual bridge across several theories or modalities, personality-guided integrationists assert that a *natural synthesis already exists within the patient.* As we better understand the configuration of traits that characterize each patient's psyche, we can better devise a treatment plan that will mirror these traits, which we believe will provide an optimal therapeutic course and outcome.

As noted previously, each *person* is a synthesized and substantive system whose distinctive meaning derives from that old chestnut, The whole is greater than the sum of its parts. The problems of persons are an inextricably linked nexus of behaviors, cognitions, intrapsychic processes, and so on. They flow through a tangle of feedback loops and serially unfolding concatenations that emerge at different times in dynamic and changing configurations. Behavioral acts, self-image cognitions, defense mechanisms, indeed, each functional and structural domain (see Chapter 4) are contextualized by and interdigitated with all others as they take on the form of a single, cohesive organism. No one domain should be segregated out and made to stand on its own. Moreover, each component of these trait configurations has its role and significance altered by virtue of its place in these continually evolving constellations. In parallel form, so should person-centered psychotherapy be conceived as a configuration of strategies and tactics in which each modality is selected not only for its efficacy in resolving particular pathological features, but also for its contribution to the overall constellation of treatment procedures of which it is but one.

In our view, current debates regarding whether technical eclecticism (Lazarus, 1981) or integrative therapy (Arkowitz, 1992) is the more suitable designation for our approach are both mistaken. *They have things backward,* so to speak, because they start the task of intervention by focusing on methodology or theory first. Integration inheres in neither treatment techniques nor in theories, eclectic or otherwise (Messer, 1986, 1992). *Natural integration exists in the person, not in theories or methodologies.* It stems from the interwoven character of the patient's traits and symptoms. Our task as therapists is not to see how we can blend discordant models of therapy, but to match the integrative pattern that is intrinsic in each patient, and *then* to select treatment goals and tactics that mirror this pattern optimally. It is for this reason, among others, that we have chosen to employ the label *personality-guided therapy* to represent this model and approach to integrative treatment.

Many investigators have begun to combine two or three theories or modalities to see how well they may improve on the effectiveness of a single approach. But combinations of techniques are in themselves meaningless, in our judgment, because they are not designed to deal with the specific dysfunctions of a specific patient. Combining cognitive and interpersonal modalities, for example, will simply muddy the water, so to speak, owing to the variety of traits and symptoms that inhere within each patient's pathology. This combination *can* be appropriate and useful if, and only if, the patients treated in this combinational fashion possess primary dysfunctions or deficiencies in both the cognitive and interpersonal realms. In our view, it is not just the notion of modality combinations nor any theoretical synthesis that will work. We contend that combinations will be effective if they are applied to the domain of dysfunctions of a specific patient. Thus, in the psychopharmacologic area, a combination of certain medications (e.g., as when treating AIDS) can prove quite effective; however, other combinations, such as when two or three drugs are taken off the bathroom shelf, so to speak, can result in dangerous consequences.

As noted previously, integration is an important concept in considering not only the psychotherapy of the individual case but also the place of psychotherapy in clinical science. For the treatment of a particular patient to be integrated, the elements of clinical science—theory, taxonomy, assessment, and therapy—should be integrated as well (Millon & Davis, 1996a). One of the arguments advanced earlier against empirically based eclecticism is that it further insulates psychotherapy from a broad-based clinical science. In contrast to eclecticism, where techniques are justified empirically, *personality-guided integration* takes its shape and character from a coordinated theory of human nature. Such "grand" theories are inviting because they attempt to explain the natural variations of human behavior; moreover, psychotherapy grows naturally out of theory. Theory does not actively disengage from technique; rather, it informs and guides it.

Murray (1983) has suggested that the field must develop a new, higher-order theory to help us better understand the interconnections among cognitive, affective, self, and interpersonal psychic systems. This is the belief of personality-guided theorists who claim that interlinked configurations of pathology can serve as the foundation of contemporary psychotherapy. We look at three models of therapy that focus primarily on the full personality pattern of the patient, viewing the person as the cornerstone for developing integrated treatment techniques.

Linehan's cognitive-behavioral dialectic.   What makes the approach of Linehan (1987, 1992, 1993) so significant is the exhaustive and systematic nature of her analysis and treatment of one specific personality disorder, the so-called borderline patient. One need not agree with all aspects of her developmental conception of the origins of the borderline, nor with each specific of her treatment technique, to appreciate the care and thoroughness with which she has examined and treated this particular personality. If each personality disorder and clinical syndrome were approached therapeutically in the manner in which Linehan approaches the borderline, we believe that treatment for all disorders and syndromes would be greatly improved.

It is Linehan's view that, at a minimum, the concept of a personality disorder requires one to assume that individual styles of functioning (including patterns of action, cognitive processes, and physiological-emotional responses) are reasonably consistent over time and circumstance. More specifically, Linehan speaks of the crucial developmental circumstances that underlie the borderline personality disorder (BPD):

> The main tenet of the biosocial theory is that the core disorder in BPD is emotion dysregulation. . . . The theory asserts that borderline individuals have difficulties in regulating several, if not all, emotions. This systemic dysregulation is produced by emotional vulnerability and by maladaptive or inadequate modulation strategies. (1993, p. 2)

Linehan defines emotional vulnerability by referring to several characteristics. A very high sensitivity to emotional stimuli, a very intense response to stimulating emotions, and a slow return to an emotional baseline once emotional arousal has occurred. In her theoretical schema, the primary source of emotional dysregulation is what she terms an *invalidating environment*. Such environments are especially destructive for young children who begin life with a high vulnerability to emotional stimuli. As she conceives it, the defining characteristic of these invalidating environments is the tendency to respond erratically and inappropriately to one's own personal experience (e.g., thoughts, feeling, sensations).

Linehan's therapeutic methodology is highly imaginative and comprehensive. In terms of goals, the first task of therapy is to orient the patient and gain his or her commitment to the treatment course. Several pretreatment sessions utilize diagnostic interviewing, formal history taking, and an analysis of targeted behaviors to serve as a focus for initial sessions. The first regular treatment stage is oriented toward having the patient attain lifestyle behaviors and capacities that are both functional and stable. Specific targets include reducing therapy-interfering behaviors, diminishing quality-of-life-interfering behaviors, and increasing various behavioral skills. During the second stage, Linehan takes a here-and-now approach. Her theoretical model asserts that previous traumatic events, especially those invalidating environments that generated emotional dysregulation, must be explored and resolved. The third stage targets the patient's self-respect; it is oriented to helping the patient to value, believe in, and validate himself or herself: "The targets here are the abilities to evaluate one's own behavior nondefensively, trust one's own responses, and hold on to self evaluations independent of the opinions of others" (1993, p. 406).

The breadth of Linehan's approach to treatment may be seen in the following:

> Strategies emphasizing acceptance are very similar to . . . strategies used in client-centered therapy and to case management outreach strategies emphasized in community psychiatry. Those emphasizing change are drawn primarily from cognitive and behavioral therapies, although the particular rendition in dialect behavior therapy overlaps considerably with both strategic and psychodynamic therapies. (1993, p. 412)

Formalizing specific treatment strategies, Linehan makes explicit a variety of methods which she combines to deal with specific personality difficulties. Among these is the use of a dialectic framework that stresses the contrast between illusory and nonrational realities and the acceptance of reality as it is. The goal here is to foster increasing reconciliations by using metaphors, paradoxes, and ambiguities and by constantly challenging and restructuring nonrational cognitions and behaviors. Especially important is what Linehan calls the validation strategy. Three steps are involved in the acceptance of one's own life beliefs: first, the patient is helped to identify relevant response patterns; second, the therapist expresses accurate empathy, showing a clear recognition of the patient's perception of his or her experiences; third and most important, the therapist communicates that these perceptions make perfect sense in the context of the person's current situation and early life experiences.

Frances/Clarkin's differential therapeutics.   John Clarkin, Allen Frances, and Samuel Perry (1992) begin their exploration of differential therapeutics by noting that present knowledge concerning their proposals is both woefully incomplete empirically as well as highly controversial theoretically. They note that most treatment assignments tend to be made routinely, based largely on customary practices and with little clinical staff discussion. They wonder why the therapeutic field has resisted the notion of selectivity among alternative treatment approaches. Analyzing the different facets of a pathological state so as to maximize the effectiveness of alternative treatments appears to them to be not only a worthy but a necessary way of thinking. As they see it, the limitations of current research evidence furnishes a good reason for openly discussing treatment selection, rather than a reason to avoid it.

In proposing *differential therapeutics,* their hope was to encourage debate and emphasize areas of ignorance concerning the complexity of typical clinical situations. Although those of a common factors persuasion contend that a good therapeutic alliance is what makes for treatment success, there is good reason to argue that different theoretical modalities can have special added applicability. As with Millon (1990), the task is to correlate the ingredients of pathology with matching therapeutic techniques employed to resolve them.

In line with the personality-guided philosophy shared with Linehan and Millon, Frances et al. write (1984):

treatment cannot be directed simply at the disorder; it must be tailored for the person and circumstances and also for the multiply interacting factors that influence how the patient is reacting to pathological processes and stressors. . . .

The limitations of psychiatric diagnosis in predicting treatment are also a function of the relative lack of available knowledge. . . . the psychiatric syndromes of *DSM-III* are for the most part no more than collections of isolated symptoms.

It must be realized, however, that although *DSM-III* has achieved remarkably increased reliability, it cannot include many variables that are crucial in deciding about the choice of treatment. It is more efficient to consider the differential advantages of the various treatments than to attempt definitive treatment plans for each psychiatric diagnosis. (p. xxiii)

In what they call *macro-treatment* planning, Frances et al. believe that the context, philosophy, and modality of treatment should be taken into account when deciding a specific approach to therapy. Thus, the setting and format of treatment addresses the environment in terms of place (hospital, office) and persons (patient, group, family) who will be present. No less significant at this level is what they term strategies and techniques, such as the technical interventions that the therapist introduces to effect change (e.g., common elements, specific techniques: cognitive, environmental, pharmacologic).

In speaking of the *micro-levels* of treatment planning, Frances et al. (1984) refer to a key element in person-centered models of integration, that is, that two people with equal levels of depressive symptomatology may be best treated by different interventions owing to the complexity and the configuration of their overall personality makeup. Thus, a histrionic may be best approached by utilizing affective modulators and cognitive techniques, whereas an avoidant person may be best approached with pharmaceutical anxiolytics and interpersonal skill training.

Although differential treatment gives special weight to the specific problem areas of the patient, most theorists and therapists pay little attention to the particular domains comprising different diagnostic categories. Frances et al. argue vigorously for considering the *configuration of personality traits* that characterize each specific patient. They recognize that current diagnostic information, such as listed in *DSM-IV,* provides only a surface coverage of the complex elements that are associated with a patient's inner and outer worlds.

Millon's personality-guided synergism.   As noted previously, whether we work with "part functions" that focus on behaviors, or cognitions or unconscious processes or biological defects, and the like, or whether we address contextual systems that focus on the larger environment, the family, the group, or the socioeconomic and political conditions of life, the crossover point, the place that links parts to contexts, is the person. The individual is the intersecting medium that brings them together.

Persons, however, are more than crossover mediums. They are the only organically integrated system in the psychological domain, inherently created from birth as natural entities rather than experience-derived gestalts constructed via cognitive attribution. Moreover, it is persons who lie at the heart of the psychotherapeutic experience, the substantive beings that give meaning and coherence to symptoms and traits—whether behaviors, affects, or mechanisms—as well as those beings, those singular entities, that give life and expression to family interactions and social processes.

The cohesion (or lack thereof) of intrinsically interwoven psychic structures and functions is what distinguishes most complex disorders of psychopathology; likewise, the orchestration of diverse yet synthesized modalities of intervention is what differentiates *synergistic* from other variants of psychotherapy. These two parallel constructs, emerging from different traditions and conceived in different venues, reflect shared philosophical perspectives, one oriented toward the understanding of mental disorders, the other toward effecting their remediation.

It is not that one-modality or school-oriented psychotherapies are inapplicable to more focal or simple syndrome pathologies, but rather that synergistically planned therapies are required for the intricate relationships that interconnect personality and clinical syndromes (whereas depression may successfully be treated either cognitively or pharmacologically); it is the very interwoven nature of the components that constitute such complex disorders that makes a multifaceted and synthesized approach a necessity.

It is our contention that integrative therapists should take cognizance of the person from the start, for the parts and the contexts take on different meanings and call for different interventions in terms of the person to whom they are anchored. To focus on one social structure or one psychic form of expression without understanding its undergirding or reference base is, as we see it, to engage in potentially misguided, if not random, therapeutic techniques.

Psychotherapy seems preoccupied with horizontal refinements. However, a search for a natural integrative schema should be based on intrinsically cohesive constructs that interweave each patient's closely related traits of structure and function. The goal—albeit a rather grandiose one—is to refashion the patchwork quilt of separate modalities into a well-tailored tapestry of uniquely integrated persons, hence permitting the development of combined techniques that mirror the diverse forms in which lives express themselves.

As stated earlier, what better sphere is there within the psychological sciences to undertake such syntheses than with the subject matter of personology and psychopathology. Persons are the only integrated system in the psychological domain, evolved through the millennia as natural entities. The intrinsic cohesion of persons is not merely a rhetorical construction, but an authentic substantive unity. Although personologic features may often be dissonant, and may be partitioned conceptually for pragmatic or scientific purposes, they are nonetheless segments of an inseparable biopsychosocial entity.

A useful metaphor derived from the philosophies of Leibniz and Whitehead, termed *holography,* may be useful as a means of explaining the widely distributed impact of life experiences. As Abroms (1993) has written:

> Holographically distributed patterns are those in which each part (e.g., . . . isolated body cell) contains information about what is stored in all other parts, thus permitting one to reconstruct . . . the entire genetic code of the organism from each of its pieces. Thus, a hologram is a representation of an object or an event in which every part contains sufficient information to characterize the whole. Each part represents the whole, and the whole implies each part. (p. 85)

In our judgment, the holographic metaphor applies with equal merit to the different conceptual realms of clinical functioning when seen idiographically in a specific patient. Each realm is a part of a single unified whole. That which may be primarily expressed cognitively, interpersonally, or intrapsychically are mere facets of the patient's total personal makeup. As therapists, we have separated these domains for scientific or clinical purposes. In "reality," what happens cognitively is also registered in the intrapsychic realm; what happens behaviorally also registers in the realm of self-image, and so on. As a result, every change that transpires in one or another trait domain will have an effect on every other. The task is to identify those traits that are most central for each patient, that is, that have a pernicious influence or pervasive impact on all other facets of the person's psychic hologram. Much of what personality-guided synergism seeks to accomplish is to identify the domains that are saliently problematic and to facilitate significant changes, both there and in all other covariant and troublesome domains.

Simply to make a platitudinous announcement that the person should serve as our integrative focus for guiding treatment, however, or that it is the natural parallel and setting for synergistic modes of therapy, is not enough. So too might it be merely sententious to speak of a personality-guided theory. In building a science of psychopathology, we must seek to discover the essential principles conducive to constructive changes and from which a corresponding synergistic therapy can be organized. For that purpose, we turn to Chapters 3 and 4.

CHAPTER THREE

Personality-Guided Synergism

In the following pages, we present a few ideas in sequence. First, that synergistic therapies require a foundation in a coordinated theory; that is, they must be more than a schema of eclectic techniques, a hodgepodge of diverse alternatives assembled de novo with each case. Second, although the diagnostic criteria that make up *DSM* syndromes are a decent first step, they must become comprehensive and comparable, that is, be systematically revised so as to be genuinely useful for treatment planning. Third, a logical rationale can be formulated as to how one can and should integrate diverse modality-focused therapies when treating complex psychopathologies.

A PHILOSOPHICAL PERSPECTIVE

Before turning to these themes, we would like to comment briefly on some philosophical issues. They bear on a rationale for developing theory-based treatment techniques, that is, methods that transcend the merely empirical (e.g., electroconvulsive therapy for depressives). It is our conviction that the theoretical foundations of our science must be further advanced if we are to succeed in constructing a personality-guided approach to psychotherapy.

Obviously, a tremendous amount of knowledge, both about the nature of the patient's disorders and about diverse modes of intervention, is required to perform personality-guided therapy. To maximize synergism among numerous modalities requires that the therapist be a little like a jazz soloist. Not only should the professional be fully versed in the various musical keys, that is, in techniques of psychotherapy that span all trait domains, he or she should also be prepared to respond to subtle fluctuations in the patient's thoughts, actions, and emotions, any of which could take the composition in a wide variety of directions, and integrate these with the overall plan of therapy as it evolves. After the instruments have been packed away and the band goes home, a retrospective account on the entire process should reveal a level of thematic continuity and logical order commensurate with what would have existed had all relevant constraints been known in advance.

The integrative processes of personality-guided therapy are dictated by the nature of personality itself. The actual content of synergistic therapy, however, must be specified on some other basis. Psychopathology, and in particular, personality, is by definition the patterning of intraindividual variables, but the nature of these variables does not follow from the definition, but must be supplied by some principle or on some basis that is "outside" the construct. In Millon's model, for example, the content of personality and psychopathology is derived from evolutionary theory, a discipline that informs but exists apart from our clinical subject. In and of itself, pathologic personality is a structural-functional concept that refers to the intraorganismic patterning of variables; it does not in itself say what these variables are, nor can it.

As stated previously (Millon & Davis, 1996a), we believe that four features signify and characterize mature clinical sciences: (a) They embody *conceptual theories* from which propositional deductions can be derived; (b) these theories should lead to the development of *coherent taxonomies* that characterize the central features of their subject domain (in our case, that of personality and psychopathology, the substantive realm within which scientific and psychotherapeutic techniques are applied); (c) these sciences possess a variety of *empirically oriented instruments* with which they can identify and quantify the concepts that make up their theories (in psychopathology, methods that uncover developmental history and furnish cross-sectional assessments); (d) in addition to theory, nosology, and diagnostic tools, mature clinically oriented sciences possess *change-oriented intervention* techniques that are therapeutically optimal in modifying the pathological elements of their domain.

Most current therapeutic schools share a common failure to coordinate these four components of an applied science. What differentiates them has more to do with the fact that they attend to different levels of data in the natural world. It is to the credit of those of an eclectic persuasion that they have recognized, albeit in a "fuzzy way," the arbitrary if not illogical character of such positions, as well as the need to bridge schisms that have been constructed less by philosophical considerations or pragmatic goals than by the accidents of history. There are numerous other knotty issues with which the nature of psychic pathology and personality-guided therapy must contend (e.g., differing "worldviews" concerning the essential nature of psychological experience). There is no problem, as we see it, in encouraging active dialectic among these contenders.

However, there are two important barriers that stand in the way of synergistic psychotherapy as a treatment philosophy. The first is the *DSM*. The idea of diagnostic prototypes was a genuine innovation when the *DSM-III* was published in 1980. The development of diagnostic work groups was intended to provide broad representation of various points of view, while preventing any single perspective from foreclosing on the others. Even some 20 years later, however, the *DSM* has yet to officially endorse an underlying set of principles that would interrelate and differentiate the Axis II constructs in terms of their deeper principles. Instead, progress proceeds mainly by way of committee consensus, cloaked by the illusion of empirical research.

The second barrier is the human habit system. The admonition that different therapeutic approaches should be pursued with different patients and different problems has become almost self-evident, but given no logical basis from which to design effective therapeutic sequences and composites, even the most self-consciously antidogmatic clinician must implicitly lean toward one orientation or another.

What specifically are the procedures that distinguish personality-guided synergistic therapy from other models of an eclectic nature?

The integrative model labeled a decade ago as *personologic psychotherapy* (Millon, 1988) insists on the primacy of an overarching gestalt that gives coherence, provides an interactive framework, and creates an organic order among otherwise discrete polarities and attributes. As noted in prior chapters, it is eclectic, but more. It is synthesized from a substantive theory whose overall utility and orientation derives from that old chestnut, the whole is greater than the sum of its parts. As stated previously, the problems our patients bring to us are often an inextricably linked nexus of interpersonal behaviors, cognitive styles, regulatory processes, and so on. They flow through a tangle of feedback loops and serially unfolding concatenations that emerge at different times in dynamic and changing configurations. Each component of these configurations has its role and significance altered by virtue of its place in these continually evolving constellations. In parallel form, so should personality-guided synergistic therapy be conceived as an integrated configuration of strategies and tactics in which each intervention technique is selected *not only* for its efficacy in resolving particular pathological attributes, but also for its contribution to the overall constellation of treatment procedures of which it is but one.

Although the admonition that we should *not* employ the same therapeutic approach with all patients is self-evident, it appears that therapeutic approaches accord more with where training occurred than with the nature of patients' pathologies. To paraphrase Millon (1969), there continues to be a disinclination among clinical practitioners to submit their cherished techniques to detailed study or to revise them in line with critical empirical findings. Despite the fact that most of our therapeutic research leaves much to be desired in the way of proper controls, sampling, and evaluative criteria, one overriding fact comes through repeatedly: Therapeutic techniques must be suited to the patient's problem. Simple and obvious though this statement is, it is repeatedly neglected by therapists who persist in utilizing and argue heatedly in favor of a particular approach to *all* variants of psychopathology. No school of therapy is exempt from this notorious attitude.

Why should we formulate a synergistic therapeutic approach to psychopathology? The answer may be best grasped if we think of the psychic elements of a person as analogous to the sections of an orchestra, and the trait domains of a patient as a clustering of discordant instruments that exhibit imbalances, deficiencies, or conflicts within these sections. To extend this analogy, therapists may be seen as conductors whose task is to bring forth a harmonious balance among all the sections as well as their specifically discordant instruments, muting some here, accentuating others there, all to the end of fulfilling the conductor's knowledge of how "the composition" can best be made consonant. The task is not that of altering one instrument, but of all in concert. What is sought in music, then, is a balanced score, one composed of harmonic counterpoints, rhythmic patterns, and melodic combinations. What is needed in therapy is a likewise balanced program, a coordinated strategy of counterpoised techniques designed to optimize sequential and combinatorial treatment effects.

If clinical syndromes were anchored exclusively to one particular trait domain (as phobias are thought of as being primarily behavioral in nature), modality-bound psychotherapy would always be appropriate and desirable. Psychopathology, however, is not exclusively behavioral or intrapsychic, confined to a particular clinical data level. Instead, they are multioperational and systemic. As noted in Chapter 1, no part of the system exists in complete isolation. Instead, every part is directly or indirectly tied to every other, such that a holographic synergism lends the whole an integrative tenacity that makes psychic pathology "real" and complex things to be reckoned with in any therapeutic endeavor. Therapies should mirror the configuration of as many trait and clinical domains as the syndromes and disorders they seek to remedy. If the scope of the therapy is insufficient relative to the scope of the pathology, the treatment system will have considerable difficulty fulfilling its adaptive goals. Both unstructured intrapsychic therapy and highly structured behavioral techniques, to note the extremes, share this deficiency.

Most psychotherapists have had the unsettling experience of developing a long-term treatment plan, only to have the patient make some startling revelation several sessions later, requiring a significant change of course. Although some therapists will always administer the same form of therapy regardless of the problem, a good theory should allow techniques across many modalities to be dynamically adapted or integrated as ongoing changes in the patient occur or as new information comes to light.

In contrast to this ideal, the state of the art in psychotherapy can be characterized as either linear but dogmatic, or eclectic but uncoordinated. Linear perspectives hail mainly from the historical schools that have dominated psychotherapy's classical past. Though major viewpoints include the psychodynamic, interpersonal, neurobiological, behavioral, and cognitive, more esoteric conceptions could also be included, including the existential, phenomenological, cultural, and perhaps even religious. Theorists within each perspective usually maintain that their content area is core or fundamental and thus serves as the logical basis for the treatment of its disorders. In the earlier, dogmatic era of therapeutic systems, psychologists strongly wedded to a particular perspective would either assert that other points of view were peripheral to their own pet contents, or just stubbornly ignore the existence of other schools of thought. Behaviorists, for example, denied the existence of the mental constructs, including self and personality. In contrast, psychodynamic psychologists held that behavior is only useful as a means of inferring the properties and organization of various mental structures, namely the id, ego, and superego, and their "drive derivatives." Theorists took this stance essentially for two reasons: First, history remembers only those that contribute significantly to the development of a particular point of view; hence, there are no famous eclectics. Second, the fact that other content areas operate according to their own autonomous principles could impugn the completeness of one's own approach. As a result, various perspectives within personality have tended to develop to high states of internal consistency, the dogmatic schools of psychotherapy, and it is not at all clear how one conceptual system might falsify another or how two systems might be put against one another experimentally. Instead, the proponents of one perspective usually seek to assimilate the variables of other domains to their own perspective, which is then put forward as the best candidate for a truly integrative model for personality and the treatment of its disorders.

In contrast to the modality- or school-oriented perspectives on personality, which appeal to organizing principles that derive from a single system of psychotherapy, we might ask whether there is any theory that honors the nature of psychopathology as the pattern of variables across the entire matrix of the person. Psychopathology is neither exclusively behavioral, exclusively cognitive, nor exclusively interpersonal, and so on, but is instead a genuine integration of each of its subsidiary domains. Far from overturning established paradigms, such a broad perspective simply allows a given phenomenon to be treated from several angles, so to speak. Even agnostic therapists, with no strong allegiance to any one point of view, may avail themselves of a kaleidoscope of modalities. By turning the kaleidoscope, by shifting paradigmatic sets, the same phenomenon can be viewed from any of a variety of internally consistent perspectives. Eclecticism becomes a first step toward synthesizing modalities that correspond to the *natural* configuration of each patient's traits and disorders.

The open-minded therapist is left, however, with several different modality combinations, each with some currency toward understanding the patient's pathology, but no real means of bringing these diverse conceptions together in a coherent model of what, exactly, to do. The therapist's plight is understandable, but not acceptable. For example, modality techniques considered fundamental in one perspective may not be so regarded within another. The interpersonal model of Lorna Benjamin and the neurobiological model of Robert Cloninger are both structurally strong approaches to understanding personality and psychopathology. Both have been subjected to confirmatory factor analysis. Yet their fundamental constructs are different. Rather than inherit the modality tactics of a particular perspective, then, a theory of psychotherapy as a total system should seek some set of principles that can be addressed to the patient's whole psyche, thereby capitalizing on the naturally organic system of the person. The alternative is an uncomfortable eclecticism of unassimilated partial views. Perhaps believing that nothing more is possible, most psychotherapists have accepted this state of affairs as an inevitable reality.

Fortunately, modality-bound psychotherapies are increasingly becoming part of the past. In growing numbers, clinicians are identifying themselves, not as psychodynamic or as behavioral, but as eclectic or integrative. As noted above, eclecticism is an insufficient guide to personality-guided therapy. As a movement, and not a construct, it cannot prescribe the particular form of those modalities that will remedy the pathologies of persons and their syndromes. Eclecticism is too open with regard to content and too imprecise to achieve focused goals. The intrinsically configurational nature of psychopathology, its multioperationism, and the interwoven character of clinical domains simply are not as integrated in eclecticism as they need be in treating psychopathology.

A THEORETICAL ORIENTATION

Before proceeding to a reasonably detailed outline of assessment and treatment techniques that will foster therapeutic synergism, we would like to make some comments in favor of the utility of a theory of the person. Kurt Lewin (1936) wrote some 60 years ago that "there is nothing so practical as a good theory." Theory, when properly fashioned, ultimately provides more simplicity and clarity than unintegrated and scattered information. Unrelated knowledge and techniques, especially those based on surface similarities, are a sign of a primitive science, as has been effectively argued by contemporary philosophers of science (Hempel, 1961; Quine, 1961).

We present a précis of the general theoretical model we have employed in analyzing personality and psychopathology (Millon, 1969; Millon & Davis, 1996a). In a way this is a digression, but it is one that we believe is only proper for our readers to reflect on, especially those who may wish to know more about the underlying evolutionary theory to which our diagnostic and treatment model adheres.

It is logically impossible for any single perspective on psychotherapy to develop constructs that embrace the *person* as a whole, that is, that has a scope and level of synthesis at which the psychopathologic phenomenon itself exists. Perspectives are necessarily analytic, whereas personality is inherently synthetic. An intrinsically synthetic treatment design is exactly what is required to transcend the hodgepodge of eclecticism. Only such a theory can allow for the construction of logically meaningful therapeutic composites and sequences.

Unfortunately, we do not as yet have an accepted, unifying theory for all human behavior. In the interim, however, we can generate fruitful microtheories that may encompass and give coherence to many of the facets that constitute our psychopathological subject domain. It is toward that end that an effort has been made to develop an integrative or unified microtheory of personality and psychopathology (Millon, 1969, 1981, 1986b, 1990, 1991, 1996; Millon & Davis, 1996a), pathologies that are themselves exemplary integrative constructs in the larger domain of mental disorders. (The reader is encouraged to read Millon and Davis for a review of the development and derivation of the disorders in a more comprehensive format.)

It is necessary to go beyond current conceptual boundaries, more specifically to explore carefully reasoned as well as "intuitive" hypotheses that draw their principles, if not their substance, from more established, adjacent sciences. Not only may such steps bear new conceptual fruits, but they may provide a foundation that can undergird and guide our own discipline's explorations. As discussed in prior chapters, much of psychopathology, no less psychology as a whole, remains adrift, divorced from broader spheres of scientific knowledge, isolated from firmly grounded if not universal principles, leading us to continue building the patchwork quilt of concepts and data domains that characterize the field. Preoccupied with but a small part of the larger puzzle, or fearing accusations of reductionism, many fail thereby to draw on the rich possibilities to be found in other realms of scholarly pursuit. With few exceptions, cohering concepts that would connect psychotherapy and psychopathology to those of its sibling sciences have not been developed.

The key lies in finding theoretical principles for psychotherapy that fall outside the field of psychology proper. Otherwise, we could only repeat the error of the past by asserting the importance of some new set of variables heretofore unemphasized, building yet another perspective inside the totality of the person but thereby missing a scientific understanding of the whole. As stated, we must go beyond current conceptual boundaries to explore hypotheses that draw their inspiration from more established, adjacent sciences.

An Evolutionary Perspective

We believe that the search for fundamental principles should begin with human evolution. Just as each person is composed of a total patterning of variables across all domains of human expression, it is the total organism that survives and reproduces, carrying forth both its adaptive and maladaptive potentials into subsequent generations. Although lethal mutations sometimes occur, the evolutionary success of organisms with "average expectable genetic material" is dependent on the entire configuration of the organism's characteristics and potentials. Similarly, psychological fitness derives from the relation of the entire configuration of personal characteristics to the environments in which the person functions. Beyond these analogies, the principles of evolution also serve as principles that lie outside personality proper, and thus form a foundation for the integration of the various historical schools that escapes the part-whole fallacy of a dogmatic past. The creation of a taxonomy of personality and psychotherapy based on evolutionary principles faces one central question: How can these processes best be segmented so that their relevance to the individual person is placed and highlighted in the foreground?

The evolutionary theory comprises three imperatives, each of which is a necessary aspect of the progression of evolution. First, each organism must survive. Second, it must adapt to its environment. Third, it must reproduce. To each of these imperatives is coupled a polarity that expresses the manifestation of that imperative in the life of the individual organism, thereby giving the theory content and putting metapsychology on a solid basis. To survive, an organism seeks to maximize pleasure *and* minimize pain, its *existential aims*. To adapt, an organism must either passively conform to the resources and constraints an environment offers, or actively reform the environment to meet its needs and make its opportunities, its *adaptation modes*. Finally, to reproduce, an organism must adopt a classically male and self-oriented strategy of producing many offspring with little further investment *or* a classically female and other-oriented strategy of producing a few or a single offspring and making a much greater investment of time and resources, its *replication strategies* (Millon, 1990). Anywhere in the universe, these are the fundamental evolutionary concerns, and there are none more fundamental.

Polarities, that is, *contrasting* functional directions representing these three phases (pleasure-pain, passive-active, other-self) have been used to construct a theoretically anchored classification system of personality styles and clinical disorders (Millon & Davis, 1996a). Such bipolar or dimensional schemes are almost universally present throughout the literatures of humanity as well as in psychology at large (Millon, 1990). The earliest may be traced to ancient Eastern religions, most notably the Chinese *I Ching* texts and the Hebrew *Kabala*.

In the life of the individual organism, each phase of evolution is recapitulated and expressed ontogenetically; that is, each individual organism moves through developmental stages that have functional goals related to their respective phases of evolution. Within each stage, every individual acquires character dispositions representing a balance or predilection toward one of the two polarity inclinations; which inclination emerges as dominant over time results from the inextricable and reciprocal interplay of intraorganismic and extraorganismic factors. For example, during early infancy, the primary organismic function is to continue to exist. Here, evolution has supplied mechanisms that orient the infant toward life-enhancing environments (pleasure) and away from life-threatening ones (pain).

The expression of traits or dispositions acquired in early stages of development may have their expression transformed as later faculties or dispositions develop (Millon, 1969). Temperament is perhaps a classic example. An individual with an active temperament may develop, contingent on contextual factors, into one of several personality styles, for example, an avoidant or an antisocial, the consequences being partly determined by whether the child has a fearful or a fearless temperament when dealt a harsh environment. The transformation of earlier temperamental characteristics takes the form of what we have called *personological bifurcations* (Millon, 1990). Thus, if the individual is inclined toward a *passive* orientation and later learns to be self-focused, a narcissistic style ensues. But if the individual possesses an *active* orientation and later learns to be self-focused, an antisocial style may ensue. Thus, early developing dispositions may undergo "vicissitudes," whereby their meaning in the context of the whole organism is subsequently re-formed into complex personality configurations.

The evolutionary model that has been presented, as well as its biosocial-learning forerunner (Millon, 1969, 1981, 1986b), has generated several new diagnostic categories, several of which have found their way into the *DSM-III* and *DSM-IV* (Kernberg, 1984). Drawing on the three key components of the polarity framework—pain-pleasure, active-passive, self-other— a series of 11 person prototypes and 3 severe variants were deduced, of which a few have proved to be original derivations in the sense that they had never been formulated as categories in prior psychiatric nosologies (e.g., portraying and coining the avoidant personality designation; Millon, 1969). Progressive research will determine if the network of concepts constituting this theory provides an optimal structure for a comprehensive nosology of personality pathology. At the very least, it contributes to the view that formal theory can lead to the deduction of new categories worthy of consensual verification.

Brief note should be made, before proceeding, to the utility of the evolutionary schema as a basis for characterizing so-called normal personal variants (Millon, 1996). Normal individuals exhibit a reasonable balance between each of the polarity pairs. Not all individuals fall at the center, of course. Individual differences in both personality features and overall style will reflect the relative positions and strengths of each polarity component. A particularly "healthy" person, for example, would be one who is high on both self *and* other, indicating a solid sense of self-worth combined with a genuine sensitivity to the needs of others.

Before proceeding to elaborate the theory-derived nosology of psychopathology, that is, Axes I and II of the *DSM*, it should be emphasized that the theory provides a basis for deriving the so-called clinical syndromes as well the personality disorders. To illustrate briefly, the most prevalent mental disorder according to recent epidemiologic studies is that of the anxiety disorders. Without explicating its several variants, a low pain threshold on the pleasure-pain polarity would dispose such individuals to be sensitive to punishments, which, depending on covariant polarity positions, might result in the acquisition of complex syndromal characteristics, such as ease of discouragement, low self-esteem, cautiousness, and social phobias. Similarly, a low pleasure threshold on the same polarity might make such individuals prone to experience joy and satisfaction with great ease; again, depending on covariant polarity positions, such persons might be inclined toward impulsiveness and hedonic pursuits, be intolerant of frustration and delay, and, at the clinical level, give evidence of a susceptibility to manic episodes.

To use musical metaphors again, *DSM-IV*'s Axis I clinical syndromes are composed essentially of a single theme or subject (e.g., anxiety, depression), a salient melodic line that may vary in its rhythm and harmony, changing little except in its timing, cadence, and progression. In contrast, the diversely expressed domains that make up Axis II seem constructed more in accord with the compositional structure known as the fugue, where there is a dovetailing of two or more melodic lines. Framed in the sonata style, the opening exposition in the fugue begins when an introductory theme is announced (or analogously in psychopathology, a series of clinical symptoms become evident), following which a second and perhaps third and essentially independent set of themes emerge in the form of "answers" to the first (akin to the unfolding expression of underlying personality traits). As the complexity of the fugue is revealed (we now have identified a full-blown personality disorder), variants of the introductory theme (i.e., the initial symptom picture) develop countersubjects (less observable, inferred traits) that are interwoven with the preceding in accord with well-known harmonic rules (comparably, mechanisms that regulate intrapsychic dynamics). This matrix of entwined melodic lines progresses over time in an episodic fashion, occasionally augmented, at other times diminished. It is sequenced to follow its evolving contrapuntal structure, unfolding a musical quilt, if you will, or better yet, an interlaced tapestry (the development and linkages of several psychological traits). To build this metaphorical elaboration further, not only may personality be viewed as a fugue, but the melodic lines of its psychological counterpoints are comprised of the three evolutionary themes presented earlier (i.e., the polarities). Thus, some fugues are rhythmically vigorous and rousing (high active), others kindle a sweet sentimentality (high other), still others evoke a somber and anguished mood (high pain), and so on. When the counterpoint of the first three polarities is harmonically balanced, we observe a well-functioning or so-called normal person; when deficiencies, imbalances, or conflicts exist among them, we observe one or another variant of the personality disorders.

Personal styles we have termed *deficient* lack the capacity to experience or to enact certain aspects of the three polarities (e.g., the schizoid style has a faulty substrate for both pleasure and pain); those spoken of as *imbalanced* lean strongly toward one or another extreme of a polarity (e.g., the dependent style is oriented almost exclusively to receiving the support and nurturance of others); and those we judge in conflict struggle with ambivalences toward opposing ends of a bipolarity (e.g., the negativistic style vacillates between adhering to the expectancies of others versus enacting what is wished for oneself).

Evolutionary theory is not undertaken for purposes of understanding alone. Its ultimate aim is to lead to intelligent remedial action. However, among the initial goals to which the theory is addressed is identification of the general personal patterns that patients possess.

Categories, Dimensions, and Prototypes

The validity of psychopathologic assessment depends on the validity of the system of categorized types and trait dimensions that might be brought to bear on the individual case. The prototype construct represents a synthesis of both categorical and dimensional models, an approach underlying the *DSM*. Prototypal models assume that no necessary or sufficient criteria exist by which syndromes and disorders can be unequivocally diagnosed. The synthetic character of the prototypal model can be seen by comparing what is saved and discarded in the three approaches. The categorical model sacrifices quantitative variation in favor of the discrete, binary judgments. The dimensional model sacrifices qualitative distinctions in favor of quantitative scores. Of the three models, the prototypal is the only one that conserves both qualitative and quantitative clinical information. Ideally, to use the model to its fullest, clinicians should ask both how and how much the patient resembles the prototypes of the diagnostic schema. Asking *how much* merely transforms the prototypes first into a set of dimensions and then into a set of categories as diagnostic thresholds are assessed. Asking *how* builds qualitative information important for the intervention into the assessment. Unfortunately, the fact that the diagnostic criteria of *DSM-IV* are noncomparable and noncomprehensive limits the utility of this approach. For example, on the basis of information that can be solicited to make a *DSM-IV* diagnosis, it is very difficult to determine which subspecies of schizoid a particular patient might be, because the criteria to discriminate among subgroups simply do not yet exist. Fortunately, the subtype descriptions given in the next section and elaborated later in the clinical chapters may be used as a descriptive supplement to the official schema.

PERSONALITY STYLES/DISORDERS: FOCUSING ON THE WHOLE PERSON

Is there a logic, perhaps evidence, for believing that certain forms of clinical expression (e.g., behaviors, cognitions, affects, defense mechanisms) cluster together as do medical syndromes—in other words, that they not only covary frequently, but make sense as a coherently organized and reasonably distinctive group of characteristics? Are there theoretical and empirical justifications for believing that the varied features of personality display a configurational unity and expressive consistency over time? Will the careful study of individuals reveal congruency among attributes such as overt behavior, intrapsychic functioning, and biophysical disposition? Is this coherence and stability of psychological functioning a valid phenomenon—that is, not merely imposed upon observed data by virtue of clinical expectation or theoretical bias?

There are reasons to believe that the answer to each of these questions is yes. Stated briefly and simply, the observations of covariant patterns of signs, symptoms, and traits may be traced to the fact that people possess relatively enduring biophysical dispositions that give a consistent coloration to their experience, and that the range of experience to which people are exposed throughout their lives is both limited and repetitive (Millon, 1969, 1981). Given the limiting and shaping character of these biogenic and psychogenic factors, it should not be surprising that individuals develop clusters of prepotent and deeply ingrained behaviors, cognitions, and affects that clearly distinguish them from others of dissimilar backgrounds. Moreover, once a number of the components of a particular clinical pattern are identified, knowledgeable observers are able to trace the presence of other, unobserved, but frequently correlated features comprising that pattern.

If we accept the assumption that most people do display a pattern of internally consistent characteristics, we are led next to the question of whether groups of patients evidence commonality in the patterns they display. The notion of clinical categories rests on the assumption that there exist a limited number of such shared covariances—for example, regular groups of diagnostic signs and symptoms that can confidently be used to distinguish certain classes of patients. (The fact that patients can profitably be classified into categories does not negate the fact that patients so classified display considerable differences as well—differences we routinely observe with medical diseases.)

Another question that must be addressed concerning the nature of personological classification concerns the covariation of clinical attributes. Why does possession of characteristic A increase the probability, appreciably beyond chance, of also possessing characteristics B, C, and so on? Less abstractly, why do particular behaviors, attitudes, mechanisms, and so on covary in repetitive and recognizable ways, instead of exhibiting themselves in a more or less haphazard fashion? And even more concretely, why should, say, behavioral defensiveness, interpersonal provocativeness, cognitive suspicion, affective irascibility, and excessive use of the projection mechanism co-occur in the same individual, instead of being uncorrelated and randomly distributed among different individuals?

First, temperament and early experience simultaneously affect the development and nature of several emerging psychological structures and functions; that is, a wide range of behaviors, attitudes, affects, and mechanisms can be traced to the same origins, leading thereby to their frequently observed covariance. Second, once an individual possesses these initial characteristics, they set in motion a series of derivative life experiences that shape the acquisition of new psychological attributes causally related to the characteristics that preceded them in the sequential chain. Common origins and successive linkages increase the probability that certain psychological characteristics will frequently be found to pair with specific others, resulting thereby in repetitively observed symptom or trait clusters.

This trend for traits to cluster is entirely consistent with studies that reflect the operation of *evolutionary convergence.* Evidence shows that fundamentally different species may acquire, over their histories, highly similar morphological features, even though their ancestry is substantially divergent. Through time, each has developed an optimal set of tools for grappling with their life's most demanding tasks. Scientists from Charles Darwin onward have described species displaying this progression of evolutionary convergence. For example, biologists have long noted the architectural parallelism of the wings of the bat, the bird, and the extinct pterodactyl; what is so significant is that these features arose independently from diverse species' origins, because they represent effective and common ways of dealing with their life circumstances.

Convergences happen ontogenetically in human behavior as well. Persons faced with similar experiences learn to cope with these experiences in parallel ways. Given that there are just so many ways of coping, the result is that persons progressively acquire highly comparable (prototypal) styles of psychic functioning. Although the potential range of adaptive (or maladaptive) coping is extremely wide and diverse, it is not one of limitless possibilities. Different personality styles reflect psychic traits in which initially divergent alternatives gradually converge into a few prepotent types. It is on these grounds that clustering concepts such as clinical syndromes and personality disorders may be understood as more-or-less coherent and common phenomena.

Despite the foregoing, not all patients with the same diagnosis can be viewed as possessing the same problem. Platitudinous though this statement may be, care must be taken not to force patients into the procrustean beds of our theoretical models and nosological entities. Whether or not they are derived from mathematical analyses, clinical observations, or a systematic theory, all taxonomies are essentially composed of prototypal classes. Clinical categories must be conceived as flexible and dimensionally quantitative, permitting the full and distinctive configuration of characteristics of patients to be displayed (Millon, 1987a). The multiaxial schema of *DSM-IV* is a step in the right direction in that it encourages multidimensional considerations as well as multidiagnoses that approximate the natural heterogeneity of patients. It is our view, however, that the atheoretical orientation of the *DSM-IV* does a disservice to assessment and psychotherapy in that it bypasses highly informative interpretations that can be generated by a comprehensive theory, be it cognitive, psychoanalytic, or evolutionary.

Applying the Polarities of the Evolutionary Model

As will be elaborated later, the *DSM* personality prototypes simply list characteristics that have been found to accompany a particular disorder with some regularity and specificity. This approach is necessary, but insufficient. The *DSM* does put forward several domains in which personality is expressed, notably cognition, affectivity, interpersonal functioning, and impulse control. However, these psychological domains are not comprehensive, nor are they comparable.

Both the nature of the person as a synthetic construct and the laws of evolution require that the stylistic domains of personality be drawn together in a logical fashion. The antagonism of competing approaches to our discipline is mainly an illusion wrought by human habits. No domain is an autonomous entity. Instead, the evolution of the structure and content of personality is constrained by the evolutionary imperatives of survival, adaptation, and reproductive success, for it is always the whole organism that is selected and evolves. To synthesize the domains of the person as a coherent unity, we draw on the boundary between organism and environment. What we call *functional* domains relate the organism to the external world, whereas other domains serve as *structural* substrates for functioning: they exist "inside" the organism. The distinction between function and structure parallels the distinction between physiology and anatomy. The basic science of anatomy investigates embedded and essentially permanent structures, which serve, for example, as substrates for mood and memory; physiology examines underlying functions that regulate internal dynamics and external transactions.

In many cases, the functional and structural domains parallel major approaches to the field. This should not be surprising, given the philosophy of science described previously, whereby progress in the soft sciences proceeds mainly through the elucidation of relevant but previously neglected sets of variables. For example, the rise of the cognitive perspective, the interpersonal perspective, and the biological perspective, all were inevitable. The particulars of history influenced the timing at which these revolutions occurred, but could not prevent their emergence. Thus, among the functional domains, we have the *expressive acts* domain representing the modern legacy of Thorndike, Skinner, and Hull, for example, and the *interpersonal conduct* domain represents the interpersonal tradition, originating with Sullivan and expressed today by Kiesler (1997), Wiggins (1982), and L.S. Benjamin (1993), among others. The *cognitive style* domain obviously represents the cognitive tradition, of which Beck and Freeman (1990a) is the most notable modern exponent, and the *regulatory mechanisms* and *object representations* domains parallel the ideas of defense mechanisms and object-relations of the psychodynamic school. All of these are legitimate approaches to personality, and through their very existence provide empirical support for the position advanced above: that person pathologies are best thought of as disorders of the entire matrix of the person. The alternative is a reduction of this complex matrix to some one perspective, be it behavioral, cognitive, or psychodynamic—in other words, to substitute part for whole.

Three treatment themes usefully illustrate the combinatorial variations among the three polarities. At the simplest level of analysis, a number of personologic consequences of a single polar extreme will be briefly noted. A high standing on the pain pole, a position typically associated with a disposition to experience anxiety, will be used for this purpose. The upshot of this singular sensitivity will take different forms depending on a variety of factors that lead to the learning of diverse styles of "anxiety-neutralizing." For example, *avoidants* learn to deal with their pervasively experienced anxiety-sensitivity by removing themselves across the board, that is, actively withdrawing from most relationships unless strong assurances of acceptance are given. The *compulsive,* often equally prone to experience anxiety, has learned that there are sanctioned but limited spheres of acceptable conduct; the compulsive reduces anxiety by restricting activities to those that are permitted by more powerful and potentially rejecting others, as well as adhering carefully to rules so that unacceptable boundaries will not be transgressed. And the anxiety-prone *paranoid* has learned to neutralize pain by constructing a semidelusional pseudocommunity (Cameron, 1963), one in which environmental realities are transformed to make them more tolerable and less threatening, albeit not very successfully. In sum, a high standing on the pain pole leads not to one but to diverse personality outcomes.

Another of the polar extremes, the passivity pole, illustrates the diversity of forms that personal styles may take as a function of covariant polarity positions. Six primary personality disorders demonstrate the passive style, but their passivity derives from and is expressed in appreciably different ways that reflect disparate polarity combinations. *Schizoids,* for example, are passive owing to their relative incapacity to experience pleasure and pain; without the rewards these emotional valences normally activate, schizoids will be devoid of the drive to acquire rewards, leading them to become rather indifferent and passive observers. *Depressive* personalities have given up on life, remaining in a passive acceptance of their misfortunes. Unwilling to make efforts to overcome their "fate," they exhibit little initiative to change their circumstances. *Dependents* typically are average on the pleasure and pain polarity, yet they are usually no less passive than schizoids or depressives. Strongly oriented to others, they are notably weak with regard to self. Passivity for them stems from deficits in self-confidence and competence, leading to deficits in initiative and autonomous skills, as well as a tendency to wait passively while others assume leadership and guide them. Passivity among *compulsives* stems from their fear of acting independently, owing to intrapsychic resolutions they have made to quell hidden thoughts and emotions generated by their intense self-other ambivalence. Dreading the possibility of making mistakes or engaging in disapproved behaviors, they became indecisive, immobilized, restrained, and passive. High on pain and low on both pleasure and self, *masochistic* personalities operate on the assumption that they dare not expect nor do they deserve to have life go their way; giving up any efforts to achieve a life that accords with their "true" desires, they passively submit to others' wishes, acquiescently accepting their fate. Finally, *narcissists,* especially high on self and low on others, benignly assume that good things will come their way with little or no effort on their part; this passive exploitation of others is a consequence of the unexplored confidence that underlies their self-centered presumptions.

To turn to slightly more complex cases, there are individuals with appreciably different personality patterns who are often characterized by highly similar clinical features. To illustrate: To be correctly judged as "humorless and emotionally restricted" may be the result of diverse polarity combinations. *Schizoids,* as noted previously, are typically at the low end of both dimensions of the pleasure-pain bipolarity, experiencing little joy, sadness, or anger; they are quite humorless and though not restricted emotionally, do lack emotional expressiveness and spontaneity. By contrast, *avoidants* are notably high at the pain polar extreme; whatever their other traits may be, they are disposed to chance neither interpersonal humor nor an emotional openness. Finally, the self-other–conflicted *compulsive* has learned to deny self-expression as a means of assuring the approval of others; rarely will the compulsive let his or her guard down, lest any true "oppositional" feelings be betrayed. A compulsive rarely is relaxed sufficiently to engage in easy humor or willing to expose any contained emotions. All three personalities are humorless and emotionally restricted, but for different reasons and as a consequence of rather different polarity combinations.

The seeming theoretic fertility of the evolutionary polarities secures but a first step toward a systematic treatment nosology. Convincing professionals of the validity of the schema requires detailed explications on the one hand, and unequivocal evidence of utility on the other. We must not only clarify what is meant by each term in the polarities—for example, identify or illustrate their empirical referents—but also specify ways in which they combine and manifest themselves clinically. It is toward those ends that the clinical chapters of the book are addressed.

As may be inferred from the foregoing, it is both feasible and productive to employ the key dimensions of the bipolar model to make the clinical features of the basic styles of personality functioning more explicit, from the actively pain-sensitive avoidant to the passively self-centered narcissist, from the actively other-oriented histrionic to the self-other–conflicted negativistic (passive-aggressive). The bias toward adaptive modes that is inherent in an evolutionary thesis does enable the identification of alternative mixtures in which these more pathological syndromes are expressed—hence, the clinical presence of frequent comorbidity, such as histrionic borderlines, sadistic paranoids, avoidant schizotypals, and passive-aggressive borderlines.

Responses to the preceding issues point to the inadequacy of any approach that links taxonomic criteria to intervention without theoretical guidance, as well as one that encompasses the functional-structural nature of the person (to be elaborated in the section on domain assessment). The argument is merely that diagnosis should constrain and guide therapy in a manner consonant with accepted standards of the theoretically derived prototypal model. The scope of the interventions that might be considered appropriate and the form of their application have been left unattended. Any set of interventions or techniques might be applied singly or in combination, without regard to the diagnostic complexity of the treated disorder. In the actual practice of therapy, techniques within a particular pathological data level, that is, psychodynamic techniques, behavioral techniques, and so on, are, in fact, often applied conjointly. Thus, systematic desensitization might be followed by in vivo exposure, or a patient might keep a diary of his or her thoughts, while at the same time reframing those thoughts when they occur in accordance with the therapist's directions. In these formulations, however, there is no strong a priori reason why any two therapies or techniques should be combined at all. As noted in the previous chapter, when techniques from different modalities are applied together successfully, it is because the combination mirrors the composition of the individual case, not because it derives its logic from the basis of a theory or the syndrome.

Personality Subtypes

At a final level of specification, existing just one level above personality traits, are what we have termed the personality subtypes. The term is used loosely and is actually somewhat of a misnomer. In fact, each of these are sub-prototypes that could easily be dimensionalized, allowing any particular individual to be described in terms of a profile. Because the evolutionary imperatives tell us only what ends must be fulfilled, but not how, the theory-derived personality disorders constructs are agnostic with respect to the controversy between categories and dimensions that currently rages in the personality literature. The categorical or dimensional nature of a personality style or disorder can be known only through clinical studies and empirical research.

The idea of subtypes recognizes two fundamental facts. The first derives from the chance side of the evolutionary equation and draws on the long descriptive tradition in psychology and psychiatry, as perhaps best expressed in the works of the turn-of-the-century nosologist Emil Kraepelin. In the ordinary course of clinical work, we find that every disorder seems to sort itself into ever finer subcategories, which rest not upon a priori basis, but instead flow from cultural and social factors and their interaction with biological influences such as constitution, temperament, and perhaps even systematic neurological defects. Accordingly, if society were different, or if the neurotransmitters chosen by evolution to bathe the human brain were different, the subtypes would be different also. Such entities are the pristine product of clinical observation, and however the boundaries drawn between them, they are unusually soft. The taxonomic controversy between the "splitters" and the "lumpers" (Widiger & Sanderson, 1995) hails from the influence of factors that give rise to disorders of no inevitability, as do the personality disorders constructs. Instead, their emergence requires an understanding of the particularities of human nature, just as knowing why there are two species of elephants rests on a knowledge of geography.

In the following two case write-ups, we wish to illustrate the fact that the personality prototype itself is often insufficient for purposes of assessing the subtleties and complexities of a case at hand. Though the first of the clinical summaries below has the histrionic style as its primary personality pattern, the secondary summary is quite different. In the first case, we see a descriptive analysis of a histrionic with obsessive-compulsive personality features. In the second case, we again have as primary a histrionic, but see as secondary a narcissistic pattern. It will be of value to note that some elements are shared in common, but others are appreciably different.

The histrionic/obsessive-compulsive personality subtype.   The profile of this man is characterized by his solicitation of attention, his search for acceptance by others, and his adherence to matters of social convention and tradition. There may be a modest fear of losing support and approval that may compel him to be compliant and obliging. At times, he may act in a superficially charming manner, seeking recognition through attention-getting behavior. Possibly naïve about world matters, he may avoid the usual give-and-take of competitive and business affairs. With interpersonal tensions, he may try to maintain buoyancy and seek to deny disturbing thoughts.

To secure his attentional and dependency needs, this essentially "normal" man is likely to be highly accommodating and responsive to the needs of others. Having learned to play socially acceptable roles, he may allow others to express their abilities and talents. There is likely to be an active soliciting of praise and a marketing of his appeal. He is likely to seek harmony with others, occasionally at the expense of his own values and beliefs. Unassertive and socially responsible, he avoids situations that involve personal conflict.

He is likely to control any oppositional feelings he may have, but his occasional frustrations may erupt at times. These resentments may stem from an awareness that he has often devalued his own intrinsic desires in favor of the wishes of others. Nevertheless, he is alert to signs of potential hostility and rejection and seeks to minimize the dangers of incurring the indifference and disapproval of others. By attending closely to their desires, he can shape his behavior to conform to their wishes and needs. Guilt, illness, anxiety, and depression may be displayed instrumentally to deflect criticism and to transform threats of disapproval into messages of support and sympathy. More extreme reactions may emerge when his security is genuinely threatened.

The histrionic/narcissistic personality subtype. The profile of this man suggests that he exhibits an inflated sense of self-worth, an air of imperturbability, and a pretense of self-satisfaction. His superficially charming personal style, noted by a seeking of recognition and attention, is usually evident in skillfully exhibitionistic, self-enhancing behaviors. His interpersonal relationships may be self-serving, shallow, and fleeting. A talent for exploiting the naïve may be present, as is a measure of delight in questioning, but adhering to, social conventions.

Although this man is aware that his facile style and occasional social exploitation may be inconsiderate and presumptuous, he gains too much to forgo them. When criticized for these behaviors, he may dismiss the charges with nonchalant innocence, charm, and, perhaps, prevarications. He is capable of feigning an air of dignity and confidence, and he may be skilled in deceiving others. These talents are usually neither hostile nor malicious in intent but are derived from a feeling of omnipotence and the assumption that he adheres only to those rules of social behavior that he finds acceptable. When others become irritated or alienated he is likely to react initially with surprise and dismay and then with flimsily substantiated rationalizations. He may project blame onto others and is likely to be especially resentful of any comments or actions that could be construed as personally derogatory. Self-righteous anger may be employed as a means of fending off detractors.

There is a measure of anxiety over being exposed and shamed; hence, rebuffs to his self-esteem may disrupt his characteristically unruffled composure and elicit a range of unpredictable behavior, such as anger, depression, anxiety, and withdrawal. If he is unable to replenish his supply of narcissistic recognition, he may employ extreme forms of coping behavior. Although he is likely to regain his typical posture of equanimity, he may revert to addictive behavior, sexual excesses, or other forms of irresponsible acting-out.

Pure antisocial personality subtype. It may be useful to characterize the synthesis of mixed characteristics for another primary personality pattern, the antisocial. The following quote describes a relatively *pure antisocial* personality, one we have titled the *covetous antisocial* (Millon & Davis, 1996a):

> In what we are terming the *covetous antisocial* we see, in its most distilled form, the essential feature we judge as characterizing the antisocial personality, the element of aggrandizement. Here we observe individuals who feel that life has not given the person their due, that they have been deprived of their rightful level of emotional support and material rewards, that others have received more than their share, and that they personally never were given the bounties of the good life. What drives these personalities is envy and a desire for retribution. These goals can be achieved by the assumption of power, and it is best expressed through avaricious greed and voracity. To usurp that which others possess is the highest of rewards for the *covetous antisocial*. Not only can he gain retribution, but he can fill the emptiness within himself. More pleasure comes from taking than in merely having. (p. 451)

Although similar in certain central characteristics to the narcissistic personality, the covetous antisocial does not manifest a benign attitude of entitlement, but an active exploitiveness in which greediness and the appropriation of what others possess are central motivating forces. Whereas the prototypal narcissist feels a sense of inner fullness and satisfaction, the covetous antisocial experiences a deep and pervasive sense of emptiness, a powerful hunger for the love and recognition absent in early life. No matter how successful, no matter how many possessions they may have acquired, these antisocials still feel empty and forlorn. Owing to the belief that they will continue to be deprived, these antisocials show minimal empathy for those whom they exploit and deceive. Much effort is expended in manipulating others to supply the services and commodities they desire—without offering any genuine reciprocation. Some may become successful entrepreneurs, exploiters of others as objects to satisfy their desires. Not expecting that people will comply willingly, the covetous antisocial must be cleverly deceptive to overcome the reluctance of their victims.

Although the chief goal of these personalities is aggrandizement through the possession of goods usurped from others, it should not be forgotten that insecurity has been central to the construction of this personality's strategy and to the avaricious character of its pathology. Like a hungry animal after its prey, covetous antisocials have an enormous drive, a rapacious outlook in which they manipulate and treat others as possessions in their power games. Although they have little compassion for the effects of their behaviors, feeling little or no guilt for their actions, they remain at heart quite insecure about their power and their possessions, never feeling that they have acquired enough to make up for their earlier deprivations. They are pushy and greedy, anxious lest they lose the gains they have achieved. Their life is openly materialistic, characterized by both conspicuous consumption and ostentatious display. Regardless of their voracious desires and achievements, they remain ever jealous and envious. For the most part, they are completely self-centered and self-indulgent, often profligate and wasteful, unwilling to share with others for fear that they will take away what was so desperately desired in early life. Hence, these antisocials never achieve a deep sense of contentment, but feel unfulfilled no matter what successes they have had, remaining forever dissatisfied and insatiable.

Antisocial/schizoid personality subtype. The next variant of the antisocial, termed the *nomadic* subtype, represents a formulation that seeks to represent a *mix* of *schizoid and antisocial* features. We wrote (Millon & Davis, 1996a):

It is commonly held that the central features that characterize "antisocials" are their overtly oppositional, hostile and negativistic behaviors, intentionally enacted to undermine the values of the larger society. Although this characterization may apply to many who are labeled antisocial, it would be incorrect to overlook other individuals whose adjustments are equally problematic from a social viewpoint. In what we are terming the *nomadic antisocial* we find individuals who seek to run away from a society in which they feel unwanted, cast aside, and abandoned. Instead of reacting antagonistically to this rejection by seeking retribution for having been denied the normal benefits of social life, these antisocials drift to the periphery of society, scavenging what little remains they can find of what they could not achieve through acceptable social means. These individuals are angry at the injustices to which they were exposed, but now feel sorry for themselves and have distanced from conventional social affairs because they feel they have little influence on others and are fearful of being further rejected. These peripheral drifters and vagrants feel jinxed, ill-fated, and doomed in life. They are gypsy-like in their roaming, itinerant vagabonds and wanderers who have become misfits or dropouts from society. Their isolation, however, is not benign. Beneath their social withdrawal are intense feelings of resentment and anger. Under minor provocation, or as a consequence of alcohol or substance abuse, these antisocials may act-out impulsively, precipitously discharging their pent-up frustrations in brutal assaults or sexual attacks upon those weaker than themselves.

A lifelong pattern of wandering and gypsy-like migrant roaming becomes more and more ingrained by the accumulation of repeated disappointments, the conviction of being worthless and useless, and possessing the feeling of being abandoned and not belonging anywhere. This pattern is not infrequently seen among adopted children who feel uneasy about their place in this world, experience being dissatisfied and lonely in their homes, and fear the possibility of total rejection. Their migrant and straying ways may be a symbolic search for what they hope may be their "true home" or their "natural parents." Many feel like misfits, dropouts from a world where they never felt fully accepted. With little regard for their personal safety or comfort, and with minimal planning, these nomadic antisocials drift from one setting to another as itinerant wanderers, homeless persons drifting often into prostitution and alcoholism as a way of life.

The urge to remain autonomous, to live as vagrants if necessary, to keep from establishing a continuous residency, is in many ways akin to the common adolescent pattern of running away from home. Insecure where they live, feeling like failures, perhaps unwilling to assume the responsibilities of family life, the vagabond style may be experienced as an optimal life strategy. Despite its problematic consequences and the necessity to live a life of petty crimes, many choose to drift aimlessly, to show little serious forethought, and to possess few if any inclinations toward serious endeavors. They exhibit what may be called a "passive asociality," a well-suited lifestyle in which one neither works nor assumes any responsibilities other than basic survival.

Most nomadics are comparatively harmless, owing to their general indifference and disengagement from life. However, in contrast to the *remote* and *affectless schizoid,* these personalities are deeply angry and resentful. Moreover, many have normal needs for life's pleasures, especially those of an erotic character. Stirred by alcohol, in the main, they may become brutal when "liberated," or engage in criminal-like sexual behaviors in lascivious assaults upon the weak and inadequate, such as children. What justifies our calling them "antisocial," therefore, is that their impulses are not benign, despite their peripheral and nomadic existence. When stirred by inner needs or environmental circumstances, their pent-up hostility will be discharged against those who are not likely to react forcefully.

The motives of the nomadic antisocial are short-term, to reduce tensions and the discomforts of everyday life. They have difficulty envisaging life beyond the moment. They can find no place to settle down; no place has ever given them the acceptance and support they have needed or wanted. This sense of "being no place" is both similar to and different than the experience of depersonalization; nomadics appear vaguely disconnected from reality, possess no clear sense of self, and seem to be transients both within themselves and their environments. (pp. 452–453)

While the concept of prototype and subtype allows the natural heterogeneity of persons to be accommodated within a classification system, there are as many ways to fulfill a given diagnosis as there are subsets of the number of diagnostic criteria required at the diagnostic threshold. For example, there are many ways to score five of a total of nine diagnostic criteria, whatever the actual syndrome. In the context of an idealized medical disease model, which Axis I approximates, the fact that two different individuals, both of whom are depressed, might possess substantially different sets of depressive symptoms is not really problematic. The symptoms may be expressed somewhat differently, but the underlying pathology process is the same and can be treated in the same way. For example, although one person gains weight and wakes early in the morning, and the other loses weight and sleeps long into the day, both may be treated with an antidepressant and cognitive therapy. From the perspective of the traditional medical model, different symptom structures are simply a nuisance that obscures the detection of the latent illness responsible for the subject's problems. Once the disease is known, any particular information about the symptoms can be discarded as an epistemological complication irrelevant to the treatment process.

Personality, however, follows a fundamentally different conceptual model. Whereas variance from the prototypal ideal is irrelevant in the medical model, it is the very essence of Axis II. The neo-Kraepelinian revolution has been most destructive to the study of the person: it encourages the view that problems of personality are diseases, which they are not. Personality styles or disorders are reified for clinical utility, but are most accurately thought of as abnormalities of personality, a phrase that communicates their clinical dimension without the erroneous connotations of disease.

The whole clinical enterprise is thereby changed. The purpose is not to classify individuals into categories, the neo-Kraepelinian position, but instead to determine how the classification system falls short in its attempt to capture the particular reality that is the person. The purpose is not to put persons in the classification system, but instead to reorient the system with respect to the person by determining how his or her unique, ontological constellation of attributes overflows and exceeds it. The classification thus becomes a point of departure for comparison and contrast, a way station in achieving a total understanding of the complexity of the whole, not a destination in itself. When in the course of an assessment the clinician begins to feel that the subject is understood at a level where ordinary diagnostic labels no longer adequately apply, the classification system is well on its way to being falsified relative to the individual, and a truly idiographic understanding of the person is close at hand, ready to be approached in a comprehensive and systematic way therapeutically.

COMPLEX SYNDROMES: FOCUSING ON SYMPTOM CLUSTERS

A historic and still frequently voiced complaint about diagnosis, whether based or not on the official classification system, is its inutility for therapeutic purposes. Most therapists, whatever their orientation or mode of treatment, pay minimal attention to the possibility that diagnosis can inform the philosophy and technique they employ. It matters little what the syndrome or disorder may be: a family therapist is likely to select and employ a variant of family therapy, a cognitively oriented therapist will find that a cognitive approach will probably work best, and so on, including integrative therapists who are beginning to become a school and join this unfortunate trend of asserting the "truth" that their approach is the most efficacious.

A clinical study that attempted to unravel all of the elements of a patient's past and present would be an exhausting task indeed. To make the job less onerous, clinicians must narrow their attention to certain features of a patient's past history and behavior that may prove illuminating or significant. This reduction process requires that clinicians make a series of discriminations and decisions regarding the data they observe. They must find a constellation of core characteristics (e.g., cognitive style, interpersonal behavior) that capture the essential personal pattern of the patient and that will serve as a framework to guide assessment and treatment.

Several assumptions are made by diagnosticians in narrowing their focus to this limited configuration of symptom domains. They assume that a patient possesses a core of interrelated behaviors, feelings, and attitudes that are central to his or her manifest pathology, that these characteristics are found in common among distinctive and identifiable groups of patients, and that prior knowledge regarding the features of these distinctive patient groups, hereby termed *complex clinical syndromes,* will facilitate clinicians' clinical responsibilities and functions.

What support is there for these assumptions? There are both theoretical and empirical justifications for the belief that people display a composite of linked characteristics and that there is an intrinsic unity among these traits over time. Careful study of individuals with complex clinical syndromes will reveal a congruency among behaviors, cognitive reports, intrapsychic functioning, and biophysical disposition. This coherence or unity of psychic functioning is a valid phenomenon; that it is not merely imposed upon clinical data as a function of theoretical bias is evident by the fact that similar patterns constituting complex syndromes are observed by diagnosticians of differing theoretical persuasions. Moreover, these findings follow logically from the fact that people possess relatively enduring biophysical dispositions that give a consistent coloration to their experiences, and that the actual range of experiences to which they have been exposed throughout their lives is highly limited and repetitive. It should not be surprising, therefore, that individuals develop a complex pattern of distinguishing, prepotent, and deeply ingrained behaviors, attitudes, and needs. Once several elements of these complex syndromes are identified, the clinician should have a fruitful basis for inferring the likely presence of other, unobserved, but frequently correlated features of the patient's life history and current functioning.

If we accept the assumption that people display covariant symptoms, we are led next to the question of whether certain patients evidence a commonality in the pattern of characteristics they display. The notion of complex clinical syndromes rests on the assumption that there are a limited number of symptom patterns that can be used profitably to distinguish certain groups of patients. The hope is that the diagnostic placement of a patient within one of these complex syndromal groups will clue the diagnostician to a wider pattern of the patient's difficulty, thereby simplifying the clinical task immeasurably. Thus, once the diagnostician identifies clusters of clinical characteristics in a particular patient, he or she will be able to utilize the knowledge learned about other patients evidencing that syndrome and apply that knowledge to the present patient.

The fact that patients can profitably be categorized into complex clinical syndromes does not negate the fact that patients, so categorized, will display differences in the presence and constellation of their characteristics. The philosopher Grunbaum (1952) illustrates this thesis:

> Every individual is unique by virtue of being a distinctive assemblage of characteristics not precisely duplicated in any other individual. Nevertheless, it is quite conceivable that the following . . . might hold: If a male child having specifiable characteristics is subjected to maternal hostility and has a strong paternal attachment at a certain stage of his development, he will develop paranoia during adult life. If this . . . holds, then children who are subjected to the stipulated conditions in fact become paranoiacs, however much they may have differed in other respects in childhood and whatever their other differences may be once they are already insane. (p. 672)

There should be little concern about the fact that certain "unique" characteristics of each patient will be lost when he or she is grouped in a complex syndrome;

differences among members of the same syndrome will exist, of course. The question that must be raised is *not* whether the syndrome is entirely homogeneous, for no complex category meets this criterion, but whether placement in the category impedes or facilitates a variety of clinically relevant objectives. Thus, if this grouping of key characteristics simplifies the task of clinical analysis by alerting the diagnostician to features of the patient's past history and present functioning that has not yet observed, or if it enables clinicians to communicate effectively about their patients, or guides their selection of beneficial therapeutic plans, or assists researchers in the design of experiments, then the existence of these syndromal categories has served many useful purposes. No single classification schema can serve all of the purposes for which clinical categories can be formed; all we can ask is that it facilitate certain relevant functions.

As noted previously, the diagnostic criteria of the *DSM-IV* have *not* been explicitly constructed to facilitate treatment, no less personality-guided psychotherapy. Criteria should do more than classify persons into categories, a rather minimalistic function. Instead, diagnostic criteria should encourage an integrative understanding of the patient across all those psychic domains in which the person's mental impairments are expressed. The *DSM-IV* criteria, disproportionately weighted in some symptom domains and nonexistent in others, cannot perform this function. At this point in time, personality-guided therapy requires that the official diagnostic criteria be supplemented by clinical judgment. Obviously, effective synergistic therapy requires a detailed assessment of all those symptom domains that can exist as constraints on system functioning. Because the *DSM-IV* therapist simply would not be cognizant of such abnormalities, techniques appropriate to those domains would not be used either combinatorially or in series. Using *DSM-IV* criteria alone as a guide to the substantive characteristics of personality and syndromes would effectively leave some systems constraints completely unobserved, free to operate insidiously in the background to perpetuate the pathological tenacity of the system as a whole. Consequently, a *DSM-IV*-based therapy is not necessarily a synergistic therapy.

We next review some of the distinctions between *complex* clinical syndromes and *simple* clinical reactions. In essence, the distinction is traceable to the interweaving of intrapsychic, cognitive, and interpersonal elements in the complex syndrome. The residuals of the past intrude on the individual's present perceptions and behaviors, often giving rise to seemingly irrational symptoms. Both complex clinical syndromes and simple reactions are classed among the *DSM-IV* Axis I disorders, an unfortunate decision that overlooks important distinctions. It is only in the complex syndromes that we see the compounding of pervasive interpersonal relations, unconscious emotions, cognitive assumptions, self-images, and so on.

Distinguishing Simple Reactions from Complex Syndromes

Simple clinical reactions, complex clinical syndromes, and personality styles/disorders lie on a continuum such that the first is essentially a straightforward singular symptom, unaffected by other clinical domains of which the person as a whole is composed (Millon, 1969). At the other extreme are personality styles and disorders that comprise an interrelated mix of cognitive attitudes and interpersonal styles, as well as biological temperaments and intrapsychic processes. Complex clinical syndromes lie in between, manifestly akin to simple syndromes but interwoven and mediated by pervasive personality traits and embedded vulnerabilities.

Clinical signs in *personality disorders* (PD) reflect the operation of a pattern of deeply embedded and pervasive characteristics of functioning, that is, a system of traits that systematically "support" one another, and color and manifest themselves automatically in all facets of the individual's everyday life. By contrast, *simple clinical reactions* (SCR) are relatively direct responses that derive from specific neurochemical dysfunctions or are prompted by rather distinctive stimulus experiences. Simple reactions operate somewhat independently of the patient's overall personality pattern; their form and content are determined largely by the character of a biologic vulnerability or the specifics of an external precipitant; that is, they are not contaminated by the intrusion of other psychic domains or forces. Simple clinical reactions are best understood, then, *not* as a function of the intricate convolutions among intrapsychic mechanisms, interpersonal behaviors, cognitive misperceptions, and the like, but as simple and straightforward responses to an endogenous liability or to adverse and circumscribed stimulus conditions. To paraphrase Eysenck (1959), there are no obscure causes that underlie simple clinical reactions, merely the reaction itself; modify the reaction, or the conditions that precipitate it, and you have eliminated all there is to the pathology.

The overt clinical features of the simple clinical reactions and the *complex* clinical syndromes (CCS) are often indistinguishable; moreover, both are prompted *in part* by external precipitants.

How, then, are they different? Complex clinical syndromes are rooted in part to pervasive personality vulnerabilities and coping styles, whereas simple clinical reactions are not. Complex syndromes usually arise when the patient's established personality equilibrium has been upset or threatened. At that point, numerous domains of expression come into play in the patient's effort to reestablish a modicum of stability. Unfortunately, as often occurs in medical diseases, the reparative process itself becomes highly problematic, creating additional difficulties. Hence, therapy must attend not only to the primary clinical domain that has begun the process, but to many of the secondary domains of expression. Complex clinical syndromes often arise in response to what objectively is often an insignificant or innocuous event; despite the trivial and specific character of the precipitant, the patient exhibits a mix of complicated responses that have minimal relationship to how normal persons respond in these circumstances. Thus, complex clinical syndromes often do not "make sense" in terms of actual present realities; they signify an unusual vulnerability and an overreaction on the part of the patient, that is, a tendency for objectively neutral stimuli to touch off and activate cognitive misperceptions, unconscious memories, and pathological interpersonal responses. Complex syndromes usually signify the activation of several traits that make up the varied facets of a personality style or disorder; that is, they are seen in individuals who are encumbered with the residues of deeply embedded past experiences or adverse life events that have led to the acquisition of problematic cognitive beliefs and behavioral habits.

As suggested, unconscious memories, self-attitudes, and interpersonal dispositions intervene in the expression of complex syndromes, complicating the connection between present stimuli and the patient's response to them. As we see it, intrusions of this nature do not occur in simple clinical reactions. In the latter, the patient's vulnerabilities are neither deep nor widespread, but restricted to a delimited class of biological vulnerabilities or environmental conditions. These pathological responses do not pass through a chain of complicated and circuitous intrapsychic and cognitive transformations before they emerge in manifest form. Thus, in addition to the restricted number of precipitants that give rise to them, simple reactions are distinguished from complex syndromes in the more or less direct route through which they are channeled and expressed clinically.

In complex syndromes, a precipitating stimulus will stir up a wide array of intervening thoughts and emotions which then take over as the determinant of the response; reality stimuli serve, then, merely as catalysts that set into motion a complex chain of intermediary processes that transform what might otherwise have been a fairly simple and straightforward response. Because of the "contaminating" intrusion of these transformations, the complex response acquires an irrational and often symbolic quality. For example, in complex phobias, the object that is feared often comes to represent something else; thus, a phobia of elevators might come to symbolize a more generalized and unconscious anxiety about being closed in and trapped by others.

Because of the frequent pervasiveness of complex syndromal vulnerabilities, thoughts and behaviors become entangled in a wide variety of dissimilar stimulus situations; for example, the feeling of being trapped may give rise to a phobia not only of elevators but also of rooms in which the doors are shut, of riding in cars in which the windows are closed, of tight clothes, and so on. Moreover, these complicated processes vary in their form and degree of intrusion; for example, a phobic patient may feel well on certain days and agree to the closing of room doors; on other days, however, all doors and windows must be wide open. Thus, the responses of complex syndromes not only are elicited by a wide variety of stimulus conditions, but these diverse responses wax and wane in their relative salience.

All this fluidity and variability in complex clinical syndromes contrasts with the relative directness and uniformity of responses found in simple clinical reactions. Uninfluenced by the intricate and circuitous transformations of other facets of the person's psyche, simple reactions tend to be consistent and predictable. They are manifested in essentially the same way each time the endogenous vulnerability or troublesome stimulus to which they have been attached occurs. Moreover, they are rarely exhibited at other times or in response to events dissimilar to the stimulus to which they were originally attached. In short, simple clinical reactions are ingrained but *isolated responses* to specific inner or outer stimulus events. They tend not to vary or be influenced by the patient's general personal makeup. They are relatively compartmentalized stimulus-response reactions that are isolated in large measure from the patient's larger and characteristic pattern of functioning. They may be narrowly focused behaviors, displaying themselves only in response to specific types of stimulus events. To use an analogy, we might speak of complex syndromes emerging from several interwoven domains of personality structure and function; they are both body and basic design of a fabric, whereas the simple reaction may be seen as an embroidered decoration that has been sewn onto it. One may remove (extinguish) the embroidery with relative ease (as conditioning therapists have done in treating the simple clinical reactions) without involving or altering the body of the cloth (personality). Simple clinical reactions, then, do not permeate and intrude on the many facets of the individual's transactions with his or her world, as do the trait covariants of complex disorders; rather, they are stimulus-specific responses to either a circumscribed inner or outer class of stimuli.

Despite the preceding, there are many similarities between simple reactions and complex syndromes. For example, anxiety can be either simple or complex. Both are characterized by feelings of tension and by a rapid increase in sympathetic nervous system reactivity (perspiration, muscular contraction, rapid heartbeat). They differ in that the origins of complex anxiety disorders are difficult to decode and are often unanchored and free-floating. In contrast, simple anxiety reactions usually are connected to a readily identifiable stimulus.

As another illustration, complex phobic syndromes and simple phobic reactions are alike in that both may be precipitated by tangible external stimuli, leading taxonomists to question whether any difference exists between them. As we conceive it, the difference is a matter of the degree and complexity of other clinical domains' contributions to the pathological response. Complex phobias, as we define them, signify that intricate and highly convoluted cognitive and emotional processes have played a determinant role in "selecting" a provocative stimulus that subjectively represents, but is objectively different from, that which may actually be feared; for example, a phobia for open places may symbolize a more generalized fear of assuming independence of others. In contrast, what we have termed a simple phobic reaction is a direct, nonsymbolic response to the actual stimulus the patient has learned to fear, for example, a fear of Asian persons that is traceable to distressing encounters in childhood with a Chinese teacher. Of course, some measure of generalization occurs in simple reactions, but the individual tends to make the simple response only to objects or events that are essentially similar or closely allied with the original fear stimulus; for example, learning to fear a cat in early life may be generalized into a fear of dogs because these are barely discriminable in the eyes of the very young. At most, then, the simple phobic reaction may reflect an uncomplicated generalization. Although often appearing irrational to the unknowing outsider, they can be traced directly to these reality-based and well-circumscribed experiences.

Complex clinical syndromes tend to occur in persons whose histories are replete with innumerable adverse experiences. Given their repeated exposure to mismanagement and faulty learning experiences, these individuals have built up an obscure psychic labyrinth, a residue of complex, tangentially related, but highly interwoven cognitions, emotions, and interpersonal behaviors that are easily reactivated under the press of new stressors. Because these intervening processes are stirred up under new stressful conditions, no simple and direct line can be traced between the overt response and its associated precipitant. The final outcome, as in complex phobias, appear often as symbolic rather than simply generalized because the associative route is highly circuitous, involving both the residuals of the past and numerous distortion mechanisms. Complex syndromes are formed, then, by the crystallization of diffusely anchored and transformed past learnings acquired in response to a wide and diverse range of faulty experiences; this pervasively adverse background and the rather circuitous sequence of distortions are what are activated among pathological persons. Because "normals" are not likely to have had such pervasively adverse experiences, they have had little reason to develop a complex of behavioral styles and defensive maneuvers to avoid the reactivation of distressing memories and emotions; as a result, what we observe in them are relatively "clean," that is, simple and direct, reactions to experiences.

It should be noted that the continuum we have drawn between simple and complex syndromes cannot be drawn with ease in describing characteristics of the first years of life. During this early period, learnings have not crystallized into ingrained, pervasive, stable, and consistent styles of life. In many respects, then, childhood personality is a loose cluster of scattered habits and beliefs learned in response to a wide variety of odds-and-ends experiences. Over time, however, as certain of the conditions that gave rise to these habits and beliefs are repeated and attached to an increasing variety of stimuli, and as the child's own self-perpetuating processes accentuate and spread the range of these events further, some of these simple reactions become more dominant than others, until they may take shape as pervasive and ingrained personality traits. Thus, early simple reactions may become the precursors of later complex syndromes and personality patterns; it is a continuous developmental process.

Psychic functions of complex syndromes.   Let us briefly recapitulate and extend several points. Coping refers to processes of instrumental activity that are learned as a function of experience. These processes enable individuals to maintain an optimum level of psychological integration by increasing the number of life-enhancing satisfactions they achieve (e.g., attention, comfort, pleasure, and status) and avoiding as many life-endangering experiences as they can (e.g., punishment, frustration, rejection, and anxiety).

Psychic pathologies utilize coping behaviors to achieve several goals, such as counteracting external precipitants that threaten to upset their equilibrium and tenuous controls; blocking reactivated anxieties and impulses from intruding into conscious awareness, thereby potentially provoking social condemnation; discharging tensions engendered by external stressors and their intrapsychic residuals; and soliciting attention, sympathy, and nurturance from others.

It is the synthesis of goals such as these that also distinguishes simple reactions from complex clinical syndromes. To dilute tensions while at the same time blocking awareness of their true sources, avoiding social rebuke and evoking social approval and support in their stead, is characteristic of the complex syndromes, a task of no mean proportions. It requires the masking and transformation of one's true thoughts and feelings by the intricate workings of several psychic mechanisms. The resulting complex syndrome symptom represents the interplay and final outcome of numerous psychic and interpersonal maneuvers. Not only have the patient's anxieties and impulses been disguised sufficiently to be kept from conscious awareness, but they also managed to solicit interpersonal attention as well as achieve a measure of cognitive resolution and tension discharge.

Alexander (1930) reports a classic case of "phobia" in which the patient's symptom achieved her goals through a complex psychic resolution:

> A young woman dreaded going into the street alone, the thought of which made her feel faint and extremely anxious. Upon clinical investigation it became clear that a forbidden and unconscious sexual impulse was associated with her phobia; each time she would go out her impulse would be stimulated by the thought that a man might "pick her up" and seduce her. The thought both excited her and caused her intense anxiety. To avoid the true character of her forbidden desire and the tension it provoked she displaced her tension to an associated and more generalized activity, that of going into the street; thus, her phobia. However, she was able to venture out quite undisturbed if accompanied by a relative. In this way she could engage in fleeting sexual fantasies as she passed attractive men, without the fear that she might be carried away and shamed by her forbidden impulse. Her symptom was extremely efficient; not only did it enable her to maintain psychological cohesion by controlling her impulse, blocking her awareness of its true source and keeping her behavior within acceptable social boundaries, but, at the same time, it solicited the assistance of others who enabled her to find some albeit skimpy means of gaining both tension and impulse release. (p. 304)

The case just described brings us to another aspect of complex clinical syndromes, the tendency for symptoms to achieve what are known as secondary gains. According to traditional theory, the primary function of clinical syndromes is the avoidance, control, and partial discharge of anxiety, or as we are inclined to call it, the elimination of a strong upsurge of negative feelings stemming from unconscious sources. But, in addition, the psychic maneuver may produce certain positive consequences; that is, as a result of his or her clinical syndrome, the patient may obtain secondary advantages or rewards. In the case noted above, for example, the woman's phobic symptom achieved a positive result above and beyond the reduction of the negatively toned anxiety; in the role of a sick and disabled person, she solicited attention, sympathy, and help from others, and was freed of the responsibility of carrying out many of the duties expected of a healthy adult. In this fashion, her symptom not only controlled and partially vented her anxieties, but enabled her to gratify a more basic dependency need.

The distinction between primary gains (anxiety neutralization) and secondary gains (positive rewards) may be sharply drawn at the conceptual level but is difficult to make when analyzing actual cases as the two processes intermesh closely in reality. However, the conceptual distinction may be extremely important. As we view it, secondary gains play no part in the formation of simple clinical reactions. Here, the patient is prompted to develop a symptom not as a means of gaining secondary or positive rewards, but as a means of avoiding, controlling, or discharging anxiety.

This sharp distinction between primary and secondary gains seems rather arbitrary and narrow. Although it is true that anxiety neutralization is centrally involved in complex syndromes, this, in itself, cannot account for the variety of symptoms that patients display (e.g., somatoform, obsessive-compulsive). We may ask: Why are certain forms of interpersonal conduct and psychic mechanisms employed by some patients and different ones by others, and why do certain symptoms rather than others emerge? If the sole purpose of syndrome formation were anxiety abatement, then any set of mechanisms could fulfill that job, giving rise to any number and variety of different syndromes.

This, however, is not the case. It seems that most complex syndrome maneuvers both neutralize anxiety (primary gain) and, at the same time, achieve certain positive advantages (secondary gain). We believe that complex clinical syndromes reflect the joint operation of both primary and secondary gain strategies (neither of which, we should note, is consciously planned). Furthermore, we propose that complex clinical syndromes, albeit different overtly, have a common and covert secondary gain characteristic that distinguishes them from simple reactions; that is, their symptoms (phobias, conversions) serve to neutralize tensions and do so without provoking social condemnation, eliciting, in its stead, support, sympathy, and nurturance.

Personality Traits Underlying Complex Syndromes

The prognostic course of simple reactions is relatively predictable and uncomplicated, assuming that the diagnosis is correct. It can safely be expected that the patient will regain normal composure and functioning shortly following the removal of the stressful inner or outer precipitant.

As noted earlier, complex clinical syndromes display themselves in such ways as both to avoid social derogation and to elicit support and sympathy from others. In the earlier example, a phobic patient manipulated members of her family into accompanying her in street outings where she gained the illicit pleasures of sexual titillation; through her unfortunate disablement, she fulfilled her dependency needs, exerted interpersonal control over the lives of others, and achieved partial impulse gratification without social condemnation. Let us look at two other examples. A depressed woman is not only relieved of family responsibilities, but through her subtly angry symptom makes others feel guilty and limits their freedom, while still gaining their concern, and yet does not provoke retribution. A hypochondriacal woman experiences diverse somatic ailments that preclude sexual activity; she not only gains her husband's compassion and understanding, but does so without his recognizing that her behavior is a subtle form of punishing him. She is so successful in her maneuver that her frustration of his sexual desires is viewed, not as an irritation or a sign of selfishness, but as an unfortunate consequence of her physical illness. Her plight evokes more sympathy for her than for her husband.

Why do the symptoms of complex clinical syndromes take this particular, devious route? Why are their anxieties or otherwise socially unacceptable impulses masked and transformed so as to appear not only socially palatable, but evocative of support and sympathy? To answer this question, we must examine which of the various personality styles and disorders tend to exhibit these clinical syndromes. When we do, we discover that they are found primarily among avoidants, depressives, dependents, histrionics, compulsives, negativists, masochists, and borderlines. More will be said when we discuss these syndromes and personalities in later chapters.

What rationale can be provided for the covariation of certain personality patterns and complex clinical syndromes? We previously stated that a clearer understanding of complex clinical syndromes is achieved by a study of the context of a patient's personality. Complex syndromes are largely an outgrowth of deeply rooted habits, vulnerabilities, and coping strategies. What events a person perceives as threatening or rewarding and what behaviors and mechanisms he or she employs in response to them depend on the history to which the person was exposed. If we wish to uncover the reasons for the particular syndromes a patient "chooses," we must first understand the source and character of the goals the patient seeks to achieve. As elaborated in Millon and Davis (1996a), the character of the symptoms a patient chooses is not a last-minute decision, but reflects a long history of interwoven biogenic and psychogenic factors that have formed his or her basic personality pattern. As noted earlier, in analyzing the distinguishing goals of complex syndromal behaviors, we are led to the following observations: susceptible patients appear especially desirous of avoiding the negative experiences (pain) of social disapproval and rejection; moreover, where possible, they wish to evoke the positive experiences (pleasure) of attention, sympathy, and nurturance.

Although individuals typifying each personality pattern (or syndrome context) have had different prior experiences, they tend to share in common a hypersensitivity to social rebuff and condemnation, to which they hesitate reacting with counteraggression. In the *dependent* patterns, for example, there is a fear of losing the security and rewards others provide; these patients must guard themselves against acting in ways that provoke disapproval and separation; rather, where feasible, they will maneuver themselves to act in ways that evoke favorable responses.

There are endless variations in the *specific* life experiences to which different members of the same personality style or disorder have been exposed. Let us compare, for example, two individuals who have been "trained" to become *compulsive* personalities. One may have been exposed to a mother who was chronically ill, a pattern of behavior that brought her considerable sympathy and freedom from many burdens. With this as a background factor, the person may be inclined to follow the model he observed in his mother when he is faced with undue anxiety and threat, thereby displaying hypochondriacal syndromes. A second compulsive personality may have learned to imitate a father who expressed endless fears about all types of events and situations. In his case, there is a greater likelihood that phobic syndromes would arise in response to stressful and anxiety-laden circumstances. In short, the specific "choice" of the complex syndrome is not a function solely of the patient's personality pattern, but may reflect more particular and entirely incidental events of prior experience and learning.

Although each complex syndrome crops up with greater frequency among certain personalities than others, they do arise in a number of different patterns. For example, *somatoform* syndromes occur most commonly among patients exhibiting a basic avoidant, dependent, histrionic, compulsive, or negativistic personality pattern; *conduct disorders* are found primarily in narcissistic, antisocial, and sadistic patterns. This observation points up the importance of specifying the basic personality style or disorder from which a complex syndrome arises. The dominant symptom a patient displays cannot, in itself, clue us well enough to the basic dispositions and vulnerabilities of the patient. In later chapters, we make it a practice to discuss complex clinical syndromes with reference to the specific pathological personality pattern from which it issues.

Three cases (of the complex clinical syndrome labeled dysthymia) are presented next to illustrate the fact that the appraisal of an Axis I syndrome should be approached in terms of the patient's larger context of personality dispositions and vulnerabilities. In the first of these cases, we write up a dysthymic syndrome in a *dependent* personality. In the second, the dysthymia will be interpreted specifically as it is likely to occur in a *negativistic* (passive-aggressive) personality. In the third dysthymic description, the characterization of the patient derives its significance in the context of a *masochistic* personality.

Dysthymia in a Dependent Personality

This woman is characteristically tense and sad; however, her apprehensiveness appears to have achieved dysphoric levels that are sufficient to classify her as experiencing a mixed anxiety and dysthymic disorder. Dependent and dejected, but also ambivalent about her relationships, she struggles to restrain her sadness and resentment, but with only partial success. The strain of her vacillations precipitates a variety of behavioral syndromes, such as restlessness and distractibility, as well as physical discomfort such as insomnia and fatigue. Holding back her dysphoric mood is stressful, but discharging it is equally problematic in that it may provoke those on whom she depends.

Dysthymia in a Negativistic Personality

A pattern of anxiety and dysthymia is likely to have emerged over time in this edgy and actively ambivalent man. Unsure of the fealty of those on whom he has learned to depend and conflicted about his neediness in this regard, he experiences strong emotions of a resentful and hostile nature. Because of his dread of rebuke and rejection, he tries to restrain these emotions, albeit only partially successfully. Rather than chance total abandonment, he turns much of his anger inward, leading to self-generated feelings of unworthiness and guilt. His increasingly hopeless feeling springs from a wide and pervasive range of events that have caused him to see his life as filled with inadequacies, resentments, fears, diminished pleasures, and self-doubts.

DYSTHYMIA IN A MASOCHISTIC PERSONALITY

The self-demeaning comments and feelings of inferiority expressed by this dysthymic woman are part of her overall and enduring characterological structure, a set of chronic self-defeating attitudes and depressive emotions that are intrinsic to her psychological makeup. Feelings of emptiness and loneliness are mixed with expressions of low self-esteem, preoccupations with ostensive failures and physical unattractiveness, and assertions of guilt and unworthiness. Although she complains about being aggrieved and mistreated, she is likely to assert that she deserves the anguish and abuse she receives. Such self-debasement is consonant with her self-image, as are her tolerance and perpetuation of relationships that foster and aggravate her misery.

Despite the short-term gains made by complex syndromal efforts, the symptoms they give rise to are frequently self-defeating in the end. By restricting their environment (e.g., phobias), limiting their physical competencies (e.g., conversions), preoccupying themselves with distracting activities (e.g., obsessions-compulsions), or deprecating their self-worth (e.g., dysthymia), patients avoid confronting and resolving their real difficulties and tend to become increasingly dependent on others. Their psychic maneuver, then, is a double-edged sword. It relieves for the moment passing discomforts and strains, but in the long run fosters the perpetuation of faulty attitudes and coping strategies.

Complex syndromal patients exhibit a blend of several traits and symptoms that rise and subside over time in their clarity and prominence. This complex and changing picture is further complicated by the fact that it is set within the context of the patient's broader personality pattern of attitudes and behaviors. In planning a treatment approach, the therapist is faced, then, with an inextricable mixture of focal and transitory symptoms that are embedded in a pattern of more diffuse and permanent traits.

Separating this complex of clinical features for therapeutic attention is no simple task. To decide which features comprise the basic personality and which represent the clinical syndrome cannot readily be accomplished because both are elements of the same system of vulnerabilities and coping strategies. Even when clear distinctions can be drawn, as when a symptom suddenly emerges in clear and sharp relief, a judgment must be made as to whether therapeutic attention should be directed to the focal symptom or to the "underlying" personality trait pattern from which it has sprung. In certain cases, it is both expeditious and fruitful to concentrate solely on the manifest clinical syndrome; in other cases, however, it may be advisable to rework the more pervasive and ingrained pattern of personality domains.

Before we proceed, let us again be reminded that the descriptive label given to each of the clinical syndromes may be misleading in that it suggests that a single symptom stands alone, uncontaminated by others. This is not the case, especially in what we have termed the complex clinical syndromes. Although a particular symptom may appear dominant at one time, it often coexists and covaries with several others, any one of which may come to assume dominance. As a further complication, there is not only covariation and fluidity in symptomatology, but each of these clinical syndromes arises in a number of different personality patterns.

Much of the confusion that has plagued diagnostic systems in the past can be attributed to this overlapping and changeability of symptom pictures. For reasons discussed in previous sections, it has been argued that greater clarity can be achieved in diagnosis if we focus on the basic personality of the patient rather than limit ourselves to the particular dominant symptom he or she manifests. Moreover, by focusing our attention on enduring personality traits and pervasive clinical domains of expression, we may be able to deduce the cluster of different symptoms the patient is likely to display and the sequence of symptoms he or she may exhibit over the course of the illness. For example, knowing the vulnerabilities and habitual coping strategies of a *paranoid* person, we would predict that he will evidence either together or in sequence both delusions and hostile mania, should he become psychotically disordered. Similarly, a *compulsive* personality may be expected to manifest cyclical swings between catatonic rigidity, agitated depression, and manic excitement, should she decompensate into a psychotic state. Focusing on ingrained personality patterns rather than transient symptoms enables us, then, to grasp both the patient's complex syndrome and the symptoms he or she is likely to exhibit, as well as the possible sequence in which they will wax and wane.

SIMPLE REACTIONS: FOCUSING ON SINGULAR SYMPTOMS

There is a close correspondence in simple clinical reactions between classical assessment *domains* (e.g., *DSM* diagnostic criteria) and modern therapeutic modalities. This concurrence greatly facilitates our understanding and selection of optimal techniques of treatment among these reactions. It addresses the long-held desire to connect diagnostic assessment with therapeutic methodology.

Unfortunately, the diagnostic criteria of the *DSM-IV* are both noncomprehensive (no real scheme for coordinating and anchoring domain attributes has been developed) and noncomparable (the criteria run the gamut from very broad to very narrow). Further, these problems exist both within and between disorders, so that different disorders evince different content distortions. Consider, for example, the obsessive-compulsive personality disorder. Criterion 5 is relatively narrow and behavioral: "Is unable to discard worn-out or worthless objects even when they have no sentimental value." In contrast, criterion 8 requires more inference: "Shows rigidity and stubbornness." In fact, the inability to discard worthless objects could well be considered simply a behavioral manifestation of the trait of rigidity. Failure to coordinate criteria across domains may also lead to redundancies. Consider, for example, the dependent personality disorder. Criterion 1 states, "Has difficulty making everyday decisions without an excessive amount of advice and reassurance from others." Criterion 2, however, says almost the same: "Needs others to assume responsibility for most major areas of his or her life." In fact, five of the eight dependent personality criteria seem oriented toward the interpersonal conduct domain, two seem oriented toward the self-image domain, and only one is concerned with cognitive style, leaving the domains of regulatory mechanisms, object representations, morphologic organization, mood/temperament, and expressive acts completely unaddressed.

Failure to multioperationalize psychopathology via comprehensive and comparable symptom domains certainly means that the content validity of the criteria sets has been compromised, quite probably contributing to diagnostic invalidity and therapeutic inefficiency. Because the *DSM* is usually taken as the "gold standard" by which other measures of psychic pathology are judged, the degree of distortion is an open question at this point—there is no gold standard for the gold standard. The worst-case scenario: Clinical wisdom states correctly that, in principle, multiple data sources and construct operationalizations should be sought as a means of obtaining convergent validity for one's assessment findings, where possible. Because the *DSM* criteria sets are noncomprehensive and noncomparable, there are substantive reasons, reasons that go beyond mere principle, for bringing extra-*DSM* notions and instruments, instruments not intended to explicitly instantiate *DSM* criteria as they may bear on the individual assessment case. To the extent that *DSM* criteria are successfully operationalized, distortions latent in these criteria are built into an instrument, providing users with information that is ostensibly confirmatory of a *DSM* diagnosis, but is in fact convergent only through redundancy. Unfortunately, test authors have usually considered conformity with the *DSM* a point of pride, so that convergence with *DSM* diagnoses yields no incremental validity, but instead is largely artifactual. Instruments embracing the same constructs but constructed independent of *DSM* considerations, that is, instruments whose findings would be truly independent and thus bear most strongly on the validity of a given diagnosis, are few and far between. Every extant instrument is to some extent contaminated by the problem. The degree to which this worst-case scenario represents clinical reality is unknown. In all likelihood, matters are not this severe, but it is wise to be aware of the possibilities. What *is* certain is that the role of clinical judgment in making diagnostic decisions has by no means been usurped by the current constellation of instrumentalities and criteria sets.

A simple reaction diagnosis focuses on which intervention(s) might be most effective. This means that in these cases, a simple syndrome diagnosis is a necessary but not sufficient basis for planning an intervention. Ideally, a diagnosis functions as a means of narrowing the universe of therapeutic techniques to some small set of choices, and within this small set, uniquely personal factors come into play between alternative techniques or the order in which these techniques might be applied.

Let us briefly examine how a few of the simple-reaction symptoms correspond to various modes of therapy; more extensive discussions will be provided later in this text.

Therapists who subscribe to the *behavioral* orientation emphasize simple reactions that can be directly observed. As a consequence, their interest centers on environmental stimuli and overt behavioral responses. Most clinical reactions are considered to be deficient or maladaptive learned behaviors. Where possible, they avoid reference to unobservable or subjective processes such as intrapsychic conflicts or cognitive attitudes. Because inner states are anathema to them, they are inclined to an action-suppressive rather than an insight-expressive process. Because the most clearly formulated schema of "behavior" change has been developed in the laboratories of learning theorists, they borrow their methods and procedures from that body of research. It follows logically, they contend, that simple reactions can best be altered by the same learning principles and procedures that were involved in their acquisition. Thus, behavior therapists design their treatment programs in terms of conditioning and imitative modeling techniques that provide selective rewards and punishments. In this way, simple syndromal behaviors that had been connected to provocative stimuli are systematically eliminated and more adaptive behavioral alternatives carefully formed.

Cognitive therapists believe that treatment for both simple reactions and complex syndromes should be conceived in terms of the patient's beliefs, assumptions, and expectancies. Because individuals react to their world in accord with their current perception of it, cognitivists contend that the goal of treatment should not be to unravel the early causes of difficulties, but to assist patients in developing a clearer understanding of how their distorted attitudes and beliefs generate and prolong their problems. As their perception of events and people is clarified, they will be able to approach life with fewer problematic assumptions and expectancies, enabling them to act in ways that will eliminate the syndrome in question.

As we know, *intrapsychic* therapists focus their efforts on the elusive and obscure data of the unconscious. To them, the crucial elements underlying most syndromes are repressed childhood anxieties and the unconscious adaptive processes that have evolved to protect against their resurgence. The task of therapy, then, is to unravel these hidden residues of the past and to bring them into consciousness, where they can be reevaluated and reworked in a constructive fashion. Shorn of insidious unconscious forces through the unfolding of self-insight and the uprooting of forbidden feelings, the patient may now be free to explore a more wholesome and productive way of life.

The concept of a system must be brought to the forefront, even when discussing reactions and syndromes. Systems function as a whole but are composed of parts. We have partitioned mental disorders into simple reactions, complex syndromes, and personality patterns, but we segregated these disorders with reference to eight structural and functional domains (Millon, 1984, 1986b, 1990; Millon & Davis, 1996a). These domains encompass the greater part of a person's makeup. As can be seen in Figure 3.2, simple reactions are essentially expressed in only one major symptom domain (e.g., affect, relationships); complex syndromes usually engage three or four clinical domains, and personality patterns are likely to comprise almost all of the symptom domains. These domains serve as a means of classifying the parts or constructs in accord with the therapeutic traditions noted in Chapter 1. In every complex syndrome, elements from several domains constrain what can exist in other domains of the system. An individual born with a phlegmatic temperament, for example, is unlikely to mature into a histrionic adult. An individual whose primary defensive mechanism is intellectualization is more likely to mature into a schizoid than an antisocial. The nature and intensity of the constraints in each of these domains limit the potential number of states that the system can assume at any moment in time; this total configuration of operative domains results in each patient's distinctive pattern of individuality. Equally significant, this pattern of domain problems serves to construct a model for what we term *synergistic treatment approaches,* a key theme to which we turn in Chapter 4.

CHAPTER FOUR

Planning Personality-Guided Treatment

There is reason for dismay with the *DSM*, especially when one observes that many clinicians are content merely to label a patient as "fitting" a category and leaving matters stand at that. The slavish adherence on the part of other clinicians to outmoded and ambiguous categories, and their resistance to changes proposed through systematic research, is further reason for dismay. But these legitimate complaints do not justify "throwing out the baby with the bathwater." The notion of diagnostic categorization should not be abolished if its products have been misused by some, or if they are only partially successful. One need not champion the features of any specific system of categories in order to recognize the merits of classification itself. Nor should we expect that any one system will encompass all the features that might prove useful to psychopathology.

A classification system of diagnostic categories, at best, is like a theory in that it serves to facilitate the search for relevant variables or characteristics. Thus, if a system enables the clinician to deduce characteristics of the patient's makeup or development that are not otherwise easily obtainable, or if they guide the clinician to a particular course of therapy, or alert him or her to potentially serious complications or any other clinical decision-making process, then the system is well worth using.

Once we accept the idea that diagnostic categories may prove useful, the question arises as to whether the system in current use fulfills as many functions as is possible, given our present theoretical and empirical knowledge. If it does not, then we may ask which features of the present system should be retained, which new features can be added to increase the clarity and utility of its syndromes, and how the system may best he reorganized.

Each person possesses a small and distinct group of primary attributes that persist over time and exhibit a high degree of consistency across situations (Mischel, 1984). These enduring (stable) and pervasive (consistent) characteristics are what we search for when we "diagnose" a personality. The multimodal therapist Arnold Lazarus (1981) and we approach the task of assessment from appreciably different perspectives. We follow a theory of personality; he adheres to an atheoretical eclectic model. Both his and our methods intersect in many ways, and their implications point to similar concerns regarding therapy interventions. The specific objectives of personality assessment will differ, of course, in different settings (psychiatric hospitals, outpatient clinics, private practice), but the central objective of all clinical assessment is to gather information that ultimately will be useful in implementing therapy and increasing a patient's well-being.

DIFFICULTIES IN CLINICAL ASSESSMENT

Significant errors and biases by even the most experienced practitioners arise in most fields of clinical science. These problems are especially prominent, however, in psychopathology. Here, clinicians possess few of the objective and quantitative instruments found in other sciences and must depend on less than optimal procedures that are unstandardized, imprecise, and subjective. Different sources of clinical data (patients' account of their illness, the observable syndromes they display, and the facts of their past history) frequently lead to contradictory clinical impressions. Conflicting judgments arise also from the tendency of different examiners to ask different questions, emphasize different features of pathology unequally, and interpret the information they have gathered in idiosyncratic and biased ways. Thus, not only is there considerable difference in the basic data from which clinical analyses are derived, but this difficulty is compounded by a lack of uniformity in clinical procedures and a low reliability in clinical judgment.

Two factors should be kept in mind by the clinician. First, there is no evidence to date indicating the unequivocal superiority of one source or one method for obtaining and interpreting clinical information. Second, there are typical errors and biases that frequently intrude and distort the data of clinical analyses. The precise skills and procedures that produce an excellent clinical study have not been established, but the pitfalls and complications that diminish clinical accuracy are well-known. In this section, we alert the reader further to some of these problems that may complicate the planning of a therapeutic program.

Intrapatient Variability

Humans are capricious creatures; their behaviors, thoughts, and feelings shift from moment to moment. Consequently, the signs of pathology observed in one context or at one point in time may not be displayed in another. In part, this variability signifies differences in the stimulating properties of the environment. To an even greater degree, however, it reflects the complex interaction of myriad internal processes, such as memories, subliminal sensations, and moods, which combine in innumerable ways to create changing surface impressions and clinical pictures.

A defective piece of electronic equipment may be a useful analogy to illustrate this point. A malfunctioning radio may, at one time, sputter and spew static; for no apparent reason, it may squeal and rumble the next; the third time the radio is on, it may perform well but lose its amplification after a few minutes. The changing symptomatology of the radio results from different defective and nondefective components combining in one way the first time, another the second, and so on. In the same manner, the inner moods, memories, and thoughts that activate overt behavior will combine to produce different clinical pictures from one time to another. To complicate matters further, research has shown that seriously disturbed persons display greater intraindividual variability than normals. This marked behavioral inconsistency among patients should warn us against giving excess weight to one-time data sources. Though rare occurrences may be a valuable clue to the patient's pathology, they tend to divert attention away from his or her more prosaic but characteristic style of functioning.

Setting, Procedure, and Timing

Basic to all psychological theory and research is the established fact that behavior is influenced by environmental conditions. Despite this knowledge, clinicians often assume that the data of their clinical assessment were not influenced by the procedures, settings, and timing of their evaluation. The assumption is unjustified; there is ample research to show the many subtle ways in which situational and interpersonal factors do influence clinical data (e.g., Masling, 1960; Sarason, 1954). The questions asked of the patient, the examiner's personality (friendly or reserved), his or her status (intern or senior staff) and physical characteristics (age and sex), the setting (outpatient clinic, hospital ward, private consultation, staff meeting), the clinical procedure (testing or interviews), and the time of evaluation (emergency admission, after drugs, or following hospital adjustment) illustrate some of the many factors that may influence and distort the character of clinical data.

To these objective situational influences, the clinician must consider the relationship among patients' motivations, their expectations, and the context of the evaluation. The behavior and feelings exhibited by patients will reflect such matters as their attitude (e.g., fears of a "mental hospital" or of psychiatrists) and the conditions that prompted the clinical study (e.g., involuntary commitment or hospital discharge planning).

The clinician should keep in mind that patients' behavior, in large measure, is a product of the situation in which they have been observed. The more clinicians are aware of these potential influences, the more certain they can be that their data are representative and their interpretations accurate.

Observational and Theoretical Biases

Psychopathologists differ in their clinical judgments because they have different orientations as to what data should be observed and how these observations should be interpreted. Despite protestations that their judgments are dispassionate appraisals of the patient, clinicians committed to a theoretical viewpoint invariably uncover and emphasize data that are consistent with their preferred theory, whereas characteristics that fit other theoretical biases are overlooked. Furthermore, by probing and asking leading questions, clinicians often evoke responses that support their expectations. Gill and Brenman (1948) described this process:

> If a therapist believes dreams are important in helping a patient, he will show interest in the patient's dreams. Merely asking if the patient has any may result in including many more dreams in the raw data than are gathered by a therapist who is not especially interested in dreams. This is on the grossest level. The subtleties of showing interests in certain kinds of material, often not consciously detected either by therapist or patient, are manifold. They may include a questioning glance, a shifting of visual focus, a well-timed "um-hum," a scarcely perceptible nod, or even a clearing of the throat.

Clearly, what a clinician "sees" often is a product of what he or she expects to see. Other observers may not record the same findings if their perceptions and behaviors have been conditioned by different theoretical beliefs. It should be obvious then, that the more clinicians look at and interpret data from alternative viewpoints, the more comprehensive and potentially accurate will be their analysis.

Interpretive Skill of the Clinician

Not all of the many inferences that clinicians make are valid or useful. They are limited by the scope of their knowledge of human functioning, and that knowledge is restricted by the incomplete state of the science. To compensate for these shortcomings, clinicians draw on an ill-defined "intuitive" sense. Unfortunately, this intuitive process is an elusive and entirely subjective act that can be neither clearly articulated to others nor examined critically.

Given the obscure nature of this intuitive process, and the notable differences in skill even among experienced clinicians, some psychopathologists have suggested that the job of interpretation should be taken out of the hands of the clinician because it can be done more reliably and validly by *actuarial* methods. In the actuarial approach, interpretation is based on statistically demonstrated correlations among such clinical data as test scores, biographical information, and behavior signs on the one hand, and a variety of relevant clinical criteria such as the future course of certain disorders and the response of patients to particular forms of therapy on the other. For example, instead of sitting down, reflecting, and intuitively deciding what certain test scores may mean, the clinician simply looks into a statistical "cookbook" and reads what these scores have been shown to correlate with empirically. With these cookbooks, the task of prediction and decision making is greatly simplified, and the accuracy of interpretations is assured at least of a modicum of validity.

The logic for the statistical or actuarial approach, sketched briefly here, has been convincingly argued by Meehl (1954, 1965) and Sarbin (1943; Sarbin, Taft, & Bailey, 1960). Both men recognize that some clinicians are especially skillful and acknowledge that the actuarial approach may be of fairly limited utility in its present state, but they note that where comparisons of the two methods have been made, the statistical approach is generally superior.

Despite impressive evidence favoring the statistical method, few actuarial formulas have been devised to handle the varied prognostic and therapeutic decisions that clinicians face daily. Furthermore, it is unlikely that all aspects of clinical judgment can be replaced by a statistical equation. Nevertheless, advances in actuarial prediction and decision making continue to be made, and the clinician should utilize the results of this work whenever feasible (Millon, Millon, & Davis, 1994).

PERSONALITY-ORIENTED ASSESSMENT INSTRUMENTS

Current tools for appraising personality and its disorders may be divided into four broad categories. Most popular today are the recently devised *self-report inventories* and *structured clinical interviews*. Although a long-established method of general assessment, the use of personality-oriented *checklists* is a contemporary development. At the other end are the well-established instruments known as *projective techniques*. These latter tools were *not* specifically designed to diagnose personality disorders; however, they can provide useful insights into their intrapsychic dynamics and interpersonal implications.

Self-Report Inventories

The self-report modality of assessment has become the most frequently employed technique for diagnosing and assessing the characteristics of psychopathology. The inventories to be described may be anchored to theory, or may reflect factorially developed empirical procedures, or may stem from careful clinical observation. Whatever origins may have prompted their construction, each of them possesses distinct and separable scales to identify the presence and magnitude of each (or most) of the *DSM* Axis-I and Axis-II disorders.

Millon Clinical Multiaxial Inventory III (MCMI-III).   The MCMI may best be considered an *objective psychodynamic* instrument in that it is composed and administered in a structured and standardized manner but is interpreted by examining the interaction of scale scores and by drawing on clinically established relationships among cognitive processes, interpersonal behaviors, and intrapsychic forces. In this regard, it is akin to the Minnesota Multiphasic Personality Inventory (MMPI) in its item format and administrative procedures, but more like the Rorschach and Thematic Apperception Test (TAT) in its interpretive style and content.

The current MCMI-III consists of 24 clinical scales, as well as three "modifier" scales available for interpretive analysis. The purpose of the modifier indices (Disclosure, Desirability, and Debasement) is to identify distorting tendencies that characterize patients and their responses. The first two clinical sections constitute all of the personality disorder scales, encompassing Axis II of both *DSM-III-R* and *DSM-IV* (i.e., including the appendixed self-defeating/masochistic and sadistic personality disorders of *DSM-III-R* and the depressive personality disorder of *DSM-IV*). The first of these sections (Scales 1 to 8B) appraises what are viewed as the moderately severe personality pathologies, ranging from the Schizoid to the Masochistic; the second section (Scales S, C, and P) represents what Millon views as the more severe or structurally defective personality pathologies, encompassing Schizotypal, Borderline, and Paranoid disorders. The next two sections cover several of the more prevalent Axis I syndromes, ranging from the more moderate to the more severe clinical syndromes. The division between the personality disorder scales on the one hand, and the clinical syndrome scales on the other is intended to make *MCMI* interpretations congruent with the *DSM*'s multiaxial logic. More important, it is especially useful when planning treatment for Axis I syndromes, in that it permits clinicians to understand the place of the syndromes in the context of the patient's specific Axis II personality pattern.

DAPP-BQ Self-Report Inventory.   There are several other, nontheoretically guided inventories that appear promising but for which supporting empirical literature is rather modest.

A thoughtful and well-developed new instrument is the Dimensional Assessment of Personality Pathology-Basic Questionnaire (DAPP-BQ) constructed by Livesley (1987) and his associates (Livesley, Jackson, & Schroeder, 1989; Livesley & Schroeder, 1990). After an extensive literature review, Livesley compiled an initial list of descriptors for each *DSM-III-R* diagnosis. Consensual judgments by knowledgeable clinicians were used to identify the most prototypical features of each diagnosis. A series of trait categories was then developed based on these prototypical features. Ultimately, each disorder was defined by a cluster of traits; for example, schizoid disorder was composed of clusters such as low affiliation, avoidant attachment, and restricted affective expression.

Wisconsin Personality Disorders Inventory (WISPI). One of the more innovative approaches to interpersonal theory is represented in L.S. Benjamin's (1974, 1984) Structural Analysis of Social Behavior (SASB). M. Klein et al. (1993) reported on the use of Benjamin's interpersonal model to guide the development of the 360-item WISPI. In a multistage strategy similar to that recommended by Loevinger (1957), interpersonal descriptors were developed for each of the *DSM-III* and *DSM-III-R* Axis II criteria.

Millon Index of Personality Styles (MIPS). Whereas the MCMI is designed to identify the personality disorders more or less directly, the MIPS (Millon, Millon, et al., 1994) focuses its scales on constructs that underlie these personality types, that is, the *latent elements* that combine to give rise to them. This 180-item inventory, useful for appraising personality *styles* as well as disorders, groups its scales to correspond directly to Millon's undergirding theory (Millon, 1990).

Structured Interview Schedules

Structured and semistructured interviews have often been thought of as the criterion standard in psychopathology. Together with the specification of diagnostic criteria and the adoption of the prototypal model in *DSM-III,* the development of interview schedules marks a watershed in the history of measurement in psychopathology.

Structured Clinical Interview for DSM (SCID). Developed originally by Spitzer, Williams, and Gibbon, (1987), each of the 120 items in this semistructured interview, phrased to accord with the language employed in the *DSM* diagnostic criteria, is usually included in a broad-based schedule designed to assess many of the Axis 1 syndromes as well. The clinician uses a 4-point measuring scale for appraising the degree to which the characteristic being examined is present. Specific probing questions are recommended to explore the extent to which the patient possesses adequate information concerning the item in question.

Structured Interview for DSM Personality Disorders IV (SIPD-IV). The SIPD-IV (Pfohl, Blum, Zimmerman, & Stangl, 1989, 1997) is a semistructured interview of approximately 160 items geared to the criteria of the *DSM-IV.* Questions are grouped into 17 topical sections, not into the *DSM* personality disorders. Questions appear at the beginning of each section; the diagnostic criteria to which they relate appear at the end. To improve interrater reliability, a 3-point scale is listed below each criterion to help anchor its level of severity.

Interviewers familiar with the instrument can administer it in 60–90 minutes. If an informant is available, 15–30 minutes of further inquiry may be necessary. Transcription of scores to the summary sheet of the interview booklet and scoring consume another 20–30 minutes. Together, these make for a minimum of about an hour and a half to a maximum of two and a half hours to complete the entire interview process.

Checklists

Checklists blur the boundaries between personality scales and diagnostic criteria. Because the intent of a checklist is to assist in making a typological or diagnostic decision, checklist items typically exist at a higher level of inference than those of self-report inventories, which may be very specific or act-oriented. In this sense, checklist items approach diagnostic criteria. A checklist, however, differs from *DSM* criteria in two important ways. First, a checklist usually provides more attributes or items than the *DSM*. Second, unlike the *DSM* personality disorders' criteria sets, these attributes or items are usually subjected to some kind of psychometric refinement and thus exhibit respectable internal consistency.

One checklist will be noted below owing to its special character. It is similar to other *simple adjective* checklists, quite popular in studies of personality traits in general. It also has the uniqueness of addressing a number of the *clinical domains* that will be presented later in this chapter. It encompasses all personality disorders and has a sound empirical history supporting its utility, especially for research endeavors.

Millon Personality Diagnostic Checklist (MPDC).   Throughout this chapter, we have stressed the need to operationalize person traits across all of the clinical domains in which styles and disorders are expressed. Eight structural and functional domains have been identified to serve as a basis of analysis. The MPDC is grouped into several categories that offer diagnosticians the opportunity to systematically assess patients in five of these eight domains: expressive acts, interpersonal conduct, cognitive style, self-image, and mood/temperament. The other three domains proved to be too difficult and inferential for clinicians to utilize with any degree of reliability or comfort.

Clinicians complete the MPDC in two stages. First, the entire checklist is surveyed, and those items judged to be characteristic of the client are marked in the first circle next to each item. Most clinicians mark between 35 and 50 items when appraising a patient they know reasonably well. Next, the marked items are reread, and for those judged "most prominent," their second circle is also marked.

Projective Techniques

Despite numerous assaults of an empirical and methodological nature, projective techniques such as the Rorschach and TAT have not only endured, but flourished, firmly grounded in the idiographic tradition. Like interviews and self-reports, projective techniques may be described as useful but not necessary for a complete personal assessment.

As with all measurement procedures, projectives involve potential gains and losses. The gain is comprehensiveness: projectives are explicitly intended to access inferential aspects of the person that exist outside of self-awareness, including the domains of object representations, regulatory mechanisms, and morphologic organization. The loss is one of precision: to the extent that the clinician's interpretation of projective material is constrained by factors outside the clinician's own awareness, the end results become as projective as the material to be interpreted. The very open-endedness that makes projectives so clinically rich in turn creates interpretational ambiguities that are inherently problematic.

PERSONALITY-GUIDED TREATMENT GOALS

Does a theoretical grounding for configurally different persons contain guidelines that can inform person-focused psychotherapy? The evolutionary principles and clinical domains (detailed later) that underlie psychopathology should, in our judgment, provide a useful framework for identifying both the goals and methods of personality-guided treatment. Notable here is the goal of balancing uneven polarities, and the use of techniques that counter thoughts, emotions, and behaviors that perpetuate the patient's difficulties (Millon & Davis, 1996a).

Balancing Polarities

As noted in Millon's model (1990), a theoretical basis is developed from the principles of evolution, to which three polarities are considered fundamental: the pain-pleasure, the active-passive, and the self-other. As a general philosophy, specific treatment techniques are selected as tactics to achieve polarity-oriented balances. Depending on the pathological polarity to be modified and the integrative treatment sequence one has in mind, the goals of therapy are (a) to overcome *pleasure deficiencies* in schizoids, avoidants, and depressive styles/disorders; (b) to reestablish *interpersonally imbalanced* polarity disturbances in dependents, histrionics, narcissists, and antisocials; (c) to undo the *intrapsychic conflicts* in sadists, compulsives, masochists, and negativists; and (d) to reconstruct the *structural defects* in schizotypal, borderline, and paranoid persons (Millon & Davis, 1996a). These are to be achieved by the use of modality tactics that are optimally suited to the clinical domains in which these pathologies are expressed (see the section below on domain assessment).

As we proceed from chapter to chapter in this text, we provide a synopsis of what may be considered the primary goals of balancing polarities according to the theoretical model. For example, therapeutic efforts responsive to problems in the pain-pleasure polarity have as their essential aim life enhancement (increased pleasure) among schizoid, avoidant, and depressive personalities. Given the probability of intrinsic deficits in this area, schizoids and depressives might require the use of pharmacologic agents designed to lift their melancholic or to activate their apathetic mood/temperament. Increments in life enhancement for avoidants, however, are likely to depend more on cognitive techniques designed to alter their alienated self-image, intrapsychic procedures to expose memories sequestered in their imagination, and behavioral methods oriented to counter their aversive interpersonal conduct. Equally important for avoidants is reducing their hypersensitivities, especially to social rejection (decreased pain); this may be achieved by coordinating the use of medications for their characteristic anguished mood/temperament with behavioral and cognitive methods geared to desensitization.

Among imbalances in the passive-active polarity, efforts may be made to increase the capacity and skills for taking a less reactive and more proactive role in dealing with life affairs (decreased passive, increased active). This would be a major goal of treatment for schizoids and depressives, for example. Interpersonal imbalances in the self-other polarity, found among narcissists and antisocials, for example, suggest that a major aim of their treatment is a reduction in their predominant self-focus and a corresponding augmentation of their sensitivity to the needs of others (increased other, decreased self). Among those with anxiety and somatoform syndromes, a major objective of therapy is to desensitize feelings and stimulate greater self-interest. For the intrapsychic conflicts that underlie the behavior and feelings of obsessive-compulsives, attention should be directed to help them recognize the nature of their ambivalences and to assist them in overcoming their inner disharmony. Similarly, the pain-pleasure discordance that undergirds the difficulties of anxious depressives will require techniques to reverse these pathological inclinations. More will be said of these "balancing" methods in each of the ensuing chapters.

Countering Perpetuating Tendencies

Continuity in personality and psychopathology may be attributed in great measure to the stability of constitutional factors and the deeply ingrained character of early experiential learning. Every behavior, attitude, and feeling that is currently exhibited is a perpetuation, a remnant of the past that persists into the present. Not only do these residuals passively shape the present by temporal precedence, if nothing else, but they insidiously distort and transform ongoing life events to make them duplicates of the past. It is this self-perpetuating re-creative process that becomes so problematic in treating psychopathology. In other words, and as we have said previously, *psychopathology is itself pathogenic*. It sets into motion *new* life experiences that are further pathology-producing.

A major goal of personality-guided psychotherapy is to stop these perpetuating inclinations, that is, to prevent the continued exacerbation and intensification of a patient's established problematic habits and attitudes. Much of what therapists must do is reverse self-pathogenesis, the intruding into the present of erroneous expectations, the perniciousness of maladaptive interpersonal conduct, and the repetitive establishing of new, self-entrapping "vicious circles." To achieve these "counteracting" effects, for example, many *dysthymics* should be guided to reduce their self-deprecating attitudes. *Dependent* persons should be encouraged to acquire adult skills. Most *avoidant* persons should be taught to reverse their habitual social detachments. *Paranoid* persons should be assisted in diminishing their fearful assumptions about the malice of others. *Depressive* persons should be helped to undo their pessimistic expectations, to enhance their mood with antidepressants, and to reappraise their negative assessments of their self-worth. Similarly, the repugnant attitudes and deceptive behaviors of those with *antisocial* patterns should be confronted and neutralized. *Sadistic* persons must be shown how to control their abusive inclinations and to identify the precipitants of their acting-out. In each of the preceding, the goal of the therapist is not only to dislodge these provocative and aggravating actions, attitudes, and feelings, but to stop them from generating new difficulties.

CLINICAL SYNDROME TREATMENT GOALS

In Part II of this text, we survey various complex clinical syndromes: phobias, conversions, anxiety, obsessive-compulsions, dysthymias, and somatoforms. With minor exceptions, this grouping corresponds to the official *DSM-IV* Axis I classification of syndromes.

Facilitating the process of dealing with complex syndromes are procedures of environmental management, biophysical treatment, supportive therapy, and counseling.

Wherever appropriate and feasible, the therapist should seek to alter the environmental conditions that prompted and now aggravate the patient's syndromal reaction; for example, in infancy, this may lead to the removal of the child from an unhealthy setting to a benevolent foster home. Not to be overlooked among available treatment measures are various biophysical techniques; for example, psychopharmacologic agents may be of immediate benefit in calming anxieties generated in civilian catastrophes or in reducing turbulent emotions following a tension-producing situation. Of note along these lines is the benefit of electroconvulsive therapy in shortening the duration of severe depressive syndromes.

Supportive therapy is often needed to assuage patients' anxieties and to shore up their flagging coping capacities. For example, a simple dysthymic reaction to a divorce may be abbreviated by the opportunity to share and discuss one's distress with a comforting and reassuring therapist. Counseling along practical lines often helps patients reorient their attitudes and plan their future in ways more congenial to mental health. For example, in both adolescent syndromes, where patients may be struggling to reorganize their self-image to meet the crisis of changing roles, a wise counselor may suggest useful future directions that are consonant with their past and may take the "sting" out of this period of painful transition.

Pharmacologic agents have become increasingly accurate in tailoring changes in patient's neurochemically driven symptoms. Various behavioral techniques, for example, systematic desensitization, seek through cognitive suggestion to pair neutral feelings and attitudes, such as relaxation, with formerly provocative stimuli. Similarly, aversive conditioning methods have been used to associate negative consequences with responses that previously were positively rewarding, for example, drugs such as Antabuse and a variety of emetics are given to alcoholics to produce intense physical discomfort in conjunction with drinking; repetition of this experience will condition pain rather than pleasure with the habit, thereby fostering its extinction. Behavior modification techniques appear especially promising as instruments for extinguishing or controlling simple syndromes and in shaping more adaptive alternative responses. Although the durability of and the ability to generalize from these beneficial effects have only recently been adequately researched, these techniques are among the most encouraging treatment approaches for both simple as well as complex syndromes. Much more will be said about all treatment methods in later chapters.

Group methods may be employed with moderate success in simple reactions that originated as a function of social imitation or that have been reinforced by group activities. Thus, alcoholics and drug addicts often benefit by extinction techniques generated in group settings, for example, Alcoholics Anonymous or Synanon for narcotic addicts. The special value of these group procedures is that the individual's habit is negatively reinforced in a setting that previously encouraged and provided positive reinforcements for it.

Cognitive, behavioral, psychodynamic, and interpersonal approaches are *all* likely to demonstrate some level of therapeutic efficacy over waiting-list controls. Even though consistently channeled through a particular bias and directed at a *particular* symptom domain, many interventions will gather enough momentum to eventually change significant portions of the entire person. In cases where the whole complex of psychic processes is reconfigured, it is not likely to be the intervention per se that produces so vast a change, but a synergistic interaction between a syndrome intervention and the personologic context in which that intervention takes place. Such changes occur, but they are often serendipitous rather than planned; it is the interdependent nature of the organismic system that compensates for the inadequacy of a single domain focus, except among simple reactions where only one or two domains are the objective. The capacity of systems to spread the effect of any input throughout its entire infrastructure is likely to be a principle reason why no major school of therapy (i.e., behavioral, cognitive, intrapsychic, biological, and interpersonal) has yet been able to consistently demonstrate an intrinsic superiority across all disorders.

Several criteria were used to select and develop the trait domains we have included in this chapter: (a) that they be varied in the features they embody, that is, not be limited to just behaviors or cognitions, but instead encompass a full range of clinically relevant characteristics; (b) that they *parallel* if not correspond to many of our profession's current therapeutic modalities (e.g., cognitively oriented techniques for altering dysfunctional beliefs, group treatment procedures for modifying interpersonal conduct); and (c) that they not only be coordinated to the official *DSM* schema of personality and syndromal prototypes, but also that most syndromes and personality patterns be able to be characterized by a distinctive characteristic within each clinical domain.

Let us recall the *symptom domain* clinical rating MPDC instrument. These domains will be elaborated shortly to illustrate their general utility. In addition to expanding the diagnostic criteria of *DSM-IV* (Millon, 1984, 1990), this approach seeks to advance the development of *clinician judgments as a mode of personality assessment*. Specifically, they comprise descriptive attributes in various clinical domains (e.g., interpersonal conduct, cognitive style) within which the polarities may be expressed and with which all of the psychopathologies may be systematically compared.

In conducting a domain-oriented assessment, especially for both simple and complex syndromes, clinicians should be careful not to regard each domain as a concretized, independent entity, and thereby fall into a naïve operationism. As discussed with regard to complex syndromes, each domain is a legitimate but highly contextualized part of an integrated whole, one absolutely necessary if the integrity of the organism is to be maintained. Nevertheless, individuals differ with respect to which and how many domains of their pathology are expressed. Patients vary not only in degree to which their domain characteristics approximate a pathologic syndrome or personality disorder, but also in the extent to which the influences of each domain shape the patient's overall functioning. Conceptualizing each form of psychopathology as a system, we should recognize that different parts of the system may be salient for different individuals, even where those individuals share a diagnosis.

This approach becomes more tangible in the following paragraphs outlining the major clinical domains, even though they may be manifested singularly, or in complex syndromes, or in personality disorders. No less important, we outline their covariant and parallel treatment modalities. For the present, our focus is on characterizing each of eight clinical domains and illustrating the eight therapeutic modalities that parallel them.

Expressive Behaviors

These attributes relate to the observables seen at the *behavioral level* of data and are usually recorded by noting how the patient acts.

Behavioral assessment domains.   Through inference, observations of overt behavior enable us to deduce either what patients unknowingly reveal about themselves or, often conversely, what they wish others to think or to know about them. The range and character of these expressive behaviors are not only wide and diverse, but they convey both distinctive and worthwhile clinical information: from communicating a sense of personal incompetence to exhibiting general defensiveness, to demonstrating a disciplined self-control, and so on. This domain of clinical data is likely to be especially productive in differentiating patients on the passive-active polarity of Millon's (1990) theoretical model.

Behavioral methods seem especially suitable to the elimination of problematic behaviors and the creation of more effective adaptations.

Listed are several brief phrases developed for the MPDC that have been researched for purposes of characterizing the *expressive behavior* of patients. Included are clinical descriptors that reflect the major observable attributes of clinical syndromes and the personality patterns:

Phlegmatic and lacking in spontaneity
Appears lethargic and lacking in vitality
Exhibits psychomotor retardation
Anxiously anticipates ridicule/
    humiliation
Scans environment for potential threats
Is being taxed by ordinary activities
Has difficulty doing things on his/
    her own

Places self in inferior or demeaning
    positions
Fails to complete tasks beneficial to self
Self-sabotaging and self-debasing
Uncooperative, contrary, and stubborn
Alternately obstructive, then acquiescent
Deliberately does poor job or works slowly
Procrastinates and puts off things

Parallel behavioral therapies.   As stated previously, behaviorists contend that "other" therapeutic approaches are method-oriented rather than problem-oriented. Nonbehaviorists are seen to proceed in a uniform and complicating fashion regardless of the particular character of the patient's difficulty, utilizing the same "psychoanalytic" or "cognitive" procedure with all forms and varieties of pathology. Not only do behaviorists claim that behavioral approaches are flexible and problem-oriented, but there is no "fixed" technique in pure behavior therapy. As we see it, behavioral techniques are extremely useful in counteracting simple clinical reactions that manifest themselves in overt behaviors. They distinguish the elements of each simple reaction and then fashion a procedure designed specifically to effect changes only in that problem. For example, if the patient complains of acute anxiety attacks, procedures are designed to eliminate just that symptom, and therapy is completed when it has been removed.

Interpersonal/Relational Conduct

A patient's style of relating to others may be captured in a number of ways, such as how his or her actions impact on others, intended or otherwise; the attitudes that underlie, prompt, and give shape to these actions; the methods by which he or she engages others to meet his or her needs; and his or her way of coping with social tensions and conflicts. Extrapolating from these observations, the clinician may construct an image of how the patient functions in relation to others, be it antagonistically, respectfully, aversively, secretively, and so on.

Interpersonal assessment domains.   Tenets of interpersonal theory, especially as encoded in the circumplex representation, make this taxonomy a promising one for the assessment of both personality traits and clusters and clinical syndromes. According to its most basic conception, each person constricts the response repertoire of others in order to evoke specifically those responses that confirm his or her perception of self and the world (Kiesler, 1982, 1997). Each party in the interpersonal system is co-opted by the other in an effort to elicit validation. Together, the parties must find a stable system state that mutually confirms and thereby maintains and perpetuates their respective self-concepts. These system states can be based on either reciprocity (on the vertical axis) or correspondence (on the horizontal axis).

Usually presented two-dimensionally, the circumplex can also be visualized as a bivariate distribution with increasing densification toward the center and increasing sparsity toward the edges. Healthy or flexible interpersonal styles appear as balanced patterns within the circle. Individuals usually possess a full range of styles by which to relate to others, regardless of the kinds of others with whom they find themselves involved. Psychic pathology can be expressed geometrically through distortions of the healthy circular and concentric pattern.

The interpersonal style of the schizoid, avoidant, dependent, histrionic, narcissistic, and antisocial personalities seem better assessed by the circumplex than do compulsive, borderline, negativistic (passive-aggressive), paranoid, and schizotypal individuals (Pincus & Wiggins, 1989). We conclude, then, that any assessment of clinical syndromes and personality that is anchored *only* in the interpersonal domain, though informative, must be regarded as incomplete. Clinicians of an interpersonal bent must balance the increased specificity gained by using an exclusively interpersonally oriented instrument with the knowledge that the paradigm itself is acknowledged to be an incomplete representation of psychic pathology.

Listed are several brief phrases from the MPDC that have been researched for purposes of characterizing the *interpersonal/relational* conduct of patients. They are grouped roughly to correspond with the features of several simple and complex clinical syndromes, as well as personality patterns:

Seems socially aloof and remote

Has no close friends or intimates

Has few social desires or human interests

Prefers peripheral roles and solitary activities

Appears indifferent to praise or criticism

Socially pan-anxious and fearfully guarded

Has lost interest in pleasurable social activities

Feels helpless or uncomfortable when alone

Creates attractive but changing social façades

Actively seeks attention and solicits praise

Seductively flirtatious and exhibitionistic

Self-centered and socially inconsiderate

Expects special favors without reciprocating

Constantly seeks recognition and admiration

Parallel interpersonal therapies.   As noted in Chapter 1, there are three major variants of treatment that focus on the interpersonal domain. The first engages one patient exclusively at a time in a dyadic patient-therapist medium, but centers its attentions primarily on the patient's relationships with others; these techniques are known as *interpersonal psychotherapy*. The second set of techniques assembles an assortment of patients together in a group so that their habitual styles of relating to others can be observed and analyzed as the interactions among the participants unfold; these techniques are known as *group psychotherapy*. The third variant is *family therapy*, where established and ostensibly problematic relationships are evaluated and treated.

To paraphrase Kiesler (1997), the essential problems of individuals reside in the person's recurrent transactions with significant others. These stem largely from disordered, inappropriate, or inadequate communications, and result from failing to attend and/or not correct the unsuccessful and self-defeating nature of these communications. The interpersonal approach centers its attention on the individual's closest relationships, notably current family interactions, the family of origin, past and present love affairs and friendships, as well as neighborhood and work relations. It is the patient's habitual interactive and hierarchical roles in these social systems that are the focus of interpersonal therapy. The dyadic treatment interaction, despite its uniqueness, is seen as paralleling other venues of human communication. The interpersonal therapist becomes sensitized to the intrusions of the patient's habitual styles of interaction by the manner in which he or she "draws out" or "pulls" the therapist's feelings and attitudes. It is these evocative responses that provides a good indication of how the patient continues to relate to others. This transactive process mirrors in many ways what psychoanalysts refer to in their concepts of transference and countertransference. More will be said on these matters when we later discuss treatment modalities oriented to modifying the patient's object relationships.

Once a past history assessment has been undertaken and its elements clarified, the task of the interpersonal therapist is to help patients identify the persons with whom they are currently having difficulties, what these difficulties are, and whether there are ways they can be resolved or made more satisfactory. Problems in the patient's current environment should be stated explicitly—for example, being intimidated on the job, arguing over trivia with a spouse, missing old friends—and shown to be derivations from past experiences and relationships.

Developed as a comprehensive modality of interpersonal treatment more than a half-century ago (e.g., Slavson, 1943), the impact of *group psychotherapy* in molding and sustaining interpersonal behaviors has been thoroughly explored in recent decades. Clearly, there are several advantages to group and also to family therapies. Perhaps most significant is the fact that the patient acquires new behaviors in a setting that is the same or similar to his or her "natural" interpersonal world; relating to family or peer group members is a more realistic experience than that of the hierarchic therapist-patient dyad. It is easier to generalize to the extratherapeutic world what one learns in family and peer-group settings because these are closer to "reality" than is the individual treatment setting.

Cognitive Modes

How the patient focuses and allocates attention, encodes and processes information, organizes thoughts, makes attributions, and communicates reactions and ideas to others represent data at the *cognitive* level, and are among the most useful indices to the clinician of the patient's distinctive way of functioning. By synthesizing these signs and symptoms, it may be possible to identify indications of what may be termed an impoverished style, distracted thinking, cognitive flightiness, constricted thought, and so on.

Cognitive assessment domains.   Beck and Freeman (1990a) have made a thoughtful contribution by illuminating the relation of maladaptive beliefs constituting the cognitive domain to complex syndromes and personality disorders. The Belief Questionnaire (1990b) is the designation they have used for the unpublished inventory developed toward this end. The questionnaire comprises nine scales, each 14 items long, assessing the avoidant, dependent, passive-aggressive, obsessive-compulsive, antisocial, narcissistic, histrionic, schizoid, and paranoid personality patterns. Unfortunately, no scales are provided for the borderline and schizotypal disorders, in spite of the fact that these disorders typically are clinically severe. While the MIPS (Millon, Millon, et al., 1994) is not explicitly intended for clinical analysis, it is nevertheless representative of the kinds of constructs that might be brought to bear to assess complex syndromes and personality functioning in the cognitive domain. It should be noted that this instrument relates to the coping *style* or *mode* of thinking, rather than to the content (beliefs, expectations) of what may be "known."

As noted in Chapter 1, and in contrast to behaviorists and in common with intrapsychic therapists, cognitivists place heavy emphasis on internal processes that mediate overt actions. Cognitivists also differ from both behavior and intrapsychic therapists with regard to which events and processes they consider central to pathogenesis and treatment. Cognitivists concern themselves with the reorientation of consciously discordant feelings and readily identifiable erroneous beliefs, and not to the modification of narrow behaviors or to disgorging the past and its associated unconscious derivatives.

Listed are several brief phrases from the MPDC that have been employed for purposes of characterizing the *cognitive mode* of patients:

Withdraws into reveries to fulfill needs
Broods about past and worries about
    future
Exhibits ingrained pessimistic outlook
Anticipates future difficulty and
    disappointment
Pollyanna attitude toward difficulties
Preoccupied with fears of being alone
Easily persuaded and gullible

Drawn to violence, injury, firearms, etc.
Unimaginative and cognitively
    constricted
Readily upset by the unfamiliar
Indecisive, can't make decisions
Preoccupied with lists, details, rules, etc.
Overly conscientious about matters of
    morality
Tends to be skeptical and cynical

Parallel cognitive therapies.   Given their emphasis on conscious attitudes and perceptions, cognitive therapists are inclined to follow an insight-expressive rather than an action-suppressive treatment process. Both cognitive and intrapsychic therapists employ the insight-expressive approach, but the focus of their explorations differs, at least in theory. Cognitivists attend to dissonant assumptions and expectations that can be consciously acknowledged by an examination of the patient's everyday relationships and activities. Therapists may not only assume authority for deciding the objectives of treatment, but may confront the patient with the irrationalities of his or her thinking; moreover, they may employ intimidating tactics to indoctrinate the patient with a value system that is considered beneficial. For example, there is the practice of *exposing* the patient's erroneous or irrational attitudes and *imposing* a particular philosophy of life in its stead. Of interest in this regard are the diametrically opposite philosophies among current cognitively oriented therapists.

As briefly noted in Chapter 1, modern *cognitive* therapy has been most clearly formulated by Ellis (1958, 1962, 1967) and Beck and Freeman (1990a), although their respective origins can be traced to the writings of earlier thinkers.

In what he terms *rational-emotive therapy*, Ellis (1967) considers the primary objective of therapy to be countering patients' tendency to perpetuate their difficulties through illogical and negative thinking. By reiterating these unrealistic and self-defeating beliefs in a self-dialogue, patients constantly reaffirm their irrationality and aggravate their distress. To overcome these implicit but pervasive attitudes, the therapist confronts patients with them and induces patients to think about them consciously and concertedly and to "attack them" forcefully and unequivocally until they no longer influence behavior. By revealing and assailing these beliefs and by "commanding" the patient to engage in activities which run counter to them, their hold on the patient's life is broken and new directions become possible.

The other highly regarded cognitive approach has been developed by Beck and his associates (Beck & Freeman, 1990). Central to Beck's approach is the concept of *schemata,* that is, specific rules that govern information processing and behavior. To Beck, the disentangling and clarification of these schemata lies at the heart of therapeutic work with psychopathology. They persist, despite their dysfunctional consequences, owing largely to the fact that they enable the patient to find ways to extract short-term benefits from them, thereby diverting the patient from pursuing more effective, long-term solutions. As with other sophisticated therapists, Beck emphasizes the therapist-patient relationship as a central element in the therapeutic process. As he notes further, considerable "artistry" is involved in unraveling the origins of the patient's beliefs and in exploring the meaning of significant past events.

Self-Image

One major configuration emerges during development to impose a measure of sameness on an otherwise fluid environment: the perception of self-as-object, a distinct, ever-present, and identifiable "I" or "me."

Self-image assessment domains.   Self-identity stems largely from conceptions formed at a cognitive level. The self is especially significant in that it provides a stable anchor to serve as a guidepost and to give continuity to changing experience. Most persons have an implicit sense of who they are, but differ greatly in the clarity, accuracy, and complexity (Millon, 1986a) of their self-introspections. Several instruments may aid in the identification of differences in self-image, including the Ego Identity Scale (EIS) and the Rosenberg Self-Esteem Scale (RSES) (Corcoran & Fischer, 1987).

The character and valuation of the self-image are often problematic, such as an unhappy and dismaying self-reality, seen in the *avoidant's* feeling of being alienated, the *depressive's* image of worthlessness, and the *negativist's* sense of self-discontent. On the other hand, there are those whose self-image is one of complacence, as is seen in the *schizoid,* or that of being gregarious among *histrionics* or admirable among *narcissists.* Thus, self-image, despite the many particulars of its character, appears to be predominantly either of a positive or a negative quality.

Listed are several brief phrases from the MPDC that have been helpful for purposes of characterizing the *self-image* of patients:

Sees self as socially isolated

Feels rejected and unwanted by others

Reports feelings of aloneness and emptiness

Feels self-pitying and sorry for self

Sees self as inept and/or fragile

Fears losing powers of self-determination

Seeks to be personally autonomous and unencumbered

Belittles own aptitudes and competencies

Notably lacking in self-confidence

Viewed as vain and self-indulgent

Has sense of high self-worth

Exaggerates achievements and talents

Especially fearful of making errors

Values restraint, prudence, and emotional control

Parallel self-image therapies. We turned in Chapter 1 to those self-actualization therapists whose orientation is to "free" the patient to develop a more positive and confident image of self-worth. Liberated in this manner, patients ostensibly learn to act in ways that are "right" for them, and thereby enable them to "actualize" their inherent potentials. To promote these objectives, the therapist views events from the patient's frame of reference and conveys both a "caring" attitude and a genuine respect for the patient's worth as a human being.

According to Carl Rogers (1942, 1951, 1961, 1967), patient "growth" is a product neither of special treatment procedures nor professional know-how; rather, it emerges from the quality and character of the therapeutic relationship. More specifically, it occurs as a consequence of attitudes expressed on the part of the therapist, notably *genuineness* and *unconditional positive regard.*

Also suitable for those who have experienced the anguish of a chronically troubled life are the philosophies and techniques of modern-day *existential therapists,* who seek to enable patients to deal with their unhappiness realistically yet in a constructive and positive manner. The existential school possesses a less sanguine view of humans' inherent fate than do Rogerians, believing that one must struggle to find a valued meaning to life; therapy, then, attempts to strengthen the patient's capacity to choose an "authentic" existence. *Self-actualizing therapists* of this latter persuasion are committed to the view that one must confront and accept the inevitable dilemmas of life if one is to achieve a measure of "authentic" self-realization. Mutual acceptance and self-revelation enables patients to find an authentic meaning to their existence, despite the profound and inescapable contradictions that life presents. These existentially oriented self-image therapies may be especially suitable for psychopathologies in which life has been a series of alienations and unhappiness, for example, avoidants, depressives, and so on. By contrast, the underlying assumption of the more humanistically oriented self-actualizing therapies, including client-centered, experiential, and Gestalt, is that we may have been too harsh with ourselves, tending to blame and judge our actions more severely than is necessary.

Intrapsychic Objects, Mechanisms, and Morphology

As noted previously, significant experiences from the past leave an inner imprint, a structural residue composed of memories, attitudes, and affects that serve as a substrate of dispositions for perceiving and reacting to life's ongoing events.

Intrapsychic assessment domains.   Analogous to the various organ systems of which the body is composed, both the character and substance of these internalized representations of significant figures and relationships of the past can be differentiated and analyzed for clinical purposes. Variations in the nature and content of this inner world can be associated with one or another complex syndrome or personality pattern and lead us to employ descriptive terms to represent them, such as shallow, vexatious, undifferentiated, concealed, and irreconcilable.

Although there are numerous informal procedures for decoding the presence and character of the inner template of *object representations,* there are few formalized procedures designed for this purpose. A potentially useful formal tool, one that focuses on object-relations characteristics among adolescents, can be adapted for use with adults as well. This instrument (Levine, Green, & Millon, 1986), called the Separation-Individuation Test of Adolescence (SITA), includes six scales: nurturance-symbiosis, engulfment-anxiety, separation-anxiety, need-denial, self-centeredness, and healthy-separation.

Listed are several brief phrases from the MPDC that have been employed for purposes of characterizing the *object representations* of patients:

Possesses strong resentments	Recurrent splittings among clashing
Possesses few tender affects	needs
Has paucity of sentimental memories	Has antithetical emotions and attitudes
Only socially approved actions	Has intense, conflict-ridden memories
permitted	Exhibits numerous illusory ideas
Memories are precisely arranged	Harbors deeply held attitudes
Forbidden impulses are tightly bound	Exhibits unyielding percepts and beliefs
Possesses concealed inner objects	Possesses unalterable inner objects

Although mechanisms of self-protection, need gratification, and conflict resolution are consciously recognized at times, they represent data derived primarily from intrapsychic sources. Because *regulatory mechanisms* also are internal processes, they are even more difficult to discern and describe than processes that are anchored a bit closer to the observable world. As such, they are not directly amenable to assessment by self-reflective appraisal in pure form, but only as derivatives many levels removed from their core conflicts and their dynamic regulation. By definition, dynamic regulatory mechanisms co-opt and transform both internal and external realities before they can enter conscious awareness in a robust and unaltered form. When chronically enacted, they often perpetuate a sequence of events that intensifies the very problems they were intended to circumvent.

Great care must be taken not to challenge or undo these intrapsychic mechanisms that regulate and balance the inner psychic system of a patient. Therapists must appraise the character of these regulatory functions so they can be quickly identified and handled in as beneficial a manner as possible. Moreover, these regulatory/defensive mechanisms may restrict the patient from dealing with difficulties in a rational and honest fashion. Unfortunately, no organizing principle has yet been found by which a periodic table or taxonomy of *defense mechanisms* might be rationally constructed (Perry & Cooper, 1989; Vaillant, 1971) and thereby put on a nonarbitrary basis. Consequently, those mechanisms ultimately selected for measurement may be conceptualized through disparate orientations and at diverse levels of abstraction, as the history of psychodynamic literature illustrates.

Although the measurement of defense mechanisms has improved through content objectification and specification, current procedures still leave something to be desired. Because the size of the correlation coefficient that can be achieved between measures is limited by their reliabilities, it is likely that external validity of defensive measures will remain more difficult to establish than that of self-report inventories.

Listed are several brief phrases from the MPDC that have been employed for purposes of characterizing the *regulatory mechanisms* employed by patients:

Utilizes introjection mechanism

Inseparable bond felt between self and another

Jettisons any independent views

Unable to cope with adult conflicts

Is firmly devoted to another

Regularly alters self-presentations

Creates a succession of changing façades

Expresses resentments by substitute means

Behaves in a forgetful manner

Displays reasonableness when anger is justified

Retracts or reverses previous acts

Nullifies assumed misdeeds or "evil thoughts"

Retreats under stress to earlier levels

Utilizes regression mechanisms

The overall architecture that serves as a framework for an individual's psychic interior may display weakness in its structural cohesion, exhibit deficient coordination among its components, and possess few mechanisms to maintain balance and harmony, regulate internal conflicts, or mediate external pressures; the concept of *morphologic organization* refers to the structural strength, interior congruity, and functional efficacy of the overall personality system. *Organization* of the mind is a concept almost exclusively derived from inferences at the intrapsychic level of analysis, one akin to and employed in conjunction with current psychoanalytic notions such as borderline and psychotic *levels,* but this usage tends to be limited, relating essentially to quantitative degrees of integrative pathology, not to qualitative variations in either integrative structure or configuration. *Stylistic* variants of this structural attribute may be employed to characterize each of the complex syndromes or personality disorder prototypes; their distinctive organizational attributes are represented with descriptors such an inchoate, disjoined, and compartmentalized.

Morphological structures represent deeply embedded and relatively enduring templates of imprinted memories, attitudes, needs, fears, conflicts, and so on, which guide experience and transform the nature of ongoing life events. Psychic structures are architectural in form. Moreover, they have an orienting and preemptive effect in that they alter the character of action and the impact of subsequent experiences in line with preformed inclinations and expectancies. By selectively lowering thresholds for transactions that are consonant with either constitutional proclivities or early learnings, one often experiences future events as variations of the past. Of course, the residuals of the past do more than passively contribute their share to the present. By temporal precedence, if nothing else, they guide, shape, or distort the character of current events and objective realities.

For purposes of definition, morphological organization represents structural domains that can be conceived as *substrates and action dispositions of a quasi-permanent nature.* Possessing a network of interconnecting pathways, this organization contains a framework in which the internalized residues of the past are cast. These structures often serve to close the organism off to novel interpretations of the world and tend to limit the possibilities of expression to those that have already become prepotent. Their preemptive and channeling character plays an important role in perpetuating the maladaptive behavior and vicious circles of pathology.

Listed are several brief phrases from the MPDC that have been researched for purposes of characterizing the *morphologic organization* of patients:

Demonstrates an inner barrenness

Manifests a marked lack of psychic clarity

Inner structures are limited and sterile

Possesses meager psychic world

Possesses inchoate psychic world

Possesses feeble drive to fulfill needs

Undeveloped adaptive abilities are evident

Exhibits immature system for life functioning

Has few channels open between affect and cognition

Psychic system is severely constricted

Psychic system is sharply partitioned

Possesses compartmentalized psychic world

Internal regulation scattered and unintegrated

Primitive thoughts are manifested frequently

Parallel intrapsychic therapies.   Readers are likely to have discussed both frequently and at length the history, rationale, and variants of intrapsychic theory (Millon, 1990). More will be said concerning this model of the mind in each of the clinical chapters later in the book; hence, there is no need to review these matters at length here. However, and despite inevitable controversies and divergences in emphasis, often appearing more divisive upon first than later examination, intrapsychic therapists do share certain beliefs and goals in common that are worthy of note and that distinguish them from other modality orientations; two will be noted below.

First, and as noted in Chapter 1, all intrapsychic therapists focus on *internal mediating* processes (e.g., regulatory mechanisms) and structures (object representations) that ostensibly underlie and give rise to overt behavior. In contrast to cognitivists, however, their attention is directed to those mediating events that operate at the *unconscious* rather than the conscious level. To them, overt behaviors and cognitive reports are merely "surface" expressions of dynamically orchestrated but deeply repressed emotions and associated defensive strategies (Magnavita, 1997), all framed in a distinctive structural morphology (Kernberg, 1984). Because these unconscious processes and structures are essentially impervious to surface maneuvers, techniques of behavior modification are seen as mere palliatives, and methods of cognitive reorientation are thought to resolve only those difficulties that are so trivial or painless as to be tolerated consciously. "True" therapy occurs only when these deeply ingrained elements of the unconscious are fully unearthed and analyzed. The task of intrapsychic therapy, then, is to circumvent or pierce resistances that shield these insidious structures and processes, bringing them into consciousness and reworking them into more constructive forms.

Second, intrapsychic therapists see as their goal the *reconstruction* of the patient's complex syndrome or personality pattern, not the removal of a single domain syndrome or the reframing of a "superficial" cognitive attitude. Disentangling the underlying structure of complex syndromes or personality pathology, forged of many interlocking elements that build into a network of pervasive strategies and mechanisms, is the object of their therapy.

Reconstruction, then, rather than repairing a simple syndrome is the option chosen by intrapsychic therapists. They set for themselves the laborious task of rebuilding those functions (regulatory mechanisms), and structures (morphologic organization) that make up the substance of the patient's psychic worlds, not merely its façade. Treatment approaches designed "merely" to modify behavioral conduct and cognitive complaints fail to deal with the root source of pathology and are bound therefore to be of short-lived efficacy. As they view it, therapy must reconstruct the *inner* structures and processes that underlie overt behaviors and beliefs. It does not sacrifice the goal of syndromal or personality reconstruction for short-term behavioral or cognitive relief. Reworking the source of the problem rather than controlling its effects is what distinguishes intrapsychic therapies as treatment procedures.

Although intrapsychic therapies may be shown to be efficacious, few patients in this day of managed care are able to devote the time or expend the funds required to pursue a full course of treatment. Assuming treatment is feasible despite these difficulties, problems arise because there are too few trained therapists to make this approach available to the masses. In short, intrapsychic therapies must be relegated to a secondary position among treatment techniques on wholly practical grounds, if on no other.

Mood/Temperament

Few observables are clinically more relevant from the *biophysical* level of data analysis than the predominant character of an individual's affect and the intensity and frequency with which he or she expresses it. The meaning of extreme emotions is easy to decode. This is not so with the more subtle moods and feelings that insidiously and repetitively pervade the patient's ongoing relationships and experiences.

Mood/temperament assessment domains.   Not only are the expressive features of mood and drive conveyed by terms such as distraught, labile, fickle, and hostile communicated via self-report, but they are revealed as well, albeit indirectly, in the patient's level of activity, speech quality, and physical appearance.

Listed are several brief phrases developed for the MPDC that have been employed for purposes of characterizing the *mood/temperament* of patients:

Is almost always sad and downcast
Is preoccupied with guilt feelings
Is characteristically gloomy and dejected
Persistently feels hopeless and gloomy
Fearful of loss or desertion
Exhibits shortsighted hedonism
Displays exaggerated and short-lived
   emotions
Is quick to be annoyed or disappointed
   in others

Provokes rejection, then feels hurt or
   humiliated
Evidences inappropriate or constricted
   affect
Is unresponsive to feelings in others
Is drawn to relationships in which
   he/she will suffer
Feels dejected or guilty after positive
   experience
Devastated when close relationships end

Parallel mood/temperament therapies.   Although the direct action of pharmacological medications is chemical and their effects formulable in terms of altered neurophysiological relationships, there are those who believe that the crucial variable is not chemical or neurophysiological, but psychological. To them, the factors that determine the patient's response are not molecular events or processes, but the patient's prior psychological state and the environment within which he or she currently functions. According to this view, biophysical changes induced by medications take on a "meaning" to the patient, and it is this meaning that determines his or her final clinical response.

Theorists of this persuasion pay less attention to specifying the mechanisms and pathways of biophysical change than to the impact of these changes on the patient's self-image, coping competencies, social relationships, and the like. To support their thesis, they note that barbiturates, which typically produce sedative reactions, often produce excitement and hyperactivity. Similarly, many persons exhibit a cheerful state of intoxication when given sodium amytal in a congenial social setting, but succumb to a hypnotic state when the drug is administered to them in a therapeutic environment.

Of even greater significance than social factors, according to this view, is patients' awareness of the energy and temperamental changes that have taken place within them as a consequence of drug action. Freyhan (1959), discussing the effect of tranquilizers in reducing mobility and drive, states that patients with *compulsive* traits, who need intensified activity to control their anxiety, may react unfavorably to their loss of initiative, resulting thereby in an upsurge rather than a decrement in anxiety. Other patients, such as *avoidants* who are comforted by feelings of reduced activity and energy, may view the drug's tranquilizing effect as a welcome relief. Thus, even if a drug produced a uniform biophysical effect on all patients, its psychological impact would differ from patient to patient, depending on the meaning these changes have in the larger context of the patient's needs, attitudes, and coping strategies.

If a drug facilitates the control of disturbing impulses or if it activates a new sense of competence and adequacy, then it may be spoken of as beneficial. Conversely, if the effect is to weaken the patient's defenses and upset his or her self-image, it may prove detrimental. The key to a drug's effectiveness then, is not only its chemical impact, but the significance of the psychological changes it activates.

SYNERGISTIC INTEGRATION

One theme that has been stressed throughout this and earlier texts is that theory, taxonomy, assessment, and intervention should be the four principal domains of an integrated clinical science (Millon, 1990, 1996). We believe that interventions based on specified theoretical principles are most likely to achieve the goals of therapy. The fact that a movement such as technical eclecticism, which explicitly advocates the disjoining of therapy and theory, can find such a wide readership suggests that the current psychiatric taxonomy has been constructed too much on the basis of piecemeal empirical observation and not enough on systematic clinical theory.

Personality-Guided Contexts

How should the author's evolutionary model inform the practice and structure of therapy? If no one subset of *DSM-IV* diagnostic criteria is necessary or sufficient for membership in a diagnostic class, and if the structure of the taxonomy and the planning and practice of therapy are to be linked in a meaningful way, it seems likely that *no* one therapy or technique can be regarded as a necessary or sufficient remediation as well. Diagnostic heterogeneity–therapeutic heterogeneity is a more intrinsically agreeable pairing than diagnostic heterogeneity–therapeutic homogeneity, which treats every person diagnosed the same way, ignoring individual differences. The argument is one of parallelism: *The palette of methods and techniques available to the therapist must be commensurate with the idiographic heterogeneity of the patient for whom the methods and techniques are intended.*

When translated into psychological terms, a theory of psychopathology should be able to generate answers to a number of key questions. For example, how do its essential constructs interrelate and combine to form specific syndromes and disorders? And, if it is to meet the criteria of an integrative or unifying schema, can it help derive all forms of personality and syndrome with the same set of constructs, that is, not employ one set of explanatory concepts for borderline personalities, another for somatoforms, a third for depressives, and so on.

One of the great appeals of early analytic theory was its ability to explain several "character types" from a single developmental model of psychosexual stages. Can the same be said for other, more encompassing theories? Moreover, can these theories provide a structure and serve as a guide for planning psychotherapy with all varieties of psychopathologies?

A major treatment implication recorded earlier in the chapter noted that the polarity schema and the clinical domains can serve as useful points of focus for corresponding modalities of therapy. It would be ideal, of course, if patients were "pure" prototypes and all expressive psychic domains were prototypal and invariably present. Were this so, each diagnosis would automatically match with its polarity configuration and corresponding therapeutic mode. Unfortunately, real patients rarely are pure textbook prototypes; most, by far, are complex mixtures, exhibiting, for example, the deficient pain *and* pleasure polarities that typify the schizoid prototype, the interpersonal conduct and cognitive style features of the avoidant prototype, the self-image qualities that characterize the schizotypal, and so on. Further, the polarity configurations and their expressive domains are not likely to be of equal clinical relevance or prominence in a particular case; thus, interpersonal characteristics may be especially troublesome, whereas cognitive processes, though problematic, may be of lesser significance. Which domains and which polarities should be selected for therapeutic intervention is not, therefore, merely a matter of making "la diagnosis," but requires a comprehensive assessment, one that appraises not only the overall configuration of polarities and domains but differentiates their balance and degrees of salience.

As noted earlier, the approach that we call synergistic therapy has its applications to a variety of simple reactions, complex clinical syndromes, and personality disorders. We seek in the following chapters to outline reasons why pathologies that reflect the interaction of clinical syndromes and personality disorders constitute that segment of psychopathology for which a synergistic form of psychotherapy is ideally and distinctively suited. The task of the therapist is to identify domain dysfunctions and to provide matching treatment modalities that derive logically from the *theory of that particular person*, that is, to put together a related combination of treatment modalities that mirror the different domains in which that specific patient's pathology is expressed and configured.

When techniques drawn from different modalities are applied together, it should be because that combination reflects the domains that comprise the individual person's characteristics, not because it is required by the logic of one or another theory or technological preference.

Although personality-guided approaches can be applied to a variety of diverse clinical conditions, it would be wise to outline some reasons why complex syndromes and personality disorders are that segment of psychopathology for which a synergistically organized model of psychotherapy is ideally suited—in the same sense as behavioral techniques may be most efficacious in the modification of simple reactions, cognitive methods optimal for reframing phenomenological distortions, and intrapsychic techniques apt in resolving unconscious processes.

As described previously, the cohesion (or lack thereof) of interwoven psychic structures (self-image, mood-temperament, interpersonal conduct) and functions is what distinguishes the complex clinical disorders of personality from simple reactions; likewise, the orchestration of diverse yet synthesized techniques of intervention is what differentiates personality-guided synergism from other variants of psychotherapy. These two parallel constructs, emerging from different traditions and conceived in different venues, reflect shared philosophical perspectives, one oriented toward the understanding of complex psychopathologies, the other toward effecting their remediation.

It is not that synergistic therapies are inapplicable to the more simple reactions, but rather that synergistic therapies are *required* for complex syndromes and personality disorders. It is the very interwoven nature of the patient's problematic domains that define syndromes and personalities that make a multifaceted and integrated approach a necessity.

Potentiating Pairings and Catalytic Sequences

What makes synergistic therapy integrated, rather than eclectic?

To restate from Chapter 2, there is a separateness among eclectically designed techniques, just a wise selectivity of what works best. In synergistic therapy, there are psychologically designed composites and progressions among diverse techniques. In an attempt to formulate them in current writings (Millon, 1988), terms such as *potentiating pairings* and *catalytic sequences* are employed to represent the nature and intent of these polarity- and domain-oriented treatment plans. In essence, they comprise therapeutic arrangements and timing series that resolve polarity imbalances and effect clinical domain changes that would otherwise not occur by the use of several, essentially uncoordinated techniques.

The first of the synergistic procedures we recommend (Millon, 1988, 1990) has been termed *potentiating pairings;* they consist of treatment methods that are combined simultaneously to overcome problematic characteristics that might be refractory to each technique if they were administered separately. These composites pull and push for change on many different fronts, so that the therapy becomes as multioperational and as tenacious as the disorder itself. A popular illustration of these treatment pairings is found in what has been referred to as cognitive-behavior therapy, perhaps the first of the synergistic therapies (Craighead, Craighead, Kazdin, & Mahoney, 1994).

In the second synergistic procedure, termed *catalytic sequences,* one might seek first to alter a patient's humiliating and painful stuttering by *behavior modification* procedures, which, if achieved, may facilitate the use of *cognitive or self-actualizing* methods to produce changes in self-confidence, which may, in its turn, foster the utility of *interpersonal* techniques in effecting improvements in relationships with others. Catalytic sequences are timing series that should optimize the impact of changes that would be less effective if the sequential combination were otherwise arranged.

A more recent example has begun to show up in numerous clinical reports. It relates to the fact that patients with depressive personalities or long-term dysthymic disorders have their clinical symptoms markedly reduced by virtue of pharmacologic medications (e.g., SSRIs). Although these patients are greatly comforted by the reduction of their clinical symptoms, depressiveness has over time become a core part of their overall psychological makeup. Because after medication their depressiveness is no longer a part of their everyday experience, many may now feel empty and confused, not knowing who they are, to what they may aspire, or how to relate to the world. It is here that a catalytic sequence of therapies may come into play constructively. Patients may no longer be depressed, but they may require therapy for their new self-image and its valuation. No less important to their subsequent treatment will be opportunities to alter their formerly habitual interpersonal styles and attitudes, substituting in their stead social behaviors and cognitions that are more consonant with their current state. Former cognitive assumptions and expectations will no longer be infused with depressogenic elements, hence, calling for substantial psychic reformulations.

As the great neurological surgeon-psychologist Kurt Goldstein (1940) observed, patients whose brains have been altered to remedy a major neurological disorder do not simply lose the function that the extirpated area subserved. Rather, the patient restructures and reorganizes his or her brain capacities to maintain an integrated sense of self. In a similar way, when one or another major domain of one's habitual psychological makeup is removed or diminished (e.g., depression), one must reorganize oneself, not only to compensate for the loss but also to formulate a new self.

Similarly, the neurologist Oliver Sacks in his 1973 book *Awakenings* describes what happens to patients who, immobile for decades by encephalitis lethargica, suddenly "unfroze" when given the drug L-Dopa. Although these patients were restored to life, they had to learn to function in a world that had long passed them by. For them, their immobile state had an element of familiarity with which they had learned to cope, miserable though it was, for 10, 20, or 30 years. With the elimination of their adaptive lifestyle, they now had to deal with the world in which they found themselves, a task that rarely can be managed without considerable guidance and encouragement. Catalytic sequences should be employed to facilitate these relearning and reintegrative processes.

Of course, there are no discrete boundaries between potentiating pairings and catalytic sequences, just as there is no line between their respective pathological analogues, that is, adaptive inflexibility and vicious circles (Millon, 1969). Nor should therapists be concerned about when to use one rather than another. Instead, they are intrinsically interdependent phenomena whose application is intended to foster increased flexibility and, hopefully, a beneficent rather than a vicious circle. As Figure 4.1 illustrates, potentiating pairings and catalytic sequences represent but the first order of therapeutic synergism. In Figure 4.2, the idea of a "potentiating sequence" or a "catalytic pairing" recognizes that these logical composites may build on each other in proportion to what the tenacity of the disorder requires.

One question concerns the limits to which the content of synergistic therapy can be specified in advance at a tactical level, that is, the extent to which specific potentiating pairings and catalytic sequences can be identified for each of the complex syndromes and personality disorders. Many of the clinical chapters of this text will contain a chart that

I: Identifying Strategic Goals
    • Restructure Polarity Imbalances
    • Counter Self-Perpetuations

II: Selecting Tactical Modalities
    • Specify Domain Dysfunctions
    • Modify Salient Domains

III: Planning Synergistic Arrangements
    • Align Potentiating Pairings
    • Design Catalytic Sequences

Figure 4.1   Synergistic psychotherapy.

presents the salience of each of the clinical domains for that syndrome or disorder. To the extent that each patient's presentation is prototypal, the potentiating pairings and catalytic sequences that are actually used should derive from modality tactics oriented to alter several of the more problematic domains. That, however, probably represents the limits to which theory can guide practice in an abstract sense, that is, without knowing anything about the history and characteristics of the *specific* individual case to which the theory is to be applied. Just as individuality is ultimately so rich that it cannot be exhausted by any taxonomic schema, synergistic therapy, ideally performed, is full of specificities that cannot readily be resolved by generalities. Potentiating pairings, catalytic sequences, and whatever other higher-order composites therapists may evolve are conducted at an idiographic rather than a diagnostic level. Accordingly,

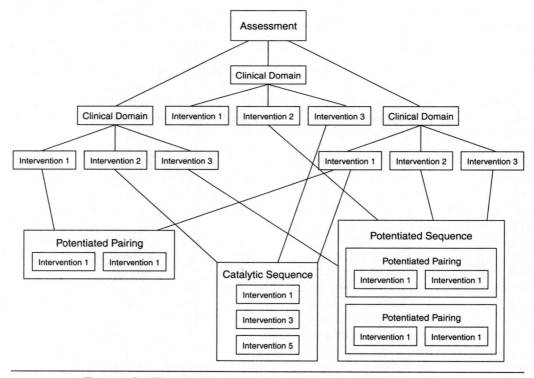

Figure 4.2   Therapy from assessment to domain to actual practice.

their precise content is specified as much by the logic of the individual case as by the logic of the syndrome or disorder itself. At an idiographic level, each of us must ultimately be artful and open-minded therapists, using simultaneous or alternatively focused methods. The synergism and enhancement produced by such catalytic and potentiating processes is what constitute genuinely innovative treatment strategies.

Probabilistic Judgments

Synergistic therapists will be more efficacious if they think about the likely utility of treatment choices in *probabilistic* terms; that is, they should make concurrent and sequential modality arrangements, knowing that the effectiveness of each component is only partial and that the probability of success will be less than perfect. To generate a high-probability estimate, therapists must gather all available assessment information and, as do mathematicians, calculate which combination of modalities will have the highest overall probability of being effective.

Note that no combinational approach can automatically be judged "best." With each new patient, a therapist should recognize that he or she is dealing with a person whose composite of dispositions and vulnerabilities has never before existed in this exact form. Moreover, it is important that the synergistic therapist never think in treatment absolutes or in black-and-white results; all treatment modalities have reasonable probabilities of success.

Treatment combinations possess complexities that add further to one's probabilistic calculations. Consideration also must be given to design programs that not only produce optimal and enduring treatment changes, but ones that anticipate and avoid potential threats (risks and resistances) to their achievement. Beyond the preceding, therapists will inevitably be faced with informational unknowns and ambiguities, as well as a host of future uncertainties.

As noted throughout the text, many therapists have a tendency to follow a fixed treatment program, either singular in its orientation (behavioral, psychodynamic) or combinational (cognitive-behavioral, pharmacologic-psychodynamic). Experience with a patient over a period of time should tell whether the treatment is working or a recalculation of probabilities is needed, that is, whether the initially chosen treatment program may best be changed to facilitate further progress should the original plan be stalled.

There will be many cases in which the pattern of a patient's characteristics does not lend itself to an intelligent estimate of treatment success probabilities. Under such circumstances, therapists should not feel that they must create a long-term or overall plan. Available options in the early stages of treatment may not provide a good, much less an excellent course of action. Such indeterminate states favor selecting a tentative or conservative course—until such time as greater clarity emerges.

It should be evident from the foregoing comments that a synergistic therapist will be challenged to make a series of difficult judgments, one more demanding and possibly with less assurance as to outcome than if the therapist routinely selected a specific modality for all or most of his or her cases. The latter course will be easier for the therapist, but not necessarily best for the patient.

The remainder of this book seeks to make the probabilistic task less indeterminate and less onerous. Each of the following chapters provides a rationale for which modalities and which combinations are likely to be most effective, given the pattern of the patient's clinical syndromes and particular disorders.

Polarity Goals

As stated earlier in the chapter, we should select our specific treatment techniques as tactics to achieve polarity-oriented goals. Depending on the pathological polarity, the domains to be modified, and the overall treatment sequence one has in mind, the goals of therapy should be oriented toward the improvement of imbalanced or deficient polarities by the use of techniques that are optimally suited to modify their expression in those clinical domains that are problematic.

Table 4.1 provides a synopsis of what may be considered the primary goals of synergistic therapy, according to the polarity model. Therapeutic efforts responsive to problems in the pain-pleasure polarity would, for example, have as their essential aim the enhancement of pleasure among schizoid, avoidant, and depressive personalities (+ pleasure). Given the probability of intrinsic deficits in this area, schizoids might require the use of pharmacologic agents designed to activate their flat mood/temperament. Increments in pleasure for avoidants, however, are likely to depend more on cognitive techniques designed to alter their alienated self-image and behavioral methods oriented to counter their aversive interpersonal inclination. Equally important for avoidants is reducing their hypersensitivities especially to social rejection (− pain); this may be achieved by coordinating the use of medications for their characteristic anguished mood/temperament with cognitive methods geared to desensitization. In the passive-active polarity, increments in the capacity and skills to take a less reactive and more proactive role in dealing with the affairs of their lives (− passive; + active) is a major goal of treatment for schizoids, depressives, dependents, narcissists, masochists, and compulsives. Turning to the other-self polarity, imbalances found among narcissists and antisocials, for example, suggest that a major aim of their treatment is a reduction in their predominant self-focus and a corresponding augmentation of their sensitivity to the needs of others (+ other; − self).

To make unbalanced or deficient polarities the primary aim of therapy is a new focus and a goal only moderately tested. In contrast, the clinical domains in which problems are expressed lend themselves to a wide variety of therapeutic techniques,

TABLE 4.1   Goals of Polarity-Oriented Personologic Therapy

Modifying the Pain-Pleasure Polarity
+ Pleasure (Schizoid, Avoidant, Depressive)
− Pain (Avoidant, Depressive)
Pain ↔ Pleasure (Self-Defeating, Sadistic)

Balancing the Passive-Active Polarity
+ Passive − Active (Avoidant, Histrionic, Antisocial, Sadistic, Negativistic)
− Passive + Active (Schizoid, Depressive, Dependent, Narcissistic, Self-Defeating, Compulsive)

Altering the Other-Self Polarity
− Other + Self (Dependent, Histrionic)
+ Other − Self (Narcissistic, Antisocial)
Other ↔ Self (Compulsive, Negativistic)

Rebuilding the Personality Structure
+ Cognitive, Interpersonal Cohesion   Schizotypal
+ Affective, Self Cohesion   Borderline
− Cognitive, Affective-Rigidity   Paranoid

the efficacy of which must, of course, continue to be gauged by ongoing experience and future systematic research. Nevertheless, our repertoire here is a rich one. For example, there are numerous cognitive-behavior techniques (Bandura, 1969; Craighead et al., 1994; Goldfried & Davison, 1976), such as assertiveness training, that may fruitfully be employed to establish a greater sense of self-autonomy or an active rather than a passive stance with regard to life. Similarly, pharmaceuticals are notably efficacious in reducing the intensity of pain (anxiety, depression) when the pleasure-pain polarity is in marked imbalance.

Domain Tactics

Turning to the specific domains in which clinical problems exhibit themselves, we can address dysfunctions in the realm of interpersonal conduct by employing any number of family (Gurman & Kniskern, 1981) or group (Yalom, 1986) therapeutic methods, as well as a series of recently evolved and explicitly formulated interpersonal techniques (Anchin & Kiesler, 1982; L.S. Benjamin, 1993; Kiesler, 1997). Methods of classical analysis or its more contemporary schools may be especially suited to the realm of object representations, as would the methods of Beck (1976) and Ellis (1970) be well chosen to modify difficulties of cognitive beliefs and self-esteem.

Tactics and *strategies* keep in balance the two conceptual ingredients of therapy. The first refers to what goes on with a particular focused intervention; the second refers to the overall plan or design that characterizes the entire course of therapy. Both are required: tactical specificity without strategic goals implies doing without knowing why in the big picture, and goals without specificity implies knowing where to go but having no way to get there. Obviously, one uses short-term modality tactics to accomplish higher-level strategies or goals over the long term.

Psychotherapies vary on the amounts of tactical specificity and strategic goals they prefer. Often, this is not merely an accident of history, but rather can be tied back to paradigmatic assumptions latent in the therapies themselves as a product of their times. Historically, the progression seems to be in the direction of both greater specificity and clearer goals. More modern approaches to psychotherapy, such as cognitive-behavioral, put into place highly detailed elements (e.g., agreed upon goals, termination criteria, and ongoing assessments) through which therapy itself becomes a self-regulating system. Ongoing assessments ensure the existence of a feedback process that is open to inspection and negotiation by both therapist and patient. The expectancy is one of action rather than talk. Talk is viewed as incapable of realizing possibilities in and of itself, but is merely a prerequisite for action, used to reframe unfortunate circumstances so that obstacles to action are removed or minimized. Action is more transactive than talk, and therapy is forward-looking and concentrates on realizing present possibilities as a means of creating or opening up new ones. Persons are often changed more through exposure and action than by focusing and unraveling the problems of the past. Insight may be a limited goal in itself.

System Transactions

The distinction between interaction and transaction points to an important element in the practice of synergistic psychotherapy. Because the goal of therapy is personality and clinical change, patient and therapist cannot be satisfied merely to interact like billiard balls and emerge from therapy unchanged. Instead, we must invent modes of therapy that maximize the transactive potential of the therapeutic process. Because of its lack of structure and feedback, traditional psychotherapy may wander around essentially indefinitely, without ever reaching termination. In fact, because patient and therapist may not have determined previously what constitutes success, it is not inconceivable that an appropriate point of termination might be reached without either the therapist or patient ever realizing it, only for new issues to be raised and the process to begin again.

Pessimistically speaking, it must be remembered that the primary function of any system is homeostasis. In an earlier book (Millon, 1981), personality was likened to an immune system for the psyche, such that stability, constancy, and internal equilibrium become the "goals" of a personality. Obviously, these run directly in opposition to the explicit goal of therapy, which is change. Usually, the dialogue between patient and therapist is not so directly confrontational that it is experienced as particularly threatening. In these cases, the personality system functions for the patient as a form of passive resistance, albeit one that may be experienced as a positive force (or trait) by the therapist. In fact, the schematic nature of self-image and object representations are so preemptive and confirmation-seeking that the true meaning of the therapist's comments may never reach the level of conscious processing. Alternatively, even if a patient's equilibrium is initially up-ended by a particular interpretation, his or her defensive mechanisms may kick in to ensure that a therapist's comments are somehow distorted, misunderstood, interpreted in a less threatening manner, or even ignored. The first is a passive form of resistance; the second an active form. No wonder then, that effective therapy is often considered anxiety provoking, for it is in situations where the patient really has no effective response, where the functioning of the immune system is temporarily suppressed, that the scope of his or her response repertoire is most likely to be broadened. Personality "goes with what it knows," and it is with the "unknown" where learning is most possible. Arguing essentially the same point, Kiesler (1966, 1997) has stated that the therapist is obliged to make the *asocial* response, one other than that which the patient is specifically trying to evoke.

If the psychic makeup of a person is regarded as a system, then the question becomes How can the characteristics that define systems be co-opted to facilitate rather than retard transactive change? A coordinated schema of strategic goals and tactical modalities for treatment that seek to accomplish these ends are what we mean by synergistic psychotherapy. Through various coordinated approaches that mirror the system-based structure of complex clinical syndromes and personality disorders, an effort is made to select domain-focused tactics that will fulfill the strategic goals of treatment.

If interventions are unfocused, rambling, and diffuse, the patient will merely "lean forward a little," passively resisting change by using his or her own "weight," that is, habitual characteristics already intrinsic to the system. Although creating rapport is always important, nothing happens unless the system is eventually "shook up" in some way. Therapists should not always be toiling to expose their patients' defenses, but sooner or later, something must happen that cannot be readily fielded by habitual processes, something that often will be experienced as uncomfortable or even threatening.

In fact, synergistic therapy appears in many ways to be like a "punctuated equilibrium" (Eldridge & Gould, 1972) rather than a slow and continuous process. The systems model argues for periods of rapid growth during which the psychic system re-configures itself into a new gestalt, alternating with periods of relative constancy. The purpose of keeping to a domain or tactical focus, or knowing clearly what you are doing and why you are doing it, is to keep the whole of psychotherapy from becoming diffused. The person-focused systems model runs counter to the deterministic universe-as-machine model of the late nineteenth century, which features slow but incremental gains. In a standard systems model, diffuse interventions are experienced simply as another input to be discharged homeostatically, producing zero change. In the machine model, in which conservation laws play a prominent role, diffuse interventions produce small increments of change, with the promise that therapeutic goals will be reached, given enough time and effort. In contrast, in the synergistic model, few therapeutic goals may be reached at all, unless something unusual is planned that has genuine transformational potential. This potential is optimized through what we have termed potentiating pairings and catalytic sequences.

Tactical specificity is required in part because the psychic level on which therapy is practiced is fairly explicit. Most often, the in-session dialogue between patient and therapist is dominated by a discussion of specific behaviors, specific feelings, and specific events, not by a broad discussion of personality traits or clinical syndromes. When the latter are discussed, they are often perceived by the patient as an ego-alien or intrusive characterization. A statement such as "You have a troublesome personality" conceives the patient as a vessel filled by some noxious substance. Under these conditions, the professional is expected to empty the vessel and refill it with something more desirable; the patient has relinquished control and responsibility and simply waits passively for the therapist to perform some mystical ritual, one of the worst assumptive sets in which to carry out psychotherapy. Whatever the physical substrates and dynamic forces involved in creating and sustaining particular traits, traits' terms are evoked as inferences from particular constituent behaviors. Behaviors can be changed; traits have a more permanent connotation.

Modality Selections

Despite the foregoing, viewing traits in an explicit way, that is, by anchoring them to real and objective events, is beneficial to both patient and therapist. Knowing what behaviors are descriptively linked to particular traits helps patients understand how others perceive them, and that these behaviors should not be repeated. Additionally, if patients are led to understand that their personality traits are, or are derived from, their concrete behaviors, there is hope, for behavior is more easily controlled and changed than is a clinical diagnosis. In this latter sense, the diagnosis or trait ascription itself may become the enemy. There is, after all, a difference between what is practically impossible, because it is at the limits of one's endurance or ability, and what is logically impossible. With support and courage, human beings can be coaxed into transcending their limitations, into doing what was before considered practically impossible. No one, however, can do what is logically impossible. When clinical syndromes and personality disorders are framed through the medical model, change is paradigmatically impossible. Individuals who see themselves as vessels for a diseased syndrome or personality should be disabused of this notion.

For the therapist, operationalizing traits as clusters of behavioral acts or cognitive expectancies can be especially beneficial in selecting tactical modalities. First, some behaviors are linked to multiple traits, and some of these traits are more desirable than others, so that some play exists in the interpretation or spin put on any particular behavior at the trait level. This play can be exploited by the therapist in order to reframe patient attributions about self and others in more positive ways. The avoidant's social withdrawal can be seen as having enough pride in oneself to leave a humiliating situation. The dependent's clinging to a significant other can be seen as having the strength to devote oneself to another's care. Of course, these reframes will not be sufficient in and of themselves to produce change. They do, however, seek a bond with the patient by way of making positive attributions and thereby raising self-esteem, while simultaneously working to disconfirm or make the patient reexamine other beliefs that lower esteem and function to keep the person closed off from trying on new roles and behaviors.

Second, understanding traits as clusters of behaviors and/or cognitions is just as beneficial for the therapist as for the patient when it comes to overturning the medical model of syndromal and personality pathology and replacing it with a synergistic systems model. One of the problems of complex syndromes and personality disorders is that their range of attributions and perceptions are too narrow to characterize the richness that in fact exists in their social environment. As a result, they end up perpetuating old problems by interpreting even innocuous behaviors and events as noxious. Modern therapists have a similar problem, in that the range of paradigms they have to bring to their syndromal and disordered patients is too narrow to describe the rich set of possibilities that exist for every individual. The belief that personality pathologies are medical diseases, monolithically fixed and beyond remediation, should itself be viewed as a form of paradigmatic pathology.

As has been outlined previously, there are *strategic goals* of therapy, that is, those that endure across numerous sessions and against which progress is measured, and there are specific *domain modality tactics* by which these goals are pursued. Ideally, strategies and tactics should be integrated, with the tactics chosen to accomplish strategic goals, and the strategies chosen on the basis of what tactics might actually achieve given other constraints, such as the number of therapy sessions and the nature of the problem. To illustrate, intrapsychic therapies are highly strategic, but tactically impoverished; pure behavioral therapies are highly tactical, but strategically narrow and inflexible. There are, in fact, many different ways that strategies might be operationalized. Just as diagnostic criteria are neither necessary nor sufficient for membership in a given class, it is likely that no technique is an inevitable consequence of a given clinical strategy. Subtle variations in technique and the ingenuity of individual therapists to invent techniques ad hoc assure that there exists an almost infinite number of ways to operationalize or put into action a given clinical strategy.

As described earlier in the chapter, a tremendous amount of knowledge, both about the nature of the patient's disorders and about diverse modes of intervention, is required to perform synergistic therapy. To quote from the prior chapter:

> To maximize this synergism requires that the therapist be a little like a jazz soloist. Not only should the professional be fully versed in the various musical keys, that is, in techniques of psychotherapy that span all personologic domains, he or she should also be prepared to respond to subtle fluctuations in the patient's thoughts, actions, and emotions, any of which could take the composition in a wide variety of directions, and integrate these with the overall plan of therapy as it evolves. After the instruments have been

packed away and the band goes home, a retrospective account on the entire process should reveal a level of thematic continuity and logical order commensurate with what would have existed had all relevant constraints been known in advance.

Ideally, in a truly integrated clinical science, the theoretical basis that lends complex syndromes and personality disorders their content, that is, the basis on which its taxonomy is generated and patients assessed and classified, would also provide the basis for the goals and modalities of therapy. Without such a basis, anarchy ensues, for then we will have no rationale by which to select from an almost infinite number of specific domain tactics that can be used, except the dogmas of past traditions. The "truth" is what works in the end, a pragmatism based on what we term synergistic integrationism.

Sociocultural Factors

The individual person represents but one structural level of life's systems; other levels of organization might also be considered and analyzed. Thus, individuals may be viewed as system units that exist within larger ecological milieus, such as dyads, families, communities, and, ultimately, cultures. Like the personality system, these higher-level systems contain homeostatic processes that tend to sustain and reinforce their own unique patterning of internal variables.

The fact that the ecology of complex clinical syndromes and personality disorders is itself organizational and systemic argues for another principle of therapy: Pull as much of the surrounding interpersonal and social contexts into the therapeutic process as possible, or risk being defeated by them. Where ecological factors are operative, therapeutic gains may be minimized and the risk of relapse increased. In the best-case scenario, family members can be brought into therapy as a group or as needed; if no latent pathologies exist, the family will cooperate in discussing characteristics of the status quo that perpetuate pathology and explore alternatives that might promote change. In the worst-case scenario, family members will refuse to come into therapy under some thin rationale, probably because nonparticipation is one way to passively undermine a change they in fact fear. If family members are not motivated to assist in the therapeutic process, it is likely that the individual is in therapy either because he or she must be, as in cases of court referral, or because family members do not want the burden of guilt that would accrue from actively refusing assistance.

EVALUATING PROGRESS

All synergistic therapies must consider several factors following the implementation of the general plan: first, progress must be evaluated on a fairly regular basis; second, problems of resistance and risk should be analyzed and counteracted; and third, efforts should be made to anticipate and prevent relapsing.

Reviewing Progress and Methods

In synergistic therapies, where things hopefully will change rapidly, treatment review should be a continuous process, every few sessions or so. The purpose of evaluating the plan is to ensure that progress is directed to achieving its strategic goals. Part of the evaluation process is intended to give the therapist a rough sense of how long treatment will be. Should progress be delayed or fail to reach a reasonable level, then it is clear that some rethinking of goals and strategies is called for. Evaluating the progress of therapy is difficult when treatment is either unstructured or when the time commitment is limited. Synergistic therapy may begin with a series of explicit goals and modalities; however, these may change over time, especially if treatment is open-ended (Bergin & Lambert, 1978).

Periodically, originally planned strategies and modalities are found lacking. Therapies start with a limited set of impressions and with only a rough notion of the more complex elements of the patient's makeup. As treatment proceeds and knowledge of the patient grows and becomes more thoroughly understood, this new information may strengthen the original plan and strategy; on the other hand, as the assessment process continues, so may the conception of the patient's psychic difficulties be altered. A fine-tuning process may be called for. The overall configuration of syndromes and disorders may require a significant shift toward the use of different domain-oriented modalities. Hence, both strategies and tactics may have to be modified to accord with this new information.

Resistance and Risk Analysis

There are numerous issues that arise with patients as therapy progresses. Some patients are highly resistant to the probing and psychic dislodging they experience in treatment. Others feel they have become "free" from their original constraints, employing treatment as a rationale to engage in increasingly risky activities.

Therapeutic resistance derives from the patient's "defensive armor," usually indicating a reluctance to voice one's feelings and thoughts to the therapist. Most *resistances* manifest themselves in a number of well-known ways: silence, lateness, becoming helpless, missing appointments, having significant memory lapses, or simply paying later and later each month. On the other hand, *risky* behaviors are likely to show themselves in a tendency to act out, to be open with regard to expressing resentments, proving the therapist is wrong, exhibiting parasuicidal behaviors, engaging in irrational behaviors, and so on. As Messer (1996) has noted, however, resistances are not the enemy of therapy but an informative expression of the way patients feel, act, and think in everyday life.

There are several choices when resistances or risks present themselves. We can insist on continuing with the original plan, we can interpret the meaning of the resistance, we can point out the consequences of risky behaviors, or we can alter aspects of the overall treatment strategy. Whatever the choice, it should be formulated as a positive and active decision. Otherwise, the whole structure of the treatment plan may be seriously compromised.

Preventing Relapses

Despite substantial progress over the treatment course, patients should leave therapy in a better state than when they entered. A worst-case scenario is when certain fundamental aspects of the patient's psychic makeup has remained unresolved at the point of treatment termination. Whether it is the patient's decision that he or she has had enough therapy, or the therapist believes that there will be diminishing returns for continuing further, it may be advisable at some point to terminate treatment.

It is the task of the good synergistic therapist to help patients anticipate potential setbacks, to avoid stress situations to which they may be highly vulnerable, and to assist them to develop problem-solving skills, as well as to strengthen their more constructive potentials.

It is not uncommon to have patients develop new psychic symptoms during the treatment process. More typically, many patients experience a reassertion of pathological thoughts and feelings following termination. As noted in an earlier section, we strongly encourage therapists to stretch the time between sessions as therapy progresses. This enables the therapist to determine which aspects of the treatment strategy have been resolved adequately, and which remain vulnerable and potentially problematic. It is our general belief that adequate synergistic therapy should continue over these periodic sessions to ensure that substantial relapses will not occur.

The reemergence of certain symptoms does not mean that the patient has deteriorated, but that the more complex elements of the patient's psyche have come together with life circumstances in an especially troublesome way. Such symptoms serve as clues to both therapist and patient, enabling them to learn and anticipate what will continue to be troublesome in the future.

In our judgment, a planned sequence of follow-up sessions is a highly successful means of reducing the likelihood of a serious relapse. Once-a-week sessions can be extended to biweekly, then monthly, then every third month, and so on for extended periods. During these follow-up sessions, patients can begin to consolidate their therapeutic gains, anticipate where setbacks are likely to occur, and develop and strengthen problem-solving skills relevant to the syndromes and disorders they faced when treatment began. In addition to these plans for preventing relapse, the author has encouraged patients who leave the area to write annual essays concerning their ongoing experiences, especially as they relate to the goals of their therapy. These essays were sent so that appraisals could be made of the progress patients experience dealing with the difficulties that once stymied their life. As an aside, we have continued to receive letters from former patients who terminated therapy more than 25 years ago.

Comment.   The system we have termed synergistic therapy may have raised concerns as to whether any one therapist can be sufficiently skilled, not only in employing a wide variety of therapeutic approaches, but also in synthesizing them and planning their sequence. The author was asked at a conference some years ago: "Can a highly competent behavioral therapist employ cognitive techniques with any measure of efficacy, and can he prove able, when necessary, to function as an insightful intrapsychic therapist? Can we find people who are strongly self-actualizing in their orientation who can, at other times, be cognitively confronting?" Is there any wisdom in selecting different modalities in treating a patient if the therapist has not been trained diversely or is not particularly competent in more than one or two therapeutic modalities?

It is our belief that the majority of therapists have the ability to break out of their single-minded or loosely eclectic frameworks, to overcome their prior limitations, and to acquire a solid working knowledge of diverse treatment modalities. Developing a measure of expertise with the widest possible range of modalities is highly likely to increase treatment efficacy and the therapist's rate of success.

In the following chapters, we provide an initial framework for utilizing the synergistic approach in a wide range of clinical syndromes and personality disorders. Part II of this text addresses those difficulties that are assigned to Axis I of the *DSM-IV,* primarily simple reactions and clinical syndromes, the latter signifying the interaction of the multiple domains, especially as they comprise personality styles. Part III addresses each of the prototypal personality disorders covered in Axis II of the *DSM-IV.* Not only is a mix of therapeutic modalities described to help disentangle and treat each of these prototypal disorders, but illustrations are presented for most personality subtypes.

PART II

Clinical Syndromes—Axis I

CHAPTER FIVE

Treating Acute, Posttraumatic, and Generalized Anxiety Syndromes

Among the most unpleasant yet common experiences is anxiety. Discomforting though it may be, anxiety plays a central role in the adaptive repertoire of all organisms; as a signal of danger, it mobilizes the individual's coping reaction to threat.

Anxiety is involved in all forms of psychopathology, either as a symptomatic expression of psychological tension or as a stimulant either to adaptive or problematic coping. Because of its universality, however, we must restrict the usage of the term to conditions in which apprehension and emotional tension are prominent features of the clinical picture.

In the *acute anxiety or panic syndromes,* as we shall describe them, the utility of anxiety as a beneficial alerting signal has been undone; the anxious patient is often unable to locate the source of apprehension; he or she experiences such unbearable distress that coping efforts become disorganized. Thus, once these anxieties are aroused, they frequently continue to mount; because the patient is unable to identify a reason for his or her fearful expectations, the anxiety generalizes and attaches itself often to entirely incidental events and objects in the environment. In this way, anxiety is not only disruptive in its own right, but it plants the seeds for its own perpetuation.

As will be evident in this chapter, pure or "simple" anxieties are a signal that patients have *not* been able to curtail the distress they feel. However, most patients do use anxiety's alerting signal to neutralize the feelings of stress. This is often done by focusing the stressful feeling on a specific external source (e.g., phobia) or transforming it into a bodily dysfunction (e.g., conversion), and so on. Anxiety syndromes, in contrast to mood disorders, *activate* the patient to seek relief. Mood disorders, such as the depressive syndromes, indicate a passive withdrawal from seeking a psychic resolution to one's difficulties, a "giving-up" mentality. Hence, there are few psychic transformations among the various mood disorders, but there are several neutralizing transformations in what we prefer to term *complex anxiety syndromes.*

161

REPRISE: THE SPECTRUM FROM SIMPLE CLINICAL REACTIONS, TO COMPLEX CLINICAL SYNDROMES, TO PERSONALITY DISORDERS

As discussed in another recent book (Millon & Davis, 1999), the behaviors and strategies that characterize personality disorders persist as permanent features of the individual's way of life and seem to have an inner momentum and autonomy of their own; they continue to exhibit themselves in a broad array of clinical domains (e.g., cognitive, interpersonal, self-image). In contrast, simple clinical reactions arise as a nonsymbolic response to distressing internal or external precipitants. Typically, they tend to be transient, that is, of brief duration, and tend to disappear soon after these precipitants subside.

The clinical domains that characterize personality disorders are highly varied and interrelate in complex ways. They are individually and widely generalized, with many attitudes and habits exhibited only in subtle and indirect ways. In contrast, behaviors that characterize the simple reactions and clinical syndromes tend to be isolated and dramatic, although they may accentuate and caricature the more prosaic features of a patient's personality style; they typically stand out in sharp relief against the background of the patient's more normal and enduring mode of functioning.

The characteristic domains constituting personality disorders "feel right" to the patient; they seem to be part and parcel of his or her makeup; the term *ego-syntonic* has been used to convey this sense of comfort, naturalness, and suitability with which patients experience their traits. In contrast, clinical reactions and syndromes often are experienced as *ego-dystonic*, that is, discrepant, irrational, and uncomfortable to patients; the behaviors, thoughts, and feelings that denote their syndrome seem strange and alien not only to others but to the patients themselves; often they feel extreme anguish, as if caught or driven by forces beyond their control.

As far as therapy is concerned, personality disorders frequently require extensive techniques because of their deep embeddedness, pervasive generality, and the automatic character in which their traits are expressed. In contrast, clinical reactions and syndromes tend to be precipitated by internal chemical vulnerabilities or external conditions of which the patient may be aware and seeking relief. Moreover, patients' motivation to get rid of their dystonic and narrowly delimited symptom works hand in hand with highly focused therapeutic methods, which we will discuss shortly, resulting in a relatively easy and effective program of reaction or syndrome extinction.

As noted previously, the symptoms of simple anxieties tend to be stimulus-specific, that is, linked primarily to specific internal or external conditions; they show themselves as isolated behaviors, largely separated from the individual's general pattern of personality functions. Although what we term complex anxiety syndromes are also prompted by internal irritabilities or external events, they are rooted in part in the overall pattern of the individual's personality characteristics; these generalized traits intrude on and complicate what otherwise might be a simple response to a stimulus precipitant.

Simple anxieties tend to be durable and unvarying, displaying themselves in a uniform and consistent way each time the precipitant occurs. This is not the case with the complex syndromes of anxiety. The diagnostic picture of complex syndromes is not only contaminated by secondary symptoms from diverse clinical domains, but entirely different expressive domains may emerge and become dominant over time. At any one point, several subsidiary domains of expression (interpersonal, cognitive) may covary simultaneously with the dominant symptom of anxiety; for example, in phobic cases, one may find, in addition to the anxiety, a mixture of painful depressions, obsessive cognitions, and a variety of psychophysiological symptoms. Over time, moreover, the dominant anxiety syndrome may subside and be replaced by previously unexpressed syndromes. This fluidity in the clinical picture of complex syndromes can be attributed to intrusions stemming from the patient's basic personality; as the varied and diverse elements of his or her habitual coping strategies become involved, waxing and waning over time, different symptoms may emerge and subside. Simple syndromes do not display these complications and fluidities because complicating realms of expression do not intrude on them.

Even in the anxiety-driven syndromes, where rather distinctive and dramatic symptoms are often present (e.g., obsession or conversion), we note that in most cases there is a coexistence of several symptoms that covary and are interchangeable over time; these symptoms wax and wane in their potency and clarity during the course of a disorder, thereby complicating efforts to assign a single symptom label to the disorder. Thus, despite the long-established tradition of referring to a disorder in terms of its most dramatic symptom, most patients exhibit *intra-individual variability,* that is, display certain symptoms at one time and place and different symptoms at other times and places.

How is the problem of symptom covariation and changeability to be resolved in the mood and schizophrenic disorders? Two directions seem reasonable toward the goal of finding a solution: (a) systematic multivariate research designed to determine which symptoms covary or cluster together in the same patient, and (b) systematic research to determine whether each of these multivariate symptom clusters are correlated with particular personality patterns whose basic traits (e.g., attitudes or coping strategies) could logically account for its correlated symptom cluster.

The clinical types to be described in later chapters, and their corresponding personality dispositions, represent the results of such an effort. Here, we have attempted to bring together the findings of multivariate cluster studies and the theoretical schema of pathological personality patterns described in Millon (1996b). Although extensive research has not been done to validate the specific typology to be presented, it may serve as a useful model for further systematic studies.

Let us note before we proceed that investigators utilizing multivariate analysis have not uncovered identical symptom clusters. This lack of correspondence arises for a number of reasons: the factorial methods they have employed have differed; the populations they have used for their respective samples often were not comparable; and the measures on which they based their data tapped different clinical features. Thus, in the grouping presented below, we have taken a measure of liberty by selecting only those clusters that logically appear to correlate with the pathological patterns described in later chapters. It will be evident in the following discussion that we have *not* asserted that a one-to-one correspondence exists between a particular personality pattern and a particular complex syndrome; rather, as the evidence of our own research suggests, certain personality patterns are *more likely* to exhibit certain syndromes than they are others. This loosely fitting model of pattern-syndrome correspondence is presented in our discussion of the anxiety-related disorders; for example, we noted that the obsessive-compulsive disorder occurred, not in one, but in several personality patterns, although with greater probability in some than in others.

As noted, simple anxiety reactions are relatively clear-cut and uncontaminated, and hence tend to be understandable and appropriate, given the nature of the external precipitant. Complex anxiety syndromes, in contrast, are often irrational, overdriven and "symbolic"; they seem unnecessarily complicated and intricate and appear to bring surplus elements to bear on minimally troublesome situations. The reason, as in obsessions, phobias, and conversions, is the intrusion of deeply rooted clinically pathological adaptive strategies. Inner forces, biophysical or learned, override present realities and become the primary stimulus to which the patient responds. Anxious behavior, then, is less a function of present precipitants than of the chemical dysfunctions and past associations they evoke. It is this primacy either or both biological sensitivity or of reactivated past experiences that gives the complex syndrome patient's clinical picture much of its irrational and symbolic quality; the bizarre or hidden meaning of a response can be understood if it is seen in terms of these inner stimulus intrusions.

In addition to eruptions of past memories and biological emotions, patients' responses are distorted in accord with their habitual style of functioning. The behaviors patients exhibit are rational and appropriate, if seen in terms of the emotions and memories that have been stirred up; however, they are quite bizarre and illogical if they are seen in terms of objective reality. In short, the patient's "symbolic" symptoms represent the direct consequences of intrusions of the past and of chemistry and the complicated strategies the patient employs to deal with them. These behavioral, cognitive, and intrapsychic convolutions contrast markedly with the relatively direct and simple responses that characterize simple anxiety reactions.

Complex syndromes represent different ways of handling anxious feelings by the use of various neutralizing methods; these methods are employed most often by persons who attempt to resolve their tensions internally, that is, by transforming them so that they are only partially distressful and do not elicit social shame or disapproval. These anxiety-related psychological and physical syndromes are discussed in Chapters 6 and 7.

Mood syndromes make up the general group of ailments to be discussed in Chapter 8. Here, the patient's melancholic inclinations and psychic struggles can find neither internal resolution nor external expression; tensions remain bound up within the individual and continue to churn away until the patient gives up trying to resolve them. The last group of clinical syndromes of Axis I is discussed in Chapter 9. These consist of what we term the cognitive-dysfunction syndromes; they reflect either extreme intrinsic vulnerabilities or the consequences of ingesting substances that markedly reduce the individual's capacity to reason and think logically and rationally.

ACUTE ANXIETY AND PANIC REACTIONS

We begin our discussion of the Axis I syndromes with a focus on anxiety because many other clinical syndromes are transformational maneuvers that patients utilize to control or diminish the experience of anxiety. In complex syndromes, patients utilize devious and often complicated behaviors or cognitions to maintain their cohesion against the upsetting and often disorganizing effects of anxiety. Should their defensive operations be deficient or without adequate compensatory measures, apprehension and tension will ensue and perhaps be accelerated.

Acute anxiety and panic attacks often are an initial reaction to impending threat; for most individuals, the precipitant subsides and the patient returns to normal functioning. However, should the source of anxiety persist, individuals will learn to cope with it in whichever way is possible and expedient; these ways of neutralizing anxiety often turn out to be the precursors of later complex syndromes. Depending on the severity and persistence of the stress the patient faces, and the coping methods available, the person may acquire either healthy adaptive strategies or pathologically maladaptive ones.

Our attention in this section will be directed to those cases of anxiety that arise relatively free of any maladaptive pattern of coping, that is, when the patient's style of functioning is relatively normal rather than routinely disrupted. Here, sources of environmental stress or neurochemical dysfunction that are normally under control have been activated and rise to the foreground. It is these cases of coping disorganization for which the *DSM-IV* should reserve the term *simple anxiety reaction*.

Acute anxieties and panic reactions are relatively episodic behaviors activated neurochemically or in response to a delimited class of ordinarily neutral stimuli; many tend to be both stimulus-specific and uniform in their expression because they are relatively free of maladaptive cognitive, interpersonal, and intrapsychic processes.

Although these simple, circumscribed, and episodic disruptions are acquired in response to the same determinants and in accordance with the same biophysical processes and learning principles as are complex syndromes, they lack the pervasiveness, generality, and complexities that characterize anxieties that are interwoven with problematic cognitive and interpersonal traits; that is, acute anxieties do not coexist with a number of traits that will permeate and color many aspects of the individual's functioning. Rather, they are a narrowly compartmentalized set of behaviors that are manifested in response to a restricted range of internal or external stimulus events.

Acute anxieties and complex anxieties are alike in that both are elicited in response either to biological dysfunctions or to external events. However, in the simple or acute anxieties, the internal or external stimulus precipitant is not merely a catalyst to activate a chain of complicating psychic processes, as it is in the more complex forms of the anxious syndrome. Rather, the stimulus evokes, directly and simply, just those responses to which it was connected by prior experiences. In other words, simple anxiety/panic syndromes are not contaminated by intervening psychic digressions and complications.

Several other types of anxiety should be distinguished. Some are transient situational anxieties that are immediate and short-lived responses to relatively brief but objectively stressful conditions. Here, the patient may possess a notable vulnerability to feeling anxious or panicky; the source of this vulnerability may be biological or experiential. The second group differs on several counts. They are relatively ingrained or permanent states of anxiety that persist long after the conditions that gave rise to them have passed. They are manifested in response not only to stressful but also to ordinarily neutral and trivial events. Thus, acute anxieties and panic reactions are emotionally charged responses precipitated by rather incidental and undramatic conditions and without evoking the intrusion of complicated cognitive and unconscious processes.

We need not elaborate the behavioral and phenomenological characteristics of acute anxiety and panic, as they are well-known. These syndromes are not considered pathological unless the response is entirely inappropriate or out of proportion to the objective seriousness of the stimulus that is associated with it, as for example in reacting fearfully to the sight of dirt on someone's dirty shoes or becoming panicky when seeing a group of Asians in a park.

As noted, there are many similarities among acute anxiety and panic reactions and what we elaborate in later chapters as complex anxiety-related syndromes; a further elaboration of these distinctions may be instructive.

Acute anxiety and panic are alike in that both are characterized by phenomeno-logical tension and by a rapid increase in sympathetic nervous system reactivity (per-spiration, muscular contraction, and rapid heartbeat). They differ from complex anxiety syndromes, which tend to be unanchored or free-floating, whereas simple anx-ieties are almost always focused on an identifiable stimuli.

Complex phobic syndromes and simple acute anxiety reactions are alike in that both tend to be focused on or anchored to a tangible external stimulus, leading many theorists to question whether any difference exists between them. As we conceive it, the difference is a matter of the degree to which and complexity with which cognitive, interpersonal, and other psychic domains contribute to shaping the pathological re-sponse. Phobias, as we define them, signify that intricate and highly convoluted psy-chic processes (self-image, cognitive style, object relations) play a determinant role in "selecting" a provocative stimulus that subjectively symbolizes but is objectively dif-ferent from that which is actually feared; for example, agoraphobia, a panic response to open places, may symbolize a generalized feeling of inadequacy or a fear of as-suming independence from others. In contrast, in what we conceive as a simple anx-iety reaction, we observe behavior that is a direct and *noncomplex* response to an actual stimulus to which the patient is highly vulnerable, or has learned to fear, for example, a fear of Asian persons that is traceable to distressing encounters in childhood with a Chinese teacher. Some measure of generalization occurs, of course, but the indi-vidual tends to make the anxious response only to objects or events that are essen-tially similar or closely associated with the original provocative stimulus; for example, learning to fear a cat in early life may be generalized into a fear of dogs as these are barely discriminable in the eyes of the very young. At most, then, acute and panic anxieties may include simple and uncomplicated generalizations based on specific earlier stressful situations. Although often appearing irrational to the unknowing outsider, they can be traced directly to a biologically based vulnerability or a well-circumscribed life experience.

As noted, this simple and direct linkage between an internal or external stimulus and a response is *not* what is meant by the concept of a complex syndrome, be it anxi-ety-driven or depressive. As stated previously, an intricate chain of intervening processes is involved in what we have termed complex disorders. They usually occur in persons whose histories are replete with numerous instances of adverse experience. Given their repeated exposure to mismanagement and faulty learning experiences, these individuals have built up an obscure psychic labyrinth, a residue of cognitively complex, tangentially related, but highly interwoven memories and mechanisms, deeply activated emotions, and interpersonal behaviors that are easily reactivated under the pressure of stressful events. Because these incidental and comorbid psychic processes are stirred up under such conditions, no simple and direct line can be traced between the complex anxious or panic response and its associated precipitants. The final out-come, as in a phobia, appears as a *symbolic* rather than as a simple *generalized* fear be-cause the associative route is highly circuitous, involving both the residuals of the past and a variety of psychic distortion processes. Complex anxieties are formed, then, by the crystallization of diffusely anchored and psychically transformed past learnings ac-quired in response to a wide and diverse range of faulty experiences; this pervasively adverse background and the rather circuitous sequence of psychic distortions that are activated are frequently found among patients with personality disorders, rather than those with normal personalities. Because "normals" are not likely to have had such pervasively adverse experiences, they have little basis for developing a complex of associated psychic complications; as a result, what we observe in them are relatively "clean," simple, and direct anxieties or panic reactions.

Let us briefly note a number of conditions that give rise to the acquisition of simple anxious and acute panic reactions. The most basic of these are situations in which a previously neutral stimulus has been paired, either intentionally or incidentally, with a noxious stimulus. For example, an anxious response may be given *naturally* to the stimulus of a sharp noise. However, as in early experiments, this anxious response was *conditioned* to the evocative stimulus by the simple process of pairing the two stimuli through temporal contiguity.

Acute or panic reactions need not have been based on direct prior experience with a fear-producing stimulus. The basis of the panic reaction of many children may be a biochemical sensitivity, a disposition to experience as anxiety-producing that is objectively neutral. Also, quite commonly, as in vicarious learning, children may have merely seen or read about the frightening qualities of certain stimuli; for example, a TV mystery in which a bloody murder occurs in a bathtub may build a persistent fear of taking a bath. In addition to visual pairings of noxious and neutral stimuli, children often acquire their anxieties through verbal association. For example, many youngsters who have never seen a snake have a dreadful fear merely of the thought of seeing one. They may have read about the "deadly poisonous" and "nauseatingly slimy" characteristics of these creatures or may have been told, in a tense and agitated voice by a fearful parent, never to go near, let alone touch one. Along similar lines, children may acquire a variety of anxious attitudes simply by observing and imitating the behaviors, ideas, and emotions of an apprehensive parental model. Thus, even though parents may never have directly told their children to be afraid of certain objects or events, children vicariously "soak in" attitudes merely by incidental observation. Through indirect associations such as these, children may acquire in their behavioral repertoire a fearful expectancy of distress to stimuli that objectively are innocuous, despite the fact that they may never have had a direct or "real" experience with them.

If we think of the many incidental stimuli and chance-like conditions under which anxiety is learned, and add to it the effects of even a simple biological proneness or stimulus generalization, we begin to understand why so many of these anxieties appear irrational and peculiar. Despite their strange, irrational, and often nonsensical quality, however, they are a simple product of learning, no more obscure in the manner of their acquisition than most of the attitudes and behaviors we take for granted as "normal."

General Clinical Picture

Acute attacks of anxiety and panic are the most common of the simple anxiety disorders, characterized by prolonged periods of moderately intense and widely generalized apprehension and strain, followed by intense feelings of dyscontrol and impending doom. The coping patterns of these patients are barely adequate to the challenges and impulses they must handle. Most frequently, patients seem on edge, unable to relax, easily startled, tense, worrisome, irritable, excessively preoccupied with fears and calamities and prone to nightmares and insomnia, have poor appetites, and suffer undue fatigue and minor but discomforting physical ailments. Many patients learn to "adjust" to their psychic state, but their lives tend to be unnecessarily limited and impoverished, restricted by the need to curtail their activities and relationships to those few they can manage with relative comfort. In panic reactions, however, there are brief eruptions of extreme and uncontrollable emotion. For varied reasons, traceable to some biochemical susceptibility or coping inadequacy, these patients feel a sense of impending disaster; they feel that they are disintegrating and powerless against forces that surge from within. These feelings often are the climax to a period of mounting distress in which a series of objectively trivial events were viewed as devastating and crushing; at some point, patients' fears and impulses are reactivated, breaking through their crumbling controls and resulting in a dramatic upsurge and discharge of emotions. As the panic attack approaches its culmination, breathing quickens, the heart races, they perspire profusely and feel faint, numb, nauseous, chilly, and weak. After a brief period, lasting from a few minutes to one or two hours, the vague sense of terror and its frightening sensations subside, and patients return to a more characteristic level of composure.

In those experiencing frequent panic attacks, especially those associated with open spaces (agoraphobia), there is a sweeping disorganization and an overwhelming feeling of terror. Controls completely disintegrate, and the patient is carried away by a rush of irrational impulses and bizarre thoughts, often culminating in sprees of chaotic behavior, terrifying hallucinations, suicidal acts, even violent outbursts of hostility, and so on. These extreme behaviors are similar to but briefer forms of a number of psychotic states. Panic, however, refers to transitory states of severe anxiety and decompensation that terminate after a few hours, or at most after one or two days, following which the patient regains "normal" equilibrium. Should these shattering eruptions linger or recur frequently and their bizarre behaviors and terrifying anxieties persist, it would be proper to categorize the impairment as a psychotic disorder.

Let us next turn to a more systematic analysis of the clinical signs of these acute anxiety and panic states.

Behavior.   The overt actions of the anxious and panicky patient are easily observed. Most appear fidgety and restless, tend to pace excessively, engage in random movements, squirm in their seats and are jumpy, on edge, irritable, and distractible. Others are overcontrolled, strained, muscularly tight; they bite their lips and exhibit minor hand tremors, facial tics, or peculiar grimaces. The tone of their voice may be tremulous and denoted by rapid shifts in tempo and loudness; speech may be voluble and hurried at one time, and quavering, blocked, distracted, and paralyzed the next, as if extreme efforts at control have waxed and waned in their effectiveness.

Cognitive reports.   Apprehension is the most notable symptom reported by these patients; there is a vague and diffuse awareness that something dreadful is imminent, an experience compounded by the fact that they may not know what they specifically dread and from where the danger may arise. This feeling of impending disaster periodically reaches intense proportions, as in the acute and panic forms of anxiety.

Apprehension and fear of the unknown distract these patients from matters of normal daily routine; they often complain of inability to concentrate and are unable to maintain interest in previously pleasurable activities and pursuits. No matter what they do, they cannot avoid this pervasive and interminable apprehension. They are unable to distinguish the safe from the unsafe, the relevant from the irrelevant; they are increasingly forgetful and irritable, and begin to view minor responsibilities as momentous and insurmountable tasks. Their distress really begins to mount when they become self-conscious of growing incompetence and tension. As this self-awareness increases, it becomes a preoccupation. Observing themselves, they experience tremors, palpitations, muscular tightness, "butterflies in the stomach," cold sweats, a feeling of foreboding, and dreadful signs of imminent collapse. The fright of self-awareness not only perpetuates itself in a vicious circle, but feeds on itself and builds to monumental proportions. Unless they are able to distract and divert their attention, their controls give way or feel torn apart; there is an upsurge of unconscious emotions and images that flood to the surface, further overwhelming the patient; at this point, we see an acute anxiety attack or panic.

Other psychic processes.   Although anxiety is experienced by all individuals, why do some persons experience it more frequently and severely than others?

To answer this question fully, we must comment on phenomena that have become so automatic that they operate implicitly or beneath the level of awareness.

Ineffective coping that leads to frequent anxiety and panic attacks is typical of the more complex forms of these disorders; they are essentially automatic and often beyond awareness, as well as deficient or adaptively inflexible. Complex anxieties typically possess implicit cognitive, interpersonal, or unconscious hypersensitivities to duplicates of a painful past. These coping inadequacies and reaction sensitivities contribute to the chronic, tenuous stability of these patients. If we extrapolate from three characteristics—coping deficits, biological and unconscious sensitivities, and tenuous stability—we may better understand why many personalities are disposed to anxiety syndromes.

First, because the coping strategies of these persons may be deficient or inflexible, they cannot mobilize themselves effectively to handle a wide range of objective environmental threats. Unable to shield themselves adequately from diverse sources of conflict and tension, patients must keep up their guard, ever alert to dangers that may upset them; as a consequence, they may remain in a constant or chronic state of tension.

Second, the residues of past problematic experiences or distinct biological susceptibilities oversensitize the person to situations that are objectively insignificant. Because patient are generally unaware of the operation of these sensitivities, they are unable to grasp the reason for or source of their frequent apprehension. They know only that their distress is grossly disproportionate to reality conditions; they do not know that the basis for their response is to be found in chemical vulnerabilities or vaguely formed derivatives of past experience, now stirred up by objectively trivial events.

Third, once reactivated, these residues upset the patient's tenuous controls; moreover, they, in turn, stimulate other emotions and impulses with which they were formerly associated. Thus, the individual not only feels a flood of seemingly unwarranted tension and fear, but also experiences a variety of other strange and unreasonable emotions, such as hostility and guilt.

Biophysical factors.   Individual patterns of somatic discomfort differ widely, but in anxiety most of these symptoms reflect sympathetic system hyperactivity. Cardiovascular signs predominate in many patients; they experience chest pains, palpitations, increased blood pressure, throbbing sensations, undue perspiration, and heat flashes. Among other visceral complaints are gastrointestinal symptoms such as nausea, vomiting, cramps, gas pains, and diarrhea. In other patients, a constriction of the musculature prevails; here we see signs of body tightness with occasional spasms, a shortness of breath, tension headaches, wry necks, and so on. A generalized picture of fatigue and exhaustion is a common residual of daily tension and is often compounded by restless sleeping and insomnia.

Most mildly anxious states, and their associated bizarre thoughts and emotions, churn close to the surface but manage to be kept under control. If these feelings overpower the patient's tenuous controls, we will observe either an acute or a panic attack. These attacks often exhibit a mixture of terror and fury. In the less severe acute attack, there is more terror than fury; violent and lascivious urges are partially controlled or neutralized in these eruptions. In panic, however, impulses rise to the behavioral foreground and account for the bizarre and turbulent picture seen during these episodes.

Although there is a marked loss of control during acute and panic episodes, these eruptions often serve as a useful safety valve. By discharging otherwise hidden and pent-up feelings, patients' tensions may subside temporarily, and they may be able to relax for a while. For a fleeting moment, they have vented emotions and engaged in acts that they dare not express in the normal course of events; chaotic and destructive as they often are, these temporary "flings" serve a minor adaptive function.

Some patients adaptively utilize their chronic moderate tensions as a source of surplus energy. These individuals may be characterized by their seeming indefatigability, their capacity to drive themselves tirelessly toward achievement and success. There are others, however, who draw on their tension surplus to intrude on and disrupt the lives of their friends and families; they often become persistent and troublesome social irritants. Whether and how these tensions will be exploited depend on the overall pattern of psychic processes that characterize the patient.

Prevailing Treatment Options

Patients suffering from simple anxiety disorders should seek a focused therapy designed primarily for the purpose of relieving their distressing symptom. Should this be the central goal, sufficient in itself to reestablish the patient's disordered equilibrium, the therapist may focus efforts appropriately, utilizing a variety of symptomatic treatment methods. Prominent among these are such psychopharmacological agents as alprazolam and diazepam. In conjunction with these, especially where objective precipitants are present, the therapist may engage in environmental manipulation, advising about, where feasible, changing jobs, taking vacations, moving, and so on. In addition, exposure procedures of behavioral and cognitive therapy may be especially effective as a means of modifying anxiety-producing reactions and attitudes; these techniques often achieve this goal in a relatively brief treatment course. A few additional words should be said regarding the efficacy of both behavioral and pharmacologic treatment.

It appears fairly clear that in vivo exposure procedures are most effective when the anxiety source can be identified. Perhaps as many as 60–75% of patients benefit from this approach (Mattick, Andrews, Hadzi-Pavlovic, & Christiensen, 1990). In general, higher degrees of success were achieved for in vivo exposure as contrasted with imaginal exposure techniques (Trull, Nietzel, & Main, 1988). The efficacy of cognitive therapeutic techniques indicates a moderate level of efficacy, perhaps equal to if not superior to medication (Roth & Fonagy, 1996). Several variations on the behavioral approach have been undertaken to evaluate their respective efficacies. Exposure treatments may be undertaken by therapists who accompany patients during their exposure experience; by contrast, exposure may be self-directed, that is, carried out by patients themselves following a manualized set of instructions. In general, the results of both are highly favorable, but therapist-guided exposure experiences appear to be slightly superior.

Combination treatment of both behavioral exposure and various medications has been undertaken (Mavissakalian & Michelson, 1986). The results of these studies suggest that combination treatment does not enhance the effectiveness of in vivo exposure alone.

Applied relaxation methods contain both behavioral and cognitive elements. In general, the results suggest that modest levels of anxiety respond rather well to applied relaxation, but have a lower level of efficacy among those patients with panic levels of the disorder (Ost, 1988).

Straightforward cognitive techniques, though more limited in their efficacy than straightforward behavioral techniques, have nevertheless been "packaged" into a Panic Control Treatment program (Beck & Emery, 1985; Hollon & Beck, 1994; Klosko, Barlow, Tassinari, & Cerny, 1990). The panic control program includes a cognitive reinterpretation of situations that are conceived as threatening, combined with an exposure to one's own introceptive cues. Some 85% of those in the PCT combination approach prove to be panic-free, whereas those who received relaxation alone were only 60% improved. At a two-year follow-up, 81% were still symptom-free with the PCT program.

Pharmacologic techniques do possess relatively rapid but temporary benefits for anxious and panicky patient populations; most notable in this regard is alprazolam. However, these medications are no more effective than psychological techniques, even for chronic and severe anxiety conditions. They should not be seen as alternatives that are preferred or can replace behavioral exposure, owing to the fact that their therapeutic effects tend to diminish rapidly when the drug is discontinued, resulting in a discomforting relapse. It should be noted that numerous other techniques, for example, self-actualizing or psychodynamic methods, may prove helpful, but at this stage of our knowledge, there are few data to support their efficacy.

Should any of the aforementioned measures of symptom removal prove successful, the patient is likely to lose incentive for further therapy; there is no reason to pursue treatment if the patient seems content and experiences no secondary complications. However, should patients desire to explore associated roots of their disorder, or should symptom-removal efforts have failed, it may be advisable to embark on more extensive and probing therapeutic techniques. Attention is directed here not to the relief of symptoms nor to teaching patients to accept and utilize their anxiety; rather, the task is to uncover the residuals of the past that have sensitized patients to anxiety (Taylor & Braun, 1988), and then to resolve or reconstruct these sustaining attitudes, relationships, and feelings. Here, therapists must proceed with caution, lest they release more of these feelings than the patient can tolerate; severe panic attacks and psychotic disorders may not be an uncommon consequence of probing and releasing too much too fast.

POSTTRAUMATIC STRESS SYNDROMES

Whereas many patients experience anxiety in conjunction with a concurrent stimulus situation, others manifest it sometime *after* the stressful event has occurred. In effect, the anxiety reemerges at a later time, a period often weeks or months after the distressing experience occurs. These have been termed in the *DSM* posttraumatic stress disorders (PTSD).

General Clinical Picture

The *DSM-IV* has sought to explicate the PTSD category by noting clearly specified criteria, such as experiencing or witnessing an event involving actual or threatened physical harm as well as events that precipitate intense fear or helplessness. Variations in the symptomatology are also noted; for example, having recurrent and unwanted recollections, having distressing dreams, or feeling and acting as if the event were reoccurring. Associated with these features is the need to avoid thoughts, feelings, or discussions about the trauma, or an inability to recall important details concerning the event. Also notable are two contrasting coping styles: some patients adapt to their distressful memories by an emotional numbing and a restriction in the range of their affective sensitivities; others exhibit hyperarousal symptoms such as difficulty in falling or staying asleep, difficulties in concentrating on the ordinary events of life, or an exaggerated startle response to modest everyday events, as well as persistent and repetitive dream flashbacks.

Traumatizing events include rape, natural disasters, and military combat in which the patient experiences or witnesses psychologically painful and/or physically harmful consequences. Epidemiologic studies suggest that some 20% of those involved in war manifest PTSD, and some 35% of victims of assault or rape likewise are subject to the syndrome (Kilpatric & Resnick, 1993). Without appropriate treatment, the disorder appears to remain for extended periods. Thus, a 40-year follow-up of World War II prisoners of war indicated that two-thirds had suffered from PTSD (Kluznik, Speed, van Valkenburg, & Magraw, 1986). Of these, some 30% fully recovered, 40% reported some symptoms, 20% showed moderate improvement, and 10% had no recovery.

Theoretical viewpoints concerning the source of the PTSD category vary considerably. Traditional psychodynamic theorists believe that PTSD occurs when the individual's coping capabilities are overwhelmed and the trauma is unresolved psychologically. They believe that trauma survivors would be best approached by techniques that strengthen the patient's defenses and coping strategies (Herman, 1992; Schwartz, 1990). Those of a behavioral orientation speak of PTSD as a conditioned fear response that can be relieved by such methods as systematic desensitization. Cognitive and cognitive-behavioral theorists understand the patient's difficulties to be a consequence of misinterpretations or distortions of the trauma. Theorists of a cognitive persuasion, in contrast to those of a more psychodynamic orientation, see the traumatic event as the direct cause of the symptoms for the PTSD syndrome, whereas dynamic theorists see it as an expression of unconscious and symbolic significance, especially those underlying forces that represent deep conflicts or guilt feelings. Although greatest efficacy has been achieved with behavioral and cognitive methods, there is no reason to assume that the PTSD syndrome could not be conceived of as a complex anxiety syndrome; that is, the cause of the disorder need not correspond theoretically with its most efficacious treatment. Many syndromes may be the result of complex psychological processes in the cognitive and intrapsychic realms, but treatment may be best achieved with behavioral procedures.

Along similar lines, there has been an increasing recognition of possible biological vulnerabilities to PTSD, suggesting that certain pharmacologic agents may be efficacious in reducing overt symptomatology. To date, little progress has taken place in the use of medications.

Prevailing Treatment Options

Pharmacologic approaches have not been notably successful in moderating the PTSD syndrome. These include double-blind studies of imipramine and amitriptyline, MAOIs, and SSRIs (Foa, Davidson, & Rothbaum, 1995).

Similarly, there appears to be limited support for the efficacy of psychoanalytically based treatment procedures. Although there is some evidence that short-term dynamic approaches result in modest improvements, the specific elements that provide for these small gains cannot be differentiated from those that are spurious (Gabbard, 1995).

It is primarily in the area of cognitive and behavioral therapy that the highest rates of success have been achieved. As with other therapeutic techniques, the exposure behavioral procedure has demonstrated a reasonably high level of efficacy (Cooper & Clum, 1989). Systematic desensitization would also appear to be useful in the PTSD syndrome. However, the limited research carried out with this treatment approach precludes definitive judgments concerning its efficacy.

Various combinations of treatment methodology have been developed, such as stress inoculation training (SIT) and anxiety management programs (AMP) (Resick & Schnicke, 1992). In studies employing the SIT model, elements of relaxation, role modeling, thought stopping, and guided self-dialogue are interwoven in an effort to overcome PTSD reactions to rape, with a modest level of efficacy achieved. Similarly, in AMP combination therapy where relaxation, biofeedback, and cognitive restructuring are employed, all facets of the PTSD syndrome have been shown to be diminished in their intensity, though only modestly. Foa et al. (1995) have sought to compare SIT alone, exposure alone, and SIT and exposure in combination. All procedures were equally effective, though the combination approach proved to be slightly more effective than those employing a single methodology. Rather interestingly, all three approaches achieved a very satisfactory level of success, but at follow-up, the groups differed substantially in terms of their level of sustained recovery; the combination group achieved a 90% recovery rate as compared to 40% and 30% of those receiving SIT and exposure procedures, respectively.

GENERALIZED ANXIETY SYNDROMES

As an introduction and perspective for the various subtypes of anxiety-related complex syndromes, it will be instructive to provide a brief comment concerning the concept.

Complex syndromes occur frequently in pathological personality styles and disorders because these persons possess a variety of comorbid trait clusters, for example, cognitive assumptions, biophysical vulnerabilities, and self-image distortions. Each of these features adds forms of expression that go beyond the classical analytic view that persons with so-called neuroses possess primarily unconscious reaction sensitivities. Intruding in their responses are not only unconscious processes but also habitual ways of relating socially and distortion-producing cognitive expectations employed in response to stressful experiences. Faced with stress sufficient to upset or "disorder" their equilibrium, they repeatedly apply their multifaceted cognitive and interpersonal as well as intrapsychic strategies. Although these symptoms are similar to those seen in the simple reactions, those of complex syndromes are also a product of reactivated self-image difficulties, unconscious feelings, and habits beyond those stemming from direct biological vulnerabilities or narrowly circumscribed learnings.

There are other important differences between acute reactions and generalized anxiety syndromes. The latter usually signify a partial ability to control overt expressions of anxiety. These individuals express some way, albeit indirect and symbolic, for discharging some of their felt or perceived tensions. In contrast, persons with acute anxieties are unable to find internal or external measures to either control, neutralize, or vent their tensions. In simple and acute anxieties, tension is uncontrolled and consciously experienced, although its biogenic or psychogenic roots often remain either ambiguous or repressed. In complex syndromes, patients can often neutralize or camouflage the true character of their emotions so as to make them personally more tolerable and socially more acceptable.

We are now ready to survey the various complex disorders labeled as generalized anxiety. With minor exceptions, this grouping corresponds to the official *DSM-IV* classification of the Axis I syndromes. Points of difference, both substantive and semantic, will be noted as our discussion proceeds.

First, it should be noted that certain classical symptoms of neuroses appear less common today than when initially formulated some century ago. Moreover, a new set of syndromes seems to be supplanting the old. For example, fewer cases of conversion or dissociation are reported today, but there are more reports of what are termed existential nonbeing, alienation, and identity diffusion. There is no way of knowing whether these changes in symptomatology are real or are linguistic and cultural, for example, changes due to new patterns of child rearing, a growing awareness of previously overlooked problems, changing social fashions, theoretical interests of modern-day clinicians, and so on.

It seems to us that these changes are both real *and* spurious. No doubt, there are differences in child-rearing practices and in the pressures and values of life, and between modern America and turn-of-the-century Europe to which early clinicians addressed their writings. We contend, however, that the basic processes and goals that underlie the formation of complex syndromes have not appreciably changed. It appears to us that the newer anxiety-related disorders are currently fashionable and acceptable ways of discharging anxieties and impulses. Symptoms such as conversion are outmoded, and perhaps even suspect, in our sophisticated post-Freudian age. Sufferers of these disorders may gain only minimal compassion and approval as a consequence of their impairment. In contrast, everyone today knows "what a difficult world we live in," and "how hard it is to break out of the ruts of modern society"; thus, symptoms of identity diffusion, feelings of meaninglessness, social alienation, and existential anxiety are likely to evoke approval and a sympathetic hearing, even though they may represent a subterfuge for dependency needs or overtly unacceptable aggressive impulses. In short, these new complex syndromes appear to reflect the same psychic maneuvers and goals as were found in more classical forms. They are expressed, however, in ways that are suitable to present-day values and conditions.

General Clinical Picture

What are the sources of generalized anxiety?

As was noted, the label simple anxiety reaction is reserved for those paniclike states found in otherwise essentially normal individuals. The primary distinction between simple and complex impairments is that the simple disorder is either stimulus-specific or chemically driven, whereas complex anxiety syndromes are precipitated also by distorted cognitions, problematic self-evaluations, or essentially unconscious processes. Thus, in complex syndromes, minor and objectively insignificant precipitants not only reactivate past memories and emotions, but stir up and unleash a variety of associated secondary thoughts and impulses. These learned or unconscious residuals of the past surge forward and become the primary stimulus that threatens the stability of the personality, giving rise, then, to a pervasive state of chronic and diffuse anxiety.

Generalized anxiety disorders (GAD) are best characterized by an oversensitivity to worry about numerous and largely incidental life events. According to *DSM-IV,* the patient's worry is difficult to control, lasts at least six months, and is accompanied by a variety of characteristic symptoms, such as an inability to relax, the experience of tension, feelings of fright, a sense of jumpiness, and a general unsteadiness. The official manual specifies that three of the following six symptoms be present: feeling on edge, concentration difficulties, fatigability, irritability, muscle tension, and sleep disturbance. Although the clinician has little difficulty in recognizing this syndrome, it has been a diagnosis with poor interrater reliability and high rates of comorbidity. Debates in the literature exhibit conflict as to whether GAD is a distinct disorder as opposed to being a subthreshold or residual state of other clinical or personality disorders. As will be noted shortly, anticipatory anxiety, or what has been termed anxiety sensitivity, appears to be a central characteristic of GAD, that is, the presence of a constant state of hypervigilance and overarousal in anticipation of potential psychic and physical threats.

As noted above, different theoretical schools advance different explanations for the causes of generalized anxiety. For example, psychoanalytic theorists propose that this ever-present anticipatory fear stems from internal impulses that evoke distress signals that punishment is forthcoming should these impulses be expressed. Hence, patients are hyperalert to their own inner threats, which then become attached to the passing events of their life. By contrast, those of a cognitive and behavioral persuasion believe that it is the patient's belief in unrealistic sources of threat, that is, misinterpretations of reality, that produce the unjustified emotional reaction. According to them, these misinterpretations of external stimuli result from actual or generalized experiences in the patient's life, but now evoke unnecessary apprehension and behavioral avoidance that are inappropriate to current life situations. Other theoretical viewpoints, such as the existential, have proposed that a state of generalized anxiety reflects an awareness of life's inherent meaninglessness; similarly, those who are more biologically oriented interpret the psychic state as reflecting inner endocrine disturbances or minor cardiovascular dysfunctions. Barlow (1988), in his usual insightful way, proposes that biological and psychological vulnerabilities combine with problematic life events, thereby activating stress-related neurobiological reactions, and then producing repetitive and persistent levels of arousal that manifest themselves in unpredictable and uncontrollable states of generalized anxiety. It is this model that we refer to shortly in noting which personality styles and disorders may be especially vulnerable to these neurobiological processes.

Generalized anxiety affects persons of both sexes, but is more frequently diagnosed in women. It frequently coexists with depression and dysthymia, and several antidepressants (SSRIs, tricyclics) appear to work well for patients with generalized anxiety.

The cases presented here, as well as those in later chapters, represent actual patients treated or supervised by Millon in the past 40+ years. Graduate students, interns, and residents contributed to a significant degree to these formulations, as well as implementing their therapeutic goals. All cases have been substantially camouflaged; changes include age, sex, and vocation. It should be noted that many precede the development of the personality-guided synergistic model and, hence, are not as comprehensive and systematic as we would have preferred.

Next, we discuss a number of the features of the GAD syndrome as they may be elicited and coped with by different personality patterns, that is, personality styles and disorders. First, let us describe a typical case.

CASE 5.1, RONNY B., 35

It is very probable that Ronny experienced an anxiety disorder. She normally kept her emotions under substantial restraint, if not totally bottled up. Lately, intense apprehensiveness had broken through her intrapsychic controls and social proprieties. This apprehensiveness could be characterized by a diffuse worrisomeness and a growing preoccupation with psychological symptoms (e.g., catastrophic forebodings, behavioral fidgetiness, hyperdistractibility) and physical symptoms (e.g., gastrointestinal pains, insomnia, fatigue, and exhaustion) that may have been prompted by the reemergence of fears of abandonment, owing to recent interpersonal difficulties, or by the upsurge of strong oppositional impulses that threaten to overwhelm her controls. Ronny struggled to regain the façade of public respectability and personal equanimity that she usually presented to the world.

No sharp line distinguishes normal styles from pathological personalities, but the differences in the pervasiveness and intensity of their respective painful past experiences make it less likely that normal personalities will subjectively distort reality or have disruptive past feelings reactivated by the presence of real threat. Relatively free of cognitive distortions and intrapsychic eruptions, normal persons rely on reality as the primary stimulus of their behavior; as a consequence, their responses are less ever-present and more anchored to objective reality than those seen in more pathological patterns.

Prevailing Treatment Options

In contrast to the simple anxiety and panic reactions, where behavioral exposure techniques appear to be maximally effective, GAD conditions seem to benefit substantially from cognitive procedures (Beck & Emery, 1985). In general, cognitive techniques, especially those with behavioral aspects added, have shown significant levels of efficacy, levels in which close to three-fourths of patients give evidence of improvement immediately upon the conclusion of therapy and at six-month follow-up (Power, Simpson, Swanson, & Wallace, 1990). By contrast, those on pharmacologic medication improve reasonably well, but drop off in their effectiveness significantly and often relapse when medication is terminated (Lindsay, Gansu, McLaughlin, Hood, & Espie, 1987; Power et al., 1990). Nevertheless, a program including the benzodiazepines (Valium, Xanax) and/or the SSRIs (Prozac, Zoloft) for long-tem use may be quite helpful. Studies employing psychodynamic therapies have not been found to be especially efficacious although the opportunity to explore childhood roots (fears, secrets) does appear to reduce anxious concerns for some patients. Moderate levels of success have been reported employing applied relaxation and nondirective or self-actualizing procedures.

Though less effective in general than cognitive methods, these latter techniques appear to be sustained to a modest degree upon 12-month follow-up (Borkovec & Costello, 1993). Also of potential utility are a number of approaches that involve teaching patients how to manage a series of self-administered relaxation procedures, graded exposure, all combined with methods of cognitive distraction and the scheduling of pleasurable life activities (Butler, Cullington, Hibbert, Klimes, & Gelder, 1987).

It appears clear that there are numerous psychic and physical features involved in the chronic states of generalized anxiety; these encompass affective, cognitive, and intrapsychic processes. Cognitive-behavioral treatments appear to successfully tap into this mix of features.

Personality-Guided Synergistic Therapy

As we have said, objective precipitants in complex syndromes play a secondary role to those that exist internally, either biological or learned. It is patients' reaction sensitivities that dispose them to these syndromes; that is, the patient transforms essentially innocuous elements of reality so that they become duplicates of a problematic past; and, as in a vicious circle, these psychic intrusions and distortions stir up a wide range of comorbid clinical domains that feed and intensify the anxiety response. To specify the source of these complex anxieties, then, we must look not only to the objective conditions of reality, though these may in fact exist, but also to the deeply rooted and clinically relevant traits that comprise the patient's personality sensitivities.

It should be noted that the task of identifying these correlated psychic and physical domains is a highly speculative one because little research has been done to explore them empirically. Nevertheless, there is a rich clinical lore that can guide us (e.g., Millon & Davis, 1996a). The best we can do is to make logical and clinically informed rationales as to which self-judgments and cognitive expectancies, for example, in each of the major personality styles and disorders are likely to give rise to an anxiety proneness; these we attempt to provide below.

It is important that we restate a central principle in planning personality-guided psychotherapy: Causes need not correspond to therapies. For example, although the underlying origins and elements of a syndrome may be largely intrapsychic and biologic, treatment may prove to be best with procedures that are cognitive or behavioral. The person is a composite of many different psychic and biologic systems. What generates and sustains a clinical syndrome may be treated best and most efficaciously by an approach that reflects only one or two parts of the overall system, ones that operate in different spheres than where the pathogenic source may stem from. To illustrate, a toothache may best be treated initially by aspirin, but the toothache may stem from a physiological infectious process; treatment may best be dealt with by relieving the symptom directly and effectively by employing the aspirin medication. If the body resolves the infection on its own, the problem has been satisfactorily dealt with. However, if the problem (the infection) persists and recurs frequently, then treatment will have to continue, perhaps in a more intense biological manner, such as being surgically cleansed. So, too, in dealing with anxiety, be it acute or generalized, cognitive and behavioral techniques may prove all that is necessary, and the evidence is strong that these techniques are often capable of settling the problem on their own. Similarly, focused pharmacologic procedures and extensive interpersonal and intrapsychic procedures may be called for when the generalized anxiety has failed to be sufficiently unraveled and dispersed by simpler and more direct procedures. As stated previously, there is no single "cause" for generalized anxiety syndromes, even in patients with highly similar personality patterns; moreover, not only do anxiety precipitants differ from patient to patient, but different sensitivities may take precedence from time to time within a single patient. Let us proceed with these cautions in mind.

GENERALIZED ANXIETY AMONG
SCHIZOID AND SCHIZOTYPAL PERSONALITIES

These personalities are characterized by their flat and colorless style; intense emotions are rarely exhibited, and states of chronic anxiety are not frequently found. Two diametrically opposite sets of circumstances, however, may undergird a persistent anxious state: unrelenting and excess stimulation, or marked understimulation. These persons may seek treatment when they feel encroached upon or when they sense that they are being surrounded by oppressive social demands and responsibilities. Similar anxiety-sustaining consequences follow from marked understimulation; here, the patient experiences feelings of depersonalization, a frightening sense of emptiness and nothingness, a state of self-nonexistence, stagnation, barrenness, and unreality.

CASE 5.2, ARTHUR L., 23

Presenting Picture: There is a reasonable probability that Arthur suffered from a generalized anxiety state. Beneath his typical surface appearance of constraint and control, he appeared to be experiencing pervasive anxieties that manifested themselves in apprehension, indecisiveness, and psychosomatic problems (e.g., insomnia, headaches, muscular tightness). Feelings of inferiority or guilt or both may have underlain and prompted Arthur's discomfort. Demands and expectations that exceeded his levels of competence and tapped his feelings of opposition and anger may recently have been experienced.

Therapeutic Course: Therapy comprised a mix of support and reassurance, processed largely in a Rogerian self-actualizing model. Although Arthur was able to resolve a number of his anxiety feelings, especially when faced with what he perceived as the demands of others, the fundamental nature of his general apprehensiveness was only modestly improved.

Synergistic Afterthoughts: Today, we would be inclined to first prescribe an appropriate anxiolytic, followed by instituting a set of cognitive-behavioral and anxiety management procedures, helping him gain insight into his tendency to distort innocuous interactions with others as signifying pressure and demands. Also important would be teaching him, through methods such as desensitization and relaxation, to moderate his distraught feelings under these circumstances.

GENERALIZED ANXIETY AMONG AVOIDANT PERSONALITIES

These persons may experience generalized anxiety as a consequence of depersonalization and encroachment, in the same manner as do their schizoid counterparts. But, in addition, their histories have made them hypersensitive to social derogation and humiliation. They have acquired a cognitive distrust of others, but lack the self-esteem to retaliate against insult and derision. When repeated deprecations occur, reactivating past humiliations and resentments, these patients cannot respond or fear responding as they would like; their frustration and tension may mount, spilling over into a generalized anxiety state.

The interpersonal abilities of avoidants are barely adequate to the social strains and challenges they must handle. As such, they characteristically seem on edge, unable to relax, easily startled, tense, worrisome, irritable, preoccupied with calamities, and prone to nightmares; and they have poor appetites and suffer fatigue and intangible physical ailments. Some avoidants "adjust" to the pervasively uncomfortable state of generalized anxiety, but their lives are thereby limited and impoverished, restricted by the need to curtail their activities and relationships to just those few they can tolerate or manage.

Phenomenological apprehension is the most notable symptom voiced by these patients. They often report a vague and diffuse awareness that something dreadful is imminent, an experience compounded by the fact that they are unsure as to what it is that they dread and from where the danger appears to arise. This persistent feeling of impending disaster periodically reaches intense proportions, often precipitated into acute states as a consequence of social encroachment. The histories of these patients have made them hypersensitive to social derogation and humiliation. Not only have they acquired a marked distrust of others, but they lack the self-esteem to retaliate against insult and derision. When repeated deprecations occur, reactivating past humiliations and resentments, avoidants are unable to respond or fear responding as they would like. As a consequence, their frustration and tension may mount beyond tolerable limits.

CASE 5.3, MARK S., 27

Presenting Picture: Mark S., employed as a clerk, normally performed his work in a nonobtrusive manner, keeping to himself and rarely speaking to anyone except to return a passing greeting. Every several weeks or so, he would be found at work in the morning sitting and quaking in a small back room, unable to calm himself or to describe why he felt as he did. Upon repeated probing, it was usually possible to trace Mark's broad-based anxiety to incidental slights he had experienced at the hands of other employees.

Therapeutic Course: Evidence indicated the presence of a prominent anxiety disorder in Mark. Widely generalized symptoms were consistent with his overall personality makeup: pervasive social disquiet, behavioral edginess, apprehensiveness over small matters, and worrisome self-doubts, the most frequent of which may have related to feelings of masculine inadequacy. Specific psychosomatic signs may have been present in addition to the more general anxious state. These signs include fatigue, insomnia, headaches, and an inability to concentrate. Especially sensitive to public reproval, yet lacking the confidence to respond with equanimity, he may have been experiencing more discomfort than usual, particularly if his resentment had been expressed against someone with whom he would rather have maintained peace or a safe distance.

Client-centered therapy was the central approach employed in dealing with Mark's course of treatment. The program was essentially supportive with considerable reassurance that his difficulties did not signify a problem of potential psychotic proportions. Treatment was supplemented by the use of the earlier anxiolytics, notably Librium and Valium. Though they appear to have reduced Mark's discomforts, they did not help undo his generalized anxious state to any appreciable degree. Albeit indirectly, a number of cognitive techniques were employed to alter his readiness to see difficulties when there was little reason to do so. Change was modest, but notable.

Synergistic Afterthoughts: If we were to approach this young man today, we would first concentrate on cognitive-behavioral methods, perhaps combined with a variety of relaxation and skill-acquisition techniques to deal with his interpersonal sensitivities. We would not avoid the use of the newer anxiolytics, but would not depend on them to the extent that many therapists appear to at this time. A secondary effort would be centered on exploring his deeper feelings so as to unburden him of his tendency to react to difficulties as intensely as he does. Here, some of the self-actualizing experiential methods would be employed to focus on affective feelings that were aroused in Mark when he contemplated potential problematic situations. This would enable us to understand a number of the sources generating his generalized anxiety; we would then again utilize methods of cognitive reorientation to help him understand that his anticipations were not as realistic as he feared them to be.

GENERALIZED ANXIETY AMONG DEPENDENT PERSONALITIES

Dependent personalities are extremely vulnerable to anxiety disorders, especially those referred to as separation anxieties. Having placed their welfare entirely in the hands of others, they expose themselves to conditions that are ripe for generalized anxieties. There may be an ever-present worry of being abandoned by their primary benefactor and left alone to struggle with what they see as their meager competencies. Another factor that may give rise to periods of generalized anxiety is the anticipation and dread of new responsibilities. Their sense of personal inadequacy and the fear that new burdens may tax their limited competencies (thereby bringing disapproval from others) may precipitate a dramatic change from a state of pseudocalmness to one of overt and marked anxiety. It should be noted, of course, that anxious displays often serve to evoke nurturant and supporting responses from others. Thus, the GAD syndrome may come to the foreground as a "tool" that enables the dependent to avoid the discomforting responsibilities of autonomy and independence.

CASE 5.4, LOUISE L., 34

Presenting Picture: Louise L. was to be married shortly; she had been overprotected throughout her life and felt generally ill-equipped to assume the various roles of a housewife. Her fiancé was a strong-willed man some 20 years her senior whose wife had died several months earlier. She was advised to see a therapist for premarital counseling; it was clear, however, that her presenting problem was that of a generalized anxiety disorder. In recent weeks, Louise was unable to sleep and woke up frightened, tense, and crying. She would sit at home in her favorite chair, anxious and fretful, preoccupied with a variety of "strange" thoughts, notably that her fiancé would die before the date of their planned marriage. She noticed that her hands trembled; she felt nauseated much of the time and had heart palpitations, feelings of dizziness, and irregularities in her menstrual cycle. These symptoms began about 10 days after her fiancé asked her to marry him, which she quickly agreed to do on the advice of her parents.

Therapeutic Course: After several cognitively oriented therapy sessions, Louise began to see that her anxiety was founded on her fear of leaving the protective security of her family and her dread that she might not be able to perform her new responsibilities in accord with her fiancé's expectations. As she gained some understanding of the roots of her generalized and acute state, and with adequate assurances of affection and support from her fiancé, her anxieties abated considerably.

Synergistic Afterthoughts: Approached from a personality-guided model, we would add to the cognitive approach such behavioral techniques as social-skill and assertiveness training, as well as methods of applied relaxation, so as to reduce the potential of reactivating early panicky experiences.

As noted, generalized anxiety in these patients often serves as a means of evoking nurturant and supporting responses from others; in addition, it may become an instrumental ploy by which they can avoid the discomforting responsibilities of autonomy and independence.

GENERALIZED ANXIETY AMONG HISTRIONIC PERSONALITIES

These persons are vulnerable to separation anxiety only to a slightly lesser extent than those with dependent personality traits; however, the specific conditions that precipitate these feelings are quite different. Histrionic personalities promote their own separation anxieties by their tendency to seek diverse sources of support and changing sources of stimulation; they quickly get bored with old attachments and excitements. As a consequence, they frequently find themselves alone, stranded for extended periods with no one to lean on and nothing to be occupied with. During these "empty" times they are "at loose ends" and experience a marked restlessness and generalized anxiety until some new excitement or attraction draws their interest. These patients experience genuine anxiety during these extended vacant periods, but they tend to overdramatize their distress as a means of soliciting attention and support; the use of anxiety histrionics as an instrumental tool of attention-getting is most notable in these patients.

CASE 5.5, ARLENE M., 35

Presenting Picture: Arlene reported experiencing the clinical signs of a generalized anxiety disorder of an uncharacteristic nature. Somewhat agitated and apprehensive, she reported physical discomfort such as headaches, fatigue, and insomnia. Also notable, Arlene displayed a variety of behavioral signs such as jitteriness, diffuse fears, and ominous presentiments. She was characteristically needy of stimulation and activity. Arlene's state was prompted by the recent loss of someone on whom she had depended, and she had a feeling of being "at loose ends," which had been precipitated by her inability to find a focus of interest or a goal. Arlene also demonstrated a proclivity to dramatize distress as an attention-getting device.

Therapeutic Course: Therapy comprised mostly supportive reassurance as an approach to dealing with her sense of emptiness and loneliness. Her fear that life had "ended" was reexamined through a series of cognitive reevaluation techniques, some of which were more directive than is usually employed with those who evidence general anxiety. Nevertheless, these procedures appear to have been quite effective, and led to a successful termination after some 20 sessions.

Synergistic Afterthoughts: A current personality-guided treatment model would center its ultimate focus on this patient's high dependency needs, especially turning to others for constant approval and attention. Cognitive techniques would be initially employed, and they would be geared to assist the patient to recognize that she is overly preoccupied with the judgments of others; in this regard, a confrontational-directive cognitive procedure would appear to be in order. A major secondary tactic would be to enhance a depleted sense of self-esteem, that is, to employ techniques geared along the lines of Rogers's client-centered approach, thereby enhancing an increased level of self-respect and self-confidence. Such techniques may reduce the likelihood that she would feel abandoned and lost whenever her interpersonal world proved problematic.

GENERALIZED ANXIETY AMONG NARCISSISTIC PERSONALITIES

These patients characteristically do not exhibit generalized anxiety disorders; however, overt anxiety may be manifested for a brief period before these patients cloak or otherwise handle the expression of these feelings. The image of "weakness" conveyed in the display of this symptom is anathema to these persons; thus, it is rarely allowed to be manifested overtly, tending to be neutralized or expressed primarily in other domains.

The source of anxiety in these patients usually reflects matters such as failures to manipulate and exploit others, or the growing disparity between their illusions of superiority and the facts of reality. Although they are not accustomed to inhibit emotions and impulses, their anxiety is manifested not in pure form but in an alloy of anxious hostility and resentment, as illustrated in the following brief history.

CASE 5.6, ROBERT A., 29

Presenting Picture.   This narcissistic man, Robert A., had been berated and his work repeatedly disparaged by his employer. In previous years, discomforting events such as these were ameliorated by his adulating mother, who assured him of the "stupidity" of others and, by contrast, his "brilliance and ability." Unfortunately, his mother passed away several months prior to this work incident. Unable to replenish his self-esteem, his feelings of anxiety began to mount. However, rather than admit his faults or "show" his inner tension, he began to criticize his boss to others in an agitated, bitter, and deprecating tone.

Therapeutic Course: Treatment was instigated by his employer owing to the desire to retain Robert as an employee but an unwillingness to experience Robert's tendency to be "arrogant and difficult." After a few sessions in which Robert's inner demons were largely ventilated, the therapist employed a variant of Glasser's Reality Therapy to help Robert realize his responsibilities and to assist him in controlling his hostile outbursts. In addition, role modeling was employed following Gestalt therapeutic techniques as a means of providing Robert with the ability to control his anger and to better understand how those on the receiving end of his outbursts will not only feel but react negatively, as in a vicious circle.

Synergistic Afterthoughts: Current treatment approaches of a personality-guided nature would closely follow that executed by Robert's original therapist. All indications are that this brief treatment (fewer than eight sessions) facilitated this young man's acquisition of a more controlled style of behaving interpersonally when he experienced a lack of emotional support and high levels of anxiety. In effect, the therapeutic approach served to curtail his tendency to act out extrapunitively when experiencing loss and generalized anxiety.

The following case is of another narcissistic man experiencing the GAD syndrome.

CASE 5.7, RICH E., 38

Presenting Picture: Rich E. was unaccustomed to experiences that characterize a generalized anxiety disorder, yet his MCMI-III responses indicated that he was undergoing this syndrome. In addition to physical indices such as a diffuse apprehensiveness, he was subjected to persistent bodily tension and muscular pains as well as undue perspiration and chest palpitations. Rich also experienced a sense of foreboding, feeling jumpy and on edge, and short periods of unexplained fatigue. Prompted by recent, unexpected failures and a sense of being a fraud underneath it all, Rich's current state stemmed from an inability to have things go his way, a reversal of his usual success in manipulating events to his liking.

Therapeutic Course: Therapy appeared to be progressing well owing to its focus on replenishing his sense of high self-worth; utilized here were supportive techniques of reassurance and the self-actualizing methods of Rogers's client-centered model. Features of Kohut's self-focused analytic techniques were also employed, as were aspects of an existential approach. Unfortunately, these techniques served to enhance his self-esteem to such a degree that he resolved to undergo his own self-therapy and, hence, withdrew from professional treatment. Subsequent to termination, the therapist learned that Rich had been hospitalized with a brief paranoid psychosis, a fact suggesting that self-enhancement may not have been a wise course with this narcissistic man.

Synergistic Afterthoughts: Recognizing the ultimately defeating character of a self-enhancing approach to these personalities suggests that a contemporary personality-guided approach should center its attention on the need to diminish the narcissist's self-focus and guide him to recognize the importance, value, and needs of others. It is here where a confrontational and reality-oriented model might prove best initially, although an early period of reassurance and acceptance might be necessary during the first several sessions.

GENERALIZED ANXIETY AMONG ANTISOCIAL AND SADISTIC PERSONALITIES

These persons experience appreciably greater and more frequent anxiety than is often claimed in the literature. The dread of attachment, of being controlled, punished, and condemned by others is intense, and events that reactivate these fears and memories evoke persistent mixtures of anxiety and hostility. Severe attacks of panic will occur if patients feel particularly powerless or at the mercy of the hostile forces they see about them; we might note that the perception of these sources of influence and persecution may become hallucinatory in patients disposed to paranoid traits, that is, projections upon the environment of the patient's own aggressive and vindictive impulses. Also notable is the fact that these patients quickly find an external source to which they can ascribe their inner discomfort.

The surplus tension and energy generated by anxiety in these patients are often transformed and utilized to spur vigorous self-assertive action. Much of the drive and aggressiveness that characterize these patients reflect the exploitation of anxious energy in the service of their goals. Many though not all of these personalities possess what we have termed the *parmic temperament* (Millon, 1969), that is, a constitutionally based fearlessness or insensitivity to threat. However, despite their relative imperviousness to anxiety, they are human, and therefore do experience intensely discomforting tensions. Nevertheless, their constitutional callousness decreases the probability of a generalized anxiety disorder.

CASE 5.8, LARRY T., 26

Presenting Picture: Unable to control deep or powerful sources of threat, and characteristically angry, conflicted, and irritable in manner, Larry was now experiencing the clinical signs of a generalized anxiety disorder. Various symptoms were evident: muscular tightness, headache, fatigue, perspiration, and chest palpitations, as well as such behavioral indices as edginess and distractibility. These experiences were probably derived from Larry's feeling of being trapped by the upwelling of uncontrollable inner conflicts and by the feeling of being exposed to events or forces that he could not counteract. His restlessness and jumpiness derived energy from the press of these unchecked sources of danger.

Therapeutic Course: Larry was encouraged to see a therapist by his mother, who recognized the sharp changes that had taken place in him in the preceding year. He was once a cocky and arrogant gang member and now was lost and filled with intense fears and premonitions of doom. Treatment was relatively brief owing to Larry's disinclination to being seen as someone in need of psychiatric treatment. Nevertheless, sufficient time was available to utilize applied relaxation techniques and to explore the sources of Larry's anxieties through cognitive and experiential techniques. It became clear that Larry had broken a central rule of the gang to which he was no longer a member. He was terribly ashamed of "squealing" and dreaded the possibility that he would be forever ostracized, if not "done in." His deeper fearfulness and shame prompted his generalized anxiety state. Although treatment was brief, he appeared to come away with a more realistic appraisal of the circumstances of his life, as well as methods of self-relaxation.

Synergistic Afterthoughts: Lacking in the therapeutic approach employed for Larry were efforts to assist him in resocialization with culturally acceptable groups. Although it was not a key part of his treatment program, owing to managed-care restrictions, participating in a therapeutic group may have aided Larry in recognizing that his difficulties were not especially unusual, nor were they justly guilt-producing. At the same time, it may have been helpful to introduce him into social skill training settings where he could learn to understand and relate comfortably with others of a non-antisocial orientation. The continued use of anxiolytics and the internalization of relaxation methodologies may also have proved useful over the long run.

GENERALIZED ANXIETY AMONG OBSESSIVE-COMPULSIVE PERSONALITIES

The pervasive presence of chronic tension should be noted as a major feature of the compulsive personality disorder; anxiety is so much a part of these persons' everyday functioning that one cannot say where personality features end and where the generalized anxiety state begins.

Along with other ambivalents, obsessive-compulsive personalities are among the most frequent candidates for generalized anxiety disorders. First, they experience a cognitive expectancy of social condemnation; every thought that may digress from an interpersonally straight and narrow path is subject to the fear of punitive reactions from external authority. Second, these cognitions and social behaviors are compounded by their deeply repressed hostile impulses, which threaten to erupt and overwhelm their controls; without these controls, the tenuous social façade and psychic cohesion they have struggled to maintain may be torn apart. Thus, ever concerned that they will fail to fulfill the demands of authority and constantly on edge lest their contrary inner impulses break out of control for others to see, these patients often live in a constant and generalized state of anxiety.

Many of these patients learn to utilize the excess energy they derive from their chronic tension to effective ends; the characteristic diligence and conscientiousness of the compulsive reflects, in large measure, the control and exploitation of anxious energy. However, should their tense and overcontrolled state be punctured, either by external social precipitants or by an acute vulnerability of internal impulses or biochemical dysfunctions, there is a high probability that a manifest anxious or panic attack will ensue.

CASE 5.9, WAYNE H., 37

Presenting Picture: Wayne has experienced a lifelong pattern of generalized anxiety. Troubled by an upsurge of inner turmoil, he usually held discomfort in check by intrapsychic controls and social conformity. Recently, however, intense apprehensiveness and edginess emerged, as noted by a worrisome preoccupation with a host of psychological symptoms (e.g., restlessness and diffuse fears) and physical symptoms (e.g., insomnia, headaches, gastrointestinal problems). These were probably prompted by the outcropping of otherwise effectively repressed impulses that threatened to erupt and overwhelm his usual controls, thereby provoking the public shame and condemnation he strove to avoid.

Therapeutic Course: A treatment program undertaken with Wayne largely comprised supportive reassurance and the use of systematic desensitization procedures. After about 10 sessions, Wayne appeared to be able to control his general state moderately well. However, after several months on his own, so to speak, he returned to treatment owing to the reemergence of his fears and his inability to successfully employ the desensitization procedure he had learned. The same procedures that were utilized initially were again utilized with a level of apparent success, although word came back that Wayne was hospitalized with a series of panic attacks several months after terminating treatment.

Synergistic Afterthoughts: If we were to approach this obsessive-compulsive person today, we would certainly want initially to employ techniques of desensitization that would be paired with those of exposure therapy. Owing to the complex nature of the intrapsychic dynamics of compulsive personalities, it would also be advisable to employ cognitive reorientation techniques in the early stages of treatment. Care, of course, would have to be taken not to expose Wayne's inner conflicts with confrontive methods that lay bare his deep ambivalences. A cognitive reframing approach should prove more efficacious and less risky. Restructuring his fears of condemnation by modest levels of reality exposure should also aid him in dealing with his erroneous anticipations of condemnation. Potentially useful also in the early stages are a variety of anxiolytic medications that should assist him in reducing his troublesome feelings.

GENERALIZED ANXIETY AMONG NEGATIVISTIC PERSONALITIES

These patients experience frequent and prolonged states of anxiety. In contrast to their compulsive counterparts, for example, their discomfort and tension are exhibited openly and are utilized rather commonly as a means either of upsetting others or of soliciting their attention and nurture; which of these two functions takes precedence depends on which facet of their ambivalence comes to the foreground.

Typically, these patients color their apprehensions with depressive complaints, usually to the effect that others misunderstand them and that life has been full of disappointments. These complaints crystallize and vent their diffuse tensions and at the same time are subtle forms of expressing intense angers and resentments. Most commonly, these patients discharge their tensions in small and frequent doses, thereby decreasing the likelihood of a cumulative buildup and massive outburst; it is only when they are unable to discharge their angry impulses or experience the threat of separation that these generally anxious patients may be precipitated into an acute anxiety attack. Having learned to utilize anxiety as an instrument of subtle aggression or as a means of gaining attention and nurture, they often complain of anxiety for manipulative purposes, even when they do not genuinely feel it.

CASE 5.10, ARNOLD S., 29

Presenting Picture: The angry, irritable, and conflicted quality that appeared to characterize Arnold's style seemed to be complicated by a tense and apprehensive quality, one suggestive of a generalized anxiety disorder. Experiencing various physical symptoms, such as muscular tightness, headaches, perspiration, and palpitations, as well as behavioral signs such as jumpiness and hyperdistractibility, Arnold felt trapped by his inability to work through his conflicts and by his powerlessness to confront what he saw as problematic forces about him. Much of his reported restlessness and edginess derived their energy from the uncontrollable and diffuse anxiety that he experienced.

Therapeutic Course: Arnold approached the therapeutic experience, one recommended by his girlfriend, with great trepidation. Efforts were made to recommend pharmacologic treatment, along with a program of systematic desensitization. He left therapy after the third session, voicing intense anger at the therapist and at therapy as a method of resolving one's personal problems.

Synergistic Afterthoughts: It is difficult to say, given the foreknowledge of Arnold's treatment experience, what would have been done synergistically had he been a new patient. The therapist may have avoided Arnold's reactions had he had assessment information (e.g., MCMI) concerning his general personality style before treatment began. It is hard not to overstate the importance of a competent psychological assessment to serve as a guide whereby the therapist can "know" enough to avoid making unnecessary misjudgments and be directed along less risky lines of approach.

GENERALIZED ANXIETY AMONG
DEPRESSIVE AND MASOCHISTIC PERSONALITIES

As part of the general dysphoric state that typifies these personalities, we often see a diffuse though usually moderate level of generalized anxiety. As with similar personalities, depressive and masochistic traits are associated with fears of loss and abandonment. The anticipation of such eventualities remain as a persistent and underlying source of concern, leaving these persons vulnerable to the fear of finding that their desperate and self-sacrificial efforts will not suffice to protect them against personal loss. States of panic may also emerge under these conditions, especially when the attachments needed to maintain their equilibrium are in serious jeopardy.

CASE 5.11, LOUIS R., 42

Presenting Picture: That Louis, an aggrieved and unhappy man, reported the symptomatology of a generalized anxiety disorder was not unexpected. Much of his run-of-the-mill existence had been fraught with discontent and suffering; hence, that he noted the diffuse fears, mental distractibility, and fatigue that typify the syndrome was not surprising. Plagued by doubts, expecting the worst, and repeatedly undoing opportunities to better his circumstances, Louis seemed to create life stressors that promoted the worries and anguish that characterized his general anxiety state.

Therapeutic Course: This man came into therapy with a mix of both generalized anxiety and dysthymia. Fears that he might be suicidal prompted the administration of the then-new SSRIs. In addition, a cognitive-behavioral approach was utilized as a means of reorienting his beliefs and expectancies about his relationships and his personal future. The focus of treatment centered on misinterpretations or exaggerations concerning significant others in his life, and his inability to behave in ways that would prove successful in achieving his aims. Similarly, the self-actualizing techniques of humanistic and experiential therapy were employed to enhance his sense of self-esteem and to acquire interpersonal styles of conduct that might prove more rewarding in the future. Also employed were brief family therapy sessions in which significant others were educated to help Louis deal with his interpersonal attitudes and difficulties.

Synergistic Afterthoughts: Much to the therapist's gratification, Louis showed considerable progress over a period of several months. Whether this progress was due to the SSRIs or the synergistic treatment modalities employed is hard to say. However, Louis's treatment suggests that a planful arrangement that utilizes several different modalities in combination or in sequence, as well as mirroring the patient's problematic domains of functioning, is more likely to be efficacious than techniques that are either piecemeal or fail to coordinate with those domains in which the patient's personality is most problematic.

GENERALIZED ANXIETY AMONG BORDERLINE PERSONALITIES

Brief eruptions of uncontrollable emotion occur in borderline patients, who often experience states of generalized anxiety. For varied reasons, traceable to particular biologic vulnerabilities or coping inadequacies, these patients repeatedly fear the omnipresence of an impending disaster or feel that they are being overwhelmed or will disintegrate from the press of forces that surge within them. A generalized anxiety may follow a period of mounting stress in which a series of objectively trivial events cumulate to the point of being experienced as devastating. At other times, it is when the patient's unconscious impulses have been activated and break through their controls that we see an upsurge of diffuse feelings, followed by an emotional discharge. After a few minutes (or at most one or two hours), the diffuse sense of fear, with its concomitant physical symptoms, begins to subside, and the patient returns to a more typical level of minor discomfort. There are other, more intense periods when a sweeping disorganization and overwhelming panic reaction may take hold. Hence, the patient is carried by a rush of irrational impulses and bizarre thoughts that often culminate in a wild spree of chaotic behavior, violent outbursts, terrifying hallucinations, suicidal acts, and so on. These extreme behaviors may be justly diagnosed as a *brief psychotic disorder,* a category listed under the schizophrenia classification. In either case, we see transitory states of both intense anxiety and ego decompensation that terminate after a few hours, or at most one or two days, following which the patient regains his or her "normal" equilibrium. Should these eruptions linger for weeks or recur frequently, with bizarre behaviors and terrifying anxieties persisting, it would be more correct to categorize the impairment as a specific psychotic disorder.

CASE 5.12, ELLEN S., 21

Presenting Picture: Ellen was typically conflicted, resentful, and irritable, and her characteristic state was complicated by the discomforting symptoms of a generalized anxiety syndrome. Headaches, insomnia, and fatigue were present, as well as behavioral symptoms such as distractibility, apprehensiveness, and presentiments of dire events. These symptoms were products of unresolved inner conflicts that had pressed to the surface, upsetting Ellen's usual ease in discharging anger and resentment. Her feeling of being at the mercy of uncontrollable inner forces did not preclude the exploitation of her anxious energies to criticize and manipulate others.

Therapeutic Course: The outpatient treatment program employed to deal with Ellen's spasmodic behaviors and persistent anxiety was insufficient to deal with her difficulty. There were periods when treatment depended on the administration of a number of antipsychotic medications; other periods sought to quiet her irritability through an existential-philosophical approach, that is, to have her recognize that much of her vacillations and explosiveness reflected the nature of our complicated and changing culture. Treatment continued on a once-a-week basis for approximately six months, at which time Ellen entered a residential treatment program at a well-known psychoanalytically oriented hospital. She remained there for approximately 18 months, and left presumably improved.

Synergistic Afterthoughts: What would we do with Ellen today? Clearly, pharmaceutical methods would be involved in the early stages to try to moderate both her underlying anxiety and depressive feelings. Much more would be needed, however, owing to the fact that pharmaceuticals have a beneficial effect while they are being taken by the patient, and lose their usefulness when they are withdrawn. As was done in Ellen's case, a brief period in a controlled environment, such as in a residential treatment program, is often necessary. Here, the main focus would be on attempting to structure her daily environment and to assist her to learn to cognitively recognize that the outside world is not as erratic and changeable as it appears to her. Synergistically, it would be wise to institute cognitive techniques (nondirective) where she could learn that her anticipations of life's changeability do not accord with objective reality. Behavioral techniques may next be utilized, especially if employed concurrently with Gestalt rehearsal procedures; these would assist her to explore how she erroneously reacts to events that previously "set her off" in one direction and then another. Owing to her erratic way of relating to others, it may be useful as a final step to institute a family therapeutic approach that would facilitate her learning that significant others in her life need not be as unpredictable as she has assumed them to be.

GENERALIZED ANXIETY AMONG PARANOID PERSONALITIES

Severe generalized anxiety disorders may take the form of diffuse apprehensions or fears of the unknown, often distracting the patient from dealing effectively with matters of daily routine. Paranoids may complain of their inability to concentrate and of being unable to enjoy previously pleasurable activities and pursuits. No matter what they do, they feel unable to avoid pervasive and interminable apprehension. They sense themselves incapable of distinguishing the safe from the unsafe. Some become notably irritable and view minor responsibilities as momentous and insurmountable tasks. Distress mounts when they become aware and self-conscious of their growing incompetence and tension. Soon, this self-awareness becomes a preoccupation. Observing themselves, paranoids sense tremors, palpitations, muscular tightness, "butterflies in the stomach," cold sweats, a feeling of foreboding, and, ultimately, the dread of imminent collapse. Their awareness of their own frailty has not only perpetuated their fright but feeds on itself until it builds to extreme proportions. Unless they can distract or divert their attention elsewhere, paranoids' controls may give way. The upsurge of otherwise controlled fears and images that flood to the surface may inundate and overwhelm them, resulting in an acute anxiety attack or panic reaction.

CASE 5.13, WILHEMINA T., 47

Presenting Picture: Irritable and depressed much of the time, Wilhemina appeared to be experiencing a level of dysphoria that was sufficient to justify characterizing her state as a generalized anxiety disorder. Behavioral symptoms such as restlessness, edginess, and distractibility coexisted with somatic signs of anxiety, such as ill-defined pains, insomnia, and exhaustion. She vacillated between keeping her dysphoric feelings in check and voicing them, thus preventing herself from stabilizing her emotions. This, in turn, precluded the opportunity for her disquiet to subside. As was consistent with her basic personality, Wilhemina attributed these discomforts to the malicious thoughts and actions of those with whom she worked and lived.

Therapeutic Course: Owing to the broad range of precipitants of her apprehensive feelings, little success was achieved in treating her from a behavioral or cognitive methodology. Efforts to use pharmacologic tools likewise appear to be of limited effect, although different medications were tried to moderate her anxiety feelings and to counter her semidelusions of persecution. It was unclear as to whether Wilhemina ever took her medications and, therefore, it was not possible to determine if they would have been beneficial to her. She terminated treatment on her own after 12 sessions, asserting that her problems were "real," and any effort to change her perceptions were not only misguided but a malicious attempt to influence her.

Synergistic Afterthoughts: Unfortunately, little progress is likely to take place in dealing with patients like Wilhemina. Their suspiciousness and feelings of inadequacy will require a combinational approach in which the patient is exposed to a variety of methods both together and sequentially. No doubt, cognitive reorientation would be the first and most likely best initial technique, were the patient willing to engage in dialogues that permit such explorations and discussions. Similarly, pending recent advances, there may be some value in dealing pharmaceutically with the patient's paranoid dimension.

CHAPTER SIX

Treating Anxiety-Related Psychological Syndromes: Phobic, Dissociative, and Obsessive-Compulsive Disorders

To discharge anxieties, while at the same time being unclear or blocking awareness of their true sources, avoiding social rebuke and evoking social approval and support in their stead, is a task of no mean proportions. It requires the masking and transformation of one's true thoughts and feelings by the intricate workings of several domains of psychic functioning, including cognitive, unconscious, and interpersonal. The resulting complex syndrome represents the interplay and final outcome of these conscious and unconscious maneuvers. Not only have the patient's emotions been disguised sufficiently to be kept from everyday awareness, but he or she often manages to solicit attention and nurturance and achieve a measure of tension discharge.

According to traditional Freudian theory, the primary function of complex, or what he termed psycho-neurotic, symptoms is the avoidance, control, and partial discharge of anxiety. Complex syndromes also may produce certain positive gains; that is, as a consequence of one's symptoms, one may obtain *secondary* advantages or rewards. For example, a woman's phobic symptom may gain positive rewards above and beyond the reduction and narrowing of anxiety precipitants; in the role of a sick and disabled person, she may solicit attention, sympathy, and help from others, as well as be freed of the responsibility of carrying out many of the duties expected of a healthy adult. In this fashion, her phobic symptom not only controls and partially vents her otherwise more diffuse anxieties, but enables her to gratify her basic dependency needs.

The distinction between primary gains (anxiety reduction) and secondary gains (positive rewards) may be sharply drawn at the conceptual level but is difficult to make when analyzing actual cases because the two processes intermesh closely in reality. However, to those who subscribe to Freudian theory, the conceptual distinction is extremely important. As they view it, secondary gains play no part in stimulating the formation of the neurotic symptom. To them, patients are prompted to exhibit their syndrome, *not* as a means of gaining secondary or positive reinforcements, but as a means of avoiding, controlling, or discharging the negative experience of anxiety.

This sharp distinction between primary and secondary gains seems rather arbitrary and narrow. Although it is true that anxiety reduction or neutralization is centrally involved in complex syndromal formations, this, in itself, could not account for the variety of complex syndromes that patients display. We may ask, Why are certain intrapsychic mechanisms, for example, employed by some patients and different ones by others, and why did certain cognitive beliefs rather than others emerge? If the sole purpose of complex symptom formation were anxiety abatement, a wide number of different intrapsychic mechanisms could fulfill that job.

This, however, is not the case. Only certain combinations of symptoms are displayed in complex syndromes, notably those that should neutralize or discharge anxiety, but do so *without provoking social condemnation,* and quite often *managing to solicit support and nurturance* as well. It would seem, then, that complex syndromes comprise a variety of psychic processes and coping maneuvers to reduce anxiety (primary gain) and, at the same time, achieve certain positive advantages (secondary gain). Thus, and in contrast to traditional clinical theory, we believe that complex syndrome formation reflects the joint operation of both primary and secondary gain strategies. Moreover, a variety of trait clusters (what we call clinical domains) evolve as deeply embedded covariants of the primary or simple anxiety syndrome, notably interpersonal style, self-image, cognitive beliefs, and others.

As noted, complex syndromes display themselves in such ways as both to avoid social derogation and to elicit support and sympathy from others. For example, an agoraphobic patient manipulated members of her family into accompanying her in street outings, where she gained the illicit pleasures of sexual titillation; through her "unfortunate" disablement, she fulfilled her dependency needs, exerted substantial control over the lives of others, and achieved partial impulse gratification without social condemnation. Let us look at two other examples. An Axis I conversion patient with psychogenic visual impairments was not only relieved of family responsibilities, but through her troubling symptom made others feel guilty and limited their freedom while still gaining their concern and yet not provoking their anger. A somatoform woman who experienced diverse physical ailments precluded sexual activity; she not only gained her husband's compassion and understanding, but did so without his recognizing that her behavior was a subtle form of punishing him; she was so successful in her maneuver that her frustration of his sexual desires was viewed, not as an irritation or a sign of selfishness on her part, but as an unfortunate consequence of her physical illness. Her "plight" evoked more sympathy for her than for her husband.

Why do the symptoms of complex disorders take this particular, devious route? Why are their hostile or otherwise socially unacceptable impulses masked and transformed so as to appear not only socially palatable but evocative of support and sympathy? To answer this question, we must examine the various clinical domains and personality styles/disorders that tend to exhibit these symptoms. Moreover, what rationale can be provided for the correspondence between certain personality patterns and complex syndromes?

We previously stated that a full understanding of complex syndromes requires the study of a patient's pattern of involved traits. The complex symptom is but an outgrowth, for example, of various deeply rooted interpersonal sensitivities and cognitive beliefs. Which events a person perceives as threatening or rewarding and which behaviors and mechanisms he or she employs in response to them depend on the entire history to which the person was exposed. If we wish to uncover the reasons for the particular symptoms a patient "chooses," we must first understand the source and character of the aims he or she seeks to achieve. The character of the aims a patient chooses has not been a last-minute decision, but reflects a long history of interwoven biogenic and psychogenic factors that have formed a basic personality pattern.

Although each of these personality patterns has had different prior experiences, most share in common a hypersensitivity to social rebuff and condemnation, to which they hesitate reacting with counteraggression. In the *dependent and histrionic patterns*, for example, there is a fear of losing the security others provide; these patients must guard themselves against acting in such ways as to provoke disapproval and separation; rather, where feasible, they will maneuver themselves to act in ways that evoke favorable responses. The *obsessive-compulsive patterns*, particularly those in whom the dependency orientation is dominant, are similarly guided by the fear of provoking social condemnation. In the *avoidant pattern*, where dependency is not a factor, as it is in other problematic personalities, there has been a painful history of social ridicule and humiliation to which they feel incapable of responding. This prompts patients to restrain or dilute their aggressive urges so as to avoid further derogation. In all personality patterns, be they stylistic or disordered, then, behaviors and impulses that might provoke social disapproval must be reworked internally. They can be vented publicly only if they have been recast by psychic distortions and subterfuge.

Several observations may be drawn from the foregoing. First, complex syndromes do not arise in one personality pattern only, normal or otherwise. Second, we would expect, in many cases, the coexistence or simultaneous presence of several symptom syndromes because they reflect the operation of the same basic coping aims and similar forms of expression. Third, we would assume that complex syndromes would be relatively transient because their underlying coping function would wax and wane as the need for them changes. And fourth, these symptoms will, in some measure, be interchangeable, with one symptom appearing dominant at one time and a different one at another.

Despite the fact that complex clinical syndromes may covary and be interchangeable, we would expect some measure of symptom dominance and durability among different personality patterns. No one-to-one correspondence should be expected, of course, but on the basis of differences in internal chemistry and lifelong habits, we would anticipate that certain personalities would be more inclined to exhibit certain symptoms rather than others. Thus, in the *obsessive-compulsive* personality, where ingrained intrapsychic mechanisms such as reaction formation and undoing have been present for years, we would expect the patient to display complex anxiety symptoms that reflect the operation of these mechanisms. Similarly, *histrionic* personalities should exhibit a more dramatic and attention-getting complex of symptoms because exhibitionistic displays have always characterized their stylistic behaviors. It seems reasonable, then, that despite the common functions achieved through symptomatic behaviors, differences will arise among personality patterns because patients will continue to draw on the habitual mechanisms they employed in the past.

There are reasons, however, not to overstate the correspondence between personality and specific complex symptoms. First, complex symptoms, typical of those exhibited by pathological personality disorders, also arise in normal persons. Second, no two members of the same personality are likely to have been exposed to precisely the same specific life experiences (Millon & Davis, 1996a). To illustrate, we might compare two separate case histories which led to *compulsive* personalities. The first may have been exposed to a mother who routinely responded with consistent and exaggerated fearfulness to a multitude of different life events and circumstances. This vicarious exposure would be likely to encourage this patient to respond to anxiety-provoking and stressful situations with phobic coping measures. Another compulsive personality, one whose mother was chronically ill, may react to similar circumstances entirely differently. This mother's dependent and helpless behavior was likely to have alleviated many typical parenthood burdens and initiated sympathy from those around her. The compulsive patient, then, may likely follow his mother's lead when faced with threat, and display hypochondriacal symptoms. To sum up, a patient's personality pattern will not dictate what clinical symptomology may arise, as syndromes may also be a function of experiential learning through individual-specific and incidental life events.

PHOBIC SYNDROMES

Pathological fears were first reported in the writings of Hippocrates. Shakespeare referred to phobic reactions in *The Merchant of Venice* when he spoke of "Some, that are mad if they behold a cat." John Locke, in the early eighteenth century, speculated on their origin in his *Essays on Human Understanding*. In 1872, Westphal reported on three cases of peculiar fears of open public places. It was not until the writings of Freud, however, that the concept of phobia was presented, not as a simple although peculiar fear reaction, but as a displacement of a psychically based internal anxiety onto an external object. Phobias were seen by Freud as the outcome of transformations and symbolic externalizations of inner tensions, whatever their source, biological or psychological. Many patients experience intense fears of an object or situation that they consciously recognize are of no real objective danger.

Different theoretical schools of thought have disagreed with the psychoanalytic model of phobic development. Biological thinkers stress the importance of certain chemical sensitivities and vulnerabilities that lead some people to avoid a wide range of phobic objects (Atwood & Chester, 1987). In further contrast to the original Freudian interpretation, cognitive and cognitive-behavioral theorists believe phobias are a result of cognitive distortions, selective and negative perceptions, overgeneralizations, and illogical thinking. Social learning theorists take a position incorporating both the notions of learning, such as conditioning and stimulus generalization, and the possibility that secondary gains may also play a part.

General Clinical Picture (Specific and Social Phobias)

Phobias are unrealistic fears; that is, they appear to be unjustified by the object or event that prompts them. For example, most people would agree on the inherent danger of and appropriateness of keeping distance from a large wild animal or from a blaze in a building that had gotten out of control. But it is not situations like these that evoke the phobic syndrome. Rather, anxiety is prompted by such innocuous events as crossing a bridge, passing a funeral home, or entering an elevator.

Specific phobias signify perhaps the most direct form of all complex syndromes and psychic transformations. Like other forms of pathological behavior, they enable the person to achieve several instrumental goals. Here, patients do not neutralize or dilute the experience of anxiety but simply displace it to a well-circumscribed and often quite manageable external source. In this way, they are able to control and focus any internal biological vulnerability, or constrain an otherwise broad-based psychological basis for its presence. By the simple act of avoiding the substitute or phobic object, they prevent themselves from experiencing a more widespread pattern of anxieties or panic attacks. As noted previously, in addition to mastering discomforting inner tensions, the behavioral symptom often achieves secondary gains such as avoiding responsibilities, gaining sympathy, controlling the lives of others, finding rationalizations for failures, and so on.

As noted earlier, entirely incidental experiences of the past may determine the particular focus of a complex syndrome. Simple conditioned learning is not sufficient in itself to account for the presence of phobias, however. Phobias arise in both normal personality styles and in pathological personalities. The objects or events to which the phobic response is displaced often have a symbolic significance; that is, the external source of fear (phobic object) crystallizes a range of widely generalized and varied clinical realms of experience. The phobic object is merely an external symbol that condenses and focuses diffusely anchored domains that characterize the patient's total psychic structure. For example, through the processes of intrapsychic condensation and displacement, patients project their diversely rooted tensions onto a simple and tangible external source, enabling them thereby to cope with it by the direct act of physical avoidance.

Whereas specific phobias are attached to a particular event or object, for example, fear of animals, heights, flying, injections, and the sight of blood, they contrast with the category of *social phobias*. The latter signifies a repetitive fear of social and performance situations, especially those in which the person's actions are subject to the scrutiny of others. These social situational fears are problematic owing to the belief that the person will act in a way that will prove embarrassing.

It is not unlikely that social phobias are a facet of a wider *avoidant personality* disorder, not only evidencing the problematic phobic response, but also displaying social skill deficits, distortions in cognitive beliefs, and a wide range of self-devaluations and interpersonal restrictions. Whereas specific phobias usually begin to develop in mid-childhood, social phobias tend to start in adolescence and early adulthood.

Prevailing Treatment Options

It is nowhere more evident than in the phobias that *causes* and *therapies* are clearly separate. Despite a variety of insightful intrapsychic interpretations that help us explain the complexity of displaced symbolic objects, the facts clearly point to the distinctly superior role of a behavioral approach in remedying these phobic difficulties. All forms of phobia appear to respond best to *exposure* procedures, be they implosive, gradual, or imaginal. The intent here is to not only reduce the anxious phobic response, but to increase the patient's psychic comfort when facing the feared stimulus. Most behavioral therapists propose that patients must be exposed to the feared stimulus long enough for their fears to be activated and then reduced, often within a few sessions (Barlow, 1993). Of course, should their phobic anxiety become very intense, patients are encouraged to leave the frightening situations, but requested to return at a later time until a measure of comfort emerges. It is under these troublesome situations that such medications as beta blockers and phenelzine may fruitfully be introduced to reduce the anxiety.

In addition to either in vivo or situational exposure therapy, there appears to be some value in utilizing supportive therapy and family counseling as strengthening elements, as long as the basic exposure procedure runs concurrently. The value of systematic desensitization should not be overlooked either (Maxmen & Ward, 1995). Here, the therapist helps the patient set up an anxiety hierarchy that reflects his or her fears in terms of their severity. Beginning with the lowest ranking of the feared objects, the therapist employs relaxation techniques to help the patient become comfortable with each level of exposure. The therapist progressively introduces higher-ranking feared objects until the patient experiences comfort with each successive level. This use of an applied relaxation technique can be done with imaginal procedures (e.g., exposure to a photo) or in vivo, that is, in direct contact with the problematic stimulus.

Cognitive techniques have also been shown to be of value, but almost invariably when in combination with behavioral procedures. As noted above, the cognitive point of view interprets these fears as being inconsistent with reality conditions, as misinterpretations maintained by erroneous and distorted appraisals of life situations (Beck & Emery, 1985).

Whereas behavioral exposure techniques for repeated phobic reactions are clearly the treatment of choice to overcome specific phobias (Schneier, Marshall, Street, Heindberg, & Juster, 1995), this approach is usually insufficient when dealing with the so-called social phobias; these latter disorders may be part of a larger constellation of psychological dysfunctions, such as seen among avoidant personality disorders. Although social phobias ostensibly signify a performance fear, and avoidant disorder a fear of intimate relationships, they are not distinct entities and, hence, often overlap in their symptomatology. Treatment for social phobias will therefore have to be multipronged, aimed not only to reduce the acute situational problem, but to seek to improve the patient's cognitive outlook, self-image, and interpersonal skills (Mattick & Peters, 1988). Optimal treatment results appear to call for a combination of in vivo exposure, cognitive reorientation, and social skill training (Chambless & Gillis, 1994).

Personality-Guided Synergistic Therapy

Let us turn next to the personality traits and patterns most susceptible to phobic syndromes and explore the precipitants that give rise to them. As previously noted, different probabilities exist as to who will exhibit these symptoms and why. The following sections survey the typical phobic precipitants of those personality styles and disorders that have a high probability of evidencing a phobic syndrome. We present these personality contexts in descending order of symptom formation probability; for example, as listed, dependents and depressives are the most vulnerable to specific phobias; as far as social phobias are concerned, avoidants are most frequent, and so on. (These rankings are based on limited observations and deductions from clinical theory, not on systematic empirical research.)

PHOBIAS AMONG DEPENDENT AND DEPRESSIVE PERSONALITIES

These personalities develop phobic symptoms when their dependency security is threatened or when demands are made, especially those that exceed their feelings of competence; both syndromes dread responsibility, particularly those that require self-assertion and independence. For similar reasons of security, they are motivated to displace or transform any internal impulse that may provoke social rebuke.

Not only does the phobic syndrome externalize anxiety and avoid further threats to its security, but by anchoring tensions to tangible outside sources the patient may prompt others to come to his or her assistance. Thus, phobias, as external threats, may be used to solicit protection. Dependents appear to be especially vulnerable to agoraphobic panic attacks. These anticipatory fears of leaving familiar and secure settings, most frequently one's home, serve well as a means of soliciting care and protection. Thus, the phobic maneuver achieves secondary gains that are fully consonant with the patient's basic orientation. In short, the phobic coping maneuver serves a variety of functions consonant with the patient's basic dependent or depressive orientation.

Although many of the clinical domains that make up a personality disorder should be addressed in planning a more synergistic treatment model, it is clear that the first order of business is to moderate the patient's phobic syndrome. Reducing that aspect of the patient's overall pattern of difficulties by exposure methods will often provide a means for exploring other correlated difficulties that are part of these personalities' makeup, that is, cognitive distortions and interpersonal deficits, as well as difficulties stemming from their low sense of self-esteem.

PHOBIAS AMONG AVOIDANT PERSONALITIES

Phobias (simple and social) among avoidant patterns tend to be private affairs. For these patients, the symptom does not serve as a means of evoking social attention, for they are convinced that attention will bring only ridicule and abuse. More commonly, it is a symbolic expression of feeling "surrounded" or of being pressured by excessive stimuli and demands. Crystallized in this fashion, these patients have created an identifiable and circumscribed phobic source that they can actively avoid and, hence, provide a feeling of competence.

CASE 6.1, HERB L., 22

Presenting Picture: Herb L., an avoidant young man, experienced sudden surges of phobic anxiety whenever reference was made to the name of a major shopping center in his hometown. Crowded areas made him feel insignificant and worthless, and also often stimulated frightening erotic and hostile impulses. For some unknown reason, the shopping center came to symbolize these unwanted feelings. By avoiding the shopping center or reference to its name, he felt that his fears and impulses could be kept in check.

Therapeutic Course: Treatment was composed entirely of progressive relaxation and the imaginal use of systematic desensitization. Although Herb's phobic anxieties diminished through these techniques, he resisted any in vivo experiences at the shopping mall. He terminated therapy after six or seven sessions when his broad-based avoidant pattern led him to feel that further exploration would provoke a serious emotional outbreak on his part.

Synergistic Afterthoughts: Today, the first course of synergistic treatment would be to utilize imaginal exposure techniques to counteract his perceptions of the shopping mall. Progressively, photos of the mall, starting with its parking lots and going to its entrance halls and then its walkways, would be presented until he experienced a reasonable measure of comfort with each step in the sequence. Next, we would bring him in vivo to the real parallels of these photos, carefully noting his levels of comfort or discomfort. It would be hoped that he could place himself in this setting in a way that he could not before. Assuming a degree of success with these exposure methods, considerable attention would turn to cognitive techniques to resolve a wide band of erroneous assumptions that are likely to have characterized his perceptions and thinking. Similarly, and as is typical of avoidant personalities, interpersonal skill training and self-actualizing methods may prove of considerable value beyond the mere elimination of his phobic syndrome.

Social phobias, of course, are so deeply ingrained and pervasive a part of the avoidant personality that it is often difficult to say where the personality pattern ends and the phobic symptom begins. Avoidant personalities may have phobic feelings about specific settings or persons that are of substantially greater magnitude than they possess toward other interpersonal situations. As noted, avoidants tend to keep their phobias to themselves. For them, the phobic symptom does not serve as a means of soliciting social attention, as it does in dependents or depressives, because they are convinced that such attentions will bring forth only ridicule and abuse. As with anxiety, phobias are an expression, albeit a symbolic one, of feeling encroached upon or of being pressured by excessive social demands. Crystallized in phobic form, they may enable avoidants to redirect their feelings of resentment, feelings that they dare not express toward the "true" object of these feelings. Dreading social rebuke, avoidants will seek some innocuous external source to keep their resentments in check. Through various psychic means, the selected phobic object may come to represent a symbolic, yet "real," basis for their anxieties and resentments.

PHOBIAS AMONG HISTRIONIC PERSONALITIES

Histrionic persons exhibit phobic symptoms somewhat less frequently than their dependent counterparts. Here, feelings of emptiness, unattractiveness, and aloneness, or the upsurge of socially unacceptable aggressive or erotic impulses, tend to serve as the primary sources for phobic transformations. These symptoms often are displayed exhibitionistically, utilized as "dramatic" vehicles to gain attention and support from others. In contrast to avoidant personalities, histrionics are quite open about their symptom and try to get as much mileage out of it as they can, as is evident in the following case history.

CASE 6.2, CARLA S., 34

Presenting Picture: Carla, a recently divorced histrionic woman, developed a phobic syndrome while driving alone in her car. She feared that she would miss her street and be lost. At home, she spent her days with her mother and two children; at work, she was busily engaged with fellow employees and customers. She was often isolated, that is, without her characteristic need for attention and support from others, when driving herself to and from work. To avoid her growing phobia about being alone, she arranged to be picked up and driven home by a man whom she "found quite attractive." Her phobia symbolized her dread of aloneness; her resolution not only enabled her to travel without anxiety, but brought her into frequent contact with an "approving" and comforting companion.

Therapeutic Course: Carla entered therapy because of a recent intense phobic attack. Fearing that she would frighten her newfound companion, she entered a therapeutic relationship in the hope that these fears could be curtailed if not extinguished. An exposure-based series of procedures were employed to help eliminate her phobic response while driving alone, as well as in a number of other circumstances that reflected a generalized phobic anxiety response. Reasonable success was achieved after about 10 sessions, portions of which dealt with relaxation and desensitization procedures. However, about six months following this first termination, Carla returned to therapy, this time feeling the need to find out why she was so vulnerable and troubled.

Synergistic Afterthoughts: The course of this second round of therapy followed a synergistic model; that is, it sought to weave together and in sequence a variety of treatment techniques to deal primarily with her personality style, that is, her histrionic need for approval, her sense of insecurity, and her low self-worth. Her social skills were of an affected nature, an aspect of her interpersonal style that was seen critically by her associates. Using cognitive methods to correct her miscalculations of how she would appear when doing this or that proved to be a helpful step in countering her personality style.

PHOBIAS AMONG COMPULSIVE PERSONALITIES

These patients develop phobias primarily as a function of three anxiety precipitants: stressful decision-making situations in which they anticipate being faulted and subjected to criticism; actual failures that they seek to rationalize or avoid facing again; and surging hostile impulses that they wish to counter, transform, or externalize lest they overwhelm the patient's controls and provoke social condemnation.

Similar to avoidants, and in contrast to dependent or histrionic persons, these patients tend to hide their phobias because their self-image would be weakened by such "foolish" and irrational symptoms. Similarly, they fear that these symptoms may provoke social ridicule and criticism. Thus, unbeknown to others, they displace their tensions onto a variety of external phobic sources. This enables them not only to deny the internal roots of their discomfort, but to make it tangible and identifiable, and thereby subject to easy control.

PHOBIAS AMONG NEGATIVISTIC AND MASOCHISTIC PERSONALITIES

These personalities tend to be more open than other personality types about discharging their erratic feelings. This ready and diffuse discharge of anxiety and emotion has its self-defeating side. By venting tensions openly and generalizing them freely to any and all aspects of their lives, these personalities increase the likelihood that many formerly innocuous objects and events will become phobic-laden. To reduce the wide range of anxiety stimuli, negativists and masochists may anchor their floating quality to just a few clear-cut precipitants, thereby reducing the extent to which they are subject to a generalized state of anxiety. Moreover, and as with other personality patterns, these patients often utilize their phobic symptoms for secondary gain: they employ them to draw attention to themselves and as a tool to control and manipulate the lives of others, as portrayed in the following case.

CASE 6.3, STELLA H., 34

Presenting Picture: Stella was a negativistic woman, with a history of two brief depressive episodes that required hospitalization. She developed an "unreasonable" dread of entering the kitchen of her home. During a series of therapeutic sessions, it became clear that her phobia symbolized her growing feeling of incompetence as a wife and enabled her to avoid facing her general fear of failure. Moreover, the phobia served to bring her sympathy and to punish her husband by forcing him to prepare most of the family's meals and to wash and dry the dishes, a chore he had always detested.

Therapeutic Course: It required no more than four sessions of in vivo exposure for her to respond with relative comfort when entering her kitchen at home. She quickly learned a variety of techniques, such as systematic desensitization, a procedure that enabled her to deal with and confront other anxiety-based difficulties in her life. Not surprisingly, after a hiatus of a year and a half, Stella decided to return to treatment, having concluded that her earlier period of therapy was incomplete, if not insufficient.

Synergistic Afterthoughts: In her second treatment experience, a more synergistic framework was developed by her therapist to deal primarily with her negativistic personality traits. The therapist decided that this focus would prove of enduring value. Hence, a mixture of treatment techniques was employed to counteract her social contrariness and her depressive and resentful behaviors. Before these modalities were employed, however, Stella was given an SSRI medication; although ultimately a positive ingredient in her treatment regimen, it took some three or four weeks before its moderating effects took hold. Also employed were cognitively oriented efforts to undo her belief that she was unappreciated and misunderstood. Similarly, self-actualizing humanistic procedures were employed to moderate her feeling that she was always going to be a discontented person. Stella continued in treatment for about nine months, having progressed in a highly satisfactory manner by the use of this combinational approach.

DISSOCIATIVE SYNDROMES

Dissociation is closely linked to phobias; in fact, they are often subsumed under the more general label of *hysteria*. Despite an overlapping in the personalities who exhibit them, as well as in the underlying strategies that give rise to them, these disorders are sufficiently distinct in other regards to justify their separation. For example, in phobias, inner tensions are displaced and discharged through a symbolic object or body part of which both the patient and others are fully conscious. In dissociation, however, patients neither crystallize their tensions into tangible forms nor give evidence of being conscious of their expression. Rather, they vent their tension through transitory behavioral acts and do so in a dreamlike state, that is, while completely unaware of what they are doing.

Since the days of the early Greeks, observations have been made of individuals who seem to "drift off" and lose contact with their surroundings for varying periods of time. Some suffer total amnesia, forgetting who they are, what they have done, and where they have been. Others experience trance-like dream states in which they engage in activities of which they have no recall.

The concept of dissociation and the first understanding of the processes involved began with the inquiries of Charcot and Janet. It was Charcot in the early 1870s who suggested that the stream of consciousness breaks up into divergent paths in cases of hysteria. He believed that this "splitting" process was traceable to a hereditary degeneration of the nervous system. Janet pursued this theme in the late 1880s in his clinical investigations of states of amnesia and somnambulism. He coined the term dissociation to represent what he viewed as the central process in these disorders. As Janet conceived it, the mental energy required to bind the diverse elements of personality had deteriorated or had been "exhausted." As a consequence, certain thoughts, feelings, and memories, which normally cohere, drift apart and become lost to the principal core of the personality.

Janet's views were extended in 1905 by Morton Prince, an American psychologist who published a series of now famous inquiries into dramatic cases of multiple personalities. Prince applied the term *co-consciousness* to represent aspects of thought that are not in the forefront of conscious attention. To him, hysteria, as found in cases of multiple personality, simply were extreme examples of independently acting co-conscious ideas.

Freud took exception to the views of both Janet and Prince, claiming that the mere process of "splitting" or "loosening" of associations, especially if attributed to neurological defects, was insufficient to account for both the timing and the content of the dissociative symptoms. He asserted that dissociation stemmed from an active process of repression in which forbidden impulses and thoughts are sealed into separate psychic compartments. These impulses are momentarily discharged during the dissociation state, providing the clinician thereby with clues into the character of the patient's repressed anxieties and conflicts. Upon a return to "normal" functioning, the memory of these ideas and emotions was again repressed and kept "out of mind."

General Clinical Picture

For our purposes, the varieties of dissociation may be grouped into several categories: relatively prolonged dreamlike states, such as events that are experienced as hazy or unreal; briefer states, such as when the individual seems divorced from self and surroundings; and, among the major forms, cases in which there is a sweeping amnesia of the past and cases known as multiple personality, in which entirely different features of the individual's psychic makeup separate and become autonomous units of functioning.

Some include experiences of *estrangement* from self or environment. Here, the patient senses familiar objects and events as strange or foreign or views the self to be unreal or unknown (depersonalization). *Trance-like states* are akin to estrangement, but here the patient's awareness is merely dimmed; he or she seems to be in a "twilight" dream-world, totally immersed in inner events and entirely oblivious of surroundings. *Somnambulism* refers to sleepwalking, a process of carrying out acts that are consistent with concurrent dream fantasies. In these states, the individual often searches for desired objects and relationships or works out tensions and conflicts that normally are unconscious. For example, a young man wanders nocturnally to the foot of the bed of his sleeping parents, seeking comfort and security; a woman runs every so often to the basement of her home to escape a nightmare fantasy of being taunted by her neighbors; a wealthy and respected man gets fully dressed, strolls into neighboring streets looking into trashcans, and then returns home to sleep. Although somnambulists are able to get to wherever they are going, their thought processes tend to be hazy and incoherent during these episodes, and they rarely recall any of the events that happened. To be included also in these more minor dissociations are *frenzied states* in which sudden, brief, and later totally forgotten bizarre behaviors erupt in the course of otherwise normal events. In these cases the person usually acts out forbidden thoughts and emotions that previously had been repressed.

The more major personalities of the dissociative group are those experiencing total *amnesia;* here, the patient usually forgets both past and identity. This may occur in conjunction with a flight from one's normal environment, an event referred to as a *fugue.* Whether or not physical flight occurs, amnesic patients have genuinely lost cognizance of their identity and the significant persons and places of their life. Most amnesic episodes terminate after several days, although a few prove to be permanent. In *dissociative identity disorders,* we now include what were formerly called multiple personalities. These are extremely rare cases in which the patient's psychic makeup is reorganized into two or more separate and autonomously functioning units; the fictional characters of Doctor Jekyll and Mr. Hyde are a dramatic and simplified portrayal of the coexistence of diametrically contrasting features that often characterize the two personality units. In most cases, the patient's "normal self" is the dominant personality unit; it periodically gives way to and is totally amnesic for a contrasting but subsidiary unit of personality functioning. Appreciably less frequent are cases in which two equally prominent personality units alternate on a regular basis and with some frequency.

What gives rise to dissociative phenomena? To answer this question, it may be useful to go back first to Janet's original thesis: a lack of power for *psychic cohesion.* Janet ascribed this deficiency to neural degeneration traceable either to hereditary weaknesses or to psychological "exhaustion." An alternative interpretation of Janet's thesis, one that is more consistent with current thinking, would assign the loss of psychic cohesion not to neural defects but to an acquired deficiency in cognitive controls. As a function of early training and experience, many individuals fail to acquire a coherent and well-integrated core of personality traits necessary for organizing their past and future experiences. We will note shortly that histrionic personalities lack an *inner identity,* are largely empty and devoid of a past, tend to be overresponsive to external stimuli, and are deficient in self-controls. It would be consistent with their ingrained patterns for these patients to be subject to the splitting or disintegration of memories, impulses, and thoughts, for they lack the equipment to bind or cohere divergent elements of their psychic makeup.

Another cause or function of dissociation may be found in the writings of Freud, who suggested that the disorder reflected the existence of strong and mutually incompatible elements of personality. Unable to contain these conflicting forces in a single cohesive unit, the personality is cleaved into separate systems, either with one system totally repressed (amnesia) or with two or more systems operating autonomously (multiple personality). This view, that dissociation reflects the preservation of the conscious self by banishing unacceptable traits from awareness, seems reasonable as another determinant of the disorder.

Not to be overlooked as a third factor are secondary gains. Janet's thesis, as modified, suggests the operation of deficient cognitive controls. The Freudian thesis focuses on primary gains, that is, the isolation of thoughts and impulses that provoke anxiety should they coexist consciously. The third hypothesis asserts that the dissociative act may provide positive reinforcements in the form of advantages such as a "new life," an escape from boredom, and the attraction of attention, affection, and nurturance.

As in most pathologies, the dissociative symptom is likely to be overdetermined, an outcome representing a compromise of several determinants. Although the prevalence of dissociative disorders has decreased this past century, there is some indication that it increased in recent decades (probably owing to the growing literature on child abuse) (Morrison, 1995). Various combinations of influence will be seen when we turn next to the personality background of dissociated patients.

Prevailing Treatment Options

Historically, work with dissociative amnesia occurred with high frequency during wartime. Therapists were quite successful in relieving the disorder by removing those effected from the front lines and giving them a feeling of protection and nurturance (Kubie, 1943).

Most dissociative disorders are difficult to treat, yet are challenging to therapists who rarely become involved with such patients (Kluft, 1994). A series of studies by Coons (1986), employing general psychotherapeutic approaches over a three-and-a-half-year period, indicated that two-thirds were appreciably improved and one-fourth had satisfactorily integrated their diverse personality components. He used a variety of treatment procedures: social skill enhancements, constructive life management, hypnosis, and abreactions. Similarly, Kluft (1984, 1988) was able to move most of his patients toward a more integrated sense of self.

Research studies on dissociative identity techniques are quite modest in scope owing to the fact that these disorders are infrequent, thereby precluding adequate numbers for statistical purposes. Nevertheless, researchers have employed with some measure of success, *homogeneous group* techniques (Caul, 1984; Caul, Sacks, & Braun, 1988), *family therapy* (L.R. Benjamin & Benjamin, 1992), several variants of *hypnosis* (Maldonado & Spiegel, 1995), and *narcosynthesis* (Baron & Nagy, 1988).

Personality-Guided Synergistic Therapy

The personality patterns disposed to dissociative episodes are generally the same as those found in other anxiety-driven complex syndromes. The theme that unifies them in this regard is their common desire to avoid social disapproval. Other personalities, both pathological and normal, may exhibit dissociative symptoms, but the probability of such episodes in these cases is rather small. Our presentation will proceed in the order of the most to the least vulnerable of the patients in whom the disorder is most frequently exhibited.

DISSOCIATION AMONG AVOIDANT PERSONALITIES

These patients experience frequent and varied forms of dissociative phenomena. Feelings of estrangement may arise as protective maneuvers designed to diminish the impact of excessive stimulation or the pain of social humiliation. These symptoms may also reflect the consequences of the patient's devalued sense of self; without patients having an esteemed and integrated inner core to which experience can be anchored, events often seem disconnected, ephemeral, and unreal. Self-estrangement, termed *depersonalization,* may be traced to a characteristic coping maneuver of cognitive interference, which not only serves to disconnect normally associated events but deprives the person of meaningful contact with his or her own feelings and thoughts. Experiences of amnesia may occur as an expression of self-rejection. Forever to be oneself is not a cheerful prospect for these persons, and life may be started anew by disowning one's past identity. Frenzied states are a common dissociative disorder in these patients. Here, for a brief period, the patient may act out frustrated and repressed impulses, as illustrated in the following case.

CASE 6.4, DOLORES J., 29

Presenting Picture: Dolores was seen after a series of "hysterical fits" at home. She lived with an elderly mother, had been unemployed for several years, and spent most of her days sitting by the window, staring blankly. Her mother reported that Dolores had always been a quiet girl. However, since her older brother left home some two years earlier, Dolores rarely spoke to anyone and often hid in her room when visitors came. Her "fits" were repeated on an average of once a week while she was hospitalized. They would begin when Dolores shouted aloud, "I don't want to, I don't want to"; she then fell on her bed, vigorously fighting an unseen assailant who, she believed, sought to rape her. As she fended off her hallucinated attacker, Dolores would begin to tear at her clothes; finally, half denuded, she submitted to his desires, enacting a rather bizarre form of masturbation. After a brief period, mixed with tears and laughter, Dolores became quiet and subdued. Conscious awareness gradually returned, with no recall of the episode.

Therapeutic Course: Treatment of Dolores had a distinct psychoanalytic air with efforts to have her freely associate her thoughts and engage in deep hypnosis. It became clear that she was enacting a number of sexual exploits with her brother over a period of several years. These were extremely distressful to her more conscious image of him. When the brother left the family home, Dolores felt bereft and was extremely needy of the care and affection that he provided for her, a feeling that no one else, she believed, could furnish in her current state. Exposing the roots of her disorder, though gradual and painful, began to release her from the powerful effects of her repressive behaviors. Some 30 sessions were required, the last portion composed largely of a cognitive-reframing procedure and a self-actualizing focus.

Synergistic Afterthoughts: The approach taken with Dolores should include a series of steps that would not only enable her to deal with her intrapsychic conflicts and impulses, but would help her learn social skills with which she could relate comfortably in the "real" social world. Many patients with dissociative disorders, such as Dolores, have segmented their self-awareness and their cognitions, leaving them lacking an appropriate range of interpersonal skills and knowledge. Although the therapist was fortunate in being involved with Dolores for 30 sessions, the need to follow up was not taken advantage of; reintegration was a primary goal, but there were parts missing, so to speak. Bringing these parts (e.g., cognitions, interpersonal style) into therapy may have provided Dolores with a wider range of competencies to create an extended psychic integration. (The reader might find it useful to turn to Chapter 11, which discusses the psychic needs of avoidant personalities.)

It is only in accord with tradition that we view these frenzied dissociative states among the less severe syndromes. There is no question but that the bizarre behavior and loss of reality evident during these episodes are severe enough to merit viewing them as psychotic. Custom and perhaps the brevity of the eruption and the rapid return to former functioning are the only justifications for placing them in the moderately severe categories.

DISSOCIATION AMONG DEPENDENT PERSONALITY DISORDERS

These persons may develop dreamlike trance states when faced with responsibilities and obligations that surpass their feelings of competence; through this maneuver, they effectively fade out of contact with threatening realities. Amnesic episodes, however, are extremely rare because these would prompt or intensify separation anxieties. Repetitive somnambulistic states are not uncommon. Here, the patient usually vents minor forbidden impulses or seeks to secure affection and nurturance.

Brief frenzied states may arise at the moderately severe level if the patient experiences an upsurge of intense hostile impulses that may threaten his or her dependency security. In this way, contrary feelings may be discharged without the patient's knowing it and therefore without having to assume blame. These irrational acts are so uncharacteristic of the patient that they tend to be seen by others as a sign of "sickness," often eliciting thereby nurturant and supporting responses.

DISSOCIATION AMONG OBSESSIVE-COMPULSIVE PERSONALITY DISORDERS

These persons succumb to dissociative episodes for a variety of reasons. Experiences of estrangement stem primarily from their characteristic overcontrol and repression of feeling. By desensitizing their emotions or withdrawing them as a part of everyday life, these patients may begin to experience the world as flat and colorless, a place in which events seem mechanical, automatic, and unreal.

Episodes of total amnesia may occur if the patient is otherwise unable to isolate and control intense ambivalent feelings. The coexistence of conflicting habits and emotions may be too great a strain. Not only will the eruption of hostile and erotic impulses shatter the patient's self-image of propriety, but they may provoke the severe condemnation he or she dreads from others. Unable to restrain these urges, patients must disown their identity and in the process obliterate all past associations and memories.

CASE 6.5, GEORGE T., 38

Presenting Picture: This rather overcontrolled and highly tense police officer had recently become involved in an extramarital affair. After a few weeks, George began to suffer marked insomnia and unbearable feelings of guilt. Unable to share his thoughts and emotions and refusing to go to confession at his church, he became increasingly disconsolate and depressed. One morning, he "forgot" who he was while driving to work, rode some 200 miles from his hometown, and was found three days later in a motel room, weeping and confused as to his whereabouts.

Therapeutic Course: Therapy was guided initially by psychodynamic methods. Hypnosis was employed to help George regain an acceptable sense of his identity. Once George was able to recognize that he was being extremely harsh on himself by forgetting who he was, and after he began to understand the basis of his amnesia, progress moved rather swiftly, enabling him to "fess up" to his transgressions and to resolve his difficulties through formal marital treatment techniques.

Synergistic Afterthoughts: The course of George's treatment was one of those occasions when therapy was not only completed successfully, but achieved in a relatively short period of time. Also notable was the focus on psychodynamic methods. As stated in prior synergistic discussions, attention in these and similar cases focused on the presenting symptom rather than the personality context within which they occurred. Should there be a desire and need to move beyond the focused treatment approach employed with George, that is, to undertake remedial steps in the cognitive and interpersonal spheres, the reader may find useful suggestions in Chapter 18.

A frenzied state may be another form of discharge when tensions become unbearable. These allow the patient to vent contrary impulses without conscious awareness. Although infrequent, dissociative identity disorders may be formed, enabling patients to retain their "true" identity most of the time while gaining periodic release through their "other" self or selves.

DISSOCIATION AMONG HISTRIONIC PERSONALITY DISORDERS

These personalities generally lack an adequate degree of personality integration, making it difficult for them even in normal times to unify the disparate elements of their lives. At times of strain and discord, this integrative deficiency may readily result in a dissociative state.

Somnambulism, a nighttime phenomenon, is not uncommon and usually takes the form of a search for attention and stimulation when these patients feel otherwise deprived. Daytime trance-like episodes are rather unusual, however, because these patients desire to be alert to their environment. Also rare are amnesic fugues and multiple personality formations. When they do occur, they usually represent an attempt to break out of a confining and stultifying environment. Faced with internal poverty and external boredom or constraint, they may seek the secondary gains of a more exciting and dramatic life in which they can achieve the attention and approval they crave.

CASE 6.6, BRENDA S., 30

Presenting Picture: This histrionic woman had begun to feel "boxed in" by her suspicious husband; she suddenly disappeared from her home and was not located for several months. Brenda was found more than a thousand miles away working as a chorus girl in a run-down burlesque house, returning thereby to her vocation prior to marriage five years earlier. Although her claim that she had "blacked out" was doubted at first, further study revealed that she was totally amnesic for her life since her marriage but recalled with great clarity her activities and relationships prior to that time.

Therapeutic Course: Therapy consisted of a combination of group treatment and family therapy. Brenda was able to openly discuss, in both venues, her sense of marital stultification, leading thereby to a number of maritally constructive discussions with her husband.

Synergistic Afterthoughts: Rather surprisingly, no effort was made to utilize psychodynamic methods to explore the deeper regions of her intrapsychic world. That Brenda was able to access the feelings and ideas that led to her amnesic experience without such inquiries was a testament to the skill of the therapist, rather than to the methodology she employed. By acting in a caring manner and exhibiting genuine empathic sensitivity, the therapist evoked from Brenda a willingness to "open up" and overcome her repressive actions, thereby bringing her less attractive attitudes into full view. (Cases of this sort might be aided with reference to Chapter 14, dealing with histrionic personalities.)

DISSOCIATION AMONG NEGATIVISTIC PERSONALITY DISORDERS

These individuals are accustomed to expressing their contrary feelings rather directly, and will exhibit dissociative symptoms only if they are unduly constrained or fearful of severe retaliation. Even under circumstances such as these, the frequency of these disorders is rather low. Temper tantrums, which approach dissociative frenzied states in their overt appearance, are rather common. However, in these eruptions, patients do not lose conscious awareness and usually vent all the emotions that well up within them.

DISSOCIATION AMONG BORDERLINE PERSONALITY DISORDERS

Borderline personalities are likely to vent brief but highly charged and angry outbursts during psychogenic fugue states. Repressed resentments occasionally take this form and erupt into the open when these patients have felt trapped and confused or betrayed. Moreover, it is not unusual for borderlines to brutalize themselves, as well as others, during these fugues. They may tear their clothes, smash their fists, and lacerate their bodies, thereby suffering more themselves than do their presumed assailants. Most frequently, these violent discharges are followed by a return to their former state. In some cases, however, borderlines may disintegrate into one or another of the more prolonged psychotic disorders. Though strange and fearsome, fugues do not come totally unexpected to friends and family members of borderlines because the symptoms of this disorder are but extremes of their long-term pattern of impulsiveness, behavioral unpredictability, and self-damaging acts.

OBSESSIVE-COMPULSIVE (AXIS I) SYNDROMES

Most people find themselves overly concerned and preoccupied when facing some real and troubling problem; they experience an inability to "get their mind off it" and turn to other matters. These events are similar to obsessive experiences, but in these cases, the idea the person mulls over is rather picayune, absurd, or irrational, yet it intrudes with such persistence as to interfere with normal daily functioning. Compulsions are similar to obsessions; however, here patients cannot resist engaging in certain acts, in performing some trivial behavioral ritual that they recognize as ridiculous, humiliating, or disgusting, but that they must execute to avoid the anxiety they experience when they fail to do it.

Both obsessions and compulsions are similar to other complex syndromes in that they reflect the operation of numerous psychic domains and physiological vulnerabilities. Each complex disorder protects the individual from recognizing the true source of upwelling anxieties, yet allows the anxiety a measure of release without damaging self-image or provoking interpersonal rebuke. In phobias, the inner tension is symbolized and attached to an external object; in conversions, it is displaced and expressed through some body part; in obsessions and compulsions, tension is controlled, symbolized, and periodically discharged through a series of repetitive acts or thoughts.

Commonalities among diverse "neurotic" symptoms were first proposed by Charcot. However, it was his student Janet who first made an effort to relate them systematically.

To Janet, all of these anxiety-neutralizing disorders were a consequence of a diminution of biological mental energies requisite to the integration of higher mental processes, a point of view that may be reexamined in light of the recent success of pharmacologic agents that help reduce the syndrome. Complex thoughts and emotions, which normally were connected and organized, drifted apart, according to Janet, into a chaotic mental anarchy when these energies diminished or were drained. As a consequence of this weakness, primitive and subsidiary forces took over the person and led to the scattering and disorganization of formerly coordinated thoughts and emotions. Obsessions and compulsions were seen in this light. They were merely incidental expressions of a basic disintegration of organized higher mental processes.

As noted earlier, Freud rejected Janet's thesis, claiming that both the timing and the choice of the symptom indicated the primacy of psychogenic rather than biogenic factors. All complex syndromes, then termed neuroses, stemmed from psychic mechanisms designed to control and alleviate anxieties traceable to early life experiences. The specific symptom reflected, symbolically, the character of the anxiety source, other facets of the patient's psychic makeup, and the maneuvers the patient employed to cope with it.

In current analytic theory, obsessions and compulsions symbolically represent the upsurging of sexual and aggressive impulses that the individual seeks to repress or inhibit. For example, the cleanliness seen in many compulsives is judged to signify a reaction formation, that is, an effort to constrain unacceptable "dirty" or aggressive impulses. Obsessions and compulsions indicated to Freud that previously repressed thoughts and feelings of hostility and guilt had been reactivated. To counteract yet give partial ventilation to these ideas and emotions, the patient employs several psychic mechanisms, namely, isolation, displacement, reaction formation, and undoing.

Through *isolation*, the patient disconnects the association that previously existed between a forbidden thought and its accompanying feeling. For example, one might have obsessional thoughts of murder without being aware of or experiencing an appropriate parallel emotion; conversely, one may feel a frightening and intense murderous urge without knowing its cause. By isolating an affect from its associated thought, the patient avoids confronting the real connection between them. Isolation may not be completely successful, however, and some residuals of the forbidden feelings and thoughts may still be experienced as distressful. *Displacement* enables the patient to find a substitute activity or thought to attach tensions to, something that camouflages the real discomfort and serves to focus attention elsewhere. Thus, one becomes obsessed with some trivial thought and thereby manages to divert oneself from true reflection. *Reaction formation* goes one step further toward self-deception; here, the individual thinks and behaves in ways that are diametrically opposite to his or her "true" but forbidden ideas and impulses. Through this mechanism, not only are feelings and thoughts disconnected and displaced, but their content is twisted into its exact opposite. Thus, instead of expressing an urge to soil and be messy, the patient becomes compulsively clean and neat. *Undoing* parallels reaction formation. Having failed to reverse their attitudes and emotions beforehand, as in reaction formation, patients find that they must rescind and gain forgiveness for their transgressions. Thus, they attempt symbolically to redeem themselves by various ritualistic acts. Through the undoing gesture, they not only pay penance for forbidden thoughts, but seek in a magical way to restore themselves to a state of purity. For example, by compulsive handwashing, patients suffer the discomfort and embarrassment of the ritual and at the same time symbolically cleanse themselves of past misdeeds and evil intentions. However, because the real source of the patient's tension was not dealt with through the undoing maneuver, relief is only temporary and he or she must repeat the ritualistic act time and again.

Recent research on obsessions and compulsions suggests that these symptoms reflect either a strong biological vulnerability or the simple overlearning of certain behaviors and thoughts or both. According to behavior theorists who eschew both neurochemical explanations and the role of unconscious processes, these acts stem from either a conditioning sequence, in which the behavior in question reduced anxiety effectively, or from repeated exposure to parental models. Learning theory, be it social or developmental, conceives obsessions and compulsions to be imitations of parental models that have been positively reinforced by virtue of their being successful in reducing anxiety. Along somewhat similar lines, interpersonal theorists suggest that obsessions may reflect underlying fears of embarrassment and humiliation; by contrast, they see compulsions as actions designed to enhance one's self-esteem. Others, viewing recent research, are disposed to support a biological basis for this disorder (Riggs & Foa, 1993).

Although learning is significantly involved in all forms of pathology, we focus our attention in this section on cases in which the symptom reflects the operation of more generalized personality traits rather than the direct and simple product of biochemical dysfunctions or overlearned behaviors. The distinction among these symptoms is a matter of the circumstances that give rise to them, and the persons in whom they appear, rather than in biological processes or how they may have been acquired.

General Clinical Picture

Because several features of the obsessive-compulsive syndrome have already been elaborated, we need only detail in more systematic fashion what has been said.

Obsessions tend to be exhibited in two forms. The first, *obsessive doubting*, represents a state of perpetual indecision in which patients interminably reevaluate a series of alternatives, rarely make a clear-cut choice, and if they do, rescind that choice only to waver again. The uncertainty they feel leads them to brood about past actions and reexamine them endlessly, to believe that they were ill-conceived or poorly executed, and then to undo or recheck them repeatedly. For example, a woman lies awake, uncertain whether she turned off the gas jets on the stove, proceeds to check them, finds them closed, returns to bed, thinks she may have inadvertently put them on, doubts that she could have done so, but must go and check again. *Obsessive thoughts* are intrusive ideas that the person cannot block from consciousness. Some are meaningless (e.g., "Where did I see a chair with one leg cut off?") and are experienced without emotion, but nonetheless are so persistent and distracting as to upset even the most routine of daily activities. Other recurrent thoughts are affect- and tension-laden, pertain to forbidden aggressive impulses or to prohibited sexual desires, and are experienced with shame, disgust, or horror. The more desperately the patient tries to be rid of these repugnant ideas, the more tormenting and persistent they become. For example, a passing thought of poisoning a wayward husband becomes fixed in a wife's mind; no matter how much she seeks to distract her attention from it, the thought returns to hound her at every meal.

Compulsions are behavior sequences, usually in the form of some ritual that is recognized by the patient as absurd or irrational, but which, if not executed, will provoke anxiety. These rituals express themselves most frequently as bizarre stereotyped acts, for example, touching one's nose with one's pinky before washing; repetition of normal acts, for example, tying one's shoelace exactly eight times before feeling satisfied with the outcome; or insisting on cleanliness and order, for example, being unduly concerned that ashtrays remain spotless or that one's books never be out of alphabetical sequence. The Freudian concepts of isolation, displacement, reaction formation, and undoing may be useful ways of referring to a principal psychic method by which the patient neutralizes anxieties and forbidden impulses.

Obsessions relieve anxiety by isolating a thought from its associated feeling. In addition, by displacing the anxiety-provoking thought to a substitute and innocuous obsessional idea, patients distract themselves, as in phobias, from the true source of tensions. Reaction formation enables them not only to disconnect but to counteract their forbidden feelings. In addition, by thinking and acting in ways that are diametrically opposite to their dangerous impulses, patients may also be able to gratify these impulses with complete impunity. For example, by actively engaging in the censoring of pornography, a patient provides himself, through his careful "examination" of this "disgusting literature," with an acceptable rationale to ventilate his otherwise repressed hostile and erotic impulses.

Compulsions achieve similar coping aims. Patients' irresistible preoccupation with a variety of absurd but "safe" activities distract them from confronting the real source of discomfort. Moreover, through reaction formation, they may be able to pursue activities that serve as a subterfuge for their socially unacceptable impulses. Symbolic acts traceable to undoing mechanisms serve not only to void past sins but to ward off anticipated future punishment and social rebuke. Thus, the self-punitive and redemptive aspects of the undoing ritual often discharge and diminish the oppressive buildup of guilt feelings. In addition, patients' insistence on order and cleanliness and the self-righteous air with which they perform these acts evoke the secondary gains of attention and approval from others. For example, the compulsively orderly and "proper" high school student will be viewed, both by parents and teachers alike, as a fine, well-disciplined, and upright young man.

Prevailing Treatment Options

Despite the fact that complex psychological disorders play a distinct role in the etiology, content, and expressive forms of obsessions and compulsions, the treatment of this syndrome has been most successful with behavioral treatment procedures and pharmacologic medications. Frequently employed are in vivo and imaginal exposure to the precipitants and maintainers of the anxiety precipitant. Response-prevention methods (e.g., thought stopping) are also likely to be helpful in deterring troubling thoughts and actions. Exposure techniques are graduated such that low-anxiety associations are dealt with initially and higher levels of anxiety are introduced step-by-step. After a patient has developed a reasonable level of comfort, he or she may be encouraged to continue exposure opportunities at home and with the help of family or friends (Greist & Jefferson, 1996).

In addition to exposure and response-prevention techniques, a number of other treatment approaches also enhance therapeutic effectiveness. Notable among these are a variety of cognitive methods designed to alter erroneous beliefs and to stop intrusive ruminations (K. Kelly, 1996). Similarly, procedures of progressive relaxation, self-management, and assertion and social skill training have proven efficacious (Roth & Fonagy, 1996).

Not to be overlooked in the recent literature is the utility of certain pharmacologic agents (chlomipramine and SSRIs) in amplifying the effectiveness of behavioral exposure and response prevention (Dattilio, 1993). Although best viewed as an adjunct to behavioral procedures, pharmacologic treatments appear to increase overall effectiveness when approached combinationally. Finally, training in relaxation methods, perhaps augmented by biofeedback procedures, should deepen the patient's capacity to deal with life's stressors in a more manageable fashion. As noted, efforts should be expended, where appropriate, to facilitate the development of "self-talk" strategies to help diminish the patient's obsessive thoughts or compulsive behaviors.

Personality-Guided Synergistic Therapy

Despite the strong role complex psychological factors play in the instigation and form in which the disorders are expressed, it is clear that many patients with this syndrome possess physiological weaknesses, as Janet argued. Identifying those disposed biologically will not be a simple task. We also know that there are intrapsychic dynamics involved in the creation of many obsessions and compulsions. Though they tend to be intellectually controversial, there is every reason to believe that they play a significant part in shaping the character and content of these disorders. Nevertheless, it is clear through research efforts that the most expedient techniques are a variety of behavioral procedures.

We turn next to the various personality styles and disorders that appear to be vulnerable to the development of obsessive-compulsive Axis I syndromes.

OBSESSIVE-COMPULSIVE SYNDROMES AMONG COMPULSIVE PERSONALITIES

These persons exhibit obsessive-compulsive symptoms with only a slightly greater frequency than most other pathological personalities. Apart from certain biochemical processes, the obsessive-compulsive symptomatology in these individuals is not so much a matter of "disordered" coping as it is a part of a deeply ingrained lifestyle strategy utilized to contain the upsurge of intense, socially forbidden impulses. Through a pattern of widely generalized reaction formations, they have learned not only to control their contrary inclinations, but to present a front of complete conformity and propriety. Note should be made again of the success of a variety of pharmacologic agents (Rauch & Jenike, 1998) in curtailing these obsessive-compulsive symptoms, suggesting that a lower threshold may exist for certain persons in permitting their expression.

Obsessive doubting may also be typical of these patients' tendencies to reevaluate and reexamine even the most trivial decisions and acts. This excessive preoccupation with minor irrelevancies enables them to distract their attention from the real source of their anxieties. Although doubting is a habitual aspect of their daily functioning, it may become quite distinctive as a symptom if there is a sudden eruption of feelings that may "give them away." Their pretense of equanimity and control is often disrupted by bizarre thoughts, usually of a hostile or erotic character. These stir up intense fears of social condemnation, which may be handled by a series of compulsive rituals. For example, each morning, by washing his face three times and knotting his tie five times, a patient assures himself of his purity; moreover, by repeating some insignificant act in which he feels competent, he strengthens his confidence in his ability to control his impulses.

OBSESSIVE-COMPULSIVE SYNDROMES
AMONG AVOIDANT PERSONALITIES

These persons develop symptoms for a variety of reasons. Obsessions may serve as substitute thoughts to distract these patients from reflecting on their "true" misery. Similarly, these thoughts may counter feelings of estrangement and depersonalization by providing avoidants with ideas and events that serve to assure them that life is "real." Compulsive acts accomplish similar aims. They "fill up" time, diverting patients from self-preoccupations; moreover, these acts keep them in touch with real events and thereby help deter feelings of depersonalization and estrangement. Certain of these repetitive and superstitious acts may reflect attempts to cope with anticipated social derision. For example, a 30-year-old avoidant patient made a complete, 360-degree turn each time prior to his walking through a door. This, he felt, would change his personality, which in turn would disincline those he subsequently met from ridiculing him. These ritualistic behaviors often signify also a bizarre method of controlling socially condemned thoughts and impulses. Thus, the patient noted above put the index finger of his right hand to his lips and then placed both hands in the back pockets of his trousers whenever he felt the urge to shout obscenities or touch the breasts of women passersby.

OBSESSIVE-COMPULSIVE SYNDROMES
AMONG DEPENDENT PERSONALITIES

These personalities are often preoccupied with obsessive doubts. These usually derive from reactivated feelings of inadequacy and are precipitated by situations in which they must assume independence and responsibility. Here, they weigh interminably the pros and cons of the situation, thereby postponing endlessly any change in the status quo of dependency. Obsessional thoughts and compulsive acts frequently are manifested when feelings of separation anxiety or repressed anger come to the fore. Here, the psychic maneuver serves, through mechanisms such as reaction formation and undoing, to counter tensions that would arise as a consequence of discharging their impulses. The symptoms displayed often take the form of "sweet" thoughts and approval-gaining acts, as illustrated in the following case.

CASE 6.7, ANNE L., 32

Presenting Picture: Anne could not rid herself of the obsessive image that her husband's face was "the most beautiful in the world"; she also took great pains each night to wash, iron, and prepare every item of clothing he planned to wear the next day. Upon clinical study, she revealed an intense fear that her husband might discover that she once allowed a neighbor to kiss her while he was away on an extended business trip. Anne's obsessive symptom enabled her to block the visualization of her neighbor's face. Her compulsive acts of caring for her husband were an attempt to "prove" her faithfulness and devotion to him.

Therapeutic Course: Her compulsive behavior abated her anxiety only minimally and, hence, she sought to enter psychotherapeutic treatment. Anne was first given a prescription for anxiolytics; this was followed by an analytically oriented exploration of her wide-ranging fears and her marital concerns. Whether a function of her medications or her analysis, Anne came to recognize her intense dependency needs and her anticipations of loss. A cognitive restructuring process was employed to help her realize the basis of several of her distorting beliefs; alternative attitudes were also encouraged. Additionally, she was invited to participate for several months in a weekly assertiveness training group program.

Synergistic Afterthoughts: The approach used to deal with Anne's distress was rather successful in that it enabled her to view life realistically as well as to learn competencies that would assist her in managing her daily responsibilities. A formal program of marital/family treatment should have been introduced; at the very least, this would have enlisted her husband in facilitating and encouraging the changes achieved in Anne's individual psychotherapy. Thought might also have been given to the early use of self-actualizing techniques, such as Rogers's client-centered modality.

OBSESSIVE-COMPULSIVE SYNDROMES AMONG HISTRIONIC PERSONALITIES

These personalities are disposed to have their thoughts and emotions rather scattered and disconnected as a function of their general deficient personality integration. They characteristically exhibit dramatic emotional feelings over matters of minimal import and significance. Conversely, they may discuss serious topics and problems with a rather cool detachment. This ease with which affect and idea can be isolated from each other is a primary factor in contributing to their obsessive symptoms. Thus, with little strain or tension, they readily disconnect an emotion from its associated content.

Quite often, these patients experience a "free-floating" erotic emotion, that is, a sexual impulse without precipitant or focus. Conversely, hostile obsessive thoughts may preoccupy them, whereas the normally associated feeling of anger remains repressed. Which behavior or emotion is expressed and which is repressed is usually guided by their basic goal of gaining social approval and minimizing social rebuke; for example, they rarely vent hostile feelings but often manifest seductive emotions and behaviors.

OBSESSIVE-COMPULSIVE SYNDROMES AMONG NEGATIVISTIC PERSONALITIES

These personalities tend to vent their contrary impulses rather openly. However, these feelings may be transformed psychically into obsessions and compulsions if they are especially intense and likely to provoke either separation anxieties or severe social reproval. Obsessive thinking is a common resolution of this conflict. For example, a normally outspoken patient was quietly obsessed with the thought that her husband's clothes were stained with lipstick and sperm; this symbolized her fear that he was having an affair and that others would discover this "fact," much to her shame. She did not dare confront him with her obsessive suspicion, dreading that he would admit it and then leave her.

OBSESSIVE-COMPULSIVE SYNDROMES
AMONG SCHIZOID PERSONALITIES

Extended social isolation, with its consequent periods of "empty" rumination, often results in obsessive thinking, which the schizoid may be unable to block from conscious intrusion. Most of these thoughts are meaningless (e.g., "Where did I see a chair with one leg?") and experienced without emotion but, nonetheless, may be so persistent and distracting as to upset the routine of daily activities. Some recurrent thoughts may become tension-laden, pertain to forbidden impulses or prohibited desires, and, hence, evoke feelings of shame, disgust, or horror. The more desperately these patients try to rid themselves of these repugnant ideas, the more persistent and tormenting they may become. For example, a passing thought of poisoning a wayward wife may become fixed in a husband's mind; no matter how much he seeks to distract his attention from it, the thought returns time and again.

OBSESSIVE-COMPULSIVE SYNDROMES
AMONG PARANOID PERSONALITIES

These patients will occasionally exhibit obsessive-compulsive syndromes as seen in an irresistible preoccupation with some absurd but "safe" activity that serves to distract them from confronting more painful sources of discomfort. Also, through reaction formation, they may pursue these activities as a subterfuge for socially unacceptable impulses. Thus, symbolic acts of compulsive undoing serve not only to void past sins but to ward off anticipated future punishment and social rebuke. Moreover, the self-punitive and redemptive aspects of the undoing ritual often diminish the oppressive buildup of guilt. For example, insistence on order and cleanliness, not especially typical of the paranoid's characteristic behavior, and the self-righteous air with which he or she performs these acts, distract others from the paranoid's previous irrationalities and often evoke a number of secondary gains.

CHAPTER SEVEN

Treating Anxiety-Related Physical Syndromes: Somatoform and Conversion Disorders

Interspersed among TV commercials for headache tablets, muscular relaxants, intestinal tonics, and the like, we manage to see a few of the other forms of entertainment provided to meet the public demand. It has often been noted that more ingenuity is invested in attracting the American populace to remedies for their nonexistent ailments than in filling their impoverished imaginations. There are many reasons for the vast and continuous commercial success of these nostrums. Primary among them is the need of millions of Americans to find magical elixirs and balms by which they hope, usually futilely, to counter their lack of energy and a bevy of minor physical discomforts. These perennial states of fatigue and the persistence of medically undiagnosable aches and pains signify another of the complex anxiety-related disorders, one that runs to endless expenditures for drugs and physicians and that disables, in one form or another, a significant portion of our populace.

Although the clinical symptoms of a heightened sensitivity to somatic distress and/or fatigue were described in early Greek medical literature, it was not until P. Briquet (1859) and George Miller Beard (1869) that a specific theory was proposed to account for them. These researchers described what we now call the somatization disorder, a stable and well-defined diagnostic category that has been recently reintroduced in the formal literature (Guze, 1967). Beard coined the term *neurasthenia* to denote what he viewed to be the outcome of nervous exhaustion in these patients. His theory rested on the assumption that nerve cells operated like an electric battery; that is, they could run down or be depleted by overwork and inadequate psychic rest.

SOMATOFORM SYNDROMES

In his early writings, Freud agreed with Beard that the neurasthenic syndrome represented a physiological dysfunction. However, he hypothesized that the difficulty lay not in the depletion of neural energy but in the cumulation of excess sexual energies, which failed to be appropriately discharged. Freud subsumed neurasthenia in a single broader syndrome, termed the *actual neuroses,* which included anxiety neuroses, neurasthenia, and hypochondriasis. As he conceived it, these three disorders were, more or less, direct outcomes of undischarged or dammed-up physiological energies.

The actual neuroses were contrasted to the *psychoneuroses,* whose origins lay in psychogenic trauma and whose tensions were transformed and discharged by the workings of various psychic transformations. Freud altered some of these views in his later writings, proposing that psychogenic factors could play a role in the actual neuroses as well as the psychoneuroses. However, he continued to speak of the actual neuroses as bound and undischarged sexual energies, but began to see them as sources of focal irritation that could serve as the base for associated symptoms. Specifically, he posited the view that neurasthenia (fatigue) might function as a somatic basis for a withdrawal from social and sexual life. Similarly, hypochondriasis, which he conceived to be a mixture of anxiety and neurasthenia, reflected the withdrawal of sexual energies from their normal external objects and their consequent attachment to narcissistically valued parts of the patient's own body.

More recent formulations of the somatoform syndromes have focused less on ostensive energy components and more on their cognitive and interpersonal roots. We base our presentation on these current viewpoints rather than on Freud's original thesis.

Somatization syndromes share with "real" medical disorders a common focus on bodily distress and discomfort. However, medical patients ostensibly have a demonstrable biological impairment that accounts for their physical discomfort; their symptomatology arises, in part, from a failure to discharge physical tensions, whereas the symptoms of somatoform patients reflect their way of discharging psychic tensions.

Somatoform patients divert part of their ambivalent feelings toward themselves, transforming their partially restrained emotions into bodily complaints. Instead of complaining to others about their psychic anger directly, for example, they camouflage and complain about it in the form of a physical substitute. By turning whatever anger they may have inward, they are distracted from the reality of their hostile impulses; this psychic maneuver prevents undue condemnation by others.

It is our belief that the subvariants of the somatoform syndrome (e.g., somatization, hypochondriasis, pain) represent different facets of the same psychic process; in one, for example, the patient complains of specific bodily ailments, and in another of pain or of a general bodily weariness. These symptoms often covary in a single patient because they serve essentially identical functions.

General Clinical Picture

The clinical features of the somatoform disorders are difficult to narrow down. Not only are the types of reported discomfort many and varied, but they almost inevitably combine with, complicate, and blend into several other domains of psychic functions (e.g., behavioral, self-image). They are given special note by the presence of prolonged periods of weariness and exhaustion, undiagnosable pain sensations, persistent insomnia, a state of diffuse irritability, and reported ailments in different, unconnected, and changing regions of the body. In general, this group of syndromes is characterized by somatic complaints or disease fears that are out of proportion to any specified medical evaluation; they likely suggest the presence of a heightened sensitivity to discomforting physical stimuli, an exaggerated fear of disease, and the possible secondary gains of adopting the patient role.

Several variants of the somatoform syndrome have been differentiated.

Somatization is the recurrence of multiple somatic complaints, often leading to frequent medical attention and treatment over a period of several years. No known general medical condition can account for the symptomatology. Somatization difficulties, previously termed Briquet's Syndrome, are not consonant with the results of physical examinations or laboratory tests; they must show up in at least four different physical locations (e.g., head, abdomen, back, joints) to be diagnosed in this category.

As part of the overall somatoform group, *hypochondriasis* signifies a preoccupation with the idea that one has a serious disease, a fear based on misinterpretations of one's own bodily symptoms. Again, as with somatization, no general medical condition can fully account for the patient's worries. Fears persist despite medical reassurances.

Pain disorders signify that the symptom is the predominant focus of the patient's clinical state; it is usually of sufficient persistence and severity to warrant clinical attention. Although the pain is not intentionally produced and is not a necessary consequence of comorbid psychiatric disorders, it is judged to be experientially "real," but exacerbated by psychological factors.

Conversion disorders will be discussed in the next section owing to this author's belief that conversions involve intrapsychic processes that are only tangentially seen in other disorders of the somatoform group.

Experientially, some patients speak of a heaviness and a drab monotony to their lives. Despite this lethargy, they are exquisitely attuned to every facet of their normal physiology and markedly concerned with minor changes in bodily functioning. Many patients, despite their preoccupation and concern with aches and pains, manage to function actively and with considerable vigor in the course of everyday life. Other patients, however, are easily exhausted and cannot perform simple daily tasks without feeling that they have totally drained their meager reserves. This state of perpetual weariness, unaccompanied by specific body anxieties or discomforts, is a very common complaint.

As has been stressed in prior chapters, anxiety-transformed symptoms reflect attempts to cope with overt anxiety and to achieve where possible a variety of secondary gains. Although coping efforts employed in these syndromes may sound as if patients plan them consciously, this is not usually the case. Strategies of coping engage deeply ingrained interpersonal habits and cognitive attitudes. These habits automatically "take over" when the patient is confronted with current situations that he or she perceives as comparable to those of the past. They persist, in part, out of sheer inertia, if nothing else.

Among the principal goals of the somatoform strategy are patients' desires to solicit attention and nurturance from others and to evoke reassurances that they will be loved and cared for despite their weaknesses and inadequacies. By their "illness," patients divert attention from the true source of their dismay, usually the lack of interest and attention shown to them by others. Thus, without complaining directly about their disappointment and resentment, they still manage to rekindle others' flagging interests and devotions. Moreover, these physical complaints are employed as a means of controlling others, making them feel guilty, and thereby retaliating for the disinterest and mistreatment patients feel they have suffered.

Prevailing Treatment Options

Of all the pathologies described, we can see the close interweaving of biological and psychological functions most clearly in the somatoform disorders. Of course, every psychopathological ailment derives in part from the operation of both psychic and somatic factors; somatoform disorders are notable in this regard only because they give evidence of this inseparable fusion in manifest physical form. What distinguishes them as disorders is not the fact that physiological processes are involved—a fact true of all disorders—but rather that they represent a failure to find a means of curtailing or dissipating the cumulation of these physiological processes. In other disorders, physiological tensions cumulate less rapidly and are discharged more efficiently. Let us turn in this section to the general therapeutic approaches that have been devised to alleviate them.

The somatic symptoms of these disorders either persist for long periods or recur at frequent intervals. This state of affairs reflects in part the occasional physical damage that often occurs in conjunction with the disorder. In addition, unless the circumstances that led to the difficulty are resolved, tensions will continue to mount and disrupt normal biological functioning. Further complications arise because many of these patients fail to recognize the psychogenic roots of their disease; some often adamantly refuse to admit that they suffer any psychological discomfort or discontent. (We must be reminded, in this regard, that not all patients exhibiting somatoform disorders suffer these ailments for psychogenic reasons; clinicians must not attempt to "convince" patients that they may be emotionally troubled unless he or she has a sound reason for believing so.) Resistance to psychogenic interpretations is found among patients who fear to "open up" or to become conscious of their forbidden or repressed feelings. In these cases, the prognosis is extremely poor because patients will shy away from therapeutic involvements that threaten to "expose" their hidden emotions. Only if their physical symptoms become extremely discomforting, frightening, or painful will they allow themselves to be subjected to psychodiagnostic scrutiny.

Therapeutic attention must be directed first to remedying whatever physical impairments have occurred in conjunction with the disorder. Body pathology, as in ulcer perforations, should be dealt with promptly by appropriate medical, nutritional, or surgical means. When the physical disease process is under adequate control, attention may be turned to the management of environmental stresses and to the modification of detrimental attitudes and habits.

As we have said, somatic symptoms arise often as a consequence of patients' inability to resolve conflicts and discharge tensions. Because of patients' dread that these emotions will overwhelm them if released, the therapist must move slowly before exposing these conflicting attitudes or "opening the floodgates" to the onrush of these repressed feelings. Quite evidently, the patient has been willing to suffer considerable physical discomfort as the price for containing unacceptable conflicts and impulses. The danger of precipitating a crisis is great if the patient gains insight too quickly or if previously hidden feelings are uncovered and unleashed too rapidly. Such exposure and release must be coordinated with a parallel strengthening of the patient's capacity to cope with these feelings.

The warning just noted points to the important role of supportive techniques in the early stages of treatment. At first, care should be taken to diminish tension and to help dissipate the cumulation of past tensions. Anxiolytics may be useful in softening the response to tension precipitants. In addition, arrangements should be made where feasible to have the patient avoid those aspects of everyday living that prompt or aggravate unresolvable anxieties and conflicts.

Turning to formal psychotherapeutic measures, the procedures of behavior modification and cognitive reorientation may be used to extinguish attitudes and habits that have generated tensions, and to build in new ones that may facilitate discharging, avoiding, or otherwise coping with them (Nathan & Gorman, 1998). Group therapy often serves as a valuable adjunct to help the pain patient explore feelings, learn methods of resolving conflicts, and liberate tensions (Turner, 1982). Hypochondriacal patients appear to benefit especially with group cognitive methods that set out to correct misinformation and exaggerated beliefs, especially those that maintain the disease fears (Barsky, Geringer, & Wood, 1988; Kellner, 1982). As was noted earlier, the probing and uncovering methods of intrapsychic therapy should not be utilized in the early phases of treatment, as they may prompt the upsurge of severely upsetting forbidden thoughts and impulses. However, should other procedures prove unsuccessful in alleviating tension or in diminishing the disturbing symptomatology, it may be necessary to employ intrapsychic processes, and to begin a slow and long-term process of reconstructing the patient's pervasive personality pattern.

Personality-Guided Synergistic Therapy

Let us turn to the various personality patterns that are susceptible to somatoform syndromes.

SOMATOFORM SYNDROMES AMONG DEPRESSIVE PERSONALITIES

In certain cases, somatoform symptoms represent a form of self-punishment, an attack on oneself disguised in the form of bodily ailments and exhaustion. The following case illuminates somatoform disorders among depressive personalities.

Case 7.1, Brian F., 46

Presenting Picture: This depressive man had recently begun to feel that his work at the office was of "measurably" less quality than that of his colleagues' and that his exhaustion at the end of the day prevented him from being a "proper" father to his children. Although Brian voiced guilt for his failures, he was unable to face the real source of his recent distressing and depressing thoughts, the fact that he believed he "faked" data to keep up with his associates. It was easier to tolerate weakness in his body than in his mind. Thus, he chose a symbolic physical substitute to punish himself for his guilt, "arthritic" pains in his fingers, that made it increasingly difficult to write or to punch the keys of a calculator. Not to be overlooked among his goals were such secondary gains as avoiding responsibilities that threatened his life pattern. Clear also was the use of his physical illness as a rationalization for his perceived inadequacies.

Therapeutic Course: In the course of the 20 or so sessions that he was seen, Brian was prescribed the then popular tricyclic medications for his depressive tone. Similarly, he was prescribed an early anxiolytic (Valium) and was engaged in a series of cognitive dialogues that sought to overcome his preoccupation with his physical difficulty. Without engaging in extensive intrapsychic probing, the combination of medications and cognitive procedures helped Brian overcome his disability. Not to be forgotten were steps that gathered information from his employer that his work was, in fact, well recognized as superior.

Synergistic Afterthoughts: Somewhat lacking in his therapeutic experience were opportunities on the part of the therapist to systematically alter Brian's self-cognitions. Rather than dislodge his intrapsychic anxieties, it may have been useful initially to refashion his low sense of self-esteem and his self-derogation; such an approach would have been of extensive value; that is, it would have carried Brian forward more effectively into the use of future procedures. A synergistic plan that arranged the sequence of treatment from an initial pharmacologic approach to that of increasing his sense of self-worth may also have reduced the likelihood of relapse. (The reader may find Chapter 12 useful in thinking through the application of the synergistic approach.)

SOMATOFORM SYNDROMES AMONG AVOIDANT PERSONALITIES

Avoidant personalities exhibit somatoform syndromes to achieve a variety of different coping goals, such as countering feelings of depersonalization. They may become alert to bodily sounds and movements to assure themselves that they exist as "real" and alive. In more severe states, and because of these patients' habitual social isolation and self-preoccupations, these bodily sensations may become elaborated into bizarre if not delusional experiences. Discomforting bodily sensations may be used also as a symbolic form of self-punishment, representing the disgust, if not hatred, that some avoidants feel toward themselves. Fatigue in these personalities may be seen as an extension of the avoidant's basic detachment strategy. Thus, physical inertia can serve instrumentally as a rationalization to justify withdrawal from social contact.

CASE 7.2, PATRICIA Y., 33

Presenting Picture: Hesitant, shy, and moody, Patricia was a troubled woman who appeared to have experienced the symptoms and preoccupations of a somatoform disorder (e.g., gastrointestinal discomfort, pain). Highly sensitive to public reproval and humiliation, as well as often feeling mistreated and aggrieved, Patricia experienced considerable bitterness toward others, which she could not express directly for fear of retribution. Hence, her inner turmoil remained bottled up, vented indirectly through multiple complaints of a physical nature as well as through hypochondriacal concerns over undefined and unconfirmed bodily diseases. Viewed psychodynamically, these complaints served as an outlet for discharging Patricia's psychic discontent, and her concerns over her bodily defects served as a symbolic displacement of her feelings of low self-esteem and self-worth.

Therapeutic Course: Over the course of her treatment, Patricia's somatoform ailments receded in their prominence. A nondirective or client-centered approach was employed to permit Patricia to express her concerns and fears and to explore the possibility that they may be an expression of her general personality traits. An informal cognitive mode was followed to assist her in recognizing her tendencies to interpret inner stimuli in the worst possible light. It became evident, however, that the wider context of her avoidant personality style would have to be treated to effect a sustainable change. Patricia began such treatment for several months, with a modicum of success regarding her somatoform syndrome.

Synergistic Afterthoughts: Several additional therapeutic modalities might have proved helpful in overcoming Patricia's approach to life. Most central would be an effort to modify her alienated self-image, that is, to help improve her self-valuation. A series of interpersonal procedures might have been utilized next to overcome her pervasive aversive behavioral style. In this regard, follow-up steps might have been taken to aid her in reducing her tendency to live largely through fantasy and imagination rather than reality. Methods of cognitive processing, in addition to altering cognitive content, might also have been helpful. For example, efforts should have been made to aid her in sorting her thoughts so that they do not interfere with one another, to guide her into feeling calmer, and to utilize a slower and more deliberate style of communication, one in which the interference of miscellaneous thoughts could be reduced. It is the clustering of Patricia's fragmented thoughts, emotional hypersensitivities, fearful behaviors, and social detachment that all contribute significantly to her current Axis I syndrome.

SOMATOFORM SYNDROMES
AMONG DEPENDENT PERSONALITIES

Dependent personalities may develop somatoform disorders as a means of controlling the upsurge of forbidden impulses. More commonly, these symptoms promote the avoidance of onerous responsibilities and help recruit secondary gains such as sympathy and nurturance. By displaying physical helplessness, dependents often succeed in eliciting the attention and care they need. Somatoform symptoms may be a form of self-punishment for feelings of guilt and worthlessness. Dependents tend, however, not to be too harsh with themselves. Their somatoform symptoms are likely to take the form of relatively mild sensory anesthesias such as a generalized numbness in the hands and feet. It is notable that their symptoms often are located in their limbs, a way perhaps of demonstrating to others that they are "disabled" and, therefore, incapable of performing even routine chores.

Among other principal goals are the dependents' desires to solicit attention and nurturance from others and to evoke assurances that they will be loved and cared for despite weaknesses and inadequacy. By their "illness," dependents divert attention from the true source of their dismay, the feeling that others are showing little interest and paying little attention to them. Without complaining directly about their disappointment and resentment, dependents still manage through their physical ailments to attract and rekindle the flagging devotions of others. Not to be overlooked also is that illness complaints may be employed to control others, make them feel guilty, and thereby retaliate for the disinterest and mistreatment dependents may feel they have suffered. In some cases, pain and nagging symptoms represent a form of self-punishment, an attack on oneself that is disguised in bodily ailments and physical exhaustion.

CASE 7.3, JEAN B., 37

Presenting Picture: Jean B. reported a pattern of undefined bodily symptoms and hypochondriacal preoccupations that typify a somatoform disorder. Although no clear organic findings could account for the full range of her ailments, she was unlikely to acknowledge the possible role emotional factors played in aggravating them. Several intrapsychic processes were involved in their maintenance. Jean used the ailments to distract attention from recent losses to her self-esteem over matters related to her attractiveness. No less plausible was the role her symptoms played in accommodating her feelings of emptiness and aloneness by compensatory self-stimulation and self-ministration. Not to be overlooked was the possibility that her symptoms were vehicles to regain the attention of significant others.

Therapeutic Course: Two treatment approaches were employed concurrently. The first was a homogeneous group composed of other dependent personalities. Discussion centered on their tendency to develop symptoms that curtailed their capacity to function effectively. Some group members were hypochondriacal, others suffered severe and recurrent pain, and the remaining gave evidence of a long-term somatization difficulty. The presence of other group members with similar "physical" ailments, as well as the willingness of members to share the possible psychological basis of their physical disorder, proved to be very useful. Overlapping with the group approach were individual cognitive treatment sessions centered on reevaluating Jean's persistent misinterpretation of her sensory signals and her irrational beliefs concerning health and illness. A high measure of success was associated with these treatment methods.

Synergistic Afterthoughts: Although problems of interpersonal habit and cognitive style were amply explored in the group format, additional realms that were given minor attention in the group setting might have been usefully introduced. Perhaps most important would be efforts to strengthen Jean's sense of self-esteem, that is, to overcome her inept self-image. Her general lack of self-confidence, added to her tendency to belittle her own competencies, left Jean with the feeling that she simply could not deal with life's exigencies on her own. A sequence of self-actualizing and skill training techniques (e.g., client-centered and behavioral learning) can be fruitfully synthesized to achieve this end. Similarly, efforts might have been made to introduce her to adult activities and responsibilities. In this regard, arrangements may have been made by the use of marital/family therapy. (The reader may turn to Chapter 13 for additional guidelines.)

SOMATOFORM SYNDROMES
AMONG HISTRIONIC PERSONALITIES

Histrionics utilize hypochondriacal and somatization symptoms as instruments for attracting attention and nurturance. To be fussed over with care and concern is rewarding for most individuals; in histrionics, it is "like a drug" that is needed to sustain them. When histrionics feel a sense of emptiness and isolation, they desperately seek a diet of constant concern and approval. Being ill is a simple solution because it requires little effort yet produces guaranteed attention. Thus, if nothing else "works," created symptoms may be depended upon as a means of achieving these ends. Moreover, if life becomes humdrum and boring, physical ailments not only evoke attention from others but provide a new preoccupation and source of stimulation.

Psychogenic pain and aches are another form of preoccupation and stimulation to fill the empty moments. Only rarely, however, do histrionics display somatic fatigue because this symptom runs counter to their active stimulus-seeking style. They prefer to use obvious and dramatic complaints to draw attention to themselves, for these behaviors enable them to continue to participate actively in social affairs.

SOMATOFORM SYNDROMES
AMONG SCHIZOID PERSONALITIES

Although only modestly prevalent, somatoform disorders will become prominent and salient features when they do occur in schizoids. With the presence of prolonged periods of weariness and exhaustion, undiagnosable physical sensations, and persistent insomnia, these patients may fall into a state of diffuse irritability and report pains in different, unconnected, and changing regions of the body. Cognitively, schizoids report experiencing a heaviness and a drab monotony to their lives. Despite this lethargy, they become fixated, exquisitely attuned to some facet of normal physiology, or uncharacteristically concerned with a minor change in their bodily functioning. These preoccupations seem to reflect a need on their part to "latch on" to something tangible about themselves, something that will assure them that they do, in fact, exist and are not insubstantial or disembodied.

SOMATOFORM SYNDROMES
AMONG NARCISSISTIC PERSONALITIES

There is a reasonable likelihood that narcissists will exhibit somatoform symptoms following the shame of a humiliating defeat or embarrassment. Unable to solicit the tribute they expect from others, narcissists become their own source of solicitude by nurturing their wounds symbolically. Their hypochondriacal concerns are a form of self-ministering, an act of providing the affection and attention they can no longer obtain from others. Not to be overlooked also among the secondary gains of these symptoms is their use as a rationalization for failures and shortcomings. Discomforting though it may be to admit to any frailty, it impugns narcissists' competence somewhat less if they can ascribe their "defeats" to a physical illness rather than to a self-implicating psychological shortcoming. Additionally, physical complaints are often a useful disguise for discharging anger and resentment. Discontent over their own inadequacies and too ashamed to express anger directly, narcissists may cloak their resentments by using their physical impairments as an excuse. Thus, they may become "household tyrants," not only by creating guilt in others for failure to attend to the needs of a "sick person," but by demanding that their claims for special status be instituted once again.

SOMATOFORM SYNDROMES
AMONG NEGATIVISTIC PERSONALITIES

These personalities often display somatization symptoms in conjunction with genuine physical disorders. Discontent, irritable, and fractious, they often use physical complaints as a weak disguise for hostile impulses, a veil to cloak their deeply felt anger and resentment. Feelings of retribution for past frustrations often underlie the excessive demands they make for special treatment. They seek not only to create guilt in others but to control the lives of family members and to cause them grief and financial cost. Although a significant proportion of these personalities may have been subjected in childhood to inconsistent parental treatment, most learned that they could evoke reliable parental attention and support when they were ill or when they complained of illness. As a consequence, when they need care and nurturance, they may revert back to the ploy of physical complaints. Some may be sufficiently aware of the maneuvers they engage in to be justly diagnosed as exhibiting a factitious disorder. Others, less successful in evoking the care and sympathy they desire, have learned to nurture themselves, that is, to tend symbolically to their own bodily needs. Disillusioned by parental disinterest or inconsistency, these patients have learned to provide a hypochondriacal ministering to themselves, ensuring thereby a consistency in self-sympathy and self-gratification that can be obtained from no one else.

Because these personalities express their feelings rather openly and directly, tension builds up more slowly than in their similarly conflicted counterpart, the compulsive personality. Moreover, when emotional tension is discharged, it is less likely to be camouflaged.

CASE 7.4, REGINA T., 44

Presenting Picture: Regina T.'s moody and conflicted bodily preoccupations and concerns were produced by both physical and psychological factors, resulting in a syndrome of features suggestive of a somatoform disorder. Enmeshed in an erratic pattern of resentment and brittle emotions, her anxious concerns about her somatic state aggravated her characteristic sullenness and led her to demand attention and special treatment. Not only did she exploit her ailments to control the lives of others, but she also liked to complain of her discomfort in ways that induced others to feel guilty.

Therapeutic Course: A rational-emotive cognitive procedure was employed to guide Regina into an awareness of her manipulative behaviors. Particularly useful was her assumption that significant others would not likely come to her assistance should she need or desire support. Her physical ailments were seen as an instrumentality to evoke such nurturant behaviors. Similarly, she was guided into recognizing not only her fears, but the anger she felt toward those she believed should be more consistent in their caring and nurturant behaviors. An early Gestalt technique was also employed to provide her with opportunities to better understand how others are likely to feel in response to her manipulations. Combined with the cognitive methodology, these "empty chair" techniques proved to be extremely helpful. Regina decided to continue treatment after her physical symptomatology abated in order to help her undo her negativistic style of functioning.

Synergistic Afterthoughts: A key element in helping Regina would be not only to alter her skeptical attitudes and contrary behaviors, but also to guide her cognitively to modify her discontented self-image. Much of Regina's diffuse unhappiness stems from her unhappiness of self. Hence, a variety of self-actualizing methods might have blended fruitfully in undercutting the psychic conflicts that inhere within her, especially those that are perpetually reinforced by her own actions and beliefs. Similarly, greater efforts should have been made to undercut her anticipation of disappointments and to help her appraise the motives and behaviors of others more accurately. Owing to the largely intrapsychic nature of her conflicts, brief variants of psychodynamic therapy might also be helpful, especially those of an object-relations variety. Should her family be intact, thought should have been given to the possibility of dealing directly with its members so as to reduce her manipulative behaviors.

As noted earlier, among the principal sources of somatoform disorders are repetitive upsets of the body's homeostatic balance and chronic failures to dissipate physiological tension. These problems arise most frequently in patients such as Regina who repeatedly find themselves in unresolvable conflict situations, such as when the discharge of tensions associated with one side of a conflict only increases the tensions engendered by the other side. This state of affairs describes the typical experience of both negativists and compulsives. They are trapped between acquiescent dependency on the one hand, and hostile or assertive independence on the other. When they submit or acquiesce to the wishes of others, they experience resentment and anger for having allowed themselves to be "weak" and having given up their independence. Conversely, if they are defiant and assert their independence, they experience anxiety for having endangered their tenuous dependency security. Although negativists do periodically discharge both sources of tension, their repetitive and chronically irritable behaviors reactivate these troublesome conflicts time and again. As a consequence, they often generate and accumulate tension faster than they can dissipate it. Moreover, because of their constantly fretful behaviors, their bodies are subjected repeatedly to vacillations in mood and emotion. As they swing from one intense feeling to another, their homeostatic equilibrium, so necessary for proper physiological functioning, is thrown off balance again and again. Not only do they experience an excess of chronic tension, then, but their systems rarely settle down into a smooth and regularized pattern. By keeping their bodies churning, they set themselves up for repeated bouts of psychosomatic discomfort.

SOMATOFORM SYNDROMES AMONG COMPULSIVE PERSONALITIES

Compulsive personalities succumb to somatic disorders, albeit infrequently, as another means of containing the upsurge of forbidden impulses. Somatoform disorders are not an easy "choice" for these patients, however, for being ill runs counter to their image of competence and self-sufficiency. Nevertheless—and in contrast to phobic symptoms, which are especially embarrassing in this regard—somatoform symptoms enable these patients to advertise their illness as one of physical origin. It allows them not only to achieve the important secondary gains of attention and nurturance but also to continue their belief that they are basically composed and proper, merely unfortunate victims of a "passing" sickness. Despite these gains, however, compulsives will feel most comfortable if they underplay their ailment, acting quite indifferent about it.

Somatization and hypochondriacal disorders are also employed by compulsives as a way of rationalizing failures and inadequacies. Fearful that they will be condemned for their shortcomings, compulsives may seek to maintain self-respect and the esteem of others by ascribing deficiencies to some ill-defined ailment or "legitimate" physical illness. This maneuver may not only shield them from rebuke but may evoke praise from others for the few accomplishments they do manage to achieve. How commendable others must think they are for their conscientious efforts, despite their illness and exhaustion. Compulsives do frequently suffer real fatigue and pain symptoms as a consequence of their struggle to control undischarged inner resentments. Bodily ailments may also represent a turning inward of repressed hostile impulses. Not infrequently, ailments such as these function as a displaced and symbolic self-punishment, a physical substitute for the guilt they feel after having expressed condemned emotions. Suffering not only discharges tension but serves as a form of expiation.

As noted previously, compulsives keep under close wraps most of the tensions generated by their inner conflicts. Through various psychic mechanisms, their resentments and anxieties are tightly controlled and infrequently discharged. As a consequence, physiological tensions are not dissipated, tend to cumulate, and result in frequent or persistent "real" somatic ailments.

CASE 7.5, ROY F., 41

Presenting Picture: Roy F. experienced a somatoform pain disorder. Unable to express disappointment with others directly or with relative equanimity, Roy turned his frustration and anger inward, thereby generating a variety of psychosomatic symptoms and disorders (e.g., tension headaches, back pain). Although a number of concomitant anxieties as well as dysthymia were evident, he resisted the suggestion that emotional factors lay at the root of his discomfort. Efforts to downplay the psychological significance of his difficulties were consistent with his personality style. Not to be overlooked was the possibility that his physical discomfort served as a form of self-punishment, a means by which he sought to expiate feelings of guilt or shame for his usually repressed oppositional and hostile urges.

Therapeutic Course: Cognitive techniques were employed to assist Roy in recognizing that much of his disorder reflected a form of self-punishment. Centrally involved in this procedure were efforts to explore his feelings of guilt and shame, and that these feelings stemmed in part from unconscious resentments and anger. Therapeutic procedures were only partially successful. For short periods of time it appeared that Roy began to "minster" to himself, experiencing less pain throughout his body. However, these periods were brief, and Roy relapsed time and time again, until he finally withdrew from psychological treatment. Some months thereafter, he entered an inpatient pain-disorder program that employed both physical and behavioral treatment methods. The outcome is not known.

Synergistic Afterthoughts: It is difficult to say whether approaches other than those employed would have resulted in Roy's continuation of therapy. Perhaps a less forceful therapeutic approach might have given him time to deal with the upsurge of his anger and resentment. It is certain that very short-term approaches, increasingly required these years, would not have sufficed to give him the opportunity to acclimate himself to the process of self-discovery. Should time have been available, a deeper and more intrapsychic approach might have been useful. In this realm, the intense conflict that Roy felt between his own wishes and those imposed upon him by others might have been sorted out; these may have been dealt with in a way to foster a more coherent set of attitudes and feelings. (The reader might be aided by additional themes discussed in Chapter 18.)

SOMATOFORM SYNDROMES AMONG MASOCHISTIC PERSONALITIES

As described in other sections of this chapter, somatoform disorders may be experienced and utilized by masochists as a decoy to diminish the likelihood that hostile actions on the part of others would be moderated in their intensity. Instrumentally, such ailments may also serve the unconscious purpose of self-depredation, a means of inducing suffering in oneself to accommodate feelings of guilt and to reflect acts of self-flagellation. Also notable is the fact that many have learned that illness is associated with genuine parental care and attention, an attitude on their part that would not otherwise be forthcoming.

CASE 7.6, ELAINE W., 31

Presenting Picture: Feeling anxious and aggrieved, this moody woman appeared to be preoccupied with physical fears and complaints that were indicative of a somatoform disorder (e.g., gastrointestinal discomfort, pain). Elaine's low self-esteem and dread of reproval and rejection prevented her from directly or consistently venting her discontent and resentment. As a consequence, her emotions remained largely bottled up, precluding her ability to relax or to give her bodily functions a chance to improve. Beyond the detrimental effects of unrelieved physical tension, Elaine's symptoms represented an assault against her body. Psychodynamically, she treated her body as an object of repudiation, a symbol of her psychic self, which she viewed as defective and undesirable.

Therapeutic Course: Medications (anxiolytics) and behavioral procedures (systematic desensitization) were employed initially. As in the case of Roy, it became clear that these procedures, as well as an early variant of cognitive reeducation, would not suffice to counter her "need" to do harm to herself. Having a measure of success in reducing her inclination to be self-destructive, therapy began to focus on her resentments and her general personality style and traits.

Synergistic Afterthoughts: Elaine's difficulties derive largely from a need to diminish if not destroy herself. This serves her efforts not only to manipulate others, but to undo memories in which she has been virtuous and kind to others. Through methods of free association and its consequent opportunities for insight development, this troubled woman should begin to recognize her tendency to repetitively recall past injustices and to intensify her expectation that life will continue to be problematic. Similarly, her unconscious objects of the past can be shown to have positive and supportive components, and not only those that have been problematic. Toward the later phases of treatment, cognitive-behavioral efforts might help her overcome her abstinent and frugal lifestyle as well as her disinclination to seek and enjoy pleasurable life experiences. If feasible, a family therapeutic approach might facilitate the modification of her self-defeating behaviors.

SOMATOFORM SYNDROMES AMONG BORDERLINE PERSONALITIES

These syndromes have as their primary goal blocking from awareness the true source of the borderline's anxiety. Despite the price these patients must pay in diminished bodily functioning, they remain relatively free of tension when they "accept" their disability. The "choice" of the symptom and the symbolic meaning it expresses reflect the particular character of an individual's underlying difficulties and the secondary gains he or she wishes to achieve. Both the problems and the gains that borderlines seek stem from their basic vulnerabilities and habitual personal style. This interplay can be illustrated with three brief examples: one borderline patient, whose pattern of life has been guided by the fear of social rebuke, develops a muscle weakness to control the impulse to strike someone whom he hates; another borderline suddenly becomes extremely hoarse for fear of voicing intense anger and resentment; a third patient loses much of her ability to hear as a way of tuning out contradictory voices, both real and imagined. Somatoform symptoms rarely are the end product of a single cause or coping function. Overdetermined, they reflect a compromise solution that blends several emotions and coping aims. Thus, a pained and immobilized arm may not only control an angry impulse but also may attract social sympathy as well as discharge the patient's self-punitive guilt feelings.

CONVERSION SYNDROMES

Aligned now with the somatoform group of syndromes, the discovery of the psychic roots of complex conversion disorders was a turning point in the history of psychopathology. The concept of conversion disorder, in which physical symptoms serve as vehicles to discharge psychological tension, may be traced to the early Greeks and Egyptians. They identified a "disease," termed hysteria, that represented a malady they believed was primarily found in women, and which they attributed to abnormal movements of the uterus (Greek *hystera*). A wandering uterus, they believed, could result either in the total loss of sensation in any of several body regions or in the experience of peculiar sensations and involuntary movements. Treatment in ancient times included the burning of incense or the rubbing of sweet-smelling ointments on the body to draw the uterus back into its proper anatomic position. Similarly, the *Corpus Hippocraticum* asserted that hysteria was more common in elderly virgins and widowers, and was the result of a lack of intimate or sexual relationships; marriage was recommended for both groups. Hysteria remained in the medical literature through the medieval period, although at that time it was attributed not to physical sources but to the operation of demonic spirits. In the sixteenth century, Lepois suggested that the disorder should not be attributed either to evil forces or to the wandering of the uterus but rather to lesions in the brain. Given this etiology, he claimed that the ailment should be found in both women and men. In the ensuing three centuries, however, no evidence of a pathological lesion was discovered, and the view persisted that the disease was limited to the female sex.

As reported earlier in this chapter, a major advance came in the late nineteenth century through the work of Charcot and the subsequent clinical studies of Janet, Breuer, and Freud. Charcot, the leading neurologist of his day, proposed that conversion symptoms were caused by a functional weakness in the brain of a vulnerable individual. Refining this view, Freud proposed the first entirely psychological theory of conversion symptom formation. On the basis of a few cases, he claimed that the symptom represented repressed emotions engendered by a traumatic incident, which failed to be discharged at the time of the trauma. These emotions and their associated thoughts were "dammed up" because they were morally repugnant to the patient's conscience. By disconnecting them from the mainstream of consciousness, the person was spared the pain of recognizing their contrary or immoral character. However, through the operation of several psychic mechanisms, these emotions could be vented in disguised form. Phobias were one outcome; here, emotional energy was detached from its original source or idea and displaced to some innocuous external object or event. In conversion hysteria, the affective energy was displaced, converted, and discharged through a body symptom; other symptoms, though often obscure in their psychic significance, do convey elements of the original unacceptable thought or impulse. To Freud, these symptoms also symbolically represented the repressed and forbidden idea.

Although Freud later altered his views on the central role played by traumatic episodes, substituting in its stead the notion of repressed sexual attachments to the opposite-sex parent (Oedipus complex), his basic formulation of the genesis of the conversion symptom remained essentially unchanged. His work on the dynamics of conversion disorders, presented at the turn of the century, became the cornerstone of his psychoanalytic contributions. About the only significant extension of his original theory of symptom formation was the concept of secondary gain, developed to account for the fact that symptoms persisted even after their repressed emotions had been ventilated.

General Clinical Picture

Among the major overt symptoms of these disorders are the following (rarely is more than one evident in any patient): (a) loss of speech—persistent mutism, repetitive laryngitis, or prolonged speech stammers; (b) muscular paralyses—loss of voluntary control of major limbs or fingers; (c) tactile anesthesias—total or partial loss of sensitivity in various external body parts; (d) visual or auditory defects—total or partial loss of sight or hearing; and (e) motor tics or spasms—eye blinks, repetitive involuntary grimaces and erratic movements, or muscular or intestinal cramps. The list can be expanded endlessly for there is a tremendous number of body parts and functions that can be used as the focus of conversion. The few we have noted are the most common and distinctive of these transformations. Other, less frequent symptoms reflect the operation of the same coping processes. What is significant in these bodily ailments is the fact that there is no genuine physical basis for the symptom.

The primary gain of the conversion maneuver is blocking from awareness the true source of anxiety. Despite the price patients must pay in diminished bodily functioning, they remain relatively free of tension by accepting their disability. The "choice" of the symptom and the symbolic meaning it expresses reflect the particular character of the patient's overall problem and the secondary gains he or she seeks to achieve. Both the problem and the gains stem from the patient's basic personality style.

It has often been reported in the literature that conversion patients evidence what is termed *la belle indifference,* that is, a rather bland lack of concern about their bodily symptom. Although this indifference to illness is found in some cases of conversion, it is by no means typical of all. It would be expected to appear in patients who for some reason do not wish to draw attention to their ailment. Thus, it may be found in compulsive and avoidant personalities, both of whom have serious doubts as to how others might react to their infirmity. Other patients, however, voice open dismay about their impairment. Such public displays of discomfort would likely be exhibited among the dependent patterns, where the desire for sympathy and nurturance may play a part. It should be especially noted also in histrionics, who characteristically seeks to draw attention to themselves.

The view has often been expressed that the frequency of conversion symptoms has been on the wane in the past half century. Systematic research, limited though it is, seems to suggest, however, that the proportion of these cases in outpatient clinics has not changed during this period (Stephens & Kamp, 1962). If there is, in fact, a decline in the reporting of this complex disorder, it may reflect changing habits of clinical diagnoses (e.g., terming these cases somatization disorder) or changing theoretical interests of psychopathologists (e.g., focusing on "more basic" symptomatic features). Not to be overlooked, however, is the possibility that patients in modern-day America express their tensions in different ways than those exposed to cultures of a century ago. Given the currently popular theme of sexual abuse, there appears to be an increase in its associated comorbid disorders; in this regard, there has been an increment in the diagnosis of one or another of the "hysterical" symptom patterns.

Another often held belief, recently reaffirmed, is that conversion is a woman's syndrome. This view persists, despite the fact that the disorder was exhibited by hundreds of soldiers during World War II and is often found today among men. There is, however, a factual basis for the belief that women exhibit conversions to a greater extent than do men. We are inclined to attribute this fact *not* to intrinsic physical characteristics that distinguish men from women but to the greater proportion of women who develop dependent personalities. Because conversions arise frequently among dependent patterns, it would follow that more women would be subject to this syndrome.

In recent decades, interpretations of conversion disorders have added possibilities other than the psychoanalytic conflict-resolution model. For example, interpersonal thinkers stress secondary gains, such as the opportunity of the patient to take advantage of the "sick role," thus enabling patients to be free of their social obligations. Another recent interpretation relates to the signal conveyed by the conversion symptom. To these theorists, the symptom signals distress regarding emotional feelings that are culturally forbidden or that may provoke retaliation should they be vented directly. Other proposals are based on behavioral learning theory. Thus, a conversion symptom, regardless of its original source in unconscious processes, may recur time and again if it is reinforced under certain conditions. For example, an accident that temporarily disables an arm may become a pseudo-neurological conversion owing to the success with which the individual gains sympathy from others or is freed from physically unpleasant activities.

Prevailing Treatment Options

Any treatment for conversion disorder should encompass three elements: (a) the possibility that certain predispositions may incline individuals to develop the syndrome, for example, underlying neurological disorders, personality traits, or impaired communication abilities; (b) an appraisal of a precipitating event of a traumatic or distressing nature, for example, an unpromising marriage, an anticipation of failure in a new job; (c) perpetuating factors should be noted to determine the possible presence of sustaining secondary gains. On the basis of this assessment, treatment may best be thought of either as the mere removal of a symptom, the resolution of a neurological dysfunction, or the reworking of intrapsychic processes.

There appears to be a minimal role for psychodynamically oriented treatment, despite the intrapsychic part these processes frequently play in generating the syndrome. Patients who utilize the conversion symptom tend not to be psychologically minded, nor are most capable of handling the costs and time required of such treatment. There may be facets of the analytic model for procedures that facilitate emotional catharses so that repressed emotions can be expressed; these cathartic expressions should be set in a context of supportive methods that may help patients orient themselves to problem solving. Other supportive and reassuring procedures may help patients recognize that their symptoms are essentially benign and are likely to be resolved with a variety of psychically oriented treatment techniques. Such supportive techniques may be used as a face-saving device so that patients may give up their symptoms with a measure of personal dignity.

Hypnosis can prove helpful for some conversion patients. The use of this altered state of consciousness may allow patients to relax their symptomatic state, be freed of unconscious defenses, and provide useful information concerning the disorder's precipitating agent or underlying psychological conflict (Swartz & McCracken, 1986). Behavioral techniques of positive reinforcement have also been reported as beneficial. Here, heavy portions of praise and approval are communicated as the patient makes increasingly successful efforts at improvement. Together with a measure of cognitive reorientations, the strong praise may reinforce a more healthy behavioral style.

Chronic pain calls for a broad-based management procedure rather than one that seeks to extinguish or to cure the disorder. Here, patients must be guided to learn skills necessary to cope with the pain, rather than being subjected to often fruitless and discomforting therapies. Cognitive-behavioral procedures, however, may prove helpful in reorienting patients' preoccupation with their disability. Similarly, through behavioral conditioning procedures, efforts may be made to introduce reinforcements that differ from the usual responses that the patient's pain has elicited, for example, being excused from social and intimate activities. In its stead, patients may be rewarded for attempts to engage in more constructive and active behaviors. Group therapeutic methods, especially in inpatient programs, also lend themselves effectively in the treatment of a variety of pain syndromes (Turner, 1982), as do cognitive-behavioral family approaches (Spence, 1989).

Personality-Guided Synergistic Therapy

We are now ready to turn our attention to correlations between personality styles/disorders and conversion syndromes. We shall bypass extensive reference to the typical precipitants of conversion syndromes. The events that trigger conversions are no different from those found in most other complex syndromes, and these have been amply referred to in prior discussions.

What does differentiate the conversion disorder from these other syndromes is the strategy patients utilize to deal with their distress. The discussion that follows focuses on psychic maneuvers and covariants that achieve significant positive gains. Which gains are sought and which strategies are used to attain them derive from a long history of experiences that have shaped the individual's overall personality pattern.

CONVERSION SYNDROMES AMONG DEPENDENT PERSONALITIES

These patients may develop conversions as a means of controlling an upsurge of forbidden impulses. However, more commonly, these symptoms serve to avoid onerous responsibilities and to recruit the secondary gains of sympathy and nurturance. By demonstrating their physical helplessness, these patients often succeed in eliciting attention and care. Conversion symptoms may also represent self-punishment in response to feelings of guilt and worthlessness. However, these patients tend not to be too harsh with themselves. As a consequence, their conversion symptoms often take the form of relatively mild sensory anesthesias such as a generalized numbness in the hands and feet. It is also notable that their symptoms are often located in their limbs; as with somatoform syndromes, this may be a means of demonstrating to others that they are "disabled" and incapable of performing even the most routine chores.

CONVERSION SYNDROMES AMONG COMPULSIVE PERSONALITIES

These persons succumb to conversion symptoms primarily as a means of containing the upsurge of hostile or other forbidden impulses. The conversion syndrome is not an easy "choice" for these patients, because being ill runs counter to their image of self-sufficiency. However, in contrast to phobic symptoms, which prove especially embarrassing in this regard, conversions enable patients to assume that their illness has a physical origin. Thus, it not only allows them to achieve the important secondary gain of dependence and nurturance, as in somatoform disorders, but it enables them to continue to believe that they are basically self-sufficient, merely an unfortunate victim of a "passing" sickness.

These patients tend to underplay their ailment, acting rather indifferent and even comfortable with it. However, because of their need to cloak the pleasure they gain in their surreptitious dependency and to rigidly seal off the intense but forbidden impulses that well up within them, the symptoms they exhibit tend to be rather severe. Thus, in these personalities we often find the *total* immobilization of some body function, for example, blindness, mutism, or complete paralysis of both legs. The severity of these symptoms not only reflects the sweeping nature of their habitual controls and the need to "prove" the seriousness and unequivocal character of their illness, but it frequently represents, in addition to self-punishment, intense guilt feelings. By becoming blind or disabling their limbs, they sacrifice a part of themselves as penance for their "sinful" thoughts and urges.

CONVERSION SYNDROMES AMONG AVOIDANT PERSONALITIES

These personalities display a wide variety of conversion symptoms, ranging from minor tics, generalized sensory anesthesias, and motor paralyses to the total loss of vision or hearing. These symptoms are not frequent, as these patients avoid situations that promote tension. Nevertheless, when they are unable to avoid censure or excessive social demands and fear expressing their tensions overtly, they may bind their anxieties in the form of a conversion symptom. These symptoms are especially likely if circumstances stir up strong impulses of counterhostility that must be contained.

The loss of vision and hearing in these patients may be seen as an extension of their habitual avoidance strategy. By eliminating all forms of sensory awareness, they no longer see or hear others deriding them. Severance of body functions, by means of either sensory anesthesia or motor paralysis, may represent the condensation and displacement of depersonalization anxieties. Rather than experience a total sense of "nothingness," patients may crystallize and contain this dreadful feeling by attaching it to one part of the body. Conversion symptoms may also reflect an act of self-repudiation. Because these patients tend to view themselves with derision and contempt, they may utilize conversion as an expression of self-rejection. By disconnecting some part of themselves, they symbolize their desire to disown their body.

CASE 7.7, NORMAN L., 20

Presenting Picture: This avoidant young man was seen for several years by his family physician in conjunction with periodic complaints of breathing difficulties associated with a numbness in the nasal region. Subsequent neurological examination proved negative, and he was referred for psychiatric evaluation. The presence of an ingrained avoidant pattern was evident. The specific referring symptom of breathing difficulty remained a puzzle. Interviews revealed that he was extremely sensitive and had frequently been taunted by his peers for his rather long and misshapen nose.

Therapeutic Course: Once he began to trust his therapist, he voiced frequent derogatory remarks about his own unattractive physical appearance, particularly the humiliation he experienced when his fellow students called him "the anteater," a term of derision designed to poke fun at his long nose. The basis for his nasal anesthesia and its attendant breathing difficulties was soon apparent. The nose symbolized the source of both social and self-rejection. By conversion desensitization, he disowned it. Breathing difficulties naturally followed the failure to use his nasal musculature. But more significantly, they represented a hidden obsessive thought that he might "breathe in" ants. After several therapeutic conditioning sessions, both conversion and obsessive symptoms receded. However, other features of his basic personality remained unmodified.

Synergistic Afterthoughts: The use of intrapsychic analysis, cognitive reorientation, and behavioral therapy have all been beneficially applied to this young man. However, little effort was made to restructure his personality style. Most significantly lacking were efforts to modify his alienated self-image, that is, his sense of isolation and his devaluation of self. Alone and feeling empty much of the time, he may have benefited substantially by the use of several self-actualizing procedures (e.g., Rogers, Maslow) to assist him in viewing himself more positively and by adopting more constructive habits and attitudes. (Here, again, the reader may find the discussions in Chapter 11 informative.)

CONVERSION SYNDROMES AMONG
HISTRIONIC PERSONALITIES

These personalities openly and dramatically exhibit physical symptoms. This is consistent with their desire to attract attention to themselves. Among the more common conversions in this personality are mutism and persistent laryngitis; this usually serves to protect against an unconscious impulse to verbalize hostile thoughts that may provoke social reproval. Moreover, these symptoms are quite eye-catching and enable patients both to dramatize their plight and to draw the total attention of others to their only means of communication, those of gesticulation and pantomime.

CONVERSION SYNDROMES AMONG
NEGATIVISTIC PERSONALITIES

These personalities express their feelings rather openly and directly; thus, there is little buildup of tension. What tension does occur is rarely camouflaged. When conversion symptoms form, they tend to be fleeting and exhibited in transitory intestinal spasms, facial tics, or laryngitis. These represent sporadic efforts to control intense anger and resentment, which typically give way to more overt outbursts. Many of these patients have been "trained" to use physical ailments as instruments for manipulating others. Complaints of vague sensations of bodily pain often draw attention and create guilt in others. These behaviors, however, are often difficult to distinguish from the other complex anxiety syndromes.

Among the principal origins of their conversion disorder are repetitive upsets of the body's homeostatic balance and chronic failures to dissipate most of their physiological tensions. These problems arise most frequently in patients who repeatedly find themselves in unresolvable conflict situations, such as when the discharge of tensions associated with one side of a conflict only increases the tensions engendered by the other side. This state of affairs describes the typical experience of ambivalent personalities. As stated previously, both compulsives and negativists are trapped between acquiescent dependency on the one hand, and hostile or assertive independence on the other. When they submit or acquiesce to the wishes of others, they experience resentment and anger for having allowed themselves to be "weak" and having given up their independence. Conversely, if they are defiant and assert their independence, they experience anxiety for having endangered their tenuous dependency security. Although negativists do periodically discharge both sources of tension, their repetitive and chronically irritable behaviors reactivate these troublesome conflicts time and again. As a consequence, they often generate and accumulate tension faster than they can dissipate it. Moreover, because of their constantly fretful behaviors, their bodies are subjected repeatedly to vacillations in mood and emotion. As they swing from one intense feeling to another, their homeostatic equilibrium, so necessary for proper physiological functioning, is thrown off balance again and again. Not only do they experience an excess of chronic tension, then, but their systems rarely settle down into a smooth and regularized pattern. By keeping their bodies churning, they set themselves up for repeated bouts of somatic discomforts.

CHAPTER EIGHT

Treating Mood-Related Syndromes: Dysthymic, Major Depressive, and Bipolar Disorders

The history of depression in its manifold forms has been known to mankind since earliest recorded history. It has remained an enigma, however. The overt manifestations of the disorder are obvious. Yet, its underlying causes and shifting expressions are debated to the present time, as evident in intense discussions during the most recent *DSM* and *International Classification of Diseases (ICD)* formulations. Does it covary with mania? Is there an irritable, explosive component associated with it? Does it wax and wane? Is there a continuous chronic state with moments of greater and lesser intensity? Is it an adaptive reaction to life circumstances or a constitutionally based temperament with genetic origins? It is questions such as these that clinicians, theorists, and empiricists have sought answers to through the ages.

Hippocrates gave the first formal medical description of depression, referring to it as *melancholia*. The four-elements model that served as the basis of the physiological doctrines of Hippocrates was initially proposed by Empedocles. These four elements—fire, water, air, and earth—were manifested in many spheres of life. As expressed in the human body, they became the groundwork for the four humors—heat (blood), dryness (phlegm), moisture (yellow bile), and cold (black bile)—found respectively and most prominently in the heart, brain, liver, and spleen. When these humors were balanced, the individual was in a healthful state; when unbalanced, illness occurred.

It was the predominance of black bile that served as the substrate for melancholia. Although Hippocrates may have been the first to provide a medical description of depression, it was Aretaeus who presented a complete and very modern portrayal of the disorder. Moreover, Aretaeus proposed that melancholia was best attributed to psychological causes, having nothing to do with bile or other bodily humors. Further, he was the first to recognize the covariation between manic behaviors and depressive moods, antedating the views of many clinical observers in the sixteenth and seventeenth centuries. Aretaeus wrote:

The characteristic appearances, then, are not obscure; for the patients are dull or stern, dejected or unreasonably torpid, without any manifest cause: such is the commencement of melancholy. And they also become peevish, dispirited, sleepless and start up from a disturbed sleep. . . . But if the illness becomes more urgent, hatred, avoidance of the haunts of men, vain lamentations are seen; they complain of life and desire to die. (Quoted in Lewis, 1934)

Although preceded by other works on melancholia in the sixteenth century, it was a layman, Robert Burton (1621/1971) who wrote a most impressive, if wandering, work entitled *Anatomy of Melancholy*. Sir William Osler judged Burton's immense and erudite work the most significant medical treatise written by a layman. It served as a guide to understanding melancholia for the next two centuries. As noted in Chapter 22 on the borderline personality, it stimulated ideas concerning one or another of the several variants of depressive disorder, most notably the writings of Bonet, Schacht, and Herschel, who, in turn, laid the groundwork for such nineteenth-century French and German clinicians as Baillarger, Falret, Feuchtersleben, Greisinger, and Kahlbaum. To illustrate, Feuchtersleben wrote (1847):

Here the senses, memory, and reaction give way, the nervous vitality languishes at its root, and the vitality of the blood, deprived of this stimulant, is languid in all its functions. Hence the slow and often difficult respiration, and proneness to sighing. . . . When they are chronic, they deeply affect vegetative life, and the body wastes away. (p. 135)

Kahlbaum (1882) was firm in the belief that mania and melancholia were a single disease that manifested itself in different forms and combinations over time. He termed the milder variant of these patterns *cyclothymia*.

Kraepelin (1896) borrowed heavily from his German predecessor Kahlbaum's formulations but separated the *personality* and *temperament* variants of cyclothymia from the manifest or clinical state of the disease. Nevertheless, he proposed the name *maniacal-depressive insanity* for "the whole domain of periodic and circular insanity," including such diverse disturbances as "the morbid states termed melancholia and certain slight colorings of mood, some of them periodic, some of them continuously morbid" (p. 161).

In this chapter, we address the periodic and relatively transient forms in which mood disorders express themselves, notably dysthymia, major depression, and bipolar disorders. We leave to a later chapter a discussion of the more enduring and characterologic style of the depressive personality.

DYSTHYMIC SYNDROMES

Dysthymic patients often alter their more intense feelings for fear that they might provoke social rejection and rebuke if openly expressed. Forbidden feelings are moderated in such ways as to recruit attention, support, and nurturance instead of reproval and condemnation. Although their "play for sympathy" may be seen through by some, these patients convey their sad plight with such genuineness or cleverness as to evoke compassion and concern from most.

General Clinical Picture

Officially, dysthymia signifies the presence of a chronically but moderately depressed mood that is present more days than not over a period of at least two years. Certain symptoms are to be expected, such as feeling "down in the dumps," having a poor appetite, experiencing insomnia and diminished energy, expressing low self-esteem, and having feelings of hopelessness. Also notable is the presence of self-criticism and self-devaluation. According to the official system, the diagnosis should not be made if the patient has ever experienced a manic episode. As will be seen when we discuss associated personality traits, these patients commonly report feelings of inadequacy, a loss of social interest, a tendency to withdraw and to feel guilt, and a brooding preoccupation about past troubling events.

The precipitants and manifest form in which dysthymia is expressed depend largely on the premorbid personality of the patient. Some exhibit their depressive mood with displays of dramatic gesture and pleading commentary; others are demanding, irritable, and cranky. Some verbalize their thoughts in passive, vague, and abstract philosophical terms. Still others seem lonely, quiet, downhearted, solemnly morose, and pessimistic. Common to all, in our judgment, is the presence of self-deprecatory comments, feelings of apathy, discouragement, and hopelessness, and a marked decline in personal initiative. Their actions and complaints usually evoke sympathy and support from others, but these reassurances provide only temporary relief from the prevailing mood of dejection.

All persons succumb, on occasion, to periods of gloom and self-recrimination, but these feelings and thoughts are usually prompted by conditions of objective stress and tend to pass as matters take a turn for the better. In contrast, dysthymia, as a pathological disorder, appears either as an uncalled for and intense response of despondency to rather trivial difficulties or as an unduly prolonged period of discouragement following an objective, distressful precipitant.

A distinction must be made between the complex syndrome of dysthymia, to be described in this section, and the psychotic-level disorder termed *major depression,* to be discussed later in the chapter. This distinction is largely a matter of degree. No sharp line can be drawn to separate what is essentially a continuum. Nevertheless, when the patient's moods and oppressive thoughts are so severe as to preclude meaningful social relationships, or to foster total invalidism and dependency, or to be accompanied by delusions and grossly bizarre behaviors, we may justly categorize the disorder as a major depression (Gotlib & Colby, 1987).

What aims are served by the patient's symptoms of morose hopelessness, ineffectuality, and self-recrimination?

First and foremost, the moods and complaints of dysthymic persons summon nurturant responses from others. They recruit from both family and friends reassurances of their lovability and value and gain assurances of faithfulness and devotion. As with other complex syndromes, the dysthymic syndrome may serve also as an instrument for avoiding unwelcome responsibilities. Dysthymia with its attendant moods and comments is especially effective in this regard because patients openly admit their worthlessness and demonstrate their state of helplessness for all to see.

Along similar lines, some of these patients develop their impairment as a rationalization for indecisiveness and failure. Here, their complaints are colored with subtle accusations, claims that others have not supported or cared for them, thus fostering their sense of futility and their ineffectuality. Overt expressions of hostility, however, are rarely exhibited by these patients, because they fear that these actions will prove offensive and lead others to rebuke or reject them. As a consequence, feelings of anger and resentment may be discharged only in subtle or oblique forms. This often is done by overplaying one's helplessness and futile state. One's "sorrowful plight" may not only create guilt in others, but cause them no end of discomfort as they attempt to fulfill one's "justified" need for attention and care.

These devious coping maneuvers may prove fruitless or may evoke exasperation in others. Under these circumstances, patients may discharge their tensions and also solicit the sympathy they otherwise failed to achieve by turning their anger on themselves and condemning their own behaviors. It is at these times that protestations of guilt and self-reproval come to the fore. These patients voice a flood of self-deprecatory comments about their shortcomings, the inordinate demands they have made of others, their irresponsibility, unworthiness, evil thoughts, and so on. Through self-derision and thinly veiled suicidal threats, they not only discharge their tensions but manage to get others to forgive them and, once more, assure them of their lovability and worthiness.

Prevailing Treatment Options

Treatment of dysthymic disorders is not different from that recommended for major depressions, to be discussed shortly, other then the fact that the latter usually requires a period of inpatient observation and treatment. For the most part, cognitive and behavior methods have been shown to be reasonably effective, as is the prescription of one or another of the SSRI medications. An interpersonal strategy, designed to achieve problem-resolution or social skills, such as assertiveness and decision making, may also prove to be beneficial (Roth & Fonagy, 1996). Important in the cognitive approach are efforts to undo cognitive misinterpretations and to develop attitudes that may overcome the patient's feelings of hopelessness (Markowitz, 1994; Seligman, 1998). Well-planned maintenance therapies should be considered to reduce the likelihood of relapse. The continued use of medication is often advisable, as long as there is ongoing physician monitoring. It seems evident that a combinational approach that encompasses both medication and psychological intervention is likely to be both effective and sustaining.

Personality-Guided Synergistic Therapy

The varieties of dysthymia exhibited in these patients reflect the particular sensitivities and coping strategies they acquired in the past. To better grasp these distinctions, we must turn to the different personality backgrounds conducive to this syndrome.

As noted previously, the common theme unifying symptom disorders is the fear of behaving or expressing thoughts and emotions that might provoke social condemnation. In addition, most of these patients seek to solicit attention, sympathy, and nurturance, as well. Patients attempt to avoid events that might precipitate a disordering of their precarious equilibrium. Toward this end also, they utilize intrapsychic mechanisms to keep disruptive and forbidden impulses from conscious awareness. Where feasible, these mechanisms are used in the service of venting these tensions and impulses in camouflage form. The strategies employed to achieve these aims are determined largely by a patient's central past experiences and learnings. Below, we survey the aims and coping styles of several of the patterns most vulnerable to dysthymia.

DYSTHYMIA AMONG DEPENDENT AND MASOCHISTIC PERSONALITIES

These personalities are especially susceptible to separation anxiety. Feelings of helplessness and futility readily come to the fore when they are faced either with burdensome responsibilities or the anticipation of social abandonment. The actual loss of a significant person almost invariably prompts severe dejection, if not psychotic depression.

Anticipation of abandonment may prompt these patients to admit openly their weaknesses and shortcomings as a means of gaining reassurance and support. Expressions of guilt and self-condemnation typically follow because these verbalizations often successfully deflect criticism from others, transforming their threats into comments of reassurance and sympathy.

Guilt may arise as a defense against the outbreak of resentment and hostility. Dependents and masochists usually contain their anger, for they dread provoking the retribution of abandonment and isolation. To prevent this occurrence, they turn their aggressive impulses inward, discharging them through self-derisive comments and verbalizations of guilt and contrition. This maneuver not only tempers the exasperation of others, but often prompts them to respond in ways that make the patient feel redeemed, worthy, and loved.

CASE 8.1, MARGARET A., 42

Presenting Picture: Clinical features of dysthymia were an integral part of Margaret's overall psychic makeup. Not only when she was notably downhearted and blue was her sorrowful and disconsolate demeanor apparent, for feelings of dejection and self-defeating attitudes were intrinsic to her life. She routinely voiced concerns over her social adequacy and personal worthiness, made repeated self-deprecatory and guilt-ridden comments about her failures and unattractiveness, and regularly complained about her inability to do things right. Although Margaret reported being aggrieved and mistreated by others, she also claimed to deserve the anguish and abuse she received, an admittance consistent with her self-image as an unworthy and undeserving person. In consonance with her unconscious dynamics, she not only tolerated relationships that aggravated her misery but also precipitated conditions and events that perpetuated it.

Therapeutic Course: Central to Margaret's depressive feelings were her intense negative self-appraisals; a major theme in therapy was to remedy these harsh judgments of self. Considerable attention was given to her distorted view of her achievements and the negative perception she had that others ridiculed her. Some exploratory work was done to uproot her habit of undoing herself. Also included were behavioral procedures designed to enhance her social and interpersonal skills. A broad-based self-actualizing procedure of a Rogerian nature was employed to enhance her sense of self-esteem. Throughout this period, Margaret had been taking a moderate dose of tricyclic antidepressants.

Synergistic Afterthoughts: Therapy for Margaret was well-organized and systematic in that it considered not only her dysthymic syndrome but the context of personality characteristics that covaried and undergirded the overt clinical syndrome. The focus on her troubled self-evaluations also assisted her in overcoming her mood disorder. Medications (today it would be the SSRIs) furnished a foundation for exploring other treatment venues of beneficial change. Not the least important among these were intrapsychic methods designed to explore her belief in her own helplessness and her fear that she could not function adequately or take care of herself. Along analytic lines also, efforts may have been extended to uproot her immature memories, to enrich them with current realities and, thereby, assist her in acquiring greater adultlike competencies.

DYSTHYMIA AMONG NEGATIVISTIC PERSONALITIES

These patients display an agitated form of dejection; they characteristically vacillate between anxious futility, despair, and self-deprecation on the one hand, and a bitter discontent and demanding attitude toward friends and relatives on the other. Accustomed to the direct ventilation of impulses, these patients restrain their anger and turn it inward only when they fear that its expression will result in total rejection. One senses a great struggle between acting out and curtailing resentments. They exhibit a grumbling and sour disaffection with themselves and with others. Moody complaints and an attitude of generalized pessimism pervade the air. These serve as a vehicle of tension discharge, relieving them periodically of mounting inner- and outer-directed hostilities.

Instrumentally, the sour moods and complaints of these patients tend to intimidate others, and enable them to gain partial retribution for past disappointments by making life miserable for others. These manipulative characteristics and their consequences are illustrated in the following case.

CASE 8.2, ANNA F., 34

Presenting Picture: Anna, a negativistic personality with dysthymic scores on the MCMI, employed a variety of complaints and intimidating maneuvers with her husband and children as a means of extracting attention and nurturance from them, but she knew that these attentions were provided without genuine affection and compassion. Moreover, these expressions of support were received by her with a mixed welcome because Anna learned all too well from the past that people were inconsistent and fickle in their affectionate overtures. The unsureness of the durability and genuineness of support, in large measure, gave her dejection its anxious and apprehensive coloring. This insecurity combined with Anna's restrained anger and mixed feelings of guilt to shape the restless and agitated character of her dejection.

Therapeutic Course: Anna approached therapy with considerable trepidation. She feared that beneficial changes might be experienced, but would be withdrawn or undone over time. Treatment focused largely on Rogerian self-actualizing methods of a nondirective type. Care was taken not to create a treatment environment that might lead Anna to view her therapist as uncaring and unsympathetic. Reassurance was used in a supportive manner, leading Anna to moderate her habitual personality inclinations of mistrust and agitation.

Synergistic Afterthoughts: Two elements should have been employed in the treatment of Anna. First, the benefits that often accrue from antidepressant medication should have been part of her treatment; here, the SSRIs or the tricyclics would have helped moderate her dysthymic affect. Second, a family treatment approach may have enabled her to learn more realistically about her resentments and manipulations, as well as to explore alternative ways of relating to those who are a part of her immediate life. Adding these two methods, one biological and one social, would have rounded out an overall synergy that might have assisted her in resolving her difficulties.

DYSTHYMIA AMONG AVOIDANT PERSONALITIES

These personalities are not viewed by most theorists as being among those who display the mood of dysthymia. This contention reflects, no doubt, the characteristic effort of these patients to flatten their affect. For purposes of self-protection, they suppress or otherwise interfere with the experience of any and all emotions. Despite the validity of this analysis, there are times when these patients sense genuine feelings of emptiness and loneliness. Periodically, they express a vague yet hopeless yearning for the affection and approval they have been denied. Adding to this mood are the contempt these patients feel for themselves, the self-deprecation they experience for their unlovability, and their failure to assert themselves and stand up for their rights. Though hesitant to express this self-contempt before others, lest it invite a chorus of further derision, close inquiry or tactful probing will frequently elicit both the self-deprecatory comments and moods of futility and dejection that we more commonly associate with other patterns.

CASE 8.3, SCOTT B., 31

Presenting Picture: Scott B. has evidence of a chronic pattern of moderate depression that was characterological in this socially awkward and introverted man. He exhibited a persistent level of downheartedness that was consistent with a dysthymic syndrome. Preoccupied with matters of personal adequacy, plagued with self-doubts, and feeling useless much of the time, he was bothered especially by the view that he was both socially unattractive and physically inferior. Periodically sad, empty, and lonely, he had deep and frustrated yearnings for social acceptance. Because of his defensive efforts to flatten his emotions as well as to hide feelings of despair, his depressive pathology was contained sufficiently to fade into his typical bland appearance. Nevertheless, self-deprecatory thoughts and attitudes of futility were readily elicited by skillful probing.

Therapeutic Course: Tricyclic medication was prescribed after the first interview with Scott. Although it took about a month before its value took hold, the interim period was used to establish a measure of therapeutic rapport, hence overcoming to some degree Scott's concern about his physical and social unattractiveness. Efforts were made to introduce an existentially based therapeutic approach. Although his basic avoidant personality pattern was moderated somewhat, the chronic dysthymic state persisted over the many months of therapy.

Synergistic Afterthoughts: As with other avoidant personalities, Scott's difficulties of the characterologic sort very often overlap with various levels of depression. Assuredly, cognitive methods to reframe his perception of events could have served very usefully in overcoming his tendency to perpetuate his misery. Equally significant would be the opportunity to be involved in either interpersonal models or group settings in which his aversive behaviors could be moderated. By altering aspects of his cognitions, his self-image, and his anguished moods, significant improvement might very well have occurred.

DYSTHYMIA AMONG BORDERLINE PERSONALITIES

Overt and direct expressions of hostility tend to be exhibited only impulsively by borderlines because they fear these actions will lead others to reject them. A major form of anger control is to turn feelings of resentment inward into mild depressive episodes. Not only may they overplay their helplessness and futile state, but the borderline's "sorrowful plight" may create guilt in others and cause them no end of discomfort as they try to meet the borderline's "justified" need for attention and care. Of course, devious coping maneuvers such as these often prove fruitless and may evoke exasperation and rebuke from others. Should such a course prevail, borderlines may turn their anger on themselves even more intensely. Protestations of guilt and self-reproval come to the fore as they voice a flood of self-deprecatory comments about their own personal shortcomings, the inordinate and despicable demands they have made of others, their history of irresponsibility, unworthiness, evil actions, and so on. Self-derision and thinly veiled suicidal threats not only discharge borderlines' anger but manage to get others to forgive them and offer assurances of their devotion and compassion.

Some borderlines display periods of *bipolar disorder* similar to *schizoaffective* states, displaying a scattering of ideas and emotions and a jumble of disconnected thoughts and aimless behaviors. In some cases, there may be an exuberance, a zestful energy and jovial mood, that is lacking among other psychotic types. Although the ideas and hyperactivity of these borderlines tend to be connected only loosely to reality, they have an intelligible logic to them and appear consonant with the predominant mood. In other cases, behaviors and ideas are fragmented, vague, disjointed, and bizarre. Here, the borderlines' moods are varied and changeable, inconsistent with their thoughts and actions and difficult to grasp and relate to, let alone empathize with. Albeit briefly, some borderlines successfully infect others for short periods with their conviviality and buoyant optimism. They may become extremely clever and witty, rattling off puns and rhymes and playing cute and devilish tricks. This humor and mischievousness rapidly drains others, who quickly tire of the incessant and increasingly irrational quality of the borderlines' forced sociability. In addition to their frenetic excitement and reckless race from one topic to another, they may display an annoying pomposity and self-expansiveness as well. Boastfulness becomes extremely trying and exasperating, often destroying what patience and goodwill these patients previously evoked from others.

DYSTHYMIA AMONG COMPULSIVE PERSONALITIES

These personalities exhibit a pattern of tense and anxious dejection that is similar to but more tightly controlled than that of their negativistic counterparts. Faced with difficult decisions but unable to obtain either clear direction or approval from others, these patients experience a strong upsurge of anger and resentment toward themselves for their weakness and toward others for their unyielding demands and their unwillingness to provide support. They are fearful, however, of exposing their personal shortcomings and hostile feelings to others. On the other hand, they have been trained well to express self-reproval and feel guilt. Thus, rather than vent their resentments toward others and suffer the consequences of severe social rebuke, these patients discharge their anger toward themselves. Severe self-reproval serves as a form of expiation for their forbidden contrary thoughts and feelings. Moreover, by being contrite, they hope that no one will be so unkind as to attack and abandon them. Unfortunately, this hope rests on a poor foundation. Compulsives have experienced severe condemnation in the past for signs of weakness and incompetence. Thus, they cannot escape the "bind" they are in, cannot free themselves from the fear that their sorrowful state ultimately will provoke rejection. Their agitated and apprehensive dejection reflects, then, both their struggle to contain the expression of resentments and their fear that weakness and contrition will prompt derision and abandonment.

On occasion, compulsives display a benign and reflective moroseness. This may arise when they realize how empty their lives have been, how much they have denied themselves, and how much they have given up as a consequence of external pressures. These "calm" periods of dejection are often interrupted by brief episodes of assertive self-determination. However, old feelings of anxiety are reactivated during these episodes, making them rather short-lived. Almost invariably, these patients revert quickly to their established conforming ways.

DYSTHYMIA AMONG HISTRIONIC PERSONALITIES

These personalities overplay their feelings of dejection, expressing them through rather dramatic gestures and in fashionable jargon. This contrasts to the flat and somber picture of the dependent, and the tense, guilt-ridden, and agitated quality seen in the negativists and compulsives. The histrionic coloring of their mood is a natural outgrowth of their basic coping style of actively soliciting attention and approval.

Episodes of dejection in these patients are prompted less by a deep fear of abandonment than by a sense of inner emptiness and inactivity. It arises most often when they feel stranded between one fleeting attachment and another, or between one transitory "exciting" preoccupation and the next. At these times of noninvolvement, they sense a lack of direction and purpose and experience a fearful void and aloneness.

Dejection in many of the histrionics tends to be expressed in popular jargon. The patient philosophizes about "existential anxiety" or the alienation that one must inevitably feel in this "age of mass society." Their use of fashionable terms provides them with a bridge to others. It gives them a sense of belonging during those moments when they feel most isolated from the mainstream of active social life in which they so desperately crave to be. Moreover, their pseudosophistication about up-to-date matters and terminology not only enables them to rationalize their sense of emptiness and confusion, but also allows them to maintain their appeal in the eyes of "interesting" people. By attaching themselves to currently popular modes of group disenchantment, they reinstate themselves as participants of an "involved" cultural subgroup and manage, thereby, to draw interested attention to themselves. These expressions of social dissent also provide an outlet for some of their resentments and tensions. However, should these feelings of hostility be discharged without group support, they are quickly rescinded and replaced by dramatic expressions of guilt and contrition.

CASE 8.4, LORI T., 34

Presenting Picture: The symptoms of a dysthymic disorder were not readily admitted by Lori on the MCMI; she is a woman who characteristically declines self-disclosure. Nevertheless, the evidence was that recent setbacks and the deprivation of her usual support sources caused her to succumb to a pattern of fearfulness of standing on her own. Increasingly preoccupied with matters of personal adequacy or attractiveness, she was both sad and irritable, self-debasing and demanding, guilt-ridden and manipulative. Shamed over humiliating outbursts, evidence of deficits, and other failures on her part, Lori felt an inner emptiness, devoid of the stimulation or support to which she was accustomed. Also noteworthy was her tendency to overplay her troubled feelings by expressing them in dramatic gestures or fashionable jargon.

Therapeutic Course: The early stages of treatment for Lori were most encouraging. She spoke of the simple fulfillment of her desire for interest and nurturance by simply being in the hands of a "famous" therapist. It was necessary, however, to bring up a number of themes in therapy that Lori would have preferred be left undiscussed. Thus, a rational-emotive approach was employed to enable Lori to recognize a number of her cognitive assumptions that were not sustainable. In addition to individual therapy, it was recommended that Lori participate in a group treatment setting. Interaction with members of this group proved to be highly useful and informative, providing Lori with an opportunity to understand how others see her and react to her. The emotional support she received from her peers appeared to carry her through her depressive period. Although Lori continued with her medication, she withdrew from individual therapy.

Synergistic Afterthoughts: The inner emptiness that characterizes Lori should have been explored early on by the cognitive methods to which she was exposed. So much of her dysthymic syndrome derived from the loss of significant others or the fear that such would be the case. Her desperate search for approval and attention stemmed in part from the feeling of emptiness she experienced throughout her life. Here, efforts should be made not only to reduce her dysthymia, but to employ methods to construct new beliefs and more sustaining relationships. Paired with an interpersonal approach (e.g., Klerman-Weissman), she could have learned to be effective not only in dealing with her depressive feelings, but in developing sustaining relationships. Also, if time would permit, an object-relations variant of analytic therapy might have been consequently employed to uncover the origins of her fears and feelings. Additionally, certain simple behavioral procedures might also have been of use, for example, opportunities to learn more effective and less provocative ways of behaving. (The reader might wish to look into Chapter 14 for further ideas in these regards.)

DYSTHYMIA AMONG NARCISSISTIC PERSONALITIES

Dysthymic disorder is perhaps the most common symptom disorder seen among narcissists. Faced with repeated failures and social humiliations, and unable to find some way of living up to their inflated self-image, narcissists may succumb to uncertainty and dissatisfaction, losing self-confidence and convincing themselves that they are, and perhaps have always been, fraudulent and phony. Kernberg (1975) has described this process of self-disillusionment well: "For them, to accept the breakdown of the illusion of grandiosity means to accept the dangerous, lingering awareness of the depreciated self—the hungry, empty, lonely primitive self surrounded by a world of dangerous, sadistically frustrating and revengeful objects" (p. 311).

Because dysthymia is not experienced as consonant with the narcissist's self-image, it rarely endures for extended periods unless the psychic blow is irreparable. More typically, we observe rapid shifts in the character of the depressive symptomatology as narcissists succumb at first to their feelings of apathy and worthlessness, and then abruptly seek to retrieve their grandiose self-confidence and reassert themselves. At one time, they may express their depressive mood dramatically; at other times, in a cranky and irritable manner; and at yet another, in a dreamy, vague, and philosophically abstract way. Not untypically, narcissists will utilize their mood as a rationalization for their increasing indecisiveness and failures. Here, their complaints are likely to be colored with subtle accusations and claims that others have not supported or cared for them, thus fostering their growing sense of futility and ineffectuality. As is more characteristic of the negativistic personality, narcissists may vacillate for a brief period between anxious futility and self-deprecation at one time, and bitter discontent and demanding attitude the next. A struggle ensues between venting and curtailing the rage felt toward others simply for being witness to their shame and humiliation. Moody and pessimistic complaints are not only genuinely expressed but are a useful outlet for mounting resentments. Moreover, depressively toned hostility often serves to intimidate others, and it thereby functions as a form of retribution or vengeance for their failure to rescue the narcissist from his or her own deficiencies.

MAJOR DEPRESSIVE SYNDROME

Numerous interpretations regarding the causes and dynamics of these severe depressive episodes have been formulated since the early work of Emil Kraepelin. As would be expected, those of the *psychoanalytic* school interpret depression as a symbolic loss of a significant or loved object, usually followed by an inward turning of anger that is felt toward the abandoning person. To analysts, self-valuation depends on the receipt of constant signs of nurturance and care on the part of others; depression results in part owing to the reality of abandonment. *Cognitivists,* in general, interpret depression as stemming from reality misinterpretations and a faulty logic that derives from their persistent pessimistic orientation. *Behavioral* theorists, by contrast, see depression as incorrectly reinforced responses; in their view, secondary gains outweigh the painful depressive experience. *Interpersonal* thinkers consider depressed individuals to have deficient social skills, hence preventing them from experiencing positive social reinforcements. To them, depressives are unusually dependent on others and have poor communication abilities in relationships. Thinkers with a *developmental* perspective see depressives as persons who experienced parental discord in childhood or insufficient levels of maternal care or were constrained by controlling parents. Finally, the more *biologically oriented* thinkers view depression to be a consequence of neurochemical dysfunctions of one of the major neurotransmitters (Atwood & Chester, 1987; Seligman, 1998).

General Clinical Picture (Retarded and Agitated Types)

There are similarities among the markedly depressed patients, but significant differences as well. Several types of depressives exhibit a generalized psychomotor inactivity, for example, heavy and lugubrious movements, slow or dragged-out speech, and

an ever-present air of fatigue and exhaustion. Careful observation, however, will uncover areas of considerable difference, even at the gross clinical level. For example,
retarded depressive patients experience deep feelings; their gloom and profound dejection are clearly conveyed as they slump with brow furrowed, body stooped, and head
turned downward and away from the gaze of others, held in their hands like a burdensome weight. Various physical signs and symptoms further enable us to distinguish these
disorders. Retarded depressives lose weight and look haggard and drained. In their
nighttime habits, they follow a characteristic pattern of awakening after two or three
hours of sleep, turn restlessly, have oppressive thoughts, and experience a growing
dread of the new day. Notable also is the content of their verbalizations, meager though
they may be. They report a vague dread of impending disaster, feelings of utter helplessness, a pervasive sense of guilt for past failures, and a willing resignation to their
hopeless fate. As will be noted shortly, retarded depressions occur most often among
dependent, avoidant, depressive, and masochistic personalities.

The features of the *agitated depressive* are rather mixed and erratic, varying in
quality and focus in accord with the patient's basic personality patterns. In many respects, it is a composite of what I have termed retarded depression and hostile manic
bipolar disorders, although not as extreme as either when their respective dominant
characteristics are prominent. In all cases, there is an incessant despair and suffering, an agitated pacing to and fro, a wringing of hands and an apprehensiveness and
tension that are unrelieved by comforting reassurances. In some cases, the primary
components are angry depressive complaints and a demanding and querulous irritability in which patients bemoan their sorry state and their desperate need for attention to manifold physical illnesses, pains, and incapacities. In other cases, the
agitated depressive picture is colored less by critical and demanding attitudes and
more by self-blame and guilt; here we see anxious self-doubting, expressions of self-
hate, a preoccupation with impending disasters, suicidal thoughts, feelings of unworthiness, and delusions of shame and sin.

Prevailing Treatment Options

The treatment of major depressive disorders establishes positive effects for a number
of antidepressant medications (tricyclics, SSRIs). The efficacy of these medications, as
well as other SSRIs coming on the market every day, are very well accepted. Safety is
often an issue with these pharmaceuticals (e.g., MAOI); here again, the SSRIs have a
wide margin of safety over the long run. Electroconvulsive therapy (ECT) should be
considered for patients who are refractory to all forms of pharmacologic and psychotherapeutic techniques.

Equally efficacious as medications for depressives are psychological treatment
techniques such as behavior therapy (Bellack & Hersen, 1981; Bellack, Hersen, &
Himmelhoch, 1983; Lewinsohn & Gotlib, 1995), cognitive-behavioral therapy (Beck,
Rush, Shaw, & Emery, 1979), and interpersonal psychotherapy (Klerman et al., 1984).
Despite their utility as explanatory schemata, intrapsychic therapies have not proven
to be comparatively more effective than those noted above (Covi & Lipman, 1987;
McLean & Hakstian, 1979; Steuer et al., 1984).

Combinational strategies that begin to approach synergistic treatment programs
have also been recommended, albeit without the reference base of differences among
patients' personality styles or disorders (Sperry, 1995). Included in these proposals are

the use of medications and group treatment (Salvendy & Joffe, 1991). Comparisons of psychotherapy and psychopharmacology suggest that combinations have the greatest efficacy (Manning & Frances, 1990; Wexler & Cicchetti, 1992). According to Manning and Frances, for example, there appears to be a U-relationship between the use of combined modalities and the severity of depression. As they see it, combinational treatment is likely best for those in the mid-range of depressive severity. Those with mild depression are likely to respond best to psychotherapeutic approaches such as cognitive-behavioral or interpersonal techniques. Those with very severe depression are best treated by hospitalization and medication until the severity abates substantially.

As to be expected, medications appear to work more rapidly than most psychotherapies. On the other hand, cognitive and interpersonal psychotherapy provide a broad base of changes that go beyond that generated by medication alone (Hollon & Fawcett, 1995). Owing to the prevalence of these disorders and their impact on family life, patients should be guided to opportunities for psychoeducation, family therapy, and homogeneous medication groups (Sperry, 1995).

Personality-Guided Synergistic Therapy

We rank the personalities that are vulnerable in approximate order of their susceptibility to depression.

RETARDED DEPRESSION AMONG DEPENDENT PERSONALITIES

Dependents are especially susceptible to this disorder; histrionics, borderlines, and depressives are only slightly less vulnerable. Each pattern manifests these symptoms in response to essentially similar precipitants, notably a loss or the anticipated loss of an important source of their dependency security, for example, the death of a parent or spouse or dismissal from a steady job. Their depression often represents a logical but overly extreme response to real or potentially threatening events. However, there is no question that the reaction is pathological; the depth of the response and the disposition to succumb to profound dejection, even before difficulties have arisen, clearly point to the presence of an unusual personality vulnerability.

Despite the genuineness of the depressive mood, dependent personalities do not forgo their coping aims in their disordered state. Their displays of contrition and the deep gravity of their mood solicit attention, support, and nurturance from others. Moreover, their coping aims enable them to avoid unbearable responsibilities and provide them with the comforts and security of dependent invalidism.

CASE 8.5, FRAN A., 34

Presenting Picture: This dependent woman was admitted to the psychiatric wing of a general hospital with her third depressive episode in eight years. When first seen, she was markedly underweight, had been "unable" to eat for weeks, and sat limply at the edge of her chair, weeping quietly and stating, over and over again, "What have I done to my family?" Fran was observed to be quiet, although downcast when she was left alone. However, as soon as someone appeared, she began to moan aloud, deprecating herself for the harm and shame she had brought to her family. Needless to say, these lamentations evoked sympathetic and reassuring responses from others.

Therapeutic Course: Within a few days of Fran's admittance to the hospital, she was begun on a series of tricyclic antidepressants. After several weeks, Fran began her daily therapeutic opportunities in a more invigorated and socially relevant manner than before. It became advisable that family therapy would prove useful in providing Fran with a sense of warmth and protection. By the time she left the hospital, some three months following admittance, Fran seemed well on her way to overcoming her depression and to face the problems that led to her prior despondency.

Synergistic Afterthoughts: Although considerable success was achieved by the employment of a thoughtful combinational approach—pharmacologic, family—little is likely to be accomplished in the long run without including additional therapeutic measures, such as those that might prepare her to deal with difficulties that stem from her lifelong personality style. It is clear that her view of herself as an inadequate and fragile person should call for self-actualizing techniques that will help build her self-esteem and confidence. Likewise, her excessive dependence on those close to her should call for efforts to overcome her interpersonal reservations and submissiveness. With the addition of these two general therapeutic approaches, the likelihood of counteracting a future relapse may be worth the effort involved.

RETARDED DEPRESSION AMONG COMPULSIVE PERSONALITIES

Both ambivalent personalities succumb with some frequency to depressions, although, more characteristically, they lean toward the agitated form of depressive expression, to be discussed later. In the retarded form, compulsives have managed to gain a measure of control over their inner conflicts and hostile impulses. This they have done by turning their feelings inward, that is, by taking out their hatred on themselves. Thus, they persist in voicing guilt and self-disparagement for their failures, antisocial acts, contemptuous feelings and thoughts. In this self-punitive depressive disorder, they manage to cloak their "real" contrary impulses, seek redemption, and ask for absolution for their past behaviors and forbidden unconscious inclinations. Moreover, their illness solicits support and nurturance from others. In a more subtle way, it also serves as a devious means of venting their hidden resentment and anger. Their state of helplessness and their protestations of self-derogation make others feel guilty and burden others with extra responsibilities and woes.

RETARDED AND AGITATED DEPRESSION AMONG AVOIDANT PERSONALITIES

Given their "detached" style, we might think that avoidants would not be among those who display affective disorders. As stated with regard to avoidants who experience dysthymia, this belief would be consistent with their characteristic effort to flatten emotions and suppress or otherwise interfere with feelings. Despite their efforts in this regard, these patients often experience *major depressions*, feeling a deep sadness, emptiness, and loneliness. Many express a yearning for the affection and approval they have been denied. Added to this melancholic tone is the contempt these patients feel for themselves and the self-deprecation they experience for their unlovability, weaknesses, and ineffectuality. Though hesitant to display this self-contempt before others, lest it invite a chorus of further derision, tactful probing will readily elicit both the self-deprecatory comments and the genuinely felt moods of futility and dejection.

CASE 8.6, CELIA L., 29

Presenting Picture: Daily feelings of dejection, apathy, and pessimism characterize Celia's socially uncomfortable and lonely life. A recurrent pattern of thoughts of death and of feeling blue, downhearted, unworthy, and unattractive suggested a major depression on the MCMI. Preoccupied with self-doubts and the perception of being physically unattractive, Celia is a shy and sad woman who has periodic thoughts of suicide. In reaction to her deep sense of personal frustration and unhappiness, she was intropunitive, self-demeaning, and hypersensitive to her own shortcomings. She evinced a diminished capacity for pleasure that was accompanied by sleep difficulties and a poor appetite that indicated an anorexic pattern. She yearned for acceptance and affection from others, but her hopes appeared to be waning rapidly.

Therapeutic Course: The first course of action for Celia was a prescription for a standard antidepressant medication, in this case, that of the SSRI, Prozac. Care was taken to decrease the possibility of suicidal action by keeping her hospitalized for a period of several weeks. It is unclear whether psychotherapeutic approaches were efficacious. Medications, by contrast, appeared to be associated with a reduction in the vegetative signs of her depression. Slow though her recovery was, Celia left the hospital, but failed to return for treatment periods designed to reduce the likelihood of relapse.

Synergistic Afterthoughts: Useful as medications may have been with this suicidally oriented avoidant personality, they are not likely to make much of a dent in those ingrained features that underlie her personality style. Most notable here would be sessions that blend cognitive and self-actualization techniques designed to counteract her interpersonal aversiveness, and to help her learn to perceive people more accurately and less in terms of the conditions she experienced early in life. Here, group therapy and social skill training may prove to be methods to forestall living solely in the past. No less important to this depressive woman is the role that can be played by self-actualization methods to, at least partially, counteract her sense of self- and social alienation. Psychodynamic methods may also be fruitfully employed to obstruct her tendencies to be lost in fantasy and to ruminate over relationships of the past that remain deeply hidden from her conscious awareness. (The reader may wish to look into Chapter 11, where aspects of this personality are discussed more fully.)

RETARDED DEPRESSION AMONG DEPRESSIVE PERSONALITIES

As should be obvious by the commonality in their label, depressive personalities are difficult to differentiate from *dysthymic* and *major depressive* disorders; this is especially evident when the dysthymic disorder is of extended duration. The essential distinction lies in the fact that the depressive personality should be demonstrated in childhood or adolescence; that is, the depressive symptomatology should be observable before it is manifested in adult pathology. Similarly, the personality disorder may be differentiated from major depressive episodes by virtue of the latter's rapid onset and intensity. Nevertheless, covariations are to be expected. Perhaps most important is the presence among depressive personalities of a wide range of characteristic cognitive, intrapsychic, and interpersonal traits that emerge as a consequence of long-standing periods of unhappiness and sadness. Hence, early onset, extended and moderate clinical symptomatology, as well as the presence of multiple trait characteristics should help in differentiating the preceding disorders.

CASE 8.7, ALLEN S., 27

Presenting Picture: A major depression characterized the daily life of Allen, a melancholic and moody man. Although he depended on others for nurturance, he also resented his neediness and what he perceived as the undependability of others. Having discharged his anger and then dreading the rebuke and rejection of others, he turned his hostility inward, thus contributing intropunitively to self-deprecation, thoughts of death, guilt, and feelings of unworthiness. He saw little to brighten his chronic depressive tone. He was filled with self-pity, felt empty and apprehensive, was sensitive to humiliation, and anticipated the worst. His mood had little reason to lift.

Therapeutic Course: Allen was approached initially by a combination of rational-emotive and psychopharmacologic treatment, both of which appeared to be constructive in lifting his mood to acceptable levels. What proved advisable was to confront Allen regarding his own behaviors that precipitated reactions that proved very troublesome to him. Thus, he was led to recognize many of the self-defeating qualities that characterized his personality style. At the same time, medications appeared to weaken the hold that his depression had taken.

Synergistic Afterthoughts: It would be wise, should managed care considerations be put aside, to engage in treatment procedures that seek to undo his self-perpetuating attitudes and behaviors. Here, cognitive procedures are likely to prove unusually helpful at first, especially in reframing his general pessimistic outlook and instituting in their stead a more accurate if not optimistic pattern. The crucial melancholic mood that typifies these patients should be counteracted with any of a variety of antidepressants so that an optimal response can be gauged. Self-actualization techniques, especially humanistic procedures and experiential therapies, should be fully explored. For example, in the experiential modality, attempts should be made to activate *positive* self-feelings and memories, and then accentuating them in a regular session-to-session sequence.

RETARDED DEPRESSION AMONG MASOCHISTIC PERSONALITIES

Separating the depressive and masochistic individuals has been a clinical issue for many therapists and theorists. As noted previously, some authors refer to a constellation termed the *depressive-masochistic* character (Kernberg, 1988). Distinctions between them have been alluded to in earlier sections of this chapter. The prime differentiating element is depressives' feeling of hopelessness and the inevitability of their affective state. By contrast, masochists, though evidently discontent and unhappy, take pains to participate in their environment, either by seeking to please or submit to others or to manipulatively "create" their own misfortunes and misery.

It is almost redundant, as it would be in the case of the depressive personality, to state that the masochistic individual is subject to mood disorders. A prolonged *dysthymia*, in particular, is in great measure an intrinsic feature of the masochistic pathology, a chronic and long-standing disposition to express as well as to feel extended periods of deep melancholy and a gloomy sadness. More than is typical of most depressives, these unhappy mood states are part of the self-sacrificial instrumental strategy employed by the masochist, a tendency to publicly display dysthymia and retarded depression as vehicles to deflect serious condemnation, to evoke guilt in its stead, to elicit sympathy, and to avoid assuming onerous responsibilities.

CASE 8.8, HELENA R., 34

Presenting Picture: Interwoven with Helena's fretful and melancholic feelings were clear signs on the MCMI of a major depression overlying a characterologic mix of dysthymic features. Notable among these were a diminished capacity for pleasure, preoccupation with lessened energy and adequacy, pessimism and suicidal ideation, a loss of confidence, feelings of worthlessness, resentment, and fears that she would vent her anger and thereby lose the little security she possessed. Unsure of the fidelity and dependability of those on whom she had previously leaned, but ambivalent about currently needing them, she not only restrained her anger toward them but turned it inward, producing judgments of self-derision and guilt. Her low self-esteem and fear of loss induced her to feel increasingly hopeless and to entertain thoughts of suicide.

Therapeutic Course: A combination of cognitive techniques, self-actualization methods, and pharmacologic medication were employed in dealing with Helena's depressive feelings. The cognitive procedures were partly those of reassurance and partly a reorientation of her self-image distortions regarding her worth. Efforts were made to build up Helena's low self-esteem by utilizing an accepting humanistic approach. No less important in the treatment mix were the tricyclic pharmaceuticals that had achieved much repute at that period.

Synergistic Afterthoughts: The approach taken with Helena appears to have been synergistically sound, employing a combination and sequence from a variety of different schools of thought in a manner that mirrored the crucial problem areas of her psychic makeup. The only technique that was not used to further her therapeutic growth was behavioral procedures that would aid her in overcoming her lack of self-confidence and her willingness to submit to the wishes of others. Here, methods to aid her in learning to assert herself and to acquire less self-destructive social habits would have strengthened her treatment program.

AGITATED DEPRESSION AMONG NEGATIVISTIC PERSONALITIES

These persons are especially prone to agitated depressions. Their disorders can be seen as an extension of their premorbid personality style, that is, complaints, irritability, and a sour grumbling discontent, usually interwoven with hypochondriacal preoccupations and periodic expressions of guilt and self-condemnation. Their habitual style of acting out their conflicts and ambivalent feelings becomes more and more pronounced, resulting in extreme vacillations between bitterness and resentment on the one hand, and intropunitive self-deprecation on the other. Self-pity and bodily anxieties are extremely common and may serve as a basis for distinguishing them from other agitated types.

CASE 8.9, ETHEL S., 53

Presenting Picture: Ethel, a negativistic personality with a prior history of several psychotic breaks, became increasingly irritable, despairing, and self-deprecating over a period of one or two months; no clear precipitant was evident. She paced back and forth, wringing her hands and periodically shouting that God had forsaken her and that she was a "miserable creature, placed on earth to make my family suffer." At times, Ethel would sit on the edge of a chair, nervously chewing her nails, complaining about the disinterest shown her by her children. Then she would jump up, move about restlessly, voicing irrational fears about her own and her husband's health, claiming that he was a "sick man," sure to die because of her "craziness."

Therapeutic Course: Ethel's agitated and fretful behavior took on a more contentious and hypochondriacal quality in the hospital to which she was brought. During a course of electroconvulsive treatments and a regimen of antidepressant drugs, Ethel's composure gradually returned, and she came home seven weeks following hospitalization. Psychotherapy during this period was composed of supportive reassurance combined with her presence in a medication group once a week.

Synergistic Afterthoughts: The probability is small that the diminished depressive pattern of Ethel would be sustained without instituting additional therapeutic modalities. Of note here might be the value of certain self-actualizing techniques (e.g., Rogers's client-centered therapy) designed to unravel and permit expression of her deep sense of discontent, not only with others, but with herself. Similarly, a cognitive-reframing method may be helpful in curtailing her tendency to view life from a skeptical and negative point of view. At the very least, such efforts may help forestall her repetitive experiences of disillusionment and disappointment. Not to be overlooked are her self-perpetuating negativistic behaviors which exasperate others and impede progress. Here, group therapy may prove to be a useful setting in which she can learn to perceive human interactions in a more constructive and cooperative fashion. (The reader should find Chapter 19 to be a useful adjunct when working with negativistic personalities.)

AGITATED DEPRESSION AMONG COMPULSIVE PERSONALITIES

Compulsive personalities exhibit the more traditional form of agitated depression noted by diffuse apprehension, marked guilt feelings, and a tendency to delusions of sin and unworthiness. These patients exhibit some of the whining and querulous qualities seen in their negativistic ambivalent counterparts. However, they turn the aggressive component of their conflict toward themselves, claiming that they deserve the punishment and misery they now suffer.

AGITATED DEPRESSION AMONG BORDERLINE PERSONALITIES

As is evident from the preceding, borderlines succumb frequently to *major depressions.* In the more retarded form of depression, borderlines gain some measure of control over their inner conflicts and hostile impulses. They do this by turning their angry feelings inward, that is, by taking out their hatred on themselves. Guilt and self-disparagement are voiced for their failures, impulsive acts, contemptuous feelings, and evil thoughts. Feelings of emptiness, boredom, and "deadness" also are frequently reported. In the more self-punitive depressions, borderlines manage to cloak their contrary impulses by seeking redemption and asking absolution for their past behaviors and forbidden inclinations. Not infrequently, this sadness and melancholy solicit support and nurturance from others. As in other symptom disorders, this is a subtle and indirect means of venting hidden resentment and anger. Helplessness and self-destructive acts make others feel guilty and burden them with extra responsibilities and woes.

AGITATED DEPRESSION AMONG
HISTRIONIC PERSONALITIES

Histrionics evidence agitated depression less frequently than do negativists. In their case, the primary precipitants tend to be anticipated losses in dependency security. They generally wail aloud and convey feelings of hopelessness and abandonment, all in the hope of soliciting support and nurturance. Their agitation does not reflect an internal struggle of hostility versus guilt, as in the case of the ambivalents, but a more direct and simple expression of worrisome apprehension.

CASE 8.10, HARRIET, 20

Presenting Picture: Recent setbacks prompted a sudden, major depression in Harriet, a usually extroverted and self-assured woman. She evinced an MCMI pattern marked by self-deprecation, diminished self-confidence, a loss of pleasure in previously rewarding activities, and a preoccupation with intrusive thoughts of suicide and death, especially in regard to matters of personal humiliation and physical attractiveness. Her discontent was expressed in an agitated manner, with sadness mixed with irritability, self-abasement combined with unreasonable demands, and guilt interwoven with efforts to exploit it for hostile purposes. Unable to tolerate constraints on her freedom and shamed over her deficits or failures, she felt an inner emptiness, viewed her life as devoid of needed stimulation and support, and saw herself as being unable to manipulate others to meet her desires. Moreover, she dramatized her discomfort as a means of drawing favorable attention and deflecting criticism.

Therapeutic Course: In addition to her antidepressant medications, begun in the first few weeks of therapy, treatment consisted largely of measures designed to enhance her self-worth and cognitive procedures designed to reduce her assumption that personal attractiveness and social charm were all that was needed to regain the attention she sought. Step-by-step, the techniques of rational-emotive cognitive therapy were employed to help her examine her false assumptions and fears. Useful also were social skill procedures employed to counteract the belief that she must constantly monitor and manipulate her world.

Synergistic Afterthoughts: As noted in prior cases, the modalities employed for this patient appear to have worked very well. At the same time, Harriet was left unchanged in certain important facets of her personality style. Interpersonally, for example, her social relationships continue to be superficial; as a consequence, her bonding to others will likely remain in constant jeopardy. Techniques of interpersonal therapy may be brought to bear to help her establish deeper and more sustaining relationships. Her social style likely derives from her superficial object-representations. A degree of analytic exploration may be called for as a means of coordinating and making more stable her habit of segregating out complex attitudes and affects. In this regard, analytically oriented procedures (e.g., transference) may assist her in recognizing the hold that her past has in shaping the way she deals with ordinary life events as well as intrapsychic conflicts. Each of these procedures should also counteract the flightiness of her cognitive style and her interpersonal attention-seeking behaviors.

BIPOLAR SYNDROMES

During their manic episodes, bipolar patients tend to be rather disorganized, scattering their ideas and emotions in a jumble of disconnected thoughts and aimless behaviors. There is an abnormally and persistently elevated mood, either of a euphoric (expansive) or hostile (irritable) character. According to the official classification system, the patient gives evidence of a number of key symptoms, such as inflated self-esteem or grandiosity, high levels of distractibility noted by flights of ideas and pressured speech, a high degree of psychomotor agitation, a search for risk-taking pleasurable activities, diminished judgment and impulse control, and a decreased need for sleep. Not uncommonly, manic patients will give evidence of mood-congruent delusions or hallucinations, resulting often in erroneous diagnoses of schizophrenia. Dysfunctional episodes are typically from two to four months in length, but may occur in periods of appreciably shorter duration. The initial episode for men is usually of a manic nature, whereas that for women is more likely to be depressive in character. Distinctions are made between Bipolar I and Bipolar II, the latter characterized by the interposition of one or more major depressive episodes.

General Clinical Picture (Euphoric and Hostile Types)

For those of the *euphoric* type, there is an exuberance, a zestful energy and jovial mood that is lacking in schizophrenically fragmented patients. Furthermore, their ideas and hyperactivity, although tending to be connected only loosely to reality, have an intelligible logic to them and are colored by a consistent mood of affability and congeniality that evoke feelings of sympathy and goodwill on the part of others. In contrast, the behaviors and ideas of the disorganized schizophrenic patients are extremely vague, disjointed, and bizarre; moreover, their emotional moods are more varied and changeable, inconsistent with their thoughts and actions, and difficult to grasp and relate to, let alone empathize with.

    Euphorics tend, albeit briefly, to infect others with their conviviality and buoyant optimism. Many are extremely clever and witty, rattling off puns and rhymes and playing cute and devilish tricks. However, their humor and mischievousness begin to drain others, who quickly tire of the incessant and increasingly irrational quality of their forced sociability. In addition to frenetic excitement and their impulsive and reckless race from one topic to another, these patients often display an annoying pomposity and self-expansiveness as well. Their boundless conceit, pretense, boastfulness, and self-aggrandizement become extremely trying and exasperating, and often destroy what patience and goodwill these patients previously evoked from others.

    Hostile excitement, one variant of the bipolar syndrome, differs appreciably from the euphoric type of this syndrome. In contrast to the rather cheerful and buoyant hyperactivity seen in euphoric excitement, these patients move about in a surly and truculent manner and explode into uncontrollable rages, during which they threaten and occasionally physically assault others with little or no provocation. They may unleash a torrent of abuse and storm about defiantly, cursing and voicing bitterness and contempt for all. Quite unpredictably, they may lunge at and assail passersby and shout obscenities at unseen hallucinated attackers and persecutors. It is this quality of irrational belligerence and fury, the frenzied lashing out, that distinguishes this disorder from others. We note parenthetically that since the advent of the major psychopharmacological drugs, the incidence of such acting-out in hospitalized patients has been markedly reduced.

Prevailing Treatment Options

There are several goals that should be kept in mind when treating bipolar disorders. The first task is to alleviate the patient's acute behavioral excesses, to remedy problems of life stemming from the disorder, and to seek to prevent future manic episodes. The behavior of bipolar patients during their manic episodes is frequently extremely severe and self-destructive; hospitalization is often called for, brief though it may be, to moderate the patient's erratic and intense moods.

Studies have been carried out to treat acute mania, to stabilize patients, and to prevent recurrences. Lithium (as well as valproate and its divalproex formulation) is clearly the standard mode of pharmacologic treatment today. Its efficacy is reasonably good (Rosenbaum, Fava, Nierenberg, & Sachs, 1995), although lithium does not achieve a sustained remission for many of these patients.

Although pharmacologic interventions appear to be the primary treatment for bipolar disorder, psychotherapeutic methods are often effective in increasing compliance to the medication regimen, reduce hospitalizations and relapse, and strengthen the ability to cope with precipitants, as well as improve the quality of life. Although therapy can be problematic during a patient's manic episode, as things come under a degree of control, attention can be directed to methods that seek to repair the difficulties the patient has created. In this regard, cognitive-behavioral approaches are often useful, as are interpersonal therapies (Rosenbaum et al., 1995; Roth & Fonagy, 1996). Where appropriate to the nature and severity of the syndrome, consideration should also be given to the use of psychoeducational, social, family, and group therapies (Dion & Pollack, 1992; Michels & Marzuk, 1993).

Personality-Guided Synergistic Therapy

Euphoric excitement occurs with reasonable frequency in several pathological patterns; in most, it tends to last for periods of less than two or three months.

EUPHORIC MANIA AMONG HISTRIONIC PERSONALITIES

Histrionic patterns are particularly susceptible to patients with this disorder because it is consistent with their characteristic gregarious style. Confronted with severe separation anxieties or anticipating a decline or loss of social approval, these personalities may simply intensify their habitual strategy until it reaches the rather forced and frantic congeniality we term euphoric mania. Here, we observe a frenetic search for attention, a release of tension through hyperactivity, and a protective effort to stave off an undercurrent of depressive hopelessness.

CASE 8.11, JERI T., 37

Presenting Picture: This histrionic woman has been living alone for several months following the breakup of an affair that had lasted for five years. Jeri had been mildly depressed for some weeks thereafter, but claimed that she "was glad it was all over with." Her coworkers at the department store in which she was employed as a buyer began to notice a marked brightening of her spirits several weeks prior to her "breakdown." Jeri's "chipper mood" grew with each passing day until it became increasingly extreme and irrational. She would talk incessantly, skipping from one topic to the next, and be uncontainable when telling lewd stories and jokes, not only to fellow employees but to customers as well. Her indiscretions and the frightening quality of her pseudoexuberance prompted her supervisor to recommend that she be seen by the store nurse, who then suggested psychiatric treatment.

Therapeutic Course: Jeri was administered the MCMI and was placed on lithium after her first session. As her hyperactive behavior slowly diminished, discussions took on a supportive, reassuring character. During this period, she was given many opportunities to ventilate, that is, to speak freely of her concerns and disappointments. Support and ventilation together, along with lithium treatment, appeared to be quite beneficial for Jeri, who terminated treatment, though not lithium, after three months.

Synergistic Afterthoughts: It is likely that Jeri will be able to be psychically sustained if she continues on her lithium medication for some time. Nevertheless, it may be useful to deal therapeutically with her excessive dependence on the approval of others. Her defensive pattern may work for her much of the time, but under stressful conditions, her manic behavior may be reactivated. Techniques of cognitive reframing and altering her interpersonal behavior may prove useful in reducing her susceptibility to troublesome life situations. Flightiness and attention seeking, as well as her dramatic expressiveness, may be dealt with through a coordinated program of relevant cognitive and interpersonal techniques.

EUPHORIC MANIA AMONG
DEPENDENT PERSONALITIES

In the dependent pattern, we see a marked, although usually temporary, reversal of these patients' more subdued and acquiescent coping style. Their effusive hyperactivity, their happy-go-lucky air, their boundless energy and buoyant optimism are a front, an act in which they try to convince themselves as well as others that "All will be well"; in short, it is a desperate effort to counter the beginning signs of hopelessness and depression, a last-ditch attempt to deny what they really feel and to recapture the attention and security they fear they have lost.

EUPHORIC MANIA AMONG
NARCISSISTIC PERSONALITIES

These personalities evidence a self-exalted and pompous variant of euphoric excitement. Faced with realities that shatter their illusions of significance and omnipotence, they become frightened, lose their perspective, and frantically seek to regain their status. No longer secure in their image of superiority, they attempt through their euphoric behaviors to instill or revive the blissful state of their youth, when their mere existence was of value in itself. Thus, narcissists are driven into their excited state in the hope of reestablishing an exalted status and not to recapture support and nurturance from others, as is the case among the dependents.

EUPHORIC AND HOSTILE MANIA AMONG AVOIDANT AND SCHIZOID PERSONALITIES

These personalities exhibit brief and rather frenzied episodes of euphoric excitement in an attempt to counter the frightening anxieties of depersonalization. Here, for a fleeting period, they may burst out of their more usual retiring and unsociable pattern and into a bizarre conviviality. The wild, irrational, and chaotic character of their exuberance tends to distinguish their euphoric episodes from those of others.

These patients often experience brief hostile episodes, usually as a consequence of excessive social demands and responsibilities or events that threaten to reactivate the anguish of the past. As in the case of the ambivalent patterns, these patients often brutalize themselves during their aggressive fury as much as they do others.

CASE 8.12, GEORGIA L., 39

Presenting Picture: This woman may be expressing the symptom cluster of a mild manic episode. Although brief spells of euphoric excitement may be understandable in this woman, such behavior is not characteristic of her personality pattern. In fact, she may appear composed, perhaps even uptight, at the motoric level; at the same time, her speech may be rushed and her thinking accelerated. Physical hyperactivity also may be exhibited at times (e.g., restless pursuit of multiple activities). Inconsistent with her typically restrained and hesitant behavioral style, hypomanic periods signify a marked reversal, a posture that she may adopt briefly as a means of nullifying, if not countermanding, the upsurge of painful thoughts and feelings that she cannot otherwise deny or neutralize.

Therapeutic Course: Georgia continued in her hyperactivity and her hypomanic speech for a three-week period following her admittance to a hospital. Lithium was prescribed in the first several days, but showed no impact for several months. Efforts were made to introduce cognitive procedures that would guide Georgia until her medications would take hold. Most important among these were opportunities to apply anger-management procedures. Although Georgia was able to remain under control for several years thereafter, word came back that she had relapsed into a manic state following a difficult and nasty breakup some three years after treatment.

Synergistic Afterthoughts: The sequence of Georgia's treatment is very typical, beginning with a dependence on medication. Significant as lithium may be, only a modest effort was included in her treatment program to reduce the likelihood that everyday precipitants can be coped with satisfactorily. As noted, an anger-management program was employed on the basis of her MCMI profile, and this proved quite helpful. What is so significant among these patients is their inability to deal with the demands of ordinary life events, the feeling that anything of more than a modest level may overwhelm and undo them. To forestall such reactions, patients must acquire methods of relaxation as well as techniques to reduce erroneous perceptions that life will be inevitably destructive to them. Here, behavioral "stop" procedures should prove helpful, as would a reorganization of their cognitive expectations.

Where feasible, the "chair" gestalt method may be of value in acclimating the patient to simulated stressful interpersonal interactions.

HOSTILE MANIA AMONG BORDERLINE PERSONALITIES

The *mood* disorder features of the borderline are rather mixed and erratic, varying in quality and focus according to the patient's special vulnerabilities. It is essentially a composite of depression and hostility, although not as extreme as either when one of these is the predominant affect. Quite often, we see an incessant despair and suffering, an agitated pacing, a wringing of hands, and an apprehensiveness and tension that are unrelieved by comforting reassurances. The primary components at these times are hostile depressive complaints and a demanding and querulous irritability. These patients may bemoan their sorry state and their desperate need for others to attend to their manifold physical ailments, pains, and incapacities. In other borderlines, the depressive picture is colored less by critical and demanding attitudes and more by self-blame and guilt. In others still, we see anxious self-doubting, expressions of self-hate, a preoccupation with impending disasters, suicidal thoughts, feelings of unworthiness, and delusions of shame and sin. Borderlines are especially prone, however, to agitated depressions. These disorders are an extension of their personality style: unstable relationships and feelings, self-destructiveness, identity confusion, complaints, irritability, and grumbling discontent, usually interwoven with expressions of guilt and self-condemnation. Their habitual style of acting out their conflicts and ambivalent feelings becomes more pronounced at these times and results in vacillations between bitterness and resentment on the one hand, and intropunitive self-deprecation on the other.

HOSTILE MANIA AMONG PARANOID PERSONALITIES

These personalities are particularly prone to this disorder because they are hypersensitive to betrayal and have learned to cope with threat by acting out aggressively. Faced with repeated failures, humiliations, and frustrations, their limited controls may be overrun by deeply felt and undischarged angers and resentments. These forces, carrying with them the memories and emotions of the past, surge unrestrainedly to the surface and break out into wild and irrational displays and uncontrollable rage.

CASE 8.13, BARRY J., 32

Presenting Picture: This paranoid personality was remanded by the court to a psychiatric hospital after attempting to run down and shoot several innocent passersby from his car. Barry was subdued after a violent struggle with several police officers who had sideswiped his auto off the road; fortunately, he had no ammunition left in his revolver at this point. For several hours after imprisonment, Barry continued to shout obscenities and to flail about in a straitjacket, finally succumbing to the effects of intravenously administered tranquilizers. No clear precipitant appeared to have set off his maniacal outburst, although it was learned that he had recently been "ditched" by a girlfriend.

Therapeutic Course: Despite the tempering effects of lithium, Barry was difficult to manage, would curse at hallucinated assailants, and periodically attempted to assault the psychiatric aides that attended him. A careful cocktail of medications was employed to attempt to deal with the psychotic elements of his clinical pattern. After Barry's manic and paranoid features diminished, an attempt was made to introduce various psychotherapeutic techniques. Group therapy did not prove useful. Efforts to bring his family into treatment likewise failed to be beneficial. Barry left treatment after several months and has not been heard from again.

Synergistic Afterthoughts: As has been found with a number of paranoid personalities, therapeutic efforts usually prove to be unsuccessful if not disillusioning to young clinicians. My own experience suggests that dealing with hostile paranoids calls for a very sympathetic and supportive role, one in which the patient is permitted to voice suspicions and anger, and to see that the therapist remains cool and collected. Concurrently, although it is not best in the long run, patients should be given an opportunity to actualize themselves, that is, to feel that the therapist is encouraging their need to protect their high self-esteem. In this manner, the hostile paranoid may begin to feel a measure of trust in the therapist, providing thereby a foundation for employing other, more specifically aimed treatment methods.

HOSTILE MANIA AMONG COMPULSIVE PERSONALITIES

These persons may exhibit brief but highly charged hostile outbursts should adverse circumstances lead them to relinquish their normal controls. The buildup of repressed resentments, concealed for years under a veneer of conformity, occasionally erupts into the open when they have felt betrayed by those in whom they have placed their faith. During their rage, it is not unusual for these patients to brutalize themselves as well as others. For example, they may tear off their clothes, smash their fists, and lacerate their bodies, thereby suffering more themselves than do their assailants and betrayers. Their violent discharge of pent-up animosity is usually followed by a return to their former controlled state. In many cases, however, these patients may begin to exhibit one of the other psychotic disorders following their hostile episode. Most common among these are the disorders labeled *motor rigidity* and *agitated depression*.

CASE 8.14, ALBERT G., 45

Presenting Picture: That this man is experiencing brief periods of hypomanic excitement is most uncharacteristic, yet possibly understandable dynamically. He may look composed, perhaps even uptight, at the behavioral or motoric level; his thoughts and verbalizations, however, may be racing ahead. At other times, he may exhibit short spells of physical hyperactivity as well. This represents a reversal of his acquiescent and subdued lifestyle, a temporary posture by which he may be struggling to deny and counteract an upsurge of troubling thoughts and feelings with which he fears he cannot cope.

Therapeutic Course: Following the administration of the MCMI, lithium treatment was introduced and Albert's hostile mania was explored through reassurance and ventilation procedures. The use of ventilation proved counterproductive; essentially, Albert did not wish to voice the very distressing thoughts and impulses he had so well under control prior to his recent manic attack. A shift in strategy directed at supporting his controls was taken, enabling the therapist to successfully seal over what was unleashed during his manic episode. Whether as a function of medication or therapeutic controls, the overall disorder that Albert experienced appeared to have resolved itself. Although more extensive treatment was suggested, Albert preferred to go back to his formerly organized and systematic lifestyle.

Synergistic Afterthoughts: Albert's angry and resentful behaviors are consonant with his unconscious impulses and constraints. As occurred during his treatment, Albert demonstrated a short-term reversal of his usual subdued and disciplined lifestyle. The best advice one can give any therapist is to do what was done during the later phases of his treatment program, that is, to seal over his violent expressive periods and to assist him in restraining the impulse to discharge his hostile feelings, lest they further complicate his life circumstances. If the patient has the funds to continue therapy for an extended period, the methods of psychodynamic therapy may be profitably employed to help the patient uncover the deep conflicts that inhere within him. Again, the process of "unpacking" the many layers of his conflicts and their resolutions must be done in a careful, step-by-step manner. (The reader is encouraged to review Chapter 18 to more fully grasp the several resistances and risks of the compulsive personality.)

HOSTILE MANIA AMONG NEGATIVISTIC PERSONALITIES

Negativists also exhibit brief episodes of hostile excitement, often associated with self-mutilation. Their behaviors, however, do not come as a total surprise to former associates because the symptoms of the disorder are but extreme variants of their lifelong pattern of hostile irritability and behavioral unpredictability. Not uncommonly, these hostile discharges covary with agitated depressions.

HOSTILE MANIA AMONG NARCISSISTIC PERSONALITIES

In these patients, we observe less of the physically vicious and cruel forms of excited hostility than is seen in the patterns noted previously. Rather, we observe an arrogant grandiosity characterized by verbal attacks and bombast. Anger and fury in these patients tend to take the form of oral vituperation and argumentativeness; there is a flow of irrational and caustic comments in which they upbraid and denounce others as inferior, stupid, and beneath contempt. This withering onslaught has little objective justification, is chaotic and highly illogical, often colored by delusions and hallucinations, and is directed in a wild, scathing, and hit-or-miss fashion in which they lash out at those who have failed to acknowledge the exalted status in which they view themselves.

CHAPTER NINE

Treating Cognitive Dysfunction Syndromes: Substance-Related and Schizophrenic Disorders

This chapter pairs schizophrenic and substance abuse syndromes, the former essentially of an *endogenous* origin, the latter resulting from *exogenous* sources. Both disorders arise as a function of brain disturbances, the former primarily built-in, so to speak, the latter stemming from drug incursions into normal brain processes.

SUBSTANCE-RELATED SYNDROMES (EXOGENOUS)

The "addiction" label has been used rather freely to describe a number of diverse preoccupations with activities such as golf, TV, and gambling. There are similarities between these normal social absorptions and those traditionally subsumed under the substance-related label (e.g., the needs they fulfill), but they differ in terms of the impact they have on "normal" brain functions. Hence, the official definition within psychopathology restricts the substance-related disorder to involvements with certain chemicals, notably alcohol and various legal and illegal drugs. We refer to these syndromes as *exogenous,* as compared to the schizophrenic group, to be discussed next, which are termed *endogenous.* We believe that the cognitive dysfunctions of the schizophrenic group are essentially generated internally, that is, derive from chemical imbalances and anatomical abnormalities. By contrast, substance-related disorders "induce" similar cognitive dysfunctions, but result from the introduction of foreign chemicals and substances into the body.

The general literature dealing with alcohol and drugs has grown rapidly in recent decades owing to their increased use among high school and college students. Along with the marked concern of parents and authorities and the fascination and intrigue that young people exhibit with regard to newer drugs, these chemicals are of major interest to psychopathologists owing to their effects on the brain. Concern and fascination notwithstanding, however, we shall deal with these substances only briefly, allying them with schizophrenia to illustrate that similar brain pathogens can be induced by exogenous agents.

Alcohol-Related Syndromes

Although early civilizations used and identified alcoholic intoxication with religious fervor and ecstasy, persistent inebriation was almost invariably condemned as a sign of moral degradation. Nevertheless, numerous figures of historical eminence were plagued with extended bouts of alcoholic indulgence, an ailment that apparently must have aided as well as impaired their attainments.

GENERAL CLINICAL PICTURE

The question arises, given the devastating effects of alcoholic addiction, why the habit persists, that is, what functions it fulfills to compensate for its many inevitable and crushing losses. In contrast to other pathological habits and their disastrous consequences, the solution to the alcoholic habit is so simple and uncomplicated: Stop drinking. What propels addicts to persist in their "foolishness" with so simple a solution at hand? Does this perverse habit reflect a deeper and more pervasive pathology? A literature review provides us with an endless number of psychological functions associated with the use of alcohol. These varied and diverse aims of the alcoholic habit can be grouped into four categories: (a) *self-image enhancement,* for example, providing a feeling of well-being and omnipotence and bolstering self-esteem and confidence; (b) *disinhibition of restraints,* for example, allowing previously controlled impulses such as hostility or extramarital and homosexual inclinations to be released without feeling personal responsibility and guilt; (c) *dissolution of psychic pain,* for example, alleviating the anguish of frustration and disappointment, as in a "dead-end" job or a hopeless marriage, or blotting out awareness of one's loneliness, meaningless existence, and feelings of futility; and (d) *masochistic self-destruction,* for example, relieving one's sense of guilt and worthlessness by destroying one's career or breaking up one's family. It is evident, then, that there is no single purpose or function to which the alcoholic habit is directed; in fact, some of them—for example, dissolution of psychic pain and masochistic self-destruction—appear at odds.

Given this diversity in alcoholic coping functions, it is not surprising that no one has been able to pinpoint an "alcoholic personality type." Some are impulsive, expansive, and hostile; others are withdrawn and introverted; still others are plagued with guilt, tension, and worry. Notable are such varied characteristics among alcoholics as schizoid traits, dependent traits, depressive traits, hostile and self-destructive impulses, and sexual immaturity. In short, research and clinical observation lead us to conclude that almost all forms of "troubled and maladjusted personalities" may be found among alcoholics, none of them distinctive or unique to alcoholism, and none of them necessarily a cause rather than a consequence of the habit. Moreover, no evidence has been adduced to tell us why alcohol rather than other means has become the primary instrument for adaptive coping in these patients.

Disentangling the web of interacting determinants in behavior habits that involve biochemical properties, such as alcoholism, is especially difficult. The interplay between predisposing constitutional factors and experiential determinants is so intricate and subtle that no one as yet has been able to trace its relations. Most studies seeking to implicate a role for biogenic influences either have been poorly designed or achieve results that lend themselves to psychogenic as well as biogenic interpretations.

Vicarious learning seems to be a universal source for the original acquisition both of drinking habits and alcohol's use as a coping instrument. Most notable in this regard is exposure to parental models and to the well-advertised image of drinking as a social lubricant and dilutor of tension. Youngsters may learn to believe that drinking is sanctioned for purposes of coping with frustration or dissolving guilt and responsibility simply by observing similar uses on the part of their parents.

Not to be overlooked among the forces of vicarious learning and imitation are common social stereotypes regarding the drinking habits of certain ethnic groups. Thus, the popular image that "the Irish are drunks" may not only serve as an implicit model to copy for youngsters of Irish descent, but also be a form of encouragement and sanction for drinking. When faced with the normal strains of life, an Irish youngster may turn to alcohol rather than to other forms of coping because he or she feels that this course of behavior is not only expected but inevitable among members of his ethnic background.

Once the practice of "normal" social drinking has become established, the powers of positive reinforcement become more significant than those of imitation. Given the presence of any of the various coping needs that alcohol can reward, drinking if practiced repetitively can become deeply ingrained as a habit. Alcohol not only serves as a useful source of reinforcement, but it is especially powerful in this regard because its effects are immediate, in contrast to the slow and delayed character of other, more complicated forms of coping. Because of this distinctive feature of immediacy, the drinking response may preempt all other coping methods. Progressively, then, the individual's alternatives for dealing with tension and discomfort are narrowed to this one preeminent response.

Of course, there are negative consequences of drinking (hangovers, spouse's complaints, and loss of job), but these negative effects are not as immediately experienced as its positive rewards. Moreover, if the person pauses to reflect on these troublesome consequences, he or she can quickly turn off these thoughts simply by taking another drink.

The final stage of alcoholism follows a long-term psychological addiction. Ultimately, there are changes in the individual's cell metabolism which result in severe withdrawal symptoms (tremors, nausea, fevers, and hallucinations) when drinking is terminated. At this stage, alcohol has become more than a psychological habit; it is a substance alcoholics crave to ward off a physiologically induced suffering. Now, as the vicious circle expands, one drinks not only for psychological reasons, but to avoid the negative reinforcements of physiological withdrawal. One is both a psychological and physiological addict.

PREVAILING TREATMENT OPTIONS

Alcohol-related disorders are ideally approached in a multipronged fashion. First, however, there is need to detoxify the patient and to outline both the goals and duration of therapy. As an initial effort, therapy should be used to increase the patient's motivations and to assess those social and interpersonal factors that sustain the continued use of alcohol. Although hospitalization may be helpful, this may be bypassed with patients who are properly motivated and can remain in their normal circumstances without encouraging further drinking (McCrady, 1993).

Unless treatment is complicated by a variety of personality factors, the primary thrust of treatment is usually behavioral, especially that carried out in like-minded groups. Efforts here seek to extinguish impulsive behavior, to identify and to cope with cues for drinking, to closely monitor drinking behaviors, and to reward abstinence (Monti, Abrhams, Kadden, & Cooney, 1989). Although groups can function with patients alone, most are structured under the guidance of a professional counselor or therapist. This is especially the case when efforts are made to deal with the reduction of anxiety and the acquisition of decision-making and assertiveness training techniques. Family therapy is often advisable, especially in helping family members share their perceptions of the patient's difficulties, as well as to reinforce the patient's healthy habits.

Except for complicating personality elements, there is little indication that intrapsychic approaches are useful. Similarly, the use of disulfiram (Antabuse) as a method of aversion therapy has not proven effective (Emmelkamp, 1994; Roth & Fonagy, 1996). On the other hand, programs based on the 12-step procedure of Alcoholics Anonymous demonstrate a reasonably high level of sobriety over extended periods (McCrady, 1993).

PERSONALITY-GUIDED SYNERGISTIC THERAPY

As before, it may be useful to illustrate some of the typical personality patterns that occur with a more-than-average frequency among alcoholics, as well as how they may best be treated synergistically.

Alcohol-Related Syndromes among Antisocial and Sadistic Personalities

These personality patterns are among the most frequent in individuals disposed to alcoholic addictions.

CASE 9.1, PETER S., 27

Presenting Picture: Alcoholism is probably part of a general substance-abuse syndrome for Peter. Set within a broad framework of hedonistic and exploitive traits, his drinking may have begun as an adolescent recreational activity, which proved consonant with his general pattern of self-indulgence and stimulus seeking. Beyond its compatibility with several of his fundamental traits, alcoholism provided an outlet for his oppositional and antiauthority attitudes; it served as a means of expressing his unwillingness to accept conventional social limits and as a way to directly flout family expectations and to exhibit his disregard for his family's feelings.

Therapeutic Course: Despite his antagonism to family efforts to help him overcome his alcohol problem, Peter was willing, for a brief period at least, to be admitted to a two-week alcohol treatment program. Detoxification and psychoeducational methods were employed primarily. Peter left the program, having learned, to a modest extent, some of the cues that stimulated his impulsive drinking. He was left to his own devices when he returned to his home life.

Synergistic Afterthoughts: Peter's course of therapy was not untypical, that is, to stop drinking and to be exposed to a surface educational reorientation. Clearly, where finances permit, a greater effort should have been expended to expose Peter to a realistic/control program such as articulated by Glasser (1965). Here, Peter might have been encouraged to examine his pattern of oppositional behavior and impulsiveness. Similarly useful would be an interpersonal approach carried out in a group setting with comparably troubled individuals; this might have assisted him in recognizing how common were his alcoholic behaviors. Along a different line, an anger management program might have assisted him in restraining his impulsive and irresponsible behaviors, as well as curtailing his long-term habit of acting-out and behaving in an unruly fashion.

Alcoholic-Related Syndromes among Negativistic Personalities

Another frequent personality pattern found among alcoholics is the ambivalent struggling negativistic person.

CASE 9.2, MARTHA C., 38

Presenting Picture: Martha was subject to periods of alcoholism, probably provoked by loneliness, disappointment, and resentment. Generally disposed to vent her brittle emotions, she was apt to create stormy scenes with destructive consequences when she was drinking heavily. Although her discontent and dissatisfaction were entwined with voiced guilt and contrition, her anger and reproach subsided infrequently. They often were aired in accusatory statements, irrational jealousies, and harsh recriminations that intimidated members of her family. Added to these denunciations was a self-destructive element that compelled her to undermine her good fortunes as well as those of others she saw as having frustrated and disillusioned her.

Therapeutic Course: Martha had been in alcohol treatment programs numerous times. Periods of improvement occurred for briefer and briefer time spans, despite her effort to become involved in Alcoholics Anonymous and other community-based therapeutic programs. Owing to her resistance and to her family's disinclination to explore more expensive long-term programs, Martha failed to improve in any significant and enduring way.

Synergistic Afterthoughts: It is clear that Martha would likely improve if she were exposed to serious and professional guidance. Because it appears that much of her alcoholic behavior represents her deeper personality style of contrariness and resentfulness, she might have benefited from cognitive methods designed to overcome her anger and social skepticism. Similarly, behavioral procedures, especially those involved in an anger management program, might have dealt with her hostile ways of relating to others. Self-actualization procedures might have proved helpful in providing her with an opportunity to explore her inner discontents and her feelings of being unappreciated and disillusioned. There are numerous comprehensive alcohol treatment programs that encompass several of the techniques just noted. Whether they in combination or sequence would suffice is unclear. Not quite as a last resort would be efforts to expose her more unconscious ambivalences, that is, the conflicts that she feels between a desire to be cared for and loved, and her need to assert her own independent impulses. (The reader may benefit from a reading of Chapter 19 when dealing with patients such as Martha.)

Alcohol-Related Syndromes among Compulsive Personalities

Alcoholism in compulsive personalities runs counter to their habitual pattern of propriety. It usually signifies a developmental sequence of imitative learning and/or the need to "break free" of the shackles they have placed on themselves.

CASE 9.3, NANCY E., 40

Presenting Picture: Nancy experienced repeated periods of alcoholism that reflected and engendered family tensions. She expressed genuine regret and self-reproach over her recurring drinking, and she made efforts to resolve the habit; however, her alcoholism was sustained and reinforced by the psychological needs it fulfilled for her. She appeared caught in an unsolvable conflict between wishing to maintain her sense of propriety and responsibility and wanting to display strong resentment toward those she felt no longer value her past dutiful efforts. Feeling unappreciated despite her devotion and conscientiousness, she was highly disappointed and resentful. Alcohol not only served to dissolve her restrictive conscience but also enabled her to discharge narcissistic impulses and embittered feelings while displacing responsibility for their consequences elsewhere.

Therapeutic Course: Combined with prescribing Antabuse, Nancy's therapist followed a Rogerian self-actualizing orientation. The combination appeared to be successful in that Nancy's alcoholism was sharply reduced for a brief period. Not unexpectedly, she adhered to the regimen that had been constructed for her and was most appreciative of the acceptance she received from her therapist. Toward the end of her formal therapeutic sessions, Nancy joined Alcoholics Anonymous, incorporating many of the techniques as well as the philosophy guiding that group. It was more than three years later that Nancy began to run into serious difficulties again. However, the course she then took was unknown, as was its outcome.

Synergistic Afterthoughts: There are many facets of Nancy's psychic makeup that remained untouched during her brief treatment course. Her world was constricted cognitively. She was overly disciplined in her behavior and was dependent on rules and regulations to keep her behavior within acceptable bounds. Rarely were her emotions brought to the surface. In each of these spheres, particularly the cognitive and interpersonally troublesome domains, she may have benefited by therapeutic methods beyond those to which she was exposed. With considerable care, it might have been possible to assist her to recognize her deep antagonisms and resentments, and to do so without resulting in an emotional explosiveness or alcoholic acting-out. Changes such as these may be fostered by analytic techniques, such as free association. The rigidity and self-denial of her inner psychic world may gradually be softened by careful probing and exposure. These methods may reduce the likelihood of her regression into alcoholism on a more or less permanent basis.

Alcohol-Related Syndromes among Avoidant Personalities

Involvement with alcohol is not unexpected among avoidant personalities owing to their anguishing life experiences and the desire to "obliterate" their reality and its residues.

CASE 9.4, RICHARD G., 43

Presenting Picture: A reasonable conclusion from his MCMI-III responses is that this man experiences repeated episodes of alcohol abuse. Anxiously troubled, lonely, and socially apprehensive much of the time, he appears to turn to alcohol to fulfill a number of otherwise difficult to achieve psychological functions. Alcohol not only may serve to medicate his social anxiety and thereby enhance his confidence, but also may help him relate more comfortably to others by bolstering his feelings of self-esteem and well-being. For him, alcohol provides a quick dissolution of psychic pain, a method for blotting out awareness of his loneliness and troubled existence.

Therapeutic Course: Richard was seen by a clinician for three sessions before being encouraged to join a hospital-based alcohol treatment program. From a therapeutic viewpoint, efforts were designed to teach him the cues that precipitated his drinking behaviors, and to have him participate in a daily group session composed of others who possessed alcohol-related problems. Upon completion of his 30-day stay at the hospital, Richard joined Alcoholics Anonymous and, from what we have heard, quickly regressed to his old drinking habits within a matter of a month or two.

Synergistic Afterthoughts: It is clear that Richard should have been approached therapeutically from several treatment orientations—cognitive, self-actualizing, and interpersonal, to name just the most suitable. It is evident from his history that Richard has utilized alcohol to reduce his social anxieties and intrapsychic tensions. Given that he fits the classical pattern of an avoidant personality, an initial effort should have been directed at increasing Richard's awareness of the functions served by alcohol. Insight into the origins of his escapist behaviors would have provided a foundation for moving secondarily into other matters of significance to him. His aversive interpersonal behavior calls for extensive behavioral and cognitive procedures. Similarly, overcoming his alienated self-image and his expectation of being rejected by others may call for extended self-actualizing methods. Of potential value also are a number of the anxiolytic medications.

Drug-Related Syndromes

Alcohol has not been the only instrument for facilitating our need to relieve pain and monotony. Drugs also have served since ancient times to moderate the discomforts of life and to expand its illusory possibilities.

Alcohol is a drug, although Western customs have guided our thinking otherwise. There are as many differences in chemical composition and effects among drugs as there are between alcohol and most drugs. In short, were it not for our customary practices, alcohol would be viewed as just one of a number of chemical substances to which people become habituated and addicted. Viewed in this way, the preceding discussion on alcohol-related syndromes applies in large measure to drug-related syndromes.

Because of condemnatory and legal attitudes toward drugs in this country, the incidence of drug abuse is somewhat less than that found with alcohol. However, in recent decades, there has been a marked rise in the usage of certain hallucinogens and stimulants, especially among adolescents of all socioeconomic groups. This increased evidence has given rise to a flood of public concern and consternation.

GENERAL CLINICAL PICTURE

Broadly speaking, two groups of patients misuse drugs: those who are in psychological or physical pain and who employ drugs as a form of self-medication, and those who use drugs for recreational purposes and appear to enjoy the experience generated by drugs (Leigh, 1985). Those who misuse drugs come from a wide range of psychological backgrounds, but most present themselves with a variety of interpersonal and occupational problems. Difficulties with impulse control is very common, particularly among those who readily experience boredom and have a need to seek excitement. We shall not go into the many varieties of drug disorders in this chapter, but touch on a few of the more prevalent in use today.

Marijuana and cocaine are among the oldest and best-known drugs used to induce temporary euphoria and relaxation (cocaine, or coke, has been listed in some quarters as an addictive drug, but it does not fulfill the criteria of physiological dependence and withdrawal symptoms). In recent years, marijuana, also known as pot or grass, has attained great popularity among "liberated" high school and college students. Here, it is used as a means of "cooling it," that is, gaining a pleasant interlude of mild euphoria to block out what are felt to be the absurd values and oppressive regulations of a dehumanized and racist society. This drug has no known harmful physical effects, but it often serves as a prelude to the use of other, less benign agents.

As was stated earlier, drugs and alcohol appear to fulfill essentially similar purposes, although perhaps in somewhat different population groups. Thus, we would include *self-image enhancement, disinhibition of restraints, dissolution of psychic pain,* and *masochistic self-destruction* among the various coping aims of drug use.

Etiological factors conducive to the development of drug habits appear, essentially, to be the same as those found in alcoholism: imitation as the source of habit origination; positive reinforcement of coping aims as a means of strengthening the habit; and body chemical changes resulting in physiological addiction. Narcotic and sedative addictions often have their origin in medical treatment; thus, morphine may have been prescribed to relieve pain, and seconal recommended to counter insomnia. The hallucinogenic habit is most commonly acquired as an incidental by-product of peer group involvement; thus, "smoking pot" or "tripping with coke" has come to be expected of everyone associated with the "alienated" adolescent subculture.

Next, we may ask if there are differences between those who become addicted to alcohol and those addicted to drugs. There is a considerable overlap, of course, but it appears that drug involvement, with the exception of sedative addictions, is primarily a problem of the young. Relatively few people over 50 are frequent users of narcotics, hallucinogens, and stimulants. This disproportionate difference between age groups reflects in part the relative recency and popularity of certain drugs. Thus, older people who were "addictively disposed" years ago would not have been exposed to these agents until well after they had been "hooked" on something else, in all likelihood alcohol. Moreover, until fairly recently, the image of the drug addict was that of a "lower-class degenerate," hardly an inviting model for the young of the past to identify with. This contrasts with the "rebellious juvenile" or "alienated intellectual hippie" images associated with current-day users, an attractive model to be emulated by ingroup high school and college students.

PREVAILING TREATMENT OPTIONS

There is no single approach that works with all varieties of drug-involved patients. If appropriate, initial steps should be taken to detoxify the patient. A basic program of drug education may also be helpful in the early phase of treatment. Where available, a measure of environmental management should be considered as a means of diminishing experiences conducive to continued drug intake. Various behavioral therapy methods should be explored to promote impulse control (e.g., reinforcement withdrawal, aversive learning). Group treatment settings, composed of a number of peer-level fellow drug patients, may be highly useful to explore their thoughts and plan methods of remediation. In these settings, styles of thought and behavioral experiences can be openly shared *without* the presence of the authority of a professional leader, hence avoiding the oppositional feelings that characterize many drug patients. Involvements with family members may be helpful, where support and reassurance may be conveyed. In general, formal cognitive and intrapsychic therapies that focus on insight have not achieved desirable levels of success.

PERSONALITY-GUIDED SYNERGISTIC THERAPY

Are there differences in personality among those who use different drugs? No clinical research or data have accumulated to provide an answer to this question. From the few unsystematic studies available, it would appear that drug choice may be influenced in part by the characteristic coping style of the individual. In other words, addicts may "select" a drug that is consonant with and facilitates their preferred mode of dealing with stress. If there is merit to this speculative hypothesis, we would expect to find a disproportionate number of schizoid and avoidant personalities among narcotic users, as these drugs would facilitate their tendencies to social withdrawal and indifference. Similarly, sedatives might be preferred among the dependent and compulsive patterns to aid in controlling impulses that can upset their equanimity and protected status. Hallucinogens, to extend this series of conjectures, might be found more commonly among narcissistic types, who characteristically turn inward to enlarge their world of experience. Stimulants may be preferred by histrionics, who seek excitement, change, and adventure, and by sadists and antisocials, who not only dread feelings of weakness but desire energy to act out their resentments and aggressive impulses.

There is a major degree of overlap between antisociality and substance-related disorders. In great measure, this covariation can be attributed to economic influences and social dynamics, rather than to intrapsychic processes that are distinctive to any specific personality. Among antisocials, the opportunities for material gain (at least for those who deal in drugs) and status enhancement are a powerful draw. For others, there are elements of dissolving feelings of guilt and self-destructiveness that may contribute some share to their intrapsychic motivation.

There is also a strong association in contemporary society between borderline personality characteristics and heavy involvement in substance abuse. The association does not appear to be an intrinsic element of these disorders, but appears to signify the borderline's desire to experience varied forms of reality and an effort to search for an identity that may give structure to divergent impulses and confusions. Hence, borderlines are inclined to be abusers of many different substances, including alcohol as well as cocaine, speed, and crack.

SCHIZOPHRENIC SYNDROMES (ENDOGENOUS)

Schizophrenic disorders are extremely severe forms of psychopathology and normally require periods of inpatient or hospital treatment. The rather baffling symptoms we observe in these patients represent extreme brain impairments plus the bizarre efforts on their part to cope with the disintegration of their thinking processes. These disorders contrast with the severe personality patterns, such as the schizotypal, in which corrosive pathological processes have permeated the entire personality structure. In schizophrenia, the pathology tends to be episodic and reversible, and not as permanent and ingrained as the personality patterns.

We refer to the schizophrenic syndromes as *endogenous* because it is our belief that this complex cluster of severe behaviors, thoughts, and feelings stem largely from internal or biological deficiencies and dysfunctions. They contrast with the substance-related disorders that were previously discussed in that the latter group suggests that external forces serve to induce the disturbed cognitive processes of the individual. In both, we see potential thought disturbances as well as irrational emotions and behavior.

General Clinical Picture

Patients are described as schizophrenic when their mental functioning is sufficiently impaired to interfere grossly with their capacity to meet the ordinary demands of life. The impairment may result from a serious distortion in their capacity to recognize reality. Hallucinations and delusions, for example, may distort their perceptions. Alterations of mood may be so profound that the patient's capacity to respond appropriately is grossly impaired. Deficits in perception, language, and memory may be so severe that patients' capacity to mentally grasp their situation is effectively lost.

The range and variety of clinical features associated with schizophrenic pathology cannot be encompassed by a summary listing. Equally difficult and problematic are attempts to classify the complex and infinitely diverse clusters into which these symptoms may form. We address some of the issues connected with specific symptom clusters in conjunction with our later presentation of personality dispositions. For the present, we note in general two distinguishing characteristics of these markedly severe states: a *diminished reality awareness* and a *cognitive and emotional dyscontrol.*

As the tide of uncontrollable neurochemicals and psychic impulses surges forward, schizophrenic patients begin to sink into a hazy and phantasmagoric world of fleeting, distorted, and dreamlike impressions in which subjective moods and images become fused with and ultimately dominate objective realities. Overt behaviors, stimulated primarily by internal biological vulnerabilities, appear purposeless, disjointed, irrational, stereotyped, and bizarre. There is a disunity and disorganization to their communications. Ideas and thoughts are conveyed in an inchoate and jumbled fashion, often taking the form of delusions or projected onto the world as hallucinatory perceptions. Controls are rendered useless or are abandoned as emotions break loose. There is no instrumental purpose or goal other than the ventilation of impulse and anxiety. Unable to grasp objective reality or coordinate feelings and thoughts, these patients regress into a totally helpless state of social invalidism.

Before we describe the various clinical types of schizophrenia, we must point out that it is extremely difficult to predict the *particular* symptoms a patient will manifest when he or she succumbs to a psychotic level. The first complication we face in this regard is the fact that the experiences of each individual are unique. Thus, the specific content and form of one's symptoms will reflect the idiosyncratic character of one's learnings. As a consequence of this individuality, no two persons will exhibit identical psychotic features. This presents a problem in organizing a classification system, because some reliable basis must be found to group together individuals who are, at least in part, dissimilar.

Certain *general* and fundamental traits give rise to similar but, in their details, often overtly different behaviors and attitudes. Enough flexibility should be built into each category to allow for considerable variability. Thus, no single behavioral symptom should be viewed to be the sine qua non of schizophrenia. References are made to specific symptoms only to illustrate the likely presence of certain fundamental characteristics.

In some cases, the schizophrenic designation does *imply* the preeminence of a *particular* clinical feature, a singular symptom that emerges in clear fashion. However, the inevitable individual variability in the symptomatic picture of these cases produces a blurring of the preeminent symptom upon which the category label is based. For example, even in anxiety-based complex syndromes, where rather distinctive and dramatic symptoms are often present (e.g., obsession or conversion), we noted in an earlier chapter that there is a coexistence of several symptoms that covary and are inter-changeable over time; these symptoms wax and wane in their potency and clarity dur-ing the course of a disorder, thereby complicating efforts to assign a single syndrome label to the disorder. Thus, despite the long-established tradition of referring to a dis-order in terms of its most dramatic symptom, most patients exhibit *intra-individual vari-ability*, that is, display certain symptoms at one time and place and different symptoms at other times and places. Nevertheless, tradition suggests the following broad cate-gories of schizophrenic subtypes.

Most striking among *withdrawn catatonic* types is their lethargy and seeming in-difference to their surroundings. They move listlessly, are apathetic and even stuporous. Clothes are drab and their faces appear lifeless and masklike. Speech is slow, labored, and often blocked, whispered, or inaudible. They seem passively withdrawn and unre-sponsive to their environment, cannot participate or feel involved, and tend to perceive the world about them as unreal and strange. There is an emotional poverty, a dreamy detachment, a tendency to stand immobile or fixed in one place for hours. They habit-ually sit in cramped, bent-over, and peculiar positions, to which they return repeatedly if they are distracted or dislodged. Some not only show a total lack of initiative, but dis-play an automatic obedience to the requests of others, even when these directives could result in severe physical discomfort or danger. Others are so profoundly detached that they fail to register reactions of distress to painful stimuli such as slaps or pinpricks.

All these behaviors signify a protective withdrawal, a retreat into indifference and a purposeful uninvolvement and insensitivity to life so as to avoid the anguish it has pro-duced. By disengaging themselves totally, they need no longer feel the painful emo-tions they experienced before, no longer suffer the discouragement of struggling fruitlessly, and no longer desire and aspire only to be frustrated and humiliated again. Faced with a sense of hopelessness and futility, they have given up, become uncaring, neutral, flat, impassive, and "dead" to everything.

Cases of *rigid catatonic* disorders are likely to display the following four dominant features: mannerisms and posturing, emotional withdrawal, motor retardation, and uncooperativeness. These patients exhibit minimal motor activity and often appear to be totally withdrawn and stuporous. (It may be of interest to note that these disorders occur primarily in passive personality patterns.) The feature that distinguishes the rigidity disorder from the others lies in the patient's purposeful recalcitrance and man-ifest uncooperativeness; one senses that beneath the quiet and restrained exterior lies a seething but controlled hostility. The patient is not only mute and immobile, then, but "bullheaded" and adamant about remaining in certain fixed and preferred positions, opposing all efforts to alter them. This rigidity and restiveness are manifest in body tension. For example, fists may be clenched, teeth gritted, and jaw locked tight and firm. Breaking periodically through this physical immobility, however, are stereotyped repetitive acts, bizarre gestures and grimaces and peculiar tics, grins, and giggles. It ap-pears that every now and then, inner impulses and fantasies emerge briefly to be dis-charged or enacted through strange symbolic expressions. Quite evidently, there are active although confused thoughts and emotions churning beneath the passive exte-rior. Periods of motor rigidity may be exhibited, in passing, by all personality patterns, but they occur rather infrequently and arise as a dominant symptom primarily in sev-eral personality types.

Disorganized schizophrenic patients are identifiable by their incongruous and dis-oriented behavior. They seem lost, scattered, confused, and unclear as to time, place, and identity. Many exhibit posturing, grimacing, inappropriate giggling, mannerisms, and peculiar movements. Their speech tends to ramble into word salads composed of incoherent neologisms and a chaotic mishmash of irrelevancies. The content of their ideas is colored with fantasy and hallucination and scattered with bizarre and fragmentary delusions that have no apparent logic or function. Regressive acts such as soiling and wetting are common, and these patients often consume food in an infantile or ravenous manner. For most patients, schizophrenic disorganization signifies a surrendering of all coping efforts. Thus, every pathological pattern may exhibit the disorder. In some personalities, however, disorganization may be an active coping maneuver, thereby increasing the likelihood of its occurrence in these types. Furthermore, some patterns are more disposed than others to surrender their controls and thus collapse into a disorganized state. In short, although all personalities may succumb to the disorganized disorder, some are more likely to do so than others.

Paranoid schizophrenics exhibit prominent delusions and auditory hallucinations, despite only a partial loss of cognitive and affective functions. Delusions are usually persecutory or grandiose, and tend to be organized around a particular theme (e.g., jealousy, religiosity, or somatization). Although the delusions may be multiple in form, they usually have a central and coherent theme to them. Many such individuals, as with their parallels among paranoid personalities, have an air of superiority and a socially patronizing style that is often formal and stilted as they interact with others. Violent possibilities exist among these schizophrenics, especially when persecutory and grandiose delusions are present. Most paranoid types tend to occur later in life than the other schizophrenias.

The *DSM* also includes a variety of mixed and short-term schizophrenic-like states: the undifferentiated type, the residual type, schizophreniform disorders, schizoaffective disorders, and delusional disorders. Not to be overlooked also are schizophrenic-related syndromes such as brief psychotic disorders, shared psychotic disorders, and substance-induced psychosis.

The various schizophrenic disorders differ in their prognoses and in their therapeutic management, but an extended discussion of these distinctions is beyond the province of this book. As a consequence, we mention only a few points applicable to the psychoses in general and report some minor observations regarding schizophrenic disorders.

Before we proceed, let us again be reminded that the descriptive label given to each of the schizophrenic disorders is misleading in that it suggests that a single symptom stands alone, uncontaminated by others. This is not the case. Although a particular symptom may appear dominant at one time, it coexists and covaries with several others, any one of which may come to assume dominance. As a further complication, there is not only covariation and fluidity in symptomatology, but each of these disorders may arise in a number of different personality patterns.

Prevailing Treatment Options

Psychotics usually are hospitalized, remaining as inpatients for periods as wide-ranging as two to three days for some and several years for others. Generally, schizophrenic syndromes run through the full course of an episode in less than a year, with a large proportion returning to their prepsychotic levels within a matter of a few months. The determination of the length of hospitalization depends, in large measure, on a variety of factors that are not intrinsic to the disorder, for example, the administrative efficiency and policies of the institution, the willingness of the patient's family to accept his or her return home, and so on. One finds all too often that patients who have recovered from their schizophrenic episode remain institutionalized because no one has made proper efforts to arrange their treatment or discharge. Many become immersed for months in the routine of the hospital as a consequence of institutional oversight or family disinterest. Today, however, approximately two-thirds of all schizophrenic patients return to live with their families after a first psychotic episode.

Practically every therapeutic modality and technique have been employed in the service of rehabilitating schizophrenic patients. In the following discussion, we note some of the measures that have been used and comment briefly on their respective merits.

Environmental management is a necessary step in the handling of schizophrenic disorders. This should consist of more than the mere removal of adverse conditions in life. Proper institutional placement should provide patients not only with a refuge from environmental stress, but also with opportunities to resolve their tensions and programs to reorient them toward social recovery. In what is termed *milieu therapy*, the patient's daily routine is scheduled to maximize both emotional support and the acquisition of attitudes and skills conducive to a better social adjustment than existed previously.

Pharmaceutical treatment methods can be of particular value in several disorders. Antipsychotic and antidepressant medications may fruitfully be utilized to stabilize patients suffering these disorders. Notable in this regard are new antipsychotic drugs, such as clozapine, rispridone, and olanzapine. Other medications are now under evaluation; progress owes to advances in our knowledge of the brain's neurochemical transmitters and receptor sites (Penn & Mueser, 1996). Each of these pharmaceutical tools is of value not only in its immediate and direct effects, but in bringing the patient to a state in which other therapeutic measures may be employed; for example, a lethargic and unresponsive patient who has been activated by drugs may now be disposed to communicate in verbal psychotherapy.

Psychological therapeutic measures have not been especially successful in the early phases of schizophrenic disorder. Cognitive and intrapsychic methods cannot be used effectively until the patient possesses a modicum of intellectual clarity and emotional quietude. Nevertheless, the sympathetic attitude, patience, and gentle manner that these procedures employ may serve to establish rapport and build a basis for further therapy.

Behavior modification techniques appear especially promising as instruments for extinguishing or controlling specific symptoms, as well as shaping more adaptive alternative responses. Especially useful are methods oriented to strengthen patients' social skills and to help them understand why they must take their drugs on a regular basis. Also useful are steps to teach them how to take appropriate self-care, to secure housing and suitable jobs by such procedures as model imitation and selective positive reinforcement (Penn & Mueser, 1996), in which patients observe others as models and repeatedly rehearse appropriate behaviors. Acquiring these very basic competencies has clearly reduced relapse rates. Although the durability of and the ability to generalize from these beneficial effects have not been adequately researched, these techniques are among the most encouraging.

Group therapeutic methods are especially efficient and adaptable to hospital settings, given the shortage of professional institutional personnel and the feasibility with which sessions can be arranged. They are particularly valuable as vehicles for resocial-izing patients and enabling them to express their confused attitudes and feelings in a highly controlled yet sympathetic environment. Family approaches can be extremely important as vehicles of resocialization and psychic stability if the family system can be adequately empathic and supportive.

Personality-Guided Synergistic Therapy

We subdivide this section to highlight several "classical" variants of schizophrenia and those personality patterns in which they most frequently occur.

An intrinsic deterrent to progress may be the schizophrenic's basic personality. Certain of the patterns possess attitudes and coping styles that undermine chances for recovery; some resist therapeutic rapport, whereas others are difficult to motivate. For example, schizoid and schizotypal personalities frequently deteriorate rapidly despite all treatment efforts. These personalities often succumb to *catatonic* states with their flat and difficult to activate qualities, or to *disorganized* disorders that, given their characteristic cognitive disorganization, are highly resistant to meaningful therapeutic communication. Other patterns are conducive to better prognoses because they provide a handle, so to speak, that the therapist can use to relate to and motivate the patient. For example, dependent and histrionic patterns are desirous of social approval and can be motivated by therapeutic attitudes of gentility and nurturance during their treatment periods. For different reasons, notably the drive to assert themselves and to reestablish their autonomy, antisocial and narcissistic personality patterns, despite *delusional* episodes, have less than promising prognostic pictures.

CATATONIC WITHDRAWAL AMONG SCHIZOID AND AVOIDANT PERSONALITIES

Catatonic withdrawal can occur in all personality patterns. The shutting off of emotions and the retreat into indifference are protective devices that can be employed easily by all individuals who have been overwhelmed by a sense of hopelessness and futility. Despite its ease as a coping maneuver, it appears with greater frequency among patients whose lifelong strategies dispose them to emotional detachment and social isolation. As a "logical" extension of their personality style, we find the catatonic withdrawn pattern arising often in avoidant and schizoid personalities. Unable to handle even minor degrees of overstimulation, whether from unexpected responsibilities, objective threat, or reactivated anxiety, they may overemploy their coping strategies and withdraw into an impassive, unresponsive, and unfeeling state. These cases can usually be identified by their total muteness and their complete "tuning out" of the world, traits that result in an inner void and a picture of masklike stupor.

CASE 9.5, ARTHUR O., 29

Presenting Picture: Arthur, a diagnosed schizoid personality on the MCMI, was admitted to the psychiatric section of a general hospital after being found by a hotel chambermaid as he sat on the edge of the bed in his room, staring vacantly at a wall. When brought to the ward, he sat impassively in a chair, was unresponsive to questioning, indifferent to his surroundings and well-being, disinterested in food, and unwilling to feed himself. He remained mute, withdrawn, and close to immobile for several days, following which he slowly began to take care of himself without assistance, although he failed to speak to anyone for almost a month.

Therapeutic Course: The essential format for treatment was short term. A modicum of time was allotted to provide Arthur with a supportive approach that, albeit slowly, brought him partially out of his shell. Whether it was the reassurance and empathy of his therapist, or the beneficial effects of Thorazine, the primary medication employed, cannot be determined. Although he was remanded to a state hospital, the general policy of the institution was to discharge patients if there were family members willing to support them.

Synergistic Afterthoughts: As many clinicians are aware, large numbers of patients are "turned around" within a few days of their admittance to a managed care hospital program. Even in those cases where patients, of necessity, must remain in a protected environment for several weeks or months, little is usually done to ensure that the patient learns to be capable of effective functioning in the outside world. Today, we have a wider range of antipsychotic drugs (e.g., Clozapine) that do not produce secondary effects such as tardive dyskinesia. Moreover, where time permits, behavioral methods designed to help patients comply with long-term pharmaceutical treatment should be an essential element in endogenously generated syndromes. The development of certain basic social competencies should also help reduce the likelihood of periodic relapses. The task of resocializing patients such as Arthur is especially problematic, however, owing to their intrinsic interpersonal deficiencies. (The reader should look into Chapter 10 for further guidance in similar cases.)

CATATONIC WITHDRAWAL AMONG DEPENDENT PERSONALITIES

These personalities succumb on occasion to catatonic impassivity, but here we often see a coloring of sadness, a tone of inner softness, an inclination to "be nice" and to acquiesce in the wishes of others in the hope of maintaining some measure of affection and support from them. It is in these patients that we often observe a cataleptic waxy flexibility, that is, a tendency to maintain bodily positions into which others have placed them. This willingness to be molded according to the whims of others signifies their total abandonment of self-initiative and their complete dependence and submission to external directives. At the heart of their acquiescent impassivity is the deep need they have to counter their separation anxieties and to avoid actions that might engender disapproval and rejection.

CATATONIC WITHDRAWAL AMONG HISTRIONIC PERSONALITIES

In the histrionic patterns, the catatonic psychosis usually reflects a collapse of their lifelong style of actively soliciting attention and approval. Rather than face failure and rejection, these patients may "retire" from their habitual strategy, disown their need for stimulation and excitement, and temporarily reverse the course of their lifestyle. Catatonia is usually of short duration in these patients, and can be relieved by genuine assurances from others of their care, interest, and affection.

CATATONIC RIGIDITY AMONG COMPULSIVE PERSONALITIES

These personalities are especially subject to this form of psychotic disorder. Their physical uncooperativeness is a passive expression of their deeply felt resentments and angers. Their body tightness reflects an intense struggle to control against the outbreak of seething hostility, and their physical withdrawal and obduracy help them avoid contact with events that might provoke and unleash their aggressive impulses. Thus, motor rigidity both communicates and controls their anger, without provoking social condemnation. It may be viewed, then, as a bizarre extension of their habitual coping style, a means of controlling contrary impulses by protective restraint and rigid behaviors. The stereotype gestures and grimaces seen in these patients usually convey symbolically an abbreviated and immediately retracted expression of their intolerable aggressive and erotic urges.

CASE 9.6, ARNOLD N., 28

Presenting Picture: Arnold, a compulsive personality, was found one morning by his wife to be "staring in a funny way" outside his bathroom window. Not only did he refuse to reply to her concerned questions regarding his health, but he remained in a rigid position and refused to budge; no amount of pleading on her part was adequate to get him to relax or lie down. A physician was called to examine him shortly thereafter, but he was equally unable to penetrate Arnold's mutism or to alter his taut and unyielding physical posture. Although Arnold did not resist being carried into an ambulance, he refused to change the body position in which his wife found him that morning.

Therapeutic Course: Arnold's physical rigidity gave way under sedation, and he spoke during these periods in a halting and confused manner. As soon as the effects of the drug wore off, however, he again was mute and resumed his immobile stance. Only after several weeks did he loosen up and begin to divulge his thoughts and feelings, both of which indicated a struggle to contain the rage he felt toward his father and his wife for the excessive demands he believed they imposed on him. As was typical during the 1970s when Arnold was first seen, the primary medication administered was Thorazine; in fact, he was given a much higher dose than was routinely recommended for patients similar to him. After a period of 9 or 10 weeks, the hospital program to which he was admitted saw "sufficient progress" to justify releasing him to his family. At that time, Arnold had reverted to his basic personality style and was capable of functioning adequately, at least vocationally.

Synergistic Afterthoughts: No effort was made to recognize that Arnold's difficulties stem from his deep-seated ambivalence toward significant others. Hence, certain cognitive and interpersonal procedures should have been utilized in tandem to provide Arnold with a basis for recognizing both the character of his ambivalences and his tendency to categorize his relationships in a black-and-white manner. Bringing him into family therapy should enable Arnold to deal with these complex feelings. Not to be overlooked are procedures to enable him to reduce provocative sources of anxiety, especially those that require excessive and rigid psychic controls. (Again, the reader may find it useful to review Chapter 18 for a fuller discussion of treatment approaches with compulsive personalities.)

CATATONIC RIGIDITY AMONG AVOIDANT PERSONALITIES

These personalities exhibit catatonic rigidity for reasons similar to those found in the catatonically withdrawn. Here, patients are motivated more by their desire to withdraw from external provocation than by the need to control aggressive impulses, not that the latter is to be overlooked as a factor. Faced with unbearable derogation and humiliation, they withdraw into a shell, resistant to all forms of stimulation that may reactivate their past misery. The grimaces and giggling often observed in these patients clue us to their rather chaotic fantasy world.

DISORGANIZED TYPE AMONG AVOIDANT PERSONALITIES

These personalities are especially inclined to this disorder not only because they can easily be overwhelmed by external and internal pressures, but because psychic disorganization is an extension of their characteristic protective maneuver of interfering with their own cognitive clarity. By blocking the normal flow of thoughts and memories, they distract themselves and dilute the impact of painful feelings and recollections. Disorganization may arise, then, as a direct product either of intolerable pressures, self-made confusion, or both. What we see as a result is a picture of "forced" absurdity and incoherence and a concerted effort to disrupt cognitive clarity and emotional rationality.

CASE 9.7, GRETA S., 22

Presenting Picture: Greta displayed an avoidant pattern ever since early adolescence. She was shy, somewhat fearful of all people, even those she had known all of her life, and preferred to spend her days at home helping her mother cook and clean for her father and younger brothers. One morning she became "silly and confused," began to talk "gibberishly," as her mother put it, became incontinent, and grimaced and giggled for no apparent reason. When the family physician arrived, he noted that Greta placed herself into a series of contorted positions on the floor, sang incoherent songs, and cried fitfully for brief periods. Greta continued this behavior, although more sporadically, for several weeks after institutionalization, following which she became quiet and withdrawn.

Therapeutic Course: Administered antipsychotic medication and participating in thrice-weekly group sessions of a supportive nature, Greta returned home and resumed her "normal" pattern of behavior about three months following hospitalization. No information is available concerning her future course.

Synergistic Afterthoughts: Given the support of her family and the general efficacy of her medications, it is likely that a brief treatment regime, such as she was exposed to, may have sufficed to stabilize her. However, barring the intrusion of managed care limitations, a serious effort should have been undertaken to reduce Greta's intense anxieties and her self-made cognitive confusions by utilizing a slowly progressive relaxation and supportive technique, notably those of ventilation and reassurance. It would not be unreasonable to expect Greta to cognitively explore her social fears and her defensive need to undermine the clarity of her thinking. Obviously, the acquisition of an enhanced sense of self-worth and interpersonal competencies would contribute measurably to her overall movement toward normality.

DISORGANIZED TYPE AMONG DEPENDENT PERSONALITIES

Dependents are disposed to fragmentation when faced with situations that seriously tax their limited capacity to function independently. Without external security and support and lacking a core of inner competence and self-determination, they may easily crumble and disintegrate, usually into regressive or infantile behaviors. Beneath their confusion and bizarre acts, we often see remnants of their former coping strategies. For example, their regressive eating and soiling may reflect a continued seeking of care and nurturance. Their stereotyped grimacing and giggling may signify a forced and pathetic effort to capture the goodwill and approval of those on whom they now depend.

DISORGANIZED TYPE AMONG COMPULSIVE PERSONALITIES

Disorganization among compulsives follows the shattering of controls previously employed to restrain deeply repressed conflicts. Unable to keep these divisive forces in check, these patients are torn apart, engulfed in a sea of surging memories and contrary feelings that now spew forth in a flood of incoherent verbalizations and bizarre emotions and acts. In their case, stereotyped grimacing, posturing, and mannerisms often signify feeble efforts to contain their impulses or to dampen the confusion and disharmony they feel.

DISORGANIZED TYPE AMONG SCHIZOTYPAL PERSONALITIES

Particularly subject to *disorganized schizophrenic* disorders, schizotypals are identifiable by their incongruous and fragmented behaviors. At these times, they seem totally disoriented and confused, unclear as to time, place, and identity. Many will exhibit posturing, grimacing, inappropriate giggling, and peculiar mannerisms. Speech tends to ramble into word salads composed of incoherent neologisms and a chaotic mishmash of irrelevancies. Ideas are colored with fantasy, illusion, and hallucination, and scattered with bizarre and fragmentary delusions that have no apparent logic or function. Regressive acts such as soiling and wetting are not uncommon, and these patients often consume food in an infantile or ravenous manner.

These psychotic states may occur after a period when the tide of unconscious anxieties and impulses has surged forward, overwhelming these patients and sinking them into a hazy world of fleeting and dreamlike impressions. Subjective moods and images become fused with and ultimately dominate objective realities. Overt behaviors are distorted and guided by primary process thinking and thereby appear purposeless, disjointed, irrational, stereotyped, and bizarre. There is a disunity and disorganization to speech and communication. Ideas are conveyed in an inchoate or jumbled fashion, reflecting delusions that are projected onto the world in hallucinatory perceptions. Controls are abandoned and random emotions break loose. No seeming purpose exists to their behaviors, other than the ventilation of momentary impulses. Unable to grasp reality or coordinate feelings and thoughts, these schizotypals may regress into a rigid and immobile catatonic state, a totally helpless form of invalidism.

PARANOID TYPE AMONG NARCISSISTIC PERSONALITIES

Under conditions of unrelieved adversity and failure, narcissists may decompensate into paranoid disorders. Owing to their excessive use of fantasy mechanisms, they are disposed to misinterpret events and to construct delusional beliefs. Unwilling to accept constraints on their independence and unable to accept the viewpoints of others, narcissists may isolate themselves from the corrective effects of shared thinking. Alone, they may ruminate and weave their beliefs into a network of fanciful and totally invalid suspicions. Among narcissists, delusions often take form after a serious challenge or setback in which their image of superiority and omnipotence has been upset. They tend to exhibit compensatory grandiosity and jealousy delusions in which they reconstruct reality to match the image they are unable or unwilling to give up. Delusional systems may also develop as a result of having felt betrayed and humiliated. Here, we may see the rapid unfolding of persecutory delusions and an arrogant grandiosity characterized by verbal attacks and bombast. Rarely physically abusive, narcissists usually display anger in the form of oral vituperation and argumentativeness. This may be seen in a flow of irrational and caustic comments in which others are upbraided and denounced as stupid and beneath contempt. These onslaughts usually have little objective justification, are often colored by delusions, and may be directed in a wild, hit-or-miss fashion in which the narcissist lashes out at those who have failed to acknowledge the exalted status in which he or she demands to be seen.

PARANOID TYPE AMONG SADISTIC PERSONALITIES

Acute delusional episodes characterized by hostile excitement may be displayed by these personalities. Particularly prone to this disorder as a result of their hypersensitivity to betrayal, they have learned to cope with threat by acting out aggressively and, at times, explosively. Faced with repeated failures and frustrations, their fragile controls may be overwhelmed by undischarged and deeply felt angers and resentments. These hostile feelings, spurred by the memories and emotions of the past, may surge unrestrained to the surface, spilling into wild and delusional rages.

PARANOID TYPE AMONG PARANOID PERSONALITIES

Paranoid personalities develop *delusional* paranoid disorders and paranoia insidiously, usually as a consequence of anticipating or experiencing repeated mistreatment or humiliation. Acute paranoid episodes may be precipitated by the shock of an unanticipated betrayal. In these acute phases, previously repressed resentments may surge to the surface and overwhelm the patient's former controls, quickly taking the form of a delusional belief, usually persecutory in nature. During these episodes, typically brief and rather chaotic, patients both discharge their anger and project it on others. Note that the resentments and suspicions of the paranoid usually do not cumulate and burst out of control. Rather, these patients continue to be persistently touchy, secretive, and irritable, thereby allowing them to vent their spleen in regular, small doses. Only if their suspicions are aggravated suddenly do they take an explosive or irrational form.

PART III

Personality Disorders—Axis II

CHAPTER TEN

Treating Schizoid
Personality Patterns

The essential features of the schizoid personality are a profound defect in the ability to form social relationships and an underresponsiveness to all forms of stimulation. Such individuals exhibit an intrinsic emotional blandness, an imperviousness to joy, anger, or sadness. Seemingly unmoved by emotional stimuli, the schizoid appears to possess a generalized inability to be aroused and activated, as well as a lack of initiative and vitality. Their interpersonal passivity, then, is not by intention or for self-protective reasons, but due to a fundamental imperceptiveness to the moods and needs of others (Millon, 1969, 1981).

Schizoid personalities typically prefer limited interpersonal contact and only a peripheral role in social and family relationships. They tend to choose interests and vocations that will allow them to maintain their social detachment. Colorless and lacking in spontaneity, they are usually perceived as unresponsive, boring, or dull in relationships. Their speech tends to be characterized by emotional flatness, vagueness, and obscurities, and there is a seeming inability to grasp the emotional components of human interactions and communications. They seem indifferent to both praise and criticism. Consistent with their interpersonal style, schizoids possess little awareness of themselves and employ only minimal introspection. Lacking in insight and relatively untroubled by intense emotions or interpersonal conflicts, the schizoid possesses limited and uncomplicated intrapsychic defenses.

Schizoid personalities' pervasive imperviousness to emotions puts them among the personality styles least susceptible to genuine depression or other affective distress. Having failed to develop an "appetite" for social stimulation (including affection and attachment), these individuals are not vulnerable to dejection resulting from object loss. In addition, because schizoids derive only limited pleasure from themselves, they are not particularly susceptible to loss of self-esteem or to self-deprecation. Emotional distress may develop, however, when faced with unusual social demands or responsibilities, or when stimulation levels become either excessive or drastically curtailed. In addition, their inner barrenness and interpersonal isolation may occasionally throw them into a fear of nonbeing or petrifaction.

On rare occasions, schizoids may exhibit brief, frenzied episodes of maniclike excitement in an attempt to counter the anxieties of depersonalization. A fleeting and erratic course of frantic and rather bizarre conviviality may then temporarily replace the schizoid's characteristic impassive, unsociable pattern. More frequently, however, the schizoid reacts to disequilibrium with increased isolation and dissociation. Lacking an investment and interest in self as well as in external events, the schizoid fails to acquire a coherent and well-integrated inner identity. Disruption to the consistency of the schizoid's lifestyle, as might result from unwanted social overstimulation or prolonged periods of social isolation, may consequently result in a kind of splitting or disintegration. During such periods of self-estrangement, schizoids may experience irrational thinking and compounding of their typical emotional poverty. Behaviorally, this might be manifested in profound lethargy, lifeless facial expressions, and inaudible speech, simulating but not reflecting a depressive mood.

Although empirical data on affective disorders in schizoid personalities are lacking, at least two of the factor analysis–generated subtypes would seem to fit the experience of depression in these individuals. *Factor Pattern A,* generated in the 1961 study by Grinker et al., is described as a depressive who is not particularly anxious, clinging, or attention seeking, but rather isolated, withdrawn, and apathetic. A slowing in thought and speech with some evidence of cognitive disturbance is also seen. The absence of large amounts of "gloomy affect," complaining, or attempts at restitution give this depressive subtype the appearance of an "empty person." Although much of this description would fit the theoretical picture of depression in the schizoid, Grinker et al. give other features of this depressive factor pattern that might be more characteristic of a compulsive premorbid personality.

The *retarded depression* discussed by Overall and Hollister (1980) might also be consistent with the symptomatic presentation of depression in the schizoid. Such depression is characterized by retardation in speech, gross motor behavior, and social interaction. A diminishment in affective responsiveness may frequently accompany the "generalized behavioral inhibition" (p. 376) that is present in this form of depression.

The restriction in the *DSM-IV* to the interpersonal and mood domains limits the range of possible useful criteria to a rather narrow band. Relevant though these domains are, the schizoid manifests a much wider scope of domain characteristics than has been included in the *DSM-IV*, for example, self-image, cognitive style, and intrapsychic structural features.

Although derived from the author's theoretical schema, an empirically and numerically derived set of factors comprising the distinguishable and partially separable traits of the schizoid personality has been developed and will be recorded in subsequent research papers. Next, however, are a few words describing the evolutionary model and theory as it pertains to the schizoid personality prototype.

The polarity schema for the schizoid (Figure 10.1) reveals that they possess a marked deficiency in the capacity to experience both psychic pleasure (enhancement) and pain (preservation). In other words, they are unmotivated to seek out joy and gratification, are unable to view life enthusiastically, and also experience none of the distressing affects of life, such as sadness, anxiety, and anger. As a consequence of these deficiencies, schizoids have little motivation to seek out rewards or to distance themselves from potentially discomforting experiences; the result is a rather passive (accommodating) individual, one ill-disposed to modify his or her life circumstances or to participate actively in life's events. Owing to these deficiencies and inclinations, there is little motivation to become involved in the affairs of others (nurturance). Hence, by default, if nothing else, they tend to be self-involved (individuated). The deductive

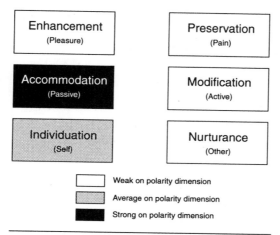

FIGURE 10.1 Status of the schizoid personality prototype in accord with the Millon Polarity Model.

model presented in this figure reflects the manner in which the theory formulates a personality disorder; it is essentially the same procedure by which Costa and Widiger (1993) articulate the components of these disorders using five quantitatively derived factors as their model, as well as the manner in which Cloninger (1986) does likewise, employing his biologically anchored tripartite schema of harm-avoidance, novelty-seeking, and reward-dependence. The key distinction between Millon's model and those of a quantitative or neurobiological character is its grounding in a theory that transcends the particular forms of expression in which personality disorders manifest themselves (lexical, biochemical). Rather, it is anchored to the deeper elements of nature, as found in principles that apply to all of the major disciplines of science.

CLINICAL PICTURE

Perhaps it is not necessary to say, but there are many variations to be seen in individuals diagnosed with the same label. Desirous though it may be to find that everyone given the same designation displays the same pattern of behaviors, feelings, and thoughts, the reality is that there are numerous and variegated forms that might be comfortably subsumed under the same label. It would not be judicious to lead the naïve reader into believing that there is a single pattern of features that typify each of our categorical classes. Hence, in the following sections, we describe the many varieties of each of the *prototypal* personality disorders, because we are convinced, for the most part, that each prototypal personality is largely an extension or more extreme variant of normal types that exhibit similar features.

Diagnostic Domains

With the foregoing as a background, this section details the clinical characteristics of the core group of prototypal schizoids in a more explicit and systematic fashion.

Reference should be made to Table 10.1 in this and later chapters; these tables summarize and highlight the different domains that characterize the prototype of each personality disorder. Also presented is Figure 10.2, which presents these same clinical domains, but highlights their relative *salience* among schizoid personalities; for example, the unengaged interpersonal conduct and the apathetic mood/temperament are the two most prominent or characteristic features that distinguish the schizoid prototype.

Impassive expressive behavior.   Most characteristic of schizoids is their lack of demonstrativeness and their deficits in energy and vitality. They appear to the observer to be unanimated and robotic; many display marked deficits in activation and spontaneity. Speech among schizoids typically is slow and monotonous, characterized by an affectless vacancy and obscurities that signify either inattentiveness or a failure to grasp

---

TABLE 10.1   Clinical Domains of the Schizoid Prototype

Behavioral Level

   (F) Expressively Impassive (e.g., appears to be in an inert emotional state, lifeless, undemonstrative, lacking in energy and vitality; is unmoved, boring, unanimated, robotic, phlegmatic, displaying deficits in activation, motoric expressiveness, and spontaneity).

   (F) Interpersonally Unengaged (e.g., seems indifferent and remote, rarely responsive to the actions or feelings of others, chooses solitary activities, possesses minimal "human" interests; fades into the background, is aloof or unobtrusive, neither desires nor enjoys close relationships, prefers a peripheral role in social, work, and family settings).

Phenomenological Level

   (F) Cognitively Impoverished (e.g., seems deficient across broad spheres of human knowledge and evidences vague and obscure thought processes, particularly about social matters; communication with others is often unfocused, loses its purpose or intention, or is conveyed via a loose or circuitous logic).

   (S) Complacent Self-Image (e.g., reveals minimal introspection and awareness of self; seems impervious to the emotional and personal implications of everyday social life, appearing indifferent to the praise or criticism of others).

   (S) Meager Objects (e.g., internalized representations are few in number and minimally articulated, largely devoid of the manifold percepts and memories of relationships with others, possessing little of the dynamic interplay among drives and conflicts that typify well-adjusted persons).

Intrapsychic Level

   (F) Intellectualization Mechanism (e.g., describes interpersonal and affective experiences in a matter-of-fact, abstract, impersonal, or mechanical manner; pays primary attention to formal and objective aspects of social and emotional events).

   (S) Undifferentiated Organization (e.g., given an inner barrenness, a feeble drive to fulfill needs, and minimal pressures either to defend against or resolve internal conflicts or cope with external demands, internal morphologic structures may best be characterized by their limited framework and sterile pattern).

Biophysical Level

   (S) Apathetic Mood (e.g., is emotionally unexcitable, exhibiting an intrinsic unfeeling, cold, and stark quality; reports weak affectionate or erotic needs, rarely displaying warm or intense feelings, and apparently unable to experience most affects—pleasure, sadness, or anger—in any depth).

F refers to Functional Domains (fluid, interactive)
S refers to Structural Domains (stable, unchanging)

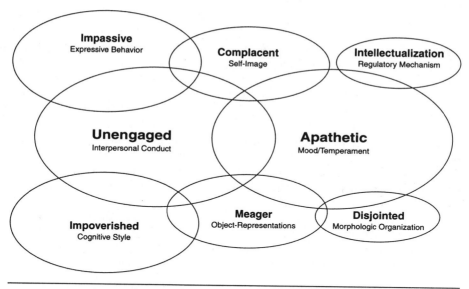

Figure 10.2   Salience of prototypal schizoid domains.

the emotional dimensions of human communication. Movements are lethargic and lacking in rhythmic or expressive gestures. They rarely "perk up" or respond alertly to the feelings of others; they are not intentionally unkind, however. They seem invariably preoccupied with tangential and picayune matters, rather passively detached from others, and drifting along quietly and unobtrusively, as if in a world of their own.

Individuals of this cast evidence underresponsiveness to all forms of stimulation. Events that normally provoke anger, elicit joy, or evoke sadness in others seem to fall on deaf ears. There is a pervasive imperviousness to emotions, and not only to those of joy and pleasure: feelings of anger, depression, or anxiety rarely are expressed. This apathy and emotional deficit are cardinal signs of the schizoid syndrome. Their generalized inability to be activated and aroused may be exhibited in a wide-ranging lack of initiative and the failure to respond to most reinforcements that prompt others into action. Thus, they are not only unmoved by emotional stimuli but seem to possess a general deficiency in energy and vitality. When they do become involved, they tend toward mental activities, such as reading or television watching, or toward physical activities that call for minimal energy expenditures, such as drawing, watch repairing, needlepoint, and so on.

Unengaged interpersonal conduct.   For the most part, schizoids seem interpersonally indifferent and remote, failing to be responsive to the emotions and behaviors of others. They prefer solitary activities, exhibit few interests in the lives of others, and tend to fade into the social background, either unobtrusive in their presence or seemingly aloof. This appears to be their preference, maintaining a peripheral role in most interpersonal settings, neither desiring nor enjoying any close relationships. The inability of schizoids to engage in the give-and-take of reciprocal relationships may readily be observed. They are rather vague and disengaged from group interactions, appearing to be involved in their own world of preoccupations. It is even difficult for them to mix with others in pleasant social activities, let alone those demanding leadership. When relating to others in a mandatory setting, as in school or at work, their social communications are expressed not in a peculiar or irrational way but in a perfunctory, formal, and impersonal manner.

For the same reasons they fail to develop intrapsychic mechanisms, schizoids also tend not to learn complex interpersonal coping maneuvers. Their drives are meager and they lack the intense personal involvement sometimes conducive to painful emotional conflicts. This is not to say that they possess no drives or discords, but that those they do experience are of mild degree and of minor consequence. One of the distinctions of the schizoid personality, then, is the paucity (rather than the character or direction) of their interpersonal coping. If any factor in their generally feeble hierarchy of motives can be identified, it is their preference for remaining socially detached. This is not a "driving" need of theirs, as it is with the avoidant personality, but merely a comfortable and preferred state. When social circumstances press them beyond comfort, they may simply retreat and withdraw into themselves. Should social discord or demands become intense or persistent, they may revert to more severe coping reactions and display various pathological disorders such as schizophrenic syndromes.

Impoverished cognitive style.   The thought processes of the schizoid tend, in general, to be rather deficient, not only in most spheres of human interest, but especially so with regard to social and personal life. Not uncommonly, their communications with others seem unfocused, conveyed in a loose or circuitous way, and occasionally wandering off the track, losing purpose or intention. Schizoid personalities rarely are introspective because the satisfactions to be found in self-evaluation are minimal for those who are incapable of experiencing deep emotions. This diminished introspectiveness, with its attendant lowering of insight, derives from another feature of the schizoid pattern. They display a vagueness and impoverishment of thought, a tendency to skim the surface of events, and an inability to convey articulate and relevant ideas regarding interpersonal phenomena.

This style of amorphous communication may be related to another trait, one referred to here as *defective perceptual scanning.* It is characterized by a tendency to miss or blur differences and to overlook, diffuse, and homogenize the varied elements of experience. Instead of differentiating events and sensing their discriminable and distinctive attributes, schizoids tend to mix them up, intrude extraneous or irrelevant features, and perceive them in a somewhat disorganized fashion. This inability to attend, select, and regulate one's perceptions of the environment seems, once again, to be especially pronounced with social and emotional phenomena.

Complacent self-image.   The schizoid appears emotionally impervious to the character of social transactions, revealing little awareness of or interest in the personal lives of others or in their own lives. They are not only indifferent to the meaning of what others convey to them, such as praise or criticism, but they exhibit little or no tendency to look into their personal feelings and attitudes. To the extent that they look inward, schizoid personalities characterize themselves as bland persons who are reflective and introversive. Most seem complacent and satisfied with their lives and are content to remain aloof from the social aspirations and competitiveness they see in others. Self-descriptions, however, tend to be vague and superficial. This lack of clarity does not indicate elusiveness or protective denial on their part, but rather their deficient powers to reflect on social and emotional processes. Interpersonal attitudes are no less vague and inarticulate. When adequately formulated, schizoids perceive themselves to be somewhat reserved and distant, lacking in much concern or care for others. Rather interestingly, they are able to recognize that others tend to be indifferent to them and their needs.

Meager object-representations.   The inner template of past experiences that are embedded in the mind of most schizoids appear to be few in number and diffusely articulated. In contrast to those of other personalities, these imprinted memories seem to be devoid of specificity and clarity. They also possess little of the dynamic interplay among drives, impulses, and conflicts that are found among well-adjusted persons. Owing to the feeble manner in which they experience events and persons, there is relatively little that imprints strongly in their minds. Low in arousal and emotional reactivity, as well as relatively imperceptive and therefore inclined to blur distinctions, their inner life remains largely homogeneous and undifferentiated. The natural variety of experiences that compose the minds of most people are unarticulated and, hence, they are unable to engage in dynamic interplay, nor are they able to change and evolve as a consequence of their intrapsychic interactions.

Intellectualization regulatory mechanism.   Schizoids describe the interpersonal and affective character of their experiences and memories in a somewhat impersonal and mechanical manner. They tend to be abstract and matter-of-fact about their emotional and social lives; when they do formulate a characterization, they pay primary attention to the more objective and formal aspects of their experiences rather than to the personal and emotional significance of these events. Schizoids engage in few complicated unconscious processes. Relatively untroubled by intense emotions, insensitive to interpersonal relationships, and difficult to arouse and activate, they hardly feel the impact of events and have little reason to devise complicated intrapsychic defenses and strategies. They do harbor segments of the residuals of past memories and emotions, but, in general, their inner world lacks the intensities and intricacies found in all other pathological personalities.

Undifferentiated morphologic organization.   As indicated earlier, the inner world of the schizoid is largely desolate, devoid of the complex emotions, conflicts, and cognitions that are harbored even in most "normal" persons. Their inner world is barren. There are minimal drives to fulfill their needs; likewise, they experience minimal pressure to resolve their internal conflicts or to deal with external demands. More than any other personality, excluding perhaps the schizotypal, the structural composition of their intrapsychic world is highly diffuse and dynamically inactive.

Apathetic mood/temperament.   Perhaps the most striking and fundamental element of schizoids is their intrinsic deficiency in affective sensibility. Not only do they report few if any affectionate or erotic needs, but they appear unable to experience these major affective states—pleasure, sadness, or anger—to any degree. They are emotionally unexcitable, exhibit the weakest level of feelings, and seem to go through life in a cold and stark manner.

Self-Perpetuation Processes

What does the future hold for the schizoid? This section explores personality features that are themselves pathogenic, that is, foster increments in the individual's difficulties. Also touched on are some of the therapeutic steps that might help reverse these trends.

The impassivity and lack of color of schizoids enable them to maintain a comfortable distance from others. But their preferred state of detachment is itself pathogenic, not only because it fails to elicit experiences that could promote a more vibrant and rewarding style of life but because it fosters conditions that are conducive to more serious forms of psychopathology. Among the more prominent factors that operate to this end are the following (see Table 10.2).

Impassive and insensitive behavior.   The inarticulateness and affective unresponsiveness that characterize schizoids do little to make them attractive to others. Most persons are not inclined to relate to schizoids for any period, tending to overlook their presence in most settings and, when interacting socially, doing so in a perfunctory and unemotional way. Of course, the fact that others consider them boring and colorless suits the asocial predilections of schizoids quite well. However, this preference for remaining apart and alone only perpetuates and intensifies their tendencies toward detachment.

Diminished perceptual awareness.   The schizoid personality not only is socially imperceptive but tends to "flatten" emotional events, that is, to blur and homogenize experiences that are intrinsically distinct and varied. In effect, these personalities project their murky and undifferentiated cognitions on discriminable and complex social events. As a consequence of this perceptual diffuseness, they preclude the possibility of learning from experiences that could lead them to a more variegated and socially discriminating life.

Social inactivity.   Passively detached schizoids perpetuate their own pattern by limiting severely their social contacts and emotional involvements. Only those activities required to perform their jobs or fulfill their family obligations are pursued with any

---

TABLE 10.2   Self-Perpetuating Processes

Schizoid

Impassive and Insensitive Behavior
   Intensifies detachment
   Inarticulate and affectively unresponsive
   Boring and colorless

Diminished Perceptual Awareness
   Flattens emotional events
   Projects undifferentiated cognitions
   Homogenizes variegated experiences

Social Inactivity
   Limits emotional involvements
   Shrinks interpersonal milieu
   Excludes life-energizing events

---

diligence. By shrinking their interpersonal milieu, they preclude new experiences from coming to bear upon them. This is their preference, of course, but it only fosters their isolated and withdrawn existence because it excludes events that might alter their style.

INTERVENTION GOALS

The prognosis for this moderately severe personality is not promising. Many appear limited by a constitutional incapacity for affective expression and physical vigor. These liabilities may be inborn or acquired as a consequence of early experience. Regardless of their origin, however, the affectivity and interpersonal deficits found in these individuals are chronic and pervasive features of their personality makeup. Coupling these ingrained traits with the characteristic lack of insight and poor motivation for change, we can only conclude that the probability is small that they will either seek or succeed in a course of remedial therapy. If their deficits are mild and if the circumstances of their life are favorable, they will stand a good chance, however, of maintaining adequate vocational and social adjustments. Given their lack of intrinsic motivators, the role of contextual factors in mobilizing therapeutic progress is paramount (see Table 10.3).

The styles that schizoids have developed to cope with the events of their everyday life are a result, in great measure, of deficits in their intrinsic capacities to experience painful and pleasurable emotions. The impact of early learning may have further weakened these dispositions over time, continuing to color all subsequent events and thereby perpetuating the initial maladaptive patterns.

Reestablishing Polarity Balances

As noted previously, the coping strategy that characterizes the schizoid's mode of relating to his or her environment can best be described as passively detached. Not only do they appear to lack the capacity to experience pleasure or pain, but they do not obtain gratification from either self or others. A major treatment goal of therapy with

TABLE 10.3 Therapeutic Strategies and Tactics for the Prototypal Schizoid Personality

STRATEGIC GOALS
Balance Polarities
   Increase pleasure/enhancing polarity
   Increase active/modifying polarity

Counter Perpetuations
   Overcome impassive behaviors
   Increase perceptual awareness
   Stimulate social activity

TACTICAL MODALITIES
   Energize apathetic mood
   Develop interpersonal involvement
   Alter impoverished cognitions

this disorder is the enhancement of pleasure, particularly to overcome the imbalance in the pain-pleasure polarity. Moreover, their passively detached nature places them near the extreme end on the active-passive polarity. This latter imbalance warrants therapeutic efforts directed toward strengthening the active end of the continuum.

Countering Perpetuating Tendencies

When schizoids do come to the attention of a therapist, the latter's initial efforts are best directed toward combating their withdrawal tendencies. A major therapeutic goal is to prevent the possibility that they will isolate themselves entirely from the support of a benign environment. The therapist should seek to ensure that they continue some level of social activity to prevent them from becoming lost in fantasy preoccupations and separated from reality contacts. However, efforts to encourage a great deal of social activity are best avoided, as their tolerance in this area is limited. Further therapeutic strategies should be oriented toward enhancing their perceptual awareness and countering their underresponsiveness to the environment. Schizoids typically display an emotional inattentiveness to others that needs to be addressed. Increasing affectivity will in turn promote more variegated social experiences.

Identifying Domain Dysfunctions

Primary domain dysfunctions can be seen in both the interpersonal conduct and mood/temperament domains. Providing the patient with opportunities for social interaction can foster improvements in the interpersonal domain and lessen social isolation. Targeting the mood/temperament domain will involve activating patients' characteristically dull mood and increasing their capacity to experience pleasurable affective states. Deficits in activation are also observed in their expressive behavior. Improvements in this area consist of elevating their energy level and enhancing their expressive abilities. Their cognitive style is rather vague and lacks richness. Intervention necessitates bringing clarity to their thought processes, helping them attend to both internal and external processes without losing focus.

Secondary dysfunctions can be seen across several other domains. Their self-image, object-representations, regulatory mechanisms, and morphological organization all lack complexity and depth. By expanding their behavioral and social repertoire and simultaneously improving their ability to attend to different stimuli, a groundwork may be provided for improving these remaining domains.

SELECTING THERAPEUTIC MODALITIES

To accomplish the goals above, a variety of therapeutic modalities can be employed to target the clinical domain dysfunctions. These techniques should then be combined and put in sequence to promote maximal growth. Because each individual possesses a unique constellation of attributes, a thorough assessment of the saliences of the clinical domains should be conducted. The formulations provided below are not foolproof, of course, and the therapist needs to be aware of the potential stumbling blocks and resistances that may loom up.

Behavioral Techniques

Techniques of behavioral modification appear to be of limited value other than to reinforce some social skills. Because schizoids commonly lack full awareness of customary ways of behaving in social spheres, social skills training and other more directive and educative measures may be employed to build a more appropriate interpersonal behavioral repertoire. Beck and Freeman (1990a) suggest setting up a hierarchy of social interaction goals that the patient may want to accomplish. Role playing and in vivo exposure can then be utilized to practice these skills. Audio-playback devices can be of some benefit in allowing patients to monitor their monotone speech. Videotaping similarly can be used in helping patients identify more subtle nuances in their own behavior.

A critical limitation of operant techniques is that there are few external sources of reinforcement that can be identified because these patients appear to have a limited capacity to experience consequent events as either rewarding or punishing. Affection and recognition, which serve as potent reinforcers for most people, are not valued. An attempt should be made to carefully analyze the patient's behavioral repertoire and past history of reinforcement to identify any operant reinforcers that might be activated at this time. Behavioral change can at times be brought about by encouraging environmental modifications (Young, 1990). Such changes may include occupational adjustments or a change in living situation.

Interpersonal Techniques

Interpersonal techniques may prove problematic because a key element in interpersonal treatment is the therapeutic relationship, a feature in the schizoid's asocial world that possesses little value. Transference reactions are less likely to occur and, if present, may only recapitulate earlier maladaptive interpersonal patterns. The therapist's empathic stance and continued acceptance of the patient may facilitate rapport building. This may prove more fruitful than an insight-oriented approach, the latter seeking with minimal success to analyze the patient's mode of interacting in the session.

By providing a supportive and trusting environment, the therapist can facilitate collaboration. The dyadic relationship can be used as a forum for practicing recently acquired interpersonal and social skills. Here, the therapist can function as a mirror, enabling the patient to gain a closer look at the self, providing a measure of confirmation and elaboration of inchoate self schemata.

If an interest is displayed in developing interpersonal relations and skills, group methods may prove useful in encouraging and facilitating the acquisitions of constructive social attitudes. In this setting, schizoids may begin to alter their self-image and increase the motivation and skills for a more effective interpersonal style. Group settings are also uniquely suited for triggering schemata of an interpersonal nature (Young, 1990). The patient is provided with the opportunity to test the accuracy of the schemata as feedback from the other group members is readily available. Leszcz (1989) suggests that the group provides an opportunity for schizoids to become involved in a nonrelating way, slowly building a feeling of trust. Here, they do not have to abandon the protection of distancing from others, but can learn how people relate to one another. Clinicians should permit this detached position until the patient learns how to relate as well as tolerate any mildly disturbing affects. Most important, schizoids learn to recognize their different responses to the other group members and learn to observe and experience their bodily responses to these differences. Yalom (1985) contends that these self-awareness goals are preferable to cathartic methods. However, the therapist will have to be extremely cautious not to expect the same degree of participation from the schizoid group member. Being in a group setting may place interactional demands on the client that might initially cause a great deal of anxiety.

It is not unlikely that schizoids do come in for therapy at the request of family members. A decision may be made to involve other members of the family system in the therapeutic process. In some cases, family and marital therapy are best directed to educating the family members with regard to their relative's potential for change. Adjusting their expectations may in turn facilitate improvements when there is more tolerance of and less intrusion in the schizoid's privacy by family members. Moreover, family members can be instrumental in cultivating reform by assisting in environmental modifications and by allowing the patient to explore newly learned social skills and modes of interacting. An in-depth assessment of the family system may, however, reveal maladaptive patterns that over time have perpetuated the personality pattern. Potential capacities for self-remediation that may have existed within the patient may have been squelched, thereby reinforcing this schizoid's image as a developmental failure.

Cognitive Techniques

Attempts to cognitively reorient the patient's attitudes may be useful for developing self-insight and for motivating greater interpersonal sensitivity and activity. The schizoid's cognitive style is markedly impoverished. Homework assignments, such as having the patient keep a daily record of dysfunctional thoughts, can help identify automatic thoughts and assist in disambiguating his or her vague cognitions. Identified automatic thoughts typically center around negative cognitions about themselves, their preference for solitude, and the feeling that they are detached observers in life (Beck & Freeman, 1990a). These records can also help patients identify their emotions, gradations in intensity, and how their emotional states affect their interactions with others (Will, 1994).

As Young and Lindeman (1992) note, it is through interpersonal experience that schemata are developed and maintained. In the case of schizoids, it may have been the absence of interpersonal experience that contributed to the observed poverty of cognitions and their characteristic low complexity of self and other object-representations. Another drawback is that therapists frequently use affective techniques to trigger schemata. The tendency of these patients to intellectualize only serves to reduce the likelihood that arousal of emotions will allow access to schemata. The automatic thoughts and schemata that revolve around beliefs that they are better off alone and that relationships have nothing to offer them can be explored. It is worthwhile for therapist and patient to examine both the functional and dysfunctional aspects of isolation in the patient's life. A more realistic goal formulation, one on which therapist and patient can agree, should be determined. For example, the schizoid is often unable to recognize and articulate subtleties of reinforcement; cognitive methods developed in conjunction with the therapist can assist the patient in identifying gradations of enjoyment obtained from a variety of experiences.

Self-Image Techniques

A major difficulty among schizoids is their lack of a sense of self; as do others, most schizoids consider themselves to be bland and uninspiring. It is a major task of therapy to attempt to stimulate the limited affective capacities of these patients. Although nondirective Rogerian techniques are not likely to be fruitful initially, they can ultimately prove helpful; similarly, little can be expected of the more humanistic-existential methods until preliminary developments of a more vibrant sense of self can be generated. Schizoids' inability to generate thoughts and feelings spontaneously owes to their natural blandness and social indifference. What may prove helpful in the early phases of treatment, however, are experiential techniques, as well as certain Gestalt procedures. The emotional insensitivity of schizoids may be counteracted by techniques that sensitize them to even the most subtle of their sensations, thereby gradually activating their capacity to become aware of how they feel. These techniques may be extremely helpful in fostering facets of experience that the patient may rarely have had. Similarly, the social indifference of schizoids may be overcome in part by procedures that engage them in role-reversal rehearsals, such as playing the role of one's wife interacting with the patient. In this manner, it may be possible to help an other orientation in what has likely been an other-indifferent orientation. Along these lines, patients may be gently urged to engage in activities where active participation is minimal at first. Progressively, further involvements with others may be encouraged, such as participation in a computer group or on a travel tour. In productive substitution (Kantor, 1992), the task is to provide patients with self-gratifying replacements for what may be missing in their everyday life. New social relationships with peers, as in a therapy group, may also substitute for a lack of social skills and worth.

Intrapsychic Techniques

Little may be expected of psychoanalytic approaches because schizoids possess a relatively uncomplicated world of intrapsychic emotions and defenses. They are not very psychologically minded and frequently lack the desire to explore their inner world. In those few cases where analytically oriented psychotherapy may be indicated, the therapist will have to take a more active role than usual. Interventions should be directed to exploring the patient's internal object-relations. The basis for intrapsychic therapy is not likely to be an interpretation of inner conflicts, but the learning that can take place by virtue of the therapeutic relationship. As Gabbard (1994) has indicated, the clinician's task is that of reducing the patient's fixed internal representations and providing a corrective experience through the everyday transference analysis. The proclivity of schizoids to be silent and unrelated can prove stressful to the clinician. The therapist must guard against proclivities to speak and act out, thereby threatening the patient when he or she needs to withdraw and disconnect. Clinicians should adopt a permissive and accepting attitude with these patients, recognizing that silence is a sign of how they typically relate to others; moreover, it need not signify treatment resistance. By sensing within themselves the countertransference feelings evoked, clinicians may obtain useful information regarding the patient's intrapsychic world. Being in therapy can provide a positive, more stable relational experience which can then be internalized (Gabbard, 1994). This new sense of relatedness may result in the patient's feeling more at ease, revealing possible hidden aspects of the self. As a result, a greater awareness of the self may ensue. Others note that enriching internal representations of self and others, increasing reality contacts, and enhancing the sense of self are primary therapeutic goals.

Pharmacologic Techniques

At the behavioral level, deficiencies are exhibited in the expressive act domain. When therapy is first initiated, schizoids' low energy level and activation deficits may render the therapeutic process ineffectual. Psychopharmacologic treatment may be called for. Trial periods with a number of stimulants can be explored to see if they "perk up" energy and affectivity. Notable in this regard may be the antidepressant bupropion (Wellbutrin), which appears somewhat effective in dealing with the schizoid's apathy and anhedonia. Low doses of rispridone and olanzapine also appear useful in a trial run to see if various negative symptoms such as anhedonia and anergia can be modulated. Clozapine may also be explored, if given in low doses to avoid the possibility of agranulocytosis. Each of these should be used with caution, however, as they may activate feelings and drive states that the patient's impoverished defensive structures and cognitive schemata are ill-equipped to handle.

MAKING SYNERGISTIC ARRANGEMENTS

It is pertinent that the patient perceives therapy as having something valuable to offer in order to prevent dropout. Therapeutic efforts with schizoids may require psychopharmacologic intervention at the onset to activate arousal systems and thereby counter their inability to experience affect or energy. This may in turn facilitate the use of other interventions that necessitate a certain amount of motivation and commitment. Such intervention, however, can be seen by the patient as a quick fix, resulting in premature termination. It may be necessary to enhance the therapeutic relationship before deciding on pharmacotherapy. The complaints that these patient do not get enjoyment out of activities and interpersonal relations can be addressed cognitively at first. Behavioral methods may be used more fruitfully after the patient's experiential repertoire has been increased or when the patient has attained a deeper level of experiencing. Group therapy can be used concurrently with individual psychotherapy, but only after the patient's desire as well as capability for social interaction has been adequately assessed. Family or marital approaches may be used conjointly and can complement individual therapy.

Illustrative Cases

As noted in an earlier chapter, the cases presented here, as well as those in later chapters, represent actual patients treated or supervised by Millon in the past 40+ years. Graduate students, interns, and residents contributed to a significant degree to these formulations, as well as implementing their therapeutic goals. All cases have been substantially camouflaged; changes include age, gender, and vocation. It should be noted that many precede the development of the personality-guided synergistic model and, hence, are not as comprehensive and systematic as we would have preferred.

Videotapes of all the personality disorder cases presented in this and the following chapters that make up the illustrative cases sections are available for teaching or professional purposes. The videos are simulations of actual patient interactions, portrayed with skill by actors, students, and professional psychologists.

The *prototypes* that constitute the body of the personality disorder chapters in this text represent derivations that are based essentially on *theoretical deduction*. They are given their descriptive characterizations from the vast literature provided by earlier clinicians and theorists, as well as from the texts of the *DSM-III, III-R,* and *IV.* What is presented is, in great part, a series of "ideal" or pure textbook conceptions of each disorder. There are numerous variations, however, of these prototypal personality disorders, divergences from the theoretically derived prototype that represent the results of empirical research and clinical experience. Although it is our belief that the deeper or underlying laws that give shape to each of the personality prototypes are best understood in terms of theory, it is wise to recognize that there are fruitful, nontheoretical sources where such information has been and can be gathered (Millon, 1987b).

In this section on adult subtypes, as well as in subsequent parallel sections, we describe variations on the core prototypal personality pattern that research and clinical observation suggests be included in our thinking about each personality disorder (see Table 10.4). We know that there is no single schizoid (or avoidant, or depressive, or histrionic) type. Rather, there are several variations, different forms in which the core or prototypal personality expresses itself. Some reflect the workings of constitutional dispositions that life experience subsequently reshapes and impacts in different ways, taking divergent turns and producing moderately different psychological characteristics. The course and character of life experiences are complexly interwoven; numerous influences have simultaneous or sequential effects, hence often producing a mixture of patterns of different personality prototypes in the same person.

It is for these and other reasons that clinicians and students in our field must learn not only the pure prototypal personalities, but the alternatives and mixtures that are seen in clinical reality. What follows in this section, therefore, are a number of these variations, or what we have termed *subtypes* (Millon & Davis, 1996a). They reflect mixtures, they reflect pure and mixed patterns of learning and experience, they reflect

TABLE 10.4   Schizoid Personality Disorder Subtypes

Affectless: Passionless, unresponsive, unaffectionate, chilly, uncaring, unstirred, spiritless, lackluster, unexcitable, unperturbed, cold; all emotions diminished.

MCMI 1 (7)

Remote: Distant and removed; inaccessible, solitary, isolated, homeless, disconnected, secluded, aimlessly drifting; peripherally occupied.

MCMI 1–2 A/S

Languid: Marked inertia; deficient activation level; intrinsically phlegmatic, lethargic, weary, leaden, lackadaisical, exhausted, enfeebled.

MCMI 1–2 B

Depersonalized: Disengaged from others *and* self; self is disembodied or distant object; body and mind sundered, cleaved, dissociated, disjoined, eliminated.

MCMI 1–S

consistent inclinations of a specific type, and they reflect conflict resolutions in which overt patterns appear quite different from that which is covert or unconscious. The author believes strongly that the reader should acquire increasing sophistication in the realm of personality *subtypes* as well as of personality *prototypes*.

There are numerous patterns that may eventuate in the schizoid personality prototype. We briefly describe presenting pictures of several of these, as well as discuss the results of a clinical assessment, the synergistic treatment plan, and the course of treatment that was employed.

It should be noted that much of what is written in the clinical assessment section of these cases go beyond what was available at the time of the initial assessment period. For this reason in part, the section on synergistic treatment plan falls short of what might have been planned, had such information been known at the time of the initial planning. Readers are likely to be faced with a similar problem in their planning, hence calling for a periodic review of their progress.

SCHIZOID PERSONALITY: LANGUID TYPE
(SCHIZOID WITH DEPRESSIVE TRAITS)

CASE 10.1, JIM S., 29

Presenting Picture: Jim S. was referred for counseling through his employee assistance program. Apparently, Jim's employer was rather fond of him, offering frequent accolades and assisting him in completion of routine tasks, but had become frustrated with his inability to motivate himself to accomplish even the simplest of tasks or communicate on any effectual level with his coworkers. "I do okay, but my boss thought I'd do better by now," was his listless perception of the situation. Not one to enjoy the company of others, Jim lived alone, didn't socialize with coworkers or others in his environment, and even failed to maintain contact with his family. This void did not bother him, he claimed. Because his existence was pretty much empty, there was nothing present with which to be dissatisfied. What was most interesting, however, was that Jim occasionally showed some affective investment, as was seen through his thoughtful pause when asked about love interests, but he just could not activate any passion regarding this or any other emotional element.

Clinical Assessment: As with other schizoids, the pattern we are calling *languid* can be traced either to life experiences or to inherent disabilities. Here, we are likely to find that Jim had been subjected to marked stimulus impoverishment in the sensorimotor-autonomy stage, leading to the underdevelopment of relevant neural substrates. It might have been a failure to receive psychic nourishment requisite to the stimulation of his inherent activation and pleasurable potentials, or perhaps a deficit that stemmed from an inborn deficiency. What we saw clinically was a mixed pattern that reflected a core schizoid makeup that had been interpenetrated with features of the depressive personality.

What was most notable about Jim was the poverty and slowness of his activation level. He was characterized by a marked inertia; rarely did we note any engagement in vigorous and energetic actions. He seemed either too comfortable or too lazy, unable to rouse himself to meet his responsibilities or to engage in even the simplest of pleasurable activities. Perhaps his nature was intrinsically phlegmatic, especially when the tempo of his behavior was uniformly slow.

A distinction should be made here between the languid and the affectless schizoids, to be discussed shortly. Although languid persons are accustomed to reacting slowly in all matters, including affectively, their affective capacities are neither shallow nor totally deficient. Some possess a reasonable measure of sentimentality, but rarely is it of considerable depth nor is it readily expressed.

As noted elsewhere (Millon, 1969), the lifestyle of patients such as Jim is typified by a quiet, colorless, and dependent way of relating to others. His introversive pattern covaried with a general lack of vitality, deficits in social initiative and stimulus-seeking behaviors, impoverished affect, and a cognitive vagueness regarding interpersonal matters. His most notable features included fatigability, low energy level, and weakness in motoric expressiveness and spontaneity.

Jim was inclined to consider himself a weak and ineffectual person. Life was experienced as uneventful, with periods of passive solitude interspersed with feelings of emptiness. There was a general deficiency in his expression of affection, which, in addition to his deficient energy level, may have stemmed from an anhedonic inability to display enthusiasm or experience pleasure. His tendency was to keep to a simple, repetitive, and dependent life pattern.

Synergistic Treatment Plan: Of primary importance was to stimulate *activity* in this very passive, discouraged man, which needed to be addressed from both the *biophysical* level, to undo constitutional depressive proclivities, as well as from *cognitive* and *interpersonal* realms, to foster greater interests in social skills. It was most important to direct attention to Jim's *passive* coping construct of gravitating toward pseudorelationships with others who expect very little or nothing from him, rather than more fulfilling attachments that require investment. *Pleasure* had become something nearly lost to Jim, just about extinct in his memory, and he needed to be able to feel engaged in life activities to make improvement. Ultimately, this was the primary thrust of his treatment; he needed to enhance *experiential* receptivity and expressivity, capabilities that certainly existed within him. The obstacle, of course, was that Jim had "shut down" these intrinsic receptors by means of listlessness, compounded by a generally pessimistic, self-denigrating disposition.

Therapeutic Course: The first major task for Jim was to augment social interests as well as improve competence in relating to others. *Psychopharmacologic treatment* was employed to increase his energy and affectivity. This treatment was used with caution, however, as such agents tend sometimes to activate problematic expectations. Although he could not be pushed beyond his fairly low tolerable limits, careful and well-reasoned *cognitive methods,* specifically those developed by Beck, served to foster the development of more precise, connected thinking styles that aided in Jim's ability to effectively associate with environmental tasks. In addition to working toward the extinction of false beliefs about himself and the attitudes of others toward him, the therapist always was ready to capitalize on those spheres of life in which Jim possessed positive emotional inclinations and encouraged him, through *interpersonal methods* and *behavior skill development* techniques, to undertake activities consonant with these tendencies.

Although the early success of these methods justified an optimistic outlook, Jim's initial receptivity caused a misleading perception that further progress would be rapid and effortless. Following early treatment success, it was imperative to monitor Jim's tendency to reestablish his "comfortable" sense of ambivalence between pursuing social acceptance and fearing vulnerability. Enabling him to forgo his long-standing expectations of disappointment and thus thwart decompensation required several sessions dedicated to bolstering previous gains following his initial successes. *Support* was provided to ease his fears, particularly his pessimistic view that his efforts were not sustainable and would inevitably result in social disapproval again.

As noted, attempts to cognitively reorient his problematic attitudes were useful in motivating interpersonal sensitivity and confidence. Likewise, short-term techniques of behavioral modification were valuable in strengthening his deficient social skills. *Group methods* were useful in encouraging and facilitating his acquisition of constructive social attitudes. In these benign settings, Jim began to alter his social image and develop both the motivation and the skills for a more effective interpersonal style. Combining short-term programs with individual treatment sessions aided in forestalling untoward recurrences of the discomfort he experienced.

Focused treatment efforts for this introversive and passive man were best directed toward countering his tendencies to shut off the outside world by subduing his cognitive-affective receptors. Minimally introspective and consistently dampening affect and energy, Jim had to be prevented from increasing his isolation from others. To exercise interactional opportunity, energy was invested to enlarge his social context, as his tendency was to pursue with any diligence only those activities required by his job or by his family obligations. He had shrunk his interpersonal milieu, thereby succeeding in precluding exposure to new experience. Of course, this was his preference, but such behavior only fostered his isolated and withdrawn existence. To prevent such backsliding, the therapist ensured the continuation of all constructive social activities as well as potential new ones. Otherwise, Jim may have become increasingly lost in asocial and fantasy preoccupations. Excessive social pressure, however, was avoided because Jim's tolerance and competencies in this area were rather limited.

SCHIZOID PERSONALITY: REMOTE TYPE
(SCHIZOID WITH AVOIDANT TRAITS)

CASE 10.2, JOHN M., 19

Presenting Picture: John M. was a college student who preferred not to socialize in any traditional sense, and had little to no desire to get to know much about the people in his immediate social context, as they were seen by John as antagonistic. He slept much of the day and spent his evenings and nights at the school's computer lab "chatting" with others over the Internet. What was of interest was that these people often sought to meet John, but he routinely declined such invitations, stating that he didn't really have any desire to learn more about them than what they shared over the computer in the chat rooms. He described a family life similar to that of his social surroundings; he was not much invested in his younger brother and sister, despite the fact that they seemed to hold him in good regard, and he had recently alienated himself entirely from his father. Though his father had a history of being hostile toward John, he had recently made a small effort to relate on a healthier and more intimate level, but John told him that he wasn't needed in his life. The only apparent investment John had in his family was with his mother, but he did not discuss this relationship substantively.

Clinical Assessment: Difficulties that can result in the isolated and withdrawn schizoid pattern have been spoken of as the *remote subtype.* John was subjected to intense hostilities and rejection by his father very early in life, and thus has protectively withdrawn in a manner so extreme as to reduce his original potential to feel and relate to the external world. Defensive maneuvers of this intensity may have been so severe as to make a child incapable of subsequent feeling and relating. We believe this to be an adaptive maneuver more typical of avoidants, but a possibility among schizoids nevertheless. As a youngster, it is likely that John was quite capable of desiring relationships and feeling emotions intensely, but he learned that such desires and emotions result in extreme anguish and disillusionment. Hence, he does not lack the capacity to feel and to relate to others, as do other schizoids, but he protectively damped down these emotions and wishes to such an extent as to be possibly unaware of them. Depending on the time and intensity of these overwhelming negative experiences, John began to exhibit signs that are more like the intrinsically deficient schizoid than the protectively avoidant pattern; we believe that he retained the wish for affective bonding, but was deeply convinced that it would not be forthcoming. Nevertheless, what we see when we examine the more moderately severe remote personalities is a commingling of both core schizoid and avoidant features.

Very severe remote schizoids give evidence of features similar to the schizotypal personality; they manifest high scores on an assessment instrument such as the MCMI-III on both the schizoid and schizotypal scales. Many are seen among the homeless, as chronically institutionalized residents of halfway houses, and in such long-term outpatient settings as VA mental hygiene clinics. A marked deficit in social interest was notable in John, as were frequent behavioral eccentricities, occasional autistic thinking, and depersonalization anxieties. At best, he had acquired a peripheral but dependent role in social and family relationships. Both stem from low self-esteem and inadequacies in autonomy and social competence. He had become a detached observer of the passing scene, was characteristically self-belittling, and possessed a self-image of being unloved and inadequate. Rather than venturing outward, he had increasingly removed himself from others and from sources of potential growth and gratification. Life was uneventful, with extended periods of solitude interspersed with occasional feelings of being disembodied, empty, and depersonalized. There was a tendency on his part to follow a meaningless, ineffectual, and idle pattern, drifting aimlessly and remaining on the periphery of social life.

A high proportion of remote schizoids such as John earn a very meager livelihood, quite frequently living a disengaged or parasitic lifestyle. He had not adapted to functioning independently. John gave the impression of possessing a weakness of will or a deficient intellectual endowment, though these features were not truly present in him. Also notable, John's career ambitions were not substantial; attendance at college was just something expected in his socioeconomic bracket, and he may have been partial to simply finding a subordinate, unskilled position, or even opted for public support and welfare. He also appeared to have very minimal sexual needs.

Synergistic Treatment Plan: An overarching goal for John was the enhancement of a seriously weakened *pleasure* polarity, which could be augmented by *self-actualizing* therapies, although these would have to be applied very judiciously and would only become central following earlier, more focused and short-term advances. The more *experiential and nondirective* approaches would be appropriate, whereas such expressive and confrontive methods as *Gestalt* therapy or *Reality/Control theory* might overwhelm him. John's perpetuating tendencies, unlike many other schizoids, had him focused *actively* on remaining on the periphery of his environment (ironically, a *passive* role), a defensive stance typical of his guarded nature. In the early stages of therapy, a careful *cognitive* approach, *nonconfrontive* in nature, was called for to reduce this vigilance toward avoiding pain, which consistently led to inertia. As trust developed and a greater sense of *self* was established, *interpersonal* and *behavioral* realms could be addressed to assure that venturing into social relationships (*other* polarity) would not always bring about pain and hostilities directed at him. With a safe measure of success in these more focused approaches, *group* methods, along with an *existential* approach in individual sessions, would be appropriate for continued growth at a comfortable pace for John.

Therapeutic Course: John's most important initial tasks were the accretion of both his contextual interests and interpersonal competence. At this early stage, it was apparent that the therapist would need to tread cautiously, as John's threshold for being "pushed" therapeutically was rather low. An *empathic* posture was crucial to develop a safe environment where John could be encouraged to explore more potent thoughts and feelings that he had successfully muted over time. As this level of trust was established, *cognitive methods* (e.g., Beck, Meichenbaum), applied prudently and judiciously, were fruitful in bringing about more balanced thought patterns and less troublesome beliefs. Beyond this routine aspect of disputing automatic thoughts, the therapist worked to encourage John, through *interpersonal methods* and *behavior skill development* techniques, to actively employ his healthier affective propensities.

Though John was quite receptive to this regimen from early in treatment, it was necessary for the therapist to guard against the likely belief that the process would be easy and expeditious. As anticipated, John was loath to take any emotional risks and perhaps preferred the safety of social alienation. It required several sessions, following this initial positive track, to undermine his tendency toward "self-fulfilling prophecies" of failure *Supportive* techniques, in this time, helped John through his pervasive belief that any improvement would be short-lived, impossible to maintain, and guaranteed to leave him once again in a state of social disapproval.

Psychopharmacologic treatment was considered, but ultimately rejected. In many cases, it is advantageous to explore several agents targeted at a patient's activity level and emotional responsiveness. With John, however, it was believed that the introduction of such agents too greatly increased the likelihood that it would trigger emotions too quickly and intensely, and this would overwhelm him. Cognitive reorientation methods, as noted earlier, facilitated self-confidence and stimulated emotional awareness. Similarly, short-term *behavioral modification* techniques augmented his deficient social skills. As adjunct to this individual modality, a *group milieu* helped John learn to utilize many of these skills as well as develop new positive attitudes toward relational tasks within a benign setting. He was able to effect changes and improvements in his interpersonal style. As he gained confidence, it became appropriate to apply some *existential* and *experiential* techniques, albeit judiciously, to enhance his sensitivity and desire for more meaningful experiences and relationships. Combining the short-term group experience with individual treatment sessions bolstered John's immunity toward his prior social discomfort.

Most important in John's treatment course was targeting his propensity to withdraw. Ill-inclined from the outset to explore psychological difficulties, and of particularly low energy and feeling, he was prevented, through these defined treatments, from fully isolating himself from others, a fate for which he seemed destined regardless of the character of those in his context. As John had a strong predilection for solitary activity and was disinclined to pursue any other activity unless it was absolutely necessary, he severely precluded any exposure to new experience or social contacts and further reinforced his isolated and withdrawn style. The therapist encouraged John's continuation in these more social tasks and activities beyond the scope of therapy, and also recommended further social explorations, as John's tendency still was to lean toward asocial and fantasy preoccupations. The byword here was *encouragement* as opposed to *pressure;* John would not have been receptive to any therapeutic "pushing," as his competence in social realms remained quite restricted. These brief and focused treatment techniques aided him in developing more skills in this area.

SCHIZOID PERSONALITY: AFFECTLESS TYPE
(SCHIZOID WITH COMPULSIVE TRAITS)

CASE 10.3, MARGARET R., 33

Presenting Picture: Margaret R., a bookkeeper in a small firm, seemed outwardly content with her quiet, unobtrusive life, and was comfortable with the fact that coworkers, family, and others in her surroundings didn't bother her. Although she did not note anything lacking in her existence, one could not help but notice that there was a disturbing lack of enthusiasm for, or even reaction to, *anything,* including activities and interests she claimed to enjoy. She stated that she was quiet even as a child, and went through school with only a few friends who joined her for homework. When asked if there might be some other occupation for which she might hold some interest, she seemed lost at first, but then remarked that she might do well in historical research. She seemed to have thought about this possibility before, but her emotional involvement in speaking of this interest remained barren.

Clinical Assessment: In what may best be termed *the affectless schizoid type,* we believe that the isolated, emotionally detached, and nonsocially communicative features of this person were likely to be a consequence in part of constitutional deficiencies. Perhaps Margaret had marked neurologic deficits in those regions of her nervous system that subserved the capacity to relate with warmth and sensitivity to others, some lesion or structural aplasia, perhaps, in relevant systems (e.g., limbic). Here, we were dealing with a person who was at the lower end of the normal distribution of affective sensibility; as noted, this diminished capacity was probably attributable largely to inborn limitations. Given her spiritless and emotionally diminished qualities, Margaret was likely to show up clinically as possessing features that interweave with those seen in obsessive-compulsive personalities.

Let us note that affectless schizoids should be distinguished conceptually from *schizotypal* personalities, where the primary defect is essentially a social/cognitive one. More precisely, in the latter syndrome, there is a marked constitutional weakness in the capacity to accurately understand the meaning of human communications. With Margaret, we saw an affective lameness, whereas in the schizotypal, we see a cognitive dysfunction. Both defects usually result in marked social difficulties. In Margaret's case, this was owing to an incapacity to connect or resonate with others affectively, whereas in the schizotypal, this can be attributed to an inability to cognitively grasp the meaning or fathom the interpersonal logic of others' thoughts and behaviors.

A few words should be said to distinguish Margaret from the *languid* schizoid subtype. In the languid, we see a primary slowness and ponderousness in energy and activation. Their deficits are largely motoric, evident in their slow movements, ready fatigue, and lack of initiative and drive. Margaret's deficiency was not motoric and behavioral, but was in the sphere of emotion and feeling. She seemed unable to activate her affect; she was affectively lame, not energetically lame. Languids are torpid, phlegmatic, unmoved, look weary and depressed; Margaret was unexcitable, unperturbed, cold, and looked restrained and dispassionate.

In former years (e.g., Kraepelin, Bleuler, Schneider), deficiencies of an affective character were often judged to underlie the "moral insanities." Possessing a social insensibility was assumed to give rise to amoral behaviors. Such relationships do occur with certain temperamental and experiential backgrounds, but the incapacity to experience praise or blame and an emotional indifference to friends and strangers alike do not necessarily result in moral depravity, much less criminality. What we see in the affectless schizoid such as Margaret is simply an inability to activate any intense emotions, be it social or antisocial in character. There is minimal warmth, but there is also minimal anger and hostility.

Synergistic Treatment Plan: Margaret's constitutional tendency was to be virtually "shut off" in affect and simply live as an automaton; that is, she did what she perceived to be her role without straying in any remarkable way or traversing any rule by involving her meager emotional life or her independent decision making. She might have been ill at ease in working with more potent emotional material, so a very empathic approach was necessary from the outset. It would be necessary to undo this very *passive,* constricted mode of existence by *cognitively* working to undo her very rigid adherence to her affectless routine, and subsequently, work to *experientially* increase *pleasure* and decrease her tendency to view herself as unable or unworthy of fulfillment via decisions that disrupt the ordinary (bolstering her *self* orientation). *Interpersonally,* Margaret needed to cultivate relationships and increase social skills and *behaviors,* tasks that were very difficult at first but that would eventuate in a strong *other* emphasis at a slightly later point in treatment.

Therapeutic Course: Margaret's fundamental goals included development of self-confidence and sociability, as well as extinguishing her trepidation over independent decision making. Early on, Margaret resisted any action toward these goals. Margaret felt, at this early stage, that the therapist's efforts to encourage responsibility and skill development equated to his rejection of her, and she became somewhat more withdrawn and pessimistic. It was necessary to be prepared for and counteract such a reaction, as failure to do so may have precipitated recurrences and squelched exploration. The alliance between the therapist and Margaret was most important, as she needed to learn how to tolerate conflicting emotions and anxieties. *Learning methods,* such as facing and controlling unstable emotions (e.g., Greenberg) were coordinated with *cognitive strengthening* (e.g., Beck) and *interpersonal methods* (e.g., Benjamin, Kiesler). The therapist provided an additional resource for learning how to approach uncertainties with reasonable poise and prevision. Had time allowed, *group* and *family* methods would have been useful in practicing these new skills and interpersonal styles in a natural but benevolent setting.

Margaret needed special care when it came to trust issues. She would not have remained in therapy long enough for any substantial improvement without a clearly empathic and understanding atmosphere. She stayed with a course of interpersonal treatment, but it tended to be somewhat inconsistent, alternating between patterns of apathy and schemes targeted at testing the therapist's sincerity. Her withdrawal tendencies as well as her uneasiness in confronting her current lethargic situation and resentful thoughts were addressed both with cognitive and interpersonal techniques. It was also necessary to impede any decompensation. Had Margaret begun to shown signs of conspicuous discouragement, alienation, or consistent melancholy, *supportive therapy* and cognitive reframing would have been apropos. *Pharmacologic agents* may have been explored as well. *Self-actualizing* and cognitive modalities were used to address periods when Margaret suffered from a sagging morale, to encourage her to continue in her social activities, to build confidence, and to combat her preoccupation with despondent feelings. She could not be pressed beyond her capabilities, however, because any failure on her part would reinforce her belief in herself as inadequate. Cognitive therapeutic methods were most effective in modifying these problematic attitudes.

SCHIZOID PERSONALITY: DEPERSONALIZED TYPE
(SCHIZOID WITH SCHIZOTYPAL TRAITS)

CASE 10.4, MARY A., 38

Presenting Picture: Mary A. presented for therapy at the insistence of her mother, with whom she had lived all of her adult life, as Mary's inactivity and lack of social context had become a source of disappointment and frustration for the mother. Mary worked in the back room of a small shop near her home, doing a rather dull, repetitive task. "Making boxes," was how she flatly described her work, and gradually it was elucidated by both her and her mother that Mary was paid "under the table" to put together small boxes for a card and gift store. Her speech in session was largely limited to one-word answers and incomplete thoughts, and even when she would begin to answer a query more substantively, her thoughts would inevitably get circumvented into something unrelated, and a more characteristic, fragmented answer would occur. Mary's free time was usually taken up watching television or renting movies. She had acquaintances at work, but had no desire to spend time with them outside of that context. It is interesting to note, too, that she did not resonate with (or even comprehend) the stories in her television and movie watching, but fixated on the particular actors who were featured.

Clinical Assessment: Mary typified this MCMI variant of the schizoid by her dreamily distant qualities. Upon initial observation, one might think that she was enjoying the contemplation of some inner vision, some inner reality that drew her more and more into her isolated state. As with other schizoids, she was extremely inattentive and disengaged from the real world. But more than the others, she had not only deteriorated into a state of obliviousness, appearing as if she were preoccupied inwardly, but, in fact, she was preoccupied with nothing in particular. Though present in the world of others, she appeared to be staring into empty space, relating neither to the actions and feelings of others nor to those that emanate from within herself. These features bring Mary into a close amalgamation with the schizotypal personality such that many of her characteristics blend and unite.

As with many others who experience depersonalization, Mary was very much an "outside observer," viewing herself as a distant object, disembodied and vacant, unconnected to her own feelings and thoughts. She had drifted into a state in which she ignored not only external phenomena but those that emanated from within herself. Disconnected from whatever is tangible and real in the world, including her own corporeal being, she was also *not* preoccupied with her own imagination and fantasies. She was much like a sleepwalker who had a physical presence but who was totally unaware of what she was doing, thinking, or feeling.

Despite her inward turning, thoughts and feelings were little more than a diffuse vagueness, an unclear and fuzzy set of disconnected ideas, an inchoate woolgathering, if you will. Not only were her internal processes undefined and diffuse, but her obscurity and inability to relate led others to sense increasingly that something might be missing within her. Not only did she seem a million miles away, unrelated and unfocused in human interactions, but her inner world appeared equally distant and obscure, if not largely absent.

Synergistic Treatment Plan: The overarching goal for Mary was to achieve some improved level of connectedness to both her intrapersonal and interpersonal worlds. Both her *self* and *other* polarities were, at the outset of treatment, diffuse and without direction. It would become necessary to disrupt her perpetuating tendencies of isolating herself, deadening her awareness of not only her social context but of her own being, and assuming an extremely *passive* stance, but these measures would need to follow a very nonthreatening period of trust enhancement through *supportive* therapy and *self-image* building that would serve to validate her. As Mary would become more engaged in her identity, it would become possible to help her reorganize and focus her *cognitive* structures and help her build *interpersonal* expressive skills. It would be possible, also, to gradually augment Mary's *pleasure*-orientation as her connnectedness as a corporeal being improved.

Therapeutic Course: In a brief or short-term approach with Mary, the primary goals focused on acquiring social skills, building confidence, and overcoming fear of self-determination. In the earliest phases, these aims were resisted. It was wise to be alert to her probable feeling that the therapist's efforts to encourage her to assume responsibility and social skills were a sign of rejection, and this may have engendered disappointment and dejection. Even reactions of rage were expected. This problematic behavior was anticipated and prepared for, however, and counteracted so that fundamental changes could be explored and rapid recurrences prevented. As a sound and secure therapeutic alliance was established, Mary learned to tolerate her contrary feelings and dependency anxieties. Learning how to face and handle her unstable emotions (e.g., Greenberg) was coordinated with the *cognitive strengthening* (e.g., Beck) of healthier attitudes and *interpersonal* relationships (e.g., Benjamin, Kiesler). Moreover, the therapist served as a model to demonstrate how feelings, conflicts, and uncertainties could be approached and resolved with reasonable equanimity and foresight. As special forms of interpersonal therapy, *group* and *family* methods were used to experiment with Mary's newly learned social skills and strategies in a more natural setting than that found in individual treatment.

Special attention was given to Mary's withdrawal tendencies and her persistent mistrust of others. This woman was not prone to sustain a therapeutic course without a heavy dose of repeated caring and empathy. Though she stayed with a course of interpersonal treatment, it often followed an inconsistent pattern, with frequent periods of indifference mixed with testing the therapist's sincerity. Clear signs of warmth and understanding were needed to ensure that treatment would not terminate before substantial improvement had occurred. Both cognitive and interpersonal techniques forestalled her habitual coping style of withdrawal and her unwillingness to face the humiliation of confronting her mix of an uneventful lifestyle and the experience of growing resentments. Efforts were made to counter her fear of activating false hopes and disappointment in therapy.

Another short-term concern was the forestalling of a decompensation process. Among the early signs of this breakdown were marked discouragement, withdrawal behavior, and persistent dejection. At this phase, *supportive* therapy, including use of *pharmacologic agents,* and cognitive reframing were especially useful. Efforts employing cognitive procedures were made to examine the basis of Mary's sagging morale, to encourage her, using interpersonal techniques, to continue to enlarge her sphere of activities, to build her self-confidence, and to deter her from being preoccupied with her melancholy feelings. Mary was not pressed beyond her capabilities, however, because failure to achieve any goals would only strengthen her conviction of her incompetence and unworthiness. These problematic attitudes were highly receptive to change with several of the classic cognitive therapeutic methods.

Resistances and Risks

The impoverished and globally undifferentiated phenomenology of the schizoid is itself a profound form of "passive resistance." Once in therapy, schizoids are not very likely to value the therapeutic relationship and may actually see the therapist as intrusive and hence shy away from therapy (Beck & Freeman, 1990a). A continuous risk is the possibility that they will drop out of therapy and revert back to their prior isolated and detached lifestyle. Even if impressive progress is made within a particular session, generalization of insight or behavior may not occur if the patient simply goes home to a solitary existence. Booster sessions to prevent regressions such as these are especially wise following termination.

Another danger is that the therapist may find interacting with such a patient unrewarding. Feelings such as frustration, helplessness, boredom, and impotence may be experienced. Therapists will need to be keenly aware that progress made with some schizoids will consist of their ability to derive greater satisfaction from solitary activities and not necessarily reduced social isolation. Even though strengthening social connectedness is a primary goal in therapy, group methods and other more interactive forms of therapy may be contraindicated. If the therapist is not careful in determining the patient's social skill level and desire for social involvement, the premature push toward interacting with others may cause discomfort, which may, in turn, reinforce existing beliefs that one is better off alone.

CHAPTER ELEVEN

Treating Avoidant Personality Patterns

Although the schizoid and avoidant personalities may appear superficially rather similar, they differ in several important ways, including their susceptibility to depression. Both personalities may appear withdrawn, emotionally flat, and lacking in communicative and social skills. The affective flatness of the avoidant, however, is typically a defensive maneuver against underlying emotional tension and disharmony. Similarly, the apparent detachment and interpersonal withdrawal of avoidants develop in response to a fear of intimacy and a hypersensitivity to rejection and ridicule. Strong desires for affection and acceptance exist in these individuals, but are denied or restrained out of apprehension and fearful mistrust of others. Not infrequently, avoidants have had experiences of painful social derogation, which resulted in an acute sensitivity and alertness to signs of ridicule and humiliation. This hypersensitivity and vigilance often result in the misperceiving of innocuous social comments or events as critical rejection (Millon, 1981, 1996).

For the most part, avoidants engage in self-imposed isolation and social withdrawal. They will, however, enter into relationships with a limited number of people if provided with strong guarantees of uncritical acceptance. Avoidants may become quite dependent on the one or two people they do allow into their lives. However, they are likely to remain rather cautious in relationships, engaging in frequent, subtle testing of their partner's sincerity.

Although the avoidant may view people in general as critical, betraying, and humiliating, they are usually very dissatisfied with the peripheral social role they feel forced to play and experience painful feelings of loneliness and alienation. Avoidants tend to be excessively self-critical, blaming themselves for their social undesirability. Consequently, they may become estranged from themselves as well as from others. They tend to resort to extreme defensive coping strategies to deal with the chronic feelings of interpersonal ambivalence and affective distress that they experience. In addition to active avoidance and withdrawal from threatening social situations, they may attempt to block and interfere with their own troubling cognitions, resulting in a fragmentation of their thoughts and disjointed verbal communications, as well as the appearance of being emotionally confused or socially irrelevant.

Avoidant types are among the most vulnerable of the personality patterns to psychiatric symptom disorders. Perhaps most frequently, the avoidant will suffer from feelings of anxiety and ruminative worry. Also, like the schizoid, prolonged estrangement from self and others can result in varied forms of dissociative disorders. Avoidants are also quite prone to feelings of deep sadness, emptiness, and loneliness. Frustrated yearnings for affection and approval, coupled with the self-deprecation they experience for their unlovability and ineffectuality, may result in a chronic melancholic tone to these personalities. Depression may nonetheless be difficult to detect in the avoidant, given their characteristic affective flattening and their typical presentation of slowness of speech and movement. Furthermore, avoidants will attempt to hide and contain their feelings of inner despair for fear that overt expressions of such weakness and suffering might render them even more vulnerable to social ridicule, humiliation, and rejection. Although major depressive episodes in these individuals may be similar to the symptomatic presentation of depressed schizoids (i.e., psychomotor retardation, extreme social withdrawal, and apathy), avoidants may also experience anxiety or obsessive ruminations with their depression.

The avoidant's susceptibility to depression can be readily explained from a cognitive-behavioral framework. First is the avoidant's tendency to view things pessimistically, that is, contempt directed at the self, fear and suspicion of others, and a sense of future despair. Next is the limited possibility the avoidant has for experiencing reinforcing events. Characteristically, these individuals tend to be inflexible, confining themselves to a small range of potentially reinforcing experiences. Although possessing the innate capacity to experience pleasure, the interpersonal anxiety felt by avoidants may cause them to deny themselves the satisfaction they could derive from others and to discount praise, compliments, and other social reinforcers. Similarly, the distorted view of self as ineffectual and unlovable precludes the possibility of pleasure coming from within.

Although the avoidant personality is a relatively new concept to psychiatric nosology (Millon, 1969), the characteristics of this pattern have frequently been cited in the literature on depression. Arieti and Bemporad (1980), in their proposal of three premorbid types of depressive personality, describe a depressive personality structure that is characterized by constant feelings of depression lurking in the background and an inhibition of an early form of gratification. Further, features of this form of chronic character structure are "A chronic, mild sense of futility and hopelessness which results from a lack of involvement in everyday activities. . . . emptiness because they do not develop deep relationships for fear of being exploited or rejected. . . . harsh, critical attitude towards themselves and others" (p. 1362).

According to the author, such depressive subtypes experience episodes of clinical depression when they are forced by some event to reevaluate their mode of existence and are confronted with the barrenness and meaninglessness of their lives.

We can review the features of the avoidant personality prototype using the theoretical model of polarities by examining Figure 11.1. As discussed in Chapter 3, we may best conceive the polarity model as a framework of ecological adaptations that represent styles of dealing with life circumstances based on constitutional dispositions and early learning. Personalities that are termed *disordered* represent different forms of maladaptation, modes of ecological functioning that are not only pathological, but also pathogenic. In some persons, such as the avoidant type, we may find an inborn sensitivity to pain, a biologically based extreme fearfulness, even in relatively benign

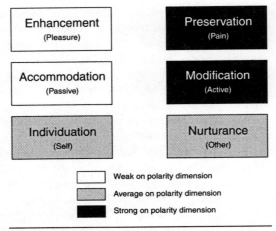

Figure 11.1 Status of the avoidant personality prototype in accord with the Millon Polarity Model.

circumstances, a tendency to feel anxiously disrupted when facing potential or actual physical or psychic stress. No less likely in the history of otherwise normally endowed youngsters is a fearful reactivity when the child had been repeatedly exposed to threatening life circumstances, such as having been reared by rejecting and hostile parents. As a result, there may be a deficiency in the capacity to experience the pleasures of life, the joys, the rewards, the means by which life is enhanced and extended. Conversely, we may see an overconcern and preoccupation with activities that center on the preservation of life, that is, avoiding the sadness and anxiety generated as emotional responses to psychic pain. What is central here is a hyperalertness to the possibility that life will likely get worse rather than better. On the one hand, there is a focus on preserving oneself, and on the other, an inattention to experiences that can make life more gratifying and pleasurable. On the second pair of polarities, we see an excessive utilization of the active mode of adaptation (modifying one's ecological niche). Interpretively, this signifies a necessary element in preserving life, a hypervigilant awareness and avoidance of events that may portend rejection, denigration, humiliation, and failure. At the third polarity level, the role of self versus others is of minimal consequence: they are only background factors in orienting and motivating the life of the avoidant. In effect, the central features of the avoidant personality are most clearly seen in their hyperalertness and reactivity to the possibility of psychic pain.

CLINICAL PICTURE

The following sections outline the major domains that provide useful information in diagnosing the prototypal variant of the avoidant personality (see Figure 11.2).

Diagnostic Domains

Avoidant personalities are acutely sensitive to social deprecation and humiliation. They feel their loneliness and isolated existence deeply, experience being "out of things" as painful, and have a strong, though often repressed, desire to be accepted. Despite their

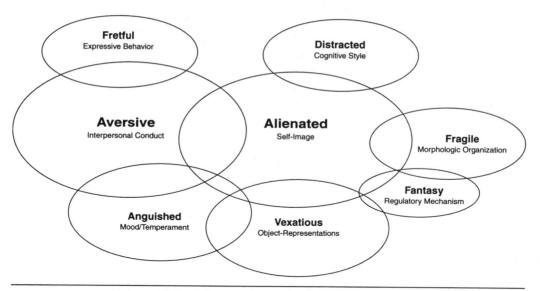

Figure 11.2   Salience of prototypal avoidant domains.

longing to relate and to be active participants in social life, they fear placing their welfare in the hands of others. Their social detachment does not stem, therefore, from deficit drives and sensibilities, as in the schizoid personality, but from an active and self-protective restraint. Although experiencing a pervasive estrangement and loneliness, they dare not expose themselves to the defeat and humiliation they anticipate. Because their affective feelings cannot be expressed overtly, they cumulate and are often directed toward an inner world of fantasy and imagination. Their need for affect and closeness may pour forth in poetry, be sublimated in intellectual pursuits, or be expressed in sensitively detailed artistic activities.

Unfortunately, isolation and protective withdrawal results in secondary consequences that further compound avoidants' difficulties. Their obviously tense and fearful demeanor often elicits ridicule and deprecation from others. Expressions of self-doubt and anxious restraint leave them open to persons who gain satisfaction in taunting and belittling those who dare not retaliate. The additional humiliation they experience thereby not only confirms their mistrust of others but reactivates the wounds of the past.

With this précis in mind, the domains of clinical data that help diagnose the avoidant pattern are detailed next (see Table 11.1).

Fretful expressive behavior.   The pervasive sense of unease and disquiet is what is most observable about avoidants. They evince a constant timorous and restive state, overreacting to innocuous experiences, hesitant about relating to events that may prove personally problematic, and anxiously judging these events as signifying ridicule or rejection from others. The speech of avoidants is generally slow and constrained. They exhibit frequent hesitations, aborted or fragmentary thought sequences, and occasional confused and irrelevant digressions. Physical behaviors tend to be highly controlled or underactive, although marked with periodic bursts of fidgety and rapid staccato movements. Overt expressions of emotion are typically kept in check, but this underresponsiveness overlays deep tension and disharmony. They exert great restraint,

TABLE 11.1   Clinical Domains of the Avoidant Personality Prototype

Behavioral Level

(F) Expressively Fretful (e.g., conveys personal unease and disquiet, a constant timorous, hesitant, and restive state; overreacts to innocuous events and anxiously judges them to signify ridicule, criticism, and disapproval).

(F) Interpersonally Aversive (e.g., distances from activities that involve intimate personal relationships and reports extensive history of social pan-anxiety and distrust; seeks acceptance, but is unwilling to get involved unless certain to be liked, maintaining distance and privacy to avoid being shamed and humiliated).

Phenomenological Level

(F) Cognitively Distracted (e.g., warily scans environment for potential threats and is preoccupied by intrusive and disruptive random thoughts and observations; an upwelling from within of irrelevant ideation upsets thought continuity and interferes with social communications and accurate appraisals).

(S) Alienated Self-Image (e.g., sees self as socially inept, inadequate, and inferior, justifying thereby his or her isolation and rejection by others; feels personally unappealing, devalues self-achievements, and reports persistent sense of aloneness and emptiness).

(S) Vexatious Objects (e.g., internalized representations are composed of readily reactivated, intense, and conflict-ridden memories of problematic early relations; limited avenues for experiencing or recalling gratification, and few mechanisms to channel needs, bind impulses, resolve conflicts, or deflect external stressors).

Intrapsychic Level

(F) Fantasy Mechanism (e.g., depends excessively on imagination to achieve need gratification, confidence building, and conflict resolution; withdraws into reveries as a means of safely discharging frustrated affectionate as well as angry impulses).

(S) Fragile Organization (e.g., a precarious complex of tortuous emotions depend almost exclusively on a single modality for its resolution and discharge, that of avoidance, escape, and fantasy; hence, when faced with personal risks, new opportunities, or unanticipated stress, few morphologic structures are available to deploy and few backup positions can be reverted to, short of regressive decompensation).

Biophysical Level

(F) Anguished Mood (e.g., describes constant and confusing undercurrent of tension, sadness, and anger; vacillates between desire for affection, fear of rebuff, embarrassment, and numbness of feeling).

F refers to Functional Domains (fluid, interactive)
S refers to Structural Domains (stable, unchanging)

not only in the control of anxiety, but in controlling feelings of confusion and in subduing the upsurge of anger.

Aversive interpersonal conduct.   Avoidants distance themselves from situations that may involve them in close personal relationships; they are strongly disinclined to become intimate unless they are certain that they will be liked and fully accepted. There is a long history of maintaining distance from others and of preferring privacy to avoid being shamed and humiliated. They report an extensive history of rejection, leading them to acquire a general distrust of others and a broad social pan-anxiety. A shy and apprehensive quality characterizes avoidants. They are not only awkward and uncomfortable in social situations but seem to shrink actively from the reciprocal give-and-take of interpersonal relations. They often impose a strain on others in face-to-face interactions. Their discomfort and mistrust often take the form of subtle testing operations, that is, guarded maneuvers by which they check whether others are sincere in their friendly overtures or are a deceptive threat to their security. Most observers who have only passing contact with avoidant personalities tend to see them as timid, withdrawn, or perhaps cold and strange—not unlike the image conveyed by the schizoid personality. Those who relate to them more closely, however, quickly learn of their sensitivities, touchiness, evasiveness, and mistrustful qualities.

Interpersonally, avoidants are best characterized as actively detached personalities. They are guided by the need to put distance between themselves and others, that is, to minimize involvements that can reactivate or duplicate past humiliations. Privacy is sought and they attempt to eschew as many social obligations as possible without incurring further condemnation. Any event that entails a personal relationship with others, unless it assures uncritical acceptance, constitutes a potential threat to their fragile security. They may deny themselves even simple possessions to protect against the pain of loss or disappointment. Efforts to comply with the wishes of others, much less to assert themselves, may have proved fruitless or disillusioning. Appeasement may have resulted in a loss of what little personal integrity they may have felt they still possessed, leading only to feelings of greater humiliation and disparagement. The only course they have learned that will succeed in reducing shame and humiliation is to back away, withdraw into themselves, and keep a watchful eye against incursions into their solitude.

In sum, these personalities avoid the anguish of social relationships by distancing themselves and remaining vigilant and alert to potential threat. This actively detached coping style contrasts markedly with the strategy of passively detached schizoids, who are perceptually insensitive to their surroundings. Avoidants are overly attentive and aware of variations and subtleties in their stimulus world. They have learned in the past that the most effective means of avoiding social rejection and deprecation is to be hyperalert to cues that forewarn their occurrence. By decreasing their relationships and diminishing their importance, they can minimize the hazards they fear surround them.

Distracted cognitive style.   It is characteristic of avoidants to scan their environment for potential threats. Also problematic is their preoccupation with intrusive and disruptive inner thoughts that seem to flood their efforts at maintaining psychic control. This upwelling from within of seemingly random and irrelevant feelings and ideas will often upset the continuity of their thoughts and interfere with their social communications. The avoidant personality is hyperalert to the most subtle feelings and intentions of others. These individuals are "sensitizers," acutely perceptive observers who scan and appraise every movement and expression of those with whom they come into contact. Although their hypervigilance serves to protect them against potential dangers, it floods them with excessive stimuli and distracts them from attending to many of the ordinary yet relevant features of their environment.

Thought processes are not only interfered with by this flooding of irrelevant environmental details but are complicated further by inner emotional disharmonies that intrude and divert avoidants' attentions. Combined with extraneous perceptions, these intrusive feelings upset their cognitive processes and diminish their capacity to cope effectively with many of the ordinary tasks of life. This cognitive interference is especially pronounced in social settings, where avoidants' perceptual vigilance and emotional turmoil are most acute.

Alienated self-image.   For the most part, avoidants see themselves as socially inept and inferior. Their self-evaluations judge them as personally unappealing and interpersonally inadequate, and they devalue whatever achievements they have attained. Most fundamentally, they find valid justifications for their being isolated, rejected, and empty. Avoidants describe themselves typically as ill at ease, anxious, and sad. Feelings of loneliness and of being unwanted and isolated are often expressed, as are fear and distrust of others. People are seen as critical, betraying, and humiliating. With so trouble-laden an outlook, we can well understand why their social behavior is characterized by interpersonal aversiveness.

Disharmonious emotions and feelings of emptiness and depersonalization are especially noteworthy. Avoidant personalities tend to be excessively introspective and self-conscious, often perceiving themselves as different from others, and they are unsure of their identity and self-worth. The alienation they feel with others is paralleled, then, by a feeling of alienation from themselves. They voice futility with regard to the life they lead, have a deflated self-image, and frequently refer to themselves with an attitude of contempt and derision more severe than they hear from others.

Vexatious objects.   The internalized residue of the past that inheres within the mind of the avoidant is composed of intense, conflict-ridden memories of problematic early relationships. These can be readily reactivated with minimal promptings. Moreover, there are limited recollections of a more rewarding nature to draw upon or to dispose one to perceive the world in an optimistic fashion. Owing to the pervasiveness of these troublesome memories, there are few opportunities to develop effective and satisfying means to bind one's impulses, to resolve one's conflicts, or to deflect external stressors. Avoidants are trapped in the worst of both worlds, seeking to avoid both the distress that surrounds them and the emptiness and wounds that inhere within them. This latter feature is especially significant to an understanding of the avoidant for it signifies the fact that turning away from one's external environment brings little peace and comfort. Avoidants find no solace and freedom within themselves. Having internalized the pernicious attitude of self-derogation and deprecation to which they were exposed in earlier life, they not only experience little reward in their accomplishments and thoughts but find instead shame, devaluation, and humiliation. In fact, there may be more pain being alone with one's despised self than with the escapable torment of others. Immersing oneself in one's own thoughts and feelings is the more difficult experience because one cannot physically avoid oneself, cannot walk away, escape, or hide from one's own being. Deprived of feelings of worth and self-respect, these persons suffer constantly from painful thoughts about their pitiful state, their misery, and the futility of being themselves. Efforts that are even more vigilant than those applied to the external world must be expended to ward off the painful ideas and feelings that well up within them. These aversive signals are especially anguishing because they pervade every facet of the avoidant's makeup. It is their entire being that has become devalued, and nothing about them escapes the severe judgment of self-derision.

Fantasy mechanisms.   The avoidant's prime, if not sole, recourse is to break up, destroy, or repress these painful thoughts and the emotions they unleash. These personalities struggle to prevent self-preoccupations and seek to intrude irrelevancies by blocking and making their normal thoughts and communications take on different and less significant meanings. In effect, and through various intrapsychic ploys, they attempt to interfere actively with their own cognitions. Similarly, the anxieties, desires, and impulses that surge within them must also be restrained, denied, turned about, transformed, and distorted. Thus, they seek to muddle their emotions also, making their affective life even more discordant and disharmonious than it is typically. To avoidants, it is better to experience diffuse disharmony than the sharp pain and anguish of being themselves. Despite their efforts at inner control, painful and threatening thoughts and feelings will periodically break through, disrupting more stable cognitive processes and upsetting whatever emotional equanimity they are able to muster.

Apart from destroying their inner cognitions, avoidants depend excessively on fantasy and imagination to achieve a measure of need gratification, to build what little confidence they may have in their self-worth, and to work out what few methods they can for resolving conflicts. Avoidants experience their feelings deeply and hence must use their daydreams and reveries as a means of dealing with their frustrated needs for affection and discharging their resentful and angry impulses. But fantasies also prove distressing in the long run because they point up the contrast between desire and objective reality. Repression of all feelings is often the only recourse, hence accounting for the avoidant's initial appearance of being flat, unemotional, and indifferent, an appearance that belies the inner turmoil and intense affect these persons truly experience.

Fragile organization. The intrapsychic structure of the avoidant is composed of a precarious complex of tortuous emotions, each of which can be reactivated and can overthrow the fragile psychic controls of these patients. What holds the structure together is a reliance, excessive in its use, on avoidance, escape, and fantasy. When faced with personal risks or unanticipated stress, the avoidant possesses few morphologic structures or dynamic mechanisms to deal with these difficulties. Similarly, there are few backup positions to which the avoidant can revert, short of regressive decompensation. Protecting oneself from real and imagined psychic pain is a paramount goal in these personalities. Avoiding situations that may result in personal humiliation or social rejection is the guiding force behind their interpersonal relationships. Of equal threat is the avoidant's own aggressive and affectional impulses. These are especially distressing because these persons fear that their own behaviors may prompt others to reject and condemn them. Much intrapsychic energy is devoted to mechanisms that deny and bind these inner urges.

Avoidant personalities are beset by several notable conflicts. The struggle between affection and mistrust is central. They desire to be close, show affection, and be warm with others, but they cannot shake the belief that such actions will result in pain and disillusion. They have strong doubts concerning their competence and, hence, have grave concerns about venturing into the more competitive aspects of our society. This lack of confidence curtails their initiative and leads to the fear that their efforts at autonomy and independence will only fail and result in humiliation. Every route toward gratification seems blocked with conflicts. They are unable to act on their own because of marked self-doubt; on the other hand, they cannot depend on others because they mistrust them. Security and rewards can be obtained, then, neither from themselves nor from others; both provide only pain and discomfort.

Anguished mood. Avoidants describe their emotional state as a constant and confusing undercurrent of tension, sadness, and anger. They feel anguish in every direction, vacillating between unrequited desires for affection and pervasive fears of rebuff and embarrassment. Not infrequently, the confusion and dysphoria they experience lead to a general state of numbness. As noted, avoidant personalities have a deep mistrust of others and a markedly deflated image of their own self-worth. They have learned to believe through painful experiences that the world is unfriendly, cold, and humiliating, and that they possess few of the social skills and personal attributes by which they can hope to experience the pleasures and comforts of life. They anticipate being slighted or demeaned wherever they turn. They have learned to be watchful and on guard against the ridicule and contempt they expect from others. They must be exquisitely alert and sensitive to signs that portend censure and derision. And, perhaps most painful of all, looking inward offers them no solace, for they find none of the attributes they admire in others.

Their outlook is therefore a negative one: to avoid pain, to need nothing, to depend on no one, and to deny desire. Moreover, they must turn away from themselves also, away from an awareness of their unlovability and unattractiveness and from their inner conflicts and disharmony. Life, for them, is a negative experience, both from without and from within.

The hyperarousal of avoidants may reflect a biophysical sensory irritability or a more centrally involved somatic imbalance or dysfunction. Using a different conceptual language to refer to this biophysical speculation, it might be hypothesized that these individuals possess a constitutionally based fearful or anxious temperament, that is, a hypersensitivity to potential threat. The conjectures suggested here may be no more than different conceptual approaches to the same thesis; for example, a fearful temperamental disposition may simply be a behavioral term to represent a biophysical limbic system imbalance.

A few speculations of an anatomical and biochemical nature may be in order. For example, avoidant personalities may experience aversive stimuli more intensely and more frequently than others because they possess an especially dense or overabundantly branched neural substrate in the "aversive" center of the limbic system. As has been described in slightly greater detail in the Millon and Davis (1996a) book's section on hypothetical biogenic factors, another plausible speculation for their avoidant tendencies is a possible functional dominance of the sympathetic nervous system. Thus, excess adrenaline owing to any one of a number of autonomic or pituitary-adrenal axis dysfunctions may give rise to the hypervigilant and irritable characteristics of this personality. Imbalances of this kind may lead also to the affective disharmony and cognitive interference found among these patients. Deficiencies or excesses in certain brain neurohormones may facilitate rapid synaptic transmission and result in a flooding and scattering of neural impulses. Such individuals will not only appear overalert and overactive but may experience the avoidant's characteristic cognitive interference and generalized emotional dysphoria.

Self-Perpetuation Processes

The coping style employed by the avoidant personality is not a matter of choice. It is the principal, and perhaps only, means these individuals have found effective in warding off the painful humiliation experienced at the hands of others. Discomforting as social alienation may be, it is less distressing than the anguish of extending themselves to others only to be rebuffed or ridiculed. Distance guarantees a measure of safety; trust only invites disillusion.

The coping maneuvers of avoidants prove self-defeating. There is a driven and frightened quality to their behaviors. Moreover, avoidants are adaptively inflexible because they cannot explore alternative actions without feeling trepidation and anxiety.

In contrast to other personalities, the avoidant coping style is essentially negative. Rather than venturing outward or drawing on what aptitudes they possess, they retreat defensively and become increasingly remote from others and removed from sources of potential growth. As a consequence of their protective withdrawal, avoidants are left alone with their inner turmoil, conflicts, and self-alienation. They have succeeded in minimizing their external dangers, but they have trapped themselves in a situation equally devastating. Several behaviors that foster and intensify the avoidant's difficulties are noted here (see Table 11.2).

Active social detachment. Avoidant personalities assume that the experiences to which they were exposed in early life will continue forever. Defensively, they narrow the range of activities in which they allow themselves to participate. By sharply circumscribing their life, they preclude the possibility of corrective experiences that might lead them to see that "all is not lost" and that there are kindly persons who will neither disparage nor humiliate them.

A further consequence of detaching themselves from others is that they are left to be preoccupied with their own thoughts and impulses. Limited to the inner world of stimuli, they reflect on and ruminate about the past, with all the discomforts it brings forth. Because their experiences have become restricted largely to thinking about past events, life becomes a series of duplications. As a consequence, avoidants are left to relive the painful experiences of earlier times rather than be exposed to new and different events that might alter their outlook and feelings. Moreover, these self-preoccupations serve only to further widen the breach between themselves and others. A vicious circle may take hold: the more they turn inward, the more they lose contact with the typical interests and thoughts of those around them. They become progressively more estranged from their environment, increasingly out of touch with reality and the checks against irrational thought provided by social contact and communication. Away from the controls and stabilizing influences of ordinary human interactions, they begin to lose their sense of balance and perspective, often feeling puzzled, peculiar, unreal, and "crazy."

TABLE 11.2 Self-Perpetuating Processes

AVOIDANT

Active Social Detachment
> Defensive narrowing precludes corrective experiences
> Preoccupations relive painful past
> Intensifies social estrangement

Suspicious and Fearful Behavior
> Evokes reciprocal disaffection
> Weakness attracts humilators
> Rebuff reinforces aversiveness

Emotional-Perceptual Hypersensitivity
> Sensitive to derogatory events
> Scanning encounters threats and fears
> Sensitivity deepens one's plight

Cognitive Interference
> Intrusive fears fragment and derail thoughts
> Ability to function is diminished
> Social communication becomes tangential and irrelevant

Suspicious and fearful behaviors.   Detached and mistrustful behaviors not only establish distance from others but evoke reciprocal reactions of disaffiliation and rejection. An attitude that communicates weakness, self-effacement, and fear invariably attracts those who enjoy deprecating and ridiculing others. Thus, the hesitant posture, suspicious demeanor, and self-deprecating attitudes of the avoidant will tend to evoke interpersonal responses that lead to further experiences of humiliation, contempt, and derogation—in short, a repetition of the past. Any apparent sensitivity to rebuff or obviously fearful and unassertive style will tend to evoke ridicule from peers, an experience that will only reinforce and intensify this personality's aversive inclinations.

Emotional and perceptual hypersensitivity.   Avoidant personalities are painfully alert to signs of deception, humiliation, and deprecation. As noted in an earlier case presentation, these patients detect the most minute traces of indifference or annoyance on the part of others and make the molehills of minor and passing slights into mountains of personal ridicule and condemnation. They are incredibly sensitive instruments for picking up and magnifying incidental actions and for interpreting them as indications of derision and rejection. This hypersensitivity functions well in the service of self-protection but fosters a deepening of the person's plight. As a result of their extensive scanning of the environment, avoidants actually increase the likelihood that they will encounter precisely those stimuli they wish most to avoid. Their exquisite antennae pick up and transform what most people overlook. In effect, their hypersensitivity backfires by becoming an instrument that brings to their awareness, time and again, the very pain they wish to escape. Their defensive vigilance thus intensifies rather than diminishes their anguish.

Intentional interference.   Avoidants must counter the flood of threatening stimuli they register as a consequence of their emotional and perceptual hypersensitivities. To assure a modicum of personal tranquillity, they engage constantly in a series of cognitive reinterpretations and digressions. They may actively block, destroy, and fragment their own thoughts, seeking to disconnect relationships among what they see, what meanings they attribute to their perceptions, and what feelings they experience in response. Defensively, then, they intentionally destroy the clarity of their thoughts by intruding irrelevant distractions, tangential ideas, and discordant emotions. This coping maneuver exacts its price. By upsetting the smooth and logical pattern of their cognitive processes, avoidants further diminish their ability to deal with events efficiently and rationally. No longer can they attend to the most salient features of their environment, nor can they focus their thoughts or respond rationally to events. Moreover, they cannot learn new ways to handle and resolve their difficulties because their thinking is cluttered and scattered. Social communications also take on a tangential and irrelevant quality, and they may begin to talk and act in an erratic and halting manner. In sum, in their attempt to diminish intrusively disturbing thoughts, they fall prey to a coping mechanism that further aggravates their original difficulties and ultimately intensifies their alienation from both themselves and others.

INTERVENTION GOALS

Avoidant disorders are among the most frequent that therapists encounter in their offices. As is evident from the preceding discussions, the prognosis for the avoidant personality is often quite poor. Not only are these persons' habits and attitudes pervasive and ingrained, as are all personality patterns, but many are trapped in environments that provide them with few of the supports and encouragements needed to reverse their lifestyles. A therapist with avoidant clients will be challenged not only to keep them in therapy but also to get beyond their tendency to reveal only what they believe will restrain the therapist from thinking ill or well of them. If the therapist manages to gain the client's trust, however, a strong alliance can be forged and progress can be made—given enough time, patience, and conscientious use of interventions.

Therapeutic intervention with avoidant patients has as its ultimate aim to reestablish balance within the pleasure-pain and active-passive polarities. The asymmetric focus within these domains leads to a clinical picture characterized by overly active avoidance of perceived threatening situations. Active search for psychic enhancement (pleasure) is notably absent. Therapeutic strategies need to be aimed at countering the patient's tendency to perpetuate a pattern of social withdrawal, perceptual hypervigilance, and intentional cognitive interference. Clinical work targeting the most salient of the domain dysfunctions can help alter their alienated self-image, aversive interpersonal conduct, vexatious object-representations, and the anguished mood that characterize these patients' psychic state (see Table 11.3).

Reestablishing Polarity Balances

Like the schizoid, the avoidant patient has marked difficulty experiencing pleasure. Unlike the schizoid, however, who has a lowered capacity to experience emotional distress as well as pleasure, the avoidant is hyperresponsive to anxiety-provoking stimuli. Avoidants' primary aim of avoiding humiliating interpersonal experiences precludes being exposed to interactions in which the affection for which they yearn can occur. Active withdrawal from situations they fear may be hurtful ensures that avoidants will rarely express their wishes even in nonintimate relationships. This leads to frustration of goals in general, as well as to feelings of loneliness. Typically, in their determination to avoid rejection and pain, avoidant personalities preclude from their repertoire of behaviors interactions that might result in personal gratification. A major therapeutic

TABLE 11.3 Therapeutic Strategies and Tactics for the Prototypal Avoidant Personality

STRATEGIC GOALS
Balance Polarities
Diminish anticipation of pain
Increase pleasure/enhancing polarity

Counter Perpetuations
Reverse social detachment
Diminish suspicious/fearful behavior
Moderate perceptual hypersensitivity
Undo intentional cognitive interference

TACTICAL MODALITIES
Adjust alienated self-image
Correct aversive interpersonal conduct
Remove vexatious objects

goal would thus be to increase avoidant patients' active focus on pleasurable stimuli, and to decrease their active avoidance of potentially painful stimuli.

Countering Perpetuating Tendencies

The characteristic active social detachment that avoidants employ as a defense against experiencing rebuff and criticism actually ensures that they experience no social interaction that serves to disconfirm their pessimistic expectations. An understanding of how their own actions solicit the very reactions from others that they so fear can help avoidants appreciate that they need to control their suspicious and fearful expectancies and behaviors in order for normal interaction to take place. Increased social contact can lead to nonthreatening encounters that can help reorganize their extreme schemata. Therapeutic intervention can provide patients with self-understanding, social skills, and the means to control or tolerate their symptoms of anxiety to help assure that their fledgling efforts to reach out for rewarding interaction will be successful.

Unfortunately, the wood that feeds the fire of withdrawal and suspicious behaviors is the very emotional and perceptual hypersensitivity that avoidants develop as a defense against potentially painful interactions. As their sensitivity escalates, all positives are seen as true positives. Their subjective identification of threat skyrockets so that avoidants spend much time and emotional energy avoiding and processing nonexistent personal assaults. An understanding of "normal" human behavior and the ability to differentiate among real, incidental, and imagined threats can allow more normal living to occur. Internal reference points according to which they can judge their own behavior need to be established so that they do not feel at the mercy of others' often unpredictable and irrational responses.

Once avoidants' hypersensitivities are reduced, they can begin to decrease their use of intentional cognitive interference as a defense against their (often misguided) painful conclusions about others' reactions. More realistic thought processes allow them to deal more effectively with their environments, learn from their surroundings, and communicate more profitably. Positive social interaction may serve, in turn, to further distract avoidants from the thoughts and impulses that preoccupy them. No longer limited to their inner world of impulses, they have material other than their past pain to ponder, and can develop more normative and adaptive attitudes toward their lives, allowing them to communicate with others and to feel less "unusual."

Identifying Domain Dysfunctions

The avoidant's predisposition and/or learning history lead to a clinical picture dominated by primary disturbances in self-image, interpersonal conduct, object-representations, and mood/temperament. The self is perceived as socially inept and self-achievements are devalued. The emotional suffering that accrues from social isolation and perceived rejection is seen as a justified natural consequence of personal inadequacy. Feelings of aloneness, and even depersonalization, are often reported. Increased social contact, assertiveness, improved social skills, and exploratory client-centered therapy can all direct the avoidant toward an improved self-image.

Aversive interpersonal conduct leads the avoidant to maintain social distance in the hope that privacy will ensure protection against anticipated humiliation and derogation. Cognitive, interpersonal, and other exploratory therapies can help the avoidant rework aversive schemata. Behavior modification programs may prove invaluable in providing avoidants with necessary social skills and incipient self-confidence. Together, these interventions help create more realistic and optimistic mental schemata about human relationships to replace the vexatious object-representations that characterize their mental framework. Pharmacologic intervention can also be considered to help ease anxiety that interferes with personal growth, effectively lowering the threshold at which avoidants may be cajoled into taking initiative with respect to their own lives.

Avoidants also need to learn to control their fretful expressive behavior in favor of a more relaxed and confident style that promotes rewarding relationships. Their distracted cognitive style interferes with fluid thinking and spontaneous communication. On an intrapsychic level, avoidants rely too heavily on fantasy as a regulatory mechanism to cope with environmental stress. Neither reveries nor isolation will promote adaptive resolution of problems or help strengthen the fragile morphologic organization of their coping system.

SELECTING THERAPEUTIC MODALITIES

It is important for the therapist working with an avoidant client to keep in mind that the avoidant will be hesitant to share feelings of shame or inadequacy with the therapist for fear of rejection. The best way to counter such client apprehension is with free-handed empathy and support. L.S. Benjamin (1993) points out that many avoidants find it particularly difficult to discuss maltreatment within their childhood family, as well as any negative feelings they have toward family members. This arises from the pressure many avoidants feel to be loyal to the family and its members, and from the accompanying transmitted belief that outsiders are "dangerous" and not to be trusted. Continued support and understanding are the therapist's only recourse against even this resistance. A protective, sanctuarylike therapeutic environment is the only one that is likely to draw the avoidant out of his or her shell.

Behavioral Techniques

At the behavioral level, avoidants manifest both aversive interpersonal conduct and fretful expressive behavior. *Behavior modification* may prove useful as a way to learn less fearful reactions to formerly threatening situations; in general, in vivo exposure is considered more effective than desensitization for symptoms of social anxiety. Behavioral management can be greatly facilitated by a variety of rather straightforward techniques, such as anxiety management, assertiveness and social skills training, and a variety of modeling opportunities, each directed at enhancing self-confidence and interpersonal skills. Before actually engaging in social interaction exercises, avoidant patients can be assigned preliminary *cognitive* tasks, such as self-monitoring of their withdrawal behavior to help clarify their inclination to avoid certain people or social situations. They can also be asked to keep a log of their self-deprecatory self-statements and physiological arousal. Anxiety management training can be very helpful. If past avoidant behavior has resulted in a failure to acquire critical social skills, then behavioral rehearsal will often improve assertiveness and behavioral fluidity. Once these tasks have been accomplished, hierarchical grading of social tasks in regard to anxiety-provoking potential (talking to a mailman vs. engaging in conversation with one's boss) can help organize the sequence of homework assignments. It is very important not to rush the patient through these steps. Initial success is critical in shifting the balance toward a more active stance with regard to procuring interpersonal pleasure and correcting aversive interpersonal conduct.

Interpersonal Techniques

The techniques above are especially useful as short-term adjunct interventions. More lasting change, however, requires additional techniques. *Interpersonal* therapy represents a prolonged effort toward healing through a *corrective emotional experience* with the therapist, ideally one that will generalize to contexts outside the therapy hour, as patients learn that they can succeed in the chances they take within treatment. Notably helpful in this regard is that most avoidants are able to relate comfortably to a select few persons. Clinicians who can model themselves to reflect the character of such "outsiders" may be able to provide the empathy and warm support needed to encourage patients to share the intimacies of their life as well as their personal feelings of shame, guilt, or inadequacy. As therapy begins to explore patients' long-term maladaptive patterns, eschewing statements or actions that expose patients' hypersensitivities, there is a reasonable likelihood that patients will also become increasingly self-accepting. The interpersonal approach outlined by L.S. Benjamin (1993) suggests a general sequence of strategic intervention the author has found to be clinically effective.

Once the patient's trust is gained through supportive reassurance and protection, the therapist can move the patient toward more functional behaviors by refusing to support avoidance and by encouraging assertive behavior. Examination of the effects of their own behavior can help avoidants sacrifice the safety of problematic patterns for the possibility of achieving enhancing experiences through more "risky" behavior, such as giving up a triangular relationship despite opening themselves up to the mercy of only one person with nowhere to turn for comfort. For example, a secret lover who provides comfort and is protective when a spouse is angry or withdrawn may be given up in favor of improving the relationship with the spouse.

Family or *couple* therapy can be very helpful for patients caught in a social environment that unwittingly supports avoidant behaviors (Carson, 1982; Kiesler, 1982). If the therapist is careful not to allow "trashing" in the name of communication to occur during the sessions, these techniques can help speed the healing process (L.S. Benjamin, 1993). *Group* approaches allow for forced exposure to strangers in an atmosphere of acceptance, and can help patients overcome painful social embarrassment in most therapeutic groups. Patients should not be forced into interacting, but rather should be allowed to observe from the sidelines until they feel ready to risk exposure. In groups that emphasize behavioral approaches, patients also have a unique opportunity to acquire and practice behavioral and social skills.

Cognitive Techniques

Avoidant patients can also profit from methods of *cognitive reorientation* designed to alter erroneous self-attitudes and distorted social expectancies. In an effort to change the dysfunctional schemata that underlie avoidant behavior, cognitive therapy focuses largely on clarifying for patients their pattern of "automatic thoughts" within the therapeutic relationship. This helps patients discover thinking errors they commit in everyday life that contribute to their dysphoria and self-defeating behaviors. These persons are notoriously difficult to engage in exploratory treatment methods in light of their strategy of avoiding fears and shames, especially their hypersensitivity to criticism. Not only do they avoid unpleasant experiences, but they also do their best not to think about matters that they experience as unpleasant or threatening. A useful step in this regard is to increase their tolerance for what they perceive as emotionally upsetting relationships or events. These difficulties arise most clearly in close or intimate relationships. Efforts should be utilized, such as through behavioral exposure, to help patients learn to tolerate minor degrees of disapproval or rejection. An important goal is enabling avoidants to recognize that difficulties in close relationships do not result in devastation and abandonment. Honest discussion of patients' feelings toward the therapist and their fears regarding the relationship are primary tools. As patients realize that the therapist (who serves as a mirror for other relationships) will not reject, abandon, or denigrate them despite exposure, they start to reformulate automatic thinking patterns and reestablish a measure of balance within their personality structure. In working toward this end, Beck and Freeman (1990a) suggest that patients can rate their therapist's feedback on a scale ranging from 0 to 100%, and thus monitor their own trust in the therapist as well as in the feedback provided. Beck and Freeman suggest that patients and therapists engage in "experiments" to evaluate the validity of their distorted cognitive schemata and automatic thoughts. For example, the therapist can ask patients if there is anything that they cannot disclose. Frequently, patients will express hesitation that can then be examined, and their fears of rejection can be confronted. Patients' fantasies about negative and rejecting therapist responses can be discussed and more realistic possibilities can be explored.

Self-Image Techniques

Considering therapy from the viewpoint of formal technique, a key approach is to assist patients in arranging a more rewarding environment, one that facilitates opportunities to enhance feelings of self-worth. In the beginning, self-enhancing therapeutic approaches of this type may be all avoidant patients can tolerate until they are capable of dealing comfortably with their more painful feelings. Early self-actualization is necessary, then, but not sufficient to produce therapeutic change. The element of trust is central to maintaining a continuous increment in feelings of self-worth. Although the client-centered/humanistic approach of Rogers can be extremely fruitful, the growth of feelings of self-esteem and self-worth must be evoked through therapist rapport-building techniques. There is some value in bringing experiential methods into play to assist patients in recognizing even the most subtle of feelings that certain circumstances elicit from them. In this way, it may be possible to demonstrate to patients which events and relationships elicit their painful and pleasurable feelings. As they rework these implicit reactions via cognitive methods, it may be possible subsequently for them to experience genuine therapeutic trust, a not insignificant element in their ultimate improvement.

Intrapsychic Techniques

Psychodynamic theories frame avoidant behavior as being driven by the shame of not measuring up to one's ego ideal, of being weak, defective, even disgusting. Treatment emphasizes a strongly empathic understanding of patients' experience of humiliation and embarrassment due to exposure both in front of the therapist and in their daily lives. Childhood memories are analyzed to clarify the roots of the disorder. Efforts are made to explore the underlying elements of the past that have led to feelings of rejection and shame. Therapy is facilitated as the patient learns to confront the source of these problematic feelings. Most patients, especially avoidants, have difficulty communicating the deeper origins of their current discomforts. Useful in this regard may be the exploration of their fantasies as they emerge in free association and transference communications. Even the slightist experience of fear or shame might be utilized to explore how the patient is "really" thinking and feeling. In this way, patients may develop a more accurate awareness of the events that provoke their dysphoric affect. Confrontation of feared situations should be attempted, as should be detailed exploration of anxiety-provoking fantasies, particularly in the context of transference feelings toward the therapist. These deeper and searching procedures of intrapsychic therapies can also be useful in reconstructing unconscious mechanisms that pervade all aspects of the patient's behavior, and of the communication style that contributes to or intensifies the avoidant's problems.

Pharmacologic Techniques

If social hypersensitivity is severe, and the fear of rejection and denigration puts the patient at risk for extreme behavioral withdrawal or the termination of treatment, possible benefits of *psychopharmacologic* intervention should be evaluated. It should be noted also that avoidant patients often shy away from medications owing to their habitual aversion to new experiences. Despite occasionally troubling side effects, there is evidence that their social anxiety may be very responsive to medications. For example, MAO inhibitors may be considered as a possible adjunct to behavioral methods, as well as other forms of psychological treatment. This medication has been found to be effective at times in controlling the symptoms of social phobia, and may allow the patient to experience a measure of initial treatment success when joined with behavioral intervention techniques. Beta blockers may also prove helpful in controlling symptoms of autonomic excitation such as sweating, trembling, and blushing, without any direct psychoactive effect. Brief episodes of panic may also be controlled with benzodiazepine anxiolytics. Serotonin uptake-inhibitor antidepressant medications may be especially effective in this regard, particularly when social anxiety symptoms are paramount. A clustering of several pharmacologic agents should be explored where possible to deal with patterns of a highly generalized nature. In this regard, a number of investigators suggest the use of benzodiazepines such as alprazolam. As will be elaborated later, many avoidants regress into psychoticlike fears and withdrawal; in these circumstances, it may prove fruitful to consider the use of an antipsychotic agent.

MAKING SYNERGISTIC ARRANGEMENTS

Any intervention plan is at risk for failure if the initial stages of the therapeutic interaction are not primarily supportive and aimed at fostering trust toward the therapist. With trust established, the therapist can help the patient to arrange for a rewarding environment and facilitate the discovery of opportunities that would enhance self-worth.

With continued therapy, the therapist can gradually shift to a slightly more confrontational style within the framework of a cognitive, interpersonal, psychodynamic, or behavioral intervention. In the course of any long-term individual exploratory psychotherapy aimed at helping patients get at the roots of their dysfunctional patterns, it is often advisable to make concomitant use of shorter-term behavioral techniques. More withdrawn patients can thus acquire the skills necessary for initial experiences of social success that instill hope and foster the motivation needed to tolerate the more painful aspects of therapy. Group therapy can be considered as a more benign and accepting social forum than avoidants normally encounter, one ripe for learning new attitudes and skills when the therapist considers the patient ready. Favorable response to anxiolytic medication may also allow highly symptomatic patients to tolerate new situations and more proactive social behavior. Especially in the initial stages, selectively combined interventions allow for positive reward gained by interacting socially in previously unthinkable ways, and for the formation of new schemata about self and others without the failure-inducing disruption caused by overwhelming anxiety.

After initial success with behavioral, interpersonal, or cognitive therapy, some patients may profit from family or couple therapy. These interventions are indicated for individuals who are embedded in social contexts that unwittingly help maintain their avoidant behavior and whose treatment may be facilitated by the development of a more supportive environment. As is suggested by Beck and Freeman (1990a), the therapist should work with the patient on a program designed to prevent relapse. Ongoing behavioral goals include establishing and improving friendships, behaving in appropriately assertive ways in different social contexts, and trying new experiences. These help maintain motivation and give patients a chance to monitor their own behavior. Patients can be taught to use anxiety as a signal to check for maladaptive automatic thoughts, to keep logs of avoidance-producing thinking and discrediting evidence against their own irrational beliefs, to plan strategies ahead of time for difficult situations, and to call the therapist for a booster session if all else fails.

TABLE 11.4   Avoidant Personality Disorder Subtypes

Hypersensitive: Intensely wary and suspicious; alternately panicky, terrified, edgy, and timorous, then thin-skinned, high-strung, petulant, and prickly.

MCMI 2A (P)

Self-Deserting: Blocks or fragments self-awareness; discards painful images and memories; casts away untenable thoughts and impulses; ultimately jettisons self (suicidal).

MCMI 2A 2B

Phobic: General apprehensiveness displaced with avoidable tangible precipitant; qualms and disquietude symbolized by repugnant and specific dreadful object or circumstances.

MCMI 2A-3

Conflicted: Internal discord and dissension; fears independence *and* dependence; unsettled; unreconciled within self: hesitating, confused, tormented, paroxysmic, embittered, unresolvable angst.

MCMI 2A-8A

Illustrative Cases

Avoidant characteristics often acquire subsidiary features as these persons begin to withdraw socially and experience critical and unsupportive responses from others. Research utilizing the MCMI (Millon, 1977, 1987b) shows that profiles including the avoidant pattern are shared most often with schizoid, dependent, depressive, negativistic, schizotypal, and paranoid personalities. When they begin to exhibit some of these associated personality features, the moods and actions that these patients manifest will provoke reactions that give a different coloration from the original traits that characterized the avoidant at the start. Insidiously developing features combine with the avoidant pattern and express themselves in a number of the subtypes discussed next (see Table 11.4).

AVOIDANT PERSONALITY: CONFLICTED TYPE
(AVOIDANT WITH NEGATIVISTIC TRAITS)

CASE 11.1, PEGGY R., 27

Presenting Picture: Peggy R., a graduate student in chemistry, was extremely uneasy regarding her teaching assistantship. Fortunately, she could "fool" everyone into believing her false confidence by spending most of her class time writing on the chalkboard, relying on her excellent knowledge of the subject matter, and "only talking when they have questions. But they *always* have questions!" Most of the time she was leading classes, she was nearly overwhelmed by the urge to run into her office and lock the door. Extremely fearful of rejection, Peggy had a great deal of difficulty, as well, relating to her peers within her program of study. Although she had several "friendly acquaintances," she stopped abruptly short of considering them friends. "If they really got to know me, they wouldn't like me," she remarked. Throughout the earlier stages of therapy, Peggy repeatedly confronted this central theme of not allowing any possible vulnerability, for everyone seemed to her to be set in her context only to judge her every move, and thereby discovering all of her inadequacies and her lack of autonomy.

Clinical Assessment: More than is typical of the ordinary avoidant, Peggy's behavior, that of a *conflicted avoidant,* was the struggle she faced between desiring detachment from others and fearing being independent. Peggy would have liked to be close and show affection, but anticipated experiencing intense pain and disillusionment. Complicating the concern about venturing into close relationships was her markedly deflated self-esteem. Thus, any effort to make a go at independence was constrained by the fear that it would fail and result in humiliation. Although she had no alternative but to depend on supporting persons and institutions, this behavior overlay deep resentments. Others had either turned against her or disapproved of her efforts to achieve autonomy. She was often petulant and negativistic, and on occasion would attack others for failing to recognize her need for affection and nurturance. The dependency security she sought was seriously jeopardized under these circumstances. To bind her conflictful feelings and anger, and thereby protect against humiliation and loss, she became anxious and withdrawn, experiencing a persistent and pervasive dysphoric mood. As evident from the foregoing, we found that Peggy's unresolvable angst was a blending of core avoidant features with those seen among negativistic personalities, both of which achieved prominent scores on the MCMI.

Peggy's discontent, outbursts, and moodiness frequently evoked humiliating reactions from others, and these rebuffs only served to reinforce her self-protective withdrawal. Every avenue of gratification seemed trapped in conflict. She could not act alone because of marked self-doubts; on the other hand, she could not depend on others because of a deep social mistrust. Disposed to anticipate disappointments, she often precipitated disillusionment through obstructive and negative behaviors. She reported feeling misunderstood, unappreciated, and demeaned by others; voiced a sense of futility about life; had a deflated self-image; and frequently referred to herself with contempt and deprecation. A depressive tone and anxious wariness are ever present, evident in erratic and conflictful displays of moodiness.

Unable to muster the wherewithal to overcome deficits and unable to achieve the support desired from others, Peggy remained embittered and conflicted, disposed to turn against herself, expressing feelings of unworthiness and uselessness. Expecting to be slighted or demeaned, she had learned to be watchful and on guard against the ridicule and contempt she anticipated from others. Looking inward offered her no solace because she saw none of the attributes admired in others in herself. This awareness intruded on her thoughts and interfered with effective behavior, upsetting her cognitive processes and diminishing her capacity to cope effectively with ordinary life tasks. During periods when stresses were minimal, she denied past resentments and attempted to portray an image of general well-being and contentment. These efforts, however, gave way readily under the slightest of pressures.

Anticipating rejection and deprecation, Peggy frequently jumped the gun with impulsive hostility. What we saw was a cyclical variation of constraint followed by angry acting-out, followed in turn by remorse and regret. These erratic emotions were not only intrinsically distressing, but they upset her capacity to cope effectively with everyday tasks. At times, unable to orient emotions and thoughts logically, she became lost in personal irrelevancies and autistic asides. This inability to order ideas and feelings in a consistent and relevant manner only further alienated her from others.

Synergistic Treatment Plan: Peggy's perpetuating tendencies included a hypervigilance that constantly searched for signs of rejection as well as the fear of inadequacy (weak in both *self* and *other* polarities). These tendencies had her constantly anticipating disappointment and avoiding an "unmasking" of what she perceived to be her pathetic shortcomings. Within this framework, it was obvious that she expended most of her energy as a sentinel, remarkably *active* in thwarting any possible damage to her already depleted and faulty image. It would be necessary to establish as safe and *empathic* an environment in therapy as possible, bolstering her *self-image* and confidence, to reduce this hypervigilance, and this would also be augmented *biophysically*. This would also give her a more favorable, controlled impression of her environment. As trust developed, it would be possible to question her defeatist *cognitive* beliefs and help her overcome *interpersonal* hostilities and instead augment social *behaviors*.

Therapeutic Course: A short-term therapy milieu was beneficial for Peggy. Though ideally she might have been guided to avoid anxiety-inducing situations, this was not possible given that these were directly related to her teaching assistantship. However, brief *supportive therapy* was successfully employed in helping Peggy with these pressures. Additionally, a *pharmacologic agent* (in this case, an anti-anxiety drug) was utilized. Defined *behavior modification* techniques were utilized to focus on socialization skills that could be augmented quickly. *Cognitive techniques* (Beck, Ellis) confronted her well-engrained inimical and disadvantageous thoughts and expectations. Peggy's relationship skills were bolstered by employing a number of *interpersonal treatment techniques* (e.g., Klerman, Benjamin), and a marked improvement was noted with her peers and students. These methods were doled out judiciously, however, as Peggy was so fearful of failure, and she tended to routinely feel guilty and depressed. It was most important to stabilize her vast mood fluctuations, as this precluded most setbacks. Also important was a diligent eye focused on the suitability of goals, as intangible aims would most likely trigger a relapse. The initial stages were directed entirely at building Peggy's trust. This was accomplished with short-term procedures aimed at directing her attention to her positive traits, thus enhancing her self-image.

A major focus with Peggy was to thwart any decompensation periods from evolving into an anxiety or depressive disorder. At the same time, vigilance was necessary in detecting any rash acting-out behavior (such as suicide gestures). Peggy was impulsive at times and sought attention via dramatic avenues. Because she entered treatment in an agitated state, the reduction of her anxieties and guilt was an early goal of short-term treatment.

Because of her confusion and indeterminance, Peggy had difficulty with trust issues, especially with the therapist. Needing reassurance but fearful of interpersonal risk, she required copious measures of warmth and attention in the therapeutic relationship. Because she was engaged in this manner from the very outset of therapy, there was little need to "test" his motives. In allying with the therapist, the collaborative effort focused on reducing stress. Family techniques were essential, and fortunately, her family was quite helpful. In situations such as Peggy's where the family is not motivated, treatment frequently calls for more intensive techniques to reduce the possibility of setbacks, and treatment must progress very quickly to ensure some measure of improvement. With Peggy, the most significant setback was her initial wish to withdraw from treatment before she was asked to confront painful feelings. This was overcome with a nurturant and empathic attitude on the part of the therapist, which moderated her belief that she would automatically be rejected. Otherwise, this belief would have led her to pull back and stifle otherwise gratifying experiences. The cognitive reorientation approach short-circuited her tendency to preliminarily defeat her chances to experience stimulating events.

AVOIDANT PERSONALITY: HYPERSENSITIVE TYPE
(AVOIDANT WITH PARANOID TRAITS)

CASE 11.2, RANDY F., 27

Presenting Picture: Randy F., a graduate student in mathematics and computer science, presented a mixed set of circumstances within his program of studies. He spent most of his time alone in the computer lab working on new programs, which was most enjoyable because he felt able to function without anyone looking over his shoulder or judging him. However, his duties also included a teaching assistantship, which was a constant source of consternation, as he felt he constantly ran the risk of being made to look like a fool in front of a large audience. This was a very difficult task, as *any* interaction was a source of frustration and worry for Randy. He lived alone, attended functions alone, and found it very difficult to make conversation with anyone. Perhaps what made Randy seek counseling was the painful awareness of his inability to socialize at a party hosted by a professor. As he watched other students in his program fraternize, he suffered in silence, wanting desperately to join his colleagues but at a loss as to how to go about doing so. The best feeling in the world, he stated, was getting out of there.

Clinical Assessment: In what has been termed the *hypersensitive avoidant* (Millon & Davis, 1996a), we see many of the general features characteristic of the basic personality core, but in an accentuated form. Randy's behavior was characterized by a high-strung and prickly manner, a hyperalertness to signs of rejection and abuse, and an excessive weariness that led to a peevish and wary attitude toward his environment. As such, he displayed a fusion of basic avoidant characteristics permeated with features more central to the paranoid personality.

In addition to his pervasive apprehensiveness, there were intense and variable moods that were noted by prolonged periods of edginess and self-deprecation. The expectancy that people will be rejecting and disparaging precipitated profound gloom at one time, and irrational negativism at another. Despite a longing to relate and be accepted, Randy constrained his needs, protectively withdrew from threats to his fragile emotional balance, and maintained a safe distance from any emotional involvements. Retreating defensively, he become remote from others and from needed sources of support. A surface apathy was exhibited in these efforts to damp down or deaden excess sensitivities. Nevertheless, intense contrary feelings occasionally broke through in peevish and immature outbursts.

Thin-skinned and deeply resentful, Randy found it difficult to bind his anger toward those whom he felt had been unsupportive, critical, and disapproving. The little security he possessed, however, was threatened when these bristly feelings and resentments were discharged. Easily offended but desiring to protect against further loss, he made repeated efforts to resist expressing anger, albeit unsuccessfully. If ever not withdrawn and drifting in peripheral social roles, he may have been unpredictable, irritably edgy, and negativistic, engaged at times in wrangles and disappointments with others, vacillating among moments of being agreeable, sullenly passive, and irritably angry. These difficulties would frequently be complicated by genuine expressions of guilt and contrition that were mixed with feelings of being misunderstood, unappreciated, and demeaned by others.

Randy had learned to be watchful, on guard against ridicule, and ever alert to signs of censure and derision. He detected the most minute traces of annoyance expressed by others and made the molehill of a minor and passing slight into a mountain of personal ridicule and condemnation. He had learned that good things don't last, that affection would capriciously end, followed by disappointment and rejection.

Synergistic Treatment Plan: Trust building was of foremost importance for this highly suspicious and very sensitive man, due to his *active* evasion of his own salient *painful* experience and others' perceived derogatory views of him. Also, it was most prudent to take measures to adjust discomforting pressures in his immediate context wherever possible. In creating this "safe haven" within therapy, it would then be feasible to begin exploring his tendencies to *cognitively* overinterpret behaviors of others, which would likely lead to a gradual discovery of a distorted *self* view as constitutionally weak, irreversibly flawed, and pervasively inadequate. As this understanding evolved, it would be crucial to remain *supportive* and continuously express an *empathic* stance, while fortifying his self-image. As confidence would grow and *pleasure* would become tangible rather than an out-of-reach abstraction, it would be a natural progression to encourage a more sociable and extroverted character with practice and experience in *behaviors* and *interpersonal* modalities.

Therapeutic Course: Short-term techniques were employed to help Randy feel secure in therapy. First, it was possible for him to avoid certain environmental pressures that aggravated his anxieties and dejection. *Supportive therapy* was employed to assuage anxiety from those sources that could not be avoided. Similarly, *pharmacologic agents* were considered, but Randy did not feel comfortable with this suggestion. Circumscribed *behavioral modification* methods were explored to focus on social behavior that could be strengthened in a relatively short time period. *Cognitive techniques,* specifically those of Beck and Ellis, were used to confront him with the obstructive and self-defeating character of his beliefs and expectations. His relations with significant others were strengthened by employing several *interpersonal* treatment techniques (e.g., Klerman, Benjamin). Such approaches had to be handled cautiously, however, as Randy frequently risked feeling that he was a failure and tended to become unduly guilt-ridden, depressed, and even suicidal. Of great benefit was to stabilize him and help him rein in his vacillations of mood and behavior. In this way, the possibility of setbacks or deterioration in his condition was diminished.

Toward the goal of reducing the likelihood of a relapse or retrogression, the therapist avoided setting goals too high or pressing changes too quickly. Initial efforts were primarily directed at building Randy's trust in the therapeutic relationship and the process of therapy. Short-term procedures designed to orient his attentions to his positive traits and to enhance his confidence and self-esteem were highly productive and worthwhile.

A major goal throughout the scope of treatment was to forestall repetitive decompensation into anxiety and depressive disorders. Also requiring focused attention was the need to anticipate suicide attempts. Randy had tendencies to act impulsively when he felt guilty, needed attention, or sought a dramatic form of retribution. The therapist guided him into recognizing the sources and character of his ambivalence and helped to establish a more realistic and optimistic outlook on life. Because he entered treatment in an agitated state, the reduction of his anxieties and guilt was an early goal of short-term treatment.

Because of an intense ambivalence between his desire for reassurance and nurturance and his fear of trusting an unknown person, Randy required a thoroughly warm and attentive attitude on the part of the therapist. Because he was engaged early on, he was not disposed to employ repetitive maneuvers to test the sincerity and motives of the therapist. Efforts were made to reduce the stressors in his environments both at home and school. Work with family members was necessary, and had they not been optimally motivated, treatment may have called for more intensive techniques to reduce the possibility of setbacks. Because of the preceding reasons, treatment had to progress more rapidly to ensure that a significant measure of remedial improvement could occur. There was also the possibility of Randy's withdrawal from treatment should he have resisted facing the humiliation of confronting painful memories and feelings. With a nurturant and empathic attitude, the therapist was able to overcome the patient's fear of reexperiencing false hopes and disappointments. The warmth and understanding of the therapist moderated Randy's expectation that others would be rejecting, leading him to pull back, thereby cutting off experiences that might have proved gratifying had they been completed. What was desired was to decrease his anticipation of loss that may have prompted him into a self-fulfilling prophecy. Without focused attention, he may have defeated the chance to experience events that could promote change and growth. It was this pattern that a cognitive reorientation treatment approach successfully interrupted.

AVOIDANT PERSONALITY: PHOBIC TYPE
(AVOIDANT WITH DEPENDENT TRAITS)

CASE 11.3, KATHERINE C., 42

Presenting Picture: Katherine C. was constantly frustrated by the plethora of little things that got in the way of her achieving goals or pursuing happiness. By little things, she was referring to unknown entities surrounding her, ranging from a frayed seat in a taxi to the multitude of strangers she dodged while walking down the street. It seemed as though anything that might take her by surprise or be construed as unusual was a source of discomfort and a reason to refrain from either a planned activity or a necessary function. Getting to the therapist's office, of course, was no exception, given the ride on the "dirty subway." However, with much effort, she arrived. She complained that this had always been the case, but it had become much worse in the past 10 years or so. It had effectively permeated nearly every facet of her life, making it impossible for her to accomplish anything from the simplest task to those she really wanted to do. Most notably, it prevented her from approaching a love interest for nearly two years. When she finally found the valor, not only was it one month prior to her moving away, but she found herself creating and finding aspects of this man that would force her into a repetitive attraction/repulsion pattern. She was continuously caught between admiring and respecting him, and finding small imperfections that would cause severe discomfort for her within the relationship.

Clinical Assessment: Phobic syndromes are seen among many and diverse personality types. Some are active and energetic, expressing their fears in rapid and dramatic ways. Those who are more constrained may show a motor restlessness, a general worrisomeness about being exposed as weak and inadequate. Personalities of a more irritable nature seem perennially on edge, even when feared objects are not present; their imagination does not permit them a moment of rest or refuge. Others, perhaps of a more compulsive variety, seek to bury their anxieties behind their public reserve but, under close observation, can be seen as tense and anxious. Katherine, a *phobic avoidant,* rarely achieved freedom from her state of generalized anxiety. Seeking to limit the many sources of her anguish, she was disposed to finding highly specific phobic precipitants that, though fewer in number, almost invariably overwhelmed her defenses and undid her psychic controls.

When faced with the phobic object, Katherine also experienced a feeling of powerlessness against forces that seemed to surge from within herself, an intense and panicky feeling of terror and disorganization. A rush of irrational impulses and bizarre thoughts would carry her away. More typically, however, there was an inability to focus, a loss in the ability to distinguish the safe from the unsafe or the relevant from the irrelevant. This distress continued to mount as she became self-consciously aware of her growing tensions and her inability to surmount them.

Phobic avoidants are usually a mixture of dependent and avoidant personalities. Both personality types are very desirous of close personal relationships, but avoidants fear or do not trust others. Dependents are not only desirous of intimate relationships, but need them and dread their loss. When facing the possibility of such loss, the anxieties of dependents become intense, even overwhelming, mirroring the everyday state in which avoidants live. Mixed avoidant/dependents such as Katherine hesitate to exhibit these fears, lest they precipitate what they dread. Instead of feeling trapped between desire and loss, she turned her attentions to finding a symbolic substitute, some object or event onto which she could displace and funnel her anxieties. These phobic objects enabled her to redirect and discharge her fears, while neither being conscious of them nor having to deal with them forthrightly. Moreover, by maintaining a distance from her trivial phobic replacement, she could tolerate the loss of the symbol that served as a substitute for what she desperately wished to keep.

As just noted, the phobic experience was likely to signify a psychic displacement and condensation of Katherine's internal and generalized anxiety onto a symbolic external object. She did not neutralize or dilute her omnipresent anxiety but merely diverted it into a well-circumscribed and potentially avoidable external source. In this way, she blocked from conscious awareness the deeper and hidden intrapsychic reason for her anxiety. Whereas this mechanism works for most other personality types, it is only partially successful in the phobic avoidant. Here, in particular, the objects or events to which Katherine displaced had a clear symbolic significance. Whereas externalization enables most patients to cope with the experience of anxiety, Katherine did so with limited success in that the symbolic object often directly represented the more pervasive sources of her anxiety. Thus, she was especially prone to experience social phobias, a fear of being exposed and humiliated in public settings. As we know, the primary source of avoidants' anxieties is their anticipation and fear of personal rejection and humiliation.

In contrast with other personalities, the phobias of avoidants such as Katherine tend to be private affairs. For her, the symptom was frequently not designed to solicit social attention and support, because she was convinced that such attentions would only bring forth ridicule and abuse. Dreading further social humiliation, she frequently searched out tangential and innocuous external objects so as to keep her phobias hidden and personal. Nevertheless, there may have been much to be gained by fearing something explicit and defined. Although she would desire to shroud her phobia in a measure of secrecy, lest she be further humiliated, where possible she might also have attempted to use her distress to gain a degree of protection and security among those who are partially supportive. In this way, Katherine may have successfully distanced herself from anxiety-producing situations, while also having a degree of forbearance from others.

Perhaps the process of finding a phobic object represented a cry for compassion for Katherine, a desire to locate little fears, self-created of course, and to make instrumental use of them as a means of deterring the rejection and abandonment threats of otherwise nonsupportive persons. Although the phobic character is viewed in the analytic literature as signifying a fear of the desired object, this intrapsychic reversal is likely to apply to personalities other than the avoidant.

Synergistic Treatment Plan: Katherine needed to be able to examine her considerable fears of social humiliation and distrust in others versus her strong need for love and attention, but had built a protective wall against facing these difficulties. Creation of an empathic environment within therapy needed to precede any further techniques, but it would not be enough for lasting change. As trust developed, Katherine's perpetuations (fearful actions and emotional hypersensitivity) could be *cognitively* challenged, and *interpersonal* and *behavioral* methods could work toward creating a feeling of autonomy and competence (balancing *self-other* difficulties as well as the conflicting *passive-active* polarities). Continued work in *self-image* techniques would form the basis for an improved *pleasure* orientation while moderating the tendency to constantly be watchful and fearful of rejection and detraction.

Therapeutic Course: A major thrust of therapy for Katherine was enhancing her social interest and competence. She was not pushed beyond tolerable limits; rather, careful and well-reasoned *cognitive methods* (e.g., Beck, Meichenbaum) fostered the development of more accurate and focused styles of thinking. In addition to working toward the extinction of false beliefs about herself and the attitudes of others toward her, the therapist was alert to spheres of life in which the patient possessed positive emotional inclinations. He encouraged Katherine, through *interpersonal methods* and *behavior skill development* techniques, to undertake activities consonant with these tendencies.

Although the success of short-term methods may have justified an optimistic outlook, Katherine's initial receptivity could have created the misleading perception that further advances and progress would be rapid. Care was taken to prevent early treatment success from precipitating a resurfacing of her established ambivalence between wanting social acceptance and fearing that she was placing herself in a vulnerable position. Enabling her to give up her long-standing expectations of disappointment required "booster" sessions following initial, short-term successes. *Support* was provided to ease her fears, particularly her feeling that her efforts may not have been sustainable and would inevitably result in social disapproval again.

Psychopharmacologic treatment was utilized in conjunction with the above approach. Trial periods with a number of agents were explored to determine whether any effectively increased her energy and affectivity. Such agents were used with caution, however, because they may have activated feelings that Katherine was ill-equipped to handle. As noted, attempts to cognitively reorient her problematic attitudes were useful in motivating interpersonal sensitivity and confidence. Likewise, short-term techniques of behavioral modification were valuable in strengthening the patient's social skills. *Group* and *family* methods may have been useful in encouraging and facilitating her acquisition of constructive social attitudes. In those benign settings, she may have begun to alter her social image and develop motivation and skills for a more effective interpersonal style. Combining these short-term programs with individual treatment sessions may have aided in forestalling untoward recurrences of the discomfort she experienced.

Focused treatment efforts for this introversive woman were directed toward countering her withdrawal tendencies. Minimally introspective and evincing diminished affect and energy, Katherine had to be prevented, through circumscribed therapies, from becoming increasingly isolated from others, were they discomforting or benign. Energy was invested to enlarge her social world owing to her tendencies to pursue with diligence only those activities required by her job or by her family obligations. By shrinking her interpersonal milieu, she precluded exposure to new experience. Of course, this was her preference, but such behavior only fostered her isolated and withdrawn existence. To prevent such backsliding and a relapse, the therapist ensured the continuation of all constructive social activities as well as potential new ones. Otherwise, Katherine may have become increasingly lost in asocial and fantasy preoccupations. Excessive social pressure, however, was avoided because Katherine's tolerance and competencies in this area were rather limited. Initial brief, focused treatment techniques aided her in developing more skills in this area.

AVOIDANT PERSONALITY: SELF-DESERTING TYPE
(AVOIDANT WITH DEPRESSIVE TRAITS)

CASE 11.4, ALLISON N., 28

Presenting Picture: Allison was a community librarian, a woman so shy that her supervisor persuaded her to seek counseling. Though most of her duties revolved around stocking books rather than patron assistance, her position was in jeopardy owing to reticence and her habit of mumbling in response to what few patron information requests she did receive. In session, the therapist inquired as to what sorts of activities she enjoyed, to which she responded, "I used to like cafes and people-watching." Allison explained that she would like to be able to talk to and relate better with others, but she was petrified to make such a connection, and initiating a conversation in such a setting was beyond hope for her. The people in such public places were going about their "fulfilling" lives, and Allison couldn't keep up. She used to imagine what these fulfilling lives must be like, as it was easier to daydream about such things than to pursue them. She also disclosed, in an early session, that she had worked for an elementary school library until recently, but found that she "couldn't escape" in such a setting. She not only felt intruded on by the children's inquisitive nature, but couldn't "escape herself" in such a setting.

Clinical Assessment: As with other personalities of this type, Allison, a *self-deserting avoidant,* drew more and more into herself as a means of avoiding the discomforts of relating to others. In so doing, she found herself increasingly aware of the psychic contents of her inner world. Whereas she may have used fantasy initially to make her life more bearable, fantasies often brought no surcease. She began to recognize that turning inward only centered her thoughts on the misery of her life and the pain and anguish of past experiences. Although spared the difficulties of public exposure and personal humiliation, she had not been successful in avoiding her inner sorrows and torment. There were moments, of course, when her fantasies provided her with fulfilling images and longings, but these became fewer and fewer over time.

Increasingly confused about where to turn, Allison felt like a melancholy outsider, not only lacking in intimate and warm relationships, but also a person of minimal value to herself. What we see in this process is the merging of avoidant and depressive personality features, an amalgamation of social aversion and self-devaluation. Although she had created a protective barrier from her real world, the inner world into which Allison had withdrawn proved to be no less problematic and disparaging. Totally interiorized, she could no longer escape from what made her withdraw into herself in the first place. Subject to her own inescapable fantasies, Allison's anguish mounted increasingly. More and more, she could not tolerate herself, and more and more, she sought to undo her own self-conscious awareness.

Seeking to ensure that nothing would get to her, Allison not only distanced from the outer world, but increasingly blocked awareness from her own thoughts and feelings. She had now become self-abandoning, increasingly neglectful of her very being, jettisoning both her psychic and physical well-being, perhaps becoming increasingly incompetent, exerting herself minimally, and ultimately failing to fulfill even the barest acts of self-care. Some self-deserting avoidants are plunged into despair and driven toward suicide, deserting their own selves in order to jettison the anguish and horror within themselves. Others, like Allison, regress into a state of affectlessness, an emotional numbness in which they become completely disconnected from themselves. This disconnection and self-desertion grew into a habitual way of life, a way of remaining in flight from both her outer and inner realities.

This flight from cognitive self-awareness resulted in a splitting of her consciousness, a breaking up into parts of what was once interconnected, a now random set of exchangeable pieces. It is at this point of self-fragmentation and cognitive disorganization that we see the blending of the avoidant style and the schizotypal structure. As these regressions and fragmentations proceeded, Allison first became an outside spectator, observing from without the drama of her transformation. She is partially connected to both herself and others by virtue of remaining a nonparticipant onlooker.

Synergistic Treatment Plan: Allison needed to be reassured *nondirectively* that by engaging in a therapeutic relationship, she would enter a secure and nurturing milieu, as her significantly diminished image of *self,* as well as her uneasy posture with *others,* made trust and confidence dubious constructs at best. As objectives of therapy would become tangible and less abstract, treatment would center on diminishing Allison's anticipation of *pain* through *cognitive* and *interpersonal* measures, eventually leading to an augmentation of *pleasure* in later stages through more *existential* modalities. It would be necessary, as well, from the very early stages of treatment, to undo Allison's perpetuating tendency to hold her environment zealously at arm's length due to her constitutional hypersensitivity to disparagement, distorted suspicions of the actions of others, and anticipations of rejection (a conflicting *active/passive* tendency).

Therapeutic Course: A first goal in therapy with Allison was to demonstrate that the potential gains of therapy were real and that they should motivate her rather than serve as a deterrent. She feared that therapy would reawaken what she viewed as false hopes; that is, it reminded her of the humiliation she experienced when she offered her trust to others but received rejection in return. By *nondirectively* acknowledging these fears, she was gradually able to find a modest level of comfort without having to distance herself from the therapist, learning to deal more effectively with her fears while maintaining a better level of adjustment than the ones to which she has become accustomed.

In a short-term *cognitive-behavioral* approach, attention was usefully directed to Allison's social hesitation, anxious demeanor, and self-deprecating actions, attitudes, and behavior that could be altered so as not to evoke the humiliation and derogation they had in the past. Cognitive efforts to reframe the basis of her sensitivity to rebuff or her fearful and unassertive behavior (e.g., Beck, Ellis) minimized and diminished not only her aversive inclinations but her tendency to relapse and regress.

More probing yet circumscribed and brief treatment procedures were useful in unearthing the roots of Allison's anxieties and confronting those assumptions and expectations that pervaded many aspects of her behavior. *Family* techniques were employed as well to moderate destructive patterns of communication that contributed to or intensified her interpersonal problems. *Interpersonal* techniques (e.g., Benjamin) and *group therapy* assisted her in learning new attitudes and skills in a more benign and accepting social setting than she normally encountered.

Focused techniques also addressed Allison's tendencies to demean her self-worth and to mistrust others. Short-term *supportive* methods were used to counteract her reluctance to sustain a consistent therapeutic relationship. As noted, maneuvers designed to test the sincerity of the therapist were evident. A warm and empathic attitude was necessary because Allison was likely to fear facing her feelings of unworthiness and because she sensed that her coping defenses were weak. The clinician drew on Allison's strengths to prevent her from withdrawing from treatment before any real gains were made. Cognitive procedures were used to explore the contradictions in her feelings and attitudes. Without proper reframing, there may have been a seesaw struggle, with periods of temporary progress followed by retrogression. Genuine short-term gains were possible, but only with careful work, a building of trust, and enhancement of Allison's sense of self-worth.

Another realm worthy of brief intervention was associated with Allison's extensive scanning of the environment. By doing this, she increased the likelihood that she would encounter those stimuli she wished to avoid. Her exquisite antennae picked up and transformed what most people overlooked. Again, using appropriate cognitive methods, Allison's hypersensitivity was prevented from backfiring, that is, becoming an instrument that constantly brought to awareness the very pain she wished to escape. Reorienting her focus and her negative interpretive habits to ones that were more ego-enhancing and optimistic in character reduced her self-demeaning outlook, intensified her positive experiences, and diminished her anguish.

Resistances and Risks

Because of their basic mistrust of others, avoidants are unlikely to be motivated either to seek or to sustain a therapeutic relationship. Should they agree to treatment, it is probable that they will engage in maneuvers to test the sincerity and genuineness of the therapist's feelings and motives. Most often, they will terminate treatment long before remedial improvement has occurred. This tendency to withdraw from therapy stems not only from their doubts and suspicions regarding the therapist's integrity, their fear of social rejection and disapproval by the therapist, but also from their unwillingness to face the humiliation and anguish involved in confronting painful memories and feelings. They sense intuitively that their defenses are weak and tenuous and that to face directly their feeling of unworthiness, much less their repressed frustrations and impulses, will simply overwhelm them, driving them into unbearable anxieties and even to (as they fear) "insanity."

To add to these fears, the potential gains of therapy may not only fail to motivate avoidants but may actually serve as a deterrent, reawakening what these personalities view as "false hopes," reminding them of the dangers and humiliations they experienced when they tendered their affections to others but received rejection in return. Having found a modest level of comfort by detaching themselves from others, they would rather let matters stand, keep to the level of adjustment to which they are accustomed, and not "rock the boat" they have so tenuously learned to sail.

When avoidants enter a therapeutic relationship, the therapist must take great pains not to push matters too hard or too fast. Among other things, patients may feel they have but a fragile hold on reality. The therapist should seek, gently and carefully, to build a sense of genuine trust. Gradually, attention may be turned to patients' positive attributes, addressing these as a means of building confidence and enhancing feelings of self-worth. Therapy is likely to be a slow and arduous process, requiring the reworking of long-standing anxieties and resentments, bringing to consciousness the deep roots of mistrust, and, in time, enabling patients to reappraise these feelings more objectively. On the other hand, the astute therapist also has to take care that warm empathic behavior does not result in patients regarding the therapeutic relationship as so satisfying that it becomes an end in itself rather than a base for learning and venturing into other relationships. A therapist must also keep in mind throughout the therapeutic process that patients' intellectual "understanding" of problems is not enough to solve them; behavioral progress must not be neglected (L.S. Benjamin, 1993).

CHAPTER TWELVE

Treating Depressive
Personality Patterns

The elucidation of the comorbidity of personality traits/disorders and mood disorders is of both theoretical and clinical importance. Major depression is among the most common reasons in the general population for seeking psychiatric help and hospitalization. Clarification of the interrelationship between personality and depressive symptomatology can have important implications in psychotherapeutic and psychopharmacologic interventions. An increased understanding of this relationship can also help clarify the heterogeneous nature of depressive illness and better delineate the ways in which these syndromes and personality disorders interact and modify each other.

The construct of a depressive personality disorder was extensively discussed in the *DSM-IV* Personality Work Group. It was concluded that the depressive personality be included as an enduring type of psychological disorder that evinces a relatively early onset, demonstrates a fairly stable and long-term course, and exhibits its many clinical features across diverse situations over time.

In prior *DSMs*, the notion of a personality variant of depressive character was conceptualized in part by the introduction of a construct termed *dysthymic disorder* (previously, the depressive neurosis). However, it was soon recognized that the dysthymic construct was rather heterogeneous, necessitating differentiations into primary and secondary, as well as early- and late-onset subtypes. Furthermore, the criteria employed for dysthymia emphasized mood symptomatology rather than a diverse set of personality traits. Moreover, the symptoms elaborated in the dysthymic category were largely of a somatic or vegetative character, rather than cognitive or interpersonal in nature. The desire was expressed that a depressively centered disorder be introduced whose symptoms were less severe, more social in character, and more prolonged, if not lifelong, as compared to those encompassed in the dysthymic diagnosis. The introduction of the *self-defeating/masochistic* disorder was provisionally made in part in *DSM-III-R* to achieve these goals. Not only has the self-defeating/masochistic personality disorder been dropped from the most recent manual, a decision not shared by the author of this book, but the depressive symptomatology it encompassed required that its features be intentionally provoked by others in response to the individual's desire to elicit punitively rejecting responses. Because of this focus, as well as other reasons, it was decided that criteria be introduced, albeit provisionally, to represent a "purer" or prototypal variant of a *depressive personality disorder*. It is to elaborate this disorder that we have chosen to include the depressive prototype in the present chapter, an inclusion the author believes to be consistent with theory, clinical observation, and an extensive literature over the past many centuries.

Millon and Davis (1996a) have recently outlined some of the key features of the disorder in terms of his polarity schema. The clinical derivations of this formulation constitute the major body of this chapter. Figure 12.1 portrays the polarity model; the text of the chapter outlines the elements of the disorder in terms of its clinical domains, predisposing background, and therapeutic interventions. A brief summary of the clinical characteristics of the disorder is noted below, following which the features of the polarity model will be portrayed:

> Characteristics include glumness, pessimism, lack of joy, the inability to experience pleasure, and motoric retardation. There has been a significant loss, a sense of giving up, and a loss of hope that joy can be retrieved. Notable is an orientation to pain, despair regarding the future, a disheartening and woebegone outlook, an irreparable and irretrievable state of affairs in which what might have been is no longer possible.
>
> This personality experiences pain as permanent with pleasure no longer considered possible. What experiences or chemistry can account for such persistent or pervasive sadness? Clearly, there are biological dispositions to take into account. The evidence favoring a constitutional predisposition is strong, much of it favoring genetic factors. The thresholds involved in permitting pleasure or sensitizing one to sadness vary appreciably. Some individuals are inclined to pessimism and a disheartened outlook. Similarly, experience can condition a hopeless orientation. A significant loss, a disconsolate family, a barren environment, and hopeless prospects can all shape the depressive character style. (p. 11)

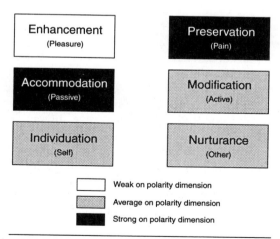

Figure 12.1   Status of the depressive personality prototype in accord with the Millon Polarity Model.

If we review the theoretically generated polarity model, as illustrated in Figure 12.1, we should note a strong representation in both the *preservation* polar extreme and the *accommodating* adaptational style. What this signifies is an overconcern with pain and anguish and secondarily, that the person has "given up," essentially succumbing to what is judged to be the inevitability of continuing suffering and misery. Despite important similarities, this depressive pattern contrasts in significant ways from the schema representing the avoidant personality. In both personality disorders there is a centering on preservation and pain reduction; similarly, in both disorders there is an inattention to the pleasures and gratifications that enhance life. The core distinction is that the avoidant actively seeks to minimize pain by anticipating its eventuality and taking steps to distance from or avoid that possibility. By contrast, the depressive no longer attempts to avoid the anguish and despair of life. Rather, he or she has accepted it as if it were inevitable and insurmountable. Depressives remain passive, resigned to the distressing reality they have suffered, no longer seeking to eschew it, but to surrender to it.

CLINICAL PICTURE

There are several aspects of the depressive personality that can be usefully differentiated for preliminary diagnostic purposes. The first phase of this assessment process attempts to delineate eight prototypal domains in which the clinical features of the depressive can be separately analyzed and described (see Table 12.1).

Prototypal Diagnostic Domains

As in all of the chapters of this text, we have sorted the various components of each disordered personality's traits and characteristics into eight domains, from those that manifest themselves in the overt behavior of the individual to those that are essentially hidden from observation but may be discerned inferentially and measured biologically (see Figure 12.2).

Disconsolate expressive behavior.   It is difficult not to recognize the disconsolate nature of depressives' appearance. Their posture conveys a deeply forlorn and heavyhearted quality. Their speech is somber, woebegone, if not grief-stricken in its character of expression. The tone of their voice seems irremediably dispirited and discouraged, and they portray a visual image of unresolvable hopelessness and wretchedness.

It can be said unquestionably that the depressive shows little initiative or spontaneity. Although answering questions posed in the interview process, depressives tend not to offer information on their own; moreover, what they do say has little variety. For the most part, speech is halting and uncertain. There is a slow, draggy element to all aspects of the depressed expressive behavior. Responses and movements take a long time, and even among those who are inclined to be agitated and irritable, there is a marked reduction in purposeful or intentional behaviors. Much of their activity appears as if in slow motion.

Defenseless interpersonal conduct.   Depressive personalities evince a constant state of feeling vulnerable, assailable, and unprotected. They act as if they were defenseless

TABLE 12.1 Clinical Domains of the Depressive Personality Prototype

Behavioral Level

(F) *Expressively Disconsolate* (e.g., appearance and posture conveys an irrelievably forlorn, somber, heavy-hearted, woebegone, if not grief-stricken quality; irremediably dispirited and discouraged, portraying a sense of permanent hopelessness and wretchedness).

(F) *Interpersonally Defenseless* (e.g., owing to feeling vulnerable, assailable, and unshielded, will beseech others to be nurturant and protective; fearing abandonment and desertion, will not only act in an endangered manner, but seek if not demand assurances of affection, steadfastness, and devotion).

Phenomenological Level

(F) *Cognitively Pessimistic* (e.g., possesses defeatist and fatalistic attitudes about almost all matters, sees things in their blackest form and invariably expects the worst; feeling weighed down, discouraged, and bleak, gives the gloomiest interpretation of current events, despairing as well that things will never improve in the future).

(S) *Worthless Self-Image* (e.g., judges oneself of no account, valueless to self or others, inadequate and unsuccessful in all aspirations; barren, sterile, impotent; sees self as inconsequential and reproachable, if not contemptible, a person who should be criticized and derogated, as well as feels guilty for possessing no priaseworthy traits or achievements).

(S) *Forsaken Objects* (e.g., internalized representations of the past appear jettisoned, as if life's early experiences have been depleted or devitalized, either drained of their richness and joyful elements, or withdrawn from memory, leaving one to feel abandoned, bereft, and discarded, cast off and deserted).

Intrapsychic Level

(F) *Asceticism Mechanism* (e.g., engages in acts of self-denial, self-punishment, and self-tormenting, believing that one should exhibit penance and be deprived of life's bounties; not only is there a repudiation of pleasures, but there are harsh self-judgments as well as self-destructive acts).

(S) *Depleted Organization* (e.g., the scaffold for morphologic structures is markedly weakened, with coping methods enervated and defensive strategies impoverished, emptied and devoid of their vigor and focus, resulting in a diminished if not exhausted capacity to initiate action and regulate affect, impulse, and conflict).

Biophysical Level

(S) *Melancholic Mood* (e.g., is typically woeful, gloomy, tearful, joyless, and morose; characteristically worrisome and brooding; low spirits and dysphoric state rarely remit).

F refers to Functional Domains (fluid, interactive)
S refers to Structural Domains (stable, unchanging)

and unshielded and, hence, beseech others to be protective and nurturant. Always fearing abandonment and desertion, their interpersonal behaviors are one of two basic varieties: that of an unprotected and inadequate individual who passively withdraws from others, or that of a needy and demanding person who seeks others to provide assurances of affection and steadfastness.

First and foremost, the moods and complaints of depressives are designed to summon nurturant responses from others. They recruit from both family and friends reassurances of their own lovability and value to them, and seek to gain assurances of others' faithfulness and devotion in turn. As with many other personality styles and disorders, depressives' symptoms may serve as an instrument for avoiding unwelcome responsibilities. This is especially effective with these personalities because they openly

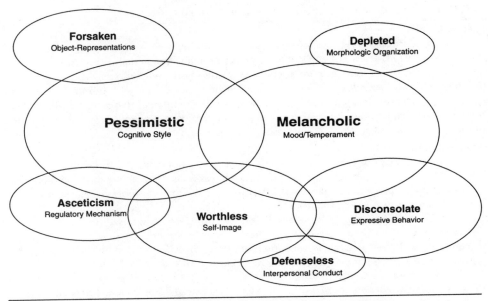

Figure 12.2   Salience of prototypal depressive domains.

admit their worthlessness and are able to demonstrate their general sense of helplessness for all to see. In this regard, their impairment serves also as a rationalization for their indecisiveness and failures. Here, their complaints may be colored with subtle accusations, claims that others have not been sufficiently supportive of them, thus fostering further their sense of futility and hopelessness. Overt expressions of hostility, however, are rarely exhibited because they fear that such actions will prove offensive and lead others to rebuke or reject them. As a result, anger and resentment are discharged only in subtle or oblique forms. This is often done by overplaying their helplessness and ineffectuality, not only creating guilt in others thereby, but causing them no end of discomfort as they attempt to meet patients' seemingly justified need for care and nurturance.

Depressives crave the love and support of others, but fail to reciprocate in ways that either gratify others or reinforce a positive relationship. Depressives' clinging behaviors, self-preoccupation, and devious coping maneuvers may ultimately evoke annoyance and exasperation from others. Under these circumstances, depressives may be persistent in soliciting the sympathy they desperately need. Failing in this regard, they may turn inward into bitter silence and guilty self-reproach. Protestations of guilt and self-condemnation may not only come to the fore, but may be unrelieved and pervasive.

Pessimistic cognitive style.   Depressives see life in its blackest form and invariably expect that the worst will happen. They give the gloomiest of interpretations about events, despairing that things will never improve in the future. They feel weighted down, discouraged, and bleak, possessing a pessimistic, defeatist, and fatalistic attitude about almost all matters. To make matters worse, depressives seem totally preoccupied with themselves and their plight, obsessively worrying about their misfortunes, both past and present.

Not only are depressives filled with remorse for their felt inadequacies, but they occasionally imagine fantasized resolutions to their difficulties that involve some magical event or omnipotent force. At heart, however, they have little hope that any solution can ever be found. Their communications with others are stereotypical and gray-colored. Efforts may be made to fight back depressive feelings and thoughts by consciously diverting ideas and preoccupations away from their depressive moods. For the most part, these new ruminations are replaced by equally troublesome ones. There is a tendency to reactivate and then to brood over minor incidents of the past. Thoughts and feelings that are *not* part of depressives' preoccupations are as clinically significant as are those with which they are preoccupied. Retrospective falsification is not uncommon: few of the pleasures of the past are remembered; only those of a painful and distressing nature are poignantly summoned. Similarly, new events are burdened retroactively, and future possibilities are prefigurations of an inevitable catastrophe.

Depressives believe that their present state is irreversible. Troublesome events today look presciently relevant to the future. Any attitude other than pessimism or gloom is merely illusory. In what has been termed the *helplessness-hopelessness* outlook, these patients assume that they are unable to help themselves and are also unlikely to be helped by outside forces (G. Engel, 1968). Most personalities can endure an astounding degree of misfortune as long as they believe that there is hope for them. In depressives, the pessimistic schemata that repeatedly shape their thoughts generate increasing levels of hopelessness, such that they are unable to imagine or plan conditions that could make things better. For depressives, life seems to create an ever deeper well of hopelessness, a wrenching fact of existence.

Worthless self-image. Depressives tend to feel guilty for possessing no praiseworthy traits or achievements. They regard themselves as valueless to self and others, inadequate and unsuccessful in all aspirations of a meaningful life. Not only do they view themselves as sterile, impotent, and of no consequential value, but they judge themselves also as reproachable, if not contemptible, as persons who *should* be criticized and derogated.

Almost any minor failure can plunge moderately unhappy depressives into a more severe state of disconsolation; such an event only proves further their state of unworthiness. Similarly, a rather harmless critical remark may set into motion obsessive worrying and brooding, further intensifying their sense of worthlessness. Even when matters are going well, there remains a deep sense of personal inadequacy, a feeling of being deficient in a host of attractive qualities, such as being popular, intelligent, physically appealing, and so on. Should adverse experiences occur, depressives will attribute their cause to some deficiency within themselves, thereby criticizing themselves for possessing the alleged defect. When difficulties become increasingly problematic, depressives are prone to blame themselves for circumstances that have no connection to them. They believe that they are incapable of taking the initiative and making decisions, reflecting their fear that they will make the wrong move or display their inadequacies for others to see.

Many depressive personalities reach so deep a level of self-denigration that they begin to take pity on themselves. When feelings of hopelessness and self-sympathy reach so low a state, there is a possibility that constructive outcomes may follow. In certain cases, depressives may feel that they have "paid their price" by sinking to the bottom of life, and that they can go no deeper into their depression than they have. Now may be a time for renewal, for an inner salvation that may be worth pursuing. On the other hand, it is at these times also that a formidable danger of self-destructiveness may take hold as well.

Forsaken object relations.   We use the term object relations to represent a series of silent, inner assumptions about the character of significant others as well as life in general. It relates to unconscious premises that give shape to how the individual interprets the transient events of everyday life. It comprises distinctly personal expectations and assumptions that are used to selectively interpret and integrate significant experiences, and contains unarticulated rules and dispositional inferences that serve both to accurately interpret observations as well as to repetitively and erroneously distort them.

In the phenomenologically oriented world of cognitive modes (Millon, Millon, et al., 1994) that are referred to with terms such as schemata, these dispositional sets relate to how events are screened, differentiated, and interpreted, largely in a conscious manner. But there is an unconscious matrix of schemata as well that refer to significant intrapsychic structures, which also selectively categorize and evaluate experiences but do so beneath the level of awareness. It is these latter schemata that we refer to when we speak of object-representations, an unconscious tendency to mold perceptions and cognitions in line with inner templates that were given shape and character earlier in life. These templates may remain inactive for periods of time, but become energized and prominent when stimulated by relevant reality experiences. Activated, they transform what is actually happening in reality to make it fit the unconscious template of expectancy and assumption. In the depressed, this template saturates ongoing experiences and thoughts with a pessimistic and negativistic tone.

In effect, the content of the depressive's inner world appears to be devitalized, jettisoned, or depleted. It appears overtly drained of its richness or joyful elements. What good things happened in the past, what happy memories and fulfillments may have been experienced, appear to have been withdrawn from memory, leaving the depressive forsaken to face the terrible complexities of life, abandoned and bereft, perhaps discarded and cast-off. These forsaken objects become the locus and metaphor of loss for many.

Ascetic regulatory mechanism.   The dynamic processes of the intrapsychic world of the depressive has as its primary goal the fulfillment of a belief that one should experience penance and be deprived of life's bounties. Through the ascetic mechanism, depressives maneuver their inner world to achieve self-denial, self-punishment, and self-tormenting. Not only is there a diminution or repudiation of pleasurable memories, but those that persist are transformed into their opposite through harsh self-appraisals and, if need be, self-destructive acts.

With so punitive an attitude toward self, depressives allow themselves minimal pleasure, if any, and constantly appraise their own actions to determine whether they have attained more joy and satisfaction than they deserve. Driven by the feeling that they deserve less rather than more, they may be "forced" to give up totally on themselves and abdicate life altogether. In a sense, they have adopted a mechanism of "playing dead" as a means of remaining alive. Self-abdication and total resignation from life have become intrapsychic maneuvers to permit them to avoid total annihilation by suicide, an act of self-jettisoning that lies but a moment ahead.

Depleted morphologic organization. The overall scaffold for the intrapsychic structures of the depressive appears markedly weakened, unable to withstand much stress without decompensating. Coping methods are enervated and dynamic strategies seem impoverished. These forces that maintain psychic cohesion appear to have been emptied or devoid of focus and vigor. As a consequence, the depressive shows a diminished if not exhausted capacity to initiate overt action or to regulate internal affects, impulses, and conflicts.

To protect against these feelings of inner ineffectuality, depressives struggle intrapsychically to keep distressing feelings at as low a level as possible, to keep them out of awareness, and to ignore both their origins and their current realities. By structuring their inner world in this manner, they can minimize the experience of psychic pain. Moreover, they may succeed in isolating their affect to such an extent that they manifest only the overt appearance and complaints of depression without experiencing its emotional undertone. In a rather circuitous manner, it is at these times that we often find patients inclined to self-destruction and suicide. Drained of feeling and life, these depressives may conclude that there is little meaning to life and that they can no longer control and direct it. Perhaps it is only when they act to kill themselves that they can regain the feeling of competence and autonomy. The occasionally observed phenomenon of improved mood just prior to taking one's life is related to this defensive maneuver. Should the preceding sentence be erroneously interpreted, let us note that suicide more commonly occurs when these patients seek to escape from painful or humiliating life circumstances.

Melancholic mood. Depressives are characteristically gloomy, morose, and tearful. Brooding and feeling inescapably worried, with low spirits and a woeful and joyless mood, their pervasive dysphoric state may persist at a moderate level of severity, remitting only on rare occasions. Their self-denigration and habitual gloom are so deeply ingrained that they have become intrinsic parts of their personality structure. Although certain subtypes may emphasize one or another aspect of the depressive constellation of symptoms—sad feelings, anguish, irritability, guilt, emptiness, longing—it is clear that these patients have a diminished interest in life, few appetites for joy and closeness, and although they go through the motions of relating, eating, sexualizing, even play, they do so with little enthusiasm. Their temperamentally based inertia and sadness may undermine whatever capacity they may have had to smile and enjoy the humor and pleasures of life.

Further reinforcing the belief that there are physiological underpinnings to this temperamental disposition are the variety of vegetative functions they display, including even lowered metabolic rates and slowed gastrointestinal functions. Most commonly, complaints include difficulty sleeping, early morning awakening, fatigue, diminished libido and appetite, as well as various bodily aches and pains. For some, the dysregulation of the hormonal substrates of mood are such that they may, for brief periods of time, become euphoric and socially driven, almost to the point in some of crossing the threshold to hypomania. More commonly, however, we are likely to observe a more persistent dysthymic or melancholic temperament.

Self-Perpetuation Process

It must be said again that chronic depressive moods often reflect the persistence of internal mood dysregulations, continuing states of unhappiness and sadness that are driven primarily by long-term neurobiologic defects and deficiencies. Not that biological forces can display themselves manifestly without being interwoven with psychological influences, but when biogenic dysfunctions are markedly persistent and penetrant, psychological factors will play a lesser role than otherwise. Given our current state of knowledge, we are unable at this time to differentiate conditions that have stronger or lesser biologic components (see Table 12.2).

Recreating experiences of suffering. Pessimistic and self-devaluing schemata influence how information and relationships are processed by depressive individuals. Retrospective recall and future anticipations are all colored by cognitive distortions and expectancies that further reinforce their unhappy state. As noted previously, depression often recruits support and nurturance; it deflects criticism and condemnation, and serves as a means of distancing from others and avoiding responsibilities about which one feels ambivalent or negative. As with the masochist, many depressives want to suffer, perhaps to suffer more than is warranted by the instrumental goals they seek to achieve.

How perverse a strategy this can be. Depressives exaggerate their misery and submerge themselves in feelings of helplessness, unhappiness, and unworthiness. One cannot help but be struck by the fact that these self-inflicted wounds deepen the abyss of misery of these persons. Again and again, the depressive magnifies minor disadvantages and failures into signs of irrevocable humiliation. As a result of these acts of self-generated despair, depressives greatly impair their ability to experience a measure of life's joy and contentment. They thereby sink into feeling helpless, needing others to care for their needs and take responsibility for their life. Although there are advantages to their disconsolation and defenselessness, they have made their already problematic situation even more tormenting. In time, fewer and fewer advantages of depression are to be gained; no persons are around to be impressed, no more sympathy is forthcoming, and there are no triumphs in asserting one's will. Life dwindles

TABLE 12.2 Self-Perpetuating Processes

DEPRESSIVE
Recreation of Suffering
    Discontents become irrevocable unhappiness
    Anguish drives support away
    Self-narcotized into total emptiness

Self-Accusation
    Invalidates self-worth
    Retroflected rage intensifies buried resentments
    Expiatory self-punishments lead to suicide

Reinforces Hopeless Feelings
    Hopelessness leads to persistent failure
    Precludes efforts to make things better
    Loss of hope leads to loss of self

to a state of nothingness and loses segments of its reality. By exaggerating their claims, depressives have driven others away. Increasingly, their feelings of misery and unworthiness begin to lose a sense of reality; even the sting of depressive pain is gradually lulled and narcotized into a feeling of emptiness.

Self-accusatory attitudes.   Although the overt expression of contrition and guilt may serve to deflect further condemnation by others, depressives further reinforce their own sense of unworthiness and despicability by these attitudes. Acts of self-accusation, by which depressives invalidate their own worth, are acts of self-derogation in which individuals become their own worst enemy. Thus, in seeking to avoid the torment of others, depressives have become their own persecutor, a critical, suspicious, and clever oppressor who knows exactly what it is that they must demean within themselves to experience a measure of relief and expiation.

At some level, depressives are aware that their retroflected rage is but a façade, a clever device to mislead their environmental tormentors, real or imagined. As such, they must assault themselves all the more severely, punish themselves deeply, not only as an act of contrition, as it may appear on the surface, but for their failure once again to be forthright and competent, that is, to say what they believe and to stand on their own. They have failed to deal again with their buried resentment toward parents and their disappointment in themselves. Their conscious remorse is recognized as a mockery of the deep and lifelong roots of helplessness and unworthiness. Elements of self-rage may be seen in refusals to eat, inability to engage in sex, and general incapacity to feel any pleasure. They may be left with only one form of self-mastery and expiatory self-punishment, that of suicide.

Reinforcing feelings of hopelessness.   The mere act of hopelessness, the ultimate product of a history of failure in eliciting care and affection, is a self-fulfilling process, an attitude that not only signifies the future persistence of failure, but alienates persons increasingly from themselves. Concluding that they are unable to be the active master of their fate, depressives lose so much faith in themselves that they give up, unwilling even to try to make matters better, to seek what is desirable; hence, they fall into a state akin to what Kierkegaard termed a "psychic death." The vicious circle has continued; the person has lost not only the hope of what could be, but the very sense of self.

INTERVENTION GOALS

Most individuals with a depressive personality disorder accept their chronic dysphoria and feeling of hopelessness as an inevitable life condition and come into therapy only after a significant other insists that something needs to be done. Sometimes it will take a major life trauma to push them into treatment. A therapist may at first focus on the presenting symptoms and conclude that the patient is suffering from a severe bout of depression, only to later realize that the patient describes having felt this way since childhood or adolescence. Patients may consider such feelings justified by life circumstance or personal failings and deny any hope that they may eventually feel better; years of experience have taught depressives that even when things look relatively bright, feelings of despair lurk right around the corner.

Fortunately, many individuals with a depressive personality disorder do respond to psychopharmacologic intervention; a therapist would do well to consider antidepressants as a first inroad into alleviating the patient's suffering. Many patients, however, who do respond to medication nonetheless continue to be skeptical about the durability of newfound improvements, having previously experienced short-lived periods of comfort. To support and consolidate gains, the therapist needs to help the patient overcome the maladaptive personality characteristics and patterns of behavior that inevitably develop as a result of the patient's chronic depression. Although overt depressive symptomatology, including downcast mood and vegetative signs, may disappear after administration of an appropriate medication, more covert personality factors may be less affected. Interpersonal behavior, self-concept, cognitive schemata, and expectancies that have been shaped by past depressive experience need to be replaced by more adaptive variants in order not to hinder the patient's optimal functioning or even undermine affective and energy gains.

Unfortunately, some patients do not respond to medication and thus have a more challenging road to travel on the way to recovery. In these cases, patient and therapist will have to rely directly on behavioral, cognitive, interpersonal, and/or other interventions to improve affect and increase pleasure as well as to reconstruct the patient's personality.

A course of therapeutic intervention for a depressive patient should aim to accomplish several parallel yet intertwined goals (see Table 12.3). The depressive's characteristic passivity needs to be replaced with more active interaction with the environment, and the affective and cognitive emphasis on pain needs to be shifted to a focus on pleasure. Unlike avoidants, who actively withdraw from potentially distressing situations, depressives have come to accept pain as unavoidable, hence their helpless immobility. Increased anticipation of pleasure could help encourage depressives to be more proactive regarding their environment. Subsequent experiences with success can help alter depressives' pessimistic cognitive style, expectations, and melancholic mood. Cognitive interventions that directly attack the dysfunction within these domains can support the personality changes that result from new experiences with the environment, and hence ultimately help restore the patient's lost sense of self-worth.

TABLE 12.3 Therapeutic Strategies and Tactics for the Prototypal Depressive Personality

---

STRATEGIC GOALS
Balance Polarities
   Diminish hopelessness/pain
   Increase pleasure/enhancing
   Stimulate active/modifying

Counter Perpetuations
   Undo pessimistic expectations
   Revive sense of self-worth
   Prompt spirited mood

TACTICAL MODALITIES
   Utilize mood antidepressants
   Retrieve forsaken object-representations
   Promote optimistic cognitive shifts

Reestablishing Polarity Balances

The hallmark of the depressive personality is his or her psychic pain and sense of hopelessness about improving the quality of life. Cognitive-behavioral interventions that encourage patients to interact in more adaptive ways with the environment can help sensitize them to experiences of success and pleasure, hence resulting in increased balance on the pain-pleasure polarity. A lessened sense of helplessness and strengthened motivation for rewarding experiences also indirectly foster more active coping strategies. These shift patients away from the depressogenic passive end of the active-passive dimension.

Countering Perpetuating Tendencies

Depressives' pessimistic expectations, lack of a sense of self-worth, and melancholic mood all serve to ensure that environmental conditions continue to reinforce their usual pattern of feeling, thinking, and behaving.

As depressives appraise the future, pessimistic expectations far outweigh hopes for success and satisfaction. Rather than exert themselves in vain and open themselves up to the possibility of further crushing failures and disappointments, depressives passively resign themselves to bear the burden of their fate. Opportunities to improve their lot are received half-heartedly, further entrenching their hopelessness and self-reproach. Experiences of success are not likely under such circumstances. Their low self-esteem and self-inflicted lack of success suggest that even if there was a road out of this empty, cold world, the depressive would not be capable of navigating around the obstacles. Believing they lack the capacity to make improvements, they may turn, in the hope of salvation, to others. Others may react to the depressive's disconsolate and defenseless behavior with initial support but, in time, often withdraw in an attempt to avoid their own feelings of frustration regarding the depressive. Aware of the effect their melancholic mood has on others yet feeling unable to behave in a more energetic and optimistic way, depressives find their pessimistic expectations fulfilled and their poor self-image reinforced. They may vow ever more forcefully to keep to themselves to avoid further pain.

The vicious circle fueled by the depressive's pessimistic expectations can be interrupted by confronting pessimism directly, by cognitive interventions that challenge assumptions, and by behavioral "experiments." Even a trickle of motivation, for some more easily mastered with the help of antidepressants, can help patients alter their depressogenic interpersonal habits, especially with social skill and assertiveness training. Tasks can be broken down into small steps easy for patients to accomplish, thus exposing them to success. Feelings of self-efficacy can bolster self-image, and supportive antidepressants may help to further lift melancholia. Cognitive techniques can teach patients to search for objective feedback in their environment rather than rely solely on emotional reasoning. Problem-solving skills allow patients to generate alternative plans in cases of genuine disappointment or failure, thus preventing them from sinking again into apathetic despair.

Identifying Domain Dysfunctions

The crux of the depressive personality's dysfunction rests in the interaction of a pessimistic cognitive style and a deeply entrenched melancholic mood. The time-tested conviction that efforts to manipulate the environment or one's mood are futile ensures that the depressive will be ineffectual in efforts to plan for change. Even on those occasions when depressives overcome feelings of inadequacy and hopelessness in an attempt to secure some reward from the environment, their resistant melancholic mood and negative interpretational bias interfere with the enjoyment of life's simple pleasures and small victories.

Psychopharmacological intervention often is a useful first inroad into the depressive's difficulties. Most depressives respond moderately well to medication, providing them with increased energy and a first inkling of optimism. With this renewed sense of hope, patients may be open to exploring and working toward changing attitudes and behaviors that contribute to their depressive pattern. Patients can be taught that helpless interpersonal behavior alienates even the most well-meaning, attracts individuals with sadistic and exploitive tendencies, and even brings out such tendencies in "regular" folks. Social skills training can teach patients to replace disconsolate expressive behavior and defenseless interpersonal conduct with more assertive and appealing alternatives. Planning tasks by breaking them down into small manageable steps can also help provide depressives with successes that, along with improved quality of social interactions, can increase their sense of self-efficacy and help bolster their worthless self-image.

Improvements in these latter domains can serve to encourage depressives to reclaim forsaken object-representations and dare to hope for (and hence find reason to work toward) something better than disappointment and failure. Increased subjective experience of pleasure can also help rejuvenate depleted morphological organization and render coping mechanisms a little more vital and productive than previously. Although depressives start out believing they can feel comfortable with only a self-denial pattern of existence, effective coping can, in fact, begin to occur as soon as hope becomes a part of their repertoire.

SELECTING THERAPEUTIC MODALITIES

In building a relationship with a depressive patient, the therapist needs to carefully balance a supportive position that satisfies the patient's dependency needs against encouraging his or her helplessness. Although most depressive patients claim to expect nothing but more unhappiness for their future, many in fact harbor a secret hope that the therapist has a magical solution that will put an end to their feelings of misery and incompetence. Patients with a depressive personality disorder have probably spent most of their time believing that life is an exhausting struggle that yields no rewards at best, and metes out disappointments and punishments as a matter of course. Yet, patients realize that life is not so cloudy for all of their peers, and they often subconsciously hope that the therapist holds the secret to joy and vitality. Whereas depressives dare not risk openly assuming that such a wish could be realized for fear of another devastating disappointment, the therapist will often be given clues about patients' dependent wishes in both subtle and more overt ways. Although the therapist will likely feel pressure to ease the patient's distress and pain, it is not advisable to assume too omnipotent a "helping" position. It is essential, however, that the therapist impart a sense of hopefulness and optimism about the possibility of the patient's achieving improved functioning and affect. It should be made clear that the patient must engage in a lot of collaborative work with the therapist to arrive at realistic but promising solutions. Because patients may wish for a "magic helper" to watch out for them, the therapist should emphasize instead developing a sense of self-efficacy and problem-solving ability.

In the beginning stages of therapy, satisfying too few of the patient's dependency needs may cause him or her to feel that the therapist is not interested or caring; this may increase the depressive's sense of futility. With very depressed patients, the therapist may find it necessary to do more than the usual amount of work to keep the session going. Many such patients feel embarrassed, incompetent, guilty, and misunderstood. They may also lack the confidence or energy to express this. Pushing the patient too quickly or even assuming a "cheerful" disposition may make patients feel that their depressive affect will not be tolerated, resulting in feelings of shame that may lead patients to terminate therapy. The truly therapeutic relationship is one in which the therapist can provide empathic support while conveying confidence in patients' capacity to learn to care for themselves.

Behavioral Techniques

Designing a useful behavioral intervention for depressive patients begins with a careful analysis of the patient's interactions with the environment. Pleasant and unpleasant events need to be identified, as do problematic patterns of behavior. By keeping a record of daily events and moods, interventions to help change depressogenic activities can be devised. Once goals have been agreed on, it is often useful for patients to choose specific reinforcers that they can employ to reward themselves when planned assignments have been carried out successfully. Interventions usually fall into one of three categories: changes in the environment (e.g., changing jobs, going to the movies), teaching new interaction skills (e.g., assertiveness training, modeling), and increasing pleasure-related actions (e.g., relaxation and pleasure training). Patients are encouraged to engage in activities that they enjoy, particularly ones that activate positive moods; they may also be taught to set time aside daily for rewarding activities. Some behavioral intervention programs include the patient's significant others to encourage communication and facilitate social interaction.

Interpersonal Techniques

Interpersonal approaches emphasize the place of the social environment in the development and maintenance of symptoms. The steps involved in treatment include reviewing symptoms and describing their usual course. Treatment is outlined, and the therapist declares the patient to have an "illness" that can be treated with cooperation. Interpersonal problems are worked out in the course of therapy. Developing positive relationships can serve to alleviate depressive symptoms by providing the patient with support, pleasure, and hope.

Depressive symptoms may be related to problems found in one or more of four general areas of dysfunction: grief overreactions, interpersonal disputes, role transitions, and interpersonal deficits. If the difficulty is a feeling of loss from a grief overreaction or a strong sense of generalized deprivation, then therapy may focus on facilitating the delayed mourning process and helping the patient substitute new relationships and interests for those that have been lost or are chronically missing. If interpersonal disputes are the issue, a plan of action and effective communication are emphasized. For patients who are having difficulties adapting to new roles, emphasis is placed on regarding the role more positively and on mastering skills needed to function effectively in the new capacity. Patients who have interpersonal deficits need to identify past positive relationships on which to base future ones, to practice skills, and to search for new promising situations and people.

A number of strengths associated with group approaches to treatment of depressive disorders have been pointed out by Yalom (1986). In group therapy, depressive patients come to realize that others experience similar difficulties and that they are not alone in their vulnerability. This realization can be therapeutic in itself. Participants can be encouraged to assist each other in solving difficulties and overcoming problems, thus helping them bolster their waning sense of self-worth and interpersonal competence. Witnessing improvement in their fellow group members' outlook can reinforce the very tenuous hope the patient has for improved functioning, and help build the motivation needed to make adaptive changes. The group format also allows for role playing, multiparticipant discussions, and behavioral interventions. Patients who lack social skills can experience corrective feedback about maladaptive behaviors. Positive reinforcement from a supportive group can give patients confidence to experiment with new behaviors outside of the therapy after practicing with members.

Family and couples approaches to treating a depressive's interpersonal relationship and functioning difficulties can focus on several areas of dysfunction. The reaction of the patient's spouse and of other family members who contribute to the patient's depressive tendencies can be explored to improve the patient's overall functioning. Family members can learn about helpful ways to react to symptomatic behavior. Cognitive patterns, whether the patient's or other family members', may contribute to the depressive's pathogenesis. Distortions in problem definition, in expectancies for self and spouse, in beliefs about change, and in attributions for behavior can be exposed and altered. Behavioral interventions can be conducted with the spouse and/or other family members to increase the patient's social skills and to demonstrate the advantages of more adaptive interaction strategies. Hostile interactions can be reduced. Often, a lack of intimacy with the spouse precipitates, exacerbates, or maintains symptomatology. Teaching the couple to interact in supportive and comforting ways can alleviate acute symptoms and help the depressive patient replace maladaptive schemata with better attitudes and coping mechanisms.

Cognitive Techniques

Cognitive techniques for treating depressive personality disorders make much use of behavioral tactics as well. Combining the two approaches is a powerful medium through which to change the patient's behavior and environmental consequences and to alter depressogenic attitudes. The cognitive approach emphasizes directly challenging the patient's depressogenic assumptions through logical reasoning as well as with environmental "data." By keeping track of events, thoughts, and moods, depressive patients can learn how much of their dysphoria is related directly to their appraisal of their environment and of themselves, as well as to their subsequent negative self-talk.

Once negative automatic thoughts have been identified, they can be evaluated and modified. When patients have a depressogenic thought, they may learn to ask themselves such questions as "What's the evidence?," "Is there any other way to look at it?," "How could alternative (less pessimistic) explanations be tested?," and "What can I do about it (to make it better)?" (Beck, 1983). The tacit beliefs on which automatic thoughts rest also need to be identified and altered for lasting change to occur and for negative thoughts not to resurface in a new form. Dysfunctional cognitive habits such as over-generalization, arbitrary inference, emotional reasoning, and dichotomous thinking can be confronted directly, allowing patients to alter their thinking and the maladaptive behaviors that logically result from faulty thought processes. A basic strategy is to help patients realize that their thoughts are inferences about the world, and not facts. Predictions can then be made and "experiments" devised to test their validity.

Behavioral exercises are used mainly as an extension of cognitive change techniques, for example, to show that optimistic appraisal of situations are justified and can be achieved. Activities can be planned as "tests" of assumptions, as well as to provide the patient with positive experiences. Cognitive rehearsal techniques can help a patient accomplish goals by imagining the steps, predicting "obstacles" and conflicts, and figuring out ways to overcome them.

Self-Image Techniques

A useful initial approach with the depressive, as with all personality disorders, is the therapist's willingness to adopt a patient-centered supportive attitude. After having lived with and "accepted" the inevitability of depressive symptoms since childhood or adolescence, the patient usually enters therapy at a time of crisis or when a relationship appears to be threatened by the patient's gloomy outlook and behavior. The first goal is to alleviate the patient's pain and to establish a solid and realistic therapeutic alliance. MacKinnon and Michels (1971) encourage the therapist to enhance patients' defenses to shield them against excessive pain. If the patient has suffered a recent interpersonal loss, the therapist can attempt to stand in for the lost figure until the patient stabilizes enough to regain some motivation and hope.

The second objective of self-actualizing therapy is to protect the patient from self-injury. The therapist must be careful to clarify the consequences of irrational, self-defeating decisions. Although the therapist cannot make decisions for the patient directly, he or she can encourage the patient to "wait till you feel better," thereby conveying concern (in itself therapeutic) and the attitude that improvement is expected. In order not to undermine the patient's self-confidence and self-efficacy, it is to be emphasized that the "sick" role and the therapist's advice are only temporary.

Depressive patients often suffer from excessive guilt. The therapist's acknowledgment of the burden of guilt and reassurance that the depressive has suffered enough can help the patient believe that "forgiveness" is possible, and that he or she finally deserves to build a better life. Some patients feel guilt about being a burden to family by not functioning adequately at work or in other roles. Anger at others may be denied because of such guilt, serving only to increase symptoms and interfere with relationships. Encouraging patients to acknowledge and work through anger can be helpful. Once patient and therapist have developed a solid alliance and the patient has realistic expectations about the advantages of working toward changes, other interventions can be initiated.

Intrapsychic Techniques

Psychodynamic approaches that involve short-term therapy are currently based on one of two premises. The first is that depression is largely caused by disturbed interpersonal relations; childhood experiences of disappointment with significant others predispose individuals to replicate depressogenic patterns. The second premise is that depressive patterns reflect difficulties in adaptive functioning that are related to inadequate self-esteem. A perceived discrepancy between aspirations and reality or what had once been and what is now (loss) is hypothesized to cause depressive symptomatology.

Analyzing the patient's transference toward the therapist, and the patient's developmental interpersonal history as the source of maladaptive emotional and cognitive distortions are the crux of dynamic treatments. Bemporad (1980) divides the process into stages. First, therapist and patient search for atavistic remnants of childhood interpersonal functioning as it presents in the relationship between them. Second, the patient works on relinquishing defenses, beliefs, and patterns that have been identified, and replaces them with more realistic and functional modes of behavior. Dreams, relationships, and feelings are all analyzed and traced to their origins. A new, mature appraisal of the patient's history and context can then help protect against continued depressive symptomatology. Healing is also promoted by supportive empathy, direct advice (when appropriate), and a positive relationship experience with the therapist.

Pharmacologic Techniques

Psychopharmacologic intervention can greatly help depressives live normal lives by uplifting their melancholic mood state. Although antidepressants may not restructure the fundamental nature of the patient's personality, it certainly can help the patient feel more optimistic and energetic enough to take risks in experimenting with new behaviors. The many antidepressants available on the market have different side effect and contraindication profiles; careful evaluation of the patient's history and sensitivities can help in deciding which one (or two) is appropriate. It is also important for the therapist to emphasize that there is a lag between the onset of medication administration and its psychoactive effects to guard against the patient's becoming discouraged during the usual two- to six-week delay.

MAKING SYNERGISTIC ARRANGEMENTS

The first inroad to be considered by the therapist when planning a treatment strategy for someone with depressive personality disorder is usually pharmacologic intervention with antidepressants. Although not every patient is willing to take medication, and although several different medications may need to be prescribed before an optimal one is found, a great many depressive patients report that they feel as though a cloud has been lifted once they take an effective drug.

For patients who take medication (as well as for those who do not), a useful initial approach is a supportive one. Alleviating the patient's pain, offering empathic understanding, and protecting him or her against bad decisions can do much to inspire the patient's hope and motivation.

Behavioral intervention may next be employed as well as combined with personality-reforming techniques, whether cognitive, interpersonal, or dynamic. Behavioral changes can help open up new experiences and reinforce more adaptive patterns. More thoroughgoing analyses of the patient's life and difficulties can help change the fabric of depressogenic attitudes and actions, thereby immunizing the patient against relapse during times of stress.

If the therapist deems adjunct family or couples intervention to be appropriate, it can begin as soon as patient and therapist feel ready. Similarly, participation in a supportive group for depressive individuals can be of benefit for several reasons. Whereas the therapist may be idolized or suspected of being supportive out of professional duty, other group members can be regarded as peers. This can result in the patient's feeling less isolated and genuinely hopeful as others in similar situations experience improved moods and lives.

An important aspect of achieving successful intervention with depressive personalities is focusing on major episodes and relapse prevention. Patients should be advised of the frequency with which most people reexperience intense dysphoric periods and should be taught strategies for feeling better and keeping active. Booster sessions can be recommended to keep patients functioning at an optimal level. Patients who are on medication need to be monitored regularly.

Illustrative Cases

Despite its recency as a formal *DSM* classification, the history of depressive syndromes is a long and rich one, many elements of which can be drawn on for the following personality presentations (see Table 12.4). Some exhibit their depressive mood with displays of dramatic gesture and pleading commentary; others are demanding, irritable, and cranky. Some verbalize their thoughts in passive, vague, and abstract philosophical terms. Still others seem lonely, quietly downhearted, solemnly morose, and pessimistic. Common to all, however, is the presence of self-deprecatory comments, feelings of apathy, and marked discouragement and hopelessness. Their actions and complaints usually evoke sympathy and support from others, but these reassurances provide only temporary relief from the prevailing mood of dejection.

TABLE 12.4   Depressive Personality Disorder Subtypes

Restive: Wrought-up despair; agitated, ruffled, perturbed, confused, restless, and unsettled; vacillatory emotions and outlook; suicide avoids inescapable pain.

MCMI 2B-2A

Self-Derogating: Disparaging self for weaknesses and shortcomings; self-deriding, discrediting, censurable, dishonorable, odious, contemptible.

MCMI 2B-3

Voguish: Suffering seen as ennobling; unhappiness considered a popular and stylish mode of social disenchantment; personal depression viewed as self-glorifying and dignifying.

MCMI 2B-4/5

Ill-Humored: Sour, distempered, cantankerous, irritable, grumbling discontent; guilt-ridden and self-condemning; self-pitying; hypochrondriacal.

MCMI 2B-8A

Morbid: Profound dejection and gloom; haggard, morose, lugubrious, macabre, drained, oppressed; intensely self-abnegating.

MCMI 2B-8B

DEPRESSIVE PERSONALITY: ILL-HUMORED TYPE
(DEPRESSIVE WITH NEGATIVISTIC TRAITS)

CASE 12.1, SHARON L., 32

Presenting Picture: Sharon L. presented for therapy after ending a relationship with her supervisor at work. From the outset, she appeared to have a guarded, edgy, "hands-off" sort of demeanor, obviously protecting herself from an environment that would inevitably cause her much distress. Sharon described her earlier life as being nomadic, as her mother frequently moved around the country, "dragging" her along. She considered herself, throughout her childhood, a "second thought" in her mother's eyes, invariably less important than her mother's current boyfriend. Notably, in her own recent relationship, she described this man as "unable to commit or to be intimate," yet it seemed obvious from her presentation, ranging from self-effacing hostility to resentful bitterness, that she may have created her own barriers.

Clinical Assessment: In cases such as Sharon's, well described by Kraepelin and Schneider, we see a constant barrage of complaints, irritability, and a sour grumbling discontent, usually interwoven with hypochondriacal preoccupations and periodic expressions of guilt and self-condemnation. Sharon's habitual style of acting out her conflicts and ambivalent feelings became more pronounced (as well as evident on the MCMI), resulting in extreme vacillations between bitterness and resentment on the one hand, and intropunitive self-deprecation on the other. She exhibited self-pity and bodily anxieties, which may serve as a basis for distinguishing her from other depressive types. A review of empirical and clinical studies suggests that the characteristics of Sharon's depressive pattern interweave with features seen most commonly among negativistic personalities.

Although not invariably gloomy, *ill-humored depressives* such as Sharon find pleasure in nothing and appear contented with nothing, taking out their grumbling negativism, not so much in a nagging and dissatisfied attitude toward others, but directing their ill disposition against themselves. She exhibited a mood composed of irritability, anxiety, and self-flagellation. There was a self-tormenting quality, a kind of scolding and hypochondriacal attitude, an extreme preoccupation with herself, and an annoying insistence that others hear her complaints and troubles. She appeared cold and selfish, irritable and critical, rejoicing in the failures of others, and never anticipating or wishing others the rewards and achievements of life.

For limited time periods, Sharon experienced an incessant despair and suffering, an agitated pacing to and fro, a wringing of hands, and an apprehensiveness and tension that were unrelieved by comforting reassurances. At times, she had hostile depressive complaints and a demanding and querulous irritability in which she bemoaned her sorry state and her desperate need for attention to her manifold physical illnesses, pains, and incapacities.

Synergistic Treatment Plan: The most pronounced of Sharon's disbalanced polarities include a strong *pain* and very weak *pleasure* orientation, which needed timely measures focused on both a *biophysical* level (reduce despairing mood) and *phenomenological* level (undo fatalistic and cynical cognitive perpetuating tendencies, as well as diminish her ongoing inclination toward hypersensitivity) in order for her to have any investment in further treatment. *Interpersonal* trust was also most important, as Sharon's faith in the actions of others toward her was nearly nonexistent, due not only to her characterologic feeling of worthlessness, but also to her view of others as malevolent. It would be necessary to very carefully rework *intrapsychic* conflicts between her weakened senses of *self* and *other* throughout treatment, but cautiously, as shifting emphasis for responsibility too quickly may be enervating to her already guilty predisposition. Also, Sharon needed to learn more effective *behaviors* that would serve more healthy functions than her frequent irresolute actions, which so often were at odds with her desires. As more functional habits would grow, it would be efficacious to dislodge Sharon's chronically low *self-image* (undo her perpetually self-defeating feelings of guilt), as well as help revive and bolster relationships with those around her.

Therapeutic Course: A *short-term* focus was helpful in aiding Sharon in therapy. First, she was guided to avoid environmental pressures that aggravated her anxieties and dejection. Brief *supportive therapy* was employed to relieve sources of anxiety. A *pharmacologic agent* (specifically, an antidepressant drug) was employed. Circumscribed *behavior modification* methods were explored to focus on social behavior that could be strengthened in a relatively short time period. *Cognitive techniques,* such as those of Beck and Ellis, were used to confront her with the obstructive and self-defeating character of her beliefs and expectations. Her relations with significant others were strengthened by employing several *interpersonal* treatment techniques (e.g., Klerman, Benjamin). Such approaches had to be handled cautiously, however, lest Sharon feel that she was a failure and become unduly guilt-ridden, depressed, or possibly even suicidal. It was of great benefit to stabilize her and help her control her vacillations of mood and behavior. In this way, the therapist diminished the possibility of setbacks or deterioration in her condition.

Toward the goal of reducing the likelihood of a relapse or retrogression, the therapist did not set goals too high or press changes too quickly. Initial efforts were directed at building the patient's trust. Short-term procedures designed to orient her attentions to her positive traits and to enhance her confidence and self-esteem were most beneficial.

A major goal throughout was to forestall repetitive decompensation into anxiety and depressive disorders. It was also necessary to monitor suicidal tendencies and anticipate possible attempts. Sharon frequently acted impulsively when she felt guilty, needed attention, or sought a dramatic form of retribution. The therapist was able to guide her into recognizing the sources and character of her ambivalence and to reinforce a more realistic and optimistic outlook on life. Because she entered treatment in a highly agitated state, the reduction of her anxieties and guilt was an early goal of short-term treatment.

Because of her intense ambivalence between her desire for reassurance and nurturance and her fear of trusting an unknown person, Sharon required an early warm and attentive attitude on the part of the therapist. She was engaged early on; thus, she was not as disposed to employ repetitive maneuvers to test the sincerity and motives of the therapist. Efforts were also made to reduce the stressors inherent in her home life. It would have been advantageous to work with family members, but they were not motivated to do so. This situation prompted more intensive techniques to reduce the possibility of setbacks. Because of the preceding reasons, treatment had to progress more rapidly to ensure that a significant measure of remedial improvement could occur. There was also the possibility of Sharon's withdrawal from treatment had she resisted facing the humiliation of confronting painful memories and feelings. With a nurturant and empathic attitude, the therapist was able to overcome Sharon's fear of reexperiencing false hopes and disappointments. What is suggested is that the warmth and understanding of the therapist moderated Sharon's expectation that others would be rejecting, leading her to pull back and thereby cut off experiences that might have proved gratifying had they been completed. What was desired was to decrease her anticipation of loss that may have prompted her into a self-fulfilling prophecy. Without focused attention, she may have defeated the chance to experience events that could promote change and growth.

DEPRESSIVE PERSONALITY: VOGUISH TYPE
(DEPRESSIVE WITH HISTRIONIC AND NARCISSISTIC TRAITS)

CASE 12.2, DEAN R., 23

Presenting Picture: Dean R., a creative writer, described the world as "phony and despicable," but simply saw this as his very accurate reflection of "seeing reality for what it is." He seemed fueled by a fascination with a perceived society in denial of its inevitable downward spiral and demise, and viewed himself as one of only a select few who chose not to be happy in the face of this disaster. As he put it, "People have to be phony to be happy; that's just not my path." Dean's written work was a self-proclaimed form of release for him, but he vacillated between describing his writing as "the truth that everyone needs to hear if they want to stop this destructive path," and his own personal release that did not need to be appreciated by anyone. This behavior had alienated him from his family, who, according to Dean, just didn't understand him. Although not stated directly, it appeared from his descriptions that the family prompted this visit.

Clinical Assessment: Both Schneider and Kraepelin noted a tendency of certain depressives to display vanity and voguishness. To Dean, suffering was seen as something noble, permitting him to feel special if not elitist. He thereby acquired a philosophical refuge that could enable him to ponder "the bitterness of earthly life." Like many *voguish depressives*, Dean displayed an aesthetic preoccupation, a way of dressing and living that gave stature to his unhappy moods. He philosophized about his "existential sadness" and the alienation that we all share in this "age of mass society." This use of fashionable language provided him with a bridge to others. It gave him a feeling of belonging during times when he was most isolated from the attachments he so desperately sought. As such, Dean was often seen to exhibit histrionic personality characteristics and, to a lesser extent, those of the narcissistic personality.

Moreover, Dean's pseudosophistication about up-to-date matters not only enabled him to rationalize his personal emptiness and confusion but also allowed him to maintain his appeal in the eyes of "interesting" people. By adopting currently popular modes of disenchantment, he reinstated himself as a participant of an "in" subgroup and thereby managed to draw attention to himself. These feeble signs of social attachment also provided a means for overcoming his deep sense of loss and isolation. However, if his expressions of connectedness failed to fulfill his attachment needs, he would have likely withdrawn quickly and replaced those expressions with soulful declarations of guilt and hopelessness.

Synergistic Treatment Plan: Dean's self-perpetuating difficulties were mostly manifest in an unbalanced *interpersonal* style: a tendency to concentrate on the perceived iniquities of the external world with little introspection (*other* orientation), yet using these perceptions to draw attention to a somewhat weaker *self*. It was as though what embodied Dean the individual was lacking, causing a damaged self-image and morose mood, and his focus on these external features would draw attention to him while keeping the critical eye of others focused elsewhere. Additionally, he perceived that his experience in chronic despondency (*pain* orientation) validated his status as a martyr. These, of course, constituted a conflicted and ineffectual adjustment, and both interpersonal and *cognitive* methods would be useful in defining these inconsistencies, building more effective social skills, and developing more genuine relationships. Equally important would be pharmacologic aids and the augmentation of a rather ambiguous self-image via cognitive and *experiential* modalities, which would remain a central theme throughout treatment.

Therapeutic Course: A primary goal of treatment with Dean was to aid him in reducing his intense ambivalence and growing resentment of others. With an empathic and brief focus, it was possible to sustain a productive, therapeutic relationship. The therapist conveyed a genuine caring and firmness, and was thus able to overcome Dean's tendency to employ maneuvers to test the sincerity and motives of the therapist. Although he was slow to reveal his resentment because he disliked being viewed as an angry person, it was eventually brought into the open and dealt with in a kind and understanding way. He was not inclined to face his ambivalence, but his mixed feelings and attitudes were to be a major focus of treatment. To prevent him from trying to terminate treatment before improvement occurred and to forestall relapses, the therapist employed brief and circumscribed techniques to counter the patient's expectation that supportive figures would ultimately prove disillusioning.

Circumscribed *interpersonal* approaches (e.g., Benjamin, Kiesler) were used to deal with the seesaw struggle enacted by Dean in his relationship with his therapist. He alternately exhibited ingratiating submissiveness and a taunting and demanding attitude. Similarly, he also solicited the therapist's affections, but when those were expressed, he rejected them, voicing doubt about the genuineness of the therapist's feelings. The therapist used *cognitive procedures* to point out these contradictory attitudes. It was important to keep these inconsistencies in focus, as otherwise, Dean may have appreciated the therapist's perceptiveness verbally but not altered his attitudes. Involved in an unconscious repetition-compulsion in which he recreated disillusioning experiences that paralleled those of the past, Dean had to not only come to recognize the expectations cognitively, but had to be taught to deal with their enactment interpersonally.

Despite his ambivalence and pessimistic outlook, there was good reason to operate on the premise that Dean could overcome past disappointments. To recapture the love and attention he only modestly expressed in childhood could not be achieved, although habits that precluded his partial satisfaction could be altered in the "here and now." Toward that end, the therapist helped him disentangle needs that were in opposition to one another. For example, he both wanted and rejected the love of those on whom he depended. Despite this ambivalence, he entered new relationships, such as in therapy, as if an idyllic state could be achieved. He went through the act of seeking a consistent and true source of love, one that would not betray him as he believed his family and friends had in the past. Despite this optimism, he remained unsure of the trust he could place in others. Mindful of past betrayals and disappointment, he began to test his new relationships to see if they were loyal and faithful. In a parallel manner, he attempted to irritate and frustrate the therapist to check whether she would prove to be as fickle and insubstantial as others had been in the past. It was here that the therapist's warm support and firmness played a significant short-term role in reframing the patient's erroneous expectations and in exhibiting consistency in relationship behavior.

Although the rooted character of these attitudes and behavior would complicate the ease with which these therapeutic procedures progressed, short-term and circumscribed cognitive and *interpersonal therapy* techniques were quite successful. A thorough reconstruction of personality was not necessary to alter the patient's problematic pattern. In this regard, *family treatment methods* focusing on the network of relationships that sustained his problems may have proven to be useful. *Group* methods may also have been fruitfully employed to help the patient acquire self-control and consistency in close relationships.

It was prudent that the therapist did not set goals too high because Dean would not have been able to tolerate demands or expectations well. Brief therapeutic efforts were directed to build his trust, to focus on positive traits, and to enhance his confidence and self-esteem.

DEPRESSIVE PERSONALITY: SELF-DEROGATING TYPE
(DEPRESSIVE WITH MASOCHISTIC TRAITS)

CASE 12.3, LINDA K., 20

Presenting Picture: Linda K. had recently dropped out of college after a relatively short duration, as she seemed to feel that she was not one cut out for any type of intellectual venture, much less the social challenges of life on campus. As she put it, "I'm not a very interesting person." What she is capable of doing, she explained, does not hold enough merit to warrant anyone else's attention. She said that she likes to write, but only for herself, as she wouldn't want to waste anyone's time with her inevitably dull ideas. When asked about relationships, she remarked that she had recently had a boyfriend, but "he was only with me because he didn't have anyone else." Furthermore, attempts at platonic relationships were evaded in favor of life in a self-created hermitage. Not atypically, her mother, who seemed to have prompted this visit, believed that Linda didn't try to make friends or to be popular, and just a small effort on her part would have made all the difference in the world. This was rejected, of course, by Linda, who continued to believe in her predetermination as a stupid individual with little or nothing to offer anyone else.

Clinical Assessment: Feelings of helplessness and futility readily come to the fore when *self-derogating depressives* such as Linda are faced either with burdensome responsibilities or the anticipation of social abandonment. The actual loss of a significant person almost invariably prompts severe dejection if not a psychotic depression. Anticipation of abandonment prompted Linda to openly admit her weaknesses and shortcomings as a means of gaining reassurance and support; these were evident in her MCMI scores. Expressions of guilt and self-condemnation typically follow because these verbalizations often successfully deflect criticism from others, transforming their threats into comments of reassurance and sympathy.

Guilt may arise as a defense against the possible expression of resentment and hostility. Linda usually contained her anger because she dreaded provoking the retribution of abandonment and isolation. To prevent this occurrence, all aggressive impulses she felt were turned inward, discharging them through self-derisive comments and verbalizations of guilt and contrition. This maneuver not only tempered the exasperation of others, but often prompted others to respond in ways that made her feel redeemed, worthy, and loved. Hence, self-derogation served not only to express her feelings, but also to solicit support from others.

Linda had managed to gain a measure of control over her feelings of loss and anger. She had done so by turning her feelings inward, that is, by diminishing her own self-worth and taking out her hatred on herself. Thus, she persisted in voicing guilt and self-disparagement for her failures, guilt-ridden actions of the past, and other shameful feelings and thoughts. Through her self-derogating depressive personality style, Linda managed to cloak whatever contrary impulses she may have felt toward others, seek redemption, and ask absolution for her past behaviors and forbidden inclinations. Moreover, her self-derogating style solicited support and nurturance from others. In a more subtle way, it also served as a devious means of venting her hidden resentment and anger. Her state of helplessness and her protestations of self-derogation made others feel guilty and burdened them with extra responsibility and woes. As should be evident from the foregoing, we may identify a fusion between depressive and masochistic features among these individuals. It is in these fused personalities that we find characteristics that have been thoughtfully described by Kernberg (1988) and others, and have been termed *depressive-masochistic* characters.

These maneuvers became problematic themselves in that Linda became increasingly dismayed and disillusioned with herself. She became aware of the fact that she had wasted a part of her life, missing opportunities and falling behind her peers. Not only was she ashamed of herself, but she came to envy others who appeared to be so much more successful and achieving than herself. Self-derogation had only intensified her sense of worthlessness. By derogating herself, she had prevented herself from exploring her life wisely as well as finding a better route to make her life more worthwhile. Through her own actions, she had diminished whatever hopes she may have had. Not only did she feel a sense of loss for what might have been, but she had alienated herself from herself, often sinking into a depressive paralysis in which she was unable to function.

Synergistic Treatment Plan: It was necessary to build some aspect of hope from the outset, a particular challenge for Linda; an empathic setting combined with a *biophysical* tactic (antidepressant) would begin the process. From there, it would be possible to address the extreme imbalance of the *pleasure* and *pain* polarities, through use of *cognitive* techniques that could undo her self-perpetuating tendencies to discredit and disparage herself and to sabotage any positive events. From an *interpersonal* view, it would also be necessary for Linda to learn more effective means of relating than to seduce others into a sense of pity for her, and a more contextual *family* intervention would serve to explore and modify the system that sustains that tendency. At that point in treatment as well, it would be fruitful to explore *behaviorally* her need to avoid challenge and remain strongly *passive*. Throughout treatment, it would be most important to maintain an empathic, trusting environment and moderate and work to build on a rather weak sense of *self*.

Therapeutic Course: Linda did not believe that any therapeutic goals were tangible, and felt that she had best not set herself up for rejection and failure. It was crucial to the success of this short-term therapy that she determine from the very first stages that these goals were achievable, in spite of the fact that these strivings might remind her, in the process, of past disillusionment and defeat. She needed to be convinced that this "comfort in familiar discontent," that is, this anxious-depressive state she lived in by removing any personal or social aspirations, did not need to symbolize her potential.

Antidepressant medication, specifically, a serotonin uptake blocker, was useful in moderating her chronic despondency and blighted hope. *Cognitive-behavioral* methods were directed at Linda's depressogenic automatic thoughts, self-effacement, and behaviors that produced melancholy, derision, and belittlement of herself in the past. These short-term and focused techniques helped control her hypersensitivity to disapproval and modify her meek interpersonal style. They were also useful in disputing her cataclysmic projections which served only to reinforce her self-defeating and depressive inclinations.

To impede possible regression, a restructuring of Linda's false beliefs and interpersonal coping strategies was necessary. Focused *interpersonal methods* such as those of Klerman and Benjamin were especially helpful. Also most effective was an adjunctive *family intervention* strategy, which unearthed troublesome communication patterns that further reinforced Linda's social difficulties. Had this strategy been unavailable, a short-term group milieu may be opted for, to gain skills and adjust certain outlooks in a benign environment.

Linda frequently left herself vulnerable to being ill-treated, owing largely to her self-devaluation. Predictably, it was difficult for her to maintain any cohesion in her relationship with the therapist, and it required an empathic and warm stance to delve into facing anything besides veneer symptomology. It was quite apparent that Linda was terrified to face her feelings of inadequacy, but an appropriate and timely supportive approach enabled her to endure treatment through genuine short-term gains as well as toward substantial inherent growth. Following self-esteem and trust improvements, brief *cognitive reframing* procedures were useful in disputing uncertainties and conflictual emotions and expectations, as well as preventing an otherwise very likely pattern of short-term gains versus ongoing recession.

Finally, Linda's orientation was toward overanalyzing her environment, emphasizing anything that might be construed as critical of her that would go unnoticed by most others, as well as extrapolating further self-affrontive elements. This hypersensitivity essentially failed in its intended purpose, as it drew attention to menacing sensations that Linda really wanted to avoid. Cognitive techniques (e.g., Beck) aimed at monitoring this overattentiveness to every negative detail helped reduce these repetitive habits and decreased her related frustration and pain.

DEPRESSIVE PERSONALITY: MORBID TYPE
(DEPRESSIVE WITH DEPENDENT TRAITS)

CASE 12.4, DONALD B., 35

Presenting Picture: Donald B., an unemployed engineer, reported that he was absolutely lost in a hopeless fog of despondency, which seemed to permeate his entire being. He stated that he didn't know where he was going and had no idea what, if any-thing, he had to look forward to in life. "I'm pathetic" was an oft-heard, self-inflicted vituperation, and he faulted himself for the path his life had taken. No change seemed possible, as he had always felt this way, and even the most concerted effort he could muster would not crack the surface of this despair. To cope with this omnipresent gloom, Donald slept as much as possible, watched television constantly, and avoided interactions with others.

Clinical Assessment: A depressive paralysis is what comes to characterize Donald, whose *morbidly depressive* personality style blends into Axis I clinical depression, both of which were clearly present on the MCMI. Donald experienced deep feel-ings, contrasting markedly with the emotional flatness of certain schizoids. The gloom and profound dejection were clearly conveyed as he slumped with brow fur-rowed, body stooped, and head turned downward and away from the gaze of oth-ers, held in his hands like a burdensome weight. Various physical signs and symptoms further enabled us to distinguish Donald from other depressive person-ality subtypes. He had lost weight and looked haggard and drained. He followed a characteristic pattern of awakening after two or three hours of sleep, turning rest-lessly, having oppressive thoughts, and experiencing a growing dread of the new day. Notable also was the content of his verbalizations, meager though they were, re-porting a vague dread of impending disaster, feelings of utter helplessness, a per-vasive sense of guilt for past failures, and a willing resignation to his hopeless fate. Features of the dependent personality permeated Donald's psychic makeup. It was his deep and pervasive sense of personal incompetence that made him feel that he was incapable of coping; moreover, given his habitual style, he did not even hope to be able to deal with his current troubled state, hence resulting in the profundity of his dejection and morbidity. By contrast, other personalities that covary with the depressive possess sufficient feelings of competence and self-worth to enable them, at the very least, to believe that they *may* ultimately cope with the difficulties they experience.

When not in a deep phase of gloom, Donald evinced a withering self-contempt. He demeaned everything about himself, saw only the worst in what he had done, caught in an obsessive pessimism, a relentless negativism in which nothing seemed as if it could get better. He spoke of being an outcast, a sort of sacrificial victim, suffering forevermore by what life had done to him and what he had done to himself. Feeling permanently dislocated and unworthy, he "knew" that others were as contemptuous of him as he was of himself. He experienced "the black dog," a sense of inner dark-ness that drained whatever hope he may have wished for into a vacuous hole. Donald's mood was one of despondency and helplessness, a state akin to what other personal-ities exhibit when experiencing a clinical depressive syndrome. But for Donald, de-spair was a persistent and unrelenting state, so much so that it pervaded every fabric of his psychic makeup.

Synergistic Treatment Plan: *Activity* stimulation was most important with Donald, as he had, in effect, reached a point where his *passive* tendency allowed him to simply remain torpid and find some skewed contentment in inertia and gloom. Along with directly addressing his *biophysically* depressed state with appropriate *antidepressants,* it would be prudent to modify environmental factors to *behaviorally* affect his lethargic and indigent tendencies. As Donald adapted to these imposed changes, it would be possible, albeit cautiously, to begin working *cognitively* and *interpersonally* to increase autonomy skills, while undermining his perpetual state of being lost in pessimistic fantasy preoccupations. He needed to learn that *others* would not take responsibility for him, and that a healthier feeling would be derived from an enhanced sense of *self*, which would be facilitated by his greater independence and feelings of competence. This would be developed throughout via an empathic *experiential* milieu as well as with the adjunct *group* milieu that would occur later in treatment.

Therapeutic Course: Active short-term techniques with Donald took advantage of introducing environmental changes to maximize growth, minimize continued dependency, and provide uplifting experiences. *Psychopharmacologic treatment* was a useful adjunct that promoted alertness and vigor and countered fatigue, lethargy, dejection, and anxiety states that inclined Donald to postpone efforts at independence and confidence building. His relationship with the therapist was explored to overcome the dominance-submission patterns that may have characterized his recent history. Both nondirective and directive *cognitive* approaches fostered growth in autonomy and self-confidence. Although *psychodynamic* approaches were utilized to rework deep object attachments and to construct a base for competency strivings, they were less effective than more focused and brief therapeutic modes. *Group therapy* eventually was pursued fruitfully as a means of learning autonomous skills and as an aid to the growth of social confidence.

Circumscribed treatment efforts were best directed toward countering the dependency attitudes and behaviors of this self-effacing man. A primary therapeutic task was to prevent Donald from slipping into a totally ineffectual state as he sought to rely increasingly on a supportive environment. Owing to his anxious and morose outlook, he not only observed real deficits in his competence but also deprecated what virtues and talents he did possess. Trapped by his own persuasiveness, he had reinforced his belief in the futility of standing on his own, and therefore, he had tried less and less to overcome his inadequacies. Cognitive methods (e.g., Ellis, Beck) were especially helpful in reframing erroneous beliefs and assumptions about himself and those he believed others had of him.

Donald's strategy had fostered a vicious circle of increased helplessness, depression, and dependency. By making himself inaccessible to growth opportunities, he effectively precluded further maturation and became more saddened and more dependent on others. Short-term techniques ensured the continuation of competence activities and the acquisition of assertive behavior and attitudes. To prevent Donald from becoming passively incompetent and lost in fantasy preoccupations, a major though short-term approach was quickly instituted. Several *behavioral modification* methods as well as *interpersonal* techniques such as those of Benjamin and Kiesler were useful in this regard. Pressure on him to show marked increases in initiative and autonomy were gradual, however, because his capacities in this area were so limited.

Effective brief, focused treatment may have created the misleading impression that progress would continue at a rapid pace. Despite initial indications of solid advances, Donald still resisted efforts to assume much autonomy for his future. Persuading him to forgo his long-standing habits may have proven to be extremely slow and arduous, but these steps had to be undertaken to move forward in this regard and to provide support. Especially problematic was the feeling he had that an increase in the expectations of others may not be met and would thereby result in disapproval. Efforts to help him build an image of competence and self-esteem was an essential step in forestalling later backsliding. A program that strengthened his attributes and dislodged his habit of leaning on others was well worth the effort it took.

DEPRESSIVE PERSONALITY: RESTIVE TYPE
(DEPRESSIVE WITH AVOIDANT TRAITS)

CASE 12.5, JOAN K., 27

Presenting Picture: Joan K., a student teacher, was referred for counseling at the suggestion of the supervising principal. Although she claimed to feel "okay," it was immediately apparent that she was holding back some anguish or agitation, as her body language and demeanor suggested that there was a great deal that she wanted to express but could not. She spoke of "better days" with some lucidity, but suggested that even then, she was something of a passive observer among others who would always plan and participate in various enjoyable activities. Lately, she admitted, she had been sad, and had become somewhat scared when she was alone, as if the isolation would not go away. She did not know what to do about this most recent state, but seemed to have an idea where it came from. Nevertheless, she only alluded to this cause cryptically, further stating that "it was a long time ago, and I shouldn't still be sad about it."

Clinical Assessment: *Restive depressive personalities* such as Joan's often covary with avoidant personalities, creating a pattern of characteristics that reflect the features of both. Typically anguished and agitated, Joan exhibited a wrought-up despair, vacillating between fretfulness and confusion at one time, and dysphoria and despair the next. She evidenced a perturbed discontent as she thought about the anguish others had caused her, venting little of the displeasure and vexation she felt. Should she ventilate her disquieted and unsettled moods, she invariably would restrain acts of irritability and disillusionment by turning them inward, manifesting a despondency and sour disaffection with herself. These shifting and vacillating attitudes were identified on the MCMI and served to discharge her tensions and relieve her of her deep unhappiness and resentfulness. Nervous, fretful, distracted, Joan manifested a sequence of brittle moods, usually short-lived and intense, affects and attitudes that ultimately became increasingly self-destructive.

Unable to get a clear hold on her feelings, she may have expressed her self-destructive acts either directly through violent suicide or through insidious behaviors such as severe alcohol or drug abuse. As she despaired that anything in life could ever become rewarding again, she might have felt she must do something to express her deeply pessimistic view of both life and herself. Feeling defeated and helpless, seeing no way to restore her participation in the good life, Joan may have been on a path to conclude that she must rid herself of the inescapable suffering she experienced. To a restive depressive such as Joan, the suicide act would not merely be a means to bring attention to herself, but a way out, a final solution to the ever-present problems she faces, a way to eliminate once and for all a persistent and painful existence. This act of self-destruction could also serve as a way of retaliating against others for not having cared enough. It would be a form of retribution, of inflicting pain on others without being either overtly hostile or having to feel guilt after the act. It is the only aspect of her life she could master. Self-annihilating though it may be, suicide could become the final act that demonstrates she can control her life.

Synergistic Treatment Plan: Joan's hypersensitivity to *pain* made it rather difficult to find inroads, as she vigilantly avoided anything that might be threatening, yet still experienced pronounced unhappiness. This, of course, made *pleasure* a very foreign concept, one that would eventually need to be restimulated. A careful and nonthreatening *cognitive* intervention would help to undo this perpetuating tendency toward hyper-sensitivity and perhaps open her receptors to more pleasing experience, as well as undo more "typical" depressive assumptions. *Behaviorally,* it would be important to address the conflicting *active* (avoidant tendency) and *passive* (depressive tendency) polarities, to find appropriate responses to environmental challenges, as well as to examine past actions that have caused discontentment. As some sense of competency is achieved, it would then be appropriate to reverse her social detachment tendency by addressing *interpersonal* issues to resolve earlier resentments toward others as well as to undo anxieties regarding relationships. Throughout, it would be important to monitor and encourage *self-image* developments and maintain an empathic, trusting therapeutic stance.

Therapeutic Course: Joan needed to understand from the outset that the goals of treatment were fully achievable and that they should motivate rather than dissuade her. Joan feared that therapy would reawaken what she viewed as false hopes; that is, it would remind her of the disillusionment she experienced when she aspired in the past and was rejected. Now that she had found a modest level of comfort by distancing herself from desires and withdrawing from others, it was important therapeutically not to let matters remain at the level of depressive-anxious adjustment to which she had become accustomed.

Antidepressant medications may have been fruitful in moderating Joan's persistent dejection and pessimism, but were not utilized. At the *cognitive-behavioral* level, therapeutic attention was usefully directed to her depressogenic assumptions, anxious demeanor, self-deprecating attitudes, and behavior that evoked unhappiness, self-contempt, and derogation in the past. Short-term and focused *cognitive* techniques such as those developed by Beck, Meichenbaum, and Ellis helped reduce her sensitivity to rebuff and her morose and unassertive style, outlooks and fears that only reinforced her aversive and depressive inclinations.

To diminish or even prevent relapse, more focused procedures were useful in reconstructing the erroneous beliefs and interpersonal mechanisms that pervaded all aspects of Joan's behavior. *Interpersonal* therapies such as those of Klerman and Benjamin were especially productive. Along the same lines, short-term *group therapy* assisted her in learning new attitudes and skills in a more benign and accepting social setting than she normally encountered. Similarly, *family* techniques may have been explored as circumscribed methods to moderate destructive patterns of communication that contributed to or intensified her social problems.

Short-term techniques also focused attention on her depressive tendencies to demean her self-worth and subject herself to the mistreatment of others. *Supportive* measures were used to counteract Joan's hesitation about sustaining a consistent therapeutic relationship. The therapist expected to see the numerous maneuvers designed to test his sincerity. A warm and accepting attitude was needed because Joan feared facing her feelings of unworthiness and because she sensed that her coping defenses were weak. With skillful supportive approaches, it was possible to prevent her proclivity to withdraw from treatment before any real gains had been made. Cognitive methods were especially useful in exploring the contradictions in her feelings and attitudes. Without reframing techniques such as these, there would have undoubtedly been a seesaw struggle, with periods of temporary progress followed by retrogression. Genuine short-term gains were achieved, but only with a building of trust and the enhancement of her shaky sense of self-worth, both of which lent themselves well to brief cognitive procedures.

Another realm worthy of short-term attention was associated with Joan's extensive scanning and misinterpretation of the environment. By doing this, she increased the likelihood that she would encounter those troubling events she wished to avoid. Moreover, her exquisite and negatively oriented antennae picked up and intensified what most people simply overlooked. In effect, her hypersensitivity backfired, becoming an instrument that constantly brought to awareness the very pain she wished to escape. Effective, focused cognitive techniques were directed at reducing her vigilance and self-demeaning appraisals and hence diminished rather than intensified her anguish.

Risks and Resistances

The high success rate of antidepressants for treating symptoms of depressive personality disorder may lead some therapists to be prematurely reassuring that difficulties will quickly abate. Some patients who fail to respond to medication may feel pressure to do so and internalize the lack of pharmacologic success as a personal failure or as confirmation that they are a hopeless case. The little motivation they had to try to improve their lot may be undone, rendering potentially helpful cognitive, behavioral, or interpersonal interventions impossible to utilize. Some patients need to try several different medications before finding one they respond to favorably. It should be understood that disappointed initial optimism can confirm their skepticism and make patients unwilling to experiment with alternatives.

Other difficulties can arise from the depressive patient's need to find a magic solution and the therapist's willingness to provide it. Some patients may interpret their therapist's confidence as the promise of a powerful helper, and attribute improvements in their condition to his or her skill and knowledge, increasing their sense of dependency on the therapist rather than their sense of self-efficacy. Still others may attribute past difficulties to a "chemical imbalance" and, encouraged by their therapist's optimistic outlook, spring into new activities and relationships without having compensated for years of interpersonal and cognitive deficits. Therapists need to keep in mind that improved affect does not necessarily imply that the patient has acquired the skills needed to successfully tackle added responsibilities and to deal with the consequences of more risky interpersonal behavior. Patients may become too bold and thereby "get in trouble." Engaging in activities that carry great emotional risks and experiencing failure before new schemata and patterns have time to develop can send the patient into a renewed crisis of despair about the futility of both life and treatment.

Encouraging patients to make the most adaptive use of increased enthusiasm and energy, and helping them develop the skills needed for more socially rewarding and personally contented lives will be productive goals. The therapist must be mindful that long-standing interpersonal patterns will have to be addressed and changed for the patient to maintain improvements, and that old cognitive schemata will need more than pharmacologic intervention in order to change. Patients should be warned that bad times and moods inevitably will come again, and should be prepared to deal with them effectively, thereby preventing full relapse. Some patients may be so apprehensive about falling back into their previous state of despair that they do not truly appreciate their improved affect and are unwilling to experiment with new behavior for fear of negative consequences. The therapist must strike a therapeutic balance between being encouraging and optimistic on the one hand, yet urging caution on the other, emphasizing that recovery is a process and making no unrealistic promises about the possibility of future perfection and happiness.

CHAPTER THIRTEEN

Treating Dependent Personality Patterns

Distinguished by their marked need for social approval and affection, and by their willingness to live in accord with the desires of others, dependent personalities are among the most likely individuals to become distressed. Characteristically, these individuals are docile, noncompetitive, and passive. Apart from requiring signs of belonging and acceptance, dependents make few demands on others. Their own needs are subordinated and their individuality denied, as these individuals assume a submissive, self-sacrificing, and placating role in relation to others. Social tension and interpersonal conflicts are carefully avoided, and troubling events are smoothed over or naïvely denied. Beneath their warm and affable presentation, however, may lie a plaintive and pessimistic quality. Dependents perceive themselves as weak, fragile, and ineffective. The recognition of their helplessness and utter reliance on others may result in self-effacement and denigration. In addition, they may become excessively conciliatory in relationships to the point of submitting themselves to intimidation and abuse (Millon, 1981).

Given their pronounced susceptibility to separation anxiety, dependent personalities are quite likely to experience any number of chronic syndromes. Frequently, the underlying characterological pessimism of these individuals lends itself to a chronic but mild depression or dysthymia. When faced with possible abandonment or the actual loss of a significant other, a major depression or panic attack may ensue. Initially, these individuals may react with clinging helplessness and pleas for reassurance and support. Expressions of self-condemnation and guilt are also likely, as such verbalizations serve to deflect criticisms and evoke sympathetic reactions. Feelings of guilt can also act as a defensive maneuver to check outbursts of resentment or hostility. Fearful that their underlying feelings of anger might cause further alienation or retribution, dependents typically turn their aggressive impulses inward, discharging them through a despondency colored by self-derisive comments and contrition. On occasion, dependent personalities may make a desperate attempt to counter or deny emerging feelings of hopelessness and depression through a temporary reversal of their typical passive, subdued style to that of hypomanic activity, excitement, and optimism. Such dramatic shifts in affective expression may resemble a bipolar disorder.

The dependent personality corresponds to the psychoanalytic "oral character" type, and more specifically, to what has been termed the *oral sucking* or *oral receptive* character. For both Abraham (1911) and Freud (1925), the orally fixated depressive or melancholic has great oral needs, manifested by sucking, eating, and insatiable demands for oral expressions of affection. Emphasis is also placed on affectional frustrations occurring during the pre-Oedipal period. In essence, the melancholic has experienced a pathological introjection or identification with the ambivalently regarded love object through the process of oral incorporation. Thus, an interpersonal conflict is transformed to an intrapsychic conflict, with the angry desire to devour the frustrating love object being turned inward and experienced as depression.

As psychoanalytic theory developed, the concept of orality was extended to include the general feelings of warmth, nourishment, and security. The dependent personality's reliance on external approval and support for maintenance of self-esteem made him or her particularly vulnerable to depression resulting from the loss of a significant other. Rado (1969) described melancholia as a "despairing cry for love," and Fenichel (1945) described the orally dependent depressive as a "love addict."

A theory of depressive subtypes, based on attained level of object-representation, has been developed by Blatt (1974; Blatt & Shichman, 1983). Of the two depressive subtypes offered, *anaclitic* and *introjective*, the anaclitic depressive would correspond most closely to the dependent personality. Individuals with this form of depression have histories of impaired object relations at the primitive, oral level of development. Anaclitic depression is associated with intense dependency on others for support and gratification, vulnerability to feelings of deprivation, and considerable difficulties in managing anger expression for fear of alienating the love object.

This negative cognitive set of the dependent, that is, poor self-concept, disparaging view of the world, and the projection of continued hardships and frustrations in the future, is central to Beck's (1974) cognitive theory of personality. Recently, Beck and Freeman (1990a) extended their cognitive formulations to include other predisposing and precipitating factors, including personality attributes that may lead to depression. They propose two basic personality modes, the *autonomous* and the *socially dependent*, and describe the respective symptom patterns of each. Individuals within the socially dependent cluster depend on others for safety, help, and gratification and are characterized by passive receiving. Such individuals require stability, predictability, and constant reassurance in relationships. As rejection is considered worse than aloneness to the socially dependent, no risks are taken that might lead to alienation from sources of nurturance (e.g., asserting oneself with others). Similarly, social dependents avoid making changes and exposing themselves to novel situations, as they feel ill-equipped to cope with the unexpected.

We next turn to the dependent personality as interpreted in Millon's polarity model; Figure 13.1 outlines the major motivational elements that undergird the ecologically adaptive style of this personality prototype. As with the majority of other personalities, the role of the enhancement (pleasure) and preservation (pain) polarities are of only modest significance. This minimal role was not found in the case of the schizoid, avoidant, and depressive personality patterns; here, the pleasure domain was notably deficient and the pain domain was prominent. In the dependent personality, primary attention may be found in the other (nurturant) and the passive (accommodating) polarities. Dependents share with the histrionic personality style a major ecological commitment to an other-oriented direction; both seek support, attention, and

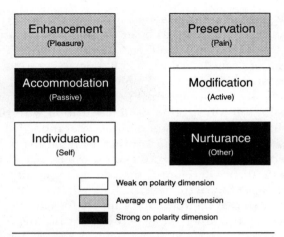

Figure 13.1 Status of the dependent personality prototype in accord with the Millon Polarity Model.

protection from others. However, for the dependent personality pattern, there is also an adaptive style of searching for guidance and support from others, a need to have them not only provide nurturance and protection but also to guide and show them how and when to achieve these security goals. This contrasts with the actively oriented ecological style of the histrionic personality, who arranges his or her life circumstances by making things happen. Histrionics may need others for attention and approval but are unwilling to accept the possibility that these might not be forthcoming; hence, they arrange and manipulate events rather than wait for others to do it for them. Histrionics take active steps to achieve their goals, effectively and reliably. By contrast, dependents entrust all to others, being passive, loyal, trustworthy, and dependable, but lacking in initiative and competence.

CLINICAL PICTURE

In the following sections, we draw on theory, clinical literature, and the *DSM*s to provide both the structure and details of the dependent personality pattern (see Table 13.1).

Prototypal Diagnostic Domains

Although the following analysis is separated into eight domains, the traits described should be seen as forming a coherent picture. Congruity among the eight descriptive realms of behavior, phenomenological report, intrapsychic processes, and biophysical temperament should be expected, as a distinguishing characteristic of a personality trait is its pervasiveness, that is, its tendency to operate in all spheres of psychological functioning. It should not be surprising, therefore, that each section provides a clinical impression similar to the others (see Figure 13.2).

TABLE 13.1 Clinical Domains of the Dependent Personality Prototype

Behavioral Level

(F) Expressively Incompetent (e.g., withdraws from adult responsibilities by acting helpless and seeking nurturance from others; is docile and passive, lacks functional competencies, and avoids self-assertion).

(F) Interpersonally Dependent (e.g., needs excessive advice and reassurance, as well as subordinates self to stronger, nurturing figure, without whom may feel anxiously alone and helpless; is compliant, conciliatory, and placating, fearing being left to care for self).

Phenomenological Level

(F) Cognitively Naïve (e.g., rarely disagrees with others and is easily persuaded, unsuspicious, and gullible; reveals a Pollyanna attitude toward interpersonal difficulties, watering down objective problems and smoothing over troubling events).

(S) Inept Self-Image (e.g., views self as weak, fragile, and inadequate; exhibits lack of self-confidence by belittling own attitudes and competencies, and hence not capable of doing things on one's own).

(S) Immature Objects (e.g., internalized representations are composed of infantile impressions of others, unsophisticated ideas, incomplete recollections, rudimentary drives, and childlike impulses, as well as minimal competencies to manage and resolve stressors).

Intrapsychic Level

(F) Introjection Mechanism (e.g., is firmly devoted to another to strengthen the belief that an inseparable bond exists between them; jettisons independent views in favor of those of others to preclude conflicts and threats to relationship).

(S) Inchoate Organization (e.g., owing to entrusting others with the responsibility to fulfill needs and to cope with adult tasks, there is both a deficient morphologic structure and a lack of diversity in internal regulatory controls, leaving a miscellany of relatively undeveloped and undifferentiated adaptive abilities as well as an elementary system for functioning independently).

Biophysical Level

(S) Pacific Mood (e.g., is characteristically warm, tender, and noncompetitive; timidly avoids social tension and interpersonal conflicts).

F refers to Functional Domains (fluid, interactive)
S refers to Structural Domains (stable, unchanging)

Incompetent expressive behavior.   Among the most notable features of dependents is their lack of self-confidence, a characteristic apparent in their posture, voice, and mannerisms. They tend to be overly cooperative and acquiescent, preferring to yield and placate rather than be assertive. Large social groups and noisy events are abhorrent, and they go to great pains to avoid attention by underplaying both their attractiveness and their achievements. They are often viewed by friends as generous and thoughtful, and at times as unduly apologetic and obsequious. Neighbors may be impressed by their humility, cordiality, and graciousness, and by the "softness" and gentility of their behavior.

Beneath their warmth and affability may lie a plaintive and solemn quality, a searching for assurances of acceptance and approval. These needs may be especially manifest under conditions of stress. At these times, dependents are likely to exhibit overt signs of helplessness and clinging behaviors. They may actively solicit and plead for attention and encouragement. A depressive tone will often color their mood, and they may become overtly wistful or mournful. Maudlin and sentimental by disposition, they may also become excessively conciliatory and self-sacrificing in their relationships.

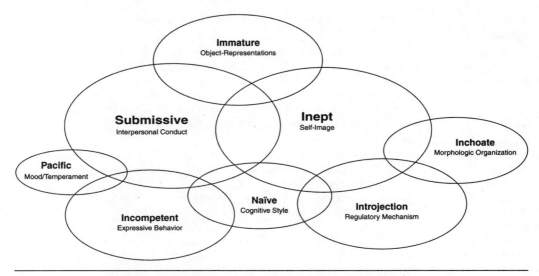

Figure 13.2 Salience of prototypal dependent domains.

Submissive interpersonal conduct.   What interpersonal behaviors do dependents use to manipulate their environment, and how do they arrange their relationships to achieve their aims?

A major problem for dependent individuals is that they not only find little reinforcement within themselves but feel that they are inept and stumbling and thus lacking in the skills necessary to secure their needs elsewhere. As they see it, only others possess the requisite talents and experience to attain the rewards of life. Given these attitudes, they conclude that it is best to abdicate self-responsibility, to leave matters to others, and to place their fate in others' hands. Others are so much better equipped to shoulder responsibilities, to navigate the intricacies of a complex world, and to discover and achieve the pleasures to be found in the competitions of life.

To achieve their goals, dependent personalities learn to attach themselves to others, to submerge their individuality, to deny points of difference, to avoid expressions of power, and to ask for little other than acceptance and support—in other words, to assume an attitude of helplessness, submission, and compliance. Moreover, by acting weak, expressing self-doubt, communicating a need for assurance, and displaying a willingness to comply and submit, dependents are likely to elicit the nurturance and protection they seek.

Naïve cognitive style.   It is characteristic of dependents to limit awareness of self and others to a narrow sphere, well within comfortable boundaries. They constrict their world and are minimally introspective and Pollyanna-like with regard to difficulties that surround them. From an introspective view, dependent personalities tend to be naïve, unperceptive, and uncritical. They are inclined to see only the "good" in things, the pleasant side of troubling events.

Inept self-image.   Dependents view themselves as weak and inadequate individuals, fragile when feeling alone or abandoned, and generally incapable of doing things on their own without the support or guidance of another. Not only do they lack a sense of self-confidence, but for reasons noted previously, they have a tendency to belittle their own competencies, beliefs, and achievements. Dependents not only see themselves as limited value to others, but prefer this image because few demands are made of inadequate persons, who are therefore often able to solicit the support and protection they desire.

From another perspective, dependents see themselves as considerate, thoughtful, and cooperative, disinclined to be ambitious and modest in their aspirations. Closer probing, however, is likely to evoke marked feelings of personal inadequacy and insecurity. Dependents tend to downgrade themselves, claiming to lack abilities, virtues, and attractiveness. They are disposed to magnify their failures and defects. When comparing themselves to others, they minimize their attainments, underplay their attributes, note their inferiorities, and assume personal blame for problems they feel they have brought on others. Of course, much of this self-belittling has little basis in reality. Clinically, this pattern of self-deprecation may best be conceived as a strategy by which dependents elicit assurances that they are not unworthy and unloved. Hence, it serves as an instrument for evoking praise and commendation.

Immature object-representations. If one is able to examine the inner world of dependents' representations of significant others, one is likely to see that these images are childlike if not infantile in character. The content of their intrapsychic world seems to be composed of unsophisticated ideas, incomplete recollections, and rudimentary aspirations. Persons are seen as they may have been years before (e.g., as parents were when the patient was a child). Most other personality types hold mixed images of the past; although initially infantile or childlike, the overlays of subsequent experiences give them a completeness, such that later impressions become part of the overall picture. For the dependent, however, there is a fixation on the past, with prominence given to more youthful impressions.

Dependents must be more than childlike if they are to secure and retain their "hold" on others. They must be admiring, loving, and willing to "give their all." Only by internalizing the role of the totally submissive and loyal can they be assured of evoking consistent care and affection. Fortunately, most dependents have learned through parental models how to behave affectionately and admiringly. Most possess an ingrained capacity for expressing tenderness and consideration, essential elements in holding on to their protectors. Also important is that most dependents have learned the "inferior" role well. They are able, thereby, to provide their "superior" partners with the feeling of being useful, sympathetic, stronger, and competent—precisely those behaviors that dependents seek in their mates. From many sources, then, dependent personalities have learned interpersonal strategies that succeed well in achieving the goals they seek.

Introjected regulatory mechanism. The inadequacies that dependents see within themselves may provoke feelings of emptiness and the dread of being alone. These terrifying thoughts are often controlled by introjection, a process by which they internalize the beliefs and values of another, imagining themselves to be one with or an integral part of a more powerful and supporting figure. By allying themselves with the competencies of their partners, they can avoid the anxieties evoked by the thought of their own impotence. Not only are they uplifted by illusions of shared competence, but through incorporation they may find solace in the belief that the attachment they have constructed is firm and inseparable.

Denial mechanisms also characterize the dependent's defensive style. This is seen most clearly in the Pollyanna quality of dependents' thoughts. Dependents are ever alert to soften the edges of interpersonal strain and discomfort. A syrupy sweetness may typify their speech, and they may persistently cover up or smooth over troublesome events. Especially threatening are their own hostile impulses; any inner feeling or thought that might endanger their security and acceptance is quickly staved off. A torrent of contrition and self-debasement may burst forth to expiate momentary transgressions.

Inchoate morphologic organization. The dependent has entrusted to others the capabilities and responsibilities for dealing with life's tasks. As a consequence, the morphologic structure of the dependent's intrapsychic world has not developed an adequate diversity of regulatory controls. What exists in this realm are either "borrowed" competencies through introjection or a melange of relatively underdeveloped and undifferentiated coping abilities. Although able to function adequately when allied or closely connected to others who can "function" for them, dependents are only weakly effective when coping on their own.

By acting in a weak and inferior manner, dependents effectively free themselves of the responsibilities they know they should assume but would rather not. In a similar manner, self-depreciation evokes sympathy and attention from others, for which dependents are bound to feel guilt. Maneuvers and conflicts such as these are difficult for dependents to tolerate consciously. To experience comfort with themselves, dependents are likely to deny the feelings they experience and the deceptive strategies they employ. Likewise, they may cover up their obvious need to be dependent by rationalizing their inadequacies, that is, by attributing them to some physical illness, unfortunate circumstance, or the like. And to prevent social condemnation, they are careful to restrain assertive impulses and to deny feelings that might provoke criticism and rejection.

Dependents' social affability and good-naturedness not only forestall social deprecation but reflect a gentility toward the self, a tender indulgence that *protects* them from being overly harsh with their own shortcomings. To maintain equilibrium, they must take care not to overplay their expressions of guilt, shame, and self-condemnation. They are able to maintain a balance between moderate and severe self-deprecation by a Pollyanna tolerance of the self, "sweetening" their own failures with the same saccharine attitude that they use to dilute the shortcomings of others.

Pacific mood/temperament. When matters are progressing well in their lives, dependents tend to be warm, tender, and noncompetitive, timidly avoiding social tensions and interpersonal conflicts. However, this pacific mood gives way under conditions of rejection and abandonment, a time period when dependents are likely to seek counseling or therapy. Underneath their initial Pollyanna veneer, these troubled dependents can no longer feel the joy of living. Once their "hair is let down," they will report deep feelings of insecurity, pessimism, discouragement, and dejection. Whatever their "suffering" may have been before, it is no longer done in silence, away from those for whom they had to appear pleased and content with life. Now that life has taken a turn for the worse, their underlying insecurities become evident in gloomy and tearful emotions.

Self-Perpetuation Processes

It may appear strange, even paradoxical, that the genuine affection and acceptance experienced in childhood by dependent personalities should dispose them to pathology. For most of these individuals, childhood was a time of warmth and security, a period marked by few anxieties that were not quickly dispelled by parental attention and care. Too much of a good thing, however, can turn bad. Excessive parental shielding may establish habits and expectancies that are detrimental in the long run because they ill prepare children to cope on their own with life. Accustomed to support from others and ill-equipped without them, dependents stand implanted, rooted to the deep attachments of their childhood. Unable to free themselves from their dependence, they face the constant danger of loss, dread desertion, and fear the abyss into which they will fall if left on their own. Beneath their pleasant and affable exterior, then, lies an extreme vulnerability, a sense of helplessness, and a fear of abandonment. Dependents' lack of resources and their self-doubts compel them to seek safe partners, trustworthy figures "like Mother," who can be depended on to assure them that they are loved and will not be deserted.

What does the future usually hold for dependents, how and why do they remain fixed in their ways, and what approaches are best when intervening therapeutically? Questions such as these are addressed, albeit briefly, in this final section of the chapter.

Dependent personalities, despite claims to ineptness and inadequacy, employ an interpersonal coping strategy that recruits the nurture and support they need. Moreover, it is a style that forestalls their sinking into deeper levels of psychopathology. By soliciting attention and affection, dependents remain in close touch with the "real" world and are exposed constantly to social relationships that keep them from straying too far into the abyss of subjective distortion. Despite the fact that dependency behaviors protect against the pernicious and decompensating effects of social withdrawal and autistic distortion, the problem remains that the coping strategy persists far beyond its origins and ultimate utility. More important, it leads the person into self-defeating vicious circles. A brief review follows of some of the features that result in the aggravation of the dependent's characteristic inadequacies (see Table 13.2).

TABLE 13.2   Self-Perpetuating Processes

DEPENDENT

Self-Depreciation
> Loss of self-respect
> Deepens image of incompetence
> Senses futility of overcoming defects

Avoids Adult Activities
> Fear of independence
> Self-restrictions diminish growth
> Becomes fixated in adolescence

Clinging Social Behaviors
> Exasperates those on whom they depend
> Reproaches self for dependence
> Continued inefficacy results in depression

Self-deprecation.   Dependents not only observe real deficits in their competence, but they deprecate what virtues and talents they may possess. This is done to prevent others from expecting them to assume responsibilities they would rather avoid. Successful as a shield against discomfort and in protecting their dependency needs, these actions are carried out at the cost of demeaning their own self-respect. Their rationalizations of inadequacy, offered for the benefit of others, have an impact on their own person. Each time dependents announce their defects, they convince themselves as well as others and thereby deepen their self-image of incompetence. Trapped by their own persuasiveness, they further reinforce their belief in the futility of standing on their own, and hence, they are likely to try less and less to overcome their inadequacies. Their strategy has fostered a vicious circle of increased helplessness and dependency.

Avoidance of adult activities.   Dependents' sense of inadequacy, fear of failure, and hesitation about antagonizing others cause them to refrain from activities that may facilitate a more mature and independent lifestyle. For example, despite ample opportunities to learn skills and to assume more "manly" roles, some dependent men shy away from these "threats," fear they could never succeed, and prefer instead to remain inept but good-natured and easy to get along with. Self-imposed restrictions will diminish short-term embarrassments and anxieties associated with failure, but they also diminish the probability that dependents will acquire competence and confidence that will enable them to function more maturely. By making themselves less accessible to growth opportunities, they effectively preclude further maturation and, hence, become ever more needful of others, resulting in clinging social behaviors. Although dependents appease others and apologize for their incompetence, their need for affection and assurance that they will not be abandoned may become so persistent as to exasperate and alienate those on whom they lean most heavily. Of course, exasperation and alienation on the part of others only serve to increase dependents' neediness. As the vicious circle persists, they may become more desperate, more ingratiating, and more urgently pleading and clinging, until they become "millstones around their partner's neck." Wearying of demands to prove fealty and love, the stronger partner may come to openly express annoyance, disapproval, and, finally, rejection. Seriously rebuffed, a cycle of decompensation may begin or take on an increased pace. Overt expressions of self-blame, self-criticism, and self-condemnation may come to the fore. Fearful of expressing hostility, lest this result in further loss, dependents are likely to turn these feelings inward—first, to reproach themselves for their shortcomings and, second, to promise to be "different" and redeem themselves for their past mistakes. The "new leaf" they plan to "turn" takes the form of promises of greater competence and less dependence, aspirations that run counter to their lifelong personality style. These goals rarely are achieved, and it is at this point that we often see the emergence of a serious symptom disorder such as a major depression.

INTERVENTION GOALS

Despite the possibilities of decompensation just noted, the prognosis for the dependent pattern is relatively good. Dependents are likely to have had a supporting relationship with at least one parent, and this provides them with a reservoir of security and a feeling of being loved and wanted. Each of these positive emotions will sustain a dependent through difficult periods. Additionally, affectionate parents serve as models for imitative learning, equipping dependents with reciprocal habits of affection and generosity. As noted earlier, dependency needs assure interpersonal contact, thereby forestalling the potentially decompensating effects of self-preoccupation and subjective distortion.

Dependents' developmental history and early learning experiences have profoundly influenced their current personality pattern. The submissive dependence on others pervades all clinical domains and has resulted in an imbalance in the polarities. Because this personality style is so ingrained and others have learned to react to the dependent in a predetermined manner, the pattern perpetuates itself. Making the dependent's life more balanced by targeting the weaker areas constitutes a major therapeutic goal for this disorder (see Table 13.3).

Reestablishing Polarity Balances

Dependents have learned that the source of pleasure and the avoidance of pain are found externally. Dependents define themselves in terms of others and therefore seek nurturance from others. Given their often extreme reliance on their partners, alteration of the other-self polarity involves countering the belief that their fate is dependent on others and fostering the self-focus as well as a diversification of coping strategies. To gain support and nurturance, dependents have learned to wait in a passive manner for others to take the lead. In the passive-active polarity, one of the main goals of therapy is to increase their active involvement in pursuing need satisfaction without excessive support from others.

Countering Perpetuating Tendencies

The dependent's deep-seated feelings of incompetency must be addressed in therapy because they contribute to the failure to develop a more independent lifestyle. Increasing self-perceptions of adequacy will provide the dependent with the courage to engage in a wide variety of social experiences and hence will preclude the possibility

TABLE 13.3   Therapeutic Strategies and Tactics for the Prototypal Dependent Personality

STRATEGIC GOALS
Balance Polarities
    Stimulate active/modifying polarity
    Encourage self-focus

Counter Perpetuations
    Reduce self-depreciation
    Encourage adult skills
    Diminish clinging behaviors

TACTICAL MODALITIES
    Correct submissive interpersonal conduct
    Enhance inept self-image
    Acquire competence behaviors

of social withdrawal and isolation. A consequence of this improvement will be a lessened need for others to provide a more stable sense of security. A decrease in clinging behaviors will help interrupt the dependent perpetuating pattern because rejection by significant others and the internalization of failure becomes less likely. Additional perpetuating factors have probably reflected childhood social stereotypes in which others have learned to selectively perceive only the person's dependent attributes and ignore efforts at independence. Changing the expectations of significant others leads to a broad range of social experiences essential for change.

Identify Domain Dysfunctions

Most notable in dependents are their deficiencies in the self-image and interpersonal conduct domains. Targeting feelings of inadequacy and fostering the development of a more competent sense of self should be considered primary goals of therapy. This will be facilitated if a concurrent attempt is made to reduce the submissive behavior that characterizes their interpersonal style. Expressively, dependents lack functional competencies, and their passivity diminishes opportunities for more diverse experiences that might promote feelings of adequacy. Therapy should further attempt to counter dependents' naïve cognitive style that emerges when confronted with interpersonal difficulties and problematic events. Helping dependents assess the validity of their beliefs about the consequences of assertive and autonomous behavior and engaging them in reality testing will clear the way for changes in this domain.

Intrapsychically, dependents defend against stress by employing introjection as a primary mechanism. They deal with their feelings of ineptness by identifying with others. This gives them a false sense of security and protects them from exposing their own relatively undeveloped adaptive style. By promoting self-control, independent thinking, and a more active attempt at acquiring mature skills, the therapist can foster improvement. Helping dependents to establish an independent personal identity will also require replacing the internalized representations of others with more realistic mature ones of their own.

SELECTING THERAPEUTIC MODALITIES

To facilitate improvements in the areas just noted, the therapist can opt to use a variety of techniques. These must be chosen and synchronized in such a manner as to allow for the optimal acquisition of independent and autonomous skills, at the same time encouraging movement between self and others. Invariably, resistance will be encountered along the way, and an understanding of the nature of these obstacles and when they are likely to occur will assist in treatment planning.

Behavioral Techniques

Dependents are rather passive and unsure of themselves, often waiting for others to provide support and guidance. Behavioral techniques can be employed after a functional analysis of behavior has been completed. This will bring to light the problem areas in the patient's life and target the avoidance behaviors that reinforce the maintenance of this pattern. A functional analysis of the dependent's style will reveal that although the immediate consequences of clinging behavior may be positive, long-term effects can run exactly counter to the desired effect and result in hostility from others.

With proper guidance, however, dependents can start to recognize the patterns of their dependency, including the events and cognitions that prompt their behavior. Setting up an anxiety hierarchy of independent and assertive behaviors for gradual implementation is a good place to begin. Both role-playing and modeling can provide the patient with basic skills for a new repertoire of behaviors. Before attempting this, it is critical to assess whether the patient actually lacks functional competencies. If this appears to be the case, some remedial training of appropriate skills should be considered. In session, reinforcement and feedback can be provided immediately contingent upon appropriate behavior. Gradual exposure can move from in-therapy situations to external settings, such as the home, social gatherings, and work, fostering generalization and maintenance of the newly acquired competencies. While the patient is working on the hierarchy, anxiety levels may temporarily rise. Teaching patients anxiety-reducing skills, such as breathing techniques and deep muscle relaxation, can help them feel more at ease and can additionally increase their tolerance for anxiety.

Dependents' reluctance to stand up for themselves can be targeted with assertiveness training and by specifically teaching skills that allow the expression of negative feelings in a constructive way. Complementary techniques include communication skills training and role-playing. Role-playing, as Klerman (1984) notes, can accomplish two goals. It provides the therapist with a more adequate sense of the patient's relationships with others and can thus be quite revealing; additionally, it allows the patient to practice increasingly assertive behaviors.

Teaching self-management techniques and behavioral contracting can be most helpful with dependents in bolstering self-reliance. Initially, the therapist will want to provide guidance when writing self-contracts to ensure that they are fair and manageable. The key to successful behavioral management here is appropriate reinforcement of the target goal, that is, increasingly independent behavior.

Interpersonal Techniques

Interpersonal techniques can be useful in treating dependents, not only because they are receptive to treatment, but also because they are disposed to seek assistance wherever they can, especially in close interpersonal relationships. The strength and authority of the therapist comforts them with a feeling of assurance that an all-powerful person will come to their rescue when needed and provide them with the kindness and helpfulness they crave. Moreover, the task of unburdening their woes to a therapist calls for little effort on their part. Although they may lack accurate insight into their difficulties, dependents will provide ample data to lead the therapist to uncover the origins of their problems. Furthermore, dependents are disposed to trust others, especially therapists, to whom they are likely to attribute great powers and the highest of virtues. As therapy progresses, dependent patients are likely to forget the primary complaint that brought them into treatment; in time, their only reason for continuing is to maintain their dependent attachment to their therapist. Many will attempt to seduce their clinician into their habits of avoiding decisions and asserting themselves. As should be evident, the clinician must resist the patient's wishes and, in a kindly way, insist that he or she give evidence of independent thoughts and actions.

It is very important that the relationship between the therapist and the dependent patient not reestablish the dominance-submission pattern that has characterized the patient's history. Interpersonally, the dependent needs to learn to separate and differentiate self from others, thereby becoming increasingly autonomous. A major challenge for the therapist is to draw patients into a pattern of behaviors that are quite different from their usual one, that is, to assist them to stop submitting to others and to learn the skills of being independent. Although this may prove difficult for dependents owing to their history of intense enmeshments with significant others, they also may lack an understanding of what it means to be separate and autonomous. From their viewpoint, they see relationships as consisting of two choices, either to dominate others or to submit to them. Because domination is considered a form of aggressive bullying, they reject it in favor of submission. The therapist can help patients explore their long-standing patterns of interacting and how these have maintained their inadequate behaviors. Analysis of dependent behaviors displayed in session may further shed light on the dynamics of this mode of interacting. The therapist, at times, may wish to communicate personal reactions to provide patients with valuable feedback. L.S. Benjamin (1993) points out that dependents have a restricted view of their interpersonal world and that they do not consider the possibility of being in charge or in control.

Group therapy may be particularly suited as an arena for learning autonomous skills and as an aid to the dependent's growth of social confidence. In this setting, patients can learn to assert themselves while receiving feedback that others will not abandon them when they display confidence and make independent decisions. Depending on the patient's level of motivation and potential for growth, either a supportive problem-solving group or a more insight-oriented group may be appropriate. Especially when patients' difficulties are deeply ingrained, problem-solving groups may be particularly beneficial, such as those oriented to assertiveness training, decision making, and social skill acquisition. In the dyadic relationship between the therapist and the dependent, some regressive behaviors may be elicited as well as negative transferences that may be counterproductive to therapeutic progress. In contrast, the group offers the advantage that when dysfunctional patterns are reactivated, feedback comes from "equals." There is a good likelihood that constructive interactions will occur between the dependent and group members. Another advantage of the group setting is that abandonment issues may arise less frequently because the dependent is not solely reliant on the therapist for nurturance.

Family or couples therapy may be helpful, especially in those cases where the family system is instrumental in maintaining the dependent pattern. These patients can often function satisfactorily if their families consistently meet their needs; they become unsettled and symptomatic when such support decreases. The family can play an important role in facilitating behavior change by not excusing the dependent from assuming adult responsibilities. The role of societal and cultural factors, however, must be kept in mind when working with dependents and their families. Independent and assertive behavior may not be sanctioned by a large segment of the system. When work on interpersonal relationships is contraindicated because of these prohibitions, other options such as environmental change may be explored to maximize growth and minimize continued dependence. Encouraging the development of outside interests, for example, may open the door to myriad opportunities the dependent would never have considered for fear of endangering his or her relationships with significant others.

Cognitive Techniques

Beck and Freeman (1990a) also note that dependent persons show dichotomous thinking with respect to independence, believing either that one is completely dependent and in need of help or totally independent and alone. There do not appear to be gradations. This may contribute to a belief that the goal of therapy is independence and consequently isolation. The patient's unrealistic expectations about the consequences of displaying more independent behavior can be addressed cognitively by helping the patient place a variety of behaviors on a continuum from dependence to independence.

Once dependents develop a more realistic perception of their internal and external environment, there will be less need to suppress or minimize resentments and potential interpersonal conflicts. Successfully challenging automatic beliefs and maladaptive schemata is a primary part of this process. The therapist may initially need to provide direct assistance in identifying more rational responses and exploring alternative modes of interacting, but at some point in therapy, the patient must be encouraged to actively explore the consequences of alternative behaviors.

The dependent's automatic thoughts are likely to interfere with progress in therapy and will be evidenced by complaints of not being able to complete homework assignments or exercises. The therapist can use this resistance productively by asking the patient to test the validity of these thoughts through in-session reality testing. Emerging feelings of anxiety may produce resistance tactics, but a moderate degree of anxiety is necessary at times for change to occur. Time-limited approaches to cognitive treatment may also prove helpful in motivating increased patient activity. Knowing at the very outset that treatment will be limited to 10 or 15 sessions may lead patients to recognize that unlimited nurturance and dependence is not sustainable, hence compelling them to confront their anxieties about abandonment and to undertake activities that may enable them to become autonomous.

Self-Image Techniques

Although there are a multitude of techniques the therapist may elect to use, the fundamental goal is to bolster dependents' self-image and encourage the use of a more active problem-solving approach in dealing with life's problems. In the course of therapy, their distorted thoughts are identified, monitored, and subsequently challenged.

Initially, dependents will likely look to the therapist to provide them with answers and to tell them what to do. Guided discovery and Socratic-type questioning can help the patient arrive at a greater understanding of what is transpiring (Beck & Freeman, 1990a). The therapist can further this course by asking patients to record their perceptions and feelings about problematic events. In this manner, patients can monitor situations that occur during the week and start gaining more insight into their automatic thoughts and associated emotions. Particular attention should be paid to the sequence of events and their consequences, including reactions from significant others. This will highlight the sustaining nature of their dysfunctional style.

Working on identifying maladaptive and perpetuating patterns will soon bring to light the automatic and demeaning thoughts of the dependent personality. Dependents are best described as naive and rather gullible. They tend to smooth over events that others would consider disturbing. Because they see themselves as unable to manage without the assistance of others, they may have developed this naïve style and Pollyanna attitude to avoid interpersonal conflict and the expected repercussions that ensue. Therapy should assist patients to substitute passive cognitions with more active ones and an improving self-image for an inept one. As Sperry (1995) has pointed out, a process of guided discovery and Socratic questioning may help these patients learn to form their own solutions and make their own decisions, reducing thereby their habitual reliance on others. Success in these techniques may become significant evidence to challenge dependents' belief in their own helplessness. Together with various behavioral experiments (e.g., assertiveness and skill training), these Socratic tasks can facilitate a transition to greater independence.

The therapist may wish to use some Gestalt techniques to facilitate schema changes at the emotional level, while simultaneously working on developing problem-solving skills. One such approach, the two-chair technique, allows for the expression of feeling without having to fear the consequences. The dependent can work on one part of the conflict while sitting on one chair and then switch chairs to play the role of adversary. The reversal technique may be especially suited to practice assertiveness skills, making the transition to facing the actual person less abrupt. The dependent can be instructed to act out the part of an uncompromising, obstinate person. A good deal of emphasis should be placed on the feelings experienced during these exercises. Suggesting that the patient write letters can further cultivate expression of emotion.

Intrapsychic Techniques

To rework deeper object attachments and to construct a base for competency strivings, it may be necessary to utilize *psychodynamic* approaches. The therapist-client relationship can be the basis for a corrective emotional experience. The patient can gradually start to internalize healthy components of this relationship, thereby replacing the immature representations currently existing. Gabbard (1994) comments on the importance of exploring the unconscious factors that might contribute to the dependence. He states that a submissive clinging stance toward others may have different meanings for each dependent: for some, it may be a defense against hostility; for others, it is a way to avoid the reactivation of traumatic experiences. Exploring the dependent's past separations and their impact is recommended. A decreased but healthier intimacy with parents will ensue as a more realistic perception of the parents emerges. With more seriously impaired personalities, the goal of therapy may be to bypass total independence and instead gear therapy toward helping them substitute dependency on the original family with a less severe dependency on the marital partner (Stone, 1993). The therapist can serve as a temporary transitional object.

It is not unlikely that during the course of therapy, some relationships will come to an end; ultimately, so will the therapeutic relationship. As with other losses, some grief work may be necessary.

As patients' exposure to mature relationships starts to increase, the therapist's interventions may address the dependent's lack of diversity in internal controls and regulatory mechanisms. Dependents will often subordinate their own needs to those of others because they fear being deprived of a supporting relationship. Moreover, their low self-esteem leads them to place excessive value on others. As a result, the dependent's primary defense mechanism is introjection. Because they have always relied on others to take care of them and solve their problems, dependents have not pursued the development of independent skills. Their deficient morphologic structure can be targeted by focusing on gradually building skills and on self-management, thereby increasing the dependent's coping abilities. As therapy progresses, the clinician should gradually increase his or her expectations of the patient's self-initiated actions and autonomous decision making. These may be "boosted" with a variety of encouraging reinforcements for increased self-management.

Pharmacologic Techniques

Psychopharmacologic treatment, notably certain antidepressants and anxiolytic agents, may occasionally prove useful in treating dependents. Because they are often plagued by fatigue, lethargy, and diffuse anxieties, states that incline them to postpone efforts at independence, these agents may be used to promote vigor and alertness. Anxiety may temporarily increase when the patient is experimenting with increasingly autonomous behaviors because the threat of rejection or abandonment is perceived as all too real. Restoring the patient's anxiety levels to normal limits may be facilitated by relaxation training. In those severe cases when extreme separation anxiety and possible panic attacks are present, SSRI and tricyclic antidepressants as well as MAOIs may be considered, with appropriate consultation and follow-up. Special care should be taken *not* to allow the patient to become overreliant on medication as well as to avoid medication with possible addictive properties. As Joseph (1997) has noted, the combination of pharmacologic agents in a broad-based psychotherapeutic model may have synergistic effects; medications may provide fairly rapid symptom relief, whereas other psychotherapies may furnish reassurance, understanding, and psychosocial coping skills.

MAKING SYNERGISTIC ARRANGEMENTS

Dependent personalities inevitably enter therapy soliciting active assistance from the therapist. As previously mentioned, the dependent is likely to feel positive about therapy and its prospects for providing nurturance, support, and guidance. Engaging the patient in therapy and establishing a long-term therapeutic alliance can be accomplished by initially giving the patient more directive feedback and engaging in acute problem solving. As Beck and Freeman (1990a) note, it may be wise to allow some dependence in the treatment, as long as the therapist consistently works to wean the patient away from that dependence. According to these authors, progress in therapy from dependence to autonomy can be fostered by changing the structure of therapy itself. Sessions can move from the therapist's providing the structure and being more directive to the patient's dictating the agenda. Moving from individual to group therapy can additionally serve to reduce the patient's dependence on the therapist. When a trusting relationship has been formed, the therapist can make use of interpersonal reinforcement to encourage the patient to experiment with increasingly independent behaviors. If a significant degree of anxiety is present, therapy may be largely confined to more supportive methods until relief occurs. Psychopharmacologic intervention may then also be considered.

Cognitive and behavioral techniques are best used concurrently to deal with the almost inevitable resistance to giving up dependent behaviors. At the domain level, it will become evident that once they successfully start to build autonomous skills, dependents' view of themselves as capable, effective human beings will be enhanced.

TABLE 13.4   Dependent Personality Disorder Subtypes

Immature: Unsophisticated, half-grown, unversed, childlike; undeveloped, inexperienced, gullible, and unformed; incapable of assuming adult responsibilities.

MCMI 3

Ineffectual: Unproductive, gainless, incompetent, useless, meritless; seeks untroubled life; refuses to deal with difficulties; untroubled by shortcomings.

MCMI 3-1

Disquieted: Restlessly perturbed; disconcerted and fretful; feels dread and foreboding; apprehensively vulnerable to abandonment; lonely unless near supportive figures.

MCMI 3-2A

Accommodating: Gracious, neighborly, eager, benevolent, compliant, obliging, agreeable; denies disturbing feelings; adopts submissive and inferior role well.

MCMI 3-4

Selfless: Merges with and immersed into another; is engulfed, enshrouded, absorbed, incorporated, willingly giving up own identity; becomes one with or an extension of another.

MCMI 3-8B

With the aid of behavioral experiments, they should gradually acquire competencies to rectify their expressive and organizational deficits. No longer "incompetent," the dependent will observe that abandonment and rejection are not imminent, thereby reducing the need for interpersonal clinging and introjection. Improvements in their self-image will in turn serve to increase the chances that they will attempt new behaviors and thereby acquire significant functional competencies.

Illustrative Cases

Although all combinations are possible theoretically, experience and research show that only certain personality types tend to overlap or coexist with the dependent disorder (Millon & Davis, 1996a). This discussion draws on the evidence of several statistical cluster studies to supplement what theoretical deduction and observation suggest as the most prevalent personality mixtures. Also included are patterns that reflect differences in the pathogenic background of the various personality subtypes (see Table 13.4).

DEPENDENT PERSONALITY: DISQUIETED TYPE
(DEPENDENT WITH AVOIDANT TRAITS)

CASE 13.1, MICHELLE K., 22

Presenting Picture: Michelle K.'s mother brought Michelle into therapy after she had an angry outburst that disrupted the household for two weeks. Michelle appeared quiet and pleasant on the surface, but she had a rather tight lip and stiff posture that belied this calmness. Underneath, fear and angry tension seemed to drive much of her behavior. Michelle lived with her mother, who structured her life for her, planned her meals, organized her recreation, and acted as her only companion. Michelle admitted to being very afraid of being left alone and tried to organize her life so that this was a rare occurrence. When she was alone in the house, she kept to her room, where she holed up with her romance novels and television. Michelle held down a part-time job as a clerk at a grocery store, where she had a coworker who mentored and supported her. Michelle's mother generally provided her with the kind of constant attention and assurance that she demanded, but on one occasion when on a business trip, she failed to telephone Michelle to inform her that she had safely arrived at her hotel. Michelle became enraged and expressed that she felt abandoned and forgotten. Her mother became increasingly resentful of the demands Michelle was making on her and insisted she come in for therapy.

Clinical Assessment: As with other dependent varieties, Michelle's behavior was characterized as submissively dependent, self-effacing, and noncompetitive. Others were leaned on for guidance and security, and a passive role was assumed in relationships. However, she gave evidence of intense apprehensiveness and fearfulness that overlay a sulking lack of initiative and an anxious avoidance of autonomy. Hence, as a *disquieted dependent,* she reflected a commingling of both the basic dependent style interwoven with those of the avoidant personality.

We may summarize some of her more distinctive features by noting that she was restlessly perturbed at times, seemed easily disconcerted and fretful, and experienced a general sense of dread and foreboding; but, as with other dependents, she was apprehensively vulnerable to fears of abandonment and experienced a sense of loneliness unless she was near nurturing figures or had access to supportive institutions.

Michelle was exceedingly dependent, not only in needing attention and support from others to maintain equanimity, but in being especially vulnerable to separation from those who provided support. Anguished and fearful of loss, she ventilated her tensions through outbursts of anger directed toward others for having failed to appreciate her needs for security and nurturance. The very security that she so desperately needed was completely undone, however, when resentments were expressed.

As a disquieted dependent, she was not only apprehensive, but acquired a pattern of withdrawing from social encounters. Further, she had built up armor to damp down and deaden excessive sensitivity to rejection. She frequently experienced loneliness and isolation. Although efforts were made to be pleasant and agreeable, as dependents often are, she experienced an underlying tension and emotional dysphoria, expressed in disturbing mixtures of anxious, sad, and guilt-ridden feelings. Insecurity and fears of abandonment underlay what may appear on the surface to be a quiet, dependent, and benign attitude toward difficulties. Despite past rebuff and fears of isolation, she continued to evidence a clinging helplessness and a persistent search for support and reassurance. Her complaints of weakness and easy fatigability may have reflected an underlying mood of depression. Having experienced continuing rebuff from others, she may have succumbed to physical exhaustion and illness. Under these circumstances, simple responsibilities demanded more energy than she could muster. She expressed the feeling that life was empty but heavy, and experienced a pervasive sense of anxiety and fatigue.

Synergistic Treatment Plan: Pivotal to timely significant change for Michelle was a focus on developing a more mature and resourceful sense of *self,* which would color the entire course of treatment, with methods ranging from focused *cognitive reframing* to more *self-actualizing* modalities *(experiential, client-centered,* etc). To achieve the necessary receptivity and vigor for such measures, it would be pragmatic to incorporate *biophysical* intervention at the outset *(anxiety medication).* Additionally, a constitutional conflict existed between her tendency to remain *passive* (protected, submissive, lethargic) in terms of autonomous functioning, and her tendency to *actively* withdraw from social settings and responsibilities. *Behavioral* and *interpersonal* techniques, following the aforementioned cognitive and self-actualizing modalities, would be fruitful in allaying these discrepancies as well as other perpetuating tendencies such as clinging behavior, hypersensitivity, and fantasy/abandonment preoccupations.

Therapeutic Course: Active short-term techniques were taken advantage of to introduce environmental changes to Michelle to encourage development, minimize continued dependency, and provide uplifting experiences. *Psychopharmacologic* treatment was utilized as a short-term treatment geared toward promoting alertness and vigor and to counter lethargy, dejection, and anxiety states that predisposed her to postpone efforts at independence and confidence building. The therapeutic relationship was examined carefully to overcome the dominance-submission patterns that so aptly characterized Michelle's history. Both *self-actualizing* and *directive cognitive* approaches fostered the growth of autonomy and self-confidence. Although *psychodynamic* approaches were attempted to rework deep object attachments and to construct a base for competency strivings, they were considerably less effective than more focused and brief therapeutic modes. *Group therapy* was pursued fruitfully as a means of learning autonomous skills and as an aid to the growth of social confidence.

Circumscribed treatment efforts were directed at countering her dependency attitudes and behavior. A primary therapeutic task was to prevent Michelle from slipping into a totally ineffectual state as she sought to rely increasingly on a supportive environment. Owing to her anxious and morose outlook, she not only fixated on real deficits in her competence but also deprecated the virtues and talents she did possess. Trapped by her own persuasiveness, she reinforced her belief in the futility of standing on her own and was therefore heavily disinclined to work at overcoming her inadequacies. Cognitive methods (e.g., Ellis, Beck) were especially helpful in reframing erroneous beliefs and assumptions about herself and those she believed others had of her.

Michelle's strategy had fostered a vicious circle of increased helplessness, depression, and dependency. By making herself inaccessible to growth opportunities, she effectively precluded further maturation and became more saddened and more dependent on others. Short-term techniques provided for the establishment and continuation of competence activities and the acquisition of skill-building behavior and assertive attitudes. To prevent Michelle from becoming passively incompetent and lost in fantasy preoccupations, a major though short-term approach was quickly instituted. Potentially useful in this regard were several behavioral modification methods as well as *interpersonal techniques* such as those utilized by Benjamin and Kiesler. Pressure on her to show marked increases in initiative and autonomy were gradual, however, because her capacities in this area were quite limited.

Brief and focused treatment created the misleading impression that progress would continue and be rapid. Despite initial indications of solid advances, Michelle resisted efforts to assume much autonomy for her future. Persuading her to forgo her long-standing habits proved to be extremely slow and arduous, but steps were undertaken to move forward in this regard and to provide support. Especially problematic was the feeling she had that an increase in the expectations of others would not be met and would thereby result in disapproval. Efforts to help her build an image of competence and self-esteem were an essential step in forestalling later backsliding. A program that strengthened her attributes and dislodged her habit of leaning on others was well worth the effort it took.

DEPENDENT PERSONALITY:
ACCOMMODATING TYPE (DEPENDENT
AND MASOCHISTIC TRAITS)

CASE 13.2, ROGER M., 35

Presenting Picture: Roger M. was a teacher in a wealthy private school who described himself as "an easy grader." He liked all of his students, claiming that they were all well-behaved, good kids. He got along exceedingly well with all of the administrators and other teachers on staff, but admitted to disliking the committee work that was required for his job. Roger didn't like taking sides if there was a disagreement among the teachers and claimed that usually he didn't even see that there *was* a real problem. He lived with a roommate who paid all of the bills, called to get repairs made, and decorated the apartment. His girlfriend of five years seemed to make the rest of the decisions in Roger's life, deciding what movie they would see and where to go to dinner. Roger was obliging to both his roommate and his girlfriend, seeming relieved that he didn't have to make such tough decisions.

Clinical Assessment: As an *accommodating dependent,* Roger showed behavior best characterized by a submissiveness, a high degree of agreeableness, and a leaning on others for affection, nurturance, and security. The fear of being abandoned led him to be overly compliant and obliging. Roger, like many other accommodating dependents, handled his fears by being socially gregarious and superficially charming, often evident in the seeking of attention and in self-dramatizing behaviors. We describe such personalities as the *appeasing histrionic,* discussed in the next chapter. These individuals possess an unusual knack for placating and conceding; as basic histrionics, they comfortably exhibit gregarious, charming, and self-dramatizing behaviors. Both accommodating dependents and appeasing histrionics are gracious, neighborly, benevolent, compliant, eager to please, that is, obliging and agreeable in their relationships with others. What differentiates them is the strong tendency of accommodating subtypes, like Roger, to be self-sacrificing, their ability to adopt not only a submissive style, but to play the role well of inferior and subordinate to others. In this regard, we see in these individuals a basic amalgamation of the dependent and the masochistic personality styles.

Roger also revealed a naïve attitude toward interpersonal problems. Critical thinking was rarely evident, and most cognitive knowledge appeared to be almost entirely undeveloped and immature. There was an effort to maintain an air of pleasantry and good spirits, a denial of all disturbing emotions, covering inner disharmonies by short-lived distractions. In part, this may have stemmed from a tendency to be genuinely docile, softhearted, and sensitive to the desires of others. Roger was more than merely accommodating and docile in efforts to secure dependency needs. He was admiring and loving, giving all to those on whom he depended. He also learned to play the inferior role well, providing partners with the rewards of feeling useful, sympathetic, stronger, and more competent. There was often an active solicitousness of praise, a willingness to demean himself, and a tendency to be self-sacrificing and virtuous.

In what way did this compliant and good-natured individual prove to be a problem to others? He always had a smile and a friendly word; he was responsive and agreeable, whatever it was that one could request; he was always willingly obliging. Difficulties arose in that Roger always said yes but rarely followed through in fulfilling what was wished of him. Unsure of himself and in many ways deficient in his competencies, Roger lacked the wherewithal to achieve what others expected of him. Adult activities called for more than good-natured agreeableness. They required concerted attention and a capacity to execute not only difficult tasks, but even those that may be enjoyable and mutually rewarding.

All that really mattered to Roger was that others liked him, were pleased by him, were willing to accept his smiles and goodwill as sufficient. Fearing that he may fail to receive acceptance and approval by attempting any "real actions," that is, by seeking to execute adult responsibilities, he restrained himself from demonstrating his weaknesses and inefficiencies, reverting again and again to sociable pleasantries. Fearing conflict and rejection, stuck with his overpowering need to be liked and accepted, he was unable to follow through on any realistic commitments, lapsing once more into his friendly and ever-promising front.

The accommodating dependent is similar to the appeasing histrionic personality in that both seek harmony with others, if necessary at the expense of their internal values and beliefs. Similarly, both are likely to actively avoid all situations that may involve personal conflict. However, to minimize distressing relationships, the accommodating dependent avoids self-assertion and abdicates autonomous responsibilities, preferring to leave matters in the hands of others. By contrast, histrionics take an active posture, maneuvering and manipulating their life circumstances rather than passively sitting by. Both types, however, owing to their preoccupation with gaining external approval, may be left without an inner identity. Accommodating and appeasing personalities value themselves not in terms of their intrinsic traits, but in terms of their relationships with others. By submerging themselves in or allying themselves with the competencies and virtues of others, these personalities not only are bolstered by the illusion of shared competence but find solace in the belief that bonds so constructed are firm and inseparable.

As noted, the accommodating dependent feels helpless when faced with responsibilities that demand autonomy or initiative. The loss of a significant source of support or identification may prompt severe dejection. Under such conditions of potential rejection or loss, he or she will openly solicit signs of reassurance and approval. Guilt, illness, anxiety, and depression are frankly displayed because these tend to deflect criticism and transform threats of disapproval into those of support and sympathy. When dependency security is genuinely threatened, the accommodating personality will manifest an anxious depressiveness covarying with other, more extreme reactions.

Synergistic Treatment Plan: As with most dependents, a central characterological feature with this man is a profound poverty in his *self*-orientation, as well as a rather heavy emphasis on *others,* perhaps more so than other individuals fitting the criteria for dependent personality disorder. It would be necessary from the outset to begin timely work on altering *cognitive dysfunctions* and *interpersonal social habits* that place all importance in the opinion of others, as this had created, in effect, a paralysis and helplessness that interfered with Roger's ability to accomplish even the simplest tasks. To foster a more *active* style, it would be necessary, as well, to bolster self-confidence and autonomy skills with the aforementioned modalities, as well as with an interactive model, such as a *group,* when Roger had advanced sufficiently to tolerate these activities. As a good measure of resistance would be expected, cautious therapeutic relationship building was initiated at the first session. Such ingrained tendencies as his reliance on public approval as well as his harboring a self-image of incompetence would be insurmountable without a safe, *self-actualizing* milieu marked with genuineness and empathy throughout the course of treatment.

Therapeutic Course: As an initial approach with Roger, certain well-known short-term methods of intervention, for example, procedures of *environmental management, psychopharmacologic treatment,* and *behavior modification,* were not of particular value. Other techniques of brief treatment were of greater utility. Erroneous beliefs about self and others were best altered with procedures of *cognitive reorientation.* Once a baseline of rapport had been established with *supportive techniques,* Roger was able to withstand directive cognitive and *interpersonal* methods designed to probe and modify his dysfunctional attitudes and ineffectual social habits. Both interventional methods, along with focused *(group)* techniques helped him view himself in a more realistic social light and aided him in learning the skills of interpersonal relatedness without fearing disapproval and shame.

Short-term therapeutic aims were more substantial than merely reestablishing former levels of functioning, especially because simply rebuilding Roger's self-protective pretensions and illusions would have proven, in the long run, to lead to frequent relapses and regression. Thus, a cognitively oriented approach assisted him in becoming more sensitive and aware of objective reality; this proved especially helpful after taking steps to strengthen his capacity to confront his weaknesses and deficiencies. When he could deal with himself on a more realistic and insightful basis than before, he was less likely to develop illusory attitudes and dysfunctional behavior.

Roger was not inclined to seek therapy, rejecting what he perceived to be the weak role of patient. Nevertheless, a short-term intervention helped convince him that he could get along in his life appreciably better with guidance to eliminate shortcomings that proved demeaning to him. Although he sought to maintain a well-measured distance from the therapist, an empathic cognitive approach minimized his resistance to the searching probes of personal exploration. By such methods, he became less perturbed over the implications of his deficiencies and was able to assume responsibility for his deficits. Reducing his evasiveness and unwillingness to face his difficulties significantly improved therapeutic progress.

With therapeutic warmth and understanding, Roger was able to maintain self-assurance and a posture of maturity without viewing therapy as a threat to his self-image. Although he was concerned about appearances, such as being well thought of by a therapist, a supportive and cognitive reframing regimen was able to overcome his inclination to resist or deny psychological interpretations. His defensiveness in these matters was honored in this short-term therapeutic approach, and probing and insight proceeded at a careful pace. Once trust and confidence had developed in the relationship, however, cognitive methods were employed to supplant his pretenses and cynicism with less defensive attitudes and behavior. However, had he been asked to confront more than he could tolerate, emotional complications leading to a relapse may have resulted; it was important to aid him in narrowing the disparity between his public front and his inner deficiencies. Every effort was made to give substance to his intellectual insights rather than have them merely serve as camouflage to deter probing by the therapist. With effective cognitive and interpersonal techniques, insight-based change was made to function more permanently than in the past. Overriding his tendency to simply pay lip service to treatment goals, Roger was led to relinquish his public posture and his defensive controls. His habitual evasiveness and discomfort with intimate issues were overcome with consistent direction and firmness. Because of his need to control matters, he was especially responsive to formal therapeutic procedures, such as cognitive and interpersonal techniques.

DEPENDENT PERSONALITY: IMMATURE
TYPE (PURE DEPENDENT)

CASE 13.3, ELENA S., 25

Presenting Picture: Elena S. was a teacher's aide working with young children. Her duties were limited to playing with the children and little else. She claimed to relate really well to the children. With her sweet, round face, her baby voice and language, and ready giggles, it was not hard to imagine her playing blocks and sandbox with the 4-year-olds. Elena was relieved that she was "not the boss" and did not have more responsibilities. She lived with her mother, who often complained of Elena's messy room, but overall Elena seemed happy with the living arrangements. Her relationship with her boyfriend was somewhat tumultuous. He complained regularly that Elena was "acting like a baby" and he was tired of dealing with her "tantrums." Overall, Elena was pleased with how her life was progressing and saw little need to change or grow.

Clinical Assessment: There is reason to believe that maturation does not follow a predetermined course in all individuals; moreover, persons differ in the speed at which certain processes develop. Similarly, there is evidence to indicate that not all persons mature in all of their capacities and functions to the same level. For example, in the intellectual realm, there are persons who appear extraordinarily talented in mathematics and music at a very early age; conversely, there are those who never achieve even a modest level of accomplishment at any point in their life in these same realms. Individual differences in the level and rapidity of maturational development are widespread across all attribute domains.

The preceding discussion also applies to the maturation of adult characteristics and capabilities. Some persons, like Elena, remain childlike throughout their lives. She preferred childhood activities, found great satisfaction relating to children, and seemed either incapable of or to abhor activities we assume are normal features of adult activity and responsibility. She was not only dependent because she was childlike in her outlook and competencies, but also because she seemed *satisfied* to remain childlike in her activities and orientation. It is individuals like Elena whom we refer to as *immature dependent* personalities. In describing Elena as an immature dependent subtype, we might say that she was undeveloped, inexperienced, unsophisticated, unformed, and unversed. Pleased and satisfied with herself in not assuming adult roles and responsibilities, she was also incapable of doing so owing to her half-grown or childlike level of maturity.

Whether she was so disposed by constitutional predilections or reinforced in early life to prefer a childlike existence cannot be determined by present scientific means. Whatever its origins, Elena seemed to prefer, felt protected by, or found her greatest satisfactions in remaining oriented to the world of childhood and adolescence. To remain undeveloped was to find a more tranquil existence than found in adulthood, with its demands, strivings, competition, and responsibilities. Elena may have simply lacked ambition and energy, hence making the expectancies of adulthood overwhelming and frightening, or she may have been overly passive and easygoing, undeveloped in the acquisition of autonomous behaviors and the confidence building crucial in the second stage of neuropsychological development. She also appeared to lack a strong gender identity and found the assumption of adult roles to be somewhat distasteful or frightening.

For the most part, Elena was pleasant and sociable—as long as she was permitted to remain preadult in her preferences and activities. She became quite problematic to others when they expected more of her or demanded that she "mature" and get down to the business of life. Unfortunately, the business of life implies being and acting like an adult. To troubled parents and friends, these behaviors were often seen as signs of irresponsibility and neglectfulness.

Synergistic Treatment Plan: *Nonconfrontive* but *focused* measures would be the most efficacious plan in treating Elena. As confrontive techniques would likely cause an emotional defensiveness, a *supportive* milieu would be an appropriate beginning. *Cognitive-behavioral* techniques would serve the dual purpose of helping define a balanced therapeutic relationship as well as adjust her perpetuations regarding herself as incompetent in order to avoid taking on adult tasks (strong *passive* and *other* orientation); *behavior modification* methods would help alleviate constitutional anxieties regarding environmental and social discomforts. As her tolerance for self-examination would grow, it would be possible to encourage Elena's *self*-orientation as well as increase her *activity* level through the use of *interpersonal* measures designed to bolster confidence and help her modify her tendency to cling to and lean on others.

Therapeutic Course: *Supportive* therapy was the best initial vehicle for treating Elena. Though *psychopharmacologic* agents were not employed in alleviating problematic periods here, it should be noted that in those cases where they are used, the level of dosage should be restricted so that the patient does not experience significant decrements in efficiency. *Behavior modification* techniques designed to desensitize Elena to discomforting or anxiety-provoking situations were useful in this brief therapeutic approach. Methods of *cognitive-behavioral* treatment designed to focus on dysfunctional self-statements also proved effectual in countering her self-demeaning judgments as well as in providing structure to what she most likely perceived as an ambiguous, elusive, and potentially threatening therapeutic relationship. Cognitive reorientation methods geared to developing insights were effective for short-term gains, but they were applied gradually and discreetly. Approaches such as these were not likely to be permanent in their accomplishments because Elena grasped her problems only at an abstract or intellectual level. Although reworking the basis of these behaviors and attitudes was necessary to diminish the likelihood of a relapse, short-term supportive and cognitive methods were helpful in restabilizing her.

An auspicious beginning to therapy was realized, but this did not signify that future progress was to be rapid. Elena sought a protective relationship with her therapist and was remarkably disinclined to acquire greater and healthier independence and autonomy. To reduce any backsliding, the therapist established the useful goal for her to relinquish her conforming and dependency habits. Efforts to assist her in building an image of true independence and self-esteem were facilitated by *interpersonally focused* programs (e.g., Klerman, Benjamin) geared toward strengthening her self-confidence and dislodging her habit of leaning on others.

It was most useful to help her reframe her tendency to observe deficits in her competence and to deprecate what virtues and talents she did possess. She did this to prevent others from expecting her to assume responsibilities she would rather avoid. Successful as a shield against discomfort and in protecting her dependency needs, these actions were carried out at the cost of forestalling the acquisition of mature abilities and self-respect. A short-term goal focused and reoriented these tendencies into more constructive modes of thought.

Owing to her need to be liked and her fear of social rebuke, Elena viewed therapy as upsetting to her overly perfectionistic and fastidious view of herself. Cognitive methods were employed to overcome her lack of insight and her inclination to resist probing and deny psychological interpretations. Her defensiveness was honored, of course, and probing interpretations were oriented to short-term goals. Given her fear of humiliation and her reluctance to expose more than she could tolerate, actions that would have directly confronted Elena would have invited emotional complications that could have potentially produced unnecessary setbacks. She sometimes voiced intellectual insights, but given her respectful if not ingratiating manner, this seemed to be a camouflage to placate the therapist. Elena's defenses were so well constructed that insight based on long-term techniques was likely to be of questionable value. Though paying lip service to treatment goals, she did not readily relinquish her defensive controls. Hence, brief and focused therapy proved to be the best option, although efforts were made to continue treatment as it was necessary to forestall probable recurrences.

DEPENDENT PERSONALITY: INEFFECTUAL TYPE
(DEPENDENT WITH SCHIZOID TRAITS)

CASE 13.4, CAROL L., 23

Presenting Picture: Carol L. completed her first year as a kindergarten teacher and was referred to therapy by her school administrator. She was reluctant to admit there were any problems at school because she got along so well with the other teachers and staff, but finally, she quietly admitted to several incidents that had happened over the course of the year. It appeared that she did not know how to handle even minor disagreements that went on between students. On several occasions, she had to call in teachers from the next room to handle routine disputes. Although she seemed undisturbed by her lack of ability to handle these situations, it was clear that it was interfering with her job. Carol shared an apartment with two other young teachers in her school. These two women made all of the household decisions, and Carol was all too content to never have to make a choice or plan of action in her life.

Clinical Assessment: As an *ineffectual dependent* type, Carol showed similarities to the *languid schizoid* pattern. Both styles exhibit a general lack of vitality, low energy level, fatigability, and a general weakness in expressiveness and spontaneity. Hence, we saw that ineffectual dependents, like Carol, reflected the intermingling of both basic dependent and schizoid characteristics, as was seen on her MCMI. However, the languid schizoid is motorically and affectively deficient. Moreover, thought processes among purer schizoid personalities, though not markedly deficient, appear unfocused, particularly with regard to interpersonal matters. Languid schizoid types also show a deficiency in the expression of affect, a defect stemming in all probability from an anhedonic temperament, inclining them to be persistently aloof from life's social interactions. By contrast, ineffectual dependents, like Carol, do not want to be isolated from close personal relationships. Although seeking to be close and caring, Carol lacked drive and staying power, was deficient in her adult skills, and seemed simply unwilling to pursue solutions to even minor problems.

Carol was possessed by a desperate need to lead a totally untroubled life and to be free of any and all responsibilities. There was a fatalism about her, a willingness to ignore the difficulties she may face by simply refusing to deal with them, tune them out, or let them be. She seemed resigned and not unhappy to accept her ineffectual fate—except for being nurtured and protected by others. However, other than seeking peace and amity with others at any price, she was unwilling to face life's difficulties squarely. She had fallen to such a level as to be unable to deal with any difficulty. If possible, she would have liked to turn her back on what she saw as a demanding world, or to bury her head as far she could in the sand. Not wanting to deal with reality, she resisted all pressures that might intrude upon her, sleepwalking through her life, increasingly disengaged and dependent. She clung to others in a childlike manner even for the most basic requirements of everyday survival. What was seen as most prominent was her total malleability and lack of will.

Synergistic Treatment Plan: Carol would need to be reassured that the therapeutic relationship and milieu would be secure, trusting, and sincere, as she had extreme characterologic anticipation of rejection, letdown, and hurt (burdensome orientation toward the importance of *others*); therefore, *supportive* therapy would be most influential in allowing Carol enough comfort to begin focused work. It would be most crucial in this case to stimulate Carol's *activity* orientation, having her assume adult activities and invest gradually in competent actions through *behavioral modification* techniques as well as alter dysfunctional *cognitions*. With an increase in activity, Carol's *pleasure* orientation would also be augmented through more meaningful experience. A *self-actualizing* focus, following earlier improvements, would assist Carol in focusing on her *self* and forming greater motivations to sustain competence.

Therapeutic Course: As a first approach in a short-term therapeutic program, an effort was made to assist Carol in arranging for a more rewarding environment and in discovering opportunities that would enhance her self-worth. *Supportive therapy* was all she could tolerate in these first sessions, that is, until she was comfortable dealing with her more painful feelings. *Psychopharmacologic* treatment was considered as a means of diminishing her depressive feelings and controlling her anxiety. *Behavior modification* was employed to help her learn competent reactions to stressful situations. As trust in her therapist developed, she became more amenable to methods of *cognitive reframing* to alter dysfunctional attitudes and depressogenic social expectations; particularly appropriate were the methods proposed by Beck and Meichenbaum. To decrease the potential of a recurrence, *focused dynamic* methods were explored to rework deep object attachments and to construct a base for competency strivings. The *interpersonal* focus proposed by Benjamin and Klerman and *group therapy* procedures also provided a means of learning autonomous skills and helped her grow in social confidence.

An important self-defeating belief that the cognitive approach sought to reframe was Carol's assumption that she must appease others and apologize for her incompetence in order to assure that she would not be abandoned. What could be shown to her was that this behavior tended to exasperate and alienate those on whom she leaned most heavily. This exasperation and alienation then served only to increase her fear and neediness. She came to recognize that a vicious circle was created, making her feel more desperate and more ingratiating. A vigorous but short-term approach that illustrated her dysfunctional beliefs and expectations was used to break the circle and reorient her actions less destructively. The combination of cognitive restructuring and the development of increasing interpersonal skills proved an effective brief course of treatment.

To restate her difficulty in different terms, not only did Carol precipitate real difficulties through her self-demeaning attitudes but she also perceived and anticipated difficulties where none, in fact, existed. She believed that good things did not last and that the positive feelings and attitudes of those from whom she sought support would probably end capriciously and be followed by disappointment and rejection. This cognitive assumption had to be directly confronted by appropriate therapeutic techniques. What had to be undone was the fact that each time she announced her defects, she convinced herself as well as others and thereby deepened her discontent and her self-image of incompetence. Trapped by her own persuasiveness, she repeatedly reinforced her belief in the futility of standing on her own and was therefore likely to try less and less to overcome her inadequacies. This therapeutic strategy aimed at undoing this vicious circle of increased despondency and dependency.

Skillful attention was also needed to alter Carol's ambivalence about dependency and her willingness to be used, if not abused. Unless checked, she had difficulty sustaining a consistent therapeutic relationship and was prone to deteriorate or relapse. Maneuvers designed to test the dependability of the therapist were often evident. Empathic warmth needed to be evident throughout to help her overcome her fear of facing her own feelings of unworthiness. Similar support levels were necessary to undo her wish to retain her image of being a self-denying person whose security lay in suffering and martyrdom. Carol needed to be guided into recognizing the basis of her self-contempt and her ambivalence about dependency relationships. She was helped to see that not all nurturant figures would habitually become abusive and exploitive. Efforts to undo these self-sabotaging beliefs paid considerable dividends in short-term and possibly more substantial long-term progress.

DEPENDENT PERSONALITY: SELFLESS TYPE
(DEPENDENT WITH DEPRESSIVE TRAITS)

CASE 13.5, DIANE M., 38

Presenting Picture: Diane M. was a third-grade student teacher with little ambition or drive of her own. She relied on her husband to take her places because she never learned to drive a car and relied on her school's principal to include her in seminars and workshops to keep her busy and entertained. Diane responded to almost every question she was asked with "Everything is okay," even when it was clear that there were significant problems. She reported that she was nervous about some of her teaching responsibilities, especially being alone with the children and having to shoulder such a big responsibility. The first time she was put in charge, she had to call in the principal to take over. She also claimed to be scared when left alone in the house. Diane reported being more "sad" than usual in recent months. She had been thinking about her older sister, with whom she had been very close and who had died two years earlier. This sister had taken care of Diane when they were younger, and Diane revered her sister and wanted to be just like her.

Clinical Assessment: Diane not only subordinated herself to others, a characteristic shared by other dependent personalities, but merged herself totally with her husband and sister such that she lost herself in the process. She willingly gave up her own identity as an independent human being to acquire a more secure sense of significance, identity, emotional stability, and purpose in life. As the process of total identification with another became established and integrated, she failed increasingly to develop any of her own personally distinctive potentials. And as her own sense of self became a less significant part of her being, whatever she did was done almost entirely in the service of extending the status and significance of another.

Whatever impulses and potentials that might have existed for her as an independent person were denied or dissociated. She had become fully merged, as if she had no self, was a nonbeing, except for her coupling with another person. Her existence was *not* denied, as occurs in some cases of the ineffectual dependent style, but became an extension of whomever she was now a part. So fused and entwined, she acted at times in ways quite divergent from what had been characteristic of her. Thus, she may have exhibited an air of confidence and self-assurance, but only as it reflected the achievements and powers of the person or institution to which she was united. Thus, she had not lost a sense of self-worth. Rather, by virtue of her alliances, she assumed that she herself now possessed many of the qualities that inhered intrinsically in those with whom she identified.

As a *selfless dependent,* Diane felt fulfilled by her associations. Not only did she willingly submit to the values and beliefs of her significant attachments, but her very sense of being depended on it. The more she fused with the idealized object, the more attached she was emotionally, and the more she felt that she herself existed as a person that had significance in the world. Another example of a selfless dependent might be a mother who lives for her children or submerges herself totally within the life of her husband. Although she may have gone overboard in her identification, losing too much of herself by so doing, Diane felt vitalized and valuable by virtue of these joinings. She had given totally of herself and had embraced fully the actions and values of another, naïvely displacing her very self for the sake of another's.

Owing to the insecurities that resulted from Diane's loss of self and the vulnerable position in which she had placed herself, she was likely to have acquired some of the features of the depressive personality, as were seen on her MCMI. She actually experienced the loss of her sister, but a selfless dependent need not experience an actual loss to develop these features. Diane and other selfless dependents learn to live on the edge of such possibilities. Experiencing the loss and consequent hopelessness that would ensue from such an eventuality, these persons infuse elements of a depressive character into their basic dependent style, interjecting expectancies and reactions that would have occurred had these losses become reality.

Synergistic Treatment Plan: Essential to a successful treatment process with this very unsure and *self*-diminished woman would be a *supportive* atmosphere, established from the outset, while trust and security were built within the therapeutic relationship. To facilitate more focused strivings, it would be prudent to address Diane's *biophysical* depressive tendencies (losing further self-worth due to the threat of abandonment) with a *pharmacologic* regimen, and gradually introduce tangible, innocuous *behavior* goals to build confidence and illustrate aspects of her own worthiness and reduce her vigilant *pain* orientation. As her poise would improve, it would be possible to begin adjusting perpetuations in *cognitive* arenas, such as her belief structure which overemphasized her dependent role with *others.* *Interpersonal* and focused *self-actualizing* measures would follow to increase *pleasure* and sense of *self* in social interactions, as well as adjusting immature object expectations.

Therapeutic Course: It was apparent almost immediately that Diane was immersed in a self-created environment that was at once comfortable and bereft of interest, and this fostered a very marginal self-image that succeeded only at masking deeper discontent. In this scenario, she was only capable, at first, of enduring a *supportive milieu.* A more demanding course of treatment at this early stage would have overwhelmed her and probably set the stage for premature termination. A *psychopharmacologic* regimen of an antidepressive (SSRI) agent was a beneficial catalyst for preparing to deal with more salient emotions. *Behavior modification* also, in this early stage, helped Diane learn to respond more effectively to environmental stressors, and the ensuing successes further enhanced her self-confidence as well as trust and investment within the therapeutic relationship and environment. As therapy progressed, she was able to tolerate *cognitive reframing* techniques, such as the methods proposed by Beck and Meichenbaum, to modify dysfunctional beliefs and expectations. Focused *dynamic methods* also were utilized to explore ingrained object attachments, enhance competency strivings, and ensure avoidance of a relapse. *Interpersonal* methods, such as those of Benjamin and Klerman, as well as an adjunctive *group* milieu, provided for further skill development and sociability.

Diane had an irrational fear of abandonment, more recently enhanced by a real loss (her sister), and constantly felt that she needed to placate others and habitually apologize for her perceived incompetence. A cognitive reframing approach helped her realize that these efforts may have actually helped cause isolation, and that this alienation spurred further anxiety and dependency. By illustrating these dysfunctional beliefs in a brief, vigorous approach, she was able to break this vicious circle and reorient her behaviors more productively. Between this combination of cognitive restructuring and interpersonal methods aimed at enhancing social and independent skills, Diane began making marked improvements.

Beyond inducing real problems with these dysfunctional habits, Diane sensed and reacted to nonexistent difficulties. She seemed to live by the maxim "Good things don't last"; specifically, the people in her life who loved and respected her would inevitably let her down and she would be abandoned. From a cognitive perspective, each time Diane proclaimed her imperfections, she further ingrained a sense of discontent and unworthiness to herself as well as others. What she was capable of was making a compelling argument for the uselessness of autonomy and, subsequently, rationalizing her failure to meaningfully pursue ambitions. This therapeutic strategy aimed at undoing this vicious circle of increased despondency and dependency. This mixed cognitive and interpersonal strategy broke down these dependent habits and helped foster more autonomous, productive skills.

Not only did Diane tend to be somewhat ambivalent about seeking autonomy, but she frequently left herself open to being used, as her perception was that servitude equated to being valued by others. She had some difficulty maintaining any consistency with the therapist, and she tested his dependability with some frequency. It was important that a therapeutic environment marked by empathic warmth be maintained to help her combat her perceptions of herself as an unworthy, incompetent woman. These measures were also necessary to undo her quest for meaning through self-denial, distress, and martyrdom. It was necessary to illustrate to Diane the foundation of her self-deprecating habits as well as her misguided motivation to sustain dependent relationships. Efforts to undo her efforts to sabotage herself were most fruitful for both short- and long-term progress.

Resistances and Risks

The dependent's receptiveness and the auspicious beginning of therapy may create a misleading impression that future progress will be rapid. Quite naturally, these patients will seek a dependent relationship with their therapist. Despite "promises" to the contrary, they will resist efforts to guide them into assuming independence and autonomy. Their goal is to elicit more nurturance and help from the therapist. All this is to be expected because their dependence is quite ego-syntonic. Assisting them in relinquishing their dependency habits will prove a slow and arduous process. Building an image of competence and self-esteem must proceed one step at a time through a program of strengthening attributes and dislodging the habit of leaning on others.

The therapist may get caught up in the patient's attempt to elicit support. After a while, excessive dependence can be exasperating. Resulting countertransference feelings of annoyance may lead to rejection once again, which in turn will intensify the dependency and clinging behaviors (Stone, 1993). Countertransference may also take the form of the therapist's allowing the patient to become emotionally dependent on him or her, resulting in reduced efforts at gaining independence. If attempts at autonomy, however, are pushed too hard initially, the anxiety may result in premature dropout.

Another potential caveat is that, in the dependent's search for approval, observed behavior changes such as enhanced assertiveness may be confined to sessions with the therapist and not exhibited elsewhere. It is important to evaluate to what degree behavior change actually has occurred outside of the therapy setting. If the patient's environment continues to foster or maintain dependency, what appears to be progress in the therapy room may not have generalized to his or her dysfunctional world.

Therapist and patient should come to an understanding of the goals of therapy. Especially when resistance is encountered, reconceptualization of the dependent's therapeutic objectives may be useful. Progress in therapy may be impeded by dependents' basic belief that they are inadequate. They may feel incompetent to utilize treatment efficiently and may attribute progress made to the therapist rather than to themselves (McCann & Dyer, 1994). Yet another potential factor that may strengthen the belief that success is attributable to external sources is reliance on medication.

Neither the therapist nor the patient must forget that the ultimate goal is not necessarily complete independence, but rather the flexibility to move between self-reliance and a healthy mutual dependence.

CHAPTER FOURTEEN

Treating Histrionic Personality Patterns

Histrionic personalities, like dependent personalities, are characterized by intense needs for attention and affection. Unlike the passive receptive stance of the dependent, however, the histrionic actively solicits the interest of others through seductive, immaturely exhibitionistic, or self-dramatizing behaviors. Toward assuring a constant receipt of the admiration and esteem that they require, histrionics develop an exquisite sensitivity to the desires and moods of those they wish to please. Although some may perceive them as being rather ingenuine or shallow, they are nonetheless typically viewed as gregarious, entertaining, and superficially charming. The histrionic's extreme other-directedness and approval-seeking results in a capricious and fickle pattern of personal relationships. Unlike the dependent's blind loyalty and attachment to one significant other, histrionics are lacking in fidelity and dissatisfied with single attachments. Their interpersonal relationships tend to be characterized by demandingness, manipulation, and at times, childish dependency and helplessness. These behaviors are particularly pronounced in heterosexual relationships, where the histrionic demonstrates a marked appetite for fleeting romantic encounters (Millon, 1981).

Histrionics tend to be emotionally overreactive and labile. Frustration tolerance is quite low and there is a proneness to immature stimulation seeking and impulsive responsiveness. Such individuals crave excitement, pleasure, and change and become easily bored with normal routines. A well-developed sense of inner identity is typically lacking in histrionics. Their perception of themselves is conceptualized in terms of their relationships and their effect on others. In contrast to their hypersensitivity to the thoughts and moods of others, such individuals are lacking insight into their own feelings. Their orientation is toward external stimuli, and only fleeting, impressionistic attention is paid to details. Their cognitive style is marked by difficulties in concentration and logical thinking. Experiences are poorly integrated and learned, and consequently, judgment is often lacking. In part, their cognitive flightiness results from their attempts to avoid potentially disrupting ideas and urges, for example, a recognition of their ravenous dependency needs and their resultant vulnerability to loss or rejection. Consequently, histrionic personalities will simply seal off, repress, or dissociate large segments of their memories and feelings.

398

Histrionics' virtually insatiable needs for attention and approval make them quite prone to feelings of dejection and anxiety should they fail to evoke the recognition they desire. Signs of indifference or neutrality on the part of others are frequently interpreted as rejection and result in feelings of emptiness and unworthiness. Unlike the dependent's flat and somber symptom picture, dysthymic disorder in histrionic personalities is characteristically overplayed in dramatic and eye-catching gestures, characteristic of the histrionic's exhibitionistic display of mood. Episodes of the milder forms of depression are usually prompted less by fear of abandonment than by a sense of emptiness and inactivity. Such dysphoria is likely to occur when histrionics find themselves stranded between one fleeting attachment and another, or between one transitory excitement and the next. At such times of noninvolvement, histrionics sense their lack of inner substance and direction and begin to experience fears of an empty life and aloneness.

Complaints among histrionic personalities tend to be expressed in current, fashionable, or intellectualized terms (e.g., "existential anxiety" or "estrangement from the mass society"). Expressing this distress through such popular jargon enables histrionics to rationalize their personal emptiness and confusion and, perhaps more important, provides them with a bridge to others at a time when they feel most isolated from the social life they so desperately seek. Such pseudosophisticated expressions of disenchantment entertain and interest others and identify the histrionic as being part of an "in" subgroup. Histrionics are also among the personality styles that may "mask" an underlying depression through physical disorders, hypochondriacal syndromes, or through acting-out behaviors such as drug abuse, overeating, or sexual promiscuity.

Depression and acute anxiety in histrionics are primarily precipitated by anticipated losses in dependency security and are more likely to be evidenced in an agitated rather than a retarded form. In the hope of soliciting support and nurturance, histrionics may wail aloud and make well-known their feelings of helplessness and abandonment. Suicidal threats or gestures are not uncommon at such times. Major depressions may also be colored with irritability and anger, although reproving reactions, especially from significant others, will cause histrionics to withdraw and substitute their anger with dramatic declarations of guilt and contrition.

Histrionic personalities may be particularly susceptible to bipolar and cyclothymic disorders, as these syndromes are consistent with their characteristic socially gregarious and exuberant style. Severe separation anxieties or the fear of losing social approval may intensify histrionics' habitual behavior pattern until it reaches the forced and frantic congeniality of hypomania. To stave off the growing feeling of depressive hopelessness, tension may be released through hyperactivity and a frenetic search for attention.

Many of the psychoanalytic writings of the depressed oral dependent's pronounced affectional needs are equally applicable to depression in the histrionic personality. Freud (1932) wrote that a "dread of loss of love" governed the behavior of hysterics, and others have referred to the predepressive's strong cravings for narcissistic gratification and low tolerance of affectional frustration.

Klein's (1977) "hysteroid dysphoria," a disturbance more frequent in women, portrays chronic, repetitive, nonpsychotic depressed moods with pronounced needs for attention, approval, and praise, especially within a romantic relationship. Extreme intolerance of personal rejection is the hallmark of this disorder. Clinical syndromes in these individuals are usually of short duration and manifested symptomatically in overeating or craving for sweets, oversleeping or extreme fatigue. Alcohol or drug abuse during brief episodes may also be common. Described as "attention junkies" with "addictions" to approval, hysteroid dysphorics possess many of the features characteristic of the histrionic personality. Hysteroid dysphorics also evidence considerably more "unstable" features (e.g., being prone to angry outbursts, impulsive acting-out, and physically self-damaging acts), which are suggestive of a more severe level of personality disorganization such as the borderline personality.

We next review the evolutionary model and theory. The polarity schema characterizing the histrionic personality is presented in Figure 14.1. The elements that stand out are a focus on others (nurturance) and on activity (modification). As is typical in most personality disorders, both the pain and pleasure polarities are not notably significant.

In a manner similar to the dependent personality, the histrionic's psychic world is centered on relationships with other persons. However, dependents and histrionics differ markedly in their mode of adaptation; histrionics actively manipulate their environment to achieve their ends; by contrast, dependents are passive, not only accommodating to their environment, but looking to others to guide and nurture them. Histrionics engage in a variety of interpersonal maneuvers to ensure that others are attentive and approving even desirous of and willingly offering tribute to them. Dependents not only seek but need others to care and nurture them, as well as to provide them with guidance. By contrast, histrionics are actively involved in giving to and even nurturing others. These latter behaviors are not altruistic, but a means of soliciting and ensuring reciprocal approval and esteem. It is the active-modifying stance that histrionics take to assure a continuous supply of admiration and fulfillment that distinguishes their style of behavior. Should this supply of reciprocal gratification fail to be forthcoming, histrionics will quickly jettison the "defective" partner, turning without much ado to locate another who will supply these needs.

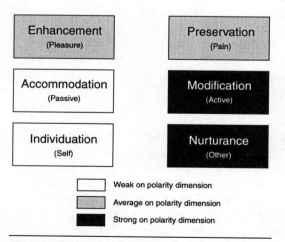

Figure 14.1 Status of the histrionic personality prototype in accord with the Millon Polarity Model.

CLINICAL PICTURE

The following sections should aid the reader in outlining a cognitive map, so to speak, of the prototypal histrionic personality disorder (see Table 14.1).

Prototypal Diagnostic Domains

Histrionic personalities often demonstrate, albeit in caricature and mild pathological form, what our society tends to foster and admire in its members: being well liked, successful, popular, extraverted, attractive, and sociable. Beneath this surface portrayal, we often see a driven quality, a consuming need for approval, a desperate striving to be conspicuous and to evoke affection or attract attention at all costs. Despite the frequent rewards these behaviors produce, they stem from needs that are pathologically inflexible, repetitious, and persistent. In this section, the histrionic picture is detailed in

TABLE 14.1 Clinical Domains of the Histrionic Personality Prototype

Behavioral Level

(F) *Expressively Dramatic* (e.g., is overreactive, volatile, provocative, and engaging, as well as intolerant of inactivity, resulting in impulsive, highly emotional, and theatrical responsiveness; penchant for momentary excitements, fleeting adventures, and short-sighted hedonism).

(F) *Interpersonally Attention-Seeking* (e.g., actively solicits praise and manipulates others to gain needed reassurance, attention, and approval; is demanding, flirtatious, vain, and seductively exhibitionistic, especially when wishing to be the center of attention).

Phenomenological Level

(F) *Cognitively Flighty* (e.g., avoids introspective thought, is overly suggestible, attentive to fleeting external events, and speaks in impressionistic generalities; integrates experiences poorly, resulting in scattered learning and thoughtless judgments).

(S) *Gregarious Self-Image* (e.g., views self as sociable, stimulating, and charming; enjoys the image of attracting acquaintances by physical appearance and by pursuing a busy and pleasure-oriented life).

(S) *Shallow Objects* (e.g., internalized representations are composed largely of superficial memories of past relations, random collections of transient and segregated affects and conflicts, and insubstantial drives and mechanisms).

Intrapsychic Level

(F) *Dissociation Mechanism* (e.g., regularly alters and recomposes self-presentations to create a succession of socially attractive but changing façades; engages in self-distracting activities to avoid reflecting on and integrating unpleasant thoughts and emotions).

(S) *Disjointed Organization* (e.g., there exists a loosely knit and carelessly united morphologic structure in which processes of internal regulation and control are scattered and unintegrated, with ad hoc methods for restraining impulses, coordinating defenses, and resolving conflicts, leading to mechanisms that must, of necessity, be broad and sweeping to maintain psychic cohesion and stability and, when successful, only further isolate and disconnect thoughts, feelings, and actions).

Biophysical Level

(S) *Fickle Mood* (e.g., displays rapidly shifting and shallow emotions; is vivacious, animated, impetuous; exhibits tendencies to be easily enthused and as easily angered or bored).

F refers to Functional Domains (fluid, interactive)
S refers to Structural Domains (stable, unchanging)

line with the four spheres of clinical observation and analysis employed in Chapter 4 for description of the dependent personality (see Figure 14.2).

Dramatic self-image.   Although not unique, there are distinctive aspects to the expressive behaviors of histrionics. They are overreactors, relating at times in a volatile and provocative manner, but usually displaying themselves in an engaging and theatrical manner. They show a tendency to be intolerant of inactivity, resulting in impulsive, capricious, and highly emotional behaviors. Similarly, there is a penchant for momentary excitements and hedonic ventures. Histrionic personalities often impress one at first meeting by the ease with which they express their thoughts and feelings, by their flair for the dramatic, and by their capacity to draw attention to themselves. These exhibitionistic and expressive talents are manifested, however, in a series of rapidly changing, short-lived, and superficial affects. Histrionic personalities tend to be capricious, easily excited, and intolerant of frustration, delay, and disappointment. Moreover, the words and feelings they express appear shallow and simulated rather than deep or real.

Attention-seeking interpersonal conduct.   Histrionics are more than merely friendly and helpful in their relationships; they are actively solicitous of praise, "market" their appeal, and are often entertaining and sexually provocative. Because affection and attention are primary goals, histrionics engage in a variety of maneuvers to elicit a favorable response. Women may behave in a charming or coquettish manner; men are typically generous in praise and, on occasion, overtly seductive. Both men and women often display an interesting mixture of being carefree and sophisticated on the one hand, and inhibited and naïve on the other. In the sphere of sexuality, for example, many histrionics are quite at ease while "playing the game" but become confused, immature, or apprehensive once matters get serious.

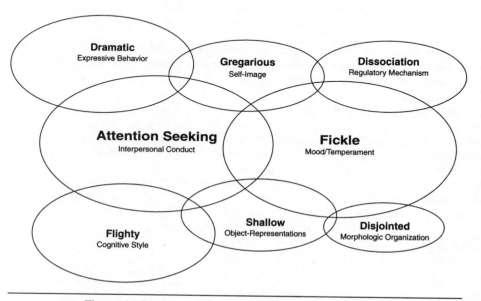

Figure 14.2   Salience of prototypal histrionic domain.

Characteristically, histrionics are unable to follow through on and sustain the initial impression of goodwill and sophistication they convey. Their social life is made up of "many acquaintances but few friends." In most areas of personal activity, they put up a good show at the start but often falter and withdraw when depth and durability in relationships are required.

It is toward the end of achieving these goals and avoiding these fears that histrionics have learned to manipulate others to their suiting. More than merely agreeable and friendly, they "sell" themselves by employing their talents and charm to elicit recognition and esteem. This is done by presenting an attractive front, by seductive pretensions, by a dilettantish sophistication, and by a show of postures and acts to impress and amuse others. Displays and exhibitions, dramatic gestures, attractive coiffures, frivolous comments, clever stories, shocking clothes, all are designed not to "express themselves" but to draw interest, stimulation, and attention. In short, histrionics use themselves as a commodity with a bag of tricks, a conspicuous "personality" that corners all of the attention of those with whom they come into contact.

Histrionic personalities not only acquire skill in sensing what is salable or will "get across" to others, but they learn to be alert to signs of potential hostility and rejection. This hypervigilance enables them to quickly adapt their behaviors to minimize indifference and disapproval. Their interpersonal facility extends, therefore, not only to evoking praise but to avoiding rejection. By paying close attention to the signals that people transmit, histrionics can fashion their reactions to conform with the desires of others. Then they need not fear indifference or desertion, for they are always ready to maneuver themselves to do things that correspond to the wishes and expectations of others.

Despite the charm and talent for pleasing others, the histrionic fails to provide them with genuinely sustained affection. All that histrionic personalities offer in return for the approval they seek are fleeting and often superficial displays of affection.

Flighty cognitive style.   Histrionics are inclined to avoid introspective thought. Lacking an integrated sense of self owing to their exteroceptive orientation, they are overly suggestible, are excessively attentive to fleeting and superficial events, and integrate their experiences poorly. This results in a widely scattered but shallow pattern of learnings, as well as a tendency to speak in impressionistic generalities and to come to essentially thoughtless judgments. The preoccupation of histrionic personalities with external rewards and approvals often leaves them bereft of an identity apart from others. They describe themselves not in terms of their own traits but in terms of their relationships and their effects on others. Histrionics behave like "empty organisms" who react more to external stimuli than to promptings from within. They show an extraordinary sensitivity to the thoughts and moods of those from whom they desire approval and affection. This well-developed "radar" system serves them well, for it not only alerts them to signs of impending rejection but enables them to manipulate the object of their designs with consummate skill.

This orientation toward external stimuli leads histrionics to pay fleeting, impressionistic, and scattered attention to details, and accounts in part for their characteristic distractible and flighty behaviors. The susceptibility of histrionics to transient events parallels their superficial cognitive style, their lack of genuine curiosity, and their inability to think in a concentrated and logical fashion. Habits of superficiality and dilettantism may represent an intellectual evasiveness and a desire to eschew troublesome thoughts or emotionally charged feelings. Part of the flightiness of histrionic personalities derives from an avoidance of potentially disruptive ideas and urges, especially those that might bring to awareness their deeply hidden dependency needs. For these and other reasons, they "steer clear" of self-knowledge and depth in personal relationships. In effect, histrionics dissociate themselves from thoughts, from people, and from activities that might upset their strategy of superficiality.

Gregarious self-image.   Histrionic personalities view themselves as sociable, friendly, and agreeable people. They consider themselves to be stimulating and charming, well liked by others, and able to be quite successful in terms of creating an exciting and interesting lifestyle. Important to them is the capacity to attract acquaintances, particularly by physical appearance, and by creating a busy and pleasure-oriented context for their social life. Many lack insight, however, failing to recognize, or admit recognizing, their deeper insecurities, their desperate need to draw attention to themselves and to be well liked. Signs of inner turmoil, weakness, depression, or hostility are almost invariably denied, suppressed so as not to be part of their sense of self.

Shallow object-representations.   Most persons seek stimulation, attention, and approval, but it is only the histrionic personality who possesses an insatiable striving for these experiences, who feels devoid of an inner self and seeks constant nourishment to fill that void. Lacking a core identity apart from others, histrionics must draw nurture from those around them. It is others who supply the sustenance of life without which histrionics will feel a deep vacancy, a fear of collapse, and a falling apart in disarray or into the empty chasm that exists within them. The internalized objects of the histrionic's intrapsychic content are composed largely of superficial memories of past relationships. Owing to the facile manner in which histrionics attach themselves to others, what comprises their inner world are random collections of transient and unconnected affects, a template of insubstantial relationships, impulses, and memories. The scattering and incidental character of these inner templates leads the histrionic to become ever more dependent on external stimulation and approval. How do histrionics manipulate their inner world to assure the stimulation and approval they require?

It may be useful before proceeding to note again that the interpersonal behaviors of most pathological personalities do not usually appear strikingly different from that seen among "normal" individuals. Their distinction lies not so much in their uniqueness or bizarreness but in their inflexibility and persistence.

Histrionics are often successful in accomplishing their aims of eliciting stimulation and captivating the attentions of others. Their strategies are considered pathological because they fail to limit their manipulations to situations in which they are appropriate. Rather, they are applied indiscriminately and persistently, seeking to attract the attentions of insignificant persons in unsuitable circumstances. Histrionics' needs for recognition and approval appear insatiable. As soon as they receive attention from one source, they turn their unquenchable thirst for approval to others. The histrionic is a bottomless pit into which esteem and tribute may be poured. Equally important is the observation that a failure to evoke attention and approval often results in dejection and anxiety. Signs of indifference or neutrality on the part of others often are interpreted as rejection and result in feelings of emptiness and unworthiness.

Having failed throughout life to develop the richness of inner feelings and lacking resources from which they can draw, histrionics have difficulty maintaining a full, meaningful, and stable relationship with another. At some level, they also sense the disparity that exists between the favorable but superficial impression they give to others and their real lack of inner substance. As a result, they are likely to shy from prolonged contact with others for fear that their fraudulence will be uncovered. In sum, the facile emotions of histrionics are shallow, fleeting, and illusory; not only are they unable to sustain close relationships, but they quickly abandon what few they may have before the "truth" becomes known.

Dissociative regulatory mechanism.   As already noted, histrionics actively seek to avoid introspection and responsible thinking. Not only are they characteristically attuned to external rather than internal events, but their lifelong orientation toward what others think and feel has prevented them from learning to deal with their own inner thoughts and feelings. As a consequence, they lack intrapsychic skills and must resort to gross mechanisms to handle unconscious emotions. What they have learned best is to simply seal off, repress, or dissociate entire segments of memory and feeling that may prompt discomfort. As a result, much of their past is a blank, devoid of the complex reservoir of attitudes and emotions they should have acquired through experiences. Histrionics regularly alter and recompose their self-presentations to create a succession of socially attractive but changing façades. By disconnecting their true selves from the theatrical pose they present to the world, they can distract themselves sufficiently to avoid reflecting on and integrating the emptiness that inheres within them or the painful thoughts and emotions that otherwise surge up into consciousness.

To the degree that histrionics possess an inner world of thought, memory, and emotion, they try to repress it and to keep it from intruding into their conscious life. This they do for several reasons. First, their own sense of worth depends on the judgment of others; there is no reason to explore the inner self, for alone they cannot appraise their personal value or provide acceptance or approval. Second, by turning attentions inward, histrionics distract themselves from attending to the outer world. This divided attention can prove troublesome because they feel they must be ever alert to the desires and moods of others.

The contrast between their pretensions and objective reality leads histrionics to repress not only one or two deficiencies within themselves but all of their inner self; it is the triviality of their entire being, its pervasive emptiness and paucity of substance, that must be kept from awareness. Repression is therefore applied across the board; it is massive and absolute.

Disjointed morphologic organization.   The morphologic structure and organization of the histrionic's inner world is loosely knit and carelessly united. Internal controls and regulations are scattered and unintegrated, with ad hoc methods used to restrain impulses, coordinate defenses, and resolve conflicts. Regulatory mechanisms must, of necessity, be broad and sweeping to maintain overall psychic stability and cohesion. Of course, when successful, these efforts only undermine psychic coherency by further disconnecting and isolating this personality's thoughts, feelings, and actions.

Having deprived themselves of past learnings, histrionics are less able to function on their own and thereby perpetuate their dependency on others. Moreover, to compensate for the void of their past, and for the guidance these learnings could provide, they remain locked in the present. In short, the intrapsychic world of the histrionic personality not only remains skimpy and insubstantial, but their preoccupation with external immediacies has led to a further impoverishment of what little richness and depth they may possess.

To preserve their exteroceptive vigilance, they must reduce "inner" distractions, especially those that may be potentially disturbing. Histrionics seek actively to blot out any awareness of the barrenness of their intrapsychic world. This inner emptiness is especially intolerable because it points to the fraudulence that exists between the impressions they seek to convey to others and their true cognitive sterility and emotional poverty.

Fickle mood/temperament.   The biological underpinnings of the histrionic personality may not be too difficult to infer. Conceived in temperamental terms, histrionic behavior suggests both a high level of energy and activation and a low threshold for autonomic reactivity. Histrionics tend, in general, to be quick and responsive, especially with regard to the expression of emotions. Feelings of both positive and negative variety come forth with extreme ease, suggesting either an unusually high degree of sensory irritability, excessive sympathetic activity, or a lack of cortical inhibition. No single temperament label readily captures the highly fickle, intense, erratic, and wide range of emotions to which they are disposed.

It would seem reasonable that histrionic adults would have displayed a high degree of emotional responsiveness in infancy and early childhood. This inference derives from the facts that constitutional traits are essentially stable throughout life and that active and responsive children are likely to foster and intensify their initial responsiveness by evoking stimulating reactions from others.

Self-Perpetuation Processes

We all engage in automatic and persistent behaviors that are "senseless" if viewed in terms of their objective utility. The difference between the persistent behaviors we consider normal and those that are pathological lies in the fact that "normal" senseless and repetitive acts do not create problems or intensify existent ones. Pathological behaviors, no matter what their immediate utility, ultimately foster new difficulties and perpetuate old ones. This section considers aspects of histrionic behaviors that foster these consequences. Three characteristics of the histrionic pattern are discussed because each tends to set up vicious circles that promote new problems (see Table 14.2).

External preoccupations.   This chapter has already recorded the observations that histrionics orient their attention to the external world and that their perceptions and cognitions tend to be fleeting, impressionistic, and undeveloped. This preoccupation with incidental and passing details prevents experiences from being digested and embedded within the individual's inner world. In effect, histrionics show little integration and few well-examined reflective processes that intervene between perception and action; behaviors are emitted before they have been connected and organized by the operation of memory and thought. The disadvantages of this hyperalertness to external stimuli may outweigh its advantages. Unless life events are digested and integrated, the individual gains little from them. Interpersonal transactions and learnings pass through the person as if he or she were a sieve. There is little opportunity to develop inner skills and few memory traces against which future experience can be evaluated. Indiscriminate and scattered responsiveness leaves the person devoid of an inner reservoir of

TABLE 14.2 Self-Perpetuating Processes

HISTRIONIC

External Preoccupations

Fleeting experiences resist internalization

Impulsive behavior lacks connection to the past

Few memory traces to evaluate future

Massive Repression

Emotional insulation precludes emotional maturation

Failure to merge new with old results in stagnation

Retains values of childhood

Superficial Relationships

Need for approval and stimulation

Needed affection and support jeopardized

Nothing exists to tide over empty times

articulated memories and a storehouse of examined ideas and thoughts. In short, an excessive preoccupation with external events perpetuates the histrionic's "empty shell" and further fosters dependence on others as the only source of guidance.

Massive repression. The tendency of histrionics to seal off, repress, and make inaccessible substantial portions of their meager inner life further aggravates their dependence on others. By insulating their emotions and cognitions from the stream of everyday life, histrionics deny themselves opportunities to learn new alternatives for their behavior, to modify their self-image, or to become more genuinely skillful and knowledgeable persons. As long as they block the merger that should occur between new and old experiences, they are likely to remain stagnant, unaltered, and impoverished. Deprived of opportunities to learn and grow, they will further perpetuate the vicious circle of dependency on others. As a consequence, the histrionic progresses little beyond childhood and retains the values and modes of behavior of an adolescent.

Superficial social relationships. The histrionic personality requires a retinue of changing events and people to replenish the need for stimulation and approval. Thus, as life progresses, histrionics move capriciously from one source to another. One consequence of these fleeting and erratic relationships is that histrionics can never be sure of securing the affection and support they crave. By moving constantly and by devouring the affections of one person and then another, they place themselves in jeopardy of having nothing to tide them over the times between. They may be left high and dry, alone and abandoned with nothing to do and no excitement with which to be preoccupied. Cut off from external supplies, histrionics are likely either to engage in a frantic search for stimulation and approval or to become dejected and forlorn. They may proceed through cyclical swings, alternating moments of simulated euphoria and excitement with longer periods of hopelessness, futility, and self-condemnation. Should deprivation be frequent or prolonged, the probability is high that these personalities will display the signs of a clear and serious affective disorder.

Despite their lack of well-developed inner resources, histrionics have a reasonably good prognosis because they possess motivation and skills for maintaining satisfactory interpersonal relationships. Given their desire to relate to others and their facility for eliciting attention and approval, the probability is slight that they will succumb to prolonged pathology.

INTERVENTION GOALS

Histrionics rarely seek therapy. When they do, it usually follows a period of social disapproval or deprivation, and with the hope that a therapist will help fill the void. Often, when the patient's social environment returns to its baseline level of reward, the patient will terminate therapy, regardless of whether any therapeutic shift in personality structure has taken place. For this reason, it is a good idea for patient and therapist to establish very specific treatment goals. This approach helps the patient remain motivated to stay in therapy despite rather vague presenting complaints such as boredom, restlessness, discontent, and loneliness. The histrionic personality also often reports a growing disaffection with his or her mate, a feeling that the vitality that supposedly characterized earlier years together has now palled. Sexual interest may have faded and the frequency of relations may have dropped due to impotence or frigidity. As disaffection intensifies, conflicts and tension rise, prompting the patient to feel a sense not only of loss but of rejection and hostility from his or her mate. Life feels as if it has taken on a purposeless and meaningless quality. The patient may begin to dramatize his or her plight, feeling that every recourse is hopeless and futile.

In planning a therapeutic intervention program, the ultimate goal is to correct the histrionic's tendency to fulfill all needs by focusing on others to the exclusion of self. This requires a shift not only on the self-other but on the active-passive polarity. Specific interventions aimed at reversing problem-perpetuating behavioral tendencies and at modifying personologic domain dysfunctions must be chosen according to the individual case (see Table 14.3).

TABLE 14.3   Therapeutic Strategies and Tactics for the Prototypal Histrionic Personality

STRATEGIC GOALS
Balance Polarities
  Diminish manipulative actions
  Moderate focus on others

Counter Perpetuations
  Reverse external preoccupations
  Kindle genuine social relationships
  Acquire in-depth knowledge

TACTICAL MODALITIES
  Decrease interpersonal attention seeking
  Stabilize fickle moods
  Reduce dramatic behaviors
  Reorient flighty cognitive style

Reestablishing Polarity Balances

Histrionic personalities operate from the basic premise that they are incapable of handling a large number of life's demands and that they need someone truly competent and powerful to do so for them. In their effort to ensure that someone powerful with these attributes is in fact around and willing to take care of all those things they "cannot," histrionics must spend emotional and mental energy focusing on others. A close vigilance of the "rescuer" must be kept so that at any sign of displeasure or potential rejection, the significant other can be placated, and thus the histrionic's survival secured. In addition, others must be charmed and impressed enough to supply a generous dose of rewards, including praise and admiration, without which the histrionic becomes anxious and depressed. These efforts, despite coming naturally to histrionics, are demanding enough that there is little resource left with which to examine their own internal state. Ironically, success at these goals obviates the need to develop instrumental competence.

To reestablish balance within the self-other polarity, histrionics must learn to turn to themselves and away from others as a means of gratification and to accomplish instrumental goals. In terms of overall adaptation, it would also serve histrionics well to shift away from their persistent attempts to ensure that the environment does indeed yield sought-for gratification, and learn to channel time and energy in more profitable ways. As they become more passive in relation to their social environment and overcome the anxiety of giving up full control over the script of their social lives, histrionics may come to enjoy the element of surprise that comes with not having to orchestrate every social interaction.

Countering Perpetuating Tendencies

In an attempt to evade the anxiety that accompanies internal exploration, histrionics engage in massive repression of their unsettled inner lives. Rather than face the existential anxiety that is an inevitable consequence of a deep appreciation of the nature of life, histrionics adopt a protective superficiality. Whatever anxieties do penetrate the shallow surface from the repressed realm of deeper experience are kept at bay through a fantasy of fusion with a powerful other. These strategies, however, involve blocking those very cognitions and emotions that would allow histrionics to process stimuli in an adaptive way. In the case of the histrionic, the lack of fruitful mental processing does not generally involve any kind of thought disorder; distraction is the histrionic's dysphoria-avoiding secret. A constant stream of social excitement and engaging (if trivial) external preoccupations must be maintained to keep histrionics from facing the hollow inner turmoil they so dread. Such a strategy requires that the histrionic be adept at creating interpersonal drama and approval. When a relationship inevitably moves past the initial "high" and into the reality of interpersonal differences that need to be worked out, the histrionic must quickly secure approval and admiration in order not to fall prey to despair. Moving onto a new relationship provides another opportunity for a "honeymoon" period, but ensures that relationships do not get past a superficial level of intimacy, leaving histrionics without solid relationships to provide support and understanding during inevitable lapses of high drama in their social lives.

In working with a histrionic, a therapist will probably find that the patient thwarts all attempts to examine thoughts and feelings. Patiently guiding the histrionic down the road to self-discovery can prove extremely helpful in reversing maladaptive patterns. If histrionics can bear to face their anxieties, they can also be convinced to give up the external preoccupations that distract them from the processing of stimuli. Allowing the mind to perform logical cognitive operations can begin to change their impressionistic and underdeveloped schemata about causal relationships among events, thoughts, and feelings. Focusing on such previously unexamined matters can result in the integration of past experiences. These, in turn, should lead to learning and the flexibility to engage in alternative and less adolescent forms of coping behavior as well as the development of a more mature level of personal independence. Self-examination can also help histrionics see the long-term futility of relationship hopping and how it serves to deprive them of the very security they crave. The value of making an effort to develop skills needed to deal with less gratifying aspects of relationships, and to tolerate times when the histrionic is not on center-stage in exchange for long-term intimacy, can then be grasped.

Identifying Domain Dysfunctions

The most salient disturbances in the prototypical histrionic personality are in the mood, interpersonal conduct, expressive behavior, and cognitive domains. Histrionics exhibit fickle mood and temperament. They overreact to environmental events, displaying dramatic but shallow emotional reactions that often lead them to behave in a less than ideal way. Constantly on an emotional seesaw between enthusiasm and irritation (anything is better than boredom), they rarely have the emotional tranquillity necessary to encourage the development of adaptive behavior. Probably one of the earliest ways to reduce their emotional hyperreactivity is to focus therapeutic sessions on their flighty cognitive style. Because avoiding introspection and obsessing about external events are habits, cognitive approaches can help histrionics learn to integrate experiences and thus forge rational schemata with which to process stimuli more completely and meaningfully. Exploratory therapy, behavioral experiments, group therapy, and cognitive exercises all can help histrionics give up a lifestyle characterized by impulsive behavior and thoughtless judgment.

The flirtatious interpersonal behavior that is the hallmark of the histrionic personality inevitably produces long-term problems despite its short-term rewards. Although others are initially easily seduced and manipulated to do and say what the histrionic wishes, ultimately the histrionic is perceived as shallow and flighty. Rarely do they experience the satisfaction of genuine intimacy and appreciation for the person they are. Once again, work in the cognitive domain can help histrionics see the advantages of limiting exhibitionistic and seductive behavior to only a few social contexts in which they are more appropriate. Behavior modification can be particularly helpful in teaching alternative behavior skills, such as more assertive communication. Because histrionics are resistant to giving up the colorful style of their demonstrative behavior that has gained them so much attention, they should be taught to discriminate when it is appropriate and when it will lead only to long-term complications and an unfavorable shallow impression. Similar interventions can prove invaluable in modifying the theatrical overresponsiveness the histrionic uses in an attempt to ward off boredom by creating momentary adventures.

The histrionic self-image is gregarious. The self is seen as charming and oriented toward a full and pleasurable social life. This would not be problematic in and of itself;

the fact is that histrionics do not know how to define themselves without reference to others. Lack of a personal identity leaves histrionics open to despair when left alone. Defining a personal identity is a major therapeutic objective. Part of this work can involve examining the historical antecedents of the development of their shallow object-representations schema and helping them see that human interactions, emotions, and conflicts can be integrated in logical, meaningful, and cohesive ways.

Intrapsychically, histrionics try to avoid stress by using dissociation as a regulatory mechanism, altering self-presentations to create a favorable response when one "persona" fails. Distraction is used to avoid painful internal experiences, even if personal identity and self-understanding must be sacrificed. Consequently, the morphologic organization of their mental coping and processing schemata and structures is weak and lacking cohesion. Without allowing themselves to think about stimuli, histrionics ensure that new behavioral strategies cannot be developed; coping will be inflexible and lack logical cohesion, mirroring the morphological structure from which it stems. A therapeutic goal is to bring this fact to the histrionic's attention, so that he or she can make informed decisions about behavior patterns. Many histrionics would indeed like to develop a stronger and less reactive sense of self.

SELECTING THERAPEUTIC MODALITIES

Most histrionic patients tend to view the therapist as a "magical" and omniscient helper who has the power to solve all the patient's problems. Chances are good that the patient will try to "charm" the therapist with entertaining stories and good looks, or "pull" for attention and nurturing with a dramatic show of distress. Two main problems arise when the therapist gives in to the patient's dependency. First, patients learn neither self-sufficient behaviors nor how to make decisions themselves; second, patients eventually discover that the therapist's care-taking capacity is indeed not superhuman, and possibly terminate therapy prematurely due to anxiety and disappointment over this inevitable discovery. It is no easy task, however, for the therapist to consistently reinforce independent and assertive behaviors in the face of the histrionic's well-practiced emotionally seductive and compelling help-seeking style.

Behavioral Techniques

Behavioral interventions can initially be most useful in relieving symptoms of emotional distress in histrionic patients; particularly helpful in this regard are relaxation training and problem-solving strategies. The more long-term objective of changing coping styles involves an array of case-specific cognitive-behavioral "experiments" that allow patients to challenge their assumptions about their fundamental lack of capacity to care for themselves. Assertiveness training can provide histrionics with behavioral alternatives to the manipulative seductive ploys they use to procure what they want and need. Encouraging patients to do just that of which they are the most afraid in small and controlled steps while carefully monitoring their reactions can lead to the acquisition of behavioral and coping skills that foster lasting changes in self-efficacy.

Whereas behavior therapy might be sufficient to help overcome dysfunctional expressive maneuvers, the shallowness that histrionics adopt to avoid the deep existential aloneness that each individual experiences requires more searching therapeutic intervention. For therapy to be successful in the long run, histrionics must come to tolerate the very existential anxiety they so successfully, but superficially, have learned to defend against.

The process, however, necessitates that histrionics be able to tolerate the identity crisis that inevitably accompanies the examination of long-term core conflicts and deep-seated anxieties. In the outline of her interpersonal therapeutic approach, L.S. Benjamin (1990) suggests that histrionics can be supported through this process by warm sympathy toward the patient's observing ego (the part of the patient that can rationally understand the ways certain behaviors can lead to problems), with whom the therapist can "gang up" against the "enemy"—that part of the patient that feels compelled to keep acting out damaging histrionic patterns.

Interpersonal Techniques

Interpersonal therapy also makes use of concrete problems and relationships as a springboard from which to examine dysfunctional patterns. Alternative behaviors are actively recommended. L.S. Benjamin (1990) summarizes the histrionic position as one in which interpersonal relationships are dominated by an overtly expressed friendly trust, accompanied by a disrespectful covert agenda of forcing nurturance and love from a powerful other. Seductive and manipulative behaviors are the means to the histrionic's coercive ends. Addressing transference issues directly through questions concerning the patient's feelings about the therapy and therapist is suggested. Revealed reactions can then be connected back to earlier history and the self-perpetuating quality of these patterns can be explored. Delineating the differences between social and therapeutic relationships (differences in reciprocity, expectations) can be used to counter romantic transference reactions. A significant challenge in the early stages of treatment is transforming the patient's conception of therapy as a way of facilitating immature fantasies to a setting where independent skills can develop. A major issue in this regard stems from histrionics' belief that if they were to become autonomous, no one would care for them, in fact, that they would be abandoned.

Interpersonal therapists suggest that couples therapy can be useful particularly for pairs whose personality styles are complementary, as has been clinically noted to be commonly the case. Histrionics often become involved with overcontrolled compulsives; intervention that focuses on role reversal can lead to more balanced personality styles as new behaviors are integrated. Couples therapy may be extremely useful following histrionics' emotional outbursts, such as threats of self-destructive behavior and/or engaging in seductive play with others in an effort to make their spouse jealous. (Harbir, 1981)

Group intervention approaches may be particularly efficacious with histrionic patients, although Slavson (1964) expressed concern that the capriciousness and unpredictability of these patients would engender unusual tensions within the group. Gabbard (1994), by contrast, finds that these patients tend to be useful group participants owing to their ability to express their feelings and thoughts openly and directly. A problematic consequence in group settings is that it may frustrate the patient's desire for the exclusive attention of the therapist. On the other hand, having an opportunity to observe individuals with similar interpersonal patterns can provide patients with a "mirror" that fosters better understanding of the impact of their own behavior on others. Multiple perspectives on the self afforded by group members can encourage patients to integrate diverse information and bolster object-representation schemata. As the group members' acquaintance with each other deepens through the process of mutual sharing and appraisal, it is doubtful that the group will continue to accept dramatic and flirtatious behavior as a substitution for genuine sharing. Group approval and encouragement of appropriate assertive behaviors and simultaneous disregard for histrionic displays can serve as powerful reinforcers that help bring about change, as long as patients do not feel so threatened by being challenged that they drop out of the group.

Cognitive Techniques

The procedures of cognitive reorientation may also prove useful in helping histrionics gain insight into their patterns and in building a richer inner life that would decrease patients' dependence on others for identity and reinforcements. Histrionics typically are motivated and cooperative. However, their rather diffuse cognitive style may not lend itself well to the highly structured nature of cognitive therapy. Hence, in the early stages of treatment, these patients may find the procedures of therapy somewhat difficult, especially when they are asked to focus their attention on one theme at a time. Also problematic is the tendency to wander about somewhat randomly, if not capriciously, crossing the boundaries set forth by the therapist. A firm and clear-cut set of agreements may usefully counter this tendency toward rather vague and diffuse goals. In time, histrionic patients may come to recognize the value of specific if short-term goals.

In the cognitive therapy approach outlined by Beck and Freeman (1990a), the initial challenge for the therapist is to maintain the patience needed to help histrionics process and perceive environmental stimuli in ways that are largely characterologically unnatural to them. Persisting despite frustration is key to successful treatment; learning the very process of cognitive therapy itself can ultimately prove to be the histrionic's greatest new tool, as new cognitive processing skills lead to novel interpretation of the environment that fosters increases in independent and competent behavior. As Beck points out, it is especially important for the therapist to consistently reinforce assertive and competent responses, so as not to encourage the dependent patterns that so often bring long-term distress despite immediate reinforcement. Because of the histrionic's lack of attention to detail, setting up specific goals can sometimes be difficult. However, insisting that histrionics establish very clear ideas about what their therapeutic objectives are (how their lives will be different) can help ensure that the goals are meaningful to patients and that termination "by boredom" is less likely.

In terms of specific interventions, cognitive authors suggest that the first step is to help patients identify their dysfunctional automatic thoughts. Histrionics have trouble with this task; they are not adept at processing environmental events, the thoughts they have, and the feelings conjured by them in logical and detailed ways. Learning this skill, however, allows patients to focus attention on their emotions and desires, identify cognitive distortions, and discover accurate causal relationships among environmental, cognitive, and emotional events. Another great advantage of focusing on learning to identify the relationship between automatic thoughts and behavior is that patients can learn to stop and try to figure out what thought they are having before reacting, thus learning to control their impulsivity. Learning to analyze these relationships in terms of a means-ends analysis can help make histrionics aware of behavioral consequences. These new insights can help persuade histrionics to undertake experiments in which they "try on" different behavioral styles for effect.

Self-Image Techniques

As difficult as it is to convince histrionics to engage in self-exploratory and logical cause-and-effect analysis, their need for approval can be taken advantage of in the initial stages of therapy by using approval and appreciation of strengths to reinforce their tentative efforts. Although direct advice giving is rarely profitable, helping patients analyze the reasons for and consequences of life choices can be invaluable. Confrontation of the dependency wish and acceptance of the fact that it inevitably cannot be satisfactorily fulfilled represent a therapeutic milestone on the road to developing a more adaptive personality structure. Once this goal is achieved, some histrionics can independently go on to make lasting changes in their lives. Others may need ongoing support as they explore new avenues to developing an identity.

One of the major changes therapy aims to support is decreased manipulation. Helping histrionics identify their authentic wants is a necessary first step in facilitating their genuine communication to others. Identifying desires can be seen as part of a larger process of discovering a sense of identity; most histrionics spend so much time focusing on others in an attempt to get their attention and approval, modifying their behavior to impact on each particular individual, that they are hardly sure of who the fundamental "I" in their "personality" is. The author suggests that making lists of things that patients know about themselves, even as basic as favorite colors and foods, is a good way to begin building a self-concept. Another important goal toward the end of increasing self-valuation is to decrease the histrionic's fear of rejection. Histrionics become paralyzed by the possibility of a relationship's ending, and often are convinced that straightforward behavior (as opposed to the "irresistible" cute, coy, or dramatic ploys they usually depend on) will be easier for others to turn their back on. The possibility of a rejection can be cognitively handled in therapy by imagining what life was like before a particular relationship, and how the patient could manage to survive in the future if a particular relationship were to end.

Intrapsychic Techniques

Psychodynamic therapies tend to be based on the premise that patients need to grasp the familial origins of their desire to have all of their needs met by a significant powerful other. The assumption is that excessive dependency is unresolved and often unconscious, and that it needs to be brought to light. Techniques include analyzing manipulative behavior and its subconscious as well as conscious goals. The futility of the histrionic's efforts needs to be made clear: it is impossible to have all of one's needs met by someone else without being prepared to tolerate loss of self-respect. These issues can all be worked on within the framework of the inevitable transference reaction. Current psychodynamic thinking frames patients' reactions toward the opposite-sex therapist in terms of their goal of manipulating the therapist to satisfy all their needs. These goals spring from patients' unconscious dependent fantasy relationship with their opposite-sex parent; nurturance—not sexual gratification—is considered the true goal of even sexually provocative behavior.

Although the classic psychodynamic therapist stance of neutrality and refusal to provide direct advice is successful with a large number of patients, those with very pronounced ego weaknesses may suffer from this particular therapist style. Weaker patients may decide that the therapist is withholding, not because of his or her desire to communicate a lack of omniscience, but rather out of principle, and try to extract these responses from the therapist at all costs. The ensuing transference drama can be more disruptive to therapy than an interested and sympathetic if noncommittal response to pleas for advice. Examination of such requests can in fact be used to point out to the patient what one can reasonably expect from other people. No intervention plan is complete without providing patients with alternative behavioral possibilities and an understanding of their possible advantages over current patterns.

Brief and short-term anxiety-provoking therapy (Sifneos, 1972) may also prove of value for those patients who exhibit higher levels of functioning and good psychological-mindedness. Not all briefer approaches are likely to be effective; thus, Mann's (1973) time-limited approach may elicit transference relationships that end too abruptly for many histrionic patients who develop intense bonds to their therapists.

Pharmacologic Techniques

Psychopharmacologic intervention with histrionics is often limited to dealing with episodes of depression. When histrionics with depression come to the attention of a therapist, the comparative degree to which symptoms are biologically based versus the extent to which they are a means to secure therapist attention needs to be evaluated. The possible advantages of taking antidepressant medication as a complement to psychotherapy should be considered. More specifically, and depending on the primary symptoms, either antidepressants or mood stabilizers may prove useful. If there is only a partial reduction of symptoms in response to the SSRIs, it may be useful to add a mood stabilizer such as lithium as an adjunctive medication. Taken in medically low dosages, symptoms of emotional sensitivity and moodiness may be diminished, with no likelihood of problematic side effects or addictive possibilities. As Joseph (1997) notes, these medications may very well improve confidence, impulse control, and frustration tolerance, thereby enabling the utility of psychosocial treatments to bring the patient to a higher level of mature functioning.

MAKING SYNERGISTIC ARRANGEMENTS

A first therapeutic step might be to curtail patients' tendency to overemotionalize and thereby aggravate their distraught feelings. Relaxation training and cause-and-effect thinking skills can be useful adjuncts to the initial phases of long-term exploratory therapies. If a histrionic presents with depression that is evaluated to be endogenous and interfering with adaptive functioning, antidepressant medication can be considered as a support to psychotherapy. However, the therapist must establish a solid alliance and specific goals before prescribing medication, because there is always the risk that as soon as the histrionic feels better, therapy will be terminated regardless of whether changes have been made.

Clients whose familial or couple environment encourages their patterns would do well to participate in specific family or couple interventions as an adjunct at some point in their individual therapy. Group therapy can also help histrionics by exposing them to others with similar behavior patterns that they may resist seeing in themselves, and

TABLE 14.4   Histrionic Personality Disorder Subtypes

Theatrical: Affected, mannered, put-on; postures are striking, eye-catching, graphic; markets self-appearance; is synthesized, stagy; simulates desirable/dramatic poses.

MCMI 4

Appeasing: Seeks to placate, mend, patch up, smooth over troubles; knack for settling differences, moderating tempers by yielding, compromising, conceding; sacrifices self for commendation; fruitlessly placates the unplacatable.

MCMI 4-3

Vivacious: Vigorous, charming, bubbly, brisk, spirited, flippant, impulsive; seeks momentary cheerfulness and playful adventures; animated, energetic, ebullient.

MCMI 4-5

Disingenuous: Underhanded, double-dealing, scheming, contriving, plotting, crafty, false-hearted; egocentric, insincere, deceitful, calculating, guileful.

MCMI 4-6A

Tempestuous: Impulsive, out of control; moody complaints, sulking, precipitous emotion, stormy, impassioned, easily wrought-up, periodically inflamed, turbulent.

MCMI 4-8A

Infantile: Labile, high-strung, volatile emotions; childlike hysteria and nascent pouting; demanding, overwrought; fastens and clutches to another; is overly attached, hangs on, stays fused to and clinging.

MCMI 4-C

---

gives them the opportunity to be rewarded for appropriate behavior from a group of people. Because others are the most powerful reinforcers for histrionics, this forum can potentially show rapid results.

Illustrative Cases

As noted in previous chapters, this section draws on extensive clinical observations as well as research on cluster and factor analysis that provide an empirical base for determining variants and coexisting personality disorders. The following sections illustrate clinical synthesis of these personality subtypes (see Table 14.4).

**HISTRIONIC PERSONALITY: THEATRICAL
TYPE (PURE HISTRIONIC TYPE)**

CASE 14.1, TOM S., 36

Presenting Picture: Tom S., a writer, seemed to always want to be performing. As a matter of fact, he was a former stand-up comic who, by his own admission, was quite good at it. He decided, however, to forgo this career choice due to a distaste for other performers in the business. He complained that the others never had an "offstage" mode to their personalities, and this made for some rather shallow characters and meaningless friendships, and he viewed himself as "above" all that. However, upon meeting Tom, it is obvious that much of what he complains about in others is present in himself! From outward behaviors such as his preoccupation with fixing his hair or his description of his chameleonlike wardrobe, to discussions that allude to the transient nature of his interpersonal context, it is obvious that Tom was aware of something in himself that did not allow others to see the "offstage" or true persona.

Clinical Assessment: Tom, a *theatrical histrionic,* is a caricature of the basic histrionic: dramatic, romantic, attention-seeking. As Fromm (1947) recognized in his description of the "marketing orientation," he is an individual who is living life as if he were a commodity, an object for sale. No personal characteristic was seen as intrinsic, that is, a stable and fundamental aspect of who he was. It is the appearance of things that was everything. Tom was adept at transforming himself into something synthesized, something that appeared in ways other than it really was. It is this readily devised image that was projected on the world, shifting from time to time as the occasion called for. He packaged himself to meet the expectations of others as closely as possible. He was a chameleon of sorts, changing his colors and shadows to fit whatever environment he found himself in. We might describe Tom as affected and mannered, one who "puts on" striking and eye-catching postures and clothes, one who markets his appearance to others, and who simulates desirable and dramatic poses that are fabricated or synthesized to create an appealing image of self.

Problems arose, however, as a consequence of this flexible image of self. Despite the charm and adaptiveness of these maneuvers, the ability to simulate all types of roles and characters, Tom was left with a sense of inner emptiness. No intrinsic quality was seen, merely a set of mirrors that reflected what would be pleasing and attractive to others. Everything was simulated and expedient, all was pragmatic and marketable. Tom was a superb manipulator of symbols that mimic reality.

Several varieties of the theatrical type are seen in society. The most visible caricature is women who encase themselves in bright jewelry, sexy clothes, and appealing perfumes. They spend much of their time putting on makeup, trying on different clothes, and reading fashion magazines. The parallel among men (Tom, of course, being no exception) is the great raconteurs and joke-tellers; also notable are those who spend an inordinate amount of time "working out," trimming and shaping their bodies to fit the latest model of the virile and vigorous man.

There are the romanticized types who complain of being disillusioned with their spouses or lovers. Living in a fantasized world of romantic aspirations, they seek to seduce and conquer those of the opposite sex. They seek to become femme fatales, bon vivants, or casanovas. By whatever means possible, they display themselves, acting as if they were lures to attract the most attractive prize available to them. They become similar to the ornaments worn on their body, a clever device to seduce the unsophisticated. Interestingly, persons of the same gender quickly size up the superficial ploys engaged in by the theatrical histrionic. Women quickly spot these behaviors and decoys; men are not as discerning, but also come to recognize the deceptive smile, the coy look, and the humorous comment. This histrionic's mode of operation is patently obvious, except to those who are in the process of being admired and seduced.

Synergistic Treatment Plan: Tom's major perpetuations included a fixation with external matters, namely, the preoccupation with attracting attention in manipulative ways (heavily unbalanced *other* orientation), as well as a narrow focus on his own less-than-attractive personal features (average but confounded *self*). Following early *supportive* measures geared toward engaging Tom with the therapeutic process, it would be necessary to work with him to reorient *cognitive* tendencies toward more grounded (less manipulatively *active*) patterns of constantly garnering attention. Likewise, it would be beneficial to address *interpersonal* difficulties by working toward a more empathic stance in relationships, that is, to assist him to acquire a more genuine, honest, "give-and-take" style of socialization. This could be further augmented by *behavior skills development,* which would serve to practice and ingrain healthier social skills. Efforts to moderate his superficial tendencies may require psychoeducational methods.

Therapeutic Course: It was obvious that Tom's investment in therapy might be fleeting, so the initial short-term goals were those that allowed him to focus on himself. This early *supportive* approach allowed him to relive a bit of his gratifying past and invest in his rather befuddled self-image. Tom quickly became active in this process, as he was quite willing to share past triumphs with the therapist, and this renewed vigor primed him for deeper, more challenging explorations. His yet uncovered, more ingrained tendencies would call for focused *cognitive* and *interpersonal* treatment approaches, which would best be achieved by combining this approach with an adjunctive *family* strategy.

The empathic and encouraging atmosphere fostered from the outset helped Tom realize that he could, in fact, secure approval and love from significant people in his life. From here, a combination of cognitive reframing (e.g., Beck) and interpersonal training (e.g., Klerman, Kiesler) proved useful to several therapy goals that were largely social in nature. It was important for Tom to build his capacity for empathy and impulse control, which would augment his ability to sustain attachments without exploitation, as well as to learn to focus on the present environment as opposed to past events. It was largely unnecessary to help Tom in means of self-expression or insight, as he showed little difficulty in these areas.

More than likely, Tom felt that seeking therapy for his difficulties was an appropriate action, but certainly he could just as well have worked matters out on his own. The caveat here is that this mindset frequently leads to diminished investment in the process of treatment and perhaps more "self-diagnosing" or resistance. This would inevitably lead to regression and repetitive social aberrations and then the resultant discontentment. Not surprisingly, Tom was reluctant to be frank and open with a therapeutic authority figure, and had to be confronted cognitively to foster more serious disclosures and discussions. Tom's tendencies included irresponsibility and impulsivity, as well as avoiding more substantial issues by wandering rather randomly among superficialities, and these trends needed to be stifled. This was accomplished by employment of *behavioral* and interpersonal treatment methods. Also, it was helpful to maintain contact with family members, as they often had an alternative take on current matters and sometimes an utterly contradictory viewpoint. Overall, treatment was most efficacious when it was focused on short-term goals, such as confronting his problematic behaviors and attitudes, restoring balance to his self-image, and bolstering those effective coping strategies he did possess.

In this regard, efforts were directed at countering Tom's self-indulgent and exploitive presentation that produced disapprobation and censure from others. Through the use of cognitive techniques, he was guided to see that this demeanor led to negative outcomes, such as estrangement, and the inability to elicit anything positive from others. As he gained interpersonal awareness (e.g., Benjamin), he became more successful at assessing situations objectively, learned how to be more clear and forthright rather than exploitive, and was able to put forth a more attractive and respected personality.

HISTRIONIC PERSONALITY: INFANTILE TYPE (HISTRIONIC WITH BORDERLINE TRAITS)

Case 14.2, Katie P., 29

Presenting Picture: Katie P. had recently been disciplined at work due to customer complaints and erratic work habits, which resulted in a change from full-time to part-time status at her job at a department store. This change prompted a rather severe and sudden anxiety (though her erratic emotionality seemed more characterological than immediate), as she now did not know if she would be able to save enough money to enroll in art school, and she really felt she needed this job to have a consistent reference on her résumé. She explained that she had had many previous jobs and that something would always happen to cause her to walk out. She described significant relationships in her life to be of a similarly fragmented nature. Although she was currently involved with a new person, Katie spoke frequently of her ex-boyfriend, who was "responsible" for her decision to go into art. He eventually moved out because he felt she was inconsistent in affect from moment to moment and regarded decisions as important one day, but discarded the next (e.g., marriage). Katie's feeling, though, was that he said he'd always be there, but as men do, "he lied." As the initial interview went on, she gradually revealed a troublesome relationship with her father, who abandoned the family in her early adolescence only to return when she was in high school with a whole new demanding attitude toward Katie. She, of course, rejected him and his new demeanor, and had viewed this ex-boyfriend as "the first healthy relationship I've ever had with a man, even though he, too, let me down."

Clinical Assessment: Katie demonstrated a compound of histrionic and borderline personality features. It is akin to what Kernberg (1967) has referred to as the *infantile personality*, noted by labile and diffuse emotions, childlike pouting, and demanding-clinging behaviors, as well as a crude and direct sexual provocativeness. In certain ways, Katie might be spoken of as a primitively developed and poorly organized histrionic. Descriptively, we might characterize her as labile, high-strung, and inclined to express volatile emotions. She displayed a childlike hysteria, typified by a pouting and demanding attachment to others; she fastened onto and clutched to significant others, seemingly fused to them, if not clinging and "hanging on."

Katie's behavior was typified by marked dependency needs, deep and varying recurring moods, prolonged periods of moodiness and self-deprecation, and episodes of high energy and impulsive, angry outbursts. There was an anxious seeking for reassurance from others to maintain equanimity. An intense fear of being abandoned led her to be overly compliant at one time, profoundly gloomy the next, behave with negativistic outbursts and tantrums, and then to engage in sexually provocative behaviors. Some saw Katie as submissive and childlike, and others as unpredictable, irritable, and irrational. She was known to portray conflicting emotions simultaneously, notably love, rage, and guilt. There appeared to be an affective-activity equilibrium that was in constant jeopardy. As a consequence, Katie vacillated between being tense and high-strung, manipulative, and moody, and was particularly sensitive to the pressures and demands of others. Her frequent vacillation between moments of childlike agreeableness, acting in an enticing and tempting manner, and being sullen or pouty was typical and frequent.

Katie often complained bitterly about the lack of care expressed by others and of being treated unfairly, behaviors that kept others constantly on edge, never knowing if they would be reacted to in a cooperative or a sulky manner. Although occasionally making efforts to be obliging, if not seductive, Katie frequently precipitated interpersonal difficulties by constantly doubting the genuineness of interest others expressed. These irritable and childlike testing maneuvers frequently exasperated and alienated those on whom she depended. Frequently, Katie exhibited seductive and clinging behaviors. However, others grew increasingly weary of these behaviors, leading her to react by vacillating erratically between expressions of gloomy self-deprecation, behaving in a sexually provocative manner, and being petulant and bitter. The struggle between childlike acquiescence and adult self-assertion constantly intruded into Katie's life, as was seen in her pattern of MCMI scale scores. The inability to regulate sexual impulses and emotional controls, the feeling of being misunderstood, and the unpredictable moods expressed, all contributed to innumerable wrangles and conflicts with others and to a persistent tense, resentful, and emotional tone.

Synergistic Treatment Plan: Katie's overall polarity structure was in a constant state of unrest, and it would be of primary importance to ease these highly volatile conflicts. Specifically, emphasis continually changed between being fully *self*-oriented (expressing and declaring her autonomy and her adult status, albeit in a naïve, resentful manner) and *other* oriented (dependent, provocative, attention-seeking, submissive). Within an empathic milieu, it would be necessary first to resolve these tendencies via *interpersonal* means designed to establish more genuine and less manipulative relationships, beginning with her relationship with the therapist. Other perpetuations to be controlled would include vacillations in *cognitive* patterns, such as perpetual motion between overvaluing safety and security (evasion of *pain*) and taking on an adolescent "indestructible" attitude (*pleasure* polarity). Throughout the course, it would be necessary to work at reducing her constitutional proclivity toward highly *active,* anxious patterns, which continually fed the conflicts between polarities.

Therapeutic Course: A primary short-term goal of treatment with Katie was to aid her in reducing her intense ambivalence and growing resentment of others. With an empathic and brief focus, it was possible to sustain a productive, therapeutic relationship. With a therapist who could convey genuine caring and firmness, she may have been able to overcome her tendency to employ maneuvers to test the sincerity and motives of the therapist. Although she would be slow to reveal her resentment because she disliked being viewed as an angry person, it could be brought into the open, if advisable, and dealt with in a kind and understanding way. She was not inclined to face her ambivalence, but her mixed feelings and attitudes were a major focus of treatment. To prevent her from trying to terminate treatment before improvement occurred and to forestall relapses, the therapist employed brief and circumscribed techniques to counter Katie's expectation that supportive figures would ultimately prove disillusioning.

Circumscribed *interpersonal* approaches (e.g., Benjamin, Kiesler) were used to deal with the seesaw struggle Katie enacted in her relationship with her therapist. She would alternately exhibit ingratiating submissiveness and a taunting and demanding attitude. Similarly, she solicited the therapist's affections, but when these were expressed, she rejected them, voicing doubt about the genuineness of the therapist's feelings. The therapist used *cognitive* procedures to point out these contradictory attitudes. It was important to keep these inconsistencies in focus or Katie would have appreciated the therapist's perceptiveness verbally but not altered her attitudes. Involved in an unconscious repetition-compulsion in which she recreated disillusioning experiences that paralleled those of the past, she had to not only come to recognize the expectations cognitively but had to be taught to deal with their enactment interpersonally.

Despite her ambivalence and pessimistic outlook, there was good reason to operate on the premise that Katie could overcome past disappointments. To capture the love and attention only modestly gained in childhood could not be achieved, although habits that precluded partial satisfaction could be altered in the here and now. Toward that end, the therapist helped her disentangle needs that were in opposition to one another. For example, she both wanted and did not want the love of those on whom she depended. Despite this ambivalence, she entered new relationships, such as in therapy, as if an idyllic state could be achieved. She went through the act of seeking a consistent and true source of love, one that would not betray her as she believed her father and others did in the past. Despite this optimism, she remained unsure of the trust she could place in others. Mindful of past betrayals and disappointments, she began to test her new relationships to see if they were loyal and faithful. In a parallel manner, she attempted to irritate and frustrate the therapist to check whether he would prove to be as "fickle" and "insubstantial" as others had in the past. It was here that the therapist's warm support and firmness played a significant short-term role in reframing Katie's erroneous expectations and in exhibiting consistency in relationship behavior.

Although the rooted character of these attitudes and behavior would complicate the ease with which these therapeutic procedures would progress, short-term and circumscribed cognitive and interpersonal therapy techniques were quite successful. A thorough reconstruction of personality was not necessary to alter Katie's problematic pattern. In this regard, *family* treatment methods that focused on the network of relationships that often sustained her problems proved to be a useful technique. *Group* methods may have also been fruitfully employed to help her acquire self-control and consistency in close relationships.

The therapist did not set goals too high because Katie may not have been able to tolerate demands or expectations well. Brief therapeutic efforts were directed to build her trust, to focus on positive traits, and to enhance her confidence and self-esteem.

HISTRIONIC PERSONALITY: VIVACIOUS TYPE (HISTRIONIC WITH NARCISSISTIC FEATURES)

CASE 14.3, HELEN S., 25

Presenting Picture: Helen S. was a flight attendant who was seemingly very satisfied with her work, as she had the opportunity to meet and interact with virtually "everybody." She was very comfortable with the brief interactions she had with a very wide audience, and even commented that one of her favorite tasks was the "performance" aspect of the emergency procedure presentation at the outset of each flight. She had recently been suspended due to several customer complaints that she had "snapped" at them, and counseling was suggested by her supervisor. Although she willingly agreed to do anything to salvage her job, an alternative career, Helen mused, might be modeling. Although quite upbeat and pert throughout the interview, it is rather interesting to note how quickly (albeit *briefly*) she shifted her affect back and forth from lively and happy to perturbed and tense at the mere mention of an unpleasant subject. She spoke of a series of men that she has dated, and in the same breath mentioned that she was married approximately two years prior to the interview for a very short duration. Helen quickly changed the subject by stating that this was a brief, unpleasant period of her life, and that there was no use dwelling on it.

Clinical Assessment: A frequent association has been found between histrionic and hypomanic features. Prevalence data indicate that this covariation occurs with considerable frequency in settings such as drug treatment programs, marital counseling clinics, and centers for handling female youth offenders.

In addition to the high level of energy and vigor that typifies hypomanic types, *vivacious histrionic* personalities such as Helen tend to be clever, charming, flippant, and capable of weaving fanciful images that intrigue and seduce the naïve. Given these latter characteristics, it should not be surprising that she also exhibited a variety of narcissistic personality traits.

Driven by a need for excitement and stimulation, this energetic and driven young woman acted impulsively, was unable to delay gratification, and evidenced a penchant for momentary excitements and fleeting adventures with minimal regard for later consequences. She was notably thrill seeking, easily infatuated, and overly but transiently attached to one thing or person following another. We might describe Helen with the following adjectives: vigorous, bubbly, spirited, brisk, and impulsively expressive. She was restlessly energetic, ebullient, seeking momentary playful and joyful adventures, without imposing constraints on where and when these were to be pursued.

For the most part, Helen's tendency was to be overly cheerful, of a lively and spirited nature, disposed to live life to the fullest in a brisk and vigorous way. She was distinguished by the animated nature of her movements, by her ill-disposition to sit still and relax for any period of time. She always seemed to be on the go, gesticulated freely and in a highly expressive manner, enjoyed conversations, and produced ideas in a quick tempo. She raced her physical and psychic engines, exhibiting vigor in her movements, as in all other aspects of her behaviors and thoughts. For the most part, she was quite cheerful, although inclined to be rather superficial in the topics she discussed. She moved from one thing to another, often in a joyous and joking manner. She almost always viewed things from an optimistic and cheerful perspective; serious and problematic matters tended to be glossed over or overlooked entirely.

Helen lacked social dependability, exhibiting a disdain for the effects of her behaviors, as she pursued one restless chase or satisfying one whim after another. There was a capricious disregard for agreements hastily assumed, and she easily may have left a trail of broken promises and contracts, squandered funds, distraught employers, and so on. Lacking inner substance and self-discipline, tempted by new and exciting stimuli, and skilled in attracting and cheerfully seducing others, Helen may have traveled an erratic course of flagrant irresponsibility and left in her wake the scattered debris of seductive and once promising hopes.

Synergistic Treatment Plan: Helen needed to be engaged and invested in the process of therapy, as she was prone to be only half-hearted, and a *supportive, self-image*–oriented milieu would serve to focus her on objective aspects of *self* that would eventually need to be *controlled* and somewhat *diminished* at a later point when she could tolerate such adjustments. It would also be necessary to moderate her constitutional tendency to be overly *active* (anxious energy), as well as her unusual *pleasure*-seeking. *Interpersonally,* she tended toward devaluing and hurting *others,* mainly through irresponsible actions (as opposed to malevolent intentions), and both interpersonal and *cognitive* measures would next be employed to develop more mature social skills as well as reevaluate and restructure basic assumptions regarding socialization, both oriented to establish more genuine, meaningful relationships. *Behavioral* interventions would be fruitful as well in reinforcing new habits and skills and establishing responsible social actions.

Therapeutic Course: Helen's interest needed to be held initially, and this was achieved by implementing short-term goals that allowed her to focus attention on herself. Further, by occasionally encouraging her indulgence in "reliving" past achievements, the therapist enabled Helen to rebuild her previously "synthetic" self-esteem. Helen became an active partner in restoring her self-confidence by recalling and elaborating on her attributes and competencies in front of the therapist. Her comfort and regained confidence were major circumscribed goals, and these were achieved in very few sessions. However, there were deeper, ingrained tendencies as well, and their modification called for focused short-term *cognitive* and *interpersonal* treatment approaches that also incorporated family and other system participants.

Helen was able to retain motivation for a short-term therapeutic regimen, but her life situation became increasingly discouraging during the earlier period of treatment when she was not working. A positive and encouraging therapeutic approach enabled her to regain the feeling that she was able to secure affection from those who mattered to her and approval from customers and coworkers. As treatment continued beyond brief intervention, the therapist directed efforts primarily toward building greater empathy and impulse control rather than seeking to achieve expressive and insight-oriented goals, toward focusing on here-and-now behavior rather than those in the past, and toward helping Helen learn how to sustain attachments through nonexploitive behavior. These were best achieved by a combination of cognitive reframing (e.g., Beck, Ellis) and interpersonal training (e.g., Klerman, Kiesler).

As the precipitant for her treatment was situational rather than internal, it is important to note that Helen did not seek therapy voluntarily. She was fully convinced that if she were just left alone, she could work out any difficulty she might have with others. This would have only led to backsliding and recurrences of her less than socially acceptable behavior. If treatment had been self-motivated, however, it may have been due to upsetting family problems, legal entanglements, social humiliation, or achievement failures. Given her surface pleasantness and exploitiveness, Helen's complaints took the form of vague feelings of boredom, restlessness, and discontent. Her tendency was to avoid major problems by wandering from one superficial topic to another, and this would inevitably lead to relapses. Hence, this had to be monitored and prevented. *Behavioral* and interpersonal treatment methods that directly addressed her irresponsibility and impulsivity were particularly helpful. Contact with family members was needed in that they frequently reported matters quite differently than did Helen. She was quite hesitant about opening up to a therapeutic authority figure and therefore had to be confronted cognitively to be persuaded to take discussions seriously. Treatment was best geared to short-term goals, such as countering her problematic stances, extinguishing questionable behavior, reestablishing psychic balance, and strengthening socially acceptable coping patterns.

In this regard, short-term efforts were made to counter Helen's characteristic self-indulgence and exploitiveness that evoked condemnation and disparagement from others. She was guided, through cognitive techniques, to see that these acts created negative consequences, and that the ensuing alienation only added to the difficulties she was facing as well as her ability to elicit positive attitudes and actions from others. Gaining interpersonal sensitivity (e.g., Benjamin), she began to assess situations objectively, thereby learning how not to be rebuffed and misunderstood, hence enhancing her attractiveness and success in her relationships with others.

HISTRIONIC PERSONALITY: APPEASING TYPE (DEPENDENT/COMPULSIVE FEATURES)

CASE 14.4, JEFF D., 26

Presenting Picture: Jeff D.'s personality might have been described by his work role, the "right-hand man." He seemed to be in a constant state of inertia, always searching for not only the best way but *every fathomable* way he might please those around him. The most conspicuous example of this behavior was Jeff's constant accommodation of his employer. From having a cup of coffee waiting at her fingertips at the precise moment she desired one, to picking up her children at their school, to wearing a pager so that she could reach him literally any time she desired, *nothing* was ever too much should it serve the potential purpose of gaining her favor. When asked about the need for such pacification, Jeff remarked that it *was* well above and beyond the call of duty, but perhaps this would make him look most favorable in his boss's eyes. He also alluded to the fact that although there had historically been no association between the two of them outside of work, "perhaps some day there would be." When asked about life outside of work, Jeff immediately began speaking of his relationship with his mother. Though he did not go into much detail, it was apparent that this relationship, too, was one geared solely toward winning approval.

Clinical Assessment: This desire to please others, to make them like him, to approve of him, to tell him that what he is doing is good, was the major driving force that motivated Jeff, an *appeasing histrionic* subtype. Approval from others was his supreme goal. Not only did Jeff want to show everyone that he loved them and that he would do anything for them, but he wanted everyone to praise and commend him in return. The search for reciprocal recognition and approval compelled and justified everything he did, as was seen in the pattern of his MCMI scores. He showed an unusual knack for pleasing people, for being thoughtful about their wishes, for making them become friends rather than mere acquaintances. What is most distinctive about histrionics such as Jeff is the need to placate others, to try to mend schisms that have taken place, and to patch up or smooth over troubling matters. He would moderate conflicts by yielding, compromising, and conceding to the wishes of others and was ready to sacrifice himself for approval and commendation. The configuration of characteristics that typify this appeasing type often encompasses an admixture of histrionic, dependent, and compulsive features.

Alert to every sign of potential indifference, Jeff quickly anticipated and avoided what might have been seen as unfavorable; rather, he appraised matters and then enacted what would make him most appealing in the eyes of others. He wished to be a faultless pleaser, invariably seen as well-intentioned, not only in a superficial and momentarily obliging way, but through acts of genuine goodwill that others could not help but appreciate. He was a magnificent flatterer, willing to sacrifice any and all signs of integrity to evoke praise and goodwill.

As a youngster, it is likely that Jeff experienced a never-satisfied parent, a person who found nothing about him that pleased, nothing that was seen as appealing or attractive or right. Such a parent probably goaded Jeff to *prove* that he was virtuous, competent, beautiful, and loving. Jeff's reaction, of course, would have been to strive fruitlessly to appease the unappeasable, to placate the unplacatable, and now he found himself investing much of his life searching for ways to elicit admiration and respect, some small measure of praise, one likely to be faint, if at all forthcoming.

Beneath his surface affability, Jeff felt, at heart, that he was a worthless or problem person, marked early in life as inferior or troublesome, consigned to a self-image of being profoundly inadequate, unloved, and unlovable. He desperately tried to compensate for his deficiencies, invariably looking for ways by which he could gain some measure of appreciation. But the unrelenting and acidlike rain of a parent's early depreciation and criticism, the sense of belittlement and dissatisfaction, remained deeply embedded, a feeling of unworthiness that could never be corrected. Admonished repeatedly not to do this or to make sure to do that, Jeff pursued an endless search for signs of warm regard and praise. No matter what he tried to do, there was nothing that would or could achieve these goals. Despite the hidden hostility felt toward the unappeasable parent, it was kept at bay, deeply suppressed, while his yearning for favorable signs of affection continued to gnaw painfully within him.

Synergistic Treatment Plan: Initial efforts with Jeff would require that his dependent, *other*-oriented pattern remain at least somewhat intact while he began exploring his difficulties, as too soon a break from this strategy would likely stifle growth and cause undue emotional stress. A *humanistic,* empathic milieu would be needed to set the stage for more focused interventions. *Interpersonal* and *cognitive* methods would be useful in working toward more genuine social skills (begin working toward a more autonomous, *self*-driven stance) and correcting the faulty self-perpetuation regarding the all-importance of winning constant approval (gradual work toward diminishing *other* orientation). It would be expected that as these skills and thoughts would be clarified and enacted by Jeff, a validation of his self-image would emerge, allowing for a more permanent, characterologic shift toward autonomy.

Therapeutic Course: To achieve significant goals employing short-term methods, environmental changes were introduced early to maximize Jeff's growth and to minimize his continued dependency. *Psychopharmacologic* treatment, notably certain antidepressants and anti-anxiety agents, may have been useful in increasing his confidence and vigor, for he seemed to be inclined to postpone efforts at changing his assumptions and acquiring a measure of independence. *Interpersonal* techniques were used in the therapeutic relationship to assure that the dominance-submission pattern that had characterized Jeff's history was not reactivated. *Cognitively* nondirective and *self-actualizing* approaches were the most likely modalities to foster the growth of autonomy in a short-term regimen.

Although Jeff was disinclined to share intimate feelings on an impersonal self-report inventory, he had little difficulty unburdening himself to the therapist under a treatment regimen that was strong in empathic caring. He did not show a high degree of insight into his difficulties, but he was quite receptive to cognitive reframing techniques (e.g., Beck, Ellis) and to various interpersonal methods (e.g., Benjamin, Klerman). Because he was disposed to trust others, he had a tendency to invest great powers and the highest of virtue in the therapist, and this facilitated progress from brief short-term procedures.

As noted, Jeff welcomed the opportunity to depend on the strength, authority, and helpfulness of the therapist. This auspicious beginning was most fortunate, but it gave a misleading impression of significant progress. Despite initial successes, Jeff resisted genuine moves to gain independence. Dependency in the therapeutic relationship was then challenged as a step toward growth and the prevention of setbacks. Without undermining his erroneous beliefs and the behavior they engendered, he may have become inactive or withdrawn from treatment, relapsing or regressing to his pretreatment level of adjustment. Only by adopting cognitive and interpersonal changes was he able to develop independence and a sense of self-worth. However, by breaking the entire dependency bond prematurely or by trying to accomplish too much too soon, therapy may have precipitated unwarranted emotions or erratic behavior.

Jeff's initial receptiveness to short-term therapy, as stated, created the misleading impression that all forms of progress would be rapid. Despite real advances, he did seek to maintain a dependent relationship with the therapist. Despite signs to the contrary, he resisted preliminary efforts to guide him into assuming independence and autonomy. Assisting him in relinquishing his dependency beliefs and habits did not, however, prove difficult, as the therapist employed a systematic program of cognitive and interpersonal methods. Efforts to help him build an image of competence and self-esteem proceeded one step at a time through a short-term program that strengthened his positive attributes and dislodged his negative habit of leaning on others.

HISTRIONIC PERSONALITY: TEMPESTUOUS TYPE
(HISTRIONIC WITH NEGATIVISTIC FEATURES)

CASE 14.5, MICHELLE T., 20

Presenting Picture: Michelle T. was referred for therapy by her physician, whom she refers to as "Jim," as she was having a great deal of difficulty with unexplainable cramps and muscular pains. Being a dancer, she did not expect her monthly cycle to be regular, but this physical problem she seemed to be having was apparently unrelated. Michelle seemed to be constantly looking for approval, seeking it from the counselor both by overtly flirtatious behaviors and direct questioning of approval. This saucy behavior, had a very guarded edge to it, as it was apparent that *no one* was allowed past this particular front. Michelle also quickly gave the impression of a resentful, angry person, very swiftly showing quite hostile underpinnings whenever she was reminded of anyone who might have behaved less than "perfectly" in her eyes. These brief outbursts would be followed immediately by a noticeable effort to regain control and the reassumption of the previous "characteristic" front.

Clinical Assessment: Michelle's *tempestuous histrionic* behavior is typified by a high degree of emotional lability and short periods of impulsive acting-out, alternating with depressive complaints, moodiness, and sulking. Her hypersensitivity to criticism, low frustration tolerance, immature behaviors, short-sighted hedonism, and excitement and stimulation seeking were also most salient. Emotions surged readily to the surface, untransformed and unmoderated, evident in a distractible, flighty, and erratic style of behavior. Whatever inner feelings may be sensed, be they guilt, anger, or desire, spilled quickly to the surface in pure and direct form. Michelle was frequently out of control, overly reactive to minor provocations, and acted out in a stormy, impassioned, and turbulent manner. When not overly wrought up, she exhibited moody complaints and sulky behaviors, but quickly reverted to an angry and inflamed response to minor events.

As with other personalities, each subtype of the histrionic exhibits a commingling of the basic personality interpenetrated with features found more typically in other personality styles. In the case of the tempestuous histrionic, we see many features of the negativistic personality and, when seen in severe form, characteristics of the borderline as well.

Michelle's moods tended to be brittle and variable, with periods of high excitement and affability alternating with a leaden paralysis, fatigue, oversleeping, or overeating. It is conceivable that this list might also have included an overuse of alcohol (though this was not directly stated). She displayed short-lived, dramatic, and superficial affects, reported a tendency to be easily excited and then quickly bored. Her mood levels were highly reactive to external stimulation. Feelings of desperation or euphoria were expressed dramatically and more intensely than justified by the situation. Michelle behaved by fits and starts, shifting capriciously down a path that appeared to lead nowhere, often precipitating wrangles with others and disappointments for self.

As noted in earlier pages, D. Klein's (1972) descriptions of the *hysteroid dysphoric* characterizes an affectively labile and shallow personality, seductive and sexually provocative, frequently love-intoxicated and giddy, inclined to think emotionally and illogically. Michelle's behaviors, likewise, were precipitous and enacted in an impetuous and excited way, and frequently created social turbulence and stormy relationships. Despite her desire to be liked, her personality generated chronic and repeated conflicts with others. She often behaved like a child: demanding, self-centered, and uncontrolled. She seemed unable to put effective limits on her emotionally impulsive and irritable behaviors, often flying off the handle and succumbing to temper tantrums.

Cut off from needed external attentions, Michelle would be likely to engage either in a frantic search for approval, become easily nettled and contentious, or become dejected and forlorn, a contradictory pattern seen in her MCMI scale scores. There might be extreme cyclical swings, alternating periods of simulated euphoria and illusory excitements, intermingled with moments of hopelessness and self-condemnation. Also likely would be angry and depressive complaints, usually to the effect that others misunderstood her and that life was full of disappointments. Over time, she might have become less and less histrionic in her behaviors and more and more disgruntled, critical, and envious of others, grudging their good fortunes with a jealous, quarrelsome, and irritable reaction to minor slights. She might have come to be preoccupied with bodily functions and health, overreact to illness, and voice unreasonable complaints about minor ailments. These symptoms would probably have been displayed exhibitionistically to regain lost attention and support.

Synergistic Treatment Plan: Michelle's self-perpetuating patterns included a strong tendency to attempt to manipulate her environment (*active, other* orientation), but also a deep-seated hostility stemming from a rather pervasive, disenchanted *self*-image, and this was a breeding ground for an internal-external conflict. It would be most useful, to begin, for the therapist to establish a firm but empathic therapeutic stance, maintaining openness and understanding but remaining impervious to her provocations. A nonconfrontive *cognitive* strategy would be aimed at examining and reevaluating her dour expectations, and *interpersonal* measures would concurrently work toward less caustic social actions. At later stages of treatment, it would be appropriate to introduce Michelle to a *group* milieu to experience some interpersonal improvements, while establishing concrete *behavioral* goals that would help her gain more effective and satisfying social skills.

Therapeutic Course: Essential to the success of a short-term approach with Michelle was the therapist's readiness to see things from her point of view and convey a sense of trust and create a feeling of alliance. To achieve reasonable short-term goals, this building of rapport could not be interpreted as a sign of the therapist's capitulation to Michelle's bluff and arrogance. Brief treatment with her required a balance of professional firmness and authority, mixed with tolerance for her less attractive traits. By building an image of a fair-minded and strong authority figure, the therapist successfully employed *cognitive* methods that encouraged Michelle to change her expectations. Through reasoned and convincing comments, the therapist provided a model for her to learn the mix of power, logic, and fairness.

Less confrontive cognitive approaches provided Michelle with opportunities to vent her anger, even in short-term therapy. Once drained of these hostile feelings, she was led to examine her habitual behavior and cognitive attitudes and was guided into less destructive perceptions and outlets than before. *Interpersonal* methods, such as those of Benjamin and Kiesler, provided a means to explore more socially acceptable behaviors. As far as *group* methods were concerned, until Michelle had incorporated changed cognitions and actions, she intruded on and disrupted therapeutic functions. On the other hand, she eventually became a useful catalyst for short-term group interaction and gained some useful insights and a few constructive skills.

A useful short-term goal for Michelle was to enable her to tolerate the experience of guilt for the turmoil she sometimes caused. Cognitive methods using a measure of confrontation helped undermine her tendency to always trace problems to another person's stupidity, laziness, or hostility. When she did accept responsibility for some of her difficulties it was important that the therapist was prepared to deal with Michelle's inclination to resent the therapist for supposedly tricking her into admitting it. Similarly, the therapist was at all times ready to be challenged and avoid efforts to outwit her. Michelle tried to set up situations to test the therapist's skills, to catch inconsistencies, to arouse ire, and, if possible, to belittle and humiliate him. Restraining impulses to express condemning attitudes was an important task for the therapist, but one that was used for positive gains, especially when tied into the application of combined cognitive (e.g., Beck, Ellis) and interpersonal interventions.

It should be noted that the precipitant for Michelle's treatment was situational rather than internal. Hence, had her physician not referred her, she would have been unlikely to have sought therapy voluntarily, and she may have even convinced herself that if she were just left alone, she could work matters out on her own. Such beliefs had to be confronted, albeit carefully. Similarly, if treatment had been self-motivated, it probably would have been inspired by a series of family problems, social humiliations, or achievement failures. Whatever its source, a firm cognitive and *behavior-change* approach would seem required. For this domineering and often intimidating woman, complaints were expressed in the form of irritability and restlessness. To succeed in her initial disinclination to be frank with authority figures, she wandered from one superficial topic to another. This inclination had to be monitored and prevented. Moreover, contact with family members was efficacious because they reported matters quite differently than did Michelle. To ensure that she took discussions seriously, she had to be confronted directly with evidence of her contribution to her troubles. Treatment was best geared toward short-term goals, reestablishing her psychic balance, and strengthening her previously adequate coping behavior with cognitive methods, unless her actions were frankly antisocial. In general, short-term approaches with Michelle were best directed toward building controls rather than insights, toward the here and now rather than the past, and toward teaching her ways to sustain relationships cooperatively rather than with dominance and intimidation.

HISTRIONIC PERSONALITY: DISINGENUOUS TYPE (HISTRIONIC WITH ANTISOCIAL FEATURES)

CASE 14.6, LANCE B., 25

Presenting Picture: Lance B., a medical school student, was referred for counseling by the school's board as a condition of his academic probation. Though he could not see an obvious reason for this referral, he did surmise that it might have had something to do with some "missing" pain medication. A seemingly affable person, Lance spoke of good relationships between himself and his peers and teachers. As he continued, however, it became apparent that much of what these others experienced must have been a salesman-like character. He spoke of his frequent manipulations of professors, how he would feign interest in particular fine points in the classroom or laboratory, regularly visit instructors during office hours to ascertain answers, and use eye contact, body language, and "charm" to get what he wanted from them. It seemed obvious that Lance did not really want to invest himself in medical training; rather, he wished to gain his credentials taking the smoothest and easiest road possible.

Clinical Assessment: Lance's *disingenuous histrionic* behavior was typified by a veneer of friendliness and sociability. Although he made a superficially good impression on acquaintances, a more characteristic unreliability, impulsive tendencies, and deep resentments and moodiness could be seen, particularly among family members and other close associates. A socially facile lifestyle could be noted by a persistent seeking of attention and excitement, often expressed in seductive behaviors. Relationships were shallow and fleeting, frequently disrupted by caustic comments and impulses that were acted on with insufficient deliberation.

Lance was irresponsible and undependable, exhibiting short-lived enthusiasms and immature stimulus-seeking behaviors. Notable also was his tendency to be contriving and plotting, to exhibit a crafty and scheming approach to life, a tendency to be insincere, calculating, and occasionally deceitful. Not likely to admit responsibility for personal or family difficulties, he manifested a cleverly defensive denial of psychological tensions or conflicts. Interpersonal difficulties were rationalized and blame was projected on others. Although egocentrically self-indulgent and insistent on attention, Lance provided others with minimal loyalty and reciprocal affection. From the foregoing picture, it should be evident that this histrionic subtype shares many of the characteristics typically seen among antisocial personalities.

Variants of the histrionic such as Lance are more egocentric and deceitful than most histrionics. He was more willful and insincere in his relationships, doing everything necessary to obtain what he needed and wanted from others. Also in contrast to other histrionics, he seemed to enjoy confrontations, gaining a degree of gratification in the excitement and tension that conflicts engender. He could be quite calculating and guileful if someone had what he wanted, be it the attentions of a person or something tangible and material. His need for the approval of others gradually eroded over time and was replaced by the means he employed to achieve approval. In effect, what is now most prominent is the style of being manipulative and cunning, that is, controlling others fully.

Lance recognized that gaining the attention and praise of others did not come without a price. Moreover, he knew that the attention and commendation of others did not come willingly, but was evoked as a consequence of his own plotting and scheming behaviors. Beneath the surface, his greatest fear was that no one would care for or love him unless he made them do so. Despite this recognition, Lance attempted to persuade himself that he was basically well-intentioned, that his insincerely motivated scheming was appreciated for its intrinsic worth. Throughout these mixed internal messages, nevertheless, Lance persisted in seeking what was most important to him, always angling and maneuvering to acquire it. He was as self-deceptive regarding his motives as he was deceptive toward others.

Synergistic Treatment Plan: As with other histrionic subtypes, it would be essential for the therapist to establish an alliance with Lance without surrendering to his characterologic arrogance and manipulation. In balancing polarities, it would be most important to foster a change toward a less *active* tendency (thwart his frequent attempts toward exploitation), as well as to adjust and clarify conflicts between *self* and *other* (typified in his perpetuations, which are inherently self-centered but also geared toward masking his knowledge that he is, in fact, causing harm). *Cognitive* tactics would include adjustment of his expectation that everyone and everything must be in his favor, and illumination of his more empathic senses through the use of experimental techniques. *Interpersonal* and *behavioral* measures would be useful in kindling more genuine and less provocative relationships and skills. As his tendencies would shift toward less malevolent behaviors, it would be likely that a *group* experience would further enhance more effective socialization.

Therapeutic Course: The therapist's ability to empathize with Lance's perspective and to convey trust and create a true therapeutic alliance was absolutely essential. However, it was also crucial that this rapport building could not be viewed in any way as the therapist's submission to Lance's deceit and insolence, nor might it smack of any other acquiescence to manipulation. This milieu required a delicate balance of professional resolution and control mixed with patience and flexibility, not to mention a high tolerance for rather ignominious behavior and attributes. After establishing himself as a fair-minded but firm therapeutic authority figure, the therapist was able to successfully utilize *cognitive* methods that were focused on Lance's selfish expectations and troublesome attitudes toward others. Through thoughtful and cogent comments, the therapist was able to demonstrate effective, fair behaviors and attitudes.

Within the framework of a short-term approach, Lance was able to vent more powerful and negative feelings much more effectively than through sly and manipulative social behaviors. This was accomplished with nonconfrontive cognitive approaches. When his hostilities had dissipated, he took a more objective look at his routine behaviors and attitudes and subsequently learned more productive strategies. *Interpersonal* methods, such as those of Benjamin and Kiesler, allowed Lance to explore more socially acceptable behavior. Although a calculated risk, Lance participated in a *group* setting as well. It was rather likely that his presence, particularly before many changes were made in his counterproductive thoughts and actions, would intrude on and disrupt the group process. Contrarily, however, this opportunity actually fostered short-term group interactions, and Lance gained several useful social skills.

A major short-term goal for Lance was to get him to accept blame and responsibility for troubles that he had caused. After the initial stages of therapy, he was able to tolerate more confrontive cognitive techniques that effectively thwarted his habit of automatically degrading and manipulating others, as well as blaming their stupidity, laziness, or hostility for his problems. As Lance began to accept responsibility for some of these difficulties, the therapist was watching for another inevitable challenge. Lance's efforts, perhaps as a function of feeling "tricked" into admitting responsibility, turned toward outwitting the therapist. This behavior ranged from a hypervigilance for any possible inconsistencies to attempts at belittling and humiliating him. It was of extreme importance to this combined cognitive and interpersonal intervention that the therapist restrain any impulse to express condemnation.

Lance clearly did not seek therapy, except to agree to it as a condition for continued enrollment in medical school. He certainly did not feel that he needed it, and was convinced that he could independently work out any problems he might have. This had to be disputed by the therapist, but delicately and skillfully. A firm cognitive and *behavior-change* approach was required. This intelligent but manipulative person meandered frequently from one triviality to the next, musing on this minor discontentment or that particular irritation, all in a rather pronounced disinclination to be frank with authority figures. This inclination had to be carefully watched and averted. Family members as well added some insight, as they rarely ever reported matters consistently with what Lance was saying. To ensure some measure of seriousness, it was pointed out to him rather clearly that his actions often contributed to his difficulties. Treatment was most effective when geared to tangible, brief goals, reestablishing balanced thought, and bolstering actions and beliefs that were not frankly antisocial. In general, Lance clearly needed controls on behavior, not a reworking of his overall internal psyche. It was also most productive to focus on present situations rather than random musings about the past, as well as learn to foster cooperative relationships rather than gain any "upper hand" through cozenage and deceit.

Resistances and Risks

A therapist whose own sense of identity and self-worth are largely satisfied by being very "helpful" to others may easily be manipulated into playing the savior role and actually repeat the patient's maladaptive experiences of significant others. Other therapists may find the flighty histrionic style annoying; hypervigilant histrionics are apt to sense the disapproval and in fact regress further into their manipulative, theatrical ways. It is important for therapists to make a real effort at empathy lest their intervention efforts be jeopardized. On the other hand, empathy should not imply playing the histrionic's game. Despite the entertaining and charming communication style, it is very important for the therapist to maintain sober and respectful attention. The playful banter that is often therapeutically helpful with other personality styles can serve in the case of the histrionic to reinforce the fact that one is always on display and must charm those around one to get attention and approval. A more serious attention, particularly a stance of respect toward the patient, helps provide the histrionic with alternative interaction schemata.

Some histrionics fear the possibility of becoming drab and dull even as they see the advantages of becoming "deeper" and adopting a more "premeditated" behavioral style. It is a good idea to encourage more constructive expression of the histrionic's natural dramatic flair (often, it can be used to advantage by enlisting the dramatic persona to work with the therapist against maladaptive cognitions and behaviors) than a complete suppression of such tendencies, which may lead to termination.

One of the frustrations a therapist might feel when working with histrionics is their tendency to have "pseudo-insights." Just when the therapist is sure that the therapy has come to a breakthrough, the vague and forgetful style of the histrionic leads to rapid disintegration of apparent gains. The tendency of the patient to want to make the therapist feel important in the hopes of thereby securing special treatment also often leads to enthusiastic agreement with the therapist, despite the lack of real internalization of the issues. Patience on the part of the therapist is a must if his or her disappointment in pseudoprogress is not itself to become disruptive.

CHAPTER FIFTEEN

Treating Narcissistic Personality Patterns

The essential feature of this personality style is an overvaluation of self-worth and a grandiose sense of self-importance and uniqueness. In seeming contradiction to the inflated self-concept is an inordinate need to be loved and admired by others. Unlike the ravenous affectional needs of histrionic and dependent personalities, however, narcissists believe that they are entitled to tribute and praise by virtue of their "specialness." These personalities also share the antisocial features of egocentricity, interpersonal exploitation, and exaggerated needs for power and success. Unlike the anger and vindictiveness of antisocials, however, narcissists are characterized by a benign arrogance and a sense that they are "above" the conventions and reciprocity of societal living. There is little real empathy for others but rather, a tendency to use people for self-enhancement and for indulging their desires. Those who satisfy their needs are idealized, and others who can serve no immediate purpose are devalued and even treated contemptuously. This shifting of overvaluation and denigration may occur frequently within the same relationship. There is an expectation of preferential treatment and special favors, without assuming reciprocal responsibilities.

Narcissistic personalities are cognitively expansive, enjoying fantasies of unrealistic goals, with a tendency to overestimate their abilities and achievements. However, these exaggerated feelings of personal importance can leave the narcissist quite vulnerable to injuries of self-esteem and pronounced feelings of unworthiness should their grandiose self-expectations not be met. Although characteristically imperturbable and insouciant, repeated failure and social humiliations may result in uncertainty and a loss of self-confidence. Over time, with the growing recognition of inconsistencies between their self-perception and their actual performance, comes self-disillusionment, feelings of fraudulence, and in some cases, a chronic state of dysthymia. In other instances, a psychic blow generated from a single event (e.g., a humiliating defeat or a public criticism) may precipitate a brief but severe depressive episode. Such states rarely endure for extended periods, as depression is not experienced as consonant with the narcissist's self-image. The symptomatology of the narcissistic depression may be quite variable, shifting between dramatic expressions of worthlessness and self-deprecation to irritable demandingness and criticism of others. These perceptions tend to be attributed to external, "universal" causes rather than to personal, inner inadequacies (Abramson, Seligman, & Teasdale, 1978). Consistent with this formulation, narcissists may subtly accuse others of not supporting or caring for them enough. At other times, hostility may be directly expressed, as narcissists become enraged at others being witness to their shame and humiliation.

Klerman (1974) described narcissistic depression as a response to fallen self-esteem, a signal of discrepancies within the self-system between "ideal expectations and practical reality" (p. 139). Depression in such individuals follows the inability to maintain the unreasonable expectations set for oneself and others. It is Kernberg (1975) who provides perhaps the most eloquent description of the process of self-disillusionment in the narcissistic: "For them, to accept the breakdown of the illusion of grandiosity, means to accept the dangerous, lingering awareness of the depreciated self—the hungry, empty, and lonely primitive self surrounded by a world of dangerous sadistically frustrating and revengeful objects" (p. 311).

According to Millon (1969, 1996), both narcissist and antisocial patterns (described in this and the next chapter) turn inward for gratification, having learned to rely on themselves rather than others for safety and self-esteem. Weakness and dependency are threatening. Because both narcissists and antisocials are preoccupied with matters of personal adequacy, power, and prestige, status and superiority must always be in their favor. They fear the loss of self-determination, proudly display their achievements, and strive to enhance themselves and to be ascendant, stronger, more beautiful, wealthier, and more important than others. In some, it is what they think of themselves, not what others say or can provide for them, that serves as the touchstone for their security and contentment.

The independent personality style has been divided into two subtypes in earlier writings (Millon, 1969): the passive-independent, or narcissistic personalities, who are confident of their self-worth and feel they need be merely themselves to justify being content and secure; and the active-independent, or antisocial personalities, who struggle to "prove" themselves, who insist on their rights and will be harsh and ruthless when necessary to retaliate or gain power over others. For the narcissistic type, self-esteem is based on a blind and naïve assumption of personal worth and superiority. For the antisocial type, it stems from distrust, an assumption that others will be humiliating and exploitive.

The narcissistic personality, in accord with Millon's ecological framework and its evolutionary model of polarities, is portrayed in Figure 15.1. What is most notable in this chart is the primacy of both passive/accommodation and self-individuation in the narcissist's adaptive style. What this translates into is the narcissist's focus on self as the center of one's existence, with a comparable indifference to others (nurturance). Owing to an unusual developmental background, in which others overvalued narcissists' self-worth by providing attention and tribute unconditionally, they fail to develop the motivation and skills ordinarily necessary to elicit these tributes. To them, merely being who they are is sufficient; one does not have to do anything, much less achieve, to elicit signs of admiration and high self-esteem. Narcissists are passive, therefore, because they expect the rest of the world to do their bidding without reciprocal efforts.

Whereas narcissists assume that others will favor them without efforts on their part, antisocial personalities make no such assumptions at all. The active/modifying polarity is preeminent in antisocials because they feel they have been mistreated and undervalued. They must actively usurp and take from others what they assume will

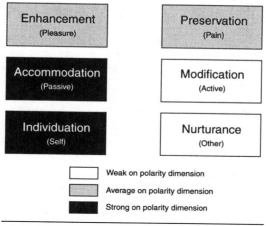

Figure 15.1   Status of the narcissistic personality prototype in accord with the Millon Polarity Model.

never be given them; nothing is voluntarily supplied by others. Whereas narcissists expect others to be freely forthcoming, antisocials expect nothing and hence must take what they can.

CLINICAL PICTURE

As in previous sections, we provide here a wide range of perspectives for observing and conceptualizing the traits of the narcissistic personality disorder (see Table 15.1).

Prototypal Diagnostic Domains

This discussion turns first to the typical characteristics of the narcissistic personality as organized in the eight clinical domains format (see Figure 15.2).

Haughty expressive behavior.   It is not uncommon for narcissists to act in an arrogant, supercilious, and disdainful manner. There is also a tendency for them to flout conventional rules of shared social living. Viewing reciprocal social responsibilities as being inapplicable to themselves, they show and act in a manner that indicates a disregard for matters of personal integrity and an indifference to the rights of others. When not faced with humiliating or stressful situations, narcissists convey a calm and self-assured quality in their social behavior. Their seemingly untroubled and self-satisfied air is viewed by some as a sign of confident equanimity. Others respond to it much less favorably; to them, these behaviors reflect immodesty, presumptuousness, pretentiousness, and a haughty, snobbish, cocksure, and arrogant way of relating to people. Narcissists appear to lack humility and are overly self-centered and ungenerous. They characteristically, but usually unwittingly, exploit others, take them for granted, and expect others to serve them, without giving much in return. Their self-conceit is viewed

TABLE 15.1 Clinical Domains of the Narcissistic Personality Prototype

Behavioral Level

(F) Expressively Haughty (e.g., acts in an arrogant, supercilious, pompous, and disdainful manner, flouting conventional rules of shared social living, viewing them as naïve or inapplicable to self; reveals a careless disregard for personal integrity and a self-important indifference to the rights of others).

(F) Interpersonally Exploitive (e.g., feels entitled, is unempathic, and expects special favors without assuming reciprocal responsibilities; shamelessly takes others for granted and uses them to enhance self and indulge desires).

Phenomenological Level

(F) Cognitively Expansive (e.g., has an undisciplined imagination and exhibits a preoccupation with immature and self-glorifying fantasies of success, beauty, or love; is minimally constrained by objective reality, takes liberties with facts, and often lies to redeem self-illusions).

(S) Admirable Self-Image (e.g., believes self to be meritorious, special, if not unique, deserving of great admiration, and acting in a grandiose or self-assured manner, often without commensurate achievements; has a sense of high self-worth, despite being seen by others as egotistic, inconsiderate, and arrogant).

(S) Contrived Objects (e.g., internalized representations are composed far more than usual of illusory and changing memories of past relationships; unacceptable drives and conflicts are readily refashioned as the need arises, as others are often simulated and pretentious).

Intrapsychic Level

(F) Rationalization Mechanism (e.g., is self-deceptive and facile in devising plausible reasons to justify self-centered and socially inconsiderate behaviors; offers alibis to place self in the best possible light, despite evident shortcomings or failures).

(S) Spurious Organization (e.g., morphologic structures underlying coping and defensive strategies tend to be flimsy and transparent, appear more substantial and dynamically orchestrated than they are in fact, regulating impulses only marginally, channeling needs with minimal restraint, and creating an inner world in which conflicts are dismissed, failures are quickly redeemed, and self-pride is effortlessly reasserted).

Biophysical Level

(S) Insouciant Mood (e.g., manifests a general air of nonchalance, imperturbability, and feigned tranquility; appears coolly unimpressionable or buoyantly optimistic, except when narcissistic confidence is shaken, at which time either rage, shame, or emptiness is briefly displayed).

F refers to Functional Domains (fluid, interactive)
S refers to Structural Domains (stable, unchanging)

by most as unwarranted; it smacks of being "uppity" and superior, without the requisite substance to justify it.

Exploitive interpersonal conduct.   As noted above, narcissists feel entitled, expecting special favors without assuming reciprocal responsibilities. Not only are they unempathic, but they take others for granted, are shameless in the process, and use others to enhance their own personal desires. Unfortunately for them, narcissists must come to terms with the fact that they live in a world composed of others. No matter how preferred their fantasies may be, they must relate and deal with all the complications and frustrations that real relationships entail. Furthermore, and no matter how satisfying it may be to reinforce oneself, it is all the more gratifying if one can arrange one's environment so that others will contribute their applause as well. Of course, true to their fashion, narcissists will seek to accomplish this with minimal effort and reciprocity on

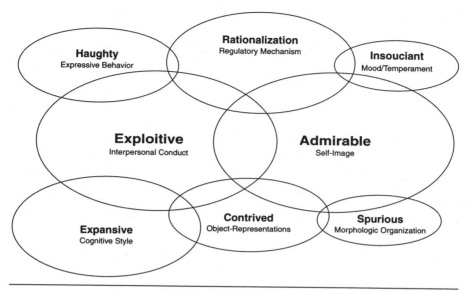

Figure 15.2   Salience of prototypal narcissistic domains.

their part. In contrast to the dependent personality, who must submit and acquiesce to evoke favorable rewards, or the histrionic, who must perform and be attractive to win praise from others, narcissists are likely to contribute little or nothing in return for the gratifications they seek. In fact, some narcissists assume that others feel "honored" in having a relationship with them, and that others receive as much pleasure in providing them with favors and attention as the narcissist experiences in accepting these tributes.

It should not be surprising that the sheer presumptuousness and confidence exuded by the narcissist often elicits admiration and obedience from others. Furthermore, narcissists typically size up those around them and quickly train those who are so disposed to honor them; for example, narcissists frequently select a dependent mate who will be obeisant, solicitous, and subservient, without expecting anything in return except strength and assurances of fidelity. It is central to narcissists' interpersonal style that good fortune will come to them without reciprocity. Because they feel entitled to get what they wish and have been successful in having others provide them with comforts they have not deserved, narcissists have little reason to discontinue their habitual presumptuous and exploitive behaviors.

Expansive cognitive style.   For the most part, narcissists exhibit an undisciplined imagination and seem preoccupied with immature and self-glorifying fantasies of success, beauty, or romance. Although nondelusional, narcissists are minimally constrained by reality. They also take liberties with facts, embellishing them, even lying, to redeem their illusions about their self-worth. Narcissists are cognitively expansive. They place few limits on either their fantasies or their rationalizations, and their imagination is left to run free of the constraints of reality or the views of others. They are inclined to exaggerate their powers, to freely transform failures into successes, to construct lengthy and intricate rationalizations that inflate their self-worth or justify what they feel is their due, quickly depreciating those who refuse to accept or enhance their self-image.

Admirable self-image.   Narcissists feel justified in their claim for special status, and they have little conception that their behaviors may be objectionable, even irrational. It is narcissists' belief that they are special if not unique persons that deserve great admiration from others. Quite frequently, they act in a grandiose and self-assured manner, often without commensurate achievements. Although they expect to be seen as meritorious, most narcissists are viewed by others as egotistic, inconsiderate, and arrogant. Their self-image is that they are superior persons, "extra special" individuals who are entitled to unusual rights and privileges. This view of their self-worth is fixed so firmly in their minds that they rarely question whether it is valid. Moreover, anyone who fails to respect them is viewed with contempt and scorn.

It is not difficult to see why the behaviors of the narcissist are so gratifying to them. By treating themselves kindly; by imagining their own prowess, beauty, and intelligence; and by reveling in their "obvious" superiorities and talents, they gain, through self-reinforcement, the rewards that most people must struggle to achieve through genuine attainments. Narcissists need depend on no one else to provide gratification; they always have themselves to "keep them warm."

Contrived object-representations.   The internalized representations of past experiences are deeply embedded and serve as a template for evaluating new life experiences. For the narcissist, these object representations are composed far more than usual of illusory and changing memories. Problematic past relationships are readily refashioned so as to appear entirely consonant with the narcissist's high sense of self-worth. Unacceptable impulses and deprecatory evaluations are quickly transformed to enable these personalities to maintain their preferred and contrived image of both themselves and their past. Fortunately for most narcissists, they were led by their parents to believe that they were invariably lovable and perfect, regardless of what they did and what they thought. Such an idyllic existence could not long endure; the world beyond home is not likely to have been so benign and accepting. As a consequence, narcissists must transform the less palatable aspects of their past to be consistent with what they wish the past was like rather than what it was in fact.

Rationalization regulatory mechanism.   What happens if narcissistics are not successful, if they face personal failures and social humiliations? What if realistic events topple them from their illusory world of eminence and superiority? What behaviors do they show and what mechanisms do they employ to salve their wounds?

While they are still confident and self-assured, narcissists deceive themselves with great facility, devising plausible reasons to justify their self-centered and socially inconsiderate behaviors. With an air of arrogance, narcissists are excellent at rationalizing their difficulties, offering alibis to put themselves in the best possible light, despite evident shortcomings or failures on their part.

If rationalizations fail, they will likely become dejected and shamed and feel a sense of emptiness. Narcissists will have little recourse other than to turn for solace to their fantasies. In contrast to the antisocial personality (described in the next chapter), most narcissists have not learned to be ruthless, to be competitively assertive and aggressive when frustrated. Neither have most acquired the seductive strategies of the histrionic to solicit rewards and protections. Failing to achieve their aims and at a loss as to what they can do next, they are likely to revert to themselves to provide comfort and consolation. It is at these times that their lifelong talent for imagination takes over. These facile processes enable them to create a fanciful world in which they can redeem themselves and reassert their pride and status. Because narcissists are unaccustomed to self-control and objective reality testing, their powers of imagination have free rein to weave intricate resolutions to their difficulties.

What the narcissist is unable to work out through fantasy is simply repressed, put out of mind and kept from awareness. As noted previously, narcissists invent alibis, excuses, and "proofs" that seem plausible and consistent and convince them of their continued stature and perfection. Flimsily substantiated rationalizations are offered but with a diminished air of confidence and authority. However, narcissists may never have learned to be skillful at public deception; they usually said and did what they liked without a care for what others thought. Their poorly conceived rationalizations may, therefore, fail to bring relief and, more seriously, may evoke scrutiny and deprecating comments from others. At these times, narcissists may be pushed to the point of employing projection as a defense as well as to begin to construct what may become rather primitive delusions.

Spurious morphologic organization.   Narcissists suffer few conflicts; their past has supplied them, perhaps too well, with high expectations and encouragement. As a result, they are inclined not to value others, but to feel confident, nevertheless, that matters will work out well for them. As will be noted in a later section, this sanguine outlook on life is founded on an unusual set of early experiences that only rarely are duplicated in later life.

The structural organization of narcissists' inner world for dealing with life tends to be quite flimsy and transparent to the discerning observer. From a surface view, one would assume that their personality organization is more substantial and dynamically orchestrated than it is in fact. Owing to the misleading nature of their early experiences, that is, that narcissists really did not have to do much to make the world work for them, they have never developed the inner skills necessary to regulate their impulses adequately, to channel their needs skillfully, or to acquire a strategy in which conflicts are resolved, failures are overcome, and a genuine sense of competence is regained following problematic experiences.

Reality bears down heavily at times. Even the routine demands of everyday life may be viewed as annoying incursions by narcissists. Such responsibilities are experienced as demeaning, for they intrude on the narcissist's cherished illusion of self as almost godlike. Alibis to avoid "pedestrian" tasks are easily mustered because narcissistics are convinced that what they believe must be true and what they wish must be right. Not only do they display considerable talent in rationalizing their social inconsiderateness, but they utilize a variety of other intrapsychic mechanisms with equal facility. However, because they reflect minimally on what others think, their defensive maneuvers are transparent, a poor camouflage to a discerning eye. This failure to bother dissembling more thoroughly also contributes to their being seen as cocksure and arrogant.

Unable to disentangle themselves from lies and inconsistencies and driven by their need to maintain their illusion of superiority, they may begin to turn against others, accusing others of their own deceptions, their own selfishness, and their own irrationalities. It is at these not very typical times that the fragility and pathology of the narcissist become clearly evident. "Breakdowns" in the defensive structure of this personality, however, are not too common. More typically, the exploitive behaviors and intrapsychic maneuvers of narcissists prove highly adaptive and provide them with the means of thwarting serious or prolonged periods of dejection or decompensation.

Insouciant mood/temperament. Roused by the facile workings of their imagination, narcissists experience a pervasive sense of well-being in their everyday life, a buoyancy of mood and an optimism of outlook—*except* when their sense of superiority has been punctured. Normally, however, affect, though based often on their semigrandiose distortions of reality, is generally relaxed if not cheerful and carefree. There is a general air of nonchalance, an imperturbability, a feigned tranquility. Should the balloon be burst, however, there is a rapid turn to either an edgy irritability and annoyance with others or to repeated bouts of dejection that are characterized by feeling humiliated and empty. Shaken by these circumstances, one is likely to see briefly displayed a vacillation between rage, shame, and feelings of emptiness.

Self-Perpetuation Processes

A major factor in the perniciousness of personality pathology is that its characterological behaviors are themselves pathogenic. Pathological personality patterns perpetuate themselves by setting into motion new and frequently more troublesome experiences than existed in the past. This section turns to a number of these self-perpetuating features.

As with all personalities, narcissists exhibit their style with persistence and inflexibility. They cannot alter their strategy because these patterns are deeply ingrained. Rather than modifying their behavior when faced with failure, they may revert more intractably to their characteristic style; this is likely to intensify and foster new difficulties. In their attempts to cope with shame and defeat, they set up vicious circles that only perpetuate their problems. Three of these are elaborated next (see Table 15.2).

Illusion of competence. Narcissists assume that the presumption of superiority will suffice as its proof. Conditioned to think of themselves as able and admirable, they see little reason to waste the effort needed to acquire these virtues. Why bother engaging

---

TABLE 15.2 Self-Perpetuating Processes

NARCISSISTIC

Illusion of Superiority
    Sees no reason to develop skills
    Views striving with contempt
    False self-image leads to feelings of fraudulence

Lack of Self-Controls
    Takes unjust liberties with social rules
    Prevaricates and fantasizes freely
    Fantasies recede from objective realities

Social Alienation
    Unable to join in social give-and-take
    Selfishness evokes condemnation
    Misinterprets others' intentions and actions

in such demeaning labors as systematic and disciplined study if one already possesses talent and aptitude? Moreover, it is beneath their dignity to struggle as others do. Because they believe that they are well endowed from the start, there is no need to exert their energies to achieve what they already have. They simply assume that what they wish will come to them with little or no effort on their part.

Many narcissists begin to recognize in time that they cannot "live up to" their self-made publicity and fear trying themselves out in the real world. Rather than face genuine challenges, they may temporize and boast, but they never venture to test their adequacy. By acting in this way, they can retain their illusion of superiority without fear of disproof. As a consequence, however, narcissists paralyze themselves. Their unfounded sense of confidence and their omnipotent belief in their perfection inhibit them from developing whatever aptitudes they may in fact possess. Unwilling to or fearful of expending the effort, they may slip increasingly behind others in actual attainments. Their deficits may become pronounced over time, making them, as well as others, increasingly aware of their shortcomings. Because the belief in their superiority is the bedrock of their existence, the disparity between their genuine and their illusory competence becomes extraordinarily painful. The strain of maintaining their false self-image may cause them to feel fraudulent, empty, and disconsolate. They may succumb to periodic depressions or may slip slowly into paranoid irritabilities and delusions.

Lack of self-controls.   The narcissist's illusion of superiority and entitlement is but one facet of a more generalized disdain for reality. Narcissists are neither disposed to stick to objective facts nor to restrict their actions within the boundaries of social custom or cooperative living. Unrestrained by childhood discipline and confident of their worth and prowess, they may take liberties with rules and reality and prevaricate and fantasize at will. Free to wander in their private world of fiction, narcissists may lose touch with reality, lose their sense of proportion, and begin to think along peculiar and deviant lines. Their facile imagination may ultimately evoke comments from others concerning their arrogance and conceit. Ill-disposed to accept critical comments about their "creativity" and needing to retain their admirable self-image, narcissists are likely to turn further to their habit of self-glorification. Lacking social or self-controls, however, their fantasies may take flight and recede increasingly from objective reality.

Social alienations.   Were narcissists able to respect others, allow themselves to value others' opinions, or see the world through others' eyes, their tendencies toward illusion and unreality might be checked or curtailed. Unfortunately, narcissists have learned to devalue others, not to trust their judgments, and to think of them as naïve and simpleminded. Thus, rather than question the correctness of their own beliefs, they assume that it is the views of others that are at fault. Hence, the more disagreement they have with others, the more convinced they are of their own superiority and the more isolated and alienated they are likely to become. These ideational difficulties are magnified further by their inability to participate skillfully in the give-and-take of shared social life. Their characteristic selfishness and lack of generosity often evoke condemnation and disparagement from others. These reactions drive narcissists further into their world of fantasy and only strengthen their alienation. And this isolation further prevents them from understanding the intentions and actions of others. They are increasingly unable to assess situations objectively, thereby failing further to grasp why they have been rebuffed and misunderstood. Distressed by these repeated and perplexing social failures, they are likely, at first, to become depressed and morose. However, true to their fashion, they will begin to elaborate new and fantastic rationales to account for their fate. But the more they conjecture and ruminate, the more they will lose touch, distort, and perceive things that are not there. They may begin to be suspicious of others, to question others' intentions, and to criticize them for ostensive deceptions. In time, narcissists' actions will drive away potential well-wishers, a reaction that will only serve to "prove" their suspicions.

Deficient in social controls and self-discipline, narcissists' tendency to fantasize and distort may speed up. Their air of grandiosity may become more flagrant. They may find hidden and deprecatory meanings in the incidental behavior of others, becoming convinced of others' malicious motives, claims upon them, and attempts to undo them. As their behaviors and thoughts transgress the line of reality, their alienation will mount, and they may seek to protect their phantom image of superiority more vigorously and vigilantly than ever. Trapped by the consequences of their own actions, they may become bewildered and frightened as the downward spiral progresses through its inexorable course. No longer in touch with reality, they begin to accuse others and hold them responsible for their own shame and failures. They may build a "logic" based on irrelevant and entirely circumstantial "evidence" and ultimately construct a delusional system to protect themselves from unbearable reality.

INTERVENTION GOALS

Despite the potential for serious decompensation, as described above, most narcissists function successfully in society if they possess even a modicum of substance and talent to back their confidence. Difficulties arise only when a marked disparity exists between their presumptions and their actual competence. Narcissists' bountiful reservoir of self-faith can withstand considerable draining before it runs dry. A particularly painful blow to their pride, however, may precipitate a depressive disorder that causes "intolerable" and unaccustomed discomfort. Such an event may entail a severe occupational failure, an embarrassing loss of public esteem, or a sudden change of attitude on the part of a previously idolizing partner. The suffering endured as a result of the crisis is often perceived as exceptional in itself and as deserving of professional attention. Once involved in treatment, however, narcissistic patients present resistances that make personality restructuring a difficult goal to realize. They persist in blaming others for all of their difficulties, adopt a position of superiority over the therapist, and perceive any attempt at constructive confrontation as humiliating criticism. If comfort and regained confidence are the goals, however, these can often be achieved in only a few sessions. The therapist can hold narcissists' initial interest by allowing them to focus attention on themselves; by further encouraging discussions of their past achievements, the therapist may enable narcissists to rebuild their recently depleted self-esteem. Not infrequently, self-confidence in narcissists is restored by talking about themselves, by recalling and elaborating their attributes and competencies in front of a knowing and accepting person.

Merely reestablishing former levels of functioning, however, especially rebuilding the narcissist's illusions of superiority, may prove over the long run to be a disservice to the narcissistic patient. Until more realistic self-evaluation is achieved, it is not likely that narcissists will be motivated to develop competencies and socially cooperative attitudes and behaviors that would lead to more gratifying and adaptive lives. If patients' capacity to confront their weaknesses and deficiencies is strengthened, they may be able to acquire greater self-control, become more sensitive and aware of reality, and learn to accept the constraints and responsibilities of shared social living (see Table 15.3).

Reestablishing Polarity Balances

Characteristic narcissistic confidence, arrogance, and exploitive egocentricity are based on a deeply ingrained, if sometimes fragile, self-image of superior self-worth. Achievements and manifest talents are often not proportional to the narcissist's presumptions of "specialness." The alternative to maintaining unsustainable beliefs of personal infallibility, that is, recognition of imperfections, limitations, and flaws, however, is tantamount to reconciliation with failure and utter worthlessness. For some narcissists, such unreal expectations for themselves stem from experiences in which otherwise doting parents became unsupportive or even abusive at the manifestation of "imperfection" in their child; others simply cannot conceive of life among the "masses." As those around narcissists "dare" not to notice their special uniqueness and then behave appropriately, narcissists turn away from attempting to secure comfort from "simpleminded" others whose place it is to tend them. Instead, they increasingly rely on themselves as a source of rewards. Turning inward provides opportunity to pamper and ponder the self and to fantasize about the great recognition that will come to shine on the narcissist one day. Thus narcissists, who start out high on the self polarity, become increasingly less other-oriented with the passage of time.

In the mind of narcissists, others are the source of all of their troubles and difficulties and are responsible for any failures to achieve fantasized goals. Not only do others have to make this up to the narcissist, but their natural inferiority dictates that they should attend to all the narcissist's whims and needs. The narcissist's exploitive

TABLE 15.3   Therapeutic Strategies and Tactics for the Prototypal Narcissistic Personality

STRATEGIC GOALS
Balance Polarities
  Stimulate active-modifying
  Encourage other focus

Counter Perpetuations
  Undo insubstantial illusions
  Acquire discipline and self-controls
  Reduce social inconsiderations

TACTICAL MODALITIES
  Moderate admirable self-image
  Dismantle interpersonal exploitation
  Control haughty behavior
  Diminish expansive cognitions

egocentricity is not the two-faced, contract-breaking, means-to-an-end exploitiveness of the antisocial. Rather than actively planning, narcissists are led by their arrogance and snobbish sense of superiority to believe that others "owe" them something, and their self-centered convictions of genuine entitlement result in the "passive" exploitation of others. The sense of superiority often results in a lack of goal-oriented behavior in general; narcissists simply believe that good things are their due, a natural by-product of their intrinsic "specialness." This nonadaptive bias toward the passive end of the active-passive dimension often results in personal, social, and professional stagnation.

A main therapeutic goal in trying to increase narcissists' other orientation and active goal-directed behaviors is to help them accept that whereas human imperfections are inevitable, they are not necessarily a sign of failure or worthlessness. If narcissists can appreciate the benefits (lack of pressure, decreased fear of criticism) of not needing to be infallible, they may be able to consider their part of the responsibility for any difficulties they may be having. Active problem solving and improved interpersonal interaction is a worthy goal.

Countering Perpetuating Tendencies

Narcissists' characteristic difficulties almost all stem from their lack of solid contact with reality. The same disdain for objectivity prevents effective coping with subsequent troubles. The problem-perpetuating cycle begins with early experiences that provide noncontingent praise that teach narcissists to value themselves regardless of accomplishments. Their inflated sense of self-worth causes them to conclude that there is little reason to apply any systematic effort toward acquiring skills and competencies when "it is so clear" that they already possess such obvious and valuable talents and aptitudes. Their natural gifts, they believe, are reason enough for them to achieve their goals and earn others' respect.

In time, narcissists come to realize that others who are expending considerable effort to achieve goals are moving ahead and receiving more recognition. Envious and resentful that the acknowledgment that is "rightfully theirs" is being bestowed on others, narcissists intensify their boasting and air of superiority. Eventually, the prospect of actually going out in the world and risking humiliating failure for all to witness becomes untenable in the face of the grand illusions of personal competence narcissists feed to themselves and others.

The problems posed by narcissistic illusions of competence feed into and are exacerbated by social alienation and lack of self-controls. The conviction that they are entitled leads narcissists to harbor disdain for social customs and cooperative living. A lack of respect for others' opinions and feelings leads to a failure to integrate normative feedback about their behaviors and illusions. In fact, the conviction that others are simpleminded and naïve causes narcissists to retreat further into their illusory and isolated world of fantasy at every hint of disapproval. Self-serving rationalizations of others' lack of adulation can escalate till complementary paranoid delusions of persecution and grandiose illusions become firmly entrenched. Were narcissists to possess some self-controls, their social isolation may not have such dire consequences. Internal reality testing, however, is as neglected as are external inputs. Rather than working to realize ambitions, threat of failure and conceit push narcissists to retain their admirable self-image through fantasy. The regard for reality that would prevent narcissists from perpetuating their psychological and coping difficulties is notably absent.

Therapeutic intervention offers an inroad into the pathological cycle through the modification of the overblown self-image. As the self is appraised more realistically, perfection is seen as unattainable, and the need to employ self-discipline to achieve goals is understood, the narcissistic patient may come to recognize and accept his or her similarity to others. As the patient begins to make genuine efforts to improve quality of life, an appreciation for others' hard work and achievements may develop and replace chronic envy and resentment. Intervention aimed directly at increasing empathic understanding can lead to a sensitivity to others' feelings that fosters motivation to adopt cooperative interpersonal behaviors. Toward this end, the narcissist can choose to learn to tolerate and make use of constructive social feedback. Day-to-day successes can eventually provide the gratification that can bolster the patient's resolve not to perpetuate nonadaptive cognitive and behavioral strategies and help control the impulse to escape into unproductive flights of fantasy. If social isolation is thus decreased, therapeutic work has led to difficult-to-realize modifications in the patient's deeply entrenched lifestyle.

Identifying Domain Dysfunctions

The most salient narcissistic dysfunctions are manifested in the self-image and interpersonal conduct domains and are expressed in the form of an admirable self-concept and unempathic, even exploitive treatment of others. At best, the narcissist confidently displays achievements and behaves in an entitled and occasionally grating manner. Facts are twisted and the line between fantasy and reality becomes blurred as narcissists boast of unsupportable personal successes and talent; at the same time, interpersonal behavior moves toward the inconsiderate, arrogant, and exploitive. Others may express irritation at the nonsubstantiated grandiosity of the narcissist's fantasies and at the inequitable nature of his or her social interactions. However, taking advantage of others to indulge desires and enhance their situation, with no consideration of reciprocal responsibilities, is considered justified owing to their sense of self-importance. As long as this self-schema is maintained, narcissists have little chance of finding motivation to effect changes in other areas. Thus, a first therapeutic intervention needs to focus on accepting a realistic self-image. As the cognitive foundation on which exploitive behavior is justified is weakened, interventions that increase empathic understanding and cooperative interactions can become the clinical focus. The possible advantages of these cognitive and behavioral modifications—warmer receptions from others and a more solid personal sense of efficacy—can then be integrated to encourage further development.

Successful intervention in the primary domains can lead to beneficial advances in secondary domains. Furthermore, resolving secondary domain dysfunctions therapeutically can also bolster progress in the more salient areas. Behavioral interventions, including role-playing, techniques of behavioral inhibition, modeling, and systematic desensitization, that elicit nonadulating therapeutic feedback can help extinguish haughty expressive behavior as well as exploitive interpersonal conduct. These in turn can result in more genuine interpersonal events that subsequently serve as useful counterexamples to unrealistic or contrived object-representations. Such exercises and the results they generate may set the groundwork for a more searching exploration of the patient's internalized schemata and their negative consequences. Illusory ideas and memories and pretentious attitudes can eventually be replaced with reality-based experiences and object-representations.

As the patient comes to grasp the nonadaptive nature of the expansive narcissistic cognitive style, preoccupation with immature fantasies may be decreased. As cognitive and behavioral dysfunctions come to be regulated, the narcissist's insouciant mood is also likely to be naturally tempered. Baseline nonchalance and buoyancy can be replaced with more context-appropriate feelings. The rages, shame, and emptiness that resulted from undeniable discrepancies between self-image and reality are often modified along with the patient's self-concept. In some cases, psychopharmacologic intervention may be indicated if a resistant depression appears to be interfering with therapeutic progress.

Ultimately, therapeutic interventions in the preceding domains can have a beneficial effect on this personality's spurious morphologic organization. Flimsy defensive strategies can be replaced by stronger coping mechanisms, and the stress-reducing regulatory mechanism of rationalization can be given up for more realistic and growth-fostering inner and outer self-representations.

SELECTING THERAPEUTIC MODALITIES

Working with narcissists is difficult for therapists who seek change in a patient's personality. L.S. Benjamin (1993) notes that the patient's presumptions of entitlement and admiration may encourage the therapist to join the patient in mutual applause, while criticizing the rest of the world. Alternatively, the patient may maintain a stance of superiority. Neither kind of therapeutic alliance helps the patient achieve more adaptive functioning. Any confrontation of the narcissist's patterns will be experienced as criticism, however, and chances are high that the patient will choose to terminate therapy. Benjamin suggests that narcissists may consider changing their interpersonal habits if they are convinced that it will lead to a more favorable response from others. Overall, best therapeutic outcomes may come from honest interpretations presented in a tone of approval and acceptance. Good therapeutic gain will result when the patient internalizes the therapist's empathic acceptance of the patient's faults and deficits. As children, most narcissists were noncontingently praised for their "perfection" and may have been led to feel like utter failures when their inevitable lack of perfection was too apparent to be ignored. The therapist's attitude that faults are inevitable and perfectly human provides an opportunity for realistic self-evaluation of self-worth that was rarely provided in the typical narcissist's early learning history. Carefully timed self-disclosures of the therapist's reactions toward the patient can also potentially lead to substantial therapeutic gain. Such information can encourage the patient's insight into the negative impact of his or her habitual behaviors on others and, if revealed with supportive skill, can foster motivation to modify these habits.

Behavioral Techniques

Behavioral approaches to treating narcissistic behaviors (e.g., sexual exploitation) and destructive habits (e.g., overspending, not working) include contingency management and behavioral response prevention. Systematic desensitization of evaluation distress and role-play reversals that increase empathic understanding of others can also prove to be useful adjuncts to individual therapy. Sperry (1995) notes that the process of disclosing personal shortcomings and social weaknesses is alien to narcissists; hence, he believes that behavioral interventions are easier to implement earlier in treatment than later because they call for less self-disclosure than do other techniques or become more frequent over time.

Interpersonal Techniques

L.S. Benjamin's interpersonal approach (1993) suggests that achieving the first crucial therapeutic objective, the patient's recognition of problematic interpersonal patterns, is particularly challenging with narcissistic patients. Although the therapist's empathic understanding is necessary in facilitating this process, the form of therapist statements needs to be carefully considered to prevent encouraging narcissistic tendencies inadvertently. Benjamin provides examples of more and less therapeutically effective statements in discussing a narcissistic patient and his dissatisfied wife. An example of a response that probably encourages a narcissistic schema is "You have been trying so hard to make things go well, and here she (your wife) just comes back with complaints." Benjamin notes that such a therapist response would probably enhance the patient's pattern of externalizing and blaming. A preferred alternative would be "You have been trying so hard to make things work well, and you feel just devastated to hear that they aren't going as perfectly as you thought." The advantage of this latter response is that it encourages the patient to examine internal processes and reaction patterns.

Many theorists believe that accurate and consistent empathic mirroring is central to effective treatment. Empathy provides a foundation for learning self-control. Similarly, patients may be able to internalize the therapist's empathic affirmation of their value. Also valuable is helping narcissistic patients learn to tolerate their realistic faults and weaknesses. This can be achieved when the therapist models behavior in which his or her own mistakes or errors are overtly acknowledged. On occasion, therapists may wish to confront, albeit gently, the patient's attitudes of grandiosity and entitlement. Care should be taken, however, not to undo the therapeutic relationship.

Present habits become clearer when their functional significance is grasped. To this end, the patient's pattern of emotional reactions such as envy and feelings of entitlement can be traced to early interactions with significant others. Internalized representations of these early figures continue to guide present functioning. As patients come to recognize which attitudes and behaviors are motivated by earlier internalizations, they may become freer to modify these. An example provided by L.S. Benjamin (1993) considers a patient that expressed anger and envy about a friend's receipt of public acknowledgment of success. The therapist shifted the patient's focus to issues underlying the envy by asking the patient how his mother would react to such news. Further discussion helped clarify to the patient that his concern about his mother's reaction of disappointment (real or internalized) supported his unpleasant envious feelings. Such insight can help the patient resolve to detach from internalized representations of such figures. Finally, it is noted that once the patient accepts that unattainable ambitions and maladaptive behaviors need to be given up in favor of more realistic and fruitful cognitive and interactive habits, the bulk of the therapeutic challenge may be well on its way; new learning may be a relatively easy undertaking thereafter.

Couples and family interventions can be a very effective way for the narcissist to learn to relate to another person in an empathic way. L.S. Benjamin (1993) points out that encouraging simple expressions of affect may serve to perpetuate rather than modify problems when working with a narcissist and his or her spouse, particularly if the spouse exhibits dependent or masochistic traits (often found to be the case). Spouses with these characteristics are prone to accept the narcissist's blame for the couple's difficulties. Instead, the complementarity of the partners' patterns needs to be confronted and collaboration from both parties secured. Agreements about reallocation of household duties and funds can help the narcissist give up the "entitled" role. Role plays and role reversals can help teach the narcissist empathic understanding that would make such transitions more palatable. Benjamin points out that in order for role-playing techniques to be successful, the narcissist's exact words and inflections must be used by the spouse; failure in exact mirroring can lead to rage and withdrawal. Properly done, however, this technique can also bring home the fact that the patient is not always at the center of the spouse's experiential field, which serves not only to decrease feelings of grandiosity and entitlement but also to reduce the perception that every instance of the spouse's failure to notice the narcissist is necessarily an insult. In broader-based family treatment settings, the therapist should function to constrain untoward affects and acted-out impulses. Moreover, every effort should be made to redirect such troublesome responses and to restore disturbed family communications to their best former levels, most notably with increased mutual support.

Group approaches can be problematic, as the patient often experiences rage and counters with withdrawal at any hint of empathic failure from other group members or from the therapist. On the other hand, sharing therapy with others provides an opportunity for the patient to constrain self-indulgences and to practice empathy. To the degree that a constructive and encouraging working relationship can be established, it may be possible to set limits on patients' less desirable characteristics and their desires for special treatment. Systematically examining patients' reactions can help provide them with insight, given that the therapist-patient relationship is strong enough for patients to tolerate the stresses of the group setting. If the group can offer unanimous strong support, patients are more likely to consider feedback about their unappealing behavior patterns. A variety of divergent factors may contribute to group effectiveness with narcissists. For the most part, feedback from peers is likely to be more acceptable than feedback from the authoritative therapist. Similarly, the intense emotion associated with personal deficits is diluted within the group, as opposed to individual treatment. As Grotjahn (1984) has noted, there are several unique elements for narcissists in group settings: an increase in the capacity to empathize with others, experiencing the mirroring of one's personal needs, and the availability of new objects for idealization.

Cognitive Techniques

The cognitive approach to treating narcissistic personality disorder outlined by Beck and Freeman (1990a) suggests that although long-term treatment goals vary with each patient, they are likely to include "adjustment of the patient's grandiose view of self, limiting cognitive focus on evaluation by others, better management of affective reactions to evaluation, enhancing awareness about the feelings of others, activating more empathic affect, and eliminating exploitive behavior" (p. 248). Beck and Freeman suggest that general interventions should be tailored to what they refer to as the three narcissistic hallmarks of dysfunction: grandiosity, hypersensitivity to evaluation, and lack of empathy.

From a cognitive perspective, narcissists' tendency to overvalue themselves is based on faulty comparisons with others, whose differences from the self are overestimated. When the comparison obviously favors another, however, narcissists tend to undervalue the self to a disproportionate extent as well. Much of these extremes in thinking can be attributed to an all-or-nothing categorical style. The therapist aims to temper extreme dualistic thinking by endorsing more realistic middle-ground positions. Another useful technique is to encourage patients to make comparisons intrapersonally rather than using others as reference points, so that progress can be internally and more honestly gauged. Searching for personal similarities with others is another cognitive exercise that can lead to improved attitudes and empathic social behavior. Beck and Freeman also note that pervasive cognitive orientations can be modified by encouraging the patient to provide evidence for case-appropriate alternative beliefs that, if integrated, help reverse narcissistic tendencies. Examples of such therapeutic positions include "One can be human, like everyone else, and still be unique"; "Colleagues can be resources, not just competitors"; "Everyone has flaws"; "Feedback can be valid and helpful. It's only devastating if I take it that way"; and "Ordinary things can be very pleasurable."

Another recommendation is to encourage narcissists to modify their fantasies. Rather than attempt to eliminate a deeply entrenched fantasizing habit, however, the typically unrealistic and unadaptive contents can be replaced with attainable gratifications and pleasures. An example provided suggests that fantasizing about singing a hit song in front of an audience of thousands can be replaced by imagining singing with a community choir. By focusing on the potential gratification of engaging in the activity itself rather than on others' positive evaluation of the performance, more realistic fantasizing can serve as a covert rehearsal of adaptive and esteem-building behavior.

Self-Image Techniques

The flip side of narcissists' craving for recognition and adulation is their hypersensitivity to criticism and their defensive grandiosity. Systematic desensitization through exposure to a hierarchy of negative feedback can be effective in reducing troublesome responses. The therapist can utilize the visualization of coping strategies that enable narcissists to deal effectively with constructive criticism. Additional exercises toward this end include learning how to decide whether a particular evaluative situation is important and how to request specific feedback from others. This can reduce the time and energy distracted from more important tasks anxiously pondering the opinions of others, even in situations of no consequence. Thought-stopping can be used to intervene with this form of obsessive rumination.

In working toward the end of increasing the narcissist's empathy, two general stages of intervention may be recommended. First, the empathic deficit needs to be brought to light. The therapist can often be helpful by drawing attention to others' feelings. If necessary, instances of inconsiderateness or exploitation should be pointed out, albeit gently. In the second stage, the patient can actively imagine how others feel, often effectively accomplished by engaging in emotion-focused role plays and role reversals. Specific new beliefs regarding the significance of others' feelings can be explored and verbalized. Behaviors that are consistent with these beliefs can be devised and rehearsed, both in therapy and outside.

Intrapsychic Techniques

Psychodynamic approaches to restructuring the narcissistic personality are generally based on one of two approaches, the first proposed by Kernberg, the second by Kohut. Kernberg formulates narcissistic grandiosity to be a result of the child's rage at mother's indifference or rejections. Kohut sees the disorder as a developmental arrest caused by a maternal failure to validate her child's developing self-worth. Kernberg's clinical recommendations include confronting the patient's conscious and subconscious anger, examining negative transference toward the therapist, and addressing the patient's use of defenses such as splitting, projection, and projective identification. According to Kernberg, symptomatic improvement is more likely to be rapid with supportive rather then expressive methods. Kohut's model encourages the therapist to assume a sympathetic and accepting stance, while addressing the objective need for the patient to accept personal limitations. Short-term methods may be especially useful for crisis intervention and to establish a bridge to more long-term treatment procedures. Binder (1979) reports on the use of a brief treatment method for increasing self-esteem, also in preparation for a longer-term program. The hope here is to increase patients' awareness of their vulnerability to shame and disappointment, as well as to increase the capacity to moderate intense affects, such as irritability and rage.

Pharmacologic Techniques

It is unclear whether the arrogance and sense of grandeur seen among narcissists lend themselves to any of the pharmacologic agents that are currently available. Of course, should the narcissist succumb to feelings of depression, consideration must be given to the use of antidepressant medications (SSRIs). Similarly, signs of hypomania or grandiosity may call for one or another of the mood stabilizers (e.g., lithium). Should the symptomatology become more severe, perhaps approaching a mild level of paranoia, low doses of several antipsychotics may prove useful (e.g., risperidone, olanzapine).

MAKING SYNERGISTIC ARRANGEMENTS

The initial phase of therapy with a narcissistic patient needs to focus almost exclusively on building a supportive working alliance. Confronting the patient's maladaptive behaviors before his or her trust and respect for the therapist are established is likely to lead to premature termination. Once this foundation has been laid, intervention focus can turn to increasing the patient's insight into his or her behavior. The developmental history and functional significance of patterns can be explored, and undesirable consequences can be clarified. Working toward helping the patient integrate more adaptive behavioral and cognitive alternatives can then begin.

At this point, the therapist can consider several adjunct interventions. If resistant depression is judged to be interfering with functioning, and the therapist judges that alleviation of acute dysphoria will not lead to abandonment of more long-term reconstructive goals, pharmacologic treatment should be carefully considered. If appropriate, group, couple, and/or family therapy may be useful concomitant approaches. Group intervention is more likely to lead to therapeutic gains if the group can provide

TABLE 15.4 Narcissistic Personality Disorder Subtypes

Elitist: Feels privileged and empowered by virtue of special childhood status and pseudoachievements; entitled façade bears little relation to reality; seeks favored and good life; is upwardly mobile; cultivates special status and advantages by association.

MCMI 5

Amorous: Sexually seductive, enticing, beguiling, tantalizing; glib and clever; disinclines real intimacy; indulges hedonistic desires; bewitches and inveigles the needy and naïve; pathological lying and swindling.

MCMI 5-4

Unprincipled: Deficient conscience; unscrupulous; amoral, disloyal, fraudulent, deceptive, arrogant, exploitive; a con and charlatan; dominating, contemptuous, vindicitive.

MCMI 5-6A

Compensatory: Seeks to counteract or cancel out deep feelings of inferiority and lack of self-esteem; offsets deficits by creating illusions of being superior, exceptional, admirable, noteworthy; self-worth results from self-enhancement.

MCMI 5-8A/2A

strong support to offset the patient's tendency to withdraw at the first hint of illusion-shattering confrontation. Couple and family therapy provide an opportunity for behavioral exercises such as role plays that increase empathy and sharpen insight into the problem-perpetuating nature of cognitive and behavioral habits specific to the patient's personal life. Guided negotiation with significant others can help break complementary patterns that support narcissistic behavior and lead to new interactions that provide gratification and bolster the patient's motivation to continue working toward adaptive change.

Illustrative Cases

Clinical experience and research employing the MCMI (Millon, Millon, & Davis, 1996a) suggest several personality blends that incorporate distinct narcissistic features. A review of the developmental background of other narcissistic personalities contributed further to the variants described below (see Table 15.4).

NARCISSISTIC PERSONALITY: UNPRINCIPLED TYPE (NARCISSISTIC WITH ANTISOCIAL TRAITS)

CASE 15.1, BILL E., 37

Presenting Picture: Bill E. was an equipment salesman who had "come up from the production line" to considerable success in the sales field. His initial impression as a self-confident man quickly gave way to a more realistic picture of an intimidating, manipulative personality. He explained that his success was largely a result of the use of "techniques" that others were afraid to employ. He saw himself as separate and apart from the crowd of salespeople, as he was one who would not get "pushed" by a customer. He also explained with a knowing grin that it was possible to butter up any deal with a little fraudulent use of the expense account. Bill saw himself as an entirely "free agent," meaning that the rules of employment, society, and perhaps life did not apply to him, and that this freedom allowed him to successfully pursue virtually anything he wanted. He went as far as to suggest that the counselor he was talking to was but a "clock puncher" and perhaps a prisoner, and assured the counselor that that was "not him, at all." Perhaps one of the most striking moments of the interview came when Bill was describing his parents. His mother, a quiet, dutiful woman, was seen by Bill as "nothing really special"; his father, on the other hand, by virtue of his beer consumption and the ability to make his point clear (with a "whipping") over a minor infraction, was seen as an impressive, revered figure. *Unprincipled narcissists* such as Bill are seen most often in these past two or three decades in drug rehabilitation programs, centers for youth offenders, and jails and prisons. Although these individuals often are successful in society, keeping their activities just within the boundaries of the law, they enter into clinical treatment rather infrequently.

Clinical Assessment: Bill's behavior was characterized by an arrogant sense of self-worth, an indifference to the welfare of others, and a fraudulent and intimidating social manner. There was a desire to exploit others, to expect special recognitions and considerations without assuming reciprocal responsibilities. A deficient social conscience was evident in his tendency to flout conventions, to engage in actions that raise questions of personal integrity, and to disregard the rights of others. Achievement deficits and social irresponsibilities were justified by expansive fantasies and frank prevarications. Descriptively, we may characterize Bill as devoid of a superego, that is, evidencing an unscrupulous, amoral, and deceptive approach to his relationships with others. More than merely disloyal and exploitive, he was likely to blend in with society's cons and charlatans, many of whom are vindictive and contemptuous of their victims. The features that were clearly seen in Bill's MCMI data support the conclusion that he was an admixture of both narcissistic and antisocial personality characteristics.

Bill evidenced a rash willingness to risk harm and was notably fearless in the face of threats and punitive action. Malicious tendencies were projected outward, precipitating frequent personal and family difficulties as well as occasional legal entanglements. Vengeful gratification was often obtained by humiliating and dominating others. He operated as if he had no principles other than exploiting others for his personal gain. Lacking a genuine sense of guilt and possessing little social conscience, he was an opportunist who enjoyed the process of swindling others, outwitting them in a game he enjoyed playing in which others were held in contempt owing to the ease with which they could be seduced. Relationships survived only as long as he had something to gain. People were dropped with no thought to the anguish they may have experienced as a consequence of his careless and irresponsible behaviors.

In many ways, this *unprincipled narcissist* is similar to the *disingenuous histrionic* (see Chapter 14). They share a devious and guileful style, plotting and scheming in their calculations to manipulate others. However, disingenuous histrionics continue to pursue their strong need for attention and love, characteristics Bill did not exhibit, where there was a basic self-centeredness and an indifference to the attitudes and reactions of others. Bill preyed on the weak and vulnerable, enjoying their dismay and anger; histrionics, by contrast, seek to hold the respect and affection of those they dismiss in their pursuit of love and admiration.

Bill displayed an indifference to truth that, if brought to his attention, was likely to elicit an attitude of nonchalant indifference. He was skillful in the ways of social influence, was capable of feigning an air of justified innocence, and was adept in deceiving others with charm and glibness. Lacking any deep feelings of loyalty, he successfully schemed beneath a veneer of politeness and civility. His principal orientation was that of outwitting others, getting power and exploiting them "before they do it to you." He often carried a chip-on-the-shoulder attitude, a readiness to attack those who were distrusted or who could be used as scapegoats. Bill attempted to present an image of cool strength, acting tough, arrogant, and fearless. To prove his courage, he may have invited danger and punishment. But punishment only verified his unconscious recognition that he deserved to be punished. Rather than having a deterrent effect, it only reinforced his exploitive and unprincipled behaviors.

Synergistic Treatment Plan: Although it would be important to garner understanding of Bill's point of view and express accurate empathy, it would be equally crucial for the therapist to maintain a steadfast posture that would remain focused on tangible interventions. It would be ill-advised to indulge in *self-image* techniques that may guide the process into digressions about his perceived grandeur. Of primary importance would be a *cognitive* reorientation to enhance Bill's alertness to the needs of *others* while diminishing his *self*-important illusion. On an *interpersonal* level, it would be necessary to adjust Bill's social outlook, which would include clarifying his *active-passive* conflict. One of his primary perpetuations was his tendency to actively exploit others, yet to maintain a laid-back, uncaring attitude regarding anyone or anything that didn't immediately affect him. A major focus of behavioral therapy for Bill would be to introduce steps to overcome his deficient controls while instilling a greater sense of empathy for others.

Therapeutic Course: Short-term methods were suitable for Bill, although *environmental management, psychopharmacologic treatment,* and *behavior modification* could be safely disqualified. The most effective course to begin changing some of his troubling attitudes and behavior was *cognitive reorientation.* As the therapeutic relationship began to develop and a modicum of comfort was established, the therapist was able to begin confronting Bill's dysfunctional beliefs and expectations (e.g., Beck, Ellis). Short-term *interpersonal* methods (e.g., Kiesler, Klerman) were also used to explore and adjust his social skills and demeanor. More expressive and time-extended techniques were not justified here, as it is more prudent in a case such as this to work at controlling Bill's illusions, rather than to foster possible grander illusions. *Group therapy* was most beneficial here, as the members provided a means for Bill to express himself without his usual arrogant front in a benevolent and non-critical environment.

Although it was very important to avoid emphasizing Bill's negative attributes, the therapeutic relationship also depended on not allowing him to assert dominance in treatment in his usual way. He fully believed himself to be perfect, and this made him notably disinclined to change any of his attitudes. He refused initially to commit to any amount of time investment in therapy, and early cession would have virtually guaranteed quick relapse. Throughout the early stages, he maintained a careful distance from the therapist and attempted to thwart any exploration of personal issues that may have implied any deficiency on his part. Cognitive confrontations were able to counter these efforts, and difficulties rooted in his evasiveness and unwillingness, though sometimes disruptive, were dealt with directly and firmly but without emitting disapproval. With this consistently honest and confrontive stance, the treatment setting went from an environment that frequently gave witness to attempts at dominance to one of relative cooperation and efficacious collaboration.

Bill routinely thought of others, regardless of their status, position, or intellect, as callow and stupid. His response to any challenge (including those he instigated) was, without question, that the other person was not only wrong but usually a stooge. A direct cognitive approach confronted this habit of assuming everyone else to be wrong and claiming superiority based on frequent arguments he could win by acumen and intimidation. Gone unchecked, this habit would have continued to encourage Bill's arrogant and presumptuous demeanor.

Bill had not sought therapy voluntarily and was convinced that there really was no problem. After all, there were no current failures or dissatisfactions on his current "scorecard," so what could be wrong? Even if he had brought himself to seek help, due perhaps to an unaccustomed loss in sales or a declining social context, it would have been unlikely that he would conceive of any trouble as linked to his actions or demeanor. It was quite transparent that entering this office put his pride on the line, and that was not a position he was inclined to take lightly. This particularly defensive stance also called for direct, firm confrontation, while maintaining a safe but honest therapeutic environment through an empathic attitude expressed by the therapist. Bill's acceptance of this environment was questionable and his attitude toward the process ambivalent until he came to respect the therapist as being forthright and not easily intimidated.

Although Bill's self-esteem needed to be augmented as a result of his being placed in the role of patient, the therapist needed to maintain his authoritative therapeutic posture. Bill easily restored his self-confidence by brief visitations to his accomplishments, a process that took no more than a session or two. It was more important, however, to work with Bill to instill a sense of empathy for others and to understand and accept the unspoken contract of restraint and responsibility in society. This measure, aimed at preventing recurrences, required that no deceptions were made by Bill and that his compliance was sincere.

NARCISSISTIC PERSONALITY: AMOROUS TYPE
(NARCISSISTIC WITH HISTRIONIC TRAITS)

CASE 15.2, STEVE G., 22

Presenting Picture: Steve G. was a bartender who enjoyed his line of work, as it was quite agreeable with his lifestyle. Tending bar in a nightclub allowed him to perform, he explained, thereby garnering much attention and attracting many potential sexual partners. He seemed quite proud of his social life and conquests, as he spoke of a quite "heavy" night the preceding evening. Although the majority of his experience had been with very short-term partners, he was actually married at one time. He described this relationship in very nonchalant terms, seeming to bestow as much importance to this six-month relationship as he would to a Saturday afternoon's activities. When questioned regarding the ending of the marriage, he faulted her jealousy, because he still drew the attention of many women at work. Although Steve seemed content and he was rather unclear in his reasons for seeking therapy, it was inferred that he sensed, albeit not consciously, some inadequacy in himself that could not be fulfilled by his exploits, or a vague tinge of guilt over some of his more dishonest manipulations.

Clinical Assessment: The distinctive feature of Steve, an *amorous narcissist,* was an erotic and seductive orientation, a building up of his self-worth by engaging members of the opposite sex in the game of sexual temptation. There was an indifferent conscience, an aloofness to truth and social responsibility that, if brought to his attention, elicited an attitude of nonchalant innocence. Though totally self-oriented, he was facile in the ways of social seduction, often feigned an air of dignity and confidence, and was rather skilled in deceiving others with his clever glibness. He was skillful in enticing, bewitching, and tantalizing the needy and the naïve. Although indulging his hedonistic desires and pursuing numerous beguiling objects at the same time, he was strongly disinclined to become involved in a genuine intimacy. Rather than investing his efforts in one appealing person, he sought to acquire a coterie of amorous objects, invariably lying and swindling as he wove from one pathological relationship to another. The qualities just outlined are strongly suggestive of the observation that narcissistic personality types such as Steve possess numerous characteristics that are primary among histrionic personalities, a fact clearly seen in his MCMI scores.

Although a reasonably good capacity for sexual athletics sustains the vanity of many individuals, narcissists or not, the need to repeatedly demonstrate one's sexual prowess is a preeminent obsession among amorous subtypes. Among these personalities are those whose endless pursuit of sexual conquests is fulfilled as effectively and frequently as their bewitching style "promises." Others, however, talk well, place their lures and baits extremely well, that is, until they reach the bedroom door; maneuvering and seduction is done with great aplomb, but performance falls short. For the most part, the sexual exploits of the amorous narcissist are brief, lasting from one afternoon to only a few weeks.

Perhaps Steve was fearful of the opposite sex, afraid that his pretensions and ambitions would be exposed and found wanting. His sexual banter and seductive pursuits were merely empty maneuvers to overcome deeper feelings of inadequacy. Although he seemed to desire the affections of a warm and intimate relationship, when he found it (assuming his marriage appeared, at first, to provide these qualities), he undoubtedly felt restless and unsatisfied. Having won someone over, he probably needed to continue his pursuit. It is the act of exhibitionistically being seductive, and hence gaining in narcissistic stature, that compels. The achievement of ego gratification terminates for a moment, but it must be pursued again and again.

It was possible that Steve left behind him a trail of outrageous acts such as swindling, sexual excesses, pathological lying, and fraud. His disregard for truth and talent for exploitation and deception were neither hostile nor malicious in intent. These characteristics appeared to derive from an attitude of narcissistic omnipotence and self-assurance, a feeling that the implicit rules of human relationships did not apply to him and that he was above the responsibilities of shared living. As with the basic narcissistic pattern, Steve went out of his way to entice and inveigle the unwary among the opposite sex, remaining coolly indifferent to the welfare of those whom he bewitched, whom he had used to enhance and indulge his hedonistic whims and erotic desires.

Caring little to shoulder genuine social responsibilities and unwilling to change his seductive ways, Steve wouldn't "buckle down" in a serious relationship and expend effort to prove his worth. Never having learned to control his fantasies or be concerned with matters of social integrity, Steve maintained his bewitching ways by deception, fraud, lying, and charming others through craft and wit as necessary. Rather than apply his talents toward the goal of tangible achievements or genuine relationships, he devoted his energies to constructing intricate lies, to cleverly exploit others, and to slyly contrive ways to extract from others what he believed was his due. Untroubled by conscience and needing nourishment for his overinflated self-image, he fabricated stories that enhanced his worth and thereby succeeded in seducing others into supporting his excesses. Criticism and punishment were likely to prove of no avail because Steve was likely to quickly dismiss these aspersions as products of jealous inferiors.

Synergistic Treatment Plan: It was expected that Steve would attempt to manipulate and monopolize the process of therapy and would need to be engaged and controlled through a firm and focused attitude on the part of the therapist. *Cognitive* and *interpersonal* strategies would focus on altering his perpetuating belief of his own importance and the devaluation of (but reliance on) *others,* and would thereby serve to establish improved social skills and more genuine relationships. Concurrently, it would also be prudent to help Steve assume a less *passive* affective stance (less nonchalant and superficial in his attitude). In addition to cognitively and interpersonally undermining Steve's irresponsible attitudes and actions, *behavioral* interventions should be fruitful in reinforcing new habits and skills as well as establishing responsible social actions. A *group* milieu might be a most beneficial adjunct, as well, in guiding Steve toward reassessing his interpersonal style and self-important attitude, establishing empathy toward others, and taking on a more responsible disposition.

Therapeutic Course: *Cognitive reorientation* seemed to be the most effective catalyst for Steve to modify some of these attitudes about himself and his socially lamentable actions in a short-term milieu. As his more affable but trite veneer gave way to increasingly more meaningful exchanges with the therapist, Steve was able to begin working on his erroneous assumptions regarding himself and his social context (e.g., Beck, Ellis). *Interpersonal* methods (e.g., Kiesler, Klerman) also were employed to examine these assumptions and reevaluate some of his less acceptable actions. These focused interpersonal methods, most notably *group therapy,* helped him reassess himself more realistically and effectively and provided a forum for him to experiment with more cooperative and sociable behaviors. For Steve, the more expressive and longer-term techniques would not have been useful, as he was prone toward self-illusions too easily reinforced by the imaginative freedom these methods foster. Likewise, several other popular short-term techniques, including *environmental management, psychopharmacologic treatment,* and *behavior modification* would not be of value in effecting change.

In the early sessions, Steve frequently attempted to dominate the therapeutic relationship, relying on his well-practiced and suave seductive tactics. This habit needed to be confronted, though delicately and honestly, as overemphasizing any shortcoming might have led to regression in establishing rapport. During this early stage, he navigated his way around any investigations into personal issues by using his "charm" and jumping from one superficiality to the next, as well as casting responsibility for himself onto others. Unless dealt with directly, yet without disapproval on the part of the therapist, his evasiveness and unwillingness would have seriously interfered with short-term gains. Cognitive confrontations that were firm but consistently honest were effective in prompting him to critically examine his own beliefs and behaviors, avoid further attempts to win dominance, and invest in the change process.

Cognitively based methods were effective at undermining faulty beliefs that prompted Steve's tendency to devalue others. It was, at first, unfathomable to him that his assumptions were askew, as he had consistently assured himself that everyone else's views were inane. That is, he simply *couldn't* be wrong, as his modus operandi seemed to work well for him, yet so many others seemed to be discontent. He needed to understand the basic tenet that disparity between himself and those more sensitive (or perhaps more accurately expressive) did not necessarily mean that his views were superior.

Generally, an illusion that calls for brief confrontive therapy with amorous narcissists is based on the fact that these patients are unlikely to seek therapy on their own. They typically believe that they will solve everything for themselves by simply being left alone. In Steve's case, where treatment was self-motivated, it may have followed an unadmitted humiliation or failure. Regardless of what his promptings were, seeking professional help harmed his pride. Though he gave lip service to accepting therapy, this attitude was rather tentative and delicate throughout the therapeutic relationship.

Although it was appropriate to help Steve rebuild this guarded, deflated self-image, the therapist could not appear submissive lest Steve revert rapidly to many of his older, problematic tactics. Rebuilding his self-confidence was a simple process, which merely involved indulging him in reminiscing about a few past conquests. An objective geared more at preventing recurrences was that of helping Steve become more empathic with others and to understand the effects of his behavior in social interactions. This required enhancing his ability to honestly scrutinize any self-deficiency. The therapist was alert in this regard not to be deceived by mere perfunctory acquiescence.

NARCISSISTIC PERSONALITY: COMPENSATORY TYPE (NARCISSISTIC WITH AVOIDANT AND NEGATIVISTIC TRAITS)

CASE 15.3, BYRON W., 34

Presenting Picture: Byron W.'s employer requested that he seek therapy. As Byron put it, however, he certainly was *not* one who needed any help. He dismissed his employer's intentions as "hatred of a visionary," which was to be expected from feeble minds such as the ones possessed by his supervisors and coworkers. He insisted that he was great at what he did, but this was not seen by the people around him, and this caused tensions. Moreover, those who worked under him seemed to feel that he could not communicate his ideas, intentions, and instructions, but Byron refused to "spell every little thing out for them," as they were all adults capable of understanding. Recently, Byron had been passed over for a promotion, which he emphatically stated that he deserved. Most interesting, however, is that when the counselor suggested the possibility of becoming his own boss, this seemed to cause a clear yet unspoken trepidation, hardly an attribute of a self-confident expert in a field.

Clinical Assessment: Byron, a *compensatory narcissist*, deviated in a fundamental way from both other narcissistic subtypes as well as from the prototypal narcissist. The origins that undergirded his overtly narcissistic behaviors derived from an underlying sense of insecurity and weakness rather than from genuine feelings of self-confidence and high self-esteem. Beneath his surface pseudoconfidence, the posture he exhibited publicly, this narcissist was driven by forces similar to those of more negativistic and avoidant personalities.

Compensatory narcissists are patients labeled narcissistic by those in the psychoanalytic community because they have suffered "wounds" in early life. Byron may have been exposed to experiences akin to the negativistic, avoidant, and antisocial types. In essence, he sought to make up or compensate for early life deprivations. He was similar to the antisocial, but sought to fill his sense of emptiness by creating an illusion of superiority and building up an image of high self-worth rather than by usurping the power and control that others possess or by accumulating material possessions.

Byron needed others to fulfill his strivings for prestige. His motive was to enhance his self-esteem, to obtain and store up within himself all forms of recognition that would "glorify" his public persona. Much to the annoyance of others, he "acted drunk" as he recounted his record of successes for others to acknowledge all forms of even minor public recognition. In effect, he actively worshipped himself; he was his own god. As this inflated and overvalued sense of self rose ever higher, he looked down on others as devalued plebeians. More and more, he acquired a deprecatory attitude in which the achievements of others were ridiculed and degraded.

For Byron, life was a search for pseudostatus, an empty series of aspirations that served no purpose other than self-enhancement. This search for these vacuous goals began to run wild, resting from its very foundation on an unsure sense of self-value that had but little contact with tangible achievements. Instead of living his own life, Byron pursued the leading role in a false and imaginary theater. Nothing he achieved in this pursuit related much to reality. His tenacious aspirations for glory, however, may have impressed the naïve and the grateful, but possessed little of a genuine or objective character.

Should these pursuits have lost their grounding in reality, becoming more and more an imaginary world, peopled with self and others as in a dream, Byron would begin to deceive himself in a manner not unlike the *fanatic paranoid* (see Chapter 23). If we draw a line between these two personality subtypes, we would see that Byron would strive for prestige in a world composed of real people; when reality recedes and fantasy comes more to the fore, fanatics act out their aspirations in solitude. One comes to the stage in front of others, in the form of exaggeration and boasting; the other stands alone in an inner world, a "pseudo-community," as Cameron (1963) has phrased it, where imagination has substantially replaced reality.

Owing to the insecure foundations on which his narcissistic displays were grounded, Byron was *hypervigilant,* to use a term employed by Gabbard (1994). He was exquisitely sensitive to how others reacted to him, watching and listening carefully for any critical judgment and feeling slighted by every sign of disapproval. Although not delusional, as are his paranoid counterparts, he was prone to feel shamed and humiliated, especially hyperanxious and vulnerable to the judgments of others. He "knew" that he was a fraud at some level, a pretender who sought to convey impressions of being in higher standing than he knew was truly the case. Despite this awareness, he did not act shy and hesitant, as one might think. Instead, he submerged and covered up his deep sense of inadequacy and deficiency by pseudoarrogance and superficial grandiosity.

Synergistic Treatment Plan: Because Byron was prone to be hostile in his general demeanor, as well as unlikely to take kindly to *insight*-oriented therapy, a first-order tactic would be to dissipate some of his anger *biophysically.* As this agitation would decrease through pharmacologic treatment as well as through *behavioral* outlets, it would be possible for him to focus on *cognitively* altering his perpetuating perception that rejection and humiliation are always one mistake away. This would alleviate the need to be *actively* scanning the environment for disapproval and constantly seeking to overcompensate for perceived inner inadequacies by establishing his narcissistic illusion of grandeur and perfection. Also, these modalities would help to clarify and alter a rather difficult, constitutional *self-other* conflict. As a more natural and genuine coping style would emerge, it would further be beneficial to incorporate *interpersonal* methods to ensure greater social sensitivities and abilities.

Therapeutic Course: Several brief therapies were considered. Among those chosen, interestingly enough, was a specific drug regimen that was useful in modulating the threshold and intensity of Byron's reactivity. *Pharmacologic agents* are not notably effective for dealing with individuals such as this, but it was worthwhile to evaluate and subsequently implement this treatment in terms of its efficacy in minimizing the frequency and depth of his hostile feelings, thereby decreasing some of the self-perpetuating consequences of his aggressive behavior. Well-directed *behavioral* approaches provided Byron the opportunity to vent some of his anger. Once his hostility had been more benignly channeled, he was led to explore his habitual expectations and attitudes and was guided through various *cognitive* techniques into less destructive perceptions and outlets than before. *Insight-oriented* procedures were not indicated because they were not likely to be of short-term utility, nor were techniques oriented to a thorough reworking of Byron's aggressive strategies. Rather, more behaviorally directed methods geared to increase restraint and control were usefully pursued. *Interpersonal* techniques (e.g., Klerman, Benjamin) may also have been fruitful in teaching him more acceptable social behavior. As far as *group* methods were concerned, the patient ended up intruding on and disrupting therapeutic functions. This modality was attempted because it was thought that he would become a useful catalyst for group interaction and possibly improve his social skills and attitudes.

The therapist was cognizant of Byron's inclination to be spoiling for a fight, almost enjoying tangling with the therapist to prove his strength and test his powers. A mixed cognitive and emotion-oriented technique (e.g., Beck, Greenberg) was employed to counter his omnipresent undertone of anger and resentment, that is, the expectation that the therapist would prove to be devious and hostile. By confronting and then venting these feelings, it was possible to dilute his inclination to repeatedly distort the incidental remarks and actions of the therapist so that they appeared to deprecate and vilify him. Similarly, a worthy brief therapeutic goal was to undo his habit of misinterpreting what he saw and heard and magnifying minor slights into major insults and slanders. Important in achieving these short-term goals was to restrain the impulse to react to Byron with disapproval and criticism. An important step beyond building rapport with him was to see things from his viewpoint. To achieve the circumscribed goals of brief therapy required that the therapist convey a sense of trust and willingness to develop a constructive treatment alliance. A balance of professional authority and tolerance diminished the probability that he would impulsively withdraw from treatment or shortly regress to prior problematic states.

Effective brief techniques were called for because Byron was not likely to be a willing participant in therapy. Specifically, he had agreed to therapy under the pressure of vocational difficulties (e.g., as a consequence of aggressive behavior on the job). One task of a cognitive approach was to get him to tolerate guilt or to accept a measure of blame for the turmoil he caused. Reframing his perceptions to ones that were more realistic countered his belief that a problem could always be traced to another person's stupidity, laziness, or hostility. Even when he accepted some measure of responsibility, he did not feel defiance and resentment toward the therapist for trying to point this out. Although he sought to challenge, test, bluff, and outwit the therapist, a strong, consistent, but fair-minded cognitive approach was successful in reducing these actions and aided him in assuming a more calm and reasoned attitude.

NARCISSISTIC PERSONALITY: ELITIST
TYPE (PURE NARCISSIST)

CASE 15.4, MIGUEL R., 31

Presenting Picture: Miguel R., a graduate student, initiated therapy at the request of his girlfriend. He described himself as an all-around expert, and projected that employment as an expert in his chosen field would be the best possible use of his time. He stated, with no hesitancy, that as an only child, he was not required to take on any family responsibility and that he had all the time he could have ever wanted to pursue and develop his own interests. He was always received as one of the brightest children in school, and he had no difficulty throughout his extensive academic career. Miguel described his relationship with his girlfriend as pleasant and satisfactory, but seemed to value her only in terms of what she could do for him. If there was any dissatisfaction prevalent, it seemed to be that Miguel had a hard time finding things to do that would be worth his very precious time, and that left much time for boredom and lethargy.

Clinical Assessment: Reich (1949) captured the essential qualities of what we are terming the *elitist narcissist* when he described the "phallic-narcissist" character as a self-assured, arrogant, and energetic person, "often impressive in his bearing . . . and . . . ill-suited to subordinate positions among the rank and file" (p. 219). As with the *compensatory narcissist,* the elitist narcissist is more taken with his inflated self-image than with his actual self. Both narcissistic types create a false façade that bears minimal resemblance to the person they really are. The compensatory narcissist, however, knows at some level that he is in fact a fraud, and that he puts forth an appearance different from the way he is. By contrast, our elitist narcissist Miguel, perhaps the purest variant of the narcissistic style, was deeply convinced of his superior self-image, albeit one that was grounded on few realistic achievements. To Miguel, it was the appearance of things that was perceived as objective reality; his inflated self-image was his intrinsic substance. Only if these illusory elements to his self-worth were seriously undermined would he be able to recognize, perhaps even to acknowledge, his deeper shortcomings.

As a consequence of his sublime self-confidence, Miguel felt quite secure in his apparent superiority. This was achieved in part by his ability to capture the attention of others and to make them take note of how extraordinary he believed himself to be. Nearly everything he did was done to persuade others of his specialness rather than to put his efforts into acquiring genuine qualifications and attainments. Miguel felt privileged and empowered by virtue of whatever class status and pseudoachievements he may have attained. He was upwardly mobile and sought to cultivate his sense of specialness and personal advantage by associating with those who possessed genuine achievements and recognition. He created comparisons between himself and others, turning personal relationships into public competitions and contests. Unrivaled in the pursuit of becoming "number one," he did not determine the grounds for this goal by genuine accomplishments, but by the degree to which he could convince others of its reality, false though its substance may have been.

As just described, many narcissistic elitists are social climbers who seek to cultivate their image and social luster by virtue of those with whom they are affiliated. To them it is not the old chestnut of "guilt by association," but rather of "status by association." Idolizing public recognition, Miguel got caught in the game of one-upmanship, a game he strove vigorously to win, at least comparatively. Status and self-promotion were all that mattered to him. To be celebrated, even famous, drove him, rather than to achieve substantive accomplishments. In whatever sphere of activity mattered to him, Miguel invested his efforts to advertise himself, to brag about achievements, substantive or fraudulent, to make anything he had done appear to be "wonderful," better than what others may have done, and better than it may actually have been.

By making excessive claims about himself, Miguel exposed a great divide between his actual self and his self-presentation. In contrast to many narcissists who recognize this disparity, he was convinced and absolute in his belief in himself. Rather than backing off, withdrawing, or feeling shame when slighted or responded to with indifference, Miguel sped up his efforts all the more, acting increasingly and somewhat erratically to exhibit deeds and awards worthy of high esteem. He may have presented grandiose illusions about his powers and future status; he may have puffed up his limited accomplishments; he may have sought competitively to outdo those who had achieved in reality.

Synergistic Treatment Plan: As Miguel was shrouded in illusion in most every sense, it would be expected that treatment would be complicated by his deep-seated beliefs. It would be essential to establish a relationship marked by candor and honesty. From a *cognitive* perspective, it would be necessary to challenge beliefs that fostered his overinflated *self*-image, but with methods less likely to cause defensive maneuvers (not overemphasizing negative traits). This approach would also include reorienting Miguel toward a more *active* stance, as most of his perceived grandeur lacked real accomplishment or initiative. *Interpersonally,* he needed to develop conscientiousness toward *others,* as he valued people only for what they could do for him. Additionally, he needed to establish social controls and discipline, tasks that would be ideally suited to *group* or *family* interventions. Throughout therapy, it would be helpful to frame interventions in terms of improved, more genuine accomplishments and interactions, rather than "corrections" or other terminology that implies deficiencies, as Miguel would tend to be guarded and resentful of such insinuations.

Therapeutic Course: Short-term methods, particularly *cognitive reorientation,* were useful in altering Miguel's illusory thoughts and socially aberrant behavior. *Environmental management, psychopharmacologic treatment,* and *behavioral modification* were not used, given that they are of limited value in effecting change in such individuals. Once therapy had begun and a foundation of trust and rapport had been established with the therapist, Miguel was able to tolerate procedures designed to confront his dysfunctional beliefs and expectations (e.g., Beck, Ellis). Short-term *interpersonal* methods (e.g., Kiesler, Klerman) were introduced next to critically reassess and modify his attitudes and social habits. More expressive and time-extended techniques were difficult to justify in that Miguel's illusions would have been reinforced too strongly by the imaginative freedom inherent in these methods. *Family* or *group therapy* may also have helped him view himself in a more realistic light and assisted him in learning the skills of sharing and cooperation.

As the therapeutic relationship was rather fragile and at risk of being jeopardized by certain types of confrontations, care was taken not to stress Miguel's deficiencies. Efforts were made, however, to not afford him a dominant position in treatment after his initial discomfort had receded. Early on, the therapist addressed Miguel's belief that he did not need to consider changing his views because he believed he was already almost perfect.

He was loath, initially, to accede to any but the briefest therapy, which increased the likelihood of early relapses. He did become involved in a short-term regimen and maintained a well-measured distance from the therapist, trying to resist the searching probes of personal exploration, especially those that implied deficiencies on his part. An effective cognitive confrontation method countered his efforts to shift responsibility for his own deficiencies to others. The therapist dealt with Miguel very directly, though without disapproval, thus thwarting his evasiveness and unwillingness, which otherwise would have seriously interfered with short-term progress. With a firm but consistently honest and confrontive technique, the treatment setting did not give witness to struggles in which he sought to outwit the therapist and assert his dominance. The therapist needed to maintain great patience and equanimity to establish a spirit of genuine confidence and respect.

A strong cognitively based method to undo distorted expectations focused on extinguishing Miguel's tendency to think of others as naïve and simpleminded. Rather than question the correctness of his own beliefs, he was habituated to assume that others' views were always to blame. The therapist called into question his habit of assuming that the more disagreements he had with others, the greater was his own superiority, which led to his becoming more arrogant and presumptuous.

Another illusion that called for brief confrontive therapy was based on the fact that Miguel would not have sought therapy voluntarily. He was convinced that, if left alone, he could solve all of his own problems. Similarly, had treatment been self-motivated, it probably would have followed a period of unaccustomed social humiliation or achievement failures. Whatever the promptings, his pride appeared to be in jeopardy in submitting to the role of patient. Though he hesitantly accepted therapy in its early stages, this attitude may have been short-lived and fragile until he came to respect the therapist as being forthright and not easily intimidated.

Although efforts needed to be made to rebuild Miguel's recently depleted self-esteem, the therapist took measures not to appear subservient in the process. His self-confidence was rapidly restored by the therapist's merely allowing him to recall past achievements and successes, a process that took but two sessions. A goal more likely to prevent recurrences, however, was that of guiding him into becoming more sensitive to the needs of others and accepting the constraints and responsibilities of shared social living. This required strengthening Miguel's capacity to face his shortcomings frankly. Care was taken in this regard not to be deceived by mere superficial compliance with these efforts.

Risks and Resistances

Narcissists are not inclined to seek therapy. Their pride disposes them to reject the imperfection-confirming "weak" role of patient. Most are convinced they can get along quite well on their own. Often, if a narcissist does accept voluntary treatment, he or she will try to enlist the therapist to support the opinion that the patient's problems are largely the result of the imperfections and weaknesses of others. Alternatively, the narcissist may adopt a stance of superiority and discredit the therapist or terminate treatment prematurely. In sum, narcissists will not accede to therapy willingly. Moreover, once involved, they will maintain a well-measured distance from the therapist, resist the searching probes of personal exploration, become indignant over implications of deficiencies on their part, and seek to shift responsibility for these lacks to others. The treatment setting may give witness to struggles in which narcissists seek to outwit the therapist and assert their dominance. Stone (1993) notes that much of the narcissistic patient's sarcasm, devaluation, and domination toward the therapist can been seen as a "test" of whether the therapist will respond in kind and therefore, like the patient's parents (who may have modeled the offensive behavior), is not to be trusted. Setting limits without resorting to an accusatory or attacking stance can prove to be invaluable aids in working with these patients. Great patience and equanimity are required to establish the spirit of genuine confidence and respect, without which the chances of achieving reconstructive personality change become even slimmer.

CHAPTER SIXTEEN

Treating Antisocial
Personality Patterns

The *DSM-IV* provides a rather detailed listing of the delinquent, criminal, and socially undesirable behaviors that may be found among antisocial personalities, but fails, in our opinion, to deal with the personality characteristics from which such antisocial behaviors stem. In adopting a focus on the "criminal personality," insufficient attention is paid to individuals with similar propensities and basic traits who have managed to avoid criminal involvement (Millon, 1981, 1996). It is our contention that antisocial personalities are best characterized by hostile affectivity, excessive self-reliance, interpersonal assertiveness, callousness, and a lack of humanistic concern or sentimentality (Millon, Simonsen, Birket-Smith, & Davis, 1998). Such individuals exhibit rebelliousness and social "vindictiveness," with particular contempt being directed toward authority figures. Other notable features in the antisocial personality include a low tolerance for frustration, impulsivity, and an inability to delay gratification. Consistent with this is a tendency to become easily bored and restless with day-to-day responsibilities and social demands. Not only are such individuals seemingly undaunted by danger and punishment, they appear attracted to it, and may actually seek it out or provoke it. Our portrayal of the antisocial personality is more consistent with the concept of the sociopathic or psychopathic personalities as depicted in the incisive writings of Cleckley (1941). These individuals are most notable for their guiltlessness, incapacity for object love, impulsivity, emotional shallowness, superficial social charm, and an inability to profit from experience (Millon et al., 1998).

An argument may also be made for a *non-antisocial* variant of the antisocial personality. Such individuals may view themselves as assertive, energetic, self-reliant, and hard-boiled, but realistic, strong, and honest. In competitive societies, these traits tend to be commended and reinforced. Consequently, such individuals may achieve positions of authority and power, which provide socially sanctioned avenues for expressing their underlying mean-spirited temperament.

Antisocials tend to be finely attuned to the feelings, moods, and vulnerabilities of others, taking advantage of this sensitivity to manipulate and control. However, they typically evidence a marked deficit in self-insight and rarely exhibit foresight. Although inner tensions, frustrations, and dysphoria inevitably occur, such discomforts are not

464

tolerated for very long, being discharged through acting-out, rather than intrapsychic mechanisms. Frequent references are made to the antisocial's active avoidance of and inability to tolerate awareness of depression (Reid, 1978).

Although the antisocial's active independence, internal locus of control, and appetite for stimulating change may militate against the impact of life stressors, these same characteristics can also make the antisocial vulnerable to occasional major clinical episodes. Precipitants for depression, for example, might include situations of forced interpersonal submissiveness or curtailed personal freedom (e.g., incarceration or required military service), as well as internal conditions (e.g., medical illness or age-related physical decline) that result in incapacitation, passivity, or immobility. It has also been suggested (Reid, 1978) that depression may ensue when antisocials are forced to confront their inner emptiness, emotional void, and tenuous object-relations. Again, this forced recognition is most likely to occur when antisocials are made to feel inadequate or weakened in a way that strips from them their "resilient shell of narcissism."

Beck (1993) proposes an "autonomous mode" characterized by a great investment in "preserving and increasing . . . independence, mobility and personal rights" (p. 272). For such action-oriented individuals, their well-being is dependent on their ability to maintain their autonomy and direct their own activities without external constraint or interference. There is little sensitivity to the needs of others with a corresponding lack of responsiveness to external feedback and corrective influences. It should be noted that the autonomous individuals described by Beck are also characterized by excessively high internalized standards and criteria for achievement, features that may be more indicative of the compulsive character structure or the noncriminal variant of the antisocial personality. Such individuals tend to experience a hostile depression characterized by social withdrawal, rejection of help, self-criticism, resistance to change, and "active" violent forms of suicide attempts.

Several major theorists have recognized the strong similarity between the antisocial and the narcissistic personality (e.g., Kernberg, 1992). As described earlier, many studies have been done investigating the attributes of these individuals, yet clarity regarding their central features seems to escape us. The evolutionary model, with its polarity schema, may provide us with insights that other approaches have only hinted at faintly but have not established firmly. Reviewing Figure 16.1, we can see the prominence assigned to both the self (individuating) and active (modifying) polarities. This suggests that antisocials are driven, first, to benefit themselves and, second, to take vigorous action to see that these benefits accrue to them. This pattern is similar to yet different from that seen in narcissists, where an unjustified self-confidence assumes that all that is desired will come to them with minimal effort on their part. The antisocial assumes the contrary. Recognizing by virtue of past experience that little will be achieved without considerable effort, cunning, and deception, the antisocial knows that desired ends must be achieved through one's own actions. Moreover, these actions serve to fend off the malice that one anticipates from others and undo the power possessed by those who wish to exploit one.

CLINICAL PICTURE

The following sections provide the reader with a systematic analysis of the prototypal domains and personality variants of the antisocial disorder (see Table 16.1).

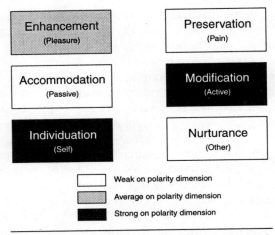

Figure 16.1   Status of the antisocial personality prototype in accord with the Millon Polarity Model.

Prototypal Diagnostic Domains

The major features of this personality pattern are approached in line with the domain levels used in previous chapters. Here, we identify characteristics that are relatively specific to the prototypal antisocial disorder (see Figure 16.2). Unless noted, the domains described should be generally applicable to most of the adult subtypes.

Impulsive expressive behavior.   Many of these personalities evidence a low tolerance for frustration, seem to act impetuously, and cannot delay, let alone forgo, prospects for immediate pleasure. They are precipitous and irrepressible, acting hastily and spontaneously in a restless, spur-of-the-moment manner. Their impulsive behaviors are short-sighted, incautious, and imprudent. There is minimal planning and limited consideration of alternative actions, and consequences are rarely examined or heeded. Antisocial types appear easily bored and restless, unable to endure the tedium of routine or to persist at the day-to-day responsibilities of marriage or a job. Others of this variant are characteristically prone to taking chances and seeking thrills, acting as if they were immune from danger. There is a tendency to jump from one exciting and momentarily gratifying escapade to another, with little or no care for potentially detrimental consequences. When matters go their way, these antisocial variants often act in a gracious, cheerful, saucy, and clever manner. More characteristically, their behavior is brash, arrogant, and resentful.

Although the preceding relates to the prototypal antisocial, it does suggest a typecasting that is somewhat misleading. There are many individuals, intrinsically antisocial in the broad sense, who appear quite conventional in appearance, manners, and styles of behavior. These nonstereotypical antisocials portray themselves in a manner consistent with their often rather conventional occupations. Hence, an aggrandizing and self-seeking physician will look and act like a physician, not like some riffraff gang member. The point to be made is that one should not be misled into assuming that antisocials advertise their inclinations by superficial appearances.

TABLE 16.1   Clinical Domains of the Antisocial Personality Prototype

Behavioral Level

(F) Expressively Impulsive (e.g., is impetuous and irrepressible, acting hastily and spontaneously in a restless, spur-of-the-moment manner; is short-sighted, incautious, and imprudent, failing to plan ahead or consider alternatives, much less heed consequences).

(F) Interpersonally Irresponsible (e.g., is untrustworthy and unreliable, failing to meet or intentionally negating personal obligations of a marital, parental, employment, or financial nature; actively intrudes on and violates the rights of others, as well as transgresses established social codes through deceitful or illegal behaviors).

Phenomenological Level

(F) Cognitively Deviant (e.g., construes events and relationships in accord with socially unorthodox beliefs and morals; is disdainful of traditional ideals, fails to conform to social norms, and is contemptuous of conventional values).

(S) Autonomous Self-Image (e.g., sees self as unfettered by the restrictions of social customs and the constraints of personal loyalties; values the image and enjoys the sense of being free, unencumbered, and unconfined by persons, places, obligations, or routines).

(S) Debased Objects (e.g., internalized representations comprise degraded and corrupt relationships that spur revengeful attitudes and restive impulses that are driven to subvert established cultural ideals and mores, as well as to devalue personal sentiments and to sully, but intensely covet, the material attainments of society denied them).

Intrapsychic Level

(F) Acting-Out Mechanism (e.g., inner tensions that might accrue by postponing the expression of offensive thoughts and malevolent actions are rarely constrained; socially repugnant impulses are not refashioned in sublimated forms, but are discharged directly in precipitous ways, usually without guilt or remorse).

(S) Unruly Organization (e.g., inner morphologic structures to contain drive and impulse are noted by their paucity, as are efforts to curb refractory energies and attitudes, leading to easily transgressed controls, low thresholds for hostile or erotic discharge, few subliminatory channels, unfettered self-expression, and a marked intolerance of delay or frustration).

Biophysical Level

(S) Callous Mood (e.g., is insensitive, irritable, and aggressive, as expressed in a wide-ranging deficit in social charitableness, human compassion, or personal remorse; exhibits a coarse incivility as well as an offensive if not reckless disregard for the safety of self or others).

F refers to Functional Domains (fluid, interactive)
S refers to Structural Domains (stable, unchanging)

Irresponsible interpersonal conduct.   It can be safely assumed that most antisocials are untrustworthy and unreliable in their personal relationships. They frequently fail to meet or intentionally negate obligations of a marital, parental, employment, or financial nature. Not only do these personalities intrude on and violate the rights of others, but they seem to experience a degree of pleasure in transgressing established social codes by engaging in deceitful or illegal behaviors.

The most distinctive characteristic of antisocials is their tendency to flout conventional authority and rules. They act as if established social customs and guidelines for self-discipline and cooperative behavior do not apply to them. In some, this disdain is evidenced in petty adolescent disobedience or in the adoption of unconventional values, dress, and demeanor. Many express their arrogance and social rebelliousness in illegal acts and deceits, coming into frequent difficulty with educational and law enforcement authorities.

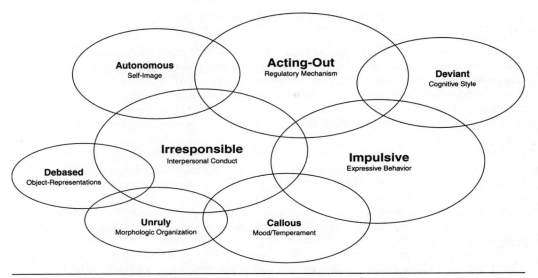

Figure 16.2   Salience of prototypal antisocial domains.

Despite the disrespect they show for the rights of others, many antisocial types present a social mask of not only civility but sincerity and maturity. Untroubled by guilt and loyalty, they develop a talent for pathological lying. Unconstrained by honesty and truth, they weave impressive tales of competency and reliability. Many are disarmingly charming in initial encounters and become skillful swindlers and impostors. Alert to weaknesses in others, they play their games of deception with considerable skill. However, the pleasure they gain from their ruse often flags once the rewards of deceit have been achieved. Before long, their true unreliability may be revealed as they stop "working at" their deception or as their need grows to let others know how clever and cunning they have been.

Deviant cognitive style.   Many antisocials construe events and interpret human relationships in accord with socially unorthodox beliefs and morals. In the main, they are disdainful of traditional ideals, fail to conform to acceptable social norms, and are often contemptuous of conventional ethics and values. It should be noted that these personalities exhibit both clarity and logic in their cognitive capacities, an observation traceable to Pinel's earliest writings. Yet, they actively disavow social conventions, show a marked deficit in self-insight, and rarely exhibit the foresight that one would expect, given their capacity to understand (at least intellectually) the implications of their behavior. Thus, despite the fact that they have a clear grasp of why they should alter their less attractive behaviors, they fail repeatedly to make such modifications. To them, right and wrong are abstractions that are irrelevant. It is not their judgment that is defective, but rather their ethics. Whereas most youngsters learn to put themselves in the shoes of others in a responsible and thoughtful way, antisocials use that awareness to their own purposes. To them, every opportunity pits their personal desires against those of others, resulting in the decision that it is they alone who deserve every break and every advantage.

It should be evident that many of these personalities are unable to change because they possess deeply rooted habits that are largely resistant to conscious reasoning. To make their more repugnant behaviors more palatable to others, antisocial types are likely to concoct plausible explanations and excuses, often those of "poor upbringing" and past "misfortunes." By feigning innocent victimization, they seek to absolve themselves of blame and remain guiltless and justified in continuing their irresponsible behaviors. Should their rationalizations fail to convince others, as when they are caught in obvious and repeated lies and dishonesties, many will affect an air of total innocence, claiming without a trace of shame that they have been unfairly accused.

Autonomous self-image.   There are two aspects to the image of self that are found among antisocials. The first and more obvious one is the sense of being unconventional and disdainful of the customs that most persons in society admire and seek to achieve for themselves. Inasmuch as antisocials reject societal values and goals, the more dissimilar they can be from "ordinary" people, the more gratified they will be with themselves. Hence, to be clever and cunning or disrespectful and deviant are both valued self-images.

Underlying these public presentations is a more fundamental desire, that of being unfettered by the constraints of personal attachments, that is, being free and unencumbered by connections and responsibilities to others. The sense of autonomy that drives this image of self is one in which the antisocial feels unconfined by persons, places, obligations, and routines. It is also important to antisocials to arrogate to themselves a sense of magisterial self-sufficiency. This independence from others often makes the antisocial too proud to ask for anything, unwilling to be on the receiving end of the kindness and care others may express. It is not only humiliating to be the recipient of the goodwill of others, but antisocials can never trust others to act out of genuine concern and interest. They must remain inviolable so that they will never be humiliated or hurt again. It is the antisocial who must be the one to intimidate and reject others.

Antisocials do what they believe is right for them, disregarding the fact that it is patently dishonest or deceptively manipulative. Rarely would they designate the term "antisocial" as applicable to themselves; rather, in their view, it is suitable to those whose actions they disdain. Should they acknowledge being involved in behaviors that skirt the spirit of the law, perhaps even exaggerating the extent of these deviations, they will defend themselves by saying that "others not only do it, but get away with it," or that "everything in society is rotten to the core." White-collar antisocials have contempt for violent antisocials, who possess the same basic personality; similarly, violent antisocials will scorn the white-collar type for being slyly devious and cowardly.

Debased object representations.   Partly a result of their past experiences and partly a result of their current opportunities, the internalized objects of the antisocial are comprised of memories and images of a degraded and corrupt nature. It is these debased objects that spur the antisocial's restive impulses and revengeful attitudes. Not only are these personalities driven to subvert established cultural ideals, but they seek to devalue personal sentiments and to sully, though they intensely covet, the material wealth that society has denied them.

Acting-out regulatory mechanism.   The inner tensions that normally accrue by postponing the overt expression of manipulative thoughts and malicious feelings are *not* constrained by most antisocials. Rather, these exploitive and resentful dispositions are discharged directly and precipitously, enacted without guilt or remorse. In contrast to most other personalities, where socially repugnant impulses and feelings are either re-fashioned or repressed, the antisocial permits them open exposure, acts them out, so to speak, despite their disingenuous and socially offensive character.

Projection is another mechanism employed by antisocials. Accustomed through-out life to anticipate indifference or hostility from others and exquisitely attuned to the subtlest signs of contempt and derision, they are ever ready to interpret the incidental behaviors and remarks of others as fresh attacks on them. Given their perception of the environment, they need not rationalize their outbursts. These are fully "justified" as a response to the malevolence of others. The antisocial is the victim, an indignant bystander subjected to unjust persecution and hostility. Through this projection ma-neuver, then, they not only disown their malicious impulses but attribute the evil to others. As persecuted victims, they feel free to counterattack and gain restitution and vindication.

Unruly morphologic organization.   Constraints that help form a structure for per-sonality organization are both few and undeveloped among antisocials. Their psychic system is poorly constructed to achieve the purposes for which the components of the intrapsychic mind are designed. As a consequence of this unruly organization, efforts to curb refractory energies and pernicious attitudes are weak or ineffectual. Controls are easily transgressed, and there is a consequential low threshold for both devious-ness and irresponsible actions, as well as for hostile and erotic discharge. There is also intolerance for delaying frustrations, unfettered self-expression, and few sublimina-tory channels developed to orient impulses of a problematic nature.

Acts that devalue their past leave a deep emptiness within antisocials. Having been jettisoned by their own actions, there is now an inner scarcity of internalized objects. And it is this inner emptiness, at least in part, that drives antisocials to their aggran-dizing behaviors. This is done with surface appearances, covering up or filling inner de-ficiencies by exploiting and usurping what others possess. Aggrandizing actions serve to make up as much for internal scarcities as for external deprivations.

The morphologic organization of antisocials is an open system possessing few val-ued components and few mechanisms for dynamic processing. It is the unruly and empty character of their intrapsychic world that necessitates aggrandizing self through superficial materialistic attainments, the big ring, the expensive and colorful car, fancy suits and shoes, and so on. Having ousted their past life from their inner world, anti-socials are alienated from themselves, unable to feel any form of experiential depth. And because nothing and no one can be trusted, neither possesses value to the antiso-cial, other than momentarily. Hence, we see a hedonistic need to experience things that provide only immediate pleasure or achieve momentary recognition and signifi-cance. These, too, will be quickly jettisoned lest they "take over" and control their lives. Nothing is permitted permanence, be it a person or a once-appealing material object.

Callous mood/temperament.   As noted, most of these personalities act out their impulses rather than rework them through intrapsychic mechanisms. Although show-ing restraint under certain conditions, there is a tendency to blurt out feelings and vent urges directly. Rather than inhibit or reshape thoughts, this personality is inclined to express them precipitously and forcibly. This directness may be viewed by some as commendable, an indication of a frankness and forthrightness. Such an appraisal may be valid at times, but this personality manifests these behaviors not as an expression of honesty and integrity, but from a desire to shock or put off others. Hence, among antisocials, we see an emotional disposition to be irritable and aggressive.

Among many antisocials, there is a wide-ranging deficit in social charitability, in human compassion, and in personal remorse and sensitivity. Beyond their lack of deeper sensitivity, many antisocials possess "a lust for life," a passion with which they are willing to pursue excitement and hedonistic pleasures. There appears also to be an impulse to explore the forbidden, an enjoyment in testing the limits of their tolerance of pain and their assertive powers. Thus, their passion appears to be for intensity and excitement, not just pleasure.

Related to their expansive and risky inclination is their seeming disdain for human compassion and sensitivity. Callousness thrives on adventures and risk rather than on concern and empathy. From these deeper temperamental sources, if we can speak of them in this manner, we see the emergence of cynicism and skepticism, their distrust of the ostensive goodwill and kindness of others. Not uncommon among less socially advantaged antisocials is a coarse incivility as well as an offensive if not reckless disregard for the safety or welfare of both self and others.

Self-Perpetuation Processes

An essential element of personality disorders is that their efforts to cope with their world are themselves pathogenic, that is, create self-defeating actions (see Table 16.2).

Distrustful anticipations. If we look at the world through the eyes of the antisocial personality—a place fraught with little love and much frustration, a place where one must be on guard against the indifference or cruelty of others—we can better understand why they behave as they do.

Their strategy is clear. You cannot trust others: they will abuse and exploit their power; they will be indifferent to your needs, even dispossess you, strip you of all gratifications, perhaps dominate and brutalize you if they can. To avoid this fate, you must

TABLE 16.2 Self-Perpetuating Processes

ANTISOCIAL
Anticipates Distrust
   Expects belittlement and exploitation
   Self-sufficiency used to forestall threat
   Provokes others to react with hostility

Vindictive Interpersonal Behavior
   Pleasure gained in usurping from others
   Scheming beneath a veneer of civility
   Elicits resentful reactions

Weak Intrapsychic Controls
   Angry feelings vented directly
   Impulsive rashness and temptation
   Sees self as victim or innocent bystander

arrogate all the power you can to yourself, you must block others from possessing the means to be belittling, exploitive, and harmful. Only by alert vigilance to disinterest, only by vigorous counteraction can you withstand and obstruct the insensitivity and hostility of others. Getting close, displaying weakness, and being willing to appease and compromise are fatal concessions to be avoided at all costs. Only by acquiring power for yourself can you be assured of gaining the rewards of life; only by usurping the powers others command can you thwart them from misusing it. Given these fears and attitudes, we can readily see why they have taken their course of action and independence. Only through self-sufficiency and decisiveness can they forestall the indifference or dangers of their environment and thereby maximize achieving the bounties of life.

Unfortunately, these self-protective attitudes set into motion a vicious circle of suspiciousness and distrust, provoking others to react in a similarly cool and rejecting fashion. Potential sources of warmth and affection become wary, creating the indifference and rejection that prompted the antisocial's distrust in the first place. Hence, antisocials have activated a repetition of their past, further intensifying their sense of isolation, their resentments, and their need for autonomy.

Vindictive interpersonal behavior. The defensive actions of antisocials serve more than the function of counteracting exploitation and indifference. They are driven by a need to vindicate themselves, a desire to dominate and humiliate others, to wreak vengeance on those who have mistreated them. Not only do they covet possessions and powers but they gain special pleasure in usurping and taking from others (a symbolic sib, for example); what they can plagiarize, swindle, and extort are fruits far sweeter than those earned through honest labor. And once having drained what they can from one source, they turn to others to exploit, bleed, and then cast aside; their pleasure in the misfortunes of others is unquenchable.

Having learned to trust only themselves, they have no feelings of genuine loyalty and may be treacherous and scheming beneath a veneer of politeness and civility. People are used as a means to an end; they are to be subordinated and demeaned so antisocials can vindicate themselves for the grievances, misery, and humiliations of the past. By provoking fear, intimidating others, and being ascendant and powerful, they will rise above the lowly caste of their childhood. Their search for power, then, is not benign; it springs from a desire for retribution and vindication.

Not only does the strategy of autonomy and domination gain a measure of release from past injustices but, as with most coping maneuvers, it proves partially successful in achieving rewards in the present. Most people find themselves intimidated by antisocials' calculated pose of resentment and provocative look, no less than the overt threat of an emotional outburst, if not physical violence. In using these terrorizing behaviors, antisocial personalities possess a powerful instrumentality for coercing others, for frightening them into fearful respect and passive submission.

Although many persons with the basic antisocial personality style find a niche for themselves in society, where their exploitive and intimidating behaviors are sanctioned, even admired, they are ultimately self-defeating, no less so than occurs among more socially troublesome antisocials. The cleverly conniving businessman, the physically brutal army sergeant, the stern and punitive school principal set into motion angry and resentful reactions from others, recreating once more what they had experienced in earlier life: a menacing and rejecting environment of persons who learn neither to trust them nor to care for them.

Weak intrapsychic control. Threats and sarcasm are not endearing traits. How does one justify them to others, and by what means does the antisocial handle the fact that these behaviors may be unjust and irrational?

As noted in an earlier section, the antisocial personality has usually rebelled against the controls parents and society have proposed to manage and guide his or her impulses. Rarely do these youngsters substitute adequate controls in their stead; as a consequence, they fail to restrain or channel the emotions that well up within them. As feelings surge forth, they are vented more or less directly; thus, we see the low tolerance, impulsive rashness, susceptibility to temptation, and acting-out of emotions so characteristic of this pattern.

Obvious and persistent acting-out and rebelliousness cannot be overlooked. To make it acceptable, antisocial individuals fabricate rather transparent rationalizations. They espouse such philosophical balderdash as "Might is right"; "This is a dog-eat-dog world"; "I'm being honest, not hypocritical like the rest of you"; "It's better to get these kids used to tough handling now before it's too late"; and "You've got to be a realist in this world, and most people are either foolish idealists, appeasers, commies, or atheists." Seeing the world in this way, antisocials feel fully justified in their actions and need not be restrained; if anything, they consider their actions more valid than ever.

Accustomed throughout life to indifference and hostility from others and exquisitely attuned to the subtlest of signs of contempt and derision, well-entrenched antisocials begin to interpret the incidental behaviors and innocent remarks of others as signifying fresh attacks on them. Increasingly, they find evidence that now, as before, others are ready to persecute, to slander, and to vilify them. Given this perception of their environment, they need not rationalize their outbursts; these are "justified" reactions to the disinterest and malevolence of others. It is others who are contemptible, slanderous, and belligerent and who hate and wish to destroy the antisocial. He or she is the victim, an innocent and indignant bystander subject to unjust persecution and hostility. Through this intrapsychic maneuver, then, antisocials not only disown and purge their own exploitive and malicious impulses but attribute this evil to others. They have absolved themselves of the irrationality of their resentful outbursts; moreover, as a persecuted victim, they are free to counterattack and to gain restitution and vindication. As expected, antisocials have now created a world, composed in their own imagination, that continues to haunt and derogate them, an inescapably malicious environment of rejection and deprecation, yet one of their own making.

INTERVENTION GOALS

Antisocials usually present for treatment as a result of an ultimatum. Therapy is often the alternative to losing a job, being expelled from school, ending a marriage or relationship with children, or giving up a chance at probation and psychological treatment. Under other circumstances, treatment is usually forced on them; most prisons and other correctional facilities require inmates to attend psychotherapy sessions. In either case, a therapist working with an antisocial personality is likely to experience frustration and exasperation regarding the patient's clear lack of insight and/or motivation to change. Antisocials do not regard their behavior as problematic for themselves, and its consequences for others, who are judged to be potentially unreliable and disloyal, are not a concern of theirs.

The patient's attitude toward the therapist will typically take one of two forms. Either the antisocial will try to enlist the therapist as an ally against those individuals who forced the antisocial to enter therapy or, alternatively, the antisocial will try to "con" the therapist into being impressed with his or her "insight" and reform in an effort to secure advantage with some legal institution. The therapist's most effective recourse is to try to impress on antisocials the ways in which their behavior is in fact disadvantageous to them in the long run. The therapist can only hope that this insight will lead to behavior that is also advantageous to those who deal with antisocials, that is, behavior that is less abusive, exploitative, and criminal. The chances are slim of antisocials changing their duplicitous patterns owing to the development of a real concern for others.

Some clinicians believe that the chances for real gains increase with the patient's age. Although the incidence of antisocial personality does decline in middle age, it is likely that this statistic reflects two factors entirely incidental to the intrinsic character of the disorder. First, those whose antisocial behaviors persist are ultimately imprisoned for prolonged periods; they are, in effect, "out of commission" by 25 or 30 years of age. Second, those who survive in the mainstream of society are likely to have learned to channel their abusive and impulsive tendencies more skillfully or into more socially acceptable endeavors. It is not probable that their basic personality has been altered, only that it expresses itself in a less obviously flagrant and public way.

Ideally, therapeutic intervention would help reestablish a reasonable equivalence between the imbalanced polarities of the antisocial personality. The goal is to help patients increase their other orientation and decrease their use of active exploitation as a means of securing rewards. This would reflect an increased sensitivity to the needs and feelings of others (see Table 16.3). More realistically, antisocials' problem-perpetuating tendencies are usually curbed only by convincing them that it is in their immediate best interests to do so.

TABLE 16.3   Therapeutic Strategies and Tactics for the Prototypal Antisocial Personality

STRATEGIC GOALS

Balance Polarities
  Shift focus more to needs of others
  Reduce impulsive acting-out

Counter Perpetuations
  Reduce tendency to be provocative
  View affection and cooperation positively
  Reverse expectancy of danger

TACTICAL MODALITIES
  Offset heedless, shortsighted behavior
  Motivate interpersonally responsible conduct
  Alter deviant cognitions

Reestablishing Polarity Balances

The underlying motive of antisocial behavior is to "exploit before being exploited." As children, antisocials typically learn that the world will treat them unfairly, if not harshly; others are perceived not as a source of rewards, but rather as potential exploiters or degraders. Antisocials defensively turn to themselves, not only to protect themselves against potential harm, but to secure gratification as well. When rewards do involve other persons, it is not in the sense that the antisocial derives pleasure from sharing and intimacy. Others are essentially treated like objects; even highly personal interactions such as friendships and sexual relations are essentially instances of simple self-gratification. Retribution for past and present injustices is sought indiscriminately, whether or not the antisocial's "victims" are among the original offenders. Compensation for past deprivations is ruthlessly sought out and taken wherever it can be obtained. This active quest for self-gain, combined with a lack of other orientation leads to the manipulative, exploitive, and often criminal behavior so characteristic of the antisocial personality.

Ideally, therapeutic intervention would lead to increased balance on the self-other polarity, where others would be perceived as relatively benign and as having the potential to meet the antisocial personality's needs without exploitation. An appreciation and respect for the feelings and desires of others might result. The active stance toward securing rewards (at the expense of others) would ideally shift toward a more socially and personally adaptive one.

Countering Perpetuating Tendencies

Antisocials learn early that they do best by anticipating and reacting to an indifferent and unreliable environment with defensive autonomy, if not suspicion and hostility. The protective shell of anger and resentment that develops also acts as a perceptual and cognitive filter well past childhood. In their effort not to overlook any signs of threat, they persistently misinterpret incidental events as evidence of the devious and untrustworthy impulses of others. Often overlooked or suspiciously dismissed, on the other hand, are signs of objective goodwill. Expressions of affection and cooperative prosocial tendencies that do not escape antisocials' awareness are demeaned so as to ensure that they do not put themselves in a "dangerously" vulnerable position. This also ensures that they do not experience their environment in a way that would encourage them to lower their defenses. In fact, antisocials feel the need to demonstrate their invulnerability, both to themselves and to potentially threatening others, by provoking them, both physically and verbally. Alternatively, antisocials may engage in illegal "beat-the-system" schemes that lead to run-ins with the law and aggressive, mean-spirited, and punitive officials. The defensive counterhostility on the part of others helps maintain the antisocial's conviction that the world is a denigrating place.

In working with an antisocial patient, the therapist would probably do well to try to impress on the patient the possible advantages (for the patient) of altering his or her socially repugnant behaviors. Despite self-interest being the primary motivator in increasing prosocial acts, the consequent decrease in abrasive social encounters may over time alter the antisocial's belief about the degree of intrinsic threat in the environment. Attempts at altering such beliefs directly would be likely to elicit disdain for the therapist, which can lead to an increased desire to "con," manipulate, or teach a lesson to the "sappy and naïve wimp."

Identifying Domain Dysfunctions

The primary domain dysfunctions of the antisocial personality are seen in the socially evident irresponsible interpersonal conduct, impulsive expressive behavior, and acting-out regulatory mechanism. The antisocial is constantly calculating how to maximize personal benefits in any given situation; broken promises, failed obligations, and illegal behaviors are the inevitable consequences of always putting one's desires before marital, parental, employment, or financial responsibilities. Expressive behavior is impulsive, incautious, and shortsighted. Consequences do not play a role in the antisocial's behavioral decisions. Intrapsychic tensions are coped with by using acting-out as a regulatory mechanism; offensive thoughts and malevolent actions are neither constrained for any length of time nor sublimated into more adaptive forms. Instead, impulses are directly expressed with no concern for the damaging effects these will have on others. Once again, teaching antisocials to consider the consequences of their actions and to see personal advantages in behaving in prosocial ways and in accordance with others' wishes is a first step in altering their dysfunctional personality style.

Changes in behavior that prove to be beneficial to the antisocial's lifestyle may have some positive effects on other dysfunctional domains. The antisocial has an autonomous self-image and enjoys seeing his or her personal freedom as unrestrained by the loyalties or social customs that "bog down" most individuals. Once again, the personal advantages in adhering to the "norms" can help shift this image somewhat toward a more adaptive interdependent one. Interventions like wilderness therapy (discussed in the following section) can also be useful in this regard. Morphologic organization of the few weak inner defensive operations antisocials possess are unruly; impulses are rarely restrained or modulated. Learning cognitive and behavioral strategies for acting as a result of consequences can help provide guidelines for some personally and societally adaptive personality traits. Antisocials' debased inner object-representations are a juxtaposition of impulses to seek revenge and subvert established mores and to demean personal sentiments and material attainments that were denied them in early life. Increased personal satisfaction and stability may lead to a decreased drive to actively rebel against "the system" and an increased motivation to work with it to their advantage.

Other dysfunctional domains are more difficult to influence. The antisocial's deviant cognitive style consists of socially unorthodox beliefs and morals, disdain for traditional ideals, and contempt of conventional rules. The characteristic callous temperament is marked by an insensitive and unempathic, even ruthless, indifference to the welfare of others. These features are more likely to be masked than changed in a majority of cases.

SELECTING THERAPEUTIC MODALITIES

Developing rapport with the patient is a real challenge for the therapist working with an antisocial. L.S. Benjamin (1993) suggests that it is virtually impossible to achieve collaboration with an antisocial patient in ordinary dyadic therapy without adjunct intervention geared toward that very aim (discussed in the following section). Power struggles need to be avoided at all costs. Frances, Clarkin, and Perry (1984) suggest that the therapist openly acknowledge the vulnerability of the therapy setting to the patient's manipulative talents. The goal is to decrease the chance that the patient feels challenged by the therapist and thus decides to become oppositional and counteract. Toward this end, it is also crucial that the therapist does not assume the role of an evaluator. This is easiest to achieve in therapeutic settings that involve a team of therapists, usually inpatient settings, where a clinician other than the primary therapist provides access to privileges. The personality style of the therapist is even more important when working with antisocial personality disorder than with most other patients. Beck and Freeman (1990a) suggest that the following therapist characteristics are particularly helpful when working with an antisocial patient: self-assurance, a reliable but not infallible objectivity, a relaxed and nondefensive interpersonal style, clear sense of personal limits, and a strong sense of humor.

Behavioral Techniques

Although the frequency of certain repugnant actions may be reduced using behavioral techniques such as aversive conditioning, gains rarely extend beyond the treatment setting and do not generalize to other equally offensive habits, much less attempt to correct the underlying causative dysfunctions. Because the vast majority of antisocial personalities have good social skills and are not impaired in their functioning by anxiety, most behavioral techniques prove of minimal value in a treatment program.

Interpersonal Techniques

The interpersonal approach to therapy outlined by L.S. Benjamin (1993) is based on the assumption that antisocials have not had a learning history with warm and caring figures that could lead to normal attachment and bonding experiences. Instead, the antisocial maintains an interpersonal position of cool detachment and autonomy that is masked by a friendly charm that gives the antisocial a good measure of interpersonal control. This superficial social ease may lead some therapists to believe that a therapeutic alliance can be achieved with this patient. Benjamin emphasizes, however, that the antisocial cannot be expected to genuinely collaborate with the therapist, and thus initial interventions cannot take the typical dyadic form of interpersonal therapy. Treatment interventions aim at providing these patients with consistent and well-modulated warmth needed to overcome their marked socialization deficits.

Benjamin suggests several methods that may facilitate this objective. One possibility is based on a milieu treatment program. This program does not try to bring antisocial patients from their suspicious and cynical baseline position with likely futile efforts of friendliness and helpfulness. Instead, the staff is advised to adopt the patient's baseline position and to ignore him or her. After the patient is familiarized with the milieu program, punishment would ensue from noncompliance. As the patient exhibits behaviors in accordance with the treatment plan, progressively greater autonomy and friendly interaction is granted by the staff.

Interventions that provide opportunities for interdependence are encouraged. The need for cooperation and deference to the group (to ensure one's ultimate welfare) can be taught in wilderness programs. Here, difficult and often dangerous group tasks require individual and group commitment. Inappropriate behavior carries with it the risk of rapid, unpleasant consequences from either hard-to-con nature or fellow antisocial participants. Exercises that require cooperation, such as getting everybody over a 14-foot sheer wall and "blind trust walks," also necessitate that participants gain trust and yield control. Benjamin reports that a group of male incest perpetrators manifested increases in self-perceived self-control after a one-day intervention of this type, whereas controls from the same population that had engaged in a day-long hike exhibited no such changes. Benjamin states that once the processes of bonding and interdependence have begun, antisocials should now have the capacity to collaborate with the therapist. At this point, self-destructive features of their lifestyle can be recognized and understood, and skills such as self-care, delay of gratification, and empathy for others can be discussed and perhaps acquired.

Family approaches are often attempted in inpatient settings. Depending on the degree of antisocial tendencies of family members, intervention can range from supportive (of baffled and often despairing relatives) to active system-change (in cases where the family inadvertently or knowingly supports or encourages antisocial habits). Success depends largely on the situation; working with families of several antisocial personalities is likely to be doomed to failure. Evidence suggests that antisocials are disinclined to become involved in family treatment. Nevertheless, the possibilities of constructive change will be enhanced to the extent that family members become engaged. Typically, one finds that spouses and other close relations have either ignored or reacted inconsistently to the antisocial's problematic behaviors. When the family learns to act consistently and to set clear limits, there is a possibility that the patient's pathological behaviors may be diminished.

Group situations allow antisocials to help learn long-term problem-solving techniques by aiding others in similar situations, and successes in the lives of other group members can serve as positive models for antisocial patients. In general, well-structured arrangements for group treatment have been shown to be reasonably effective with these patients. Exploratory and nondirective groups, composed of heterogeneous personality styles, do not work nearly as well as those that are put together by the therapist and are homogeneous with regard to their antisocial characteristics. Here, the therapist should be in charge of both the content and the interactional process. It is advisable, where feasible, that two therapists work together with these patients. This model should help preclude the possibility that a single group leader would become an easy target for isolation or attack. As Walker (1992) has noted, two group leaders not only enable a second source of identification for patients to emulate, but permit the therapists to adopt a "good guy/bad guy" approach.

Cognitive Techniques

Cognitive techniques are outlined in Beck and Freeman (1990a), and are based on the assumption that changes in affect and behavior can be brought about by the patient's reevaluation of basic assumptions regarding key problem areas in his or her life. Beck and Freeman note that this model does not try to improve moral and social behavior through the induction of shame or anxiety, but rather through enhancement of cognitive functioning. They suggest that the treatment plan be based on a cognitive-growth-fostering strategy: helping the patient move from concrete operations and self-determination to abstract thinking and interpersonal thoughtfulness (formal operations).

A thoroughgoing review of the patient's life needs to be undertaken to identify special problem areas. The patient's significant others can be particularly helpful in this regard. Cognitive distortions related to each problem area need to be identified; these frequently include (a) justifications—"Wanting something or wanting to avoid something justifies my actions"; (b) thinking is believing—"My thoughts and feelings are completely accurate, simply because they occur to me"; (c) personal infallibility—"I always make good choices"; (d) feelings make facts—"I know I am right because I feel right about what I do"; and (e) the impotence of others—"The views of others are irrelevant to my decisions, unless they directly control my immediate consequences." Such assumptions are self-serving and minimize future consequences. The goal of therapy is for patients to recognize the implications of their behavior and how it affects others, and for long-range consequences to be considered. This does not represent real "moral" development, but rather constitutes a change from not caring what others think or feel to caring what they think or feel, because their reactions can be for or against the antisocial's advantage. The chances of an antisocial patient truly caring about others' welfare is very slim.

Beck and Freeman (1990a) offer suggestions about how to overcome antisocials' resistance to enter and stay with therapy. Antisocial behavior should be described as a "disorder"; the chances of the patient feeling accused thereby diminishes, thus increasing the probability of cooperation. The so-called disorder can further be framed as causing long-term negative consequences for the afflicted individual, such as incarceration, physical harm from others, and broken contact from friends and family. An initial "experimental" trial can be suggested, in which therapy can be explained as "a series of meetings that take place with an interested observer for the purpose of evaluating situations that might be interfering with the patient's independence and success in getting what he or she wants" (p. 156). Noncompliance with therapy guidelines such as missing sessions, not doing homework, or being hostile or noncommunicative despite the therapist's stance as a "helper" warrants discussion about the patient's feelings about therapy.

Therapeutic intervention includes helping the patient set clear priorities and examine a full range of possibilities and consequences before drawing a conclusion about appropriate behavior. The choice review exercise is very useful in this regard. A problem situation is rated on a scale of 1–100 to represent the patient's satisfaction. A series of behavioral responses to the problem are then listed, each with a rating of 1–100 in terms of their effectiveness in solving the problem. Advantages and disadvantages of all the alternatives are listed, and a final decision can be made on the basis of the overall attractiveness of the consequences of each choice. Persistent choices of ineffective alternatives indicate a need to examine particular skill deficits or undetected dysfunctional beliefs.

Patients who have demonstrated appreciable progress may still be susceptible to later relapse. In the very late stages of treatment, every effort should be made to alert these antisocials to those life situations that are prone to trigger their misbehaviors and misthinking. The therapist will thereby have an opportunity to strengthen the patient's coping when facing life's inevitable and unpredictable pressures.

Self-Image Techniques

The troublesome nature of the antisocial's characteristic behaviors suggest that self-actualizing techniques should be dealt primarily through methods proposed by Glasser (1990). In contrast to the majority of other self-enhancing procedures, Glasser's Reality/Control Therapy is well suited to counteract the patient's irresponsibility, self-centeredness, and social insensitivity. A confrontational and strong-willed posture on the part of the therapist may be necessary to make patients aware that their actions have more negative than positive consequences. Similarly, various Gestalt methods may be employed to help the patient recognize that others are not as positively reinforcing as he or she may be inclined to think they are. Both Glasser's and Gestalt procedures can also be employed to guide patients toward a more realistic appraisal of themselves, as well as how others react to their behavior.

Intrapsychic Techniques

There is a widespread pessimism as to whether intrapsychic therapy can produce significant changes within the antisocial. The problem is stated well by Gabbard (1990), who raises the question of whether such patients with uncertain outcomes are worth expending the time and money required by this approach to therapy. Meloy (1988) notes several contraindications to any form of therapy with these patients: violence toward others, absence of remorse, inability to develop emotional attachments, intense countertransference fears on the part of the therapist. The last of these also relate to the difficulties associated in forming a therapeutic alliance.

Moreover, psychodynamic approaches tend to be difficult to undertake because antisocials are not apt to internalize therapeutic "insights" without external controls or interventions, even if they do stay in treatment more than a few sessions. If severe limits are put on the antisocial personality (such as in highly controlled incarceration settings), anxiety and depression may lead some patients to be more amenable to change. Almost any other treatment orientations would have a greater (if limited) chance at success given the antisocial's lack of insight and low tolerance for boredom or slowly progressive changes.

Pharmacologic Techniques

No known pharmacologic techniques appear to be available to counteract the difficulties and emotions spurring the antisocial's behaviors. There are preliminary studies that suggest that the SSRIs may reduce both impulsive behavior and outbursts of aggressiveness.

MAKING SYNERGISTIC ARRANGEMENTS

If the resources are at all available, a therapist working with an antisocial would do well to involve the patient in an adjunct intervention that explores the diversity of human interdependence: wilderness therapy or supervised "nurturant" role exposure (working with children or animals) can activate cooperative schemata that may increase the chances of a real relationship developing between patient and therapist. In the case of aggressive antisocial patients, the therapist can consider evaluating the appropriateness of psychopharmacological intervention to help control physically abusive behavior. Group therapy with other antisocial patients can provide the patient with an opportunity to come in contact with credible role models; potential benefits of changing the antisocial behavioral style can be observed in others' positive experiences. Helping people with similar life difficulties come up with solutions can also help provide insight about behavioral consequences in the patient's own life. Another adjunct that may in some cases prove to be a helpful addition to dyadic therapy is family intervention, particularly in cases where family dynamics inadvertently support antisocial behavior.

Illustrative Cases

The combinations to be described below appear to constitute the great majority of so-called antisocial personality types. Although the focus in this section is on those features that distinguish the various antisocial amalgams, it should be noted that all combinations exhibit certain commonalities, most notably their marked self-centeredness and disdain for others. Security and gratification are achieved primarily by attending to oneself; the interests and needs of others are given incidental consideration, if attended to at all. Each of these personality mixtures views the world at large as composed of opportunities for exploitation and self-aggrandizement.

Psychopaths, sociopaths, sadists, and antisocial personalities have been lumped together in various ways in the past century. Each has been described by a parade of both common and contradictory characteristics. Some clinicians have described them as sharing a number of features, such as being impulsive, immature, naïve, aimless, and flighty. No less frequently, it has been said that they are sly, cunning, and well-educated sorts who are capable of making clever long-range plans to deceive and exploit others. To complicate the clinical picture further, they have been noted for their cruel aggressiveness and for the keen pleasure they derive in disrupting and intimidating others. At still other times, they are pictured as lacking true hostility and are believed to feel considerable discomfort when their actions prove harmful to others. This confusion stems in part from a failure to recognize that these repugnant behaviors may spring from appreciably different personality combinations or mixtures. In this section, we limit ourselves to variants that have at their core the aggrandizing elements that we believe are central to the antisocial personality pattern (see Table 16.4).

TABLE 16.4   Antisocial Personality Disorder Subtypes

Covetous: Feels intentionally denied and deprived; rapacious, begrudging, discontentedly yearning; envious, seeks retribution, and avariciously greedy; pleasure more in taking than in having.

MCMI 6A

Nomadic: Feels jinxed, ill-fated, doomed, and cast aside; peripheral drifters; gypsylike roamers, vagrants; dropouts and misfits; itinerant vagabonds, tramps, wanderers; impulsively not benign.

MCMI 6A-1/2A

Risk-Taking: Dauntless, venturesome, intrepid, bold, audacious, daring; is reckless, foolhardy, impulsive, heedless; unblanched by hazard; pursues perilous ventures.

MCMI 6A-4

Reputation-Defending: Needs to be thought of as unflawed, unbreakable, invincible, indomitable; formidable, inviolable, intransigent when status is questioned; overreactive to slights.

MCMI 6A-5

Malevolent: Belligerent, mordant, rancorous, vicious, malignant, brutal, resentful; anticipates betrayal and punishment; desires revenge; truculent, callous, fearless; guiltless.

MCMI 6A-6B/P

ANTISOCIAL PERSONALITY: COVETOUS TYPE
(ANTISOCIAL WITH NARCISSISTIC TRAITS)

CASE 16.1, DAN B., 32

Presenting Picture: Dan B. began treatment as an alternative to incarceration after repeated infractions involving petty theft. He was anything but apologetic for his actions, explaining that his philosophy of life was simply to "make it happen," meaning that he would do anything he needed to get what material possessions and money he wanted. Growing up poor in an affluent community and experiencing his father's abandonment at the age of 8, he was frequently the brunt of his peers' jokes and considered it "poetic justice" when he began selling them drugs in late high school. Dan felt that the world was a hard place, and one had to be deceitful to get one's fair share. Throughout the years since high school, he held a number of menial jobs, once going into business for himself (a cleaning service that served as a front for theft), and always supplementing his income and fulfilling his needs through dishonest schemes and practices. Dan liked to consider himself a "big spender," frequently picking up the tab for large social gatherings, mainly as a way of flaunting his attainments. He also mentioned that his girlfriend, who was a "decent, loving person," was someone who needed a bit of "training" to fulfill his needs.

Clinical Assessment: Dan is an example of what we are terming the *covetous antisocial.* In this most distilled form, we see the essential feature we judge as characterizing the antisocial personality, the element of aggrandizement. Here we observe an individual who feels that life has not given him his due, that he has been deprived of his rightful level of emotional support and material rewards, that others have received more than their share, and that he personally was never given the bounties of the good life. What motivated Dan was envy and a desire for retribution. These goals could be achieved by the assumption of power, and it was best expressed through avaricious greed and voracity. To usurp what others possessed was the highest reward he could attain. Not only could Dan then gain retribution, but he could fill the emptiness within himself. More pleasure came from taking than in merely having.

Although similar in certain central characteristics to the narcissistic personality, Dan did not manifest a benign attitude of entitlement, but an active exploitiveness in which greediness and the appropriation of what others possessed were central motivating forces. Whereas the prototypal narcissist feels a sense of inner fullness and satisfaction, a covetous antisocial such as Dan experiences a deep and pervasive sense of emptiness, a powerful hunger for the love and recognition he did not receive early in life. No matter how successful, no matter how many possessions he may have acquired, Dan still felt empty and forlorn. Owing to the belief that he will continue to be deprived, he showed minimal empathy for those whom he exploited and deceived. Much effort was expended in manipulating others to supply the services and commodities he desired—without offering any genuine reciprocation. Dan was, at times, a successful entrepreneur, an exploiter of others as objects to satisfy his desires. Not expecting that people will comply willingly, he was cleverly deceptive to overcome the reluctances of his victims.

Although Dan's chief goal was aggrandizement through the possession of goods usurped from others, it should not be forgotten that insecurity had been central to the construction of his strategy and to the avaricious character of his pathology. Like a hungry animal after its prey, Dan had an enormous drive, a rapacious outlook in which he manipulated and treated others as possessions in his power games. Although he had little compassion for the effects of his behaviors, feeling little or no guilt for his actions, he remained at heart quite insecure about his power and his possessions, never feeling that he had acquired enough to make up for earlier deprivations. Dan was pushy and greedy, anxious lest he lose the gains he had achieved. His life was openly materialistic, characterized by both conspicuous consumption and ostentatious display. Regardless of his voracious desires and achievements, he remained ever jealous and envious. For the most part, he was completely self-centered and self-indulgent, often profligate and wasteful, unwilling to share with others for fear that they would take again what was so desperately desired in early life. Hence, Dan never achieved a deep sense of contentment, felt unfulfilled no matter what successes he had, remaining forever dissatisfied and insatiable.

Synergistic Treatment Plan: Dan's most salient characterologic features revolved around retribution driven by an inner emptiness and faulty *cognitive schemata* regarding unfairness; therefore, an extremely *self*-driven style (completely forsaking *others*) emerged. This extremely angry man expended an enormous amount of energy (*active* orientation) scheming and manipulating, reaping as much (if not more) satisfaction from the chase as the catch. It would first be necessary to dispel anger, through several possible modalities (e.g., *behavioral, pharmacologic, experiential*), before concentrating on such perpetuating tendencies as the aforementioned deviant thoughts, shortsighted social conduct, and destructive actions. Directive *cognitive* and *interpersonal* interventions, with a strong focus on developing more *empathic* and responsible thoughts and actions, would be most beneficial in establishing a more appropriate style.

Therapeutic Course: Several brief therapies were considered. Among them were *pharmacologic agents* that may have been explored for modulating both the threshold and intensity of Dan's reactivity. These agents are not notably effective in such cases, but it may have been worthwhile to evaluate a few in terms of their efficacy in minimizing the frequency and depth of his hostile feelings and thereby decreasing some of the self-perpetuating consequences of his aggressive behavior. Well-directed *behavioral* approaches provided Dan with opportunities to vent his anger. Once drained of hostility, he was led to explore his habitual expectations and attitudes and could be guided through various *cognitive* techniques into less destructive perceptions and outlets than before. *Insight-oriented* procedures were attempted, but were not of short-term utility, nor were techniques oriented to a thorough reworking of his aggressive strategies. More behaviorally directed methods geared to increase restraint and control were most effective. *Interpersonal* techniques (e.g., Klerman, Benjamin) were also fruitful in teaching him more acceptable social behaviors. As far as *group* methods were concerned, Dan intruded on and disrupted therapeutic functions in early stages of group process, but later became a useful catalyst for group interaction and was able to gain some constructive social skills and attitudes.

The therapist needed to be cognizant of Dan's inclination to be spoiling for a fight, almost enjoying tangling with the therapist to prove his strength and test his powers. A mixed cognitive and emotion-oriented technique (e.g., Beck, Greenberg) was employed to counter his omnipresent undertone of anger and resentment (i.e., the expectation that the therapist may prove to be devious and hostile). By confronting and then venting these feelings, it may have been possible to dilute his inclination to repeatedly distort the incidental remarks and actions of the therapist so that they appeared to deprecate and vilify him. Similarly, a worthy brief therapeutic goal was to undo his habit of misinterpreting what he saw and heard and to magnify minor slights into major insults and slanders. Important in achieving these short-term goals was to restrain the impulse to react to Dan with disapproval and criticism. An important step beyond building rapport was to see things from his viewpoint. To achieve the circumscribed goals of brief therapy required that the therapist convey a sense of trust and willingness to develop a constructive treatment alliance. A balance of professional authority and tolerance diminished the probability that Dan would impulsively withdraw from treatment or regress to prior problematic states.

Effective brief techniques were called for because Dan was not a very willing participant in the process of therapy. He agreed to therapy only under the pressure of legal difficulties. One task of a cognitive approach was to get him to tolerate guilt or to accept a measure of blame for the turmoil he caused. Reframing his perceptions to ones that were more realistic countered Dan's belief that a problem could always be traced to other people's circumstances. Even when he accepted some measure of responsibility, he did not need to feel defiance and resentment toward the therapist for trying to point this out. Although he sought to challenge, test, bluff, and outwit the therapist, a strong, consistent, but fair-minded cognitive approach reduced these actions and aided him in assuming a more calm and reasoned attitude.

ANTISOCIAL PERSONALITY: REPUTATION-DEFENDING TYPE (ANTISOCIAL WITH SADISTIC TRAITS)

CASE 16.2, EMMANUEL A., 36

Presenting Picture: Defensive and agitated, yet maintaining an affable façade, Emmanuel A. was seen for therapy following a dispute at work. A dispatcher for a small shipping firm, Emmanuel enjoyed his work and the authority it provided. In his position, quite a few drivers had to listen to him and follow his directives. The particular incident that brought him into treatment involved a physical altercation "provoked by the other guy." When asked about home life, he explained that he generally had a good marital relationship, but occasionally his wife would be disrespectful and he would have to respond physically. He defined mutual respect as a quid pro quo, whereby if someone earned a close relationship with him, he would "take care of them," but he was not to be trifled with. He made it clear that honor was central to having a healthy life, citing his "no-good, alcoholic, cheating" father, whom he wasn't going to emulate. However, he could recall, as a child, defending his father against neighborhood derogation and disrespect, regardless of what he really thought. "It wasn't my opinion that was important," he explained, "it was the family's honor."

Clinical Assessment: Not all antisocials desire to fill their sense of emptiness by pursuing material acquisitions. For some, it is their reputation and status that they wish to defend or enlarge. For Emmanuel, antisocial acts were primarily defensive, designed to ensure that others recognized him as a person of substance who should not be "toyed with." He needed to be thought of as an invincible and formidable individual, indomitable and inviolable, and that others should be aware that he possessed qualities of strength and invulnerability. In these latter features, we see a strong amalgamation between the characteristics of the *reputation-defending antisocial* and those of the sadistic personality.

Emmanuel wished to convey to others that he was a tough and potent person, that he could not be pushed around, and that no one would get away with anything that would slight his status. He reacted with great intensity when his status and capabilities were questioned. He was perpetually on guard against the possibility that others would denigrate or belittle him. He would react instantaneously to a slight, though it should be noted that other reputation-defending antisocials may brood and work themselves up until the proper moment arises to act defensively and assertively.

Emmanuel's reputation defending, especially during his adolescence, reflected his social position and group status. He needed to overcome past deficits that made him particularly sensitive to signs of indifference and disinterest as well as of criticism. Both an expression of his internal needs and of his public reputation, Emmanuel did things that demonstrated to his peers that he was a "contender," a person of potential significance. This also required acts of aggressive leadership or risk-taking behaviors, sometimes of a violent or perhaps a criminal nature. A notable example of this behavior with other reputation-defending antisocials is the high prevalence of drug involvement and turf wars among gangs. The strengthening of one's reputation is often a by-product of these acts. What was initially intended as a defensive step to protect one's standing may become a major drive and aim in itself. But for Emmanuel and many others with such a characterological makeup, being tough and assertive, proving his strength among his peers, remains largely a reputation-defending act and not a hostile one, as is often the case in the pure sadistic personality type.

Synergistic Treatment Plan: As with the other antisocials, a major aspect of therapeutic intervention would be renegotiating a balance on the subject-object polarity more in favor of *other* and less of *self,* but perhaps nowhere else is this more true than in this subtype. The central issue in Emmanuel's life was dominance directly over others, not muddled by representations such as material possession. A first order of intervention would be to establish an empathic yet firm therapeutic relationship not characterized by defensiveness or disapproval, where his hostilities could be explored *experientially. Cognitive* strategies would be focused on establishing a clear sense of the implications of his chronically competitive proclivity, and a reorientation toward cooperation. From *behavioral* and *interpersonal* perspectives, it would be most important to diminish provocations (i.e., encourage more *passive* orientation), as well as establish a basis for more genuine and balanced social relationships.

Therapeutic Course: Although short-term methods were likely to be suited to Emmanuel, the techniques of *environmental management, psychopharmacologic treatment,* and *behavior modification* would be of limited value in effecting change. Altering his attitudes toward himself and his less than socially acceptable behavior was best brought about through procedures of *cognitive reorientation.* Once a baseline of rapport had been established, Emmanuel was able to withstand methods that confronted his dysfunctional beliefs and expectations (e.g., Beck, Ellis). The introduction of short-term *interpersonal* methods (e.g., Kiesler, Klerman) was employed next to probe and modify his attitudes and social habits. More expressive and time-extended techniques were not applicable in this case, as they were difficult to justify in that the patient's illusions may have been reinforced too strongly by the imaginative freedom these methods foster. Focused interpersonal methods, such as *group* and *family* therapy, helped him view himself in a more realistic light and assisted him in learning the skills of sharing and cooperation.

With a brief therapeutic focus, care was taken not to stress Emmanuel's deficiencies because this might have endangered the therapeutic relationship. Efforts were made, however, not to allow him to assume a dominant posture in treatment after his initial discomfort had receded. What needed to be confronted early on was Emmanuel's belief that he need not consider changing his views because he believed himself to be already almost perfect. In sum, he was hesitant to accede to any but the briefest therapy, hence increasing the likelihood of early relapses. He did become involved in a short-term regimen, but maintained a well-measured distance from the therapist, trying to resist the searching probes of personal exploration, especially those that implied deficiencies on his part. An effective cognitive confrontation method countered his efforts to shift responsibility for his own deficiencies to others. Unless dealt with directly yet without disapproval on the part of the therapist, Emmanuel's evasiveness and unwillingness may have seriously interfered with short-term progress. With a firm but consistently honest and confrontive technique, the treatment setting did not give witness to struggles in which he sought to outwit the therapist and assert his dominance. The therapist maintained great patience and equanimity in establishing a spirit of genuine confidence and respect.

A strong cognitively based method to undo distorted expectations focused on extinguishing his tendency to devalue others, not to trust their judgments, and to think of them as naïve and simpleminded. Rather than question the correctness of his own beliefs, he assumed that the views of others were at fault. What was questioned was his habit of assuming that the more disagreements he had with others, the greater was his own superiority, and so the more arrogant and presumptuous he was likely to become.

Another illusion that called for brief confrontive therapy was based on the fact that Emmanuel was unlikely to have sought therapy voluntarily. Hence, he was convinced that, if left alone, he could solve his own problems. Similarly, if treatment had been self-motivated, it probably would have followed a period of unaccustomed social humiliation or achievement failures. Whatever the promptings, Emmanuel's pride was in jeopardy by submitting to the role of patient. Though he accepted therapy in its early stages, this attitude may have been short-lived and fragile, unless he came to respect the therapist as being forthright and not easily intimidated.

Although efforts were made to rebuild his recently depleted self-esteem, the therapist took care not to appear subservient to Emmanuel in the process. His self-confidence was rapidly restored by merely allowing him to recall past achievements and successes. This was achieved very rapidly. A goal more likely to prevent recurrences, however, was that of guiding Emmanuel into becoming more sensitive to the needs of others and accepting the constraints and responsibilities of shared social living. This required strengthening his capacity to face his shortcomings frankly. Care was taken in this regard not to be deceived by mere superficial compliance with these efforts.

ANTISOCIAL PERSONALITY: RISK-TAKING TYPE
(ANTISOCIAL WITH HISTRIONIC FEATURES)

CASE 16.3, DENNIS N., 28

Presenting Picture: Dennis N. was a man always testing the limits of his own existence. Originally from a small Midwestern town, he moved to New York City in an effort to join the "independent-minded." He appeared to have a great deal of contempt for people living a quieter life, stating directly that those people were "rotting," living only vicariously through the television set. His preferred activities included skydiving and drag racing, and he always tended to be the most intemperate character among other risk-takers. Most sponsors of these events, as a matter of fact, eventually removed him from events for this reason. To hear Dennis explain it, this was all reasonably normal, and he felt sorry for those who cannot push these "human limits" for it requires "a little death in life for existence to be truly savory." At first, Dennis might have seemed simply adventurous and healthy, but it quickly became apparent that his routine flirtations with death via life-endangering stunts, as well as his preference to die "in pieces on a runway" rather than by a meaningless heart attack, were manifestations of something more maladaptive.

Clinical Assessment: Risk taking is often carried out for itself, for the excitement it provides, for the sense of feeling alive and engaged in life, rather than for purposes such as material gain or reputation defending. As noted elsewhere in this chapter, there are people who respond before thinking, act impulsively, behaving in an unreflective and uncontrolled manner. Beyond this inability to control his behaviors and feelings, Dennis, a *risk-taking antisocial,* appeared to be substantially fearless, unblanched by events that most people experience as dangerous or frightening. He gave evidence of a venturesomeness that appeared blind to the potential of serious consequences. His riskiness seemed foolhardy, not courageous. Yet, he persisted in a hyperactive search for hazardous challenges and for gambling with life's dangers. Descriptively, we may characterize Dennis as being dauntless, intrepid, bold, and audacious. Perhaps more significantly, he was recklessly foolhardy, seemed unblanched by genuine hazards, and was disposed to pursue truly perilous ventures. What we see here was an MCMI admixture and commingling of both antisocial and histrionic features.

In contrast to other antisocials, where the basic motivations are largely aggrandizement and revenge, Dennis was driven by the need for excitement and stimulation, for momentary and fleeting adventures that are intrinsically treacherous. He was, in effect, a thrill seeker, easily infatuated by opportunities to test his mettle or open his possibilities. What makes him antisocial is the undependability and irresponsibility of his actions, his disdain for the effects of his behaviors on others as he pursued a restless chase to fulfill one capricious whim or another.

Dennis's actions were driven by the feeling of being trapped and burdened by responsibilities, by feeling suffocated and constrained by routine and boredom. Unwilling to give up his need for autonomy and independence, lacking the habits of self-discipline, unsure that he could ever achieve or fulfill the emptiness he felt within himself in the real world, he was tempted to pursue the potentials that may be found in new and exciting ventures, traveling on a dilatory and erratic course of chancy and hazardous activities.

Synergistic Treatment Plan: Early treatment would need to be focused on establishing a more grounded *cognitive* style that would allow Dennis to view choices on more than just a superficial level, as well as establish a solid, empathic (but not submissive) working alliance with the therapist. It would be necessary, from both a cognitive and *interpersonal* framework, to stimulate a more mature *other* orientation, one that would appreciate the experience of the people around him. Dennis's perpetuations, additionally, included a highly *active* orientation that refused to allow him to assume any sort of "take it as it comes" stance (meager *passive* orientation), and *behavioral* and *experiential* treatments would be appropriate for working toward a more balanced activity polarity. These measures would also be geared toward instilling a greater sense of trust, reducing his vindictive inclinations, and bolstering his responsible actions and thoughts through adjustments in his *self* orientation.

Therapeutic Course: It was absolutely essential for the therapist to be open to see things from Dennis's point of view and to convey a sense of trust. To achieve reasonable short-term goals, this relationship building could not be interpreted as a sign of the therapist's capitulation to his bluff and arrogance; rather, it needed to be very clear that this was to be a therapeutic establishment of rapport and alliance. Brief treatment with Dennis required a balance of professional firmness and authority mixed with tolerance for his less attractive traits. By establishing himself as a fair-minded and consistent authority figure, the therapist was able to successfully employ *cognitive* methods that encouraged Dennis to change his expectations. Through reasoned and convincing comments, the therapist provided a learning model for Dennis in terms of the mix of power and logic.

Less confrontive cognitive approaches provided Dennis with opportunities to disengage his anger, even in short-term therapy. Once his hostility was dissipated, he was led to examine his habitual behavior and cognitive attitudes and was guided into less destructive outlets than before. *Interpersonal* methods, such as those of Benjamin and Kiesler, provided a means to explore more effective behavior. As far as *group* methods were concerned, until Dennis had incorporated changed cognitions and actions, he may have intruded on and disrupted therapeutic functions. Surprisingly, he became a useful catalyst for short-term group interaction and gained some useful insights as well as a few constructive social skills.

A useful short-term goal for Dennis was to enable him to tolerate the experience of guilt and to accept blame for the turmoil he frequently caused. Cognitive methods employing a measure of confrontation helped undermine his tendency to always trace problems to another person's stupidity or laziness. When he did accept responsibility for some of his difficulties, it was important that the therapist was primed to deal with Dennis's inclination to resent the therapist for supposedly tricking him into admitting it. Similarly, Dennis frequently attempted to outwit the therapist, and the therapist had to be ready to be challenged and to avoid these efforts. Whenever possible, Dennis set up situations to test the therapist's abilities, to catch inconsistencies, to arouse his ire, and to belittle and denigrate him. Restraining impulses to express condemning attitudes was a major task for the therapist, but one that was used for positive gains, especially when tied into the application of combined cognitive (e.g., Beck, Ellis) and interpersonal interventions.

It should be noted that the precipitant for Dennis's treatment was situational rather than internal. Hence, he did not seek therapy voluntarily, and he was convinced that if he were just left alone, there wouldn't be a problem. Such beliefs had to be confronted expediently, though with caution. Similarly, if treatment had been self-motivated, it would probably have been inspired by a series of legal entanglements or achievement failures. Whatever its source, a firm cognitive and *behavior-change* approach was required.

For this rather domineering and somewhat intimidating man, complaints were usually manifest in the form of agitation and discontentment. To succeed in his overall disinclination to be candid with authority figures, he meandered from one trivial subject to the next. This inclination had to be monitored and prevented. Moreover, contact with family members may have been advisable because they may have reported matters quite differently than did Dennis. To ensure that he took discussions seriously, he had to be confronted directly with evidence of his contribution to his troubles. Treatment was best geared to short-term goals, reestablishing his psychic balance, and strengthening his previously adequate coping behavior with cognitive methods, except where his actions were frankly antisocial. In general, short-term approaches with Dennis were best directed toward building controls rather than insights, toward the here and now rather than the past, and toward teaching him ways to sustain relationships cooperatively rather than with dominance and intimidation.

ANTISOCIAL PERSONALITY: NOMADIC TYPE
(ANTISOCIAL WITH AVOIDANT OR SCHIZOID FEATURES)

CASE 16.4, GLEN S., 29

Presenting Picture: Glen S. was attending therapy involuntarily, due to a drug possession charge. He described himself as one who "makes his own rules" and "goes where he wants." At the time of this interview, he was living with a woman whom he had met several weeks earlier, and whom he described as "nice" and "less demanding." Usually, he said, the women he met became more and more demanding, requesting that he get a job, help around the house, or not sleep with other women. For the time being, it appeared as though Glen would be able to live off of this woman's salary and not have to make any immediate changes. Historically, the longest such arrangement lasted nine months, and he could "never do that again." Glen was unemployed at the time of the initial interview and had no direct plans to pursue employment. Apparently, he was fired for taking days off without notice and coming in late, but Glen saw this as unfair, because he *did* his work when he was there. He began describing his upbringing, which included an alcoholic mother and a rule-following father. He seemed to hold contempt especially for his father, as his adherence to society's norms got him absolutely nowhere.

Clinical Assessment: It is commonly held that the central features that characterize antisocials are their overtly oppositional, hostile, and negativistic behaviors, intentionally enacted to undermine the values of the larger society. Although this characterization may apply to many who are labeled antisocial, it would be incorrect to overlook individuals such as Glen whose adjustments are equally problematic from a social viewpoint. Glen, a *nomadic antisocial,* sought to run away from a society in which he felt unwanted, cast aside, and abandoned. Instead of reacting antagonistically to this rejection by seeking retribution for having been denied the normal benefits of social life, Glen drifted to the periphery of society, scavenging what little remains he could find of what he could not achieve through acceptable social means. He had been angry at the injustices to which he was exposed, but at the time of therapy felt sorry for himself and had distanced from conventional social affairs because he felt he had little influence on others and was fearful of being further rejected. A peripheral drifter, Glen felt jinxed, ill-fated, and doomed in life. He was gypsylike in his roaming, an itinerant vagabond who had become a misfit or dropout from society. His isolation, however, was not benign. Beneath his social withdrawal were intense feelings of resentment and anger. Under minor provocation or as a consequence of alcohol or substance abuse, he might have acted out impulsively, precipitously discharging his pent-up frustrations in brutal assaults or sexual attacks on those weaker than himself.

In certain respects, this nomadic antisocial represents a mixture of antisocial characteristics and those of either or both the schizoid or avoidant personalities; he scored high on all three scales of the MCMI. A lifelong pattern of wandering and gypsylike migrant roaming becomes more and more ingrained by the accumulation of repeated disappointments, the conviction of being worthless and useless, and possessing the feeling of being abandoned and not belonging anywhere. This pattern is not infrequently seen among adopted children who feel uneasy about their place in this world, experience being dissatisfied and lonely in their homes, and fear the possibility of total rejection. Their migrant and straying ways may be a symbolic search for what they hope may be their "true home" or their "natural parents." Many feel like misfits, dropouts from a world where they never felt fully accepted. With little regard for their personal safety or comfort and with minimal planning, these nomadic antisocials drift from one setting to another as itinerant wanderers, homeless persons drifting often into prostitution and alcoholism as a way of life.

The urge to remain autonomous, to live as a vagrant if necessary, to keep from establishing a continuous residency, are in many ways akin to the common adolescent pattern of running away from home. Insecure where he lives, feeling like a failure, perhaps unwilling to assume the responsibilities of family life, Glen had adopted the vagabond style perhaps as an optimal life strategy. Despite its problematic consequences and the possible necessity to live a life of petty crimes, he chose to drift aimlessly, to show little serious forethought, and to possess few if any inclinations toward serious endeavors. He exhibited what may be called a "passive asociality," a lifestyle in which one neither works nor assumes any responsibilities other than basic survival.

Glen was comparatively harmless, owing to his general indifference and disengagement from life. However, in contrast to the *remote* and *affectless schizoid,* he was deeply angry and resentful. Moreover, he had normal needs for life's pleasures, especially those of an erotic character. Stirred by alcohol, in the main, he might become brutal when "liberated" or engage in criminal-like sexual behaviors in lascivious assaults on the weak and inadequate, such as children. What justifies our calling him antisocial, therefore, is that his impulses are not benign despite his peripheral and nomadic existence. When stirred by inner needs or environmental circumstances, his pent-up hostility will be discharged against those who are not likely to react forcefully.

Glen's motives were short term: to reduce tensions and the discomforts of everyday life. He had difficulty envisaging life beyond the moment. He could find no place to settle down; no place had ever given him the acceptance and support he needed or wanted. This sense of "being no place" is both similar to and different from the experience of depersonalization; Glen appeared vaguely disconnected from reality, possessed no clear sense of self, and seemed to be a transient both within himself and his environment.

Synergistic Treatment Plan: Glen was possessed of a fundamental hypersensitivity to disapproval, and his primary coping strategy was to *actively* detach; therefore, it would be necessary to begin building the therapeutic relationship by trust and reassurance that he was not subject to "harsh" societal criticisms (*pain* orientation typical of the avoidant). As Glen would begin to accede to this unfamiliar sort of relationship, it would be possible to *cognitively* reassess some of the sources of his hostility and begin viewing *interpersonal* aspects of his environment with more effective attitudes (adjustment toward greater *other* orientation, clarification of a somewhat befuddled sense of *self*). *Behavioral* modalities, specifically *social modeling,* would also serve to demonstrate and reinforce the potential to live in a more satisfying manner by implementing a more responsible style. It should be noted, too, that throughout treatment, it would be crucial to monitor Glen's *biophysical* proclivity toward unstable moods and be prepared to intervene with a *pharmaceutical* regimen, should it become necessary.

Therapeutic Course: Efforts to alter Glen's current symptoms and basic psychopathology were attempted by employing focused and short-term techniques. Primary goals in brief therapy included the facilitation of autonomy, the building of confidence, and the overcoming of fear of self-determination. As was to be expected, there was a period of initial resistance. As part of a short-term approach, it was important to counter Glen's feeling that the therapist's efforts to encourage him to assume responsibility and self-control were a sign of rejection. A warm and empathic building of trust helped prevent disappointment, dejection, and even rage. These potential reactions were anticipated, given his characteristic style, and they needed to be responded to with equanimity if fundamental changes were to be explored and relapses prevented. When a sound and secure therapeutic alliance had been established, Glen learned to tolerate his contrary feelings and dependency anxieties. Learning how to face and handle his unstable emotions was coordinated with the strengthening of healthier attitudes through *cognitive* methods such as those of Beck and Meichenbaum, as well as through *interpersonal* procedures such as those of Kiesler and Benjamin. Additionally, the therapist served as a *social learning* model to demonstrate how feelings, conflicts, and uncertainties could be approached and resolved with reasonable equanimity and foresight. An area worthy of exploration would have been *family* methods, had there been members available, that may have been used to test these newly learned attitudes and strategies in a more natural setting than that found in individual treatment.

As implied by his affective instability and self-deprecation, Glen avoided confronting and resolving his real interpersonal difficulties. His coping maneuvers were a double-edged sword, relieving passing discomfort and strains but perpetuating faulty attitudes and strategies. These distorted attitudes and faulty behavior were the main targets of cognitive and interpersonal therapeutic interventions (e.g., Safran and Segal).

Special care was called for in a short-term treatment regimen to counteract the possibility that Glen's hold on reality would disintegrate and his capacity to function wither. Similar care was necessary when the attention and support that he required was withdrawn or when his strategies proved wearisome and exasperating to others, possibly precipitating their anger. *Pharmacologic* agents would have been considered had he begun to succumb to depression or to erratic surges of hostility. Particular attention would have been necessary to anticipate and quell the danger of suicide during these episodes. A major concern during these early periods was the forestalling of a persistent decompensation process. Among the early signs of such a breakdown would have been marked discouragement and melancholic dejection. At this phase, *supportive therapy* and cognitive reorientation methods would have been actively implemented. Efforts were made to boost the patient's sagging morale, to encourage him to continue in his usual sphere of activities, to build his self-confidence, and to deter him from being preoccupied with his melancholy feelings. He was not pressed beyond his capabilities, however, for his failure to achieve any goals would only have strengthened his conviction of his incompetence and unworthiness. Properly executed cognitive methods oriented to correcting erroneous assumptions and beliefs were especially helpful.

ANTISOCIAL PERSONALITY: MALEVOLENT TYPE (ANTISOCIAL WITH PARANOID AND/OR SADISTIC TRAITS)

CASE 16.5, JANICE S., 26

Presenting Picture: Janice S. was arrested for buying cocaine and chose to attend counseling as an alternative to the ordinary penalty of community service. Her attitude about this consequence could be summed up in her statement, "You think I wanted to walk old ladies across the street? I ain't no seeing-eye dog. I figured this was easy. Come in, sit down, and talk to some jerk." Janice didn't see the sense in being punished for something that didn't hurt anyone else, and felt that she should be able to make up her own rules regarding what she did to herself. However, on speaking with her further, it became apparent that the thought of hurting others was really of very little significance to her. Janice felt as though the entire world was out to victimize her, so she may as well do it first. This attitude carried over into her interactions with others, most notably her boyfriend. "He pays my bills. Other guys get demanding, and tell you what you can't do," she said, describing relationships that had ended previously because of her engaging in intercourse with multiple partners. It was very difficult to establish any kind of rapport with Janice, as she had the attitude that anything said would come back against her. Thus, she did not allow the therapist to gain her trust, and she attempted repeatedly to sabotage the therapist's control over the interview.

Clinical Assessment: Janice epitomized this vindictive, hostile, and least attractive of the antisocial variants we term the *malevolent antisocial.* Her impulse toward retribution was discharged in a hateful and destructive defiance of conventional social life. Distrustful of others and anticipating betrayal and punishment, she acquired a cold-blooded ruthlessness, an intense desire to gain revenge for the real or imagined mistreatment to which she was subjected in childhood. Here we saw a sweeping rejection of tender emotions and a deep suspicion that the goodwill efforts expressed by others were merely ploys to deceive and undo her. She assumed a chip-on-the-shoulder attitude, a readiness to lash out at those whom she distrusted or those whom she could use as scapegoats for her seething impulse to destroy. Descriptively, we may summarize her traits with the following adjectives: belligerent, mordant, rancorous, vicious, malignant, brutal, callous, truculent, and vengeful. She was distinctively fearless and guiltless, inclined to anticipate and search out betrayal and punitiveness on the part of others. Her primary antisocial characteristics may have been seen as features that blend with either or both the paranoid or sadistic personality, reflecting not only a deep sense of deprivation and a desire for compensatory retribution, but intermingling within her an intense suspiciousness and hostility.

Dreading the thought that others may view her as weak or may manipulate her into submission, Janice rigidly maintained an image of hard-boiled strength, carrying herself truculently and acting tough, callous, and fearless. To "prove" her courage, she routinely courted danger and punishment. But punishment would only verify her anticipation of unjust treatment. Rather than being a deterrent, it reinforced her rebelliousness and her desire for retribution. When she gained power in a social context, she would brutalize others to confirm her self-image of strength. If faced with persistent failure, beaten down in efforts to dominate and control others, or finding aspirations far outdistancing her luck, her feelings of frustration, resentment, and anger would only mount to a moderate level, rarely to a point where her controls gave way to a raw brutality and vengeful hostility, as is seen in the *tyrannical sadist.* Spurred by repeated rejection and driven by an increasing need for power and retribution, Janice's aggressive impulses would surge into the open. At these times, her behaviors became outrageously and flagrantly antisocial. Not only would she show minimal guilt or remorse for what she had done, but she was likely to display an arrogant contempt for the rights of the others.

What distinguishes the malevolent antisocial from the tyrannical sadist is the former's capacity to understand guilt and remorse, if not necessarily to experience it. Janice was capable of giving a perfectly rational explanation of ethical concepts; that is, she *knew* what was right and what was wrong, but she seemed incapable of feeling it. We could not ascertain whether this experiential deficit was constitutionally built in or consequential to deficiencies in early learning. Nevertheless, there appeared to be a defect in the capacity to empathize with the rightness or wrongness of her actions. As with the tyrannical sadist, Janice may have come to relish menacing others, to make them cower and withdraw. She was combative and sought to bring more pressure on her opponents than her opponents were willing to tolerate or to bring against her. She made few concessions and was inclined to escalate as far as necessary, never letting go until others succumbed. In contrast to the tyrannical sadist, however, Janice recognized the limits of what could be done in her own self-interests. She did not lose self-conscious awareness of her actions and would press forward only if her goals of self-aggrandizement were likely to be achieved. Her adversarial stance was often contrived, a bluffing mechanism to ensure that others would back off. Infrequently were actions taken that may have led to a misjudgment and counterreaction in these matters.

Synergistic Treatment Plan: As Janice would be ill-disposed to cooperate, it was imperative that she at least be intellectually aware of the pragmatic implications of therapy (namely, that her presence would be necessary, but it would be her choice as to whether the time would be worthwhile). Her constitutional hostility and defensiveness would need to be dissipated and/or channeled more effectively, and this would be most effectively addressed with a *biophysical* and *behavioral* regimen to reduce her highly *active* agitation and impulsive behavior. Very gradually, it would become possible to begin exploring more personal constructs through carefully executed *cognitive* strategies aimed at questioning her perpetuations of malevolent attitudes, distrust, and vengefulness, and her frequent tendency to court outside hostilities. Other behavioral interventions, in addition to those mentioned previously, would also be used toward the goal of establishing controls. Toward this end as well, group *interpersonal* methods might be useful in improved socialization, as a more harmonious balance would be struck with an increase in *other* orientation, as well as an adjustment toward clarifying and, in some ways, diminishing aspects of *self*.

Therapeutic Course: A *pharmacologic* regimen was attempted at the outset with Janice, targeted at modulating both the threshold and intensity of her reactivity. This approach was not notably effective in this case, though it is sometimes efficacious in easing the occurrence and intensity of hostile emotions that so often lead to negative consequences as a result of externalized behavior. Well-directed *behavioral* approaches provided a venue for expression of more potent feelings. As her anger dissipated through this modality, she became more amenable (though *gradually*) to some personal explorations. *Cognitive* techniques helped her examine and reevaluate her propensity toward problematic expressions and assumptions. From there, it was possible for her to very pragmatically develop less destructive thoughts and reactions than before. *Insight-oriented* procedures, along with more extended approaches focused on elaborately restructuring her aggressive strategies, were not used, as Janice was not likely to withstand an elongated, probing strategy. Behavioral methods providing expressive outlets (as mentioned earlier) as well as those that reinforced social restraint, were employed. *Interpersonal* techniques (e.g., Klerman, Benjamin) also were effective in instilling less destructive social behaviors. *Group* methods were rejected, as Janice was likely to intrude on and disrupt therapeutic functions. On the other hand, she may have become a useful catalyst for group interaction and possibly could have gained constructive social skills and attitudes.

The therapist was cognizant of Janice's strong proclivity toward altercations, as she gained a much relished sense of dominance from "acting tough." A cognitive-emotive approach (e.g., Beck, Greenberg) systematically challenged and discharged those hostilities and served to undermine her chronically irritable, choleric undertone and eased her tendency to continually misinterpret the therapist's incidental remarks and behaviors as vexing and aspersive. Similarly, another important therapeutic goal was to confront her

494 Personality Disorders—Axis II

habit of perceiving nearly everything around her as slanderous to her, and to magnify even the most minor indignity into a near declaration of war. To achieve these goals, it was important that the therapist suppress any impulse to show disapproval. It was of absolute importance to demonstrate an ability to create a sense of trust, convey a strong alliance, and most important, to show the ability to empathize with Janice. This approachable posture, combined with a firm, professional, and forthright stance, allowed Janice to gradually invest in therapy and alleviated concerns that she would prematurely withdraw from treatment.

Effective brief techniques were called for, as Janice was highly unlikely to be a model patient and would never have tolerated a time-extended treatment. She had agreed to therapy, as stated before, under the pressure of a legal entanglement. One important cognitive task, in order to make any progress, was to get Janice to accept some measure of responsibility for her difficulties. Through reframing toward a more realistic perspective, it was possible to counter her ingrained belief that her problems were always the fault of some lazy, stupid, or hostile person elsewhere. With a strong, consistent, and fair attitude, the therapist was able to help Janice cognitively rework these assumptions in a way that was acceptable and nonthreatening. Her acceptance of blame did not turn into resentment of the therapist for "tricking" her or bringing this to her attention.

Risks and Resistances

Despite the therapeutic focus on the disadvantages of the antisocial lifestyle, many emotional and material advantages mitigate against possible therapeutic headway. Feelings of control, power, and even rage can produce a "high" that the patient is understandably not willing to give up. Unlike other personality types who experience considerable discomfort in association with their symptoms, the antisocial's dysfunctional behaviors are rewarded more often than punished, and consequences are contingent on reactions of others and tend not to be immediate. Because neither antisocial "symptoms" nor their consequences generate immediate and internally generated discomfort, they do not serve to directly extinguish antisocial behavior. A cooperative and congenial attitude often is a mask for evasive behavior that is adopted to gain advantage with the therapist and legal authorities. Some antisocial patients who come to therapy as an alternative to jail may clearly not be participating in therapy. Therapists may feel compelled to continue with the intervention process to "rescue" the patient from incarceration, but in fact unwittingly reward antisocial behavior and support the lifestyle by helping the patient avoid the legal consequences of his or her choices. This can also undermine the very purpose of the legal system: to protect innocent society members from harm.

A different kind of countertransference reaction can lead to animosity that can interfere with potential therapeutic gains; therapist suspiciousness and anger about being lied to and manipulated, feelings of frustration and helplessness about apparent lack of intervention success, and disdain and disgust for the antisocial patient and his or her lifestyle are common. Therapy with this group can prove to be highly frustrating and nongratifying, and in the opinion of many therapists, generally unsuccessful. As antisocials are very sensitive to negative evaluation, power struggles and evaluation of the patient by the therapist should be avoided if at all possible. This is easier to achieve in inpatient settings because a clinician other than the therapist can be responsible for providing access to privileges; the primary therapist should not be viewed by the patient as an evaluator, but rather as a strategic helper. However, the therapist should resist intervening on the patient's behalf.

Many therapists are discouraged by the conviction that even when some behavioral changes are secured, it is highly unlikely that they reflect any change in moral character. Rather, they represent an accommodation to the constrains of society to yield a more profitable lifestyle for the antisocial individual. Some therapists try to keep in mind that circumscribed goals that decrease problems for those around these patients as well as for the patients themselves are valid. Others worry that a veneer of socialization may lead to disastrous personal consequences for people who would have been less likely to be "duped" by antisocials had therapy not been undertaken and the patients not learned to present themselves well in the short term.

Treating Sadistic
Personality Patterns

At the most fundamental level, the primary motives that guide the lives of sadistics conflict directly with one another. No matter what their other inclinations may be, their internal orientations move in opposing ways; to remain at war with themselves is intrinsic to their psychic makeup. Not only do these multiple perspectives fail to resolve internal conflicts, but they are likely to intensify them. Thus, if the defendant wins the case, the prosecutor must lose, and vice versa. In the masochistic personality, for example, these individuals consciously hold high expectations of others, who, of course, almost invariably fail to meet them. As a consequence, masochists unconsciously wish retribution and to derogate others, but, if they were to do so, they would assault the very persons they desire will love and care for them. As the saying goes, these personalities can't win for losing, nor can they lose for winning.

More specifically, in both the sadistic and masochistic types, the conflict between the pain-pleasure polarities represents a transposition such that normally pleasurable experiences are viewed as painful, and normally painful experiences are felt as pleasurable. In the compulsive and negativistic personalities, it is the self and other polarities that are in conflict; that is, the more they are disposed toward one component of the polarity pair, the more they are inclined to reverse themselves and turn toward the second. In sum, in the sadistic and masochistic types we find a psychic *dissonance* between the survival functions of pain and pleasure.

The notion of an abusive, explosive, and violent character type (individuals who are destructive to life) long preceded the decision of the *DSM* to introduce the sadistic personality disorder in 1987. The official proposals at that time coalesced viewpoints of numerous theorists and clinicians. As is well-known, the introduction in the *DSM-III-R* was shortly followed by the deletion of the disorder in *DSM-IV*. In reviewing its history in the *DSM,* it should be self-evident that our society has become increasingly preoccupied with matters of public violence and private abuse (Millon et al., 1998). Some commentators have characterized our times as a period when incivility and crudeness have come to the fore not only as inevitable products of a declining society, but also as sanctioned, encouraged, and even admired qualities of life. One need not look very far to see the pervasive nature of this "plague" of murder and mayhem in our daily news, in films, and on TV, as well as in the lyrics of our popular songs. And yet, at this point in time, the *DSM-IV* Task Force saw fit to delete the characterization of a violence-prone personality. Offering rationalizations galore, the Task Force sought to justify the decision to delete the sadistic disorder from the nomenclature. Having been privy to these justifications, the author of this text cannot help but conclude that the true motive for this decision was essentially a political one, a decision to sweep under the rug what was difficult to sustain in the face of unrelenting criticisms by a small minority of mental health professionals. How ludicrous it will appear to clinicians in the next decade when they reflect on a course of action that essentially "ran away" from perhaps the most significant personality problem of the 1990s.

It should be noted that sadistic behaviors are not limited to the actions of violent psychopaths who are seen only in the back wards of state prisons, those crudely vicious and brutalizing members on society's periphery. Through sublimation, if nothing else, many such individuals may be found at the center of everyday society. They are seen, for example, in the harsh moralism of members of congress whose truculence is "justified" by the "arrogant demands" of "alien" immigrant groups. Such behavior is evident in the machinations of politicians whose façade of so-called good intentions cloaks a lust for power that leads to repressive and socially demeaning legislation. Less dramatically, and more frequently, these individuals participate in the ordinary affairs of life: the harshly punitive and abusive father; the puritanical, fear-inducing minister; the vengeful dean; and the irritable, guilt-producing mother.

We turn our attention to the evolutionary model, specifically viewing the polarity schema as presented in Figure 17.1. As can be seen, primary focus for the aggressive/sadistic centers in the pain (preservation) and active (modifying) polarities. At first glance, one might be inclined to note that the polarity focus is essentially the same as seen in the avoidant personality, where both pain and active polarities are preeminent as well. However, the avoidant actively anticipates and escapes from abuse, whereas the sadistic actively assaults and degrades others. Both are active, but one imposes pain,

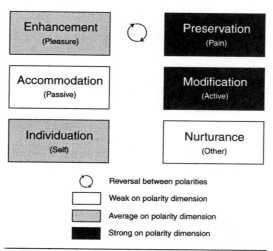

Figure 17.1 Status of the sadistic (aggressive) personality prototype in accord with the Millon Polarity Model.

whereas the second avoids pain. The reversal sign in the sadistic/aggressive figure signifies that sadists engage in behaviors that are discordant given evolution's progression through life enhancement, that is, seeking joy, optimism, and pleasure in relating to one's environment. In its stead, the sadistic acts in a hostile and malevolent manner, actively working toward harmful and ruinous ends. Rather than uplifting and preserving life, the sadist is actively evil, violent, and deadly, assaulting and demeaning others instead of encouraging and enhancing them.

CLINICAL PICTURE

As in prior chapters, we furnish the reader with a variety of sources to assist in the appraisal of the sadistic personality, first noting how their features show up in eight clinical domains and then describing the several subtypes in which they express themselves (see Table 17.1).

TABLE 17.1   Clinical Domains of the Sadistic Personality Prototype

Behavioral Level

(F) Expressively Precipitate (e.g., is disposed to react in sudden abrupt outbursts of an unexpected and unwarranted nature; recklessly reactive and daring, attracted to challenge, risk, and harm, as well as unflinching, undeterred by pain, and undaunted by danger and punishment).

(F) Interpersonally Abrasive (e.g., reveals satisfaction in intimidating, coercing, and humiliating others; regularly expresses verbally abusive and derisive social commentary, as well as exhibiting vicious if not physically brutal behavior).

Phenomenological Level

(F) Cognitively Dogmatic (e.g., is strongly opinionated and closed-minded, as well as unbending and obstinate in holding to preconceptions; exhibits a broad-ranging authoritarianism, social intolerance, and prejudice).

(S) Combative Self-Image (e.g., is proud to characterize self as assertively competitive, as well as vigorously energetic and militantly hardheaded; values aspects of self that present pugnacious, domineering, and power-oriented image).

(S) Pernicious Objects (e.g., internalized representations of the past are distinguished by early relationships that have generated strongly driven aggressive energies and malicious attitudes, as well as by a contrasting paucity of sentimental memories, tender affects, internal conflicts, shame or guilt feelings).

Intrapsychic Level

(F) Isolation Mechanism (e.g., can be cold-blooded and remarkably detached from an awareness of the impact of own destructive acts; views objects of violation impersonally, as symbols of devalued groups devoid of human sensibilities).

(S) Eruptive Organization (e.g., despite a generally cohesive morphologic structure composed of routinely adequate modulating controls, defenses, and expressive channels, surging powerful and explosive energies of an aggressive and sexual nature threaten to produce precipitous outbursts that periodically overwhelm and overrun otherwise competent restraints).

Biophysical Level

(S) Hostile Mood (e.g., has an excitable and irritable temper that flares readily into contentious argument and physical belligerence; is cruel, mean-spirited, and fractious, willing to do harm, even persecute others to get own way).

F refers to Functional Domains (fluid, interactive)
S refers to Structural Domains (stable, unchanging)

Prototypal Diagnostic Domains

The major features of this personality pattern are approached in line with the domain levels used in previous chapters. Identifying characteristics often are similar to what we noted in our discussion of the antisocial personality inasmuch as they frequently covary as personality mixtures (see Figure 17.2).

Precipitate expressive behavior.   Many people shy away from these personalities, feeling intimidated by their brusque and belligerent manner. They sense them to be cold and callous, insensitive to the feelings of others, gaining what pleasure they can by competing with and humiliating everyone and anyone. These aggressively oriented personalities tend to be argumentative and contentious. Not infrequently, they are abrasive, cruel, and malicious. They often insist on being seen as faultless, invariably are dogmatic in their opinions, and rarely concede on any issue despite clear evidence negating the validity of their argument. Most behave as if the "softer" emotions were tinged with poison. They avoid expressions of warmth and intimacy and are suspicious of gentility, compassion, and kindness, often seeming to doubt the genuineness of these feelings.

They have a low tolerance for frustration and are especially sensitive to reproachful or deprecating comments. When pushed on personal matters or faced with belittlement, they are likely to respond quickly and to become furious and vindictive; easily provoked to attack, their first inclination is to demean and to dominate. In sum, sadists are disposed to react suddenly and abruptly, evidencing outbursts of an unexpected and unwarranted nature. Although it is not true of all sadists, there is a tendency to be recklessly reactive and daring, to be unflinching and undeterred by pain, as well as undaunted by danger and punishment.

Abrasive interpersonal style.   Sadistic personalities, by definition, reveal satisfaction in intimidating, coercing, and humiliating others. Some are experts in expressing verbally abusive and derisive social comments. Others exhibit physically vicious and

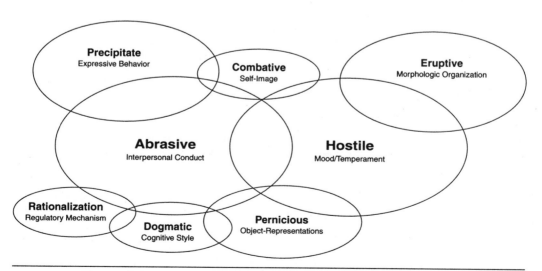

Figure 17.2   Status of the prototypal aggressive (sadistic) domains.

brutal behaviors. Still others are sexually abusive, enjoying the process of demeaning members of their own or the opposite sex.

Not only does the strategy of assertion and domination gain release from past injustices, but, as with most coping maneuvers, it often proves successful in achieving current psychological rewards. Because most persons are intimidated by hostility, sarcasm, criticism, and threats of physical violence, the aggressive demeanor of these personalities is a powerful instrument for coercing others and for frightening them into fearful respect and submission. Moreover, some sadistic/aggressive personalities frequently find a successful niche for themselves in roles where their hostile and belligerent behaviors are not only sanctioned but admired. The ruthless and cleverly conniving businessman, the intimidating and brutalizing sergeant, the self-righteous and punitive headmistress, the demanding and dominating surgical chief, all illustrate roles that provide outlets for vengeful hostility cloaked in the guise of a socially responsible and admirable function.

Dogmatic cognitive style.   Despite their seemingly crude and callous actions, many sadistics are finely attuned to the subtle elements of human interaction. A minor segment within this group may be constitutionally gross and insensitive, but the great majority, though appearing to be coarse and unperceptive, are in fact quite keenly aware of the moods and feelings of others. Their ostensive insensitivity stems from their tendency to use what weaknesses they see in others for the purpose of upsetting the other's equilibrium. In short, they take advantage of their perception of the foibles and sensitivities of others to manipulate and be intentionally callous.

It would not be inconsistent to find that most aggressives/sadistics are strongly opinionated and closed-minded with regard to their beliefs and values. Once they have a point of view, they will not change it. Hence, they tend to be unbending and obstinate in holding to their preconceptions. Of additional interest is the disposition of these personalities to a broad-ranging social intolerance and prejudice, especially toward envied or derogated social groups, ethnic, racial, or otherwise.

Of special note is the sadist's unusual sensitivity to signs of derision and derogation from others. Owing to their expectation of disparagement and belittlement, they are likely to see it in the most neutral and incidental of remarks or "looks." Should they be unable to vent the rage that such poor-mouthing and denigration evoke within them, it is probable that their fury will be discharged toward the first person they meet—most typically, after a few drinks, toward members of their immediate family.

Combative self-image.   The majority of sadistic personalities are likely to view themselves as assertive, energetic, self-reliant, and perhaps hardboiled, but honest, strong, and realistic. If we accept their premise that ours is a dog-eat-dog world, we can understand why they would prefer a self-image of being tough, forthright, and unsentimental rather than malicious and vindictive. Hence, these personalities seem proud to characterize themselves as competitive, vigorous, and militantly hardheaded. Some value aspects of themselves that present a pugnacious, domineering, and power-oriented image, all of which enhances their sense of self and gives a favorable interpretation to their malevolent behaviors.

Pernicious object-representations.   The inner templates that guide the perceptions and behaviors of the sadistic personality are composed of aggressive feelings and memories and images comprising harsh relationships and malicious attitudes. Hence, whatever they experience in life is immediately recast to reflect the expectancy of hostility and the need to preempt it. Not to be overlooked, also, is the fact that there is a marked paucity of tender and sentimental objects, and an underdevelopment of images that activate feelings of shame or guilt. In their deeply imbued jungle philosophy of life, where "might makes right," the only course to which they are disposed is to act in a bold, critical, assertive, and ruthless manner.

The harsh and antihumanistic dispositions of the sadistic personality are manifested in a number of ways. Some are adept at pointing out the hypocrisy and ineffectuality of so-called do-gooders. They rail against the devastating consequences of international appeasement. They justify their toughness and cunning by pointing to the hostile and exploitive behavior of others. Contemptuous of the weak and the underprivileged, they do not care at all if they are looked on with disfavor. They claim that "good guys come in last," and so on. To them, the only way to survive in this world is to dominate and control it.

Isolation regulatory mechanism. Intrapsychically and dynamically, the most distinctive transformations of the sadist's inner world are those processed by the isolation mechanism. Many of these personalities are remarkably and cold-bloodedly detached from an awareness of the impact of their destructive acts. For example, their wives and children are perceived as objects devoid of human feeling and sensibility. The painful consequences of their cruel behaviors are kept from mind. In the same manner, sadists who engage in group scapegoating view the objects of their violations impersonally, merely as despised symbols of a devalued people, devoid of human sensibilities and feelings.

Despite the relative openness with which aggressives voice their thoughts and feelings, they have learned that there are times when it is best to restrain and transmute them. One cannot function effectively in society if one constantly bursts forth with hostility. To soften and redirect these urges, these individuals depend primarily on three mechanisms: rationalization, sublimation, and projection. The simplest means of justifying one's aggressive urges is to find a plausible and socially acceptable excuse for them. Thus, the blunt directness that characterizes the aggressive's social behavior is rationalized as signifying frankness and honesty, a lack of hypocrisy, and a willingness to face issues head-on—as being realistic and not mealy-mouthed and softheaded. More long-range and socially sanctioned resolutions of hostile urges are seen in the occupations to which these aggressive personalities gravitate. Many sublimate their impulses in highly competitive business enterprises, military careers, the legal profession, and so on. Disposed to ward off threat by aggressive counteraction, this type accentuates the disapproval they anticipate from others by projecting their own hostility onto them. This act enables these personalities to justify their aggressive actions because they perceive themselves to be the object of unjust persecution.

Eruptive morphologic organization. In the main, the morphologic structure of the sadist's inner world is composed of routinely adequate modulating controls, reasonable defensive operations, and numerous expressive channels. Nevertheless, there are powerful and explosive energies of an aggressive and sexual nature that are so forceful as to periodically overwhelm and overrun these otherwise competent restraints. As a consequence, periodic eruptions are manifested, resulting in the harsh and cruel behaviors we see among these personalities.

Similarly, the psychic organization of sadists possesses intense and explosive emotions derived from the nature of their early life experiences. Rather than backing off and restraining these internalized experiences and objects, they become quickly or persistently manifested in overt actions. Furthermore, these personalities dread the thought of being vulnerable, of being deceived, and of being humiliated. They assume they will receive no greater kindness from others than they have in the past. Others are seen as potentially threatening, and sadists claim they must be aggressive to defend themselves. Their principal task is to gain power over others before others can outfox and dominate them. People are seen as ruthless. It is this "fact" that makes them act as they do. They must outmaneuver others at their own game. Personal feelings are a sign of weakness and of maudlin and sloppy sentimentality. No one can make it in this life if he or she lets feelings get in the way.

Hostile mood/temperament.   Many sadists have an excitable and irritable temper that flares readily into contentious arguments and physical belligerence. Others are notably mean-spirited and fractious, willing to do harm, perhaps even to persecute others as a means of getting their own way. Beyond their callous disdain for the rights of others, these personalities may be deficient in the capacity to share tender feelings, to experience genuine affection and love for another or to empathize with their needs. Among the more vicious types, pleasure is gained in both the thought and process of hurting others and in seeing them downtrodden and suffering pain. Thus, many sadistic personalities are not only devoid of guilt or remorse for their malicious acts, but they may obtain a perverse and cruel satisfaction thereby. To achieve these malevolent ends, sadists may go out of their way to intimidate and harm others, enjoying not only the tangible fruits of their abuse and deceit but the distress and misery they leave in their wake.

Self-Perpetuation Processes

Despite the fact that behavioral strategies have been learned to optimize positive experiences, they produce, as do all pathological strategies, certain self-defeating actions. They are not only adaptively inflexible and thereby ineffective in dealing with novel challenges, but they rest on a rather tenuous and easily upset psychic balance. Perhaps their most destructive consequence is that they foster rather than resolve problems (see Table 17.2).

Perceptual and cognitive distortions.   Most of what is communicated and experienced in life is fragmentary in nature: a few words, an intonation, a gesture. On the basis of these suggestive but incomplete messages, we come to some conclusion or inference as to what others seek to convey. We constantly "read between the lines" on the basis of past experiences, enabling us thereby to give these incidental cues their coherence and meaning. Among the determinants of what we "fill in" are our moods and anticipations. If we expect someone to be cruel and abusive, we are likely to piece together the hazy elements of the communication in line with this expectancy. If we feel downhearted some days, it appears that the whole world is downcast and gloomy with us. Because the outlook and moods of most of us are episodic and temporary, these intrusions tend to be counterbalanced. That is, we may be suspicious of certain persons

TABLE 17.2 Self-Perpetuating Processes

SADISTIC
Perceptual-Cognitive Distortions
   Others seen as devious and derogatory
   Unable to recognize objective goodwill
   Creates imagined dangers

Contempt for Warmth and Affection
   Empathy seen as repugnant
   Tender feelings subvert hardheaded realism
   Abusive manner blocks others' affections

Creates Realistic Antagonisms
   Intentionally provokes conflict
   Seeks challenges and dangers
   Imagined humiliations become reality

but overly naïve with others; we may feel "blue" some days but cheerful and optimistic on others.

This pattern of variability and balancing of mood and attitude is less typical of pathological than "normal" personalities. In the aggressive/sadistic individual, for example, there is an ever-present undertone of anger and resentment, a persistent expectation that others will be deviously denigrating, if not openly hostile. Because these moods and expectancies endure, these personalities are likely to repeatedly distort the incidental remarks and actions of others so that they appear to deprecate and vilify them. They persist in misinterpreting what they see and hear and magnify minor slights into major insults and slanders.

Despite the fact that this personality's aggressive reaction to external threat is understandable, given past experience, it promotes repetitive self-defeating consequences. For example, by perceiving derogation from others where none exists, these individuals prevent themselves from recognizing and appreciating the objective goodwill of others when it is there. Their reality is what they perceive, not what objectively exists. Thus, their vulnerability to deprecation blocks them from recognizing the presence of experiences that might prove gratifying and thereby change the course of their outlook and attitudes. Moreover, their distortion aggravates their misfortunes by creating, through anticipation, fictitious dangers and humiliations that duplicate those of the past. Rather than avoiding further pain and abuse, the antisocial's hypersensitivity to derogation uncovers them where they do not exist. In essence, their moods and defenses have fabricated dangers from which sadists cannot escape because they derive from within themselves.

Demeaning of affection and cooperative behavior.   This personality is not only suspicious of but tends to depreciate sentimentality, intimate feelings, tenderness, and social cooperativeness. These individuals lack sympathy for the weak and oppressed and are often contemptuous of those who express compassion and concern for the "underdog." Given their past, there is little reason to expect that sadistic personalities would be empathic and sentimental. What affection and consideration did they enjoy in childhood? They learned too well that it is best to trust no one. Why be sympathetic and kindly? Should they chance again the rebuffs they believe they suffered at the hands of their parents and later, in the case of the several subtypes, from society as a whole? Will not others undo them and infringe on the fragile self-esteem that they so desperately seek to uplift, and that is so vital to them?

By denying tender feelings, they protect themselves against the memory of painful parental rejections. Furthermore, feelings of sympathy would be antithetical to the credo they have carved for themselves as a philosophy of life. To express the "softer" emotions would only undermine the foundations of their coping strategy and reactivate feelings that they have rigidly denied for years. Why upset things and be abused and exploited again? Sympathy and tender feelings only "get in the way," distract and divert one from being the hardheaded realist one must be. Of course, this very attitude creates a vicious circle. By restraining positive feelings and repudiating intimacy and cooperative behaviors, these personalities provoke others to withdraw from them. Their cold and abusive manner intimidates others and blocks them from expressing warmth and affection. Once again, by their own action, they create experiences that only perpetuate the frosty, condemning, and rejecting environment of their childhood.

Creating realistic antagonisms.   Both the sadistic personality and the malevolent antisocial subtype evoke counterhostility, not only as an incidental consequence of their behaviors and attitudes but because they intentionally provoke others into conflict. They carry a "chip on their shoulder," often seem to be spoiling for a fight, and appear to enjoy tangling with others to prove their strength and test their competencies and powers. Having been periodically successful in past aggressive ventures, they feel confident of their prowess. They may seek out dangers and challenges. Not only are they unconcerned and reckless, but they appear poised and bristling, ready to vent resentments, demonstrate their invulnerability, and restore their pride.

Unfortunately, as with their perceptions and attitudes, these aggressive, conflict-seeking behaviors only perpetuate their fears and misery. More than merely fostering distance and rejection, they have now provoked others into justified counterhostility. By spoiling for a fight and by precipitous and irrational arrogance, they create not only a distant reserve on the part of others but intense and well-justified animosity. Now they must face real aggression, and now they have a real basis for anticipating retaliation. Objective threats and resentments do exist in the environment now, and the *vicious* circle is perpetuated anew. Their vigilant state cannot be relaxed; they must ready themselves, no longer for suspected threat and imagined hostility, but for the real thing.

INTERVENTION GOALS

The prognostic picture for this personality cannot be viewed as promising, unless the person has found a socially sanctioned sphere in which to channel his or her energies and hostilities. Even though a large majority of these individuals are able to disguise their pathological character by selecting vocations and hobbies that provide a socially acceptable outlet for their aggressive impulses, the persistent nature of their condition will eventually get them into trouble. At work, such individuals may have misused their status, and at home, domestic violence may have escalated. The strain on coworkers and family members has become so great that, as a last resort, these personalities are "forced" to seek help.

In other cases, the criminal justice system may have caught up with the transgressor. Violent and controlling behaviors that earlier were sanctioned are likely to have deteriorated into vengeful actions against arbitrary victims. These acts may no longer be tolerated, because the transgressions have become so blatant that the public can no longer claim ignorance, and societal pressures force law enforcers to take an active stance.

Not uncommonly, sadists lack insight into the nature of their interpersonal difficulties and the emotional distress they cause. More often, they simply do not care. Capacity for insight, however, is not a guarantee that treatment will succeed. Because it is impossible to force collaboration and coerce these patients to truly engage in treatment, it is unlikely that much of the underlying personality structure will be altered by the therapeutic process.

Cardinal aims of personologic therapy with the sadistic personality are to balance the polarities by reversing the discordance of pain-pleasure and reducing the active self-focus. Other important goals of treatment are to increase interpersonal sensitivity and reduce the sadistic's hostile and, at times, volatile moods. Improvements in these and other domains are central to reversing the perpetuation of the maladaptive pattern (see Table 17.3).

Reestablishing Polarity Balances

The sadistic personality's primary mode of relating to others is by inflicting pain. The humiliation and victimization of others allows sadists to discharge pent-up anger and their own psychic pain. For some, this is experienced as pleasurable, even though it objectively runs counter to life enhancement. Sadists actively engage in behaviors that will allow them to control and display dominance over others. Ideally, therapeutic intervention would assist these personalities in recognizing that rewards can be obtained from interpersonal relationships devoid of destructive elements and thereby remediate the reversal in the pain-pleasure polarity.

TABLE 17.3   Therapeutic Strategies and Tactics for the Prototypal Sadistic (Aggressie) Personality

STRATEGIC GOALS
Balance Polarities
  Reverse discordance of pain-pleasure polarity
  Reduce active self-focus

Counter Perpetuations
  Control abusive behaviors
  Identify precipitants of acting-out
  Modify macho-truculent image

TACTICAL MODALITIES
  Moderate hostile moods
  Undo interpersonal abrasiveness
  Control precipitous behaviors

The active approach of these personalities takes the form of manipulative schemes, venomous acts of cruelty, and, at times, reckless outbursts of hostility without control. The therapist must work with the sadistic personality to move him or her toward the passive end of the continuum and facilitate the acquisition of greater restraint and compassion. Sadistics are generally unmoved by the hurtful consequences of their malicious intentions. Balancing the self-other polarity can be promoted by augmenting sadists' ability not only to empathize with others, but to encourage them to engage in acts that lead to the preservation rather than the destruction of life.

Countering Perpetuating Tendencies

Given their early hurtful experiences, it is not surprising that sadists have come to expect abuse from others. However, this expectancy is often unrealistic in their current environment. These personalities have learned to selectively attend to stimuli from their surroundings that tend to support their distorted beliefs. Most of their current experiences are malevolently colored and the benign motives of others are misconstrued. It is therefore important that therapeutic strategies focus on increasing accurate perceptual judgments and reducing cognitive distortions. Gradually, aiding the sadistic personality to interpret the environment in a more realistic manner will be an important step in exposing the person to potentially gratifying experiences and reversing the maladaptive pattern.

Sadists have further learned to be wary and distrustful of others. Displaying sentiments and responding sympathetically to others are interactional styles they carefully avoid to protect themselves from anticipated humiliation and abuse. Although this rigid coping style allows these individuals to practice great restraint in displaying emotions, others tend to be intimidated by this "macho" image and are likely to withdraw as a result. To prevent the re-creation of earlier unloving and hostile experiences, sadistic personalities must learn to be more emotionally involved in their relationships with others. This will be facilitated if they allow their softer side to emerge. Intervention must stress further social cooperation rather then personal individuation.

A vital component of the vicious circle that sadistics have created for themselves is their hostile and belligerent mode of interacting. One of the rewards of this interactional style is the feeling of self-importance. Not surprisingly, their aggressive and reckless ventures provoke counterhostility, and what once was an imagined foe, may now be an actual adversary. Sadists must learn to put down their weapons and let down their guard. Assisting these individuals in finding alternative avenues for self-enhancement without "attacking" others may provide a link to a new chain of positive reactions. Their image will gradually improve once the acting-out behaviors are under control.

Identifying Domain Dysfunctions

The most salient dysfunctions in the sadistic personality are in the mood and interpersonal conduct domains. Hostile moods and an abrasive interpersonal style are central characteristics of this cruel and abusive personality. To these individuals, coercion and intimidation are instrumental in providing rewards and a sense of personal control. Teaching sadists alternative styles of interacting that will enhance their self-efficacy, as well as encouraging them to sublimate their aggression more appropriately, may have important therapeutic implications.

Other prominent dysfunctions are observed in the expressive behavior and morphological organization domains. Uncontrolled outbursts of aggressive impulses will sporadically wipe out otherwise adequate control mechanisms. Sadists, however, are undeterred by the consequences of their explosive reactions. This lack of regard for possible negative repercussions is one of the reasons these domains are so difficult to influence. One of the goals of personologic therapy with this disorder is to facilitate the acquisition of more prosocial behaviors. This includes teaching sadists to display greater restraint when impulses threaten to overwhelm them. Helping these individuals gain control over their eruptive behavior will facilitate work in other domains.

Sadists will be hard-pressed to give up those behaviors that have been instrumental for so long. Not only do their internalized representations of the past contain mainly destructive elements, but sadists also lack those sentiments that would allow them to show compassion for others and feel remorse for any harm done. Instead, they regard others merely as impersonal objects not worthy of respect. In contrast, most sadists view themselves as strong, hardheaded, and competitive. These personality features will be difficult to alter because their dogmatic and rigid cognitive style is likely to interfere with efforts to modify other domain dysfunctions. Cognitive restructuring can aid these individuals to broaden their perspective and enable them to make more accurate attributions.

Therapeutic efforts to improve cognitive as well as other areas of functioning should draw on the self-serving motives that underlie the sadistic's behavior. Although it is unlikely that treatment will transform such individuals into compassionate, self-sacrificing human beings, if they perceive that displaying such behaviors is in their best interest, progress can be made.

SELECTING THERAPEUTIC MODALITIES

The treatment of the sadistic personality presents quite a challenge for the therapist. Often, these individuals enter the therapeutic arena involuntarily and will comply only superficially to satisfy others' demands. The therapist will have to be careful not to be conned into believing that actual therapeutic gains have been achieved when they have not. Sadistic patients will be hard-pressed to recognize and admit their contribution to the presenting problem; instead, they will blame their victims.

Of therapeutic relevance are the resources available to the therapist and the patient's level of motivation. For example, a more controlled setting such as an institution allows the therapist to exercise greater control over the patient's immediate environment. Similarly, if family members or significant others can be targeted for intervention as well, the chances of maintaining progress are greater. It is unlikely that interventions that target only specific symptoms will have long-range effects if the context or source of the sadist's problems remains as before.

Behavioral Techniques

Behavioral intervention may be employed to target both aggressive and impulsive symptomatology. Appropriate methods should be selected depending on the function these behaviors serve. For some, explosive outbursts of violence signify a release of pent-up anger. Teaching these individuals impulse management techniques may enhance their ability to keep their anger under control. Relaxation training can help reduce the frustration that tends to escalate and overwhelm them. Once the therapist has gained a greater understanding of the situations that tend to elicit anger, a hierarchy of anger-arousing stimuli can be set up as part of systematic desensitization. Anger management efforts may also involve social skills training with an emphasis on improving less hostile forms of assertiveness, as well as making environmental modifications to help the patient avoid upsetting stimuli.

For other sadistic patients, aggression serves an instrumental purpose. The therapist may have to deal more directly with the calculated nature of their maliciousness by impressing on these patients that adverse consequences will be imminent. These individuals are, however, unlikely to benefit solely from aversive conditioning. Teaching them self-management techniques may be beneficial if the rationale is presented that they exert more control this way.

It is clear that sadistic personalities represent a rather heterogeneous group; interventions will have to be carefully selected to reflect the therapist's conceptualization of each patient's problems. A behavioral formulation based on a detailed functional analysis will aid the therapist in gaining a more accurate understanding of the contextual determinants that are instrumental to the maintenance and perpetuation of aggressive behaviors.

Unfortunately, the effectiveness of behavioral methods is questionable. Some methods, such as contingency management programs, are best utilized in institutional settings where more control can be exercised over the distribution of reinforcers. Unfortunately, treatment gains rarely extend far beyond the therapy setting. The problems with behavior generalization and maintenance may be due to the lack of environmental consistency. Working with the patient's spouse or family whenever possible may enhance treatment efficacy.

Interpersonal Techniques

Interpersonal techniques, such as those recommended by L.S. Benjamin (1993) for the treatment of the antisocial personality, can also be utilized with sadistic patients. Unfortunately, collaboration, a vital component of the interpersonal approach, is hard to achieve. Benjamin suggests several alternative methods for eliciting collaboration and fostering bonding. One example is placing the patient in an institutional setting where more control can be exercised over the interpersonal messages from staff members. As a result, one of the links in the perpetuating chain, that of others reinforcing aggressive-sadistic acts, is broken. Another goal of these interventions is to set up alternative bonding experiences as well as situations that promote collaboration. Exposing sadistic patients to a variety of "life-enhancing" experiences may fuel their desire to give up controlling and exploitive behaviors. Benjamin stresses, however, that unless the link between violent acts and the consequent "highs" that they may generate has been broken, sadistic individuals will see little reason to end their practices.

Group therapy may be indicated because for many sadists, this setting may present a less emotionally threatening environment than does individual therapy. The most effective groups are probably those in institutional settings where more control can be exerted over stable attendance, an important factor in the development of a cohesive group. Members in the group can exert pressure on the patient to express resentments and anger verbally, thereby reducing acting-out behavior. Gabbard (1994) notes that in some specialized settings, such as the Patuxtent, treatment is enhanced by the homogeneous compositions of the residents. This program uses group confrontation by peers who may be more effective in engaging the sadistic patient owing to their considerable familiarity with the manipulative and cunning schemes he or she employs.

Family and couples therapy may be indicated when those individuals in the sadist's immediate surroundings are experiencing extreme discomfort. The family may inadvertently support the sadist's maladaptive patterns. Fostering growth of the family unit as a whole may depend on the cooperation of the other members. When working with families and couples, the therapist must take care to investigate both partners' history of abuse. A wife who has been abused in the past may have come to expect revictimization. As Stone (1993) notes, unhappy marriages often consist of a victimizer-victim pairing. He further points out that the therapist may have difficulty empathizing with the more openly abusive partner. If these countertransference feelings persist, it may be wise to use a cotherapist. The therapist can help family members communicate more clearly with each other without criticism and derisive commentary.

Cognitive Techniques

Cognitive techniques, such as those proposed by Beck and Freeman (1990a) for the treatment of the antisocial personality, may also prove useful with sadistic patients. Cognitive therapy can help them shift their thinking from a rigid closed-mindedness to a broader range of cognitions that may generate greater tolerance for the beliefs and values of others.

The sadist's dysfunctional belief system includes the assumption that because he or she has been hurt in the past, similar treatment can be expected in the future. Therefore, it is best not to trust anyone. If others are out to get you, why not beat them first. Maladaptive schemata also include the belief that one should feel pleased with venting one's "powers," regardless of the damage done to others. When exploring these faulty assumptions, the therapist must take care not to "attack" the patient, yet must be sure to communicate that harmful actions are not acceptable. One of the goals of cognitive therapy is to assist patients in reevaluating the consequences of their aggressive behavior and how it adversely impacts everyone in the long run.

Utilizing a cognitive-behavioral approach may be especially helpful with sadists who lack impulse control or act out in a harsh manner with others. Thus, behavioral anger-management techniques may be employed to control patients' impulses and to fully recognize the awful consequences of their behaviors. From this, patients may also acquire a measure of comfort when the former triggers for such action are present. As a consequence, patients may become less inclined to act out problematic thoughts and feelings, acquiring thereby a less intense and hostile inner world.

Furthermore, by learning to engage in prosocial behaviors, patients will avoid the adverse consequences of hostility and, most important, may be able to obtain constructive rewards from more agreeable behaviors. The therapist can aid patients in evaluating the advantages and disadvantages of various options available. Beck and Freeman (1990a) have suggested using a structured format when reviewing different problem areas in the patient's life, and evaluating the "risk-benefit ratio" of various choices. Ideally, cognitive interventions with the sadistic patient will result in a higher level of thinking and moral reasoning, one characterized by tolerance for others, capacity for guilt, and open-mindedness.

Self-Image Techniques

The deep ambivalence that characterizes sadists results in a conflicting set of self-images. On the one hand, sadists express intense hostility by abusing and destroying others; they know this to be a true element of themselves. On the other hand, most sadists feel a considerable measure of shame and guilt for the havoc they wreak. Although these contradictory images of self coexist, the patient may try, albeit unsuccessfully, to bring them together into a synthetic oneness. Several self-actualizing procedures may prove helpful; for example, a Rogerian method may assist patients to express their contradictory feelings, enabling the therapist to have patients see how their sense of self is conflictful. These methods may also be productive in providing opportunities for imaginal ventilation and, hence, reducing to some degree the actuality of their feelings of anger. Similarly, a dialogue of an existential-humanistic nature may provide patients with an opportunity to recognize that their sadistic urges are not as reprehensible as they may feel them to be. Along another line, Glasser's Reality/Control methods may be employed to teach patients to face the destructive consequences of their behaviors, as well as to develop constructive attitudes to replace those of a more destructive nature. Also of potential use are experiential techniques that may help patients to become aware of the prodromal cues that signify a desire to discharge anger before they reach an explosive extreme.

Intrapsychic Techniques

Psychodynamic approaches may prove useful if the patient is sincerely engaged in the therapeutic process. One of the goals of analytically oriented intervention is to help patients recognize their own contribution to their difficulties and to minimize the use of defenses such as isolation, rationalization, and projection. Sadistic patients must relinquish claims that they deserve rewards for their behavior. There may be times that countertransference feelings such as impatience, annoyance, hatred, and riddance wishes will be elicited (Stone, 1993). If perceived as such by the patient, such feelings recreate the atmosphere of early home life. The therapist must contain his or her feelings instead of acting on them, thereby providing the patient with a new object relationship. Stone notes that, in time, patients may come to understand how the attack mode elicits defensiveness and counterattack from others. Eventually, they may be able to recognize that their preconceptions about others may be partially incorrect. These benevolent experiences may overpower the internal images of significant figures from the past as being malevolent.

Blackburn (1993) notes that it is unlikely that therapy will have favorable results unless the patient is able to express emotions. Strong affect will appear only after the patient has been in treatment for a prolonged period of time. These new feelings are bound to be alien to the sadistic patient and may induce anxiety. The therapist must therefore continually provide encouragement.

Pharmacologic Techniques

Pharmacotherapy plays a minor role in the treatment of the sadistic personality. To these personalities, the use of medications may be viewed as a threat to self-control and may further signify weakness. The utility of lithium may be evaluated when aggressive and impulsive behaviors predominate or when violent mood swings occur. To gain collaboration, the therapist must emphasize to the patient how the medication can increase self-control.

MAKING SYNERGISTIC ARRANGEMENTS

Although each of the approaches discussed previously has its own merits, those programs that rely on a combination of techniques are more likely to influence the different domain dysfunctions. Interventions where the therapist has more control over the patient's environment should be considered if the resources are available. In these controlled settings, patients will experience less difficulty in gaining control over their hostile impulses. Anger-arousing stimuli can also be kept to a minimum. Growth in this area can then facilitate work in other domains.

If the sadistic personality becomes involved in individual psychotherapy first, it is imperative that he or she perceive possible gains from treatment. Otherwise, the patient is likely to drop out. Once again, the therapist will have to emphasize that the techniques employed are in the patient's best interest. For example, gaining control over one's volatile nature will reduce others' tendency to withdraw or react with counterhostility. Adjuncts such as group and family methods should be considered from the onset, because they promote system change rather than individual change. Family therapy may increase empathy and emotional involvement with the other members of the system, thereby promoting the development of trust and tolerance for others. Over time, interpersonal and psychodynamic approaches may aid the patient in developing more secure object relations.

Illustrative Cases

It may seem strange in this text to discuss subtypes of the sadistic personality, given the fact that the broader construct of a sadistic personality type has itself been deleted

TABLE 17.4   Sadistic Personality Disorder Subtypes

Explosive: Unpredictably precipitous outbursts and fury; uncontrollable rage and fearsome attacks; feelings of humiliation are pent-up and discharged; subsequently contrite.

MCMI 6B

Spineless: Basically insecure, bogus, and cowardly; venomous dominance and cruelty is counterphobic; weakness counteracted by group support; public swaggering; selects powerless scapegoats.

MCMI 6B-2A

Enforcing: Hostility sublimated in the "pubic interest"; cops, "bossy" supervisors, deans, judges; possess the "right" to be pitiless, merciless, coarse, and barbarous; task is to control and punish, to search out rule breakers.

MCMI 6B-7

Tyrannical: Relishes menacing and brutalizing others, forcing them to cower and submit; verbally cutting and scathing, accusatory and destructive; intentionally surly, abusive, inhumane, unmerciful.

MCMI 6B-8A/P

from the official *DSM-IV* classification system. One might ask, Why bother describing multiple variants of a personality disorder that is no longer part of the *DSM?* As noted earlier, it is the belief of the author that the sadistic personality prototype should have remained as part of the official classification. Hence, the recognition that several varieties of the disorder are likely to exist seems to be a reasonable position. In the following sections, we describe some of the central features that may differentiate the major subtypes of this disorder (see Table 17.4).

SADISTIC PERSONALITY: EXPLOSIVE TYPE
(SADISTIC WITH BORDERLINE FEATURES)

CASE 17.1, JOE T., 33

Presenting Picture: Joe T. seemed to lose control without warning. He sought therapy mainly at of the insistence of his girlfriend, but also expressed an interest in understanding and changing his outbursts, though it was unclear as to how genuine this motivation was. Typically, he stated, he would be involved in a nonphysical, seemingly unemotional argument with his girlfriend, and very suddenly and without much warning, he would be overcome with a "blind rage" and would hit her. He described the sensation of his entire body becoming "hot," but this would only occur a few seconds before the explosion. He stated that he did not like anyone telling him what to do or what he can or cannot do, and he described a long history of anger, dating back to childhood. His parents frequently slapped him, and when he grew older, he eventually slapped them back. By the age of 15, he had run away from home. He stated that this was certainly not the first time he had been physically hostile in a relationship, but this was the first instance when he sought to change this pattern.

Clinical Assessment: It is the unpredictability and sudden emergence of hostility that differentiates Joe, an *explosive sadist,* from other variants of this personality type. Joe manifested adult tantrums, uncontrollable rage, and fearsome attacks on others, most frequently against members of his family or his girlfriend. Before its intensive nature could be identified and constrained, there was a rapid escalation of fury in which unforgivable things were said and unforgettable blows were struck.

Explosive behaviors erupted precipitously. Feeling thwarted or threatened, Joe responded in a volatile and hurtful way, bewildering others by the abrupt change that had overtaken him. As with children, tantrums were instantaneous reactions to cope with frustration or fear. Often effective in intimidating others into silence or passivity, this explosive behavior was not primarily an instrumentality, but rather an outburst that served to discharge pent-up feelings of humiliation and degradation.

Disappointed and feeling frustrated in life, Joe lost control and sought revenge for the mistreatment and deprecation to which he felt subjected. In contrast to other sadists, Joe did not move about in a surly and truculent manner. Rather, his rage burst out uncontrollably, often unpredictably, and with no apparent provocation. In periods of explosive rage, he unleashed a torrent of abuse and stormed about defiantly, cursing and voicing bitter contempt for all. It is this quality of sudden and irrational belligerence and the frenzied lashing out that distinguishes this form of sadistic disorder from the others. Many such as Joe are hypersensitive to feelings of betrayal or may be deeply frustrated by the futility and hopelessness of their lives.

Faced with repeated failures, humiliations, and frustrations, Joe's limited controls were quickly overrun by deeply felt and undischarged resentments. Once released, the fury of the moment drew on the memories and emotions of the past that were surging unrestrained to the surface and breaking out into a wild, irrational, and uncontrollable rage. From the preceding descriptions, it would not be unreasonable to hypothesize that Joe possessed beneath his surface controls a wide-ranging pattern akin to what we describe as borderline. Periodically under control, but lacking the cohesion of psychic structure to maintain these controls, Joe periodically erupted with the precipitous and vindictive behaviors that signify his sadistic personality style.

Whether justified or not, certain persons came to symbolize for Joe the sense of frustration and hopelessness he felt and that sparked his explosive reactions. In his eyes, these symbolic figures had to be obliterated. Unable to resolve the real sources of his resentment and frustration, these symbols of his feelings of futility and hopelessness *had to* be removed from the scene, lest they block all avenues of escape. Feeling trapped and impotent, Joe would be provoked into a panic and blind rage. His violence was a desperate lashing out against symbols rather than reality.

The physical assaults Joe meted out during these periods were likely to be the product of a verbally unskilled individual seeking to terminate an altercation in which he felt incapable of responding effectively. Unable to verbalize what and why he felt the way he did, sensing being outmaneuvered and humiliated, he responded in the only way he could to remove the irritation he felt. Impotence and personal failure were the sources from which the aggressive act drew its impetus.

The violence of the attack served to release accumulated tensions. In many ways, the identity of the victim was rather incidental and arbitrarily selected. The explosions were not so much a social response as an emotional release. However, social indifference accounts for but a small portion of explosive abuse. In the main, and as noted previously, the sadist has established "safe partners" for abuse, a person who has come to symbolize their failures and frustrations, someone who "knows" of their inadequacies. With minimal prompting, a full rush of hostile feelings are directed at the symbol of the sadist's discontent. Precipitous abuse is unleashed with minimal justification and minimal provocation. To the explosive sadistic nature of Joe, however, the mere presence of the symbol stirred his deep feelings of failure and reminded him of the violations that life had done to his hopes and his integrity. Although insidious in its development, once "another person" had come to represent his frustrations and life's impossibilities, little was required to prompt an explosive reaction.

Synergistic Treatment Plan: Whether or not Joe's "self-motivated" reasons for seeking treatment were genuine, it was most beneficial that he agreed to therapy, as this aided in rapport and trust building, which is often very difficult with this subtype. Within the context of this therapeutic relationship building, Joe became oriented to a more logical model of interaction. The possibility of becoming sensitive to cues that portend an explosive outburst may lend itself to *experiential* therapy. *Cognitively*, it would be important to identify and reevaluate such precipitants of his "explosions" as his characterological disillusionment, hopelessness, and sense of failure, as well as examine his perceived satisfaction with "obliterating" those people close to him (adjusting the discordance between *pain* and *pleasure*). Rather than regressing into a more primitive stance as a reaction to stress, Joe would be encouraged *interpersonally* to begin exploring improved options for more satisfying relationships and conflict resolution, through a reduction in his engrained *active self*-focus.

Therapeutic Course: Essential to the success of a short-term approach with Joe was the therapist's readiness to see things from his point of view and to convey a sense of trust and create a feeling of alliance. Brief treatment with Joe required a balance of professional firmness and authority, mixed with tolerance for his less attractive traits. By building an image of a fair-minded and strong authority figure, the therapist was able to successfully employ *cognitive* methods that encouraged Joe to change his expectations. Through reasoned and convincing comments, the therapist provided a model for Joe to learn the mix of power, logic, and fairness.

Less confrontive cognitive approaches provided ample opportunities for Joe to vent his anger, even in short-term therapy. Once drained of these hostile feelings, he was led to examine his habitual behavior and cognitive attitudes and was guided into less destructive perceptions and outlets than before. *Interpersonal* methods, such as those of Benjamin and Kiesler, provided a means to explore more socially acceptable behavior. As far as *group* methods were concerned, until Joe had incorporated changed cognitions and actions, he intruded on and disrupted therapeutic functions. This particular therapeutic risk was attempted because he might have become a useful catalyst for short-term group interaction and gained some useful insights and a few constructive skills under slightly different circumstances.

A useful short-term goal for Joe was to enable him to tolerate the experience of guilt or to accept blame for the turmoil he caused. Cognitive methods employing a measure of confrontation helped undermine his tendency to always trace problems to another person's stupidity, laziness, or hostility. When he accepted responsibility for some of his difficulties, it was important that the therapist was prepared to deal with his inclination to resent the therapist for supposedly tricking him into admitting it. Similarly, the therapist was ready to be challenged and to avoid Joe's efforts to outwit him. Joe may have tried to set up situations to test the therapist's skills, to catch inconsistencies, to arouse ire, and, if possible, to belittle and humiliate the therapist. Restraining impulses to express condemning attitudes could have been a major task for the therapist, but one that could have been used for positive gains, especially if tied into the application of combined cognitive (e.g., Beck, Ellis) and interpersonal interventions.

It should be noted that the precipitant for Joe's treatment was more situational than it was internal. Until this most recent incident, he was unlikely to have sought therapy, and he may have been convinced that if he were just left alone, he would work matters out on his own. Such beliefs had to be confronted, albeit carefully. Although this treatment appeared to be self-motivated, it was inspired by a series of family and relationship problems, and quite possibly other social humiliations, legal entanglements, or achievement failures. Whatever its source, a firm cognitive and behavior-change approach was required. For this domineering and often intimidating man, complaints were often expressed in the form of irritability and restlessness. To succeed in his initial disinclination to be frank with authority figures, he wandered from one superficial topic to another. This inclination had to be monitored and prevented. Moreover, contact with the significant people in Joe's life was efficacious, as they sometimes reported matters quite differently than did Joe. To ensure that he took discussions seriously, he had to be confronted directly with evidence of his contribution to his troubles. Treatment was best geared to short-term goals, reestablishing his psychic balance, and strengthening his previously adequate coping behavior with cognitive methods, except for those actions that were frankly antisocial. In general, short-term approaches with Joe were best directed toward building controls rather than insights, toward the here and now rather than the past, and toward teaching him ways to sustain relationships cooperatively rather than with dominance and intimidation.

SADISTIC PERSONALITY: TYRANNICAL TYPE (SADISTIC WITH NEGATIVISTIC AND PARANOID FEATURES)

CASE 17.2, CRAIG F., 41

Presenting Picture: Craig F. was seen as part of a routine screening program for municipal workers. The head of a fire station, Craig was proud that whereas other stations resembled "fraternity houses," his was consistently awarded for top-level discipline, a standard he would do anything to maintain. A former military sergeant, he admitted getting a sort of "high" from pushing his crew's limits in training that went far beyond protocol. When they would reach the point of no further tolerance, Craig mused, he would push them further to break their spirit entirely in order to rebuild it in "his" way. He also liked to find the "runt" of any group and make an example of him. It was brought to his attention that he was the least popular of all station chiefs, to which he responded, "I don't want them to like me." Recently divorced due to "irreconcilable differences," Craig spoke little of his personal life outside of work, mentioning briefly that he was the youngest of four brothers (in response to a direct question) and not close with any of them. In his spare time, he liked to "hole up" in his cabin, where he lived by himself, and paint. Most of his paintings, he said, were of solid architecture, as he liked impermeable structure.

Clinical Assessment: Along with the malevolent antisocial, *tyrannical sadists* such as Craig are among the most frightening and cruel of the personality disorder subtypes. Both subtypes relate to others in an attacking, intimidating, and overwhelming way, both accusatory and abusive and almost invariably destructive. At times, Craig was crudely assaultive and distressingly vulgar, and at other times he was physically restrained yet unrelentingly critical and bitter. There was a verbally or physically overbearing character to his assaults, and even minor resistances or weaknesses stimulated him, encouraging his attack rather than deterring and slowing him down. His forcefulness, his unrestrained character, and his indiscriminate anger were most notable. Descriptively, we may note that Craig appeared to relish the act of menacing and brutalizing others; forcing them to cower and submit seemed to provide him with a special sense of satisfaction. When he was not physically brutal, we saw verbally cutting and scathing commentaries that were both accusatory and demeaning. He frequently intentionally heightened and dramatized his surly, abusive, inhumane, and unmerciful behaviors. Although Craig was in many respects the purest form of the psychopathic sadist, he did exhibit some features of other personality types, most notably the negativistic and/or the paranoid, as was evident in his MCMI scale scores.

What is also especially distinctive was Craig's desire and willingness to go out of his way to be unmerciful and inhumane in his violence. More than any other personality, he derived deep satisfaction in creating suffering and in seeing its effect on others. His mean-spirited disposition led him to abandon universally held constraints that limit the viciousness of one's personal actions. In contrast to the explosive sadist, for whom hostility serves primarily as a discharge of pent-up feelings, Craig employed violence as an intentionally utilized instrument to inspire terror and intimidation. Moreover, he could self-consciously observe and reflect on the consequences of his violence, and do so with a deep sense of satisfaction. Many other sadists, by contrast, would experience second thoughts and feel a measure of contrition about the violence they had produced.

Often calculating and cool, Craig was selective in his choice of victims, identifying scapegoats who were not likely to react with counterviolence. He employed violence to secure cooperation and obeisance from his victims. Quite frequently, he displayed a disproportionate level of abusiveness and intimidation to impress not only the victim but those who observed his own unconstrained power. Circumstances such as these are often seen not only in settings such as Craig's (e.g., settings with formal protocol, military operations) but also in the behavior of street gangs and prisons.

Much of what motivated Craig was his fear that others may recognize his inner insecurities and low sense of self-esteem. To overcome these deeply felt inner weaknesses, he learned that he could feel superior by overwhelming others by the force of his physical power and brutal vindictiveness: "I am superior to you. I can defeat you in all things that matter. I will triumph over you despite your past achievements and superior talents. In the end, I will be the victor." Once unleashed, the power of vindication drew on deep fantasies of cruel and unmitigated revenge. There were no internal brakes to constrain him until his fury was spent. There was little remorse for the fury of his violence and the destructive consequences he created.

Synergistic Treatment Plan: Immediate attention needed to be focused on drawing Craig into the process of treatment, as he was undoubtedly going to be quite resistant. *Cognitive* strategies would be the most appropriate choice, in initial stages, to develop a therapeutic alliance. Further cognitive and *interpersonal* methods would address his constitutional anger, examine and correct his perpetuating need to dominate *others,* and acclimate him to appreciate the difficult experience of the people around him. It would be necessary to work toward a dissipation of his *active-pain* orientation as well as an augmentation of his empathy for *others. Behavioral* techniques of anger management would be used throughout the course of treatment as a useful procedure to achieve these goals.

Therapeutic Course: A short-term and circumscribed focus was optimally suited to Craig. Directive *cognitive techniques,* such as those of Meichenbaum and Ellis, were used to confront him with the obstructive and self-defeating character of his expectations and his personal relations. Formal *behavior modification* methods were fruitfully explored to achieve greater consistency and interpersonal harmony in his social behavior. Although the deeply rooted character of these problems impeded the effectiveness of most therapeutic procedures, it was fruitful to explore the more confrontive and incisive techniques of both cognitive and *interpersonal* therapies (e.g., Benjamin, Kiesler). A thorough reconstruction of personality was not the only means of altering Craig's deeper pathologies. In support of short-term interpersonal techniques, *family* treatment methods were utilized to focus on the complex network of relationships that sustained his personality style. Together with cognitive reframing procedures, this proved to be among the most useful techniques to help him recognize the source of his own hurt and angry feelings and to appreciate how he provoked hurt and anger in others.

Not surprisingly, Craig actively resisted exploring his motives. Although he did not start out an active and willing participant in therapy, a strong and persuasive cognitive approach drew him into the therapeutic process. He submitted to therapy under the press of vocational discord, but he learned to see the benefits of reframing his attitudes and the consequences of doing so. For example, he may have been in trouble as a consequence of aggressive or abusive behavior or as a result of incessant quarrels, but each of these was diminished by viewing his behavior differently and by acquiring other means of fulfilling the needs that drove them. With confronting methods, Craig learned not to assume that a problem was always traceable to another person's stupidity or laziness. As he found it possible to accept a measure of responsibility for his difficulties, he did not conclude that the therapist tricked him into admitting it. In this situation, the therapist restrained any impulse to react to him with general disapproval or criticism. An important step in building rapport with Craig was to see things from his viewpoint. If success was to be achieved in a short-term intervention, the therapist needed to convey a sense of trust and a willingness to develop a constructive alliance. A balance of professional authority and tolerance was useful to diminish the probability that he would relapse or impulsively withdraw from treatment.

As noted, Craig did not start out a willing participant in therapy, and agreed to treatment under the pressure of vocational difficulties. A strong and determined attitude overcame his desire to outwit the therapist by setting up situations to test the therapist's skills, to catch inconsistencies, to arouse ire, and, if possible, to belittle and humiliate the therapist. For the therapist, restraining the impulse to express a condemning attitude was not a difficult task. Goal-directed in a brief treatment program, the therapist was able to check any hostile feelings, keeping in mind that Craig's difficulties were not fully under his control. Nevertheless, Craig may have actively impeded his progress toward conflict resolution and goal attainment, undoing what good he had previously achieved in treatment. A combination of cognitive and interpersonal techniques was employed with behavioral anger management to counteract his contrary feelings and his inclination to retract his more kindly expectations of others and quickly rebuild the few advances that he and the therapist had struggled to attain. A committed and professional approach prevented relapses by confronting the ambivalence that stood to rob him of what steps he had secured toward progress.

SADISTIC PERSONALITY: ENFORCING TYPE (SADISTIC WITH COMPULSIVE FEATURES)

CASE 17.3, JACK B., 39

Presenting Picture: Complaints from employees prompted a counselor's visit for Jack B., a midlevel supervisor for a debt-collection agency. He mused that the visit was designed by his boss to give him a "bad rap," and that he was fearful of Jack's taking his job, a feat Jack had every confidence that he eventually would succeed in doing. He described himself as a fair supervisor, but he *expected* a full workday out of everyone, with no slacking off, chatter, coming in late, or excuses for not getting tasks done. "I check 'em *in,* and I check 'em *out,* every day!" he emphasized with a great deal of pride. He did not work with "problem" employees; he simply fired them, as they probably did not have what it took for his line of work. Debt collection was something Jack was very proud of as well. He said that he loved the power of his job, the aspect of telling others what to do, but he most enjoyed collecting debts. With immense satisfaction, he described one case where he prompted a debtor to run, then chased her across the country, doing anything he saw fit to keep her involved in the "chase," and eventually catching up with her in California.

Clinical Assessment: Jack fell within the subtype we term the *enforcing sadist,* where he is in the company of certain military sergeants, cops on the beat, deans in universities, and judges who sit on the bench, to name just a few others whose hostile inclinations are employed ostensibly in the public interest. He was an individual who felt he had the right to control and punish others, who knew when rules had been broken, and how these violators should have been dealt with, even violently and destructively. Operating under the guise of a sanctioned role to meet the common interest, the deeper motives that spurred his actions were of questionable legitimacy owing to the extraordinary force with which he meted out condemnation and punishment. As a socially sanctioned referee, he searched out rule-breakers and perpetrators of incidental infractions who fell within his role and exercised whatever powers he possessed to the most severe degree. Rather interestingly, he permeated within his configuration of characteristics some of the major features of the compulsive personality, one who was a stickler for rules, but who, as an enforcing sadist, could openly discharge his otherwise deeply repressed angers against the weak and condemnable.

In all societies and cultures throughout history, from the most primitive to the most civilized, there are persons who are empowered to control and punish their fellow members should they stray from the customs that have been set forth as proper. These powers often are executed with fairness and balance. Unfortunately, they also provide for individuals such as Jack the opportunity to exercise that power in a vicious and unjustified manner. He became a sadistic enforcer, one who imposed his will and malicious inclinations on others who had ostensibly "crossed the line." To meet Jack was to do so at one's peril. Because his position had been authorized by society, he could execute within his immense domain the means to prevail over and destroy others. Because he had permission "to be just," he was able to enforce with a single-minded and steely determination the rights of society as he had been empowered to execute them. In carrying out his duties, he treated others in an inhumane and destructive manner. Despite his responsibility to be fair and balanced, he was not able to put limits on the emotions that drove his sadistically vicious behaviors. Dominating everything and everyone becomes his goal.

What differentiates these sadists from others is their built-in and socially sanctioned power base, a power base that allows them to exert any and all forms of control over others. Jack swaggered about as a prideful "enforcer of the law"; the more he dominated and discharged his venom, the more pridefully he swaggered and the more he felt righteously empowered. The more he discharged his hostility and exercised his will, the more he displayed his dominance and fed his sadistic urges, the more he felt justified in venting his anger. Power had gone to his head. Jack began to dehumanize his victims, further enlarging the sphere and intensity of his aggressive destructiveness. Increasingly opportunistic and manipulative, he also sought to usurp whatever he could from others. Beneath his ostensible good intentions lay a growing deceptive viciousness, a malicious inclination that eventually produced the very destructiveness he had been authorized to control.

Synergistic Treatment Plan: Underpinning Jack's need to "seek justice" in this most extreme manner was an extremely volatile collection of anger and hostility that would need to be dispelled in order to begin work, a task that could be approached *behaviorally* and possibly also *biophysically*. As a modicum of peacefulness would be established (less *active* orientation) and Jack's tension would dissipate, it would be possible to *cognitively* confront several basic assumptions that served to create this embittered personal context. This would also serve to remedy the confusion regarding his reversed *pleasure-pain* continuum. As some of these basic assumptions would come into question and his perpetuating circles would be disrupted, *interpersonal* methods would be employed to stimulate a stronger *other* orientation, to develop healthier socialization, and, together with behavioral methods, to establish a basic set of emotional and behavioral controls derived from a healthier characterologic context. Each of these steps may be facilitated by the use of self-actualizing techniques such as the *experiential* methods of sensitizing Jack to prodromal cues and *Gestalt* procedures to enable him to see the other's point of view.

Therapeutic Course: Several brief therapies were worth considering. Among them were specific *pharmacologic agents* that were explored for modulating the threshold and intensity of Jack's reactivity. These drugs are not notably effective for dealing with individuals such as Jack, but it was worthwhile to evaluate a few in terms of their efficacy in minimizing the frequency and depth of his hostile feelings, thereby decreasing some of the self-perpetuating consequences of his aggressive behavior. Well-directed *behavioral* approaches provided the patient with opportunities to vent his anger. Once drained of hostility or having it more benignly channeled, he was able to explore his habitual expectations and attitudes and was guided through various *cognitive* techniques into less destructive perceptions and outlets than before. *Insight-oriented* procedures were not of short-term utility, nor were techniques oriented to a thorough reworking of Jack's aggressive strategies. Rather, more behaviorally directed methods geared to increase restraint and control were most useful. *Interpersonal* techniques (e.g., Klerman, Benjamin) were also fruitful in teaching him more acceptable social behavior. As far as *group* methods were concerned, Jack ran the risk of intruding on and disrupting therapeutic functions, but fortunately enough become a useful catalyst for group interaction and possibly improved various constructive social skills and attitudes.

The therapist was always cognizant of Jack's inclination to be spoiling for a fight, almost enjoying tangling with the therapist to prove his strength and test his powers. A mixed cognitive and emotion-oriented technique (e.g., Beck, Greenberg) was employed to counter his omnipresent undertone of anger and resentment, that is, the expectation that the therapist would prove to be devious and hostile. By confronting and then venting these feelings, it was possible to dilute his inclination to repeatedly distort the incidental remarks and actions of the therapist so that they appeared to deprecate and vilify him. Similarly, a worthy brief therapeutic goal was to undo his habit of misinterpreting what he saw and heard and magnifying minor slights into major insults and slanders. Important in achieving these short-term goals was to restrain the impulse to react to the patient with disapproval and criticism. An important step beyond building rapport with this man was to see things from his viewpoint. To achieve the circumscribed goals of brief therapy required that the therapist convey a sense of trust and willingness to develop a constructive treatment alliance. A balance of professional authority and tolerance was able to diminish the probability that Jack would impulsively withdraw from treatment or shortly regress to prior problematic states.

Effective brief techniques were called for because Jack was not likely to be a willing participant in therapy. He had agreed to therapy initially only under the pressure of vocational difficulties (e.g., as a consequence of aggressive and abusive behavior on the job). One task of a cognitive approach was to get him to tolerate guilt or to accept a measure of blame for the turmoil he may have caused. Reframing his perceptions to ones that are more realistic countered his belief that a problem could always be traced to another person's stupidity, laziness, or hostility. Even when he accepted some measure of responsibility, he did not feel defiance and resentment toward the therapist for trying to point this out. Although he sought to challenge, test, bluff, and outwit the therapist, a strong, consistent, but fair-minded cognitive approach reduced these actions and aided him in assuming a more calm and rea- soned attitude.

SADISTIC PERSONALITY: SPINELESS TYPE (SADISTIC WITH AVOIDANT FEATURES)

CASE 17.4, CARL D., 34

Presenting Picture: Carl D., an adult adoptee, described being "pushed around" frequently as a child, both by other children and his father, but he no longer suffered from such prob- lems due to various tactics he had embraced. He was a small child who went through a late onset of puberty and always wanted to "be a man." His father, who was a Marine, seemed disgusted by him and frequently insulted and attacked him. As an adult in therapy, however, Carl stated that this was all under control, as he *had* become a man, had gone through mil- itary training, and would be the first to "make it clear" that he would not allow *anyone* to threaten him. He was a gun enthusiast and worked in a gun and ammunition store, where he was not afraid to fire into the ceiling to shake up a "suspicious" customer. Very defen- sive and bigoted, Carl seemed *extremely* discomforted by anyone who appeared to be dif- ferent or who appeared to threaten his freedom or his expression. He did disclose that he relied on the fact that he would never "come to blows" with anyone, for as long as he showed he was tougher, the "other guy" was really the coward. Not surprisingly, he lived a very guarded, prisonlike life, which was anything but the free life he worshipped, and he showed all sorts of signs of cowardly, underhanded behavior.

Clinical Assessment: Not all sadists are intrinsically powerful and vicious executors of oth- ers. The explosive type acts so only periodically, and is often troubled and contrite about the consequences of his or her irrational actions. The tyrannical and enforcing varieties more closely fit the prototype of the sadist. However, a type such as Carl is deeply insecure and ir- resolute, often faint-hearted and cowardly, in fact. For him, his sadistic actions were responses to felt dangers and fears. His aggression signified an effort to show others that he was *not* anxious nor ready to succumb to the inner weaknesses and external pressures he experienced. Carl, who essentially was a craven and cowardly type, we are calling a *spine- less sadist.* Carl committed violent acts as a means of overcoming his fearfulness and need to secure refuge. He was basically an insecure, bogus, and cowardly person whose venom and cruelty was essentially a counterphobic act. Anticipating real danger, projecting his hostile fan- tasies, he struck first, hoping thereby to forestall his antagonist and ask questions later. An analysis of his psychic structure indicated that his overt hostility and abuse mapped onto a covert pattern of avoidant personality characteristics, as was shown on his MCMI profile.

When Carl's fantasy was peopled with powerful and aggressive enemies, when he felt precariously undefended, he gained moments of peace by counteracting the dangers he saw lurking about him. Experiencing panic, he counteracted his assaultors by engaging in the very acts he deeply feared. Subjected early on to repeated physical brutality and intimida- tion, Carl had learned to employ these instrumentalities of destruction and turn them against others who seemed threatening and abusive. It is in situations such as these that we see the fearful and spineless nature of a sadist such as Carl, who copes with his fears not by with- drawing, but with a preemptive attack.

For Carl, aggressive hostility was a message to others that he was neither anxious nor intimidated. Hostility served intrapsychically to diminish and control his real inner feelings, as well as to publicly display their opposite. As noted, his behavior was counterphobic, as the analysts have pointed out so clearly. Not only did this mechanism serve to enable him to master his personal fears, but it served to divert and impress the public by his false sense of confidence and self-assurance. With Carl we saw the publicly swaggering spineless type, a belligerent and intimidating variant who wanted the world to know that he "could not be pushed around." As with many other sadists, public aggressiveness is not a sign of genuine confidence and personal strength, but a desperate means to try to feel superior and self-assured. Neither naturally mean-spirited nor intrinsically violent, Carl became a caricature of swaggering tough guys and petty tyrants.

Many spineless sadists join groups that search for a shared scapegoat, a people or ethnic population that has been "sanctioned to hate," so-called outsiders of all varieties. What makes these groups so special as an object of hate is that they presumably embody the very weaknesses that these sadists feel within themselves. In a perverse twist of psychic logic, by assaulting the scapegoat, these sadists assault the very elements within themselves that they wish and seek to purge or deny.

Synergistic Treatment Plan: Carl's self-perpetuations were situated in a constant state of protectiveness, and his constitutional proclivity was to ward off, in "hex sign" fashion, any possible perceived threat with a false macho demeanor (an ineffective *active-pain* construct). A first measure would be to approach Carl with a *cognitive* milieu that would serve to question the logic behind his characterological fears and suspicions as well as alleviate long-developed hostilities. As a more reasonable understanding of these fears was established, it would be possible to work *interpersonally* to augment greater understanding of and empathy for *others,* as well as develop effective and more satisfying interactional skills and contexts. A further adjunct that would be effective in establishing comfort in this unfamiliar style of interaction would be a *family* or *group* milieu. Also, it should be noted that owing to the volatility of Carl's emotions, it would be well advised to be alert for signs of decompensation and to be prepared to intervene *biophysically* if necessary.

Therapeutic Course: Focused techniques were used to alter Carl's symptoms and basic psychopathology. Primary goals in brief therapy included the facilitation of autonomy, the building of confidence, and the overcoming of fears of self-determination. There was, not surprisingly, a period of initial resistance. As part of a short-term approach, it was important to counter Carl's feeling that the therapist's efforts to encourage him to assume responsibility and self-control were a sign of rejection. A warm, trusting, and empathic atmosphere was established to prevent disappointment, dejection, and even rage. These potential reactions were anticipated, given his characteristic style, and they needed to be responded to with equanimity if fundamental changes were to be explored and relapses prevented. When a sound and secure therapeutic alliance had been established, Carl learned to tolerate his contrary feelings and dependency anxieties. Learning how to face and handle his unstable emotions was coordinated with the strengthening of healthier attitudes through *cognitive* methods such as those of Beck and Meichenbaum, as well as through *interpersonal* procedures such as those of Kiesler and Benjamin. Additionally, the therapist served as a model to demonstrate how feelings, conflicts, and uncertainties could be approached and resolved with reasonable equanimity and foresight. *Family* methods were also used to test these newly learned attitudes and strategies in a more natural setting than that found in individual treatment. As implied, by his affective instability and self-deprecation, Carl avoided confronting and resolving his real interpersonal difficulties.

His coping maneuvers were a double-edged sword, relieving passing discomfort and strains but perpetuating faulty attitudes and strategies. These distorted attitudes and faulty behavior were the main targets of cognitive and interpersonal therapeutic interventions (e.g., Safran, Segal).

Special care was called for in a short-term treatment regimen to counteract the possibility that Carl's hold on reality could disintegrate and his capacity to function wither. Similar care was taken when the attention and support that he required was withdrawn and when his strategies proved wearisome and exasperating to others, precipitating their anger. *Pharmacologic agents* were used, as he at one point began to succumb to depression. Particular attention was given to anticipate and quell the danger of suicide during this time. A major concern during this early period was the forestalling of a persistent decompensation process. Among the early signs of such a breakdown were marked discouragement and melancholic dejection. At this phase, *supportive* therapy was called for, and cognitive reorientation methods were actively implemented. Efforts were made to boost Carl's sagging morale, to encourage him to continue in his usual sphere of activities, to build his self-confidence, and to deter him from being preoccupied with his melancholy feelings. He could not be pressed beyond his capabilities, however, for his failure to achieve any goals would only strengthen his conviction of his incompetence and unworthiness. Properly executed cognitive methods oriented to correcting erroneous assumptions and beliefs were especially helpful.

Resistances and Risks

The aggressive pattern will not be readily altered because mistrust is both chronic and deep. Moreover, these individuals will resist exploring their motives, and their defenses are resolute. One of the major challenges the therapist faces is to gain collaboration. It is an understatement to say that these personalities are not willing participants in therapy. The submissive and help-seeking role of patient is anathema to these power-oriented people. When they "submit" to therapy, it is usually under the press of severe marital discord or work conflicts. For example, they may be in a jam as a consequence of aggressive or abusive behavior on the job or as a result of incessant quarrels and brutality toward their spouse or children. Rarely do they experience guilt or accept blame for the turmoil they cause. To them, the problem can always be traced to the other person's stupidity, laziness, or hostility. Even when they accept a measure of responsibility for their difficulties, one senses an underlying resentment of their "do-gooder" therapist, who tricked them into admitting it.

Not uncommonly, these personalities will challenge therapists and seek to outwit them. They will set up situations to test the therapist's skills, to catch inconsistencies, to arouse ire, and, if possible, to belittle and humiliate the therapist. It is no easy task for the therapist to restrain the impulse to "do battle" or to express a condemning attitude; great effort must be expended at times to check these counterhostile feelings. Therapists must avoid getting in a power struggle with these patients. Beck and Freeman (1990a) note that therapists may actually gain credibility if they acknowledge the patient's skill in manipulating others, including the therapist. Therapists may have to remind themselves that these patients' plight was not of their own doing, that they were the unfortunate recipients of a harsh upbringing, and that only by a respectful and sympathetic approach can they be helped to get on the right track.

To accomplish this goal, therapists must not only be ready to see things from the patient's point of view but must convey a sense of trust and create a feeling of sharing an alliance. It is important, however, that the building of rapport not be interpreted by the patient as a sign of the therapist's capitulation, of the latter's having been intimidated by bluff and arrogance. Attempts to build rapport must not exceed personal boundaries, and the therapist must set clear limits. A balance of professional firmness and authority, mixed with tolerance for the patient's less attractive traits, must be maintained. By building an image of a fair-minded and strong authority figure, the therapist may encourage these patients to change their expectancies. Through quiet and thoughtful comments, the therapist may provide a model for learning the mix of power, reason, and fairness. By this process, patients may develop more wholesome attitudes toward others and be led to direct their energies more constructively than in the past.

CHAPTER EIGHTEEN

Treating Compulsive Personality Patterns

The most prominent features of the compulsive personality include excessive emotional control and interpersonal reserve; preoccupation with matters of order, organization, and efficiency; indecisiveness; and a tendency toward being overly conscientious, moralistic, and judgmental. It is our belief that much of the personality organization of the compulsive individual arises in reaction to marked feelings of interpersonal ambivalence. Like passive-aggressive (negativistic) personalities, compulsive personalities are torn between their leanings toward submissive dependence on the one hand and defiant autonomy on the other (Millon, 1969, 1981). Unlike the overt emotional lability and chronic vacillation of negativists, however, compulsive personalities bind and submerge their rebellious and oppositional urges through a rigid stance of overcompliance, conformity, and propriety. By clinging grimly to rules of society and insisting on regularity and uniformity in relationships and life events, these individuals help restrain and protect themselves against their own aggressive impulses and independent strivings. Although this behavioral and cognitive rigidity may effectively shield the individual from intrapsychic conflict as well as social criticism, it may also preclude growth and change, cause alienation from inner feelings, and interfere with the formation of intimate and warm relationships.

To others, compulsives appear to be industrious and efficient but lacking in flexibility, imagination, and spontaneity. They may also be viewed as stubborn or stingy and picayune, with a tendency to get lost in the minutiae rather than appreciate the substance of everyday life. Compulsives are easily upset by the unfamiliar or by deviations from their accustomed routines. Their perfectionistic standards and need for certainty may result in a tendency toward indecisiveness and procrastination. Although the social behavior of compulsives is typically polite and formal, there is a definite tendency to relate to others on the basis of their rank or status. Compulsives require considerable reassurance and approval from their superiors and consequently may relate to them in a deferential, ingratiating, and even obsequious manner. In contrast, compulsives may be quite autocratic and condemnatory with subordinates, using their authority and the rules they represent to justify the venting of considerable hostility and criticalness.

Compulsives devalue self-exploration and exhibit little or no insight into their motives and feelings. Beset with deep ambivalence and contrary feelings, they employ extensive defensive maneuvers to transmute or seal off frightening urges from conscious awareness. Rigid moralism and behavioral conformity bind much of their hidden feelings of defiance and anger, and these individuals also find it necessary to compartmentalize or isolate their emotional responses to situations. They may particularly attempt to block or otherwise neutralize reactions to stressful events for fear that signs of emotional weakness may become apparent and lead to embarrassment or disapproval.

Despite their elaborate defensive strategies, compulsives tend to be among the personality styles that are most troubled by clinical syndromes. Their cognitive and behavioral organization make them particularly susceptible to anxiety and affective disorders of virtually every type. Plagued by their own exacting standards as well as the high expectations that they perceive others to hold for them, compulsives frequently feel as though they have fallen short of their criteria for acceptable performance. Although angry at themselves for being imperfect and resentful toward others for their unyielding demands, compulsives dare not expose either their own shortcomings or their anxious hostility toward others. Rather than voicing their defiance or venting their resentment and thereby being subject to social rebuke, they turn their feelings inward, discharging their anger toward themselves. In this regard, the compulsive's propensity for experiencing guilt, expressing self-reproval, and acting contrite serves as a form of expiation for hidden, unacceptable feelings while preventing humiliation or condemnation from others. The anger-guilt, anxiety, and self-degradation sequence may occur quite frequently in compulsives, resulting in a chronic, mild depression or dysthymic disorder. Major depressive states may be quite common among compulsives in later life, usually following a period of reflection and self-evaluation. At such times, compulsives are confronted with the realization that their lofty life goals and long-held standards of excellence have not been attained, and further, that rigid conformity to external values has yielded a rather barren existence with the denial of a multitude of potentially satisfying experiences. Severe clinical syndromes in compulsives tend to have an agitated and apprehensive quality, marked by feelings of guilt and a tendency to complain about personal sin and unworthiness. The tense and anxious coloring of their symptoms may be a reflection of their struggle to contain their hostility and resentments, as well as their fear that contrition and despondency will prompt derision and condemnation from others.

As with other personality disorders, compulsive personality traits have held a prominent place in the psychoanalytic literature. Kolb, in his 1973 revision of Noyes's original text, provides the following description of the premorbid personality of a depressed-type manic-depressive:

> Many have been scrupulous persons of rigid ethical and moral standards, meticulous, self-demanding, perfectionistic, self-depreciatory, prudish, given to self-reproach, and sensitive to criticism. Their obsessive-compulsive tendencies have doubtless been defensive mechanisms for handling hostility, which characteristically they cannot express externally. (pp. 372–373)

An important distinction must be made between compulsive personality traits and obsessive-compulsive symptoms as they occur in depression. Although there is some evidence that obsessions, ruminative worry, and compulsive behaviors are more likely to occur in individuals with obsessive or compulsive premorbid personalities (Vaughan, 1976), these same symptoms are frequent accompaniments of syndromal episodes in a variety of other personality types. Studies that have attempted to carefully tease apart clinical symptomatology from enduring characterologic traits, however, have revealed considerable differences with respect to the intensity and duration of obsessive-compulsive symptoms.

Of particular interest is the suggestion among some of these studies that obsessional symptoms and traits serve as a defense against depression. Wittenborn and Maurer (1977) hypothesize that intensification of obsessionalism and denial of anger at the onset of a clinical episode may serve a defensive function among individuals feeling overwhelmed by environmental stressors and sensing an impending loss of control. Some authors suggest that marked premorbid obsessionalism seemed to offer protection against the development of manic episodes. Von Zerssen (1977), in his review of the literature, postulates that many of the obsessive traits result from the tendency to build defenses against the negative emotions involved in depression. He cites as an example the melancholic's strivings toward self-confirmation in performance as a strategy to avoid a lack of self-esteem. Consistent with this line of thought, Akiskal (1981) noted: "The psychoanalytical literature has suggested that the anankastic traits of orderliness, guilt and concern for others are a defense against the depressive's tendency for disorganization, hostility and self-preoccupation" (p. 86).

A brief summary of the obsessive-compulsive personality pattern as interpreted by the evolutionary model is portrayed in the polarity schema of Figure 18.1. Notable here is the dominance of the passive (accommodating) and other (nurturing) polar extremes. Worthy of note also is the arrow that is placed between the self and other boxes, which signifies the conflict experienced between these two orientations. As has been described previously, and as will be elaborated in later pages, the compulsive is one of two "ambivalent" personality disorders; both compulsives and negativists struggle between doing the bidding of others versus doing their own bidding. The compulsive

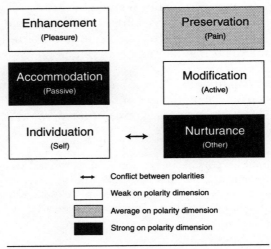

Figure 18.1 Status of the obsessive-compulsive personality prototype in accord with the Millon Polarity Model.

resolves this conflict by submerging all indications of self-interest and instead devoting all efforts toward meeting the desires of others. The weak intensity seen in the self/individuating polarity and the contrasting strong intensity in the other/nurturing polarity represent this resolution. To ensure that their unconscious self-desires do not become overtly manifest, compulsives are extraordinarily accommodating, never taking the initiative about matters, always awaiting signals from others as to what they should do. Notable also in the polarity figure is the relative strength of the preservation focus over that of enhancement. This difference signifies the strong interest on the part of compulsives to protect themselves against potential harm and criticism and a contrasting indifference to the experience of pleasure and joy; it is here where we can see the grim and cheerless demeanor that typifies these personalities.

CLINICAL PICTURE

Our analysis of the characteristics of obsessive-compulsive personalities may be usefully differentiated in several ways, notably in accord with the several domains in which their pathology is manifested and in the several subtypes in which their prime features are displayed (see Table 18.1).

Prototypal Diagnostic Domains

The major characteristics of the compulsive personality are organized in terms of the usual eight clinical domains (see Figure 18.2).

Disciplined expressive behavior.   The grim and cheerless demeanor of compulsives is often quite striking. This is not to say that they are invariably glum or downcast but rather to convey their characteristic air of austerity and serious-mindedness. Posture and movement reflect their underlying tightness, a tense control of emotions that are kept well in check. Most significantly, their emotions are kept in check by a regulated, highly structured, and carefully organized life. They appear emotionally tight, displaying features that signify an inner rigidity and control. There is a tendency for them to speak precisely, with clear diction and well-phrased sentences. Clothing is formal and proper, consistent with current fashions but restrained in color and style. Perfectionism limits the alternatives they consider in their everyday actions, often interfering with their ability to make choices and complete ordinary tasks.

Respectful interpersonal behavior.   Compulsives display an unusual adherence to social conventions and proprieties, preferring to maintain polite, formal, and "correct" personal relationships. Most are quite scrupulous about matters of morality and ethics. In a similar vein, they usually insist that subordinates adhere to their personally established rules and methods of conduct. The social behavior of compulsives may be characterized as formal. They relate to others in terms of rank or status; that is, they tend to be authoritarian rather than egalitarian in their outlook. This is reflected in their contrasting behaviors with "superiors" as opposed to "inferiors." Compulsive personalities are deferential, ingratiating, and even obsequious with their superiors, going out of their way to impress them with their efficiency and serious-mindedness. Many seek the reassurance and approval of authority figures, experiencing considerable anxiety when

TABLE 18.1   Clinical Domains of the Obsessive-Compulsive Personality Prototype

Behavioral Level

(F) Expressively Disciplined (e.g., maintains a regulated, highly structured, and strictly organized life; perfectionism interferes with decision making and task completion).

(F) Interpersonally Respectful (e.g., exhibits unusual adherence to social conventions and proprieties, as well as being scrupulous and overconscientious about matters of morality and ethics; prefers polite, formal, and correct personal relationships, usually insisting that subordinates adhere to personally established rules and methods).

Phenomenological Level

(F) Cognitively Constricted (e.g., constructs world in terms of rules, regulations, schedules, and hierarchies; is rigid, stubborn, and indecisive and notably upset by unfamiliar or novel ideas and customs).

(S) Conscientious Self-Image (e.g., sees self as devoted to work, industrious, reliable, meticulous, and efficient, largely to the exclusion of leisure activities; fearful of error or misjudgment and, hence, overvalues aspects of self that exhibit discipline, perfection, prudence, and loyalty).

(S) Concealed Objects (e.g., only those internalized representations, with their associated inner affects and attitudes that can be socially approved, are allowed conscious awareness or behavioral expression; as a result, actions and memories are highly regulated, forbidden impulses sequestered and tightly bound, personal and social conflicts defensively denied, kept from awareness, maintained under stringent control).

Intrapsychic Level

(F) Reaction-Formation Mechanism (e.g., repeatedly presents positive thoughts and socially commendable behaviors that are diametrically opposite deeper contrary and forbidden feelings; displays reasonableness and maturity when faced with circumstances that evoke anger of dismay in others).

(S) Compartmentalized Organization (e.g., morphologic structures are rigidly organized in a tightly consolidated system that is clearly partitioned into numerous, distinct, and segregated constellations of drive, memory, and cognition, with few open channels to permit interplay among these components).

Biophysical Level

(S) Solemn Mood (e.g., is unrelaxed, tense, joyless, and grim; restrains warm feelings and keeps most emotions under tight control).

F refers to Functional Domains (fluid, interactive)
S refers to Structural Domains (stable, unchanging)

they are unsure of their position. These behaviors contrast markedly with their attitudes toward subordinates. Here, the compulsive is quite autocratic and condemnatory, often appearing pompous and self-righteous. This haughty and deprecatory manner is usually cloaked under regulations and legalities. Not untypically, compulsives will justify their aggressive intentions by recourse to rules or authorities higher than themselves.

The compulsive person is extraordinarily careful to pay proper respect to those in authority. These individuals are not only correct and polite but ingratiating and obsequious. Their conduct is beyond reproach; they are ever punctual and meticulous in fulfilling the duties and obligations expected of them. These behaviors serve a variety of functions beyond gaining approval and the avoidance of displeasure. For example, by allying themselves with a "greater power," compulsives gain considerable strength and authority for themselves. Not only do they enjoy the protection and the prestige of

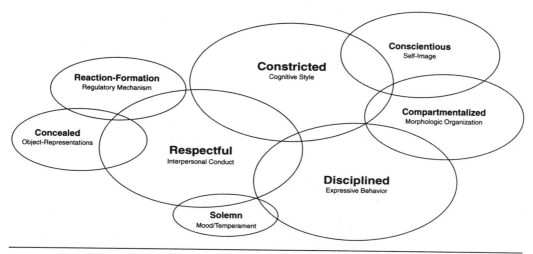

Figure 18.2 Salience of prototypal obsessive-compulsive domains.

another, but by associating their actions with the views of an external authority, they relieve themselves of blame should these actions meet with disfavor. Of course, by submerging their individuality and becoming chattels of some other power or person, compulsives alienate themselves, preclude experiencing a sense of true personal satisfaction, and lose those few remnants of personal identity they may still possess.

As noted, compulsives are usually uncompromising and demanding in relationships with subordinates. This they do to bolster their deep feelings of inadequacy. Disrespect and disloyalty on the part of subordinates remind them all too painfully of their own inner urges and weaknesses. Moreover, this power over others provides them with a sanctioned outlet to vent hostile impulses. Should the others fail to live up to their standards, they feel just in reprimanding and condemning them.

Constricted cognitive style. The thinking of compulsive personalities is organized in terms of conventional rules and regulations as well as personally formulated schedules and social hierarchies. They tend to be rigid and stubborn about adhering to formal schemata for constructing and shaping their lives. Notable also is the ease with which they can be upset by having to deal with unfamiliar customs and novel ideas. In these circumstances, compulsives feel unsure of what course of action should be taken, often ending up immobilized and indecisive. Especially concerned with matters of propriety and efficiency, compulsives tend to be rigid and unbending about regulations and procedures. These behaviors often lead others to see them as perfectionistic, officious, and legalistic.

Compulsives are contemptuous of those who behave "frivolously and impulsively"; emotional behavior is considered immature and irresponsible. To them, people must be judged by "objective" standards and by the time-proven rules of an organized society. Reactions to others must be based on "established" values and customs, not on "personal" judgments. What compulsives invariably fail to recognize is that they seek to judge others in accord with rules that they themselves unconsciously detest. They impose harsh regulations on others largely to convince themselves that these rules can, in fact, be adhered to. If they succeed in restraining the rebellious impulses of others, perhaps they can be confident of successfully restraining their own.

Compulsives are viewed by others as industrious and efficient, though lacking in flexibility and spontaneity. Many consider them to be stubborn, stingy, possessive, uncreative, and unimaginative. As noted previously, they tend to procrastinate, appear indecisive, and are easily upset by the unfamiliar or by deviations from routines to which they have become accustomed. Content with their "nose to the grindstone," many work diligently and patiently with activities that require being tidy and meticulous. Some judge these behaviors to be a sign of being orderly and methodical; others see it as reflecting a small-minded and picayune nature.

Conscientious self-image.   These personalities see themselves as devoted to work and as industrious, reliable, meticulous, and efficient individuals. They tend to minimize the importance of recreational and leisure activities in favor of those that signify productive efforts. Fearful of being viewed as irresponsible or slack in their efforts or being seen as one who fails to meet the expectancies of others or is error-prone, compulsives overvalue those aspects of their self-image that signify perfectionism, prudence, and discipline.

Compulsives are good "organization men," typifying what we have termed the *bureaucratic* personality type. The compulsive's self-image is that of a conscientious, selfless, loyal, dependable, prudent, and responsible individual. Not only do these individuals willingly accept the beliefs of institutional authorities, but they believe that these authorities' demands and expectations are "correct." Compulsives identify with these strictures, internalizing them as a means of controlling their own repressed impulses and employing them as a standard to regulate the behavior of others. Their vigorous defense of institutional authorities often brings them commendation and support, rewards that serve to reinforce their inclination toward public obedience and moral self-righteousness.

It is characteristic of compulsives to be as harsh in their self-judgments as they are with others. In addition, they voice a strong sense of duty to others, feeling that they must not let others down and, more significantly, not engage in behaviors that might provoke their displeasure. Although compulsives feel self-doubt or guilt for failing to live up to some ideal, they have no awareness that it is often their own ambivalence about achieving, their own unconscious desire to defy authority, that blocks them from attaining their public aspirations. They may rationalize their indecisiveness by the "wisdom" of "looking before one leaps," of delaying action until one is sure of its correctness, and of "aiming for high standards," which, of course demand the most careful and reflective appraisal. These philosophical clichés merely cloak an unconscious desire to undo the rigid mold into which compulsives have allowed their life to be cast.

Concealed object-representations.   It is of special importance to the compulsive that only those internalized representations of the past that are socially acceptable be permitted into conscious awareness or given expression behaviorally. Inner impulses and attitudes as well as residual images and memories are all highly regulated and tightly bound. Forbidden impulses are sequestered in the unconscious. Similarly, current personal difficulties and social conflicts anchored to past experiences are defensively denied, kept from conscious awareness, and maintained under the most stringent of controls.

Compulsives take great pains to avoid recognizing the contradictions between their unconscious impulses and their overt behaviors. This they do by devaluing self-exploration. Thus, compulsives often exhibit little or no insight into their motives and feelings. To bolster this defensive maneuver, they demean the "personal equation," claiming that self-exploration is antithetical to efficient behavior and that introspection only intrudes on rational thinking and self-control. Protectively, then, they avoid looking into themselves and build a rationale in which they assert that analyses such as these are signs of immature self-indulgence, traits that they view as anathema to civilized life.

Reaction-formation regulatory mechanism. Compulsives engage in numerous "mechanisms of defense" to keep a tight rein on their contrary feelings and dispositions. More than any other personality, they actively exhibit a wide range of regulatory actions. Most distinctive, perhaps, is their use of reaction-formation. This is seen in their repeated efforts to present a positive spin on their thoughts and behaviors, to engage in socially commendable actions that are, in fact, diametrically opposite their deeper forbidden and contrary feelings. Hence, they tend to display publicly a mature reasonableness when faced with circumstances that would evoke dismay or irritability in most persons. The ingratiating and obsequious manner of many compulsives, especially in circumstances that normally evoke frustration and anger in others, may be traced to a reversal of their hidden and oppositional urges. Not daring to expose their true feelings of defiance and rebelliousness, they bind these feelings so tightly that their opposites come forth.

Two of the most effective techniques for transforming negative impulses yet finding outlets for them at the same time are identification and sublimation. If compulsives can find a "punitive" model of authority to emulate, they can "justify" venting their hostile impulses toward others and perhaps receive commendation as well. For example, in one case, the author observed that a child identified with his parents' strict attitudes by "tattling" on and reproaching his brother; this enabled the child to find a sanctioned outlet for his otherwise unacceptable hostility. Much of the compulsive's self-righteous morality reflects the same process. Mechanisms of sublimation serve similar functions. Unconscious feelings of hostility that cannot be tolerated consciously are often expressed in socially acceptable ways through occupations such as judge, dean, soldier, or surgeon. Fiercely moralistic fathers and "loving" but overcontrolling mothers are more common roles of restraint that often camouflage hidden hostility.

There are two other intrapsychic mechanisms—isolation and undoing—that do not provide an outlet for submerged rebellious impulses but do serve to keep them in check. Compulsive individuals also compartmentalize or isolate their emotional response to a situation. They block or otherwise neutralize feelings that are normally aroused by a stressful event and thereby ensure against the possibility of reacting in ways that might cause embarrassment and disapproval. Should compulsives trespass the injunctions of authority figures or fail to live up to their expectations, they may engage in certain ritualistic acts to "undo" the evil or wrong they feel they have done. In this manner, they seek expiation for their sins and thereby regain the goodwill they feared was lost.

Compartmentalized morphologic organization. The structure of the compulsive's mind is rather distinctive among the personality patterns. To keep oppositional feelings and impulses from effecting one another and to prevent ambivalent images and contradictory attitudes from spilling forth into conscious awareness, the organization of compulsives' inner world must be rigidly compartmentalized. There is a tightly consolidated system that is clearly partitioned into numerous, distinct, and segregated constellations of dispositions, memories, and feelings. Crucial is that these compartments be tightly sealed, hence precluding any open channels through which these components can interrelate.

Appearing deliberate and poised on the surface, compulsives sit atop this tightly constrained but internal powder keg. Beset by deep ambivalences and conflicts, their inner turmoil threatens to upset the balance they have so carefully wrought throughout their lives. They must preserve that balance and protect themselves against the intrusion into both conscious awareness and overt behavior of their intensely contrary impulses and feelings. They must carefully avoid events that could dislodge and unleash these forces, causing them to lose favor with those in authority. Having opted for a strategy in which rewards and security are granted to those in power, they must, at all costs, prevent losing the powerful's respect and protection. To achieve this, they must take no risks and operate with complete certainty that no unanticipated event will upset their equilibrium. Avoiding external disruptions is difficult enough, but their greatest task is that of controlling their own emotions, that is, restraining the impulses that surge from within and from which they cannot escape. Their only recourse for dealing with these intrusive and frightening urges is either to transmute them or to seal them off. As noted previously, they do this by the extensive use of intrapsychic mechanisms. Because of the depth of their ambivalence and the imperative nature of its control, compulsive personalities employ more varied defensive mechanisms than any of the other pathological patterns.

A major force behind the tightly structured world of compulsives is their fear of disapproval and their concern that their actions will not only be frowned upon, but severely punished. This fear can be understood given their likely history of exposure to demanding, perfectionistic, and condemnatory parents. One would assume that by "toeing the line" and behaving properly and correctly, compulsives could put this concern aside and be relaxed and untroubled. But this does not prove to be possible because their conformity and propriety are merely a public façade behind which lurk deeply repressed urges toward defiance and self-assertion. The ever-present threat that their rebellious and angry feelings will break into the open intensifies their fear of provoking condemnation. At some level, they sense the pretentiousness and insincerity of their public behavior. Thus, their fantasies may be a constant reminder of the disparity that exists between the front they present to others and the rebelliousness they feel beneath. No matter how perfect their behavior may be in fact, no matter how hard they may attempt to prove themselves, this inner ambivalence remains. They must be alert to the possibility of detection at all times. Condemnation is a constant threat because their "true" feelings may be readily uncovered. To cope with both their fears and their impulses, compulsives engage in the characteristic control mechanisms and formal interpersonal behaviors that have been addressed in previous sections.

Solemn mood/temperament.   It is typical to find compulsives to be unrelaxed, tense, joyless, and grim. Most restrain warm and affectionate feelings, keeping their emotions under a measure of firm control. Some compulsives exhibit a marked diminution in activity and energy, attributable in all probability to their lifelong habit of constraint and inhibition. Few evidence a lively or ebullient manner; most are rigidly controlled and emotionally tight, and their failure to release pent-up energies is likely to dispose them to psychophysiologic disorders. Any speculation that the ambivalence of compulsives might reflect some intrinsic antagonism between opposing temperamental dispositions would seem presumptuous. Yet we do observe an opposition between intense fear and intense anger among these individuals. Both tendencies may be great and may account in part for their frequent indecisiveness and immobilization. Given their grim and joyless quality, we might also conjecture that many possess a constitutionally based anhedonic temperament. Translating these notions into tangible substrates, it might be hypothesized that regions of the limbic system associated with both fear and anger may be unusually dense or well branched; conflicting signals from these areas might underlie the hesitancy, doubting, and indecisive behaviors seen in these patients. Similarly, the substrate for experiencing pleasure may be poorly developed, leading to the compulsive's typical stern countenance. Speculations such as these are highly conjectural.

Self-Perpetuation Processes

As in previous chapters, this section addresses the features that perpetuate the personality style—that is, are themselves pathogenic of the pattern—followed by a brief exploration of some of the remedial steps that may prove useful in modifying the problem.

Given the conflicts and anxieties engendered by their strategy, why do compulsives resist exploring alternative coping methods? One answer, of course, is that they experience less pain by continuing, rather than changing, their style of behavior. Thus, discomforting as the strategy may be, it is less anguishing and more rewarding than any other they can envisage. Another answer is that much of what they do is merely the persistence of habit, the sheer continuation of what they have learned in the past. Thus, compulsives persevere, in part at least, not because their behavior is instrumentally so rewarding but because it is deeply ingrained, so much so that it persists automatically. None of this is unique to the compulsive personality. It is true of all personality patterns. Each style fosters a *vicious* circle such that the individual's adaptive strategy promotes conditions similar to those that gave rise initially to that strategy. Pathological personality traits are traps, self-made prisons that are perniciously self-defeating in that they promote their own continuation. The following looks at three of these self-perpetuating processes (see Table 18.2).

Pervasive rigidity. Compulsives dread making mistakes and fear taking risks lest they provoke disapproval. Defensively, they learn to restrict themselves to situations with which they are familiar and to actions they feel confident will be approved. They keep themselves within narrow boundaries and confine themselves to the repetition of the familiar. Rarely do they wander or view things from a different perspective than they have in the past. Moreover, compulsives are characteristically single-minded, have sharply defined interests, and can stick to "the facts" without deviation. To avoid the unknown—that is, the potentially dangerous—they maintain a tight and well-organized approach to life. They hold onto the "tried and true" and keep their nose to old and familiar grindstones. The price paid for this rigid and narrow outlook is high. Subtle emotions and creative imagination are simply incompatible with the deliberate and mechanical quality of the compulsive's style. Further, repetitiously going over the same dull routine prevents these persons from experiencing new perceptions and new ways

---

TABLE 18.2   Self-Perpetuating Processes

COMPULSIVE
Pervasive Rigidity
 Repeats the familiar and approved
 Imagination incompatible with mechanical lifestyle
 Resists exposure to novel events

Guilt and Self-Criticism
 Lifestyle constrained by punitive introjects
 Persecutes self for deviant thoughts
 Persistent doubt prevents exploration of the new

Creates Rules and Regulations
 Uncovers tangential legalities and standards
 Irrelevant precepts shrink choices
 Excessive structure counters fear of losing control

---

of approaching their environment. By following the same narrow path, compulsives block their chances of breaking the bonds of the past. Their horizons are confined as they duplicate the same old grind.

Guilt and self-criticism.   By the time compulsives attain adolescence, they are likely to have fully incorporated the strictures and regulations of their elders. Even if they could "get away with it" and be certain that no external power would judge them severely, they now carry within themselves a merciless internal conscience, an inescapable inner gauge that ruthlessly evaluates and controls them, one that intrudes relentlessly to make them doubt and hesitate before they act. The proscriptions of "proper" behavior have been well learned and they dare not deviate irresponsibly. The onslaughts of guilt and self-recrimination are adamant and insidious. External sources of restraint have been supplanted with the inescapable controls of internal self-reproach. Compulsives are now their own persecutor and judge, ready to condemn themselves not only for overt acts but for thoughts of transgression as well. These inner controls stop them from exploring new avenues of behavior and thereby perpetuate the habits and constraints of the past.

Creation of rules and regulations.   Most persons strive to minimize the constraints that society imposes. Laws are the price for a civilized existence, but we prefer as few as necessary. Compulsives are different. Not only do they live by rules and regulations, but they go out of their way to uncover legalities, moral prescriptions, and ethical standards to guide themselves and judge others. This attitude is understandable, deriving from their intense struggle to control raging impulses toward defiance that well up within them. The more restrictive the injunctions they find in legalities and external authority, the less effort they must expend on their own to control these contrary urges. Once more, they trap themselves in a self-defeating circle. By creating or discovering new percepts to heed, they draw the noose even tighter around themselves and shrink their world into an ever-narrowing shell. Opportunities for learning new behaviors or to view the world afresh and more flexibly are further curtailed. Their own characteristic habits have increasingly narrowed their boundaries for change and growth.

INTERVENTION GOALS

Compulsive personalities often seek therapy as a result of psychophysiologic discomforts. These symptoms are the psychosomatic manifestations of the difficulty compulsives have in discharging internal tensions caused by repressed emotions that churn within them. Symptoms often include attacks of anxiety, spells of immobilization, sexual impotence, and excessive fatigue. The therapist is enlisted to help the compulsive cope as the symptoms begin to be perceived as a threat to the efficient and responsible lifestyle that defines the compulsive's identity. This is not to say, however, that compulsives believe their symptoms are of a psychological nature. Compulsives are in fact so well defended against distressing emotions that they are typically oblivious to the possibility that internal ambivalence and repressed resentments exist, much less that they underlie the very symptoms they genuinely believe to be caused by an isolated (if unidentifiable) "disease."

Given the complex and ambivalent character of the compulsive's inclinations, what goals should the therapist keep in mind to guide his or her strategies?

Compulsive's subconscious conviction about the dire consequences of facing desires and discontent leads them to repress "inappropriate" feelings. Although this serves to keep the compulsive stable, it also makes the emotional insight needed to reestablish balance in the self-other polarity and the active-passive dimension difficult for the therapist to elicit in the patient. Focused and steady work on countering emotional and behavioral rigidities that perpetuate problems and lead to clinical domain dysfunctions can ultimately lead to the self-examination and risk-taking that can help provide increased balance in the personality structure (see Table 18.3).

Reestablishing Polarity Balances

What polarity imbalances underlie the compulsive's difficulties?

A typical early learning history of being punished for rule transgressions and praised for virtually nothing results in compulsives operating from the basic premise that their own wishes and desires are "wrong" and that expressing them leads to

TABLE 18.3 Therapeutic Strategies and Tactics for the Prototypal Compulsive Personality

STRATEGIC GOALS
Balance Polarities
Identify and stabilize self-other conflict
Encourage decisive actions

Counter Perpetuations
Loosen pervasive rigidity
Reduce preoccupation with rules
Moderate guilt and self-criticism

TACTICAL MODALITIES
Alter constricted cognitive style
Adjust perfectionistic behaviors
Brighten solemn-downcast mood

intimidation and punishment. Unlike the negativistic personality style, whose resentment at having to concede to the wishes of others is at times all too clear, the compulsive personality internalizes others' strictures as true. Feelings of hostility about having wishes and desires conflict with those of "powerful" others are unconsciously repressed in an attempt to avoid further social disapproval and punishment. The conflict between turning to others rather than self for approval has been termed the *ambivalent pattern*. Normal personalities more or less balance their efforts at securing rewards between both alternatives. Compulsives, who deal with their ambivalence by forcing it out of consciousness, exhibit their ambivalence passively. Although they are characterized by overt diligence and conscientious work patterns, most compulsives' efforts are a response to the demands and expectations of others, real or imagined. Compulsives are almost exclusively reactive (passive) in relation to their environment. Initiative to actively change their circumstances is rarely exhibited due to their excessive fear of making a mistake. Because of this obsessive need to achieve perfection, tasks are often turned into paralyzing chores marked by indecision and delay. Even more fundamental to the passive style of compulsives is being out of touch, not only with their unconscious oppositional feelings, but with most of their emotions. Even if hesitation were not a behavioral obstacle to self-exploration, the inability to identify what they really feel and want certainly would be.

To reestablish balance within the self-other polarity, compulsives must work toward establishing an identity that differentiates their own feelings and desires from those they judge are expected of them. Before this can be accomplished, repressed anger and fear of disapproval must become conscious and emotionally worked through. Ultimately, both the expectations of others and the needs of self should be recognized and taken into consideration as valid. The resurrection of a personal self composed of genuine feelings and desires can set the groundwork for a shift in the active-passive polarity. Once wishes are acknowledged as acceptable, only perfectionism stands between the compulsive and a more active goal-seeking style. Therapeutic work undermining impossibly high standards can help put an end to inertia.

Countering Perpetuating Tendencies

The compulsive decides early on in life that making mistakes leads to punishment. The only way to avoid disapproval is to be "perfect." By the time a compulsive comes to the attention of a therapist, parental injunctions have been internalized, and the simple yet foolproof mechanism of potential guilt prevents any deviation from the firmly entrenched rules. Self-criticism functions in much the same manner; by engaging in internal reprimands, compulsives feel that they "prove" their good intentions and obviate the need for disapproval from external sources. In familiar or straightforward situations, compulsives can ward off anxiety and self-reprisals by "doing the right thing." In new or ambiguous situations, however, they are paralyzed by indecision and anxiety because the consequences of different potential responses are unknown. At best, compulsives can decide how to react based on an educated guess; however, this does not satisfy their need for complete control. To avoid anxiety-provoking ambiguity, compulsives become pervasively rigid. As they stick to a well-rehearsed routine, they encounter few confusing stimuli. Even thinking becomes limited to the realm of the tried and "acceptable" and does not evoke guilty intrusions of conscience. To further ensure that they are not caught off guard in an unknown (threatening) situation, compulsives become extraordinarily sensitive to conventions, regulations, laws, and rules that can help them control unacceptable impulses, guide thinking, dictate behavior, and ensure that they are always beyond reproach.

These behavioral patterns, although allowing compulsives to control their guilt and anxiety over social disapproval, severely narrow their thinking and limit their experiences. Compulsives have no opportunity to explore new ways of approaching and integrating stimuli in their environment, and thus adaptive learning cannot occur. More personally satisfying habits cannot be acquired and relationships remain restricted. Helping compulsives loosen their unattainable standards of perfection for themselves and others is a basic therapeutic goal that lays the foundation for experimentation with more spontaneous behavior and mental ventures into uncharted, "dangerous" cognitive territory. As the constant fear of making a mistake dissipates, restrictive behavior patterns can be varied and more profitable modes can be discovered. Overreliance on rules can be restricted, and creativity, given freer rein, allows for flexible behavior that can prove to be gratifying in and of itself. The possibility of enjoying non-task-oriented activities, including relationships, may then open up.

Identifying Domain Dysfunctions

The compulsive personality is characterized by primary dysfunctions in the domains of cognitive style, expressive behavior, and interpersonal conduct. The compulsive handles life's ambiguities and internal anxieties by adopting a constricted cognitive style that relies on rules, regulations, schedules, and hierarchies for their resolution. Unfortunately, unfamiliar situations and ideas are emotionally and cognitively disruptive because creative mental processes are not available to deal with and integrate novel stimuli. Exploratory therapies that examine the historical development of cognitive rigidities, as well as cognitive approaches that confront the validity of the compulsive's assumptions, can help the patient develop a more fluid and creative cognitive style that allows both more adaptive and more rewarding interaction with the environment.

More fluid thinking can also help compulsives recognize that their disciplined expressive acts lead to limited experiences. Rather than make the most of each situation, compulsives adhere to structured and organized life patterns, regardless of whether they are optimally suited to the context. Insisting that all those around them behave in the same way ensures that exposure to alternative ways of doing or thinking about things is minimal. Once again, exploratory work that challenges internalized strictures and that helps dissolve fears about the "terrible consequences" of possibly making a mistake can help patients experiment with alternative behaviors.

Overly respectful interpersonal relations again reflect the compulsive's reliance on rules; propriety guarantees that the compulsive is always beyond reproach. Lack of interpersonal imagination, however, also leads others to find the compulsive boring and uptight, and the compulsive rarely enjoys rich and rewarding interpersonal feedback. As fears about being judged and punished decrease, the therapist may be able to convince the compulsive to try more spontaneous and potentially gratifying interaction styles, despite initial anxiety. Couples and sex therapy approaches can be particularly effective as adjuncts to individual therapy in helping the compulsive develop a healthier and more fruitful relationship.

Improvements in functioning in the primary dysfunctional domains can be bolstered by therapeutic intervention in the domains of self-image and object-representations. The compulsive's self-image is conscientious; the self is seen as industrious, reliable, meticulous, and efficient. Fear of making an error and a bad impression leads the patient to fixate on discipline, perfection, prudence, and loyalty. Exploratory work can help the patient get in touch with deep-seated aspects of the self that have been repressed, and cognitive work can help the compulsive realize that although these traits are indeed attractive and valuable, other repressed tendencies can balance them and lead to a more functional, healthy, and appealing persona. Similarly, object-representations are concealed, and only socially approved affects, attitudes, and actions are acknowledged. As a wider range of internal experiences come to be tolerated, the therapist can encourage a wider range of expressive communication and sociability. Intrapsychic coping mechanisms can get stronger as compulsives acknowledge the existence of the deeper emotional experiences they have been unconsciously repressing. The compulsive deals with these ("unacceptable") feelings by using the regulatory mechanism of reaction-formation and thus will display exactly the opposite emotion. For example, a compulsive who believes that anger is a weakness will suppress these feelings, even when they would be appropriate.

As work in the other domains helps patients develop an individual identity, there will no longer be as much need as previously to present themselves in a socially proper light. The compartmentalized morphologic organization of the compulsive's personality may also become more fluid and integrated; distinct and segregated memories, cognitions, and drives can be drawn on in various contexts and profitably applied. The typically solemn emotional affect should become sunnier as the need to control every aspect of behavior and environment diminishes. Decreased obsessive behavior and lessened concern with outcomes can increase the patient's enjoyment of the process of living.

SELECTING THERAPEUTIC MODALITIES

As they do in all of life's undertakings, compulsives want to perform "perfectly" in therapy. To this end, they may desire highly structured therapeutic approaches that provide a yardstick against which to measure "progress." Successful intervention with this personality style, however, entails the encouragement of open and spontaneous communication. Not only does this approach provide no specific procedural framework, but spontaneity terrifies the compulsive, in itself resulting in a host of possible resistances and transference reactions with which the therapist must cope. As the compulsive's deep-seated fear of "losing control" is inevitably kindled by the therapy process (which threatens to disequilibrate the much labored-for balance the patient has achieved), so is the ever-present rage that is activated by the pressure to maintain (unattainable) perfection. Some patients may express their resentments and anger by becoming openly critical of themselves, the therapy, or the therapist; justification for all interventions may be demanded of the therapist. Patients who view anger as an unacceptable form of expressing displeasure may become so "busy" at work that they are "forced" to miss sessions. In either case, as L.S. Benjamin points out (1993), therapists can make use of the compulsive's intellectual curiosity to secure cooperation where emotional guardedness would cause the patient to flee. A therapist's initial kindly and logical discussion of some of the patient's behaviors and their causes, if they ring true to the patient, can foster the trust in the therapist that is an essential requirement for success. Without this trust, few compulsives are likely to accept as viable such therapeutic goals as increasing interpersonal openness and warmth.

Behavioral Techniques

Behavioral methods are useful in treating many of the undesirable manifestations of the compulsive personality disorder, particularly phobic avoidance and ritualistic or highly restrictive and rigid behavior. Treatment involves desensitizing the patient to the anxiety-provoking stimuli (whatever these may be for a particular compulsive) that promote the problematic behavior. The first step involves establishing a hierarchy of stimuli within a relevant context, followed by relaxation training. Covert desensitization can then be carried out. Other effective techniques used with these disorders, according to Salzman (1989), include flooding, modeling, response prevention, satiation training, and thought stopping. Important in this regard also is a clear-cut agenda, such as prioritized problem specifics, and a systematic problem-solving approach designed to overcome indecisiveness and procrastinating behaviors. Also useful are formal relaxation procedures to modulate underlying tensions and anxieties. However, Turkat (1990) concluded that behavioral techniques alone are usually not sufficient to undo the long-term habit system of these patients. A measure of social skills training, combined with an effort to reduce their commitment to constant work, may occasionally be efficacious.

Interpersonal Techniques

Obsessive-compulsive personalities possess traits that create difficulties in all forms of therapeutic technique. Developing a collaborative relationship may be difficult to achieve owing to their high levels of rigidity, their persistent defensiveness, their resistance to emotional expression, and their tendency to devalue interpersonal relationships that are not based on clear hierarchy of status. Progress on interpersonal approaches will require, therefore, the establishment of rapport, contingent largely on the patient's respect for the therapist's competence and genuineness.

One of the techniques that approaches treatment by working on causative factors is the interpersonal approach. L.S. Benjamin (1993) assumes that the majority of compulsive patterns are acquired as a response to a cold and demanding parent that the child must placate to avoid verbal or physical punishment. Constant frustration of the desire for parental love and approval is transformed into an identification with the critical parent, followed by the internalization of self-criticisms. The first step toward emotional healing is to enable the patient to openly recognize the character of these early learning experiences and to develop a measure of empathy, if not compassion, for the child he or she once was. Perfection and absolute control need to be exposed and accepted as the unrealizable aims that they are. More realistic and less frustration-producing standards can then be integrated. The inevitable anxiety produced by failing to live up to such lofty early goals can then begin to dissipate. Benjamin also suggests employing cognitive techniques (outlined later in this discussion) to help the compulsive recognize that black-and-white values and relationships are best seen as variegated and multidimensional phenomena.

Couples therapy is also recommended as useful. The sexual arena is one in which many of the compulsive's patterns can be easily identified. Power struggles manifest themselves in the female compulsive's inability to give up sexual control (and frequent consequent anorgasmia). The male compulsive patient will be likely to interpret any lack of submission to his sexual overtures as a seizure of control, if not rejection, on the part of his partner. The therapist can help mediate communication and clarify that sexual (as well as other) reluctance can in fact result from differences in desire, and not necessarily from a will to control or put down. Sexual therapy may help some compulsives interact in a less controlling and more open way through the practice of sexual "exercises." Prescribed by the therapist, these procedures require the patient to follow instruction (which the compulsive is good at) and thus paradoxically yield control to his or her partner (as the doctor ordered!).

A common aim of compulsive patients is to finally come to an understanding with their "critical parent." Family therapy generally represents an attempt to bring members together, straighten out misunderstandings, and allow for the expression of long-stifled sentiments. Most often, satisfactory resolution of long-standing issues does not occur. Talking about relationship difficulties can be problematic here, as compulsives have a tendency to dominate other family members, and problems may even be aggravated. The compulsive needs to give up the wish for harmonious understanding before any structural changes in personality can occur. A different form of family therapy can occur in the compulsive's current family. Better success may be had where playful contact is encouraged between the patient and his or her spouse and children in an effort to emphasize the rewards inherent in even non-task-oriented activity and in being warm and spontaneous.

Group therapy can prove to be virtually fruitless with many compulsive patients, as they will often ally themselves with the therapist, refusing to participate wholeheartedly with other group participants. Unable to share thoughts and feelings spontaneously, compulsives have been termed "monopolists" by Yalom (1985), a designation to signify their tendency to dominate and control group discussions. Group leaders may be called on to modulate power struggles in which the compulsive patient seeks to assume a stance of authority in the peer relationship. On the other hand, group therapy may successfully diffuse the compulsive person's tedious and problematic impact. Also of value are opportunities to explore the compulsive's real problems, rather than merely talking about them. A useful model proposed by Wells and Giannetti (1990) has been designed to obviate certain contraindications for this approach among compulsives, as well as to resolve developmental issues that often lie at the core of their difficulties. Nevertheless, compulsives often develop contempt for the other patients in the group, or suffer extreme anxiety if forced to relinquish their defenses and expose their feelings in front of others.

Cognitive Techniques

Cognitive reorientation methods are particularly well suited to the compulsive, who tends to overintellectualize in an effort to ward off emotional reactivity. The cognitive therapy approach offered by Beck and Freeman (1990a) suggests that helping patients alter their basic cognitive assumptions about themselves and the world will lead to a therapeutic shift in emotions and behaviors. These assumptions include: (a) "There are right and wrong behaviors, decisions, and emotions"; (b) "To make a mistake is to have failed, to be deserving of criticism"; (c) "Failure is intolerable"; (d) "I must be perfectly in control of my environment as well as of myself; loss of control is intolerable and dangerous"; (e) "I am powerful enough to initiate or prevent the occurrence of catastrophes by magical rituals or obsessional ruminations"; and (f) "Without my rules and rituals, I'll collapse into an inert pile." At the onset of therapy, the patient is taught the cognitive theory of emotion, and specific goals related to the compulsive's difficulties are established. Goals are ranked according to solvability and importance; some easily resolved difficulties should be put at the top of the list to motivate the patient with experiences of therapeutic success. The automatic thoughts that interfere with the attainment of goals should be identified. Thoughts, feelings, and behaviors related to specific goals are monitored during the week so that the compulsive can become aware of anxiety-provoking stimuli and the cognitive assumption they elicit. Finally, after the negative consequences of these assumptions have been grasped, patient and therapist can work at refuting them in a way that makes sense to the patient.

Self-Image Techniques

If the main goal of therapy is to help patients stabilize following unsettling circumstances, the therapist may wish to help patients identify the troublesome consequences of their actions, but also help them refute their role in creating them and thereby regain a sense of control. A procedure of cognitive dissonance and reorganization may be well received by compulsive persons owing to their preference for structured and problem-centered solutions, their focus on the here and now, and their undergirding of characteristic defenses.

One of the more useful behavioral approaches is teaching patients how to truly relax. A common problem in convincing compulsives to make use of helpful relaxation techniques is that they are perceived as a waste of productive time. Adopting a stance of short-term behavioral experimentation, where patients assess the helpfulness of relaxation exercises in their lifestyle, helps overcome resistances. If a patient is afraid of giving up worrying, due to an irrational conviction that it is somehow useful in preventing disaster, he or she may agree to try limiting worry behavior to a particular time of the day. Beck and Freeman (1990a) also suggest that patients be warned about the likelihood of relapse and the probable need for booster sessions; in this way, it may be possible to minimize patients' tendency to want to be perfect, thereby avoiding feelings of shame over their "failure" that may prevent them from requesting a needed session.

Rogers's procedures may be helpful in showing patients that the therapist, an authority figure, displays a measure of high self-regard, a willingness to permit patients to express their deeper feelings of hostility and not be repudiated for them. Of value also are experiential procedures that may be a first step in illustrating for patients how readily their defensive façade can be pierced by deep feelings of an implicit character. Equally valuable among experiential techniques is their anti-intellectual character, their focus on the concrete realities of subtle feelings and emotions.

Intrapsychic Techniques

Psychodynamic approaches focus on interpreting displaced and repressed elements that result in overt symptoms. Compulsive patients, however, strongly resist abandoning their defenses initially, fearing a loss of control and the upsurge of untoward thoughts and emotions. Slowly, as they become aware of the therapist's support and their increasing confidence in themselves, compulsives may not only abandon their defensive patterns but begin to recognize that they may function more effectively without their protective façade. Progress is usually evident as patients learn to decrease their self-expectations and to supplant them with worthy but realistic and achievable ones. Rather than intellectualize and discuss matters cognitively, an effort should be made to promote an increase in risk taking and emotionally based decision making. Here, the therapist's task is to undo the patient's need for absolutes and certainties.

The transference relationship can be used as a starting point for exploring earlier relationships that may have been causative in the development of symptoms. Early traumas may be investigated. Dreams and free association can be helpful in getting past the patient's intellectual guard to deep-seated fears and feelings; often, the patient is surprised at the blatant and emotionally revealing content of his or her dreams. The patient's fantasies about a relaxed and flexible approach to life can also be explored. As fears and feelings of shame become conscious, they can be productively worked through. Although the valuable aspects of compulsivity need to be acknowledged by the therapist, its creativity-blocking and frequently inefficient aspects need to be pointed out.

Pharmacologic Techniques

Pharmacologic intervention with compulsive patients, if indicated, usually involves the use of anxiolytic and antidepressant medications, but only as an adjunct to psychotherapy. Relieving the anxiety and depression that help maintain compulsive symptoms often leads to more cooperative patients, enabling therapists to make inroads into the rigid structure of this personality. The utility of various medications with the Axis I obsessive-compulsive syndromes does not extend to the obsessive-compulsive personality disorders of Axis II (Jenike, 1991).

MAKING SYNERGISTIC ARRANGEMENTS

After establishing treatment goals and a solid alliance with the patient, behavioral techniques such as relaxation training, desensitization, and thought-stopping can prove to have good early results as an adjunct to the cognitive or interpersonal individual therapies. The possible benefits of anxiolytic or antidepressant medication can then be evaluated for the specific individual, as premature administration can lead, as with every personality disorder, to temporary alleviation of emotional symptoms and termination before longer-term reconstructive work can be done. Once some initial insight and behavior change is achieved by the patient in the course of individual treatment, the therapist may decide that couple, sex, or, less commonly, family therapy may further increase self-understanding and help provide environmental conditions that bolster the process of reorganizing the functional structure of the compulsive personality.

Illustrative Cases

With perhaps three or four notable exceptions (particularly antisocials, borderlines), compulsives have been found to blend with almost every other personality type. The variants described below reflect these combinations in part, but they are mostly accentuations of a number of the more prominent clinical domains of the prototypal obsessive-compulsive personality (see Table 18.4).

TABLE 18.4   Compulsive Personality Disorder Subytpes

Conscientious: Rule-bound and duty-bound; earnest, hardworking, meticulous, painstaking; indecisive, inflexible; marked self-doubts; dreads errors and mistakes.

MCMI 7

Parsimonious: Miserly, niggardly, tight-fisted, ungiving, hoarding, unsharing; protects self against loss; fears intrusions into vacant inner world; dreads exposure of personal improprieties and contrary impulses.

MCMI 7-1

Bureaucratic: Empowered in formal organizations; rules of group provide identity and security; is officious, high-handed, unimaginative, intrusive, nosy, petty, meddlesome, trifling, closed-minded.

MCMI 7-5

Bedeviled: Ambivalences unresolved; feels tormented, muddled, indecisive, befuddled; beset by intrapsychic conflicts, confusions, frustrations; obsessions/compulsions condense and control contradictory emotions.

MCMI 7-8A

Puritanical: Austere, self-righteous, bigoted, dogmatic, zealous, uncompromising, indignant, and judgmental; grim and prudish morality; must control and counteract own repugnant impulses and fantasies.

MCMI 7-P

COMPULSIVE PERSONALITY: CONSCIENTIOUS TYPE (COMPULSIVE WITH DEPENDENT TRAITS)

CASE 18.1, JAMES S., 43

Presenting Picture: James S. was a supervisor for a driver's license examination site who sought therapy after an idle comment of "You need help" was made by a colleague. Regimented and automated in his mannerisms and work ethics, he seemed entirely rule-bound and completely driven by a desire to make everything in his life conform to "upper authorities." It was not sufficient that he kept a smooth-running operation at his job; rather, he made sure that he was the first to arrive and last to leave every day, took his lunch break at his desk, and double- and triple-checked the other examiners' assignments to ensure that everyone knew exactly what they were doing each day. Although the others were quite experienced and knowledgeable about their work, he kept an extensive schedule of rotations and flow charts for the unit, taking absolute responsibility for everyone and everything involved with the site. He saw this as doing the bare minimum expected of him, though to his colleagues, this was entirely beyond protocol. However, should situations arise that would *require* autonomous or flexible thought or action, James would be highly ineffectual. So long as absolute order was maintained at all times, however, James could continue to derive much satisfaction from his work.

Clinical Assessment: This behavior of the *conscientious compulsive* is typified, more than any other compulsive type, by a conforming dependency, a compliance to rules and authority, and a willing submission to the wishes and values of others. James had a tendency to be self-effacing and noncompetitive, as well as a fear of independent self-assertion and a surface compliance to the expectations and demands of others. He voiced a strong sense of duty, feeling that others must not have their expectations unmet. His self-image, on the surface, was that of being a considerate, thoughtful, and cooperative person, prone to act in an unambitious and modest way. He possessed deep feelings of personal inadequacy as he tended to minimize attainments, underplay tangential attributes, and grade his abilities by their relevance to fulfilling the expectations of others. We might characterize James by the following descriptive adjectives: earnest, duty-bound, hard-working, meticulous, painstaking, and rule-bound. Dreading the consequences of making errors or mistakes, he reacted to situations that were unclear or ambiguous by acting indecisively and inflexibly, evincing marked self-doubts and hesitations about taking any course of action. From the foregoing, we can see that the basic compulsive structure of individuals such as James combine in a variety of significant ways with features associated primarily with the dependent personality.

James was overly respectful, even ingratiating with those in authority. The fear of failure and of provoking condemnation created considerable tension as well as occasional expressions of guilt. Submissive behavior with those in authority may also be traced to a reversal of hidden rebellious feelings. Lurking behind the front of propriety and restraint may have been intense contrary feelings that occasionally broke through their controls. Rarely daring to expose these feelings, James bound them so tightly that life became overorganized in an anxiously tense and disciplined self-restraint. As a consequence, he lacked spontaneity and flexibility, was often indecisive, and was easily upset by deviations from routine. There was a marked denial of discordant emotions and a tendency to neutralize feelings normally aroused by distressful events.

James's marked self-doubts and deflated sense of self-esteem were given support by attaching himself to an institutional organization. In this way, he sought to associate his actions by identifying them with those in authority. Efforts were made to maintain a behavioral pattern that was consistent and unvarying, one in which independent actions were restrained and the strictures of approved rules were rigidly complied with. The conscientious tendency to perfection and a preoccupation with minor irrelevancies distracted his attention from deeper sources of anxiety, inadequacy, and anticipated derogation.

Most central to James's psychic makeup, as deduced from his MCMI responses, were the dread of making mistakes and the fear of taking risks. There was a persistent reworking of things, a feeling of never being satisfied with the results of his efforts, and a concomitant anxiety of being unprepared for any new task. His conscientiousness reflected a deep sense of inadequacy, potential failure, and ultimate exposure for inner deficiencies and untenable impulses.

James was meticulous and fastidious, not because the tasks facing him required such conscientious behavior, but because he anticipated criticism and derogation: What can I do to prevent others from seeing how empty and shallow I am? What can I do to make sure that no one sees beneath my surface proprieties to the obnoxious and immoral impulses that keep welling up within me? Fearing to commit himself and make a mistake, James kept within a narrow rut, unwilling to gamble with the possibility that he may choose wrong. Totally lacking in the gambling spirit, he was unwilling to chance placing his destiny in unpredictable events. To avoid misguided transgressions and to obviate the unknown and potentially dangerous, James sought to convey a front of equanimity and social agreeableness. He displayed minimal introspection and a rigorous internal conscience, inner gauges that served to counter any oppositional urges and unacceptable thoughts.

Synergistic Treatment Plan: As James would likely be ill-suited to effectively handle deep *insight-oriented* therapy and *dynamic* reconstructions, a focus on immediate manifestations would be in order, but as always, from a systematic, personologic perspective. It would be necessary, first, to work toward *behaviorally* and *biophysically* adjusting his anxieties regarding possible "slip-ups" and the consequences of imperfections (decrease *pain* orientation). As his vigilance became diminished, it would then be useful to address, in a nonconfrontive manner, James's *cognitive* self-perpetuations that established rules are infallible and that he must rely on and abide by these constructs in all circumstances (a rigid *passive-other* orientation). Additionally, it would be necessary to enhance his very meager *self* picture, as James's self-deprecating attitudes continually enforced the notion that he lacked the mere ability to function with any free will. An approach that would meld interventions addressing these faulty cognitions with an *interpersonal* focus would help to achieve a more *active-other* personal style.

Therapeutic Course: Short-term *supportive* therapy was the major initial vehicle for treating James. *Psychopharmacologic agents* were beneficial in the early periods of this patient's difficulties, but the level of dosage employed was not such as to cause significant decrements in his efficiency and alertness. Also useful as part of a focused treatment approach were *behavior modification* techniques designed to desensitize James to currently discomforting or anxiety-provoking situations. *Group* and *family therapy* techniques were not utilized because he probably would have wanted to ally himself with the therapist and therefore may not have participated wholeheartedly as a patient. Long-term techniques that may have forced him to relinquish his defenses and expose his feelings in front of others may have produced an unwanted deterioration in his condition.

Among his reasons for seeking therapy were unanticipated attacks of anxiety, spells of immobilization, and excessive fatigue. Because symptoms such as these threatened his public style of efficiency and responsibility, it was especially useful to employ circumscribed and focused short-term methods of treatment. Because he viewed his symptoms as products of an isolated physical disease, failing to recognize that they may have represented the outcropping of his inner psychological dynamics (e.g., ambivalence and repressed resentments), a less expressive and more concise approach suited James best. Certainly, for every piece of defensive armor removed, the therapist had to bolster the patient's confidence twofold. To remove more defenses than the patient could tolerate may have prolonged the treatment plan extensively. Fortunately, James was well guarded, such that careful inquiries by the therapist fostered growth without a problematic relapse. Caution was the byword with this patient.

Owing to his anxious conformity and his fear of public ridicule, James viewed therapy as a procedure that would expose his feelings of inadequacy. Tense, grim, and cheerless, he preferred to maintain the status quo rather than confront the need to change. His defensiveness was honored, and probing and insight proceeded at a careful pace. Once a measure of trust and confidence had developed in the relationship, the therapist used *cognitive* and *interpersonal* methods to stabilize anxieties and foster change. Because James preferred to restrict his actions and thoughts to those to which he was accustomed, therapeutic procedures did not confront more than he could tolerate. Goals of this nature focused on changing assumptions, noted by Beck and others, such as the fear that any shortcoming would result in a catastrophe or that not performing at the highest level would result in a humiliating failure. Unless his problematic beliefs were explicitly addressed, he may have voiced pseudo-insights, but this would have been a façade to placate the therapist. His habitual defenses were so well constructed that general insight-based interpretations were likely to be temporary at best. Genuine progress necessitated brief, focused techniques to modify problematic self-statements and assumptions. Without these concrete and short-term techniques, James would have paid lip service to treatment goals, expressing guilt and self-condemnation for his past shortcomings, but he may not have readily relinquished his defensive controls. Empathy alone may likewise have been only modestly useful because of his evasiveness and his discomfort with emotion-laden materials. Owing to his need to follow a rigid and formalized lifestyle, he was likely to respond better to short-term cognitive or interpersonal methods that were specific in their procedures rather than to more expressive or *nondirective* techniques. To diminish the occurrence of setbacks, efforts were made to strengthen his will to give up maladaptive beliefs such as unrelenting self-criticism and the unyielding correctness of authority-based rules and regulations.

COMPULSIVE PERSONALITY: PURITANICAL TYPE (COMPULSIVE WITH PARANOID FEATURES)

CASE 18.2, LAUREN A., 27

Presenting Picture: Lauren A., a church youth group leader, had been troubled by both insomnia and "impure thoughts" that someone like her should "certainly not have." Very high-strung and seemingly at her wit's end, Lauren broke into tears at the mere thought of a slip-up in front of the youth group adolescents (in her case, accidentally using a "foul" word), and any minor deviation from perfect order in and around her environment was enough to ruin an entire day's schedule. For example, the thought of a dish towel not replaced in the rack after she had left for a therapy appointment constituted her dwelling on being in "disarray," and she was left with the agitation over the decision of whether to right this "terrible" wrong or to be punctual for her appointment. Lauren had learned certain routines that helped combat insomnia prior to starting therapy, but it seemed as though *nothing* could possibly help with her impure thoughts. She could not bring herself to speak these thoughts, for she feared the result would be to act on them. Equally troubling for her was the fact that she was seeing a therapist, something that she did not think was moral, and something that she did in absolute secrecy. Lauren's most salient vulnerability seemed to be her fear of being *shamed*, whether to herself or in front of her fellow congregants.

Clinical Assessment: Lauren, a *puritanical compulsive*, could be described as possessing an austere, self-righteous, highly controlled, but deeply conflictful conformity to the conventions of propriety and authority. Her intense anger and resentment are given sanction, at least as she sees it, by virtue of the fact that she is on the side of righteousness and morality. Evident are periodic displays of suspiciousness, irritability, obsessional ideation, and severe judgmental attitudes. There is a tendency toward denial, with an extreme defensiveness about admitting emotional difficulties and psychosocial problems. However, despite the preceding efforts, there are clear signs that Lauren is unusually tense and high-strung. Anticipating public exposure and humiliation, periods of self-deprecation and self-punishment give way to outbursts of extrapunitive anger and persecutory accusations. This conflictual struggle against expressing emotions and directing anger endangered her efforts at maintaining control.

In addition to her harsh judgments of the behavior of others, Lauren made efforts to maintain a disciplined self-restraint; she rarely relaxed or let down a guarded defensiveness. She typically appeared grim and cheerless, exhibited an anxiously tense and serious-minded prudish morality. Beneath a cooperative and controlled façade were marked feelings of personal insecurity, and she was vigilantly alert to avoid social transgressions that may have provoked humiliation and embarrassment. This puritanical variant of the compulsive shows distinct features of the paranoid personality, notably the bigoted, dogmatic, and zealous characteristics.

Lauren avoided situations that may have resulted either in personal censure or derision, and she dreaded making mistakes or taking risks, lest these provoke disapproval. As a defensive maneuver, she restricted activities, operated within narrow boundaries, and confined herself to a rigid and, at times, self-righteous conformity to rules and regulations. By adhering vigorously to propriety and convention, by following the straight and narrow path, she sought to minimize criticism and punitive reactions, particularly from persons in authority.

Lauren's conforming style had been undermined repeatedly, and there was a consequent tendency to be argumentative, resentful, and critical of others. Lurking behind her façade of propriety was a growing bitterness and disillusionment, features clearly present in her MCMI profile. These animosities churned within her. They would either break through to the surface in angry upsurges or be countered in ritualistic precautions or obsessive ruminations. Guilt and self-condemnation may have been periodically exhibited, as when she turned her feelings inward and imposed severe punitive judgments and actions on herself. Despite the tension it generated, such self-reproval was likely to serve as a release for her hostile and forbidden feelings. However, ambivalence was constantly present. On the one hand, there were strong desires to discharge hostility and, on the other, a constant fear that such expressions would prompt derision and rejection. As a residual of this ambivalence, she had a history of persistent tensions, possibly evident in psychosomatic symptoms.

Beneath the surface, Lauren felt the press of irrational impulses, including what she judged to be repugnant impulses and sexual desires. Her puritanical attitudes had developed as a protection against her own as well as the world's uncontrollable passions. Rather than allowing these impulses to wreak public havoc should she ever have let loose and allowed expression, Lauren kept them tightly under control, resisted their emergence, and ensured that such emotions be kept from desirable objects. Her ascetic and austere lifestyle, her constraint of herself and others, served as a method of prohibiting her own darker impulses and fantasies.

Indignant and judgmental about the lack of perfection in others, Lauren's puritanical attitudes were seen by others as abrasive and irritating. These behaviors intimidated others at first, and then provoked them into acts of defiance and disobedience. Progressing over time from acts of an impersonal propriety and politeness, Lauren deteriorated into an acerbic dogmatism, a harsh and opinionated style that sought constantly to fix the mistakes of others and to endlessly criticize as inadequate or improper that which others had done. Upright and straitlaced, she quickly lost her temper over matters of a trivial nature. She had become a harsh and stern disciplinarian, a fault-finding and moralistic prig. Not only did she have to prove others wrong and immoral, but she judged them as deserving punishment. Because others were seen as sinners and perpetrators of immoral acts, she could justly condemn without guilt. Justice requires a punitive attitude; morality sanctions it. Hence, Lauren, who had feared condemnation in the past, had now become the merciless condemnor. Once concerned with just treatment for herself, she had become the perpetrator of injustices herself.

Synergistic Treatment Plan: As a first measure, it would be necessary to modify Lauren's *behavioral* and *biophysical* proclivities toward tense hypervigilance against imperfections, and the resultant anger and disillusionment (decrease *pain* orientation). Measures to adjust *cognitive* self-perpetuations would follow, specifically addressing the ambivalent schemata that constantly thwart disapproval (a rigid *passive-other* orientation). Lauren's statute-centered morality routinely set up impossible catch-22 conflicts and perceived antagonisms, such that she could never measure up to her imposed standards; this characterological flaw fed into an already depleted sense of *self*. Furthermore, she lived in constant fear of acting-out based on these conflicts. A cognitive reframing approach, combined with an *interpersonal* focus on less stressful, healthier interactions, would foster a greater *active-self* personologic style.

Therapeutic Course: *Supportive* therapy was necessary to begin this process with Lauren. A *psychopharmacologic* agent was suggested for this early stage in treatment, and after much deliberation and hesitancy over the "moral implications" of such an intervention and a thorough discussion of the physiological reasoning behind the use of this drug, she accepted this treatment. As Lauren was able to establish a baseline of comfort with these "unusual" (from her perspective) conditions, *behavior modification* techniques were introduced to help Lauren cope with current stress-provoking issues. *Group* and *family therapy* techniques were not an option; she most likely would tend to "cling" to the therapist in such a situation and avoid, at all costs, shaming herself in front of anyone. Likewise, time-extended therapies aimed at making her relinquish her aegis and leaving her feeling vulnerable in front of the therapist (much less anyone else) would have proved counterproductive.

Lauren sought therapy because she was now ineffectual in her life; her preoccupations with perfection and purity in every conceivable facet of her life had, in effect, undermined her capacity to perform those duties she expected of herself. She was now stricken with chronic panic attacks, periods of emotional and effectual paralysis, and excessive fatigue. Because these symptoms were at odds with her public persona, it was most practical to utilize short-term focused techniques. Lauren was not oriented toward exploring her difficulties as a manifestation of troubled or repressed internal psychological functions; rather, she viewed these symptoms as physical ailments that needed to be fixed. As she would have strongly resisted extensive *insight-oriented* therapies that were at odds with her considerable moral and religious investment, it was best to work from a concise and focused milieu. Even with this cautious and targeted intervention, defenses had to be removed, and the therapist needed to keep the old therapeutic axiom in mind: "Don't take anything away unless you have something to replace it." Lauren, by her nature, was quite well guarded, and appropriate, nonintrusive probings and suggestions provided for positive motion and limited setbacks in treatment.

Owing to her zealous conformity and her terror at the thought of being "shamed," Lauren had a tendency to view therapy as an instrument whose inherent design was to uncover and humiliate her by proving her inadequate. Consistently wrought with worry, she was not oriented toward fundamental change, but toward alleviation of difficulty with minimal personal modification. This desire was honored, and inquiries and suggestions were undertaken carefully. As the therapeutic relationship was built and began to gain effectiveness, the therapist used *cognitive* and *interpersonal* methods to effect the necessary changes as well as alleviate anxiety syndromes. Lauren's tolerance was always kept in mind when confrontive methods were used, as it was only safe for her to work with familiar behaviors and attitudes. As noted by Beck and others, tangible goals in this realm included disputing fears such as the inevitability of a particular shortcoming resulting in a catastrophe, or that performing at less than perfection would result in devastating failure. Explicitly addressing these problematic assumptions and self-statements with concrete and short-term techniques short-circuited most attempts to placate the therapist with false insights and empty talk. Although the early employment of these focused methods were effective, the therapist needed to continue to be alert for half-hearted expression of culpability, as Lauren tended to use this tactic to obscure and salvage unrelinquished defensive controls. A caveat should be issued, as well, that empathy by itself would have fostered evasiveness and most likely would have been ineffective due to her uneasiness with more personal, affective issues. In sum, her quite rigid style was best suited to focused cognitive or interpersonal methods rather than nondirective, expressive modalities.

COMPULSIVE PERSONALITY: BUREAUCRATIC TYPE (COMPULSIVE WITH NARCISSISTIC FEATURES)

CASE 18.3, CATHERINE F., 35

Presenting Picture: Catherine F. was an assistant high school principal, which she was happy to describe as "no small job at all." Though her tasks at work were quite numerous, she seemed to relate most closely to her task of maintaining discipline throughout the school. Conformity, to Catherine, was very comforting, and she derived a great deal of satisfaction ensuring that the school would run at peak efficiency, with a very homogeneous "standard" of behavior for students. Interestingly enough, however, certain intrinsic features of the job caused distress. Although she claimed to enjoy maintaining discipline, Catherine lacked the flexibility to shift her daily routine to approach a misbehaving student unexpectedly. When this would happen, she said, she would be out of sorts the remainder of the day. What was particularly notable with Catherine was her description of her "significant relationship." Though she did not go into great detail, she did itemize the process of decision making within the relationship, describing the *sensible* nature of both parties and that all decisions that affected both parties went through a rather stringent ratification process.

Clinical Assessment: Not unlike other compulsive personalities, Catherine, a *bureaucratic compulsive,* found that an alliance with time-tested traditional values, established authorities, and formal organizations worked extremely well for her. Instead of feeling angered and oppressed by authoritarian and organizational rules, she felt strengthened and comforted by these associations. Being part of a group or a bureaucracy made her feel that she was not alone and that her ability to act firmly and decisively had thereby been empowered. She felt that her alliance with the school system fortified her self-esteem. The group not only provided a powerful identification, but an established set of rules and values that gave her a framework and a direction for action. Moreover, it was of great comfort to her to have the structure and goals of her group organize her life and show her what really mattered in life. Fearful that she could not constrain her inner impulses, she sought firm boundaries that would guide her to make proper decisions. At the deepest level, therefore, she believed that by following the rules of the organization, no one could fault and punish her. She did what she was told to do. Although obedience limited the range of her opportunities, it freed Catherine from the anxiety of taking responsibility for making decisions on her own.

The hierarchy of authorities and subordinates enabled Catherine to clearly define her place and responsibilities in the system. Once established, she became extremely loyal and dependable. Now that she knew she was protected, she could give of herself freely within the boundaries the organization had established. Moreover, knowing what was expected of her and knowing that others also had clearly defined roles and expectancies as well enabled her to feel secure within the organization. Not only did she feel that she was no longer alone, but she was less fearful of being abandoned by the system. For Catherine, union with others provided secure and deep identifications; the bureaucracy became an important index of who she was, giving her both a sense of identity and a purpose for being. As long as she stayed within the organization, she knew that she would be highly valued. To reciprocate, she was a loyal, trustworthy, and diligent group member, faithfully committed to the community's goals and values.

More than most members of a formal hierarchical organization (church, police, union, university, company), bureaucratic compulsives such as Catherine are rigid adherents to the structure of the organization. She was a "stickler" for following the details and aspirations of the system. Rules were set out precisely, lists and plans were formed to arrange her work, she knew who was above and below whom, and she kept to precise time schedules. Punctual and meticulous, Catherine adhered to the so-called Protestant work ethic, had a hierarchical or authoritarian schema for evaluating and ranking others on an explicit rating system. Personal inclinations were put aside; such inclinations were always suspect in that they might have come to override the goals and values of the system. As in totalitarian societies, Catherine denied her individuality and submitted to the impersonal values of the system.

As a consequence of this narrow and rigid adherence to bureaucratic policies and rules, she was often seen as officious, high-handed, unimaginative, closed-minded, as well as intrusive, nosy, and meddlesome. It is petty and trifling bureaucrats such as Catherine that often make dealing with public agencies so trying and tiresome.

Owing to the status and security she gained by her alliance with institutional standing and perquisites, this otherwise rigid and constrained individual exhibited a public sense of pride and self-importance. As a consequence, she might have displayed overt features that appear similar to those seen among narcissistic personalities. However, in contrast to prototypal narcissists, her air of superiority and status was but skin deep.

Synergistic Treatment Plan: Catherine's well-established defenses would be difficult to traverse, and it would be important to work at a cautious pace to adjust these ingrained coping strategies. A *supportive* milieu would begin the process, with exploration into *biophysical* aspects of her difficulties. As a more comfortable therapeutic environment was established, it would then be appropriate to begin introducing *interpersonal* and *cognitive* intervention schemes. Catherine's perpetuations included rigid assumptions regarding the "outlandish" characteristics of the people in her environment, and holding everyone and everything at arm's length to herself (*passive* orientation). She viewed herself in a superior role, but placed a great deal of importance on others' response to her authority (*self-other* conflict); therefore, instilling a more empathic attitude and establishing social skills that would allow for more parallel relationships would be beneficial. Additionally, *behavioral* measures would work toward adjusting habits, the ultimate objective being a less perfectionistic style. An increase in her sensitivity to her own moods would likely be helpful by employing several *experiential* methods.

Therapeutic Course: For Catherine, *supportive* therapy was the major initial vehicle for treatment. Several *psychopharmacologic agents* were considered for alleviating tense feelings, but these were ultimately rejected. However, some of the more recent SSRI agents may have been helpful in this case, had they been available at the time. Various *interpersonal* techniques (e.g., Benjamin, Klerman) designed to counteract the patient's tendency to feel and act superior to problematic situations were useful. *Cognitive reorientation* methods geared to reframing assumptions about herself and the expectations of others were also used gradually and with discretion. Care was taken to accomplish the purposes of altering these dysfunctional beliefs, especially because Catherine may have grasped the point of these methods only at an abstract or intellectual level. To rework the foundations of her lifestyle did not require long-term procedures. Rather, circumscribed and focused approaches offered significant personality reconstruction in a condensed and fruitful way. Although interpersonal methods that focused on the patient alone were successful, she was not amenable to *group* or *family* therapy. That is, she displayed extreme resistance in relinquishing her defenses and would have been ill-equipped to expose her feelings in front of others.

In general, Catherine was prone to regard therapy, either brief or extended, as a threat to her defensive armor. Although it was possible to readily relieve her symptoms, she tried to avoid self-exploration and self-awareness. Her defensiveness was deeply protective and needed to be honored by the therapist; probing proceeded no faster than she could tolerate. Only after building trust and confidence in the therapeutic relationship could the therapist begin to bring cognitive and interpersonal methods into the open. For every piece of defensive armor removed, however, the therapist needed to bolster the patient's sense that the treatment process would be constructive and self-enhancing. Removing more defenses than the patient could handle was avoided to prevent relapse. She was sufficiently well guarded and self-assured to ignore or intellectualize distressing confrontations, but nonetheless, caution was the byword.

As noted, Catherine was not only somewhat suspicious of therapy and psychology but also tended to denigrate sentimentality, intimate feelings, and tenderness. Her narcissistic streak led her to lack sympathy for the weak and oppressed. The therapist could not allow the entire therapeutic enterprise to be hostage to her indifference. A directive cognitive approach was necessary to lead her to recognize that dealing with the softer emotions would not necessarily undermine the foundations of her interpersonal style or reactivate feelings buried for years. Her assumption that sympathy and tender feelings only distracted and diverted people from being correct and successful was confronted cognitively. Her exploitive inclinations, propriety, and conventional regulations were examined and counteracted by combining cognitive and interpersonal therapies.

COMPULSIVE PERSONALITY: PARSIMONIOUS TYPE (COMPULSIVE WITH SCHIZOID FEATURES)

CASE 18.4, PAT F., 44

Presenting Picture: Pat F., the head of the billing department for a large law firm, seemed to live life planning for a rainy day. She took pride in her hard work, though she stated, "I don't know that I necessarily have to like the work," and that at least she didn't *dislike* it. It seemed as though there was no room in Pat's life for any pleasure or excesses; her entire being was focused on making sure that what she had achieved was not lost, with particular emphasis on finances. For example, in her daily commute, she would walk two miles from the train stop to the office, her only intention being to save the bus fare. Additionally, she kept the vast majority of her money in a safe in her basement, and would only open a bank account after interviewing the president of the bank. Although Pat stated that she was happy with this particular lifestyle, there was a notable dearth of enthusiasm, as if to say that relative safety was the only necessity of life, and true happiness was something best left alone.

Clinical Assessment: Fromm's (1947) discussion of the "hoarding orientation" gets close to the characterization of Pat, a *parsimonious compulsive*. What is most notable in Pat was her miserliness, the protective wall she placed between herself and the outer world, keeping tight to that which she possessed, being ungiving and unsharing. She was notably niggardly, tight-fisted, and penny-pinching. Her parsimony, as we viewed it, reflected a wariness against the possibility of loss, a self-protective stance in which exposure permitted the possibility of loss.

Another aspect of the parsimonious compulsive relates to property and possessions. Pat's behavior conveyed the attitude What is mine is mine and what is yours is yours; I will leave alone what you possess as long as you do likewise with mine. Just as she learned in her struggle with parental restrictions to find a small sphere of behavior that was safe and above reproach, so too did she, as an adult, gather and hold tight to her limited body of rights and possessions. As Fromm (1947) puts it, she would hoard and protect against all intrusions those few prized belongings she had struggled to acquire for herself. Having been deprived of so many wishes and desires in childhood, she nurtured and protected what she had achieved. She fortified herself and staved off those vultures who wished to deprive her of her resources. She was miserly and ungiving and acted as if her "fortune" could never be replenished. In this latter regard, we saw the basis for clinical observations that indicated that Pat shared a number of significant features more typically seen in the schizoid personality: a cool distancing and an apparent self-protectiveness from external intrusions.

There was a deeper and more devious basis for Pat's demand that her possessions and privacy be secure. She dared not permit anyone to explore the emptiness of her inner self, the truly barren quality of her attainments and competencies. Of even greater import, she dreaded that others would uncover her rebellious urges, those angry and defiant feelings that lurk beneath her cloak of respectability and propriety. She had to quickly stop others from exploring and possibly exposing the pretense of her very existence. Respect was a way of maintaining distance, then, a means of hiding what she must keep from others and from herself.

Synergistic Treatment Plan: Rigid adherence to the status quo was an intractable rule in Pat's life, along with a distaste for sharing or interacting (*passive* orientation), and these principles needed to be respected throughout the course of therapy, with interventions and increasingly confrontive measures proceeding at *her* pace. It would be most beneficial to begin with a *supportive* milieu, gradually broaching the possibilities of clear-cut *biophysical* and *behavioral* perspectives and tactics. As her considerably fortified barriers were relaxed, she would become more prepared to begin exploring those *cognitions* of hers that led to self-perpetuations. Again, at *her* pace, the focus would be on such assumptions that everyone else is either incompetent or antagonistic, or that some possible flaw in herself would inevitably lead to catastrophe (*pain* orientation, conflicting and salient *self-other* imbalance). As some attitudes were clarified, it would be possible *interpersonally* to adjust self-imposed barriers, encourage socialization, and work toward a new appreciation of enjoyment (increase *pleasure*).

Therapeutic Course: *Supportive therapy* and *behavior modification* techniques were useful in initiating a focused treatment approach, as they set the stage for a less disconcerting therapeutic atmosphere and helped desensitize Pat to currently discomforting and anxiety-provoking situations. Introduction of a *psychopharmacologic agent,* in a suitable dosage that did not intrude on her effectiveness in daily tasks, also proved beneficial in preparing Pat for more confrontive methods that would follow. She also participated in a *group therapy* milieu, but this was not a successful venture. Pat's considerable discomfort with expressing personal issues caused her to retreat, seeking protection with the therapist and refusing to participate effectively with the group. Likewise, more expressive *insight-oriented* and *nondirective* techniques that would have prompted her to abandon her defense strategies or exhibit more potent emotions would have provided a breeding ground for setbacks and decompensation.

Pat's concerns included unanticipated panic attacks, brief lethargic periods, and constant exhaustion. As these symptoms were discordant with her structured and consistently paced lifestyle of efficiency and responsibility, focused short-term treatment techniques were most appropriate. Pat was unlikely to entertain the notion that her difficulties stemmed from inner psychological dynamics (e.g., ambivalence and repressed resentments); rather, she was convinced that these were symptoms analogous to a singular physical disease, if not a direct manifestation of a physical problem. Therefore, a less exploratory and more direct plan suited this case best. Of course, as the therapist removed Pat's troublesome coping strategies, he needed to provide extra measures of support and help her replace those obsolete strategies with more effective skills. He exercised caution consistently, as removing more defenses than she could tolerate would have been extremely counterproductive. Hypervigilance to her sensitivities, however, was *not* necessary, as her well-established defenses were able to tolerate careful inquiries and appropriate disputes.

Pat's hypervigilance, on the other hand, was geared primarily toward avoiding any vulnerability to expose her inadequacy. Rigid and implacable, any thoughts of fulfillment were overshadowed by a need to maintain the status quo. This defensive nature was respected, and more intrusive and expressive approaches were avoided in the earlier stages. As the therapeutic relationship developed and a more genuine trust emerged, short-term *cognitive* and *interpersonal* methods began to be employed. As Pat preferred to maintain her usual boundaries and regulations, these procedures proceeded at a comfortable pace, as determined by her. During this period, the work focused on modifying beliefs and schemata (imperfection begets catastrophe, half-hearted performance results in failure and denigration, etc.). One of Pat's habitual coping strategies was to voice pseudo-insights in attempts to cloak the need for change, and this required a watchful eye on the part of the therapist. Her defenses were rather immutable, unlikely to have been swayed by her own or the therapist's insights. A *nondirective* approach, relying primarily if not solely on the therapist's empathic posture, would have been only modestly useful, as Pat most likely would have used her evasive tactics in dodging emotionally charged issues. Genuine progress required tangible methods that worked rapidly enough in modifying problematic assumptions to provide consistent incentive to remain invested in therapy. She responded best to short-term cognitive and interpersonal methods that were specific in their procedures, as abstraction, pondering, and exploring were an ill fit for her regimented style.

COMPULSIVE PERSONALITY: BEDEVILED TYPE
COMPULSIVE WITH NEGATIVISTIC FEATURES)

CASE 18.5, NEIL S., 29

Presenting Picture: Neil S. was referred for therapy by his physician after an unexplainable bout with dreams that would wake him up screaming. Remarkably tense and agitated, he seemed always to be in conflict with himself, desiring an outlet for his emotional life that just couldn't exist within the logical order. As he explained, he was "the only person who could do certain things" in his role at work, and this carried forth into his role in society, as well. However, Neil was not without fantasies. He could vividly describe the "ideal vacation," one that would take him across the country at 150 miles per hour in a foreign sports car. The pleasure and temporary relaxation that permeated his tense being were obvious, but he was swiftly brought back into his "reality" when the fantasy approached feasibility. He was trapped between very powerful desires and the need to keep "compartmentalized" for the greater sake of order.

Clinical Assessment: As with some variants of both negativistic and compulsive ambivalent personality types, Neil, a *bedeviled compulsive,* possessed an amalgamation of both prototypes. He experienced a deep struggle beneath the surface between the need to comply with the wishes of others at one moment, and the desire to assert his own interests the next, features in clear evidence on his MCMI profile. Contending somewhat unsuccessfully with this ambivalence was what undermined him. For the most part, compulsives' strategy of self-denial works reasonably well for them; they submerge their oppositional desires and put forth a proper and correct front. For a bedeviled subtype such as Neil, however, this strategy did not hold. Although he appeared on the surface to be in psychic control, underneath he was going around in circles, unable to decide which course to follow, increasingly unsure of who he was and what he wanted to do. When he was expected to act decisively, he oscillated and procrastinated, felt tormented and befuddled, became cautious and timid, delaying decisions and using complex rationales to keep his inner confusion under control. Unable to get a hold of who he was, feeling great pressure to meet his obligations, he began to doubt what it was that he believed and what it was that he wanted. Caught in his upsurging ambivalence, with one part of himself accelerating in one direction and the other part resisting movement, he became exhausted, grumpy, and discontent but, more than anything else, perplexed and confused, driven by thoughts and impulses that could no longer be contained and directed. He felt overwhelmed by both his will and his better knowledge. Thoughts and impulses that were usually contained and that adhered to guiding principles seemed contradictory and uncontrolled. Inner uncertainties came to the fore, arising from unknown conflictual attitudes and feelings.

The persistence of these oscillating directions resulted in Neil's tendency to engage in *self-torture,* to create a self-punitive resolution that sought to undo the powerful emotions that bedeviled him. The emergence of obsessions and compulsions may be seen as a futile attempt to control irrational thoughts and feelings. It also signifies, however, that his habitual controls were crumbling. It was at these times that Neil may have felt possessed by demons. Unable to acknowledge what was upsetting him, that is, the ambivalences of his inner life, he sought through obsessions and compulsions to provide an outlet for his contradictory emotions, hoping thereby that these irreconcilable feelings would not undermine or overwhelm him. The eruption of untoward thoughts and distressing impulses made him feel as if he were caught in the grip of an unresolvable state. Most troublesome during this time was the recognition that he might be driven by temptations that would overwhelm his moral strength. He could not have it both ways. He saw himself as succumbing to corruption, perhaps controlled by the devil himself. Constrained and deformed by these contradictory tendencies, he felt as though he were on the edge of psychic dissolution.

Synergistic Treatment Plan: Though Neil would be prone to exhibit those tendencies toward avoiding change that are characteristic of the prototype compulsive personality, an important feature in this case was Neil's emerging realization that there indeed was a *need* for treatment, as the therapist would be able to draw on the momentum inherent in this quality. Prior to countering and disputing Neil's perpetuations, it would be necessary to alleviate his most salient agitations and anxieties (hypervigilance to avoid *pain*) through *behavioral* outlets as well as possible *biophysical* remedies. As Neil's ambivalence regarding therapy would dissipate, the next phase of treatment would be directively confronting such faulty and conflicting *cognitions* as his need to conform, juxtaposed against his desire to release (strong and conflictual *passive-active* stance) and to correct *interpersonal* imbalances (less salient but still conflictual *self-other*), such as a strong tendency to distrust and devalue others mixed with a negative and condemning self-view. As these conflicts become clarified, the therapist would be able to strengthen Neil's *pleasure* orientation, a construct that was present but thoroughly denied.

Therapeutic Course: A short-term and circumscribed focus was the most optimally suited treatment for Neil. Formal *behavior modification* methods were productive in achieving greater consistency and interpersonal harmony in his social behavior. Directive *cognitive techniques,* such as those of Meichenbaum and Ellis, were also used to confront Neil with the obstructive and self-defeating character of his expectations and his personal relations. Although the deeply rooted character of these problems undoubtedly impeded the effectiveness of treatment, it was most fruitful to explore the more confrontive and incisive techniques of both cognitive and *interpersonal* therapies (e.g., Benjamin, Kiesler). A thorough reconstruction of personality, then, was not the only means of altering his deeper pathologies. In support of short-term interpersonal techniques, *family* treatment methods were used as an adjunct to individual modalities and were rather successful in examining the complex network of relationships that sustained his personality style. Together with cognitive reframing procedures, these methods proved to be among the most useful in helping the patient recognize the source of his own hurt and angry feelings and in appreciating how he provoked hurt and anger in others.

Although Neil was, at heart, committed to the therapeutic process, he did show resistance to actively and fully participating in more vulnerable areas by intellectualizing and "testing" the therapist. A strong and persuasive cognitive approach was required to draw him more effectively into the therapeutic process. As he began to understand and invest in his treatment, he learned to see the benefits of reframing his attitudes and the consequences of doing so. With confronting methods, he learned not to assume that a problem could always be traced to another person's stupidity, laziness, or hostility. As he found it possible to accept a measure of responsibility for his difficulties, he didn't need to conclude that the therapist tricked him into admitting it. In this situation, the therapist restrained any impulse to react to him with general disapproval or criticism. An important step in building rapport with Neil was to see things from his viewpoint. As success needed to be achieved in a short-term intervention, the therapist had to convey a sense of trust and a willingness to develop a constructive alliance. A balance of professional authority and tolerance was useful in diminishing the probability that he would relapse or impulsively withdraw from treatment.

As noted, Neil was not initially fully cooperative in therapy. The therapist's strong and determined attitude overcame his desire to outwit the therapist by setting up situations to test the therapist's skills, to catch inconsistencies, to arouse ire, and, if possible, to belittle and humiliate the therapist. For the therapist, restraining the impulse to express a condemning attitude could not be a difficult task. Goal-directed in a brief treatment program, the therapist was able to check any hostile feelings, keeping in mind that the patient's difficulties were not fully under his control. Nevertheless, the patient may have actively impeded his progress toward conflict resolution and goal attainment, undoing what good he had previously achieved in treatment. A combination of cognitive and interpersonal techniques was employed to counteract his contrary feelings and his inclination to retract his more kindly expectations of others and quickly rebuild the few advances that he and the therapist had struggled to attain. The therapist's committed and professional approach prevented relapses by confronting the ambivalence that often robbed Neil of what steps he had secured toward progress.

Risks and Resistances

In the early phases of treatment, it is particularly important for the therapist to keep in mind that compulsives, even more than other personality-disordered patients, perceive change as a possible route to danger and increased vulnerability. Security and stability for them depend on a simple and well-ordered life. Should the unanticipated occur, or should stress supersede their defenses, equanimity may falter. They may vacillate between diffuse anxiety, explosive outbursts, expressions of doubt and contrition, and any number of bizarre compulsions. If pressure mounts or continues over prolonged periods, compulsives may decompensate into a florid disorder.

Compulsive personalities are likely to regard therapy as an encroachment on their defensive armor. They seek to relieve their symptoms, but at the same time want desperately to prevent self-exploration and self-awareness. The patient's defensiveness is deeply protective and must be honored by the therapist; probing should proceed no faster than the patient can tolerate. Only after building trust and self-confidence may one chance bringing to the open the patient's anger and resentment. It is important for therapists who are trying to establish rapport with compulsive patients in the initial phases of therapy not to push a close emotional relationship too quickly. Although this is a valid therapeutic technique for the later phases of treatment, anything but a respectful, problem-focused therapist manner may cause the compulsive enough discomfort to lead to premature termination.

Insight may be a first step, but it is not a guarantee that patients will consent to take risks, either in or out of therapy. For every piece of defensive armor removed, the therapist must be sure to bolster the patient's autonomy twofold. To remove more defenses than the patient can tolerate is to invite disaster. Fortunately, compulsives themselves are usually so well guarded that precipitous movement by the therapist is often ignored or intellectualized away. The therapist's best recourse against excessive hesitation is to reiterate often that life offers no guarantees, and that taking risks, although opening one up to the possibility of pain, disappointment, and failure, is also the only chance one has at real reward and success. Discussion of how the patient would cope were things to turn out badly may give the patient a modicum of security even in the face of threatening new situations.

Therapists often experience exasperation at a compulsive patient's focus on detail, particularly when the details come to obscure the larger picture. Sometimes, the patient is perceived as boring and dry. Frustration often results from compulsives' tendency to avoid significant emotional issues; rather than examine the anxiety that underlies their actions, compulsives often justify their behavior as the best response to confusing goals or, alternatively, to the psychological problems of others. Anger is a common reaction when the patient's need for control manifests itself through passive refusal to do assignments. The astute therapist will manage to use his or her own reactions as a tool in understanding the patient's resistances, and will keep in mind that a power struggle will do little to help the patient. Polarity conflicts and perpetuating tendencies should always remain the focus of therapy.

CHAPTER NINETEEN

Treating Negativistic
Personality Patterns

The overt picture of the *DSM-IV*'s negativistic syndrome is strikingly *dissimilar* from that of the compulsive personality. According to Millon (1969, 1981, 1990), however, both share an intense and deeply rooted ambivalence about themselves and others. Compulsives deal with this ambivalence by vigorously suppressing the conflicts it engenders, and they appear as a consequence to be well controlled and single-minded in purpose; their behavior is perfectionistic, scrupulous, orderly, and quite predictable. In contrast, the negativist fails either to submerge or to otherwise resolve these very same conflicts; as a consequence, the ambivalence of negativists intrudes constantly into their everyday life, resulting in indecisiveness, fluctuating attitudes, oppositional behaviors and emotions, and a general erraticism and unpredictability. They cannot decide whether to adhere to the desires of others as a means of gaining comfort and security *or* to turn to themselves for these gains; whether to be obediently dependent on others *or* defiantly resistant and independent of them; whether to take the initiative in mastering their world *or* to sit idly by, passively awaiting the leadership of others. They vacillate, then, like the proverbial donkey, moving first one way and then the other, never quite settling on which bale of hay is best.

The erratic pattern of behaviors observed in negativistics is similar to that employed by young children who explore, through trial and error, various actions and strategies in the hope of discovering which succeed for them. In this exploratory phase, children display considerable spontaneity, shifting in an almost random fashion from assertion to submission to avoidance to exploitation to obstinacy, and so on. Most children meet with fairly stable parental responses to their varied behaviors, and, as a consequence, most learn to discern which actions and attitudes are acceptable and help to achieve their goals. This predictability in gauging the consequences of one's behaviors is not learned by future negativists, for these children experience little in the way of parental consistency. Because they cannot discern a clear pattern of consequences for their behaviors, they continue on an erratic, "childish" course. The persistence of these childlike and capriciously unpredictable behaviors accounts in part for the frequency with which these personalities are referred to in adulthood as "emotionally immature."

Referred to as negativistic personalities, these individuals are noted for their general contrariness and disinclination to doing things that others wish or expect of them. But beyond this passive-resistance, there is a capricious impulsiveness, an irritable moodiness, a grumbling, discontented, sulky, unaccommodating, and fault-finding pessimism that characterizes their behaviors. They not only obstruct but dampen everyone's spirits as sullen malcontents and perennial complainers whose very presence demoralizes others. Although anguished and discontent with themselves, they never appear satisfied with others either. Even in the best of circumstances, they always seem to seek the "dark lining in the silver cloud." If they find themselves alone, they would prefer to be with others; if they are with others, they prefer to be alone. If someone gives them a gift, they dislike being obligated; if they fail to receive one, they feel slighted and rejected. If they are given a position of leadership, they complain bitterly about the lack of support they get from others; if they are not allowed to lead, they become critical and unsupporting of those who are.

The broader formulation of the passive-aggressive or negativistic personality here is consistent with the oral sadistic melancholic described in the writings of early psychoanalysts. Characterized by deep-seated and pervasive ambivalence, consequent to difficulties arising in the oral biting stage, these individuals have been described as spiteful, petulant, and overdemanding with a pessimistic mistrust of the world (Menninger, 1940).

The characteristic vacillation, discontentment, and socially maladaptive behaviors of passive-aggressive personalities almost inevitably result in varying states of interpersonal conflict and frustration as well as emotional confusion and distress. Consequently, such individuals are highly susceptible to psychiatric symptomatology, including anxiety, somatoform disorders, and especially depression. Although major depressive episodes are not uncommon, passive-aggressive personalities are probably most likely to experience chronic forms of dysthymic disorder. Typically, these individuals display an agitated form of dysphoria, shifting between states of anxious futility, self-deprecation, and despair, to demanding irritability and bitter discontent. They may struggle between their desire to act out defiantly and their social sense that they must curtail their resentments. Although passive-aggressive personalities are accustomed to directly venting their feelings, anger will be restrained and turned inward should they sense that such expression might result in rejection or humiliation. Their grumbling, moody complaints, and sour pessimism, however, serve as vehicles of tension discharge, relieving them periodically of mounting inner- and outer-directed anger. A secondary but important function of these behaviors is to intimidate others and induce guilt, which provides passive-aggressives with some sense of retribution for the miseries others have caused them in the past. After a time, however, the sullen moodiness and complaining of the passive-aggressive may tend to annoy and alienate others. Although the piteous distress of these depressed individuals may inhibit others from directly expressing their frustration and annoyance, their exasperation is readily perceived by the hypersensitive passive-aggressive and taken as further evidence of the low esteem in which others hold him or her.

A final commentary in this introductory section on the negativistic personality refers to the evolutionary model and the polarity characterization represented in Figure 19.1. Little stands out in this portrayal, other than the element of conflict and ambivalence signified by the double-pointed arrow between the self and other polarities. What this indicates is the inability of negativistic personalities to find a comfortable ground between acting on their own behalf versus acting for others. They cannot find

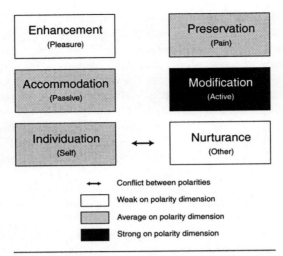

Figure 19.1   Status of the negativistic (passive-aggressive) personality prototype in accord with the Millon Polarity Model.

a consistent, single-minded purpose. As a consequence, they shift erratically back and forth, manifesting fluctuating attitudes and unpredictable behaviors. If they move toward the fulfillment of what others desire, they become irritated and annoyed with themselves for doing so, quickly shifting their thoughts and feelings in favor of doing their own thing. In so doing, however, they jeopardize the security and support they need from others, leading them quickly to become contrite and to reverse their position again. Negativists are active, not passive, shifting from one moment to the next in their behaviors, thoughts, and feelings. Little joy is experienced in this process; fear and self-preservation predominate. Whichever direction they take, there are discomforting consequences to pay. It is this unsettled character of the self-other orientation that keeps negativists in a perpetual state of discontent and dysphoria.

CLINICAL PICTURE

The following sections serve to provide the reader with several perspectives on the negativistic personality. As in prior chapters, we first organize clinical data sources in line with the eight domains (see Table 19.1).

Prototypal Diagnostic Domains

This section discusses the central features of the so-called negativistic pattern, detailing these characteristics in accord with the major domains of clinical analysis utilized in earlier chapters (see Figure 19.2). As noted previously, the traits of the negativistic are more broadly conceived here than in the *DSM-IV* appendix, and it is thereby conceptualized as a comprehensive personality disorder. This extended formulation is guided by the personality pattern described as the "negativistic" type by Millon in 1969.

TABLE 19.1   Clinical Domains of the Negativistic Personality Prototype

Behavioral Level

(F)   Expressively Resentful (e.g., resists fulfilling expectancies of others, frequently exhibiting procrastination, inefficiency, and obstinate as well as contrary and irksome behaviors; reveals gratification in demoralizing and undermining the pleasures and aspirations of others).

(F)   Interpersonally Contrary (e.g., assumes conflicting and changing roles in social relationships, particularly dependent and contrite acquiescence and assertive and hostile independence; conveys envy and pique toward those more fortunate, as well as actively concurrently or sequentially obstructive and intolerant of others, expressing either negative or incompatible attitudes).

Phenomenological Level

(F)   Cognitively Skeptical (e.g., is cynical, doubting, and untrusting, approaching positive events with disbelief and future possibilities with pessimism, anger, and trepidation; has a misanthropic view of life, is whining and grumbling, voicing disdain and caustic comments toward those experiencing good fortune).

(S)   Discontented Self-Image (e.g., sees self as misunderstood, luckless, unappreciated, jinxed, and demeaned by others; recognizes being characteristically embittered, disgruntled, and disillusioned with life).

(S)   Vacillating Objects (e.g., internalized representations of the past comprise a complex of countervailing relationships, setting in motion contradictory feelings, conflicting inclinations, and incompatible memories that are driven by the desire to degrade the achievements and pleasures of others, without necessarily appearing so).

Intrapsychic Level

(F)   Displacement Mechanism (e.g., discharges anger and other troublesome emotions either precipitously or by employing unconscious maneuvers to shift them from their instigator to settings or persons of lesser significance; vents disapproval by substitute or passive means, such as acting inept or perplexed or behaving in a forgetful or indolent manner).

(S)   Divergent Organization (e.g., there is a clear division in the pattern of morphologic structures such that coping and defensive maneuvers are often directed toward incompatible goals, leaving major conflicts unresolved and full psychic cohesion often impossible by virtue of the fact that fulfillment of one drive or need inevitably nullifies or reverses another).

Biophysical Level

(S)   Irritable Mood (e.g., frequently touchy, temperamental, and peevish, followed in turn by sullen and moody withdrawal; is often petulant and impatient; unreasonably scorns those in authority and reports being annoyed easily or frustrated by many).

F refers to Functional Domains (fluid, interactive)
S refers to Structural Domains (stable, unchanging)

Resentful expressive behavior.   One of the problems that arise when focusing on the distinctive characteristics of a pathological personality type is that the reader is led to believe, incorrectly, that these individuals always display the features that have been described. This is not the case. Most personalities behave "normally" much of the time; that is, their behaviors are appropriate to the reality conditions of their environment. What a text such as this seeks to stress are those features that, by virtue of their frequency and intensity, *distinguish* certain personalities. Thus, "resentfulness" may be used as a descriptor to characterize the negativist. But almost everyone behaves resentfully sometimes, and the negativistic is not resentful much of the time. What distinguishes negativists is the ease with which they can be made to act in a resentful manner and the regularity with which this behavior is manifested. With this qualification in mind, the discussion turns to a brief note of the resentful feature as typically found in the negativist.

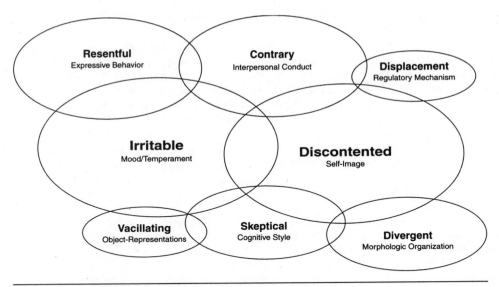

Figure 19.2   Salience of prototypal negativistic domains.

As seen in these personalities, resentfulness is manifested in a variety of forms that signify their resistance to fulfilling the expectancies of others. Thus, they exhibit procrastination, inefficiency, and obstinate as well as contrary and socially irksome behaviors. These actions also reflect the gratification that negativists feel in demoralizing and undermining the pleasures and aspirations of others.

Contrary interpersonal conduct.   Most persons acquire styles of relating to others that enable them to achieve an optimal level of satisfaction and security, as well as to maintain a reasonable degree of self-harmony. So-called normals may be differentiated from pathological personalities by the variety and character of the strategies they employ to achieve these goals. Healthy personalities draw on their strategies flexibly as they face changing demands and pressures. Psychologically impaired individuals, however, tend to be inflexible. They approach different events as if they were the same and utilize the same strategies they acquired in childhood, even though these are presently inappropriate. Once having learned a particular style that has worked for them, it continues to be used as if it were a sacred rule book for navigating the future.

The problem that faces negativists (and borderlines also) is quite different from that of most pathological personalities. Their difficulties stem *not* from the rigid character of their coping style but from its exaggerated fluidity. They are actively and overtly ambivalent, unable to find a satisfactory direction or course for their behavior. They vacillate and cannot decide whether to be dependent or independent of others and whether to respond to events actively or passively. Their dilemmas do not arise from an overcommitment to one strategy but from a lack of commitment. As a consequence, they vacillate indecisively in a tortuous and erratic manner from one mood and one course of action to another. They behave by fits and starts, shifting capriciously down a path that leads nowhere and precipitates them into endless wrangles with others and disappointments with themselves.

The contrary character seen in this domain of the negativistic personality takes the form of changing and conflicting social relationships. Most notable is the contrast between dependent and contrite acquiescence on the one hand, and assertive and hostile independence on the other. They exhibit envy and pique toward those they see as more fortunate, and are actively obstructive toward those with whom they must relate regularly, expressing either critical or incompatible attitudes toward them.

It would appear from the foregoing that the ambivalence and erratic course of negativists would fail to provide these individuals with any satisfactions or security. If this were the case, we would expect them to decompensate quickly. Few do. Hence, we are forced to inquire as to what gains and supports these individuals do achieve in the course of behaving in their vacillating and ambivalent manner.

Quite simply, being "difficult," quixotic, unpredictable, and discontent will produce certain rewards and avoid certain discomforts. The following are examples, drawn from the sphere of marital life, of the ingenious, though unconscious, mechanisms these personalities employ.

> A negativistic man, who is unwilling or unable to decide whether to "grow up" or remain a "child," explodes emotionally whenever his wife expects "too much" of him. Afterward, he expresses guilt, becomes contrite, and pleads forbearance on her part. By turning toward self-condemnation, he evokes her sympathy, restrains her from making undue demands, and maneuvers her into placating rather than criticizing him.
>
> A woman, feeling the ambivalence of both love and hate for her husband, complains bitterly about his loss of interest in her as a woman. To prove his affections, he suggests that they go on a "second honeymoon," that is, take a vacation without the children. To this proposal, she replies that his plan only proves that he is a foolish spendthrift; in the same breath, however, she insists that the children come along. No matter what he does, he is wrong. She has not only trapped him but confused him as well. Her ambivalence maneuvers him first one way and then the other. It forces him to be on edge, always alert to avoid situations that might provoke her ire, yet he can never quite be sure that he has succeeded.

The negativistic's inconsistent strategy of being discontent and unpredictable, of being both seductive and rejecting, and of being demanding and then dissatisfied is an effective weapon not only with an intimidated or pliant partner but with people in general. Switching among the roles of the martyr, the affronted, the aggrieved, the misunderstood, the contrite, the guilt-ridden, the sickly, and the overworked is a tactic of interpersonal behavior that gains negativists the attention, reassurance, and dependency they crave, while, at the same time, allowing them to subtly vent their angers and resentments. For all its seeming ineffectuality, vacillation recruits affection and support on the one hand, and provides a means of discharging the tensions of frustration and hostility on the other. Interspersed with self-deprecation and contrition, acts that relieve unconscious guilt and serve to solicit forgiveness and reassuring comments from others, this strategy proves *not* to be a total failure at all.

Skeptical cognitive style.   It is typical for negativists to be cynical, doubting, and untrusting, approaching most events in their life with a measure of disbelief and skepticism. Future possibilities are viewed with a degree of trepidation, if not pessimism and suspicion. Most negativists display a misanthropic view of life, tend to appraise matters in a whining and grumbling manner, and voice disdain and caustic comments toward circumstances and persons that appear to be experiencing good fortune.

It should also be noted that negativists are usually quite articulate in describing their subjective discomforts. Only rarely, however, are they willing to explore or to admit any insight into its roots. In talking about their sensitivities and difficulties, they will *not* recognize that these reflect, in large measure, their own inner conflicts and ambivalences. Self-reports alternate between preoccupations with personal inadequacies, bodily ailments, and guilt feelings on the one hand, and social resentments, frustrations, and disillusionments on the other. They will voice dismay about the sorry state of their life, their worries, their sadness, their disappointments, their "nervousness," and so on. Although most will express a desire to be rid of distress and difficulty, they seem unable, or perhaps unwilling, to find any solution.

Ambivalence also characterizes the thinking of these persons. No sooner do they "see" the merits of approaching their problems one way than they find themselves saying, "But . . ." Fearful of committing themselves and unsure of their own desires and competencies, they find their thoughts shifting erratically from one solution to another. Because of their intense ambivalences, they often act precipitously, on the spur of the moment. Any other course for them would lead only to hesitation or vacillation, if not total immobility.

Discontented self-image. Negativists often assert that they have been trapped by fate, that nothing ever "works out" for them, and that whatever they desire runs aground. These negativistic persons express envy and resentment over the "easy life" of others. They are frequently critical and cynical with regard to what others have attained, yet covet these achievements themselves. Life, negativists claim, has been unkind to them. They feel cheated and unappreciated. Whatever they have done has been for naught. Their motives and behaviors have always been misunderstood and they are now bitterly disillusioned. The obstructiveness and pessimism that others have attributed to them are only a reflection, they feel, of their "sensitivity" or the pain they have suffered from physical disabilities or the inconsiderateness that others have shown toward them. But here again, the negativist's ambivalence intrudes. Perhaps, they say, it has all been a consequence of their own unworthiness, their own failures, and their own "bad temper." Maybe it is their own behavior that is the cause of their misery and the pain they have brought to others. Among these personalities, the ambivalent struggle between feeling guilt and feeling resentment permeates every facet of thought and behavior.

Vacillating object-representations. The inner templates of the past among negativistic personalities are composed of complexly conflicting images and memories. Few components of this template are composed of internally consistent qualities. Most internalized objects are associated with contradictory feelings, countervailing inclinations, and incompatible memories. Hence, the foundation of dispositions that serve to organize the negativist's ongoing perceptions and personal relationships are divergently oriented and in a constant state of flux. Adding to these internally vacillating objects is the fact that they are generally colored by negative emotions, resulting in a disposition to undermine the pleasures and achievements of self and others, without necessarily appearing to do so.

The behaviors of these overtly ambivalent personalities are even more erratic and vacillating than we might expect from their reinforcement history. They appear to have labored under a double handicap. Not only were they deprived of external consistency and control in childhood but, as a consequence of these experiences, they never acquired the motivation and competencies of internal control. Unsure of what their environment expects of them and unable themselves to impose self-discipline and order, these persons seem adrift in their environment, bobbing up and down erratically from one mood to another.

As will be noted later, these individuals failed to experience consistent parental discipline. What they did acquire was largely through implicit modeling. In essence, they imitated the contradictory or capricious style of their parents. Deprived of conditions for acquiring self-control and modeling themselves after their opposing or erratic and ambivalent parents, these personalities never learn to conceal their moods for long and cannot bind or transform their emotions. Whatever inner feelings well up within them—guilt, anger, or inferiority—they spill quickly to the surface in pure and direct form.

Displacement regulatory mechanism.   A distinguishing clinical feature of negativists is their paucity of intrapsychic controls and mechanisms. Their moods, thoughts, and desires tend not to be worked out internally. Few unconscious processes are employed to handle the upsurge of feelings, and, as a consequence, these come readily to the surface, untransformed and unmoderated. These negativistic persons are like children in that they often react spontaneously and impulsively to passing emotions. As a result, there is little consistency and predictability to their reactions.

Perhaps the most consistent mechanism seen among negativists is their use of displacement, that is, their tendency to shift their anger both precipitously and unconsciously from their true targets (e.g., persons or settings) to those of lesser significance. Thus, through their passive-aggressive maneuvers, negativists will vent their resentments by substitute means, such as acting inept or perplexed or behaving in a forgetful or indolent manner.

Displacement, and the confusion of attitudes and feelings that this creates, is paralleled by a variety of other, often erratic and contradictory mechanisms. Sometimes, patients will turn their externally directed, hostile feelings back toward themselves, a mechanism termed introjection by some, the converse of projection. For example, hatred felt toward others may be directed toward the self, taking the form of guilt or self-condemnation. True to form, however, the negativist will alternate between introjection and projection. At one time, by projection, these persons will ascribe their destructive impulses to others, accusing the others, unjustly, of being malicious and unkind to them. At other times, by introjection, they will reverse the sequence, accusing themselves of faults that justifiably should be ascribed to others.

Thus, even in the use of unconscious mechanisms, the negativist behaves in a vacillating and contradictory manner. Those at the receiving end of these seemingly bizarre intrapsychic processes cannot help but conclude that the person is behaving in an irrational way and exhibiting uncalled for outbursts and emotional inconsistencies.

Divergent morphologic organization.   The pattern of morphological structures in the negativistic personality exhibits a clear division among its components. Hence, controls and defensive maneuvers are often employed to achieve incompatible goals and purposes. Major conflicts may remain unresolved, therefore, and full psychic cohesion may become impossible to achieve by virtue of the fact that the fulfillment of one goal or purpose will nullify or undo and reverse another.

Weakness of intrapsychic control would not prove troublesome if the negativist's feelings were calm and consistent, but they are not. Rooted in deep personal ambivalences, negativists experience an undercurrent of perpetual inner turmoil and anxiety. Their equilibrium is unstable. Their inability to anticipate the future as consistent or predictable gives rise to a constant state of insecurity. The frustration and confusion they feel turn readily to anger and resentment. Guilt often emerges and frequently serves to curtail this anger. In short, the actively ambivalent suffers a range of intense and conflicting emotions that, because of weak controls and lack of self-discipline, surge quickly and capriciously to the surface.

Irritable mood/temperament.   This personality pattern is best characterized by the rapid succession of changing behaviors and moods. Much of the time, these patients seem restless, unstable and erratic in their feelings. They are easily nettled, offended by trifles, and readily provoked into being sullen and contrary. There is often a low tolerance for frustration. Many are chronically impatient and irritable and fidgety unless things go their way. There are periods when they vacillate from being distraught and despondent at one moment, to being petty, spiteful, stubborn, and contentious the next. At other times, they may be enthusiastic and cheerful, but this mood is usually short-lived. In no time, they are again disgruntled, critical, and envious. They often begrudge the good fortunes of others and are jealous, quarrelsome, and easily piqued by signs of indifference or minor slights. Their emotions are "worn on their sleeves." Many are excitable and impulsive. Others suddenly burst into tears and guilt at the slightest upset. Still others often discharge anger or abuse at the least provocation. The impulsive, unpredictable, and often explosive reactions of these personalities make it difficult for others to feel comfortable in their presence or to establish rewarding and enduring relationships with them. Although there will be periods of pleasant sociability and warm affection, most acquaintances of these personalities often feel "on edge," waiting for them to display a sullen and hurt look or become obstinate or nasty.

Negativists do not exhibit a distinctive or characteristic level of biologic activation. There is reason, however, to believe that they may possess an intrinsic irritability or hyperreactivity to stimulation. They seem easily aroused, testy, high-strung, thin-skinned, and quick-tempered. Minor events provoke and chafe them. They become inflamed and aggrieved by the most incidental and insignificant acts of others. Of course, these hypersensitivities could stem from adverse experiences as well as constitutional proclivities. We may speculate further that these personalities possess some unusual mixture of temperaments. Their behavioral ambivalences may reflect the back-and-forth workings of conflicting dispositions and result in the erratic and contradictory emotional reactions they characteristically display. The reader must note that there is no substantive evidence to warrant placing confidence in these biogenic conjectures.

The negativistic pattern may be more prevalent among women than among men. Although speculative as a thesis, women are subject to hormonal changes during their menstrual cycle that could regularly activate marked, short-lived, and variable moods. Rapid changes in affect such as these may set into motion erratic behaviors and interpersonal reactions that lead to both the acquisition and perpetuation of an ambivalently oriented pattern. Whereas obstreperous and uncontrolled characteristics among men are likely to be judged as a sign of being "tough-minded," these same characteristics among women may be viewed as being "bitchy" and "negativistic." Note again that conjectures such as these are no more than unconfirmed speculations.

Self-Perpetuation Processes

Most pathological personalities feel some measure of stability and self-content with the lifestyle they have acquired. This is not typical among negativistic personalities. Their feelings, attitudes, and behaviors allow for little internal equilibrium or consistent external gratification. They frequently live in a phenomenological state of discontent and self-dissatisfaction. Their irritability provokes them to behave unpredictably and to appear restless, sullen, and obstructive much of the time. Not only do they suffer an ever present sense of inner turmoil, but they act out their discontent for all to see.

The following sections describe three aspects of the negativistic style that perpetuate and intensify the troublesome behaviors and attitudes acquired in childhood (see Table 19.2).

Negativistic and unpredictable behaviors.   Acting erratically, vacillating from one course to another, is a sheer waste of energy. By attempting to achieve incompatible goals, these persons scatter their efforts and dilute their effectiveness. Caught in their own crosscurrents, they cannot commit themselves to one clear direction, swinging indecisively back and forth, performing ineffectually, and experiencing a sense of paralyzing inertia or exhaustion.

In addition to the wasteful nature of ambivalence, negativists may actively impede their own progress toward conflict resolution and goal attainment. Thus, they frequently undo what good they previously had done. Driven by contrary feelings, they retract their "kind words" to others and replace them with harshness, or they undermine achievements they struggled hard to attain. In short, their ambivalence often robs them of what few steps they secured toward progress. This inconstant "blowing hot and cold" behavior precipitates others into reacting in a parallel capricious and inconsistent manner. By prompting these reactions, negativists re-create the very conditions of their childhood that fostered the development of their unstable behaviors in the first place.

Most people weary of the sulking and stubborn unpredictability of these actively ambivalent personalities. Others are frequently goaded into exasperation and confusion when their persistent efforts to placate the negativist so frequently meet with failure. Eventually, everyone is likely to express both anger and disaffiliation, reactions that serve then only to intensify the negativist's dismay and anxiety.

TABLE 19.2   Self-Perpetuating Processes

NEGATIVISTIC

Unpredictable Behaviors
   Erratic actions scatter efforts
   Inconstant behavior impedes progress
   Sulking goads exasperation

Anticipation of Disappointment
   Good fortune will end abruptly
   "Jumps gun" to avoid disillusionment
   Vented discontentment provokes hostility

Recreation of Disillusioning Experiences
   Striving followed by testing behavior
   Ultimately drives others to anger
   Creates vicious circles of expected betrayal

Anticipating disappointment.   Not only do negativists precipitate real difficulties through their negativistic behaviors, but they often perceive and anticipate difficulties where none in fact exist. They have learned from past experience that "good things don't last," that positive feelings and attitudes from those whom they seek love will end abruptly and capriciously and be followed by disappointment, anger, and rejection.

Rather than be disillusioned and embittered, rather than allowing themselves to be "led down the primrose path" to suffer the humiliation and pain of having their hopes dashed again, it would be better to put a halt to illusory gratifications and to the futility and heartache of short-lived pleasures. Protectively, then, negativists may refuse to wait for others to make the turnabout. Instead, they "jump the gun, " pull back when things are going well, and thereby cut off experiences that may have proved gratifying had they been completed. The anticipation of being set back and left in the lurch prompts negativists into a self-fulfilling prophecy. By their own hand, they defeat their chance to experience events that could have promoted change and growth.

By cutting off the goodwill of others and by upsetting their pleasurable anticipations, negativists gain the perverse and negative gratification of venting hostility and anger. These acts, however, prove to be Pyrrhic victories; not only do they sabotage their own chances for rewarding experiences, but they inevitably provoke counterhostility from others and increased guilt and anxiety for themselves. Their defensive action has instigated responses that perpetuate the original difficulty, setting into motion a vicious circle in which they feel further discontent and disappointment.

Recreating disillusioning experiences.   As noted earlier, interpersonal vacillation does gain partial gratification for the negativist. And partial reinforcements, as we know from experimental research, strengthen habits and cause them to persist and recur. In the negativist, this appears to take the form of unconscious repetition-compulsions in which the individual recreates disillusioning experiences that parallel those of the past.

Despite their ambivalence and pessimistic outlook, negativists operate on the premise that they can overcome past disappointments and capture in full measure the love and attention they only partially gained in childhood. Unfortunately, their search for complete fulfillment can no longer be achieved because they now possess needs that are in fundamental opposition to one another; for example, they both want and do not want the love of those on whom they depend. Despite this ambivalence, negativists enter new relationships as if a perfect and idyllic state could be achieved. They go through the act of seeking a consistent and true source of love, one that will not betray them as their parents and others have in the past. They venture into new relationships with enthusiasm and blind optimism: this time, all will go well. Despite this optimism, they remain unsure of the trust they really can place in others. Mindful of past betrayals and disappointments, they begin to test their newfound loves to see if they are loyal and faithful. They may irritate others, frustrate them, and withdraw from them, all in an effort to check whether they will prove as fickle and insubstantial as those of the past. Soon, these testing operations exhaust the partner's patience; annoyance, exasperation, and hostility follow. The negativist quickly becomes disenchanted; the "idol" has proved to be marred and imperfect, and the negativistic is once more disillusioned and embittered. To vent their resentment at having been naïve, these persons may turn against their "betrayers," disavow and recoil from the affections they had shown, and thereby complete the vicious circle. These experiences recur repeatedly, and with each recurrence, negativists further reinforce their pessimistic anticipations. In their efforts to overcome past disillusionment, they have thrown themselves into new ventures that have led to further disillusion.

INTERVENTION GOALS

The impression that negativists convey is that of childlike rebellion. They are likely to come to therapy at the request of others because their oppositional behavior has interfered with their marital, parental, or occupational responsibilities. Relationships with authority figures tend also to be problematic. This personality's characteristic negative outlook on life is likely to extend to therapy as well; therefore, it is improbable that they have entered the therapeutic arena voluntarily. Convinced that others are to blame for their misfortunes, they avoid taking responsibility for altering their provocative behaviors.

Progress in therapy is not promising. These personalities appear compliant on the surface, yet covertly they resist and manage to undermine the therapist's efforts. It may be difficult for these patients to see the therapist as a collaborator rather than an adversary.

The goals of therapy are to guide negativistic patients to recognize the source and character of their ambivalences toward themselves and others and to reinforce a more consistent approach to life. Treatment must further attempt to mitigate the negativist's tendency to overreact in an obstructive and sullen manner. Recognition of the factors that foster the cyclical and recurrent nature of their interactions with others will assist in planning interventions, especially those oriented to the mood/temperament and self-image domains (see Table 19.3).

Reestablishing Polarity Balances

The conflictual coping style of negativistic personalities is manifested by extreme vacillations between submission to others and gratification of self needs. They may seek to obtain nurturance from others without examining their own adaptive capabilities. Not uncharacteristically, they may shift gears and quickly turn against those from whom

TABLE 19.3 Therapeutic Strategies and Tactics for the Prototypal Negativistic (Passive-Agressive) Personality

STRATEGIC GOALS

Balance Polarities
Diminish self-other conflict
Stabilize erratically changing actions

Counter Perpetuations
Reduce anticipation of disappointment
Moderate unpredictable behaviors
Prevent creation of disillusionment

TACTICAL MODALITIES
Reverse discontented self-image
Moderate irritable moods
Alter skeptical cognitive style
Undo contrary/resentful behaviors

they sought assistance. This self-other conflicted orientation provokes others to respond angrily in return. Assisting these patients in finding a comfortable balance within these bipolar orientations should be considered a major goal of therapy. Negativists need to learn to differentiate between self and others and to adopt coping mechanisms that will allow them to move flexibly from fulfilling their own desires without guilt, to being oriented toward others without resentment.

Unlike the obsessive-compulsive, who is overly controlled and represses urges to act out, the negativist employs an active mode of adaptation, displaying both erraticism and hyperreactivity. In these efforts to avoid distress, these personalities enact behaviors that not only upset others but also harm themselves. The observed imbalance in the active-passive polarity must be attenuated. It would be beneficial for negativists to take a more passive stance, especially in ambiguous situations, where carefully exploring options and gathering more evidence when needed are more adaptive than reacting impulsively and erratically.

Countering Perpetuating Tendencies

The inconsistencies to which negativists were exposed in childhood reinforced the belief that disappointments are inevitable in life. In anticipation of this, they may withdraw prematurely from potentially gratifying experiences, upsetting their focus and changing their goals, only to repeat the same dysfunctional cycle. This behavior not only alienates others but also induces guilt in themselves. To interrupt this pattern, negativists must learn not only to commit to a specified plan of action, but to actively follow through as well. Acquiring control over their impulses is a paramount therapeutic goal.

Through their erratic and oppositional behaviors, negativistic personalities place themselves in double-bind situations, vacillating between incompatible goals and unable to commit and fulfill personal needs. Scornful, moody, and unpredictable emotional displays tend to exasperate others, causing them to react in a similar fashion. This, in turn, intensifies the negativist's beliefs that others cannot be relied on and will generate new conflictual behaviors. A major goal of personologic therapy with this disorder is to temper the volatile expression of behaviors and affect. When these patients learn to appropriately express their discontent, resentful encounters will give way to more mature interactions.

It is in the realm of interpersonal relations that the erratic cycle is played out in its full form. Not knowing whether they can rely on their partners, negativists proceed to test their fidelity and trustworthiness, eventually exasperating even the most compliant partner. Unable to find security and disillusioned once again, they will turn to their next victim. To prevent this recapitulation of past experiences, the dyadic relationship between therapist and patient may serve as a stable model to emulate, a starting block from which the patient can learn new ways of connecting.

Identifying Domain Dysfunctions

Central to this disorder are dysfunctions in the mood/temperament and self-image domains. Negativists feel that the world does not understand them and fear there is little hope they will ever receive fair treatment. Their discontent is manifested through fickle and volatile emotional displays. Therapeutic efforts must be directed toward balancing the emotional seesaw, helping these patients gain control over the expression of negative affects. These personalities vacillate between blaming others and attributing the cause of their woes to themselves. Therapeutic goals include strengthening a consistent self-image as well as improving their perceptions of the real basis of their misfortunes.

Negativists have a very pessimistic outlook on life, believing that good things don't last. This skepticism often leads them to pull back and choose an opposite course of action when things seem to be going their way, thereby causing their predictions to come true. Therapy must assist these patients to challenge the faulty assumptions and allow them to actively test reality. This negative outlook expresses itself particularly in interpersonal relationships. Believing that personal needs will never be met satisfactorily and that they will not be treated fairly, negativists develop a conflictual interpersonal style. They also resent others' good fortune, feeling personally deprived when observing what others may have received. Therapy must strive to help patients regulate contrary behaviors and develop tolerance for others so that their social behaviors will be more charitable and consistent.

Problems in relatedness began early in life and characterize their domain of inner object-representations. Experiences from the past have left a residue of internalized dispositions that are essentially ambivalent. Intervention must work toward replacing these conflictual and vacillating objects with more stable, dependable ones.

When expressing discontent and troublesome feelings, the negativist quite often fails to recognize their original and primary unconscious source. More direct and consciously assertive ways of voicing discontent should be explored in real life. As noted, the internal morphological structures of negativists are divergent, consisting of coping mechanisms that are directed toward incompatible goals. The ultimate therapeutic objective in this area is a more consistent coping strategy as well as a commitment to follow through in achieving its goal, that of psychic cohesion.

SELECTING THERAPEUTIC MODALITIES

The therapist must seek to demonstrate the effectiveness of therapy to these patients, whose skeptical nature is likely to discount the possibility of progress ever being achieved. When everything seems to be moving along well and progress is made steadily, these patients may suddenly decide to discontinue therapy, stating that it is a waste of time. Major life issues that were brought up just prior to the end of the previous session may be discounted by the next meeting. The therapist will have to go with the flow, so to speak, keeping in mind the plan of action, not giving into countertransference feelings or reactions. Much therapy time will be devoted to exploring resistances, and a slow pace of progression with many ups and downs can be expected.

Behavioral Techniques

Formal behavior modification methods may be fruitfully explored to achieve greater consistency in social behaviors. Lacking appropriate role models in childhood, some negativists may have learned that goals may be achieved only through indirect means. The thought of dealing with matters in a straightforward way is anxiety arousing. During the course of therapy, negativists will be asked to engage in behaviors that are likely to raise anxiety levels. Teaching anxiety management techniques can help them tolerate the expected discomforts and frustrations that normally would cause them to change their mode of action.

Controlling untimely expressions of anger may require impulse control and assertiveness skills training. These patients need to learn to "count to 10." By encouraging the direct expression of appropriate anger, the negativist will be less inclined to displace resentments to substitute objects. Within the therapeutic context, role-playing and videotaped playback of interactions may facilitate an understanding of the negativist's dysfunctional interpersonal style. A functional analysis will reveal that there are contextual determinants to the negativist's behavior. Stimulus control procedures, such as removal of environmental pressures that aggravate the patient's anxieties, may be explored and appropriate modifications should be made.

Engaging the patient in behavioral contracting at the onset of treatment may foster compliance with therapy. Contracts should initially be short-term and concise to avoid giving the negativist an opportunity to use ambiguity as an excuse for not following through. Accomplishing the stated goals in the contract will help the patient develop a view of the self as competent. Self-management procedures are generally contraindicated as a first approach because these patients believe that others are to blame for their misfortunes.

Interpersonal Techniques

Interpersonal techniques can be used to help these patients gain insight into the origin of their destructive behaviors and how these early learning experiences are played out in their current relationships. The transference reactions manifested in therapy will shed light on these patterns. Gradually, the therapist can start pointing out possible connections between the patient's early experiences and his or her current style of interacting. It is vital that the therapist point out the commonalities between the patient's behavior in the family of origin and his or her behavior in treatment, so that therapy will not recapitulate them or end in premature termination (L.S. Benjamin, 1993). Most important is to establish a collaborative therapeutic relationship, one in which the patient is permitted to act out capriciously, if not assertively, without fear of provoking therapeutic retribution. Discussions can be centered on the patient's habit of seeking help but then refusing it when offered. Care must be taken on the part of the therapist to protect against his or her own countertransference reactions to a patient who has provoked and felt neglected by former caregivers. Little progress should be expected until the negativist's hidden agenda of therapeutic abuse and incompetence has been relinquished.

As noted, interpersonal work with negativists is a slow and arduous process. L.S. Benjamin (1993) states that for negativists to recognize their maladaptive patterns, they must be partly adept at blocking these cycles and must have some desire to give up their mode of interaction. Successfully working through the obstructive behaviors in therapy will provide a corrective emotional experience. The therapist may be the first person who has not expressed criticism or counterreacted with hostility.

Because family and marital treatment methods focus on the complex network of relationships that often sustain this personality style, these may prove to be among the most useful techniques available. When negativists come in for marital therapy, it is not unusual for the identified patient in the dyad to be the victim of misplaced hostility. Quite commonly, however, each partner has his or her own conflicts and dysfunctional style, and each in turn perpetuates the other's pathology. The negativist often projects undesirable traits onto the marital partner and subsequently expresses dismay, yet proceeds to behave in a manner to actually generate this behavior in the partner. In couples therapy, it is not uncommon that improvement in one member of the dyad may result in increased symptomatology in the other. The therapist must be attuned to this possibility.

Group methods may be fruitfully employed to assist the patient to acquire more self-control and consistency in social situations. When group members share their reaction to the obstructiveness of negativistic persons, recognition of their pathological patterns may be facilitated. Unfortunately, premature dropout may ensue, especially in the early phases. Because their interactions are consistently negative, these patients do not usually obtain positive responses from others. Yalom (1985) describes these patients as "help-rejecting complainers" from which other participants experience repeated confusion and frustration in response to their vacillating patterns. According to Yalom, negativists are among the most difficult group therapy patients. Care must be taken by the therapist to restrain his or her role as a rescuer, that is, to avoid expressions of encouragement and giving explicit advice. By listening to reactions from other group members, negativists can be led to recognize their behaviors' effect on others. Of course, negativists may intentionally or inadvertently hold others responsible for their own misfortunes, or may speak or act in other ways to sustain the pattern. Therapists should be especially alert when group members occasionally combine their forces against the negativist.

Cognitive Techniques

More directive cognitive techniques may be used to confront these patients with the obstructive and self-defeating character of their interpersonal relations. Cognitive approaches must be handled with caution, however, lest the patient become unduly guilt-ridden, depressed, and suicidal. The greatest benefit derived through these approaches is to stabilize these patients, to "set them straight," and to put reins on their uncontrollable vacillations of mood and behavior, very much like what must be done with borderline personalities.

Beck and Freeman (1990a) highlight a number of cognitive interventions with this disorder. From the onset, patients need to be engaged in a collaborative and practically oriented series of tasks. Because negativists are extremely resistant to external control, the therapist must take special care to actively involve them in treatment planning, reinforcing the autonomy they so desire. The therapist must avoid challenging the accuracy of their dysfunctional beliefs too directly or prematurely.

Important in this therapeutic technique is assisting patients to become more aware of the assumptions and expectancies that shape their dysfunctional thoughts and behaviors. Central to this model is an analysis and reorientation of their conflicting cognitive schemata about autonomy and self-interest versus submissiveness and other-focus. Also important is that clear-cut rules and limits be set and maintained consistently. Another cognitive approach recognizes negativists' inclination to defy authority and to engage in meaningless power struggles. Here, it is wise to lead patients to recognize that they are making cognitive selections and choices rather than being externally abused and manipulated by others. As Beck and Freeman (1990a) note, the therapist should encourage patients to select in-session topics for discussion. Also useful are cognitive experiments that can be tested in reality to examine the accuracy of the patient's beliefs and assumptions.

Self-Image Techniques

Typical automatic thoughts of the negativistic person include "Nothing ever works out for me in life"; "I never get what I deserve"; and "How dare others tell me how to lead my life." These faulty statements can be explored and subsequently challenged. A dysfunctional thought record will be useful to help identify the automatic thoughts and accompanying emotions. The validity of the negativist's thinking can then be determined by setting up alternative hypotheses and trials to test them. Reality testing will provide patients with more precise information about the probability of anticipated misfortune, hence taking the edge off their skepticism.

Another important strategy is maintaining consistency in treatment. Negativists will inevitably try to blame lack of progress on the therapist, but with strict rules, structured sessions, and clear rationales for each intervention, the ambiguity that provides an excuse for their lack of responsibility should be reduced via Glasser's Reality/Control procedures. It is also important to examine which of the negativistic's assumptions contribute to his or her success in obtaining satisfactions from others, exploring both pros and cons as well as short-term versus long-term gains. A Rogerian model, one that permits patients to listen to their own verbalizations, may lead them to recognize the character of their own inner struggles, thereby opening up the opportunity to develop a coherent rather than conflictual sense of self.

Intrapsychic Techniques

Because of the deeply rooted character of these problems and the high probability that unconscious resistances will impede the effectiveness of other therapeutic procedures, it may be necessary to explore the more extensive and prolonged techniques of psychodynamic therapy. On the other hand, working with negativists is often so toxic for many therapists that they readily refer them to others who may be more tolerant or less likely to express negative countertransferences (e.g., anger, annoyance). The talent of these patients to criticize and rebut the therapist's efforts serves as a major defense against deeper self-awareness. As the negativist becomes more willing to accept guidance from the therapist, a searching exploration may begin to trace the early roots of the negativist's conflictual psyche that developed in childhood, inconsistently rewarding at times and frequently punishing. Most notable in this personality disorder is how these patients undermine themselves repeatedly. As Gabbard (1990) suggests, a frank statement about the consequences of the patient's behaviors on the therapist should be made clear, for example, "I sense you are trying to make me angry with you."

A thorough reconstruction of personality may be the only means of altering the pattern. An awareness of the origins of their paradoxical behavior should enhance negativists' understanding of how the same behaviors are played out in negative transference responses to the therapist. The neutrality of responses with which the therapist engages the patient can be a major corrective force. Once these personalities see that they can express their anger overtly, without disapproval and rejection from this authority figure, a more consistent model and self-image may then be internalized.

Replacement of the vacillating objects with stable ones will allow negativists to view their interactions with others as consistent and as safe ground.

Unless there is a greater harmony in the negativist's internal structural elements, coping and defensive maneuvers will continue to be used to fulfill contradictory goals. The therapist must help patients understand that their behavior actually serves to exacerbate conflicts. Encouraging patients to make sense of the confused mix of emotions they carry inside will help them be in touch with internal stimuli. Once they understand these feelings, the internal confusion may no longer be overwhelming. Patients can then sort through their internal reserves to select appropriate coping mechanisms.

Stone (1993) notes that dream analysis can be helpful to get at the heart of the central conflicts. If the therapist can work through the patient's resistance, underlying feelings of impotence and unworthiness may be exposed and examined. Stone further points out that the patient has received primarily conditional love in the past, and enters treatment with the belief that the therapist will not be much different. When the therapist communicates an understanding of the issues important to the patient and provides support rather than telling him or her what to do, the negativistic personality can start to develop a more secure self-image.

Pharmacologic Techniques

As noted previously, negativists are quite vulnerable and react with strong feelings when under stress (anxiety, depression). Their internal conflicts comprise feelings of inadequacy on the one hand, and hostility toward those on whom they are dependent on the other hand. Intense anxieties frequently preoccupy patients in the early phases of treatment. Pharmacologic anxiolytic agents may prove helpful in their relief. If depressive features predominate, antidepressant drugs may be prescribed. However, the therapist must be aware of the potential for the misuse of medication, such as the patient's inclination to be oppositional and noncompliant. Attention should also be given to the proclivity of these patients to suicide via the use of medications.

MAKING SYNERGISTIC ARRANGEMENTS

Therapy must initially help the negativistic personality to settle down and calm his or her erratic emotions. Supportive techniques may be used as a first approach, especially if combined with pharmacologic intervention. Without curtailing the patient's emotional lability, other interventions are not likely to prove beneficial. Behavioral techniques can be of use to desensitize the patient to established anxiety-arousing stimuli. These methods should promote increasingly autonomous behavior, allowing the patient to feel more in control. This will subsequently decrease the resentfulness and contrariness displayed in interpersonal situations. Concurrent modifications in these patients' cognitive style will help them attend in more detail to attitudes and assumptions about themselves and others.

Throughout the therapy process, the use of interpersonal techniques will facilitate negativists' recognition of their interactive patterns. Understanding their own contributions to interpersonal difficulties may pave the way for a transition in object-relatedness. Only when therapy has progressed for some period of time, will dynamic

TABLE 19.4   Negatisitic Personality Disorder Subtypes

Circuitous: Opposition displayed in a roundabout, labyrinthine, and ambiguous manner, e.g., procrastination, dawdling, forgetfulness, inefficiency, neglect, stubbornness; indirect and devious in venting resentment and resistant behaviors.

MCMI 8A (3)

Vacillating: Emotions fluctuate in bewildering, perplexing, and enigmatic ways; difficult to fathom or comprehend own capricious and mystifying moods; wavers, is in flux, and is irresolute both subjectively and intrapsychically.

MCMI 8A (C)

Discontented: Grumbling, petty, testy, cranky, embittered, complaining, fretful, vexed, and moody; gripes behind pretense; avoids confrontation; uses legitimate but trivial complaints.

MCMI 8A-2B

Abrasive: Contentious, intransigent, fractious, and quarrelsome; irritable, caustic, debasing, corrosive, and acrimonious; contradicts and derogates; few qualms and little conscience or remorse.

MCMI 8A-6B

techniques be able to help patients get in touch with their innermost fears and contradictions. Understanding and acknowledgment of these feelings will significantly reduce the need for displacement and other externalizing defenses. Gradually, the careful application of the above-mentioned techniques can result in psychic cohesion.

Illustrative Cases

In contrast to the *DSM-III* and *DSM-III-R* formulations, the passive-aggressive/negativistic personality has been introduced into the appendix of *DSM-IV* to represent a comprehensive pattern of traits. This wider-ranging concept of the disorder will result in part in overlaps and combinations with other personality disorders. As such, we should anticipate finding amalgams and mixtures that display the features of several personalities, a number of which are described below (see Table 19.4).

NEGATIVISTIC PERSONALITY: CIRCUITOUS TYPE
(NEGATIVISTIC WITH DEPENDENT TRAITS)

CASE 19.1, FRANK B., 38

Presenting Picture: Frank B., a substitute high school math teacher, seemed always to be one step behind in life, a trait he traced back to childhood, where he was the least talented among six talented siblings, as well as overachieving parents. His wife, a successful corporate lawyer, had given him an ultimatum, stating that he needed help after losing a substantial amount of her money to his passive hobby of playing the stock market online. Highly dependent on her for income, Frank enjoyed the freedom inherent in substitute teaching, though he indicated that he might take a permanent job "for the rest of the year, anyway," to appease his wife. From his wife as well as administrators he heard complaints of his repressed hostility, grumbling, habit of giving incomplete answers, and forgetful ("incompetent") resistance to finishing even simple tasks. He admitted that there was a shred of truth there, as "you can keep your workload minimized by being smart and acting a little stupid." Currently, Frank admitted that there was a "woman friend" at the school where he was thinking about taking a semipermanent job, though it was unclear as to what, exactly, was the nature of this new friendship.

Clinical Assessment: Frank, a *circuitous* subtype of the negativistic personality disorder, closely corresponded to the classification previously labeled the passive-aggressive personality disorder. Here, we saw a prominent if not singular feature that was characterized by a resistance to the expectations of others, a resistance that was expressed indirectly rather than directly. Despite the passive nature of his resentments, Frank clearly was grumbling and oppositional, habitually angry at those who demanded of him a level of performance that he was deeply unwilling to carry out. As noted, his oppositional behaviors were displayed indirectly and, as the descriptive label suggests, in a circuitous fashion through maneuvers such as procrastination, dawdling, stubbornness, forgetfulness, and a general but intentional inefficiency.

If we can recall the early *DSM* history of the passive-aggressive designation, we will remember that this label had been grouped together with the passive-dependent type in the *DSM-I*. It is this circuitous variant of the negativistic (passive-aggressive) personality that reflects the alliance that had been proposed in the early manual. To state the matter more directly, Frank was largely a psychic blend of both negativistic and dependent traits.

Unwilling or fearing to express resentments directly and overtly, Frank often fulfilled the requirements set forth by others, but with a foot-dragging slowness and a bumbling inefficiency. Resistance was usually expressed in areas in which others could not easily conclude that he was acting in an intentionally oppositional manner and, hence, could not readily criticize his behavior. Despite these frequently successful maneuvers at self-protection, he had effectively, if unconsciously, sacrificed his own opportunities for achievement. He retaliated against the rejection and depreciation he had felt in the past in a way that ultimately undid him in the present. He paid a severe personal penalty, therefore, for expressing his anger through a stubborn and oppositional style of behavior. In seeking to undo others, he efficiently undid himself.

Frank was not consciously aware of the problems he had caused. He resisted facing the guilt feelings and interpersonal conflicts he would have to deal with were he not protecting himself against conscious awareness. Moreover, by maintaining a high degree of repression, his neglectfulness and disagreeable behaviors could remain impervious to efforts to pressure him to change. Frank became highly defensive with others who wished to expose his maneuvers or sought to force him to do anything, and he resolutely denied resisting on a conscious or intentional basis.

Frank could not deal with the internal tension and external pressure created by his own indirectly retaliatory behaviors. It was an exhausting process to put on the brakes constantly. On the one hand, he had to relate to others who either implored him to function better or were furious at him for his repeated incompetencies and deficiencies. On the other hand, he had to control his own intensely conflictual and smoldering impulses that were surging in his unconscious. Though some of these negativists feel dismayed over their obvious negligence and failures, Frank was spared from dealing with these feelings by his successful repressive efforts. Many, however, realize that their lack of success and failure of self-fulfillment result from their own inactions, a decision that cannot be undone, nor perhaps even remedied.

Synergistic Treatment Plan: Because of Frank's pessimism and lack of feelings of competence, a safe and empathic environment would need to be established, along with *interpersonal* measures to ensure that familiar but ineffective relationship patterns would not become troublesome within the context of therapy. As these patterns would emerge, however, it would be possible to address them both interpersonally and on a *cognitive* basis, thus creating a concurrent intellectual understanding and personal resonance. Self-perpetuating issues that would follow and would need to be confronted in a similar manner would include strong tendencies toward *active* and *passive* orientations (e.g., expending much energy scheming to be inefficient, lazy, bumbling), as well as conflicting *self-other* tendencies (e.g., expressing more negative feelings by letting others down, yet ruining his own interests in so doing). As these deeply conflictual characterologic strategies would become clarified, it would be beneficial to employ measures that afforded the opportunity to build and implement effective *behaviors,* such as a *group* or *family* intervention.

Therapeutic Course: A primary short-term goal of treatment with Frank was to aid him in reducing his intense ambivalence and growing resentment of others. With an empathic and brief focus, it was possible to sustain a productive, therapeutic relationship. With a therapist who could convey genuine caring and firmness, Frank was able to overcome his tendency to employ maneuvers to test the sincerity and motives of the therapist. Although he was slow to reveal his resentment because he disliked being viewed as an angry person, it was brought into the open and dealt with in a kind and understanding way. He was not inclined to face his ambivalence, but his mixed feelings and attitudes were a major focus of treatment. To prevent him from trying to terminate treatment before improvement occurred and to forestall relapses, the therapist employed brief and circumscribed techniques to counter Frank's expectation that supportive figures would ultimately prove disillusioning.

Circumscribed *interpersonal* approaches (e.g., Benjamin, Kiesler) were used to deal with the seesaw struggle enacted by Frank in his relationship with the therapist. He alternately exhibited ingratiating submissiveness and a taunting and demanding attitude. Similarly, he solicited the therapist's affections, but when these were expressed, he rejected them, voicing doubt about the genuineness of the therapist's feelings. The therapist used *cognitive* procedures to point out these contradictory attitudes. It was important to keep those inconsistencies in focus or Frank may have appreciated the therapist's perceptiveness verbally but not altered his attitudes. Involved in an unconscious repetition-compulsion in which he re-created disillusioning experiences that paralleled those of the past, the patient not only came to recognize the expectations cognitively but was taught to deal with their enactment interpersonally.

Despite his ambivalence and pessimistic outlook, there was good reason to operate on the premise that Frank could overcome past disappointments. To capture the love and attention only modestly gained in childhood could not be achieved, although habits that precluded partial satisfaction could be altered in the here and now. Toward that end, the therapist helped him disentangle needs that were in opposition to one another. For example, he both wanted and did not want the love of those on whom he depended. Despite this ambivalence, he entered new relationships, such as in therapy, as if an idyllic state could be achieved. He went through the act of seeking a consistent and true source of love, one that would not betray him as he believed his parents and others did in the past. Despite this optimism, he remained unsure of the trust he could place in others. Mindful of past betrayals and disappointments, he began to test his new relationships to see if they were loyal and faithful. In a parallel manner, he attempted to irritate and frustrate the therapist to check whether he would prove to be as fickle and insubstantial as others had in the past. It was here that the therapist's warm support and firmness played a significant short-term role in reframing Frank's erroneous expectations and in exhibiting consistency in relationship behavior.

Although the rooted character of these attitudes and behavior complicate the ease with which these therapeutic procedures will progress, short-term and circumscribed cognitive and interpersonal therapy techniques were quite successful. A thorough reconstruction of personality was not necessary to alter Frank's problematic pattern. In this regard, *family* treatment methods that focused on the network of relationships that often sustained his problems proved to be a useful technique. *Group* methods were also fruitfully employed to help Frank acquire self-control and consistency in close relationships.

The therapist did not set goals too high because Frank may not have been able to tolerate demands or expectations well. Brief therapeutic efforts were directed to build the patient's trust, to focus on positive traits, and to enhance his confidence and self-esteem.

NEGATIVISTIC PERSONALITY: ABRASIVE TYPE (NEGATIVISTIC WITH SADISTIC TRAITS)

CASE 19.2, MARGE H., 33

Presenting Picture: Marge H. was referred to an employee assistance program following several coworker complaints regarding her interpersonal attitude. One coworker reported being frightened by her aggressive, critical demeanor. Despite good reports regarding the quality of her work, the report stated, her job was in jeopardy due to these difficulties. "Everyone annoys me and I get angry," Marge explained. "What am I supposed to do? Not react?" The idea of being friendly or establishing some kind of camaraderie with people in her work environment seemed a very foreign notion to her. Reporting very few friends outside of work, no history of relationships that had become substantial, and living alone, Marge also stated that even her cat annoyed her. "He's always getting sick, so I stop feeding him and he doesn't get sick all over the place." Questions regarding her childhood and family of origin met the expected aggressive defense of "What does this have to do with my job?" She did mention, however, that she was the younger of two siblings of rather elderly parents. Her father had died when she was young, and her mother was always disgruntled by the fact that she had to work so hard to support her daughter, who was an "accident," at her advanced age.

Clinical Assessment: In contrast to circuitous negativists, who exhibit their struggle between doing what others wish and doing what they wish in an oblique if not passive manner, Marge, an *abrasive negativist,* acted in an overtly and directly contentious and quarrelsome way. An irascible and derogating personality, Marge used everything and anyone as sounding boards for discharging her inner irritabilities, as readily available objects for nagging and assaulting. More than merely irritable in a general way, she was intentionally abrasive and antagonistic. Not surprisingly, Marge exhibited features usually associated with the sadistic personality prototype.

Marge had incessant discords with others, discords that magnified every minor friction into repeated and bitter personal struggles. The following descriptive adjectives characterize her: contentious, intransigent, fractious, irritable, caustic, debasing, quarrelsome, acrimonious, and corrosive. She also appeared to have few qualms and little conscience or remorse about contradicting or derogating even her most intimate associates.

Marge insisted that her quarrelsomeness was dedicated to certain high principles; though a kernel of truth may be found in her belief, these higher principles corresponded to positions she herself held, never to those taken by others. Others were unquestionably wrong; she was unquestionably right. Fault-finding and dogmatic, she achieved special delight in contradicting and derogating others. Her pleasure was greatest, not so much in the legitimacy and logic of her argument, but in the fact that it served to demean others and retaliate against them.

Patterns akin to the abrasive personality are seen among adolescents who seek to establish their separateness and individuality, acting in ways that clearly oppose those of their parents. Thus, boys will let their hair grow long, and girls will wear their skirts short; the children of deeply committed conservatives will favor highly liberal or socialistic values, whereas the teenagers of liberal parents will adopt intensely conservative points of view. But the rebellion of adolescents against the customs and standards of their parents is largely time-limited, a stage of development in which strategies of self-assertion are appropriate. Once a sense of independence is achieved, oppositional teenagers will likely drop this style of behavior, not infrequently reverting to the parental customs they previously sought to overturn. The hostile and opposing manners of an abrasive negativist such as Marge, however, are part of the core of her being. Her knack of belittling and denigrating anyone in the name of whatever principle she happened to espouse was well rehearsed and persistent. Derogation of others was "good for them." Believing that she derived no personal satisfaction in telling people off or in having ulterior motives for doing so, she felt unconstrained, free to say and do anything she pleased "to set people right."

It is evident to those with whom Marge related that her pretentions of principled behavior were but a thin veneer. Faced with any opposition, especially from persons she considered of lesser stature than herself, she would spew forth bitter complaints of how she had been ill-treated by others and how unappreciated she had been. As a result of these direct attacks, the deeper origins of her personality style were reactivated. Recriminations and counteractions are refueled. She claimed that anything personal she had done to others did not really reflect her character, but was merely a justified reaction to the uncaring treatment to which she had been exposed. She felt justified in what she said and did, with no qualms of conscience and little remorse for having acted in a most obnoxious way.

Synergistic Treatment Plan: Initially, Marge would be unlikely to accede to a therapeutic focus that would seek to explore aspects of herself, as she rejected the premise that she was responsible for current difficulties. *Behaviorally,* she would need to establish a less impulsive style of interacting (balance toward diminishing *active,* encouraging *passive* style), which would be a pragmatic and concrete goal with which she could resonate. This would serve as a preamble to focus on *cognitions,* which would counter perpetuations such as her perception that she needed to be defensive and antagonistic in response to what she felt was ambivalent and perhaps harmful treatment from others, and what was most likely brought on by her abrasive style (clarification of *self-other* conflict). From here, it would be useful to explore less caustic *interpersonal* styles, which would encourage empathy, and alleviate her salient *pain* orientation.

Therapeutic Course: A short-term and circumscribed focus was optimally suited for Marge. Formal *behavior modification* methods were fruitfully explored to achieve greater consistency and interpersonal harmony in her social behavior. Directive *cognitive* techniques, such as those of Meichenbaum and Ellis, were used to confront Marge with the obstructive and self-defeating character of her expectations and her personal relations. Although the deeply rooted character of these problems certainly impeded the effectiveness of most therapeutic procedures, it was fruitful to explore the more confrontive and incisive techniques of both cognitive and *interpersonal* therapies (e.g., Benjamin, Kiesler). A thorough reconstruction of personality was not necessarily the only means of altering her deeper pathologies. In support of short-term interpersonal techniques, *family* treatment methods were used to focus on the complex network of relationships that sustained her personality style. Together with cognitive reframing procedures, this combination proved to be highly useful in helping Marge recognize the source of her own hurt and angry feelings and to appreciate how she provoked hurt and anger in others.

Not at all surprisingly, Marge quite actively resisted exploring her motives. Although she was unlikely to be an active and willing participant in therapy, a strong and persuasive cognitive approach eventually drew her into the therapeutic process. She submitted to therapy only under the press of her employer, but she did learn to see the benefits of reframing her attitudes and the consequences of doing so. For example, she was facing difficulty as a consequence of aggressive behavior and incessant quarrels, but these were diminished by viewing her behavior differently and by acquiring other means of fulfilling the needs that drove them. With confronting methods, she learned not to assume that a problem could always be traced to another person's stupidity, laziness, or hostility. As she found it possible to accept a measure of responsibility for her difficulties, she did not find it necessary to conclude that the therapist tricked her into admitting it. In this situation, the therapist restrained any impulse to react to her with general disapproval or criticism. An important step in building rapport with Marge was to see things from her viewpoint. If success was to be achieved in a short-term intervention, the therapist needed to convey a sense of trust and a willingness to develop a constructive alliance. A balance of professional authority and tolerance was useful in diminishing the probability that Marge would relapse or impulsively withdraw from treatment.

As noted, Marge was hardly a willing participant in therapy initially, agreeing to treatment only under the pressure of vocational difficulties. The therapist's strong and determined attitude overcame her desire to outwit him by setting up situations to test his skills, to catch inconsistencies, to arouse ire, and, if possible, to belittle and humiliate him. For the therapist, a most important aspect of the therapeutic relationship was restraining any impulse to express a condemning attitude. Goal-directed in a brief treatment program, the therapist was able to check any hostile feelings, keeping in mind that the patient's difficulties were not fully under her control. Nevertheless, Marge may have actively impeded her progress toward conflict resolution and goal attainment, undoing what good she had previously achieved in treatment. A combination of cognitive and interpersonal techniques was employed to counteract her contrary feelings and her inclination to retract her more kindly expectations of others and quickly rebuild the few advances that she and the therapist had struggled to attain. The therapist's committed and professional approach prevented relapses by confronting the ambivalence that often robbed her of what steps she had secured toward progress.

NEGATIVISTIC PERSONALITY: DISCONTENTED TYPE
(NEGATIVIST WITH DEPRESSIVE TRAITS)

CASE 19.3, FRAN D., 31

Presenting Picture: Fran D. appeared so fully exasperated with basic questions that she turned on the counselor when asked what was most important to change and exclaimed,

"Listen, you're the doctor. I don't even know what's going on!" As she gained some initial control of her affect, it emerged that she wanted the first order of business to be fixing her relationship with her husband. She claimed that she was unable to gain emotional space within this relationship. She then mused, "I must drive him crazy, but that's me." She seemed entirely unconcerned that her corrosive and antagonistic behaviors might cause unrest for anyone but herself. Highly defensive and entirely unwilling to cooperate in responding to very general questions, Fran stated bitterly, "You get personal, *fast*." It was immediately apparent that she was entirely ill at ease with exploring any aspects of her needs or behaviors, and it would inevitably be too much to ask of her to modify any of her own viewpoints and expectations.

Clinical Assessment: Somewhere between the circuitous and abrasive negativist lies Fran's pattern, which we have termed the *discontented negativist*. Fran was embittered, complaining, and pessimistic, but she was neither indirect in her expression of disillusion and displeasure nor was she intentionally contentious and abrasive. This negativist is the consummate griper. She did not assault others in a harsh and brutal fashion; rather, she attacked under cover, from behind some pretense, one not readily transparent, from which she took piecemeal potshots, evincing niggling and annoying criticisms and complaints. There was a nonplayful teasing, a not-too-subtle dig, and various clever innuendoes. Fran would leave her object of criticism somewhat unprotected, often with no clear response to make. Descriptively, we might note this discontented variant of the negativist as testy, cranky, petty, complaining, vexed, and fretful, one who would avoid direct confrontation but who would constantly gripe with marginal and trivial complaints. Fran exhibited features akin to depressive personalities, especially those of the ill-humored subtype, with its sour and grumbling qualities.

Owing to the clever camouflage she employed, one had the impression that Fran had something worthwhile to say, a recommendation or observation that justified her comments and criticisms. These complaints, however, essentially reflected her hidden resentments and deep discontents about life. She rarely provided real solutions to the problems she would gripe about. Hence, her apparently worthwhile observations were merely sly ways to discharge her personal dissatisfactions, ways that ultimately intensified problems rather than resulting in their resolution.

As with the circuitous negativist, Fran was not so unwise as to risk open battles and confrontations. Rather, she sought to undercut her adversaries, to make them look inept or ridiculous, hence reaffirming the correctness of her own views without directly endangering herself or being overwhelmed by the counteractions of others. She had learned to choose a subtle and hidden rather than a frontal attack. She used small darts and stones rather than cannons and tanks. Having a distaste for and a fear of confrontational scenes, Fran used the cover of minor and tangential slights to avoid being exposed and punished. Whereas the circuitous negativist hides completely behind a veneer of seeming indifference and passivity, Fran was open but not confrontational, using "small cuts" rather than coarse and abrasive actions.

Fran was a malcontent who griped about everything, found fault with all matters of things, while appearing to have legitimate complaints that she sought to bring to someone's attention. As noted, these complaints were merely safe ploys to discharge her deeper discontents, struggles, and conflicts. She acted as if she were exasperated with the problems at hand, giving evidence thereby of being a person of goodwill and good intentions who has had to struggle with the inefficiencies and ineptitude of others. Hence, she could not be criticized for her "occasionally" unpleasant behaviors and attitudes. There was a sense of puzzlement, if not bewilderment, among those who perceptively recognized her underlying anger. Should they try to examine the legitimate problems about which Fran had complained, or should they confront her for being an annoyingly persistent crank and grumbler? The talent of the discontented was that she could quickly turn the tables on those to whom she complained, putting them on the defensive rather than on the offensive. Minor though the charges may have been, they were frequently real and justified, though often trivial and tangential.

Fran rarely dumped personal accusations on significant others. Rather, she complained to them about the awful and terrible characteristics of associates and relatives, accusing them of being incompetent and negativistic, precisely those attributes she possessed herself. Not able to fulfill her own wishes successfully nor to discharge her resentments directly, Fran demeaned the power and stature of competing others and thereby appeared to rise up in relative stature. She claimed that it was others who had fallen short; she, personally, was blameless and innocent. Now that Fran had brought problems to the forefront, it was up to others to right the wrongs that she had pointed out. Unable to fulfill her own strivings or to settle within herself the struggle between self and others, she had to derogate competitors, often in an avaricious and greedy manner. Desiring the privileged status of self-fulfillment, she sought to be honored by those in power, yet was resentful of those who possessed that power. Hence, Fran was caught again in a conflict between her need for self-expression and her resentment of those who had achieved it. This clash between envying others and being repulsed by them further intensified the inner conflict that gave rise to her fundamental problem between self and other.

Synergistic Treatment Plan: Early treatment would focus on establishing a trusting, empathic, and supportive environment, as the source of much of Fran's discontent was perceived shortcomings. As more directed interventions would be called for, a note of caution would be prudent, for she would be likely to suffer setbacks and possible depressive episodes if her coping mechanism of *displacement* of troublesome emotions was altered too quickly. It would be wise to consider *biophysical* and *behavioral* modalities to alleviate disgruntled moods and establish more effective social skills. *Cognitive* strategies would then be appropriate for altering such perpetuations as chronic pessimism and creation of disillusionment and resentfulness toward others (reduction of *pain* orientation). More efficient *interpersonal* strategies, in tandem with these cognitive goals, would strengthen the patient's troubled social network and create more satisfying interactions. In other words, this would constitute a clarification of *self-other* issues as well as enhance *pleasure.*

Therapeutic Course: Short-term techniques were helpful in aiding Fran in therapy. First, she was guided to avoid environmental pressures that aggravated her anxieties and dejection. Brief *supportive* therapy was employed to relieve sources of anxiety. Another option considered, but not utilized at this time, was *pharmacologic agents* (such as anti-anxiety or antidepressant drugs). Circumscribed *behavioral modification* methods were explored to focus on social behavior that could be strengthened in a relatively short time period. *Cognitive* techniques, such as those of Beck or Ellis, were used to confront Fran with the obstructive and self-defeating character of her beliefs and expectations. Strengthening her relations with significant others was benefited by employing a number of *interpersonal* treatment techniques (e.g., Klerman, Benjamin). Such approaches were handled cautiously, however, lest she feel that she was a failure and become unduly guilt-ridden, depressed, and possibly even suicidal. Of great benefit was to stabilize Fran and help her put reins on her vacillations of mood and behavior. In this way, the possibility of setbacks or deterioration in her condition was diminished.

Toward the goal of reducing the likelihood of a relapse or retrogression, the therapist did not set goals too high or press changes too quickly. Initial efforts were directed to build Fran's trust. Short-term procedures designed to orient her attentions to her positive traits and to enhance her confidence and self-esteem were well worth the effort involved.

A major goal throughout was to forestall repetitive decompensation into anxiety and depressive disorders. Also requiring focused attention was the need to anticipate suicide attempts. Fran acted impulsively when she felt guilty, needed attention, or sought a dramatic form of retribution. The therapist guided her into recognizing the sources and character of her ambivalence and reinforced a more realistic and optimistic outlook on life. Because she entered treatment in an agitated state, the reduction of her anxieties and guilt was an early goal of short-term treatment.

Because of an intense ambivalence between her desire for reassurance and nurturance and her fear of trusting an unknown person, Fran required an early warm and attentive attitude on the part of the therapist. Because she was engaged early on, she was not disposed to employ repetitive maneuvers to test the sincerity and motives of the therapist. Efforts were made to reduce the stressors of her home life. Working with family members was necessary. Had they not been optimally motivated, treatment may have called for more intensive techniques to reduce the possibility of setbacks. Because of the preceding reasons, treatment had to progress more rapidly to ensure that a significant measure of remedial improvement occurred. There was also the possibility of Fran's withdrawal from treatment should she have resisted facing the humiliation of confronting painful memories and feelings. With a nurturant and empathic attitude, the therapist was able to overcome her fear of re-experiencing false hopes and disappointments. What is suggested is that the warmth and understanding of the therapist moderated Fran's expectation that others would be rejecting, which would have led her to pull back, thereby cutting off experiences that might have proved gratifying had they been completed. What was desired was to decrease her anticipation of loss that may have prompted her into a self-fulfilling prophecy. Without focused attention, she may have defeated the chance to experience events that could promote change and growth. It was this pattern that a cognitive reorientation treatment approach successfully interrupted.

NEGATIVISTIC PERSONALITY: VACILLATING TYPE (NEGATIVISTIC WITH BORDERLINE TRAITS)

Case 19.4, Ann G., 26

Presenting Picture: Ann G. was an art student who was enjoying her course of study quite considerably. At first very guarded and defensive about pursuing a bachelor's at a "nontraditional" age (she began by telling the therapist that it was none of his business), then quite apologetic a few moments later for her harshness, Ann seemed to sway between several different moods without any apparent provocation. Her elongated college career was a result of many changes in major courses of study. She would start very enthusiastically, but as she reached more advanced coursework and varying moods struck, she would lose interest. Equally difficult was the tight schedule of the "nine-to-five" world, as it lacked the flexibility for her "off-times." Although she had found contentment in studying art, where adherence to schedule was more secondary, her husband prompted a visit to the therapist's office. She admitted that she often took her frustrations and sour moods out on him, but then would try to make it up to him. This bewildered her husband, as his stress stemmed from never knowing how Ann was going to be.

Clinical Assessment: Although Ann's primary characteristic is seen among most negativists, the quality of rapid fluctuation from one emotional state or interpersonal attitude to another is particularly notable in *vacillating negativists.* Ann was experienced by others, particularly her husband, as upsetting and frustrating because of her sharp and frequent reversals of mood and behavior. At times she was affectionate, predictable, interesting, and charming. Then suddenly, she became irritable, oppositional, and disagreeable. The next moment, she was self-assured, decisive, and competent; but before one could get accustomed to these behaviors, she reverted to being dependently clinging and childlike. Tantrums were quite common, frequently moving to the foreground and evidencing her characteristic recalcitrant behaviors and emotional instabilities. She could become almost childlike in other ways, being disagreeably disobedient one moment, and submissively conforming the next. Most characteristic, however, were her bewildering and enigmatic emotions, her inability to fathom her own capricious and mystifying moods, and her subjective wavering and intrapsychic fluctuations.

Ann was difficult to understand for most people. Few felt comfortable around her; not only was she enigmatic to herself, but she was invariably baffling to those with whom she lived and worked. It was her contradictory qualities and the ease with which she oscillated in her behaviors and attitudes that distinguished her from "run-of-the-mill" negativists. She was actively ambivalent. Her oscillation was rapid, with extremes of emotion. What made her difficult to grasp was that her behaviors and emotional states were unpredictable, changing from one moment to the next for no obvious reason. Ann's ambivalence was not only a matter of public appearance, that is, seen in overt emotions and manifest interpersonal behaviors, but her conflict was also internal. For example, her self-image shifted rapidly: she disparaged herself at one time and acted pleased and superior the next.

In many ways, Ann's vacillating negativistic personality is a dilute variant of the borderline personality. However, the ambivalence of the borderline is exhibited in all spheres of expression, between being passive or active, between seeking pleasure or pain, and being self-focused one moment and other-focused the next. By contrast, Ann's struggle was centered largely on the polarity of self versus other. As a result, her intrapsychic ambivalence was more limited in its underlying scope and makeup, resulting in a less severe form of pathology than seen in the borderline.

Synergistic Treatment Plan: Before more directive methods could be utilized, Ann needed to view the therapeutic environment as a safe and trusting atmosphere, and an *empathic* but steadfast posture from the therapist would help Ann begin to interact in a way that would not require her characteristic defenses and hostilities. As her comfort in-session would increase, *cognitions* would be emphasized, specifically those undermining her confidence and underlying her erratic and impulsive emotions, which frequently were used instrumentally. Her *interpersonal* strategies would be examined in conjunction with her disbalanced thought structures to further clarify her conflicts between *self* and *other,* as well as to lessen her very *active* stance in continually expecting disappointment and disillusionment and warding off these difficulties with impulsive and inefficient tactics.

Therapeutic Course: Serious efforts to alter Ann's current symptoms and basic psychopathology were attempted by employing focused and short-term techniques. Primary goals in brief therapy included facilitating autonomy, building confidence, and overcoming fears of self-determination. As anticipated, there was a period of initial resistance. As part of a short-term approach, it was important to counter the patient's feeling that the therapist's efforts to encourage her to assume responsibility and self-control were a sign of rejection. A warm and empathic building of trust prevented disappointment, dejection, and even rage. These potential reactions were to be expected, given Ann's characteristic style, and they would have needed to be responded to with equanimity if fundamental changes were to be explored and relapses prevented. When a sound and secure therapeutic alliance was established, the patient learned to tolerate her contrary feelings and dependency anxieties. Learning how to face and handle her unstable emotions needed to be coordinated with the strengthening of healthier attitudes through *cognitive* methods such as those of Beck and Meichenbaum, as well as through *interpersonal* procedures such as those of Kiesler and Benjamin. Additionally, the therapist was able to serve as a model to demonstrate how feelings, conflicts, and uncertainties could be approached and resolved with reasonable equanimity and foresight. Also fruitful were *family* methods that were used to test these newly learned attitudes and strategies in a more natural setting than that found in individual treatment.

As implied, by her affective instability and self-deprecation, Ann avoided confronting and resolving her real interpersonal difficulties. Her coping maneuvers were quite the double-edged sword, relieving passing discomfort and strains but perpetuating faulty attitudes and strategies. These distorted attitudes and faulty behaviors were the main targets of cognitive and interpersonal therapeutic interventions (e.g., Safran and Segal).

Special care was called for in a short-term treatment regimen to counteract the possibility that Ann's hold on reality might disintegrate and her capacity to function wither. Similar care would have been taken had the attention and support that she required been withdrawn or had her strategies proved so wearisome and exasperating to others that they precipitated their anger. *Pharmacologic agents* might have been considered had she begun to succumb to depression or to an erratic surge of hostility. Particular attention would have been given to anticipate and quell the danger of suicide during episodes such as these.

A major concern during these early periods was the forestalling of a persistent decompensation process. Among the early signs of such a breakdown would have been marked discouragement and melancholic dejection. At this phase, *supportive* therapy would have been called for, and cognitive reorientation methods would have been actively implemented. Efforts would need to be made to boost Ann's sagging morale, to encourage her to continue in her usual sphere of activities, to build her self-confidence, and to deter her from being preoccupied with her melancholy feelings. She could not be pressed beyond her capabilities, however, because her failure to achieve any goals would only strengthen her conviction of her incompetence and unworthiness. Properly executed cognitive methods oriented to correcting erroneous assumptions and beliefs would have been especially helpful.

Resistances and Risks

Negativistic patients frequently decompensate into anxiety and depressive disorders. Therapists must be on guard to anticipate suicidal attempts because ambivalent personalities can act quite impulsively when they feel guilt, need attention, or seek a dramatic form of retribution. Because these patients often enter treatment in an agitated state, an early treatment task is to calm their anxieties and fears. Relieved of tension, many will lose the incentive to continue treatment. Motivating them to pursue a more substantial course of therapy may call for considerable effort on the part of the therapist because these personalities are deeply ambivalent about dependency relationships. They desire to be nurtured and loved by a powerful parental figure, but such submission poses the threat of loss and undermines the desire to maintain independence.

A seesaw struggle is often enacted between patient and therapist; the negativist is likely to exhibit an ingratiating submissiveness on one occasion, and a taunting and demanding attitude on another. Similarly, these patients may solicit the therapist's affections, but when these are expressed, the patient rejects them, voicing doubt about the genuineness of the therapist's feelings. When the therapist points out these contradictory attitudes, patients may verbally appreciate the therapist's perceptiveness but not alter their attitudes at all. It becomes clear that the roundabout tactics negativists employ to air their grievances can take many different forms in the therapeutic setting. Delaying payments, late arrivals, forgetting appointments, not remembering to do homework, poor boundaries, and anger projection are just a few examples of the many resistances encountered. These patients are likely to use the ambiguity inherent in the therapeutic setting as an excuse for withdrawing or enacting passive-aggressive maneuvers.

If therapy has moderated the negativist's pathology to the point where he or she can satisfactorily fulfill social and occupational obligations without causing friction, treatment should be considered successful. Only in select cases can therapy become a major corrective force for more fundamental personality change.

CHAPTER TWENTY

Treating Masochistic Personality Patterns

Although clinical inclinations of a self-abasing character have been observed for centuries, it failed to gain official recognition as a personality disorder until 1987. An effort to include the psychoanalytic construct *masochistic personality disorder* was made in early discussions of the *DSM-III* (American Psychiatric Association [APA], 1980). Given the antitheoretical orientation of that manual's Task Force, the concept of masochistic behaviors, originally conceived as a potential Axis II disorder, was formulated instead as a feature of the Axis I *affective* group of syndromes. Soon after the appearance of *DSM-III*, several clinical theorists continued to press for an Axis II category that would encompass the self-abusive and self-undoing qualities of a *depressive/masochistic* personality. This proposal was taken seriously by the Work Group assigned the task of revising the *DSM-III*. The proposal quickly generated both professional and public controversy. To minimize substantive objections and harassing debates, the label was changed from masochistic to *self-defeating*. The initially proposed criteria were then modified to rule out depressive symptomatology, as well as to minimize gender biases, for example, to exclude from the list abusive relationships in which women victims were in effect blamed for ostensibly precipitating the abuse. It was then decided to place the diagnosis of a self-defeating personality in the *DSM-III-R* appendix (American Psychiatric Association [APA], 1987), along with the sadistic personality diagnosis, owing to the fact that they were "new" disorders and hence required further clinical and empirical study.

Although the original label masochism acquired a somewhat confusing array of meanings (e.g., a sexual perversion, a moral character type), the selection of self-defeating as an alternative did not achieve either clarity or precision in its potential usage. Moreover, all personality disorders are essentially self-defeating in that they all set into motion self-perpetuating behaviors and reactions that further intensify the very problems that gave rise to them in the first place. Any number of terms would have proved more apt, we believe, for example, self-abasing, deferential, obsequious, abject, servile, self-denigrating, and so on. The need to clarify the meaning of the construct, which we prefer to label again masochistic personality disorder, is a central task for those who wish to extend the boundaries of the *DSM-IV* (American Psychiatric Association [APA], 1994) and from which the disorder has been deleted.

The reason for describing the masochistic/self-defeating prototype in this text is to broaden the reader's perspective by including in the scope of their clinical work a constellation of cohering self-abasive and self-undoing personality characteristics. With such knowledge in hand, clinicians should be able to better understand and treat their patients. It is true that all labeling and diagnoses possess the potential for misuse, but we cannot bypass our studies because interpretations given these disorders may at times be fallacious and misguided. Personality disorders of all stripes result from interacting biogenic, psychogenic, and sociogenic factors. It is especially regrettable that such complexly formed pathologies are interpreted by some solely in terms of their potential social and political implications. We must obviate all such interpretations lest mental disorders be recast, as they have been in Germany and Russia this past century, as social defects rather than as *intrinsic clinical phenomena,* in this case as one of the several persistently chronic and widely pervasive pathologies of persons.

Horney's (1945) formulation of "masochistic phenomena" bridges the theme of ambivalence first posited as central to these personalities by Abraham (1911/1968) and the notion of spiteful suffering proposed by Reich (1933). As she views it, the masochist establishes "a value in suffering" as a means of defending against fears associated with a sense of intrinsic weakness and insignificance, both of which leave the person with an inordinate need for affection and an extraordinary fear of disapproval.

In subsequent writings, Horney (1950) recognized that the suffering of the masochist often serves the defensive purpose of avoiding recriminations and responsibilities; that is, it is a way of expressing accusations in a disguised form. For some, it is a way of demanding affection and reparations. For others, it is a virtue that justifies claims for love and acceptance.

As in prior chapters, brief notes will be made of the evolutionary theory as a framework for explicating the key elements of the masochistic/self-defeating pattern that were included in the *DSM-III-R* appendix (APA, 1987). Figure 20.1 provides a visual picture of

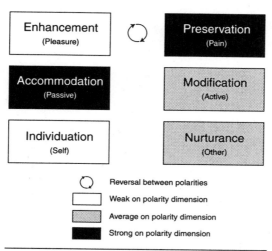

Figure 20.1   Status of the masochistic (self-defeating) personality prototype in accord with the Millon Polarity Model.

the strength of the three major bipolarities of the theory. As can be seen, the major pathologic component is the reversal between the pain and pleasure segments of the first polarity. This signifies that the individual has learned to experience pain in a manner that makes it preferable to experiences of pleasure. Of course, this preference may be a relative one; that is, the individual may be willing to tolerate significant discomfort and abuse as long as it is the lesser of greater degrees of anguish and humiliation. To be moderately distressed and disheartened may be better than to be severely pained and demoralized.

The self-defeating disorder is passive and accommodating in a manner similar to the depressive personality. The distinction is a fine one, but one that is significant nevertheless. In the depressive, passivity indicates an acceptance of one's fate, a sense that loss and hopelessness are justified and that depression is inevitable; further, that these experiences can never be overcome and, hence, one should accept one's depressive state and the irretrievability of happiness. In the self-defeating, there is a measure of both control and desirability in giving in to one's suffering and discomfort. For these individuals, a measure of moderate anguish may be a preferable state; that is, it may be the best of all possible alternatives available. Passivity, therefore, indicates an acceptance of pain as a realistic choice given one's inescapable options, not a final and irretrievable state of hopelessness.

CLINICAL PICTURE

The following sections encompass several perspectives in our attempt to illuminate the major characteristics of the prototypal masochistic (self-defeating) personality pattern (see Table 20.1).

Prototypal Diagnostic Domains

This section discusses the central features of the so-called masochistic (self-defeating) pattern, detailing these characteristics in accord with the major domains of clinical analysis utilized in earlier chapters (see Figure 20.2).

Abstinent expressive behavior.   Overtly, masochistic personalities are inclined to act in a self-effacing and unpresuming manner. For public consumption, they place themselves in an inferior light or abject position, reluctant to seek pleasurable experiences and refraining from exhibiting signs of enjoying life. For the most part, they present themselves as being nonindulgent, frugal, and chaste. Some appear shabby in public; their clothes are designed to signify poverty or a disinterest in common forms of attractiveness. Others may actually abuse their bodies in ways that lead to self-starvation and anorexia. Most merely fail to dress up and appear appropriate given their socioeconomic status.

What we see in these abstinent behaviors is an active expression of self-denigration, an act of frustrating personal choices and self-respect. There is a taboo on most forms of enjoyment and self-enhancement. Masochists are saying, in effect, that they do not wish to gain pleasure or gratification, that good things are not good for them, that any form of self-indulgence is best forbidden and denied. Some of these self-taboos are cast in the form of social concern and altruism. To them, self-denial is a sign of social

TABLE 20.1 Clinical Domains of the Masochistic Personality Prototype

Behavioral Level

(F) Expressively Abstinent (e.g., presents self as nonindulgent, frugal, and chaste; is reluctant to seek pleasurable experiences, refraining from exhibiting signs of enjoying life; acts in an unpresuming and self-effacing manner, preferring to place self in an inferior light or abject position).

(F) Interpersonally Deferential (e.g., distances from those who are consistently supportive, relating to others where one can be sacrificing, servile, and obsequious, allowing if not encouraging them to exploit, mistreat, or take advantage; renders ineffectual the attempts of others to be helpful and solicits condemnation by accepting undeserved blame and courting unjust criticism).

Phenomenological Level

(F) Cognitively Diffident (e.g., hesitant to interpret observations positively for fear that, in doing so, they may not take problematic forms or achieve troublesome and self-denigrating outcomes; as a result, there is a habit of repeatedly expressing attitudes and anticipations contrary to favorable beliefs and feelings).

(S) Undeserving Self-Image (e.g., is self-abasing, focusing on the very worst personal features, asserting thereby that one is worthy of being shamed, humbled, and debased; feels that one has failed to live up to the expectations of others and hence, deserves to suffer painful consequences).

(S) Discredited Objects (e.g., object-representations are composed of failed past relationships and disparaged personal achievements, of positive feelings and erotic drives transposed into their least attractive opposites, of internal conflicts intentionally aggravated, of mechanisms for reducing dysphoria being subverted by processes that intensify discomfort).

Intrapsychic Level

(F) Exaggeration Mechanism (e.g., repetitively recalls past injustices and anticipates future disappointments as a means of raising distress to homeostatic levels; undermines personal objectives and sabotages good fortunes so as to enhance or maintain accustomed level of suffering and pain).

(S) Inverted Organization (e.g., owing to a significant reversal of the pain-pleasure polarity, morphologic structures have contrasting and dual qualities—one more or less conventional, the other its obverse—resulting in a repetitive undoing of affect and intention, of a transposing of channels of need gratification with those leading to frustration, and of engaging in actions that produce antithetical if not self-sabotaging consequences).

Biophysical Level

(S) Dysphoric Mood (e.g., experiences a complex mix of emotions, at various times anxiously apprehensive, forlorn and mournful, anguished and tormented; intentionally displays a plaintive and wistful appearance, frequently to induce guilt and discomfort in others).

F refers to Functional Domains (fluid, interactive)
S refers to Structural Domains (stable, unchanging)

conscience and responsibility, by which material gains would be ill-gotten were they not shared equally by others. In its most extreme form, the determination to deny oneself can generate feelings of panic if one realizes that one has failed to jettison an attractive trait or material possession.

Deferential interpersonal conduct. These personalities prefer relationships in which they can be self-sacrificing, even servile and obsequious in manner. The tendency to place themselves in a general deferential position is notable. It is not untypical for them to allow if not encourage others to be exploitive, mistreating, even to take advantage of them. Equally problematic is a tendency to distance from those who are

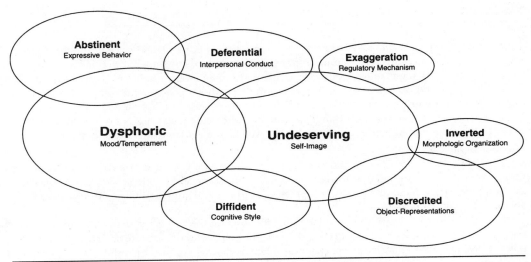

Figure 20.2   Salience of prototypal masochistic domains.

supportive and helpful. At times, they may render ineffectual the attempts of others to be kindly and of assistance. Most pathologic is their inclination to solicit condemnation from others and to accept undeserved blame, as well as to court unjust criticism for their actions and performance.

By self-sacrifice, the masochist aims to arouse guilt in others, and such self-denigration helps explain relationships that would otherwise seem perplexing. Rather puzzling is the fact that this pattern of repetitive self-flagellation persists even when a hurtful partner shows no sign of guilt or remorse. Instead, masochists continue to humiliate themselves before their denigrating partner. By intensifying their self-disparagement, they hope ultimately to provoke their unprincipled partner not only to admit his or her acts of dishonor and exploitation, but to feel contrite and loving. This signifies, in effect, masochists' belief that they must submit and denigrate themselves in order to be loved and cared for by another.

The self-contempt that masochists feel necessitates that they assume an inferior and contemptible role with others. Hence, even when making an appropriate request, masochists feel that they may be taking undue advantage of another. Either they refrain from the request or make the request apologetically and deferentially. Along this line, they will fail to defend themselves when treated in an insulting and derogatory fashion. They behave as if they were defenseless, easily exploitable, a ready prey for those who seek to take advantage.

There is an inverse ratio, as Horney (1950) has put it, between success and inner security. Achievements in relationships or in their occupation do not make masochists more secure, but more anxious. Fearing retribution, even total annihilation for their presumption of possessing worthy gains, they will neither stand up for their rightful awards nor counter any expression of anger and resentment directed at them. Their dismay can only be expressed in disguised or denied forms. Only in the most extraordinary circumstances will they reprimand, reproach, or accuse others, even in a joking or sarcastic way. Of course, to be self-effacing, to suffer and restrain oneself from success and self-assertion provides an alibi for not achieving much in life. Masochists can thereby save face, both in their mind and in the eyes of others, for their self-induced deficiencies and failings.

Diffident cognitive style. Masochists are unsure of themselves, reluctant to assert their views, and tend to be self-effacing and restrained in their interpretation of life events. Disposed to construe events as troublesome and problematic, they are hesitant to see life in a positive light for fear that optimism will ultimately result in troublesome and self-denigrating aftermaths. As a result, masochists bring to their interpretive inclinations a habit of expressing views and anticipations that are pessimistic in orientation and contrary to favorable consequences. Not only do they express pessimistic and negative feelings, but whatever positive attitudes may be engendered are likely to be voiced without any genuine enthusiasm.

One might wonder how this singularly heavy outlook can be maintained without one's being devastated or collapsing under its weight. What is surprising is that masochists appear never to be undone by their persistent apologetic and self-deprecating attitudes. Observation over a period of time is likely to find that these self-reproachful attitudes are largely overdone, artificial, and forced, presenting an exaggerated façade of simulated communications. In great measure, their public posture of inadequacy, their voiced deficiencies and sense of demoralization are designed (unconsciously) to deflect or defeat those who they believe may assault and demean them. The fabled forest wolf, who has concluded that continuing a fight to the finish would result in its annihilation, effectively thwarts its enemy by admitting its inadequacy, exposing its jugular vein and thereby exhibiting that it is no longer a threat to its enemy. Similarly, by overtly exaggerating their weaknesses and ineffectuality, masochists turn away the aggression of others.

Undeserving self-image. Masochists are overtly self-abasing, inclined in public to focus on their very worst personal features. As they see it, they have failed to live up to the expectations of others, despite their repeated efforts at self-sacrifice. Hence, they deserve to suffer painful consequences and, thereby, should feel shamed, humbled, and debased. In some masochists, this self-effacing, nondeserving image is so extreme as to lead them to conclude that anything that exemplifies personal achievement or competence could only have been the result of good luck or the contributions of others. To have a strong personal conviction or opinion is potentially endangering, a position that the masochist will quickly yield when facing an opposing viewpoint or interpretation. A public commendation of their work is usually judged to have been mistaken, an erroneous observation that fails to recognize their core deficiencies and inadequacies. Masochists do not seek to strive, to reach out for more than they have, because to do so challenges fate and exposes them to potential humiliation and denigration. Nothing should ever be done just for oneself. Requiring little keeps them in a small and protective shell, one in which they can maintain to a minimum any ridicule and deprecation.

As in the section above on cognitive style, we find on closer examination that many self-sacrificing and unassertive masochists are preoccupied not with the welfare of others, but with their own suffering and resentments. What appears on the surface to be a sympathetic and self-sacrificial attitude often cloaks a lack of genuine empathy and a distrust of others.

Discredited object-representations.   Reflecting on aspects of their past experience, but even more so by transforming their memories, the inner template of their objects and events comes to have a distinctly negative tone. As masochists retrospectively view it, their past relationships are recast to signify problematic failures, and their own personal achievements are disparaged. Affectionate and erotic feelings of the past are transposed to their least attractive opposites. Adding further insult to these transmutations of past realities, unmodified internal conflicts are intentionally aggravated. In a similar fashion, mechanisms for reducing dysphoric feelings are subverted by processes that intensify the discomfort level of the masochist's recollections.

Owing to their early life experiences, masochists are likely to assume that all close relationships contain at their root the potential of new frustrations and deprecations. In the main, they transmute their current everyday experiences to reproduce the frustrations and cruelty that remain from the past in their intrapsychic world. Some recognize that there are genuinely caring persons in their environment, but they judge it to be the invariable misfortune with which they are cursed in life that such persons are not the people to whom they relate.

As part of their intrapsychic dissonance, masochists struggle between internal images of being a tormentor themselves on the one hand, and an innocent and abused victim on the other. Thus, the self and other objects of their inner world are split into opposing elements, one convinced that others will continue to seek to destroy them, the other that they themselves wish to destroy others. Incapable of resolving this schism and thereby provide a genuinely positive attitude, the masochist bends over backward, as in a reaction-formation, attempting with every resolve to be an unambivalently reliant and ever sacrificing partner.

Exaggeration regulatory mechanism.   Whereas regulatory mechanisms are internal dynamic processes designed to resolve or soften the psychic pain of objective realities, these processes are inverted in the masochist, at least for public consumption. Rather than lessen their public discomforts, these personalities recall and exaggerate past injustices to raise their overt experience of distress. Similarly, they go out of their way to anticipate and magnify likely future disappointments as a means of raising their expectation of distress to levels consonant with their negative orientation. Furthermore, masochists often undermine their personal plans and sabotage their good fortunes so as to maintain or enhance the level of suffering and pain to which they have become accustomed.

As noted by Shapiro (1981), these patients dwell on their misfortunes, not only for public purposes but to manage their personal discomfort and private suffering. Despite the melodramatic public fashion in which they exaggerate the incidental grievances of the past, exaggeration reflects the operation of a useful defensive maneuver in that it enables masochists to control and recast their sources of bitterness. By repetitively re-creating in their mind early humiliations and injustices, masochists are able to diminish the actual pain and deprecation they suffered. As in the implosive therapeutic technique, excessive exposure to painful and threatening stimuli ultimately diminishes their impact and power. So too is exaggeration an inverted form of self-protection and pain diminution. By exaggeration, masochists have diminished their suffering. They can now control it, compartmentalize it, bring it up at will, transform and moderate it; in effect, they can now be in charge of their past discomforts, play them out, manipulate them, make them less painful than they may have been, should that be their intrapsychic desire.

Inverted organization.   As is typical of personalities who are intrapsychically ambivalent or discordant, masochists' morphological structures possess contrasting and dual qualities. One segment of their inner world is structured in a more or less conventional fashion; the other reflects opposing or contradictory components. Thus, masochists exhibit a reversal of the pain-pleasure polarity, experiencing pleasure when pain would be more appropriate and vice versa. As a consequence, they exhibit a repetitive undoing of intention and affect. There is a frequent transposition of channels of need-gratification so that frustration results. Most problematic, their inverted structural organization and dynamic processes result in actions that produce perplexing, often antithetical if not self-undoing consequences.

As with most complex phenomena, the structure of personality undergirds many functions in the economy of the mind. Conventionally structured, the components of the mind serve to gratify instinctual drives, impose social constraints by means of psychic expiation and punishment, and provide methods of adapting to life's realities. As in the case of the sadist, the compulsive, and the negativistic, the masochist possesses intrapsychic structures that are in intrinsic opposition. For example, structural inversion of the basic polarities results in masochists assuming that they are loved most when they suffer most, generating the conviction that when love is desired, they must first seek to suffer. Rather than pursue affection in a straightforward fashion, masochists may need to engage in a form of "naughtiness," hoping thereby to elicit a rejecting or scolding response from the significant other; the assumption that carries them forward is the belief that forbidden behaviors will ultimately evoke love in return.

It is often quite puzzling and perplexing to track these reversals of what are usually straightforward and natural orientations. By defeating themselves, masochists seek not only to avoid being beaten and humiliated, but to elicit nurturance and affection. The direct pursuit of pleasure threatens them by evoking experiences of anxiety and guilt. Whether these processes stem from "internalized bad objects" is an interesting way to formulate the problem. This simply means that the person has internalized a punitive system that must be enacted when normal affectional desires are sought. One must suffer, therefore, to be loved.

Dysphoric mood.   Masochists experience a complex of countervailing emotions. At times, they are anxiously apprehensive; at other times, they are forlorn and mournful. Many are disposed to feel anguished and tormented; these same individuals may exhibit a socially pleasant and engaging manner at other times. Some intentionally display a plaintive and wistful appearance, features that seem designed to induce discomfort and guilt in others.

Suffering among masochists is not invariably designed to impress others; it serves as much to ennoble themselves. Once established, masochists effectively accuse others and excuse themselves. They seek in every way possible to dampen their own spirits as well as those of others. At times of deepening distress, however, masochists are strongly tempted to simply "let things go," just giving up what is felt to be a hopeless struggle for consistent and reliable love, for meeting the self-sacrificial demands imposed on themselves, to be free of the terror of everyday life. All of these feelings can create a sense of ultimate triumph, a way to escape forever, to be "done with it all." The broad dysphoric mix of emotions we often see in masochists serves to glorify their ultimate state of misery, providing proof of the fundamental nobility of their suffering.

Self-Perpetuation Processes

As the interim label for masochistic personality clearly indicates, these individuals are self-defeating; that is, what they do further intensifies their difficulties and undoes any promising advances they may have made in their lives. Although the very notion of self-perpetuation is therefore intrinsic to the masochistic construct, it may be useful to specify some of the more explicit ways in which these personalities undermine their own healthful progress (see Table 20.2).

Demeaning of self.   Masochists are specialists in "beating themselves down," disparaging, belittling, ridiculing, and being contemptuous of themselves. Although there are considerable differences among masochists in the degree to which they are aware of these denigrating processes, they all add up to diminishing their capacity to take anything that they do seriously; they are surprised, if not astonished, when others judge their opinions and attitudes to be of consequence. Not only are they unable to appreciate their own talents and achievements but, as has been stated previously, they seek to undo whatever good fortune may accidentally have come their way.

As a consequence of demeaning their own self-worth, these individuals greatly impair themselves, preclude any form of spontaneous self-assertive behavior, exaggerate their difficulties and, in effect, submerge themselves in a pervasive feeling of helplessness and ineffectuality. Not only do these behaviors undermine their competence and self-esteem, but they throw masochists into an abyss of lifelong misery that is quite disproportionate to the circumstances that their life's experiences would justify. Hence, through their own actions and exaggerations, they place themselves repeatedly in positions of almost irrevocable disgrace and contempt.

TABLE 20.2   Self-Perpetuating Processes

MASOCHISTIC
Demeaning of Self
    Undoes good fortunes
    Takes nothing about self seriously
    Persists in being ineffectual and hopeless

Dependence on Others
    Self-worth determined by others' judgments
    Fears abandonment when uncertain of support
    Tolerates abuse for fear of abandonment

Intensifies Abuse
    Believes disparagement is deserved
    Increasingly accusatory of others' treatment
    Becomes righteously indignant at wrongs perpetuated

Dependence on others.   In a manner similar to the dependent personality, masochists have devalued themselves to such an extent that it is only others who can judge their self-worth. Their psychic state rises or falls with the attitudes that others have of them. Devaluing themselves has made them entirely dependent on others for judging the adequacy with which their self-sacrificial behaviors have met others' desires. This self-minimization forces them to turn to others to provide them not only with feelings of security, but with a sense of salvation. Should their self-denigrating and self-abasing behaviors fail to be recognized, their search for appreciation may begin to take on a frantic character, further reducing their sense of self-esteem.

Masochists' fear of being abandoned and isolated becomes prominent at times when they are unsure of their value in the eyes of significant others. They are unable to be alone for any length of time, and feel lost and rejected, cut off from the stream of life. Fearful as these insecurities may be, they can be overcome by any form of connection to others; abuse can be tolerated as long as it is kept within extreme limits. As long as masochists can remain connected and needed, regardless of how much abuse they receive, they will not feel the nameless terror of being totally abandoned. Hence, they must keep attached at all costs, regardless of the humiliation and derogation they experience. To be alone is the ultimate proof that they are not only unwanted and rejected, but disgraced and forsaken.

Intensifying self- and other-abuse.   Although masochists have undoubtedly experienced troublesome early relationships, we know that they also transform new life events to conform with those of the past. This distorting process creates a series of unrealities. Not only do they suffer anguish, shame, and guilt for every shortcoming or failure in their lives, but they are hyperscrupulous about their own behaviors and circumstances, such that everything they do or observe deserves to be ridiculed and disparaged. They are "injustice collectors," seeing unfairness if not derogation in those who do not appreciate their self-sacrificial behaviors.

A problem that may arise here is a growing indignation felt toward those whom they see as having humiliated them. This reversal from self-denial into a more openly critical and negative attitude toward others reflects a desire to quiet their idealized self-image and conscience. Although they judge themselves to be unworthy, they do not judge themselves so unworthy as to continue to have abuse heaped upon them *in spite of* their willingness to carry undue burdens and to persist in their self-sacrifice. As this reversal of characteristic behaviors becomes intensified, masochists begin to discharge their misery and to begin to assert a feeling of entitlement, a confused and disillusioned state that leads them to want others to make up for the injuries they feel have been perpetrated on them throughout their life.

No longer are masochists merely self-pitying persons who feel unfairly treated, but they now rise up in a rather pathetic form of righteous indignation. The more they distort the actions of others as being accusatory and abusive, the more frantically are they likely to exaggerate the wrongs that have been done to them and the more deeply they feel that recompense is their due. Should their vindictive anger break into consciousness, it will mar their idealized image of being virtuous and magnanimous, violating their inner image of being self-sacrificing and all-forgiving. Hence, the expression of previously repressed resentments becomes a disruptive element of considerable magnitude. In addition to the inner turmoil it creates, masochists may have provoked others into rejecting them even further, leading them thereby to be doubly ignoble, both victim and perpetrator.

INTERVENTION GOALS

Although the masochistics' self-defeating behavior pervades all aspects (personal, social, and occupational) of their functioning, the self-sabotaging tendencies are seen primarily in the area of interpersonal relationships. Despite relatively adaptive adjustment in some spheres of life, there often exists a long history of abusive relationships that combines with an apparent lack of understanding of their role in inviting maltreatment. Although patients may lament years of undeserved victimization and suffering, they often continue to behave in excessively deferential and self-demeaning ways, making no attempt to constructively alter the dynamics of exploitive relationships. The therapist may marvel as a patient sabotages potentially positive interactions and rejects opportunities for involvement with caring and considerate individuals, dismissing them as boring or otherwise inappropriate companions.

Lacking the experience of deriving rewards from behaving in an interpersonally competent and self-respecting manner, and having no coherent personal identity other than victim, masochists are threatened with a loss of self in giving up their usual ways of relating. Suffering provides masochists with an identity, a sense of value, and predictable interactions. The therapist working with a masochist has to keep in mind that much work will have to be done to provide the patient with the foundations of a healthier self-concept. Resistance to adopting new modes of interaction will be reduced as self-respecting behavior can be meaningfully incorporated, rather than posing a threat to the only identity he or she has known. The therapist must point out behaviors that provoke hostile reactions from others, as well as to empathize with the patient's tendency to perpetuate his or her victimization. Eventually, the patient may come to internalize the therapist's empathy and positive regard, making the patient more amenable to change.

Much of their difficulty is based on a pain-pleasure discordance that draws masochists to situations and individuals that cause them pain. Reestablishing a balance on this polarity can help patients acquire more adaptive behaviors. Also, a shift on the active-passive dimension can lead to constructive rather than self-defeating attitudes and actions.

Intervention within the masochist's dysfunctional domains are intertwined with the former objectives. Cognitive interventions that produce change within the patient's cognitive style, exploring the developmental history of the patient's difficulties, and behavioral interventions that teach assertiveness and social skills may allow him or her to replace customary interpersonal deference with respect-fostering relationships. Strategic plans of action, as well as increased insight, can help patients reduce their tendencies to allow others to abuse them (see Table 20.3).

Reestablishing Polarity Balances

To accomplish the goal of restructuring the masochist's disordered personality, a balance needs to be established on the pain-pleasure and active-passive polarities. A major problem of masochists is their distorted and inverted focus on life-preserving experiences. The tendency to perpetuate unpleasant situations stems from the fact that the

TABLE 20.3   Therapeutic Strategies
and Tactics for the Prototypal
Masochistic Personality

STRATEGIC GOALS
Balance Polarities
Reverse pain-pleasure discordance
Strengthen active-self focus
Counter Perpetuations
Stop willingness to be abused
Avoid self-demeaning experiences
Prevent the undoing of positive events
TACTICAL MODALITIES
Moderate dysphoric moods
Revoke undeserving self-image
Unlearn interpersonal deference

masochist's identity is intertwined with suffering and the victim role. As described throughout the chapter, many masochists learned in childhood to misidentify abuse as love. To modify their self-sabotaging and abuse-perpetuating behavior, they first need to clarify and internalize the difference between loving and abusive behavior, that is, between pleasure and pain. Work must also be done to help the masochist develop a more adaptive and positive self-image. Interventions aimed at cognitive reorientation can be effective in this regard.

Once patients become cognizant of and begin to overcome their victimized self-image and self-inflicted pain, they may be ready to start overcoming their self-defeating passivity. Behavioral intervention, including assertiveness and social skills training, can prepare patients to relate to others in a more equity-fostering way. Patients can be taught to set time aside daily to engage in pleasurable activities and can reward themselves in prespecified ways for appropriate interactions.

Countering Perpetuating Tendencies

A therapist working with a masochistic personality would be well-advised to focus efforts on helping the patient become aware of and change his or her problem-perpetuating behaviors. Goals here are to counter the patient's willingness to be abused, to be involved in self-demeaning experiences, and to engage in self-sabotage through the undoing of positive events.

Cognitive interventions and exploratory therapies can help patients expand their understanding of a fuller range of human interactions, allowing patients to conceive of relational experiences that can work without victimization. Some masochists have learned to feel important or validated when others are hostile toward them. Masochists learn that a significant other's cruelty relents when they are suffering, and from that conclude that their value increases with increments in their unhappiness. A growing understanding of this process may encourage patients to adopt new attitudes and interaction styles. Bolstering the patient's self-esteem will further increase the likelihood that self-demeaning experiences will be avoided as they become less consistent with a changed and more positive self-image.

Some patients may benefit from pharmacologic intervention as an adjunct to dyadic treatment. Antidepressants may bolster improvements in self-esteem and reduce guilt. In conjunction with new ways of thinking about themselves and their environments, decreased guilt can help patients prevent the undoing of positive events that in the past had served as self-punishment for failings, at the same time preserving their sense of identity.

Identifying Domain Dysfunctions

Central to masochistic personalities' characteristic difficulties are their undeserving self-image and their dysphoric mood. Convinced that they have failed to achieve others' expectations, masochists genuinely believe they deserve to be shamed and punished. Suffering is actively sought to ease their sense of guilt about perceived failings. Consistent with this self-image, the masochist's mood is dysphoric and ranges from anxiety to anguish. After years of believing themselves to be both inadequate and victimized, masochists display extreme self-denial and deferential interpersonal conduct. These modes of expressing themselves and relating interpersonally serve a preconscious purpose: they help maintain consistent and predictable internal and external representations of the self as a suffering, inferior individual. By behaving in a self-effacing and unpresuming manner, and by declining to participate in pleasant activities and denying any experiences of joy, masochists can also "atone" for inadequacies and render themselves beyond reproach.

Convinced that pleasure and fun are undeserved and in fact beyond their capacity, masochists find that suffering not only eases their guilt but is the only feeling they can allow that is better than the prospect of an inner nothingness. Not only do these patients feel unjustified in attempting to feel better, but their suffering and helplessness serve to provide a tangible identity and social role. The role of depression in the patient's dysphoric mood should be carefully evaluated. Psychopharmacologic intervention in the form of antidepressants may be indicated for some patients. Improved affect and self-esteem can help provide motivation to continue working toward more permanent structural personality changes.

For some masochists, the tendency to be self-sacrificing, even to invite exploitation and accept undeserved blame, have other self-serving functions. Experiences with punitive adults in childhood may lead to equating maltreatment with love, leading some masochists to search out powerful and oppressive others and to play the complementary part to satisfy their need for affection. Others have learned that a punitive parent was in fact most loving, or at least less cruel, when the masochist's suffering was most evident. Overt expressions of suffering in adulthood may thus serve to appease significant others or, as the only weapon in the masochist's arsenal, to punish them and make them feel guilty for not meeting his or her needs.

A therapist working with a masochistic personality is going to encounter much resistance in trying to modify the patient's poor self-concept. Methods of cognitive reorientation can help patients realize that their diffident cognitive style maintains their difficulties. Self-effacing and unsure of themselves, masochists construe events as troublesome and problematic for fear that optimism will ultimately result in disappointing and self-denigrating aftermaths. More adaptive ways of thinking can help to alter the basis on which these masochistic behaviors are built. In time, the patient may stop repetitively recalling past injustices, anticipating future disappointments, and undermining personal objectives and good fortune to maintain his or her accustomed level of suffering and pain.

Insight-oriented therapy can help identify the developmental causes of the masochist's discredited object relations. The patient can learn that although his or her parents confused love and abuse, not all people do. Behavioral interventions can teach assertive social skills that provide the patient with new modes of interacting. Successful therapeutic intervention should help reorganize the patient's personality structure so that its organization is no longer inverted. Once the pain-pleasure polarity has been rebalanced, the channels of need gratification and frustration should no longer be transposed. This adjustment can help the patient strive for reward rather than pain, resulting in more adaptive behaviors.

SELECTING THERAPEUTIC MODALITIES

Masochistic patients are likely to elicit a number of antitherapeutic countertransference reactions from their therapists. However, a consistently warm and empathic alliance can provide a prototype for self-evaluation that the masochist can internalize over time and draw on in working to overcome self-defeating tendencies.

Behavioral Techniques

Behavioral interventions can help masochists change their tendency to be victimized in relationships. Social skills training can expand their interactional repertoire beyond their typical abuse-inviting and self-denigrating subservience. Assertiveness training can help patients learn how to enforce personal limits that prevent abuse. Learning to express their desires allows masochists to have their needs fulfilled directly and obviates the need for passive-aggressive behaviors as well as manipulative displays of martyrdom and suffering. Helping the patient overcome individual self-defeating behaviors begins with a careful analysis of the patient's interactions. Masochistic behaviors need to be identified, as do the circumstances that trigger them. Enjoyable and esteem-building events and activities should also be noted. By keeping a record of daily events, behaviors, and moods, interventions to help change self-sabotaging tendencies can be devised. The patient's dysphoric mood also needs to be targeted. Esteem-building activities, as well as material reinforcers, can be used as rewards for behaving more adaptively and for carrying out assignments successfully.

Interpersonal Techniques

Some behavioral intervention programs include the patient's significant others, who are drawn upon to facilitate communication and to guide and support interactions in the patient's natural environment. Toward this end, interpersonal approaches can highlight the role of the patient's own actions in initiating and maintaining self-defeating patterns. In interpreting the patient's behavior, the therapist needs to keep in mind that many masochists are not fully aware that they have contributed to their own abuse, nor that their own behavior leads them to fall repeatedly into the victim role. The process by which they seek abusive partners and by which they provoke benign others to denigrate them is largely unconscious. Although it is important for the therapist to point out to patients that their parent's punitive attitudes have been internalized in the form of self-criticism, outright blaming by the therapist of the parents may create patient resistance that may interfere with therapeutic progress. Guilt over anger at idealized parents can be too much for some patients to bear. The therapist can point out to patients their victim role in present relationships. The value of asserting one's rights and of learning skills to avoid or stop maltreatment needs to be emphasized. More adaptive modes of interaction should be explored.

Including masochistic patients in treatment groups can be helpful in providing the patient both with support and with assertive role models. However, the group therapist should watch out for the possibility that patients will sacrifice their own needs for the benefit of other members and inadvertently be reinforced for the "martyr" role. Alternatively, group members may become frustrated when, after hours of attempting to find solutions for these individuals' difficulties and providing overt support, masochists continue to protest that their situation is hopeless and that they are also hopeless. The unpleasant feedback may be destructive to a newly burgeoning sense of self.

Couples intervention can be helpful if the partner is willing to cooperate, but we know that masochists often pair up with a range of abusive types. If the partner is willing, role playing and role reversals can help both understand the dynamics of their interaction and how it perpetuates self-defeating tendencies.

Cognitive Techniques

Cognitive approaches in the treatment of the masochistic personality are similar to those employed for reducing depressive symptomatology, and emphasize directly challenging the patient's self-sabotaging assumptions through logical reasoning. By keeping track of events, thoughts, and moods, masochistic patients can learn how much of their suffering is directly related to their appraisal of their environment and of themselves, and how much to their self-demeaning attitudes and behaviors.

Once negative automatic thoughts have been identified, they can be evaluated and modified (Beck & Freeman, 1990a) by teaching patients to ask themselves such questions as "What's the evidence?"; "Is there any other way to look at it?"; "How could alternative (less pessimistic) explanations be tested?"; and "What can I do about it (to make it better)?" The tacit beliefs on which automatic thoughts rest also need to be identified and altered for lasting change to occur and for negative thoughts not to resurface in a new form. Past experiences that have led to the patient's poor self-image can be discussed, and the role of dysfunctional cognitive habits such as overgeneralization, arbitrary inference, emotional reasoning, and dichotomous thinking in maintaining the poor self-image can be confronted directly. A basic strategy is to help patients realize that their thoughts are inferences and not facts about themselves and the world. Predictions can then be made and "experiments" devised to test their validity.

Self-Image Techniques

A useful initial approach with the masochist, as with all personality disorders, is the adoption of a supportive orientation. Most masochistic patients will anticipate rejection and/or humiliation by the therapist and will provoke him or her to fulfill expectations. Establishing a therapeutic alliance in which the therapist expresses sympathy for the patient's tendency to elicit negative reactions from others, and thus punish himself or herself can help the patient adopt a less harsh self-concept. This should help the patient understand that he or she does not deserve to suffer and hence contribute to building a more positive identity.

Much like depressive patients, masochists often suffer from excessive guilt. The therapist's sympathetic reassurance that the patient has suffered enough can mobilize the patient to work toward a more adaptive and satisfying way of life. Also like depressives, masochists may deny or repress their resentment of others and fail to recognize that hostility and a desire to punish others is guilt-inducing and reactivates the vicious circle that leads to personal suffering. Helping patients to acknowledge their feelings of resentment and to express them more directly can make it easier for them to develop a self-concept that is inconsistent with the victim role. Once patients come to trust that the therapist's supportive empathy toward their self-destructive tendencies will not be transformed into abusive derision, the probability of their benefiting from other interventions is greatly increased.

Intrapsychic Techniques

Psychodynamic approaches to treating masochistic personalities tend to conceptualize patients' behavior to be a result of their childhood relationship to a withholding or cruel parent. The child defended against his or her greatest fear—abandonment by the parent—by assuming a self-deprecating and defeated position that served to complement the parent's behavior. As in most other approaches, the importance of the patient-therapist relationship is emphasized. Although the classic psychodynamic therapist stance is neutral and reserved, it has been suggested that this approach with masochistic patients may create an atmosphere of inequality that is too conducive to masochistic transference reactions reminiscent of the parent-child relationship. It has also been suggested that a conscious self-presentation as a fallible human being by the therapist may help prevent the patient from trying to act out the unconscious wish for submission to avoid abandonment.

Regardless of the therapist's sensitivity, masochistic patients will likely seek to frustrate the therapist's efforts with negative therapeutic reactions, as well as to challenge the therapist by claiming that nothing can help them (sometimes even blaming the therapist for making them worse). Brenner (1959) sees masochistic tendencies as serving four separate functions: repetition of the patient's reactions to childhood conflict; defense against feelings of loss or helplessness; expiation; and unconscious gratification. Persistent yet sympathetic interpretations of the patient's self-defeating attitudes are recommended, as objective statements are likely to leave the patient feeling criticized and worthless. The realistic need to point out the patient's less attractive tendencies should be balanced by a warm and relatively self-revealing therapeutic stance so as to avoid having the patient internalize the therapist's interpretations as insults. Berliner (1947) suggests that the therapist begin to bring patients' self-defeating behaviors to their awareness through examination of relationships outside of therapy. By pointing out that patients' accusations and complaints all relate to individuals these masochists love or care about, the therapist can avoid an intense transference reaction that might lead to excessive acting-out. Once patients achieve some insight into their own masochistic patterns, any acting-out that does occur in the context of the therapy becomes easier to interpret.

Berliner (1947) suggests that patient and therapist can then proceed to work through the patient's identification with the aggressor. The patient can thus come to appreciate how much of his or her self-criticism is due to external reinforcement, and

604 **Personality Disorders—Axis II**

can thus learn to differentiate between love and cruelty. Eisenbud (1967) suggests that another avenue that leads to therapeutic success is to target the masochist's feelings of inadequacy and need for efficacy.

Pharmacologic Techniques

Self-defeating personalities often develop depression after years of abuse and self-sabotaging, which then serves to maintain the masochistic tendencies. Evaluating the appropriateness of psychopharmacologic intervention for the patient may serve as a useful first step to regulate mood. It is also important for the therapist to emphasize that there is a lag between the onset of antidepressant medication and its psychoactive effects so as to guard against the patient's giving up in the interim.

MAKING SYNERGISTIC ARRANGEMENTS

Masochistic patients tend to have negative reactions to therapy and to resist change, making a supportive stance a useful way for the therapist to establish initial rapport. Patience and consistency, despite the patient's provocations, can aid in solidifying the masochist's trust that the therapist will not abuse his or her "superior" position in the relationship. If after careful evaluation the patient is judged to be suffering from a concomitant depression, appropriate antidepressant medication can help provide him or her with motivation to persevere through more anxiety-provoking exploratory and cognitive work.

If the patient's partner is amenable to entering couple's therapy, it can help provide the patient with a supportive home environment and insight into interaction patterns. Behavioral couples intervention can teach the couple more adaptive ways of relating. Group treatment is another potential adjunct that can help increase the patient's social appropriateness and assertiveness skills. If deemed preferable, behavioral interventions can also be integrated into the primary dyadic therapy.

Illustrative Cases

As noted previously, there has been considerable controversy concerning the concept of a masochistic or self-defeating personality disorder. The decision to delete this personality pattern from the *DSM-IV* nosology is an unfortunate one, as we perceive it. That the original formulation was interpreted in a specific and narrow manner by psychoanalytic thinkers early in this century was also unfortunate. The intense reaction by feminists to the original psychoanalytic formulation was justified. The solution favoring dropping the disorder from the official classification, however, was not a wise one, in our estimation. A better solution would have been to illustrate the many routes individuals travel to become manifestly *self-defeating*, only one of which reflects the developmental theme proposed by analytic thinkers.

Almost all of the personality disorders are self-defeating in the sense that they engage in self-perpetuating patterns that foster the continuation of their already established pathologies. Hence, we have also argued that the original term assigned this personality type, that of masochistic, would be the better choice of the two designations. As we have stressed, the original analytic conception describes only one of several types

TABLE 20.4   Masochistic Personality Disorder Subtypes

Self-Undoing: Is "wrecked by success"; experiences "victory through defeat"; gratified by personal misfortunes, failures, humiliations, and ordeals; eschews best interests; chooses to be victimized, ruined, disgraced.

MCMI 8B (3)

Oppressed: Experiences genuine misery, despair, hardship, anguish, torment, illness; grievances used to create guilt in others; resentments vented by exempting self from responsibilities and burdening "oppressors."

MCMI 8B-2B

Virtuous: Proudly unselfish, self-denying, and self-sacrificial; self-ascetic; weighty burdens are judged noble, righteous, and saintly; others must recognize loyalty and faithfulness; gratitude and appreciation expected for altruism and forbearance.

MCMI 8B-4

Possessive: Bewitches and ensnares by becoming jealously overprotective and indispensable; entraps, takes control, conquers, enslaves, and dominates others by being sacrificial to a fault; controls by obligatory dependence.

MCMI 8B-8A

---

of masochistic behavior. Its developmental dynamics are manifold, and it is the purpose of the following to illustrate a number of the subtypes of the personality, subtypes that differ not only in the descriptive picture they manifest, but in the developmental course that leads to the clinical state (see Table 20.4).

**MASOCHISTIC PERSONALITY:
SELF-UNDOING TYPE
(MASOCHISTIC WITH AVOIDANT TRAITS)**

CASE 20.1, JANEANE H., 32

Presenting Picture: Janeane H. was referred through her employee assistance program after a period of chronic tardiness and failure to complete important projects. The company valued her as an employee because of her outstanding input on group tasks or those she did not head, but she could not manage to get her own work accomplished. She routinely became agitated and teary-eyed in therapy at the mere thought of completing a task for which she might receive accolades, and this extended to duties from the mundane to the sublime. Whether it was an important document that she wouldn't turn in because she was "too intensely involved with it to call it finished just because of a deadline," or her disorderly apartment that she would get almost perfectly clean before returning it to a state of disarray, Janeane found extraordinary discomfort in anything remotely resembling success. As therapy continued, Janeane disclosed various problematic encounters with her parents, particularly with her mother. It seemed that by various exchanges, her mother had instilled in Janeane a sense of guilt for taking any credit for an accomplishment when someone else helped, but also had routinely rewarded sickly behavior.

Clinical Assessment: The classical psychoanalytic conception of the masochist represents individuals who have actively and repetitively, although unconsciously, sought out circumstances that led to their own suffering, if not destruction. These behaviors do not necessarily bring pleasure, but may be the less distressing choice of two painful states. What is most notable is that these persons ostensibly create or provoke circumstances in which they will experience misfortune or abuse. They achieve what Reik (1941) called "victory through defeat" or what Freud (1916/1925) had earlier described as patients "wrecked by success." They appear, at least from an outsider's perspective, to be gratified by experiencing their own personal misfortunes, failures, humiliations, or ordeals. They eschew their own best interests, choosing instead to be disgraced, victimized, even ruined.

A major manifestation of these behaviors is found in what has been termed the "success neurosis"; here, the deeper layers of psychic experience react to being successful by provoking intense anxieties and guilt rather than pleasure and happiness. Success is responded to as if it were a horrible disaster. Rather than suffering these consequences, individuals undo themselves, behaving in ways that provoke failure, humiliation, or punishment. This process of undoing one's good fortunes is what characterizes Janeane, a *self-undoing masochist*. In effect, she repetitively does the opposite of what objectively is in her best interest. Although striving to achieve and perform her best, she stops short of its attainment, quickly proves herself insufficient to the task or undeserving of its rewards. As Schneider (1923) wrote in describing his "depressive psychopath," individuals such as Janeane "overtly express distress, but are covertly gratified at the prospect of the satisfaction they could bring from their misfortune."

For Janeane, there was more relief in sharing her troubles and failures than in experiencing the pressure of trying to live up to being successful and happy. In many regards, she was akin to avoidant personalities in that avoidants anticipate that they will ultimately fail or be disillusioned, even when matters appear to be going well for the moment. Rather than be disappointed when things "inevitably" would turn sour, Janeane quickly undid herself before she could be undone by others. She would rather be seen as a victim of unfortunate circumstance, largely self-created of course, than as someone who had sought rewards and gains and was expected thereby to maintain them and to behave in a valued and prideful way.

Moreover, in her developmental background, her life had been better for her when she was suffering than when things were going well for her. Thus, as a young child, Janeane learned that her otherwise mean-spirited and critical mother stopped her abusive behaviors when she was ill, and she also learned that being ill was the more comfortable state. She acquired a general belief that suffering was greatest when things were apparently going well, rather than when she manifested pain and discomfort. Hence, when faced in later life with opportunities for achievement and happiness, Janeane stepped back from these possibilities, fearing that more suffering would happen in "good" circumstances than when things were apparently problematic.

Synergistic Treatment Plan: Janeane would exhibit difficulty accepting rapid challenges to her deeply ingrained coping mechanisms which kept her in a comfortable state of helplessness and disillusionment, and concrete goal-setting would need to follow an establishment of comfort and empathy, as well as *biophysical* treatment of her dysphoric mood. *Behavioral* measures could be utilized carefully in these early stages to begin exposing Janeane to competent responses rather than self-sabotage. As her level of comfort would increase, a focus on faulty *cognitions* would follow to reverse her expectations of failure and catastrophe (*actively* circumventing pressures to succeed), as well as perpetuating her view of *self* as unworthy or undeserving of happiness. In later stages, *dynamic* approaches would be beneficial to reexamine objects that she had assimilated as discrediting, as well as further correct her reversed *pain-pleasure* spectrum. Concurrently, *interpersonal* processes would be strengthened to bolster social confidence and satisfaction in relationships (enhancement of *self* and *other*).

Therapeutic Course: As a first approach in a short-term therapeutic program, an effort was made to assist Janeane in arranging for a more rewarding environment and in discovering opportunities that enhanced her self-worth. *Supportive* therapy was all she could tolerate in the very first sessions, that is, until she was comfortable dealing with her most painful feelings. *Psychopharmacologic* treatment was employed, following appropriate consultation, as a means of diminishing her depressive feelings and controlling her anxiety. *Behavior modification* also was utilized to help her learn competent reactions to stressful situations. As trust in her therapist developed, she became amenable to methods of *cognitive* reframing to alter dysfunctional attitudes and depressogenic social expectations; particularly appropriate were the methods proposed by Beck and Meichenbaum. To decrease the potential of a recurrence, focused *dynamic* methods were explored to rework deep object attachments and to construct a base for competency strivings. The *interpersonal* focus proposed by Benjamin and Klerman and *group therapy* procedures provided means of learning autonomous skills and the growth of social confidence.

An important self-defeating belief that a cognitive approach sought to reframe was Janeane's assumption that she must appease others and apologize for her incompetence to assure that she would not be abandoned. What could be shown to her was that this behavior exasperated and alienated those on whom she leaned most heavily. This exasperation and alienation then served only to increase her fear and neediness. She then came to recognize that a vicious circle was created, making her feel more desperate and more ingratiating. A vigorous but short-term approach that illustrated her dysfunctional beliefs and expectations was used to break the circle and reorient her actions less destructively. The combination of cognitive restructuring and development of increasing interpersonal skills proved an effective brief course of treatment.

To restate her difficulty in different terms, not only did Janeane precipitate real difficulties through her self-demeaning attitudes, but she also perceived and anticipated difficulties where none in fact existed. She believed that good things did not last and that the positive feelings and attitudes of those from whom she sought support would probably end capriciously and be followed by disappointment and rejection. This cognitive assumption was directly confronted by appropriate therapeutic techniques. What had to be undone was the fact that each time she announced her defects, she convinced herself as well as others and thereby deepened her discontent and her self-image of incompetence. Trapped by her own persuasiveness, Janeane repeatedly reinforced her belief in the futility of standing on her own and was therefore likely to try less and less to overcome her inadequacies. This therapeutic strategy aimed at undoing this vicious circle of increased despondency and dependency.

Skillful attention was also needed to alter Janeane's ambivalence about dependency and her willingness to be used, if not abused. Unless checked, she had difficulty sustaining a consistent therapeutic relationship and was prone to deteriorate or experience relapses. Maneuvers designed to test the dependability of the therapist were frequently evident. To prevent such setbacks, empathic warmth was expressed to help her overcome her fear of facing her own feelings of unworthiness. Similar support levels were necessary to undo her wish to retain her image of being a self-denying person whose security lay in suffering and martyrdom. She needed to be guided into recognizing the basis of her self-contempt and her ambivalence about dependency relationships. She was helped to see that not all nurturant parental figures would habitually become abusive and exploitive. Efforts to undo these self-sabotaging beliefs paid considerable dividends in short-term and possibly more substantial long-term progress.

MASOCHISTIC PERSONALITY:
POSSESSIVE TYPE
(MASOCHISTIC WITH NEGATIVISTIC FEATURES)

CASE 20.2, ROSE B., 36

Presenting Picture: Rose B. had been experiencing acute dissatisfaction with many significant relationships in her life, but she seemed doggedly determined only to change those around her rather than look at her own expectations and behaviors. Most of her dissatisfaction centered around her husband, whom she described as "the perennial sloppy student." Rose claimed to have been single-handedly responsible for his timely completion of an advanced degree, and seemed quite convinced (albeit resentful) that her indispensable contributions as caretaker, confidant, personal secretary, homemaker, and "adult nanny" allowed him to be the man he was. At the same time, she was quite skilled at making sure her influence was known to him, and that certain aberrations from the norm would not occur. For example, Rose was quite instrumental in her husband's sabotage of a lengthy friendship he had with another woman. Similar behavior occurred outside of the marriage as well. A notable example was her choice of employment as a personal assistant to a "clueless and slovenly" business executive. "All men are like little boys" seemed to be her catch-phrase, and at the same time, determined her role in life as an underappreciated "Gal Friday." She revealed that she had honed her caretaking skills as a child herself, as her father left when she was an adolescent, her mother had to work to support the family, and she had to assume the role of mother for several little brothers. She felt that this was a role that kept repeating itself throughout many years and situations.

Clinical Assessment: As with other masochists, Rose was constantly giving of herself, although insinuating herself may be perhaps a more descriptive and pertinent way of describing her actions. She was unable to let go of those to whom she was attached. Her need to be indispensable was so intensely self-sacrificial that others were unable to withdraw from her without feeling irresponsible, unkind, or guilty. Rose entrapped others, drew them into a reciprocal dependency, disarmed by the depth of concern and interest she felt for them. Sacrificial to a fault, she found ways to make others feel simultaneously needy and fulfilled, less capable of functioning without the kindness and labors she would engage in to meet their narcissistic desires. In effect, she controlled others by an obligatory dependence. Moreover, she was jealously overprotective and an indispensable collaborator, dominating those she possessed by sacrificing herself in every way they desired. This pattern of behaviors is seen in personality admixtures composed of core masochistic components permeated by characteristics most common to the negativistic style; this pattern corresponded to her MCMI profile.

Rose made ostentatious sacrifices, intruding herself repeatedly into the daily affairs of her spouse, friends, and employer. She made it her business always to be there, to be a vital and necessary contributor and advice giver. She meddled into all areas of the possessed person's activities: love life, health, job situation, any and all problems in which she felt she could help and insinuate herself. In this way, she sought to induce so profound a sense of obligation on the part of others that they would be unable either to repay her fully or to function effectively without her. This stratagem was effective; it created an emotional and obligatory dependence that forced others to be both submissive and yielding by virtue of psychic need and personal guilt.

As a result of her maneuvers, Rose believed she had proprietary rights and was justified in enveloping and possessing others. She had suffered and had been kind and giving, all for the benefit of others. Whatever this possessive masochist had done had been done for others, so she said; her kindnesses were intended to advance and better rather than to control and dominate their lives. On the surface, what she did appeared to be the opposite of what her ulterior motives may have been. In essence, Rose bribed others to love her, gave to others to control them, and became indispensable and hence possessive of them.

Synergistic Treatment Plan: Rose's initial strategy of externalizing blame but seeming to "thrive" on her martyr status suggested that she was discomforted by the notion of focusing on herself, and a *supportive* approach would gradually help her feel more at ease. As Rose would became more invested in processing personal issues, the therapist would begin to focus on faulty *cognitive* perpetuations, such as automatically interpreting events as negative or arranging expectations in ways she knew would fail (*pain-pleasure* discordance). *Behavioral* fallacies would be modified, providing healthier responses and interactions. Rose's *self-other* conflict, typical of her negativistic qualities, would require examination of her *interpersonal* deference and corrective techniques that would be facilitated by including others in restructuring habits (e.g., group or family methods).

Therapeutic Course: A first goal in therapy with Rose was to demonstrate that the potential gains of therapy were real and that they should motivate her rather than serve as a deterrent. Rose feared that therapy would reawaken what she viewed as false hopes; that is, it reminded her of the humiliation she experienced when she offered her trust to others but received rejection in return. By nondirectively acknowledging these fears, she was able to find an adequate level of comfort without having to distance herself from the therapist, learning to deal more effectively with her fears while maintaining a better level of adjustment than that to which she had become accustomed.

In a short-term *cognitive-behavioral* approach, attention was usefully directed to Rose's social hesitation, anxious demeanor, and self-deprecating actions, attitudes, and behavior that could be altered so as not to evoke the humiliation and derogation they had in the past. Cognitive efforts to reframe the basis of her sensitivity to rebuff or her fearful and unassertive behavior (e.g., Beck, Ellis) minimized and diminished not only her aversive inclinations but her tendency to relapse and regress.

More probing yet circumscribed treatment procedures were useful in unearthing the roots of her anxieties and confronting those assumptions and expectations that pervaded many aspects of her behavior. *Family* techniques were employed as well to moderate destructive patterns of communication that contributed to or intensified her relationship problems. *Interpersonal* techniques (e.g., Benjamin) and *group therapy* may also have assisted her in learning new attitudes and skills in a more benign and accepting social setting than she normally encountered.

Focused techniques also addressed Rose's tendencies to demean her self-worth and to mistrust others. Short-term *supportive* methods were used to counteract her ill-disposition to sustain a consistent therapeutic relationship. As noted, maneuvers designed to test the sincerity of the therapist were evident. A warm and empathic attitude was necessary because the patient was likely to fear facing her feelings of unworthiness and because she sensed that her coping defenses were weak. Commendable skills of hers were drawn on to prevent her from withdrawing from treatment before any real gains were made. Cognitive procedures were used to explore the contradictions in Rose's feelings and attitudes. Without proper reframing, there may have been a seesaw struggle, with periods of temporary progress followed by retrogression. Genuine short-term gains were attained, but only with careful work, a building of trust, and enhancement of her sense of self-worth.

Another realm worthy of brief intervention was associated with Rose's extensive scanning of the environment. By doing this, she increased the likelihood that she would encounter those stimuli she wished to avoid. Her exquisite antennae picked up and transformed what most people overlooked. Again, using appropriate cognitive methods, her hypersensitivity was prevented from backfiring, that is, becoming an instrument that constantly brought to awareness the very pain she wished to escape. Reorienting her focus and her negative interpretive habits to ones that were more ego-enhancing and optimistic in character reduced her self-demeaning outlook, intensified her positive experiences, and diminished her anguish.

MASOCHISTIC PERSONALITY: OPPRESSED TYPE (MASOCHISTIC WITH DEPRESSIVE TRAITS)

CASE 20.3, CATHY T., 28

Presenting Picture: Cathy T. viewed life as if it were her destiny to be punished. Continually downtrodden and discouraged by repeated "failed" attempts to do anything well, she always assumed that the efforts of others to assist her were simply tactics utilized to make her go away. She expressed this very thought to the therapist, and when it was made clear that this was not the case, she very flatly and "automatically" expressed that she knew that the therapist, indeed, wanted to help her pursue happiness. She remarked that her husband (who had prompted the visit) seemed to place blame on her for not being a better homemaker and, by association, for their lack of friends. She continued on to elucidate that she did *nothing* well, be it work at home, duties as a wife, or tasks at her job. Furthermore, despite her constant efforts to improve herself and her abilities, she felt that no one seemed to like her and that she was predisposed to failure and suffering in all of her undertakings.

Clinical Assessment: *Oppressed masochists* such as Cathy make use of all kinds of psychic symptoms and physical diseases to dominate and make their families and friends feel guilt. Anyone who was not responsive to the maneuver of psychological or medical illness was quickly prompted to fall in line by her guilt-inducing moans and groans, saying, in effect, Don't let my suffering make you think twice about me; overlook my suffering if you will and do only what you think is best for you. Ultimately, the ostensive victim, that is, Cathy, effectively triumphs over her true victims by making them feel guilty and obligated. Let us not be misled into thinking that she was merely feigning her anguish; she experienced genuine misery and despair, felt tormented, and was often physically ill. However, these grievances were used secondarily, but quite effectively, to create guilt in others, enabling this masochist to vent the resentments she felt, and exempting her from responsibilities she may normally have been asked to carry out. As can be inferred from the preceding, Cathy formed an amalgam with features seen most prominently in the depressive personality disorder, accounting in part for her frequently judged coalescence by knowledgeable clinicians (Kernberg, 1988).

Hypochondriacal manipulations came to the fore when no other method of gaining love and dependence had been successful. Symptoms of illness were an effective and reliable way of assuring the receipt of attention and appreciation. Becoming a sorrowful invalid was a rather pathetic solution, a genuine but self-created suffering that forced others to be caring and nurturing. Cathy did not actually enjoy her state of suffering; it was merely a necessary if discomforting instrumentality to produce small benefits. By exaggerating real but minor discomforts, she was not merely making them public but, in effect, intensifying and making her suffering greater. It was the small secondary gains that made the process somewhat worthwhile.

Not to be overlooked was the fact that the state of being oppressed enabled Cathy to be exempt from fulfilling responsibilities and also to discharge resentments toward others for not having been sufficiently caring or supportive in the past. Feeling victimized by the ingratitude of others, she sought to make them feel guilty and to act responsibly and caring, attitudes and feelings they had failed to demonstrate previously. She exaggerated her plight by moping about helplessly, placing added burdens on others and causing them not only to be attentive and nurturing, but to suffer and feel guilty while doing so.

Synergistic Treatment Plan: Cathy's depressogenic state required immediate *biophysical* measures, as it would be extremely difficult to mobilize her from her presenting *passive,* lethargic orientation and dysphoric mood. A safe, empathic, and *supportive* stance from the therapist would be required from the outset, continuing throughout the therapeutic process. As the relationship would develop and Cathy would demonstrate her ability to focus on more difficult schemata inherent in her characterologic makeup, a *cognitive* approach would address her perpetuating tendency to consider herself worthless and cast aspersions inward, as well as the assumption that it is safer and more comfortable to be *passively* discontent (reduce *pain* orientation, strengthen *self*). *Behavioral* interventions would focus on learning more competent skills and reducing the frequency of sabotaging positive events. *Interpersonal* measures, which would possibly include contextual *group* or *family* techniques, would focus on development of social skills, leading to more positive interactions.

Therapeutic Course: In her thoroughly disconsolate state, Cathy feared that therapy might reawaken what she viewed as false hopes; that is, it might remind her of the disillusionment she experienced when she aspired in the past and was rejected. It was of primary importance to illustrate that therapeutic goals were, in fact, achievable, and that they could serve as motivation. As she had now found at least a perceived modest level of comfort by distancing herself from desires and withdrawing from others, it was important therapeutically not to let matters remain at the level of depressive-anxious adjustment to which she had become accustomed.

Antidepressant medications were utilized to moderate her persistent dejection and pessimism. At the *cognitive-behavioral* level, therapeutic attention was usefully directed to Cathy's depressogenic assumptions, anxious demeanor, self-deprecating attitudes, and behavior that may have evoked unhappiness, self-contempt, and derogation in the past. Short-term and focused *cognitive* techniques such as those developed by Beck, Meichenbaum, and Ellis helped reduce her sensitivity to rebuff and her morose and unassertive style, outlooks and fears that only reinforced her aversive and depressive inclinations.

To diminish the potential for or even prevent relapse, more focused procedures were useful in reconstructing the erroneous beliefs and interpersonal mechanisms that pervaded all aspects of Cathy's behavior. *Interpersonal* therapies such as those of Klerman and Benjamin were especially productive. Along the same lines, *family* techniques may have been employed as circumscribed methods to moderate destructive patterns of communication that contributed to or intensified her social problems. Similarly, short-term *group therapy* may have assisted her in learning new attitudes and skills in a more benign and accepting social setting than she normally encountered.

Short-term techniques also focused attention on her depressive tendencies to demean her self-worth and subject herself to the mistreatment of others. *Supportive* measures were used to counteract her hesitation about sustaining a consistent therapeutic relationship. Maneuvers designed to test the sincerity of the therapist were frequently evident. A warm and accepting attitude was needed because Cathy feared facing her feelings of unworthiness and because she sensed that her coping defenses were weak. With skillful supportive approaches, it was possible to prevent her tendency to withdraw from treatment before any real gains were made. Cognitive methods were especially useful in exploring the contradictions in her feelings and attitudes. Without reframing techniques such as these, there would have been a seesaw struggle, with periods of temporary progress followed by retrogression. Genuine short-term gains were achieved, but only with a building of trust and an enhancing of her shaky sense of self-worth, both of which lent themselves well to brief cognitive procedures.

Another realm worthy of short-term attention was associated with Cathy's extensive scanning and misinterpretation of the environment. By doing this, she increased the likelihood that she would encounter those troubling events she wished to avoid. Moreover, her exquisite and negatively oriented antennae picked up and intensified what most people simply overlooked. In effect, her hypersensitivity backfired, becoming an instrument that constantly brought to awareness the very pain she wished to escape. Effective, focused cognitive techniques were directed at reducing her vigilance and self-demeaning appraisals and hence diminished rather than intensified her anguish.

MASOCHISTIC PERSONALITY: VIRTUOUS TYPE (MASOCHISTIC WITH NARCISSISTIC TRAITS)

CASE 20.4, JOANNE W., 33

Presenting Picture: Joanne W., a nun, had recently left her order and had promised her Mother Superior that she would seek counseling, though it was unclear as to why she had been asked to do this. While in the order, Joanne had started a soup kitchen as her own "pet project." To hear her describe the venture, it seemed as though the organization wanted nothing to do with this project until it started receiving very good press. At that point, Joanne claimed, the sisters wanted to make it their own, to "take over," as it were, and this seemed to be the major cause of their rift. She had taken great pride in the amount of work that went into creating a service that expansive, and she marveled to the therapist about how she would serve all three daily meals, thereby making her commitment one that ran 24 hours a day. She went on to describe how the patrons of the kitchen had it easier than even she did, emphatically stating that "they had coats before *I* had a coat." A thank you from the order, Joanne said, was just "simply too much to ask." As she continued to describe the circumstances surrounding the rift, her rancor became remarkably apparent.

Clinical Assessment: Masochists such as Joanne are *proudly* unselfish and self-sacrificial. Her self-denial and asceticism was judged, at least by herself, as noble and righteous acts that signified that she was, in essence, meritorious, if not saintly. Rather than negate her altruism, depreciate her esteem in the eyes of others, and accept the inferior status that typifies most other masochists, this prideful or *virtuous masochist* asserted a sense of specialness and the high status and veneration in which she should have been held. Had she not consistently demonstrated her concern for the welfare of others? Had she not deprived herself of the good life? Had she not sacrificed herself at the altar of others?

Turning her life pattern on its heels, she cried out that others had been ungrateful and thoughtless and should be mindful of how faithful and loyal and giving she had been to them. In effect, she, the self-sacrificing servant, should have been seen as the master, the one to receive a constant stream of gratitude and attention, deserving to be repaid for her lifelong sacrifices, real or imagined. The overt demonstration of self-sacrifice was turned periodically into a display of pride and egocentrism. Having submerged herself and been indispensable to others, she praised herself and became self-congratulatory: I am good and virtuous; I am special and deserve special considerations, she said to herself. However, the depth of these narcissistic displays was shallow. Beneath the surface, there remained a low sense of self-esteem and an unsureness about her self-assertions that whatever recognition she got was manipulated and solicited rather than genuinely felt by others. For reasons consistent with the foregoing, Joanne would, at times, exhibit overt narcissistic features and, at other times, appeared more like a dependent. Hence, despite her self-approval and self-congratulatory tone, she continued to be self-sacrificing, persistently doing for others what she wished others would do for her—but more genuinely so.

Synergistic Treatment Plan: A rather depleted *self*-orientation was what was most striking with Joanne; her desperation for fulfillment needed immediate *support,* as well as some *environmental* adjustment that would allow her to feel meaningful. *Biophysically,* Joanne appeared rather edgy, yet seemed as though she would just allow that anxious demeanor to thrive (*passive* stance), and it would be advantageous to explore *behavioral* response alternatives that would be more effective. Joanne had a perpetuating tendency to invite abuse, yet she also garnered attention through her "downtrodden" plight (reversed *pain-pleasure* tendency). *Cognitive* and *interpersonal* measures, possibly including a *group* milieu, would be useful at a pace that would allow Joanne to reorganize these fallacies and develop less dependent, autonomous skills. In looking toward permanency in change, it would be necessary to gradually introduce *dynamic* techniques to reorganize objects and internal structures in a more realistic and mature fashion.

Therapeutic Course: The first strategy utilized with Joanne was a contextual one: arrange for a more rewarding environment that might help her with image-enhancing opportunities. Until some aspects outside of the therapeutic relationship were under control, *supportive* therapy was all she could tolerate. As her environmental situation improved, she became more comfortable dealing with her painful feelings. *Psychopharmacologic* treatment was considered as a means of diminishing her anxious feelings, but eventually, Joanne opted against this intervention. *Behavior modification* was employed to help her choose more effective responses to environmental stress. As the therapeutic relationship became more secure, she was able to tolerate *cognitive reframing* methods, specifically those proposed by Beck and Meichenbaum, to alter problematic attitudes and social expectations. To decrease the likelihood of regression, *psychodynamic* methods were used to focus on modifying deep object attachments. Benjamin and Klerman's *interpersonal* techniques, as well as *group therapy* procedures, provided for the development of autonomy skills and self-confidence.

One of Joanne's most damaging schemata, though not directly expressed, was that she needed to always appease others and compensate for her perceived inabilities so that she would never be abandoned. This was confronted by demonstrating how this behavior ended up alienating others as they became exasperated by her actions, and this served only to increase her fear and neediness. She came to recognize this perpetuating cycle and became invested in a vigorous intervention to break the circle and reorient her actions less destructively. Combining cognitive restructuring and interpersonal skill building proved most effective.

To emphasize another facet of Joanne's overall picture, not only did she bring real problems to herself through her self-destructive actions, but she also sensed and predicted difficulties when they were nonexistent. Her axiom might as well have been "Good things don't last"; in other words, positive feelings and attitudes of those around her were but fleeting fantasies that would end, ultimately, in abrupt rejection. This assumption needed to be confronted by undoing the habit of announcing her defects and convincing herself (as well as others) of her worthlessness. She could be quite persuasive, as a matter of fact, and would have been successful in fully convincing herself of the futility of self-sufficiency, had this not been disputed and the circle not been broken.

Of particular note, attention needed to be directed at altering her tendency to invite abuse. Unless checked, Joanne would have assumed a very subservient role in therapy, and this would have eventually made her prone to relapse. It was quite obvious, at times, that she would "test" the therapist's reliability. An empathic stance was expressed consistently to help her overcome her fear of addressing uncomfortable feelings. Similar support was necessary to undo her image of herself as one whose security relied entirely on martyrdom. She was alerted as to the basis of her self-deprecating tactics, as well as her ambivalence toward dependency. Efforts to undo her self-sabotage were most fruitful in terms of both short- and long-term growth.

Risks and Resistances

Most therapists may initially be able to empathize with the patient's low self-esteem and complaints of years of abuse. However, as the patient's tendency to arrange situations to ensure the continuation of pain becomes increasingly evident, the therapist may come to harbor the suspicion that the patient enjoys suffering. The patient's pathetic self-presentation and ineffectual implementation of the therapist's suggestions begin to call forth an almost sadistic therapeutic style. Many provoke defensiveness by devaluing both the therapeutic process and the therapist. Many a well-meaning therapist can be seduced in this manner to complement the masochistic patient's role with subtly punishing comments.

Although a defensive reaction on the part of the therapist is understandable, challenging the masochist's negative distortions too early in the therapeutic process may be counterproductive. Such confrontation may prove too threatening to the patient's undeserving self-image, which requires that anything the patient is involved in must not be very good, including therapy. If the therapist can resist the temptation to insist that his or her therapy may be very helpful or valuable, the patient will not be as threatened by the possibility of being judged a failure by the "superior" therapist. Countertransferential anger is often also provoked as constructive suggestions are met with replies that the patient's suffering cannot be overcome, that he or she is passively helpless, and so the patient succumbs to a defensive sullenness. Even worse, the patient's negative therapeutic reactions and regressions may be interpreted as being staged to serve as "proof" that the therapist is doing more harm than good.

To prevent this antitherapeutic interaction from developing, it is important for therapists to understand that masochists' apparent need to suffer is based not in their perverse enjoyment of pain, but rather in their belief that they will experience less of it by doing what they do. Defensiveness only confirms and perpetuates the patient's expectation that all significant others are cruel and insensitive. Conversely, being overly encouraging rarely serves to "snap" patients out of their masochistic behavior or into taking a more assertive and confident stand for themselves.

Therapists working with these patients should also remember that pushing the patient too fast can precipitate too much distress, possibly resulting in a psychotic decompensation.

Before masochists can give up their self-defeating patterns, a slow process of building up a new identity and new attitudes must first take place. Negating these patients' problematic sense of identity without offering integratable alternatives can leave a psychic void that may foster even more difficulties than they already have. Pitying patients and harboring "rescue" fantasies toward them can also lead to disappointment when these patients fail to live up to the therapist's expectations. Countertransference reactions toward patients' resistance or slow progress often include defensiveness and hostility. Harm to patients can be avoided by sympathizing with their tendency to sabotage their own potential, and by keeping in mind that success threatens masochists' identity and instigates strong feelings of guilt. Patients should not be blamed for their failures.

CHAPTER TWENTY-ONE

Treating Schizotypal
Personality Patterns

The hallmark of this disorder is a variety of peculiarities of behavior, speech, thought, and perception that are not severe enough to warrant the diagnosis of schizophrenia. There is considerable variability in the presentation of this syndrome (e.g., magical thinking, ideas of reference or suspiciousness, illusions, depersonalization, and hypersensitivity with undue social anxiety), and no single feature is invariably present. It is our contention that the schizotypal disorder is most frequently an advanced dysfunctional personality (akin in severity to the borderline or paranoid types), and that it is often best understood as a more pathological variant of the schizoid and avoidant patterns. Such a framework allows a greater appreciation of the schizotypal characteristics of social impoverishment and the tendency toward distant rather than close interpersonal relationships. In fact, the observed oddities in behavior and thought, such as paranoid ideation, magical thinking, and circumstantial speech stem, in part from the schizotypal's withdrawn and isolated existence. Without the stabilizing influences and repetitive corrective experiences that come with frequent human contact and social interactions, individuals may lose their sense of behavioral judgment and gradually begin the process of acting, thinking, and perceiving in peculiar and eccentric ways. In the advanced stages of such a dysfunctional progression, schizotypals may merely drift aimlessly from one activity to another, leading meaningless and ineffectual existences and remaining on the periphery of societal life.

Depending on which of the two *detached patterns* (i.e., schizoid or avoidant) the schizotypal resembles, he or she may be emotionally flat, sluggish and apathetic, or hypersensitive, anxious, and socially apprehensive. In a similar fashion, schizotypal personalities' vulnerability to depression or other symptom disorders is, in part, dependent on whether they have evolved from the sensitive and suffering avoidants or the innately bland, unfeeling schizoids.

Clearly manifest in the schizotypal personality are a variety of persistent and prominent eccentricities of behavior, thought, and perception. These characteristics mirror—but fall short of, in either severity or peculiarity—features that would justify the diagnosis of clinical schizophrenia. It is the author's contention (Millon, 1969) that these "odd" schizotypal symptoms contribute to and are derivatives of a more fundamental and profound social isolation and self-alienation. Although the schizotypal syndrome should be seen as an advanced form of structural pathology, akin in severity to both the borderline and paranoid types, it may also be understood as a more grave form of the pathologically less severe schizoid and avoidant patterns.

As noted, these three syndromes—schizoid, avoidant, and schizotypal— are characterized by an impoverished social life, a distancing from close interpersonal relationships, and an autistic but nondelusional pattern of thinking. To paraphrase what was stated in an earlier chapter, the more individuals turn inward, the more they lose contact with the styles of behavior and thought of those around them. As they become progressively estranged from their social environment, they lose touch with the "conventions of reality" and with the checks against irrational thought and behavior that are provided by reciprocal relationships. Increasingly detached from the controls and stabilizing influences of repetitive, though ordinary, human affairs, they may lose their sense of behavioral propriety and suitability and gradually begin the process of acting and thinking in unreal and somewhat "crazy" ways—hence, their manifest and prominent eccentricities.

The *DSM-III* text and criteria for the syndrome were based on a study carried out and reported by Spitzer, Endicott, and Gibbon (1979) to clarify distinctions that might be drawn between what were then tentatively termed in the deliberations of the *DSM-III* Task Force the *unstable (borderline)* and *schizotypal* personalities. Following guidelines established earlier by relevant Task Force members, Spitzer et al. consulted other theorists and researchers at work in the field for further advice toward the goal of constructing two subsets of potentially discriminating criterion item lists. Although procedures for data gathering, analyzing, and cross-validating these criterion sets were carried out with exceptional diligence, the final item lists were found to highly correlate when utilized with a heterogeneous patient population. However, within a select group of more disturbed or dysfunctional patients, borderline and schizotypal item subsets did show a high degree of independence.

As an illustration of contemporary proposals, we turn briefly to the evolutionary polarity model as presented in Figure 21.1. The primary theme illustrated is the vacancy or weakness that exists in each of the six polarity boxes. Notable, however, are the reversal signs between each of the three pairs. In essence, this signifies that none of the survival motives and aims of the schizotypal have a firm grounding. Rather, they are feeble in their intensity and focus, and can be easily reversed or distorted in their usual objectives and goals. The figure portrays their rather ineffectual existence, as well as the meaningless and eccentric character of their activities. Possessing little spark or drive, these individuals become increasingly estranged from social conventions, resulting in the purposeless nature of their behaviors, the curious character of their thoughts, and the frequent inappropriateness of the emotions they express.

In line with the view that the severe personality disorders are largely structural pathologies rather than stylistic ones, an understanding of these patients requires that we combine the particular structural pathology of the patient with the less severe personality style with which it is fused. Schizotypals usually demonstrate either a schizoid or an avoidant stylistic pattern. The features of these less severe pathological styles then conflate with the pathology of structure that typifies the schizotypal, thereby producing the particular configuration of characteristics of the patient under study.

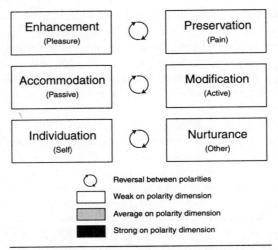

Figure 21.1   Status of the schizotypal personality prototype in accord with the Millon Polarity Model.

CLINICAL PICTURE

Several clusters of symptoms are found in common among patients classed in the schizotypal category; these will be noted before arranging them into clinical domains and specifying characteristics that differentiate the two major subvarieties. Three aspects of the schizotypal picture will be described in this and following sections: (a) the source of anxiety that tends to prompt psychotic episodes; (b) characteristic cognitive processes and preoccupations; and (c) general mood and behavior.

Depersonalization anxiety. The deficient or disharmonious affect of these patients deprives them of the capacity to relate to things or to experience events as something different from flat and lifeless phenomena. Schizotypals suffer a sense of vapidity in a world of cold and washed-out objects. Moreover, they feel themselves to be more dead than alive, insubstantial, foreign, and disembodied. As existential phenomenologists might put it, schizotypals are threatened by "nonbeing." Detached observers of the passing scene, these patients remain uninvolved, looking in from the outside not only with regard to others but with regard to themselves as well.

Many people may have experienced moments of inner void and social detachment at one time or another, but the feeling of estrangement and depersonalization is an ever present and insistent feature of schizotypals' everyday existence. This persistent detachment or disavowal of self distinguishes the unreal and meaningless quality of their life, and may give rise to a frightening sense of emptiness and nothingness. Every so often, the schizotypal may be overwhelmed by the dread of total disintegration, implosion, and nonexistence. These severe attacks of depersonalization may precipitate wild psychotic outbursts in which the patient frantically searches to reaffirm reality.

Cognitive autism and disjunctiveness. The slippage and interference in thought processes that characterize the milder detached patterns are even more pronounced in schizotypals. When motivated or prompted to relate to others, they are frequently unable to orient their thoughts logically and become lost in personal irrelevancies and tangential asides that have no pertinence to the topic at hand. Schizotypals lack "touch" with others and are unable to order their ideas in terms relevant to reciprocal, social communication. This pervasive disjunctiveness, this scattered and autistic feature of thinking, only further alienates them from others.

Deficient social behaviors and impoverished affect. Examination of the developmental achievements of the typical schizotypal will indicate an erratic course in which the person has continually failed to progress toward normal social attainments. School and employment history of these patients shows marked deficits and irregularities, given their intellectual capacities as a base. Not only are they frequent dropouts, but they drift from one source of employment to another, and, if married, often are separated or divorced. This deficit in social competence and attainment derives from, and in part contributes to, their lack of drive and their feelings of unworthiness.

The colorfulness of personality is lost in the schizotypal; there is a blandness of affect, a listlessness and a lack of spontaneity, ambition, and interest in life. These patients are able to talk about only a few relatively tangible matters, usually things that demand immediate attention; rarely do they initiate conversation or pursue it beyond what is necessary to be civil. Not only do they lack the spark to act and participate, but they seem enclosed and trapped by some force that blocks them from responding to and empathizing with others. This inability to take hold of life leaves them nonmembers of society, unable to invest their energies and interests in the world of others.

Clinical Domains

Although important distinctions exist among subvariants of the schizotypal syndrome, they do share a number of features, and it is these to which attention is directed in the following sections (see Table 21.1 and Figure 21.2).

Eccentric expressive behavior. What is most distinctive about schizotypal personalities is their socially gauche and peculiar mannerisms and their tendency to evince unusual actions and appearances. Many dress in strange and unusual ways, often appearing to prefer a "personal uniform" from day to day, for example, wearing a baseball cap with the visor in the back and invariably dressed in a horizontally striped T-shirt, always draped over a khaki pants belt. The tendency to keep to peculiar clothing styles sets them distinctively apart from their peers. As a consequence of their strange behaviors and appearances, schizotypals are readily perceived by others as aberrant, unobtrusively odd, curious, or bizarre.

Some schizotypals are aloof and isolated and behave in a bland and apathetic manner because they experience few pleasures and have need to avoid few discomforts. It would appear, then, that they should have little reason to acquire instrumental behaviors. Other schizotypals more actively control expressions of intense affect because

TABLE 21.1 Clinical Domains of the Schizotypal Prototype

Behavioral Level

(F) Expressively Eccentric (e.g., exhibits socially gauche and peculiar mannerisms; is perceived by others as aberrant, disposed to behave in an unobtrusively odd, aloof, curious, or bizarre manner).

(F) Interpersonally Secretive (e.g., prefers privacy and isolation, with few, highly tentative attachments and personal obligations; has drifted over time into increasingly peripheral vocational roles and clandestine social activities).

Phenomenological Level

(F) Cognitively Autistic (e.g., capacity to "read" thoughts and feelings of others is markedly dysfunctional; mixes social communications with personal irrelevancies, circumstantial speech, ideas of reference, and metaphorical asides; often ruminative, appearing self-absorbed and lost in daydreams with occasional magical thinking, bodily illusions, obscure suspicion, odd beliefs, and a blurring of reality and fantasy).

(S) Estranged Self-Image (e.g., exhibits recurrent social perplexities and illusions as well as experiences of depersonalization, derealization and dissociation; sees self as forlorn, with repetitive thoughts of life's emptiness and meaninglessness).

(S) Chaotic Objects (e.g., internalized representations consist of a piecemeal jumble of early relationships and affects, random drives and impulses, and uncoordinated channels of regulation that are only fitfully competent for binding tensions, accommodating needs, and mediating conflicts).

Intrapsychic Level

(F) Undoing Mechanism (e.g., bizarre mannerisms and idiosyncratic thoughts appear to reflect a retraction or reversal of previous acts or ideas that have stirred feelings of anxiety, conflict, or guilt; ritualistic or magical behaviors serve to repent for or nullify assumed misdeeds or "evil" thoughts).

(S) Fragmented Organization (e.g., possesses permeable ego boundaries; coping and defensive operations are haphazardly ordered in a loose assemblage of morphologic structures, leading to desultory actions in which primitive thoughts and affects are discharged directly, with few reality-based sublimations, and significant further disintegrations into a psychotic structural level, likely under even modest stress).

Biophysical Level

(S) Distraught or *Insentient Mood* (e.g., excessively apprehensive and ill at ease, particularly in social encounters; agitated and anxiously watchful, evincing distrust of others and suspicion of their motives that persists despite growing familiarity); *or* (e.g., manifests drab, apathetic, sluggish, joyless, and spiritless appearance; reveals marked deficiencies in face-to-face rapport and emotional expression).

F refers to Functional Domains (fluid, interactive)
S refers to Structural Domains (stable, unchanging)

they fear being humiliated and rejected. They are inexpressive and socially isolated for protective reasons. Their constricted affect and interpersonal reserve do not arise because of intrinsic emotional or social deficits but because they have bound their feelings and relationships to protect against the possibility of rebuff.

Secretive interpersonal conduct.   Perhaps as a consequence of their unusual cognitive dysfunctions, schizotypals may have learned to prefer privacy and isolation. Unable to achieve a reasonable level of interpersonal comfort and satisfaction, they may have learned to withdraw from social relationships, to draw increasingly into themselves, with

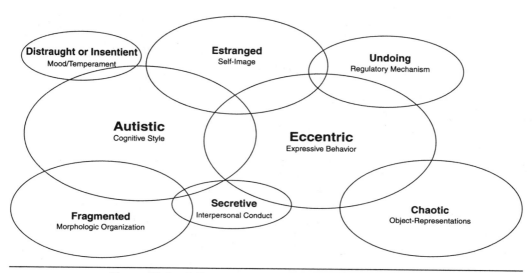

Figure 21.2 Salience of prototypal schizotypal domains.

just a few very tentative attachments and personal obligations. Depending on the difficulty they have experienced in these limited social relationships, they may have drifted over time into increasingly peripheral vocational roles, finding a degree of satisfaction in unusual and clandestine social activities.

The social achievements of the typical schizotypal usually indicate an erratic course in which the person has failed to make normal progress. School and work histories show marked deficits and irregularities, given their intellectual capacities as a base. Not only are they frequent dropouts, but they tend to drift from one job to another and are often separated or divorced, if they ever married. Their deficits in achievement competence derive from and, in part, contribute to their social anxieties and feelings of unworthiness. Moreover, there is a listlessness and a lack of spontaneity, ambition, and interest in life.

Schizotypals are able to talk about only a few relatively tangible matters, usually those things that demand their immediate attention. If they do sustain a conversation, they may press it beyond the appropriate or suitable, digressing into highly personal, odd, or metaphorical topics. More commonly, they lack the spark to initiate action or to participate socially, seemingly enclosed and trapped by some force that blocks them from responding to and empathizing with others. This inability to take hold of life to become a member of a "real" society and to invest their energies and interests in a world of others lies at the heart of their pathology.

Disorganized cognitive style. Crucial to the pathology of schizotypals is their inability to organize their thoughts, particularly in the realm of interpersonal understanding and empathy. They interpret things "differently" than do most of us. The capacity to differentiate what is salient from what is tangential seems lacking in these personalities. They attribute unusual and special significance to peripheral and incidental events, construing what transpires between persons in a manner that signifies a fundamental lack of social comprehension and logic. They do *not* evince a *general* deficit in cognitive capacity, one that is pervasively awry or is broadly deficient. Rather, their distortions and deficiencies appear limited to the interpersonal facets of the cognitive domain. As a consequence of their misrenderings of the meaning of human interactions, they construct idiosyncratic conceptions regarding the thoughts, feelings, and actions of others. They are unable to grasp or resonate to the everyday elements of human behavior and thought.

Daily transactions are transformed in bizarre ways, rendering them odd and peculiar to most observers. In sum, the capacity to "read" the thoughts and feelings of others is markedly distorted. They interpose personal irrelevancies, circumstantial speech, ideas of reference, and metaphorical asides in ordinary social communications. Lacking in the ability to implicitly understand the give-and-take that coheres interpersonal transactions, they may gradually withdraw from such transactions, becoming highly ruminative, self-absorbed, lost in daydreams. Owing to their problematic information gathering and disorganized processing, their ideas may result in the formation of magical thinking, bodily illusions, odd beliefs, peculiar suspicions, and cognitive blurring that interpenetrates reality with fantasy.

Why else do they develop superstitions, referential ideas, and illusions, and engage at times in frenetic activity and vigorous coping? In essence, schizotypals have enough awareness of the fruits of life to realize that other people do experience joy, sorrow, and excitement, whereas they, by contrast, are empty and barren. They desire *some* relatedness, *some* sensation, and *some* feeling that they are part of the world about them. Although avoiding more than they can handle comfortably, they also feel considerable discomfort with less than they need, especially because less brings them close to nothing. Their recurrent illusions, their magical and telepathic thinking, and their ideas of reference may be viewed as a coping effort to "fill the spaces of their emptiness," the feeling that they are "going under" and are bereft of all life and meaning.

Alienated from others and themselves, they may sense the terror of impending nothingness and of a barren, depersonalized, and nonexistent self. Such feelings prompt them to engage in bizarre behaviors, beliefs, and perceptions that enable them to "reaffirm reality." It is for this reason among others that we observe the ideas of reference, the clairvoyance, the illusions, and the "strange" ideation that typify the schizotypal.

Owing to their unsatisfactory social and cognitive dysfunctions, most schizotypals evidence recurrent social perplexities as well as self-illusions, depersonalization, and association. Many see themselves as alienated from the world around them, as forlorn and estranged beings, with repetitive ruminations about life's emptiness and meaninglessness. The deficient cognitions and disharmonious affects of schizotypals deprive them of the capacity to experience events as something other than lifeless and unfathomable phenomena. They suffer a sense of vapidness in a world of puzzling and washed-out objects. Many schizotypals see themselves as more dead than alive, insubstantial, foreign, and disembodied. As existential phenomenologists might put it, they are threatened by "nonbeing." Detached observers of the passing scene, these patients remain uninvolved, looking in from the outside not only with regard to others but with regard to themselves as well. Many pathological personalities experience periods of inner void and social detachment, but the feeling of estrangement and depersonalization is an ever-present and insistent feature of the schizotypal's everyday existence.

Chaotic objects.   The inner world of the schizotypal is grounded in a piecemeal jumble of early memories, perceptions, and feelings. The inner template that comprises this chaotic melange of objects, impulses, and thoughts is almost random, resulting in an ineffective and uncoordinated framework for regulating the patient's tensions, needs, and goals. Perhaps for the greater part of their lives, these internalized representations have been only fitfully competent for accommodating to their world, binding their impulses, and mediating their interpersonal difficulties.

When motivated or prompted to relate to others, schizotypals are frequently unable to orient their inner dispositions in a logical manner; as noted previously, they become lost in personal irrelevancies and in tangential asides that seem vague, digressive, and with no pertinence to the topic at hand. They are "out of touch" with others and are unable to order their ideas in terms relevant to reciprocal, social communication. The pervasive disjunctiveness of their inner templates, the scattered, circumstantial, and autistic elements of their thinking, only further alienate these patients from others.

Undoing mechanism. It appears that many of the bizarre mannerisms and idiosyncratic thoughts of the schizotypal reflect a retraction or reversal of previous acts or ideas. Intrapsychically, this regulatory mechanism may serve to counteract feelings of anxiety, conflict, or guilt. By utilizing this dynamic process, the patient "repents for" or nullifies the ostensive misdeed or "evil thought." The outcropping of this undoing process may be seen in magical beliefs and ritualistic behaviors.

This persistent undoing mechanism, combined with schizotypals' periodic disavowal of self, may come to characterize the unreal and meaningless quality of their lives and may give rise to their frequent and frightening sense of emptiness and nothingness. As already noted, schizotypals are often overwhelmed by the dread of total disintegration, implosion, and nonexistence—feelings that may be countered by imposing or constructing new worlds of self-made reality, an idiosyncratic reality composed of superstitions, suspicions, illusions, and so on. The more severe attacks of depersonalization may precipitate psychotic episodes, irrational outbursts in which these patients frantically search to build a sense of reality to fill their vacant existence.

Fragmented organization. If one looks into the intrapsychic organization of the schizotypal's mind, one is likely to find highly permeable boundaries among psychic components that are commonly well segregated. There is a haphazardly ordered and loose assemblage of morphologic structures. As a consequence of these less than adequate and poorly constructed defensive operations, primitive thoughts and impulses are usually discharged in a helter-skelter way, more or less directly and in a sequence of desultory actions. The intrinsically defective nature of the schizotypal's internal structures results in few reality-based sublimations and few successful achievements in life. These defects make the patient vulnerable to further decompensation, even under modest degrees of stress.

The inner structures of the schizotypal may be overwhelmed by excess stimulation. This is likely to occur when social demands and expectations press hard against their preferred uninvolved or withdrawn state. Unable to avoid such external impositions, some schizotypals may react either by "blanking out," drifting off into another world, or by paranoid or aggressive outbursts. Undue encroachments on their complacent world may lead them to disconnect socially for prolonged periods, during which they may be confused and aimless, display inappropriate affect and paranoid thinking, and communicate in odd, circumstantial, and metaphorical ways. At other times, when external pressures may be especially acute, they may react with a massive and psychotic outpouring of primitive impulses, delusional thoughts, hallucinations, and bizarre behaviors. Many schizotypals have stored up intense repressed anxieties and hostilities throughout their lives. Once released, these feelings burst out in a rampaging flood. The backlog of suspicions, fears, and animosities has been ignited and now explodes in a frenzied cathartic discharge.

Distraught or insentient mood.   Although variable in nature, schizotypals tend to display one of two predominant affective states. *Insipid* schizotypals, to be discussed shortly, manifest a drab, apathetic, sluggish, and joyless demeanor, a pattern of behaviors that appears to overlie an intrinsically spiritless and affectless temperament. Rarely do they display an ease in emotional expression; as a consequence, they exhibit marked deficiencies in their face-to-face rapport with others. Whether this deficit derives from some inborn constitutional disposition or a lack of affective-attachment experiences in early life cannot be ascertained readily; more will be said regarding this matter in a later section.

A contrasting predominant mood may be seen among patients labeled *timorous* schizotypals; these actively detached persons exhibit many features of the avoidant personality as well. These schizotypals are excessively apprehensive and ill at ease, particularly in social encounters, and evidence a generally agitated and anxious watchfulness. Many exhibit a distrust of other persons and are suspicious of their motives, a disposition that rarely recedes despite growing familiarity.

Self-Perpetuation Processes

The future of the schizotypal syndrome is perhaps the least promising of all personality types. This section briefly summarizes factors that contribute toward the downward progression (see Table 21.2).

In the preceding discussion, we referred to several of the strategies employed by the schizotypal personality. This reflects the assertion that the adaptive efforts utilized by pathological personalities are themselves pathogenic, that is, that many of their coping strategies are self-defeating and foster new difficulties; all pathological patterns are alike in this regard. The central distinction between the more and less severe patterns is the fact that the strategies of the former group are instrumentally less successful and more self-defeating than those of the latter, either because they were never

TABLE 21.2   Self-Perpetuating Processes

SCHIZOTYPAL

Faltering Controls
Dormant thoughts and impulses become overt
Feels dead and empty
Senses pressure and encroachment

Compensates for Depersonalization
Flight into chaotic ideas to avoid nothingness
Bizarre outbursts counter loss of self
Terrified by impending nonexistence

Deflects Overstimulation
Drifts off into confusion
Experiences prolonged physical disappearance
Outbursts of protective aggression

learned adequately or because they have faltered under persistent and cumulative stress. Because their adaptive facilities are instrumentally so deficient, it seems best to focus on the restitutive and defensive efforts these patients employ; thus, these patients are distinguished from their milder counterparts, not in their strategies but in what they do to shore up these strategies when they begin to crumble, albeit to minimal avail.

As formerly effective strategies begin to falter, the schizotypal may be driven to engage in a variety of extreme and frequently dramatic restitutive maneuvers; these are often displayed in the form of brief psychotic episodes in which previously dormant or controlled thoughts and impulses break into consciousness, producing primary process symptoms of bizarre ideation and behavior. If sufficient tension is discharged during these upsurges, and if environmental pressures are adequately relieved, the individual may regain composure and equilibrium; his or her temporary "disordered state" has ended, and the person returns to his or her previous level of pathological personality functioning. For the present, we focus our attention on the coping aims schizotypals seek to achieve, that is, what they attempt to do to cope with stress now that their former strategies have failed them.

Earlier, we noted two sets of conditions that precipitate schizotypals into temporary psychotic disorders. One occurs when they feel a frightening sense of petrifaction, "deadness," depersonalization, and emptiness, that is, a degree of outer and inner stimulation that is much *less* than that to which they are accustomed. The second occurs when they feel an oppressive sense of being encroached upon, pressured and obligated to others, that is, a degree of external stimulation that is much *more* than that to which they are accustomed. Let us next discuss the restitutive measures they employ to deal with these conditions.

Depersonalized disintegration.   To cope with depersonalization, the schizotypal frequently bursts into frenetic activity, becomes hyperactive, excited, and overtalkative, spews forth a flight of chaotic ideas and is unrestrained, grabbing objects and running hurriedly from one thing to another, all in an effort to reaffirm his or her existence, to validate life, to avoid the catastrophic fear of emptiness and nothingness.

Insipid (schizoid style) schizotypals generally behave in a bland and apathetic manner because they experience few positive reinforcements and seek to avoid few negative reinforcements. As a result, they have little reason to acquire instrumental behaviors. Why then do they become active, frenetic, and feverish and engage in vigorous coping efforts?

Insipid schizotypals have enough awareness of the fruits of life to realize that other people do experience joy, sorrow, and excitement, whereas they, by contrast, are empty and barren. They seek to maintain the modest level of sensation and feeling to which they have become accustomed; although they avoid more than they can handle comfortably, they also feel considerable discomfort with less than they need, especially because less brings them close to nothing. Their frantic, erratic, and bizarre outbursts may be viewed, then, as a coping effort to counter the feeling that they are "going under," bereft of all life and meaning.

Timorous (avoidant style) schizotypals control expressions of affect because they fear humiliation and rejection; they are bland and socially withdrawn, then, for protective reasons. Their overt appearance is similar to the insipid schizotypal, not because of an intrinsic affectivity deficit, but because they have bound their emotions against possible rebuff. However, the consequences of their coping strategy are the same as those experienced by the insipid schizotypal. Alienated from others and themselves, they may sense the terror of impending nothingness and of a barren, depersonalized, and non-existent self. Such feelings prompt them to engage in a frenetic round of behaviors to reaffirm reality.

Deflecting overstimulation.   At the other extreme, both insipid and timorous schizotypals may be faced with excess stimulation.

Unable to avoid external impositions, *insipid schizotypals* may react either by "blanking out," drifting off into another world, or by wild and aggressive outbursts. Undue encroachments on their complacent world may lead them to disappear for prolonged periods of time, during which they seem confused and aimless, and which they later only vaguely recall. At other times, where pressure may be especially acute, they may instrumentally turn away these pressures by reacting with a massive outpouring of primitive impulses, delusional thoughts, hallucinations, and bizarre behaviors.

As with insipid schizotypals, external pressures may be too great for *timorous schizotypals*, going beyond their tolerance limits and leading them also either to "drift out" or to become wild and uncontrollable. During these outbursts, the probability of delusions, hallucinations, and bizarre and aggressive behaviors is even greater than that found in the insipid schizotypal. The timorous schizotypal has stored up intense repressed anxieties and hostilities throughout life. Once released, they burst as in a rampaging flood; the person's backlog of fears and animosities has been ignited and now explodes in a frenzied, cathartic discharge.

INTERVENTION GOALS

Schizotypal individuals are one of the easier personality disorders for clinicians to diagnose. Odd speech, cognitive slippage, peculiar mannerisms, and even unusual dressing patterns give hints about the correct personality diagnosis. Confusion can sometimes arise, however, in attempting to differentiate between a schizotypal experiencing a temporary psychotic break and a diagnosis of schizophrenia. In general, however, schizotypals do not exhibit the delusions, hallucinations, and loose associations of either the schizophreniform or schizophrenic disorder.

Therapists working with schizotypals are likely to find themselves giving a lot more "advice" to schizotypals than to other patients. Whereas some therapists believe that the aim of therapy is to help patients help themselves, many schizotypals have trouble generalizing from one situation to another and hence need repeated "lessons" about similar life circumstances. Despite the probability that personality reconstruction is not a likely outcome, except with mild cases of the disorder, many schizotypal patients benefit from the therapeutic relationship owing to the limits it provides on reality-distorting social isolation, and for the lessons it teaches about more adaptive functioning.

When formulating the therapeutic goals for a particular patient, the therapist would do well to keep in mind that schizotypals can be either active or passive regarding their characteristic social isolation and detachment; the cognitive dysfunctions and behavioral eccentricities that are the hallmark of the disorder usually map onto less pathological avoidant or schizoid personality disorders. Although the avoidant variant is more likely to be seen clinically, the therapist needs to distinguish between the two types to maximize treatment goals and strategies (see Table 21.3).

TABLE 21.3 Therapeutic Strategies
and Tactics for the Prototypal
Schizotypal Personality

STRATEGIC GOALS
Balance Polarities
 Stabilize erratic pain-pleasure polarities
 Stabilize erratic self-other polarities

Counter Perpetuations
 Prevent social isolation
 Undo excessive dependency
 Reduce fantasy preoccupations

TACTICAL MODALITIES
 Alter eccentric behaviors
 Reverse autistic cognitive style
 Reconstruct estranged self-image

Reestablishing Polarity Balances

As one of the three more severe and structurally defective personality disorders, schizotypals are burdened with disturbances in several polarity realms. As discussed previously, the constellation of these disturbances falls into one of two general patterns, the active-detached (avoidant/timorous) and the passive-detached (schizoid/insipid) variants. Those who fall into the passive category are unlikely to be motivated by either pain or pleasure: the capacity for feelings appear to be markedly reduced. Those of the actively detached type, on the other hand, are highly sensitive to environmentally produced and intrapsychically generated painful experiences, leading them to feel self-alienated and to withdraw from social interactions. Internally, however, anxiety and shame unremittingly continue to intrude. Neither active nor passive variants balance their social disengagement with an adaptive self-strategy. Daydreaming, magical thinking, and ideas of reference serve either to replace the turmoil and anxiety of the timorous schizotypal or to fill the frightening inner void of the insipid variant.

 An increase in an adaptive other-oriented focus can be achieved with behavioral interventions such as social skills training and modeling. A first potential benefit is to limit cognitive distortions through socially provided reality controls. Quality of life may be improved by increasing sensitivity to pleasure. Should these goals be realized, the passive subtype will probably also shift toward the active end of the active-passive dimension, and the active subtype will likely channel energy into more gratifying goals and may become more passive in relation to avoiding potential (mostly illusory) threats. In the case of timorous schizotypals, decreasing their fear of rejection or insult may be achieved by making them aware of the common and usual mutually rewarding rules of social exchange.

Countering Perpetuating Tendencies

Both social isolation and dependency training not only perpetuate the schizotypal personality style, but in fact intensify deficits in cognitive organization and social skills. Environmental conditions that foster dependency can develop easily in the schizotypal's home, where well-intentioned family members may, with the best intentions for the patient's welfare, inadvertently coddle and patronize him or her. Schizotypals who relinquish their activities and learn to depend on others too much are likely to regress further into an amotivated and isolated state. Patients who remain in understaffed hospitals for extended periods of time are likely to end up in a similar condition. In the latter case, this is likely to result from staff neglect and a failure to encourage involvement with friends, relatives, fellow patients, and staff, even while basic needs are provided for. Finally, many schizotypals contribute to their own deterioration by consistently avoiding social interactions that could provide the stimulation and feedback that can keep them functional.

One main objective when working with a schizotypal patient is to encourage the development and maintenance of relatively normal social relationships through social skills training, cognitive reorientation, and environmental management. Patients should be taught basic skills and encouraged to do as much for themselves as possible. Contact with a therapist is in itself helpful in preventing deterioration. Compensating for isolation through fantasy can sustain schizotypals for but brief periods before preoccupations turn to past misfortunes and injustices. Unable to escape misery by turning inward, they may disavow their own existence, scramble what organization there is between thoughts and feelings, and sink into nothingness.

Identifying Domain Dysfunctions

The schizotypal's most salient personologic domain dysfunctions are evidenced in cognitive style and expressive behavior. Disorganized cognitive functioning underlies disturbances in almost all of the other domains. Schizotypals mix social communication with personal irrelevancies, perceive the environment as imbued with material that feeds their ideas of reference and their metaphorical mental tangents. Nonproductive daydreaming often supports magical thinking and irrational suspicions and obscures the line between reality and fantasy. Such thinking is the foundation for aberrant expressive behavior. This, paired with a lack of human interaction that could provide normalizing feedback about thinking and behavior, leads the schizotypal to exhibit socially gauche habits and peculiar mannerisms. The estranged self-image contributes to permeable ego-boundaries and increases the tendency to be perplexed by social interactions and to experience depersonalization, derealization, and dissociation. A preference for privacy and isolation tends to drive the schizotypal toward clandestine activities and peripheral roles. A result of this secretive interpersonal conduct is that others usually find the schizotypal odd, although unobtrusive.

As a result of consistent misperception of the world (and of possible early abusive experiences), the schizotypal's object-representations tend to be chaotic. Schizotypals' main stress-reducing regulatory mechanism is bizarre mannerisms and idiosyncratic thoughts that reflect a retraction or reversal of previous acts or ideas that have stirred conflict or anxiety. Their ritualistic or magical thinking is meant to counteract "evil" thoughts and deeds, both of themselves and of others. All of these dysfunctions contribute to the fragmented morphologic organization of the schizotypal's personality. Few reality-based sublimations bind primitive thoughts and affect. Mood is typically distraught in active schizotypals and insentient in passive. Complaints of being ill at ease, agitated, and watchful of others' motives is typical of active variants. Drab, apathetic, or otherwise markedly deficient face-to-face rapport and emotional expression is typical of passive variants.

In the case of the insipid schizotypal, a primary goal is to help the patient identify those spheres of life toward which some positive inclination exists. Even if enthusiasm is not likely, increased participation in such activities can decrease the need for bizarre internal gratifications. It may also provide a window of reality-based experiences through which to objectively examine cognitive dysfunctions and distorted object-relations. Psychopharmacologic intervention can be helpful in increasing affectivity and laying the groundwork on which increased motivation and active adaptation can be based. Group and/or behavioral interventions can help the patient develop social and other skills, leading to more satisfying social interactions that may strengthen other-oriented and active behaviors. Vocational and other areas of functioning can be enhanced, even if real intimacy with others is not likely to be achieved.

Interventions that foster feelings of self-worth and that encourage active schizotypals to realistically appraise their positive attributes and capacities can help provide patients with an improved self-image and motivation. Energy previously channeled into avoidance strategies can now be more productively directed into securing pleasure via much craved-for social contact and/or vocational accomplishments. Improved social skills and increased self-esteem can help prevent extreme isolation and the cognitive distortions that result from the subsequent lack of socially provided reality checks, difficulties that so readily lead to decompensation.

SELECTING THERAPEUTIC MODALITIES

Most schizotypals seen by therapists are of the active-detached or timorous variant. Their extreme social anxiety and frequent paranoia can make it difficult for the therapist to establish a solid relationship, for patients will try to defensively distance themselves. Many schizotypals interpret the therapist's behavior in unusual ways that may not be conducive to a positive therapeutic alliance. Because schizotypal patients often believe that they can read minds or influence others through telepathic means, the therapist would do well to inquire about the patient's therapy experience to make sure that the patient's perception mirrors reality.

Behavioral Techniques

Many of the behaviors of schizotypals are amenable to behavioral interventions. Marked peculiarities of speech, dress, and mannerism can be reduced through modeling, social skills training, and simple advice. Especially useful for schizotypals in inpatient settings are techniques such as aversive learning and selective positive reinforcement. No less helpful are social skill training procedures. Here, the therapist may serve as a model the patient can imitate in order to function more skillfully and efficiently than heretofore. Peculiarities of belief may be dealt with either behaviorally or cognitively. In the behavioral strategy, efforts can be employed to counteract extreme and irrational anxieties by the use of imaginal or in vivo exposure procedures.

Interpersonal Techniques

Benjamin's (1993) outline for interpersonal intervention with schizotypal patients focuses largely on the role of undoing aspects of schizotypals' histories. Magical thinking is seen as being provoked by placement in situations in which the young child was led to believe that he or she had control when in fact he or she had none. In other circumstances, the child may have been given undue or inappropriate responsibility, for example, being led to believe that abuse could be prevented by certain behaviors that did not achieve this end. It is suggested that the patient needs to see how the content of such ideas mirrors past interpersonal dynamics before he or she will be willing to attempt to interpret and cope with life differently.

In the early stages of therapy, a supportive approach may be the only kind of therapy that a schizotypal patient can handle. Although other approaches can be used concomitantly, a realistic positive outcome may involve increasing the patient's pleasure in living rather than changing fundamental aspects of personality style or structure. The therapist's acceptance, empathic understanding, and benevolent advice can serve to realize this aim. The therapist may need to serve as the patient's "reality-testing auxiliary ego" for a very long time. As a consequence of establishing a genuine sense of rapport, the schizotypal patient might develop sufficient trust to give up magical and ritualistic beliefs.

Cognitive Techniques

Cognitive approaches are more directly focused on altering the content of schizotypals' thoughts. Beck and Freeman's (1990a) outline of cognitive intervention procedures for treating schizotypal personality disorders suggests that a first therapeutic step is to identify the patient's dysfunctional automatic thoughts. Examples of such thoughts include: "Is that person watching me?"; "I can feel the devil in her"; and "I am a nonbeing." Dysfunctional thoughts generally fall into one of four categories: (a) ideas of reference in which patients believe that unrelated events are related to them; (b) paranoid ideation; (c) magical thinking, such as a conviction that a dead relative is present; or (d) experiencing illusions, such as seeing people in shadows. Another common cognitive distortion seen among schizotypals is emotionally-generated reasoning, which causes them to believe that emotions are "evidence" about circumstances: if they feel bad, they believe that there is necessarily a problem, and vice versa. Schizotypals also engage in personalization, in which they believe that they are responsible for external circumstances, when in fact they are not.

Teaching schizotypals to recognize when they are distorting reality can be done within the context of the therapeutic relationship, as these patients usually harbor unrealistic ideas about the therapist's communication and intent. Many schizotypals may even fear that harm will befall the therapist because of the therapeutic association. As ideas and predictions are countered, more realistic thinking can be learned. As new cognitive skills are learned, maladaptive patterns can be altered as the patient gives up the pathogenic wish, which Benjamin (1993) sums up as "the wish to magically protect the self and others while maintaining loyalty to early abusers" (p. 110). Interpreting symptomatic behavior, such as suicidal fantasies that reflect this underlying wish, can help the patient realize the function of these behaviors. Benjamin's example of such an interpretation is: "Well, he (abusive father) would sure be happy to see what a good job you are doing of punishing yourself this time. This will prove that you love him and want to stay with him forever" (p. 112). As long as the therapist consistently displays sympathy for patients' "terror of defying the internalized wishes and fears implanted by abusers" (p. 111), as well as convincing schizotypals that they can think about themselves and others differently than previously, more adaptive patterns may come to replace the old.

An important first step is to establish a good therapeutic alliance. In the context of a solid relationship, patients are less likely to be handicapped by the deleterious effect of social isolation on their reality testing and more likely to be receptive to cues and interventions to improve social appropriateness. Social skills training, including modeling of appropriate behavior and speech, can be very helpful in reducing patients' social anxiety and awkwardness. Beck and Freeman (1990a) suggest that a group setting can be ideal for identifying and challenging automatic thoughts about social functioning, as well as for learning and practicing new skills. They also point out that keeping the session structured is helpful with these patients, as their rambling cognitive style can result in little getting accomplished.

Teaching patients to evaluate their thoughts against environmental evidence, rather than against their feelings, can help reduce emotional reasoning and drawing incorrect conclusions about life circumstances. Although dysfunctional thoughts are not likely to disappear, it may be possible for the patient to learn to disregard them, rather than to respond either emotionally or behaviorally. Instead, a cognitive coping statement can be employed to counter the dysfunctional one. An example of such a statement is: "There I go again. Even though I'm thinking this thought, it doesn't mean that it's true." A particularly useful suggestion is to keep track of the patient's predictions and systematically to test them. The patient can then see that emotion does not predict or necessarily reflect circumstance. Communication style problems, whether they include circumstantiality, tangentiality, or fixation on or exclusion of detail, can usually be reduced when the patient can identify the reason the particular style is used. It is also recommended that patients be taught practical ways to improve their life, whether this means learning about personal hygiene, finding employment, or initiating relationships.

Self-Image Techniques

A primary focus of therapy is to enhance these patients' self-worth and to encourage them to recognize their positive attributes. Pride in self and valuing one's constructive capacities are necessary in rebuilding patients' motivation. No longer alienated from themselves, they will have a basis for overcoming their alienation from others. With a sense of self-worth, these patients may be guided by the therapist to explore positively rewarding social activities. Initiating such experiences may be crucial in preventing what otherwise might be a downward progression.

Schizotypals often discuss problematic early experiences without expression of any affect. It is recommended that sympathizing and empathizing with others who experienced similar treatment can help lead patients to understand their own position, as well as to generate appropriate affect. Also possible with these patients is a tendency to do the opposite of what was intended therapeutically, for example, identifying with the perpetrator of aggression and experiencing guilt or feeling the need for punishment as a result of having traitorous thoughts, or what they interpret as their part in instigating an abusive situation. Alternatively, the feelings can be projected on the therapist, who may be seen as an enemy.

It has been suggested further that the process of forging a good relationship can be greatly aided by the therapist's respect for the schizotypal patient's particular sensitivities. Not pushing the patient too hard or too fast can prevent the patient from experiencing severe anxiety and paranoid reactions. Schizotypals' peculiar and rambling cognitive style can make it difficult for them to maintain focus in therapy sessions. Providing well-structured interventions and sessions can be very helpful with this group of individuals.

Others recommend that group therapy is appropriate for schizotypals who do not display prominently eccentric behavior, thereby causing other group members too much discomfort. Similarly, if the patient has paranoid features, these attributes may cause more turmoil than desirable. If the patient is appropriate for group therapy, the experience can help the schizotypal overcome social anxiety and awkwardness by providing a supportive environment and an opportunity to realize that others have similar insecurities.

Intrapsychic Techniques

Psychodynamic approaches focus on the need for the schizotypal patient to internalize a healthy, "related" bond with another person, often the therapist. Gabbard (1994) suggests that the therapist should expect the patient to react to increased closeness with silence and emotional distance. This silence should be accepted as a legitimate part of the patient's personality. It is also suggested that the patient may then begin to reveal hidden aspects of the self and integrate them in adaptive ways. Offering classic psychodynamic interpretations to patients about their behavior, however, is not likely to be very successful in helping them. Most schizotypals find psychotherapy to be quite challenging and stressful. There is great need, according to analytic thinkers, to adopt a very permissive and tolerant attitude with these patients. Rather than viewing their silence as a form of resistance, it should be seen as a generalized style of "nonrelating." When the schizotypal's communications are confusing, or when silence is prolonged, the therapist must guard against his or her own frustrated feelings and potentially troublesome countertransferences.

Pharmacologic Techniques

Psychopharmacologic intervention can prove very helpful in controlling many of the symptoms of the schizotypal personality disorder. Illusions, ideas of reference, phobic anxiety, obsessive-compulsive symptoms, and "psychoticism" have all been shown to respond favorably to low doses of clozapine, risperidone, or olanzapine without serious side effects (Goldberg et al., 1986; Joseph, 1997; Serban & Siegel, 1984). Anxiolytics in modest doses appear to be advisable in patients who experience distinct anxious feeling during the early stages of treatment (Akiskal, 1981). Amoxipine, a combination antidepressant and antipsychotic, has been recommended for schizotypal patients with depressive symptomatology. Some patients, however, appear to tolerate such medications poorly due to excessive sedation. The SSRIs may also reduce concurrent depressive symptoms, interpersonal sensitivities, and paranoid ideation, as well as improve "peculiar" secondary features such as obsessions and compulsions.

Stone (1993) recommends that patients who show relatively good functioning and exhibit only the milder signs of the disorder (cognitive slippage, odd speech) probably need no or few medications at most times in their treatment. Institutionalization, when necessary, should be brief. Hospital settings too often breed isolation, reward "quiet" behaviors, and provide models of eccentric belief and perception, each of which can lead to increased detachment and bizarre preoccupations.

MAKING SYNERGISTIC ARRANGEMENTS

Establishing a good relationship with a schizotypal patient is a necessary first objective. In fact, providing a healthy, steady relationship is therapeutic in and of itself. A good alliance is most likely to result from an initial, almost exclusively supportive therapist stance. Silence may need to be tolerated, empathy expressed, and encouragement of participation in "pleasurable" activities emphasized. The therapist's practical advice can often provide structure and foster improvements in the patient's life. When patients come to trust the therapist, cognitive and behavioral interventions can help them learn to identify distortions in their interpretation of the environment and provide the skills necessary for more enhancing relationships. As noted earlier, patients who evidence psychotic thinking above and beyond the oddities of speech and mannerism may benefit from low doses of neuroleptics. This is likely to be more true of timorous than of insipid schizotypals. If behavioral eccentricities are not too great, the patient may also benefit from group therapy, particularly if a major presenting problem is social anxiety and a lack of social skills. Unfortunately, most schizotypals are not likely to undergo substantial changes in the structure of their personality or in the level of intimacy involved in their relations with others. Gains are more likely to be made, however, in nonintimate interactions, in reality testing, and in participation in activities that the schizotypal can "enjoy."

Illustrative Cases

There are two major variants of the defective schizotypal personality. The first derives from the *passive-detached style,* termed the schizoid personality; the second reflects an *active-detached style* and has been termed the avoidant personality. Although there are several adult subtypes of each of these broad personality styles (e.g., "languid" and "remote," to represent two of the schizoid subtypes), we limit our discussion to the two broad variations of the defective-schizotypal disorder (see Table 21.4).

TABLE 21.4 Schizotypal Personality Disorder Subtypes

Insipid: Sense of strangeness and nonbeing; overtly drab, sluggish, inexpressive; internally bland, barren, indifferent, and insensitive; thoughts obscure, vague, and tangential; bizarre telepathic powers.

MCMI S-1/2B/3

Timorous: Warily apprehensive, watchful, suspicious, guarded, shrinking; deadens excess sensitivity, alienated from self and others, intentionally blocks, reverses, or disqualifies own thoughts.

MCMI S-2A/8A

SCHIZOTYPAL PERSONALITY:
INSIPID TYPE
(SCHIZOTYPAL WITH SCHIZOID FEATURES)

CASE 21.1, RICK N., 37

Presenting Picture: Rick N., a night watchman at a warehouse, seemed entirely disconnected from himself and his surroundings. He liked his work because he could be by himself in a quiet atmosphere, away from anyone else. He described this empty warehouse, surprisingly enough, as "homey." Throughout the initial interview, Rick remained aloof, never once looking at the counselor, answered questions with either one-word responses or very short phrases, and usually waited to respond until a second question was asked. He described, in these short, bizarre answers, a life devoid of almost any human interconnectedness, with about his only tangible contact being his brother, whom he saw only during major holidays. Living alone, he could only remember one significant "relationship," and that was with a girl in high school. Very simply, he stated, "We graduated, and then I didn't see her any more." He expressed no apparent loneliness, however, and appeared entirely emotionless regarding any aspect of his life.

Clinical Assessment: Notably insensitive to feelings, Rick, an *insipid schizotypal* personality, often experienced a separation between his mind and his physical body. There was a strange sense of nonbeing or nonexistence, as if his floating conscious awareness carried with it a depersonalized or identityless human form. Behaviorally, his tendency was to be drab, sluggish, and inexpressive. He possessed a marked deficit in affectivity and appeared bland, indifferent, unmotivated, and insensitive to the external world. Cognitive processes seemed obscure, vague, and tangential. He was either impervious to, or missed the shades of, interpersonal and emotional experience. Social communications were responded to minimally or with inappropriate affect or peculiar ideas, or in a circumstantial and confused manner. Speech was often monotonous, listless, or inaudible. Most people considered him to be an unobtrusive and strange person who drifted on the periphery of life or who faded into the background, self-absorbed, wool gathering, and lost to the outside world. Most typically, Rick derives from and coalesces with the schizoid pattern. In a very modest number of cases such as his, we might see a fusion with depressive and dependent personality features, though this was not in evidence in his MCMI scores, nor did they seem apparent here.

Rick would occasionally experience the awesome terror of feeling "dead," nonexistent, petrified. Detached from the world and insensitive to his own feelings, he may have become terrified by a frightening sense of "nothingness," of passing through a barren, cold, lifeless existence. The disaster of losing self, of becoming a walking automaton, a petrified object without meaning or purpose, may have occasionally overwhelmed him, driving him into a bizarre psychotic state in which he created tangible illusions to which he could relate, self-referential ideas that gave him a significance he otherwise lacked. Bizarre "telepathic" powers enabled him to communicate with mythical or distant others, all in a desperate effort to reaffirm his existence in reality. Sinking into a lifeless void, he would catch himself struck by a sense of becoming a thing and not a being. This dread, this catastrophic sense of nothingness, caused him to grasp at anything, real or fantasized, by which he could convince himself that he did, in fact, exist. On the brink of feeling totally annihilated, he struggled desperately to confirm his being, clinging tenaciously to whatever meaning and feeling he could find in or impute to his surroundings. As in his pure schizotypal counterpart, these eccentricities were attempts to forestall the void of oblivion and nothingness.

Schizotypals such as Rick occasionally succumb to psychotic disorders when faced with too much rather than too little stimulation. Painfully uncomfortable with social obligations or personal closeness, Rick felt encroached on when pressed into responsibilities beyond his limited tolerance. During these periods, he may have exploded, bursting into frenetic activity to block the intrusions forced on him. More likely, in Rick's case, he simply "faded out," became blank, lost conscious awareness, and "turned off" the pressures of the outer world.

Synergistic Treatment Plan: To work toward reorienting Rick to the here and now and away from bizarre fixations, it would be necessary first to demonstrate connectedness within the therapeutic relationship as a safe and realistic construct through *supportive* and *behavioral* interventions, and possibly with *biophysical* remedial approaches. A less wavering *active* orientation then would be fostered by addressing *cognitions* that perpetuated fantasies and indifference to his context by requiring a "deadened" approach to perceived dejection (wavering *pain-pleasure* polarity conflict). His tendency to retract and undo previous associations, typical of his *passive* nature, would be countered *interpersonally,* and more effective social skills would be encouraged. More effective and steadfast orientations toward *self* and *other* would be encouraged, as well, through this combined cognitive and interpersonal strategy.

Therapeutic Course: The first nuance Rick needed for this treatment to work was the notion that realistic goals were not only desirable but fully achievable, and that they need not be impossible fantasies. Rick feared that therapy may reawaken what he viewed as false hopes; that is, goal setting may remind him of the frustration he experienced with previous ambitions. Now that he had found a perceived level of comfort by distancing himself from desires and withdrawing from others, it was important therapeutically not to let matters remain at the level of depressive-anxious adjustment to which he had become accustomed.

Antidepressant medication was a useful targeted instrument in moderating his persistent dejection and pessimism. At the *cognitive-behavioral* level, therapeutic attention was usefully directed to Rick's depressogenic assumptions, anxious demeanor, self-deprecating attitudes, and behavior that may have evoked unhappiness, self-contempt, and derogation in the past. Short-term and focused *cognitive* techniques such as those developed by Beck, Meichenbaum, and Ellis helped reduce his sensitivity to rebuff and his morose and unassertive style, outlooks and fears that only reinforced his aversive and depressive inclinations.

To diminish or even prevent relapse, more focused procedures were used in reconstructing the erroneous beliefs and interpersonal mechanisms that pervaded all aspects of Rick's behavior. *Interpersonal* therapies such as those of Klerman and Benjamin were especially productive. Similarly, short-term *group therapy* assisted him in learning new attitudes and skills in a more benign and accepting social setting than he normally encountered. Along the same lines, *family* techniques may have been employed as circumscribed methods to moderate destructive patterns of communication that contributed to or intensified his social problems.

Short-term techniques also focused attention on his depressive tendencies to demean his self-worth and subject himself to the mistreatment of others. All supportive measures were used to counteract Rick's hesitation about sustaining a consistent therapeutic relationship. Maneuvers designed to test the sincerity of the therapist were sometimes evident. A warm and accepting attitude was needed because Rick feared facing his feelings of unworthiness and because he sensed that his coping defenses were weak. With skillful supportive approaches, it was possible to prevent his tendency to withdraw from treatment before any real gains were made. Cognitive methods were especially useful in exploring the contradictions in his feelings and attitudes. Without reframing techniques such as these, there would have been a seesaw struggle, with periods of temporary progress followed by retrogression. Genuine short-term gains were achieved, but only with a building of trust and the enhancing of his shaky sense of self-worth, both of which lent themselves well to brief cognitive procedures.

Another realm worthy of short-term attention was associated with Rick's extensive scanning and misinterpretation of the environment. By doing this, he increased the likelihood that he would encounter those troubling events he wished to avoid. Moreover, his exquisite and negatively oriented antennae picked up and intensified what most people simply overlooked. In effect, his hypersensitivity backfired, becoming an instrument that constantly brought to awareness the very pain he wished to escape. Effective, focused cognitive techniques were directed to reduce his vigilance and self-demeaning appraisals and hence diminished rather than intensified his anguish.

SCHIZOTYPAL PERSONALITY: TIMOROUS TYPE (SCHIZOTYPAL WITH AVOIDANT TRAITS)

CASE 21.2, MARK K., 29

Presenting Picture: Mark K., from the very outset, appeared to be entirely displaced from reality. Little could be made at first of his short utterances and disjointed thoughts, but it soon became apparent that he was indulging in a self-constructed fantasy that provided temporary shelter from reality, and also drew outside stimuli from others that validated him as someone real. He was brought to therapy by the police, whom Mark said were always on his case. He further remarked that he could feel their desire to "bust his head," and that they were typical of everyone and everything in their desire to be antagonistic. Mark's stream-of-conscious utterances seemed constructed with the intention of confusing and bewildering others, and he seemed to take some peace and solace in the realization that he was alone in this fantasy, a place where no one else could invade, for the time being. By these bizarre withdrawal tactics, he not only disconcerted others, but managed to evoke unusual responses that fed his need to be validated.

Clinical Assessment: As with his less severe avoidant counterparts, Mark, a *timorous schizotypal* personality, was restrained, isolated, apprehensive, guarded, and shrinking. Protectively, he sought to "kill" his feelings and desires, bind his impulses, and withdraw from social encounters, thereby defending himself from the pain and anguish of interpersonal relationships. His surface apathy and seeming indifference was not, as it is in the insipid schizotypal, owing to an intrinsic lack of sensitivity but to his attempt to restrain, damp down, or deaden excessive sensitivity. In addition to his social isolation, Mark depreciated his self-worth. There was an abandonment of self and a disowning and remoteness from feeling and desire. His "real" self had been devalued and demeaned, split off, cast asunder, and rejected as humiliating or valueless. Not only was he alienated from others, then, but he found no refuge or comfort in turning to himself. His isolation thus was twofold. So little was gained from others, and only a despairing sense of shame was found within himself. Without the rewards of self or others to spur him, Mark drifted into personal apathy and social isolation. As described previously, his timorous schizotypal pattern either emerged from or was interwoven with the more basic avoidant personality style.

Having little hope of gaining affection and security, Mark learned that it was best to deny real feelings and aspirations. Cognitive processes were intentionally confused in an effort to disqualify and discredit rational thinking. In their stead were substituted fantasy worlds that provided some respite from the anguish of realistic thought. But this, too, held brief interest because the outer world kept intruding and "shamed" him back to reality.

Disharmonious affects, irrelevant and tangential thoughts, and an increasingly severe social bankruptcy forced Mark to build an ever tighter armor around himself. His characteristic eccentricities derived from this wall of isolation and insularity that he had constructed. Like the insipid schizotypal, he was subject to the devastating terror of "nothingness," the feeling of imminent nonexistence. By insulating himself, shrinking his world, and deadening his sensitivities, he laid the groundwork for feeling emptiness and unreality. To counter the anxieties of depersonalization and derealization, he was driven into excited and bizarre behaviors, contrived peculiar and hallucinating images, and shouted utterly unintelligible but beseeching sounds, all in an effort to draw attention and affirm his existence as a living being. He maneuvered irrationally just to evoke a response from others, created a stir simply to prove that he was real and not a mirage of an empty, floating automaton such as he sensed himself to be. Failing in this effort to quiet his anxieties, as is likely, he turned to a "make-believe" world of superstitions, magic, and telepathy—anything that he could fashion from imagination that would provide him with a "pseudocommunity" of fantasized persons and objects to which he could safely relate.

Synergistic Treatment Plan: Establishment of a safe environment would be a primary goal in the initial phases of treatment for Mark, as he demonstrated a very high *active-pain* orientation that manifested in very erratic reactions. *Biophysical* treatment would be in order to decrease the frequency and intensity of phobic anxieties and illusory scenarios. A *self-image* focus, nondirective in nature, would begin the process toward more focused milieus. As trust would develop, the therapist would work gradually towards undermining perpetuating autistic *cognitions* that kept him in a constant state of actively withdrawing. Efforts would be made toward enhancing *self,* as well, through combined cognitive and *interpersonal* measures, which would also encourage autonomy and social interaction. Possible adjunctive treatments, especially as Mark would become less disjointed and increase his investment in an *other* orientation, might also include *group* and *family* therapy.

Therapeutic Course: A first goal in therapy with Mark was to demonstrate that the potential gains of therapy were real and that they should motivate him rather than serve as a deterrent. Mark feared that therapy would reawaken what he viewed as false hopes; that is, it would remind him of the humiliation he experienced when he offered his trust to others but received rejection in return. By nondirectively acknowledging these fears, the therapist was able to guide Mark to a modest level of comfort without having to distance himself from the therapist, thus learning to deal more effectively with his fears while maintaining a better level of adjustment than that to which he had become accustomed. Additionally, a *pharmacologic* (neuroleptic) regimen helped to alleviate anxiety-producing illusions.

In a short-term *cognitive-behavioral* approach, attention was usefully directed to Mark's social hesitation, anxious demeanor, and self-deprecating actions, attitudes, and behavior that could be altered so as not to evoke the humiliation and derogation they had in the past. Cognitive efforts to reframe the basis of his sensitivity to rebuff and his fearful and unassertive behavior (e.g., Beck, Ellis) minimized and diminished not only his aversive inclinations but his tendency to relapse and regress.

More probing yet circumscribed and brief treatment procedures were useful in unearthing the roots of Mark's anxieties and confronting those assumptions and expectations that pervaded many aspects of his behavior. *Family* techniques may also have been employed to moderate destructive patterns of communication that contributed to or intensified his withdrawal and sheltering behaviors. *Interpersonal* techniques (e.g., Benjamin) and *group* therapy may have assisted him in learning new attitudes and skills in a more benign and accepting social setting than he normally encountered.

Focused techniques also addressed Mark's tendencies to demean his self-worth and to mistrust others. Short-term *supportive* methods were used to counteract his ill-disposition to sustain a consistent therapeutic relationship. As noted, maneuvers designed to test the sincerity of the therapist were frequently evident. A warm and empathic attitude was necessary because the patient was likely to fear facing his feelings of unworthiness and because he sensed that his coping defenses were weak. The clinician drew on the client's strengths to prevent him from withdrawing from treatment before any real gains were made. Cognitive procedures were used to explore the contradictions in his feelings and attitudes. Without proper reframing, there may have been a seesaw struggle, with periods of temporary progress followed by retrogression. Genuine short-term gains will be possible, but only with careful work, a building of trust, and enhancement of the patient's sense of self-worth.

Another realm worthy of brief intervention was associated with Mark's extensive scanning of the environment. By doing this, he increased the likelihood that he would encounter those stimuli he wished to avoid. His exhibited a hypersensitivity to what most people simply overlooked or were not even aware of. Again, via appropriate cognitive methods, his extreme sensibility was prevented from backfiring, that is, becoming an instrument that constantly brought to awareness the very pain he wished to escape. Reorienting his focus and his negative interpretive habits to ones that were more ego-enhancing and optimistic in character reduced his self-demeaning outlook, intensified his positive experiences, and diminished his anguish.

Risks and Resistances

Both insipid and timorous schizotypals have poor prognostic prospects. Although great therapeutic gains can be made with some mildly affected individuals, many more do not alter their core personality. The pattern is deeply ingrained, if not strongly genetically predisposed. These patients rarely live in an encouraging or supportive environment. Probing into personal matters is experienced as painful or even terrifying. Schizotypals distrust close personal relationships such as occur in most forms of psychotherapy. Therapy sets up what they see as false hopes and necessitates painful self-exposure.

Most would rather let matters be, keep to themselves, and remain insulated from the potential of further humiliation and anguish. Should they enter treatment, timorous schizotypals tend to be guarded, constantly testing the therapist's sincerity. Excessive probing into the patient's sensitivities or another "false move" is likely to be interpreted as an attack or as verification of the disinterest and deprecation the patient has learned to anticipate from others.

Trust is therefore essential. Without a feeling of confidence in the genuineness of the therapist's motives, these patients will block the therapist's efforts and, ultimately, terminate treatment. Equally important is that the patient find a supportive social environment. Treatment will be difficult enough, a long and uphill battle, unless external conditions are favorable.

CHAPTER TWENTY-TWO

Treating Borderline Personality Patterns

From our perspective, the borderline concept is best used to represent a structurally defective and severe level of functioning that may occur in virtually any of the personality disorders (perhaps with the exception of the schizoid and compulsive styles). Most frequently, however, the borderline personality appears as an advanced dysfunctional variant of the dependent, histrionic, antisocial, sadistic, and, most commonly, the negativistic personality. Regardless of the background personality history, borderlines are characterized by intense, variable moods and irregular energy levels, both of which frequently appear to be only moderately related to external events. The affective state characteristically may be either depressed or excited or noted by recurring periods of dejection and apathy, interspersed with episodes of anger, anxiety, or euphoria. There is a notable fear of separation and loss with considerable dependency reassurance required to maintain psychic equilibrium. Dependence on others is colored with strong ambivalent feelings, such as love, anger, and guilt. Chronic feelings of anxiety may be present as borderlines struggle between feelings of anger and shame at being so dependent, and fears that self-assertion will endanger the security and protection they so desperately seek. In an attempt to secure their anger and constrain their resentment, borderlines often turn against themselves in self-critical, condemnatory manner, which at times may lead to self-mutilating and suicidal thoughts as well as self-damaging behaviors.

As a result of their instability of both affect and behavior, borderlines are prone to rather checkered histories in their personal relationships and in school and work performance. Most exhibit repeated setbacks, a lack of judgment and foresight, tendencies to digress from earlier aspirations, and failures to utilize their natural aptitudes and talents. For the most part, despite their setbacks, borderlines manage to recoup and regain their equilibrium before slipping into a more pernicious and serious decompensation. At times, however, when overwhelmed with mounting internal pressures, the borderline's tenuous controls may break down, resulting in an eruption of bizarre behaviors, irrational impulses, and delusional thoughts. These minipsychotic episodes tend to be brief and reversible and seem to assist borderlines in regaining their psychic balance. Afterward, such episodes are usually recognized by the individual as being peculiar or deviant.

As noted earlier, overt and direct expressions of hostility in borderlines tend to be exhibited only impulsively, for fear that such actions might result in abandonment or rejection. A characteristic form of anger control in these individuals is to turn feelings of resentment inward into hypochondriacal disorders and mild depressive episodes. Borderlines tend to overplay their helplessness and anguish, employing their depression as a means of avoiding responsibilities and placing added burdens on others. Their exaggerated plight causes guilt and discomfort among family and friends, as they try to meet the borderline's "justified" need for attention and care. As with negativistic personalities, the dour moods and excessive complaints of the borderline may evoke exasperation and rebuke from others. In this event, borderlines may turn their anger on themselves even more intensely, voicing a flood of self-deprecatory comments about their worthlessness, evilness, and their inordinate demands on others. This self-derision may be accompanied by thinly veiled suicidal threats, gambling, drug abuse, or other impulsively self-damaging acts that not only serve to discharge anger, but often succeed in eliciting forgiveness and reassurance if not compassion from others.

Agitated depressions are common, with the borderline exhibiting an apprehensive and tense despondency, accompanied by a querulous irritability and hostile depressive complaints. Some borderlines may demonstrate a more intropunitive, self-deprecatory depression, manifest by expressions of self-doubt, feelings of unworthiness, delusions of shame and sin, and suicidal thoughts. In other borderlines, a retarded form of depression is expressed, where guilt and self-disparagement is accompanied by lethargy, feelings of emptiness, boredom, and "deadness."

As borderlines' moods are quite changeable and inconsistent with their thoughts and actions, it is virtually impossible for others to comprehend or empathize with their experiences. In their more euphoric moments, borderlines' zestful energy and joviality may temporarily engage and entertain others. The irrational, self-expansive quality of borderlines' forced sociability, along with their lapses into irritability, eventually exasperate and drain others, however, destroying any patience or goodwill that was previously evoked.

One group of contemporary biological researchers, led by Akiskal (1981, 1983), has also argued strongly for the inclusion of the borderline syndrome within the subaffective spectrum. On the basis of affective family history, positive dexamethasone suppression test findings, major affective episodes, and high risk of suicide during prospective follow-up, Akiskal (1983) has suggested that approximately 50% of patients with severe characterologic disturbances subsumed under the "borderline" rubric seem to suffer from lifelong affective disorders. He suggests that although about one-fifth of borderline patients do suffer severe, primary characterological pathology in the form of somatization disorder and sociopathy, the largest group of borderlines exhibit "atypical, chronic and complicated forms of affective disorder with a secondary personality dysfunction" (Akiskal, 1981, p. 31). Akiskal argues that although such patients may superficially present the picture of a personality disorder, an underlying biological affective illness may be "masked" by characterologic disturbances. He proposes a variety of subaffective disorders that may fall within the borderline realm. According to Akiskal, subaffective disorders, as opposed to major affective disorders, manifest only subsyndromal and intermittent (often lifelong) affective psychopathology, which only infrequently crystallizes into discrete syndromal episodes. The mood changes associated with such disorders may be quite subtle, with behavioral and interpersonal disturbances (in part having resulted from the affective instability) dominating the clinical picture.

Both Akiskal (1981) and Millon (1981) have proposed that the unstable sense of self that is characteristic of the borderline may be less an ego development problem and more a consequence of a constitutional affective disorder with associated unpredictable, uncontrollable mood swings. It is further suggested that the borderline's relatively poor response to psychotherapy may result, in many cases, from a failure to provide pharmacologic treatment of the underlying affective disorder. Stone (1980) also cites the similarities of the two disorders, observing that a large number of cyclothymic patients, in addition to having depressive and hypomanic bouts, favorably respond to lithium, and that relatives with bipolar or unipolar illness also exhibit characteristics that meet the criteria for borderline personality disorder.

As described by Akiskal (1981), the borderline personality features an unstable sense of self, stemming from disturbances in the individuation-separation phase of development:

> The disorder is conceptualized in characterologic terms and defined by impulsivity, drug-seeking behavior, polymorphous sexuality, affective lability (i.e., display of unmodulated affects such as rage and panic), boredom, anhedonia, bizarre attempts at self-harm and "micropsychotic episodes." (p. 25)

It will be of interest to review the borderline personality construct with reference to the evolutionary model presented in the polarity schema of Figure 22.1. Worthy of note is that all of the usual motives and aims reflected in the model are present, albeit to a moderate degree. What is most significant is that all three pairs of polarities are in conflict, as indicated by the double-pointed arrows between them. This signifies the intense ambivalence and inconstancy that characterize borderlines, their emotional

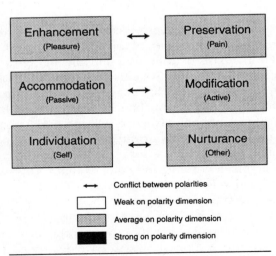

Figure 22.1   Status of the borderline personality prototype in accord with the Millon Polarity Model.

vacillation, their behavioral unpredictability, and the inconsistency they manifest in their feelings and thoughts about others.

This conflictual pattern contrasts with the other two severe or structural pathologies, the schizotypal and paranoid. The borderline possesses distinct inclinations, but they clash and are disharmonious; hence, the borderline switches back and forth, going from one direction to its opposite. By contrast, the intensity of the polarity inclinations in schizotypals is diffuse and undirected, hence producing the randomness and eccentricity that characterizes their thoughts, feelings, and behaviors. In paranoids, the structural problem is one of rigidity and compartmentalization; there is an unbending and unvarying character to their polarity inclinations, an unwillingness to change their attitudes, behaviors, and emotions despite good reasons to do so. No such difficulty is evident in borderlines. In their case, each polarity position is but a temporary one, quickly jettisoned for its opposite.

As has been noted, the severe or structural pathologies, which include the schizotypal, paranoid, and borderline disorders, almost invariably coexist with one or another of the stylistic personality disorders: avoidant, histrionic, negativistic, and so on. Hence, in evaluating a patient with distinct but conflictual structural defects that characterize the borderline, it is necessary to consider which stylistic personality pattern is also present. The polarity model requires the integration of both stylistic polarity features and structural borderline defects. A fusion of the two, style and structure, is necessary for a thorough and accurate assessment.

CLINICAL PICTURE

Patients categorized as borderline personalities display an unusually wide variety of clinical symptoms (see Table 22.1). However, certain elements stand out and are common to most; these will be noted shortly. As with the preceding structurally defective personality, the schizotypal, we introduce these features first by dividing them into three broad categories: primary source of anxiety; cognitive processes and preoccupations; and general mood and behavior. Further differentiations will be made in terms of the eight basic clinical domains (see Figure 22.2).

Separation anxiety. Borderline personalities are exceedingly dependent; not only do they require a great deal of protection, reassurance, and encouragement from others to maintain their equanimity, but they are inordinately vulnerable to separation from these external sources of support.

Separation and isolation can be terrifying not only because borderlines do not value themselves or use themselves as a source of positive reinforcement, but because they lack the wherewithal, know-how, and equipment for independence and self-determination. Unable to fend for themselves, they not only dread signs of potential loss but anticipate it and distort their perceptions so that they see loss where, in fact, there is none. Moreover, because borderlines devalue their own self-worth, it is difficult for them to believe that others can value them; as a consequence, they are exceedingly fearful that others will depreciate them and cast them off.

With so shaky a foundation of self-esteem and lacking the means for an autonomous existence, these patients remain constantly on edge, prone to the

TABLE 22.1 Clinical Domains of the Borderline Personality Prototype

Behavioral Level

(F) Expressively Spasmodic (e.g., displays a desultory energy level with sudden, unexpected, and impulsive outbursts; abrupt, endogenous shifts in drive state and inhibitory controls; not only places activation and emotional equilibrium in constant jeopardy, but engages in recurrent suicidal of self-mutilating behaviors).

(F) Interpersonally Paradoxical (e.g., although needing attention and affection, is unpredictably contrary, manipulative, and volatile, frequently eliciting rejection rather than support; frantically reacts to fears of abandonment and isolation, but often in angry, mercurial, and self-damaging ways).

Phenomenological Level

(F) Cognitively Capricious (e.g., experiences rapidly changing, fluctuating, and antithetical perceptions or thoughts concerning passing events, as well as contrasting emotions and conflicting thoughts toward self and others, notably love, rage, and guilt; vacillating and contradictory reactions are evoked in others by virtue of one's behaviors, creating, in turn, conflicting and confusing social feedback).

(S) Uncertain Self-Image (e.g., experiences the confusions of an immature, nebulous, or wavering sense of identity, often with underlying feelings of emptiness; seeks to redeem precipitate actions and changing self-presentations with expressions of contrition and self-punitive behaviors).

(S) Incompatible Objects (e.g., internalized representations comprise rudimentary and extemporaneously devised but repetitively aborted learnings, resulting in conflicting memories, discordant attitudes, contradictory needs, antithetical emotions, erratic impulses, and clashing strategies for conflict reduction).

Intrapsychic Level

(F) Regression Mechanism (e.g., retreats under stress to developmentally earlier levels of anxiety tolerance, impulse control, and social adaptation; among adolescents, is unable to cope with adult demands and conflicts, as evident in immature if not increasingly infantile behaviors).

(S) Split Organization (e.g., inner structures exist in a sharply segmented and conflictful configuration in which a marked lack of consistency and congruency is seen among elements; levels of consciousness often shift and result in rapid movements across boundaries that usually separate contrasting percepts, memories, and affects, all of which leads to periodic schisms in what limited psychic order and cohesion may otherwise be present, often resulting in transient, stress-related psychotic episodes).

Biophysical Level

(S) Labile Mood (e.g., fails to accord unstable mood level with external reality; has either marked shifts from normality to depression to excitement, or has periods of dejection and apathy, interspersed with episodes of inappropriate and intense anger, as well as brief spells of anxiety or euphoria).

F refers to Functional Domains (fluid, interactive)
S refers to Structural Domains (stable, unchanging)

anxiety of separation and ripe for feelings of inevitable desertion. Any event that stirs up these feelings may precipitate a psychotic episode, most notably that of depression or excitement.

Cognitive conflict and guilt. Matters are bad enough for borderlines, given their separation anxiety, but these patients are also in conflict regarding their dependency needs and often feel guilt for having tried to be self-assertive. In contrast to their mildly pathological counterparts who have found a measure of success utilizing their strategies, borderline patients have been less fortunate, and have

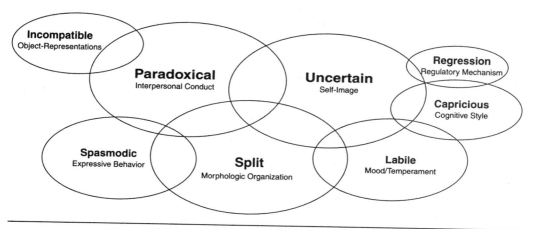

Figure 22.2   Salience of prototypal borderline domains.

struggled hard to achieve the few rewards they have sought. Moreover, in their quest for security and approval, most of them have been subjected to periods of isolation and separation; as a result, many have acquired feelings of distrust and hostility toward others.

Borderlines cannot help but be anxious. To assert themselves would endanger the rewards they so desperately seek from others and perhaps even provoke others to totally reject and abandon them; yet, given past experiences, borderlines know they can never fully trust others nor hope to gain all the affection and support they need. Should they be excessively anxious about separation and therefore submit to protect themselves against desertion, they will still feel insecure; moreover, they will experience anger toward those on whom they depend because of these others' power over them, for "forcing" them to yield and acquiesce. To complicate matters, this very resentment becomes a threat to borderlines; if they are going to appease others as a means of preventing abandonment, they must take great pains to assure that their anger does not get out of hand. Should these resentments be discharged, even in so innocuous a form as displays of self-assertion, their security may be undermined and severely threatened. Thus, borderlines find themselves in a terrible bind: Should they "go it" alone, no longer depending on others who have been so unkind, or should they submit for fear of losing what little security they can eke out?

To secure their anger and constrain their resentment, borderlines often turn against themselves and are self-critical and self-condemnatory. They begin to despise themselves and to feel guilty for their offenses, unworthiness, and contemptibility. They impose on themselves the same harsh and deprecatory judgments they anticipate from others. Thus, we see in these patients not only anxiety and conflict but overt expressions of guilt, remorse, and self-belittlement.

Mood and behavior vacillation. The most striking feature of borderlines is the intensity of their moods and the frequent changeability of their behaviors. These *rapid* swings from one mood and behavior to another are *not* typical of the borderline; they characterize periods in which there is a break in control or what we have referred to as a psychotic episode. More commonly, these patients exhibit a single dominant mood, usually a self-ingratiating and depressive tone that, on occasion, gives way to brief displays of anxious agitation, euphoric activity, or outbursts of hostility.

Prototypal Diagnostic Domains

Patients categorized as borderline personalities display a wide variety of clinical features. Certain elements do stand out as relatively distinct and these are the prime focus in this section. As in prior chapters, these characteristics are separated into several domains of clinical significance.

Spasmodic behavior.   Although the erratic qualities of the borderline are conceived as primarily of an emotional character, it is in all aspects of their behavior that we see high levels of inconsistency and irregularity. Their dress and their voice show this pattern of vacillation and changeability. One day they are dressed quite appropriately and attractively; the next they are sloppy and disheveled. One day their voice has a spirited and energetic quality to it; the next they are hesitant, slow, and monosyllabic. Borderlines display a desultory energy level, occasioned at times by sudden, unexpected, and impulsive outbursts. Their activation and emotional equilibrium seem to be in constant jeopardy, with endogenous shifts in mood, drive, and inhibitory controls. Given this lack of control and the intensity of their emotional states, it should not be surprising that they are vulnerable to recurrent suicidal or self-mutilating impulses.

It is the unpredictability and the impetuous, erratic, and unreflected impulsivity that characterizes the borderline's tempers and actions, rather than the presence of a pattern of smoothly and repetitively swinging emotions that go from one end of the affective continuum to the other. This brittle, labile, and unsustainable quality contrasts with the cyclical regularity of contrasting moods that is often believed to typify these patients.

Paradoxical interpersonal conduct.   Although borderlines need attention and affection, they act in an unpredictably contrary, manipulative, and volatile manner in their interpersonal relationships. These paradoxical behaviors frequently elicit rejection rather than the support they desperately seek. In an unpredictable and frantic reaction to their fears of abandonment and isolation, borderlines become mercurially angry and explosive, hence damaging their security rather than eliciting the care they seek.

As a secondary consequence of their unsure or unstable self-identities, borderlines have become exceedingly dependent on others, if they were not so already. Not only do they need protection and reassurance to maintain their equanimity, but they become inordinately vulnerable to separation from these external sources of support. Isolation or aloneness may be terrifying not only because borderlines lack an inherent sense of self but because they lack the wherewithal, know-how, and equipment for taking mature, self-determined, and independent action. Unable to fend adequately for themselves, they not only dread potential loss but often anticipate it, seeing loss where, in fact, there is none.

The borderline is more ambivalent about relationships with others than are most personality syndromes. Moreover, these individuals have been less successful in fulfilling their dependency needs, suffering thereby considerably greater separation anxieties. Their concerns are not simply those of gaining approval and affection but of not submitting to others, yet preventing further loss. Because they already are on shaky ground, borderlines' actions are directed less toward accumulating additional reserves of support and esteem than toward preserving the little security they still possess.

At first, borderlines will employ their characteristic coping styles with increased fervor in the hope that they will regain their footing. Some may become martyrs, dedicated and self-effacing persons who are "so good" that they are willing to devote or sacrifice their lives for some greater purpose. The usual goal of these borderlines is to insinuate themselves into the lives of others who will not merely "use" them but need them and therefore not desert them. Self-sacrificing though they may appear to be, these borderlines effectively manipulate others to protect against the separation they dread. Moreover, by "sacrificing" themselves, they not only assure continued contact with others but serve as implicit models for others to be gentle and considerate in return. Virtuous martyrdom, rather than being a sacrifice, is a ploy of submissive devotion that strengthens the attachments borderlines need.

The intolerance of being abandoned and the feeling of emptiness and aloneness consequent to the borderline's failure to maintain a secure and rewarding dependency relationship cumulate into a reservoir of anxiety, conflict, and anger. Like a safety valve, these tensions must be released either slowly or through periodic and often impulsive outbursts against others. Because borderlines seek the goodwill of those on whom they depend, they will try to express their inner tensions subtly and indirectly *at first.* Depression is among the most common of these covert expressions. Thus, the pleading anguish, despair, and resignation voiced by borderlines serve to release tensions and to externalize the torment they feel within themselves. For some, however, depressive lethargy and sulking behavior are a means primarily of expressing anger. Depression serves as an instrument for them to frustrate and retaliate against those who have "failed" them or "demanded too much." Angered by the "inconsiderateness" of others, these borderlines employ their somber and melancholy sadness as a vehicle to "get back" at others or "teach them a lesson." Moreover, by exaggerating their plight and by moping about helplessly, they effectively avoid responsibilities, place added burdens on others, and thereby cause their families not only to take care of them but to suffer and feel guilt while doing so. In addition, the dour moods and excessive complaints of these borderlines infect the atmosphere with tension and irritability, thereby upsetting what equanimity remains among those who have "disappointed" them. Similarly, suicidal threats, gambling, and other impulsively self-damaging acts may function as instruments of punitive blackmail, a way of threatening others that further trouble is in the offing and that they had best "make up" for their prior neglect and thoughtlessness.

Capricious cognitive style. It is characteristic of borderlines to experience rapidly changing, fluctuating, and antithetical perceptions and thoughts concerning persons and passing events. Not only do they experience contrasting emotions, but they have ambivalent attitudes toward themselves and others; for example, they may perceive a spouse with love one moment, feel rage the next, and then experience guilt thereafter. Most problematic is that their vacillating and contradictory perceptions evoke in others similarly conflicting and confusing feedback. This perpetuates the vicious circle of experiencing again and again that which prompted them to their actions in the first place.

A major problem for borderlines is the lack of a consistent purpose or direction for shaping attitudes, behaviors, or emotions. Unable to give coherence to their existence, they have few anchors or guideposts to either coordinate their actions, control their impulses, or construct a goal-oriented means for achieving their desires. Feeling scattered and unintegrated, they vacillate, responding as a child would to every passing interest or whim and shifting from one momentary course to another. In effect, borderlines appear to have deteriorated increasingly toward primary-process thinking. Under the press of upsurging affects and their inability to maintain a clear focus, there is a regression to a psychoticlike thought process, occasionally reflected in quasiparanoid ideation and severe dissociated symptoms.

Uncertain self-image.   It is typical of borderlines to experience the confusions of an immature, nebulous, or wavering sense of identity, often with underlying feelings of emptiness. They have considerable difficulty maintaining a stable sense of "who they are," conveying rapidly shifting presentations of self, or in formulating any clear sense of their personal image. They remain aimless, unable to channel their energies or abilities, incapable of settling down on some path or role that might provide a basis for fashioning a unified and enduring sense of self. Seeking to redeem their precipitate actions and changing self-presentations accounts in part for their expressions of contrition and for their self-punitive behaviors. Likewise, borderlines demonstrate highly contradictory self-representations. These reflect their lack of inner cohesion and the so-called splitting maneuvers that they employ. Portions of their schismatic psyche may be split off and projected onto others as a means of bewildering or controlling them, a defensive maneuver designed in part to create confusion in others that mirrors their own inner ambivalences.

Incompatible objects.   Inferring the internalized representations of the borderline on the basis of their thoughts and behaviors suggests that their inner objects comprise rudimentary and extemporaneously derived dispositions and images. Early learnings regarding significant others are likely to have been repetitively aborted, resulting in conflicting memories, discordant attitudes, contradictory needs, erratic impulses, and clashing strategies for conflict resolution. In effect, their inner templates for perceiving and thinking about current events are composed of complex antithetical dispositions.

Because borderlines are very likely to devalue their self-worth, it is difficult for them to believe that those on whom they have depended in the past could ever have thought well of them. Consequently, at a deep intrapsychic level, they are exceedingly fearful that others will inevitably depreciate them and perhaps cast them off. With so unstable an inner template of self-esteem, and lacking the means for assuring their autonomous existence, borderlines remain constantly on edge, prone to the anxiety of separation and ripe for anticipating inevitable desertion. Being anchored to these internalized objects stirs up deep fears that efforts at restitution such as idealization, self-abnegation, and attention-gaining acts of self-destruction or, conversely, self-assertion and impulsive anger, will inevitably fail. As a result of the schisms that characterize both their overt and covert psychic processes, borderlines fail to recognize that other persons possess a mix of both positive and negative feelings and attitudes. Instead, the inner templates of borderlines are sharply divided, split, so to speak, into polar extremes; that is, others are seen as either totally good or totally bad.

Consequentially, as life experiences progress with significant others, borderlines may alternate on a regular basis between idealizing these persons and then abruptly devaluing them, a process that both reflects their inner schisms and creates erratic shifts in the reactions of others.

Matters are bad enough for borderlines, given their identity diffusion and separation anxieties, but their internalized images and impulses are in intense conflict regarding dependency needs. Not only do they feel guilt for past attempts at self-assertion and independence, but these quests for self-determination and self-identity may have been subjected to ridicule and isolation, resulting in increased feelings of distrust and resentment toward others. Moreover, should they seek to become close to another, two contrasting but distressful consequences come to mind. First, they fear that they will be engulfed by the person, thereby losing what little sense of autonomy and identity they possess. On the other hand, there is the fear that they will, without forewarning, be precipitously abandoned.

Regression mechanism. What is most significant among the regulatory mechanisms employed by the borderline is the tendency to retreat under stress to developmentally earlier levels of anxiety tolerance, impulse control, and social adaptation. Among adolescents who exhibit borderline tendency, we find an inability to cope with adult demands and life's conflicts, as evident in immature, if not increasingly infantile behaviors.

The hostility expressed by borderlines poses a serious threat to their security. To experience resentment toward others, let alone to vent it, endangers them because it may provoke the counterhostility, rejection, and abandonment they fear. Angry feelings and outbursts must not only be curtailed or redirected toward impotent scapegoats but may be intrapsychically reversed and condemned. To appease their conscience and to assure expiation, they may reproach themselves for their faults and purify themselves to prove their virtue. To accomplish this regulatory goal, their hostile impulses may be dynamically inverted. Thus, aggressive urges toward others may be turned upon themselves. Rather than vent their anger, they will openly castigate and derogate themselves and voice exaggerated feelings of guilt and worthlessness. These borderlines become notably self-recriminating. They belittle themselves, demean their abilities, and derogate their virtues, not only as a means of diluting their aggressive urges but to assure others that they themselves are neither worthy nor able adversaries. The self-effacement of these borderlines is an attempt, then, both to control their own hostility and to stave off hostility from others.

Among other borderlines, where hostile impulses are more deeply ingrained as a form of self-expression, these feelings must be counteracted more forcefully. Because these patients are likely to have displayed their anger more frequently and destructively, they must work all the harder to redeem themselves. Instead of being merely self-effacing and contrite, they will often turn on themselves viciously, claiming that they are despicable and hateful persons. These condemnatory self-accusations may at times reach delusional proportions, and such patients may reject every rational effort to dissuade them of their culpability. In these cases, it is the struggle to redeem themselves that often leads to self-mutilation and physical destruction.

Split organization. The structural concept termed *split* is especially apt in characterizing the intrapsychic organization of borderlines. Their mind comprises inner structures that exist in sharply segmented and conflictful configurations. There is a marked lack of systematic order and congruency among the elements of the mind. Levels of consciousness often shift to and fro. Similarly, rapid movements take place across boundaries that should separate contrasting perceptions, memories, and affects. This lack of control and cohesion produces periodic but serious schisms in psychic order and cohesion, resulting in a susceptibility to transient, stress-related psychotic episodes.

Borderlines cannot help but be intrapsychically ambivalent. To assert themselves endangers the security and protection they desperately seek from others by provoking the latter to reject and abandon them. Yet, given their past, they know they can never entirely trust others nor fully hope to gain the security and affection they need. Should their anxiety about separation lead them to submit as a way of warding off or forestalling desertion, they expose themselves to even further dependency and, thereby, an even greater threat of loss. Moreover, they know they experience intense anger toward those on whom they depend, not only because it shames them and exposes their weakness but also because of others' power in having "forced" them to yield and acquiesce. This very resentment becomes then a threat in itself. If they are going to appease others to prevent abandonment, they must take pains to assure that their anger remains under control. Should this resentment be discharged, even in innocuous forms of self-assertion, their security will be severely threatened. They are in a terrible bind. Should they "strike out" alone, no longer dependent on others who have expected too much or have demeaned them, or should they submit for fear of losing what little security they can gain thereby?

To secure their anger and to constrain their resentment, borderlines often turn against themselves in a self-critical and self-condemnatory manner. Despising themselves, they voice the same harsh judgments they have learned to anticipate from others. They display not only anxiety and conflict but overt expressions of guilt, remorse, and self-belittlement. It is these feelings that occasionally take hold, overwhelm them, and lead to the characteristic self-damaging and periodic self-destructive acts.

Labile mood.   The most striking characteristic of borderlines is the intensity of their affect and the changeability of their actions. Most fail to accord their unstable mood levels with external reality. They tend to show marked shifts from normality to depression to excitement. There are periods of dejection and apathy, interspersed with episodes of inappropriate and intense anger, followed by brief spells of anxiety or euphoria.

Rapid shifts from one mood and attitude to another are not inevitable aspects of the everyday behavior of the borderline, but they do characterize extended periods when there has been a break in control. Most borderlines exhibit a single, dominant outlook or frame of mind, such as a self-ingratiating depressive tone, which gives way periodically, however, to anxious agitation or impulsive outbursts of temper or resentment. Self-destructive and self-damaging behaviors, not too infrequent, are usually recognized subsequently as having been irrational and foolish.

Self-Perpetuation Processes

As in prior chapters, this section describes how aspects of the behavioral style of the personality pattern under discussion perpetuate and intensify the difficulties that characterize that personality.

It is difficult to see the utility of any of the borderline's characteristic behaviors, let alone to grasp what gains the patient may derive by vacillating among them. Clinging helplessness, resentful stubbornness, hostile outbursts, pitiable depression, and self-denigrating guilt seem notably wasteful and self-destructive. Although these genuinely felt emotions are instrumentally useful in eliciting attention and approval, releasing tensions, wreaking revenge, and avoiding permanent rejection by redeeming oneself through contrition and self-derogation, they ultimately intensify and subvert the borderline's efforts for a better life.

Despite short-term gains, these behaviors are self-defeating in the end. By their affective instability and self-deprecation, these patients avoid confronting and resolving their real interpersonal difficulties. Their coping maneuvers are a double-edged sword, relieving passing discomforts and strains, but in the long run fostering the perpetuation of faulty attitudes and strategies. It will be instructive to outline several of the dysfunctional efforts the borderline exhibits in seeking to overcome his or her difficulties (see Table 22.2).

Countering separation.   In contrast to their milder counterparts, borderlines have been less successful in fulfilling dependency needs, suffering, thereby, considerably greater separation anxieties. As a consequence, their concerns are not simply those of gaining approval and affection, but of preventing further loss; because they are already on shaky ground, their actions are directed less toward accumulating a reserve of support and esteem than of preserving the little security they still possess.

At first, borderlines will employ their characteristic strategies with even greater vigor than usual. Whichever style typifies their established personality pattern will be applied with increased fervor in the hope of regaining footing with others. Thus, borderlines with *self-destructive* and *discouraged* styles may begin to view themselves as martyrs, dedicated and self-effacing persons who are "so good" that they are willing to sacrifice their lives for a higher or better cause. This they do, but not for the reasons they rationalize. Their goal is to insinuate themselves into the lives of others, to attach themselves to someone who will not only "use" them, but need them, and therefore not desert them. Self-sacrificing though they may appear to be, these borderlines have effectively manipulated the situation so as to assure against the separation they dread. Furthermore, by demeaning themselves, they not only assure contact with others, but

---

TABLE 22.2   Self-Perpetuating Processes

BORDERLINE

Countering Separation
> Insinuates self into lives of others
> Demeans self to gain empathic attention
> Repeatedly reverses coping strategies

Releasing Tensions
> Externalizes inner fright and torment
> Sulking expresses anger and retaliation
> Moping makes others feel guilty

Redemption through Self-Derogation
> Resentments may provoke abandonment threats
> Reproaches self to achieve expiation
> Castigates self to justify worthless feelings

often stimulate them to be gentle and considerate in return. Virtuous martyrdom, rather than being a sacrifice, is a means of exploiting the generosity and responsibility of others, a ploy of submissive devotion that strengthens attachments.

But what if the borderline's efforts fail to counter the anxiety of separation? What occurs when exaggerations of his or her characteristic strategy fail to produce or strengthen the attachments the borderline needs?

Under these conditions, we often observe a brief period in which patients renunciate their lifelong coping style. For example, *discouraged* borderlines, rather than being weak and submissive, may reverse their more typical behaviors and assert themselves, becoming frivolous, demanding, or aggressive. They may employ a new and rather unusual mode of coping as a substitute method for mastering the anxiety of separation. Unable to quiet their fears, faced with situations that refuse to be solved by their habitual adaptive style, and discouraged and annoyed at the futility of using them, discouraged borderlines disown them, divest themselves of these deficient coping devices, and supplant them with dramatically new instrumentalities. Their goal remains the same, that of denying or controlling anxiety, but they have "found" a new strategy by which to achieve it, one that is diametrically opposed to that used before. It is this shifting from one strategy to another that in part accounts for the variable or borderline pattern observed in these patients.

These novel efforts are not only often bizarre, but typically even less effective in the long run than these patients' more established strategies. They have sought to adopt attributes and behaviors that are foreign to their more "natural" self; unaccustomed to the feelings they try to simulate and the behaviors they strive to portray, patients act in an "unreal," awkward, and strained manner with others. The upshot of this reversal in strategy is a failure to achieve their goals, leading to increased anxiety, frustrations, dismay, or hostility. Not only have their simulations alienated them from their real feelings, but the pretensions they display before others have left them vulnerable to exposure and humiliation.

Releasing tensions. The ever present fear of separation and the periodic failure of the borderline to achieve secure and rewarding dependency relationships cumulate an inner reservoir of anxiety, conflict, and hostility. Like a safety valve, these tensions are released either slowly and subtly or through periodic and dramatic outbursts.

Because borderlines seek to retain the goodwill of those on whom they depend, they try at first to express indirectly the inner tensions they experience. Dejection and depression are among the most common forms of such covert expression. The pleading, the anguish, and the expressed despair and resignation of borderlines serve to release inner anxieties and to externalize and vent the fright and torment they sense within themselves.

Of even greater importance, depressive lethargy and sulking behaviors are means of expressing anger. In certain borderline styles, for example, depression may serve as an instrument to frustrate and retaliate against those who now seek to buoy borderlines' spirits. Angered by others' previous failure to be thoughtful and nurturant, these borderlines employ their somber depression as a vehicle to "get back" at others or to "teach them a lesson." By exaggerating their plight and moping about helpless and exhausted, borderlines effectively avoid responsibilities, place added burdens on others, and thereby causes their families not only to care for them, but to suffer and feel guilt while doing so.

Impulsive (histrionic) borderlines vent their anger in similar ways. Because others are accustomed to their gregarious and affable manner, their glum moroseness and sluggish and gloomy manner become doubly frustrating. By withdrawing into a dismal and sullen attitude, they construct a barrier between themselves and others so that others can no longer experience the pleasures of these borderlines' dramatic and cheerful behaviors. Thus, in the form of recalcitrant depression, they gain revenge, punish, sabotage, and defeat those who have failed to appreciate them.

Other borderlines are equally adroit in venting their tensions and expressing their angers. Their frequent fatigue and minor somatic ailments force others not only to be attentive and kind, but, by making them carry excess burdens, to suffer as well. Moreover, the dour moods and excessive complaints of these borderlines infect the atmosphere with tension and irritability, thereby upsetting the equanimity of those who have disappointed them. In the same way, these borderlines' cold and stubborn silence may function as an instrument of punitive blackmail, a way of threatening others that further trouble is in the offing or a way of forcing others to "make up" for the inconsiderations previously shown.

Despite the temporary gains achieved by these indirect forms of tension and hostility discharge, they tend to be self-defeating in the long run. The gloomy, irritable, and stubborn behavior of this borderline wears people down and provokes them to exasperation and anger, which, in turn, will only intensify the anxieties, conflicts, and hostilities the patient feels.

As these more subtle means of discharging negative feelings prove self-defeating, these patients' tensions and depressions mount beyond tolerable limits and they may begin to lose control. Bizarre thoughts and psychotic behaviors may burst forth and discharge a torrential stream of irrational emotion. For example, they may shriek that others despise them, are seeking to depreciate their worth, and are plotting to abandon them. Inordinate demands for attention and reassurance may be made; they may threaten to commit suicide and thereby save others the energy of destroying them slowly. Under similar circumstances, the usually restrained preborderline may burst into vitriolic attacks on his or her loved ones, as deep and previously hidden bitterness and resentment surge into the open. Not unjustifiably, the preborderline accuses others of having aggressed against him or her, protesting that others are contemptuous of and unjustly view him or her as a deception, a fraud, and a failure. Utilizing the distorting process of intrapsychic projection, this patient ascribes to others the weakness and ineptness felt within; it is "they" who have fallen short and who should be punished and humiliated. With righteous indignation, the patient rails outward, castigating, condemning, and denouncing others for their frailty and imperfections.

Redemption through self-derogation.   Borderlines' hostility poses a serious threat to their security. To experience resentment toward others, let alone to vent it, endangers patients because it may provoke the counterhostility, rejection, and abandonment they dread. Angry feelings and outbursts must be not only curtailed but condemned. To appease their conscience and to assure expiation, borderlines must reproach themselves for their faults, purify themselves, and prove their virtue. To accomplish this goal, hostile impulses are inverted; thus, aggressive urges toward others are turned upon themselves. Rather than express their anger, they castigate and derogate themselves and suffer exaggerated feelings of guilt and worthlessness.

Many borderlines are notably self-recriminating; they belittle themselves, demean their competence, and derogate their virtues, not only in an effort to dilute their aggressive urges, but also to assure others that they are neither worthy nor able adversaries. The self-effacement of these borderlines is an attempt, then, to control their hostile outbursts, and to stave off aggression from others. Among other borderlines, where hostile urges are profound and enduring, patients must counteract them more forcefully. Furthermore, because they have displayed anger more frequently and destructively, they must work all the harder to redeem themselves. Instead of being merely self-effacing and contrite, they may turn on themselves viciously, viewing themselves as despicable and hateful. Condemnatory self-accusations may reach delusional proportions in these patients; moreover, they often reject rational efforts to dissuade them of their culpability and dishonor. In some cases, the struggle to redeem themselves may lead to self-mutilation and destruction.

INTERVENTION GOALS

Borderlines are notoriously difficult patients for therapists. They run through the whole gamut of emotions in therapy, and their erratic and frequently threatening behaviors stir countertransference responses in many therapists. Because the risk of burnout is so high, therapists should limit the number of borderline patients in their caseload, if possible. This having been said, however, it should be noted that working with a borderline can prove to be a gratifying experience. Unlike working with some personalities, such as antisocials or schizotypals, with whom the therapist can hope at best only for modestly increased levels of adaptive behavior, borderline disturbances are much more amenable to personality change and reorganization. Many borderlines have a range of highly developed social skills, along with the intrinsic motivation to restrain contrary and troublesome impulses. Therapeutic gains can lead to extended periods of productive functioning and interpersonal harmony in the patient's life, and can provide the therapist with an unusual if not satisfying relationship, as well as the opportunity to see therapeutic goals realized.

As noted previously, and before gauging the patient's prognostic picture and recommending a remedial course of therapy, it is well to remember that borderlines, despite their common defining characteristics, are frequently more severe variants of other personality disorders, notably the negativistic, depressive, histrionic, antisocial, sadistic, and avoidant. As a result, they are even less homogeneous a classification than are other personality disorder categories. Some are well-compensated; most are not. Some are bolstered by supportive families; others face destructive environmental conditions. Despite symptom commonalities, these differences in the clinical picture must be attended to closely to produce effective remedial intervention (see Table 22.3).

Reorganizing the structure of the borderline personality is no trivial undertaking. The clinical picture represents a state of imbalance on all four of the passive-active, other-self, pain-pleasure, and thinking-feeling polarities. Not only are the personality's coping mechanisms ineffective and problem perpetuating, but the lack of consistency leads to identity confusions as well. Personologic domain dysfunctions include the morphological structure of the personality itself, handicapping the borderline above and beyond the difficulties presented by disturbances in the other domains. These many deviations from optimal functioning make the borderline,

TABLE 22.3   Therapeutic Strategies
and Tactics for the Prototypal
Borderline Personality

STRATEGIC GOALS
Balance Polarities
   Reduce conflict between active-passive polarities
   Reduce conflict between pain-pleasure polarities
   Reduce conflict between self-other polarities

Counter Perpetuations
   Reduce capricious emotionality
   Moderate inconsistent attitudes
   Adjust unpredictable behaviors

TACTICAL MODALITIES
   Stabilize paradoxical interpersonal conduct
   Rebuild unstable self-image
   Steady labile moods

along with the schizotypal and paranoid personalities, one of the three more severe disorders of personality. The borderline's characteristic desire for gratifying relationships (unlike the schizotypal) and flexibility in the personality structure (unlike the paranoid), however, work to the borderline's advantage and give this personality an edge over the other two severe variants.

Reestablishing Polarity Balances

Borderlines vacillate between being motivated by pain and pleasure, turning to others and to self for gratification, and taking an active and passive stance in regard to manipulating their environments. Although most borderline patients do have fundamental tendencies toward particular orientations within the polarities, they often adopt diametrically opposed strategies when they find that their usual behavior patterns are not resulting in the desired consequences. For example, a borderline that tends toward dependency can become suddenly aggressive and independent in an effort to "bully" the partner into caretaking behavior. Fluctuation between extremes of dependency and aggression are not likely to produce desired results, however, as they tend to leave significant others confused, frightened, or worse. Additionally, such behavior on the part of the borderline leads to repeatedly undoing and even reversing previous actions. This leaves the patient with distress from failing to secure nurturing responses from others, and increasing feelings of emptiness and confusion from being without a clear sense of who he or she is.

Therapeutic interventions help patients to moderate their vacillations between extreme polarity behaviors until they are stabilized in a more adaptive balance between the active-passive, self-other, and pain-pleasure polarities. An important first step is to gently illustrate the inevitably unfavorable consequences of extreme behaviors, and to help the borderline patient learn more moderate and adaptive coping strategies. Consideration of the particular environmental context, whether deciding between relying on self or others or between passive and active strategies, can prove to be an invaluable skill. Ultimately, a decrease in vacillation between extremes can serve to stabilize not only the borderline's life, but his or her uncertain self-image, providing thereby a more solid grounding to prevent painful and disruptive breaks with reality.

Countering Perpetuating Tendencies

Teaching the borderline patient to overcome the tendency to engage in deeply ingrained problem-perpetuating behavioral strategies is only a first step; the therapist faces the additional challenge of overcoming the largely "unnatural" behaviors that borderlines desperately adopt when their more or less typical behaviors fail to produce desired results. The tactic of reversing their habitual attitudes and roles, whether these be clinging helplessness, resentful stubbornness, hostile outbursts, pitiable depression, or self-denigrating guilt, serves to alienate borderlines even further from their fragile sense of self and their relationships with others. In addition, most people can sense the "unreal" quality of these dramatic behavioral changes, and often fail to respect or respond to the borderline's needs. Even when these momentary reversals provide the patient with attention and support, the long-term effect of these "forced" strategies will likely wear down and exasperate others. Borderlines sense the growth of these unpleasant sentiments in others, becoming thereby more conflicted about what they should do and leading them to be increasingly anxious about potential abandonment.

Once the counterproductive nature of the patient's strategies is grasped, a major therapeutic goal is to help borderlines tolerate the anxiety that causes them to switch from one extreme behavior to another. These extremes represent a frantic desire to discharge anxiety. Learning to contain these feelings long enough to delay responses will provide the time to evaluate whether the perceived threat is real and to choose a healthier response. This serves to eliminate the negative effects of failing to cope adequately with consequent diminished self-esteem and interpersonal dislocations. A painful and disruptive break with reality thereby becomes less likely, extreme reactions more moderate, and opportunities for healthier emotional experiences more probable.

Identifying Domain Dysfunctions

The three most salient domain dysfunctions of the borderline personality are paradoxical interpersonal conduct, split morphologic organization, and uncertain self-image. Borderlines' paradoxical interpersonal conduct is the hallmark of the disorder, the immediate source of the chaos and uncertainty that typifies their life. Although borderlines' overwhelming motivation is to secure attention and nurturance, a fundamental split in the morphologic organization of their personality leads to nonintegrated emotional functioning and cognitive black-and-white thinking. The result is often inconsistent and paradoxical behaviors, such as seen in displays of anger when the prospect of separation is threatened. Although such hostile acts sometimes elicit the desired nurturance in the short term, they greatly increase the probability of abandonment over time.

Such erratic tendencies are further aggravated by the borderline personality's uncertain self-image. This tentative sense of identity creates confusion regarding what behavior is appropriate. When behavioral strategies do not yield desired results, borderlines intensify them; that is, they will try harder, but not necessarily more wisely.

Ultimately, failure compels them to redeem themselves with expressions of contrition and self-punitive behaviors that seek to forestall further rejection. Unfortunately, they also negate important aspects of the self, intensify the uncertainty about their identity, and reinforce the vicious circle of personality decline.

Therapeutic interventions that aim to solidify patients' identity can indirectly lead to decreases in the anxiety produced by the threat of abandonment, and thus can serve to undermine maladaptive behaviors at their source. A stable and solid self-image can also provide grounding and security needed for borderlines to risk exploring the validity of long held and ingrained assumptions, to face the futility of their behavioral patterns, and to motivate them to tolerate useful interventions that may produce temporary increases in anxiety. One consequence of helping patients tolerate anxiety long enough to explore inner conflicts and to experiment with moderate behaviors can be the integration of the many splits within the morphological structure of the personality. Tolerance for unpleasant reactions can also diminish the tendency to regress to earlier modes of coping and anxiety reduction.

Improvements in the primary domain dysfunctions can be bolstered by intervention into the secondary dysfunctional domains. Focusing on altering borderlines' capricious style will help them assess whether the anxiety-provoking environment is actually a product of their own misperceptions and misinterpretations. Life events have been perceived in contradictory ways, leading to inconsistent responses. In turn, individuals associated with the patient have also responded in conflicting ways, leaving the patient with the distressing reality of an unpredictable and seemingly irrational world. Coming to realize that the world is not structured in black-and-white categories is a large part of overcoming the tendency to overreact. If people are seen as either all good or all bad, the appropriate reaction is to either love or hate them; if they do one imperfect thing to negate their goodness, they must by default be bad, and need to be treated as such. Extreme and categorical behavior is thus built on the foundation of extreme categorical thinking. The borderline's incompatible object-representations are an example of such thinking. Examining early memories can lead to insight into antithetical emotions, contradictory needs, and readily aborted schemata about others. Spasmodic expressive acts that reflect impulsive outbursts and abrupt endogenous shifts in drive state can be stabilized also by the former interventions. Although the borderline's labile temperament can often be somewhat stabilized with medication, therapeutic gains in other domains help bring about stability in the structure of the personality that will be reflected in less fluctuating mood states.

SELECTING THERAPEUTIC MODALITIES

Despite changes in the borderline diagnostic conceptions and definitions over time, one aspect has remained stable: therapists have many difficulties dealing with borderline patients. And despite the near inevitability of therapist frustrations, the importance of a solid alliance between therapist and patient cannot be overestimated. More than other personality disorders, borderlines have erratic interpersonal relationships that take a great toll on their lives and that will be mirrored in their relationship with a therapist. These patients' strong positive and negative reactions and rapidly fluctuating attitudes toward the therapist can evoke powerful countertransference responses. The patient may have bouts with therapist idealization and devaluation, threats of legal repercussions, suicidality, self-harm, and other uncontrollable behaviors, each of which may evoke empathy, anger, frustration, fear, and inadequacy feelings.

In the course of either of these troublesome sequences, the therapist may experience a blurring of personal boundaries, an invasion of privacy that leaves him or her at a loss as to what to do. Borderlines may not hesitate to intrude into the therapist's space, ask the therapist for lunch, call him or her at home at off hours, or use abusive tactics to manipulate and "set the therapist up." The patient may plead for inappropriate intimacies and then turn the tables and accuse the therapist of taking advantage of his or her more powerful position. These difficulties should be avoided as much as possible by making it clear at the beginning of therapy that the goal of treatment is to foster independence, and that limits will have to be set to aid its achievement. This does not imply that the therapist should refuse to help or provide support in a crisis, but rather that help should also support the goal of strength building; instead of long hand-holding phone calls and special arrangements, the therapist should offer a supportive but brief reminder of treatment goals, contracts, and gains in therapeutic work. In short, clear limits should be set in the first few sessions. Then the therapist should be as responsive and supportive as possible *within* those clear limits. A failure to be responsive will lead to accusations of abandonment and hypocrisy; overstepping agreed-on boundaries will lead to further testing of the therapist by the patient. Some clients may decide from the beginning that they need a therapist to provide a more nurturant position.

If the patient accepts the therapist's terms, the two can begin working on building an alliance. A good therapeutic relationship can take quite some time to develop. Much can be gained therapeutically as the borderline realizes that not all individuals are dangerous and that not all self-disclosure necessarily leads to being judged unacceptable and worthy of abandonment. Beck and Freeman (1990a) note that the patient's difficulty trusting the therapist cannot be resolved quickly and easily. Explicit acknowledgment of the patient's difficulty with trust, special care to communicate clearly, assertively, and honestly, and especially the maintenance of congruity between verbal and nonverbal cues by the therapist can all help. The importance of a basic attempt to behave in a trustworthy manner cannot be overestimated. Although it may not be appropriate for the therapist to flood clients with information regarding his or her reactions, any strong emotions that the therapist fails to contain should be partially acknowledged, lest the patient find reason to mistrust the therapist.

Many borderlines are uncomfortable with intimacy (due to their basic mistrust of others) and can become quite anxious in therapy if their boundaries are overstepped. It is suggested by Beck and Freeman (1990a) that the therapist solicit clients' feedback regarding how to make therapy more comfortable for them. Many borderlines experience greater comfort with the intimacy involved in the therapeutic process if they feel that they have some control over the pace and the topics discussed.

It is very important to make clear from the beginning of therapy that getting better will not mean that the patient will be thrown out of treatment, and that termination will be a mutual decision. Otherwise, the therapist will be faced with the threat that the patient will feel the need to regress or resist progress to get attention from the therapist. Benjamin (1993) suggests that in the event of such manipulation by the client, whether in the form of lethal attacks or seductive gestures, the appropriate response is to be firm yet nonattacking. The terms of the therapy and its goals should be stated clearly and in a supportive tone, giving patients safe ground despite their habitual emotional turmoil.

Behavioral Techniques

Dialectic behavior therapy (Linehan, 1987, 1992) is conceptually related to several cognitive approaches in that it emphasizes a dialogue between patient and therapist that seeks through persuasion to bring the patient's worldview in line with that of the therapist. To this end, therapist self-disclosure is considered a valid and useful technique. The ultimate goal of therapy is to create a "responsible autonomy" in the patient's attitudes and behaviors; this aim is arrived at gradually by moving through a series of hierarchical steps designed to prevent suicidal and self-injurious behavior, secure a therapeutic alliance, deal with symptoms that disrupt functioning (e.g., substance abuse), counter less disruptive problems in living, and finally, contend with the patient's cognitive schemata (hopes, ambitions, beliefs) and explore healthy psychic reorganization. Linehan's outline for individual therapy includes adjunct group therapy in which behavioral interventions such as skill training, rehearsal, and didactic analysis aim to decrease dependency and improve tolerance for negative feedback and affect.

Proposing an alternative behavioral formulation, Turkat (1990) centers his efforts on strengthening the "problem-solving deficiencies" among borderlines; for example, he recommends systematic training in concept formation, processing speed, and skill training in developing well-structured categories.

Interpersonal Techniques

L.S. Benjamin (1993) sees the interactional pattern of borderline relationships as deriving from the patient's long history and expectation of abandonment, and as a recent consequence of therapist burnout after prolonged but failed attempts to effect significant therapeutic changes. It is when the patient realizes that the therapist will never be able to provide enough nurturance that desperate and extreme behaviors, such as suicidal gestures, cause the therapist to begin to withdraw. The borderline in turn accuses the therapist of not caring and often "ends" therapy in a dangerous and dramatic way. At times, the therapist is held responsible or even threatened with lawsuits. If the patient decides to return to treatment, the therapist may have lost enthusiasm but fear legal repercussions or charges of professional irresponsibility. The vicious circle for continued failure is now set. Another possible pattern is one in which patients start to get better but fear that improvements will lead to being "kicked out" of therapy. They will therefore preemptively regress.

The approach outlined by L.S. Benjamin (1993) places great emphasis on the development of a solid alliance. The next therapy objective is for the patient to recognize his or her maladaptive patterns. Dream analysis, free association, role-plays, and discussion may all help achieve this goal. Helping the borderline understand the connection between his or her present symptomatic behavior and early history can bring relief and generate motivation. Validating the patient's sense of reality about having been victimized (often refuted by family members) can also help set the patient on the path toward healing. Any guilt the borderline feels needs to be acknowledged as normal, although his or her role in supposedly "asking for" early abuse needs to be clarified as being patently false. Once the maladaptive patterns are recognized, therapist and patient need to work on blocking them. The therapist can point out to the borderline that a "nose dive" often follows periods when things go well in therapy. Plans can be made for averting or at least minimizing damaging actions. The reasons for self-destructive behavior can be uncovered by examining internal fantasies; parents are appeased, and abusers realize that they are still loved and will be good to the patient. Benjamin suggests strengthening the will to resolve old attachments by asking penetrating questions such as "Do you still love your brother (or any significant other) enough to give him this (self-destructive result)?"

Family intervention is often useful when the borderline has frequent interaction with parents or other family members who are overinvolved but not supportive of the patient's individual therapy. In these cases, borderlines often feel guilty about being disloyal to the family and terminate therapy prematurely. Involving the family in helping the patient with his or her "problem" by not reinforcing dependent behavior can help tremendously in meeting treatment objectives. In families where abuse and/or incest has led to symptomatology (more common), there is often strong resistance to participate. Independent meetings with the parents may be required to emphasize that family intervention will be focused on increasing the patient's independence, not on blaming parents or other family members.

Group approaches have some benefits that are not provided by dyadic therapy and, therefore, often serve as a useful adjunct to individual intervention. A peer group is less likely than an individual therapist to be accused of being controlling or of having bad intentions when confronting maladaptive patterns. This rich interpersonal setting also provides a wealth of opportunities for these persons to act out and be identified as erratic and labile. On the other hand, new behaviors can often be actively encouraged by the group and can be practiced in this generally supportive setting. However, the borderline may need individual therapeutic support to deal with group-generated stress, as well as to internalize the feelings the group often provokes. It is not uncommon for borderlines to be scapegoated owing to their behavioral and emotional inconsistencies; also troublesome are competitive and envious feelings regarding the presumed success of others in attracting the leader's affections. Some theorists suggest that the individual therapist *not* be the group therapist in order to reduce the likelihood that fantasies of favoritism may be engendered. Also wise is that groups be heterogeneous, preferably with most of the members being higher-functioning individuals than is the borderline. On the other hand, some therapists suggest that homogeneous groups composed entirely of borderlines may also prove successful.

Cognitive Techniques

In their book outlining cognitive interventions with personality disorders, Beck and Freeman (1990a) note that one of the initial setbacks in working with borderlines is that their lack of clear identity makes it difficult for them to set goals and maintain priorities from week to week. Beck and Freeman suggest that a focus on concrete behavioral goals is a useful initial therapeutic intervention for several reasons. The patient does not need to reveal deeply personal thoughts and feelings before trust can be established, and initial success can provide motivation to continue in therapy. As therapy shifts to more extensive goals, the therapist may find that the patient's concerns and goals change from week to week; discussion about the advantages of keeping focused, or about setting aside time in each session for immediate as well as long-term problems can be very helpful. The therapist should make a special effort to point to underlying commonalities among problems as they come up, attempting thereby to illustrate the presence of persistent behavioral and cognitive patterns to the patient.

It is sometimes difficult to convince borderline patients to complete homework assignments. Discussing advantages and disadvantages of trying out new behaviors often helps patients feel as though the therapist is not trying to control or manipulate them. Asking patients to pay attention to their thoughts at those times when they decide *not* to do their homework can help identify what may be disturbing or obstructing progress. Sometimes, therapists find that they are ascribing incorrect intentions to patients, thinking that they do not want to get better. Careful consideration of the meaning of noncompliance for the patient may need to be evaluated before it can be overcome.

A main therapeutic focus of cognitive therapy with borderline clients is decreasing their dichotomous thinking. Borderlines tend to think in terms of discrete categories such as "good," "bad," "reliable," and "unreliable" rather than more realistic, continuous dimensions. Beck and Freeman (1990a) recommend pointing out to patients examples of their black-and-white thinking, and then asking them to consider whether in their experience it is reality-based. One example provided involves asking a patient to provide a description of the salient polarities "trustworthy" and "not trustworthy." After the patient defines these extremes operationally, therapist and client examine whether people actually exhibit constant trustworthy or untrustworthy behavior, and the patient realizes that although some may be more trustworthy than others, very few are always or never reliable. Examination of the patient's own behavior and motivation can help clarify that not all instances of so-called unreliable behavior are motivated by bad intentions or lack of concern for others.

Effecting a decrease in dichotomous thinking leads to a decrease in the intensity and vacillation of moods, as problem situations are not evaluated in such extreme terms. Additional methods to control nonadaptive emotional symptoms can also be taught. Many borderlines believe that if they express anger or other unpleasant emotions, they will be jeopardizing their relationships. They suppress those feelings until they erupt in ways that generate negative consequences and reinforce the conviction that expressing emotions causes problems. The therapist can encourage the patient to express negative feelings in moderate ways and provide feedback and consequences that help speed the accomplishment of therapeutic goals.

Building a collaborative relationship is most difficult with these emotionally unstable patients. Fostering this goal depends on the therapist's willingness to both acknowledge and accept the patient's untrusting attitude. Therapists should communicate their thoughts honestly and clearly, as well as display consistency by following through on all implicit or explicit agreements. Believing that the world is an inconsistent and troublesome place, most borderlines fear that they will inevitably be abandoned by others. Despite the borderline's inconsistent behaviors and erratic emotions, change should be pressed, but only in a series of small steps. Fears about treatment termination may be cloaked in a stream of antagonistic comments and actions, but these fears derive from a long-established sense of potential abandonment. The patient should be led to recognize that abandonment fears often set off a sequence of self-destructive behaviors, such as self-mutilation or suicidal acting-out. In helping the patient learn to control impulses, it is important to first address the borderline's need *not* to be under the control of anyone, including the therapist. Once patients understand ways to control their own impulses and can thereby improve their life, they are less likely to be resistant to cognitive intervention. Therapist and patient need to work on identifying the first hints of impulsive inclinations; through self-instructional training (Meichenbaum, 1977), useful steps can be taken to help patients implement new and appropriate attitudes and feelings. Self-destructive impulses, particularly, need to be addressed cognitively. Once intent and tendencies toward acting-out are understood, other means to the same ends can be developed. Hospitalization may have to be considered if the impulse to self-mutilate or to suicide is strong.

Self-Image Techniques

An empathic approach is often the best intervention strategy in the beginning phases of therapy. Therapist sympathy, reassurance, education about interpersonal dynamics, advice, limit-setting, and safeguarding of the patient's self-disclosure and secrets make up the larger body of patient-therapist interactions within this initial approach.

All the following interventions should help strengthen the borderline's sense of identity and point out strengths and accomplishments that will serve to further this goal. Discussions about what constitutes self can also be helpful. Basic beliefs about life's inherent dangers and the borderline's helplessness can also be addressed through behavioral experiments and the development of new coping skills. Certain ideas can be confronted using contrary evidence from the patient's own life. Most borderline patients strongly believe that self-disclosure will lead to inevitable rejection. The therapeutic relationship can serve as a good example that this assumption is not universally true. Discussion of fear of rejection and helping the patient understand that a certain amount of rejection is a normal part of living can help the patient feel less singled out and that rejection or personal slight need not be testimony to inherent flaws.

Although efforts should be made to counteract the patient's diffuse sense of self, as with Rogerian or Gestalt procedures, progress in strengthening a more cohesive self-image may have to wait for other transformations to occur first. While the patient is freely moving from one labile state to another, there is little that can be done to create the kind of structure required for a distinctive self-image to occur.

Intrapsychic Techniques

Intrapsychic therapists believe that the borderline will give up self-destructive behavior if he or she can "divorce" the "internalized abusive attachment figure." A dislike of the internalization can be fostered, or an attachment to someone else can serve to replace it. The therapist can become an "emotional cheerleader" who encourages healthy life choices and behaviors; direct attachment to the therapist as a significant other, however, should be avoided. On the other hand, if patients can permit themselves to trust the therapist enough, they can internalize the therapist's compassion for them as a young abused child and help build self-protective and self-nurturing inclinations. If direct blaming of the abuser is avoided, borderlines can dare for the first time to be "disloyal" to the abuser by emotionally detaching from his or her internalized figure. Pushing the borderline in this direction too quickly, however, can precipitate great anxiety, self-sabotaging behavior, and withdrawal from therapy. The therapist should make it clear that the goal of therapy is for patients to make their own decisions, and know that they can stay on good terms with the abusive person(s) if needed, as long as their welfare is not jeopardized.

Approaches of a psychodynamic character emphasize the need to monitor and control countertransference reactions. Borderline patients tend to have intense negative as well as positive reactions toward the therapist that can easily disrupt the therapeutic process. These must be properly handled. Controversy abounds regarding how strict the therapist's personal limits should be, how to handle crises appropriately, and how soon and how much confrontation is effective. Classic approaches such as free association and minimal therapist action are tolerated quite poorly by most borderline patients, who have poorly structured psychic boundaries. Their natural proclivity toward psychoticlike episodes may be prompted by such methods. The usual length of treatment by psychodynamic techniques appears to be needlessly time-consuming given the availability of equally effective alternatives.

Pharmacologic Techniques

Psychopharmacologic medications are often prescribed to borderline personalities in line with their multiple symptom disorders. Depression is a common presenting complication. A study by Soloff et al. (1986) suggests that different presenting depressions warrant different classes of antidepressant medication: irritable and hostile patients may do better when treated with MAOIs; others may do just as well, if not better, on SSRIs or tricyclic medications or low doses of antipsychotics (olanzapine, clozapine, risperidone). The latter appear to be most useful when depression, hostility, and anxiety are accompanied by psychoticlike symptoms such as illusions, ideas of reference, derealization, and depersonalization. Anxiety and panic may be controlled with benzodiazepines, though some borderlines become more irritable when taking these anxiolytics (Cowdry & Gardner, 1988). In general, polypharmacy is not wise and perhaps should be avoided, if at all possible. The mixture of diverse and changing symptoms among these patients often invites the clinician to organize medication combinations that mirror but may intensify the imbalanced emotions of these patients. Where possible, only one or two major symptom groups should be considered primary; most attention should be directed to modulate their specific upsetting effects.

Discretion must be exercised when prescribing any medications. For example, when evaluating the possible benefits of MAOIs for suicidal patients, it is particularly important to consider that they are lethal in overdose. Another factor therapists should keep in mind when prescribing medications is that many borderlines are noncompliant; others often report feeling worse when the medications seem objectively to be fostering improvements. One possible explanation is that borderlines may feel that they will be "abandoned" by the therapist if they truly get better; another reason suggests that decreases in anxiety and/or depression may lead to disinhibited behavioral controls.

MAKING SYNERGISTIC ARRANGEMENTS

The most important first step in helping a borderline begin progress toward adaptive personality change is to establish a solid working alliance that can help alter the patient's schema about the inherent dangers of relationships. Supportive interventions are a useful way to accomplish this first goal. To bolster motivation without delving into anxiety-provoking self-exploration, helping patients realize behavioral goals may provide them with an initial success in treatment. Severe anxiety and depression can then be evaluated as candidates for psychopharmacologic intervention. Behavioral interventions, in conjunction with psychopharmacologic agents, may then help bring about a measure of predictability in the borderline's social relationships. At this point, the therapist may decide that a group approach would be a useful adjunct. Here, objective feedback and a supportive environment can help keep the patient from feeling attacked as more searching cognitive and emotional work begins. When the therapist feels that the patient has a grasp of some of the main issues, family therapy can help speed the healing process and solidify control over the patient's maladaptive and erratic patterns.

Illustrative Cases

Both theory (Millon, 1969, 1981, 1990) and research (Millon, 1977, 1987b) show that the borderline pattern overlaps almost invariably with every other personality disorder; the schizoid and compulsive types are about the only significant exceptions; narcissists and avoidants are also infrequent covariants of the borderline structure. Among the other stylistic personality disorders, it often develops insidiously as a structurally advanced or structurally more defective pattern.

However, what we observe in a number of personality styles are brief episodes of impulsivity and affective instability that mimic the more intrinsic and persistent traits of the borderline. A key notion here is brevity, that is, the evanescent nature with which these covariant symptoms exhibit themselves. Impulsive anger, affective instability, and self-destructive acts are not, nor do they appear to become, integral character traits of these nonborderline personalities. Some succumb to these behaviors fleetingly following severe psychic deflation, that is, a loss of a significant source of status or fantasized self-esteem; during these transitory episodes, they will appear borderline, but only until they can regain their more benign composure. Others may also succumb to the borderline's more overtly exhibitionistic symptoms following a painful psychic blow. However, these personalities are much more apt to decompensate, if at all, along schizotypal or paranoid lines. They intensify at these times their established pattern of social anxiety and isolation, their self-created cognitive interference, and their flat and constricted affect. The discussion returns now to those subtypes of the borderline that share its prime features in a more enduring and integrated fashion.

It is the author's contention that we will find the same complex of determinants in the borderline syndrome as we do in several of its less structurally defective variants: the avoidant, depressive, dependent, histrionic, antisocial, sadistic, and negativistic personalities. The primary differences among them are the intensity, frequency, timing, and persistence of a host of potentially pathogenic factors. Those who function at the borderline level may begin with less adequate constitutional equipment or be subjected to a series of more adverse early experiences. As a consequence of their more troublesome histories, they either fail to develop an adequate coping style in the first place or decompensate slowly under the weight of repeated and unrelieved difficulties. It is the author's view that most borderline cases progress sequentially through a more adaptive or higher level of functioning before deteriorating to the structurally defective state. Some patients, however, notably childhood variants, never appear to "get off the ground," and give evidence of a borderline pattern from their earliest years.

TABLE 22.4   Borderline Personality Disorder Subtypes

Discouraged: Pliant, submissive, loyal, humble; feels vulnerable and in constant jeopardy; feels hopeless, depressed, helpless, and powerless.

MCMI C-2A/2B/3

Self-Destructive: Inward-turning, intropunitively and angry; conforming, deferential, and ingratiating behaviors have deteriorated; increasingly high-strung and moody; possible suicide.

MCMI C-2B/8B

Impulsive: Capricious, superficial, flighty, distractible, frenetic, and seductive; fearing loss, becomes agitated and then gloomy and irritable; potentially suicidal.

MCMI C-4/6A

Petulant: Negativistic, impatient, restless, as well as stubborn, defiant, sullen, pessimistic, and resentful; easily slighted and quickly disillusioned.

MCMI C-8A

The borderline's typical, everyday mood and behavior reflect his or her basic personality pattern. Below, we note some of the clinical features that differentiate the several subtypes of the disorder (see Table 22.4).

BORDERLINE PERSONALITY: DISCOURAGED TYPE (BORDERLINE WITH DEPENDENT AND AVOIDANT TRAITS)

CASE 22.1, SHANNON E., 25

Presenting Picture: Shannon E., a graduate student in biochemistry, sought professional help due to her self-proclaimed lack of social ability. Although she enjoyed her solitary activities in the lab, she was acutely aware that she lacked any kind of social context. She tried very hard to create a favorable impression on her peers, but she noted that others really didn't show any interest in her. More expressively, at one point, she stated, "They don't want me around." Intensely uncomfortable in her physical being as evidenced by her closed posture and her incessant arm rubbing, she approached her teaching assistantship with great dread of "all those people looking at me!" Living off campus by herself in a small apartment, she did almost nothing socially and longed for companionship, but continued her secluded activities in a self-induced vacuum that, to her, seemed very much impervious to change.

Clinical Assessment: *Discouraged borderlines* such as Shannon typically have been pliant and submissive individuals who shun competition, are lacking in initiative, and are frequently chronically sad or depressed. She had previously attached herself to one or two other persons on whom she depended, with whom she had been able to display affection and thoughtfulness and to whom she had been loyal and humble.

However, Shannon's strategy of quiet cooperation and compliance, in contrast to the less pathological dependent or depressive personalities, had not been notably successful. She may have put all her eggs in one basket, a specific loved one to whom she was excessively attached. But this attachment did not prove secure; her lifeline was connected to an unreliable anchor and her psychic equilibrium was in constant jeopardy. As a consequence, she exhibited a perennial preoccupation and concern with security; her pathetic lack of inner resources and her marked self-doubts led her to cling tenaciously to whomever she could find, and to submerge every remnant of autonomy and individuality she possessed. As can be expected from the preceding, the features just outlined demonstrate traits likely to be seen in mixed clinical pictures composed of deteriorated dependent and avoidant and structurally defective borderline personalities.

This insecurity experienced by Shannon precipitated conflict and distress. She easily became dejected and depressed and felt hopeless, helpless, and powerless to overcome her fate. Everything became a burden; simple responsibilities demanded more energy than she could muster; life seemed empty but heavy; she could not go on alone; and she began to turn on herself, feeling unworthy, useless, and despised. As her sense of futility grew, she regressed to a state of marked depression and infantile dependency, requiring others to tend to her as if she were a baby.

At times, Shannon reversed her habitual strategy and sought actively to solicit attention and security. For short periods, she would become exceedingly cheerful and buoyant, trying to cover up and counter her sense of underlying despondency. Another possible coping ploy may have been to disown her submissive and acquiescent past and display explosive though brief outbursts of angry resentment, a wild attack on others for having exploited and abused her and for failing to see how needful she had been of encouragement and nurturance. At these times, a frightening sense of isolation and aloneness might have overwhelmed and panicked her, driving her to cry out for someone to comfort and hold her, lest she sink into the oblivion and nothingness of self.

Shannon appeared to be an extreme variant of the less pathological conforming and depressive personalities. Both have been conscientious and proper persons; they overcomply with the strictures of society, display an air of propriety, are overly respectful and deferential to authority, and tend to be grim and humorless. They have learned to look to others for support and affection, but such rewards are contingent on compliance and submission. However, Shannon was less certain than their less disturbed counterparts that she would receive support for compliant behaviors. Try as she may have, she no longer had confidence that diligence and acquiescence would forestall desertion, and that she would not be left adrift, alone, and abandoned even when she submitted and conformed.

For a person such as Shannon, insecurity may have stemmed from several sources; for example, she may have been reproached unfairly by perfectionistic parents, or may not have been told with sufficient clarity "exactly" what was expected of her. Whatever the source, her compliant and conscientious strategies had not always paid off, and she was justly distressed and resentful; the pact she had made with her parents and other authorities had been abrogated too often, and they had failed to fulfill their share of the bargain.

The resentment and anger Shannon felt for having been coerced into submission and then betrayed churned within her and pressed hard against her usually adequate controls. Periodically, these feelings broke through to the surface, erupting in an angry upsurge of fury and unbridled vituperation. This anger drew its strength not only from immediate precipitants but from her deep reservoir of animosity, filled through years of what was experienced as constraint. These outbursts of venom usually were directed toward weaker persons, innocent subordinates or children who, by virtue of their powerlessness, could not retaliate.

Whether resentments were discharged overtly or kept seething near the surface, Shannon experienced them as a threat to her equanimity; feelings such as these signified weakness and emotionality, traits that were anathema to her self-image of propriety and control. Moreover, contrary impulses created anxiety because they jeopardized her security, that is, her basic dependency on others. Hostility was doubly dangerous; not only may it have led to an attack on the very persons on whom she depended, thereby undermining the strength of those to whom she looked for support, but it may have provoked their wrath, which may have resulted in outright rejection and desertion by these important persons.

To counter these hostile impulses, Shannon became excessively constrained. Guilt and self-condemnation frequently became dominant features. Struggling feverishly to control her aggressive impulses, she would likely turn her feelings inward and impose on herself severe punitive judgments and actions. Accusations of her own unworthiness were but mild rebukes for the guilt she felt. Self-mutilation and suicide, symbolic acts of self-desertion, may have been a means of controlling her own expressions of resentment or punishing herself for her anger.

Synergistic Treatment Plan: Early treatment with Shannon would require a consistent, genuine, and empathic *self-image* approach, establishing a safe and supportive environment that would contradict her disappointment expectation. Also effective in this early stage would be *interpersonal* examination of her wavering dominant-submissive patterns of reacting, as well as investigation and possible *biophysical* remediation of her mood shifts, which ran paradoxical to her perceived needs. As Shannon's emotional stability increased, the aforementioned self-image modality as well as *cognitive* pattern inconsistencies could be monitored and modified. Such perpetuations that would be countered in this manner included erroneous and inconsistent assumptions regarding herself and the futility of seeking autonomy (lability of *self-other* polarities derived from a dearth of self-value). Also, changes in *behavioral* and interpersonal patterns, such as her manipulative helplessness and isolation, would be appropriate in this working stage (stabilizing an *active-passive* split as well as a tendency to avoid *pain*). These combined approaches would be an effective preamble to more effective, permanent pattern changes.

Therapeutic Course: Active short-term techniques took advantage of introducing Shannon to environmental changes to maximize growth, minimize continued dependency, and provide uplifting experiences. *Psychopharmacologic* treatment was initiated as a useful short-term technique geared to promote alertness and vigor and to counter fatigue, lethargy, dejection, and anxiety states that may have inclined the patient to postpone efforts at independence and confidence building. The relationship between therapist and patient was explored to overcome the dominance-submission patterns that may have characterized Shannon's recent history. Both nondirective and directive *cognitive* approaches fostered growth in autonomy and self-confidence. Although *psychodynamic* approaches were used to rework deep object attachments and to construct a base for competency strivings, they were less effective than more focused and brief therapeutic modes. *Group therapy* may also have been pursued as a means of learning autonomous skills and as an aid to the growth of social confidence.

Circumscribed treatment efforts were directed toward countering the dependency attitudes and behavior of this self-effacing woman. A primary therapeutic task was to prevent Shannon from slipping into a totally ineffectual state as she sought to rely increasingly on a supportive environment. Owing to her anxious and morose outlook, she not only observed real deficits in her competence but also deprecated what virtues and talents she possessed. Trapped by her own persuasiveness, she reinforced her belief in the futility of standing on her own and was therefore inclined to try less and less to overcome her inadequacies. *Cognitive* methods (e.g., Ellis, Beck) were especially helpful in reframing erroneous beliefs and assumptions about herself and those she believed others had of her.

Her strategy had fostered a vicious circle of increased helplessness, depression, and dependency. By making herself inaccessible to growth opportunities, she effectively precluded further maturation and became more saddened and more dependent on others. Short-term techniques ensured the continuation of competence activities and the acquisition of assertive behavior and attitudes. To prevent Shannon from becoming passively incompetent and lost in fantasy preoccupations, a major though short-term approach was quickly instituted. Potentially useful in this regard were several *behavioral modification* methods as well as *interpersonal* techniques such as those of Benjamin and Kiesler. Pressure on her to show marked increases in initiative and autonomy was gradual, however, because her capacities in this area were limited.

Effective brief, focused treatment may have created the misleading impression that progress would continue and be rapid. Despite initial indications of solid advances, Shannon still resisted efforts to assume much autonomy for her future. Persuading her to forgo her long-standing habits proved to be extremely slow and arduous, but it was important that steps were undertaken to move forward in this regard and to provide support. Especially problematic was the feeling she had that an increase in the expectations of others would not be met and would thereby result in disapproval. Efforts to help her build an image of competence and self-esteem were an essential step in forestalling later backsliding. A program that strengthened her attributes and dislodged her habit of leaning on others was worth the effort it took.

BORDERLINE PERSONALITY: IMPULSIVE TYPE (BORDERLINE WITH HISTRIONIC AND ANTISOCIAL TRAITS)

CASE 22.2, DARREN V., 27

Presenting Picture: Darren V. was at a crossroad in his life, where he was coming to realize that he was getting older, and that it might be time to do something more "logical" with himself. He had been something of a drifter, doing pretty much whatever he felt like doing from day to day. Although very much aware of his predicament, his ideas concerning future plans were markedly without much forethought. At one moment, he spoke of his desire to go back to school to study medicine, but within seconds, he was speaking of continuing to "ramble" throughout the world, as there was much he had yet to see. This concern that Darren had regarding these decisions seemed only to be something to which he paid lip service, and to which he could assign only limited importance. Also notable was his agitation with the therapist, as he dismissed the questions regarding his plans as "pretty dumb." He liked to describe himself as someone with a "short fuse," not possessed of great tolerance. Obviously defensive about his decision making, Darren seemed to want to "brush over" the issues as quickly as possible, thereby not necessitating any deep exploration.

Clinical Assessment: *Impulsive borderlines* such as Darren are typically structurally defective variants of certain of their less pathological counterparts, primarily the histrionic and antisocial personalities. Each is capricious, evasive, superficial, and seductive. This was clearly evident in his MCMI score profile. However, at the borderline level, strategies are instrumentally less successful than heretofore. As a consequence, we observed more extreme efforts to cope with events, many of which served only to perpetuate and deepen his difficulties. For example, Darren may not have mastered the techniques of soliciting approval and ensuring a stream of support and encouragement; because of an excessively flighty and capricious style of personal relationships, he may have experienced long periods in which he lacked a secure base and a consistent source of attention.

Deprived of the attentions and rewards he sought, Darren may have intensified his strategy of seductiveness and irresponsibility. He evidenced extreme hyperactivity, flightiness, and distractibility. At moments, he exhibited a frenetic gaiety, an exaggerated boastfulness, and an insistent and insatiable need for social contact and excitement. Frightened lest he lose attention and approval, he at times displayed a frantic conviviality, an irrational and superficial euphoria in which he lost all sense of propriety and judgment and raced hypomanically from one activity to another. With Darren's stronger antisocial history, he may have engaged in a series of restless, spur-of-the-moment acts, failing to plan ahead or to consider more pragmatic alternatives, much less to heed the consequences of his actions. For him, the struggle to free himself from the restrictions of social customs resulted in impetuous and irresponsible behaviors.

At times, Darren experienced repeated rebuffs; at others, his efforts to solicit attention simply proved futile. Fearing a permanent loss of attention and esteem, he eventually succumbed to periods of hopelessness and self-depreciation. Having lost confidence in his seductive or exploitive powers, dreading a decline in vigor, charm, and youth, he began to fret and worry, to have doubts about his worth and attractiveness. Anticipating desertion and disillusioned with self, he began to ponder his fate. Because worry begets further worry and doubts raise more doubts, his agitation eventually turned to gloom, to increased self-derogation, and to feelings of emptiness and abandonment; ultimately, he began to distort reality so that everything, no matter how encouraging or exciting it formerly was, seemed bleak and barren.

Synergistic Treatment Plan: Immediate attention in treating Darren would center around building the therapeutic relationship as a model of parallel alliance, particularly challenging given his generally negative view of others. A combined *supportive self-image* and *interpersonal* approach would begin the process of adjusting social patterns to a less agitative, defensive style, and would continue throughout treatment. *Cognitive* techniques would then be incorporated, as his characterologic defenses would diminish and he could tolerate confrontive measures. Darren's need to dominate relationships from moment to moment and his assumption of others' ignorance (*self-other* discordance, deriving from earlier disparagement, leading to an unsturdy but overemphasized assertion of *self*) would be a perpetuating construct worthy of challenge. Additionally, it would be beneficial to confront his flighty, carpe diem approach to his circumstances (*active-pleasure* tendency) in favor of less impulsive, more security-oriented interactional *behavioral* strategies of coping with his environment.

Therapeutic Course: Essential to the success of a short-term approach with Darren was the therapist's readiness to see things from the patient's point of view, to convey a sense of trust, and to create a feeling of alliance. To achieve reasonable short-term goals, this building of rapport could not be interpreted as a sign of the therapist's capitulation to his bluff and arrogance. Brief treatment required a balance of professional firmness and authority mixed with tolerance for Darren's less attractive traits. By building an image of a fair-minded and strong authority figure, the therapist successfully employed *cognitive* methods that encouraged Darren to change his expectations. Through reasoned and convincing comments, the therapist provided a model for him to learn the mix of power, logic, and fairness.

Less confrontive cognitive approaches provided Darren with opportunities to vent his anger, even in short-term therapy. Once drained of these hostile feelings, he could be led to examine his habitual behavior and cognitive attitudes and was guided into less destructive perceptions and outlets than before. *Interpersonal* methods, such as those of Benjamin and Kiesler, provided a means to explore socially more acceptable behavior. As far as *group* methods were concerned, until Darren had incorporated changed cognitions and actions, he may have intruded on and disrupted therapeutic functions. On the other hand, taking this therapeutic risk may have been a useful catalyst for short-term group interaction, and he may have gained some useful insights and a few constructive skills.

A useful short-term goal for Darren was to enable him to tolerate the experience of guilt or to accept blame for the turmoil he may have caused. Cognitive methods employing a measure of confrontation helped undermine his tendency to always trace problems to another person's stupidity, laziness, or hostility. When he accepted responsibility for some of his difficulties, it was important that the therapist was prepared to deal with Darren's inclination to resent the therapist for supposedly tricking him into admitting it. Similarly, the therapist had to be ready to be challenged and to avoid the patient's efforts to outwit him. Darren consistently tried to set up situations to test the therapist's skills, to catch inconsistencies, to arouse ire, and, if possible, to belittle and humiliate the therapist. Restraining impulses to express condemning attitudes was a major task for the therapist, but one that was used for positive gains, especially when tied into the application of combined cognitive (e.g., Beck, Ellis) and interpersonal interventions.

It should be noted that the precipitant for Darren's treatment was as much situational as it was internal. Hence, he did not seek therapy voluntarily, and he was fairly convinced that had he been simply left alone, he would work all matters out on his own. Such beliefs were confronted, albeit carefully. Similarly, had treatment been self-motivated, it probably would have been inspired by a series of legal entanglements, family problems, social humiliations, or achievement failures. Whatever its source, a firm cognitive and behavior-change approach seemed required. This domineering and often intimidating man readily expressed complaints in the form of irritability and restlessness. To succeed in his initial disinclination to be frank with authority figures, he wandered from one superficial topic to another. This inclination had to be monitored and prevented. Moreover, contact with family members may have been fruitful because they may have reported matters quite differently than did Darren. To ensure that he took discussions seriously, he was confronted directly with evidence of his contribution to his troubles. Treatment was best geared to short-term goals, reestablishing his psychic balance, and strengthening his previously adequate coping behavior with cognitive methods, unless his actions were frankly antisocial. In general, short-term approaches with this patient were best directed toward building controls rather than insights, toward the here and now rather than the past, and toward teaching him ways to sustain relationships cooperatively rather than with dominance and intimidation.

BORDERLINE PERSONALITY: PETULANT TYPE
(BORDERLINE WITH NEGATIVISTIC TRAITS)

CASE 22.3, STEPHANIE H., 24

Presenting Picture: Stephanie H. had been referred for counseling following a series of unfortunate events culminating in her jumping out of her boyfriend's moving car. "I just wanted to see what would happen" was her simplistic rationalization of this event, also remarking that she was high at the time and felt nothing, so she figured that this might be a way of feeling *something.* Prior to the incident, Stephanie had dropped out of school, raising her boyfriend's ire and inciting him to put pressure on her to "get her act together." Apparently, following the incident, her boyfriend removed himself from the picture. What had Stephanie visibly upset, however, was that her father, who had been markedly absent emotionally for much of her life, suddenly appeared at the hospital with her stepmother. "They sent me away to boarding school at age 14," she complained. "Why the hell do they care now?" Throughout her life, it seemed, people would leave Stephanie just when she needed them, or when she was just developing stronger bonds with them. Friends from boarding school also fit this pattern; they could not be relied on in times of need. Thus, she had a very difficult time trusting anyone or allowing anyone to become close, as this compromised her safety.

Clinical Assessment: *Petulant borderlines* such as Stephanie are often difficult to distinguish from certain of their less structurally defective counterparts, most notably the negativistic personality. Simply stated, we can say that Stephanie's overt symptoms were more intense and that psychotic episodes occurred with somewhat greater frequency than in the negativist. She may have been best characterized by her extreme unpredictability and by her restless, irritable, impatient, and complaining behaviors. Typically, she was defiant, disgruntled, and discontent, as well as stubborn, sullen, pessimistic, and resentful. Enthusiasms were short-lived; she was easily disillusioned and slighted, tended to be envious of others, and felt unappreciated and cheated in life.

Despite her anger and resentment, Stephanie feared separation and was desirous of achieving affection and love; in short, she was ambivalent, trapped by conflicting inclinations to "move toward, away or against others," as Horney (1950) might have put it. She oscillated perpetually, first finding one course of action unappealing, then another, then a third, and back again. To give in to others was to be drained of all hope of independence, but to withdraw was to be isolated.

Stephanie always resented her dependence on others and hated those to whom she had turned to plead for love and esteem. In contrast to other borderline subtypes, she did not have even a small measure of consistency in the support she received from others; she had never had her needs satisfied on a regular basis and had never felt secure in her relationships. She openly registered her disappointments, was stubborn and recalcitrant, and vented her anger only to recant and feel guilty and contrite. She was erratic and continued to vacillate between apologetic submission on the one hand, and stubborn resistance and contrariness on the other.

Unable to get a hold of herself and unable to find a comfortable niche with others, Stephanie became increasingly testy, bitter, and discontent. Resigned to her fate and despairing of hope, she oscillated between two pathological extremes of behavior. For long periods, she expressed feelings of worthlessness and futility, became highly agitated or deeply depressed, developed delusions of guilt, and was severely self-condemnatory and perhaps self-destructive. At other times, her habitual negativism crossed the line of reason, broke out of control, and drove her into maniacal rages in which she distorted reality, made excessive demands of others, and viciously attacked those who had trapped her and forced her into intolerable conflicts. However, following these wild outbursts, she would turn her hostility inward, became remorseful, plead for forgiveness, and promise "to behave" and "make up" for her unpleasant and miserable past. One need not be too astute to recognize that these "resolutions" were short-lived.

Synergistic Treatment Plan: Before any challenges could be made to Stephanie's maladaptive strategies and extremely volatile inner conflicts, the therapist would need to assure, through an empathic, *self-image*–oriented posture, that she would consider this therapeutic relationship resilient and secure. It would also be prudent from the beginning, and throughout the process, to be alert to signs of *biophysical* mood decompensation that may occur unexpectedly, and be ready to respond to possible depressive or psychotic episodes in a timely and effective manner. Her need to "test" others in her environment and her expectation that they would fail due to her unworthiness (conflictual *self-other* tendency) was a key perpetuating feature in her characterologic makeup. Combining careful *cognitive* and *interpersonal* approaches, instilling healthier and less *active-pain*–oriented attitudes and strategies would be a most fruitful approach. As greater levels of comfort would be achieved, other constructs that might be addressed in this combined approach would include interaction patterns from a *family dynamic* perspective, which would examine and dispute long-term patterns that perpetuated this flawed interpersonal style.

Therapeutic Course: Serious efforts to alter Stephanie's current symptoms and basic psychopathology were attempted by employing focused and short-term techniques. Primary goals in brief therapy included the facilitation of autonomy, the building of confidence, and the overcoming of fears of self-determination. There was, not surprisingly, a period of initial resistance. As part of a short-term approach, it was important to counter Stephanie's feeling that the therapist's efforts to encourage her to assume responsibility and self-control were a sign of rejection. A trusting, warm, and empathic atmosphere was absolutely necessary to prevent disappointment, dejection, and even rage. These potential reactions were anticipated, given Stephanie's characteristic style, and they were appropriately responded to with equanimity as fundamental changes needed to be explored and relapses prevented. When a sound and secure therapeutic alliance had been established, she learned to tolerate her contrary feelings and dependency anxieties. Learning how to face and handle her unstable emotions was coordinated with the strengthening of healthier attitudes through *cognitive* methods such as those of Beck and Meichenbaum, as well as through *interpersonal* procedures such as those of Kiesler and Benjamin. Additionally, the therapist needed to serve as a model to demonstrate how feelings, conflicts, and uncertainties could be approached and resolved with reasonable equanimity and foresight. Also, the exploration provided in *family* methods was useful in testing these newly learned attitudes and strategies in a more natural setting than that found in individual treatment.

As implied, by her affective instability and self-deprecation, Stephanie avoided confronting and resolving her real interpersonal difficulties whenever possible. Her coping maneuvers were a double-edged sword, relieving passing discomfort and strains but perpetuating faulty attitudes and strategies. These distorted attitudes and faulty behaviors were the main targets of cognitive and interpersonal therapeutic interventions (e.g., Safran and Segal).

Special care was called for in this short-term treatment regimen to counteract the anticipated occurrence that Stephanie's hold on reality would disintegrate and that her capacity to function would wither. Similar care was taken as the attention and support that she required were withdrawn and when her strategies proved wearisome and exasperating to others, precipitating their anger. *Pharmacologic agents* were employed as she began to succumb to depression and occasional erratic surges of hostility. Particular attention was given to anticipate and quell the danger of suicide during these episodes. A major concern during these early periods was the forestalling of a persistent decompensation process. Among the early signs of breakdown were marked discouragement and melancholic dejection. At this phase, *supportive* therapy was called for, and cognitive reorientation methods were actively implemented. Efforts were made to boost Stephanie's sagging morale, to encourage her to continue in her usual sphere of activities, to build her self-confidence, and to deter her from being preoccupied with her melancholy feelings. She was not pressed beyond her capabilities, however, because her failure to achieve any goals would only strengthen her conviction of her incompetence and unworthiness. Properly executed cognitive methods oriented to correcting erroneous assumptions and beliefs were especially helpful.

BORDERLINE PERSONALITY: SELF-DESTRUCTIVE TYPE (BORDERLINE WITH MASOCHISTIC AND DEPRESSIVE TRAITS)

CASE 22.4, CHERYL H., 23

Presenting Picture: Cheryl H. came to therapy after a friend noticed scars on her arms. As she explained, though, she was only scratching herself, and this was not indicative of a suicide attempt *this time.* She had a long history of therapy, her tendency to hurt herself dating back to childhood. Many times previously, she had wanted to die. Cheryl was thoroughly convinced that she was a bad person, and that people were always leaving her due to her unworthiness as a human being. Most recently, her boyfriend had left after what Cheryl described as a "pretty long relationship" (three months) because she needed too much from him and was no fun any more. This pattern of people "leaving" and her self-accusations led directly back to her father, who had left after Cheryl had stood up to him for the first time for his long history of physical and sexual abuse of her and her mother. "I wasn't a good daughter" is how she conceptualized this. From then on, she had sensed that her mother was angry with her for ruining her marriage, and that she tormented her with new boyfriends that her mother always seemed to leave her alone with. Throughout therapy, the theme of "better off dead" pervaded. At the outset of therapy, when the counselor asked for a commitment not to harm herself, she immediately responded with defensiveness, projecting that he would throw her out of therapy "just like all the others." However, rather bitterly, she gave this commitment and began work.

Clinical Assessment: As with other borderline subtypes, Cheryl, a *self-destructive borderline,* vacillated perpetually, first finding one course of action unappealing, then another, then a third, and back again. To give in to others was to lose hope of independence, but to withdraw was to be isolated. She had always resented her dependence on others and often hated those to whom she had turned to seek security, love, and esteem. As with other borderline subtypes, she was indecisive and oscillated between apologetic submission and stubborn resistance and contrariness. In a manner similar to the petulant borderline, she was unable to "get a hold of herself" and find a comfortable niche with others. However, in contrast to the petulant type, she did not become increasingly testy and bitter over time. Although expressing her discontent in an erratic and changeable manner, she became more inward turning, and expressed her anger in an intropunitive way. She had a long history of depressive and masochistic traits, and these features interpenetrated her defective psychic structure.

In the past, Cheryl's surface appearance may have presented a veneer of sociability and conformity. Beneath this superficial front, however, was a fear of genuine autonomy and a deeply conflictual submission to the expectations of others. This social propriety cloaked deep and increasingly intense but suppressed antagonisms. To control these oppositional tendencies, there was a struggle to maintain a self-restraint and a self-sacrificial affability, both elements in evidence in her MCMI responses. She evinced a long-standing pattern of being deferential and ingratiating with superiors, going out of her way to impress them with her adherence to their expectations and her serious-mindedness.

Failures to evoke needed emotional support and approval led to periods of depression and chronic anxiety. Cheryl became high-strung and moody, straining to express attitudes contrary to her inner feelings of tension, anger, and dejection. To avoid these discomforts, she became overly sensitive to the moods and expectations of others. Although viewing herself as self-sacrificial and submissive, the extreme other-directedness utilized in the service of achieving approval resulted in an increasingly unstable lifestyle. Whereas in earlier years she successfully learned to be alert to signs of potential hostility and rejection, her success rate had diminished appreciably. In the past, she paid attention to the signals that others transmitted and thereby usually avoided disapproval. The pattern of adapting her behaviors to comply with the desires of others had been central to her lifestyle. Not only had this preoccupation become less and less successful over time, but it resulted in a growing sense of personal impotence and social dependency.

Cheryl sought to deny awareness of her inner deficiencies, for admission would point up the fraudulence that existed between the overt impressions she sought to create and her internally felt sterility and emotional poverty. This tendency to seal off and deny the elements of her inner life further intensified her dependence on others, a dependency that had become increasingly insecure. As noted, deep resentments toward those to whom she had sacrificed herself began to emerge. These antagonisms periodically broke through their surface constraints, erupting in outbursts of anger and resentment, followed by sorrowful expressions of guilt and contrition. These vacillations between periods of submissive compliance and depressive negativism further compounded her discomforts.

Moreover, public displays of inconsistency and impulse expression contrasted markedly with Cheryl's self-image. She had bitter complaints about being treated unfairly, of expecting to be disillusioned and disapproved by others, and of no longer being appreciated for her diligence, submissiveness, and self-sacrifice. With the persistence of these ambivalent feelings, Cheryl began to suffer somatic discomforts, voicing growing distress about a wide range of physical symptoms. Increasingly upset, labile in mood and impulse, she turned her anger inward, seeking to maintain her earlier image of propriety and responsibility. Anger became intropunitive rather than extrapunitive. She rarely expressed her deep antagonisms and resentments. More and more we began to see a depressive, self-abnegating tone to her verbal and emotional expressions. Although abrupt outbreaks of contrary feelings occasionally emerged, for the most part we observed an increasingly self-destructive and self-depreciating pattern of behaviors and attitudes. The possibility of suicide was almost always present.

Synergistic Treatment Plan: Consistency and genuineness in attitude would be most important on the part of the therapist, as Cheryl would likely approach the therapeutic relationship as she might any other significant bond, with the conviction that it would ultimately disappoint and fail. The therapist would need to be mindful of Cheryl's submissive (extreme *passive-other*–oriented) habit, which was "routinized," as she might tend to play a well-rehearsed role rather than invest in a process. With this posture as a backbone, the therapist would begin by addressing perpetuating *cognitions* that undermined Cheryl's already poor sense of *self:* viewing assertiveness as causing disparagement, making impulsive judgments about events, being hypersensitive to rebuff, and so on. *Behavioral* and *interpersonal* changes, such as modifying her habit of setting up disappointments as well as responding submissively to social engagement and following with considerable resentment, along with the aforementioned cognitive milieu, would work toward providing more realistic expectations and *active* autonomous skills. These changes would also foster an orientation more open to enhanced *pleasure.*

Treatment Course: A first goal in therapy with Cheryl was to demonstrate that the potential gains of therapy were real and that they should motivate her rather than serve as a deterrent. Cheryl feared that therapy would reawaken what she viewed as false hopes; that is, it would remind her of the humiliation she experienced when she offered her trust to others but received rejection in return. By implicitly acknowledging these fears, she was able to find a modest level of comfort without having to distance herself from the therapist, learning to deal more effectively with her fears while maintaining a better level of adjustment than that to which she had become accustomed.

In a short-term *cognitive-behavioral* approach, attention was usefully directed to Cheryl's social hesitation, anxious demeanor, and self-deprecating actions, attitudes, and behavior that could be altered so as not to evoke the humiliation and derogation they had in the past. Cognitive efforts to reframe the basis of her sensitivity to rebuff and her fearful and unassertive behavior (e.g., Beck, Ellis) should minimize and diminish not only her aversive inclinations but her tendency to relapse and regress.

More probing yet circumscribed and brief treatment procedures were useful in unearthing the roots of her anxieties and confronting those assumptions and expectations that pervaded many aspects of her behavior. *Family* techniques may also have been employed to moderate destructive patterns of communication that contributed to or intensified personal problems. *Interpersonal* techniques (e.g., Benjamin) and *group therapy* assisted her in learning new attitudes and skills in a more benign and accepting social setting than she normally encountered.

Focused techniques also addressed Cheryl's tendencies to demean her self-worth and to mistrust others. Short-term *supportive* methods were used to counteract her ill-disposition to sustain a consistent therapeutic relationship. As noted, maneuvers designed to test the sincerity of the therapist were frequently evident. A warm and empathic attitude was necessary because the patient was likely to fear facing her feelings of unworthiness and because she sensed that her coping defenses were weak. Her commendable skills were drawn on to prevent her from withdrawing from treatment before any real gains were made. Cognitive procedures were used to explore the contradictions in her feelings and attitudes. Without proper reframing, there would have been a seesaw struggle, with periods of temporary progress followed by retrogression. Genuine short-term gains were possible, but only with careful work, a building of trust, and enhancement of Cheryl's sense of self-worth.

Another realm worthy of brief intervention was associated with Cheryl's extensive scanning of the environment. By doing this, she increased the likelihood that she would encounter those stimuli she wished to avoid. Her exquisite antennae picked up and transformed what most people overlooked. Again, using appropriate cognitive methods, her hypersensitivity was prevented from backfiring, that is, becoming an instrument that constantly brought to awareness the very pain she wished to escape. Reorienting Cheryl's focus and her negative interpretive habits to ones that were more ego-enhancing and optimistic in character reduced her self-demeaning outlook, intensified her positive experiences, and diminished her anguish.

Risks and Resistances

If borderlines find an emotionally nurturant environment and are reinforced in their need for acceptance and attachment, they can live in relative comfort and tranquility, maintaining a reasonably secure hold on reality. However, should the attention and support that borderlines require be withdrawn, and should their strategies prove wearisome and exasperating to others, precipitating others' anger and unforgiveness, then their tenuous hold on reality often disintegrates and their capacity to function withers.

Many therapists worry that somber depression and explosive hostility, which often signify acute breaks with reality, can lead to a more permanent decompensation process. Among the early signs of a growing breakdown are marked periods of discouragement and a persistent dejection. At this phase, it is especially useful to employ supportive therapy and cognitive reorientation. Efforts should be made to boost these patients' sagging morale, to encourage them to continue in their usual sphere of activities, to build their self-confidence, and to deter them from being preoccupied with their melancholy feelings. Of course, they should not be pressed beyond their capabilities nor told to "snap out of it," for their failure to achieve these goals will only strengthen their growing conviction of their own incompetence and unworthiness. Should depression be the major symptom picture, it is advisable to prescribe any of the suitable antidepressant agents as a means of buoying the patient's flagging spirits. Should suicide become a threat, or should the patient lose control or engage in hostile outbursts, it may be advisable to arrange for brief institutionalization in the hope of obviating future needs for more serious institutional intervention.

Some therapists may overreact to a borderline patient's tendency toward psychoticlike experiences or actual breaks with reality. In order not to bias therapeutic work against the client it is important for the therapist to remember that brief hospitalizations should not be interpreted by patients as a sign that they are "crazy" and that outpatient therapeutic work is futile. When a therapist does feel that his or her efforts are futile or feels threatened by a patient's behavior, countertransference reactions can include a variety of problematic reactions. Therapists who realize they are experiencing such feelings need to examine them to ensure that they do not bias their interaction with the patient against the patient's best interest. It may be best for the therapist to seek consultation with a colleague if this becomes a pattern in therapy with a particular client.

On the other hand, some patients become excessively dependent owing to the lack of responsibilities during a period of hospitalization. Therapists working with such borderline behaviors can help break this dependency by suggesting to the patient that hospitalization is not a cure, but just a "life preserver" that will keep the patient from sinking. Not conducting therapy while the patient is hospitalized can help the patient view hospitalization as a temporary solution to problems, and thereby strengthen the will to return to a more functional lifestyle.

CHAPTER TWENTY-THREE

Treating Paranoid Personality Patterns

The paranoid personality may be viewed as a more structurally defective and dysfunctional variant of the antisocial, sadistic, compulsive, and narcissistic patterns, with each sharing a preoccupation with matters of adequacy, power, and prestige. Among the more prominent features of paranoid personalities are a pervasive and unwarranted mistrust of others, hypersensitivity to signs of deception or malevolence, and restricted affectivity. These individuals are fearful of external sources of influence and may be resistant to forming intimate relationships for fear of being stripped of their power of self-determination. In spite of their air of self-importance, invincibility, and pride, paranoid personalities tend to experience extreme jealousy and envy at the "good fortune" of others. To justify these feelings of resentment, they constantly search for signs of deception and actively construct situations to "test" the sincerity of others. Inevitably, their provocative and abrasive behaviors elicit the very signs of malice that they project on others. Even the slightest, most trivial cues are seized upon and magnified to justify their preconceptions. Data that contradict their perceptions are ignored, with paranoids accepting no responsibility or blame for their role. This distortion of events, although personally logical, is irrational and at times verges on delusional.

In their attempts to remain constantly on guard and mobilized, paranoids may exhibit an edgy tension, irritability, and rigid defensive posture. To protect themselves from the sadistic treatment and betrayal they anticipate, these individuals maintain an interpersonal distance and attempt to desensitize themselves from tender and affectionate feelings toward others. They become hard and insensitive to the suffering of others, as well as alienated from their own emotions and inner conflicts.

Although dysfunctionally rigid, this stance of social withdrawal, callousness, and projection of personal malevolence and shortcomings onto others provides the paranoid with a glorified self-image and relative freedom from intrapsychic distress. In circumstances of real or imagined threats to their autonomy or challenges of their competency, however, paranoids' tenuous sense of self-determination and superiority can be badly shaken. Initially, these individuals may construct new "proofs" to fortify their persecutory fantasies, while vigorously struggling to reestablish their former autonomy and esteem.

During the course of their self-assertion, considerable hostility may be unleashed on others. In paranoids with prominent narcissistic features, threats to their illusion of omnipotence and superiority may elicit a self-exalted and pompous variant of manic disorder. With an exaggerated cheerfulness, excitement, and buoyancy, reminiscent of their former state of complacency, these individuals are frantically driven to recover their lost exalted status. In some instances, their previous sense of self-determination and confidence cannot be easily reconstructed. Time and again, paranoids' competencies have been shown to be defective, and they have been made to look foolish. Defeated and humiliated, their past arrogance and self-assurance now submerged, a deep sense of helplessness and major depression may ensue.

A feature that justifies considering paranoids among the more structurally defective personalities is the inelasticity and constriction of their coping skills. The obdurate and unyielding structure of their personality contrasts markedly with the lack of cohesion and instability of the borderline personality. Whereas borderlines are subject to a dissolution of controls and a fluidity in their responsiveness, paranoids display such inflexible controls that they are subject to having their rigid façade shattered.

Entirely insignificant and irrelevant events are often transformed by paranoids so as to have personal reference to themselves. They may begin to impose their inner world of meanings on the outer world of reality. As Cameron put it (1963), they create a "pseudo-community" composed of distorted people and processes. Situations and events lose their objective attributes and are interpreted in terms of subjective expectations and feelings. Unable and unwilling to follow the lead of others and accustomed to drawing power within themselves, paranoids reconstruct reality so that it suits their dictates. Faced with a world in which others shape what occurs, they construct a world in which they determine events and have power to do as they desire. In contrast to their less structurally defective counterparts, paranoids' need for autonomy and independence has been undermined often and seriously. These personalities counter the anxiety their experiences create by distorting objective reality and constructing in its stead a new reality in which they can affirm their personal stature and significance.

Stone (1993) brings together a number of features of several varieties of the paranoid disorder. In his usual insightful and descriptively articulate manner, he writes:

> The *grandiosity* . . . may be either secret or blatant, [and reflects] the paranoid person's intense fear of dissolution of self (loss of identity) as a central dynamic. . . .
>
> The characteristic *hypervigilance* of paranoid persons has relevance both to their hostility and to their fear of boundary-loss. The need for a wide psychological and even geographical space between paranoid persons and those with whom they interact is a reflection of both (a) fear of hostile invasion by others (for which real distance has survival value) and (b) fear of being "unduly" influenced by others, to the point of losing a sense of separate self (for which extra psychological "space"—not getting intimate with others—is a solution). (p. 200)

We turn to contemporary conceptions by referring to the evolutionary model of the paranoid personality, as seen in Figure 23.1. What is most notable here is the presence of a "block" between each pair of the polarity groups. This signifies the rigid compartmentalization of paranoids' thoughts and feelings about themselves and others, as well as the unyielding and constricted nature with which they perceive and relate to the

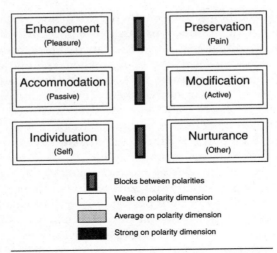

Enhancement (Pleasure)		Preservation (Pain)
Accommodation (Passive)		Modification (Active)
Individuation (Self)		Nurturance (Other)

Blocks between polarities

Weak on polarity dimension

Average on polarity dimension

Strong on polarity dimension

Figure 23.1   Status of the paranoid personality prototype in accord with the Millon Polarity Model.

world. Whatever motives and aims they have developed in life remain firmly fixed, unchangeable and uninfluenced by life circumstances.

It is the obduracy and inelasticity of their polarity inclinations that characterizes paranoids, and distinguishes them from the two other severe/structural pathological types, the schizotypal and borderline. Despite commonalities in the eccentricity of their beliefs and attitudes, the schizotypal comes to this characterization by virtue of excessive structural fluidity, whereas in the paranoid it reflects an unwillingness to adapt to external realities, a fixity in psychic structure that is unbending and inelastic. Similarly, paranoids' inflexibility and rigidity differs from borderlines' extraordinary inconstancy and changeability.

As with the two other severe/structural pathologies, the paranoid disorder almost invariably covaries with one or more of the usually less severe personality "styles." In reviewing MCMI cases of most paranoids, we are likely to see a conflation of paranoid structural pathologies combined with a stylistic disorder, for example, paranoid-avoidant, paranoid-antisocial, paranoid–obsessive-compulsive. The task of the clinician is not to disentangle these components, but to recognize that they almost invariably coexist as a stylistic/structural fusion. It is these mixtures that result in what we have described as prototypal variants or subtypes.

CLINICAL PICTURE

Certain symptom characteristics are shared in common among paranoids (see Table 23.1). As in the two previous structurally defective patterns, we divide these characteristics initially into three broad areas of clinical significance: primary sources of anxiety; cognitive processes and preoccupations; and typical moods and behaviors. Five of the major subtypes that develop into variants of the paranoid personality are discussed in detail later. Characteristics that will further aid in distinguishing the prototypal

TABLE 23.1   Clinical Domains of the Paranoid Personality Prototype

Behavioral Level

   (F) Expressively Defensive (e.g., is vigilantly guarded, alert to anticipate and ward off expected derogation, malice, and deception; is tenacious and firmly resistant to sources of external influence and control).

   (F) Interpersonally Provocative (e.g., not only bears grudges and is unforgiving of those of the past, but displays a quarrelsome, fractious, and abrasive attitude with recent acquaintances; precipitates exasperation and anger by a testing of loyalties and an intrusive and searching preoccupation with hidden motives).

Phenomenological Level

   (F) Cognitively Suspicious (e.g., is unwarrantedly skeptical, cynical, and mistrustful of the motives of others, including relatives, friends, and associates, construing innocuous events as signifying hidden or conspiratorial intent; reveals tendency to read hidden meanings into benign matters and to magnify tangential or minor difficulties into proofs of duplicity and treachery, especially regarding the fidelity and trustworthiness of a spouse or intimate friend).

   (S) Inviolable Self-Image (e.g., has persistent ideas of self-importance and self-reference, perceiving attacks on own character not apparent to others, asserting as personally derogatory and scurrilous, if not libelous, entirely innocuous actions and events; is pridefully independent, reluctant to confide in others, highly insular, experiencing intense fears, however, of losing identity, status, and powers of self-determination).

   (S) Unalterable Objects (e.g., internalized representations of significant early relationships are a fixed and implacable configuration of deeply held beliefs and attitudes, as well as driven by unyielding convictions that, in turn, are aligned in an idiosyncratic manner with a fixed hierarchy of tenaciously held by unwarranted assumptions, fears, and conjectures).

Intrapsychic Level

   (F) Projection Mechanism (e.g., actively disowns undesirable personal traits and motives and attributes them to others; remains blind to own unattractive behaviors and characteristics, yet is overalert to and hypercritical of similar features in others).

   (S) Inelastic Organization (e.g., systemic constriction and inflexibility of undergoing morphologic structures as well as rigidly fixed channels of defensive coping, conflict mediation, and need gratification create an overstrung and taut frame that is so uncompromising in its accommodation to changing circumstances that unanticipated stressors are likely to precipitate either explosive outbursts or inner shatterings).

Biophysical Level

   (S) Irascible Mood (e.g., displays a cold, sullen, churlish, and humorless demeanor; attempts to appear unemotional and objective, but is edgy, envious, jealous, quick to take personal offense and react angrily).

F refers to Functional Domains (fluid, interactive)
S refers to Structural Domains (stable, unchanging)

paranoid in accord with our schema of eight clinical domains immediately follow this section (see Figure 23.2).

   Attachment anxiety. Paranoids detest being dependent not only because it signifies weakness and inferiority, but because they are unable to trust anyone. To lean on another is to expose oneself to ultimate betrayal and to rest on ground that will only give way when support is needed most. Rather than chance deceit, paranoids aspire to be the maker of their own fate, free of entanglements and obligations.

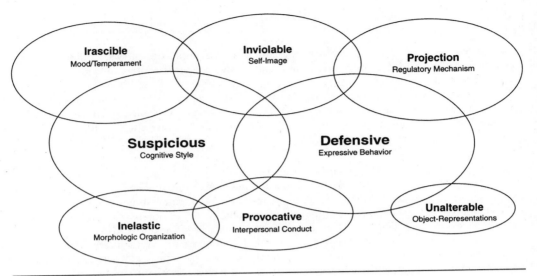

Figure 23.2   Salience of prototypal paranoid domains.

It is bad enough to place one's trust in others; even worse is to be subject to their control and to have one's power curtailed and infringed upon.

To be coerced by external authority and attached to a power stronger than themselves provoke extreme anxiety. Paranoid are acutely sensitive to threats to autonomy, resist all obligations, and are cautious lest any form of cooperation be a subtle ploy to seduce them and force their submission to the will of others. It is this attachment anxiety, with its consequent dread of losing personal control and independence, that underlies paranoids' characteristic resistance to influence. Ever fearful of domination, they watch carefully to ensure that no one robs them of their will.

Any circumstance that prompts feelings of helplessness and incompetence, decreases their independence and freedom of movement, or places them in a vulnerable position subject to the powers of others may precipitate a psychotic episode. Trapped by the danger of dependency, struggling to regain integrity and status, and dreading deceit and betrayal, paranoids may strike out aggressively, accuse others of seeking to persecute them, and ennoble themselves with grandiose virtues and superiority. Should they find that they think, feel, and behave in ways that are alien to their preferred self-image, paranoid's will claim that powerful sources have manipulated and coerced them to submit to others' malicious intent. That these accusations are pathological is evident by their vagueness and irrationality; for example, paranoids safely locate these powers in unidentifiable sources such as "they," "a voice," "communists," or "the devil."

Paranoids' dread of attachment and fear of insignificance are similar to the anxieties of schizotypals. Both shy from close personal relationships and are vulnerable to the threat of "nothingness." These commonalities account, in part, for the difficulties that clinicians have faced in differentiating between these syndromes. There is, however, a crucial difference. Schizotypals find little reinforcement in themselves; their fantasies generate feelings of low self-worth.

Moreover, they turn away from others *and* from themselves; thus, they are neither attached nor possess a sense of self. Though paranoids turn away from others, as do schizotypals, they find reinforcements within themselves. Accustomed to self-determination, they use their active fantasy world to create a self-enhanced image and rewarding existence apart from others. Faced with the loss of external recognition and power, they revert to internal sources of supply. Thus, in contrast to schizotypals, their inner world compensates fully for the rebuffs and anguish of experience; through delusional ideation, they reconstruct an image of self that is more attractive than reality.

Cognitive suspicions and delusions. Paranoids' lack of trust colors their perceptions, thoughts, and memories. No doubt all people selectively perceive events and draw inferences based on their needs and past experiences. But the feelings and attitudes generated in the life history of paranoids have produced an intense mistrust of others, creating within them a chronic and pervasive suspiciousness; they are oversensitive, ready to detect signs of hostility and deception, tend to be preoccupied with such signs, and actively pick up, magnify, and distort the actions and words of others so as to confirm their expectations. Moreover, they assume that events that fail to confirm their suspicions "only prove how deceitful and clever others can be." In their desire to uncover this pretense, they explore every nook and cranny to find justification for their beliefs, constantly testing the "honesty" of their friends. Finally, after cajoling and intimidating others, the paranoid provokes them to exasperation and anger.

In short, the preconceptions of paranoids rarely are upset by facts; they disregard contradictions, confirm their expectations by seizing on real, although minute and irrelevant facts, or create an atmosphere that provokes others to act as they anticipated.

The unwillingness of paranoids to attach themselves to others or to share others' ideas and points of view leaves them isolated and bereft of the reality checks that might restrain their suspicions and fantasies. Driven to maintain independence, paranoids are unable to see things as others do. Apart from others and with no one to counter the proliferations of their imagination, they concoct events to support their fears or wishes, ponder incessantly along a single deviant track, put together the flimsiest of evidence, reshape the past to conform to their beliefs, and build an intricate logic to justify their anxieties and desires. Thus, left to their own devices, they cannot validate their speculations and ruminations; no difference exists in their mind between what they have seen and what they have thought; fleeting impressions and hazy memories become fact; a chain of unconnected facts is fitted together; conclusions are drawn. The inexorable course from suspicion to supposition to imagination has given birth to a delusion; a system of invalid and unshakable beliefs has been created.

Delusions are a natural outgrowth of the paranoid personality pattern. Two conditions, dependence on self for both stimulation *and* reinforcement, are conducive to the emergence of minidelusions. Insistent on retaining independence, paranoids isolate themselves and are unwilling to share the perspective and attitudes of others. They have ample time to cogitate and form idiosyncratic suppositions and hypotheses; these then are "confirmed" as valid because it is they *alone* who are qualified to judge them.

The delusions of the paranoid differ from those seen in other pathological patterns. Accustomed to self-reinforcement and independent thought and "convinced" of their competence and superiority, paranoids are both skillful in formulating beliefs and confident in their correctness; their delusions tend, therefore, to be systematic, rational, and convincing. In contrast, the occasional delusions of the schizotypal and borderline appear illogical and unconvincing, tending to arise under conditions of unusual emotional duress; moreover, in further distinction, they are usually bizarre, grossly irrational, scattered, and unsystematic.

Defensive vigilance and veiled hostility. Paranoids are constantly on guard, mobilized and ready for any emergency or threat. Whether faced with real dangers or not, they maintain a fixed level of preparedness, an alert vigilance against the possibility of attack and derogation. There is an edgy tension, an abrasive irritability, and an ever present defensive stance from which they can spring to action at the slightest hint of threat. This state of rigid control never seems to abate; rarely do they relax, ease up, or let down their guard.

Beneath the surface mistrust and defensive vigilance in the paranoid lies a current of deep resentment toward others who have "made it." To paranoids, most people have attained their status unjustly; thus, paranoids are bitter for having been overlooked, treated unfairly, and slighted by the "high and mighty," "the cheats and the crooks" who duped the world. Only a thin veil hides these bristling animosities.

Unable to accept their own faults and weaknesses, paranoids maintain their self-esteem by attributing their shortcomings to others. They repudiate their own failures and project or ascribe them to someone else. They possess a remarkable talent for spotting even the most trifling of deficiencies in others; both subtly and directly, they point out and exaggerate, with great pleasure, the minor defects they uncover among those they despise. Rarely does their undercurrent of envy and hostility subside; they remain touchy and irascible, ready to humiliate and deprecate anyone whose merits they question and whose attitudes and demeanor evoke their ire and contempt.

There are no universal attributes that may be spoken of as the "essence" of the paranoid personality. The great majority of these patients evidence the constellation of anxieties, cognitions, and behaviors described above, but we must be careful not to let our focus on these common symptoms obscure the variety of forms into which this impairment unfolds or the different coping patterns that underlie them. In the illustrative cases below, we describe some of the features that differentiate five basic subtypes of the paranoid personality. Despite the distinctions we draw, we must be mindful that distinctions are not well defined in reality; there are overlappings, with traces of the more distinctive features of each subvariety found often in the others. Few "pure" textbook cases ever are met.

Prototypal Diagnostic Domains

As in prior chapters, the presentation of the characteristics of the personality under review is divided into the eight domains that are this text's standard format.

Defensive behavior. Paranoids appear tense and guarded. Eyes tend to be fixed, sharply focused on whatever facet of their worldview draws their attention. It is not uncommon for them to make quick movements, should they hear or see something they view as untoward; otherwise, they are likely to remain fixed and unmovable. These characteristics represent the vigilant quality of paranoids' attention to their environment. They are notably alert to anticipate and to ward off any potential malice, deception, or derogation of themselves. It also signifies that they are tenaciously and firmly resistant to external influence and control. Paranoids are constantly mobilized, ready for any real or imagined threat. Whether faced with danger or not, they maintain a fixed level of preparedness, an alert vigilance against the possibility of attack and derogation. They exhibit an edgy tension, an abrasive irritability, and an ever present defensive stance from which they can spring into action at the slightest offense. Their state of rigid control never seems to abate, and they rarely relax, ease up, or let down their guard.

Provocative interpersonal conduct. Paranoids not only bear grudges and are unforgiving of those with whom they have related in the past, but are also likely to display a quarrelsome, fractious, and disputatious attitude toward recent social acquaintances. Interpersonally, they tend to be provocative in their transactions with others, precipitating exasperation and anger by testing others' loyalty and by intrusive and searching preoccupations with possible hidden motives. Beneath the obvious mistrust and defensive vigilance of the paranoid stirs a current of deep resentment toward those who have "made it." To paranoids, most people have attained their status and esteem unjustly. To make matters worse, they feel that they have been personally overlooked and are bitter for having been treated unfairly and slighted by those "high and mighty cheats and crooks" who dupe the world. Only a thin veil hides these bristling animosities.

Every trivial rebuff is a painful reminder to paranoids of their past, part of a plot whose history can be traced back to early mistreatments. Trapped in what they see as a timeless web of deceit and malice, the fears and angers of paranoids may mount to monumental proportions. Should their defenses fall into shambles, their controls dissolve, and their fantasies of doom run rampant, their underlying dread and fury may surge into the open. A flood of hostile energies may erupt, letting loose a violent and uncontrollable torrent of vituperation and aggression. These psychotic outbursts are usually brief. As the surge of fear and hostility is discharged, these patients typically regain their composure and seek to rationalize their actions, reconstruct their defenses, and bind their aggression. This subsiding of bizarre emotions does not lead to a "normal" state but merely a return to their former personality pattern.

Suspicious cognitive style. Perhaps the most distinctive feature of paranoids is their pervasive suspiciousness. Moreover, they are unwarrantedly skeptical, cynical, and mistrustful of the motives of others, including relatives, friends, and associates. Innocuous events are construed as signifying hidden or conspiratorial intent. Most reveal tendencies to search for hidden meanings in completely benign matters and to magnify tangential or minor difficulties into proofs of duplicity or treachery, especially regarding the fidelity of a spouse or intimate friend.

All of us are selective in what we perceive and infer, based on our pattern of needs and past experiences. Unfortunately, the learned feelings and attitudes of paranoids produce a deep mistrust and pervasive suspiciousness of others. They are notoriously oversensitive and disposed to detect signs everywhere of trickery and deception; they are preoccupied with these thoughts, actively picking up minute cues, then magnifying and distorting them so as to confirm their worst expectations. To complicate matters further, events that fail to confirm their preformed suspicions "only prove how deceitful and clever others can be." In an effort to uncover the assumed pretense, they will "test" others and explore every nook and cranny to find some justification for their beliefs. These preconceptions rarely are upset by facts. Paranoids dismiss contradictions and confirm their expectations by seizing on real, although trivial or irrelevant, data. Even more problematic is that they create an atmosphere that provokes others to act as they anticipated. After testing the "honesty" of their friends and constantly cajoling and intimidating others, paranoids will provoke almost everyone into exasperation and anger.

The unwillingness of paranoids to trust sharing their doubts and insecurities leaves them isolated and bereft of the reality checks that might restrain their suspicions. Driven to maintain secrecy, they become increasingly unable to see things as others do. Lacking closeness and sharing, and with no one to counter the proliferations of their imagination, they concoct events in support of their fears or wishes, pondering incessantly over deviant ideas, putting together the flimsiest of evidence, reshaping the past to conform to preconceptions, and building an intricate logic to justify their distortions. Left to their own devices, paranoids are unable to validate their speculations and ruminations. Little difference exists in their mind between what they have seen and what they have thought. Momentary impressions and hazy memories become fact. Chains of unconnected facts are fitted together. An inexorable course from imagination to supposition to suspicion takes place, and soon a system of invalid and unshakable beliefs has been created.

Inviolable self-image.   The majority of paranoids have persistent ideas of self-reference and self-importance. They perceive attacks on their character not apparent to others, asserting as personally derogatory and scurrilous, if not libelous, entirely innocuous actions or events. As a consequence, they seek to be inviolable, are pridefully independent-minded, reluctant to confide in and be dependent on others. This highly insular attitude derives from their intense fear of losing their identity and, more important, their powers of self-determination.

Paranoids detest being dependent, not only because it signifies weakness and inferiority but because they dare not trust anyone. To lean on another is to be exposed to ultimate betrayal and to rest on ground that will give way when support is needed most. Rather than chance deceit, paranoids strive to be the makers of their own fate, free of all personal entanglements and obligations. It is bad enough to trust others; even worse is to be subject to their control.

As a further means of assuring self-determination, paranoids assume an attitude of invincibility and pride. Convincing themselves that they have extraordinary capacities, they can now master their fate alone, as well as overcome every obstacle, resistance, and conflict. All traces of self-doubt are dismissed, and they repudiate all nurturant overtures from others. Thus assured, they will never dread having to need or to depend on anyone.

To be coerced by a power stronger than themselves provokes extreme anxiety. Paranoids are acutely sensitive to any threat to their autonomy, resist all obligations, and are cautious lest any form of cooperation be but a ploy to seduce them and force their submission to the will of others. This attachment anxiety, with its consequent dread of losing personal control and independence, underlies much of the paranoid's characteristic resistance to influence. Fearful of domination, these personalities watch carefully to ensure that no one robs them of their will. Circumstances that prompt feelings of helplessness and incompetence, or decrease their freedom of movement, or place them in a vulnerable position subject to the powers of others may precipitate a sudden and ferocious "counterattack." Feeling trapped by the dangers of dependency, struggling to regain their status, and dreading deceit and betrayal, they may strike out aggressively and accuse others of seeking to persecute them. Should others accuse them accurately of thinking, feeling, or behaving in ways that are alien to their self-image, they are likely to claim that powerful and malevolent sources have coerced them with malicious intent. These accusations may become grossly pathological and signify the presence of an incipient psychotic disorder, as when they locate these powers among an unidentifiable "they" or as a "voice," "communist," or "devil."

Unalterable objects. The internalized representation of significant early relationships among most paranoids are limited and rigidly fixed. There is an implacable configuration of objects representing firmly held images, beliefs, and attitudes. These intrapsychic components are driven to yield unwarranted convictions regarding the attitudes and dispositions of others with whom they interact in their current world. What is most notable about this inner template of objects is their idiosyncratic character and the fixed and tenaciously held assumptions of which they are comprised.

The experiential history of paranoids often gives them reason to be mistrustful and to fear betrayal or sadistic treatment. To counter these sources of threat, they have learned to distance themselves from others and to remain strong and vigilant, not only as a protective stance but as a means of vindication and triumph over potential attackers. To assure their security, they go to great pains to avoid any weakening of their resolve and to develop new and superior powers to control others.

As must be evident from the foregoing, the confidence and pride of paranoids cloak a hollow shell. Their arrogant pose of autonomy rests on insecure internal footings. Extremely vulnerable to challenge, their defensive façade is constantly weakened by real and fantasized threats. In their efforts to reassert their power and invincibility, they will resort to any course of action that will shore up their defenses or thwart their detractors.

Projection mechanism. Perhaps second only to suspiciousness as a sign of the paranoid disorder is their use of the projection regulatory mechanism. These personalities actively disown their undesirable personal traits and motives, attributing them freely to others. Not only are they blind, therefore, to their own unattractive behaviors and characteristics, but they are hyperalert to similar features that may be present to a limited degree in others. Thus, troubled by mounting and inescapable evidence of inadequacy and hostility, paranoids are driven to go beyond mere denial. They not only disown these personally humiliating traits but throw them back at their real or imagined accusers. Through the mechanism of projection, they are able to claim that it is others who are stupid, malicious, and vindictive, and they who are the innocent and unfortunate victim of the incompetence and malevolence of others.

Unable to accept faults and weaknesses within themselves, paranoids maintain their self-esteem by attributing their shortcomings to others. Repudiating their own failures, they project or ascribe them to someone else. They possess a remarkable talent for spotting the most trifling deficiencies in others. Both indirectly and directly, they point to and exaggerate the minor defects they uncover among those they learn to despise. Rarely do their envy and hostility subside. They are touchy and irritable, ready to humiliate and deprecate anyone whose merits they question and whose attitudes and demeanor evoke their ire or contempt. By a simple reversal, paranoids not only absolve themselves of fault but find a "justified" outlet for their resentment and anger. If paranoids are found to have been in error, others should be blamed for their ineptness. If they have been driven to become aggressive, it is only because the evil of others has provoked them. They are innocent, and justifiably indignant, unfortunate and maligned scapegoats for the blundering and the slanderous.

Faced with persistent derogation and threat, paranoids will seek vigorously to redeem themselves and reestablish their sense of autonomy and power. However, they may have no recourse to achieve these ends except fantasy. Unable to face their feelings of inadequacy and insignificance, they may begin to fabricate an image of superior self-worth. Left to ruminate alone, they may construct proofs of their eminence through intricate self-deceptions. Renouncing objective reality, they supplant it with a glorified self-image. They endow themselves with limitless powers and talents, and hence need no longer be ashamed of themselves or fear others. They can now "rise above" petty jealousies, "understanding all too clearly" why others seek to undermine their stature and virtue. The meaning of the malicious and persecutory attacks of others is obvious; it is the paranoid's eminence and superiority that they envy and seek to destroy.

Inelastic organization.   The structural organization of the intrapsychic world of the paranoid is composed of highly controlled and systematically arranged images and impulses. Particularly notable is its constriction and inflexibility such that channels for defensive coping are few and persistently employed; similarly, processes for conflict mediation and need gratification are fixed and immutable. This inelastic structure creates an overstrung and taut frame that is so uncompromising in its accommodation to changing circumstances that unanticipated stressors are likely to precipitate either explosive outbursts or inner shatterings. In contrast to other severe personality disorders, the defective nature of the paranoid's structural organization is *not* its lack of cohesion, but rather its overly constrained and rigid character.

To preclude the possibility of external outbursts or internal shatterings, paranoids seek to transform the ongoing events of their everyday life to make them fit their interior structures and objects. As noted previously, they utilize the projection mechanism and its variants (e.g., projective identification) to achieve these ends. Moreover, even those patients who are noted for their rigidity and their hyperalertness to the environment may begin to lower their controls and loosen their usually firm boundaries between reality and fantasy. This latter process of blurring formerly segregated features of their psychic world will inevitably create new and troublesome consequences.

Irascible mood.   Underlying many of the paranoid's more general characteristics appears to be a cold, sullen, churlish, and humorless temperament. Whether learned or constitutionally based, the paranoid personality tends to be unemotional and "objective" in outlook. On the other hand, they are typically edgy, envious, jealous, and quick to take personal offense, reacting angrily with minimal provocation. One of their major goals is to desensitize their tender and affectionate feelings. They become hard, unyielding, immune, and insensitive to the suffering of others. By so doing they protect themselves against entrapment and against being drawn into a web of anticipated deceit and subjugation. To assume a callous and unsympathetic stance is not difficult for paranoids. Not only is it a successful defensive maneuver against entrapment, but it also allows them to discharge their resentments and angers.

Hostility for the paranoid serves both defensive and restitutive measures. Not only is it a means of countering threats to their equilibrium, but it helps restore their image of self-determination and autonomy. Once released, this hostility draws on a reserve of earlier resentments. Present angers are fueled by animosities from the past. Desire for reprisal and vindication spurred by prior humiliations is brought to the surface and discharged into the stream of current hostility.

Self-Perpetuation Processes

The instrumental behaviors of the structurally defective patterns are less adaptive and more self-defeating than those of the less severely ill. Moreover, they are more vulnerable to the strains of life and are easily precipitated into psychotic disorders. Situations that promote the anxieties of attachment, expectations of sadistic treatment, or the loss of self-determination result in defensive vigilance, withdrawal, and ultimately in the delusions that are so characteristic of the paranoid personality. Not infrequently, the isolation and fantasy ruminations of the patient become deeply entrenched, leading to more permanent psychotic habits and attitudes. Here, we discuss the coping efforts of paranoids, that is, the means by which they seek to prevent further decompensation, but that only intensify their difficulties (see Table 23.2).

Countering attachment. Paranoids have reason to be mistrustful and to fear betrayal and sadistic treatment. To counter these sources of anxiety, they have learned to keep their distance from others and to remain strong and vigilant, not only as a protective stance but as a means of vindication and triumph over potential attackers. To assure their security, they engage in a variety of measures both to prevent the weakening of their own resolve and to generate new powers for controlling others.

TABLE 23.2 Self-Perpetuating Processes

PARANOID

Countering Attachment
    Distances from dependence on others
    Desensitizes or denies tender feelings
    Repudiates overtures of kindness

Discharging Hostility
    Hostility protects jeopardized autonomy
    Anger fueled by resentment of past injustices
    Pent-up anger leads to violent discharges

Reconstruction of Reality
    Disowns objectionable traits, projects onto accusers
    Creates an inescapable hostile environment
    Fabricates superior self-worth

One of the major steps in this quest is a desensitization of tender and affectionate feelings. Paranoids become hard, unyielding, immune, and insensitive to the suffering and pleading of others. By so doing they secure themselves against entrapment and against being drawn into a web of deceit and subjugation. Assuming a callous and unsympathetic posture is not difficult for paranoids; not only does it serve as a defensive maneuver against attachment, but it also allows for the discharge of resentments and angers.

As a further means of affirming self-determination, paranoids assume an air of invincibility and pride. They convince themselves that they have extraordinary capacities, that they can master their fate alone, and overcome every obstacle, resistance, and conflict. They dismiss all traces of self-doubt and repudiate the nurturant overtures of others; in this way, they need never dread having to lean on anyone.

But paranoids' autonomy is spurious. They maintain an illusion of superiority by rigid self-conviction and exaggerated bluff. Time and again, their competencies are proved defective and they are made to look foolish; thus, their precarious equilibrium, their self-appointed certainty and pride are upset too easily and too often. To redeem their belief in their invincibility, paranoids begin to employ extreme and grossly pathological measures. Rather than accepting their obvious weaknesses and faults, they assert that some alien influence is undermining them and causing them to fail and be humbled before others. Frailty, ineffectuality, shame, or whatever predicament they find themselves in must be attributed to an irresistible destructive power. As paranoids' suspicion of a "foreign force" grows and as their vigilance against belittlement and humiliation crumbles, they begin increasingly to distort reality. Not only can they not accept the fact that their failures are self-caused, but they are unwilling to ascribe these failures to "pedestrian" powers and events; rather, their loss reflects the malicious workings of devils, x-rays, magnetism, poisons, and so on. Their delusions of influence and persecution signify, then, both their dread of submission and their need to bolster pride by attributing their shortcomings to the action of insidious deceits or supernatural forces.

Discharging hostility.   As just noted, the confidence and pride of paranoids are hollow shells; their pose of independence stands on insecure footings. They are extremely vulnerable to challenge, and their defensive façade is constantly weakened by real and delusional threats. To reassert their power and invincibility, they must resort to some course of action that will shore up their defenses and thwart their attackers. Hostility in paranoids is a defensive and restitutive measure, a means of countering threats to their equilibrium and a means of reestablishing their image of self-determination and autonomy.

Once released, paranoids' hostility draws on a deep reserve of earlier resentments. The fires of present angers are fed by animosities reactivated from the past; intense impulses for reprisal and vindication are brought to the surface and discharged into the stream of current hostility. Every trivial rebuff by others is a painful reminder of the past, part of a plot whose history is traced back to early humiliations and mistreatments. Trapped in this timeless web of deceit and malice, paranoids may multiply their fears and angers to monumental proportions. With defenses down, controls dissolved, and fantasies of doom running rampant, dread and fury increase. A flood of frantic and hostile energies may erupt, letting loose a violent discharge, an uncontrollable torrent of vituperation and aggression.

These psychotic outbursts are usually of brief duration. As the swell of fear and hostility is discharged, the patient regains composure and seeks to rationalize actions, reconstruct defenses, and bind aggression. But this subsiding of bizarre emotions does not lead to "normality"; rather, the patient merely returns to his or her former paranoid personality pattern.

Reconstructing reality. Paranoids transform events to suit their self-image and aspirations; delusions may be seen as an extreme form of this more general process of reality reconstruction. Even the passive-ambivalent, noted for excessive rigidity, exhibits this lowering of controls, this loosening of boundaries between what is real and what is fantasized. These reconstructions take many forms, but it will suffice for us to describe the two that are most commonly found among paranoids: denial of weakness and malevolence, and their projection on others; and aggrandizement of self through grandiose fantasies.

Troubled by the mounting and inescapable evidence of their inadequacy and hostility, paranoids must go further than mere denial; they not only disown these objectionable traits, but throw them back at their real or imagined accusers. It is others who are stupid, malicious, and vindictive; paranoids, in contrast, are the innocent and unfortunate victim of the ineffectuality and malevolence of others. With this simple reversal, paranoids not only absolve themselves of fault, but find an outlet and a justification for their resentment and anger. If they are in error, others should be blamed for their ineptness; if they have been aggressive, it is only because the evil in others has provoked them. They have been an innocent, and justifiably indignant, scapegoat for the blundering and the slanderous.

But the gains of the projection maneuver are short-lived; moreover, it ultimately intensifies the paranoid's plight. By ascribing slanderous and malevolent urges to others, paranoids now face threat where none in fact existed; thus, by subjective distortion, they have created an ever present hostile environment that surrounds them and from which there is no physical escape. Furthermore, their unjust accusations are bound to provoke in others feelings of exasperation and anger; thus, their strategy of projection has transformed what may have been overtures of goodwill from others into the hostility they feared.

Faced with genuine derogation and threat, paranoids must redeem themselves and reestablish their sense of autonomy and power. Once more, they may have no recourse but to turn to fantasy. Unable to confront feelings of inadequacy and insignificance, they fabricate an image of superior self-worth and importance. Left alone to ruminate, they unfold proofs of their eminence through intricate self-deceptions. They renounce or distort objective reality and supplant it with a glorified image of self. Having endowed themselves with limitless virtues, powers, and talents, they need not now be ashamed of themselves or fear anyone; they can "rise above" petty jealousies and can "understand all too clearly" why others seek to undermine and persecute them. The meaning of others' malicious attacks is obvious; it is the paranoid's eminence—his or her infinite superiority—that others envy and seek to destroy.

Step by step, paranoids' self-glorifications and persecutory delusions form into a systematic pattern; the "whole picture" comes into sharp relief. One delusion feeds on another, unchecked by the controls of social reality. Fabrications, employed initially to cope with the despair of reality, become more "real" than reality itself; it is at this point that we see the clear emergence of a psychotic phase.

INTERVENTION GOALS

Not unlike other structurally defective personality patterns, the future prospects for paranoids are not promising. Their habits and attitudes are deeply ingrained and pervade the entire fabric of their functioning. Modest improvements are possible, of course, but these are likely merely to diminish the frequency of troublesome episodes rather then revamp the basic personality style. Impairment in the paranoid is more likely to be of an interpersonal than an intrapsychic nature, and tends to be less disturbing to the patient than to others. Most paranoid personalities do not succumb to serious and persistent delusions and tend to come in contact with psychological services only at the request of others or when their defenses crumble, triggering the onset of a more severe condition. They are regarded by most associates as suspicious and testy people. A very small number do attain considerable success, especially if they are unusually talented or happen by good fortune to attract a coterie of disciples.

Despite difficult social relationships, the long-range prognosis for paranoids is not as poor as that of the schizotypal, one of their structurally defective counterparts. Paranoids can obtain satisfactions from themselves; schizotypals do not. Faced with external derogation, paranoids can nurture themselves until their wounds are sufficiently healed. Schizotypals, lacking faith both in themselves and others, remain empty-handed. Compared to borderlines, their other structurally defective counterpart, paranoids have both a disadvantage and an advantage insofar as prognosis is concerned. Borderlines characteristically maintain reasonably good, if erratic, interpersonal relations; paranoids do not. As a consequence, borderline personalities may gain some of the support and encouragement they need. Furthermore, unlike the paranoid, they turn to others during difficult periods, often soliciting enough affection and security to forestall a further decline. In contrast, paranoids tend to remain socially difficult and keep to themselves when relationships turn sour. Behaviors such as these increase their isolation, not only resulting in an intensification of their suspicions and secretiveness but giving rise to further social estrangement. To borderlines' disadvantage is their lack of internal reserve, which leads them to slip into a state of helplessness should they fail to evoke external support. This is not the case with paranoids. Not only will they refuse to submit to weakness and indolence, but they will struggle to "pull themselves up by their own bootstraps."

Despite each patient's unique combination of presenting complaints, reasons for entering therapy, and personality presentation, a cardinal aim of synergistic therapy with paranoid personalities is to loosen up the extreme constriction and inflexibility that pervades all clinical domains (see Table 23.3). Concurrently, an attempt must be made to balance the confused mix of polarity reversals that may have contributed to perpetuating the paranoid pattern. If paranoids can learn to let down their guard and obtain satisfaction and reinforcement from interpersonal relationships, instead of being constantly on the defensive, they may open themselves up to many life-enhancing experiences.

Reestablishing Polarity Balances

Paranoid personalities display an extreme sensitivity to psychic pain, anticipating rejection and humiliation at every turn. For this reason, they try to avoid situations that are aversive or negatively reinforcing. Always wary of what others can do to hurt them

TABLE 23.3   Therapeutic
Strategies and Tactics for the
Prototypal Paranoid Personality

STRATEGIC GOALS
Balance Polarities
 Reduce polarity
 Increase polarity

Counter Perpetuations
 Stop provocations of rejection
 Modify rigid minidelusions
 Undo self-protective withdrawals

TACTICAL MODALITIES
 Alter inviolable self-image
 Moderate irascible mood
 Reorient cognitive suspiciousness

and fearful of external control, paranoids have learned to withdraw from others and turn to themselves. Therapy thus should begin to focus on reducing the predominant self-orientation as well as attenuating the extreme insensitivity to the needs of others. Countering vigilant paranoid mistrust of others is fundamental to balancing the pain-pleasure polarity. Gradually aiding patients in identifying possible rewards from interactions with others will fuel their desire to seek positive experiences within the realm of interpersonal contact.

Countering Perpetuating Tendencies

The suspicious nature and extreme distrust of others are at the core of this personality's problems. Paranoids remain so vigilant to signs of rejection that they inevitably uncover them. Accusations and provocations, combined with projection of personal insecurities onto others, cannot help but antagonize people. Interrupting the cycle that perpetuates these tendencies may best be accomplished in an indirect manner. Beck and Freeman (1990a) suggest increasing the paranoid's sense of self-efficacy. This in turn will reduce the likelihood that projection will be employed as a defense. Empowering the self may take the edge off the extreme hypervigilance the paranoid uses to scan the environment for expected signs of hostilities.

 As a result of these delusional thought patterns, paranoids tend to turn from others to avoid rejection and rebuff. Withdrawal thus serves a self-protective function, yet it also makes them more susceptible to reality distortions, leaving them to ruminate and construct elaborate fabrications without the necessary reality checks. Inadequate reality testing combined with a suspicious attitude toward others fosters the development of delusional thought processes. A major goal of personologic therapy with this disorder is to minimize paranoids' tendency to engage in self-protective withdrawal by encouraging them to gather additional information from the environment before reevaluating assumptions about others. When it is established that paranoids' perceptions about the dangers in their surroundings are largely inaccurate, the use of self-protective withdrawals may decrease, thereby further attenuating their pathology.

Identifying Domain Dysfunctions

The paranoid personality displays prominent dysfunctions in the cognitive style and expressive behavior domains. Paranoids' suspicious nature extends rigidly, inflexibly, and virtually indiscriminately to all situations encountered. Helping them see that most fears are imaginary and invalid will assist in alleviating the guardedness. It also will diminish the need to engage in self-protective withdrawal.

The projective thinking displayed by paranoids not only protects their self-image, it often elicits attack and rejection. As personal faults are disavowed and attributed to others, the belief that the source of all misery lies in the malevolent nature of their adversaries becomes stronger. Therapeutic efforts must aim to strengthen paranoids' self-sufficiency, gradually encouraging patients to accept minor faults in themselves. Affectively, paranoids display a touchiness and irritability that, combined with their interpersonally provocative style, will be experienced as abrasive even by otherwise affable individuals. Interventions must teach paranoids to express anger and criticism in a more subtle, socially accepted manner, as well as encourage the expression of positive emotions.

Early relational experiences have been internalized and have left paranoids with a set of fixed, unyielding, and unwarranted beliefs about others. The systemic constriction and inflexibility of their morphological organization and their tenacious and unalterable coping styles present a major dilemma. Work in this area must emphasize the acquisition of more diverse coping mechanisms. It is also essential that new relational experiences be encountered.

SELECTING THERAPEUTIC MODALITIES

Essentially, the therapist must build trust through a series of slow and progressive steps. A quiet, formal, and genuine respect for the patient as a person must be shown. The therapist must accept, but not confirm, patients' unusual beliefs and allow them to explore their thoughts and feelings at a pace that can be tolerated. The major initial goal of therapy is to free paranoids of mistrust by showing them that they can share their anxieties with another person without the humiliation and maltreatment to which they are accustomed. If this can be accomplished, paranoids may learn to look at the world not only from their own perspective but through the eyes of others. If they can trust the therapist, they can begin to relax, relinquish their defenses, and open themselves to new attitudes. Once they have accepted the therapist as someone they can trust, they may be able to lean on him or her and accept his or her thoughts and suggestions. This may become a basis for a more generalized lessening of suspicions and for a wider scope of trusting and sharing.

Behavioral Techniques

The goals of behavioral treatment have been designed to diminish paranoids' hypersensitivity to criticism and to modulate their behavioral reactions (Turkat & Maisto, 1985). A variety of information-processing and social skills training programs may be employed with paranoids who appear particularly resistant to advice-giving cognitive approaches. Skills training may include such techniques as role playing, behavioral rehearsals, and modeling via videotape methods. Central to this task is having the patient learn to interpret what others say in a nondefensive and noncounteracting way.

Behavioral interventions can be of use to target paranoids' need to be constantly on guard, actively resisting sources of external control. Because they are so fearful of being externally influenced, behavioral techniques will need to emphasize personal control. Contingency management programs that rely on others to provide reinforcement are likely to fail and should be avoided. In situations where others represent a threat to their autonomy, paranoids may lash out aggressively in an attempt to regain control and relieve anxiety. The immediate gains, however are, temporary, and ultimately serve only to perpetuate the paranoid style. Achieving a reduction in defensiveness, however, as well as enhancing feelings of competence and self-control, can be achieved through assertiveness training. The therapist may have to educate the patient about the differences between aggression and assertiveness. Teaching paranoids that they can express thoughts in a constructive manner, without the intensity of the negative affect, will take the edge off their explosive nature. Relaxation training can help them feel more at ease and may also lessen the need for alternative modes of relaxation such as substance abuse.

A functional analysis often will reveal particular environments or people that promote paranoid reactions. Impulse control can be strengthened by assisting the patient to recognize these contextual determinants and subsequently avoid them if the situation cannot be handled. If possible, environmental irritants should be removed. To gain the patient's cooperation, the therapist can use verbal reinforcers, emphasizing that the skills to be acquired would enhance self-control.

Some behaviorists focus on diminishing the patient's anxiety about criticism. Components of the anxiety reduction approach include construction of a fear hierarchy, teaching progressive muscle relaxation, and developing a repertoire of adaptive cognitions in response to fear-eliciting stimuli. Criticism and negative feedback may be the result of deficits in interpersonal skills; therefore, anxiety management training procedures should be followed by social skills training. Paranoids are often extremely self-absorbed, unable to tune in to others' thoughts and feelings. Assisting them in overcoming this inattentiveness can be accomplished by communication skills training. The therapist can engage the client in role playing, providing immediate feedback. In summary, treatment with these patients is aimed at diminishing hypersensitivity to social evaluation and eliminating those behaviors that invite criticism.

Interpersonal Techniques

Interpersonal approaches may be well suited to establish a collaborative relationship between the paranoid and the therapist. An important goal of interpersonal therapy with this disorder is to facilitate what L.S. Benjamin (1993) calls pattern recognition. She notes, however, that paranoids often are hesitant to discuss family history. This reluctance is thought to stem from fear that talking about family issues will elicit punishment. Nevertheless, paranoid patients need to learn that, although the expectations of attack are understandable considering early learning experiences, they are no longer appropriate or adaptive in their current environment. Especially in the therapeutic relationship when a genuine collaboration takes place, much of paranoid thinking begins to wane; that is, the patient no longer perceives the therapist as being judgmental and critical. The task of all therapists is to convey a kindness and patience that does not suggest either criticism or appeasement. With a solid basis of trust, patients may begin to recognize that the expectation of hostility from others is no longer appropriate and that their own feelings of anger and hostility only provoke counter-hostility from others.

The abuse and harassment paranoids suffered at the hands of parents can have a profound impact on child-rearing practices; if intervention does not target this area, future generations may repeat the pattern of abuse. L.S. Benjamin (1993) suggests helping paranoids recall how it felt to be abused; this in turn can foster a more empathic attitude toward their own children. Substituting maladaptive patterns requires paranoids to shift from identification with to differentiation from aggressors, while rechanneling the anger that often has been misdirected. Central in achieving the goal of reducing patients' fearfulness and hostility is recognition that their behavior signifies the internalization of childhood figures who were excessively controlling and abusing. One tactic suggested by Benjamin is to help patients see that they are now acting like their despised parent; this observation may prompt some paranoids to try to be different.

The therapist may at times have to draw back to allow for interpersonal breathing space. Intensive therapy, as Stone (1993) notes, encourages self-revelation and transference reactions that are extremely anxiety provoking. Allowing more space between appointments may prevent premature dropout. Once patients feel safe, there are opportunities to help them learn about trust and to think more benignly about present life matters.

Assisting patients to recognize that past perceptions of danger were not always accurate will additionally facilitate the development of a more flexible interpersonal style. Reluctance to engage in close relationships can be addressed by encouraging patients to explore the benefits of being alone versus having intimate relationships. When paranoids can accept that interactions with others may actually have something positive to offer, an important step in reducing isolation has been achieved.

With most personality disorders, group therapy can provide an ideal forum for reality testing. Yet, because of paranoids' obstinate and accusatory attitudes, as well as their intrinsic mistrust, rigidity, and refusal to examine interpersonal distortions, group methods are generally contraindicated (Yalom, 1985). The tendency to misinterpret feedback or contributions from other group members may provoke hostility, putting a strain on the group's cohesion and placing the paranoid at risk for premature dropout. Paranoids may, however, benefit from examining group processes while maintaining a secure distance. Allowing the paranoid to be a passive observer can encourage the patient to examine different hypotheses for people's behavior, without actually having to defend his or her own actions.

Similarly, marital and family techniques may run aground if careful attention is not paid to paranoid processes. Paranoids may question the fidelity and trustworthiness of their partners and may see the therapist as combining forces with other family members; therefore, it is wise to use cotherapists. The predominance of negative affect in family dynamics as well as in interactions with others must be counterbalanced by encouraging patients to express more positive statements and emotions. On the other hand, it is often wise, once patients have achieved a reasonable level of impulse control, to support the nonparanoid spouse to stand up for his or her beliefs, if not to directly challenge the pervasive mistrust of the paranoid.

Cognitive Techniques

Cognitive techniques can additionally help paranoids gain insight into their dysfunctional behaviors. This personality style is maintained by the core beliefs and schemata that others cannot be trusted and will intentionally try to hurt them. Interventions should aim to modify the individual's basic assumptions, as these are the root cause of this disorder; yet schema-driven cognitive distortion must not be directly challenged because confrontation will be seen as a personal attack. Beck and Freeman (1990a) note that modifications of patients' basic assumptions would require patients to relax enough to reduce their hypervigilance and defensiveness. However, increasing paranoids' sense of self-efficacy must precede attempts to modify other aspects of their automatic thoughts, interpersonal behavior, and basic assumptions. These authors propose two ways of accomplishing this goal: (a) if the paranoid overestimates the threat posed by the situation, or underestimates his or her capacity to solve the problem, interventions that promote a more realistic appraisal of coping ability will increase the patient's sense of self-efficacy; (b) if it is determined that the appropriate skills to contend with the situation are lacking, interventions that cultivate coping skills will serve to increase self-efficacy.

The paranoid's suspicious cognitive style manifests itself in cognitive errors frequently characterized by dichotomous thinking and overgeneralizations; for example, others are likely to be viewed as either trustworthy or untrustworthy, fully competent or entirely incompetent. Such beliefs are reinforced by paranoids' tendency to reason backwards from preconceived ideas to the evidence. Several techniques can be employed to help establish a new perspective on others. Initially, the patient can be instructed to monitor interpersonal experiences along with the cognitions and emotions that accompany these interactions. Gathering more information can help fill in the inevitable gaps that exist in the paranoid's fund of knowledge about others' motives. Alternative explanations can then be explored. The therapist must take care not to interpret the assumptions as being faulty, but must seek instead to shift the weight of probability the paranoid attributes to the alternative hypotheses. The therapist should strive to introduce an element of doubt in the paranoid's mind regarding the validity of his or her beliefs (Stone, 1993).

Self-Image Techniques

Beneath the flimsy exterior that conveys a sense of grandiosity and self-importance, paranoids carefully shelter a fragile self-image. Unable to admit to personal faults, they project them onto others. Cognitive interventions can address the patient's need to blame others and utilize projection as a defense. Toward the end of therapy, some theorists suggest that the therapist can help patients refine their interpersonal skills by improving the ability to empathize with others and see things from others' perspective. This can be done by asking patients to anticipate the impact of their actions on others and to imagine what it would feel like to be in another's shoes. The validity of patients' belief about the feelings and thoughts of others can be examined by investigating how closely their conclusions match the available evidence. Especially valuable in this regard may be the introduction of an existentially based perspective, one that helps patients recognize that some of their suspicions and their fearful outlook may have a measure of merit. However, the therapist can use the patient's growing sense of affirmation as a vehicle to explore distinctions between past and contemporary realities.

Regarding specific modes of therapy, it is simplest to say that technique is secondary to building trust. There are, however, a variety of procedures that can be employed along the way. Regardless of the particular approach used at any given time, the therapist can avoid arousing further suspicion by carefully explaining each move to the patient. The treatment rationale should be straightforward and clear, and treatment planning must acknowledge the paranoid's need for control. At no time should the patient be directly confronted with his or her delusions.

Intrapsychic Techniques

Gabbard (1994) highlights the goals of psychodynamic interventions with this disorder as helping patients shift their beliefs about the origin of their problems from an external cause to an internal one. This will be no mean feat, however; the therapist's willingness to tolerate paranoids' distortions and hostile feelings, as well as his or her empathic sensitivity, may provide a basis for developing genuine rapport. As the therapist asks for patients' life details, he or she must avoid challenging patients' perception of events. Most important, the therapist must restrain from reacting in a problematic countertransferential way. Salzman (1980) states that the patient should come to see the therapist as a benign and friendly helper.

Letting go of their rigid defensive structure can free up patients' energy to acquire more satisfying interpersonal relationships. Paranoids also spend a great deal of energy on ruminating about the past and feeling that they should receive retribution for perceived wrongs. Goals in this area center on having patients accept reality. Frustrations are an inevitable part of everyone's life, and paranoids must relinquish these claims at compensation. As the paranoid's defenses gradually ease up, feelings of vulnerability, inferiority, and worthlessness come to the foreground. Depression may result, calling for a shift in the focus of therapy to resolve these depressive components.

At times, the therapeutic balance may be challenged by the patient's attempts to elicit a counterreaction from the therapist. Gabbard (1994) emphasizes that the therapist must contain feelings instead of acting on them, thereby providing the patient with a new object relationship unlike those previously encountered. Gradually, these new experiences may be internalized.

Pharmacologic Techniques

Despite the relative paucity of research reporting therapeutic benefit from pharmacologic intervention, trials with medication may be indicated when the paranoid's characterologic defenses fail and specific symptoms such as anxiety or depression occur. Often useful in this regard are SSRI antidepressants (e.g., fluoxetine, sertraline) and low-dose regimens of one or another benzodiazepine (e.g., alprazolam, diazepam). Only when contact with reality worsens and a psychotic breakdown is imminent are low dosages of antipsychotics called for (e.g., risperidone, olanzapine). Medication may represent a threat to the paranoid's need for internal control and as a result resistance can be expected. With medications, as with other therapeutic efforts, the therapist must involve the patient in treatment planning, outlining in detail the potential benefits as well as the possible side effects. To gain collaboration, the therapist must emphasize to the patient how the medication can help increase self-control and moderate feelings of tension.

MAKING SYNERGISTIC ARRANGEMENTS

Early on in therapy, focus should be on developing the therapeutic relationship. Other techniques will have the desired effect only when the patient has developed enough trust in the therapist and when the alliance has stabilized. Nondirective cognitive approaches that focus on increasing self-efficacy may be indicated as a first course of action, to be followed, where appropriate, by other measures. The choice of second-stage therapeutic methods depends on both practical and ultimate goals. At best, therapy is likely to control or moderate rather then reverse the basic personality pattern.

Developing a trusting relationship and increasing the patient's feelings of self-esteem will lay the groundwork for other therapeutic modalities and have profound effects across clinical domains. Feeling more secure with their own strengths, for example, will lessen patients' need to engage in projective defense. Other cognitive techniques can subsequently be employed to target paranoids' unrealistic perception of their environment. Creating an element of doubt in the patient's mind about the accuracy of beliefs will encourage him or her to explore potentially positive characteristics of others in interpersonal relationships. At the same time, behavioral methods can teach patients to be less defensive and to inhibit expressions of hostility. Equipped with a better outlook on life and the potential for obtaining reinforcement from others, these patients may be able to handle the more searching psychodynamic procedures. Rebuilding the paranoid's basic personality structure necessitates the careful utilization and sequencing of these techniques, and must proceed slowly and carefully to uncover unconscious elements.

If it is determined that the family contributes to the paranoid pattern or that the marital partner bears the brunt of the malicious accusations, marital or family therapy should be pursued concurrently. In the course of therapy, medication should be considered when anxiety crops up or when the paranoid becomes extremely hostile or starts acting out. Institutionalization may be required if reality controls break down. At this point, the carefully orchestrated therapeutic efforts that may have led to some progress previously will have to be put on hold. If the patient decides to continue therapy, the therapist will, quite likely, have to start from scratch rebuilding the fragile, trusting bond that may have been severed by the therapist's decision to institutionalize the patient.

Illustrative Cases

There are several attributes that may be spoken of, somewhat loosely, as the core features of the paranoid personality. The great majority of these patients evidence the constellation of anxieties, cognitions, and behaviors described in prior sections, but we must be careful not to let our focus on these common symptoms obscure the variety of forms into which this disorder unfolds. In what follows, we describe some of the features that differentiate five adult subtypes of the paranoid personality (see Table 23.4). Despite the distinctions we draw, we must be mindful that distinctions are

TABLE 23.4   Paranoid Personality Disorder Subtypes

Insular: Reclusive, self-sequestered, hermitical; self-protectively secluded from omnipresent threats and destructive forces; hypervigilant and defensive against imagined dangers.

MCMI P-2A

Malignant: Belligerent, cantankerous, intimidating, revengeful, callous, and tyrannic; hostility vented primarily in fantasy; projects own venomous outlook onto others; persecutory delusions.

MCMI P-6B

Obdurate: Self-assertive, unyielding, stubborn, steely, implacable, unrelenting, dyspeptic, peevish, and cranky stance; legalistic and self-righteous; discharges previously restrained hostility; renounces self-other conflict.

MCMI P-7

Querulous: Contentious, caviling, fractious, argumentative; fault-finding, unaccommodating, resentful, choleric, jealous, peevish, sullen, endless wrangles, whiny, waspish, snappish.

MCMI P-8A

Fanatic: Grandiose delusions, irrational and flimsy; pretentious, expansive; supercilious contempt and arrogance toward others; lost pride reestablished with extravagant claims and fantasies.

MCMI P-5

not well defined in reality; there are overlappings, with traces of the more distinctive features of each subvariety found often in the others. Few "pure" textbook cases ever are met.

PARANOID PERSONALITY: FANATIC TYPE (PARANOID WITH NARCISSISTIC TRAITS)

Case 23.1, Elizabeth R., 47

Presenting Picture: With her flamboyant style and flare for the dramatic, Elizabeth R. felt from an early age that she had a "special destiny." Considering herself a visionary, she painted portraits "from her soul," where she had special insights into people. She could paint people's faces with a deep understanding of who they were even if she had never spoken with them. She also had a special sensitivity to light that she discovered while studying art in Italy. In Europe, she became aware of a "natural ability" that set her apart from the teaming masses of artists she studied with. Reluctantly admitting that her commissions for paintings were drying up and that she had few prospects on the horizon, she was quick to add that others were still jealous of her extraordinary talents. The problem was that she was just too brilliant and forward-thinking for others to understand her. After all, "a great artist must suffer," and this was her time for suffering. This did not dissuade her from continuing to pursue her mission and fulfill her calling to be a great artist.

Clinical Assessment: Fanatic paranoids are similar to their less structurally defective parallel, the narcissistic personality, with whom they are often interwoven. Both seek to retain their admirable self-image, act in a haughty and pretentious manner, are naïvely self-confident, ungenerous, exploitive, expansive, and presumptuous, as well as display an air of supercilious contempt and benign arrogance toward others.

In contrast to the narcissist, who achieves a modicum of success with an optimistic veneer and exploitive behaviors, Elizabeth had run hard against reality. Her illusion of omnipotence had periodically been shattered, toppling her from her vaulted image of eminence. Accustomed to being viewed as the center of things and to being a valued and admired figure, at least in her own eyes, she could not tolerate the lessened significance circumstances had now assigned to her. Her narcissism had been profoundly wounded.

Not only did Elizabeth have to counter the indifference, the humiliation, and the fright of insignificance generated by reality, but she needed to reestablish her lost pride through extravagant claims and fantasies. Upset by assaults on her self-esteem, she reconstructed her image of herself and ascended once more to the status from which she fell. To do this, she endowed herself by illusory self-reinforcement with superior powers and exalted competencies. She dismissed events that conflicted with her newly acquired and self-designated importance; flimsy talents and accomplishments were embellished, creating a new self-image that supplanted objective reality.

Because Elizabeth lacked internal discipline and self-control, she allowed her reparative fantasies to embroider a fabric of high sheen and appeal, caring little for the fact that her claims were unwarranted. These grandiose assertions, clearly evident in her MCMI protocol, became fixed and adamant; they were too important to Elizabeth's need to regain importance and to become a person of significance and esteem. She went to great lengths to convince herself and others of the validity of her claims, insisting against obvious contradictions and the ridicule of others that she deserved to be catered to and that she was entitled to special acknowledgment and privileges.

But the evidence in support of Elizabeth's assertions was as flimsy as a house of cards, easily collapsed by the slightest incursion. Unable to sustain this image before others and rebuffed and unable to gain the recognition she craved, she turned more and more toward herself for salvation. Taking liberties with objective facts and wandering further from social reality and shared meanings, she concocted an ever more elaborate fantasy world of grandiose delusions. Not in an uncommon pattern, she began to assume the role and attributes of some idolized person, someone whose repute could not be questioned by others. As this identification took root, Elizabeth asserted her new identity as an awesome and talented genius. Grandiose missions were proposed for "saving the world," plans were made for solving insurmountable perplexities, and so on. These schemes were worked out in minute detail, corresponding to objective needs and formulated with sufficient logic to draw at least momentary attention and recognition from others.

Synergistic Treatment Plan: Elizabeth would be likely to show marked resistance in therapy, given that the probable reason for her seeking treatment was to find a counselor who would validate what she already "knew" to be the correct course of action. A genuine, trusting, and honest posture would be required from the beginning, though a measure of steadfast nondefensive confrontiveness would accompany this stance. The primary modality with Elizabeth would be working toward identifying faulty perpetuating *cognitions,* including her synthetic belief of her own grandiosity and withdrawal from the "common folk," which masked a lacking sense of *self,* while protecting her from *pain.* Not surprisingly, these actions provoked greater levels of rejection from others; her *interpersonal* tendency to devalue and distrust others needed to be modified for her to engage in more parallel, give-and-take social relations.

Therapeutic Course: Whereas short-term methods were optimally suited to Elizabeth, the techniques of *environmental management, psychopharmacologic treatment,* and *behavior modification* would not be of substantive value in effecting change. Altering her attitudes toward herself and her less than socially acceptable behavior were best brought about through procedures of *cognitive reorientation.* Once a baseline of rapport had been established, Elizabeth was able to withstand methods that confronted her dysfunctional beliefs and expectations (e.g., Beck, Ellis). Short-term *interpersonal* methods (e.g., Kiesler, Klerman) were employed next to probe and modify her attitudes and social habits. More expressive and time-extended techniques may have been useful in some ways, but they would have been difficult to justify in that the patient's self-illusions may have been reinforced too strongly by the imaginative freedom these methods foster. Focused interpersonal methods, such as brief *group* and *family* therapy, may also have helped her view herself in a more realistic social light and assisted her in learning the skills of social sharing and cooperation.

With a brief therapeutic focus, care was taken not to stress Elizabeth's deficiencies because this may have endangered the therapeutic relationship. Efforts were made, however, not to allow her to assume a dominant posture in treatment after her initial discomfort had receded. Confronted early on was her belief that she did not need to consider changing her views because she believed herself to already be almost perfect. In sum, she was loath to accede to any but the briefest therapy, hence increasing the likelihood of early relapse. She did, however, become involved in a short-term regimen and maintained a well-measured distance from the therapist, trying to resist the searching probes of personal exploration, especially those that implied deficiencies on her part. An effective cognitive confrontation method countered her efforts to shift responsibility for her own deficiencies to others. Unless dealt with directly, yet without disapproval on the part of the therapist, her evasiveness and unwillingness seriously interfered with short-term progress. With a firm but consistently honest and confrontive technique, the treatment setting did not give witness to struggles in which she sought to outwit the therapist and assert her dominance. The therapist maintained great patience and equanimity to establish a spirit of genuine confidence and respect.

A strong cognitively based method to undo distorted expectations focused on extinguishing her tendency to devalue others, not to trust their judgments, and to think of them as naïve and simpleminded. Rather than question the correctness of her own beliefs, she assumed that the views of others were always at fault. Confronted was her habit of assuming that the more disagreements she had with others, the more she was convinced of her own superiority and thus the more arrogant and presumptuous she was likely to become.

Unusual for a problem of this nature, Elizabeth's treatment was self-motivated, though it followed a period of unaccustomed achievement failures. More typically, brief confrontive therapy would be called for to counter the belief that, if left alone, a fanatic paranoid such as Elizabeth would be able to solve her own problems. Whatever the promptings, her pride appeared to be in jeopardy in submitting to the role of patient. Though she accepted therapy in its early stages, this attitude was rather fragile and tenuous until she came to respect the therapist as forthright and not easily intimidated.

Although efforts were made to rebuild Elizabeth's recently depleted self-esteem, the therapist took care not to appear subservient in the process. Elizabeth's self-confidence was able to be restored rapidly by merely allowing her to recall past achievements and successes, and this was attained in a few sessions. A goal more likely to prevent recurrences, however, was that of guiding Elizabeth into becoming more sensitive to the needs of others and accepting the constraints and responsibilities of shared social living. This required strengthening her capacity to face her shortcomings frankly. In this regard, the therapist was careful not to be deceived by mere superficial compliance with these efforts.

PARANOID PERSONALITY:
MALIGNANT TYPE
(PARANOID WITH SADISTIC TRAITS)

CASE 23.2, ARNOLD K., 46

Presenting Picture: Arnold K. seemed at first to be settling into a new lifestyle, prompted by an employment change. Until recently, he had worked for a moving company, but decided that he wanted to freelance, using his own truck to move or repossess items. His new business arrangements required that customers be people he knew and that they pay cash at the outset of the agreement. Arnold explained that he did not have reason to trust outsiders, and that even so-called trusted friends could be unscrupulous. As he continued to explain his motivation for these "protective" measures, it became clear that Arnold, having a childhood marked by oppressive parents, was suspicious of everyone and believed that there was an ulterior motive to every action. Above and beyond self-driven motives, according to him, people had a desire to persecute him. These delusions carried with them a strong desire for retribution, and Arnold envisioned that there would come a day when all these people would "get theirs," and that he would see to this personally.

Clinical Assessment: *Malignant paranoids* such as Arnold tend be structurally defective variants of the sadistic personality, whose features frequently commingle and blend with those of the paranoid. He would be best characterized by his power orientation, his mistrust, resentment, and envy of others, and by his autocratic, belligerent, and intimidating manner. Underlying these features was a ruthless desire to triumph over others, to vindicate himself for past wrongs by cunning revenge or callous force, if necessary.

In contrast to his less structurally defective counterpart, Arnold had found that in his efforts to abuse and tyrannize others, he had only prompted further hostility and harsh punishment of the sort to which he was subjected in childhood. His strategy of arrogance and brutalization had backfired too often, and he sought retribution, not as much through action as through fantasy.

Repeated setbacks confirmed Arnold's expectancy of aggression from others; by his own hand, he evoked further hostility and disfavor. Because of his argumentative and chip-on-the-shoulder attitudes, he provoked ample antagonism from others. Isolated and resentful, he increasingly turned to himself, to cogitate and mull over his fate. Left to his own ruminations, he began to imagine a plot in which every facet of his environment played a threatening and treacherous role. Moreover, through the intrapsychic mechanism of projection, he attributed his own venom to others, ascribing to them the malice and ill will he felt within himself. As the line drew thin between objective antagonism and imagined hostility, the belief took hold that others intentionally persecuted him; alone, threatened, and with decreasing self-esteem, Arnold's suspicions had been transformed into delusions. Not infrequently, persecutory delusions combined with delusions of grandeur; however, these latter beliefs played a secondary role with Arnold, in contrast to their primacy among fanatic paranoids.

Arnold needed to retain his independence; despite all adversity, he held tenaciously to the belief in his self-worth. This need to protect his autonomy and strength was seen in the content of his persecution delusions. Malevolence on the part of others was viewed neither as casual nor random; rather, it was designed to intimidate, offend, and undermine his self-esteem. "They" were seeking to weaken his "will," destroy his power, spread lies, thwart his talents, conspire to control his thoughts and to immobilize and subjugate him. Arnold dreaded losing his autonomy; his persecutory themes were filled with fears of being forced to submit to authority, of being made soft and pliant, and of being tricked to surrender his self-determination, each feature of which was seen in his MCMI scale scores.

Synergistic Treatment Plan: Averse to self-exploration, Arnold would need to begin with very concrete and tangible social goals accomplished through modifying *behaviors*. As these methods would provide less troublesome social interactions, the therapist would be able to begin engaging him in deeper exploration through *cognitive* challenges, aimed at his retribution-oriented fantasies. Such perpetuations as Arnold's perceived satisfaction from exerting power over others and causing them duress (*active-pain* orientation, devaluation of *other*) would be addressed cognitively in this manner. It would follow that the diminishing of his chip-on-the-shoulder attitude would create a more affable persona and decrease the likelihood of being confronted by a troublesome attitude from others. *Interpersonal* change, as well, would serve to alleviate Arnold's constant perception of danger from others and help bolster healthier, positive social interactions.

Therapeutic Course: A short-term and circumscribed focus optimally suited Arnold. Formal *behavior modification* methods were fruitfully explored to achieve greater consistency and interpersonal harmony in his social behavior. Directive *cognitive techniques,* such as those of Meichenbaum and Ellis, were used to confront him with the obstructive and self-defeating character of his expectations and his personal relations. Although the deeply rooted character of these problems impeded the effectiveness of most therapeutic procedures, it was fruitful to explore the more confrontive and incisive techniques of both cognitive and *interpersonal* therapies (e.g., Benjamin, Kiesler). A thorough reconstruction of personality was not the only means of altering his deeper pathologies. In support of short-term interpersonal techniques, *family* treatment methods were utilized to focus on the complex network of relationships that sustained Arnold's personality style. Together with cognitive reframing procedures, they proved to be among the most useful techniques to help him recognize the source of his own hurt and angry feelings and to appreciate how he provoked hurt and anger in others.

Not surprisingly, Arnold entered therapy actively resisting any exploration of his motives. Although he was not initially an active and willing participant in therapy, a strong and persuasive cognitive approach eventually drew him into the therapeutic process. He submitted to therapy under the press of extrinsic reasons, but he learned to see the benefits of reframing his attitudes and the consequences of doing so. For example, he experienced interpersonal difficulty as a consequence of aggressive behavior and incessant quarreling, but these tendencies were diminished by viewing his behavior differently and by acquiring other means of fulfilling the needs that drove him. With confronting methods, Arnold learned not to assume that a problem could always be traced to another person's hostility. As he found it possible to accept a measure of responsibility for his difficulties, he didn't need to conclude that the therapist tricked him into admitting it. In this situation, the therapist restrained any impulse to react to him with general disapproval or criticism. An important step in building rapport with Arnold was to see things from his viewpoint. If success was to be achieved in a short-term intervention, the therapist needed to convey a sense of trust and a willingness to develop a constructive alliance. A balance of professional authority and tolerance was useful in diminishing the probability that he would relapse or impulsively withdraw from treatment.

As noted, Arnold was not a willing participant in therapy and agreed to treatment only under the pressure of external difficulties. A strong and determined attitude was able to overcome his desire to outwit the therapist by setting up situations to test the therapist's skills, to catch inconsistencies, to arouse ire, and, if possible, to belittle and humiliate the therapist. For the therapist, a most important task was to restrain the impulse to express a condemning attitude. Goal-directed in a brief treatment program, the therapist was able to check any hostile feelings, keeping in mind that Arnold's difficulties were not fully under his control. Nevertheless, Arnold may have actively impeded his progress toward conflict resolution and goal attainment, undoing what good he had previously achieved in treatment. A combination of cognitive and interpersonal techniques were employed to counteract his contrary feelings and his inclination to retract his more kindly expectations of others and quickly rebuild the few advances that he and the therapist had struggled to attain. The therapist's committed and professional approach was able to prevent relapses by confronting the ambivalence that often robbed him of what steps he had secured toward progress.

PARANOID PERSONALITY: OBDURATE TYPE (PARANOID WITH OBSESSIVE-COMPULSIVE TRAITS)

CASE 23.3, ROBERT M., 30

Presenting Picture: Robert M., a high school teacher, was zestfully self-assertive and assiduous in his manner, yet had nearly flat affect. His school administrators requested an evaluation because, as Robert perceived it, they wanted an excuse to find him incompetent and they couldn't find another way to do it. Robert had his own set of rules and policies that he expected his students to follow. Unfortunately, they often collided head on with the district's policies. Robert believed that the school's standards were too lax and that he was entitled to enforce his own more stringent rules for the good of his students. Robert was also convinced that through practice, he had sharpened his senses to the point where he had developed extrasensory perception. He could "sense" others' motives and feelings and felt justified in grading his students based on the feelings he got from them. He used his ESP to discover that other teachers and administrators were jealous of him and were motivated to "break him down" and get him fired.

Clinical Assessment: *Obdurate paranoids* such as Robert are more pathological variants of the less structurally defective obsessive-compulsive personality disorder, whose rule-bound and rigid characteristics typically mesh and unite with those of the paranoid. However, in contrast to their compulsive counterparts, who retain the hope of achieving gratification and protection through the good offices of others, Robert broke his self-other conflict, renounced his dependency submission, and took on a stance of self-assertion. Despite his growing hostility and his repudiation of conformity as a way of life, he retained his basic rigidity and perfectionism; he remained grim and humorless, tense, controlled and inflexible, small-minded, unyielding and implacable, dyspeptic, peevish and cranky, legalistic and self-righteous. These features of his basic psychic makeup were deeply embedded, internalized as a fixed system of habits, feelings, and thoughts. Though he found it necessary to discard others as his primary source of security, the remnants of his lifelong habits of overcontrol and faultlessness were not so readily abandoned; the basic personality style remained immutable.

Robert continued to seek the clarity of rules and regulations; he could not tolerate suspense and had to create an order and system to his life. Deprived of the customary guidelines he spurned, he learned to lean increasingly on himself and to be his own ruthless slave driver in search of order, power, and independence. This led to an obsessive concern with trivial details and an excessive intellectualization of minor events, all to the end of obtaining internal perfection and faultlessness. These features were notable on both his MCMI and Rorschach scores.

With this independence, he freed himself from the constraints of submission and propriety. He began to discharge the reservoir of hostility he previously had repressed and imposed his self-created standards on others, attacking them with the same demands and punitive attitudes to which he himself was earlier subjected. Impossible regulations set for others allowed him to vent hostilities and condemnation for their failures to meet them. He could give to others what he himself had received. He despised and hated them for their weaknesses, their deceits, and their hypocrisy—precisely those feelings he previously had experienced within himself, had once sought to repress, and now tried to conceal by condemning them in others.

Despite his overt repudiation of conformity and submission, Robert could not free himself entirely of conflict and guilt; despite efforts to justify his newfound hostility, he was unable to square these actions with his past beliefs. Furthermore, his arrogance reactivated past anxieties; he could not escape the memories of retaliation that his own hostile actions provoked in the past.

Deep within Robert, then, were the remnants of guilt and the fear of retribution; these two elements gave rise to persecutory delusions. First, Robert learned from past experience to anticipate disfavor and criticism in response to contrary and nonconforming behaviors; thus, as he looked about him, he saw, in the movements and remarks of others, the hostility he anticipated. Second, to deny or justify his behaviors, he projected his anger on others; this mechanism, however, caused him to find hostile intent where none, in fact, existed. Last, his inner feelings of guilt reactivated his self-condemnatory attitudes; thus, part of him felt that he deserved to be punished for his resentments and behaviors. Thus, as a result of anticipation, projection, and guilt, he began to believe that others were "after him," seeking to condemn, punish, belittle, and undo him.

There are certain encapsulated and well-defined delusions that often exist apart from the main body of a patient's "normal" beliefs. These rare delusional systems have been referred to as cases of classical *paranoia* in the past. When they are seen, they tend to be found among these obdurate paranoid types. The overly rigid and tightly controlled thought processes of these paranoids often enable them to segment their beliefs and to keep them as separate and compartmentalized units. Thus, the patient may appear to function much of the time in a normal manner; however, once a topic associated with the delusion is broached, his or her irrational, but normally hidden and encapsulated, belief becomes manifest.

Synergistic Treatment Plan: Owing to Robert's excessive *pain* orientation, early efforts in treatment would be limited to *supportive* strategies, combined with a *biophysical* approach to altering his irascible mood. Gradually, *behavioral* techniques would be introduced, in pace with Robert's ability to loosen his well-constructed defenses, which would concentrate on desensitization from fantasized hostilities in his environment. *Cognitive* tactics would follow, aimed at self-perpetuations such as his beliefs that he could "keep the wolves at bay" by projecting anger, exhibiting extreme self-assertion, and positioning himself in a power role to maintain control (break from *self-other* conflict, as he had forsaken *other* and overemphasized *self*). As defenses would relax, these cognitive strategies would be accompanied by *interpersonal* techniques, which would serve to alleviate his feeling worthy of punishment and help him explore less defensive social interactions.

Therapeutic Course: The initial major vehicle used with Robert was short-term *supportive* therapy. *Psychopharmacologic* agents were also beneficial in the early period of his difficulties, but the level of dosage employed was not such as to cause significant decrements in his efficiency and alertness. Also useful as part of a focused treatment approach were *behavior modification* techniques designed to desensitize Robert to currently discomforting or anxiety-provoking situations. *Group* and *family* therapy techniques were not considered, as he most likely would have wanted to ally himself with the therapist and may not have participated wholeheartedly as a patient. Similarly, long-term techniques that would force him to relinquish his defenses and expose his feelings in front of others may have produced an unwanted deterioration in his condition.

Robert's notable symptoms included unanticipated attacks of anxiety, spells of immobilization, and excessive fatigue. Because symptoms such as these threatened his public style of efficiency and responsibility, it was especially useful to employ circumscribed and focused short-term methods of treatment. Because he probably viewed his symptoms as products of an isolated physical disease, failing to recognize that they represented the outcropping of his inner psychological dynamics (e.g., ambivalence and repressed resentments), a less expressive and more concise approach was best. Certainly, for every piece of defensive armor removed, the therapist bolstered Robert's confidence twofold. Removing more defenses than he could tolerate may have prolonged the treatment plan extensively. Fortunately, he was so well guarded that careful inquiries by the therapist fostered growth without a problematic relapse. Caution was the bywordwith Robert.

Owing to his anxious conformity and his fear of public ridicule, Robert viewed therapy as a procedure that would expose his feelings of inadequacy. Tense, grim, and cheerless, he greatly preferred to maintain the status quo rather than confront the need to change. As noted above, his defensiveness had to be honored, and probing and insight proceeded at a careful pace. Once a measure of trust and confidence had developed in the relationship, the therapist used *cognitive* and *interpersonal* methods to stabilize anxieties and foster change. Because Robert preferred to restrict his actions and thoughts to those to which he was accustomed, therapeutic procedures could not confront more than he could tolerate. Goals of this nature focused on changing assumptions, noted by Beck and others, such as the fear that any shortcoming would result in a catastrophe or that not performing at the highest level would result in a humiliating failure. Before his problematic beliefs were explicitly addressed, he voiced pseudo-insights, especially because he was well educated, but this was most frequently a façade to placate the therapist. His habitual defenses were so well constructed that general insight-based interpretations were temporary at best. Genuine progress necessitated brief, focused techniques to modify problematic self-statements and assumptions. Without these concrete and short-term techniques, he would tend to pay lip service to treatment goals, expressing guilt and self-condemnation for his past shortcoming, but not readily relinquishing his defensive controls. Empathy alone likewise was only modestly useful because of his evasiveness and his discomfort with emotion-laden materials. Owing to his need to follow a rigid and formalized lifestyle, he responded better to short-term cognitive or interpersonal methods that were specific in their procedures rather than to more expressive or nondirective techniques. To diminish the occurrence of setbacks, efforts were made to strengthen his will to give up maladaptive beliefs such as unrelenting self-criticism and the unyielding correctness of authority-based rules and regulations.

PARANOID PERSONALITY: QUERULOUS TYPE
(PARANOID WITH NEGATIVISTIC TRAITS)

CASE 23.4, TONY A., 32

Presenting Picture: Tony A. was court-ordered to seek therapy. Tony's wife was filing for divorce and was requesting alimony payments. He vociferously denounced his wife, claiming he knew she had been cheating on him since the beginning of their relationship. This, despite acknowledging that he had no actual proof of her infidelity, he "just knew." Tony was extremely argumentative and would constantly shoot quick, furtive side glances. He also had an odd and inappropriate laugh that rang hollow and peculiar. His defensive nature could clearly been seen as he asked in accusing tones "Why are you asking me that?" and "Are you recording what I say?"

Clinical Assessment: These personalities may be differentiated from several of their less structurally defective counterparts by the presence of both overt hostility and frank delusions. Along with their milder variants, such as the negativistic style with whom shared characteristics continue to coexist, *querulous paranoids* are noted by their discontent, pessimism, stubbornness, and vacillation. However, at this defective structural level, the pathology is more aggressively negativistic and faultfinding, sullen, resentful, obstructive, and peevish at all times, and openly expressive of feelings of jealousy, of being misunderstood, and of being cheated. As a consequence, querulous paranoids rarely can sustain good relationships, creating endless wrangles wherever they go. Demoralized by these events, they forgo all hopes of gaining affection and approval from others, and decide to renounce these aspirations in preference for self-determination. Notable as characteristics distinguishing the querulous paranoid are the following adjectives: contentious, fractious, resentful, choleric, jealous, waspish, and whiny.

Despite the strength with which they assert their newfound independence, querulous paranoids remain irritable, dissatisfied, and troubled by discontent and ambivalence. They rarely forget their resentments, their feelings of having been mistreated and exploited. Not uncommonly, they begin to perceive the achievements of others as unfair advantages, preferential treatments that are undeserved and that they have been denied. Their disgruntlement and complaints mount; their fantasies expand and weave into irrational envy; their grumbling turns to anger and spite; each of these feed into the central theme of unjust misfortune, and are whipped, bit by bit, into delusions of resentful jealousy.

Erotic delusions are not uncommon among these patients. Although consciously repudiating their need for others, querulous paranoids still seek to gain affection from others. Rather than admit to these desires, however, they defensively project them, interpreting the casual remarks and actions of others as subtle signs of amorous intent. However, querulous paranoids are unable to tolerate these "attentions" because they dread further betrayal and exploitation. Thus, in conjunction with their erotic delusions, these paranoids protest that they must be "protected"; they may accuse innocent victims of committing indignities, of making lewd suggestions, or of molesting them.

Synergistic Treatment Plan: Tony's minimal investment and interest required focused measures from the beginning of treatment. *Behavioral* interventions would serve to adjust and temper Tony's impulsive and unpredictable social interactions, reducing his *active*-oriented characterologic mannerisms. As such inquiries could be tolerated, therapy would begin to focus on *cognitions* that helped perpetuate Tony's *active pain*–oriented style and continually placed his *self-other* orientation in conflict. These thought patterns included his overemphasis on resentment, and his view (which lead to minidelusions) that he was a victim of unjust misfortune. *Interpersonal* measures, in tandem with these cognitive strategies, would assist in examining social perpetuations of difficulties and would work toward implementing changes in Tony's interaction style.

Therapeutic Course: As Tony obviously had little to no belief in therapeutic process and was attending only due to a court order, a short-term, circumscribed focus was needed to optimize the limited time and investment of this patient. Formal *behavior modification* methods were employed to control his inconsistent temperament and style and to modify his discordant social actions. Directive *cognitive techniques* (e.g., Meichenbaum, Ellis) addressed his distrusting attitudes toward others, confronting the destructive character of this perspective. Though these problems were very entrenched, obstructing most therapeutic inroads, the more confrontive and incisive techniques of both cognitive and *interpersonal* therapies (e.g., Benjamin, Kiesler) were of merit. Thus, as might otherwise have been expected, a thorough reconstruction of personality, which would have been a formidable task, was not the only means of modifying deeper pathologies. *Family* treatment methods would have been a fruitful adjunct to Tony's individual milieu, to explore and treat the complex network of relationships that sustained his personality style. Unfortunately, the family was unwilling to participate. Together with the cognitive reframing procedures previously described, this combination may have proven to be among the most useful interventions in helping Tony recognize the sources of his inconsistent affect and understand how the manifestations of those feelings may have caused harm to his family.

Not at all surprisingly, Tony actively resisted exploring his motives. As this referral was not of his free will, Tony was not disposed toward actively pursuing therapeutic goals. To this end, a rather persuasive cognitive approach helped draw him in and invest him in the therapeutic process. He had submitted to therapy, initially, under the press of family discord and legal problems, but he eventually learned to see that reframing his attitudes and assumptions had positive results. Through methods of cognitive confrontation, he learned that most of his problems were not a result of the "hostile" and "duplicitous" people around him. As he began accepting responsibility for some of his problems, he did not fall into the common trap of thinking the therapist tricked him into admitting this. Throughout the course of treatment, it was important in building rapport that the therapist not only avoided disapproval or criticism, but also that he was able to see things from Tony's viewpoint. There needed to be signs of success from an early stage of this intervention, and the therapist needed to convey that not only was this intervention potentially helpful, but he was willing to develop a trusting and effective alliance. A balance of professional authority and tolerance was useful in establishing this vital atmosphere that prevented any impulsive withdrawal from treatment.

As noted, Tony was not prone to be a willing participant in therapy, agreeing to treatment only under legal pressure. A strong and determined attitude on the part of the therapist was necessary to overcome Tony's desire to "test" him by setting up traps for inconsistencies and trying to intellectually corner him. It was essential that the therapist restrain any impulse to express a condemning attitude toward Tony. Goal-directed in this short-term treatment program, the therapist was able to check any hostile feelings, always keeping in mind that Tony could not always control these tendencies. Nevertheless, at times, Tony impeded his progress, sometimes undoing the good he had previously achieved in treatment. Cognitive and interpersonal techniques were used to counteract his disharmonious feelings and his proclivity to retract his new, positive expectations of others. Timely intervention quickly rebuilt the advances that he and the therapist had struggled to attain. This committed, balanced approach helped prevent relapses by confronting Tony's ambivalence, a force that too often stood to undo his progress.

PARANOID PERSONALITY: INSULAR TYPE (PARANOID WITH AVOIDANT TRAITS)

CASE 23.5, LeeAnn B., 33

Presenting Picture: LeeAnn B. was an intense woman, a bookkeeper who was convinced her coworkers were trying to get her fired. She claimed to have great abilities to understand numbers and to see patterns in numbers that others did not understand. For LeeAnn, numbers took on significance beyond the ordinary. Odd numbers were good, even numbers bad. If her evening out started at 7:22, it was doomed from the start and could not be salvaged. If a word had six letters, it was divisible by three, which was good, but only twice (an even number), so ultimately, it was bad. Her superstitions about numbers interfered with every aspect of her life, including dictating the number of locks on her front door and how many hours a week she could work. LeeAnn was convinced her coworkers were slipping wrong numbers into her piles to throw off her patterns because they didn't like her. From an early age, her mother had ingrained in her the idea that LeeAnn had to protect herself because others were out to take advantage of her and wanted to laugh at her. Her mother, "a widow, ripe for picking," was very concerned that others were out to get her money. LeeAnn had extremely limited contact with other people, never allowing others to visit or call because she did not like others entering her apartment and she was worried about her phone being bugged.

Clinical Assessment: LeeAnn was notably hypervigilant. As an *insular paranoid type,* she was extremely moody and apprehensive, overly reactive to criticism, particularly in response to judgments made of her status, beliefs, and achievements. In earlier stages of her pathology, she resembled an avoidant personality, frequently withdrawn from the world, increasingly reclusive and isolated. Extremely vulnerable, she sought solace in a variety of self-focused ways; for example, she engaged in abstruse intellectual activities to enhance her fantasied self-esteem. Other insular paranoids indulge in alcohol or drugs as a way of calming the frightening nature of troublesome fantasies, and still others pursue sexual escapades with prostitutes, not only to provide a measure of physical relief from their insular state, but also to purchase a willing ear to listen to their fears and grandiosities.

More than other paranoid types, LeeAnn, as an insular variant, sought to protect herself from a world she judged to be both threatening and destructive. She apparently spotted problems in their earliest stages, quickly anticipated what could be troubling, and defended herself against both real and imagined dangers. As evident in the preceding paragraphs, self-protective insular types such as LeeAnn share certain core features with the avoidant personality, well demonstrated in her MCMI scale pattern. LeeAnn was prone to coming to premature conclusions about rather incidental and trivial events, events that were given meaning largely by projecting her own anxieties and hostility. The natural complexities of her social world were narrowed to signify one or two persistent and all-embracing ideas; in this way, LeeAnn could effectively deal with the problems she faced by "knowing" that everything represented basically one or two variants of the same thing.

Part of the reason for insulating herself stemmed from her need to prevent anything or anyone from influencing her. LeeAnn had an unusual fear of being controlled. Not only did she seek to divert or preclude external sources of influence, but there was a strong desire to remain autonomous, to keep to herself and to rely solely on her own ideas and beliefs. Ultimately, this isolation, this unwillingness to check her thoughts against reality resulted in her becoming more and more out of touch with reality. As a consequence of believing that the only reality was the one she had created, LeeAnn had no defense against external forces because her world was a product of her own imagination. Hence, she not only had difficulty in accurately observing external reality, but there was no escape from the false reality that inhered within herself.

As with the avoidant personality, LeeAnn's inner thoughts became so painful and terrifying that she had to undo or destroy them. Her intense feelings of insecurity and threat escalated as a consequence of her own defensive actions. Everything was now seen as part of a general assault intended to destroy her. But the conspiracies and the persecution she perceived were self-created. To defend against these frightening feelings, she intentionally disrupted her own thoughts, seeking to distance herself from her own mind. Her inner world became a void, a chaotic mélange of distorted and incidental thoughts. It was at this point that she regressed into the decompensated paranoid state. She became detached from herself, an empty vessel devoid of the cohesion and focus that dominated her life, until her own imagination made existence so painful as to require that it be ultimately purged.

Synergistic Treatment Plan: Primary efforts with LeeAnn would involve reducing her *active-pain* orientation toward avoiding a perceived harsh and cruel external world, and bolstering *self* and *other,* in order to attain greater social abilities, thus also enhancing *pleasure.* It would be beneficial to explore *biophysical* underpinnings to her mood and demeanor. *Cognitive* exploration would include reorganization of thought habits that led LeeAnn to impulsively overemphasize trivial environmental concerns, as well as examine her fear of being controlled. To break perpetuating cycles, both *interpersonal* and *behavioral* realms would be explored to begin putting into motion those skills and actions consonant with her emotional spheres that desire healthy interaction.

Therapeutic Course: A major thrust of brief therapy for LeeAnn was to enhance her social interest and competence. Although she could not be pushed beyond tolerable limits, careful and well-reasoned *cognitive* methods (e.g., Beck, Meichenbaum) fostered the development of more accurate and focused styles of thinking. In addition to working toward the extinction of false beliefs about herself and the attitudes of others toward her, the therapist was alert to spheres of life in which LeeAnn possessed positive emotional inclinations and encouraged her, through *interpersonal* methods and *behavior skill development* techniques, to undertake activities consonant with these tendencies. Although the success of short-term methods may have justified an optimistic outlook, LeeAnn's initial receptivity created the misleading perception that further advances and progress would be rapid. Care had to be taken to prevent early treatment success from precipitating a resurfacing of her established ambivalence between wanting social acceptance and fearing that she was placing herself in a vulnerable position. Enabling her to give up her long-standing expectations of disappointment required booster sessions following initial, short-term success. Support was provided to ease her fears, particularly her feeling that her efforts were not sustainable and would inevitably result in social disapproval again.

With appropriate consultation, *psychopharmacologic* treatment was employed. Trial periods with a number of agents were explored to determine whether any effectively increased her energy and affectivity. Such agents had to be used with caution, however, because they could activate feelings that LeeAnn was ill-equipped to handle. As noted, attempts to cognitively reorient her problematic attitudes were useful in motivating interpersonal sensitivity and confidence. Likewise, short-term techniques of behavioral modification were valuable in strengthening her social skills. *Group* and *family* methods may also have been useful in encouraging and facilitating her acquisition of constructive social attitudes. In these benign settings, she would begin to alter her social image and develop the motivation and skills for a more effective interpersonal style. Preceding or combining short-term programs with individual treatment sessions may have aided in forestalling untoward recurrences of the discomfort she experienced.

Focused treatment efforts for this introversive and passive woman were best directed toward countering her withdrawal tendencies. Minimally introspective and evincing diminished affect and energy, she was prevented, through circumscribed therapies, from becoming increasingly isolated from others, whether discomforting or benign. Energy was invested to enlarge her social world owing to her tendency to pursue with diligence only those activities required by her job or by her family obligations. By shrinking her interpersonal milieu, she precluded exposure to new experience. Of course, this was her preference, but such behavior only fostered her isolated and withdrawn existence. To prevent such backsliding and a relapse, the therapist ensured the continuation of all constructive social activities as well as potential new ones. Otherwise, she may have become increasingly lost in asocial and fantasy preoccupations. Excessive social pressure, however, was avoided because the patient's tolerance and competencies in this area were limited. Initial brief, focused treatment techniques aided her in developing more skills in this area.

Resistances and Risks

Therapeutic work with paranoids is a touchy proposition at best. Few come willingly for treatment. Therapy to them signifies weakness and dependency, both of which are anathema. When they do come in, the therapeutic work may be complicated because paranoids' suspicious and distrustful nature guards them against revealing emotional and interpersonal difficulties, making it extremely difficult to examine internal processes.

Many therapists fall into the trap of disliking these patients because their suspicions and hostility readily provoke discomfort and resentment. Therapists must resist being intimidated by the arrogance and demeaning comments of these patients. Weakness is not a trait paranoids can accept in someone in whom they have placed their trust. Other problems can complicate the therapeutic effort. Excessive friendliness and overt sympathies often connote deceit to these patients, a seductive prelude to humiliation and deprecation. As paranoids tend to view it, they have suffered pain at the hands of deceptively "kind" people. A comfortable distance must be maintained. Nor can therapists question these patients directly about their distorted attitudes and beliefs. This may drive them to concoct new rationalizations. It may intensify their distrust and destroy whatever rapport has been built. Conceivably, it may unleash a barrage of defensive hostility or precipitate an open psychotic break. Their beliefs, self-confidence, and image of autonomy and strength should not be directly challenged. These illusions are too vital a part of their style; to question them is to attack these patients' fragile equilibrium.

Despite the risks involved and therapeutic modifications required in working with these personalities, it is possible to put them on the road to recovery, providing them with a glimpse of a positive, healthy way of relating that might ultimately draw them further into the process of therapy.

References

Abraham, K. (1968). Notes on the psychoanalytic investigation and treatment of manic-depressive insanity and allied conditions. In *Selected papers of Karl Abraham*. London: Hogarth. (Original work published 1911)

Abramson, L., Seligman, M., & Teasdale, J. (1978). Learned helplessness in humans: Critique and reformulation. *Journal of Abnormal Psychology, 87*, 49–74.

Abroms, E.M. (1993). *The freedom of the self: The bio-existential treatment of character problems*. New York: Plenum Press.

Ackerman, N.W. (1958). *The psychodynamics of family life*. New York: Basic Books.

Ackerman, N.W. (1966). *Treating the troubled family*. New York: Basic Books.

Adler, A. (1929). *Problems of neurosis*. New York: Harper & Row.

Agras, S., Leitenberg, H., & Barlow, D.H. (1968). Social reinforcement in the modification of agoraphobia. *Archives of General Psychiatry, 19*, 423–427.

Akiskal, H.S. (1981). Subaffective disorders: Dysthymic, cyclothymic, and bipolar II disorders in the "borderline" realm. *Psychiatric Clinics of North America, 4*, 25–46.

Akiskal, H.S. (1983). Dysthymic disorder: Psychopathology of proposed chronic depressive subtypes. *American Journal of Psychiatry, 140*, 11–20.

Akiskal, H.S. (1984). Characterologic manifestations of the affective disorders: Toward a new conceptualization. *Integrative Psychiatry, 2*, 83–88.

Alexander, F. (1930). The neurotic character. *International Journal of Psychoanalysis, 11*, 292–313.

Alexander, F., & French, T. (1944). *Psychoanalytic therapy*. New York: Norton.

American Psychiatric Association. (1980). *Diagnostic and statistical manual of mental disorders* (3rd ed.). Washington, DC: Author.

American Psychiatric Association. (1987). *Diagnostic and statistical manual of mental disorders* (3rd ed., Rev.). Washington, DC: Author.

American Psychiatric Association. (1994). *Diagnostic and statistical manual of mental disorders* (4th ed.). Washington, DC: Author.

Anchin, J.C., & Kiesler, D.J. (1982). *Handbook of interpersonal psychotherapy*. New York: Pergamon Press.

Arieti, S., & Bemporad, J.R. (1978). *Severe and mild depression*. New York: Basic Books.

Arieti, S., & Bemporad, J.R. (1980). *Severe and mild depression: The psychotherapeutic approach*. London: Tavistock.

Arkowitz, H. (1992). Integrative theories of therapy. In D.K. Freedhein & H.J. Freudenberger (Eds.), *History of psychotherapy: A century of change* (pp. 261–303). Washington, DC: American Psychological Association.

Arkowitz, H. (1997). Integrative theories of therapy. In P.L. Wachtel & S.B. Messer (Eds.), *Theories of psychotherapy: Origins and evolution* (pp. 227–288). Washington, DC: American Psychological Association.

Atwood, J.D., & Chester, R. (1987). *Treatment techniques for common mental disorders.* Northvale, NJ: Aronson.

Ayllon, T., & Michael, J. (1959). The psychiatric nurse as a behavioral engineer. *Journal of the Experimental Analysis of Behavior, 2,* 323–334.

Bach, G.R. (1954). *Intensive group psychotherapy.* New York: Ronald Press.

Bandura, A. (1962). Social learning through imitation. In M.R. Jones (Ed.), *Nebraska Symposium on Motivation.* Lincoln: University of Nebraska Press.

Bandura, A. (1969). *Principles of behavior modification.* New York: Holt, Rinehart and Winston.

Bandura, A., & Walters, R.H. (1965). *Social learning and personality development.* New York: Holt, Rinehart and Winston.

Barlow, D.H. (1988). *Anxiety and its disorders: The nature and treatment of anxiety and panic.* New York: Guilford Press.

Barlow, D.H. (1993). *Clinical handbook of psychological disorders* (2nd ed.). New York: Guilford Press.

Baron, D.A., & Nagy, R. (1988). An amobarbital interview in a general hospital setting: Friend or foe? A case report. *General Hospital Psychiatry, 10,* 220–222.

Barsky, A., Geringer, E., & Wood, C.A. (1988). A cognitive-educational treatment for hypochondriasis. *General Hospital Psychiatry, 10,* 322–327.

Beard, G.M. (1869). *Our home physician: A new and popular guide to the art of preserving health and treating disease; with plain advice for all the medical and surgical emergencies of the family.* New York: E.B. Treat.

Beck, A.T. (1964). Thinking and depression: II. Theory and therapy. *Archives of General Psychiatry, 10*(6), 561–571.

Beck, A.T. (1970). Cognitive therapy: Nature and relation to behavior therapy. *Behavior Therapy, 1,* 184–200.

Beck, A.T. (1974). *Coping with depression.* New York: Institute for Rational-Emotive Therapy.

Beck, A.T. (1976). *Cognitive therapy and the emotional disorders.* New York: International Universities Press.

Beck, A.T. (1983). Cognitive therapy of depression: New perspectives. In P. Clayton & J. Barrett (Eds.), *Treatment of depression.* New York: Raven Press.

Beck, A.T. (1991). Cognitive therapy: A 30-year retrospective. *American Psychologist, 46,* 368–375.

Beck, A.T. (1993). *Cognitive therapy of depression.* Aberdeen: Scottish Cultural Press.

Beck, A.T., & Emery, G. (1985). *Anxiety disorders and phobias.* New York: Basic Books.

Beck, A.T., & Freeman, A. (1990a). Belief questionnaire. In A.T. Beck & A. Freeman (Eds.), *Cognitive therapy of personality disorders.* New York: International Universities Press.

Beck, A.T., & Freeman, A. (1990b). *Cognitive therapy of personality disorders.* New York: Basic Books.

Beck, A.T., Rush, A.J., Shaw, B.F., & Emery, G. (1979). *Cognitive therapy of depression.* New York: Guilford Press.

Beitman, B.D. (1992). Integration through fundamental similarities and useful differences among the schools. In J.C. Norcross & M.R. Goldfried (Eds.), *Handbook of psychotherapy integration* (pp. 202–230). New York: Basic Books.

Bellack, A., & Hersen, M. (1981). *Behavioral assessment: A practical handbook.* New York: Pergamon Press.

Bellack, A., Hersen, M., & Himmelhoch, J.M. (1983). A comparison of social-skills training, pharmacotherapy and psychotherapy for depression. *Behavior Research and Therapy, 21,* 101–107.

Bellak, L., & Siegal, H. (1983). *Handbook of intensive brief and emergency psychotherapy* (B.E.P.). Larchmont, NY: C.P.S.

Bellak, L., & Small, L. (1978). *Emergency psychotherapy and brief psychotherapy* (2nd ed.). New York: Grune & Stratton.

Bemporad, J.R. (1980). Review of object relations theory in light of cognitive development. *Journal of the American Academy of Psychoanalysis, 8,* 57–75.

Benjamin, L.R., & Benjamin, R. (1992). An overview of family treatment in dissociative disorders. *Dissociation, 5,* 236–241.

Benjamin, L.S. (1974). Structural analysis of social behavior. *Psychological Review, 81,* 392–425.

Benjamin, L.S. (1984). Principles of prediction using structural analysis of social behavior. In R.A. Zucker, J. Aronoff, & A.I. Rabin (Eds.), *Personality and the prediction of behavior.* New York: Academic Press.

Benjamin, L.S. (1990). Interpersonal analysis of the cathartic model. In R. Plutchick, H. Kellerman, et al. (Eds.), *Emotion, psychopathology, psychotherapy. Emotion: Theory, research, and experience* (Vol. 5, pp. 209–229). San Diego: Academic Press.

Benjamin, L.S. (1993). *Interpersonal diagnosis and treatment of personality disorders.* New York: Guilford Press.

Benson, H. (1975). The forgotten treatment modality in bipolar illness: Psychotherapy. *Diseases of the Nervous System, 36,* 634–638.

Bergin, A.E., & Lambert, M.J. (1978). The evaluation of therapeutic outcomes. In S.L. Garfield & A.E. Bergin (Eds.), *Handbook of psychotherapy and behavior change* (2nd ed.). New York: Wiley.

Berliner, B. (1947). On some psychodynamics of masochism. *Psychoanalytic Quarterly, 16,* 459–471.

Berne, E. (1961). *Transactional analysis in psychotherapy.* New York: Grove Press.

Berne, E. (1964). *Games people play: The psychology of human relationships.* New York: Ballantine Books.

Bernstein, D.A., & Borkovec, T.D. (1973). *Progressive relaxation training: A manual for the helping professions.* Champaign, IL: Research Press.

Beutler, L.E. (1979). Values, beliefs, religion and the persuasive influence of psychotherapy. *Psychotherapy: Theory, Research, and Practice, 16,* 432–440.

Beutler, L.E. (1981). Differential psychotherapy outcome among depressed and impulsive patients as a function of analytic and experiential treatment procedures. *Psychiatry, 44,* 297–306.

Beutler, L.E. (1983). *Eclectic psychotherapy: A systematic approach.* New York: Pergamon Press.

Beutler, L.E. (1986). Individualized outcome measures of internal change: Methodological considerations. *Journal of Consulting and Clinical Psychology, 54,* 48–53.

Beutler, L.E. (1991). Have all won and must all have prizes? Revisiting Luborsky et al.'s verdict. *Journal of Consulting and Clinical Psychology, 59,* 226–232.

Beutler, L.E., & Clarkin, J. (1990). *Selective treatment selection: Toward targeted therapeutic interventions.* New York: Brunner/Mazel.

Beutler, L.E., Consoli, A.J., & Williams, R.E. (1994). Psychotherapy with women in theory and practice. In B.M. Bongar & L.E. Beutler (Eds.), *Comprehensive textbook of psychotherapy: Theory and practice.* New York: Oxford University Press.

Binder, J. (1979). *Choosing the appropriate form of time-limited dynamic psychotherapy*. Charlottesville: University of Virginia Medical Center.

Binswanger, L. (1942). *Grundformen und erkenntnis menschlichen daseins*. Zurich: Niehaus.

Binswanger, L. (1947). *Ausgewählte vorträge und aufsätze*. Berne: Francke.

Binswanger, L. (1956). Existential analysis and psychotherapy. In F. Fromm-Reichmann & J.L. Moreno (Eds.), *Progress in psychotherapy* (Vol. 1). New York: Grune and Stratton.

Birk, L. (1970). *Group psychotherapy for homosexual men by male–female cotherapists*. Copenhagen: Munksgaard.

Blackburn, R. (1993). *The psychology of criminal conduct*. Chichester: Wiley.

Blatt, S.J. (1974). Levels of object representation in anaclitic and introjective depression. *Psychoanalytic Study of the Child, 29*, 107–157.

Blatt, S.J., & Shichman, S. (1983). Two primary configurations of psychopathology. *Psychoanalysis and Contemporary Thought, 6*, 187–254.

Bloom, B.L. (1981). Focused single-session therapy: Initial development and evaluation. In S.H. Budman (Ed.), *Forms of brief therapy* (pp. 167–216). New York: Guilford Press.

Bloom, B.L. (1992). *Planned short-term psychotherapy*. Boston: Allyn & Bacon.

Borkovec, T.D., & Costello, E. (1993). Efficacy of supplied relaxation and cognitive-behavioral therapy in the treatment of generalized anxiety disorder. *Journal of Consulting and Clinical Psychology, 61*, 611–619.

Boss, M. (1957). *Psychoanalyse und daseinsanalytik*. Berne: Hans Huber.

Boss, M. (1963). *Psychoanalysis and daseinsanalysis*. New York: Basic Books.

Bowen, M. (1976). Theory in the practice of psychotherapy. In P.J. Guerin, Jr. (Ed.), *Family therapy: Theory and practice* (pp. 42–90). New York: Gardner Press.

Bowen, M. (1978). *Family therapy in clinical practice*. New York: Aronson.

Breger, L., & McGaugh, J.L. (1965). Critique and reformulation of "learning-theory" approaches to psychotherapy and neurosis. *Psychological Bulletin, 63*, 338–358.

Brenner, C. (1959). The masochistic character: Genesis and treatment. *Journal of the American Psychoanalytic Association, 7*, 197–266.

Briquet, P. (1859). *Traite clinique et therapeutique a l'hysterie*. Paris: J.B. Balliere et Fils.

Budman, S.H. (1981). Looking toward the future. In S.H. Budman (Ed.), *Forms of brief therapy* (pp. 461–467). New York: Guilford Press.

Budman, S.H., & Gurman, A.S. (1988). *Theory and practice of brief therapy*. New York: Guilford Press.

Burton, R. (1971). *Anatomy of melancholy*. New York: Da Capo Press. (Original work published 1621)

Butler, G., Cullington, A., Hibbert, G., Klimes, I., & Gelder, M. (1987). Anxiety management for persistent generalized anxiety. *British Journal of Psychiatry, 151*, 535–542.

Cameron, N. (1963). *Personality and psychological development*. New York: Houghton-Mifflin.

Carson, R.C. (1982). Self-fulfilling prophecy, maladaptive behavior, and psychotherapy. In J.C. Anchin & D.J. Kiesler (Eds.), *Handbook of interpersonal psychotherapy*. New York: Pergamon Press.

Cashdan, S. (1988). *Object relations therapy: Using the relationship*. New York: Norton.

Caul, D. (1984). Group and videotape techniques for multiple personality. *Psychiatric Annals, 14*, 43–50.

Caul, D., Sacks, R.G., & Braun, B.G. (1988). Group psychotherapy in treatment of multiple personality disorder. In B.G. Braun (Ed.), *Treatment of multiple personality disorder* (pp. 145–156). Washington, DC: American Psychiatric Press.

Chambless, D.L., & Gillis, M.M. (1994). Cognitive therapy of anxiety disorders. *Journal of Consulting and Clinical Psychology, 61*, 248–260.

Clarkin, J., Frances, A., & Perry, S. (1992). Differential therapeutics: Macro and micro levels of treatment planning. In J.C. Norcross & M.R. Goldfried (Eds.), *Handbook of psychotherapy integration.* New York: Basic Books.

Cleckley, H. (1941). *The mask of sanity.* St. Louis, MO: Mosby.

Coons, P.M. (1986). Treatment progress in 20 patients with multiple personality disorder. *Journal of Nervous and Mental Disease, 174*, 715–721.

Cooper, N.A., & Clum, G.A. (1989). Imaginal flooding as a supplementary treatment for PTSD in combat veterans: A controlled study. *Behavior Therapy, 20*, 381–391.

Corcoran, K., & Fischer, J. (1987). *Measures for clinical practice: A sourcebook.* New York: Free Press.

Corsini, R.J. (Ed.). (1981). *Handbook of innovative psychotherapies.* New York: Wiley.

Covi, L., & Lipman, R.S. (1987). Cognitive-behavioral group psychotherapy combined with imipramine in major depression. *Psychopharmacology Bulletin, 23*, 173–176.

Cowdry, R.W., & Gardner, D.L. (1988). Pharmacotherapy of borderline personality disorder: Alprazolam, carbamazepine, trifluperazine and trancypromine. *Archives of General Psychiatry, 45*, 111–119.

Craighead, L.W., Craighead, W.E., Kazdin, A.E., & Mahoney, M.J. (Eds.). (1994). *Cognitive and behavioral interventions: An empirical approach to mental health problems.* Boston: Allyn & Bacon.

Dattilio, F. (1993). A practical update on the treatment of obsessive-compulsive disorder. *Journal of Mental Health Counseling, 15*, 244–259.

Davanloo, H. (1978). *Basic principles and techniques in short-term dynamic psychotherapy.* New York: Spectrum.

Davanloo, H. (Ed.). (1980). *Short-term dynamic psychotherapy.* Northvale, NJ: Aronson.

Davison, G.C. (1968). Systematic desensitization as a counterconditioning process. *Journal of Abnormal Psychology, 73*, 91–99.

Dejerine, J., & Gaukler, E. (1913). *Psychoneurosis and psychotherapy.* Philadelphia: Lippincott.

deShazer, S. (1982). *Patterns of brief family therapy.* New York: Guilford Press.

deShazer, S. (1988). *Clues: Investigating solutions in brief therapy.* New York: Norton.

Deutsch, M. (1948). *The effects of cooperation and competition upon group process.* Cambridge: Massachusetts Institute of Technology.

Dies, R.R. (1986). Practical, theoretical, and empirical foundations for group psychotherapy. In A.J. Frances & R.E. Hales (Eds.), *The American Psychiatric Association annual review* (Vol. 5, pp. 659–667). Washington, DC: American Psychiatric Press.

Dion, G.L., & Pollack, W.S. (1992). A rehabilitation model for persons with bipolar disorder. *Comprehensive Mental Health Care, 2*, 87–102.

Dollard, J., & Miller, N.E. (1950). *Personality and psychotherapy.* New York: McGraw-Hill.

DuBois, P. (1909). *The psychic treatment of mental disorders.* New York: Funk & Wagnell.

Dunlap, K. (1932). *Habits: Their making and unmaking.* New York: Liveright.

D'Zurilla, T.J., & Goldfried, M. (1971). Problem solving and behavior modification. *Journal of Abnormal Psychology, 78*, 107–126.

Eisenbud, J. (1967). Why psy? *Psychoanalytic Review, 53*, 47–163.

Eldridge, N., & Gould, S. (1972). Punctuated equilibria: An alternative to phyletic gradualism. In T. Schopf (Ed.), *Models in paleobiology.* San Francisco: Freeman.

Ellis, A. (1958). *How to live with a neurotic.* New York: Crown.

Ellis, A. (1962). *Reason and emotion in psychotherapy.* New York: Stuart.

Ellis, A. (1967). *A guide to rational living.* Englewood, NJ: Prentice-Hall.

Ellis, A. (1970). *The essence of rational psychotherapy: A comprehensive approach to treatment.* New York: Institute for Rational Living.

Ellis, A. (1979). *Theoretical and empirical foundations of rational-emotive therapy.* Monterey, CA: Brooks/Cole.

Ellis, A. (1980). Rational-emotive therapy and cognitive behavior therapy: Similarities and differences. *Cognitive Therapy and Research, 4,* 325–340.

Emmelkamp, P.M.G. (1994). Behavior therapy with adults. In A.E. Bergin & S.L. Garfield (Eds.), *Handbook of psychotherapy and behavior change* (4th ed., pp. 247–379). New York: Wiley.

Engel, G. (1968). A life setting conducive to illness. *Bulletin of the Menninger Clinic, 32,* 355–368.

Engel, L. (1962). *Psychological development in health and disease.* Philadelphia: Saunders.

Eysenck, H.J. (1952). The effects of psychotherapy: An evaluation. *Journal of Consulting Psychology, 16,* 319–324.

Eysenck, H.J. (1959). *The structure of human personality.* New York: Wiley-Interscience.

Farrelly, F., & Brandsma, J.M. (1974). *Provocative therapy.* Fort Collins, CO: Shields.

Fenichel (1945). *The psychoanalytic theory of neurosis.* New York: Norton.

Ferenczi, S. (1921). *Psycho-analysis and the war neuroses.* Vienna: International Psycho-Analytic Press.

Ferenczi, S. (1926). *Further contributions to the theory and technique of psychoanalysis.* New York: Basic Books.

Ferster, C.B. (1958). *Control of behavior in chimpanzees and pigeons by time out from positive reinforcement.* Washington, DC: American Psychological Association.

Ferster, C.B. (1964). Positive reinforcement and behavior deficits in autistic children. In C.M. Franks (Ed.), *Conditioning techniques in clinical practice and research.* New York: Springer.

Feuchtersleben, E. (1847). *Lehrbuch der arztlichen Seelenkunde.* Vienna: Gerold.

Flaherty, J.L. (1952). *A study of the effect of operational factors on secondary school instruction.* Washington, DC: Catholic University of America Press.

Foa, E.B., Davidson, J., & Rothbaum, B.O. (1995). Posttraumatic stress disorder. In G.O. Gabbard (Ed.), *Treatments of psychiatric disorders* (pp. 1499–1520). Washington, DC: American Psychiatric Press.

Foulkes, S.H., & Anthony, A.E. (1965). *Group psychotherapy.* Baltimore: Penguin Books.

Frances, A.J., Clarkin, J.F., & Perry, S. (1984). *Differential therapeutics in psychiatry.* New York: Brunner/Mazel.

Frank, J.D. (1961). *Persuasion and healing.* Baltimore: Johns Hopkins University Press.

Frank, J.D. (1968). Methods of assessing the results of psychotherapy. In R. Porter (Ed.), *The role of learning in psychotherapy* (pp. 38–60). Boston: Little, Brown.

Frank, J.D. (1973). Persuasion and healing (Rev. ed.) Baltimore: Johns Hopkins University Press.

Frank, J.D. (1984). The psychotherapy of anxiety. In L. Greenspoon (Ed.), *Psychiatry update: The American Psychiatric Association Annual Review* Vol. III (pp. 418–426). Washington, DC: American Psychiatric Press.

Frank, J.D., & Frank, J.B. (1991). *Persuasion and healing.* Baltimore: Johns Hopkins University Press.

Frankl, V.E. (1955). *The doctor and the soul: An introduction to logotherapy.* New York: Knopf.

Frankl, V.E. (1965). *The doctor and the soul: From psychotherapy to logotherapy.* New York: Knopf.

French, T.N. (1933). Interrelations between psychoanalysis and the experimental work of Pavlov. *American Journal of Psychiatry, 89,* 1165–1203.

Freud, S. (1925). Some character-types met with in psychoanalytic work. In J. Strachey (Ed. and Trans.), *The standard edition of the works of Sigmund Freud* (Vol. 14, pp. 310–333). London: Hogarth. (Original work published 1916)

Freud, S. (1932). *The interpretation of dreams* (3rd ed.). New York: Macmillan.

Freyhan, F.A. (1959). Clinical and integrative aspects. In N.S. Kline (Ed.), *Psychopharmacology frontiers*. Boston: Little, Brown.

Fromm, E. (1947). *Man for himself*. New York: Holt, Rinehart and Winston.

Gabbard, G.O. (1990). *Psychodynamic psychiatry in clinical practice*. Washington, DC: American Psychiatric Press.

Gabbard, G.O. (1994). *Psychodynamic psychiatry in clinical practice*. Washington, DC: American Psychiatric Press.

Gabbard, G.O. (Ed.). (1995). *Treatments of psychiatric disorders*. Washington, DC: American Psychiatric Press.

Garfield, S.L. (1957). *Introductory clinical psychology: An overview of the functions, methods, and problems of contemporary clinical psychology*. New York: Macmillan.

Garfield, S.L. (1992). Eclectic psychotherapy: A common factors approach. In J.C. Norcross & M.R. Goldfried (Eds.), *Handbook of psychotherapy integration* (pp. 169–201). New York: Basic Books.

Garfield, S.L., & Bergen, A.E. (Eds.). (1994). *Handbook of psychotherapy and behavior change* (4th ed.). New York: Wiley.

Gendlin, E.T. (1979). Experiential psychotherapy. In R. Corsisi (Ed.), *Current psychotherapies* (2nd ed., pp. 340–373). Itasca, IL: Peacock.

Gill, M., & Brenman, M. (1948). Research in psychotherapy. *American Journal of Orthopsychiatry, 18*, 100–110.

Glasser, W. (1961). *Mental health or mental illness? Psychiatry for practical action*. New York: Harper.

Glasser, W. (1965). *Reality therapy*. New York: Harper & Row.

Glasser, W. (1990). *The control theory–reality therapy workbook*. Canoga Park, CA: Institute for Reality Therapy.

Goldberg, S.C., Schultz, S.C., Schultz, P.M., Resnick, R.J., Hamer, R.M., & Friedel, R.O. (1986). Borderline and schizotypal personality disorders treated with low dose thiothoxine versus placebo. *Archives of General Psychiatry, 43*, 680–686.

Goldfried, M.R. (1971). Systematic desensitization as training in self-control. *Journal of Consulting and Clinical Psychology, 37*, 228–234.

Goldfried, M.R. (1980). *Some views on effective principles of psychotherapy*. New York: Plenum Press.

Goldfried, M.R. (1991). Research issues in psychotherapy integration. *Journal of Psychotherapy Integration, 1*, 5–25.

Goldfried, M.R., & Davison, G.C. (1976). *Clinical behavior therapy*. New York: Holt, Rinehart and Winston.

Goldfried, M.R., & Padawer, W. (1982). Current status and future directions of psychotherapy. In M.R. Goldfried (Ed.), *Converging themes in psychotherapy: Trends in psychodynamic, humanistic, and behavioral practice*. New York: Springer.

Goldstein, A.P., & Dean, S.J. (1966). *The investigation of psychotherapy: Commentaries and readings*. New York: Wiley.

Goldstein, K. (1940). *Human nature in the light of psychopathology*. Cambridge, MA: Harvard University Press.

Gotlib, I.H., & Colby, C.A. (1987). *Treatment of depression*. New York: Pergamon Press.

Gottschalk, L.A., & Auerbach, A.H. (1966). *Methods of research in psychotherapy*. New York: Appleton-Century-Crofts.

Greenberg, J.A., & Mitchell, S.A. (1983). *Object relations in psychoanalytic theory.* Cambridge, MA: Harvard University Press.

Greenberg, L.S., North, R.L., & Elliott, R. (1993). *Facilitating emotional change: The moment-by-moment process.* New York: Guilford Press.

Greenberg, L.S., & Safran, J.D. (1987). *Emotion in psychotherapy.* New York: Guilford Press.

Greist, J.H. (1993). *Panic disorder and agoraphobia: A guide.* Madison, WI: Dean Foundation for Health, Research, and Education.

Greist, J.H., & Jefferson, J.W. (1996). Obsessive-compulsive disorder. In G.O. Gabbard & S.D. Atkinson (Eds.), *Synopsis of treatments of psychiatric disorders* (pp. 627–635). Washington, DC: American Psychiatric Press.

Grinker, R.R. (1961). A demonstration of the transactional model. In M. Stein (Ed.), *Contemporary psychotherapies.* Glenco, IL: Free Press.

Grinker, R.R., Werble, B., & Drye, R.C. (1968). *The borderline syndrome.* New York: Basic Books.

Grotjahn, M. (1984). The narcissistic person in analytic group therapy. *International Journal of Group Psychotherapy, 34,* 234–256.

Grunbaum, A. (1952). Causality and the science of human behavior. *American Scientist, 26,* 665–676.

Gurman, A.S., & Kniskern, D. (Eds.). (1981). *The handbook of family therapy.* New York: Brunner/Mazel.

Guze, S. (1967). The diagnosis of hysteria: What are we trying to do? *American Journal of Psychiatry, 124,* 491–498.

Haley, J. (1963). *Strategies of psychotherapy.* New York: Grune & Stratton.

Haley, J. (1973). *Uncommon therapy: The psychiatric techniques of Milton H. Erikson, M.D.* New York: Norton.

Haley, J. (1987). *Problem-solving therapy.* San Francisco: Jossey-Bass.

Hamilton, E.W., & Abramson, L.Y. (1983). Cognitive patterns and major depressive disorder: A longitudinal study in a hospital setting. *Journal of Abnormal Psychology, 92,* 173–184.

Hamilton, M. (1980). Rating depressive patients. *Journal of Clinical Psychiatry, 41,* 21–24.

Hempel, C.G. (1961). Introduction to problems of taxonomy. In J. Zubin (Ed.), *Field studies in the mental disorders.* New York: Grune & Stratton.

Herman, J.L. (1992). *Trauma and recovery.* New York: Basic Books.

Hoch, P.H., & Zubin, J. (1964). *The evaluation of psychiatric treatment: The proceedings of the fifty-second annual meeting of the American Psychopathological Association held in New York City, February, 1962.* New York: Grune & Stratton.

Hollander, E., Liebowitz, N.R., Winchel, R., Klumker, A., & Klein, D.F. (1989). Treatment of body dysmorphic disorder and serotonin reuptake inhibitors. *American Journal of Psychiatry, 146,* 768–770.

Hollon, S.D., & Beck, A.T. (1994). Cognitive and cognitive-behavioral therapies. In A.E. Bergin & S.L. Garfield (Eds.), *Handbook of psychotherapy and behavior change* (4th ed.). New York: Wiley.

Hollon, S.D., & Fawcett, J. (1995). Combined medication and psychotherapy. In G.O. Gabbard (Ed.), *Treatments of psychiatric disorders* (pp. 1222–1236). Washington, DC: American Psychiatric Press.

Horner, A.J. (1990). *The primacy of structure: Psychotherapy of underlying character pathology.* Northvale, NJ: Aronson.

Horney, K. (1945). *Our inner conflicts: A constructive theory of neurosis.* New York: Norton.

Horney, K. (1950). *Neurosis and human growth.* New York: Norton.

Horowitz, M., Marmar, C., Krupnick, J., Wilner, N., Kaltreider, N., & Wallerstein, R. (1984). *Personality styles and brief psychotherapy.* New York: Basic Books.

Hunt, J. McV. (1952). Toward an integrated program of research on psychotherapy. *Journal of Consulting Psychology, 16,* 237–246.

Jacobson, E. (1929). *Progressive relaxation.* Chicago: University of Chicago Press.

Jacobson, E. (1964). *The self and the object world.* New York: International Universities Press.

Jenike, M. (1991). *Understanding obsessive-compulsive disorder (OCD): An international symposium held during the eighth World Congress of Psychiatry, Athens, Greece, October 1989.* Lewiston, NY: Hogrefe & Huber.

Joseph, S. (1997). *Personality disorders: Symptom-focused drug therapy.* New York: Haworth Press.

Kahlbaum, K.L. (1882). *Uber zyklisches irresein, irrenfreund.* Berlin: Springer.

Kahn, M.M. (1960). Clinical aspects of the schizoid personality: Affects and techniques. *International Journal of Psychoanalysis, 41,* 430–437.

Kanfer, F.H., & Saslow, G. (1965). Behavioral analysis: An alternative to diagnostic classification. *Archives of General Psychiatry, 15,* 114–127.

Kantor, M. (1992). *Diagnosis and treatment of the personality disorders.* St Louis, MO: Ishiyaku Euroamerica.

Kaslow, F.W. (1996). *Handbook of relational diagnosis and dysfunctional family patterns.* New York: Wiley.

Kellner, R. (1982). Psychotherapeutic strategies in hypochondriasis: A clinical study. *American Journal of Psychotherapy, 36,* 146–157.

Kelly, J.A. (1955). *The psychology of personal constructs.* New York: Routledge & Kegan Paul.

Kelly, J.A. (1985). Group social skills training. *Behavior Therapist, 8,* 93–95, 102.

Kelly, K.R. (1996). Review of clinical mental health counseling process and outcome research. *Journal of Mental Health Counseling, 18,* 358–375.

Kernberg, O.F. (1967). Borderline personality organization. *Journal of the American Psychoanalytic Association, 15,* 641–685.

Kernberg, O.F. (1975). *Borderline conditions and pathological narcissism.* Northvale, NJ: Aronson.

Kernberg, O.F. (1984). *Severe personality disorders.* New Haven, CT: Yale University Press.

Kernberg, O.F. (1988). Object relations theory in clinical practice. *Psychoanalysis Quarterly, 57,* 481–504.

Kernberg, O.F. (1992). *Aggression in personality disorders and perversions.* New Haven, CT: Yale University Press.

Kiesler, D.J. (1966). Some myths of psychotherapy research and the search for a paradigm. *Psychological Bulletin, 65,* 110–136.

Kiesler, D.J. (1982). The 1982 interpersonal circle: A taxonomy for complementarity in human transactions. *Psychological Review, 90,* 185–214.

Kiesler, D.J. (1986a). Interpersonal methods of diagnosis and treatment. In J.O. Cavenar (Ed.), *Psychiatry* (Vol. 1, pp. 1–23). Philadelphia: Lippincott.

Kiesler, D.J. (1986b). The 1982 interpersonal circle: An analysis of *DSM-III* personality disorders. In T. Millon & G. Klerman (Eds.), *Contemporary directions in psychopathology.* New York: Guilford Press.

Kiesler, D.J. (1997). *Contemporary interpersonal theory and research.* New York: Wiley.

Kilpatric, D.G., & Resnick, H.S. (1993). PYSD associated with exposure to criminal victimization in clinical and community populations. In J.R.T. Davidson & E.B. Foa (Eds.), *PTSD in review: DSM-IV and beyond.* Washington, DC: American Psychiatric Press.

Klein, D.F. (1972). *Psychiatric case studies: Treatment, drugs, and outcome.* Baltimore: Williams & Wilkins.

Klein, D.F. (1977). Psychopharmacological treatment and delineation of borderline disorders. In P. Hartcollis (Ed.), *Borderline personality disorders* (pp. 365–383). New York: International Universities Press.

Klein, M.H., Benjamin, L.S., Rosenfeld, R., Treece, C., Husted, J., & Griest, J.H. (1993). The Wisconsin personality disorders inventory: Development, reliability, and validity. *Journal of Personality Disorders, 7,* 285–303.

Klerman, G.L. (1974). Treatment of depression by drugs and psychotherapy. *American Journal of Psychiatry, 131,* 186–191.

Klerman, G.L. (1984). Ideologic conflicts in combined treatments. In B. Beitman & G.L. Klerman (Eds.), *Combining pharmacotherapy and psychotherapy in clinical practice* (pp. 17–34). New York: Guilford Press.

Klerman, G.L. (1986). Drugs and psychotherapy. In S.L. Garfield & A.E. Bergin (Eds.), *Handbook of psychotherapy and behavior change* (pp. 777–818). New York: Wiley.

Klerman, G.L. (1991). Ideological conflicts in integrating pharmacotherapy and psychotherapy. In B.D. Beitman, G.L. Klerman, et al. (Eds.), *Integrating pharmacotherapy and psychotherapy* (pp. 3–19). Washington, DC: American Psychiatric Press.

Klerman, G.L., & Weissman, M.M. (1982). Interpersonal psychotherapy theory and research. In A.J. Rush (Ed.), *Short-term psychotherapies for depression* (pp. 88–106). New York: Guilford Press.

Klerman, G.L., Weissman, M.M., Rounsaville, B.J., & Chevron, E.S. (1984). *Interpersonal psychotherapy of depression.* New York: Guilford Press.

Klosko, J.S., Barlow, D.H., Tassinari, R., & Cerny, J.A. (1990). A comparison of alprazolam and behavior therapy in treatment of panic disorder. *Journal of Consulting and Clinical Psychology, 58,* 77–84.

Kluft, R.P. (1984). Aspects of the treatment of multiple personality disorder. *Psychiatric Annals, 14,* 51–55.

Kluft, R.P. (1988). The dissociative disorders. In J.A. Talbot, R.E. Hales, & S.C. Yudofsky (Eds.), *Textbook of psychiatry* (pp. 557–585). Washington, DC: American Psychiatric Press.

Kluft, R.P. (1994). Treatment trajectories in multiple personality disorder. *Dissociation, 7,* 63–75.

Kluznik, J.C., Speed, N., Van Valkenburg, C., & Magraw, R. (1986). 40 year follow-up of United States prisoners of war. *American Journal of Psychiatry, 143,* 1443–1446.

Kohut, H. (1971). *The analysis of self.* Madison, CT: International Universities Press.

Kohut, H. (1977). *The restoration of the self.* New York: International Universities Press.

Kolb, L. (1973). *Modern clinical psychiatry.* Philadelphia: Saunders.

Kraepelin, E. (1896). *Psychiatrie: Ein Lehrbuch* (5th ed.). Leipzig: Barth.

Kubie, L.S. (1943). Manual of emergency treatment for acute war neuroses. *War Medicine, 4,* 582–598.

Lambert, M.J. (1992). Psychotherapy outcome research: Implications for integrative and eclectic therapists. In J.C. Norcross & M.R. Goldfried (Eds.), *Handbook of psychotherapy integration* (pp. 94–129). New York: Basic Books.

Lazarus, A.A. (1965). Behavior therapy, incomplete treatment, and symptom substitution. *Journal of Nervous and Mental Diseases, 140,* 80–86.

Lazarus, A.A. (1971). *Behavior therapy and beyond.* New York: McGraw-Hill.

Lazarus, A.A. (1973). Multimodal behavior therapy: Treating the "BASIC ID." *Journal of Nervous and Mental Disease, 156,* 404–411.

Lazarus, A.A. (1976). *Multimodal behavior therapy.* New York: Springer.

Lazarus, A.A. (1981). *The practice of multimodal therapy: Systematic, comprehensive, and effective psychotherapy.* New York: McGraw-Hill.

Lazarus, A.A. (1986). Multimodal therapy. In J.C. Norcross (Ed.), *Handbook of eclectic psychotherapy* (pp. 65–93). New York: Brunner/Mazel.

Lazarus, A.A., & Messer, S.B. (1991). Does chaos prevail? An exchange on technical eclecticism and assimilative integration. *Journal of Psychotherapy Integration, 1,* 143–158.

Leigh, G. (1985). Psychosocial factors in the etiology of substance abuse. In T.E. Bratter & G.G. Forrest (Eds.), *Alcoholism and substance abuse* (pp. 3–48). New York: Free Press.

Leszcz, M. (1989). Group psychotherapy of the characterologically difficult patient. *International Journal of Group Psychotherapy, 39,* 311–335.

Levine, J.B., Green, C.J., & Millon, T. (1986). The separation-individuation test of adolescence. *Journal of Personality Assessment, 50,* 123–137.

Levitt, E.E. (1957). The results of psychotherapy with children: An evaluation. *Journal of Consulting Psychology, 21,* 186–189.

Lewin, K. (1936). *Principles of topographical psychology.* New York: McGraw-Hill.

Lewinsohn, P.M., & Gotlib, I.H. (1995). Behavioral theory and treatment of depression. In E.E. Becker & W.R. Leber (Eds.), *Handbook of depression* (pp. 352–375). New York: Guilford Press.

Lewis, A. (1934). The story of unreason. In A. Lewis (Ed.), *The state of psychiatry.* London: Routledge & Kegan Paul.

Lindsay, W.R., Gansu, C.V., McLaughlin, E., Hood, E.M., & Espie, C.A. (1987). A controlled trial of treatments for generalized anxiety. *British Journal of Clinical Psychology, 26,* 3–15.

Linehan, M.M. (1987). Dialectical behavior therapy for borderline patients. *Bulletin of the Menninger Clinic, 51,* 261–276.

Linehan, M.M. (1992). Behavior therapy, dialectics, and the treatment of borderline personality disorder. In D. Silver & M. Rosenbluth (Eds.), *Handbook of borderline disorders* (pp. 415–434). Madison, CT: International Universities Press.

Linehan, M.M. (1993). *Cognitive-behavioral therapy of borderline personality disorder.* New York: Guilford Press.

Livesley, W.J. (1987). Theoretical and empirical issues in the selection of criteria to diagnose personality disorders. *Journal of Personality Disorders, 1,* 88–94.

Livesley, W.J., Jackson, D.N., & Schroeder, M.L. (1989). A study of the factorial structure of personality pathology. *Journal of Personality Disorders, 3,* 292–306.

Livesley, W.J., & Schroeder, M.L. (1990). Dimensions of personality disorder: The *DSM-III* cluster-A diagnoses. *Journal of Nervous and Mental Disorders, 178,* 395–401.

Loevinger, J. (1957). Objective tests as instruments of psychological theory. *Psychological Reports, 3,* 635–694.

London, P. (1964). *The modes and morals of psychotherapy.* New York: Holt, Rinehart and Winston.

MacKinnon, R.A., & Michels, R. (1971). *The psychiatric interview in clinical practice.* Philadelphia: Saunders.

Magnavita, J.J. (1997). *Restructuring personality disorders: A short-term dynamic approach.* New York: Guilford Press.

Mahoney, M.J. (1974). *Cognition and behavior modification.* Cambridge, MA: Ballinger.

Mahoney, M.J. (1977). Reflections on the cognitive-learning trend in psychotherapy. *American Psychologist, 32,* 5–13.

Mahrer, A.R. (1996). *The complete guide to experiential psychotherapy.* New York: Wiley.

Malan, D.H. (1963). *A study of brief psychotherapy.* London: Tavistock.

Malan, D.H. (1980). The most important development in psychotherapy. In H. Davenloo (Ed.), *Short-term dynamic psychotherapy.* Northvale, NJ: Aronson.

Maldonado, J.R., & Spiegel, D. (1995). Using hypnosis. In C. Classen (Ed.), *Treating women molested in childhood* (pp. 163–186). San Francisco: Jossey-Bass.

Mann, J. (1973). *Time-limited psychotherapy.* Cambridge, MA: Harvard University Press.

Manning, D.W., & Frances, A. (1990). *Combined pharmacotherapy and psychotherapy for depression.* Washington, DC: American Psychiatric Press.

Marececk, J., & Hare-Mustin, R.T. (1987). *Feminism and therapy: Can this relationship be saved?* Unpublished manuscript.

Markowitz, J.C. (1994). Psychotherapy of dysthymia: Is it effective? *American Journal of Psychiatry, 151,* 1114–1121.

Marks, I.M., Swinson, R.P., Basoglu, M., Kuch, M., Noshirvani, H., O'Sullivan, G., Lelliot, P.T., Kirby, M., McNamee, G., Sengun, S., & Wickwire, K. (1993). Alprazolam and exposure alone and combined in panic disorder with agoraphobia. *Journal of Psychiatry, 162,* 776–787.

Masling, J. (1960). The influences of situational and interpersonal variables in projective testing. *Psychological Bulletin, 57,* 65–85.

Mattick, R.P., Andrews, G., Hadzi-Pavlovic, D., & Christiensen, H. (1990). Treatment of panic and agoraphobia: An integrative review. *Journal of Nervous and Mental Diseases, 178,* 567–576.

Mattick, R.P., & Peters, L. (1988). Treatment of severe social phobia: Effects of guided exposure with and without cognitive restructuring. *Journal of Consulting and Clinical Psychology, 56,* 251–260.

Mavissakalian, M., & Michelson, M. (1986). Two year follow-up of exposure and imipramine treatment of agoraphobia. *American Journal of Psychiatry, 143,* 1106–1112.

Maxmen, J.S., & Ward, N.G. (1995). *Essential psychopathology and its treatment* (2nd ed.). New York: Norton.

May, R. (Ed.). (1958). *Existence.* New York: Basic Books.

May, R., & Van Kaam, A. (1963). Existential theory and therapy. In J.H. Masserman (Ed.), *Current psychiatric therapies* (Vol. 3). New York: Grune & Stratton.

McCann, J., & Dyer, F. (1994). *Forensic assessment with the MCMI-III.* New York: Guilford Press.

McCrady, B.S. (1993). Alcoholism. In D.H. Barlow (Ed.), *Clinical handbook of psychological disorders* (2nd ed., pp. 362–395). New York: Guilford Press.

McLean, P.D., & Hakstian, A.R. (1979). Clinical depression: Comparative efficacy of outpatient treatments. *Journal of Consulting and Clinical Psychology, 47,* 818–836.

Mead, G.H. (1934). *Mind, self, and society.* Chicago: University of Chicago Press.

Meehl, P.E. (1954). *Clinical versus statistical prediction: A theoretical analysis and a review of the evidence.* Minneapolis: University of Minnesota Press.

Meehl, P.E. (1965). Seer over sign: The first good example. *Journal of Experimental Research in Personality, 1,* 27–32.

Meichenbaum, D. (1971). Examination of model characteristics in reducing avoidance behavior. *Journal of Personality and Social Psychology, 17,* 298–307.

Meichenbaum, D. (1977). *Cognitive-behavioral modification: An integrative approach.* New York: Plenum Press.

Meloy, J.R. (1988). *The psychopathic mind.* Northvale, NJ: Aronson.

Menninger, K. (1940). Character disorders. In J.F. Brown (Ed.), *The psychodynamics of abnormal behavior* (pp. 384–403). New York: McGraw-Hill.

Messer, S.B. (1986). Eclecticism in psychotherapy: Underlying assumptions, problems, and trade-offs. In J.C. Norcross & M.R. Goldfried (Eds.), *Handbook of eclectic psychotherapy* (pp. 379–397). New York: Brunner/Mazel.

Messer, S.B. (1992). A critical examination of belief structures in integrative and eclectic psychotherapy. In J.C. Norcross & M.R. Goldfried (Eds.), *Handbook of psychotherapy integration* (pp. 130–165). New York: Basic Books.

Messer, S.B. (1996). Concluding comments. *Journal of Psychotherapy Integration, 6,* 135–137.

Michels, R., & Marzuk, P.M. (1993). Progress in psychiatry: II. *New England Journal of Medicine, 329,* 628–638.

Miller, G.A., Galanter, E., & Pribam, K.H. (1960). *Plans and structures of behavior.* New York: Holt, Rinehart and Winston.

Millon, T. (1969). *Modern psychopathology: A biosocial approach to maladaptive learning and functioning.* Philadelphia: Saunders. (Reprinted 1985, Prospect Heights, IL: Waveland Press)

Millon, T. (1977). *Millon clinical multiaxial inventory manual.* Minneapolis: National Computer Systems.

Millon, T. (1981). *Disorders of personality: DSM-III, Axis II.* New York: Wiley-Interscience.

Millon, T. (1984). On the renaissance of personality assessment and personality theory. *Journal of Personality Assessment, 48,* 450–466.

Millon, T. (1986a). Personality prototypes and their diagnostic criteria. In T. Millon & G.L. Klerman (Eds.), *Contemporary directions in psychopathology: Toward the DSM-IV* (pp. 671–712). New York: Guilford Press.

Millon, T. (1986b). A theoretical derivation of pathological personalities. In T. Millon & G.L. Klerman (Eds.), *Contemporary directions in psychopathology: Toward the DSM-IV* (pp. 639–669). New York: Guilford Press.

Millon, T. (1987a). *Millon clinical multiaxial inventory manual: II.* Minneapolis: National Computer Systems.

Millon, T. (1987b). On the nature of taxonomy in psychopathology. In C. Last & M. Hersen (Eds.), *Issues in diagnostic research* (pp. 3–85). New York: Plenum Press.

Millon, T. (1988). Personologic psychotherapy: Ten commandments for a post eclectic approach to integrative treatment. *Psychotherapy, 25,* 209–219.

Millon, T. (1990). *Toward a new personology: An evolutionary model.* New York: Wiley-Interscience.

Millon, T. (1991). Classification in psychopathology: Rationale, alternatives, and standards. *Journal of Abnormal Psychology, 100,* 245–261.

Millon, T. (1996). *Personality and psychopathology: Building a clinical science.* New York: Wiley-Interscience.

Millon, T., & Davis, R.D. (1996a). *Disorders of personality: DSM-IV and beyond.* New York: Wiley.

Millon, T., & Davis, R.D. (1996b). An evolutionary theory of personality disorders. In J. Clarkin & M. Lenzenweger (Eds.), *Major theories of personality disorder.* New York: Guilford Press.

Millon, T., & Davis R.D. (1999). *Abnormal personalities: The study of contemporary personality disorders.* New York: Wiley-Interscience.

Millon, T., Millon, C., & Davis, R.D. (1994). *Millon clinical multiaxial inventory-III.* Minneapolis: National Computer Systems.

Millon, T., Simonsen, E., Birket-Smith, M., & Davis, R. (Eds.). (1998). *Psychopathy: Antisocial, criminal, and violent behavior.* New York: Guilford Press.

Millon, T., Weiss, L., Millon, C., & Davis, R. (1994). *MIPS: Millon index of personality styles manual.* San Antonio, TX: Psychological Corporation.

Minuchin, S. (1974). *Families and family therapy.* Cambridge, MA: Harvard University Press.

Minuchin, S., & Fishman, H.C. (1981). *Family therapy techniques.* Cambridge, MA: Harvard University Press.

Mischel, W. (1984). Convergences and challenges in the search for consistency. *American Psychologist, 39,* 351–364.

Monti, P.M., Abrhams, D.B., Kadden, R.M., & Cooney, N.L. (1989). *Treating alcohol dependence: A coping skills training guide.* New York: Guilford Press.

Moreno, J.L. (1934). *Who shall survive? A new approach to the problem of human interrelations.* Washington, DC: Nervous and Mental Disease.

Moreno, J.L. (1946). *Group psychotherapy: A symposium.* New York: Beacon House.

Morrison, J. (1995). *DSM-IV made easy.* New York: Guilford Press.

Mowrer, O.H. (1961). *The crisis in psychiatry and religion.* Princeton: Van Nostrand.

Mowrer, O.H. (1966). Learning theory and behavior therapy. In B. Wolman (Ed.), *Handbook of clinical psychology.* New York: McGraw-Hill.

Mowrer, O.H. (1965). Integrity therapy: A self-help approach. *Psychotherapy, 3,* 14–19.

Murray, E.J. (1983). Beyond behavioural and dynamic therapy. *British Journal of Clinical Psychology, 22,* 127–128.

Murray, E.J. (1986). Possibilities and promises of eclecticism. In J.C. Norcross (Ed.), *Handbook of eclectic psychotherapy.* New York: Brunner/Mazel.

Nathan, P.E., & Gorman, J.M. (Eds.). (1998). *A guide to treatments that work.* New York: Oxford University Press.

Neisser, U. (1967). *Cognitive psychology.* Englewood Cliffs, NJ: Prentice-Hall.

Norcross, J.C., & Goldfried, M.R. (Eds.). (1992). *Handbook of psychotherapy integration.* New York: Basic Books.

O'Hanlon, W.H. (1987). *Shifting contexts: The generation of effective psychotherapy.* New York: Guilford Press.

O'Hanlon, W.H., & Weiner-Davis, M. (1989). *In search of solutions: A new direction in psychotherapy.* New York: Norton.

Ost, L.G. (1988). Applied relaxation vs. progressive relaxation in the treatment of panic disorder. *Behaviour Research and Therapy, 26,* 13–22.

Overall, J.E., & Hollister, L.E. (1980). Phenomenological classification of depressive disorders. *Journal of Clinical Psychology, 36,* 372–377.

Paivio, A. (1971). *Imagery and verbal processes.* New York: Holt, Rinehart and Winston.

Parloff, M.B. (1968). Analytic group psychotherapy. In J. Marmor (Ed.), *Modern psychoanalysis* (pp. 492–531). New York: Basic Books.

Pavlov, I.P. (1928). *Lectures on conditioned reflexes.* London: Lawrence & Wishart.

Penn, D.L., & Mueser, K.T. (1996). Research update on the psychosocial treatment of schizophrenia. *American Journal of Psychiatry, 153,* 607–617.

Perry, J.C., & Cooper, S.H. (1989). An empirical study of defense mechanisms. *Archives of General Psychiatry, 46,* 444–452.

Perry, S., Frances, A.J., & Clarkin, J.F. (1985). *A DSM-III casebook of differential therapeutics: A clinical guide to treatment selection.* New York: Brunner/Mazel.

Pfohl, B., Blum, N., Zimmerman, M., & Stangl, D. (1989). *Structured interview for DSM-III-R personality (SIDP-R).* Iowa City: University of Iowa, Department of Psychiatry.

Pfohl, B., Blum, N., Zimmerman, M., & Stangl, D. (1997). *Structured interview for DSM-IV personality (SIDP-IV).* Iowa City: University of Iowa, Department of Psychiatry.

Phillips, E.L. (1956). *Psychotherapy: A modern theory and practice.* Englewood Cliffs, NJ: Prentice-Hall.

Pincus, A.L., & Wiggins, J.S. (1989). Conceptions of personality disorders and dimensions of personality. *Psychological Assessment, 1,* 305–316.

Power, K.G., Simpson, R.J., Swanson, V., & Wallace, L.A. (1990). A controlled comparison of cognitive-behavior therapy, diazepam, and placebo, alone and in combination, for the treatment of generalized anxiety disorder. *Journal of Anxiety Disorders, 4,* 267–292.

Prochaska, J.O. (1984). *Systems of psychotherapy: A transtheoretical analysis* (2nd ed.). Homewood, IL: Dorsey.

Prochaska, J.O. (1995). An eclectic and integrative approach: Transtheoretical therapy. In A.S. Gurman & S.B. Messer (Eds.), *Essential psychotherapies: Theory and practice.* New York: Guilford Press.

Prochaska, J.O., & DiClemente, C.C. (1982). Transtheoretical therapy: Toward a more integrative model of change. *Psychotherapy: Theory, Research & Practice, 19*(3), 276–288.

Prochaska, J.O., & DiClemente, C.C. (1983). Stages and processes of self-change in smoking: Toward an integrative model of change. *Journal of Consulting and Clinical Psychology, 5,* 390–395.

Prochaska, J.O., & DiClemente, C.C. (1984). *The transtheoretical approach: Crossing traditional boundaries of therapy.* Homewood, IL: Dow Jones–Irwin.

Prochaska, J.O., & DiClemente, C.C. (1985). Common processes of change in smoking, weight control, and psychological distress. In S. Shiffman & T. Wills (Eds.), *Coping and substance abuse.* New York: Academic Press.

Quine, W.V.O. (1961). *From a logical point of view* (2nd ed.). New York: Harper & Row.

Rado, S. (1928). The problems of melancholia. *International Journal of Psychoanalysis, 9,* 297–313.

Rado, S. (1969). *Adaptational psychodynamics.* New York: Science House.

Raimy, V. (1975). *Misunderstandings of the self.* San Francisco: Jossey-Bass.

Rank, O. (1936). *Will therapy: An analysis of the therapeutic process in terms of relationship.* New York: Knopf.

Rauch, S.L., & Jenike, M.A. (1998). Pharmacological treatment of obsessive compulsive disorder. In P.E. Nathan, J.M. Gorman, et al. (Eds.), *A guide to treatments that work* (pp. 358–376). New York: Oxford University Press.

Reich, W. (1933). *Character analysis.* Leipzig: Verlag.

Reich, W. (1949). *Character analysis* (3rd ed.). New York: Farrar, Strauss and Giroux.

Reid, W.H. (1978). *The psychopath: A comprehensive study of antisocial disorders and behaviors.* New York: Brunner/Mazel.

Reik, T. (1941). *Masochism and modern man.* New York: Farvar and Rinehart.

Resick, P.A., & Schnicke, M.K. (1992). Cognitive processing therapy for sexual assault victims. *Journal of Sex and Marital Therapy, 7,* 184–194.

Riggs, D.S., & Foa, E.B. (1993). Obsessive-compulsive disorder. In D.H. Barlow (Ed.), *Clinical handbook of psychological disorders* (2nd ed., pp. 189–239). New York: Guilford Press.

Rogers, C.R. (1942). *Counseling and psychotherapy.* Boston: Houghton Mifflin.

Rogers, C.R. (1951). *Client-centered therapy.* Boston: Houghton Mifflin.

Rogers, C.R. (1959). A theory of therapy, personality, and interpersonal relationships, as developed in the client-centered framework. In S. Koch (Ed.), *Psychology: A study of a science* (Vol. 3). New York: Basic Books.

Rogers, C.R. (1961). *On becoming a person.* Boston: Houghton Mifflin.

Rogers, C.R. (Ed.). (1967). *The therapeutic relationship and its impact.* Madison: University of Wisconsin Press.

Rogers, C.R., & Dymond, R.F. (1954). *Psychotherapy and personality change.* Chicago: University of Chicago Press.

Rosenbaum, J.F., Fava, M., Nierenberg, A., & Sachs, G.S. (1995). Treatment-resistant mood disorders. In G.O. Gabbard (Ed.), *Treatments of psychiatric disorders* (pp. 1275–1328). Washington, DC: American Psychiatric Press.

Rosenthal, D., & Frank, J.D. (1956). Psychotherapy and the placebo effect. *Psychological Bulletin, 53,* 294–302.

Rosenzweig, S. (1936). Some implicit common factors in diverse methods of psychotherapy. *American Journal of Orthopsychiatry, 6,* 412–415.

Roth, A., & Fonagy, P. (1996). *What works for whom? A critical review of psychotherapy research.* New York: Guilford Press.

Rotter, J.B. (1954). *Social learning and clinical psychology.* Englewood Cliffs, NJ: Prentice-Hall.

Rotter, J.B. (1962). An analysis of Adlerian psychology from a research orientation. *Journal of Individual Psychology, 18*(1), 3–11.

Rubinstein, E.A., & Parloff, M.B. (Eds.). (1959). *Research in psychotherapy, proceedings.* Washington, DC: American Psychological Association.

Rutan, J.S., & Stone, W.N. (1984). *Psychodynamic group psychotherapy.* Lexington, MA: Collamore Press.

Sacks, O. (1973). *Awakenings.* New York: Harper & Row.

Safran, J.D. (1984). Assessing the cognitive-interpersonal cycle. *Cognitive Therapy and Research, 8*(4), 333–347.

Safran, J.D., & Segal, Z.V. (1990). *Interpersonal process in cognitive therapy.* New York: Basic Books.

Salter, A. (1949). *Conditioned reflex therapy: The direct approach to the reconstruction of personality.* New York: Creative Age Press.

Salvendy, J.T., & Joffe, R. (1991). Antidepressants in group psychotherapy. *International Journal of Group Psychotherapy, 41,* 465–480.

Salzman, L. (1980). *Treatment of the obsessive personality.* Northvale, NJ: Aronson.

Salzman, L. (1989). Compulsive personality disorder. In T. Karasu (Ed.), *Treatments of psychiatric disorders* (pp. 2771–2782). Washington, DC: American Psychiatric Press.

Sarason, S.B. (1954). *The clinical interaction, with special reference to the Rorschach.* New York: Harper.

Sarbin, T.R. (1943). A contribution to the study of actuarial and individual methods of prediction. *American Journal of Sociology, 48,* 593–602.

Sarbin, T.R., Taft, R., & Bailey, D.E. (1960). *Clinical inference and cognitive theory.* New York: Holt, Rinehart and Winston.

Satir, V. (1972). *Peoplemaking.* Palo Alto, CA: Science and Behavior Books.

Satir, V., & Baldwin, M. (1983). *Satir step by step: A guide to creating change in families.* Palo Alto, CA: Science and Behavior Books.

Schacht, T.E. (1984). Clinical problem solving and therapeutic noncompliance: A heuristic for enhancing the clinician's generation of alternatives. *Cognitive Therapy & Research, 8*(1), 19–28.

Scharff, D.E., & Scharff, J.S. (1991). *Object relations family therapy.* Northvale, NJ: Aronson.

Schneider, K. (1923). *Psychopathic personalities.* London: Cassell.

Schneier, F.R., Marshall, R.D., Street, L., Heindberg, R.G., & Juster, H.R. (1995). Social phobia and specific phobia. In G.O. Gabbard (Ed.), *Treatments of psychiatric disorders* (pp. 1453–1476). Washington, DC: American Psychiatric Press.

Schwartz, L.S. (1990). A biopsychosocial treatment approach to post-traumatic stress disorder. *Journal of Traumatic Stress, 3,* 221–238.

Sechrest, L., & Smith, B. (1994). Psychotherapy is the practice of psychology. *Journal of Psychotherapy Integration, 4,* 1–29.

Seligman, L. (1998). *Selecting effective treatments: A comprehensive, systematic guide to treating mental disorders.* San Francisco: Jossey Bass.

Selvini-Palazzoli, M., & Viaro, M. (1988). The anorectic process in the family: A six-stage model as a guide for individual therapy. *Family Process, 27*(2), 129–148.

Serban, G., & Siegel, S. (1984). Response of borderline and schizotypal patients to small doses of thiothixene and haloperidol. *American Journal of Psychiatry, 141,* 1455–1458.

Shapiro, D. (1981). *Autonomy and rigid character.* New York: Basic Books.

Shlien, J.M. (1968). *Research in psychotherapy: Proceedings of the third conference, Chicago, IL, May 31–June 4, 1966.* Washington, DC: American Psychological Association.

Sifneos, P.E. (1967). Two different kinds of psychotherapy of short duration. *American Journal of Psychiatry, 123,* 1069–1074.

Sifneos, P.E. (1968). Learning to solve emotional problems: A controlled study of short-term anxiety-provoking psychotherapy. In R. Porter (Ed.), *The role of learning in psychotherapy* (pp. 87–99). Boston: Little, Brown.

Sifneos, P.E. (1972). *Short-term psychotherapy and emotional crisis.* Cambridge, MA: Harvard University Press.

Skinner, B.F. (1938). *The behavior of organisms: An experimental analysis.* New York: Appleton-Century.

Skinner, B.F. (1953). *Science and behavior.* New York: Macmillan.

Slavson, S.R. (1943). *An introduction to group therapy.* New York: Commonwealth Fund.

Slavson, S.R. (1964). *A textbook in analytic group psychotherapy.* New York: International Universities Press.

Soloff, P.H., George, A., Nathan, R.S., Schulz, P.M., Ulrich, R.F., & Perel, J.M. (1986). Progress in the psychopharmacology of borderline disorders: A double blind study of amitriptyline, haloperidol, and placebo. *Archives of General Psychiatry, 43,* 691–697.

Spence, S. (1989). Cognitive-behavior therapy in the management of chronic, occupational pain of the upper limbs. *Behavior Research and Therapy, 27,* 435–446.

Sperry, L. (1995). *Handbook of diagnosis and treatment of the DSM-IV personality disorders.* New York: Brunner/Mazel.

Spitzer, R.L., Endicott, J., & Gibbon, M. (1979). Crossing the border into borderline personality and borderline schizophrenia. *Archives of General Psychiatry, 36,* 17–24.

Spitzer, R.L., Williams, J.B.W., & Gibbon, M. (1987). *Structured clinical interview for the DSM-III-R personality disorders (SCID-II).* New York: New York Psychiatric Institute.

Stampfl, T.G., & Levis, D.J. (1967). Essentials of implosive therapy: A learning-theory based psychodynamic behavioral therapy. *Journal of Abnormal Psychology, 72,* 496–503.

Stephens, J.H., & Kamp, M. (1962). On some aspects of hysteria. *Journal of Nervous and Mental Disease, 134,* 305–315.

Steuer, J., Mintz, J., Hammen, C., Hill, M.A., Jarvik, L.F., McCarley, T., Motoike, P., & Rosen, R. (1984). Cognitive-behavioral and psychodynamic group psychotherapy in treatment of geriatric depression. *Journal of Consulting and Clinical Psychology, 52,* 180–192.

Stollak, G.E., Guerney, B.G., & Rothberg, M. (Eds.). (1966). *Psychotherapy research: Selected readings.* Chicago: Rand McNally.

Stone, M.H. (1980). *The borderline syndromes.* New York: McGraw-Hill.

Stone, M.H. (1993). Long-term outcome in personality disorders. In P. Tyrer & G. Stein (Eds.), *Personality disorder reviewed.* London: Gaskell.

Stricker, G., & Gold, J. (Eds.). (1993). *Comprehensive handbook of psychotherapy integration.* New York: Guilford Press.

Strupp, H.H., & Luborsky, L. (1962). *Research in psychotherapy: Proceedings of a conference, Chapel Hill, North Carolina, May 17–20, 1961.* Washington, DC: American Psychological Association.

Sullivan, H.S. (1953). *The interpersonal theory of psychiatry.* New York: Norton.

Sullivan, H.S. (1954). *The psychiatric interview.* New York: Norton.

Swartz, M.S., & McCracken, J. (1986). Emergency room management of conversion disorders. *Hospital and Community Psychiatry, 37,* 828–832.

Talmon, M. (1990). *Single-session therapy: Maximizing the effect of the first (and often only) therapeutic encounter.* San Francisco: Jossey-Bass.

Taylor, S., & Braun, J.D. (1988). Illusion and well-being. *Psychological Bulletin, 103,* 193–210.

Taylor, S., & Hyer, S.E. (1993). Update on factitious disorders. *International Journal of Psychiatric Medicine, 23,* 81–94.

The Quality Assurance Project. (1990). Treatment outlines for paranoid, schizotypal, and schizoid personality disorders. *Australian and New Zealand Journal of Psychiatry, 24,* 339–350.

Thorne, F.C. (1944). A critique of nondirective methods of psychotherapy. *Journal of Abnormal and Social Psychology, 39,* 459–470.

Thorne, F.C. (1948). Principles of directive counseling and psychotherapy. *American Psychologist, 3,* 160–165.

Thorne, F.C. (1950). *Principles of personality counseling: An eclectic viewpoint.* Brandon, VT: Journal of Clinical Psychology.

Thorne, F.C. (1961). *Personality: A clinical eclectic viewpoint.* Brandon, VT: Journal of Clinical Psychology.

Thorne, F.C. (1967). The structure of integrative psychology. *Journal of Clinical Psychology, 23*(1), 3–11.

Thorne, F.C., & Pishkin, V. (1968). The ideological survey. *Journal of Clinical Psychology, 24*(3), 263–268.

Trull, T.J., Nietzel, M.T., & Main, A. (1988). The use of meta-analysis to assess the clinical significance of behaviour therapy for agoraphobia. *Behavior Therapy, 19,* 527–538.

Turkat, I.D. (1990). *The personality disorders.* New York: Pergamon Press.

Turkat, I.D., & Maisto, S.A. (1985). Personality disorders: Application of the experimental method to the formulation of personality disorders. In D.H. Barlow (Ed.), *Clinical handbook of psychological disorders.* New York: Guilford Press.

Turner, J. (1982). Comparison of group progressive-relaxation training and cognitive-behavioral group therapy for chronic low back pain. *Journal of Consulting and Clinical Psychology, 50,* 757–765.

Vaillant, G.E. (1971). Theoretical hierarchy of adaptive ego mechanisms. *Archives of General Psychiatry, 24,* 107–118.

Vaughan, M. (1976). The relationship between obsessional personality obsessions in depression, and symptoms of depression. *British Journal of Psychiatry, 129,* 36–39.

von Bertalanffy, L. (1933). *Modern theories of development: An introduction to theoretical biology.* New York: Harper.

von Bertalanffy, L. (1950). An outline of general system theory. *British Journal for the Philosophy of Science, 1,* 134–165.

von Meduna, L.T. (1935). Versuche uber die biologische Beeinflussung des Ablaufes der Schizophrenie. *Zeitschrift fur die gesamte Neurologie und Psychiatrie, 152,* 235–262.

von Neumann, J., & Morgenstern, O. (1944). *The theory of games and economic behavior.* New York: McGraw-Hill.

Von Zerssen, J. (1977). Premorbid personality and affective psychosis. In G.D. Burrows (Ed.), *Handbook of depression.* Amsterdam: Excerpta Medica.

Wachtel, E.F. (1992). An integrative approach to working with troubled children and their families. *Journal of Psychotherapy Integration, 2*(3), 207–224.

Wachtel, P.L. (1973). Psychodynamics, behavior therapy and the implacable experimenter: An inquiry into the consistency of personality. *Journal of Abnormal Psychology, 82,* 324–334.

Wachtel, P.L. (1977). *Psychoanalysis and behavior therapy: Toward an interpretation.* New York: Basic Books.

Wachtel, P.L. (1984). On theory, practice, and the nature of integration. In H. Arkowitz, S. Messer, et al. (Eds.), *Psychoanalytic therapy and behavior therapy: Is integration possible?* (pp. 31–52). New York: Plenum Press.

Wachtel, P.L., & Wachtel, E.F. (1986). *Family dynamics in individual psychotherapy: A guide to clinical strategies.* New York: Guilford Press.

Walker, R. (1992). Substance abuse and B-cluster disorders: II. Treatment recommendations. *Journal of Psychoactive Drugs, 24,* 233–241.

Walton, D. (1960). Drug addiction and habit formation: An attempted integration. *Journal of Mental Science, 106,* 1195–1229.

Wells, R., & Giannetti, V. (Eds.). (1990). *Handbook of brief psychotherapies.* New York: Plenum Press.

Werner, H. (1940). *Comparative psychology of mental development.* New York: Follett.

Wessler, R.L. (1993). "Constructivism and rational-emotive therapy: A critique of Richard Wessler's critique": Reply. *Psychotherapy, 30*(3), 533–534.

Wexler, B.E., & Cicchetti, D.V. (1992). The outpatient treatment of depression: Implications of outcome research for clinical practice. *Journal of Nervous and Mental Disease, 180,* 277–286.

Whitaker, C.A., & Keith, D.V. (1981). Symbolic-experiential family therapy. In A.S. Gurman & D.P. Kniskern (Eds.), *Handbook of family therapy* (pp. 187–225). New York: Brunner/Mazel.

Whitaker, C.A., & Malone, T.P. (1953). *The roots of psychotherapy.* New York: Blakiston.

Widiger, T., & Sanderson, C. (1995). Toward a dimensional model of personality disorder in *DSM-IV* and *DSM-V.* In W.J. Livesley (Ed.), *The DSM-IV personality disorders.* New York: Guilford Press.

Wiggins, J.S. (1982). Circumplex models of interpersonal behavior in clinical psychology. In P. Kendall & J. Butcher (Eds.), *Handbook of research methods in clinical psychology.* New York: Wiley-Interscience.

Will, H. (1994). Zur phanomenologie der depression aus psychoanalytischer sicht: The phenomenology of depression: A psychoanalytic view. *Psyche Zeitschrift fur Psychoanalyse und ihre Anwendungen, 48,* 361–385.

Winston, A., Laikin, M., Pollack, J., Samstag, L.W., McCullough, L., & Muran, J.C. (1994). Short-term psychotherapy of personality disorders. *American Journal of Psychiatry, 151,* 190–194.

Wittenborn, J.R., & Maurer, H.S. (1977). Persisting personalities among depressed women. *Archives of General Psychiatry, 34,* 968–971.

Wolberg, L.R. (1965). *Short-term psychotherapy.* New York: Basic Books.

Wolberg, L.R. (1967). *The technique of psychotherapy* (2nd ed.). New York: Grune & Stratton.

Wolberg, L.R. (1980). *Handbook of short-term psychotherapy.* New York: Thieme-Stratton.

Wolf, A. (1949). The psychoanalysis of groups. *American Journal of Psychotherapy, 3,* 525–558.

Wolf, A. (1950). The psychoanalysis of groups. *American Journal of Psychotherapy, 4,* 16–50.

Wolf, A., & Schwartz, E.K. (1962). *Psychoanalysis in groups.* New York: Grune & Stratton.

Wolpe, J. (1958). *Psychotherapy by reciprocal inhibition.* Stanford, CA: Stanford University Press.

Worell, J., & Remer, P. (1992). *Feminist perspectives in therapy: An empowerment model for women.* New York: Wiley.

Yalom, I.D. (1980). *Existential psychotherapy.* New York: Basic Books.

Yalom, I.D. (1985). *The theory and practice of group psychotherapy.* New York: Basic Books.

Yalom, I.D. (1986). *The theory and practice of group psychotherapy* (3rd ed.). New York: Basic Books.

Young, J.E. (1990). *Cognitive therapy for personality disorders: A schema-focused approach.* Sarasota, FL: Professional Resource Exchange.

Young, J.E., & Lindeman, M.D. (1992). An integrative schema-focused model for personality disorders. *Journal of Cognitive Psychotherapy, 6,* 11–23.

Zubin, J. (1953). Evaluation of therapeutic outcome in mental disorders. *Journal of Nervous and Mental Diseases, 117,* 95–111.

Author Index

Subject Index